TALIS 2013 Results

AN INTERNATIONAL PERSPECTIVE ON TEACHING AND LEARNING

O))OECD

BETTER POLICIES FOR BETTER LIVES

This work is published on the responsibility of the Secretary-General of the OECD. The opinions expressed and arguments employed herein do not necessarily reflect the official views of the OECD member countries.

This document and any map included herein are without prejudice to the status of or sovereignty over any territory, to the delimitation of international frontiers and boundaries and to the name of any territory, city or area.

Please cite this publication as:

OECD (2014), *TALIS 2013 Results: An International Perspective on Teaching and Learning*, OECD Publishing. http://dx.doi.org/10.1787/9789264196261-en

ISBN 978-92-64-21133-9 (print)
ISBN 978-92-64-19626-1 (PDF)

Note by Turkey: The information in this document with reference to "Cyprus" relates to the southern part of the Island. There is no single authority representing both Turkish and Greek Cypriot people on the Island. Turkey recognises the Turkish Republic of Northern Cyprus (TRNC). Until a lasting and equitable solution is found within the context of the United Nations, Turkey shall preserve its position concerning the "Cyprus issue".

Note by all the European Union Member States of the OECD and the European Union: The Republic of Cyprus is recognised by all members of the United Nations with the exception of Turkey. The information in this document relates to the area under the effective control of the Government of the Republic of Cyprus.

The statistical data for Israel are supplied by and under the responsibility of the relevant Israeli authorities. The use of such data by the OECD is without prejudice to the status of the Golan Heights, East Jerusalem and Israeli settlements in the West Bank under the terms of international law.

Photo credits:
© Andersen Ross/Inmagine LTD
© Digital Vision/Getty Images
© Feng Yu/Stocklib
© Hero Images/Corbis
© Michael Brown/Stocklib
© Monkey Busines/Fotolia
© Pressmaster/Shutterstock
© Vetta Collection/iStock
© Tyler Olson/Shutterstock

Corrigenda to OECD publications may be found on line at: *www.oecd.org/publishing/corrigenda*.

Foreword

The skills that students need to contribute effectively to society are in constant change. Yet, our education systems are not keeping up with the fast pace of the world around us. Most schools look much the same today as they did a generation ago, and teachers themselves are often not developing the practices and skills necessary to meet the diverse needs of today's learners.

The OECD Programme for International Student Assessment (PISA) is broadening the discussion about improving national education systems beyond government and research institutions. Parents want the best education for their children to ensure their success later in life. But beyond the influence of parents and other factors outside the school, teachers provide the most important influence on student learning. Thus, teachers and teaching are facing growing scrutiny due to a general agreement that improvements in teaching can lead to better learning and more effective education system.

The OECD Teaching and Learning International Survey (TALIS) is the largest international survey of teachers. TALIS began in 2008 and gives teachers and school leaders around the world a voice to speak about their experiences. The survey emphasises the themes that research tells us can influence effective teaching. Teachers report on their initial training and the professional development they receive, the feedback they get on their teaching, the climate in their classrooms and schools, their own satisfaction with their jobs, and their feelings about their professional abilities.

This report shares findings from the most recent cycle of the survey. TALIS 2013 results show that we need to put teachers on a path to success immediately. Those professionals whose initial education included content, pedagogy and practice elements specifically for the subjects that they teach report feeling better prepared for their work than their colleagues without this kind of training. This is relevant information for systems of initial teacher preparation in all countries.

If teachers are now expected to prepare students to become lifelong learners, TALIS tells us that they themselves need to learn and develop throughout their careers. Teachers not only need to be able to use the latest tools and technologies with their students, but they also need to take advantage of the latest research on learning, pedagogies and practices. Part of making this happen requires access to high-quality professional development. But access alone is not enough. TALIS shows that teachers report higher participation rates in professional development activities in those countries where they also report higher levels of both monetary and non-monetary support for this development.

Furthermore, teachers want to improve their skills and receive feedback that will help them improve. According to TALIS, more than six in ten teachers report that appraisal leads to positive changes in their teaching practices. Also, more than half of all teachers surveyed report that such feedback leads to positive changes in both their use of student assessments and their classroom-management practices.

While teaching has often been thought of as an isolating profession, where teachers retreat into their classrooms and simply close the door, the TALIS data also show that this is no longer the case. The survey illustrates the importance of collaboration between teachers, to the extent that those who participated in collaborative professional learning activities at least five times a year also reported being significantly more confident in their own abilities. Teachers' use of collaborative teaching practices five times a year or more also increases both their reported levels of self-efficacy and their job satisfaction.

We are aware that making substantial changes to develop the teaching profession is not an easy endeavour, but countries, schools and teachers are not alone in this critical task. Further to this volume, the OECD will produce several additional reports and policy briefs with new analyses of this rich data on teachers and schools, as well as policy recommendations based on those findings. Recognising that education is the great equaliser in society, the challenge for all of us is to equip all teachers with the skills and tools they need to provide effective learning opportunities for their students.

Angel Gurría
OECD Secretary-General

Acknowledgements

The OECD Teaching and Learning International Survey (TALIS) is the outcome of a collaboration among the participating countries, the OECD Secretariat, the European Commission and an international consortium led by the International Association for the Evaluation of Educational Achievement (IEA). The report was prepared by Olusola O. Adesope, Bruce Austin, Julie Bélanger, Brian French, Chad Gotch, Maria Luisa Hidalgo Hidalgo, Ben Jensen, Simon Normandeau, Mathilde Overduin, José Ignacio García Pérez, Heather Price, Charles Ungerleider, Kristen Weatherby and Zohreh Zadeh with help from Michael Davidson, Francesca Borgonovi, Tracey Burns, Dirk Van Damme, Tadakazu Miki, Gabriella Moriconi, Deborah Nusche, Beatriz Pont, Andreas Schleicher and Pablo Zoido.

Communications assistance was provided by Elizabeth Del Bourgo, Cassandra Davis and Sophie Limoges. Administrative assistance was provided by Delphine Versini with help from Brigitte Beyeler, Elisa Larrakoetxea, Elizabeth Morgan, Isabelle Moulherat and Diana Tramantano.

The development of the report was steered by the TALIS Board of Participating Countries, chaired by Anne-Berit Kavli (Norway). Annex D of this report lists the members of various TALIS bodies as well as the individual experts and consultants who have contributed to TALIS in general.

Table of Contents

BOXES

FIGURES

TABLES

This book has...

StatLinkS

A service that delivers Excel® files from the printed page!

Look for the *StatLinks* at the bottom left-hand corner of the tables or graphs in this book.
To download the matching Excel® spreadsheet, just type the link into your Internet browser,
starting with the *http://dx.doi.org* prefix.
If you're reading the PDF e-book edition, and your PC is connected to the Internet, simply
click on the link. You'll find *StatLinks* appearing in more OECD books.

Executive Summary

Our view of teachers is coloured by our own experience as students. This firsthand – and often dated – knowledge is augmented by the portrayal of teachers and their working conditions in the media. Thus, in many countries, the traditional view of teaching is one in which teachers work alone in classrooms, behind closed doors, often with larger numbers of students than they can realistically handle. In some countries, teaching is seen as a job without real career prospects that young people enter if they cannot get into a better one. The fact that pay tends to be lower than that of other college graduates is compensated for by the fact that teachers often enjoy more holiday time and are seen as working fewer hours than their colleagues in other fields.

The OECD Teaching and Learning International Survey (TALIS) asks teachers and school leaders about the conditions that contribute to the learning environments in their schools. In so doing, it also verifies – and dispels – many of the myths that exist about teachers today. For example, when teachers are asked about class size and whether it has any detrimental effects on their job satisfaction or feelings of effectiveness as a teacher, their responses reveal that it is not the number of students in a class but the type of students (such as students with behavioural issues) that has the strongest association with the teacher's job satisfaction and feelings of self-efficacy.

TALIS data also indicate that most teachers are still teaching largely in isolation, as over half of teachers report very rarely or never team-teaching with colleagues, and two-thirds report the same rates for observing their colleagues teach. Some 46% of teachers report never receiving feedback on their teaching from their school leader, and 51% have never received feedback from other members of the school management. Only slightly more than a third of teachers in TALIS countries report that the feedback they receive on their teaching leads to a moderate or large positive change in the likelihood of career advancement. Similarly, less than a third of teachers believe that if a teacher is consistently under-performing, he or she would be dismissed.

Teachers also report that they work an average of 38 hours per week across countries, which could be considered an average work week for many fields. On average, half of teachers' time is spent teaching and half is spent on all of the other daily tasks that are required of teachers.

WHO ARE OUR TEACHERS AND WHERE ARE THEY WORKING?

The majority of lower secondary teachers are women in all countries surveyed, except for Japan. In fact, in 22 countries, at least two-thirds of teachers are women. While the average age of teachers across countries is 43, several countries may face significant teacher shortages as large numbers of teachers approach retirement age.

On average, teachers are well-educated, with the majority reporting that they completed university or equivalent education and a programme to prepare them for becoming a teacher. In addition, teachers whose formal training included the specific content, pedagogy and classroom practice of the subjects they teach report feeling better prepared for teaching.

Today's learning environments are, on average, well-resourced and relationships reported amongst the teaching staff and between teachers and students are generally positive. However, more than a third of teachers work in schools with significant staffing shortages of qualified teachers, teachers for students with special needs, and support personnel.

WHO ARE OUR SCHOOL LEADERS AND WHAT DO THEY DO?

In contrast to the population of lower secondary school teachers, half of the school leaders in TALIS schools are men. Principals are also well-educated, with the majority reporting that they completed tertiary education. At least three-quarters of principals report that this education included programmes in school administration, teacher preparation or instructional leadership.

While principals report spending the most time (41%), on average, managing human and material resources, planning, and reporting, they increasingly distribute leadership and decision-making tasks, which can benefit both the teachers and the principals themselves. Indeed, principals with heavy workloads who distribute tasks and decision making less also report lower levels of job satisfaction.

Distributing leadership also saves principals valuable time for what some consider the most important task: instructional leadership. Principals who report more instructional leadership tend to spend more time on curriculum and teaching-related tasks and are more likely to observe classroom teaching as part of the formal appraisal of teachers' work. In some countries, these principals more often report using the results of student performance and evaluations to develop the school's educational goals and programmes.

TO WHAT EXTENT DO TEACHERS PARTICIPATE IN PROFESSIONAL DEVELOPMENT ACTIVITIES?

As with the first cycle of TALIS in 2008, most lower secondary teachers report that they participate in professional development activities. In TALIS 2013, an average of 88% of teachers in lower secondary education report engaging in professional development in the previous year. The reasons most often cited by teachers for not participating in professional development activities are conflicts with work schedules and the absence of incentives for participation. In general, teachers report higher participation rates in professional development in countries where they also report higher levels of financial support. In some cases, even when monetary support is not offered, teachers who are offered non-monetary support, such as scheduled time for activities during the school day, report participating in professional development.

Formal teacher induction programmes are also shown to be important activities for teachers, although many teachers aren't taking advantage of this opportunity. TALIS data show that teachers' participation in formal induction programmes is an important predictor of their participation in professional development in later years. In addition, in 17 countries and economies, teachers who report having participated in a formal induction programme in the past are more likely to report that they currently act as a mentor for other teachers. However, even though most school principals report that induction programmes are available, not even half of teachers, on average, report that they participated in one during their first regular teaching job.

HOW ARE TEACHER APPRAISALS AND FEEDBACK USED?

Formal performance appraisal and feedback on practice help teachers improve. Teachers surveyed in TALIS agree that appraisals are helpful, as more than six in ten teachers report that appraisals lead to positive changes in their teaching practices, and more than half report that appraisals lead to positive changes in both their use of student assessments and their classroom-management practices. More than eight in ten teachers work in schools where formal appraisals at least sometimes lead to teacher development or training plans.

Yet the outcomes or impact of appraisal seem less apparent to the teachers surveyed in TALIS. Almost half of teachers report that appraisal and feedback are undertaken simply to fulfil administrative requirements. Annual increments in teacher pay are awarded regardless of the outcome of formal teacher appraisal in all but about one-fifth of schools. Some 44% of teachers work in schools whose principal reports that formal teacher appraisal never results in a change in a teacher's career advancement.

TALIS teachers receive formal or informal feedback on their practice in a variety of ways, from a variety of sources. Almost 80% of teachers report receiving feedback following classroom observation, and nearly two-thirds report receiving feedback following an analysis of student test scores. Nearly nine in ten teachers report that student performance, teachers' pedagogical competency in their subject, and classroom management are strongly emphasised in the feedback they receive.

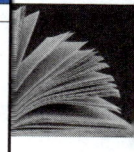

WHAT HAPPENS BEHIND CLASSROOM DOORS?

It is perhaps reassuring to learn that teachers in TALIS report that the majority of their classroom time is actually spent teaching. While teachers report spending about 80% of their time on teaching and learning, on average, approximately one in four teachers in more than half of the participating countries report losing at least 30% of their time to classroom disruptions and administrative tasks.

In spite of these disruptions, roughly two-thirds of teachers report a positive classroom climate, and these teachers are more likely to use active teaching practices, such as small group work, projects requiring more than a week for students to complete, and information and communication technologies. Teachers who report participating in professional development activities involving individual and collaborative research, observation visits to other schools, or a network of teachers are also more likely to use these practices.

WHAT GIVES TEACHERS GREATER JOB SATISFACTION?

As might be expected, in most TALIS countries and economies, teachers with more than five years of teaching experience report a stronger belief in their ability to teach (self-efficacy), as do teachers who work with their colleagues. In almost all countries, teachers who report participating in collaborative professional learning at least five times a year report notably greater self-efficacy.

TALIS findings show that, in nearly all countries, when teachers perceive that appraisal and feedback lead to changes in their teaching practice, they also report greater job satisfaction. When teachers believe that appraisal and feedback is performed only for administrative purposes they report less job satisfaction. In addition, teachers who report that they participate in decision making at school also report greater job satisfaction. Indeed, although fewer than a third of teachers believe that teaching is a valued profession in their country, those teachers who report that they can contribute to school decisions are more likely to report that teaching is valued in their society.

Teacher-student relations have an exceptionally powerful influence over teachers' job satisfaction. In almost all countries, when teachers have more students with behavioural problems, they report significantly less job satisfaction.

Reader's Guide

Statistics and analysis

This report presents statistics and analysis derived from the survey responses of teachers of lower secondary education (level 2 of the International Standard Classification of Education (ISCED-97)) and the principals of their schools.

Classification of levels of education

The classification of the levels of education is based on the revised International Standard Classification of Education (ISCED-97). ISCED is an instrument for compiling statistics on education internationally and distinguishes among six levels of education:

- Pre-primary education (ISCED level 0).
- Primary education (ISCED level 1).
- Lower secondary education (ISCED level 2).
- Upper secondary education (ISCED level 3).
- Post-secondary non-tertiary level of education (ISCED level 4).
- Tertiary-type A education (ISCED level 5A).
- Tertiary-type B education (ISCED level 5B).
- Advanced research qualifications (ISCED level 6).

While ISCED 2011 is now available, the first data collection based on the new classification will begin in 2014, meaning it was not available at the time of the TALIS 2013 data collection.

Data underlying the figures

The data referred to in this volume are presented in Annex C and in greater detail, including some additional tables on the web. These additional tables either contain more detail than similar tables that are published in the main report or refer to domains referred to but not examined in the report.

A *StatLink* URL is provided under each figure and table. Readers using the PDF version of the report can simply click on the relevant *StatLink* URL to either open or download a Microsoft Excel® workbook containing the corresponding figures and tables. Readers of the print version of this report can access the Excel® workbook by typing the *Statlink* URL into their internet browser.

Calculation of international average

TALIS averages were calculated for most indicators presented throughout this report. TALIS averages are calculated as the mean of the data values of the TALIS countries and economies included in the table. TALIS averages therefore refer to an average of data values at the level of the national systems.

Symbol for missing data

The following symbol is employed in the tables and charts to denote missing data:

a   The category does not apply in the country concerned. Data are therefore missing.

Abbreviations used in this report

The following abbreviations are used in this report:

ISCED	International Standard Classification of Education
rxy	Correlation coefficient
(S.E.)	Standard error

Rounding of figures

Because of rounding, some figures in tables may not exactly add up to the totals. Totals, differences and averages are always calculated on the basis of exact numbers and are rounded only after calculation.

All standard errors in this publication have been rounded to one decimal place. Where the value 0.00 is shown, this does not imply that the standard error is zero, but that it is smaller than 0.005.

Country Coverage

The TALIS 2013 publications feature data on 34 countries and economies, including 24 OECD countries and 10 partner countries and economies. The complete list of countries that participated in TALIS 2013 is listed in Chapter 1.

The data from the United States are located below the line in selected tables in this report and are not included in the calculations for the international average. This is because the United States did not meet the international standards for participation rates. See Annex A for more information.

The statistical data for Israel are supplied by and under the responsibility of relevant Israeli authorities. The use of such data by the OECD is without prejudice to the status of the Golan Heights, East Jerusalem and Israeli settlements in the West Bank under the terms of international law.

There are four subnational entities participating in TALIS 2013. They are referred to throughout the report in the following manner, consistent with other OECD publications:

- The province of Alberta, in Canada, is referred to as Alberta (Canada).
- The Flemish Community of Belgium is referred to as Flanders (Belgium).
- The nation of England is referred to as England (United Kingdom).
- The emirate of Abu Dhabi is referred to as Abu Dhabi (United Arab Emirates).

Two notes were added to the statistical data related to Cyprus.

1. Note by Turkey: The information in this document with reference to "Cyprus" relates to the southern part of the Island. There is no single authority representing both Turkish and Greek Cypriot people on the Island. Turkey recognises the Turkish Republic of Northern Cyprus (TRNC). Until a lasting and equitable solution is found within the context of the United Nations, Turkey shall preserve its position concerning the "Cyprus issue".

2. Note by all the European Union Member States of the OECD and the European Union: The Republic of Cyprus is recognised by all members of the United Nations with the exception of Turkey. The information in this document relates to the area under the effective control of the Government of the Republic of Cyprus.

Further documentation

For further information on TALIS documentation, the instruments and methodology see the *TALIS 2013 Technical Report* and the TALIS website (*www.oecd.org/edu/school/talis.htm*).

1

Overview of TALIS

This chapter introduces the Teaching and Learning International Survey (TALIS) and provides information about the participating countries and economies and the teachers and schools surveyed. It describes the objectives of TALIS as well as the main themes covered by the survey and this report, and provides information to explain why these themes were chosen as a policy focus for this study. This chapter also provides an outline of the report to follow.

WHAT IS TALIS?

The OECD Teaching and Learning International Survey (TALIS) is an international, large-scale survey that focuses on the working conditions of teachers and the learning environment in schools. TALIS aims to provide valid, timely and comparable information to help countries review and define policies for developing a high-quality teaching profession. It is an opportunity for teachers and school leaders to provide input into educational policy analysis and development in key areas and is a collaboration between participating countries, the OECD, an international research consortium, social partners and the European Commission.

Understanding that recruiting, retaining and developing teachers is a priority in school systems worldwide, TALIS examines the ways in which teachers' work is recognised, appraised and rewarded. TALIS assesses the degree to which teachers' professional-development needs are being met. The study provides insights into the beliefs and attitudes about teaching that teachers bring to the classroom and the pedagogical practices that they adopt. Recognising the important role that school leadership plays in fostering an effective teaching and learning environment, TALIS describes the role of school leaders and examines the support that they give their teachers. Finally, TALIS examines the extent to which certain factors may relate to teachers' feelings of job satisfaction and self-efficacy.

The first cycle of TALIS was conducted in 2008 and surveyed teachers and school leaders of lower secondary education in 24 countries. The initial report, *Creating Effective Teaching and Learning Environments: First Results from TALIS*, published in 2009, provided valuable findings that are still being used today. Two thematic reports were also written using the TALIS 2008 data. They were *The Experience of New Teachers: Results from TALIS 2008* and *Teaching Practices and Pedagogical Innovation: Evidence from TALIS*.

TALIS 2013

TALIS 2013 has expanded to include additional countries (Figure 1.1). While maintaining the focus on lower secondary education (ISCED level 2, as classified by the International Standard Classification of Education [ISCED 1997], which identifies comparable levels of education across countries), TALIS 2013 also gave countries the option of surveying teachers in their primary (ISCED level 1) and upper secondary (ISCED level 3) schools. Some countries chose to gain additional insights by conducting the survey in schools that participated in the 2012 Programme for International Student Assessment (PISA) through an option that is referred to as the TALIS-PISA link. (Figure 1.2 shows a complete list of countries and economies participating in all TALIS 2013 options.)

■ Figure 1.1 ■
Countries and economies participating in TALIS 2013

OECD Countries and Economies			Partner Countries and Economies
Alberta (Canada)	Flanders (Belgium)[1]	Netherlands	Abu Dhabi (United Arab Emirates)
Australia	France	Norway	Brazil
Chile	Iceland	Poland	Bulgaria
Czech Republic	Israel[1]	Portugal	Croatia
Denmark	Italy	Slovak Republic	Cyprus[2, 3]
England (United Kingdom)	Japan[1]	Spain	Latvia
Estonia	Korea[1]	Sweden	Malaysia[1]
Finland	Mexico	United States[4]	Romania
			Serbia[1]
			Singapore[1]

Note: Cells shaded in light blue indicate countries and economies that also participated in TALIS 2008.

1. See Annex A for notes about interpreting the data from these countries.

2. Note by Turkey: The information in this document with reference to "Cyprus" relates to the southern part of the Island. There is no single authority representing both Turkish and Greek Cypriot people on the Island. Turkey recognises the Turkish Republic of Northern Cyprus (TRNC). Until a lasting and equitable solution is found within the context of the United Nations, Turkey shall preserve its position concerning the "Cyprus issue".

3. Note by all the European Union Member States of the OECD and the European Union: The Republic of Cyprus is recognised by all members of the United Nations with the exception of Turkey. The information in this document relates to the area under the effective control of the Government of the Republic of Cyprus.

4. The data from the United States are located below the line in selected tables in this report and is not included in the calculations for the international average. This is because the United States did not meet the international standards for participation rates. See Annex A for more information.

■ Figure 1.2 ■
Countries and economies participating in TALIS options

ISCED 1	ISCED 3	TALIS-PISA link
Denmark	Abu Dhabi (United Arab Emirates)	Australia
Finland	Australia	Finland
Flanders (Belgium)	Denmark	Latvia
Mexico	Finland	Mexico
Norway	Iceland	Portugal
Poland	Italy	Romania
	Mexico[1]	Singapore
	Norway	Spain
	Poland	
	Singapore[1]	

1. See Annex A for notes about interpreting the data from these countries.

THE AIMS OF TALIS

The overall objective of TALIS is to provide robust international indicators and policy-relevant analysis on teachers and teaching in a timely and cost-effective manner. These indicators help countries review and develop policies in their efforts to promote conditions for high-quality teaching and learning. Cross-country analyses provide the opportunity to compare countries facing similar challenges to learn about different policy approaches and their impact on the learning environment in schools.

The guiding principles underlying the survey strategy are as follows:

- *Policy relevance*. Clarity about key policy issues and a focus on the questions that are most relevant for participating countries are both essential.
- *Value added*. International comparisons should be a significant source of the study's benefits.
- *Indicator-oriented*. The results should yield information that can be used to develop indicators.
- *Validity, reliability, comparability and rigour*. Based on a rigorous review of the knowledge base, the survey should yield information that is valid, reliable and comparable across participating countries.
- *Interpretability*. Participating countries should be able to interpret the results in a meaningful way.
- *Efficiency and cost-effectiveness*. The work should be carried out in a timely and cost-effective way.

The population surveyed

The international sampling guidelines and other operational parameters applied in TALIS for the core (ISCED 2) survey are shown in Box 1.1. Further details, including teacher and school participation rates by country, are given in Annex A.

Box 1.1. **The TALIS Design**

International target population: Lower secondary education teachers and leaders of mainstream schools.

Target sample size: 200 schools per country; 20 teachers and 1 school leader in each school.

School samples: Representative samples of schools and teachers within schools.

Target response rates: 75% of the sampled schools, together with a 75% response rate from all sampled teachers in the country. A school is considered to have responded if 50% of sampled teachers respond.

Questionnaires: Separate questionnaires for teachers and school leaders, each requiring between 45 and 60 minutes to complete.

Mode of data collection: Questionnaires filled in on paper or on line.

Survey windows: September-December 2012 for Southern Hemisphere countries and February-June 2013 for Northern Hemisphere countries.

The sample size for the ISCED 1 and ISCED 3 options is the same as the sample size for ISCED 2: 200 schools per country and 20 teachers and 1 school leader per school. For the TALIS-PISA link, 150 schools per country were surveyed, with an oversample of mathematics teachers in each school. The target response rates for all TALIS survey options were the same as those for the core ISCED 2 sample, delineated in Box 1.1. Further details on the sample for all target populations can be found in Annex A.

Who is a TALIS teacher?

TALIS defines a teacher as one whose primary or major activity in the school is student instruction, involving the delivery of lessons to students. Teachers may work with students as a whole class, in small groups or one-to-one inside or outside regular classrooms. They might also share their teaching time among more than one school.

For the purposes of TALIS, the definition of a teacher does not include the following school-staff categories:

- Teacher aides: Non-professional or paraprofessional staff who might support teachers in providing instruction to students.
- Pedagogical support staff: Those who provide services to students to support the instructional programme, such as librarians or guidance counsellors.
- Health and social support staff: Health professionals such as doctors, nurses, psychiatrists, psychologists, occupational therapists and social workers.

The following profiles of teachers are also excluded from the target population of teachers: substitute, emergency or occasional teachers; teachers teaching adults exclusively; and teachers on long-term leave. However, different from TALIS 2008, eligible teachers in TALIS 2013 also include teachers in regular schools who instruct students with special needs.

TALIS 2013 policy themes

The themes selected for study in the second cycle of TALIS were chosen as part of a priority rating exercise by the countries participating in TALIS 2013. Countries decided to retain some topics that were covered in TALIS 2008 and added some new questions and indicators as well. The participating countries chose the following policy themes for TALIS 2013:

- School leadership, including new indicators on distributed or team leadership.
- Teacher training, including professional development and new indicators on initial teacher education.
- Appraisal of and feedback to teachers.
- Teachers' pedagogical beliefs, attitudes and teaching practices, including new indicators on the profile of student-assessment practices.
- Teachers' reported feelings of self-efficacy, their job satisfaction and the climate in the schools and classrooms in which they work.

A conceptual framework was developed by subject-matter experts, the international research consortium and the OECD Secretariat and was approved by participating countries. The purposes of the conceptual framework were to steer development of the TALIS instruments and serve as a guide for future TALIS cycles.

The *Teaching and Learning International Survey: Conceptual Framework* (OECD, 2013) is based on the concept of effective teaching and learning conditions. According to the OECD, effectiveness refers to the extent to which the stated objectives of a given activity are met (OECD, 2007). Thus, the concept of effectiveness is simultaneously broad and dependent on context. In the case of TALIS, effective teaching and learning environments are environments that contribute to student learning. The TALIS 2013 themes and the individual items that they comprise represent the elements that participating countries and economies agree contribute to student learning. These include some elements that have yet to be proven to be related to positive student outcomes. Of course, effective teaching and learning may include many other factors that cannot be examined through TALIS or any self-reported instrument.

An Instrument Development Expert Group (IDEG) was established to translate the policy priorities into questionnaires to address the policy and analytical questions agreed to by the participating countries and economies. Separate questionnaires for teachers and school leaders were prepared. Considerable effort was devoted to achieving cultural and linguistic validity of the survey instruments, and stringent quality assurance mechanisms were applied both for their translation and for the sampling and data collection. (See the *TALIS 2013 Technical Report* [OECD, 2014] for more details.)

Administering TALIS

The development of TALIS has been the result of productive co-operation between the participating member countries of the OECD and partner countries. A Board of Participating Countries, representing all of the countries and economies taking part in TALIS, set out the policy objectives for the survey and established the standards for data collection and reporting. A key partner in both cycles of TALIS has been the European Commission, which has provided not only support for European Member States participating in TALIS but also expertise and further analyses of the TALIS data in particular areas. Engagement with bodies representing teachers and regular briefings and exchanges with the Trade Union Advisory Committee (TUAC) at the OECD have been very important in the development and implementation of TALIS. In particular, the co-operation of the teachers and school leaders in the participating schools has been crucial in ensuring the success of TALIS.

Participating countries implemented TALIS at the national level through National Project Managers (NPMs) and National Data Managers (NDMs), who adhered to rigorous technical and operational procedures. The NPMs played a crucial role in helping to secure the co-operation of schools, validate the questionnaires, manage the national data collection and process and verify the results from TALIS. The NDMs co-ordinated the data processing at the national level and aided in the cleaning of the data.

The co-ordination and management of implementation at the international level was the responsibility of the appointed contractor, the International Association for the Evaluation of Educational Achievement (IEA). The study's implementation was led by the IEA's Data Processing and Research Center (DPC). The IEA Secretariat was responsible for overseeing the verification of translations and for quality control of the data collection. Statistics Canada, as a subcontractor of the IEA, developed the sampling plan, advised countries on its application, acted as the sampling referee, calculated the sampling weights and advised on the calculation of sampling errors.

The OECD Secretariat had overall responsibility for managing the programme, monitoring its implementation on a day-to-day basis and serving as the secretariat of the Board of Participating Countries. (See Annex D for a list of contributors to TALIS.)

Interpretation of the results

TALIS results are based on self-reports from teachers and school leaders and therefore represent their opinions, perceptions, beliefs and accounts of their activities. This is powerful information because it provides insight into how teachers perceive the learning environments in which they work, what motivates teachers and how policies that are put in place are carried out in practice. But, as with any self-reported data, this information is subjective and therefore differs from objectively collected data. The same is true of school leaders' reports about school characteristics, which may differ from descriptions provided by administrative data at a national- or local-government level.

In addition, as a cross-sectional survey, TALIS cannot measure causality. For instance, in examining the relationship between school climate and teacher co-operation, it is not possible to establish whether a positive school climate depends on good teacher co-operation or whether good teacher co-operation depends on a positive school climate. The perspective taken in the analysis – i.e. the choice of predicted and predictor variables – is based purely on theoretical considerations, as laid out in the analytical framework. When a reference is made to "effects", the reference should be understood in a statistical sense – i.e. an effect is a statistical parameter that describes the linear relationship between a predicted variable (e.g. job satisfaction) and a predictor variable (e.g. participation in professional development activities) – taking effects of individual and school background as well as other independent variables into account. Thus, the effects reported are statistical net effects even if they do not imply causality.

Additionally, the cross-cultural validity of the results is an important feature of the analysis, particularly with regard to the international scales and indices (see Annex B). The analysis indicates the extent to which the scales can be compared among countries; where there appear to be limitations on the comparability of the scales, this is noted in the text. Full details of the cross-cultural validity analysis are provided in the *TALIS 2013 Technical Report* (OECD, 2014).

Finally, even for those countries that participated in the TALIS-PISA link, the intention of TALIS is not to measure the effects of teaching on student outcomes. Neither the design of PISA nor the design of TALIS is amenable to analyses of teacher and teaching effectiveness, and the purpose of the TALIS-PISA link is to use school-level data from PISA to contextualise teachers' responses in TALIS. Because TALIS cannot measure teaching effectiveness directly, it looks at themes that are not only policy priorities for participating countries but have also been shown in the research literature to be associated with high-quality teaching.

Organisation of the report

The following chapters of this report present the analyses, results and policy recommendations emerging from TALIS 2013. The report aims to tell a story that begins with the profiles of teachers and school leaders and continues with the reports of the conditions in which they work and the factors influencing their work, with an aim of providing a more detailed picture of the learning environments in these countries. While this report focuses mainly on lower secondary teachers, each chapter also presents some data and analyses for key indicators from primary and upper secondary teachers as well.[1]

- Chapter 2 presents a description of the characteristics of the lower secondary teacher populations and the schools in which they work. In doing so, it provides an important context for the later analytical chapters.

- Chapter 3 has at its centre the key role played by school leaders in ensuring that teachers receive the support they need to be as effective as possible. It will look at the profile of leaders in these teachers' schools and will also set the stage for the introduction of key factors in supporting teachers in their work.

- Chapter 4 looks at the issue of professional development as a tool to improve teaching and studies the data on teachers' experiences with professional development, whether they still have development needs and how any unsatisfied needs for professional development might be met.

- Chapter 5 examines the importance of the appraisal and feedback that teachers receive on their teaching along with the impact it has on their practice.

- Chapter 6 focuses on the teaching itself by exploring the relationships between various factors and a teacher's reported practices. It makes connections between many of the themes in previous chapters and how they influence the way a teacher teaches. Teachers' beliefs about student learning and instruction are also investigated.

- Chapter 7 returns to the various factors examined in the previous chapters and describes how they can come together to influence the teaching and learning environment. It looks at the effects of these and other factors on a teacher's feelings of self-efficacy and levels of job satisfaction.

Note

1. The TALIS-PISA link survey option will be discussed in a separate report. A full report on the ISCED 1 and 3 options will be released separately.

A note regarding Israel

The statistical data for Israel are supplied by and under the responsibility of the relevant Israeli authorities. The use of such data by the OECD is without prejudice to the status of the Golan Heights, East Jerusalem and Israeli settlements in the West Bank under the terms of international law.

References

Jensen, B. et al. (2012), *The Experience of New Teachers: Results from TALIS 2008,* OECD Publishing, Paris, *http://dx.doi.org/10.1787/9789264120952-en*

OECD (2014), *TALIS 2013 Technical Report, www.oecd.org/edu/school/TALIS-technical-report-2013.pdf.*

OECD (2013), *Teaching and Learning International Survey: Conceptual Framework, www.oecd.org/edu/school/TALIS%202013% 20Conceptual%20Framework.pdf.*

OECD (2009), *Creating Effective Teaching and Learning Environments: First Results from TALIS*, OECD Publishing, Paris, *http://dx.doi.org/10.1787/9789264072992-en*

OECD (2007), *Glossary of Statistical Terms*, OECD, Paris. Retrieved from: *http://stats.oecd.org/glossary/index.htm.*

Vieluf S. et al. (2012), *Teaching Practices and Pedagogical Innovation: Evidence from TALIS,* OECD Publishing, Paris, *http://dx.doi.org/10.1787/9789264123540-en*

2

Teachers and their Schools

This chapter provides background information about the teachers surveyed as part of the OECD Teaching and Learning International Survey (TALIS) and the schools in which they work. The first part of the chapter focuses on demographic characteristics such as the age and gender of teachers, their formal education and their previous work experience. The second section of the chapter provides a profile of the schools in which teachers work, with particular emphasis on school background information, resources, composition of students at the school, the level of autonomy enjoyed at the school level and school climate. In addition, this chapter begins to look at issues of equity in education systems by examining the distribution of teachers across the systems and also provides a basis for analyses conducted in subsequent chapters of this volume.

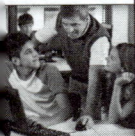

Highlights

- Teachers who benefited from formal education that included content, pedagogy and practical components for the subjects they teach feel better prepared for their work than their colleagues whose formal education did not contain these elements.

- More than half of lower secondary teachers in all TALIS countries and economies except Japan are women, and in 22 countries two-thirds or more of teachers are women. Furthermore, several countries may face the prospect of significant teacher shortages as a result of large numbers of teachers reaching retirement age.

- More than a third of teachers work in schools where the school principal reported a significant shortage of qualified teachers. Additionally, almost half of teachers work in schools where there is a reported need for teachers of students with special needs and a need for support personnel.

- Across most TALIS countries and economies, the majority of teachers work in environments with a positive professional climate among the teaching staff. This positive climate is characterised by a common set of beliefs, mutual respect for colleagues' ideas, a culture of sharing success, high levels of co-operation between the school and the local community and the ability to have open discussions about difficulties.

- Most teachers work in schools in which there is little to no authority at the school level for making decisions related to teacher pay. In almost all countries, however, a large proportion of teachers work in schools that enjoy a high level of autonomy for establishing student disciplinary procedures or selecting the learning materials used.

INTRODUCTION

Teachers play a crucial role in education systems – they are the front-line workers responsible for engaging students and promoting their learning. It is now widely accepted that within schools, teacher- and teaching-related factors are the most important factors that influence student learning (e.g. Darling-Hammond, 2000; Konstantopoulos, 2006; Rivkin, Hanushek and Kain, 2005; Rockoff, 2004; Scheerens, Vermeulen and Pelgrum, 1989; Scheerens, 1993; Willms, 2000). As such, countries are especially interested in learning more about their own teaching workforce and making comparisons with other countries in order to develop more effective policies to improve teaching and learning. This chapter provides a profile of lower secondary teachers (referred to simply as "teachers" unless otherwise specified), looks at the extent to which they are distributed equitably across their education system and describes the schools in which they work.

The analyses presented in this chapter and Chapter 3 (on school principals and school leadership) not only provide a picture of the teaching workforce and the contextual school environment in which teachers work across TALIS countries and economies, but also set the scene for the analyses in subsequent chapters of this volume.

This chapter is divided into two main sections. The first section focuses on teacher characteristics and provides a profile of lower secondary teachers (with selected information provided for primary and upper secondary teachers). Analyses in this section focus on demographic characteristics such as the age and gender of teachers, their employment status, their formal education and their previous work experience. This chapter also looks at these characteristics in relation to how teachers are distributed across a system, in rural or urban areas or in schools deemed to be in more or less challenging environments. Profiles of school principals are examined in Chapter 3.[1]

The second section of this chapter provides a profile of the schools in which teachers work, with particular emphasis on school background information, human and material resources, the composition of students at the school, school autonomy and school climate. Because TALIS focuses on teachers and teachers' working conditions, it is important to note that, as in the first cycle of TALIS, most of the tables and charts in this section and in most of the report are presented from a teacher perspective. This focus becomes particularly apparent in the second section of this chapter, where the data represent the *proportion of teachers who work in schools* with certain characteristics rather than the *proportion of schools* with certain characteristics.[2] In cases where the policy issue is most interesting at the school level in particular (especially in Chapter 3), analyses were performed accordingly (*proportion of schools*), and this is clearly noted under the tables in question.

WHO IS TEACHING IN LOWER SECONDARY SCHOOLS?

While some countries have staffing surveys or census information that provide a profile of teachers in the school system, the TALIS survey offers an international comparison of teacher characteristics across the participating countries and economies. Teachers were asked to provide background information on themselves, their education and work experience, their current employment status and the kind of training (if any) they received in the process of joining the teaching profession.

Teachers' gender and age

The demographic characteristics of teachers are of interest to policy makers and researchers in their own right. The potential impacts of gender imbalance in the teaching profession on issues such as student achievement, student motivation, teacher retention and others represent policy concerns in a number of countries where very few males are attracted to the profession (Drudy, 2008; OECD, 2005, 2009). This gender imbalance seems to be common in many regions of the world. It is most prominent in pre-primary and primary education, though the differences persist well into secondary education in many countries (OECD, 2013a; UNESCO Institute for Statistics, 2006, 2009). There is little evidence that a teacher's gender has an impact on student performance (e.g. Antecol, Eren and Ozbeklik, 2012; Holmlund and Sund, 2008), although there is some evidence that female teachers' attitudes towards subjects such as mathematics can have an impact on their female students' achievement (Beilock et al., 2009). Finally, some evidence suggests that male teachers stay in the profession longer (Ingersoll, 2001), while other research conducted in Finland suggests the opposite (Blomqvist et al., 2008).

■ Figure 2.1 ■
Gender and age distribution of teachers

Percentage of lower secondary education female teachers and age of teachers

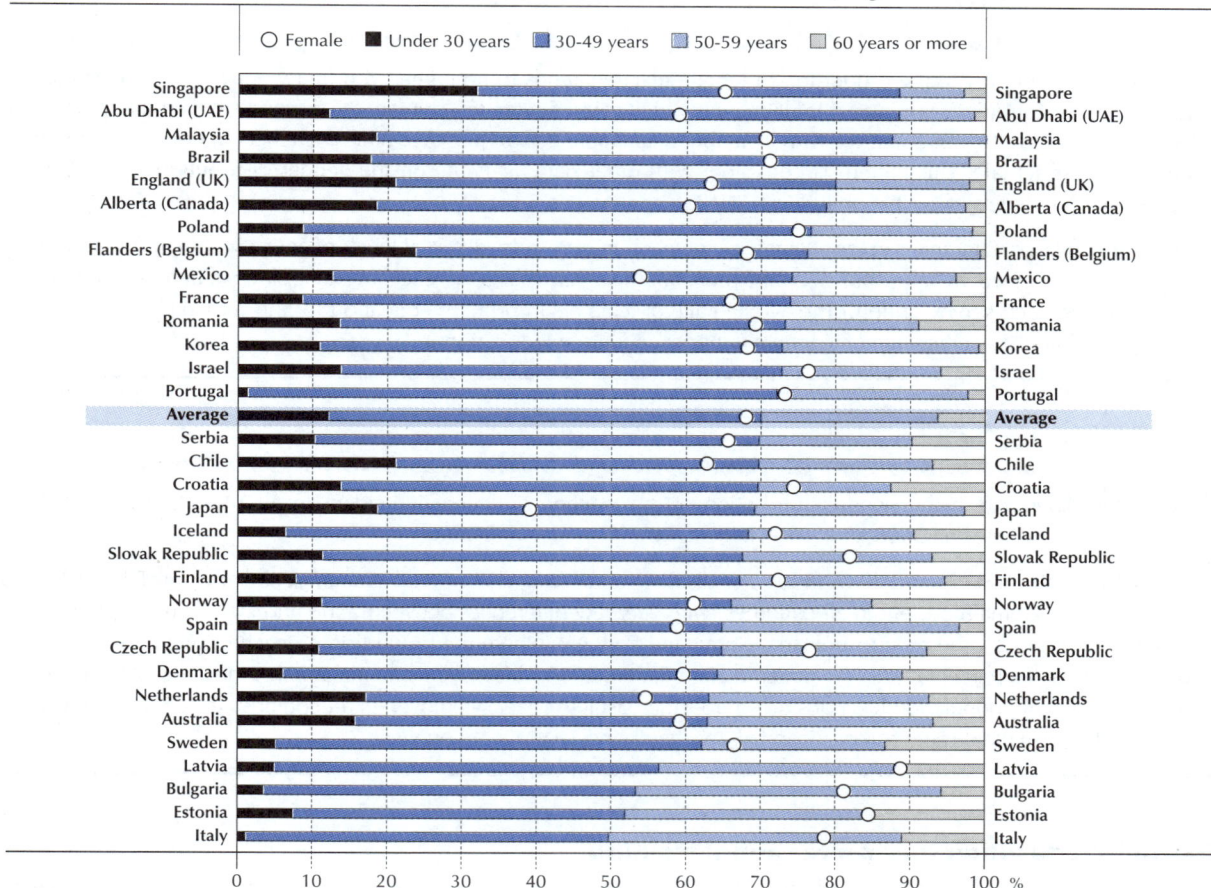

Countries are ranked in descending order, based on the percentage of teachers aged 49 or younger.
Source: OECD, TALIS 2013 Database, Table 2.1.
StatLink ▇▇▇ http://dx.doi.org/10.1787/888933041117

Gaining information about the age distribution of the teaching workforce is also valuable to policy makers. Some countries face important challenges related to their aging teacher workforce, with a high proportion of teachers nearing retirement age (OECD, 2009, 2013a). The age of teachers has also been found to be related to teacher attrition in schools: Attrition rates tend to be higher in the first few years of teaching and decline the longer that teachers are in the profession (OECD, 2005; Ingersoll, 2001).

Table 2.1 and Figure 2.1 examine gender and age distribution of teachers, and Box 2.1 examines data for primary and upper secondary education in the countries that implemented the survey for these teacher populations. Box 2.2 compares data from countries that also participated in TALIS 2008.

In all TALIS countries and economies, with the exception of Japan, more than half of the lower secondary education teaching workforce is made up of women. On average, 68% of all teachers are female. More than eight out of ten teachers in secondary education are female in Bulgaria (81%), Estonia (84%), Latvia (89%) and the Slovak Republic (82%). On the other side of the spectrum, fewer than six out of ten teachers are women in Australia (59%), Japan (39%), Mexico (54%), the Netherlands (55%), Spain (59%) and Abu Dhabi (United Arab Emirates) (59%).

Given concerns in many countries about an aging teacher population, it is significant that, on average, only 12% of secondary teachers are younger than 30 years, while 30% are 50 or older. The average age of lower secondary teachers in TALIS countries and economies is 43 years. Singapore has the youngest teacher workforce with an average age of 36 years while Italy has the oldest teacher population with an average age of 49 years.

Estonia and Norway have the highest proportions of teachers aged 60 or more (16% and 15%, respectively), while in a number of countries, nearly half of the teachers are 50 years or older (Bulgaria, Estonia and Italy). On the other hand, Singapore has the largest proportion of teachers aged below 30 years (32%).

Box 2.1. **Gender and age distribution of primary and upper secondary education teachers**

As shown in Table 2.1.a, the proportion of female teachers tends to be higher in primary education. On average across the six countries with available data, nearly eight out of every ten primary teachers are female. In contrast, on average across the ten countries with available data (Table 2.1.b), just over half of teachers in upper secondary education are female. This pattern is consistent with other data available on the gender distribution of teachers across different levels of education (OECD, 2013a).

There are no large differences in the average age of teachers across the different levels of education. (Any differences in the average need to take into account the countries that make up each average since different countries implemented each survey option.) The average age of teachers in primary education for the six TALIS countries is 43 years, while the average age of teachers in upper secondary education is 45 years.

Box 2.2. **Comparisons of gender and age distribution with TALIS 2008 data**

Very little difference in the gender distribution of the teacher workforce is evident in all TALIS countries with comparable data between 2008 and 2013 (Table 2.1.c).

TALIS 2008 showed large variations in the age distribution of teachers between countries. As shown in Table 2.1.c, these variations remain present in all countries, with very few differences between 2008 and 2013. An exception to this general trend can be seen in Bulgaria, Korea and Portugal, where the proportion of teachers aged 50 years or older is at least ten percentage points higher in 2013 than in 2008. This may be an indicator that the aging of the lower secondary teacher population has not slowed over the past few years. Moreover, in all countries except for Norway, there is also a smaller proportion of secondary teachers aged 30 years or younger.

Teachers' education and professional training

Teachers' pre-service education and training are just the beginning of their professional continuum of learning (European Commission, 2012; OECD, 2005; Ward et al., 2013). Indeed, the extent, the content and the quality of teachers' education can influence their future in-service learning needs. The research literature presents inconsistent findings

regarding the impact of teacher education and experience on student achievement. Some studies have shown limited or no relationship between teacher educational attainment, teacher qualifications and student outcomes (Buddin and Zamarro, 2009; Croninger et al., 2007; Harris and Sass, 2011; Larsen, 2010). Other studies and reviews have shown positive relationships between initial education (either in terms of its level or its content) or the process of obtaining teacher certification and teaching effectiveness (Clotfelter, Ladd and Vigdor, 2007, 2010; Darling-Hammond et al., 2005; Monk, 1994; Ronfeldt and Reininger, 2012). For example, Ronfeldt and Reininger (2012) found that the quality (rather than the duration) of the practical component of teacher education programmes can have positive impacts on select outcomes of pre-service teachers, such as their perception of preparedness, their efficacy and their career plans.

Table 2.2 summarises the highest level of formal education completed by secondary teachers. This table presents the percentages of teachers with various levels of education, as defined by the International Standard Classification of Education (ISCED 1997), which identifies comparable levels of education across countries. ISCED 5 represents the first stages of tertiary education and is split between ISCED levels 5A and 5B. ISCED level 5B programmes are generally more practically oriented and shorter than programmes at ISCED level 5A. ISCED level 5A typically includes Bachelor's degrees and Master's degrees from universities or equivalent institutions. ISCED level 6 represents further education at the tertiary level that leads to an advanced research qualification such as a Doctorate degree.

As shown in Table 2.2, in most countries, the great majority of teachers report having obtained formal education at the level of ISCED 5A. An exception to this is Flanders (Belgium), where 85% of the teachers have completed ISCED level 5B. Country differences often reflect the differences in qualification requirements among countries. In Flanders (Belgium), an ISCED level 5B education is required to be fully certified to teach in secondary education. On average, very few teachers (2%) have not completed tertiary education, although teachers with less than a tertiary education were most commonly found in Iceland (10%) and Mexico (9%).

Box 2.3 examines the educational attainment of primary and upper secondary teachers in those countries that have implemented TALIS for those populations, and Box 2.4 compares findings from TALIS 2008 and TALIS 2013 for countries with available data.

Box 2.3. **The educational attainment of primary and upper secondary teachers**

Tables 2.2.a and 2.2.b show that teachers' educational attainment levels are similar at the primary and upper secondary levels; the great majority of teachers in all participating countries completed ISCED level 5A (79% of primary teachers and 91% of upper secondary teachers on average).

Box 2.4. **Comparisons of lower secondary teachers' educational attainment with TALIS 2008**

As Table 2.2.c shows, overall, the proportion of teachers who have completed each level of education and training is very similar between 2008 and 2013 (less than three percentage points difference at each ISCED level). It is interesting to point out that some countries, such as Brazil and Bulgaria, have seen a slight decrease in their proportion of teachers without tertiary education (below ISCED level 5).

Table 2.3 shows that in all TALIS countries and economies, the majority of teachers report having completed a teacher education or training programme, ranging from 62% in Mexico and 71% in Serbia to at least 98% in Australia, Bulgaria, Poland, Singapore, Alberta (Canada) and Flanders (Belgium).

The structure, content and emphasis of initial teacher education all vary greatly across countries (Darling-Hammond and Lieberman, 2012; OECD, 2005), but teacher formal education usually includes opportunities for the development of practical experience alongside subject-matter training and pedagogical training. Table 2.3 also presents the percentage of teachers who report that these elements of teaching were included in their formal education for all or for some of the subjects they teach (see also Figure 2.2).

On average, 72% of teachers report having received formal education that included content for all the subjects they currently teach. A further 23% of teachers report having received prior content training for at least some of their subjects.

In Iceland and Alberta (Canada), less than half of the teachers (42% and 44%, respectively) report that their formal education included content for *all* the subjects they teach, which indicates a high proportion of teachers who are teaching subjects for which they may not have been specifically prepared as part of their formal education (Figure 2.2, right panel).

With respect to pedagogy, on average 70% of secondary teachers report that their formal education included pedagogy for all the subjects they teach and nearly one-quarter (23%) for some of the subjects they teach. Proportions are similar for practical components: On average, 67% of teachers report that their formal education included classroom practice in all of the subjects they teach, while 22% report it included practice in some of the subjects they teach. On one hand, Italy stands out, with only 35% of its teachers reporting that they had practical components for all the subjects they teach and an additional 12% for some of the subjects they teach. On the other hand, at least eight in ten teachers in Bulgaria (84%), Croatia (86%), Latvia (80%), the Netherlands (82%), Poland (88%), Romania (82%), Singapore (83%) and England (United Kingdom) (81%) report that their formal education included classroom practice for all the subjects they teach. TALIS data show, then, that overall, a majority of teachers have indeed received formal content and pedagogical training and a practical component for some or all of the subjects they currently teach (Figure 2.2).

■ Figure 2.2 ■
Teachers' feelings of preparedness for teaching

Percentage of lower secondary education teachers who feel "very well prepared", "well prepared", "somewhat prepared" or "not at all prepared" for the content and the pedagogy of the subject(s) they teach and whether these were included in their formal education and training

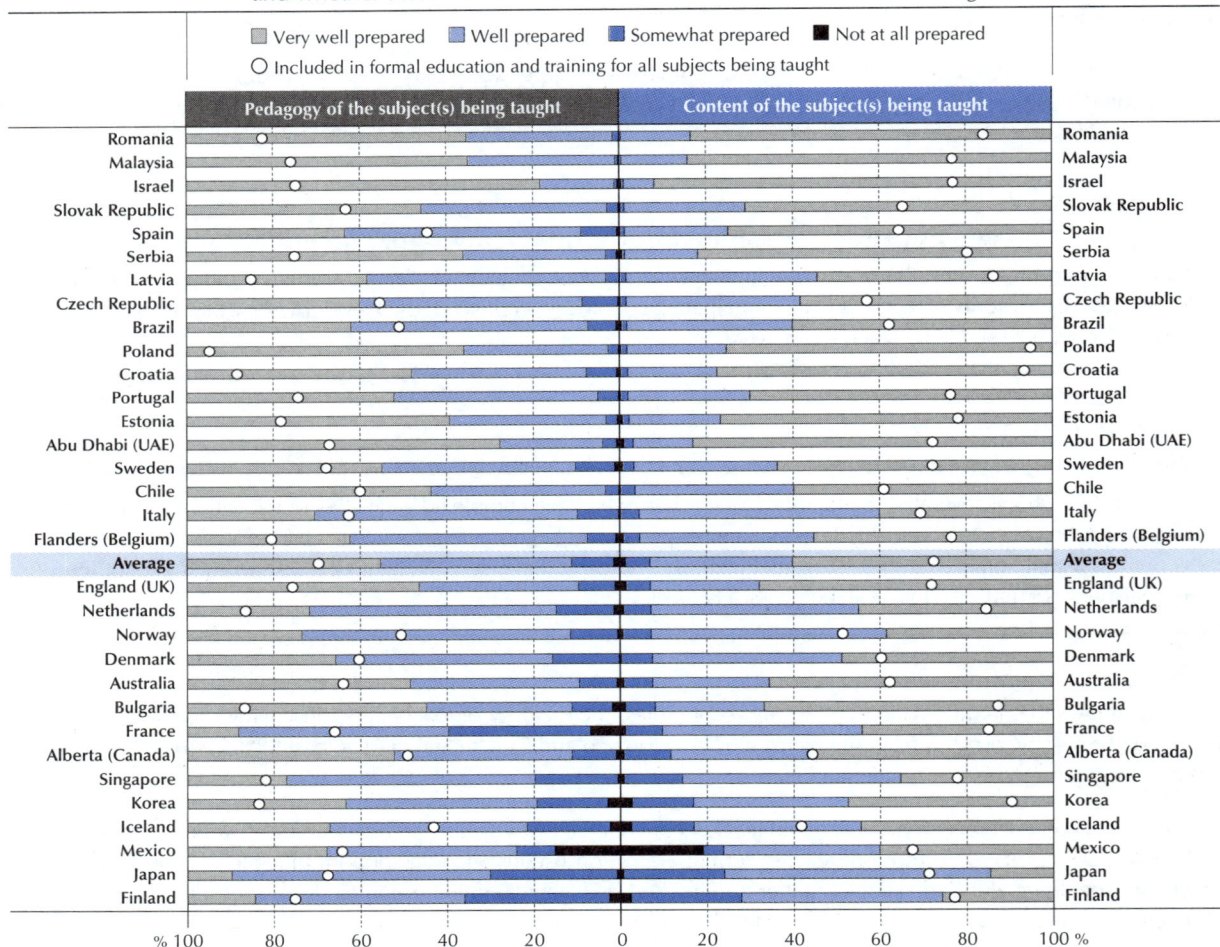

Countries are ranked in ascending order, based on the percentage of teachers who feel "not at all prepared" or "somewhat prepared" for the content of the subject(s) being taught.
Source: OECD, TALIS 2013 Database, Tables 2.3 and 2.4.
StatLink ᵐˢᵖ http://dx.doi.org/10.1787/888933041136

In general, teachers find that their formal education prepared them well for their work as teachers (Table 2.4 and Figure 2.2). On average, 93% of teachers report being well or very well prepared to teach the content of the subjects they teach, and 89% feel well or very well prepared in terms of the pedagogy and the practical components of the subjects they teach. However, it is striking that around a quarter or more of teachers in Finland, Japan and Mexico do not feel prepared or feel only somewhat prepared to teach the content, pedagogy and practical components of the subjects they teach (Figure 2.2).

What is it about a teacher's formal education, then, that makes the teacher feel more or less prepared for teaching? Country-level logistic regression analyses (described in Box 2.5) were performed to examine the relationship between specific elements included in teachers' formal education or training and how prepared teachers feel when encountering those elements in their teaching (Table 2.5). For some countries, the overall percentage of teachers not feeling prepared is too low to draw conclusions (Table 2.4),[3] so only those countries in which a minimum of 5% of the teachers report not feeling prepared for these elements are further elaborated upon here. In all of these countries, the components of teachers' education and training seem to matter: Teachers are more likely to report feeling prepared for the content, pedagogy or classroom practice element of their teaching if this element was included in their formal training for some or all of the subjects they teach. As one would expect, the upward trend of feeling prepared is even stronger if teachers received this formal training for *all* of the subjects they teach (as opposed to only *some* of the subjects they teach).

When it comes to content matters, teachers in six countries are at least four times more likely to report feeling prepared if they received formal training in the content of all of the subjects they teach than if they had not. This effect is most pronounced for teachers in Bulgaria and France. In 13 countries, teachers trained in pedagogy are also at least four times more likely to feel prepared for these elements in their teaching. The countries that stand out in this area are Norway and, again, Bulgaria, where teachers are 9 and 18 times more likely (respectively) to feel prepared compared with teachers who had not received such training. Finally, in seven countries teachers are again at least four times as likely to feel prepared for classroom practice if this was included in their formal training. In Bulgaria, this association is even more dramatic, as teachers there are 15 times more likely to feel prepared for these aspects if these practical elements were included in the teachers' education for all of the subjects they teach than if they had not been included.

What these data show is that not only does a teacher's formal education (including teacher initial education) help them feel better prepared for their work as a teacher, but the specific elements included in that training, such as content and pedagogical training and classroom practice, can make a significant difference as well.

Box 2.5. **Description of logistic regression analysis**

Logistic regression analysis enables the estimation of the relationship between one or more independent variables (predictors) on categorical dependent (predicted) variables with two categories (binary logistic regression) or more than two categories (multinomial logistic regression). (Multinomial logistic regression compares multiple groups through a combination of binary logistic regressions.) Logistic regression analyses were carried out for each country separately because prior analysis showed noticeable differences in regression coefficients between countries. When a logistic regression is calculated, the statistical software (SPSS) output generates first the regression coefficient (ß), which is the estimated increase in the log odds of the *outcome per unit increase* in the value of the *predictor variable*. Additionally, the exponential function of the regression coefficient (exp(ß)) is obtained, which is the odds ratio (OR) associated with a one-unit increase in the predictor variable. The transformation of log odds (ß) into odds ratios (exp(ß); OR) makes the data more interpretable in terms of probability. Three outcomes are possible for the odds ratios:

- OR = 1 Predictor variable does not affect odds of outcome

- OR > 1 Predictor variable associated with higher odds of outcome

- OR < 1 Predictor variable associated with lower odds of outcome

...

In the text, the language of odds ratios was made more accessible by reformulating and rounding up in terms of likelihood and probabilities.

In odds ratios, categories are compared with a predetermined reference category. For example, the combined "not at all/somewhat" prepared group was chosen as a reference category for the analysis examining the extent to which teachers feel that the contents of their formal education prepared them for their current work. Odds ratios can be interpreted in such a way that for a unit change in the predictor variable (e.g. having received formal training of content components for ALL of the subjects teachers teach, for SOME of the subjects teachers teach, or for NONE of the subjects teachers teach), the odds ratio of the outcome variable (e.g. feeling "well/very well" prepared for the content elements in the subjects teachers teach) relative to the reference category (e.g. feeling "not at all/somewhat" prepared) is expected to change by a factor of the respective parameter estimate, given that the variables in the model are held constant. In this particular analysis, the background variables included as control variables were teacher's gender, years of experience, subjects taught and level of education.

Note that with cross-sectional data such as the TALIS data, no direction of impact can be established. Hence, it is not possible to distinguish empirically between, for example, a model that describes teachers feeling prepared for the content of subjects they teach as dependent on teachers' formal education and a model that describes teachers' formal education as dependent on the teachers feeling prepared for the content of subjects they teach. The perspective taken – i.e. the choice of independent and dependent variables – is entirely based on logic, experience and theoretical considerations.

Work experience of teachers

Along with teacher educational attainment, teachers' work experience helps shape their skills and competencies. A teacher's tenure may also affect his or her willingness to implement innovative practices or reforms (Goodson, Moore and Hargreaves, 2006).

The relationship between teacher experience and student achievement has been repeatedly examined in empirical studies (Clotfelter, Ladd and Vigdor, 2007, 2010; Croninger et al., 2007; Leigh, 2010). In Hanushek and Rivkin's (2004) review, 41% of methodologically sound studies showed positive relationships between teacher experience and student achievement, while in 56% the results were positive but non-significant. Years of experience may especially matter early in a teacher's career. Some evidence shows that each additional year of experience is related to higher student achievement, especially during a teacher's first five years in the profession (Rockoff, 2004; Rivkin, Hanushek and Kain, 2005; Harris and Sass, 2011).

Table 2.6 presents the number of years that teachers report working as a teacher, working in other educational roles and working in other jobs (see also Figure 2.3 and Table 2.6.Web). It shows that across TALIS countries, teachers have on average 16 years of teaching experience, 3 years of experience in other educational roles and 4 years of experience in other types of jobs. On average across TALIS countries, one-third of all lower secondary teachers have more than 20 years of teaching experience. This represents a substantial proportion of teachers with considerable experience. In Bulgaria, Estonia and Latvia, this situation is even more pronounced, as more than 50% of the teachers have more than 20 years of teaching experience, while on the other side of the spectrum, 20% of the teachers in Singapore is in the first 2 years of teaching.

Box 2.6. **Work experience of primary and upper secondary teachers**

Tables 2.6.a and 2.6.b show teachers' previous work experience for primary and upper secondary teachers. The average years of work experience as a teacher, in other educational roles and in other jobs are quite similar to those of lower secondary school teachers. Very few country differences emerge between the different educational levels, suggesting that teachers in primary, lower secondary and upper secondary education in all countries with comparable data have similar levels of previous work experience.

■ Figure 2.3 ■

Work experience of teachers

Lower secondary education teachers' average years of work experience

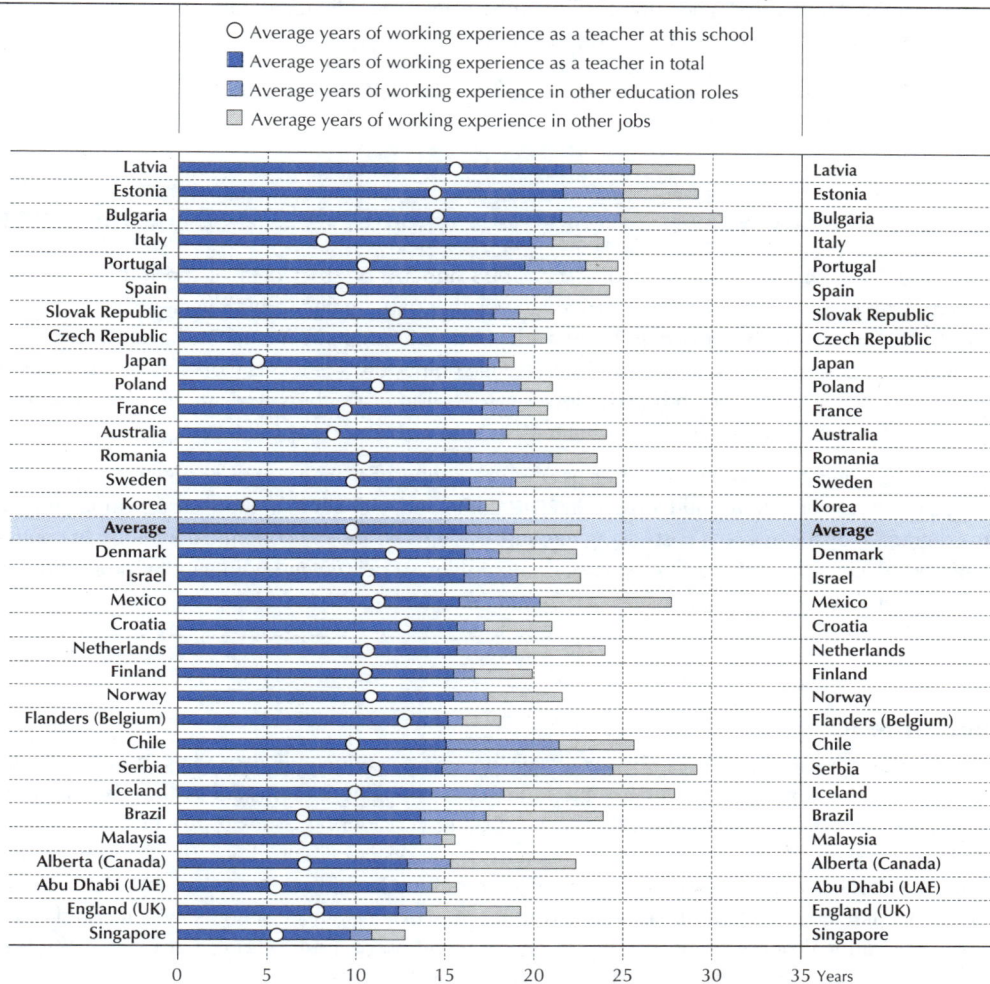

○ Average years of working experience as a teacher at this school
■ Average years of working experience as a teacher in total
▨ Average years of working experience in other education roles
▨ Average years of working experience in other jobs

Countries are ranked in descending order, based on the average years of working experience as a teacher in total.
Source: OECD, TALIS 2013 Database, Table 2.6.
StatLink ᵃᵃˢᵖ http://dx.doi.org/10.1787/888933041155

Employment status

Employment status can be an indication of job security (through long-term or permanent contracts) but also of job flexibility (through the possibility of choosing to work part time), and it is therefore an important factor in attracting teachers to the profession and retaining them (OECD, 2005). TALIS asked teachers whether they are permanently employed at their current school or whether they are employed on a fixed-term contract basis. The TALIS survey also asked teachers whether they work full time or part time across all their teaching jobs. Table 2.7 examines the distribution of lower secondary teachers who work full time and part time (defined as 90% or less of full-time hours), and Table 2.8 examines the proportion of teachers with permanent employment and with fixed-term contracts (of more or less than one school year).

On average, 83% of teachers across countries are employed permanently[4] and 82% are employed full time.[5] Only 12% are on fixed-term contracts of less than one school year. There are large variations between countries in the type of employment contracts (permanent or not). The lowest proportions of teachers with permanent employment status are found in Chile (63%), Romania (69%) and Abu Dhabi (United Arab Emirates) (50%), while all teachers in Malaysia are permanently employed at their current school.[6]

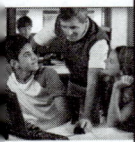

Of the 18% of teachers who work part time, nearly half indicate that they did not have an option to work full time. In Croatia, Mexico, Poland, Portugal and Serbia, these figures are even higher; between 81% and 96% of part-time teachers in these countries indicate that their employment status is the result of the absence of full-time opportunities. On the other hand, in Australia, Denmark, France, the Netherlands, Norway and England (United Kingdom), the vast majority of part-time teachers (85-90%) have chosen to work part time.

Box 2.7 compares findings on teachers' employment status from TALIS 2008 and TALIS 2013 for countries with available data.

Box 2.7. **Comparing teachers' employment status, TALIS 2008 and TALIS 2013**

Tables 2.7.c and 2.8.c show comparisons of TALIS 2008 and TALIS 2013 data of the full-time, part-time and permanent employment status of teachers across countries that participated in both cycles. On average, countries do not show big differences in the types of full-time and part-time arrangements teachers have. The largest difference between both cycles is found in Brazil, where 11 percentage points fewer teachers work full time in 2013 compared with 2008. In contrast, Mexico, which had the lowest proportion of teachers working full time in 2008, at 35%, shows a 5 percentage points increase in 2013, with 40% of teachers working full time.

With respect to permanent or fixed-term contracts, the proportion of teachers with permanent contracts is at least 10 percentage points lower in Korea and Mexico in 2013 compared with 2008. In these cases, employing teachers on fixed-term contracts may have been a cost-saving measure during a period of economic downturn. In contrast, during this same period in Iceland, there was an increase of more than 10 percentage points in the proportion of teachers with permanent contracts.

Distribution of teachers

An important issue to consider is the distribution of teachers across educational systems. Across countries, schools vary in terms of their location (rural vs. urban), the kinds of challenging circumstances they face and the particular subject areas for which they need teachers. Many countries are considering issues of teacher distribution as they try to find the right teachers to fill the needs in different areas of the system (Schleicher, 2012). Teacher distribution also becomes relevant in conversations about creating equity across an education system. A number of studies have found that teachers with weaker qualifications are more likely to teach in disadvantaged schools, which could lead to potential discrepancies in educational opportunities for the student population of these schools (Jackson, 2009; Bonesronning, Falch and Strom, 2005; Boyd et al., 2008; Lankford, Loeb and Wyckoff, 2002).

Are teachers equitably distributed across schools with different student composition?

TALIS data enable an examination of the distribution of teachers by their level of educational attainment (categorised as ISCED level 5A and above and ISCED level 5B and below) and their experience as teachers, separating more experienced teachers (those with more than five years teaching) from their less-experienced colleagues (five years or less of teaching experience). The following analyses look at the distribution of these teachers within schools with different types of student populations. School principals were asked to estimate the proportion of their student population with certain characteristics. For this analysis, schools are classified as more challenging if the principal indicated that their school was made up of more than 10% of students with a native language different from the language of instruction; more than 10% of students with special needs; or more than 30% of students from socioeconomically disadvantaged homes.[7]

Tables 2.9 to 2.11 present the overall proportion of teachers who work in these more challenging schools, as well as the distribution of more experienced and more highly educated teachers among these three types of more and less challenging schools. There is considerable variation between countries in the proportion of teachers who work in more challenging schools (see the first column in Tables 2.9 to 2.11). It should be noted that the range of countries participating in TALIS 2013 is quite broad, and within these countries there might exist substantial variation in the overall populations of students who can be said to have these challenging characteristics. Nonetheless, regardless of the prevalence of these schools, an important policy consideration is how to ensure that teachers with the most experience and qualifications are teaching where they are most needed. Figure 2.4 illustrates the extent to which this happens across countries.

■ Figure 2.4 ■

Distribution of experienced teachers in more and less challenging schools

Proportion of lower secondary education teachers working in more challenging schools and difference in the proportion of more experienced teachers working in more and in less challenging schools[1,2]

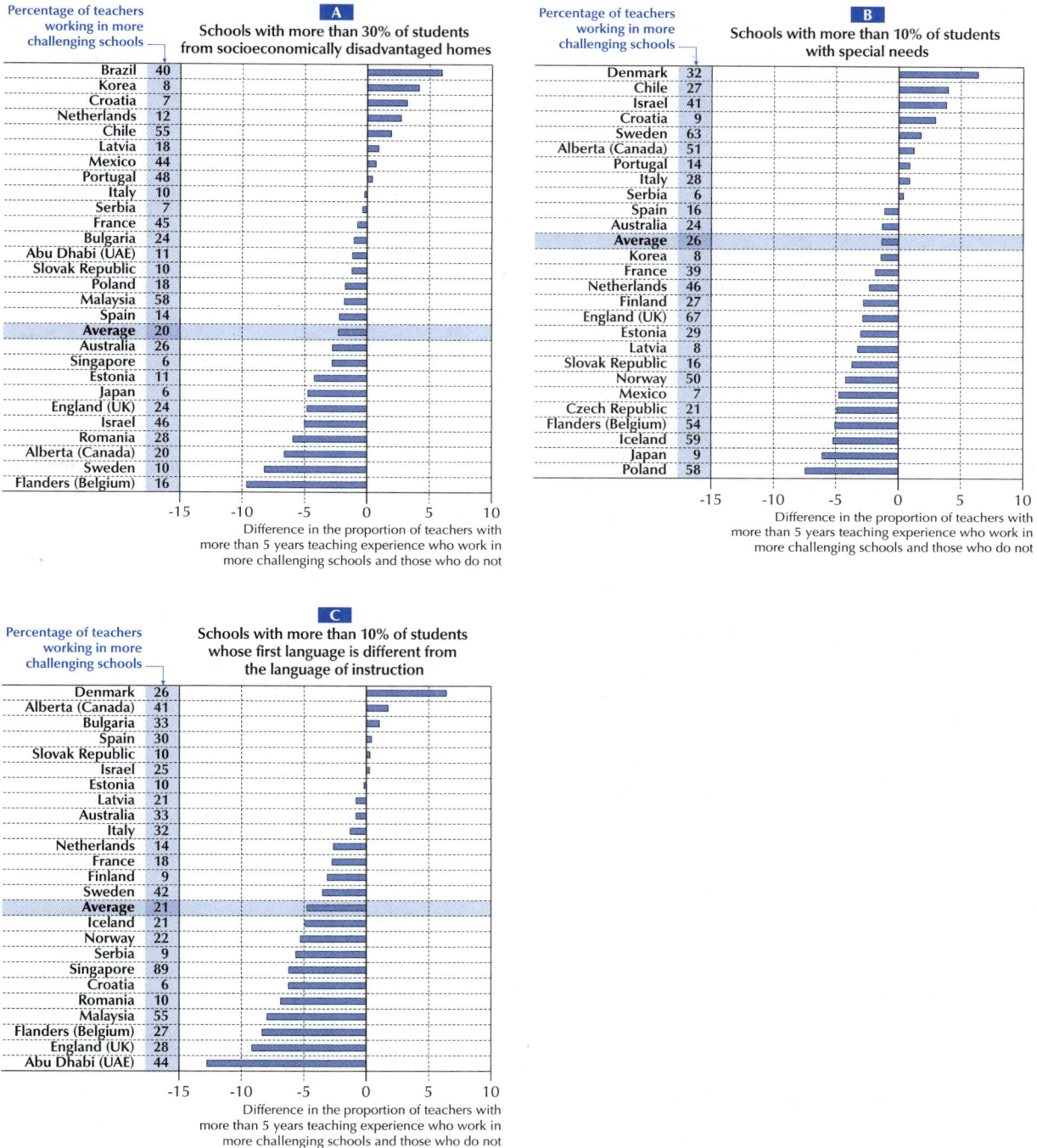

A — Schools with more than 30% of students from socioeconomically disadvantaged homes

Percentage of teachers working in more challenging schools:

Country	Percentage
Brazil	40
Korea	8
Croatia	7
Netherlands	12
Chile	55
Latvia	18
Mexico	44
Portugal	48
Italy	10
Serbia	7
France	45
Bulgaria	24
Abu Dhabi (UAE)	11
Slovak Republic	10
Poland	18
Malaysia	58
Spain	14
Average	20
Australia	26
Singapore	6
Estonia	11
Japan	6
England (UK)	24
Israel	46
Romania	28
Alberta (Canada)	20
Sweden	10
Flanders (Belgium)	16

Difference in the proportion of teachers with more than 5 years teaching experience who work in more challenging schools and those who do not

B — Schools with more than 10% of students with special needs

Percentage of teachers working in more challenging schools:

Country	Percentage
Denmark	32
Chile	27
Israel	41
Croatia	9
Sweden	63
Alberta (Canada)	51
Portugal	14
Italy	28
Serbia	6
Spain	16
Australia	24
Average	26
Korea	8
France	39
Netherlands	46
Finland	27
England (UK)	67
Estonia	29
Latvia	8
Slovak Republic	16
Norway	50
Mexico	7
Czech Republic	21
Flanders (Belgium)	54
Iceland	59
Japan	9
Poland	58

Difference in the proportion of teachers with more than 5 years teaching experience who work in more challenging schools and those who do not

C — Schools with more than 10% of students whose first language is different from the language of instruction

Percentage of teachers working in more challenging schools:

Country	Percentage
Denmark	26
Alberta (Canada)	41
Bulgaria	33
Spain	30
Slovak Republic	10
Israel	25
Estonia	10
Latvia	21
Australia	33
Italy	32
Netherlands	14
France	18
Finland	9
Sweden	42
Average	21
Iceland	21
Norway	22
Serbia	9
Singapore	89
Croatia	6
Romania	10
Malaysia	55
Flanders (Belgium)	27
England (UK)	28
Abu Dhabi (UAE)	44

Difference in the proportion of teachers with more than 5 years teaching experience who work in more challenging schools and those who do not

1. Categorisation of more challenging schools is based on principals' estimates of the broad percentage in the schools of: *a)* students from socioeconomically disadvantaged homes, *b)* students with special needs, and *c)* of students whose first language is different from the language of instruction.
2. Country data for categories representing fewer than 5% of the cases are not presented in this figure.
Countries are ranked in descending order, based on the difference in the proportion of experienced teachers who work in more challenging schools and those who do not.
Source: OECD, TALIS 2013 Database, Tables 2.9, 2.10 and 2.11.
StatLink ᴬᴵˢᴾ http://dx.doi.org/10.1787/888933041174

In countries and economies found at the top of each chart in Figure 2.4 (with positive differences), experienced teachers are more likely to be working in more challenging schools than in less challenging schools. This is the case for Brazil (for schools with high proportions of students from socioeconomically disadvantaged homes) and for Denmark (for schools with higher proportions of students with special needs and with a first language different from the language of instruction). These graphs show that for a majority of countries, however, the opposite is true. Negative difference scores on these graphs indicate that a larger proportion of more experienced teachers teach in less challenging schools compared to more challenging ones. In Flanders (Belgium) this is the case with respect to schools with larger proportions of students from socioeconomically disadvantaged backgrounds; in Poland this is true with respect to schools with higher proportions of students with special needs; and in Abu Dhabi (United Arab Emirates) this is the case with respect to schools with higher proportions of students whose first language is different from the language of instruction.

These descriptive distributions of teachers across challenging schools are informative, but are a teacher's level of educational qualification and work experience significant predictors of teaching in a more or less challenging school, when controlling for key variables such as gender and subjects taught? In other words, across countries, are teachers more likely to work in challenging schools if they have lower levels of education and less teaching experience? Or is the opposite the case? Country-specific binary logistic regressions were performed (see Box 2.5), with ISCED level 5B and below for education and less than five years for the work experience variable as reference categories. However, for some countries the percentage of teachers in each category is too low to draw conclusions (indicated by shaded cells in Table 2.12). Thus, only those countries with a minimum of 5% of teachers in the categories of interest for the analysis will be further elaborated upon here.

Most TALIS countries do not show a strong association between teachers' highest level of education or years of teaching experience and the distribution of teachers across schools with potentially more challenging student populations. In other words, in most countries the distribution of more experienced teachers is not different in more or less challenging schools. Nonetheless, in some countries, some significant and substantial associations are apparent for education level and for years of teaching experience (Table 2.12).

For example, in Bulgaria, teachers with higher educational attainment are 50% less likely to work in schools where more than one in ten students speak a mother tongue different from the language of instruction. Teachers from Chile who have more education are also more than 50% less likely to work in schools with more socioeconomically disadvantaged students. Similarly, teachers with higher levels of education are 40% less likely to work in schools with higher percentages of special-needs students in the Czech Republic and Serbia.

Yet the opposite relationship can be seen in other TALIS countries, where teachers with higher levels of education are more likely to work in schools characterised as more challenging. In Flanders (Belgium), teachers with higher education levels are 30% more likely to work in schools with a larger population of students with special needs, more than twice as likely to work in more linguistically diverse schools and nearly twice as likely to work in schools with higher proportions of students from socioeconomically disadvantaged homes (Table 2.12). In Singapore, these teachers are 60% more likely to work in more linguistically diverse schools.

Similar patterns can be observed with respect to teaching experience. In some countries, teachers with more than five years of teaching experience are less likely to teach in schools that could be considered more challenging. For example, in Abu Dhabi (United Arab Emirates), these teachers are 60% less likely to work in schools with higher proportions of students from diverse language backgrounds. In Sweden, teachers with more experience are half as likely to work in schools with larger proportions of students from socioeconomically disadvantaged homes.

In a smaller number of countries, more experienced teachers are actually more likely to work in schools that may be considered more challenging. Notably, in Denmark, these teachers are 70% more likely to work in schools with higher proportions of linguistic diversity in the student body, and they are 80% more likely to work in schools with higher proportions of students with special needs. In Brazil, more experienced teachers are 50% more likely to work in schools with higher proportions of students from socioeconomically disadvantaged homes.

These results suggest that at least in some TALIS countries, the distribution of teachers is somewhat more equitable than what is sometimes described in the literature, in that less-experienced teachers are not necessarily being placed in more challenging circumstances (Akiba and Liang, 2014; Clotfelter et al., 2007; Darling-Hammond, 2004). This isn't the case in all locations, however, and evidence from the cycle of the Programme for International Student Assessment (PISA)

in 2012 suggests that socioeconomically disadvantaged schools tend to have great difficulty in attracting qualified and/or quality teachers (OECD, 2013b). Even in those countries or economies in which teachers are free to choose where they work and are not placed in particular areas (either for their first assignment or as experienced teachers), there are policy implications for these findings. Governments can provide incentives to attract highly educated or experienced teachers to more disadvantaged schools or challenging locations. Strategies that are not tied to salary can also be employed, such as less class time or smaller class sizes for teachers who are teaching in difficult areas or have larger proportions of students with special educational needs. In addition, see Chapter 7 for a discussion on how issues of school climate relate to teacher job satisfaction.

Are teachers equitably distributed across schools located in rural and urban areas?

To ensure equity within an education system, but also to ensure that teachers work in contexts where they can receive the support they need to be successful, countries are also concerned with the distribution of less-experienced and less-educated teachers across urban and rural areas (Table 2.13). Following the same procedure as described in Box 2.5, country-specific regressions were performed to see whether teachers with lower levels of education or less experience are more or less likely to work in schools located in bigger cities than in small towns. In contrast to the analyses presented in the previous section, the analyses in this section use ISCED level 5A and above for education and five years or more for the work experience as reference categories. Again, for some countries the percentage of teachers in each category is too low to draw conclusions (indicated by shaded cells in Table 2.14). Thus, only those countries with a minimum of 5% of teachers in the categories of interest for the analyses will be further elaborated upon here. For the purpose of these analyses, school location was divided into three categories: schools located in areas with less than 15 000 people (towns), 15 000-100 000 people (small cities) and more than 100 000 people (large cities). In the regression analyses, small cities and large cities are compared with the reference category "towns".

The analyses show that in a number of countries, education and/or teaching experience are indeed related to the likelihood of teaching in more populated areas (see Table 2.14, significant results in bold). In most countries, compared with teachers with higher levels of education and experience, those with lower levels of education and fewer years of teaching experience are less likely to work in areas that are more urban (both small and large cities), as opposed to more rural (towns with 15 000 or fewer inhabitants). For example, in Brazil and Bulgaria, teachers with lower educational qualifications are roughly 60% less likely to work in large cities as opposed to towns. Similarly, in Australia, Croatia, Romania, Serbia and Spain, teachers with fewer years of teaching experience are 40% to 70% less likely to teach in small and/or large cities than in towns. Policy makers in these countries and economies will want to explore the reasons underlying why less-experienced or less-educated teachers are more likely to teach in more rural areas. It might be that it is more difficult to attract teachers to these jobs or locations. Governments will also want to ensure that teachers in more rural areas have access to the same level of support, including development and resources, that they would if they worked in more urban locations.

Opposite associations appear for Latvia, however, where teachers with less experience are 2.5 times more likely to work in cities as opposed to towns. Similarly, teachers with lower levels of education and/or more teaching experience are at least 40% more likely to work in small and/or large cities than in towns in France, Norway, Poland, the Slovak Republic, Sweden, Abu Dhabi (United Arab Emirates) and Flanders (Belgium).

Are teachers teaching subjects for which they have been well prepared to teach?

Because of shortages of qualified teachers in specific areas, individuals can be assigned to teach subjects for which they have not been adequately prepared. Alternatively, it is also possible to have a pool of teachers who are not currently teaching subjects for which they have received formal education or training. One indication of these situations is an examination of the mismatch between the education and training for teaching specific subjects and the subjects that are currently taught within countries (Figure 2.5).

Table 2.15 shows the percentages of teachers who currently teach in selected subject categories and indicates whether they have received formal education or training in these subjects. In general, for subjects such as reading, writing and literature, mathematics, science, and foreign languages, only small proportions of teachers (11% or less) seem to be teaching subjects in which they have not received formal education at ISCED level 4 or higher or at the in-service professional development stage. This overall average, however, hides important variation between countries and between subjects. A closer examination of Tables 2.15 and 2.15.Web reveals a number of countries where larger proportions of teachers did not report receiving formal education or training in the subjects they teach.[8]

■ Figure 2.5 ■

Teacher training mismatch and teacher resource allocation

Percentage of lower secondary education teachers who report teaching the following subjects without having received formal education or training for this subject and teachers who report that the following subjects were included in a subject specialisation as part of their teacher training but who do not currently teach this subject

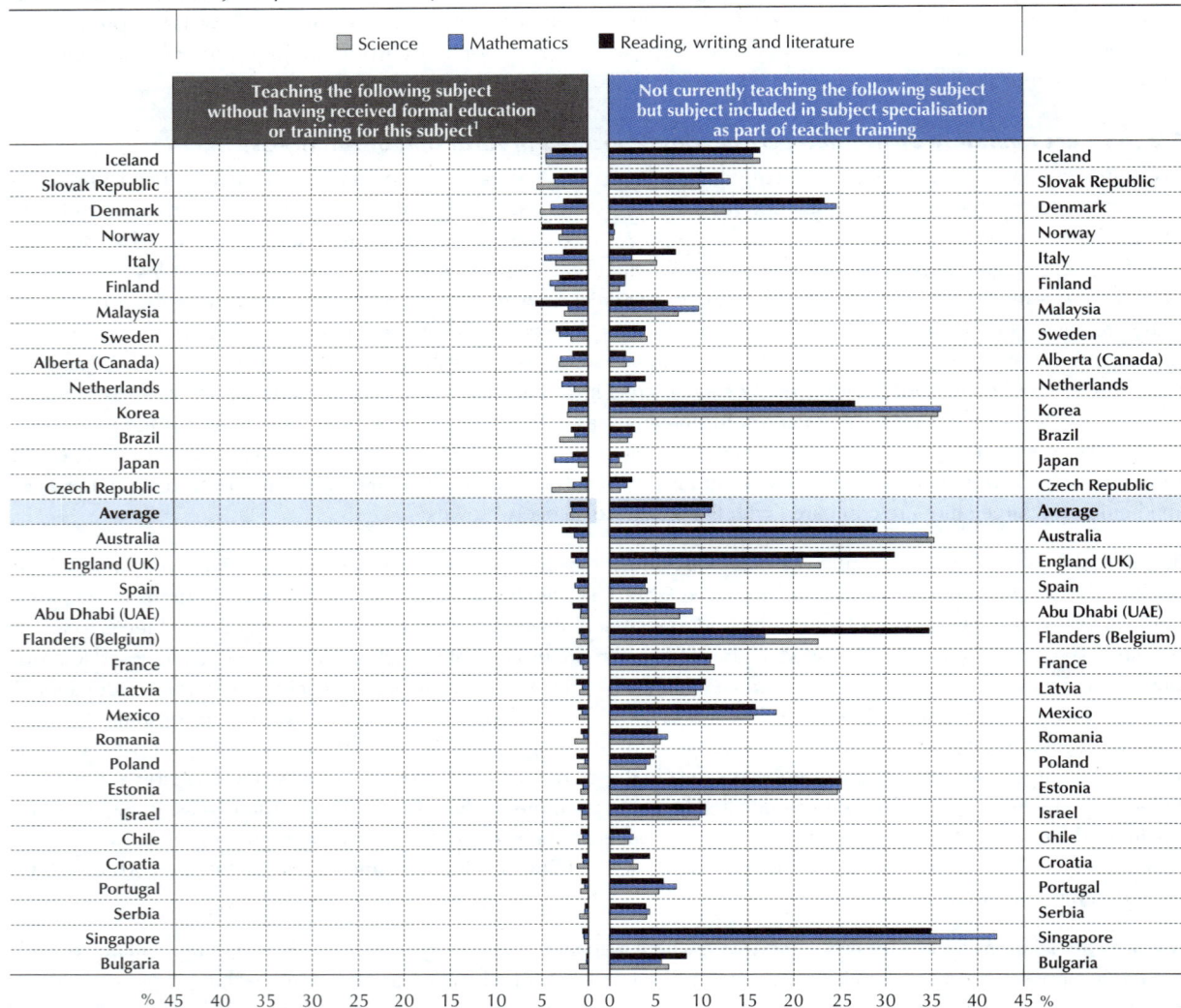

□ Science ■ Mathematics ■ Reading, writing and literature

	Teaching the following subject without having received formal education or training for this subject[1]	Not currently teaching the following subject but subject included in subject specialisation as part of teacher training	
Iceland			Iceland
Slovak Republic			Slovak Republic
Denmark			Denmark
Norway			Norway
Italy			Italy
Finland			Finland
Malaysia			Malaysia
Sweden			Sweden
Alberta (Canada)			Alberta (Canada)
Netherlands			Netherlands
Korea			Korea
Brazil			Brazil
Japan			Japan
Czech Republic			Czech Republic
Average			Average
Australia			Australia
England (UK)			England (UK)
Spain			Spain
Abu Dhabi (UAE)			Abu Dhabi (UAE)
Flanders (Belgium)			Flanders (Belgium)
France			France
Latvia			Latvia
Mexico			Mexico
Romania			Romania
Poland			Poland
Estonia			Estonia
Israel			Israel
Chile			Chile
Croatia			Croatia
Portugal			Portugal
Serbia			Serbia
Singapore			Singapore
Bulgaria			Bulgaria

% 45 40 35 30 25 20 15 10 5 0 0 5 10 15 20 25 30 35 40 45 %

1. This category includes those teachers who responded to the question but who did not select one of the response options ("in ISCED level 4 or 5B", "in ISCED 5A or above", "in subject specialisation as part of the teacher training", or "at the in-service or professional development stage") for that particular subject.
Countries are ranked in descending order, based on the sum of teachers teaching "reading, writing and literature", "mathematics" and "science" without having received formal education or training for these respective subjects.
Source: OECD, TALIS 2013 Database, Tables 2.15 and 2.16.
StatLink ᐛᔑᐠ http://dx.doi.org/10.1787/888933041193

For example, in the Netherlands, approximately one fifth of the teachers who currently teach reading, writing and literature or mathematics have not received formal education or training to teach these subjects. Approximately one-fifth of science teachers in Iceland have not received formal science education or training. This type of allocation issue for science is not apparent in Bulgaria, Chile, Estonia, France, Israel, Mexico, Portugal, Serbia, Singapore and Abu Dhabi (United Arab Emirates).

Finally, on average, one in ten foreign-language teachers have not received formal education or training in foreign languages. This percentage is much higher in Denmark (21%), Iceland (22%) and Malaysia (20%), indicating a potentially high need in these countries for teachers with specific training to teach foreign languages.

In some countries, the data show similarly high potential needs for teachers trained to teach subjects from other subject categories, such as social studies, technology, arts, physical education, religion and/or ethics, and practical and vocational skills. The overall average of teachers teaching subjects in these categories who have not received formal education or training at the ISCED level 4 or higher, or at the in-service professional development stage in these subjects, ranges from 9% for physical education to 23% for teaching practical and vocation skills (Table 2.15.Web).

At the same time, there are significant proportions of teachers who do not currently teach in subject categories that were included in a subject specialisation as part of their teacher training (Tables 2.16 and 2.16.Web). In some cases at least, these teachers might represent a potential resource that could be used to more efficiently address the apparent teacher shortages in some subject categories as highlighted previously. The right panel of Figure 2.5 shows this potential pool of teachers that could alleviate the shortages experienced in some subject categories (as shown on the left panel of Figure 2.5). Looking at Iceland's data, for example, nearly 5% of Iceland's teachers currently teach mathematics but have not received formal education or training at ISCED level 4 or above or at the professional development stage in this subject, while nearly 15% of Iceland's teachers are not currently teaching mathematics but report that this subject was included in their teacher training. Similar situations are seen for other subject categories in some countries.

A PROFILE OF SCHOOLS WHERE TEACHERS WORK

This section explores the school-level background information provided by principals that describes the schools in which lower secondary education teachers work. This kind of data can provide important contextual information to consider both on its own and in relation to teachers' work and the working conditions that teachers perceive enable them to function effectively in their roles. This section looks at the size and location of schools, the resources to which they have access, the quality of the school climate and the level of autonomy they have in decision making.

School type and school composition

Teachers work in schools that can vary greatly in terms of their location (rural or urban environment), their sector (publicly or privately funded), their size and the characteristics of their student population. All of these factors are important aspects of teachers' work environment and can interact with other aspects of teachers' work.

The ideal school size has also been a topic of debate for over a century. In two recent reviews of empirical studies that researched the effects of school size on various student and organisational outcomes, smaller schools are concluded to be favourable. In larger schools, teacher-student relations can be more difficult to develop and socioeconomically disadvantaged students or students with learning difficulties tend to be overlooked (Leithwood and Jantzi, 2009; Ready, Lee and Welner, 2004). However, some evidence suggests that larger schools are better in nurturing the achievement of academically successful senior high school students (Schreiber, 2002). Also, some studies indicate that greater costs are involved to educate a student in a small school compared with a large school (Barnett et al., 2002; Bowles and Bosworth, 2002).

Overall, working in a public school appears to be the norm for the average teacher. On average, 82% of TALIS teachers work in public schools, and 77% of teachers work in schools (public or private) that compete with one or more schools for students (Table 2.17). Nevertheless, in a number of countries, fewer than half of the teachers work in public schools, notably Chile (40%), the Netherlands (22%), Abu Dhabi (United Arab Emirates) (45%) and Flanders (Belgium) (27%).[9]

As can be seen in Table 2.18, the average school size across TALIS countries is 546 students.[10] Countries with average student bodies over 1 000 are Malaysia, Portugal and Singapore. While the overall TALIS average number of teachers per school is 45, the averages for the aforementioned countries are much higher and range from 83 to 110. The average class size across countries is 24.[11] Larger class sizes are seen in Brazil, Chile, Japan, Korea, Malaysia, Mexico and Singapore, each with more than 30 students in the classroom.

Box 2.8. **School type and school composition in primary and upper secondary schools**

Tables 2.17.a and 2.17.b show the proportion of primary and upper secondary teachers who work in public and private schools. As was the case for lower secondary, the vast majority of teachers work in public schools (83% for primary school teachers and 82% for upper secondary school teachers). Notable exceptions to this overall finding are Flanders (Belgium), where only 39% of primary teachers work in public schools, and Australia and Abu Dhabi (United Arab Emirates), where only 56% and 43% of upper secondary teachers work in public schools.

Across all TALIS countries, the average student-teacher ratios vary. [12] In Estonia, Iceland, Norway, Poland and Flanders (Belgium), the ratio is 8 students for every teacher. The ratio is 19 students per teacher in Brazil and 20 students per teacher in Chile and Japan (Table 2.18). The ratio of teachers to support personnel also varies significantly across countries. [13] On average, there is one pedagogical support person for every 14 teachers in a school. For Italy and Malaysia, this ratio is much higher; on average in Italy there is one support person for every 60 teachers, and in Malaysia there is one for every 53 teachers. For Iceland, Alberta (Canada) and England (United Kingdom), support personnel is provided for every four teachers. It is noteworthy that ratios of teachers to school administrative or management personnel[14] tend to be lower, perhaps showing a greater emphasis on providing administrative rather than pedagogical support. On average, there is one administrative or management support person for every six teachers in the school (though the number of teachers is roughly double for Croatia, Finland, Italy and Sweden).

Box 2.9. **Primary and upper secondary school and class size**

Tables 2.18.a and 2.18.b show the average school and class sizes in primary and upper secondary in countries with available data. Unsurprisingly, the average number of students is much lower, with 248 students, in schools where primary teachers work than in schools where upper secondary teachers work (788 students on average). Similarly, there are more than three times as many teachers on average in schools where upper secondary teachers work (69) than in schools where primary teachers work (20).

The average primary school class size (20 students) is somewhat smaller than in lower secondary schools (24 students) or upper secondary schools (24 students). In some countries, it is possible to compare between ISCED levels. The only country where the average class size is larger in primary education than in lower secondary education is Flanders (Belgium), although it is a very small difference of just one student. The average class size is smaller in upper secondary education than in lower secondary education in Australia (19 vs. 25), Norway (19 vs. 23), Singapore (33 vs. 36) and Abu Dhabi (United Arab Emirates) (24 vs. 25).

The overall average student-to-teacher ratios are very similar between all levels of education. In specific countries, however, more important differences emerge. For example, in Mexico, the student-to-teacher ratio is much less favourable in primary education (24 students for each teacher) than in lower secondary education (15 students per teacher) or upper secondary education (16 students per teacher). In a few countries there are slightly more favourable ratios in upper secondary education compared with lower secondary education, namely in Finland (10 vs. 13 students per teacher) and Iceland (8 vs. 12 students per teacher).

In a few countries, there is also evidence of more pedagogical support for teachers in primary than in lower and/or upper secondary schools. Such a case is found in Finland (5 additional pedagogical support staff for every teacher), Mexico (6 additional pedagogical support staff) and Flanders (Belgium) (16 additional pedagogical support staff). In Denmark and Iceland, the teacher-to-pedagogical-support ratios are less favourable in upper secondary schools than in lower secondary schools (39 vs. 10 and 20 vs. 4, respectively). In contrast, teachers in Italy benefit from much more pedagogical support in upper secondary (18 teachers per pedagogical support) than in lower secondary schools (60 teachers per pedagogical support).

School resources

Although there is great policy interest in improving educational outcomes around the world, there remains even greater uncertainty as to how to achieve this. Countries often enact education policies that look at increasing or making a more equitable distribution of resources to schools. Resources, as defined by TALIS, could be teaching staff (especially targeted at specific student or subject needs) or material resources, such as instructional materials, computers or computer software. A variety of studies suggest that resource-only policies are unlikely to be effective (Hanushek, 2006; OECD, 2010). Resource policies should have links to specific incentives, for example targeting those schools with many socioeconomically disadvantaged or special-needs students. PISA also shows that the more school principals perceive that resource shortages hinder instruction, the lower student performance in that school (OECD, 2007: 263).

Research does show that across different countries, headteachers and principals generally have great concerns over teacher shortage and inadequacy as well as teacher turnover. These concerns are supported empirically by some research (Akiba and Liang, 2014; Clotfelter et al., 2007; Darling-Hammond, 2004) and by the analysis of the distribution of teachers earlier in this chapter, although other research suggests that neither location, school size nor selection

policies of schools have any noticeable effect on the likelihood of principals reporting problems with either teacher shortage, inadequacy or turnover (White and Smith, 2005). This section investigates the relationship between school characteristics and resources issues for the TALIS countries.

Table 2.19 presents the proportion of teachers who work in schools with different types of shortages that principals felt hindered the provision of quality instruction in their school (see also Figure 2.6). More than a third of lower secondary teachers work in schools where principals indicate that there is a significant shortage of qualified and/or well-performing teachers. This figure varies based on the kind of teacher that is needed. On average, less than 20% of teachers work in schools with a reported shortage of vocational teachers, but nearly half work in schools where there is a need for teachers of students with special needs or support personnel. In particular, a significant proportion of teachers in Japan (80%), the Netherlands (71%) and Abu Dhabi (United Arab Emirates) (60%) work in schools with a shortage of qualified and/or well-performing teachers. Conversely, this is less of an issue in some countries, where less than one-fifth of teachers work in schools where the principal reports this issue (Denmark, 15%; Finland, 17%; Iceland, 14%; Poland, 13%).

■ Figure 2.6 ■

Lack of resources hindering the school's capacity for quality instruction

Percentage of lower secondary education teachers whose school principal reports that the following resource issues hinder the school's capacity to provide quality instruction in their school

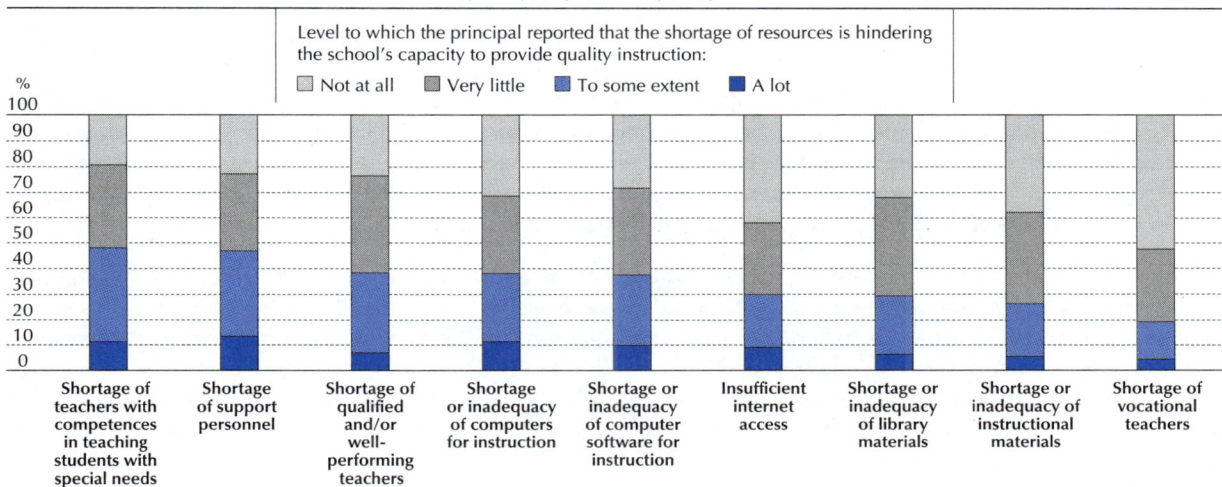

Items are ranked in descending order, based on the percentage of teachers in lower secondary education whose school principal reported that the shortage of resources is hindering "a lot" or "to some extent" the school's capacity to provide quality instruction in their school.
Source: OECD, TALIS 2013 Database, Table 2.19.
StatLink ⫘ http://dx.doi.org/10.1787/888933041212

As for shortages of materials, between 26% and 38% of teachers across TALIS countries work in schools where principals report a shortage of or inadequate instructional materials, computers or computer software for instruction, internet access and library materials (as reported by their principals). Romania and the Slovak Republic are the most under-resourced in terms of adequate instructional material, with roughly 80% of teachers working in schools where principals report a deficit in this area. Romania and Mexico show particularly high concerns about the availability and quality of computers, computer software and internet access (64%-76%). More than half of the teachers in Mexico and Romania also work in schools where library materials are a concern for principals in providing quality instruction (Table 2.19).

School climate

The concept of school climate is not a new one; its relevance and importance have been recognised for 100 years (Cohen et al., 2009; Thapa et al., 2013). Over the past three decades, however, researchers and educators alike have recognised the influence of school climate on other parts of, or players in, the learning environment. School climate comprises quality of school life and includes factors such as safety issues (bullying or verbal or physical abuse of teachers or students); late arrivals to school, absenteeism by teachers or students, or cheating; criminal behaviours (vandalism or drug and alcohol possession or use); and discrimination. But school climate also includes the overall culture of the school in terms of the quality of the relationships between staff and between staff and students and the levels of co-operation, respect and sharing that are present.

Research shows that a positive school climate is a powerful influence on many elements affecting both students and teachers in a school. Most importantly, perhaps, school climate has been shown to be related to student academic achievement at all levels of schooling (MacNeil, Prater and Busch, 2009; Sherblom, Marshall and Sherblom, 2006; Stewart, 2008). Constructive teacher-student relationships associated with a positive school climate not only affect teaching and learning but have also been shown to influence other student-related factors, such as the prevention of bullying or violence in a school (Eliot et al., 2010) and the motivation of students to learn (Eccles et al., 1993). A healthy school climate has been shown to be related to teachers' confidence that they can influence student learning (Hoy and Woolfolk, 1993) and to aid in teacher retention (Fulton, Yoon and Lee, 2005; Weiss, 1999).

The TALIS data look at the student and teacher behaviours contributing to school climate separately. Of all factors included in school climate, weekly absenteeism and late arrival to school by students are by far the most commonly occurring across TALIS countries (Table 2.20). Fifty-two percent of teachers work in schools where principals report that students arrive late on a weekly basis, and 39% of teachers work in schools where absenteeism of students occurs every week across countries. Yet in Chile, Finland, the Netherlands, Sweden and Alberta (Canada), the problem is more severe, with 70% or more of teachers working in schools where principals report that students arrive late on a weekly basis. In these countries and economies, absenteeism of students is also reported as significantly higher than the TALIS average. In particular, in Finland, Sweden and Alberta (Canada), more than 60% of teachers work in schools where school principals report that this behaviour in students occurs on a weekly basis.

The occurence of the more serious infractions of cheating, vandalism and theft, and intimidation or verbal abuse among students varies widely across TALIS countries (Table 2.20). Whereas approximately one-third of teachers in Croatia, Estonia and Latvia work in schools where principals report that cheating occurs at their school, in the Netherlands this number is 58% and in Poland it is 40%. In contrast, in more than one-third of TALIS countries, 5% or less of teachers work in schools where principals report that cheating occurs in their schools. Moreover, the most serious infractions of vandalism and thefts are not reported frequently. Only in Brazil, Malaysia and Mexico did more than 10% of teachers work in schools where principals report experiencing incidents of vandalism or theft on a weekly basis.

Furthermore, almost a third of teachers in Brazil, Mexico, Sweden and Flanders (Belgium) work in schools with reported intimidation or verbal abuse occurring among their students on a weekly basis (Table 2.20). This percentage is smaller, at 5% or less, for teachers in the Czech Republic, Japan, Singapore and the Slovak Republic. Finally, fewer teachers in all TALIS countries work in schools where physical injury caused by violence among students and use/possession of drugs and/or alcohol is reported. The same is true for intimidation or verbal abuse of teachers or staff in all countries except Australia, Brazil and Estonia, where 10% or more of the teachers work in schools where their principals declare that intimidation or verbal abuse of teachers or staff occurs at least weekly.

Table 2.21 presents the proportion of teachers who work in schools where the climate is negatively impacted by certain teacher behaviours (as reported by principals). The degree to which teachers work in schools where teachers arrive late varies widely across countries. Yet there seem to be fewer teachers who work in schools where teacher absenteeism or discrimination is a problem. On average across TALIS countries, 11% of teachers work in schools where principals report that teachers arrive late at least weekly. This type of climate is more widespread in Brazil, Chile, Mexico and Flanders (Belgium), encompassing a quarter or more of teachers. A significant proportion of teachers in Australia, Brazil, Chile and Mexico (between 16%-21%) work in schools where principals report problematic teacher absenteeism.

Teachers' work is also greatly influenced by the professional climate in the school. It is important to consider to what extent school staff share a common set of beliefs about schooling, the degree to which staff have open discussions about difficulties, the extent to which there is mutual respect for colleagues' ideas and whether there is a culture of sharing success. It seems that in these areas, most teachers across TALIS countries work in environments with a positive professional climate among the teaching staff. As can be seen in Table 2.22, 87% of teachers across TALIS countries work in schools where principals report that their school staff share a common set of beliefs, although this is reported by principals of only 57% of Croatian teachers. A further three-quarters of teachers work in schools where principals report high levels of co-operation between their school and the local community, though this is less than half for Denmark (46%), the Netherlands (21%), Norway (41%) and Sweden (33%). Finally, between 90% and 93% of all teachers across TALIS countries work in schools where principals report that their staff have open discussions about difficulties, mutual respect for colleagues' ideas and a culture of sharing success.

A final indicator of school climate in TALIS is the quality of student-teacher relations. Table 2.23 provides an overview of teachers' and principals' views on several important indicators of student-teacher relations. On average, 98% of

principals across all TALIS countries report good relations between teachers and students, with no notable exceptions. Furthermore, the vast majority of teachers (between 91% and 96%) report positive teacher and student relations at their schools. It is only in the area of providing students with extra support that any variation is observed. In Brazil (77%), Korea (77%), Mexico (72%) and Sweden (74%), fewer than eight in ten teachers report that students get extra support if they need it.

Box 2.10 compares findings from TALIS 2008 and TALIS 2013 for countries with available data.

Box 2.10. **Comparing teacher-student relations in lower secondary education, TALIS 2008 and TALIS 2013**

Table 2.23.c provides a comparison of TALIS 2008 and TALIS 2013 data on teacher-student relations in education for those countries that participated in both cycles. It can be seen that across indicators, average scores have not changed much, though a small difference was observed across countries for teachers and students getting along better. In 2013, 8 percentage points more teachers in Estonia report that teachers in their schools have an interest in what students have to say. Conversely, in 2013, teachers in Korea were less likely (76%) than in 2008 (86%) to report that students in need of extra assistance in their schools are provided with such assistance.

School autonomy

TALIS asks school principals about their level of school autonomy, or the degree to which the responsibility for decision making in certain areas is held at a school level, as opposed to at a local or national government level. It is possible for schools to have autonomy in some areas but not others. For example, schools may have the power to appoint or hire teachers but may not be able to determine their starting salaries or set pay scales. They may be able to determine course content or choose which learning materials are used, but the decision as to which courses are offered may not be made at a school level.

Increased school autonomy is being considered in more countries and school systems, and we see charter schools and other independent school models promising autonomy for schools and further decentralisation of systems (Finnegan, 2007). Indeed, a general reading of the research seems to show that greater levels of autonomy for schools would also improve learning outcomes. However, upon closer inspection, it is evident that the impact of autonomy on student achievement varies across countries (Hanushek, Link and Woessmann, 2013). The kinds of decisions that are devolved to a school level also make a difference; some studies show the importance of curricular and assessment decisions being made at a school level (OECD, 2010), while others emphasise the benefits of process and personnel decisions being decentralised (Wößmann, 2007). There are other possible benefits for autonomy in developing the roles of school leaders, for example, if their decisions are supported and their responsibilities are well defined (Pont, Nusche and Moorman, 2008).

Table 2.24 provides a snapshot of the proportions of teachers across countries who work in schools where certain key responsibilities lie at the school level (as reported by their principal). Tasks that principals reported on were hiring and dismissal of teachers, teacher pay issues, budgeting within the school, establishing student discipline, assessment and admission and any curricular issues. There are a few countries where a large proportion of teachers work in schools where principals report a high level of autonomy across all areas. In the Czech Republic, Estonia, the Netherlands, the Slovak Republic and England (United Kingdom) almost all teachers work in schools where principals report that all listed tasks are completely decided upon at the school level. For the remaining countries, teachers tend to work in schools where the level of autonomy varies per task. Teachers in Malaysia and Mexico seem to work in schools where principals report consistently low levels of autonomy.

Across countries, almost all lower secondary teachers work in schools where principals report that the schools have significant responsibility for establishing student disciplinary policies and procedures and choosing which learning materials are used (Table 2.24). In contrast, less than 40% of teachers, on average, work in schools where principals report that the school is empowered to make decisions on pay issues (such as establishing teachers' starting salaries, setting pay scales and determining teachers' salary increases). The areas with the most variation between countries include hiring and dismissing or suspending teachers. In more than half of the TALIS countries, 90% or more of teachers work in schools where school principals say they have significant autonomy at a school level for hiring or appointing

teachers. Yet less than a third of teachers in France (31%), Japan (18%), Malaysia (7%), Mexico (31%) and Spain (27%) work in schools where principals report that the school enjoys this privilege. When it comes to dismissing or suspending teachers, the school-level authority decreases further, with less than a third of teachers in France (16%), Japan (17%), Korea (33%), Malaysia (6%), Mexico (29%) and Spain (26%) working in schools having this authority.

SUMMARY AND MAIN POLICY IMPLICATIONS

The background information presented in this chapter about teachers and the schools in which they work offers a basis for the analyses and policy recommendations in subsequent chapters of this report but is of interest on its own as well. While there are, of course, variations across countries, the TALIS data provide a picture of the "typical" teacher of lower secondary education across TALIS countries.

According to TALIS, the typical lower secondary teacher:

- is a woman;
- is 43 years old;
- has completed university or other equivalent higher education (ISCED 5A);
- has completed a teacher education or training programme;
- has 16 years of experience as a teacher; and
- is employed on a full-time basis with a permanent contract.

Likewise, the TALIS data give a description of the school environment in which the typical lower secondary school teacher works. This is a school that:

- is public;
- competes with other schools for students;
- has 546 students, 45 teachers and an average class size of 24 students;
- employs one pedagogical support personnel for every 14 teachers in the school and 1 administrative or management personnel for every 6 teachers;
- has adequate material and staffing resources;
- experiences students arriving late to school on a weekly basis; and
- enjoys good relations between teachers and students.

When presented only with the average situation across countries, the state of lower secondary education looks quite positive. In a very general sense, teachers seem experienced and educated and have stable employment. Teachers enjoy positive classroom climate, reasonable class sizes and principals report adequate staffing support and material resources. However, there are exceptions to each of these averages, both between countries and within countries. It is in the deviation from these averages that the opportunities for reform lie. Looking across countries at the "typical" teacher reveals potential challenges and opportunities for governments and school leaders in particular.

Provide extra support to less experienced or more experienced teachers in the workforce, based on their specific needs

The TALIS data note that some countries, such as Italy, may have a more experienced but aging teaching workforce, while others, such as Singapore, might have a generally younger but somewhat less experienced teaching workforce. There are impacts on and opportunities for policies to help shape the teaching profession in both of these instances. If a country has a young teaching force, as is the case in Singapore, initial teacher education will have a greater influence on the practices occurring in the classroom. (See Chapter 6 for a further discussion of the TALIS data on teaching practices.) The aging teacher population in Italy and other countries requires more emphasis on continued professional development to help teachers adapt to changing demands. (See Chapter 4 for further analysis of the TALIS data on teacher professional development.)

Review the allocation of teachers across the system and develop policies to attract teachers to more challenging schools

When considering the data on the distribution of teachers, it is clear that a number of countries face challenges in matching their supply of teachers to their needs. Some countries do not have an equitable allocation of more experienced teachers across the education system, in both more and less challenging schools (Figure 2.4). Some countries have had a great deal of success in attracting teachers to schools with challenging circumstances. For example, PISA 2012

data show Portugal, Poland and Finland as the top three OECD countries in terms of allocating a higher proportion of qualified teachers to socioeconomically disadvantaged schools than to advantaged schools.

The data discussing whether teachers have received training for the subjects they teach are also revealing of a potential resource allocation issue within some countries (Figure 2.5). In some countries, significant percentages of teachers are currently teaching subjects for which they have had no formal education or training, while equally important percentages of teachers are not teaching subjects for which they have received training. In these countries, it would be well worth looking at the reasons behind this mismatch and perhaps developing policies designed to attract experienced teachers where they are most needed, whether this is in more challenging locations or where teacher shortages in specific subjects are more prevalent.

Ensure that schools are given more autonomy in the right areas, for the right reasons

Finally, issues of school autonomy are important to consider as well. While TALIS data identify in which countries principals report that their school enjoys less autonomy for certain tasks, this does not necessarily indicate that more autonomy is needed in all of these areas. For example, the individual actors within the system may not have the capacity for certain kinds of decision-making responsibility. Further, as data from the OECD PISA indicate, schools tend to perform better when higher levels of autonomy in certain areas are also paired with higher levels of accountability (OECD, 2010). In other words, policies that grant schools more autonomy without providing support or accountability mechanisms are not the answer.

Notes

1. For more information on the questions that were asked of teachers and school principals, see the TALIS questionnaires in the TALIS 2013 Technical Report.

2. To clearly understand the reasoning behind this analytical decision, it is important to remember that the main purpose of TALIS is to gather data on teachers and their working conditions. If issues are examined on a school-level only, the number of teachers at the school is not taken into account. A problem of particular policy interest might plague 25% of schools in a country, but these could be the smallest schools in the country, and thus this problem would affect only a small minority of the teachers in that country. If analyses are conducted at a teacher level, however, they provide a more accurate picture of the percentage of the country's teacher population that is affected by a particular issue, and thus enable policy decisions to be made that more accurately reflect the teacher issues at stake.

3. The reference category is the combination of teachers who answered "not at all prepared" or "somewhat prepared".

4. The questionnaire asked teachers to refer to their employment in the school that was selected to participate in TALIS 2013 and not include employment at any other schools in which they may work.

5. The questionnaire asked teachers to refer to all their current teaching jobs combined.

6. Only government-controlled schools were included in the Malaysian sample.

7. To determine the cut-off points for the percentages of students needed to form these categories of more challenging schools, the overall distribution of teachers in schools with certain proportions of students with each type of characteristic was examined. These thresholds of more than 10% or more than 30% were chosen because in each one of these cases, fewer than one-fifth of the teachers overall work in schools characterised as being more challenging.

8. In some countries, teachers who teach mostly or entirely special-needs students may not have received training to teach a particular subject.

9. In this survey, the school types were defined as either publicly managed or privately managed. Note that in some countries, the privately-managed-schools category includes schools that receive significant government funding (government-dependent private schools).

10. The data used for the number of students, number of school staff and ratio presented in this section are reported by principals and are means of the schools where lower secondary teachers worked. The education provision in these schools may extend across ISCED levels (e.g. in schools that offer both lower and upper secondary education) and therefore may not apply only to teachers or students in lower secondary education.

11. Class-size data are reported by teachers and refer to a randomly chosen class they currently teach from their weekly timetable.

12. Based on head counts reported by principals.

13. Support personnel include teacher aides or other non-teaching professionals who provide instruction or support teachers in providing instruction, professional curriculum/instructional specialists, educational media specialists, psychologists and nurses.

14. School administrative personnel include receptionists, secretaries and administrative assistants, and school management personnel include principals, assistant principals and other management staff whose main activity is management.

A note regarding Israel

The statistical data for Israel are supplied by and under the responsibility of the relevant Israeli authorities. The use of such data by the OECD is without prejudice to the status of the Golan Heights, East Jerusalem and Israeli settlements in the West Bank under the terms of international law.

References

Akiba, M. and **G. Liang** (2014), "Teacher qualification and the achievement gap: A cross-national analysis of 50 countries", in J.V. Clark (ed.), *Closing the Achievement Gap from an International Perspective: Transforming STEM for Effective Education,* Springer, New York.

Antecol, H., O. Eren and **S. Ozbeklik** (2012), "The effect of teacher gender on student achievement in primary school: Evidence from a randomized experiment", IZA Discussion Paper, No. 6453, *http://ftp.iza.org/dp6453.pdf.*

Barnett, R.R. et al. (2002), "Size, performance and effectiveness: Cost-constrained measures of best-practice performance and secondary-school size", *Education Economics,* Vol. 10, pp. 291-310.

Beilock, S.L. et al. (2009), "Female teachers' math anxiety affects girls' math achievement", *Proceedings of the National Academy of Science of the United States of America-PNAS,* Vol. 107/5, pp.1860-1863.

Blomqvist et al. (2008), *Att välja eller välja bort läraryrket. Manliga klasslärares karriärval (To choose or to avoid choosing teacher profession. Male class teachers' selection of career)* Publikation 15/2008, Pedagogiska fakulteten, Åbo Akademi (Faculty of Education, Åbo Akademi University), Turku.

Bonesronning, H., T. Falch and **B. Strom** (2005), "Teacher sorting, teacher quality, and student composition", *European Economic Review,* Vol. 49, pp. 457-483.

Bowles, T.J. and **R. Bosworth** (2002), "Scale economies in public education: Evidence from school level data", *Journal of Education Finance,* Vol. 28, pp. 283-300.

Boyd, D. et al. (2008), "Who leaves? Teacher attrition and student achievement", *NBER Working Paper,* No. 14022.

Buddin, R. and **G. Zamarro** (2009), "Teacher qualifications and student achievement in urban elementary schools", *Journal of Urban Economic,* Vol. 66, pp. 103-115.

Clotfelter, C.T., H.F. Ladd and **J.L. Vigdor** (2010), "Teacher credentials and student achievement in high school: A cross-subject analysis with student fixed effects", *The Journal of Human Resources,* Vol. 45/3, pp. 655-681.

Clotfelter, C.T., H.F. Ladd and **J.L. Vigdor** (2007), "Teacher credentials and student achievement: Longitudinal analysis with student fixed effects", *Economics of Education Review,* Vol. 26/6, pp. 673-682.

Clotfelter, C.T. et al. (2007), "High poverty schools and the distribution of principals and teachers", *CALDER Working Paper 1,* CALDER Urban Institute, National Center for Analysis of Longitudinal Data in Education Research, Washington, DC.

Cochran-Smith, M. and **K. Zeichner** (eds.) (2005), *Studying Teacher Education: The Report of the AERA Panel on Research and Teacher Education,* Lawrence Erlbaum Publishers, Mahweh, NJ.

Cohen, J. et al. (2009), "School climate: Research, policy, practice and teacher education", *Teachers College Record,* Vol. 111/1, pp. 180-213.

Croninger, R.G. et al. (2007), "Teacher qualifications and early learning: Effects of certification, degree, and experience on first-grade student achievement", *Economics of Education Review,* Vol. 26, pp. 312-324.

Darling-Hammond, L. (2004), "Inequality and the right to learn: Access to qualified teachers in California's public schools", *Teachers College Record,* Vol. 106/10, pp.1936-1966.

Darling-Hammond, L. (2000), "Teacher quality and student achievement: A review of state policy evidence", *Education Policy Analysis Archives,* Vol. 8/1, *http://epaa.asu.edu/epaa/v8n1.*

Darling-Hammond, L. and A. Lieberman (eds.) (2012), *Teacher Education around the World,* Routledge, Abingdon.

Darling-Hammond, L. et al. (2005), "Does teacher preparation matter? Evidence about teacher certification, Teach for America, and teacher effectiveness", *Education Policy Analysis Archives,* 13(42), *http://epaa.asu.edu/epaa/v13n42/.*

Drudy, S. (2008), "Gender balance/gender bias: The teaching profession and the impact of feminisation", *Gender and Education,* Vol. 20/4, pp. 309-323.

Eccles, J.S. et al. (1993), "Negative effects of traditional middle schools on students'motivation", *Elementary School Journal,* Vol. 93, pp. 553-574.

Eliot, M. et al. (2010), "Supportive school climate and student willingness to seek help for bullying and threats of violence", *Journal of School Psychology,* Vol. 48, pp. 533-553.

European Commission (2012), "Supporting the teaching professions for better learning outcomes", [SWD(2012) 374 final], European Commission, November 2012, p. 58, Strasbourg.

Finnegan, K. (2007), "Charter school autonomy: The mismatch between theory and practice", *Educational Policy,* Vol. 21/3, pp. 503-526.

Fulton, K., I. Yoon and C. Lee (2005), "Induction into learning communities", *http://nctaf.org/wp-content/uploads/NCTAF_Induction_Paper_2005.pdf*

Gates, S.M. et al. (2006), "Mobility and turnover among school principals", *Economics of Education Review,* Vol. 25, pp. 289-302.

Goodson, I., S. Moore and A. Hargreaves (2006), "Teacher nostalgia and the sustainability of reform: The generation and degeneration of teachers' missions, memory and meaning", *Educational Administrative Quarterly,* Vol. 42, pp. 42-61.

Hanushek, E.A. (2006), "School resources", in E.A. Hanushek and F. Welch (eds.), *Handbook of Economics of Education,* Vol. 2, pp. 866-908, Amsterdam.

Hanushek, E.A., S. Link and L. Woessmann (2013), "Does school autonomy make sense everywhere? Panel estimates from PISA", *Journal of Development Economics,* Vol. 104, pp. 212-232.

Hanushek, E.A. and S.G. Rivkin (2004), "How to improve the supply of high-quality teachers", *Brookings Papers on Education Policy,* Vol. 7, pp. 7-25.

Harris, D.N. and T.R. Sass (2011), "Teacher training, teacher quality and student achievement", *Journal of Public Economics,* Vol. 95, pp. 798-812.

Holmlund, H. and K. Sund (2008), "Is the gender gap in school performance affected by the sex of the teacher?", *Labour Economics,* Vol. 15, pp. 37-53.

Hoy, W.K. and A.E. Woolfolk (1993), "Teachers' sense of efficacy and the organizational health of schools", *The Elementary School Journal,* Vol. 93, pp. 355-372.

Ingersoll, R.M. (2001), "Teacher turnover and teacher shortages: An organizational analysis", *American Educational Research Journal,* Vol. 38/3, pp. 499-534.

Jackson, K. (2009), "Student demographics, teacher sorting, and teacher quality: Evidence from the end of school desegregation", *Journal of Labor Economics,* Vol. 27, pp. 213-256.

Konstantopoulos, S. (2006), "Trends of school effects on student achievement: Evidence from NLS:72, HSB:82, and NELS:92", *Teacher College Record,* Vol. 108/12, pp. 2550-2581.

Lankford, H., S. Loeb and J. Wyckoff (2002), "Teacher sorting and the plight of urban schools: A descriptive analysis", *Educational Evaluation and Policy Analysis,* Vol. 24/1, pp. 37-62.

Larsen, S.E. (2010), "Teacher MA attainment rates, 1970-2000", *Economics of Education Review,* Vol. 29, pp. 772-782.

Leigh, A. (2010), "Estimating teacher effectiveness from two-year changes in students' test scores", *Economics of Education Review,* Vol. 29, pp. 480-488.

Leithwood, K. and D. Jantzi (2009), "A review of empirical evidence of school size effects: A policy perspective", *Review of Educational Research,* Vol. 79, pp. 464-490.

MacNeil, A., D. Prater and S. Busch (2009), "The effects of school culture and climate on student achievement", *International Journal of Leadership in Education: Theory and Practice,* Vol. 12/1, pp.73-84.

Monk, D.H. (1994), "Subject area preparation of secondary mathematics and science teachers and student achievement", *Economics of Education Review,* Vol. 13/2, pp.125-145.

OECD (2013a), *Education at a Glance 2013: OECD Indicators*, OECD Publishing, Paris, *http://dx.doi.org/10.1787/eag-2013-en*.

OECD (2013b), *PISA 2012 Results: Excellence through Equity: Giving Every Student the Chance to Succeed (Volume II)*, PISA, OECD Publishing, Paris, *http://dx.doi.org/10.1787/9789264201132-en*.

OECD (2010), *PISA 2009 Results: What makes a school successful? Resources, Policies and Practices (Volume IV)*, PISA, OECD Publishing, Paris, *http://dx.doi.org/10.1787/9789264091559-en*.

OECD (2009), *Creating Effective Teaching and Learning Environments: First Results from TALIS*, OECD Publishing, Paris, *http://dx.doi.org/10.1787/9789264072992-en*.

OECD (2007), *PISA 2006: Science Competencies for Tomorrow's World: Volume 1: Analysis*, PISA, OECD Publishing, Paris, *http://dx.doi.org/10.1787/9789264040014-en*.

OECD (2005), *Teachers Matter: Attracting, Developing and Retaining Effective Teachers*, Education and Training Policy, OECD Publishing, Paris, *http://dx.doi.org/10.1787/9789264018044-en*.

Pont, B., D. Nusche and H. Moorman (2008), *Improving School Leadership, Volume 1: Policy and Practice,* OECD Publishing, Paris, *http://dx.doi.org/10.1787/9789264044715-en*.

Ready, D.D., V.E. Lee and K.G. Welner (2004), "Educational equity and school structure: School size, overcrowding, and schools-within-schools", *Teachers College Record,* Vol. 106, pp. 1989-2014.

Rivkin, S., E. Hanushek and J. Kain (2005), "Teachers, schools, and academic achievement", *Econometrica,* Vol. 73/2, pp. 417-458.

Rockoff, J.E. (2004), "The impact of individual teachers on students' achievement: Evidence from panel data", *American Economic Review*, Vol. 94/2, pp. 247-252.

Ronfeldt, M. and M. Reininger (2012), "More of better student teaching?", *Teaching and Teacher Education,* Vol. 28, pp. 1091-1106.

Scheerens, J. (1993), "Basic school effectiveness research: Items for a research agenda", *School Effectiveness and School Improvement*, Vol. 4/1, 17-36.

Scheerens, J., C.J.A.J. Vermeulen and W.J. Pelgrum (1989), "Generalizability of instructional and school effectiveness indicators across nations", *International Journal of Educational Research*, Vol. 13/7, pp. 789-799.

Schleicher, A. (ed.) (2012), *Preparing Teachers and Developing School Leaders for the 21st century: Lessons from Around the World,* OECD Publishing, Paris, *http://dx.doi.org/10.1787/9789264174559-en*

Schreiber, J.B. (2002), "Institutional and student factors and their influence on advanced mathematics achievement", *The Journal of Educational Research,* Vol. 95/5, pp. 274-286.

Sherblom, S., J. Marshall and J. Sherblom (2006), "The relationship between school climate and math and reading achievement", *Journal of Research in Character Education,* Vol. 4/1-2, pp. 19-31.

Stewart, E. (2008). "School structural characteristics, student effort, peer associations, and parental involvement", *Education and Urban Society,* Vol. 40/2, pp. 179-204.

Thapa, A. et al. (2013), "A review of school climate research", *Review of Educational Research,* Vol. 83/3, pp. 357-385.

UNESCO Institute for Statistics (2009), *Global Education Digest 2009: Comparing Education Statistics Across the World*, UNESCO Institute for Statistics, Montreal.

UNESCO Institute for Statistics (2006), *Teachers and Educational Quality: Monitoring Global Needs for 2015*, UNESCO Institute for Statistics, Montreal.

Ward, L. et al. (2013), "Teacher preparation to proficiency and beyond: Exploring the landscape", *Asia Pacific Journal of Education,* Vol. 33/1, pp. 68-80.

Weiss, E.M. (1999), "Perceived workplace conditions and first-year teachers' morale, career choice commitment, and planned retention: A secondary analysis", *Teaching and Teacher Education*, Vol. 15/8, pp. 861-879.

White, P., and E. Smith (2005), "What can PISA tell us about teacher shortages?", *European Journal of Education,* Vol. 40, pp. 93-112.

Willms, J.D. (2000), "Monitoring school performance for standards-based reform", *Evaluation and Research in Education*, Vol. 14, pp. 237-253.

Wößmann, L. (2007), "International evidence on school competition, autonomy, and accountability: A review", *Peabody Journal of Education,* Vol. 82/2-3, pp. 473-497.

3

The Importance of School Leadership

Unlike other chapters of this volume, which take the teachers' perspective in the analyses, the data in this chapter focus on principals and the schools in which they work. This chapter provides details about the increasingly demanding role of school principals; their responsibilities; the instructional leadership they provide; their demographic characteristics, formal education, prior work experience, and engagement in professional development; and their satisfaction with their work. Findings from the cross-national comparisons are used to draw inferences for policy and practice.

Highlights

- Principals in countries and economies taking part in the OECD Teaching and Learning International Survey (TALIS) have a demanding and far-ranging set of responsibilities. On average, principals spend the most time (41%) managing human and material resources, planning, reporting and adhering to regulations.

- In some countries, principals who show high levels of instructional leadership are more likely to report using student performance and student evaluation results to develop the school's educational goals and programmes and to report working on a professional development plan for their school.

- Principals with higher levels of instructional leadership tend to spend more time on curriculum and teaching-related tasks, and in most countries they are more likely to directly observe classroom teaching as part of the formal appraisal of teachers' work in their school.

- The gender distribution of principals differs from the distribution of teachers. Although the majority of teachers in all but one country are women, the proportion of female principals is generally lower.

- Across TALIS countries and economies, principals are well educated. The majority of principals have completed formal education at the tertiary level, which, on average, included participation in school administration or principal training programmes, teacher preparation programmes or instructional leadership training.

- On average across TALIS countries and economies, school principals have 21 years of teaching experience.

- While principals who report high levels of distributed leadership and instructional leadership also report higher job satisfaction, heavier workloads and lack of shared work and decision making have a negative relationship with principals' job satisfaction.

INTRODUCTION

School principals are often the connection between teachers, students and their parents or guardians, the education system and the wider community in which a school exists. Although principals have always occupied this intersection, the profession has become increasingly challenging over time. Some principals say they confront incompatible demands, referring to the challenge of meeting the demands of teachers, students and parents or guardians on the one hand, while addressing the expectations placed upon them by the systems in which they work and the communities in which schools are located on the other. In the contexts in which most decision-making authority has been devolved to the school level, principals can be especially challenged by the number and variety of demands they face. These demands can include increasing social diversity, the inclusion of students with special needs, an emphasis on retaining students until graduation, and ensuring that students have the knowledge necessary to be able to participate in an increasingly competitive economy. These demands require that principals manage human and material resources, communicate and interact with individuals who occupy a variety of positions, make evidence-informed decisions and provide the instructional leadership to teachers necessary for helping students succeed in school.

Thus, school leadership is increasingly a priority for many countries concerned about improving student achievement results (Pont, Nusche and Moorman, 2008; Robinson, Hohepa and Lloyd, 2009) and in improving schools that are underperforming or failing (Branch, Hanushek and Rivkin, 2013). Many see principals as contributing to student achievement through their impact on the school, its organisation and climate and especially upon teachers and teaching. Hallinger and Heck (1996) observed that the relationship between principal leadership and student achievement was difficult to establish empirically. One reason for this is that the role of the school principal is not particularly well understood. Marzano, Waters and McNulty (2005) assert that, contrary to what one might expect, there is no clear, well-articulated body of research about the role of the principal and school leadership. They reference the historical line of literature arguing that leadership at the school level is linked to the existence and clarity of a school's mission and goals, the climate that prevails in the school as well as in individual classrooms, teachers' attitudes, the practices that teachers employ in the classroom, the way that curriculum and instruction are organised and the opportunity that students have to learn.

The principal's influence on students is often indirect, which can make it difficult to understand ways in which principals' leadership or decisions might affect student achievement. (see, for example, Ross and Gray, 2006). School leadership

and a school's success are linked, mediated by the impact that principals have on the organisation of teachers' work, school organisation and relationships between the school and the wider community (Aydin, Sarier and Uysal, 2013; Lucas et al., 2012; Chin, 2007; Bell, Bolam and Cubillo, 2003; Hallinger, Bickman and Davis, 1996). In other words, principals influence the climate and organisation of their school and its staff and the conditions under which the staff, especially teachers, work.

In a number of contexts, principals are being accorded much greater decision-making authority than they have enjoyed in the past. Sometimes described as the "devolution revolution" (Baker and LeTendre, 2005), this movement has given schools in some countries more relative autonomy for the management and control of education. While the forms and names of such entities differ across countries and sometimes even within countries (local educational authorities, charter schools and local school councils, for example), greater autonomy typically includes increased principal decision-making authority and increased demands for results. It is not surprising that in almost every country, the demands on and responsibilities of school principals are greater today than at any time in the past.

The TALIS data add to the collective understanding of principals' roles and their leadership in the varied policy contexts represented among the countries taking part in TALIS 2013 and of principals' potential for improving schools and student achievement. This chapter begins by discussing the increasingly complex and demanding work in which contemporary principals engage, including their development of school goals and programmes and professional development plans. The chapter is then devoted to what many regard as the most important professional responsibility that principals carry out: instructional leadership.

The chapter's next section provides a profile of principals in TALIS countries and economies, including information about gender and age distribution, formal education, leadership training, practical experience and continued professional development of the principals who responded to the survey. The chapter then describes the relationships between principals' leadership styles and a variety of other factors previously discussed in the chapter. These factors include the impact of instructional leadership on principals' work setting goals and programmes, their work on professional development planning, outcomes of teacher appraisals and the time principals spend on curriculum and teaching-related tasks. The chapter concludes with a discussion of principals' job satisfaction and implications for policy and practice that can be drawn from all of the data examined.

THE PRINCIPAL'S WORK

The work of a principal is demanding (see, for example, Day et al., 2008), and the time for meeting the demands is limited. The TALIS data provide a useful starting point for understanding the work of principals and how they prioritise their time.

Box 3.1. **Principal working time in primary and upper secondary schools**

Tables 3.1.a and 3.1.b contain the data on time distribution for principals in primary (ISCED 1) and upper secondary (ISCED 3) schools. In general, the way that principals distribute their time is similar across education levels. There are, however, a few notable exceptions.

In Finland and Mexico, primary school principals report spending a smaller proportion of their time on administrative and leadership tasks and meetings (40% and 32%, respectively) than their lower secondary colleagues (48% and 38%, respectively). In contrast, primary school principals in Finland report spending more of their time on curriculum and teaching-related tasks (29%) than lower secondary school principals (18%).

In upper secondary schools, administrative and leadership tasks consume even more time for principals in Finland, who report spending more than half (55%) of their time on these tasks and meetings. This proportion is similar to the average in Denmark (51%) and Iceland (50%). Upper secondary principals in Denmark, Finland and Iceland report spending about half as much time as their colleagues in lower secondary schools interacting with parents (4-5% versus 10-11%). In contrast, principals tend to report spending more time interacting with local and regional community, businesses and industry partners in upper secondary as compared with lower secondary education. This is particularly the case in Finland (10% compared with 5% of their time) and in Norway (18% compared with 12% of their time).

■ Figure 3.1 ■

Principals' working time

Average proportion of time lower secondary education principals report spending on the following activities

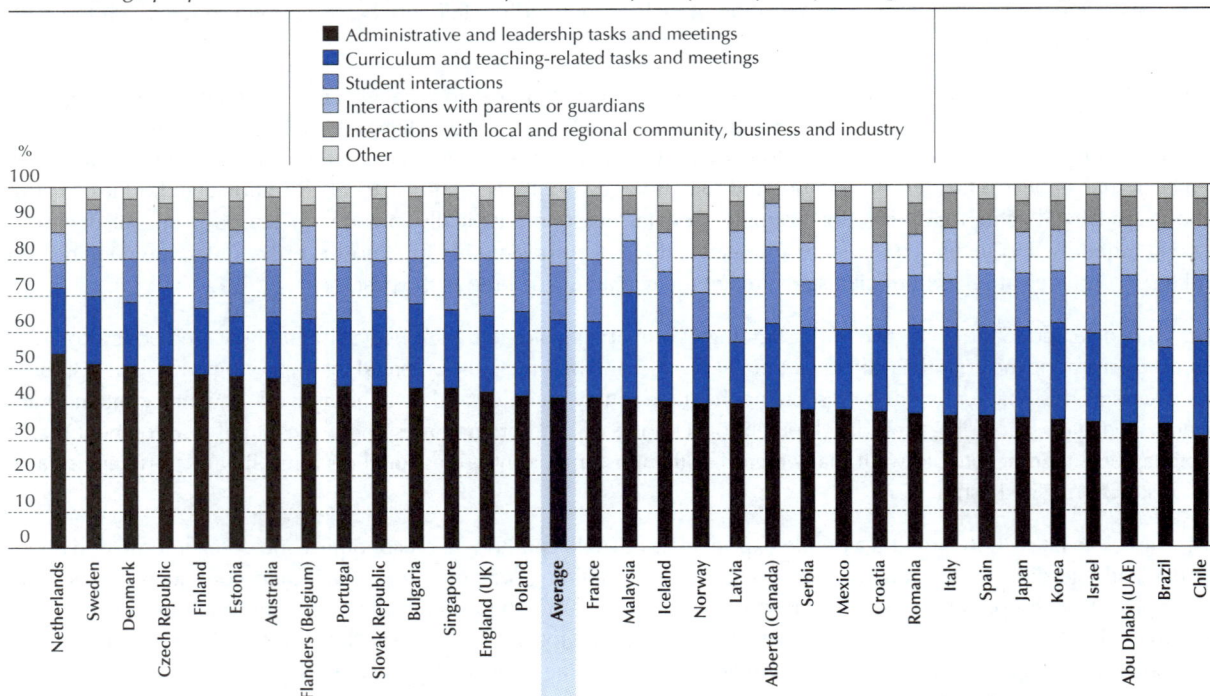

Countries are ranked in descending order, based on the percentage of time principals spend on administrative and leadership tasks and meetings.
Source: OECD, TALIS 2013 Database, Table 3.1.
StatLink ⬛⬛⬛ http://dx.doi.org/10.1787/888933041231

Respondents to the TALIS 2013 survey were asked how they distribute their work time. As Table 3.1 and Figure 3.1 indicate, on average, principals devote 41% of their time to administrative and leadership tasks and meetings; 21% of their time to curriculum and teaching-related tasks and meetings; 15% to interactions with students; 11% to interactions with parents or guardians; and 7% to interactions with local and regional community, businesses and industries. While there is definitely variation between countries for each of these tasks, Figure 3.1 shows that nearly two-thirds of principals' time, on average, is spent on administrative and leadership and curriculum and teaching. While this can be seen as the main business of the school and main responsibility for principals, it leaves very little time for principals to carry out other tasks. Box 3.1 shares the data on working time for principals of primary and upper secondary schools in the countries with data for these populations.

The work of principals includes a variety of administrative activities that, if not performed, could impede the effective operation of the school. The TALIS survey asked principals about the leadership activities in which they engaged during the preceding 12 months. Table 3.2 and Figure 3.2 present data about the proportion of principals who report having engaged "frequently" in particular leadership activities.[1]

Among the most challenging of a teacher's responsibilities is maintaining a productive and orderly environment in which teachers can teach and students learn (see, for example, MacNeil and Prater, 1999). Students cannot learn and teachers cannot teach if students are unruly. Collaboration between principals and teachers to solve classroom discipline problems varies significantly across countries. Malaysia and Romania are on one end of the spectrum, where more than 90% of principals report high-frequency collaboration with teachers to solve discipline problems. Australia, Estonia, Iceland, Japan, the Netherlands and England (United Kingdom) are at the other end of the spectrum, where more than half of principals (58%-72%) report infrequent collaboration with teachers to solve classroom discipline problems (Table 3.2). It is important to keep in mind that the patterns reported here may reflect differences in disciplinary issues among countries rather than differences in the attention that principals pay to disciplinary matters. Further investigation is necessary to determine the significance of these differences.

 TALIS 2013 RESULTS: AN INTERNATIONAL PERSPECTIVE ON TEACHING AND LEARNING

■ Figure 3.2 ■
Principals' leadership
Percentage of lower secondary education principals who report having engaged in the following leadership activities, and the frequency in which they engaged, during the 12 months prior to the survey

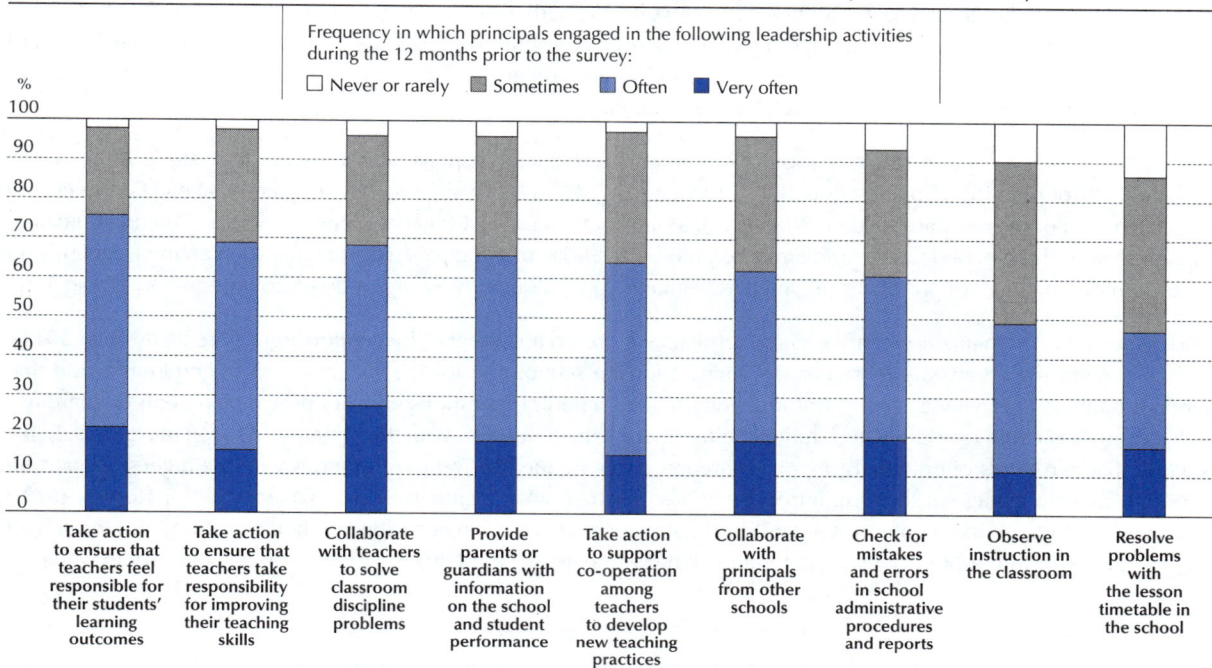

Leadership activities are ranked in descending order, based on the percentage of principals who engaged "often" or "very often" in a specific leadership activity during the 12 months prior to the survey.
Source: OECD, TALIS 2013 Database, Tables 3.2 and 3.2.Web.
StatLink ⟨⟩ http://dx.doi.org/10.1787/888933041250

In addition to the help principals may provide to teachers in solving disciplinary problems, principals can observe instruction and provide teachers with feedback based on their observations (OECD, 2013; see also Chapter 5). Veenman, Visser and Wijkamp (1998) provide evidence from a programme for training Dutch principals in coaching skills, showing, among other things, that principal coaching helped to strengthen teacher autonomy, enabling teachers to reflect on the effectiveness of their instruction and to formulate action plans for improving their teaching. Improving instructional effectiveness and improving teaching should, in turn, help to improve student learning outcomes.

The average proportion of principals who say they frequently observe instruction in the classroom is more evenly divided. On average, nearly half (49%) of school leaders say they make observations frequently. Frequently observing instruction in the classrooms is more commonly reported among principals in Bulgaria (89%), Malaysia (88%), Romania (82%) and Abu Dhabi (United Arab Emirates) (88%) and substantially less commonly reported among principals in Estonia (7%), Finland (11%), France (8%), Iceland (15%) and Portugal (5%).

Another challenge that teachers face is maintaining the currency of their knowledge and practice. By encouraging teachers to learn from one another, principals help teachers remain current in their practice and may also help to develop more collaborative practices between teachers in their schools (see Chapter 7). Principals were asked about taking action to support co-operation among teachers to develop new teaching practices. As Figure 3.2 indicates, on average 64% of principals report taking such action frequently (ranging from 34% in Japan to 98% in Malaysia) (see also Table 3.2.Web). In Chile, Malaysia, Romania, Serbia, the Slovak Republic and Abu Dhabi (United Arab Emirates), principals report the highest incidence (between 80% and 98%) of frequently supporting co-operation among their teachers around the development of new teaching practices. In Denmark, Estonia, Japan, the Netherlands and Flanders (Belgium), more than half of principals report never, rarely or only sometimes doing this. It would be interesting to learn whether this is simply a lack of action on the part of principals in these countries or whether it is simply unnecessary because teachers in these schools might have cultures of co-operation already.

Students' achievement depends on the experience and skills their teachers possess (Jepsen and Rivkin, 2009; Huang and Moon, 2008; Biniaminov and Glasman, 1983; Veldman and Brophy, 1974). Principals can play an important part in ensuring that teachers take responsibility for improving their teaching skills. Table 3.2 and Figure 3.2 show that on average a majority of principals (69%) take this action frequently (ranging from 39% in Japan to 95% in Malaysia). Bulgaria (88%), Chile (88%), Malaysia (95%), Romania (85%), Serbia (82%), Singapore (84%) and Abu Dhabi (United Arab Emirates) (93%) are among the high-incidence countries where principals frequently act in this regard. Finland (60%), Japan (61%), Norway (53%), Sweden (56%) and Flanders (Belgium) (59%) are the countries where more than half of principals report doing this never or rarely or only sometimes.

Many principals also remind teachers about the importance of taking responsibility for what their students learn. On average, 76% of principals (ranging from 33% in Japan to 100% in Malaysia) say they frequently take action to ensure that teachers feel responsible for their students' learning outcomes. In Bulgaria, Chile, Malaysia, Poland, Romania, Singapore and Abu Dhabi (United Arab Emirates), more than 90% of principals report taking such action frequently. In contrast, more than half of principals in Denmark, Finland, Japan and Norway report doing so infrequently (Table 3.2).

Student success is enhanced when the efforts of teachers are complemented by support from parents (Jeynes, 2011). Parents play an important role in expressing support for the school and for the success of their children, a role that depends upon parents having accurate information from the school. The responsibility for providing parents or guardians with information about the school and student performance sometimes rests with the principal. As seen in Figure 3.2, this is a task that two-thirds of principals on average report doing frequently. The five countries with the highest proportion of principals who engage in this task infrequently are Croatia (62%), Denmark (72%), Finland (75%), Norway (63%) and Sweden (70%). In these countries, it could be that parents are not being provided with information from the school very frequently or the responsibility for communicating with parents could lie elsewhere (with teachers, for example).

Box 3.2. **Activities in which primary and upper secondary principals engaged in the 12 months prior to the survey**

Table 3.2.a and Table 3.2.b present data on the percentage of principals who report engaging often or very often in a number of leadership activities for those countries that implemented TALIS in their primary (ISCED 1) or upper secondary (ISCED 3) schools.

For many of the activities examined, principals across different education levels do not differ greatly. In many of these cases, this may indicate that these activities are considered important whether a principal works in a primary, a lower secondary or an upper secondary school. This is the case for activities such as supporting co-operation among teachers to develop new teaching practices or ensuring that teachers feel responsible for their students' learning.

There are, however, activities that primary school principals in some countries are less likely than their lower secondary colleagues to identify as being an important part of their work. This is the case in Norway, where primary school principals are much less likely to report that they collaborate with teachers to solve classroom disciplinary problems (48%) than their colleagues in lower secondary schools (78%). Primary school leaders in Poland, on the other hand, are more likely to say that they collaborate with principals in other schools (79%) as compared with principals in lower secondary schools (61%).

There is also a divergence in practice between lower secondary and upper secondary school principals. In Denmark, Finland, Iceland, Norway and Poland, principals in upper secondary schools are much less likely to report that they collaborate with teachers to solve classroom discipline problems than those in lower secondary schools. A smaller proportion of upper secondary principals in Mexico and Norway say that they observe instruction in the classroom (48% and 6%, respectively) compared with their lower secondary peers (64% and 21%, respectively). In half of the countries with comparable data (Denmark, Finland, Iceland, Mexico and Norway, specifically), principals in upper secondary schools are less likely to provide parents with information on school and student performance than principals in lower secondary schools. Upper secondary principals in Mexico and Norway are also less likely to collaborate with principals from other schools (44% and 56%, respectively) than their lower secondary peers (57% and 71%, respectively).

Identifying and correcting errors in administrative procedures or reports and resolving problems with the school's timetable of lessons are two of the many administrative tasks that principals perform. On average, 61% of principals say they check frequently for mistakes and errors in school administrative procedures and reports. On average, slightly less than half of principals (47%) say they frequently resolve problems with the lesson timetable in the school. In Chile, Finland, Malaysia, Romania and Abu Dhabi (United Arab Emirates), 74-84% of principals say they frequently resolve timetable problems, while in the Czech Republic, Estonia, Japan, Latvia and England (United Kingdom), between 80% and 91% of school principals say they resolve school timetable problems infrequently. Both of these administrative tasks are important, yet in some countries principals are much freer from this administrative burden than in others. It would be interesting to learn how and whether these tasks are distributed to other members of the staff in these countries.

Collaboration between principals from different schools is one way that principals can learn from and support one another. The TALIS data in Table 3.2 also provide an indication of the extent to which such collaboration occurs (see also Table 3.2.Web). On average, 62% of principals indicate that they collaborate with principals in other schools frequently. Large proportions of the principals in Finland (82%), Malaysia (89%), the Netherlands (86%), Romania (87%) and Serbia (96%) say they collaborate with principals from other schools frequently. In contrast, significant proportions in Brazil (10%), Chile (18%), Israel (8%) and Spain (9%) say they never or rarely collaborate with principals in other schools. Box 3.2 presents the data on the activities that primary and upper secondary principals reported participating in for the countries with available data.

A strong school leader establishes a climate conducive to teaching and learning and fosters community support for the efforts of the teaching staff. In many countries, concern about improving student achievement results has made strong school leadership a priority (Pont, Nusche and Moorman, 2008; Branch, Hanushek and Rivkin, 2013). The literature devoted to principal leadership is replete with examples of the ways that principals exert leadership (see especially Chapter 4 in Robinson, Hohepa, Lloyd, 2009), including planning the school's goals and programme (Grissom, Loeb and Master, 2013) and its professional development plan (OECD, 2013); collaborating with teachers to solve classroom discipline problems (MacNeil and Prater, 1999); observing instruction (Veenman, Visser and Wijkamp, 1998); encouraging teachers to take responsibility for improving their teaching and for student learning; and providing parents or guardians with information about the school and about student performance (Jeynes, 2011).

Planning school goals, programmes and professional development

As data have become more available to principals over the last quarter century, there has been a transition from reliance on a principal's own knowledge in making decisions to making choices informed by the use of more readily available data. This transition has been accompanied by increased demands for accountability (Vanhoof et al., 2014). Today, more than at any time in the past, principals are responsible for the development of the school's educational goals and programmes and for the use of student performance and student evaluation results to develop those goals and programmes.

Data about principals' participation in activities related to a school development plan appear in Table 3.3 and Figure 3.3. Nearly nine in ten principals on average across TALIS countries report using student performance and student evaluation results (including national or international assessments) to develop the school's educational goals and programmes. The proportions of principals who reported using student performance and student evaluation results to develop the school's educational goals and programmes was lowest in Croatia (75%), Finland (74%) and Flanders (Belgium) (58%) and nearly universal in Malaysia (99%), Norway (98%), Singapore (99%), Alberta (Canada) (97%) and England (United Kingdom) (99%). It would be interesting to learn whether the actions of school leaders in the latter five locales are influenced by a national policy in this regard.

In addition to the development of their school's goals and programmes, principals are increasingly responsible for working on a professional development plan for their school. Although this plan is an important facet of a principal's work, on average the proportion of principals working on such a plan is nearly ten percentage points lower (79%) than the average proportion of principals who report using student performance and student evaluation results to develop the school's educational goals and programmes. Figure 3.3 shows that this pattern is found in most countries. The proportion of principals who report working on a professional development plan for their school is lowest in Finland and Spain (40%) and almost comprehensive in Malaysia (97%), Singapore (99%), Abu Dhabi (United Arab Emirates) (97%) and Alberta (Canada) (98%). Box 3.3 presents principals' reported activities related to school development plans in primary and upper secondary education for countries with available data.

■ Figure 3.3 ■

Principals' participation in a school development plan

Percentage of lower secondary education principals who report having engaged in the following activities related to a school development plan in the 12 months prior to the survey

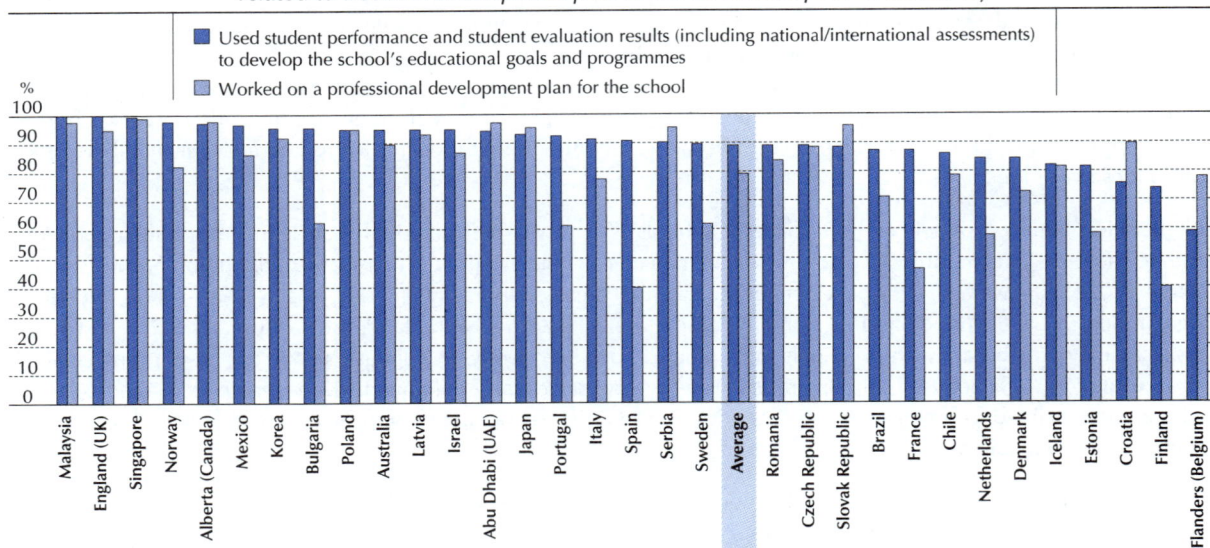

■ Used student performance and student evaluation results (including national/international assessments) to develop the school's educational goals and programmes
■ Worked on a professional development plan for the school

Countries are ranked in descending order, based on the percentage of principals who used student performance and student evaluation results (including national/international assessments) to develop the school's educational goals and programmes.
Source: OECD, TALIS 2013 Database, Table 3.3.
StatLink ■■■■ http://dx.doi.org/10.1787/888933041269

Box 3.3. Activities related to a school development plan in primary and upper secondary schools

Tables 3.3.a and 3.3.b show the percentages of principals at the primary (ISCED 1) and upper secondary (ISCED 3) levels who report engaging in activities related to a school development plan in the 12 months prior to the survey.

Primary school principals in Finland report working on a professional development plan for the school and using student performance and student evaluation results to develop the school's educational goals and programmes at lower rates (32% and 56%, respectively) than the other countries for which data on primary education are available (overall average of 74% and 82%, respectively). Compared with the average, primary school principals in Denmark and Flanders (Belgium) are also less likely to say that they use student performance and evaluation results to develop the school's educational goals and programmes (75% and 74%, respectively). In contrast, almost all primary principals in Mexico, Norway and Poland report doing so.

As was the case at the other levels, principals in upper secondary schools in Finland report working on a professional development plan at a lower rate than do principals in other countries for which these data are available (54% versus 84%). However, this proportion is higher for upper secondary principals in Finland than for principals in lower secondary schools in Finland. Although all or almost all upper secondary principals in Norway and Singapore report using student performance and student evaluation results to develop the school's educational goals and programmes, those in Denmark (78%), Finland (76%) and Iceland (79%) report doing so at slightly lower rates than average (89%).

Sharing responsibilities

Because of its complexity, the work of the school and especially the work of the principal are increasingly recognised as responsibilities that are or should be more broadly shared. The increased responsibility and accountability demanded of school principals suggests that to meet their responsibilities, principals would be prudent to share their work among others inside and outside the school (Schleicher, 2012).

Chapter 2 examines issues of school autonomy, looking at the percentage of teachers whose school leader reported that considerable responsibility for certain tasks was held at a school level (see Table 2.24). This chapter looks at those principals who do have significant responsibility for tasks such as appointing, hiring, suspending and dismissing teachers; determining the allocation of a school's resources; approving student admission; establishing the school's disciplinary and assessment policies; and determining which courses the school offers, the course content, and the instructional resources. Table 3.4 displays the percentage of principals who have significant responsibility for such tasks and who also report a shared responsibility. When a principal reports that the responsibility for a task is shared, this indicates that an active role is played in decision making by the principal and other members of the school management team, teachers who are not part of the school management team, a school's governing board or a local or national authority.

The data reveal a wide variation among countries in the extent to which principals share responsibility for various tasks (Table 3.4). For example, the percentage of principals in Croatia, Denmark, and the Netherlands reporting shared responsibility for the appointment of teachers is 75% or more, and for Bulgaria, France, Japan, Korea, Malaysia and Mexico, it is 20% or less (the overall average being 39%). More than half of the principals in Croatia, Denmark, the Netherlands, Serbia and England (United Kingdom) report sharing responsibility for dismissing or suspending teachers from employment. Yet, in many countries (Bulgaria, the Czech Republic, France, Japan, Korea, Malaysia, Mexico, Poland, Spain and Sweden), 20% or less of the principals report sharing this responsibility (the overall average being 29%). Fewer principals report a shared responsibility for establishing teachers' salaries and pay scales (14% on average) or determining teachers' salary increases (18% on average). In only two countries (Latvia and England [United Kingdom]) do more than half of the principals indicate that they share responsibility for establishing teacher salaries and pay scales. Similarly, only in Estonia, Latvia and England (United Kingdom) do more than half of the principals share responsibility for determining salary increases for teachers.

On average, nearly half of the principals (47%) report a shared responsibility for deciding on budget allocation within the school. In some countries, however, fewer than one in four principals report this (Chile, Korea, Mexico, Romania and Abu Dhabi [United Arab Emirates]). In contrast, more than three-quarters of principals report this in Denmark and Latvia.

Overall, more principals report a shared responsibility with regard to the management of student discipline policies (61% on average) and assessment policies (52% on average). Of the principals in Denmark and Singapore, 80% or more report sharing responsibility for establishing student disciplinary policies and procedures, whereas less than half of the principals in Chile, Japan, Korea, Malaysia, Mexico, Sweden and Abu Dhabi (United Arab Emirates) report doing so. Again, more than 80% of the principals in Denmark and Singapore report that they share responsibility for establishing student assessment policies. However, in Korea, Malaysia and Spain, less than 30% say that this responsibility is shared with others.

Many principals report a shared responsibility for tasks related to choosing which learning materials are used (45%), determining course content (35%) and deciding which courses are offered (52%). At least eight of ten principals in Denmark and the Netherlands report sharing responsibility for determining the courses that their schools offer, whereas less than a quarter of their peers in Croatia, Japan and Korea report sharing this responsibility. In the Czech Republic and the Slovak Republic, 70% or more of the principals report that they share responsibility for determining the content of courses, while less than 10% of their counterparts in France, Malaysia and Flanders (Belgium) report doing so.

The variations in the extent to which particular responsibilities are shared are likely a reflection of both the policy contexts in which principals work and the proclivities of principals regarding the distribution of their responsibility. As pointed out in Chapter 2, schools may have autonomy in some areas but not in others. For example, teachers may be appointed by principals in some contexts, but salaries and increases may be determined by collective agreements negotiated outside the context of the local school.

Finally, more than a third of principals report a shared responsibility for approving students for admission to the school (37%). This is especially common in the Netherlands, where more than 80% of principals report this, while fewer than 20% of principals report this in Japan, Korea, Malaysia, Poland and Sweden.

Collaborative school culture for decision making: Distributed leadership

In addition to looking at the tasks that a principal may or may not share with colleagues, TALIS 2013 also asked principals about whether there was a collaborative culture for making decisions in the school. When school decisions involve not only the principal but others in the school who do not occupy the formal post of principal, including other members

of the school's management team, vice-principals, and classroom teachers, this can be referred to as *distributed leadership* or *distributed decision making* (see, for example, Harris, 2008; Harris, 2012; Leithwood, Mascall and Strauss, 2009; Smylie et al., 2007). Figure 3.4 indicates the distribution of responses to five items on school decisions and school collaborative culture (some of which make up the distributed leadership index). As Figure 3.4 shows, on average across TALIS countries, the vast majority of principals (more than nine in ten) agree that there is a collaborative school culture in their schools (which is characterised by mutual support) or that the school provides staff with opportunities to participate in decisions. Along those same lines, only about a third of principals agree that they make important decisions on their own. This would indicate that, according to school leaders, most schools in TALIS countries enjoy some level of distributed leadership for decision making. Box 3.4 details the items that principals responded to regarding who makes decisions at their schools and describes the index that was constructed from these items.

■ Figure 3.4 ■

School decisions and collaborative school culture

Percentage of lower secondary education principals who "strongly disagree", "disagree", "agree" or "strongly agree" with the following statement about their school

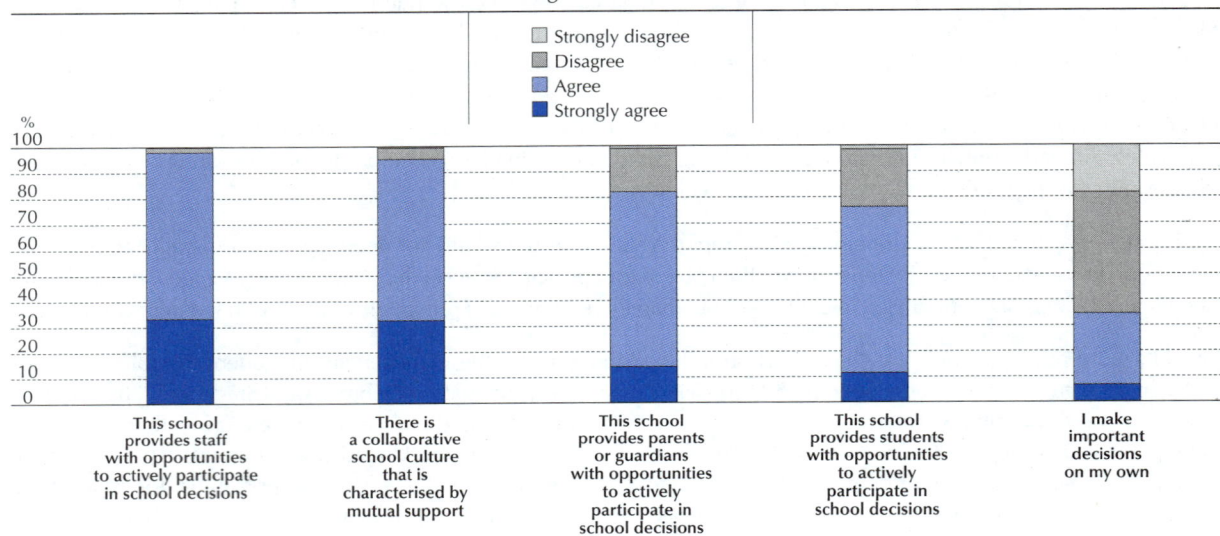

Items are ranked in descending order, based on the percentage of principals who "disagree" or "strongly disagree" with the statement about their school.
Source: OECD, TALIS 2013 Database, Table 3.35.Web.
StatLink ⌗ http://dx.doi.org/10.1787/888933041288

Box 3.4. Description of the principal distributed leadership index

To measure distributed leadership, TALIS asked principals how strongly they agreed or disagreed with these statements regarding decision-making responsibilities at their school:

- This school provides staff with opportunities to actively participate in school decisions.
- This school provides parents or guardians with opportunities to actively participate in school decisions.
- This school provides students with opportunities to actively participate in school decisions.

See Annex B for more details on the construction and validation of this index.

The relationships of principal and school characteristics to principal distributed leadership (shown in Tables 3.5 and 3.6, respectively) were explored, though no consistent significant relationships were apparent across countries (see Box 3.5 for a description of multiple linear regression analyses used to examine relationships in this chapter). However, consistent relationships were found between distributed leadership and school climate. Principals in 23 countries report using higher levels of distributed leadership when working in schools with a positive school climate characterised by mutual respect,

openness and sharing among colleagues (Table 3.7). It would make sense, then, that sharing decision making might be easier in a climate such as this or, conversely, that sharing decision making might help develop a school climate such as this. (TALIS data do not allow us to report on the direction of the relationship.) Moreover, principals who report higher levels of distributed leadership also tend to report higher levels of job satisfaction in just over half (17) of TALIS countries (Table 3.19). If governments – and school principals themselves – are interested in higher levels of principal job satisfaction, this might provide another reason to encourage more distribution of leadership in schools.

Box 3.5. **Description of multiple linear regression analysis in TALIS**

In this chapter, multiple linear regression analysis was employed to determine the extent to which various factors (independent variables) contribute to instructional leadership or distributed leadership (dependent variables). The technique provides a better understanding of how the value of the dependent variable changes when any one of the independent variables varies (while all other independent variables are held constant).

A regression coefficient represents the change in the dependent variable that is associated with a change in the predictor variable when all other variables are held constant. For example, if the regression coefficient for a dependent variable (for example, a mark on a test) is 0.5, this means that a change of one (1.0) in an independent variable (for example, hours of study) is associated with a change of 0.5. If two students differed in the amount of study by one hour, then one could predict that the students would differ in their test marks by (1)(0.5) = 0.5. If, on the other hand, their study time differed by 30 minutes, one would predict that the students' marks would differ by (0.5)(0.5) = 0.25.

When interpreting multiple regression coefficients, it is important to keep in mind that each coefficient is influenced by the other independent variables in a regression model. The influence depends on the extent to which predictor variables are correlated. Therefore, each regression coefficient does not explain the total effect of independent variables on dependent variables. Rather, each coefficient represents the additional effect of adding that variable to the model, if the effects of all other variables in the model are already accounted for.

Readers should keep in mind that no adjustments were made to correct for the multiple analyses, increasing the likelihood that a relationship will be considered significant simply by chance. It is also important to note that because cross-sectional survey data were used in these analyses, no causal conclusions can be drawn. The perspective taken – i.e. the choice of independent and dependent variables – is entirely based on theoretical considerations.

For more details about these analyses as well as about the control variables used in these analyses, see Annex B.

The TALIS data serve to confirm what is already known: The job of the principal encompasses a wide range of complex tasks and responsibilities. When comparing the TALIS data across countries, the extent of participation in various administrative and leadership activities by principals is found to differ significantly, either by choice, circumstance or authority. However, a majority of principals in all countries work to develop their school's educational goals and programmes, and in some countries the number of principals doing so approaches 100%. A lower number – but still sizable in many countries – work to prepare a school's professional development plan. Principals are aided in both these endeavours by the increasing availability of student performance and evaluation data. Finally, the extent to which principals share responsibility for tasks or decisions also varies by country as well as by the nature of the specific task or decision. The TALIS data in this area serve as an interesting profile of the profession of a principal and could be used to support the development of standards for the profession as well as to help identify the kinds of initial training or professional development that might be required for this role.

WHO ARE TODAY'S SCHOOL LEADERS?

As illustrated previously, the TALIS data confirm the extensive responsibilities that principals have in many areas. These responsibilities include planning for and managing human resources, complying with regulations, reporting, managing finances, setting school goals and planning the school's programmes, preparing timetables, developing curriculum, teaching, making classroom observations, evaluating students, mentoring teachers, encouraging teacher professional development and the like. TALIS data further help answer important questions about today's school principals: Who are the individuals who assume responsibility for such an extensive and significant range of responsibilities?

What formal preparation and experience have they had for such responsibilities? What do they do to grow or develop their professional practice? By learning more about the background, skills and experience of school leaders and examining the tasks that are required of them, countries can better understand where gaps in skills or experience might lie.

Age and gender of principals

The typical lower secondary school leader in the countries participating in TALIS 2013 is approximately 50 years of age (Table 3.8). Given that principals are often recruited from the ranks of teachers, it is not surprising that the proportion of principals younger than 40 years of age is small, with some notable exceptions. As shown in Figure 3.5, in Brazil and Romania, for example, around 30% of school principals are younger than 40. In Italy and Korea, nearly half of the school leaders are 60 years of age or older.

■ Figure 3.5 ■

Gender and age distribution of principals

Percentage of lower secondary education female principals and age of principals

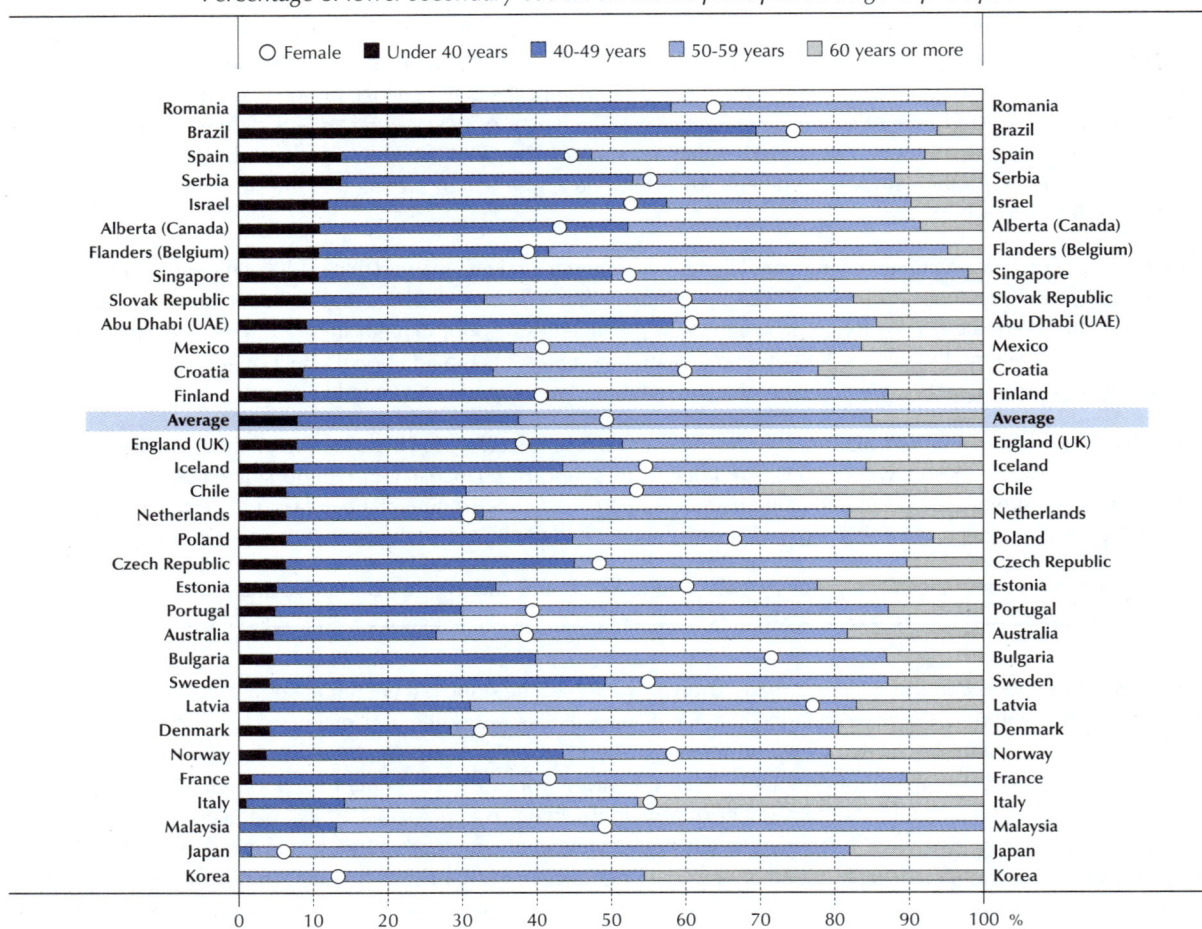

Countries are ranked in descending order, based on the percentage of principals who are under 40 years old.
Source: OECD, TALIS 2013 Database, Table 3.8.
StatLink ⬛⬛⬛ http://dx.doi.org/10.1787/888933041307

As was evident in TALIS 2008, the gender distribution of principals in lower secondary schools differs from the distribution of teachers. In all TALIS countries but Japan, more than half of the lower secondary education teaching workforce is made up of women (see Chapter 2). On average, 68% of all teachers are female (see Table 2.1). The percentage of women principals is generally lower: 49% of principals in lower secondary schools in the TALIS countries are female, although the ratio of males to females is within a 40/60 to 60/40 spectrum. There are a few exceptions to this. In Brazil, Bulgaria and Latvia, school leadership positions are primarily occupied by women (75%, 71% and 77%, respectively),

while in Japan and Korea, men predominate (94% and 87%, respectively). Box 3.6 provides data on the gender and age distribution of principals in primary and upper secondary schools for those countries with data for these populations. Box 3.7 looks at data on the gender and age of principals for those countries that participated in TALIS 2008 and TALIS 2013.

Box 3.6. **Gender and age distribution of primary and upper secondary principals**

Tables 3.8.a and 3.8.b reveal that the percentages of male and female principals in primary (ISCED 1) and upper secondary (ISCED 3) education are similar to their colleagues in lower secondary schools. In all countries with data available for both primary and lower secondary education, there are higher proportions of female principals in primary schools than in lower secondary schools. The difference is particularly large in Flanders (Belgium), where more than half (59%) of the principals are female in primary education compared with 39% in lower secondary education.

In Denmark, a slightly higher proportion of upper secondary principals are women (46%) compared with their peers in primary (37%) and lower secondary (32%) schools. In Norway and Poland, fewer women are principals in upper secondary schools compared with both primary and lower secondary (however, the percentage of female principals at both school levels is relatively high in Poland).

In Iceland, Italy and Abu Dhabi (United Arab Emirates), there is a higher proportion of female principals in lower secondary school as compared with upper secondary.

The mean age of principals tends to be similar across all three levels of education. The largest difference is in Mexico, where principals tend to be younger on average in primary (45 years) and upper secondary (46 years) education than in lower secondary education (52 years).

Box 3.7. **Comparing gender and age distribution, TALIS 2008 and TALIS 2013**

Table 3.8.c compares the gender and age distributions of lower secondary principals for those countries that participated in both TALIS 2008 and TALIS 2013. Overall, the average proportion of principals who are women reached 50% in 2013 (compared with 47% in 2008). There are some large differences in gender between these countries, however. In Korea the proportion of female principals is comparatively small (13%), while in Brazil and Bulgaria the proportion is comparatively large (75% and 71%), and in all three countries there has been little change from 2008 to 2013.

In comparison with the other countries for which data are available, large proportions of principals in Italy (47%) and Korea (46%) are 60 years of age or older, which is an increase of 12 and 10 percentage points, respectively, since 2008. Although it is slightly lower in 2013 compared with 2008, the proportion of principals younger than 40 remains high in Brazil (30%).

Formal education of school principals

In the same way that the knowledge and skills students obtain from their schooling is influenced by the quality of the preparation and the conduct of teachers, the quality of a nation's schools relies heavily upon the preparation and conduct of its school leaders. Branch, Hanushek and Rivkin (2013) argue that because school leaders affect the achievement of all the students in a school, improving the quality of school leadership is more important than improving the quality of a *single* teacher's practice.

Given the complexity of the position and the fact that most principals typically begin their careers as teachers, it is not surprising that the majority (92% on average) of principals have formal education at ISCED level 5A (Table 3.9). (ISCED level 5A typically includes Bachelor's degrees and Master's degrees from universities or equivalent institutions. See Chapter 2 for a description of the ISCED levels of classification.) In Chile (25%), Croatia (18%), France (13%) and Flanders (Belgium) (40%), there are relatively large proportions of principals whose highest level of education is at ISCED level 5B. These types of programmes are generally more practically oriented and shorter than programmes at ISCED level 5A.

Box 3.8 describes the formal education of principals in primary and upper secondary schools in those countries with available data. Box 3.9 compares data on principals' educational preparation in 2008 and 2013 for those countries that participated in both cycles of TALIS.

Box 3.8. **Educational preparation of principals in primary and upper secondary education**

The educational attainment of principals in primary (ISCED 1) and upper secondary (ISCED 3) schools is similar to their lower secondary colleagues with a few noteworthy differences (see Tables 3.9.a and 3.9.b).

In Flanders (Belgium), 10% of principals in primary education have achieved ISCED level 5A and 90% have achieved ISCED level 5B, compared with 59% and 40%, respectively, in lower secondary education. In Mexico, 14% of the principals in primary education have completed education below ISCED level 5 compared with 1% in lower secondary education.

In Finland, 11% of principals in upper secondary schools reported their level of education at ISCED level 6,[2] while the proportion is lower (5%) in lower secondary education.

Box 3.9. **Educational preparation of principals in TALIS 2008 and in TALIS 2013**

Table 3.9.c contains data comparing the educational preparation of principals in 2008 and in 2013. Overall, similar patterns prevailed among countries participating in both cycles, although there were some notable differences. In Australia, Iceland and Spain, the proportions of principals at ISCED level 5A are noticeably larger in 2013 than they were in 2008. In Italy and Portugal, the proportions of principals at ISCED level 5A are noticeably smaller, primarily as a consequence of the larger proportions of principals who report that their highest level of education is ISCED level 6.[3]

Further to examining the level of education achieved by school principals, TALIS 2013 inquired about the nature of the education that school leaders have received, asking about participation in school administration or principal training programmes or courses, teacher preparation programmes or courses and instructional leadership training or courses (Table 3.10). Although one might assume that principal preparation would typically include these types of programmes or courses, one of the most striking findings, as shown in Figure 3.6, is the large proportions of school leaders in some countries who report that their preparation did not include these experiences.

Looking at participation in a school administration programme or course, on average across TALIS countries, a quarter of principals report having undertaken such preparation prior to assuming the position, 37% after being appointed to the position and 22% that they began such preparation prior to taking up the position but continued the preparation after being assigned as a principal. However, in Croatia, and Serbia, at least half of the school principals say that they have never participated in a school administration or principal training programme or course.

The data from Table 3.10 indicate that typical preparation of principals includes participation in a teacher training or education programme. For the majority of principals, participation occurs prior to assuming responsibilities of the position. A substantial proportion of individuals undertake some formal preparation as teachers after they assume the principal's position (8%) or cumulatively before and after assuming that position (18%). However, 32% of the principals in the Czech Republic and 45% of the principals in Portugal indicate that they have never participated in a teacher training programme or course.

In a similar fashion, preparation of principals typically includes preparation in instructional leadership. On average, 24% of principals report undertaking such preparation prior to assuming the position, 31% after being appointed to the position and 23% that they began such preparation prior to taking up the position but continued the preparation after becoming a principal. However, more than half of the principals in Poland and Serbia indicate they have never had such preparation.

■ Figure 3.6 ■

Elements not included in principals' formal education

Percentage of lower secondary education principals who report that the following elements were not included in their formal education

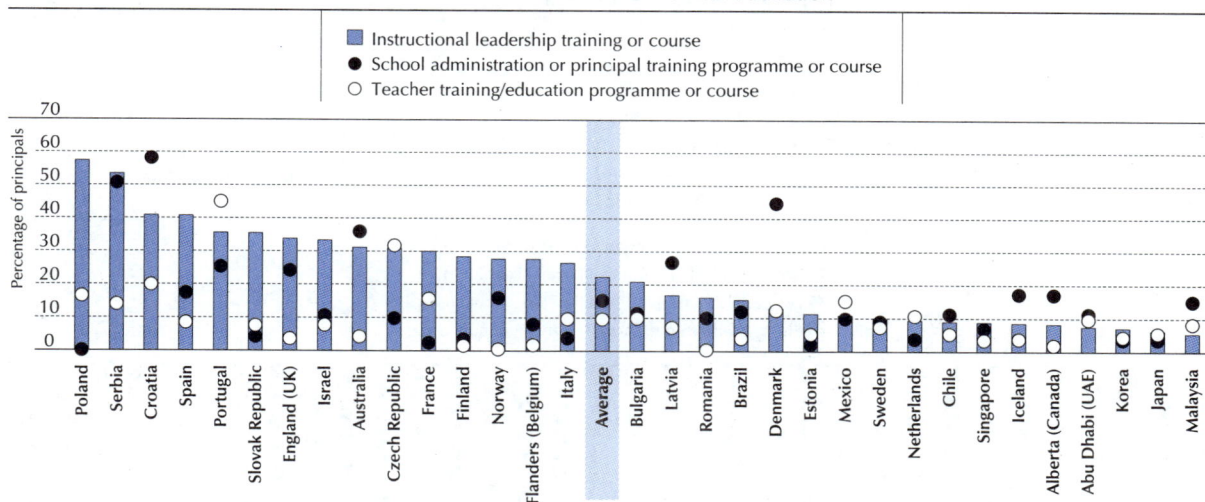

Countries are ranked in descending order, based on the percentage of principals for whom instructional leadership training or course were not included in their formal education.
Source: OECD, TALIS 2013 Database, Table 3.10.
StatLink ⬛ http://dx.doi.org/10.1787/888933041326

Box 3.10 includes data on the elements included in the formal education of primary and upper secondary principals for those countries with available data.

Box 3.10. Elements included in primary and upper secondary principals' formal education

Tables 3.10.a and 3.10.b contain data on the formal education of principals in primary (ISCED 1) and upper secondary (ISCED 3) schools, respectively. On average, only 8% of principals in primary schools have never undertaken teacher education in any form. But the average is distorted by Denmark and Poland, where 13% and 23% of primary principals, respectively, have never undertaken any kind of teacher education. More than a third (36%) of the principals in Denmark also report that school administration or principal training programmes or courses were not included in their formal education. Two-thirds of the principals in Poland have never had formal education that included instructional leadership training or courses.

Nearly half (46%) of the principals at the upper secondary school level in Mexico and 22% of the principals in Denmark have never undertaken teacher education in any form, which is substantially above the average of 11% for all ten countries surveyed. The average of the principals in the participating countries who say they never had school administration or principal training programmes or courses as part of their formal education (21%) is raised because of the rates of 61% of the upper secondary principals in Denmark and 34% of the principals in Iceland. More than half of the principals at the upper secondary level in Poland have never had formal education that included instructional leadership training or courses.

Comparing principals who did not receive administration training across education levels, in Iceland, the proportion of principals who report not having administration training is double in upper secondary (34%) than in lower secondary (17%). As for teacher training, in both Denmark and Norway, the proportion of principals who did not receive teacher training is approximately ten percentage points higher in upper secondary than in lower secondary education. With regard to instructional leadership, a higher percentage of principals in primary education lack the training compared with the lower secondary level in all countries with available data for both education levels. Differences between lower and upper secondary levels are less consistent across countries, but slightly higher proportions of upper secondary principals in Denmark, Iceland and Mexico report lacking this training compared with their peers in lower secondary.

Principals' leadership training

In addition to the data about the level and type of formal training principals report having received, TALIS also measures the level or intensity of the leadership training that principals report was included in their formal education. Table 3.11 and Figure 3.7 show the percentages of principals who report receiving no, weak, average or strong leadership training as part of their formal education. The level of leadership training is measured using the leadership training index, explained in Box 3.11.

■ Figure 3.7 ■

Principals' formal education, including leadership training

Percentage of lower secondary education principals who report having received leadership training in their formal education[1]

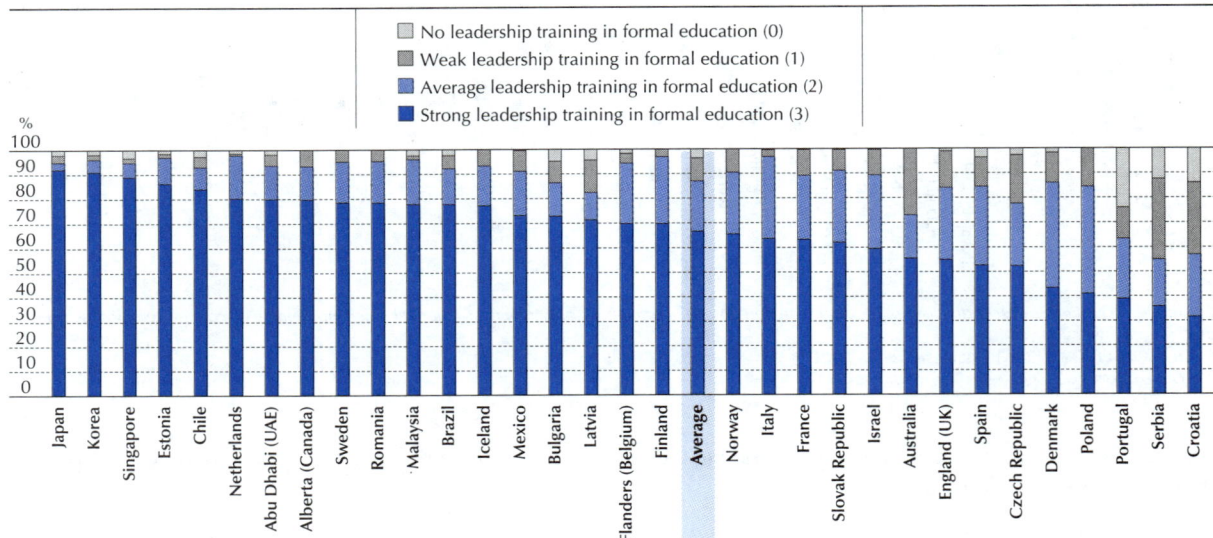

1. Leadership training index was constructed from the following variables: *i)* school administration or principal training programme or course, *ii)* teacher training/education programme or course, and *iii)* instructional leadership training or course. Responses indicating "never" were coded as zero (0) and responses indicating that the training had occurred "before," "after," or "before and after" were coded as one (1). Each respondent's codes were summed to produce the following categories: 0 (no training), 1 (weak leadership training), 2 (average leadership training) and 3 (strong leadership training). *Countries are ranked in descending order, based on the percentage of principals who received a strong leadership training in formal education.*
Source: OECD, TALIS 2013 Database, Table 3.11.
StatLink ⬛⬛⬛ http://dx.doi.org/10.1787/888933041345

Box 3.11. **Construction of the leadership training index**

The leadership training index presented in Table 3.11 was constructed from the question asking whether a principal's formal education included the following elements and whether this was before or after taking up duty as principal:

- School administration or principal training programme or course
- Teacher training/education programme or course
- Instructional leadership training or course

Responses indicating never were coded as zero (0), and responses indicating that the training had occurred before, after or before and after were coded as one (1). Each respondent's codes were summed to produce the following categories:

- 0 (no training)
- 1 (weak leadership training)
- 2 (average leadership training)
- 3 (strong leadership training)

For further information on the construction of this index, see Annex B.

More than 80% of principals in Chile, Estonia, Japan, Korea, the Netherlands and Singapore report having had strong leadership preparation as part of their formal education. The smallest proportions of principals reporting strong leadership preparation are found in Croatia (32%), Denmark (43%), Poland (41%), Portugal (40%) and Serbia (36%), including a number that indicated no formal administrative or principal training preparation as part of their formal education.

While there is merit in fostering different pathways to the goal of achieving excellence in preparation for school principals, policy makers would find advantages in developing such programmes based upon the characteristics of exemplary programmes. As Box 3.12 indicates, the Stanford Educational Leadership Institute study of exemplary programmes for the development of strong leaders identified common characteristics that provide a useful starting point for the conduct and appraisal of leadership preparation programmes.

Box 3.12. **Characteristics of exemplary leadership programmes**

Commissioned by the Wallace Foundation, a study by the Stanford Educational Leadership Institute examined eight exemplary pre-service and in-service programme models that develop strong educational leaders. All of the programmes of initial preparation that were characterised as exemplary shared the following characteristics:

- A comprehensive and coherent curriculum aligned with professional standards

- A philosophy and curriculum that explicitly focus on instructional leadership and school improvement

- Student-centered instruction that integrates theory and practice and stimulates reflection

- Faculty knowledgeable about their subject areas and experienced in school administration

- Social and professional support in the form of a cohort structure and formalised mentoring and advising by expert principals

- Vigorous, targeted recruitment and selection to seek out expert teachers with leadership potential

- Well-designed and supervised administrative internships under the guidance of expert veterans.

Source: Darling-Hammond et al. (2007).

PRINCIPALS' WORK EXPERIENCE

Regardless of the level or type of education that a principal might have, there is sometimes no substitute for experience. No amount of education can prepare a person for some of the situations that might be encountered in a school, and these experiences can shape a principal's behaviour and actions.

Figure 3.8 and Table 3.12 provide evidence about the work experience that principals bring to their responsibilities. The data indicate that across TALIS countries, school principals have an average of 9 years of experience in the role (ranging from 3 years in Korea to 13 years in Denmark and Latvia). Comparatively large proportions of the principals in Korea (47%) and Portugal (39%) have less than 3 years of experience in the role. Bulgaria, Chile, Estonia and Italy are at the other end of the distribution, with approximately one-fifth of their principals having more than 20 years of experience.

School principals bring a variety of prior experiences to their roles as principals, including working in other school management roles, prior work as teachers and experience in other jobs. On average, lower secondary school principals have spent 6 years in other management roles, with a range from 2 years (Bulgaria and Poland) to 12 years (England [United Kingdom]). The TALIS data confirm that experience as a principal is typically built upon a foundation of teaching experience. On average, principals have 21 years teaching experience. The countries with principals who have the highest average years of teaching experience are Australia (27 years), Japan (30 years) and Korea (29 years). Those with the fewest years of experience (less than 15 years) are Brazil, France, Iceland, Serbia, Singapore, Sweden and Abu Dhabi (United Arab Emirates). Box 3.13 details the work experience of school principals in primary and upper secondary education for those countries with available data.

■ Figure 3.8 ■
Work experience of principals

Percentage of lower secondary education principals with the following average years of experience in each role

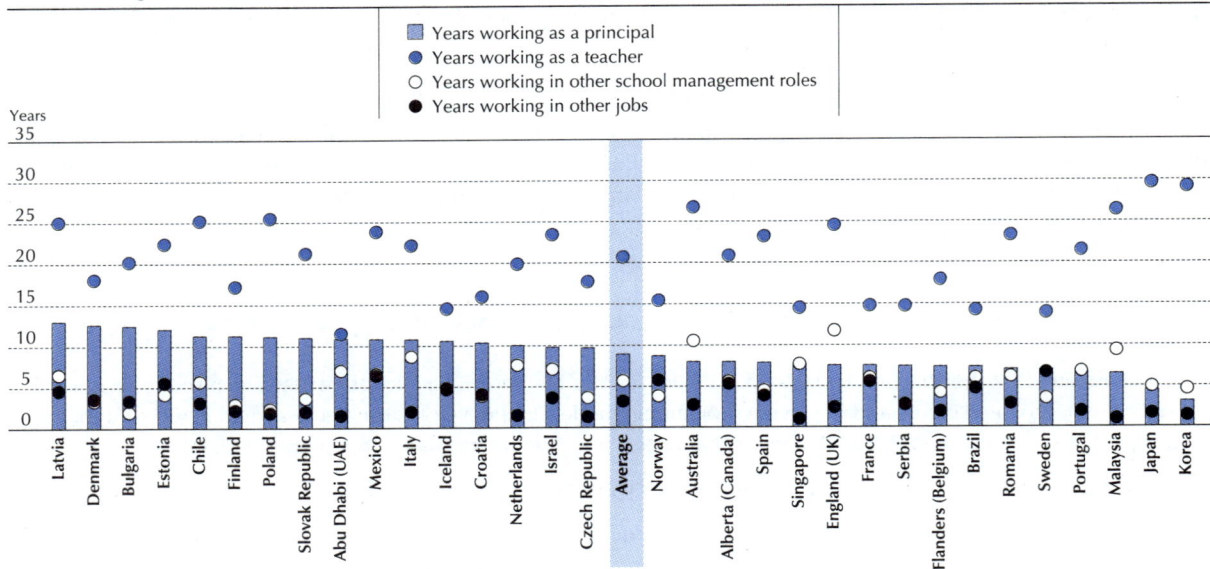

Legend:
- Years working as a principal
- Years working as a teacher
- Years working in other school management roles
- Years working in other jobs

Countries are ranked in descending order, based on the years of working experience as a principal.
Source: OECD, TALIS 2013 Database, Table 3.12.
StatLink http://dx.doi.org/10.1787/888933041364

Box 3.13. **Work experience of primary and upper secondary principals**

Tables 3.12.a and 3.12.b present the work experience of principals in primary (ISCED 1) and upper secondary (ISCED 3) education, respectively. The average years of work experience for primary principals across countries surveyed is 11 years. For upper secondary principals in these ten countries, it is nine years. In none of the countries with comparable data between the different education levels are there large differences in the number of years principals have been in their roles.

In primary education, principals have between two and four years of experience, on average, in other management roles. Principals in upper secondary education tend to have slightly more experience in other management roles than those in lower secondary. Upper secondary principals in Australia have the most experience in other school management roles, with 12 years.

With regard to principals' teaching experience, principals in primary schools tend to have slightly more years of teaching experience on average than principals in lower secondary (with the exception of Mexico). In upper secondary schools, principals tend to have fewer years of teaching experience than in lower secondary (except in Norway).

Leading and teaching are both demanding responsibilities. Table 3.13 contains data about the teaching obligations of principals. At one end of the spectrum are nine countries in which more than 90% of the principals are employed full time (90% of their time) as principals, without the responsibilities of teaching. At the other end are countries in which 90% or more of the principals employed full time must balance their work as principals and as teachers (Bulgaria, the Czech Republic, Malaysia, and the Slovak Republic). The proportions of principals employed on a part-time basis in Romania and Spain who must balance their responsibilities as principals with the responsibilities of a teacher are 29% and 19%, respectively. While it is true that principals who must also carry the workload of a classroom teacher will undoubtedly have many extra tasks to accomplish, retaining some teaching responsibilities also keeps them closer to the core job of the school. They are able to maintain a different kind of relationship with students – and possibly with teaching staff – and can even test some of the policies they are trying to enact at a school level.

PROFESSIONAL DEVELOPMENT FOR PRINCIPALS

The application of specialised knowledge is one of the hallmarks of professionalism (Goode, 1969; Larson, 1977; Epstein and Hundert, 2002; Gerrard, 2012). School leaders, as professionals, acknowledge their need for further development of their skills or competencies and actively engage in such endeavours. Table 3.14 and Figure 3.9 provide data about the percentage of principals who participated in a professional network, mentoring or research activity; courses, conferences or observation visits; or other types of professional development activities in the 12 months prior to the survey. On average in TALIS countries, principals spent 20 days participating in a professional network, mentoring or research activity; 13 days in courses, conferences or observation visits; and 10 days in other types of professional development activities.

■ Figure 3.9 ■
Principals' recent professional development

Participation rates and average number of days of professional development reported to be undertaken by lower secondary education principals in the 12 months prior to the survey

	Percentage of principals who participated in the following professional development activities in the 12 months prior to the survey	Average number of days of participation among those who participated
Percentage of principals who participated in courses, conferences or observation visits	83%	13
Percentage of principals who participated in a professional network, mentoring or research activity	51%	20
Percentage of principals who participated in other types of professional development activities	34%	10

Items are ranked in descending order, based on the percentage of principals participating in professional development activities in the 12 months prior to the survey.
Source: OECD, TALIS 2013 Database, Table 3.14.
StatLink http://dx.doi.org/10.1787/888933041383

As a consequence of school improvement efforts, it is increasingly common for professionals in education to participate in collaborative professional learning opportunities, the defining characteristic of which is professionals working together to examine their professional practice and to acquire new knowledge (DuFour, 2004). The percentages of principals across TALIS countries who have engaged in professional networks, mentoring or research activities during the preceding 12 months and the average numbers of days spent by those who participated are quite varied. Small proportions of principals in the Czech Republic (28%), Portugal (11%), Romania (29%), Serbia (21%) and Spain (28%) report taking part in a professional network, mentoring or research activity during the preceding 12 months, in contrast to the large proportions of principals in Australia (84%), the Netherlands (87%) and Singapore (93%) who say they took part in such activities. The amount of time spent on these activities varies as well. For example, in 11 countries principals spent fewer than 10 days on such activities. However, the proportions of principals in these 11 countries who were engaged in these activities – even though for a short amount of time – ranged from 42% in Sweden to 84% in Australia.

Australia provides an interesting example of developing a standard for the role of the principal that takes into account the overarching goals held for schooling and the cultural context in which schooling occurs (Box 3.14). The adoption of such a standard could, over time, help elevate the status of the principal and provide guidance to their preparation, conduct and professional development.

The percentages of principals who participated in courses, conferences or observation visits ranged from 54% in France to 99% in Singapore. For other types of professional development activities, percentages ranged from 15% in Bulgaria to 58% in Malaysia. The range of the average number of days spent in each activity was modest, from an average of 4 days (France) to 37 days (Brazil) in courses, conferences or observation visits, and from 4 days (Australia, Croatia, Finland, Japan and England [United Kingdom]) to 37 days (Mexico) for other types of professional development. While participation in professional development is generally supported for school leaders and teachers alike, spending 37 days away from school each year attending courses or conferences or making observation visits may prove to be excessive given a principal's busy schedule.

Box 3.14. **Strengthening the role of the principal by developing a national standard: Australia**

Australia has formally recognised the importance of the role of the principal in raising student achievement, "promoting equity and excellence, creating and sustaining the conditions under which quality teaching and learning thrive, influencing, developing and delivering community expectations and government policy, contributing to the development of a 21st century education system at local, national and international levels" (Australian Institute for Teaching and School Leadership, 2011: 2). Australia has adopted a National Professional Standard for Principals (the Standard). The Standard is intended to "define the role of the principal and unify the profession nationally, to describe the professional practice of principals in a common language and to make explicit the role of quality school leadership in improving learning outcomes" (Australian Institute for Teaching and School Leadership, 2011: 1). The Standard is founded on requirements in three domains – vision and values, knowledge and understanding, and personal qualities and social and interpersonal skills – and represented in five areas of professional practice: leading teaching and learning; developing self and others; leading improvement, innovation and change; leading the management of the school; and engaging and working with the community.

Source: Australian Institute for Teaching and School Leadership (2011).

Participation in professional development depends upon a variety of factors, including the availability of opportunities that are perceived to be relevant, the availability of time and other resources that would permit someone to take advantage of professional development, employers who are supportive and the necessary qualifications to be able to benefit from the opportunities available. These concepts are discussed further in relation to teachers in Chapter 4. Figure 3.10 looks at the barriers to professional development that principals report experiencing.

■ Figure 3.10 ■

Barriers to principals' participation in professional development

Percentage of lower secondary education principals who "strongly disagree", "disagree", "agree" or "strongly agree" that the following items present barriers to their participation in professional development

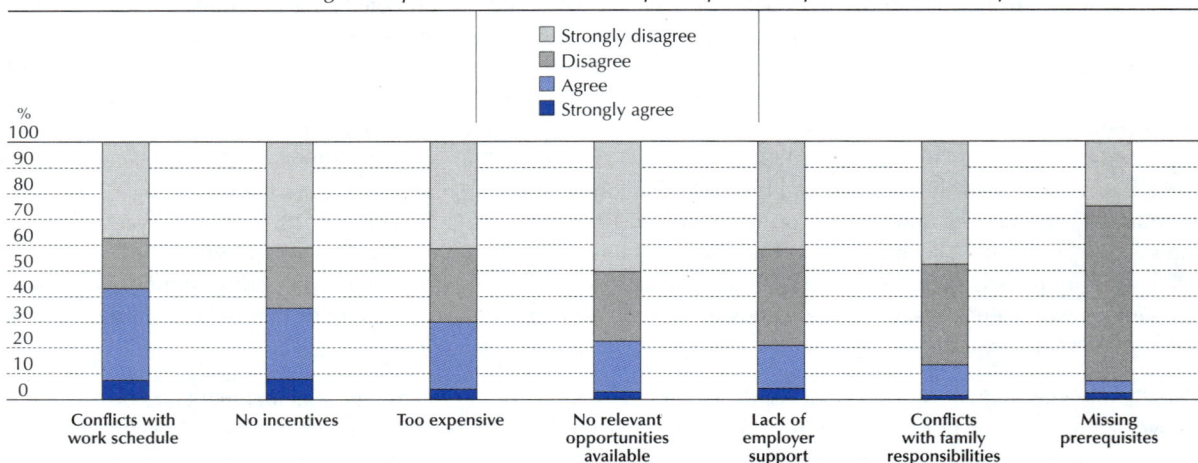

Items are ranked in descending order, based on the percentage of principals in lower secondary education who "strongly agree" or "agree" that the item presents a barrier to their participation in professional development.
Source: OECD, TALIS 2013 Database, Tables 3.15 and 3.15.Web.
StatLink http://dx.doi.org/10.1787/888933041402

Table 3.15 indicates that the proportion of principals who stated that there were no relevant opportunities available for professional development is quite high in some countries, such as Chile (44%), Italy (52%), Mexico (37%), Poland (37%), Portugal (54%), Serbia (41%) and Spain (53%). While principals in many countries indicated that there were no incentives for participation in professional development activities, large proportions of school leaders in Bulgaria (54%), Chile (59%), Italy (73%), Mexico (48%), Portugal (71%), Serbia (55%), Spain (79%) and Abu Dhabi (United Arab Emirates)

(51%) indicated that there were no incentives for participation in professional development activities. The perception that employer support for professional development is lacking is evident among a number of countries, with the largest proportions of school leaders reporting this lack of support in Italy (58%), Mexico (47%), Portugal (82%) and Serbia (40%).

In 13 countries more than half of the school leaders agreed that their work schedule conflicted with opportunities for professional development, including 5 countries at more than 60% (Australia, Japan, Korea, Sweden and Alberta [Canada]). For "conflicts with family responsibilities", the rate is much lower than for "conflicts with work schedule" (overall average of 13% vs. 43%). More than 20% of the school leaders in Australia, Chile, Iceland, Israel, Spain and Alberta (Canada) agreed that family responsibilities conflicted with opportunities for participation in professional development. In Chile, Croatia, Japan, Poland, Portugal, Romania, Serbia and Abu Dhabi (United Arab Emirates), 40% or more of the school leaders perceived that the expense of professional development was a barrier to their participation. In Chile, Japan, Korea, Malaysia, Mexico and Portugal, 10% or more of the school leaders agreed that lacking prerequisites was a barrier to their participation in professional development.

Principals' engagement in professional development activities is an indicator of the value placed upon maintenance and development of professional knowledge by the individual principal and by those who employ the principal. As mentioned earlier in the chapter, because principals can affect the achievement of all the students in a school, improving the quality of school leadership is more important than improving the quality of a single teacher's practice (Branch et. al., 2013). It is thus important to stimulate interest in and opportunities for continuing professional development for principals as well as to remove the personal and professional barriers to principal participation in such activities.

Thus the profile of school principals regarding age, educational attainment and gender is relatively consistent across countries. Although principals are often former teachers, a profession in which, on average across TALIS countries, 68% of all teachers are female, the percentage of women principals is generally lower than the proportion that are men. It is in the areas of preparation to be a principal and participation in professional development that a wide variability between countries occurs. In some countries, many principals report being afforded no, little, or weak preparation for assuming that role. In addition, either through lack of opportunity, interest, time, prerequisites, incentives, or encouragement, the participation by principals in professional networks, mentoring or research activities is low in many countries. Time spent in courses, conferences or observation visits is also modest. Given the increasing recognition of the importance of school leadership, countries may want to place additional emphasis on preparation to be a principal and on continuing professional development.

PRINCIPALS' LEADERSHIP: PROVIDING DIRECTION TO THE SCHOOL AND SUPPORTING TEACHERS

Schools have multiple responsibilities, chief among them equipping students with the knowledge and dispositions they need to assume the responsibilities that come with adult citizenship. Improving student achievement, while always an important goal of schooling, has become more prominent as a consequence of increased international economic competition. The pressure to ensure that students possess an education required for a competitive economy and the accompanying demand for greater accountability for results have increased the emphasis on the principal's instructional leadership. Instructional leadership is evident in much of the work that principals do, including ensuring that the goals of the school are well articulated, that the school's environment is one that is safe and conducive to learning and that teachers' effort are focused on instruction and their own instructional improvement. This section explores the impact of instructional leadership on the work principals do setting goals and programmes, their work on professional development planning and the time they spend on curriculum and teaching-related tasks. Box 3.15 discusses how instructional leadership is measured in TALIS.

Box 3.15. **Description of the instructional leadership index**

To measure instructional leadership, TALIS asked principals to indicate how frequently they engaged in the following activities in their school during the preceding 12 months. Response options ranged from never or rarely to very often.

- I took actions to support co-operation among teachers to develop new teaching practices
- I took actions to ensure that teachers take responsibility for improving their teaching skills
- I took actions to ensure that teachers feel responsible for their students' learning outcomes

For more information on the construction and validation of this index, see Annex B.

Instructional leadership and principals' engagement in school and teacher development

Important responsibilities that fall on principals include providing educational direction for the school and ensuring that teachers' appraisals provide them with tools to be successful. Principals can meet these responsibilities in part by using student performance and evaluation results to develop educational goals and programmes and by working on a professional development plan for the school. The former is about establishing the school's focus and aligning its programme with those goals. The latter is concerned with ensuring that the school's staff has the capacity to reach the goals established by implementing the school's programmes. Further, principals can ensure that the outcomes of teachers' appraisals are meaningful. This section examines whether the extent to which principals engage in these school and teacher development roles is related to their level of instructional leadership. Box 3.5 describes the technical details of the analyses used in this section (see also Annex B).

As Table 3.16 indicates, in six countries, principals who show high levels of instructional leadership tend to be more likely to say that they use student performance and student evaluation results to develop the school's educational goals and programmes. Similarly, in 13 countries, principals with higher levels of instructional leadership are more likely to report working on a professional development plan for their school. In addition, in six TALIS countries (Australia, Denmark, Israel, the Netherlands, Sweden and Flanders [Belgium]), principals with higher levels of instructional leadership tend to spend more time on curriculum and teaching-related tasks (Table 3.17). Moreover, in 20 countries, principals with higher levels of instructional leadership are more likely to directly observe classroom teaching as part of the formal appraisal of teachers' work in their school (Table 3.16). What this shows is that principals who report higher levels of instructional leadership also report that they spend more time on tasks directly related to teaching, learning and development of their teachers' practices.

TALIS data also indicate that instructional leadership is related to some of the actions taken following teacher appraisal. Principals have a range of actions they can take following an appraisal of a teacher's performance, including the development of plan for further development, appointing a mentor or imposing negative sanctions.

In nine countries, principals who exhibit higher levels of instructional leadership more frequently report that a development or training plan is created for their teachers following their appraisal (Table 3.16). Similarly, the association between instructional leadership and the appointment of a mentor to help the teacher improve is positive in ten countries.

Higher levels of instructional leadership do not appear to be related to the likelihood of imposing material sanctions such as reductions in a teacher's salary after teacher appraisals, and only in five countries is instructional leadership related to the likelihood of making a change in teachers' work responsibilities after teacher appraisal (Table 3.16).

In six countries higher levels of instructional leadership are associated with reports that changes in the likelihood of a teacher's career advancement occur after teacher appraisals. The dismissal or non-renewal of a contract following teacher appraisal is more likely to be reported by principals with higher levels of instructional leadership only in Bulgaria, Malaysia and Spain, while the opposite is the case in Chile (Table 3.16).

Chapter 5 discusses the impact and outcome of teacher appraisals from teachers' points of view, which provides an interesting comparison with the data from principals presented in this section. What the data described here show is that while the relationship between instructional leadership and appraisal outcomes is not positive in all countries, in certain countries principals who exhibit higher levels of instructional leadership are more likely to follow up a teacher's formal appraisal with an action that can seriously impact a teacher's job and career. Given that, as Chapter 5 indicates, teachers value the appraisal they receive but often find it to be merely an administrative exercise, increasing the skills of principals in instructional leadership may help appraisals to become more meaningful for teachers as well.

Instructional leadership and school climate

Chapter 2 showed that in most TALIS countries the majority of teachers work in environments with a positive professional climate among the teaching staff. Data from the principal questionnaire indicate that principals share this feeling of a positive climate. Table 3.18 examines the relationship between instructional leadership and principals' reports on the factors that contribute to school climate, such as shortages of school resources (materials and personnel), delinquency in the school, the degree of mutual respect and an indication of the ratio of administrative and support staff in the school. (See Box 3.5 and Annex B for details about the analyses performed in this section.)

In 17 countries, principals with higher levels of instructional leadership tend to work in schools that are reported to have more positive school climates characterised by high levels of mutual respect. As was seen earlier in the discussion of distributed leadership, this could mean either that the climate of mutual respect already existing in a school makes instructional leadership easier or that the instructional leadership exerted by the principals promotes a school climate of mutual respect. Either way, the school benefits. The other school climate variables examined do not appear to have consistent relationships with principals' instructional leadership.

PRINCIPALS' JOB SATISFACTION

Two aspects related to principals' job satisfaction were measured in TALIS: One is their satisfaction with their current work environment, and the other is their satisfaction with the profession. Because the two were highly correlated, analyses were performed using the overall measure of principal job satisfaction, which combined these two aspects. Box 3.16 describes the measures of job satisfaction in TALIS.

Box 3.16. **Description of the principal job satisfaction indices**

Two aspects of principal job satisfaction were measured in TALIS: Satisfaction with current work environment and satisfaction with the profession. Specifically, principals were asked to indicate how strongly they agreed or disagreed with the following statements as applied to their job. Response options raged from strongly disagree to strongly agree.

The first aspect (satisfaction with current work environment) was measured with the following items:

- I enjoy working at this school
- I would recommend my school as a good place to work
- I am satisfied with my performance in this school
- All in all, I am satisfied with my job

The second aspect (satisfaction with the profession) was measured with the following items:

- The advantages of this profession clearly outweigh the disadvantages
- If I could decide again, I would still choose this job/position
- I regret that I decided to become a principal

Note that because these two aspects of job satisfaction are highly related to each other and perhaps overlap (see Table 3.37.Web), the overall job satisfaction scores are used in the analyses rather than the scores for each construct separately. See Annex B for more details about the construction and validation of this scale.

Figure 3.11 looks at principals' reported levels of job satisfaction by country and, as indicated in Box 3.16, divides the responses in terms of principals' satisfaction with the profession as compared with their satisfaction with their current work environment (see also Table 3.26.Web). It is interesting to note that across countries, there is more variation in principals' feelings about their profession than in their reported satisfaction with their schools. Across countries, close to nine in ten or more principals are satisfied with their jobs overall and generally feel positive about their school working environment. Moreover, when questioned about the profession of principal overall, more than 80% of principals in all countries feel confident in their choice of career and do not regret becoming a principal. Although more than eight principals in ten report that the advantages of the position clearly outweigh the disadvantages, in Bulgaria, Italy, Japan, Romania, Serbia and the Slovak Republic, only between 60% and 70% of school leaders report this. Similarly, although nearly nine principals in ten report that they would still choose to become a principal if they could decide today, only between 60% and 70% of school leaders feel this way in Japan and Serbia.

The TALIS data were analysed to determine the relationship between instructional leadership and distributed leadership and principals' job satisfaction. Table 3.19 contains data about the relationship between both aspects of leadership and principal job satisfaction. Principals exhibiting higher levels of instructional leadership tend to be more satisfied with their job in 20 countries, and principals exhibiting higher levels of distributed leadership tend to be more satisfied with their jobs in 17 countries.

■ Figure 3.11 ■
Principal job satisfaction

*Percentage of lower secondary education principals who "agree" or "strongly agree"
with the following statements*

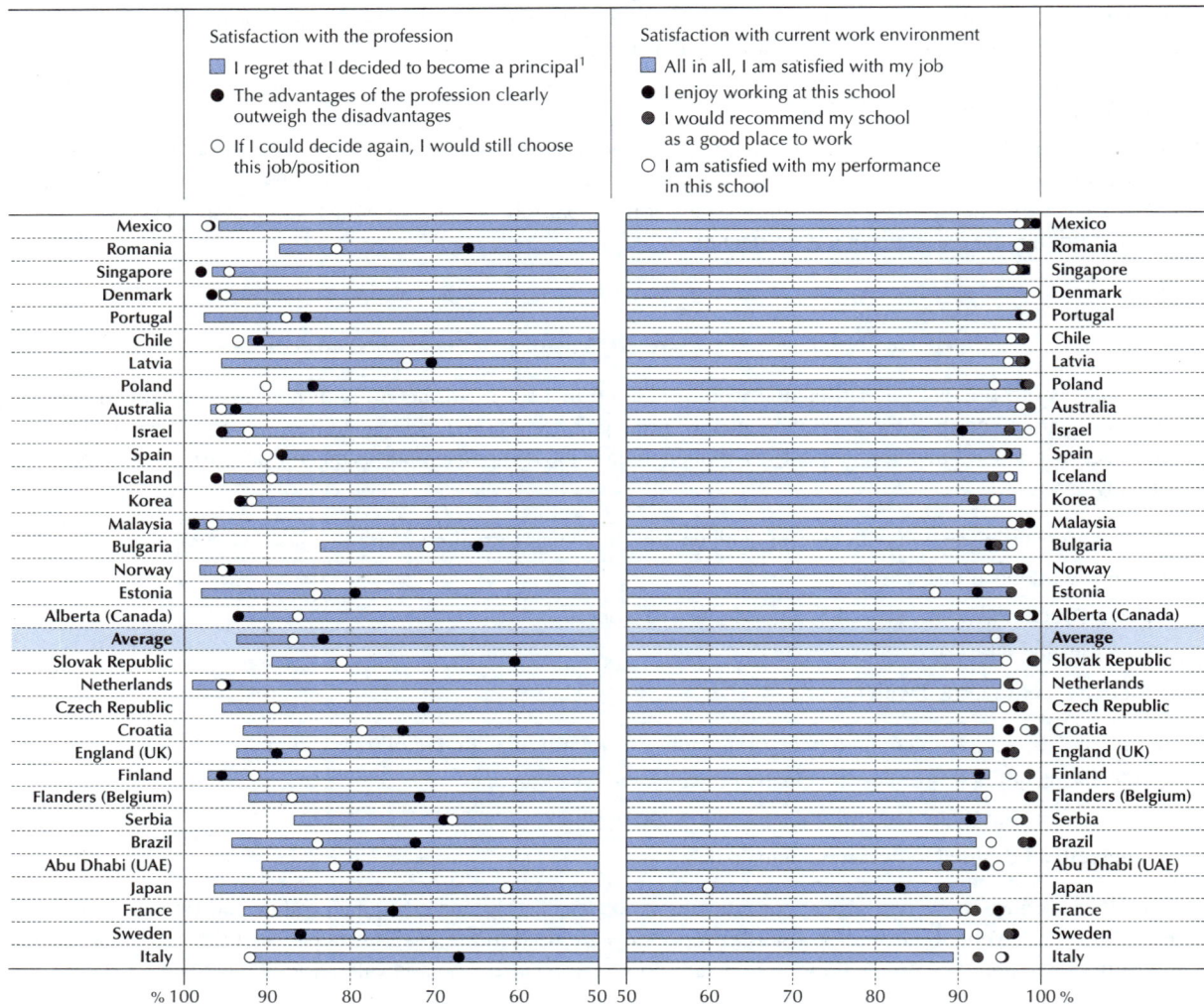

Satisfaction with the profession
- I regret that I decided to become a principal[1]
- The advantages of the profession clearly outweigh the disadvantages
- If I could decide again, I would still choose this job/position

Satisfaction with current work environment
- All in all, I am satisfied with my job
- I enjoy working at this school
- I would recommend my school as a good place to work
- I am satisfied with my performance in this school

1. For the item "I regret that I decided to become a principal", the percentage represents the principals who answered "strongly disagree" or "disagree" because of the nature of the question.
Countries are ranked in descending order, based on the percentage of principals who "agree" or "strongly agree" that all in all, they are satisfied with their job.
Source: OECD, TALIS 2013 Database, Table 3.26.Web.
StatLink ᐧᐧᐧ http://dx.doi.org/10.1787/888933041421

Additional factors affecting principals' job satisfaction were explored using multiple regression analyses with principal job satisfaction as the dependent variable and demographic background (Table 3.20) and school background (Table 3.21) as independent variables.

Table 3.20 examines the relationship between job satisfaction and principal characteristics, including gender, age and years of experience as a principal and as a teacher. For most countries, these variables were not related to principals' job satisfaction. A few exceptions include Italy, Poland, the Slovak Republic, Abu Dhabi (United Arab Emirates) and Alberta (Canada), where female principals are more likely to have higher levels of job satisfaction. Conversely, in France and Malaysia, male principals report higher levels of job satisfaction. In Croatia, Italy, the Slovak Republic and Spain, principals with more experience as a principal have higher levels of job satisfaction. In the Netherlands, Romania and Abu Dhabi (United Arab Emirates), those principals with more years of experience as teachers have higher job satisfaction, while the opposite relationship was found in Japan.

Table 3.21 examines the relationship between job satisfaction and school characteristics such as school locality, school type (public/private, source of funding), school size (number of staff and number of students) and student composition (percentage of students whose first language is different from the language of instruction, percentage of students with special needs and percentage of students from socio-economically disadvantaged homes). Again, while in most countries these variables were not related to job satisfaction, in a few countries some relationships emerged. For example, in Estonia, Alberta (Canada) and England (United Kingdom), principals working in schools with higher proportions of students with special needs tended to have lower levels of job satisfaction. The reverse is true in Australia and the Czech Republic. Furthermore, in Australia, principals working in schools with higher proportions of students from socio-economically disadvantaged homes showed lower levels of job satisfaction. Policy makers in these countries might want to consider the support that they are providing to principals in schools with these more challenging circumstances, with the objective of helping to improve the job satisfaction of the leadership and the staff as a whole.

Analyses were also performed to examine the relationship between job satisfaction and principals' reports of shortages of school resources (materials and personnel), principals' reports of delinquency in the school, the degree to which the school climate is characterised by mutual respect and an indication of the ratio of administrative and support staff in the school (Table 3.22). The most pronounced relationship found was between having a school climate of mutual respect and principals' job satisfaction. Mutual respect is positively associated with principal job satisfaction in all TALIS countries except Iceland, Latvia and Sweden. This means principals tend to be satisfied with their job when there is a high level of mutual respect in school.

Given that between one in five and one in two principals reported resource needs in the schools in which they work (see Chapter 2), it was surprising that resources do not seem to matter in many countries when it comes to principals' job satisfaction. Only in Bulgaria, Latvia, Serbia and Abu Dhabi (United Arab Emirates) do principals who report that a lack of material resources in their schools is a bit of a problem also report lower levels of job satisfaction. Perhaps not surprisingly, in a number of countries (Brazil, Denmark, Finland, France, Japan and Abu Dhabi [United Arab Emirates]), principals who report higher levels of delinquency in their schools also report lower levels of job satisfaction.

The data in Table 3.23 allow a further examination of the relationship between principals' job satisfaction and nine potential barriers to a principal's effectiveness. These barriers include inadequate school budget and resources, government regulations and policy, teachers' absences, lack of parent involvement, teachers' career-based wage system, a lack of opportunities and support for principals' professional development, a lack of opportunities and support for teachers' professional development, a heavy workload and high level of responsibility, and a lack of shared leadership with other school staff members.

The one factor most commonly related to principals' job satisfaction is a heavy workload and high level of responsibility. In 14 countries, principals who identified higher workloads as a barrier to their effectiveness also showed lower levels of job satisfaction. Furthermore, a lack of distributed leadership with other school staff members and principals' job satisfaction are negatively related in nine countries. The relationship between principals' job satisfaction and their perception of other barriers were inconsistent and affected fewer countries.

Few factors consistently relate to job satisfaction for principals across countries. One that does is an atmosphere of mutual respect within the school. The most common cause of job dissatisfaction is, not surprisingly, a heavy workload. It is difficult to point with confidence to other factors consistently leading to principal job satisfaction when, for instance, higher proportions of students from socio-economically disadvantaged homes or many students with special needs correlates with job satisfaction for some and job dissatisfaction for others. Further investigation into the reasons for these inconsistent attitudes might reveal important differences in the measure of support principals receive in more challenging circumstances.

SUMMARY AND MAIN POLICY IMPLICATIONS

As the literature and the data presented in this chapter indicate, the demands upon school leaders are many and diverse, requiring considerable administrative acumen and knowledge of teaching and learning. It is difficult to imagine that one person could have the expertise in all areas needed to successfully run a school, especially as some school systems continue to devolve and schools become more independent. School leaders must be visionary leaders who can inspire, motivate and develop their staff; experts in the latest teaching, learning and assessment practices; and sensitive and adept human resource managers who are able to provide feedback to staff that encourages them to grow. In addition to this, today's school principal must be able to bring together parents, community stakeholders, students, teachers and support

staff into a community dedicated to the well-being of the school's students and may, in some systems, even be required to be a savvy businessperson, able to creatively use the school's funds for the most efficient and effective outcomes. Countries must consider how to train and develop people to be successful in such a challenging role, and school leaders themselves must endeavour to find balance between their various responsibilities. The TALIS data in this chapter reveal findings that can aid in policy or programme development in these areas.

Develop formal programmes to prepare school leaders to enter the profession

There is wide variability within countries with regard to participation in school administration or principal training programmes or courses, teacher preparation programmes or courses and instructional leadership training or courses. Many principals report that their preparation did not include these experiences. On average, a quarter of principals participate in a school administration or principal training programme prior to becoming a principal. An additional 37% participate after being appointed to the position, and 22% indicate that they began such preparation prior to taking up the position but continued the preparation after being assigned as a principal.

Over time, countries are likely to reap benefits in terms of school improvement and student achievement from the development of quality professional preparation programmes for their school principals. The responsibilities of principals are many and complex. Attention to the principals' participation in teacher preparation programmes, school administration or principal training programmes and instructional leadership training should produce tangible benefits for students and increased professionalism for principals.

Provide opportunities and remove barriers for continuing professional development for principals

Maintaining the currency and applicability of one's professional knowledge is affected by many different factors, including the opportunities that are available, having the time and qualifications necessary to take advantage of the opportunities and so on. The percentages of principals who have engaged in collaborative professional development activities during the preceding 12 months and the average numbers of days spent by those who participated are quite varied. Large proportions of the principals in many countries say there were no relevant opportunities available for professional development and no incentives for participation. In more than a dozen countries, principals said their work schedules conflicted with opportunities for professional development. Countries should strive to minimise obstacles to professional development for principals, align state-supported opportunities with the country's long-term educational goals (OECD, 2013) and set standards for high-quality professional learning. Because what they do affects the achievement of all the students in a school, principals must make improving the quality of their practice a priority and must take advantage of the opportunities afforded.

There are several high-priority areas for professional development. For example, principal instructional leadership can improve student achievement by:

- Establishing what school outcomes are essential for all students

- Ensuring that these outcomes are expressed clearly in the curriculum and are supported with appropriate instructional material

- Holding students, parents and teachers accountable for those outcomes

- Encouraging and coaching teachers' use of teaching strategies that increase learning outcomes for all students

- Assessing student progress in the areas of importance at different times over their school careers (Ungerleider, 2006; Ungerleider, 2003; Willms, 2000; Willms, 1998; Woessman 2001).

Encourage the use of distributed leadership among school principals

Given a principal's importance to the school's operations and a principal's impact on instruction, it is important that being a principal be, and remain, a satisfying position. Principals who feel their schools have climates of mutual respect also exhibit higher levels of job satisfaction. Principals, through the work they do and the relationships they establish with teachers, staff and students, help to create a positive, mutually supportive climate that, in turn, contributes to their satisfaction. This is likely why personal qualities and social and interpersonal skills are one of the important areas upon which successful professional practice is based. But, as Australia's standard for principals appreciates (Box 3.13), personal qualities and social and interpersonal skills must be complemented by vision and values as well as by knowledge and understanding and be realised in leading learning and teaching, the development of one's self and others, improving and innovating, managing the school, and engaging and working with the community.

The TALIS data confirm that the position of principal is very demanding both in terms of the breadth of its responsibilities and the time that those responsibilities consume. As the connection between teachers, students, their parents or guardians, the educational system and the wider community in which the school exists, principals often feel pulled in different directions by demands that they see as incompatible. One strategy for addressing those demands is to share the work and decision-making authority with others (Schleicher, 2012). Principals who do so enjoy the climate of mutual respect they perceive in their schools and greater job satisfaction.

Ensure that principals receive training in and have opportunities to employ instructional leadership

It could be said that instructional leadership – focusing on the teaching and learning that takes place in the school – is the most important of all of the principal's tasks. In addition, the TALIS data demonstrate that when principals exhibit higher levels of instructional leadership, they are also more likely to develop a professional development plan for their school (13 countries), observe teaching as part of a teacher's formal appraisal (20 countries) and report there is high level of mutual respect among colleagues at the school (17 countries). Principals with higher levels of instructional leadership tend to spend more time on curriculum and teaching-related tasks and exhibit higher levels of job satisfaction.

Thus it is obvious that instructional leadership is important in a variety of ways. Yet of all the elements that principals reported as being included in their formal education, fewer principals report taking part in instructional leadership training than in any other. More than one in five (22%) principals report never having participated in instructional training, and 31% have had this training only after they became a principal.

Countries need to review the training that is provided to principals on instructional leadership and how that leadership is actually enacted at a school level. As recommended previously, there is an opportunity for additional professional development to be provided on instructional leadership, but principals need to be made aware of its importance and be familiar with its practices during their initial principal training as well.

Notes

1. In the analyses, the categories "often" and "very often" were collapsed into one category, called "frequently". The categories "never or rarely" and "sometimes" were combined into one category, called "infrequently".

2. ISCED level 6 represents further education at the tertiary level that leads to an advanced research qualification such as a Doctorate degree.

3. In Portugal, the principals with a "Pre-Bologna Master's degree" are counted as ISCED level 6. The way the question is presented prevents the disaggregation between "Pre-Bologna Master's degree" and "Doctorate degree".

A note regarding Israel

The statistical data for Israel are supplied by and under the responsibility of the relevant Israeli authorities. The use of such data by the OECD is without prejudice to the status of the Golan Heights, East Jerusalem and Israeli settlements in the West Bank under the terms of international law.

References

Australian Institute for Teaching and School Leadership (2011), *National Professional Standard for Principals*, Education Services Australia, *http://www.aitsl.edu.au/verve/_resources/NationalProfessionalStandardForPrincipals_July25.pdf*.

Aydin, A., Y. Sarier and **S. Uysal** (2013), "The effect of school principals' leadership styles on teachers' organizational commitment and job satisfaction", *Educational Sciences: Theory & Practice*, Vol. 13/2, pp. 806-811.

Baker, D. and G. LeTendre (2005), *National Differences, Global Similarities: World Culture and the Future of Schooling*, Stanford University Press, Palo Alto, CA.

Bell, L., R. Bolam and **L. Cubillo** (2003), "A systematic review of the impact of school leadership and management on student outcomes", in *Research Evidence in Education Library*, EPPI-Centre, Social Science Research Unit, Institute of Education, London.

Biniaminov, I. and **N.S. Glasman** (1983), "School determinants of student achievement in secondary education", *American Educational Research Journal*, Vol. 20/2, pp. 251-268.

Branch, G.F., E.A. Hanushek and **S.G. Rivkin** (2013), "School leaders matter: Measuring the impact of effective principals", *Education Next*, Vol. 13/1, pp. 63-69.

Chin, J.M. (2007), "Meta-analysis of transformational school leadership effects on school outcomes in Taiwan and the USA", *Asia Pacific Education Review*, Vol. 8/2, pp. 166-177.

Darling-Hammond, L., et al. (2007), *Preparing School Leaders for a Changing World: Lessons from Exemplary Leadership Development Programs*, Stanford Educational Leadership Institute, Stanford University, Stanford, CA.

Day, C., et al. (2008), "Research into the impact of school leadership on pupil outcomes: Policy and research contexts", *School Leadership & Management* (formerly *School Organisation*), Vol. 28/1, pp. 5-25.

DuFour, R. (2004), "What is a professional learning community?", *Educational Leadership*, Vol. 61/8, pp. 6-11.

Epstein, R.M. and **E.M. Hundert** (2002), "Defining and assessing professional competence", *Journal of the American Medical Association*, Vol. 287/2, pp. 226-235.

Gerrard, S. (2012), "A response to raven", *The Psychology of Education Review*, Vol. 36/1, pp. 27-30.

Goode, W.J. (1969), "The theoretical limits of professionalism", in *The Semi-Professions and Their Organizations: Teachers, Nurses, and Social Workers*, A. Etzioni (ed.), Free Press, New York, NY.

Grissom, J.A., S. Loeb and **B. Master** (2013), "Effective instructional time use for school leaders: Longitudinal evidence from observations of principals", *Educational Researcher*, Vol. 42/8, pp. 433-444.

Gunter, H.M. and **T. Fitzgerald** (2013), "New Public Management and the modernisation of education systems", *Journal of Educational Administration and History*, Vol. 45/4, pp. 303-305.

Hallinger, P., L. Bickman and **K. Davis** (1996), "School context, principal leadership, and student reading achievement", *The Elementary School Journal*, Vol. 96/5, pp. 527-549.

Hallinger, P. and **R.H. Heck** (1996), "Reassessing the principal's role in school effectiveness: A review of empirical research, 1980-1995", *Educational Administration Quarterly*, Vol. 32/1, pp. 5-44.

Harris, A. (2012), "Distributed leadership: Implications for the role of the principal", *Journal of Management Development*, Vol. 31/1, pp. 7-17.

Harris, A. (2008), *Distributed Leadership: Developing Tomorrow's Leaders*, Routledge, London.

Huang, F.L. and **T.R. Moon** (2009), "Is experience the best teacher? A multilevel analysis of teacher characteristics and student achievement in low performing schools", *Educational Assessment, Evaluation and Accountability*, Vol. 21, pp. 209-234.

Jepsen, C. and **S. Rivkin** (2009), "Class reduction and student achievement: The potential tradeoff between teacher quality and class size", *Journal of Human Resources*, Vol. 44/1, pp. 223-250.

Jeynes, W.H. (2011), *Parental Involvement and Academic Success*, Routledge, New York, NY.

Larson, M.S. (1977), *The Rise of Professionalism: A Sociological Analysis,* University of California Press, Berkeley, CA.

Leithwood, K., B. Mascall and **T. Strauss** (2009), *Distributed Leadership According to the Evidence*, Routledge, London.

Lucas, O., et al. (2012), "School principal's leadership style: A factor affecting staff absenteeism in secondary schools", *Journal of Emerging Trends in Educational Research and Policy Studies*, Vol. 3/4, pp. 444-446.

MacNeil, A.J. and **D. Prater** (1999), "Teachers and principals differ on the seriousness of school discipline: A national perspective", *National Forum of Applied Educational Research Journal*, Vol. 12/3, pp. 1-7.

Marzano, R.J., T. Waters and **Brian A. McNulty** (2005), *School Leadership That Works: From Research To Results*. Association for Supervision and Curriculum Development, Alexandria, VA.

Møller, J. and **G. Skedsmo** (2013), "Modernising education: New Public Management reform in the Norwegian education system", *Journal of Educational Administration and History*, Vol. 45/4, pp. 336-353.

OECD (2013), *OECD Reviews of Evaluation and Assessment in Education. Synergies for Better Learning: An International Perspective on Evaluation and Assessment*, OECD Publishing, Paris, *http://dx.doi.org/10.1787/9789264190658-en*.

Pont, B., D. Nusche and **H. Moorman** (2008), *Improving School Leadership, Volume1: Policy and Practice*, OECD Publishing, Paris, *http://dx.doi.org/10.1787/9789264044715-en*.

Robinson, V., M. Hohepa and **C. Lloyd** (2009), *School Leadership and Student Outcomes: Identifying What Works and Why: Best Evidence Synthesis Iteration*, University of Auckland and the New Zealand Ministry of Education.

Robinson, V.M.J., C.A. Lloyd and **K.J. Rowe** (2008), "The impact of leadership on student outcomes: An analysis of the differential effects of leadership types", *Educational Administration Quarterly*, Vol. 44/5, pp. 635-674.

Ross, J.A. and **P. Gray** (2006), "School leadership and student achievement: The mediating effects of teacher beliefs", *Canadian Journal of Education*, Vol. 29/3, pp. 798-822.

Schleicher, A., (ed.) (2012), *Preparing Teachers and Developing School Leaders for the 21st Century: Lessons from around the World*, OECD Publishing, Paris, *http://dx.doi.org/10.1787/9789264174559-en*.

Smylie, M.A., et al. (2007), "Trust and the development of distributed leadership", *Journal of School Leadership*, Vol. 17/4, pp. 469-503.

Ungerleider, C.S. (2006), "Reflections on the use of large-scale student assessment for improving student success", *Canadian Journal of Education*, Vol. 29/3, pp. 873-888.

Ungerleider, C.S. (2003), "Large-scale student assessment: Guidelines for policy-makers", *International Journal of Testing*, Vol. 3/2, pp. 119-128.

Vanhoof, J., et al. (2014), "Data use by Flemish school principals: Impact of attitude, self-efficacy and external expectations", *Educational Studies*, Vol. 40/1, pp. 48-62.

Veenman , S., Y. Visser and **N. Wijkamp** (1998), "Implementation effects of a program for the training of coaching skills with school principals", *School Effectiveness and School Improvement: An International Journal of Research, Policy and Practice*, Vol. 9/2, pp. 135-156.

Veldman, D.J. and **J.E. Brophy** (1974), "Measuring teacher effects on pupil achievement", *Journal of Educational Psychology*, Vol. 66/3, pp. 319-324.

Willms, J.D. (2000), "Monitoring school performance for 'standards-based reform'", *Evaluation and Research in Education*, Vol. 14/3 and 4, pp. 237-253.

Willms, J.D. (1998), "Assessment strategies for Title I of the improving America's Schools Act", report prepared for the Committee on Title I Testing and Assessment of the National Academy of Sciences.

Woessmann, L. (2001), *Schooling, Resources, Educational Institutions, and Student Performance: The International Evidence*, Kiel Institute of World Economics, Kiel.

4

Developing
and Supporting Teachers

This chapter focuses on the professional development experiences of teachers. Professional development refers to activities that aim to advance teachers' skills and knowledge, with the ultimate aim of improving their teaching practice. The chapter looks at what studies say about the importance of professional development and then discusses reports from teachers about the different types of development opportunities they receive (including induction and mentoring programmes). It also examines the range of variables related to teachers and schools that might influence the amount of professional development that a teacher undertakes. The discussion then moves to the development needs that teachers identify and the barriers that prevent teachers from getting the professional development they desire. It concludes with recommendations for policy makers, school leaders and teachers.

Highlights

- In the participating countries and economies, an average of 88% of teachers in lower secondary education report engaging in professional development in the past year. Slightly lower participation rates are found among males and especially among non-permanent teachers. Having taken part in formal induction programmes in the past appears to be an important predictor of teachers' participation in professional development in later years.

- Although school principals report that induction programmes are currently available at their schools, on average, not even half of teachers report taking part in some induction practice in their first regular employment.

- The level and intensity of participation in professional development activities are influenced by the types of support that teachers receive to undertake them. In general, teachers report higher participation rates in professional development activities in countries where they also report higher levels of financial support. However, in some cases participation rates in professional development activities is high even though monetary support is not offered. In these cases, non-monetary support for teacher development is provided through scheduled time for activities that take place during regular working hours at the school.

- Teachers report that the areas of most critical need for professional development are in teaching students with special needs and developing information and communication technology (ICT) skills for teaching. One in five lower secondary teachers identified the former to be especially important for them, which implies that teachers do not feel fully prepared to cope with this challenge.

- Across the participating countries and economies, teachers' most commonly reported reasons for not participating in professional development activities are conflicts with work schedules and the absence of incentives for participation.

INTRODUCTION

Ensuring that millions of teachers around the world have the essential competencies they require to be effective in the classroom is one of the keys to raising levels of student achievement. Education systems, therefore, seek to provide teachers with opportunities for developing and extending their competencies in order to achieve or maintain a high standard of teaching and to develop or retain a high-quality teacher workforce.[1]

Since the time when many of today's more-experienced teachers undertook their initial teacher education or training, knowledge about learning and teaching has deepened and expanded (see European Commission, 2012b). As noted at the International Summit on the Teaching Profession (Schleicher, 2012), teachers' tasks need to be expanded to include providing students with both cognitive and non-cognitive skills. These skills include ways of thinking and working (creativity, critical thinking, communication and collaboration), tools for working (including information and communications technologies) and skills related to citizenship and personal and social responsibility for succeeding in today's societies.

In-service professional development programmes aim to introduce new tools or skills or update those that teachers already possess. The professional development of teachers is defined in the relevant literature in many different ways. However, at the core of such definitions is the understanding that professional development is about teachers learning procedures, learning how to learn and transforming their knowledge into practices that benefit their students' growth (Avalos, 2011). The OECD Teaching and Learning International Survey (TALIS) adopts a broad definition of professional development (see the TALIS framework, 2013). Specifically, professional development is defined as activities that aim to develop an individual's skills, knowledge, expertise and other characteristics as a teacher.

This definition recognises that development can be provided in many ways, ranging from the most formal (such as courses or workshops) to more informal approaches (such as collaboration with other teachers or participation in extracurricular activities).[2] Professional development can be provided through external expertise in the form of courses, workshops or formal qualification programmes or through collaboration between schools or teachers across schools (in the form of observational visits to other schools) or within schools where teachers work. Professional development within schools can be provided through coaching or mentoring, collaborative planning and teaching and sharing good practices.

Indeed, according to recent evidence (Jackson and Bruegmann, 2009), the teachers whose students experience larger achievement gains are precisely those who have more effective colleagues (based on estimated value-added results). Box 4.1 summarises the types of professional development activities considered by TALIS.

Box 4.1. **Types of professional development**

The TALIS questionnaire asked teachers about the professional development they participated in during the 12 months prior to the survey. Teachers were asked to indicate whether they had participated in any of the following activities:

- **Courses/workshops** (on subject matter or methods and/or other education-related topics).
- **Education conferences or seminars** (where teachers and/or researchers present their research results and discuss education problems).
- **Observation visits to other schools**.
- **Observation visits to business premises, public organisations, or non-governmental organisations.**
- **In-service training courses** in business premises, public organisations or non-governmental organisations.
- **Qualification programmes** (e.g. a degree programme).
- **Participation in a network of teachers** formed specifically for the professional development of teachers.
- **Individual or collaborative research** on a topic of professional interest.
- **Mentoring and/or peer observation and coaching** as part of a formal school arrangement.

In addition to asking teachers about their professional development activities during the 12 months prior to the survey, TALIS also asked teachers about the support they received for undertaking these activities, their effect, the areas of their work that they found most in need of further development and the barriers they felt had prevented them from undertaking additional development activities. Teachers were also asked about their participation in induction and mentoring activities. For the purposes of TALIS, induction activities refer to activities completed during the teacher's first regular employment. In addition, TALIS asked school principals about the availability of induction and mentoring programmes in their schools. Figure 4.1 presents the elements of teacher professional development examined in TALIS.

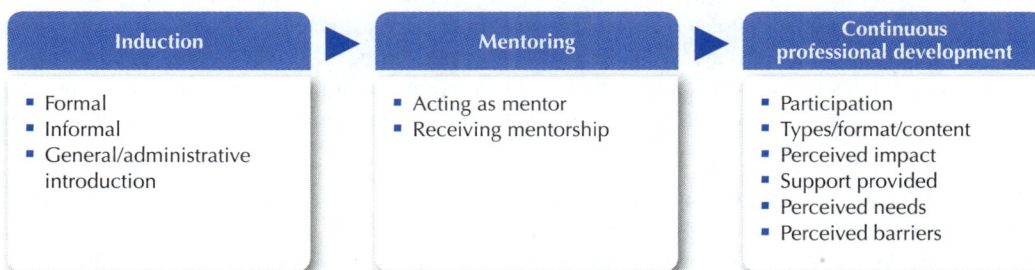

■ Figure 4.1 ■
Elements of teacher professional development examined in TALIS

Induction	Mentoring	Continuous professional development
▪ Formal ▪ Informal ▪ General/administrative introduction	▪ Acting as mentor ▪ Receiving mentorship	▪ Participation ▪ Types/format/content ▪ Perceived impact ▪ Support provided ▪ Perceived needs ▪ Perceived barriers

It is crucial to keep in mind two important limitations of the present analyses while interpreting the results. First, because TALIS is a cross-sectional survey, it does not show how individual professional development participation evolves or how it adapts or responds to policy changes. Second, because of the self-reporting nature of TALIS, teachers' responses regarding their participation in induction, mentoring and professional development activities are subject to the limitations of memory and perception. Nevertheless, these responses might be considered good proxies for the registered participation rates. The proposed measure of the degree of effectiveness of professional development activities is again a subjective one. However, teachers' perceptions are important as well and can be expected to influence their behaviour (see, among others, Rockoff and Speroni [2011] for recent evidence on the positive impact of subjective evaluations of teacher effectiveness on the achievement gains made by teachers' future students).

Following the structure highlighted in Figure 4.1, this chapter begins by looking at the profile and degree of teachers' participation in induction and mentoring programmes and the variation within and between countries. The objective in this section is to identify characteristics that may explain a teacher's participation in these programmes so as to provide some insight into the distribution of development opportunities.

The chapter continues by looking at the range of individual and/or school variables that may explain the intensity and diversity of teachers' participation in professional development. The diversity of professional development refers to the different types of activities that a teacher undertakes, and the intensity reflects the duration of the professional development activities. The focus is on understanding what factors may influence teachers' decisions about diversity of participation in certain professional development activities.

The third part of the chapter discusses teachers' professional development needs. It compares the extent of unsatisfied demand within and between countries and identifies the areas of teachers' work for which they report the greatest development need. This section concludes by considering how levels of unsatisfied demand relate to the professional development that teachers have received.

The last part of the chapter considers the main barriers that teachers report for not participating in professional development. This analysis is based on teachers' reports of the factors that prevent them from engaging in more professional development than they did. The final section discusses the policy implications arising from the analysis.

INDUCTION AND MENTORING PROGRAMMES

No matter how good initial teacher education is, it cannot be expected to prepare teachers for all the challenges they face during their first regular employment as a teacher. As the European Commission noted in its recent handbook for policy makers on induction (European Commission, 2010, pp.13-16):

> Effective induction programmes can avoid some of these problems ("praxis-shock" by newly-qualified teachers and consequent early drop-out from the profession) by providing all new teachers with systematic personal, social and professional support in the early years of their career. They can therefore also help improve school and teacher performance. Induction provides a vital link in the continuum of teacher education that runs from Initial Teacher Education through induction to career-long continuing professional development.

TALIS defines induction programmes for teachers as a range of structured activities at a school to support teachers' introduction into the school (or into the teaching profession for new teachers). These activities could include peer work or mentoring. This chapter first examines the policies and practices at the school level that are intended to support teachers who are either new to the profession or new to the school. Induction and mentoring programmes may help new teachers cope with initial difficulties and challenges associated with teaching. Ingersoll and Strong (2011) reviewed empirical studies on the effects of support, guidance and orientation programmes (that is, induction programmes) for beginning teachers. They found that most of the studies provide empirical evidence for the claim that support and assistance for beginning teachers have a positive influence on several outcomes, such as teachers' commitment and retention and students' achievement (Fuller, 2003; Cohen and Fuller, 2006; Fletcher, Strong and Villar, 2008).[3] In particular, empirical evidence shows that students taught by teachers who receive comprehensive induction support demonstrate learning gains that are larger than those experienced by students taught by teachers who do not receive such support (see, for instance, Glazerman et al., 2010).

TALIS 2013 sought to learn through two channels the extent to which induction and mentoring programmes for new teachers exist in lower secondary schools. First, school principals were asked whether induction and mentoring were available for teachers new to the school or new to teaching. Second, teachers were asked about their participation in induction programmes in their first regular employment as a teacher and their current participation in mentoring activities (either as a mentor or a recipient of mentoring). The following section examines what percentage of teachers has access to induction programmes in their schools in a variety of formats.

Availability of induction programmes

Figure 4.2 and the first columns of Table 4.1 show country-level availability of induction programmes for the lower secondary teacher population. On average across participating countries, 44% of teachers work in schools where principals report the availability of formal induction programmes for all new teachers to the school, and 22% work in schools where induction programmes are available only for teachers new to teaching. In total, more than three-quarters of teachers (76%) work in schools with informal induction programmes. Finally, some 86% of teachers work in schools where school principals report the availability of general and/or administrative introduction programmes. However, there is great variation among countries.

As shown in Figure 4.2, in general, those countries with a greater number of formal induction programmes are also those with more informal ones. A possible explanation for this pattern (which, unfortunately, cannot be addressed with TALIS data) could be that schools in these countries consider these programmes to be complementary instead of substitutes for one another. This could be the case if, for example, formal induction programmes are offered during a limited time period, whereas informal induction activities are not. However, the Czech Republic, Estonia, Finland, Iceland, Latvia, Poland and Portugal show quite large differences between both types of induction programmes. In particular, the informal induction activities in these countries are much more frequent than formal induction programmes. Finally, there are also large differences in Japan, but in contrast to the previous case, the formal induction programmes in Japan are much more frequent than informal induction activities.

In some countries, most teachers work in schools that don't have a formal induction programme. This is the case in Brazil, Mexico, Poland, Portugal and Spain, where between 70% and 80% of teachers work in schools that do not have an induction programme. The situation in these countries contrasts sharply to that in Australia, Malaysia, the Netherlands, Singapore, England (United Kingdom) and Flanders (Belgium), where formal induction programmes are virtually universal for all new teachers to the school. In Singapore and England (United Kingdom), only a small fraction of teachers (less than 1%) are in schools that lack any formal induction programme.

■ Figure 4.2 ■

Access to formal and informal induction programmes or activities

Percentage of lower secondary education teachers whose school principal reports the existence of formal and informal inductions

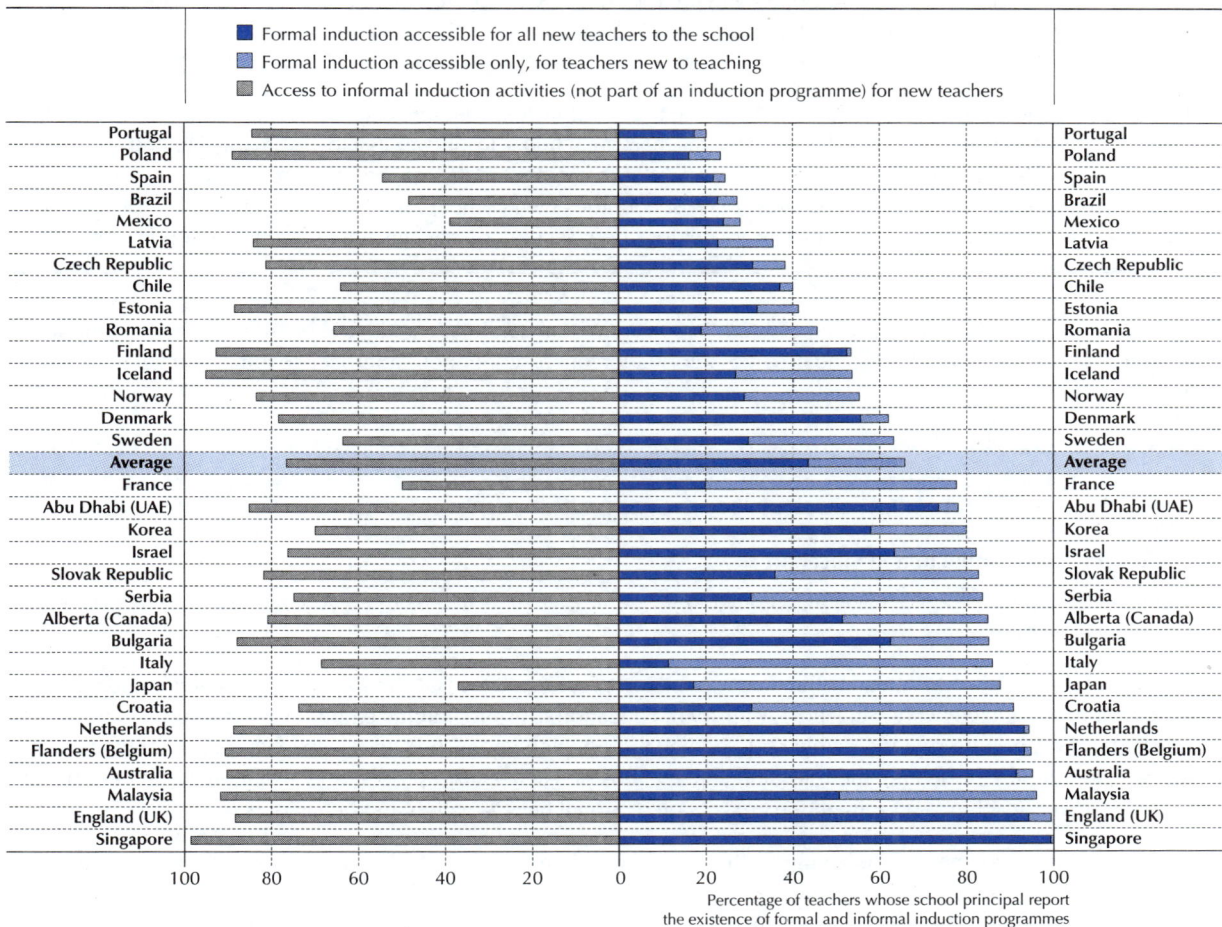

- Formal induction accessible for all new teachers to the school
- Formal induction accessible only, for teachers new to teaching
- Access to informal induction activities (not part of an induction programme) for new teachers

Percentage of teachers whose school principal report the existence of formal and informal induction programmes

Countries are ranked in ascending order, based on the cumulative percentage of teachers whose school principal reports access to formal induction programmes for all new teachers to the school and for only teachers new to teaching.

Source: OECD, TALIS 2013 Database, Table 4.1.

StatLink ⟨⟩ http://dx.doi.org/10.1787/888933041440

As with formal induction, informal induction activities are also available for most new teachers in Australia (90%), Flanders (Belgium) (91%), Finland (93%), Iceland (95%), Malaysia (92%) and Singapore (99%). However, informal induction activities are less frequent in Japan and Mexico, where only 37% and 39% of teachers, respectively, are in schools where these are available.

Finally, general and/or administrative introductions for new teachers are very common in most countries: On average, 86% of teachers are in schools where these activities are in place. Only in Mexico do no more than 50% of teachers work in schools in which any particular one of the three types of induction activities are offered.

Box 4.2 examines the availability of induction programmes for primary and upper secondary teachers in those countries that have implemented TALIS for those populations.

Box 4.2. **Availability of induction in primary and upper secondary education**

Tables 4.1.a and 4.1.b show the country-level availability of induction programmes for the primary (ISCED 1) and upper secondary (ISCED 3) teacher populations, respectively, in those countries with available data.

Table 4.1.a shows that, in general, primary teachers report slightly less access to induction programmes than their lower secondary colleagues. More primary teachers are in schools with no induction programmes in Finland, Mexico and Flanders (Belgium). In addition, in Mexico and Flanders (Belgium), the percentage of primary teachers who are in schools where principals report the availability of informal induction activities or general introduction programmes is lower than the corresponding figure for lower secondary teachers. In other words, in the countries listed here, teachers in primary education are more likely than teachers in lower secondary education to work in schools with no induction programmes (either formal or informal) or without general introduction programmes.

For upper secondary teachers, Table 4.1.b shows that, as for lower secondary teachers, formal induction practices are virtually universally available for all new teachers in schools in Singapore. In Denmark, Finland, Mexico and Norway, for example, there is greater availability of formal induction programmes for upper secondary teachers than for lower secondary teachers. In most countries with comparable data, the availability of general or administrative introduction programmes is greater for upper secondary teachers than for lower secondary ones.

Box 4.3 describes details of the education system in Singapore that can help explain the broad availability of induction programmes for new teachers there, and provides information on the continuous approach to initial teacher training and induction in France.

Box 4.3. **Induction programmes in Singapore and France**

The central role of induction in Singapore

Upon completion of preservice teacher education, beginning teachers in Singapore undergo induction at both the national and school levels.

At the national level, they attend a three-day induction programme, called the Beginning Teachers' Orientation Programme, conducted by the Singapore Ministry of Education. This programme emphasises the importance of the role of teachers in nurturing the whole child and enables beginning teachers to consolidate their learning at the teacher institute. By presenting the roles and expectations of teachers, this programme also inducts new teachers into Singapore's teaching fraternity in the areas of professional beliefs, values and behaviours.

During the first two years of teaching, further guidance is provided to beginning teachers via the Structured Mentoring Programme. This programme enables them to learn practical knowledge and skills from assigned mentors who are experienced or senior teachers at the school. The school has the autonomy to customise the programme according to the learning needs of the new teachers. Besides practical skills, the programme helps to deepen the understanding of new teachers about the values and ethos of the teaching profession.

...

Box 4.3. **Induction programmes in Singapore and France** (cont.)

Induction as part of a consecutive model of teacher education in France

From the early 1990s to 2010, France had a consecutive model of teacher education. Training in academic subjects was largely predominant, which led to a high level of specialisation in secondary education teaching. After a bachelor degree or more, students had a competitive examination for recruitment. Successful candidates received one year of training and were assigned a tutor. Since the early 2000s, new teachers have been mostly enrolled in formal induction programmes during their first year of regular employment, with scheduled time for activities. These specific programmes take place outside the schools, and they are based especially on classroom practices to help new teachers manage a full-time job.

Launched in 2010, the reform called "mastérisation" made access to the teaching profession conditional upon completing a master's degree. A new structure of initial teacher education has been elaborated under the education act of July 2013 and is effective since the start of the 2013/14 school year. Within graduate schools of professorship and education (*Écoles supérieures du Professorat et de l'Enseignement,* ESPE), which are integral parts of the universities, the study programmes combine academic subject studies, theoretical pedagogy and practical teaching experience to ensure a progressive start to the teaching profession. Induction programmes still exist, but they are now reduced and included in other in-service teacher training activities. If available, they are often focused on classroom management in order to respond to new teachers' needs, especially those assigned to difficult areas.

Sources: Ministry of Education, Singapore; Ministry of Education, France.

Participation rates in induction programmes

The previous section explored the availability of induction programmes in schools across TALIS countries and economies. This section examines TALIS data about teachers' reported participation in such programmes. The last columns in Table 4.1 show country-level participation for lower secondary school teachers in formal induction, informal induction and general introduction activities, as reported by teachers. For each of the activities, almost 50% of teachers on average report participation. Hence, important differences exist between the availability of induction programmes or activities and participation rates. Even though participation rates in some countries exceed availability (for example, in Mexico this occurs for both formal and informal induction programmes), Table 4.1 shows that in most countries, teachers' participation rates are generally lower than the reported availability levels. This last finding might be an indication of low engagement of teachers in these activities, in spite of their availability, but it might also reflect that teachers are asked about their participation in these activities in their first employment as a teacher, whereas principals report on the current availability of such activities in their school (i.e. the reference period for these responses may or may not overlap).

When participation rates are compared across countries, some notable differences are evident. In Japan, Malaysia and Singapore, participation in induction programmes is extensive, with 80% or more of teachers reporting participation in a formal induction programme. This contrasts with Finland, Norway and Sweden, where only 10% to 16% of teachers report having participated in a formal induction programme. With respect to informal induction activities, the largest participation rates are in Bulgaria, Korea, Malaysia, Poland, Romania and Singapore (around 60% in each country).

Box 4.4. **Participation in induction in primary and upper secondary education**

Table 4.1.a and Table 4.1.b show country-level participation in induction programmes for primary (ISCED 1) and upper secondary (ISCED 3) school teachers. The largest difference between participation rates for primary and lower secondary teachers in any type of induction programme occurs in Flanders (Belgium). On average, among all primary education teachers in the participating countries, only 30% participated in formal induction programmes, while 42% report having participated in informal induction and 35% report having engaged in general introduction activities.

On average for countries with data for lower and upper secondary education, the reported participation rates in each type of activity are very similar for these levels of education (averages are about half of the teachers). In Denmark, upper secondary teachers report much greater participation than their lower secondary colleagues in each of the two induction programmes (formal and informal) and also in general/administrative introduction activities. A similar pattern is observed in Mexico even though the difference between both types of teachers is not as important.

Similarly, in Bulgaria, Malaysia and Singapore, a large majority (more than 80%) of teachers report taking part in general or administrative introduction activities. This is different from the situation in Norway, Portugal, Spain and Sweden, where less than a quarter of teachers say they participated in general or administrative inductions. As explained previously, some countries offer their teachers more informal induction activities than formal induction programmes. However, in the majority of countries in which teachers indicate a high participation in formal programmes, there is also high participation reported in informal activities.

Box 4.4 examines participation rates in induction programmes for primary and upper secondary teachers in those countries with available data.

Table 4.2 shows the characteristics of teachers who report having participated in formal induction programmes in their first regular employment as a teacher. There are no important differences in participation between male and female teachers. Similarly, differences in participation rates between permanent and fixed-term teachers are not very large, on average. There are, however, some countries where these differences are more important. First, in France, Japan and Serbia, approximately twice as many permanent teachers as fixed-term teachers report having participated in induction programmes. In Italy, permanent teachers are more than six times more likely than teachers with fixed-term contracts to report having participated in formal induction. The reverse occurs in the Netherlands, Norway, Sweden and Flanders (Belgium). For example, among permanent teachers in Sweden, only 10% report participating in induction programmes, compared with 19% among fixed-term teachers. (The percentages are 37%, 42% and 9% for permanent teachers and 68%, 64% and 19% for fixed-term teachers, respectively, in Flanders (Belgium), the Netherlands and Norway.) Although in some countries, years of teaching experience seems to be an important factor in teachers' reports of having participated in induction programmes, more experienced teachers on average are only slightly less likely to report having participated (about 5 percentage points, on average) in these types of programmes. This difference is more pronounced in Israel, Singapore and Flanders (Belgium), although the proportion of more-experienced teachers in Singapore who report participating in induction (69%) is relatively high compared with other countries. This might indicate a trend toward required participation or just greater availability of formal induction programmes in recent years. Again, some countries present the opposite behaviour: Less-experienced teachers seem to participate less than experienced teachers in Italy and Japan, even though in Japan, participation rates are still not that low. In particular, the participation rates in Italy and Japan for teachers with more than five years of teaching experience are 52% and 88%, respectively, whereas the participation rates in these countries of teachers with less than five years of teaching experience are 19% and 66%. Since different participation patterns emerge in different countries, it seems important to study the country-specific profile of teachers who report undertaking induction to better understand those who do not participate in these programmes.

As noted earlier, the current availability of induction programmes as reported by school principals is larger than past participation in induction programmes reported by teachers. Empirical evidence shows that students taught by teachers who receive comprehensive induction support demonstrate learning gains that are greater than those experienced by students taught by teachers who did not receive such support (Glazerman et al., 2010).

Figure 4.3 depicts new teachers' access to and participation in induction programmes. Note that to accurately examine the association between the availability of and participation in induction programmes, the participation rate of teachers who have access to induction programmes at the time they are eligible for such programmes (i.e. at the beginning of their career or when they join a new school) is needed. Unfortunately, TALIS did not gather such data, and thus an approximation approach has been taken. In particular, the analysis focuses on teachers who have less than three years of experience as a teacher and who have been working in their current school for less than three years. Restricting the sample to these less-experienced teachers reduces the time period that may have elapsed since their eligibility for induction programmes and increases the chances that these teachers are still working in their first school (for which data about principals' reports on the availability of induction programmes are available).

As shown in Figure 4.3, whereas on average 70% of these less-experienced teachers work in schools where principals report that induction programmes are available, only slightly more than half of these teachers report having taken part in such programmes. This means that some teachers who have access to such programmes may not be taking advantage of them. Teachers' reported participation in induction programmes appears to match principals' reports on their availability in schools in the Czech Republic, Malaysia, Romania, Singapore and England (United Kingdom), suggesting that most teachers are taking advantage of the available induction programmes.

■ Figure 4.3 ■

New teachers' access to and participation in formal induction programmes

Percentage of lower secondary education teachers who have less than three years of experience at their school and less than three years of experience as a teacher who are working in schools where the principal reports the following access to formal induction programmes and the percentage of teachers with the same characteristics who report having participated in formal induction programmes[1,2]

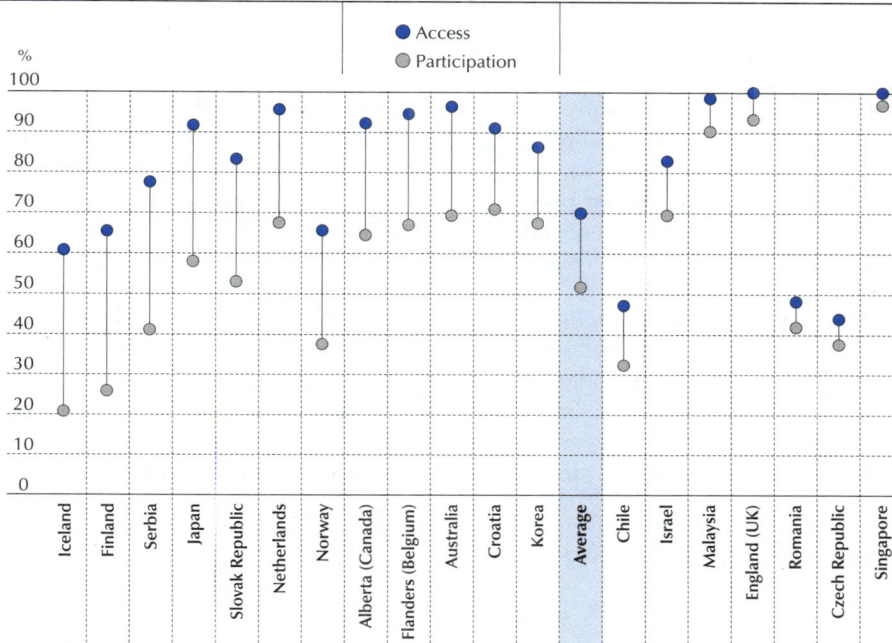

1. Data on access to induction programmes are derived from the principal questionnaire, while data on participation are derived from the teacher questionnaire. Teachers were asked about their participation in an induction programme in their first regular employment as a teacher.
2. Data presented in this graph are for formal induction programmes only, meaning they do not consider participation in or access to informal induction activities not part of an induction programme or a general and/or administrative introduction to the school.
Countries are ranked in descending order, based on the gap between access to and participation in induction programmes. Countries are not presented in this graph if the percentage of teachers with less than three years of experience at their school and less than three years of experience as a teacher is below 5%.
Source: OECD, TALIS 2013 Database, Table 4.28.Web.
StatLink ⌗ http://dx.doi.org/10.1787/888933041459

Availability of mentoring programmes

Another often-discussed method of professional development is mentoring, which in TALIS is defined as a support structure in schools where more-experienced teachers support less-experienced teachers. This structure might involve all teachers in the school or only new teachers.

The literature similarly defines mentoring as personal guidance, usually provided by more- experienced teachers to beginning teachers. Recently, mentoring programmes have become a dominant form of teacher induction (Strong, 2009). Indeed, as Hobson et al. (2009) recognise, many countries have seen a massive increase in the number of formal programmes of school-based mentoring for beginning teachers. The overall objective of teacher-mentoring programmes is to give newcomers a local guide, but the character and content of these programmes varies widely. In addition, evidence shows that teachers who receive more hours of mentoring have higher student achievement gains than those who had fewer hours of mentoring (Rockoff, 2008).

Across TALIS countries, one-quarter of teachers on average work in schools where principals report that no mentoring programme is available (Table 4.3). Yet for the other three-quarters of teachers, a huge heterogeneity exists in the access to mentoring programmes across countries (that is, whether such access is offered only to teachers new to the school, only to those new to teaching or to all new teachers). In general, there are important differences in availability rates across countries. Some countries have a large percentage of teachers with no access to such programmes (Chile, Finland, Mexico, Portugal and Spain), whereas others (Australia, Croatia, England [United Kingdom], the Netherlands, Serbia and Singapore) offer these programmes to almost all teachers.

The target teacher population for mentoring programmes also differs across countries. For example, in Croatia, France and Serbia, more than two-thirds of teachers work in schools where principals report that mentoring programmes are directed only at teachers who are new to teaching. On the contrary, in Flanders (Belgium) nearly two-thirds of teachers work in schools where the principals report that these programmes are available for all teachers who are new to the school. Finally, in Brazil, the Netherlands, Romania, and Abu Dhabi (United Arab Emirates), more than half of teachers work in schools where the principals report that mentoring programmes are available for all teachers in the school.

Evidence supports the idea that the quality of the mentor also influences the impact of these programmes on outcomes such as teachers' classroom practices. For example, Evertson et al. (2000) found that teachers with trained mentors had better classroom organisation and students were more engaged. A characteristic of mentoring programmes that might capture their quality to some extent is whether the subject field of the mentor is the same as that of the teacher being mentored. This alignment between the subject field expertise of the mentor and the teacher being mentored has been shown to influence the impact of teachers on students (Dee, 2005). That congruence is shown in the middle part of Table 4.3. On average, 68% of teachers who work in schools with a mentoring system work in schools where the principal claims that most of the time, the subject field of the mentor was the same as that of the teacher being mentored.

In Croatia, the Czech Republic, France, Israel, Italy, Poland, Portugal, Serbia, Singapore and the Slovak Republic, the subject field of the mentor is mostly the same as that of the teacher being mentored (in particular, the percentage of teachers who work in schools with a mentoring system and where the principal claims that the subject field of the mentor and the mentee is the same most of the time is above 80%). This is not the case in the Netherlands and Flanders (Belgium), where about one-third of teachers who work in schools with a mentoring system also work in schools where the subject field of the mentor is rarely or never the same as that of the teacher being mentored.

Box 4.5 examines the reported availability of mentoring programmes for primary and upper secondary teachers in those countries that have implemented TALIS for those populations.

Box 4.5. **Availability of mentoring programmes in primary and upper secondary education**

Tables 4.3.a and 4.3.b show country-level availability of mentoring programmes for primary (ISCED 1) and upper secondary (ISCED 3) teacher populations. This availability is lower on average for primary teachers than for lower secondary teachers (when comparing those countries with data for both populations). In Flanders (Belgium) and Mexico, the rate of teachers working in schools whose school principals report no availability of mentoring programmes is much larger for primary than for lower secondary teachers. However, the concordance between subject fields of mentor and mentored teachers is larger for primary teachers than for lower secondary teachers in Norway and Flanders (Belgium). The reverse is true for Denmark.

The availability of mentoring programmes for upper secondary teachers is similar to that for lower secondary teachers. In countries such as Denmark and Norway, there is a larger percentage of schools where mentoring programmes are available for upper secondary teachers than for the lower secondary ones. Finally, the concordance between mentor and mentoring subject field(s) among upper secondary teachers is also much greater in these two countries.

Participation rates in mentoring programmes

As with the discussion of induction programmes, now that the availability of mentoring programmes has been examined, the following sections turn to teachers' participation rates in these programmes. Table 4.3 also shows teachers' participation in mentoring programmes as either mentor or mentee. On average across TALIS countries, 14% of teachers report serving as mentors for other teachers. This rate is much higher in Korea (34%), Singapore (39%) and England (United Kingdom) (31%). Participation in mentoring programmes as mentees varies significantly across countries. In 19 countries, less than 10% of teachers report that they currently have an assigned mentor to support them. This contrasts with countries such as Brazil (34%), Japan (33%), Malaysia (27%), Singapore (40%) and Abu Dhabi (United Arab Emirates) (52%), where these figures are above 25%.

Box 4.6 examines participation rates in mentoring programmes for primary and upper secondary teachers in those countries that have implemented TALIS for those populations.

Box 4.6. **Participation in mentoring programmes in primary and upper secondary education**

Tables 4.3.a and 4.3.b show country-level participation in mentoring programmes for primary (ISCED 1) and upper secondary (ISCED 3) school teachers. Again, participation rates in mentoring programmes (either as a mentor or as a mentee) among primary teachers are only slightly lower, on average, than among lower secondary teachers.

On average, 8% of teachers report having a mentor assigned to them in lower secondary schools versus 15% in upper secondary schools. In addition, a higher percentage of teachers reports acting as a mentor in upper secondary schools (19%) compared with lower secondary schools (9%). In particular, the proportion is almost three times as large for upper secondary (25%) than for lower secondary (9%) teachers in Denmark.

■ Figure 4.4 ■

Availability of and participation in mentoring activities

Percentage of lower secondary education teachers whose school principal reports that mentoring is available for all teachers in the school and the percentage of teachers who report presently having an assigned mentor

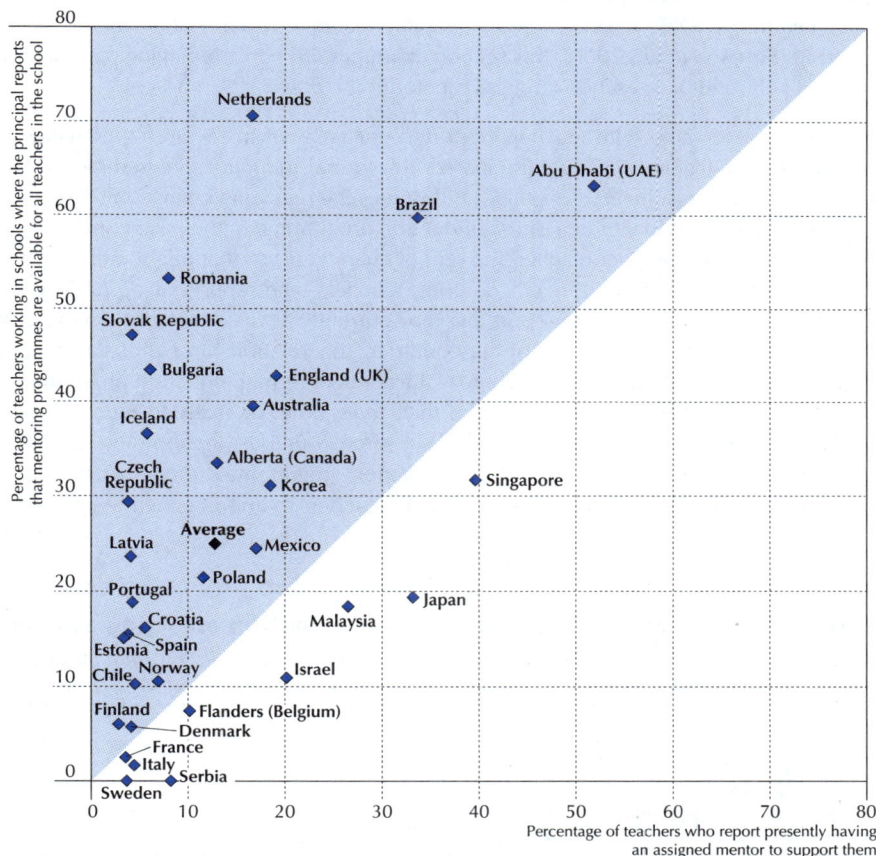

Source: OECD, TALIS 2013 Database, Table 4.3.
StatLink ⫘ http://dx.doi.org/10.1787/888933041478

Tables 4.4 and 4.5 show the characteristics of teachers who report receiving mentoring and of those who report serving as mentors. First, with a few exceptions (namely, Brazil, Japan, Korea, Poland and Abu Dhabi [United Arab Emirates]), no notable differences exist between the percentages of male and female teachers who report either serving as a mentor or receiving mentoring. However, and quite reasonably, teachers with more experience tend to report acting as mentors more and tend to report receiving mentoring less. Likewise, permanent teachers are more likely to report serving as mentors, whereas fixed-term teachers tend to report receiving less mentoring.

Figure 4.4 presents the availability of mentoring programmes for all teachers in the school for each country, along with the percentage of teachers who report having an assigned mentor. This figure shows a clear positive correlation between the reported availability of mentoring for all teachers in schools and the percentage of teachers who report having an assigned mentor. In most countries, a larger proportion of teachers work in schools where the principal reports the availability of mentoring programmes for all teachers than do teachers who report having a mentor (indicated by the shaded area in Figure 4.4). This suggests that not all teachers in schools with mentoring programmes for all teachers report having mentors. This result may not be surprising given that we should not expect all teachers in these schools to have mentors (at the very least, some teachers in these schools act as mentors). In some countries, however, there is a very large difference between the proportion of teachers who work in schools with mentoring programmes for all teachers and the proportion of teachers who report having a mentor. In the Netherlands, although 71% of teachers work in schools where the principal reports the availability of mentoring programmes, only 17% of teachers report having a mentor. In Romania, these percentages are 53% and 8%, respectively. As previously noted, mentoring programmes can have an important impact on teachers' classroom practices and students' outcomes (Rockoff, 2008). Thus, it is important to identify these countries – or schools within a country – where in spite of the high availability of mentoring programmes, participation rates among teachers are not high. School leaders need to highlight the benefits of such programmes for teachers and remove any barriers to access to ensure that teachers can actively engage in these activities and reap the positive outcomes that will ensue.[4]

Teachers' past participation in induction programmes improves their performance and thus might better prepare them to serve as mentors. Based on empirical evidence that shows the importance of the quality of the mentor on modulating the positive effects of mentoring (Evertson et al., 2000), this section examines the effect of having participated in induction activities in the past on the likelihood of a teacher acting as mentor in the present.

Analyses examined the factors associated with teachers' reported engagement in mentoring activities.[5] Of particular interest here is the association of a teacher having participated in a formal induction programme in the past with the teacher's current probability of acting as a mentor.[6] Figure 4.5 illustrates the predicted change in the probability of acting as a mentor for those teachers who participated in a formal induction programme in the past, compared with those who did not, while controlling for a number of other teacher and school characteristics that might influence this relationship (see also Table 4.29.Web). The results show that in 17 countries, teachers who report having participated in a formal induction programme in the past are more likely to report that they currently act as a mentor than those who report not having participated in such programmes (for the rest of the countries, this relationship is not statistically significant.)[7] This effect is, however, highly varied across countries. Whereas the effect of formal induction programmes is quite large in Chile, Latvia and Portugal, where these teachers are more than three times as likely to report being a mentor, the relationship is not significant in 11 countries (Table 4.29.Web). In some countries, therefore, these results suggest that early policy interventions, as, for example, participating in an induction programme during the first employment, might have a long-term impact on teachers' later willingness to help other teachers to improve their teaching capacities.

■ Figure 4.5 ■
Predicted effect of formal induction programme participation on acting as a mentor

Probability for lower secondary education teachers who report having participated in a formal induction programme to report acting as a mentor versus teachers who report not having participated such programmes[1]

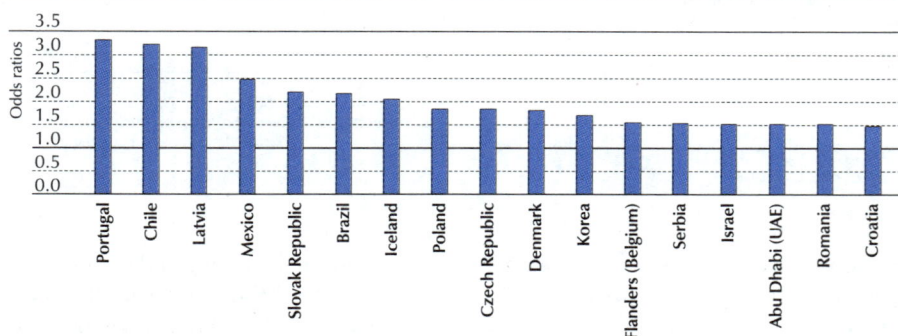

1. Countries for which the odds ratio is not statistically significant at 5% or where data are representing less than 5% of the cases are not presented in this figure. *Countries are ranked in descending order, based on the predicted effect of participating in any induction programme on the probability of acting as a mentor.*
Source: OECD, TALIS 2013 Database, Table 4.29.Web.
StatLink http://dx.doi.org/10.1787/888933041497

In sum, the TALIS data show that while various types of induction programmes are spread across participating countries, there are important differences between the reported availability and participation rates. Regarding mentoring programmes, data indicate that even though the availability of these programmes is a source of concern in some countries, availability is greater than participation rates in many countries. Hence, this suggests a need not only to support schools to ensure the availability of both programmes but for policy makers and school leaders to ensure that teachers engage in these supporting programmes.

WHY TEACHERS PARTICIPATE IN PROFESSIONAL DEVELOPMENT

As previously noted, the role of education and teaching is expanding in today's societies. Therefore, teachers today need to be able to constantly reflect on and evaluate their work and to innovate and adapt accordingly. These skills will give them the flexibility to modify classroom practices to respond to students' needs. As emphasised in European Commission (2012b: 8-9):

> Teaching competences are thus complex combinations of knowledge, skills, understanding, values and attitudes, leading to effective action in situation. [...] The range and complexity of competencies required for teaching in actual societies is so great that any one individual is unlikely to have them all, nor to have developed them all to the same high degree. [...] Teachers' continuous professional development is, thus, highly relevant both for improving educational performance and effectiveness and for enhancing teachers' commitment".

Meanwhile, empirical evidence increasingly shows the positive impact of teachers' professional development on students' scores. Yoon et al. (2007) provide a review of several research studies on this issue. They conclude that professional development that includes a substantial number of hours spread out over 6 to 12 months shows positive and significant effects on student achievement gains. Hill, Beisiegel and Jacob (2013) also provide a review of evidence based on key questions in the literature of professional development, providing similar results to the ones commented on above. All these findings, together with additional evidence regarding the impact of teachers' competences on students' achievement,[8] have led policy makers around the world to support the relevance and quality of career-long opportunities for professional development.

Participation rates

This section analyses teachers' participation rates in various professional development activities. Participation rates are measured in terms of the percentage of teachers who participated in any of the activities described in Box 4.1 during the 12-month period prior to the survey.

Table 4.6 shows country-level participation rates in professional development for lower secondary teachers. On average across participating countries, about 88% of teachers report engaging in some professional development (defined as having taken part in at least one activity in the previous 12 months) over the survey period. This finding reinforces the similar finding in TALIS 2008 (which showed an average participation rate of 89%) and thus suggests that participation in professional development is a fairly common feature in the professional careers of most teachers in the participating countries (OECD, 2009).

Nevertheless, notable differences are found among participation rates across countries. Participation rates are greater than 95% in Australia, Croatia, Latvia, Malaysia, Mexico, Singapore and Alberta (Canada), but this rate is below 75% in Chile (72%) and the Slovak Republic (73%). The relatively high rates of non-participation in these countries could be a source of concern for all agents participating in their educational system, from teachers and school leaders to education policy makers.

The second column in Table 4.6 shows the proportion of teachers who did not receive any type of support for their participation in professional development. On average across participating countries, less than 6% of teachers undertook professional development activities without receiving any type of support. Nevertheless, in some countries this proportion is well above average, as is the case in Portugal (29%) and Romania (21%). This fact might reflect a high commitment of teachers in these countries to improving their effectiveness and performance, which leads them to undertake professional development activities without any kind of support.

The last three columns of Table 4.6 represent the financial commitments associated with those professional development activities. On average, about two-thirds of teachers who participated in professional development during the 12 months prior to the survey reported that they did not have to pay personally for the professional development activities they

participated in. There are, of course, differences among countries. On the one hand, most of these activities are basically costless for teachers in Singapore and England (United Kingdom). On the other hand, some countries have a higher proportion of teachers (compared with the overall average of 9%) who claimed that they had to pay all the costs – Brazil (20%), Chile (17%), Portugal (33%) and Romania (28%).

Figure 4.6 illustrates the positive correlation between the percentage of teachers who reported not having to pay for any of the professional development they engaged in and teachers' reported participation in professional development. Countries in the bottom-left quadrant of the figure (Chile, Japan, Romania, the Slovak Republic and Spain) show both lower-than-average proportions of teachers who say they did not have to pay for any of their development activities and below-average participation rates in professional development. The figure clearly shows that teachers are willing to assume at least some of the cost of their professional development. Eleven countries can be found in the lower-right quadrant in the figure. In these countries, although fewer teachers than average report that they had to pay for none of their development activities, there are higher-than-average participation rates in professional development.

Box 4.7 examines participation rates in professional development programmes for primary and upper secondary teachers in those countries that have implemented TALIS for those populations.

■ Figure 4.6 ■

Teachers' recent participation in professional development, by their personal financial cost

Participation rates and reported personal financial cost of professional development activities undertaken by lower secondary education teachers in the 12 months prior to the survey

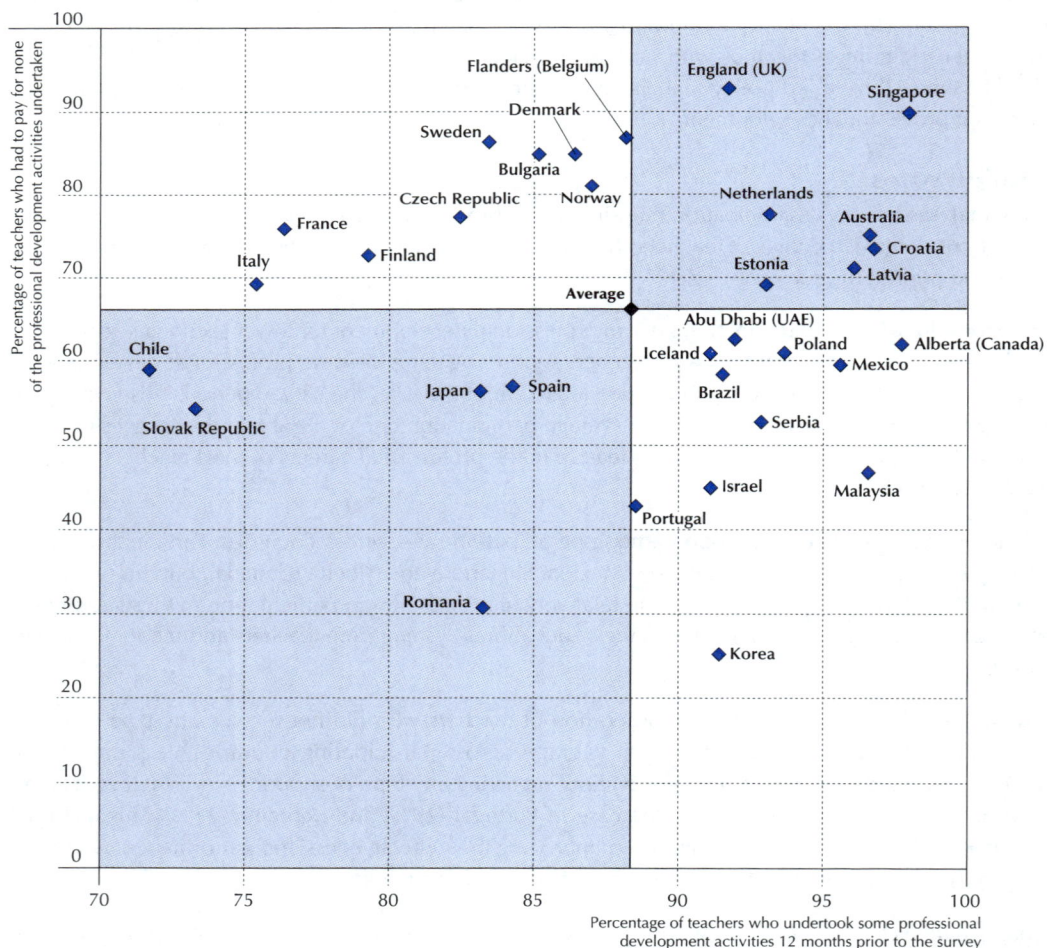

Source: OECD, TALIS 2013 Database, Table 4.6.
StatLink ᴍᴸᴾ http://dx.doi.org/10.1787/888933041516

Box 4.7. **Participation in professional development activities
in primary and upper secondary education**

Tables 4.6.a and 4.6.b show country-level participation in professional development activities for primary (ISCED 1) and upper secondary (ISCED 3) teachers. There are no large differences between primary and lower secondary teachers' participation rates. However, in Finland, Mexico and Norway, a higher percentage of primary teachers than lower secondary teachers report that they did not have to pay. In general, participation rates among upper secondary teachers are slightly greater than among lower secondary teachers, with the exception of Iceland. Regarding the personal payment for these activities, there are no important differences between the proportions of primary and upper secondary teachers who report paying for all or none of their activities and their lower secondary teacher counterparts.

Different types of professional development activities require different levels of investment. Figure 4.7 represents the levels of personal payment among teachers in relation to the type of professional development in which they participated. In general, more than half of the teachers who participated in professional development activities said that they paid nothing regardless of the type of programme (with the exception of qualification programmes), and 10% or less of teachers said that they paid the full cost. Qualification programmes tend to require more involvement (both in terms of time and money) and tend to be organised outside the confines of the school (i.e. at a university or college). It is not surprising, therefore, that these programmes are also those for which teachers are more likely to pay some or all of the cost. A very similar result was found in TALIS 2008 (see Box 4.8).

■ Figure 4.7 ■

Level of personal payment for teachers' professional development participation

Percentage of lower secondary education teachers who report having participated in the following professional development activities and who "paid no cost", "paid some cost" or "paid all cost" for the activities they participated in[1]

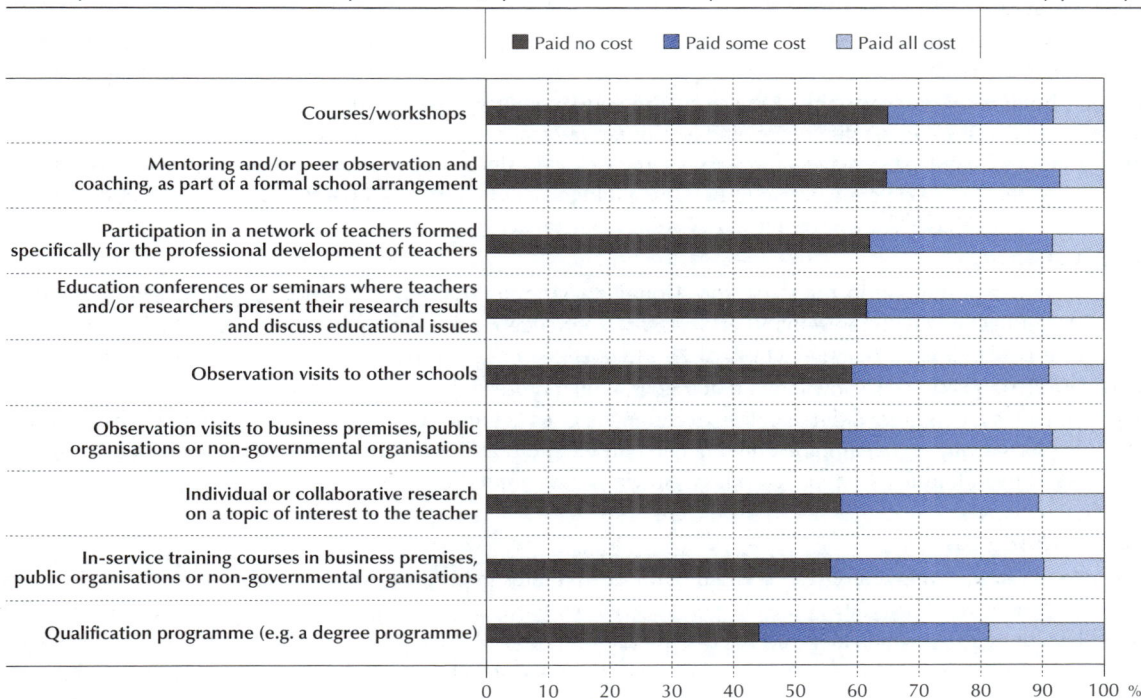

1. Teachers can participate in more than one professional development activity at the same time. Teachers were not asked about the level of personal payment for each activity but rather for their general level of personal payment for all the professional development activities they participated in. Therefore, the percentages presented in this figure should be interpreted as the level of general personal payment reported by the teachers who participated in each type of professional development activity.

Professional development activities are ranked in descending order, based on the average percentage of teachers who reported paying no cost.

Source: OECD, TALIS 2013 Database, Tables 4.6 and 4.9.

StatLink ᵃᵢˢᵖ http://dx.doi.org/10.1787/888933041535

Box 4.8. **Comparing lower secondary teachers' participation in professional development activities, TALIS 2008 and TALIS 2013**

The first two columns of Table 4.6.c list the participation rates in professional development activities of lower secondary teachers across the countries that participated in both TALIS 2008 and TALIS 2013.[9] The results shown in this table indicate that the average participation rate is very similar for both cycles. However, some differences emerge across countries. For example, participation in professional development activities is lower in 2013 in Spain (100% vs. 84%) and Italy (85% vs. 75%). This contrasts with higher participation rates observed in 2013 in Denmark (76% vs. 86%) and Iceland (77% vs. 91%).

Finally, the remaining columns in Table 4.6.c show the differences in the financial aspects of those professional development activities. There is no clear pattern in the differences between both cycles of the survey in the percentage of teachers who report paying for these professional activities. For example, looking at those countries whose participation rates in professional development activities are higher in 2013 than in 2008 (Denmark and Iceland), it can be observed that whereas in Denmark the percentage of teachers who report not paying is higher by 8 percentage points in 2013, in Iceland the percentage of teachers who report paying none of the full cost is lower in 2013 (61%) than in 2008 (68%).

How does participation vary by teacher and school characteristics?

To better understand the differences in participation rates in professional development activities, this section provides an analysis of the characteristics of teachers who participate in professional development activities and of the schools in which they work.[10] The results shown in Tables 4.7 and 4.8 are related to lower secondary teachers who took some professional development in the survey period. The teacher and school characteristics chosen for the comparison are those that were the most significant in the country regression analyses shown in Table 4.21.Web.

Gender differences

On average across participating countries, reported participation rates in professional development are slightly greater among women than men (89% on average for female teachers compared with 87% for male teachers; this difference being the same when holding all other variables constant).[11] In some countries, the reported participation rates were nearly equal for both genders. The largest differences in favor of female teachers were found in Italy and the Slovak Republic (on average, nine and eight percentage points more, respectively). In a few countries, male teachers report higher participation rates, the largest difference being Abu Dhabi (United Arab Emirates) (5 percentage points). (Table 4.7.)

Teaching Experience

On average, reported participation rates in professional development activities do not vary much with teaching experience: 89% of teachers with more than five years of experience report participating in professional development versus 87% of less-experienced teachers (Table 4.7). However, some countries and economies, such as Iceland or Abu Dhabi (United Arab Emirates), show larger differences, with more-experienced teachers participating in professional development activities much more often than less-experienced ones (a difference of 13 percentage points). In contrast, it is interesting that in Norway and Spain, the difference in participation rates is in favor of less-experienced teachers, who seem to be more active in professional development activities than are more-experienced teachers.

Work status differences

On average across participating countries, reported participation rates in professional development activities are lower among non-permanent teachers (Table 4.7). In general, permanent teachers claimed that they participated more in professional development activities than did fixed-term teachers (89% compared with 85% respectively, on average). The country with the largest difference between these two groups of teachers is Iceland, where the participation rate among teachers on fixed-term contracts is 15 percentage points lower than their permanent counterparts. There might be several explanations for the pattern found for permanent and non-permanent teachers. For instance, these two types of teachers might also differ in other characteristics, such as initiative and commitment to the profession, that affect both their employment status and professional development participation. Unfortunately, as TALIS data cannot provide information in this regard, further conclusions must be approached with caution. Nevertheless, countries and schools may want to consider ensuring that professional development is also made available to non-permanent teachers.

Teachers who work more than 30 hours per week report participating in professional development activities more than teachers who work less than 30 hours per week. The largest difference in favor of teachers working more than 30 hours per week is in Japan (16%).

Differences between public and private schools

Table 4.8 shows the main characteristics of the schools in which teachers who undertake professional development activities work. On average for all countries considered, participation rates in professional development activities are slightly greater among teachers working in public schools than in private ones. (See Chapter 2 for a complete definition of both types of schools.) The largest differences in favour of public school teachers are in Japan (17 percentage points) and France (9 percentage points). There are also some differences in favour of private school teachers in Portugal, the Slovak Republic and Spain (between 4 and 6 percentage points). In the case of Portugal, the difference could be related to the fact that more teachers say they have to pay for their professional development activities there. But it could also be that the supply of activities differs among public and private schools in some countries. (See further discussion in the subsection about barriers to participation.)

School location differences

As with the findings in TALIS 2008 (see OECD, 2009), on average the participation rate of teachers in professional development activities is very similar regardless of whether the schools in which they work are located in a village, town or city. Even though some variation occurs across countries, differences are not large (Table 4.8).

For example, in Chile and Romania, teachers in less urban areas (with 15 000 or fewer inhabitants) took part in slightly fewer professional development activities compared with their counterparts in other types of communities (a participation rate of about 10 percentage points more). In these two countries, participation rates increase with the size of the population in the school's locality. The reverse occurs in Brazil, Italy and Japan. On average, however, the geographic location of the school does not have a significant impact on lower secondary teacher's participation in professional development activities. (See Table 4.21.Web for the estimated effect of this variable on the probability of participating in professional development activities.)

HOW MUCH PROFESSIONAL DEVELOPMENT DO TEACHERS GET?

This section analyses the intensity and diversity of participation in professional development activities across the lower secondary teacher population. In other words, it looks at how much professional development teachers are actually receiving. Diversity of participation is measured in the number of different types of professional development activities undertaken during the 12-month period prior to the survey (see Box 4.1). Intensity of participation is measured by the average number of teachers' days during the 12-month period prior to the survey. Some empirical evidence shows a positive relationship between the total number of hours of professional development and students' achievement gains (see Yoon et al., 2007). Nevertheless, it must be emphasised here that intensity of participation is not equivalent to quality of professional development.

To better understand factors related to the intensity of participation in professional development activities and gain insight into potential policy making, TALIS 2013 expands on the reporting done in the first cycle of TALIS, in 2008, on the intensity of professional development participation. TALIS 2013 starts by asking teachers about various activities, ranging from more organised and structured to more informal and self-directed learning, all of which are listed in Box 4.1 and Table 4.9. The type of professional development activity most often mentioned was attending courses or workshops, with 71% of teachers on average reporting that they participated in this activity during the survey period. Indeed, in virtually all countries, this development activity was most frequently reported, with a participation rate around 80% in several countries and greater than 90% in Malaysia, Mexico and Singapore.

After courses and workshops, the most frequently reported activities on average are attending education conferences or seminars (44%) and participation in a teacher network (37%). The least common types of professional development activities were observation visits to businesses or other organisations (13%) and in-service training courses at these same organisations (14%).[12] However, there are some interesting patterns emerging across countries:

- **Courses and workshops:** Participation rates in general are quite common, except for the cases of Italy (51%), Romania (52%) and particularly the Slovak Republic (39%).

- **Education conferences and seminars:** More than two-thirds of teachers report participating in this activity in Croatia and Alberta (Canada) (79% and 74%, respectively). However, participation was 25% or less in the Czech Republic (22%), France (20%), the Slovak Republic (25%), Spain (24%) and Flanders (Belgium) (23%).

- **Observation visits to other schools:** Participation rates are less than 20% on average. However, more than half of the teachers in Iceland, Japan and Latvia report undertaking observation visits to other schools. This contrasts with reported participation rates in Denmark (6%) and the Slovak Republic (4%).

- **Observation visits to business premises:** Fewer teachers report participation in observation visits to businesses (13% on average). The country in which the most teachers report participation is Portugal (39%).

- **In-service training courses in business premises, public organisations and non-governmental organisations:** Brazil has the highest participation rate, 38%, in contrast to countries such as France or Italy, where participation is around 3%.

- **Qualification programmes:** Bulgaria has the greatest participation rate (almost one-half), but this area was much less a feature of teachers' professional development in Croatia, France and Japan (6% in all three countries).

- **Participation in a network:** Nearly two-thirds of teachers report engaging in this activity in Croatia and Alberta (Canada) (63% in both), but it was much less common in the Czech Republic (17%), France (18%) and Portugal (19%).

- **Individual or collaborative research:** Almost one-half of teachers (49%) participated in this activity in Mexico, Abu Dhabi (United Arab Emirates) and Alberta (Canada). This contrasts with Finland, where only 8% of teachers report engaging in this kind of professional development.

- **Mentoring and peer observation as part of a formal school arrangement:** More than half of teachers in Singapore (65%), Abu Dhabi (United Arab Emirates) (61%), England (United Kingdom) (57%) and Korea (53%) report having participated in this activity. The country with the lowest reported participation was Finland, where only 5% of teachers said they engaged in this activity in the past 12 months.[13]

Box 4.9 presents more information about the development of teachers in Finland.

Box 4.9. **Teacher development in Finland**

In Finland, professional development of teachers is seen as a comprehensive process, which begins with initial teacher education. Teacher education has been available in universities since 1971, and a Master's degree is a requirement, including a Master's thesis. This kind of teacher education leads to teachers becoming reflective professionals who actively develop their own work and professional skills and methods, as researchers do, having had this research-based initial education.

Finland does not have a nationally organised induction system. Education providers and individual schools have autonomy over arranging support for new teachers, and therefore there are notable differences between schools in ways of implementing induction. However, there is awareness of the increasing need for support for new teachers, and already many different applications of mentoring practices are in place. A specific model of peer-group mentoring has been developed and is being disseminated by the Finnish Network for Teacher Induction ("Osaava Verme"), which is part of a seven-year national Osaava programme (2010-16) funded by the Ministry of Education and Culture. The objective of the programme is to motivate education providers and individual institutions to take greater responsibility and a proactive approach to their own staff development activities with the help of networking activities and mutual co-operation.

Source: Ministry of Education, Finland, 2014.

Figure 4.8 shows both the type and the intensity of participation for all types of professional development activities. On average, of all the types of professional development, teachers report spending the greatest number of days in courses and workshops (eight days). There is wide variation both between countries and, in some cases, within countries in the number of days spent on this type of activity, as shown in Figure 4.9. This figure shows the number of days reported by teachers in the 25th to 75th percentile. There is much wider variation in the reported number of days in Korea, Mexico, Romania and Spain than in other countries.

■ Figure 4.8 ■

Professional development recently undertaken by teachers, by type and intensity

Participation rates and average number of days for each type of professional development reported to be undertaken by lower secondary education teachers in the 12 months prior to the survey

	Percentage of teachers who participated in the following professional development activities in the 12 months prior to the survey	Average number of days of participation among those who participated
Courses/workshops	71%	8
Education conferences or seminars where teachers and/or researchers present their research results and discuss educational issues	44%	4
Observation visits to other schools	19%	3
In-service training courses in business premises, public organisations or non-governmental organisations	14%	7
Observation visits to business premises, public organisations or non-governmental organisations	13%	3
Participation in a network of teachers formed specifically for the professional development of teachers	37%	
Individual or collaborative research on a topic of interest to the teacher	31%	
Mentoring and/or peer observation and coaching, as part of a formal school arrangement	29%	
Qualification programme (e.g. a degree programme)	18%	

Items are ranked in descending order for each block, based on the percentage of teachers who report having participated in professional development activities in the 12 months prior to the survey.
Source: OECD, TALIS 2013 Database, Tables 4.9 and 4.9.Web.
StatLink http://dx.doi.org/10.1787/888933041554

■ Figure 4.9 ■

Professional development recently undertaken by teachers, by intensity of participation in courses and workshops

Percentiles of lower secondary education teachers who report having participated in courses/workshops based on the number of days of participation in the 12 months prior to the survey[1]

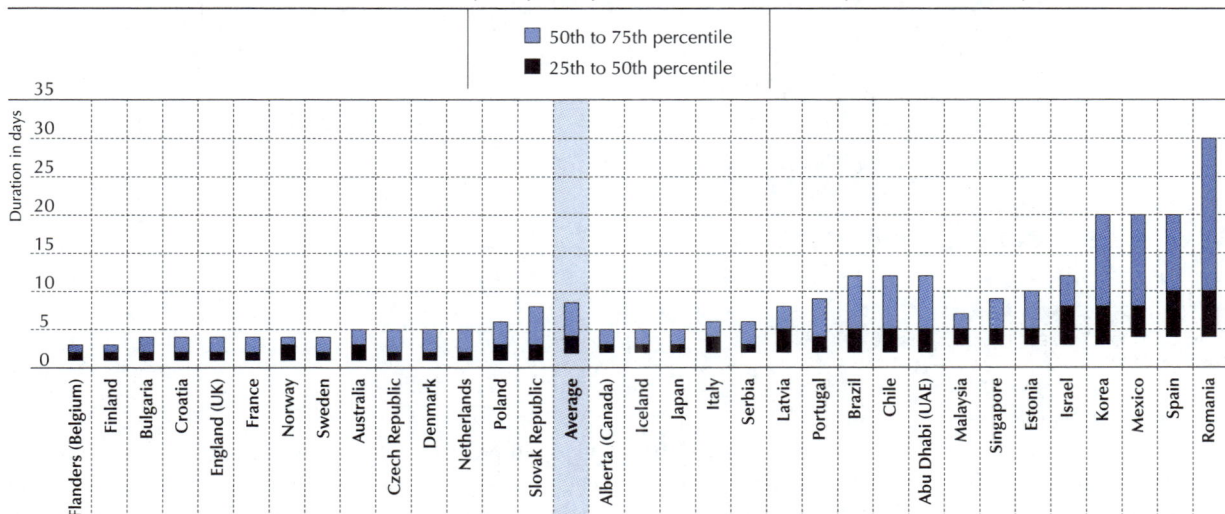

- 50th to 75th percentile
- 25th to 50th percentile

1. Percentiles presented in this figure are only for teachers who participated in courses/workshops in the 12 months prior to the survey. For example, in Romania 25% of teachers who participated in courses/workshops in the 12 months prior to the survey reported spending between 10 to 30 days on this type of professional development activity. Another quarter of teachers reported spending between 4 to 10 days on this activity over the same period.
Countries are ranked in ascending order, based on the 25th percentile of number of reported days of participation among teachers who participated in courses/workshops.
Source: OECD, TALIS 2013 Database, Table 4.9.Web.
StatLink http://dx.doi.org/10.1787/888933041573

Figure 4.10 shows the system-level relationship between the level and intensity of participation in courses and workshops, the professional development activity with the highest participation rates on average. Some interesting contrasts become apparent. First, countries found in the top-right quadrant in the figure are those countries where both the intensity and the level of participation are above the TALIS average. As in TALIS 2008, Mexico particularly stands out in this respect, with about 90% of Mexican teachers reporting that they have used this professional development activity for an average of 19 days in the past 12 months. At the other extreme, countries in the lower-left quadrant of the figure are those countries where teachers report lower participation rates and fewer days of professional development. In particular, teachers in France, Italy, the Slovak Republic and Sweden report using this activity in a less-intensive way (reported participation below 60% and average number of days below the average of nine). Finally, in countries such as Brazil, Chile and Romania, the participation is low, but the intensity of those participating is particularly high, with 20 days or more of reported participation. In contrast, countries in the upper-left quadrant show higher reported participation rates than average but a lower number of days of professional development.

■ Figure 4.10 ■

Professional development recently undertaken by teachers in days

Percentage of lower secondary education teachers who report having participated in courses/workshops in the 12 months prior to the survey and the number of reported days they participated in courses/workshops over the same period

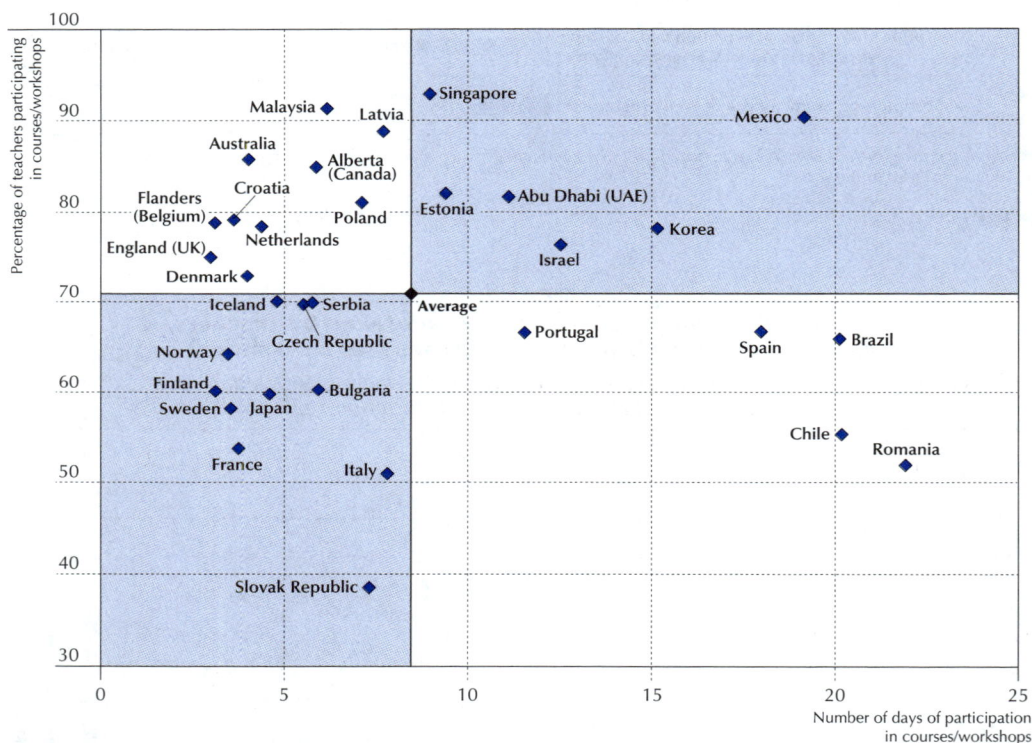

Source: OECD, TALIS 2013 Database, Table 4.9.Web.
StatLink ⬛ http://dx.doi.org/10.1787/888933041592

To better understand factors related to the diversity of participation in professional development activities and provide insight for potential policy development, a logistic model for each country was estimated. In this analysis, the diversity of participation is measured by examining the variety of activities teachers report having participated in. This variety is defined as teachers participating in three or more different professional development activities, among the nine activities identified in Box 4.1.[14] This participation is related to teachers' past participation in formal induction activities. Figure 4.11 shows the country-level predicted effect of teachers' reported past participation in induction programmes on their probability of reporting that they participated in three or more different types of professional development activities over the past 12 months (compared with those teachers who report having participated in two types of activities or less).[15]

For the 26 countries and economies illustrated, teachers who report having participated in induction programmes are more likely to report participating in three or more different types of professional development activities. This is especially apparent in Brazil, Chile, Mexico, the Slovak Republic and Abu Dhabi (United Arab Emirates), where teachers who participated in induction programmes are at least twice as likely to report this.

Although the results should be viewed with caution,[16] the significant positive relationships shown in Figure 4.11 could be an indication that promoting induction programmes is an instrument to encourage teachers' future participation in professional development activities. Similarly, and from the teachers' perspective, being involved in induction activities might spark teachers' interest in remaining up to date through further learning opportunities.

■ Figure 4.11 ■

**Predicted effect of formal induction programme participation
on professional development participation**

*Probability of participation in three or more professional development activities
for lower secondary education teachers who report having participated in a formal induction programme
versus teachers who report not having participated in such programmes[1]*

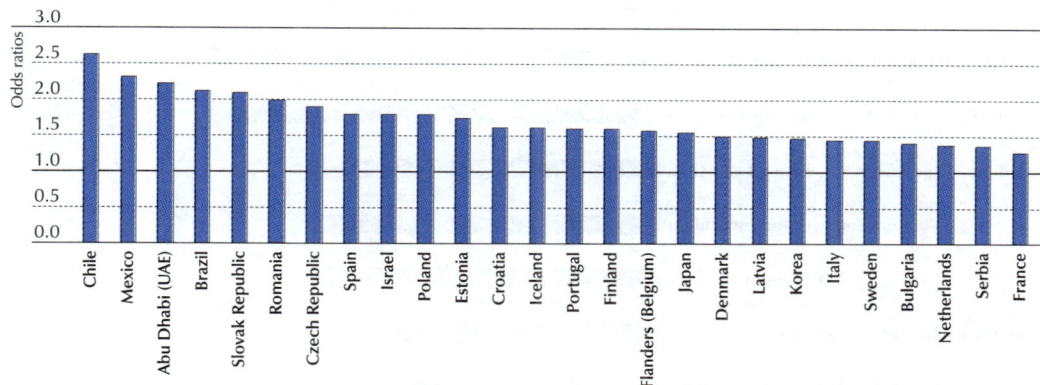

1. Countries for which the odds ratio is not statistically significant at 5% or where data are representing less than 5% of the cases are not presented in this figure. Countries are ranked in descending order, based on the predicted effect of having participated in any induction programme on the reported number of professional development activities.
Source: OECD, TALIS 2013 Database, Table 4.30.Web.
StatLink ⟲ http://dx.doi.org/10.1787/888933041611

Thus, the TALIS data highlight the importance of teachers' participation in formal induction programmes not only for its potential impact on teachers' decision to act as mentors to new teachers (see previously) but also for its potential influence on teachers' future participation in a wider variety of professional development activities. The effects vary between countries, suggesting that the ways in which induction and professional development policies are structured within each country and the kinds of support provided for these programmes are important factors to consider. Moreover, a number of other factors that are not measured by TALIS are likely playing an important role in these relationships, such as teachers' motivation and interest in participating in these types of activities.[17]

TALIS 2008 found that there was not a strong relationship between the presence of induction programmes in schools and the extent of teachers' professional development (OECD, 2009). The results presented in this chapter do not contradict that finding because the present analysis is focused on participation in formal induction rather than on the availability of formal induction programmes as a predictor of participation in professional development. This variable, measured at the individual level, better captures individual decisions of teachers. Furthermore, it could also be the case that teachers participated in a formal induction programme in a different school than the one where they are currently working, so the effect of availability of induction programmes cannot be properly evaluated here.

TEACHERS' PERCEPTIONS ABOUT THE EFFECTIVENESS OF THEIR PROFESSIONAL DEVELOPMENT

Data on teachers' perceptions about the positive impact of their professional development are presented in Table 4.10 and Figure 4.12 (see also Table 4.10.Web). TALIS asked teachers whether their professional development covered each of 14 specific topics (such as pedagogical competencies in teaching the subject field, student evaluation and assessment

practices, approaches to individual learning and teaching students with special needs) and if so whether it had a positive impact on their teaching. This self-reported measure of effectiveness is important because teachers' perception of the effectiveness of certain professional development activities may affect their future participation in such activities.

Although the reported participation rates in professional development vary widely across the different areas of focus (between 16% to 73% of teachers on average report having participated in professional development covering any one of these areas), teachers generally indicate that their professional development has a moderate or large positive impact on their teaching, regardless of the area covered (between 76% and 91% of teachers on average report that their professional development in these areas had a positive impact on their teaching).

■ Figure 4.12 ■

Content and positive impact of professional development activities

Percentage of lower secondary education teachers who report having participated in professional development with the following content in the 12 months prior to the survey and who report a moderate or large positive impact of this professional development on their teaching[1]

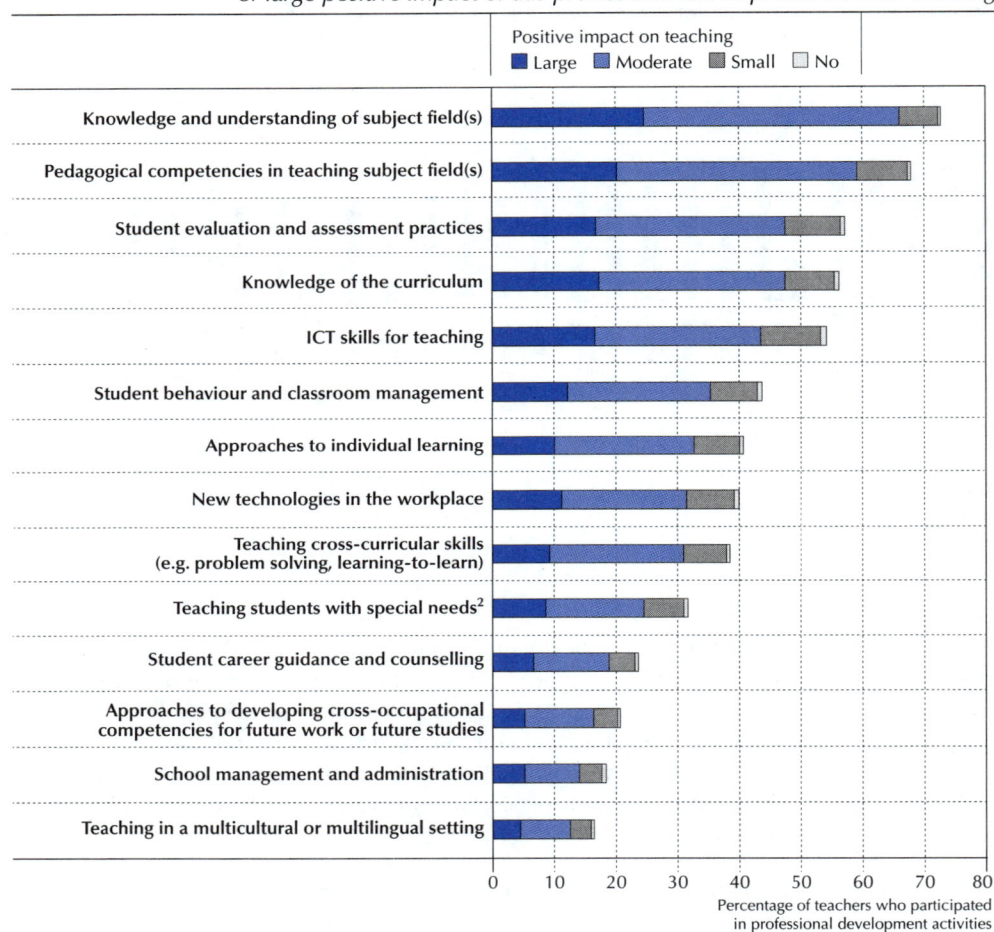

1. The percentages presented in this graph do not have the same denominator. The percentages presented on the perceived impact are based on answers from teachers who indicate that the topic was covered in their professional development activities, while the percentages of teachers reporting that the topic was covered in their professional development activities are based on answers from all the teachers who report having participated in professional development activities.

2. Special needs students are not well defined internationally but usually cover those for whom a special learning need has been formally identified because they are mentally, physically or emotionally disadvantaged. Often special needs students will be those for whom additional public or private resources (personnel, material or financial) have been provided to support their education. "Gifted students" are not considered to have special needs under the definition used here and in other OECD work. Some teachers perceive all students as unique learners and thus having some special learning needs. For the purpose of this survey, it is important to ensure a more objective judgment of who is a special needs student and who is not. That is why a formal identification is stressed above.

Items are ranked in descending order, based on the percentage of lower secondary education teachers who report having participated in this professional development activity.

Source: OECD, TALIS 2013 Database, Tables 4.10 and 4.10.Web.

StatLink ᵐˢ⁹ http://dx.doi.org/10.1787/888933041630

Specifically, Figure 4.12 shows that larger proportions of teachers on average report having undertaken professional development that focused on their knowledge and understanding of their subject field (73%) and on their pedagogical competencies in teaching their subject field (68%). In contrast, fewer teachers report having taken part in professional development that focused on approaches to developing cross-occupational competencies for future work or studies (21% on average), on teaching in a multicultural setting (16% on average) or on school management (18% on average). In almost all participating countries, of the various contents of professional development, teachers are most likely to report that content that focuses on their knowledge and understanding of their subject field and on their pedagogical competencies for teaching their subject field has a moderate or large positive impact on their teaching (on average, 91% and 87% of teachers who participate in such professional development report this, respectively). The professional development activities that lower proportions of teachers (albeit still more than three-quarters of teachers on average) identified as having a positive impact on their teaching are those related to school management (76%), teaching students with special needs (77%) and teaching in a multicultural or multilingual setting (77%).

These results highlight that although most teachers view their professional development in all these areas to be helpful in improving their teaching, professional development that focuses on content and pedagogical knowledge in the teachers' subject field – the content focus of the professional development in which they participate the most – seems to be particularly helpful to teachers, and teachers are actively seeking these types of development opportunities.

HOW TEACHERS' PROFESSIONAL DEVELOPMENT IS SUPPORTED

The level and intensity of participation in professional development activities are in part a function of the types of support that teachers receive to undertake them (Avalos, 2011; Jurasaite-Harbison and Rex, 2010). Support can take many forms, and the TALIS questionnaire asked teachers about forms of support ranging from scheduled time for activities to a salary supplement to other non-monetary support. TALIS distinguished between financial support (mentioned previously) or salary supplements for undertaking these activities and non-monetary support for activities outside working hours (reduced teaching time, days off, study leave, etc.).[18] Figure 4.13 presents data on how teachers report that their professional development is supported. In most participating countries, financial measures are the most common forms of support given to teachers for professional development, followed by scheduled time for activities taking place at the school during working hours.

■ Figure 4.13 ■

Professional development participation by level of personal cost and support

Percentage of teachers who report paying for none of the professional development activities undertaken and level of support received for the three following elements in lower secondary education

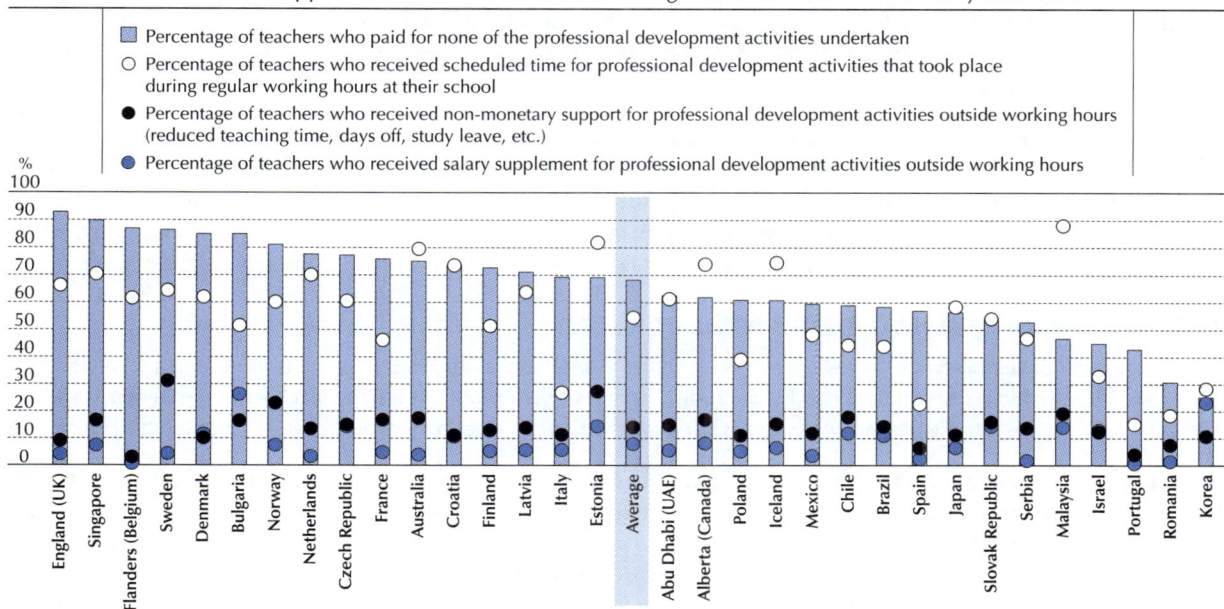

Countries are ranked in descending order, based on the percentage of teachers who report paying for none of the professional development activities undertaken.

Source: OECD, TALIS 2013 Database, Tables 4.6 and 4.11.

StatLink ᕫᕬᔕᕟ http://dx.doi.org/10.1787/888933041649

Indeed, in most countries, the percentage of teachers who claimed that they paid for none of the professional activities they undertook is above 50%. When teachers engage in professional development without bearing the burden of paying for it, this might reflect the monetary support they enjoy from various sources (e.g. the ministry, schools, external organisations, etc.). There are some countries and economies – Estonia, Iceland, Malaysia and Alberta (Canada) in particular – that focus more on an alternative method of support, such as scheduling time for activities to take place during regular working hours at the school.

The following sections examine the different types of support based on the data shown in Table 4.11. The first important message from these data, when examined in relation to the level of participation in professional development activities shown in Table 4.6, is that those countries or economies with higher participation rates also exhibit high levels of both monetary and non-monetary support. The best examples are Alberta (Canada) and Singapore, where more than 97% of teachers report participating in professional development activities, and, at the same time, more than 70% indicate having access to support in the form of scheduled time and more than 17% say they have access to other forms of non-monetary support.

Scheduled time

More than half of teachers on average received scheduled time to take part in development activities. However, the percentage varies substantially across countries, from well over three-quarters in Australia (79%), Estonia (82%) and Malaysia (88%), to less than 20% in Portugal (15%) and Romania (18%).

Financial support: Salary supplements

Salary supplements are not a common means of support for professional development, with only 8% of teachers on average receiving them for activities they had taken part in during the survey period. This is a somewhat more common means of support in Bulgaria (26%) and Korea (23%), but in a lot of countries this policy is practically unused: It is less than 2% in Portugal, Romania, Serbia and Flanders (Belgium).

Non-monetary support

In addition to formal non-monetary support of professional development in the form of scheduling time for activities to take place during regular working hours at school, TALIS also asked teachers whether they received non-monetary support (such as reduced teaching, days off, study leave, etc.) for activities outside working hours. Table 4.11 indicates that this is not a common practice, although it is generally more widespread than providing salary supplements. On average across participating countries, 14% of teachers who participated in professional development over the 12 months prior to the survey claim to have received this type of support. These results are very similar across countries, with the exceptions of Estonia and Sweden, which have approximately double the average percentage of all other countries (27% and 31%, respectively). In contrast, only 4% of teachers in Portugal and 3% of teachers in Flanders (Belgium) received this type of non-monetary support.

Table 4.11 also shows that some countries have relatively high levels of all three forms of support (teachers in Estonia, Malaysia and Alberta [Canada] report above average support in all three measures). In contrast, the level of support that teachers report receiving in Portugal, Romania and Spain is well below average on all three measures. It is important for policy makers from all countries, but these countries in particular, to consider a variety of support and incentives (including non-monetary ones) that teachers receive to help them improve their practice throughout their career.

TEACHERS' PROFESSIONAL DEVELOPMENT NEEDS

The professional development that teachers report receiving in TALIS does not always meet the needs of teachers. Teachers were asked to rate their development needs for various aspects of their work, and many teachers report needs in specific areas. Table 4.12 presents the percentage of teachers who report a high level of need in various aspects of their work.

Consistent with findings from TALIS 2008 (OECD, 2009), across all participating countries, the aspect most frequently cited by teachers as an area of high development need is related to teaching students with special needs.[19] As highlighted in Figure 4.14, about 22% of teachers on average report that they need more professional development for this specific aspect of teaching, with 60% of teachers in Brazil and 47% in Mexico indicating needs here. As discussed in the previous section, only 32% of teachers identify having taken part in professional development that focused on teaching students with special needs (Table 4.10). Moreover, of the 14 areas of focus of professional development examined earlier, teaching students with special needs was one of the least likely on average to be identified by teachers as having a positive impact on their teaching (Figure 4.12). These findings may point to some problems with the adequacy of support provided.

■ Figure 4.14 ■

Teachers' needs for professional development

Percentage of lower secondary education teachers indicating they have a high level of need for professional development in the following areas

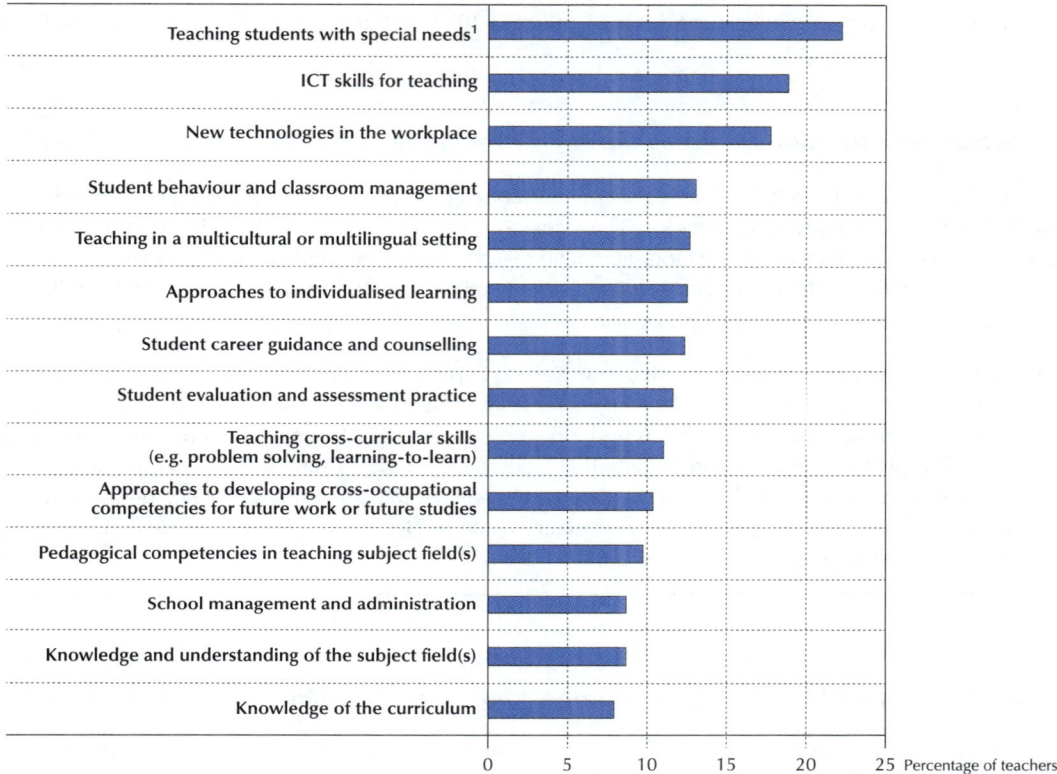

1. Special needs students are not well defined internationally but usually cover those for whom a special learning need has been formally identified because they are mentally, physically or emotionally disadvantaged. Often, special needs students will be those for whom additional public or private resources (personnel, material or financial) have been provided to support their education. "Gifted students" are not considered to have special needs under the definition used here and in other OECD work. Some teachers perceive all students as unique learners and thus having some special learning needs. For the purpose of this survey, it is important to ensure a more objective judgment of who is a special needs student and who is not. That is why a formal identification is stressed above.

Items are ranked in descending order, based on the percentage of teachers indicating they have a high level of need for professional development.

Source: OECD, TALIS 2013 Database, Table 4.12.

StatLink ▆▆▆ http://dx.doi.org/10.1787/888933041668

Professional development on using ICT

On average, the second and third most important professional development needs teachers report are related to teaching with information and communication technology (ICT) skills (19% of teachers) and to using new technologies in the workplace (18% of teachers), two items closely related to each other. Teachers from all TALIS countries identify these two needs to be especially important for them, and the need is even stronger for teachers in Brazil (27% and 37%, respectively), Italy (36% and 32%, respectively) and Malaysia (38% and 31%, respectively). Given that these technologies are continuously evolving and changing, the identification of this specific need by teachers may be signaling the increasing challenge for teachers and schools to fully exploit them for the benefit of teaching and learning (Drent and Meelissen, 2008).

The other needs shown in Table 4.12 are less important on average, but they nonetheless represent specific and important areas of needs in some countries. For example, in Japan and Korea, more than 40% of teachers report a high level of need for professional development on student career guidance and counseling. Furthermore, the data notably show that teachers in Japan indicate a high level of need in areas including knowledge and understanding of the subject field(s) (51%), pedagogical competencies in teaching subject field(s) (57%), student behaviour and classroom management (43%),

student evaluation (40%) and how to approach individualised learning (40%). Finally, teaching in a multicultural or multilingual setting seems not to be an important issue in European countries, but it is a significant concern for Latin American countries and Italy, where more teachers consider this an important need for professional development (46% of Brazilian teachers, 24% of Chilean teachers, 27% of Italian teachers and 33% of Mexican teachers).

Box 4.10 presents the reported needs for professional development for teachers in primary and upper secondary schools. Box 4.11 compares the needs of lower secondary teachers in 2008 and 2013 for the countries that participated in both cycles.

Box 4.10. **Professional development needs among primary and upper secondary teachers**

Table 4.12.a shows that compared with their lower secondary colleagues, primary (ISCED 1) teachers have a higher need for ICT skills, particularly in Denmark (23%), Mexico (24%) and Norway (25%). In addition, high percentages of teachers report a professional development need regarding teaching students with special needs in Denmark (34%) and Mexico (42%). In Mexico, the percentage of teachers with this specific need is a bit smaller among primary teachers than it is for lower secondary ones.

Table 4.12.b shows that in Denmark, Iceland, Mexico and Norway, upper secondary (ISCED 3) teachers report lower needs for ICT skills than do lower secondary teachers. It also shows fewer needs for lower secondary teachers in Denmark, Finland, Iceland, Italy, Mexico and Singapore in terms of teaching students with special needs. This difference is especially important in Denmark (17 percentage points), Italy and Mexico. Finally, in Italy, more upper secondary teachers than lower secondary teachers have indicated a demand for professional development in the area of new technologies in the workplace, while in Denmark, Iceland and Mexico, fewer upper secondary teachers have indicated so.

Box 4.11. **Comparing professional development needs, TALIS 2008 and TALIS 2013**

The differences between teachers' needs in 2008 and 2013 can be examined for the countries that participated in TALIS in both years (Table 4.12.c).

In general, and for countries participating in both studies, the two major areas of needs highlighted earlier (teaching students with special needs and ICT skills) seem to be less important among lower secondary teachers in 2013 than they were in 2008. Indeed, on average, the percentage of teachers identifying a need for skills to teach students with special needs is 30% in 2008 compared with 24% in 2013.[20] The difference is much larger in Malaysia, Norway, Poland, Portugal and Spain, where it is more than 14 percentage points. On the contrary, more secondary teachers in Denmark, Korea and Mexico identified this need in 2013 in comparison with their counterparts in 2008. The same pattern can be seen for the need for ICT teaching skills. There are, however, some exceptions, as in Iceland, Italy, Korea and the Slovak Republic. On average in participating countries, the need for professional development for knowledge and understanding of the subject field is identified less in 2013 than in 2008. The difference in the identification of this need is especially large in Italy (-18 percentage points), Malaysia (-28 percentage points), Poland (-15 percentage points) and Flanders (Belgium), where the difference is -14 percentage points.

Finally, on average for countries participating in both studies, the need for skills in teaching in a multicultural setting is about the same in terms of importance for lower secondary teachers in 2008 and 2013. However, for Brazil, Korea and Mexico, this specific need is more important in 2013 than it was in 2008 by more than eight percentage points, and this specific need is less important in 2013 than in was in 2008 in Malaysia (20 percentage points fewer teachers report this as a high level of need).

Table 4.13 presents results of the effect of two indices of professional development needs (described in Box 4.12) on participation in different professional development activities. One index measures the need for professional development for teaching for diversity (index of need for teaching for diversity, from here on), and one index measures the need for professional development in subject matter and pedagogy (index for pedagogical needs, from here on).

Box 4.12. **Indices of professional development needs**

To assess the level of professional development needs identified by teachers in the areas of teaching for diversity and pedagogical aspects of teaching, TALIS asked teachers to rate their level of need in the following areas:

Need for teaching for diversity

- Approaches to individualised learning
- Teaching students with special needs
- Teaching in a multicultural or multilingual setting
- Teaching cross-curricular skills
- Approaches to developing cross-occupational competencies for future work or future studies
- Student career guidance and counselling

Pedagogical needs

- Knowledge and understanding of my subject field(s)
- Pedagogical competencies in the specific teacher field(s)
- Knowledge of the curriculum
- Student evaluation and assessment practice
- Student behaviour and classroom management

See Annex B for more information about the construction and validation of these indices.

Table 4.13 shows the significant relationships between these two indices and participation in seven different professional development activities per country.[21] The first column presents the significant effects of these two indices on an individual teacher's decision to participate in courses, workshops and conferences. A plus (+) sign indicates an increase in the likelihood of participating in courses, workshops and conferences. In 23 countries, pedagogical needs show a significant and positive relationship with this decision. In other words, in these countries, teachers are more likely to participate in courses, workshops and conferences if they have reported a high level of professional development need (on the pedagogical scale). The reported need for professional development for teaching for diversity is also associated with this decision in 17 countries.

The second column in Table 4.13 captures professional development participation in observation visits to other schools, business premises, public organisations and non-governmental organisations. For this specific activity, the importance of the reported need for professional development for teaching for diversity seems to be large: In 17 countries this need is related to higher participation rates related to observational visits. (See Table 4.13.Web for detailed results.) The index for pedagogical needs seems to be less important in affecting participation decisions for this professional development activity.

The same result is obtained when analysing the effect of these two indices on the probability of participating in training courses, mentoring and/or peer observation and coaching: The effect of the reported need for teaching for diversity is more important as a determinant for choosing these professional development activities, as shown in Table 4.13.Web. The same can be seen with the probability of participating in a network of teachers and in engaging in individual or collaborative research. Finally, it is interesting to note that the index of need for teaching for diversity shows a small but significant negative effect for Brazil and Mexico in some of the activities analysed, which means that in these cases, a high level of need is associated with lower participation rates.

BARRIERS TO PARTICIPATION

To better understand participation in professional development and provide insight into potential policy implications, TALIS asked teachers to indicate barriers to their participation. The average responses from this question are presented in Table 4.14 and Figure 4.15. Across participating countries, the reasons that teachers cited most commonly as barriers to professional development are a conflict with the work schedule (51% of teachers) and a lack of incentives for participating in professional development (48%).

■ Figure 4.15 ■

Barriers to professional development participation

Percentage of lower secondary education teachers who "strongly disagree", "disagree", "agree" or "strongly agree" that the following elements represent barriers to their participation in professional development activities

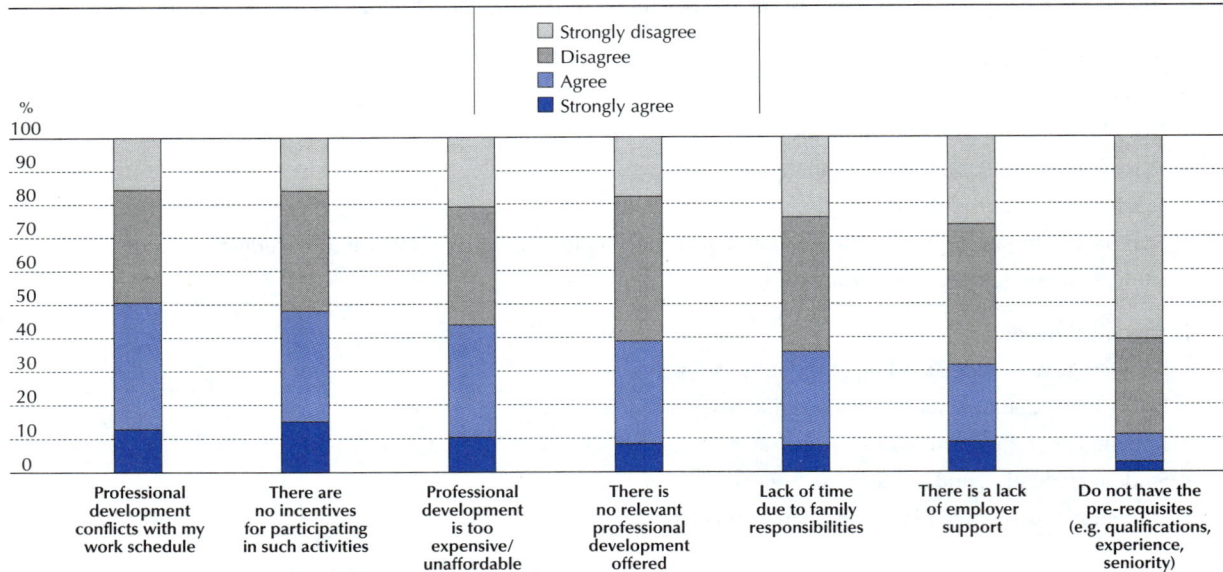

Barriers to teachers' participation in professional development activities are ranked in descending order, based on the percentage of teachers who "agree" or "strongly agree" that the element represents a barrier to their participation in professional development activities.
Source: OECD, TALIS 2013 Database, Tables 4.14 and 4.14.Web.
StatLink ⬛🔢 http://dx.doi.org/10.1787/888933041687

Conflict with work schedule

As mentioned above, the most commonly reported barrier to participation in professional development activities is a conflict with work schedules. As the data in Table 4.14 show, this is reported by three quarters or more of the teachers in Japan (86%), Korea (83%) and Portugal (75%). On the contrary, fewer teachers in Croatia (22%), Latvia (29%) and Serbia (27%) indicate that conflicts with work schedules are barriers to participation in professional development. This might be explained, at least for teachers from the last two countries, by the high percentage of teachers receiving support through scheduled time during regular working hours: 73% in Croatia and 64% in Latvia (Table 4.11). However, across all countries there is no distinct relation between these two variables. For instance, about 58% of teachers in Australia report that a conflict with their work schedule is a barrier for participating in professional development, yet 79% report that they received scheduled time for professional development. This situation might indicate only that the scheduled time was insufficient or not very well aligned with the types of professional development that teachers wanted.

Lack of incentives for participation

TALIS data suggest that the problem of not receiving enough incentives for participating in professional development is a substantial issue for teachers in Italy (83%), Portugal (85%) and Spain (80%) (Table 4.14). This is important because participation rates in professional development are below average in Spain and at average in Portugal (Table 4.6). Given that a higher percentage of teachers in these two countries reported paying for at least some of their professional development activities, this could help explain their low participation rates (Figure 4.6). This should be of special concern from a policy perspective in these countries.

Participation is too costly

A substantial proportion of teachers consider professional development activities to be too expensive (44% on average), which is also very relevant from a policy perspective. As mentioned previously, there is a positive relationship between the percentage of teachers who pay for none of their professional development activities and their participation rate (Figure 4.6). This is especially relevant for teachers in Chile (73%) and Portugal (81%). In contrast, this seems to be much less important in Singapore (20%) and Flanders (Belgium) (17%).

Other barriers

Finally, teachers not having access to a relevant supply of professional development activities in their country is also a barrier that deserves more attention from a policy perspective. Although on average fewer teachers (by 12 percentage points) report this as a barrier compared with work schedule conflicts, this issue is important in Chile (64%), Italy (67%), Portugal (68%) and Spain (61%). These are countries where lower secondary teachers, especially in public schools (Table 4.8), actually participated in professional development activities less often than average during the survey period. This might be interpreted as evidence of the association between the perceived lack of suitable professional development activities and the participation rates of teachers.

SUMMARY AND MAIN POLICY IMPLICATIONS

This chapter has reviewed current patterns of availability and participation in induction, mentoring and professional development activities for lower secondary education teachers. Teachers' continuous professional development is at the core of most education policy debates because it has been found to be highly relevant both for improving educational performance and effectiveness and for enhancing teachers' commitment to their work (Angrist and Lavy, 2001). This study and other references cited earlier in this chapter may be inspiring many policy makers who support the relevance of career-long opportunities for professional development.

As shown in Chapter 2, new teachers often report feeling unprepared for various aspects of their work, even after completion of an initial teacher preparation programme. Professional development and support is necessary not only to fill in the gaps in the skill sets of new teachers, but also to continue to develop the expertise of teachers throughout their career. Teachers are meant to develop students as lifelong learners. To achieve this lofty goal in today's rapidly changing world, teachers must be continuously learning themselves. Professional development at all points in a teacher's career is necessary to keep the teacher up to date with the changing research, tools, practices and student needs that teachers face with every passing year.

The TALIS data provide findings that have implications for policies related to professional development at all stages of a teacher's career.

Encourage schools to offer formal induction programmes for new teachers and urge teachers to attend

Induction programmes for new teachers have a stronger influence on teachers' future behaviour than previously realised. TALIS data show that in many countries, teachers who report participating in a formal induction programme in the past are more likely to have a higher level of participation in professional development, to the extent that they participate in three more professional development activities than teachers who did not attend formal induction programmes. In other words, those teachers who start their first teaching roles with access to development in the form of induction move on to take advantage of a variety of induction opportunities. Further, participation in an induction programme during a teacher's first employment is also positively related to a teacher's decision to help other teachers by acting as a mentor.

TALIS data also indicate that in many countries, induction programmes are readily available and yet teachers are not participating.[22] It is clear that it is important not only for schools to offer formal induction programmes to their teachers but for teachers to attend. Policy makers and school leaders should seek to understand what is preventing teachers from attending such programmes, when they are available, and should ensure that programmes are offered for all new teachers. Some additional examination is needed into what content is most effective in such programmes, since, as this chapter indicates, early support activities for teachers may have significant long-term influence over their future professional development activities. Indeed, participation in an induction programme during a teacher's first employment is positively related not only to the later decision to help other teachers by acting as a mentor but also to more intensively undertake professional development activities.

Support teachers' participation in mentoring programmes at all levels of their careers

Clear evidence shows that teachers with mentoring support have higher student achievement gains (Rockoff, 2008). However, TALIS 2013 shows that, on average for all countries, one-quarter of teachers work in schools where principals report that there is no mentoring programme, with some countries showing larger percentages of no access. Further, TALIS findings suggest that even when mentoring is available at schools, not all teachers take part is these opportunities. Mentoring provides teachers with a way to build relationships with colleagues (further discussed in Chapter 7) and to collaborate to improve their teaching practice. It is an inexpensive form of professional development that is ongoing and can take place anytime within the teacher's own school context. Policy makers should provide schools with support to develop mentoring programmes, which might include the latest research on best practices

for successful implementation. School leaders should provide teachers with time and arrange for successful pairings of teachers who have common subject areas. And teachers should participate, both as mentors and as recipients, regardless of their level of work experience (it might be that a young teacher could mentor a more-experienced teacher in the use of ICT, for example).

Ensure availability of and participation in professional development for all teachers

TALIS looks at teachers' participation in a broad range of professional development activities, and the data show that on average across participating countries almost 90% of teachers report taking part in some sort of activity. However, in some countries as many as a quarter of teachers report not participating in any professional development activities in the past year.

The level and intensity of teachers' participation in professional development activities are influenced by, among other factors, the types of support that teachers receive to undertake them. Some countries provide relatively high levels of support for teachers, including paying any necessary fees, scheduling time for training during a teacher's school day and other types of non-monetary support. In other countries, this kind of support is not available to teachers.

The solution to these issues seems simple: If it is a priority to policy makers and school leaders that teachers take part in professional development in order to improve their teaching, then support (both financial and otherwise) that enables all teachers to do this needs to be provided. However, this is not as easy as it sounds. Because a school leader will have a full staff of teachers who all need development in a given year, the budget and time away from class required to pursue these development opportunities may be stretched thin. In addition, while in some areas there might be a surplus of professional development offerings available, teachers might not always be able to identify the most appropriate, highest-quality activity that fits both their needs and their schedule.

This might be a further opportunity for schools to develop and use mentoring programmes or other within-school or between-school development opportunities for teachers. Creating a professional development plan that is tied to a teacher's individual needs for development might also help teachers pinpoint the best offerings for them (see Chapter 5). Encouraging participation in professional development activities that boost collaboration among teachers might not only provide teachers with new skills, but could also help build relationships between teachers in or outside the school (see Chapter 7).

Remove barriers to teachers' participation in professional development

Finally, the main reasons that teachers report for not participating in professional development activities are a conflict with their work schedule and the absence of any incentives for participating in such activities. In many countries, a significant number of teachers also report that they simply do not have access to professional development offerings relevant to their needs. Any one of these barriers could explain lower participation rates of professional development in specific countries. If teachers do not have the time or flexibility in their work schedule or if there are no offerings available, it will be very difficult for them to participate. The absence of incentives for participation, such as monetary or non-monetary rewards, is equally serious. Incentives could also include recognition in front of colleagues or a connection to a teacher's development plan that might further motivate them to seek professional development. Teachers' time is valuable, especially when it takes them away from their most important role, teaching their students. Teachers may need extra encouragement to understand and identify professional development activities that can provide the most benefit to their work.

Notes

1. See Chetty, Friedman and Rockoff (2011) for a brief review of the debate about the best way to measure and improve teacher quality.

2. See Broad and Evans (2006) for a large set of examples of both formal and informal professional development activities.

3. See also Helms-Lorenz, Slof and van de Grift (2012) for a more recent study with similar findings.

4. Reasons other than teacher interest or willingness or lack of understanding of the benefits of mentoring may be underlying low participation rates. For example, in some cases, mentoring programmes may be available only for teachers newly appointed on permanent contracts. It is possible, for example, that low teacher turnover (perhaps due to economic downturn) has led to fewer permanent contract appointments in recent years, thus explaining low availability and low participation in mentoring.

5. Individual logistic models have been estimated for each country to identify the basic determinants of the teacher's probability of acting as a mentor. See Box 2.5 in Chapter 2 for a basic explanation of these discrete choice models and Annex B for more technical information about these analyses.

6. A more general analysis of the main variables associated with teachers acting as mentee found that past participation in induction programmes was an important factor. This type of analysis might open a possible further avenue of research.

7. There might be other factors, such as teachers' motivation and interest in participating in activities aimed at further learning and development of their profession, that might also influence both induction participation and acting as a mentee. Unfortunately, TALIS data do not provide these types of additional control variables. Therefore, results presented here must be interpreted within these limitations.

8. For example, Rivkin, Hanushek and Kain (2005) found that up to three-quarters of school effects on student outcomes can be explained by teacher effects.

9. In TALIS 2008, the reference period for participation in professional development activities was 18 months. However, during the TALIS 2013 field trial phase, information on participation was collected from teachers in two segments: for the last 12 months and for the previous 6 months. These data showed no significant difference in overall participation rates over the last 12 months and over the wider 18-month window. It was determined that the results for participation in professional development would be comparable despite the different reference periods. The reference period used in the main survey was therefore changed to the "last 12 months" in the TALIS 2013 teacher questionnaire.

10. Variables other than teacher and school characteristics, such as the existence of compulsory participation policies at country level, might affect teachers' participation in professional development activities. Unfortunately, TALIS data do not provide these types of variables. Therefore, results in this section must be interpreted with this limitation in mind.

11. This difference as it is shown in Table 4.21.Web is statistically significant for most of the countries analysed.

12. A possible explanation for this pattern may be related to which type of activities teachers consider to be most useful. See later sections for analyses on this issue.

13. Some discrepancies might arise between the participation rates in mentoring shown in Tables 4.9 and 4.3. These differences might be due to the period of time to which each of them refer: Participation rates shown in Table 4.3 refer to current mentoring activities that teachers are involved in, whereas those presented in Table 4.9 refer to mentoring activities teachers participated in during the 12-month period prior to the survey. In addition, Table 4.9 includes "peer observation and coaching" together with mentoring activities.

14. The median in the distribution across teachers in all countries participating in TALIS 2013 is three, that is, 50% of teachers participated in three or more professional development activities during the 12-month period prior to the survey. Furthermore, additional models have been estimated to analyse the number of activities teachers participate in. The results from these models show that the basic difference, in terms of the differential effects of most of the explanatory variables used, is between one to two and three or more activities. This is the main reason why three was chosen as the cut-off point defining variety in participation.

15. As in Figure 4.5, this figure shows the odd ratios of the probability of participating in three or more professional development activities, comparing those teachers who have participated in a formal induction programme in the past with those with no participation in such programmes. The estimated coefficient for this variable is presented in Table 4.31.Web.

16. As noted in several places in the chapter, no causality can be established with cross-sectional data such as that provided by TALIS (see Box 2.5 in Chapter 2 for further explanation).

17. The results remain qualitatively similar for the relationship highlighted in Figure 4.11 when some proxies for teachers' motivation (individual job satisfaction and a measure of intensive involvement in planning or preparing lessons) are also included in the estimated model.

18. There might be other types of non-monetary support, such as providing recognition, appreciation, new challenges, and access to mentors. Unfortunately, TALIS data do not provide this information.

19. As described in Table 4.12, special needs students are not well defined internationally but usually cover those for whom a special learning need has been formally identified because they are mentally, physically or emotionally disadvantaged.

20. This might be an especially surprising result considering that teachers teaching only special needs students in sampled schools were excluded from TALIS in 2008 but not in 2013.

21. These participation decisions are estimated by means of a logit model (see Table 4.13.Web for the regression coefficients). These models are controlling for the individual and school characteristics described in Table B2.5 in Annex B. The results are almost unchanged when teacher's motivation, support and perceived barriers to participation are also taken into account with proxy measures.

22. This imbalance between availability and participation may also be due to the gap between the present day and the time at which some teachers, especially older ones, participated in this type of programme.

A note regarding Israel

The statistical data for Israel are supplied by and under the responsibility of the relevant Israeli authorities. The use of such data by the OECD is without prejudice to the status of the Golan Heights, East Jerusalem and Israeli settlements in the West Bank under the terms of international law.

References

Angrist, J.D. and **V. Lavy** (2001), "Does teacher training affect pupil learning? Evidence from matched comparison in Jerusalem public schools", *Journal of Labor Economics*, Vol. 19/2, pp. 343-369.

Avalos, B. (2011), "Teacher professional development in *Teaching and Teacher Education* over ten years", *Teaching and Teacher Education,* Vol. 27/1, pp. 10-20.

Broad, K. and **M. Evans** (2006), "A review of literature on professional development content and delivery modes for experienced teachers", Ontario Institute for Studies in Education, University of Toronto.

Chetty, R., J.N. Friedman and **J.E. Rockoff** (2011), "The long-term impacts of teachers: Teacher value-added and student outcomes in adulthood", NBER Working Paper, No. 17699.

Cohen, B. and **E. Fuller** (2006), "Effects of mentoring and induction on beginning teacher retention", paper presented at the annual meeting of the American Educational Research Association, San Francisco, CA.

Dee, T. (2005), "A teacher like me: Does race, ethnicity or gender matter?", *American Economic Review*, Vol. 95/2, pp. 158-165.

Drent, M. and **M. Meelissen** (2008), "Which factors obstruct or stimulate teacher educators to use ICT innovatively?" *Computers and Education*, Vol. 51/1, pp. 187-199.

European Commission (2012a), "Supporting the teaching professions for better learning outcomes", SWD (2012) 374 final.

European Commission (2012b), "Supporting teacher competence development for better learning outcomes", *http://ec.europa.eu/ education/school-education/doc/teachercomp_en.pdf*.

European Commission (2010), "Developing coherent and system-wide induction programmes for beginning teaching staff – a handbook for policymakers", SEC (2010) 538 final.

Evertson, C.M. and **M.W. Smithey** (2000), "Mentoring effects on protégés' classroom practice: An experimental field study", *Journal of Educational Research*, Vol. 93, pp. 294-304.

Fletcher, S.H., M. Strong and **A. Villar** (2008), "An investigation of the effects of variations in mentor-based induction on the performance of students in California", *Teachers College Record*, Vol. 110, pp. 2271-2289.

Fuller, E. (2003), "Beginning teacher retention rates for TxBESS and non-TxBESS teachers", unpublished manuscript, State Board for Educator Certification, Austin, TX.

Glazerman, S. et al. (2010), *Impacts of Comprehensive Teacher Induction: Final Results from a Randomized Controlled Study*, NCEE 2010-4027, National Center for Education Evaluation and Regional Assistance, Institute of Education Sciences, U.S. Department of Education, Washington, D.C.

Helms-Lorenz, M., B. Slof and **W. van de Grift** (2012), "First year effects of induction arrangements on beginning teachers' psychological processes", *European Journal of Psychology of Education,* forthcoming.

Hill, H.C, M. Beisiegel and **R. Jacob** (2013), "Professional development research consensus, crossroads, and challenges", *Educational Researcher,* Vol. 1/42, pp. 476-487.

Hobson, A.J. et al. (2009), "Mentoring beginning teachers: What we know and what we don't", *Teaching and Teacher Education: An International Journal of Research and Studies,* Vol. 25, No. 1, pp. 207-216.

Ingersoll, R.M. and **M. Strong** (2011), "The impact of induction and mentoring programs for beginning teachers: A critical review of research", *Review of Educational Research,* Vol. 81/2, pp. 201-233.

Jackson, C.K. and **E. Bruegmann** (2009), "Teaching students and teaching each other: The importance of peer learning for teachers", *American Economic Journal: Applied Economics,* Vol. 1/4, pp. 85-108.

Jurasaite-Harbison, E. and **L.A. Rex** (2010), "School cultures as contexts for informal teacher learning", *Teaching and Teacher Education,* Vol. 26/2, 267-277.

OECD (2013), *Teaching and Learning International Survey: Conceptual Framework,* www.oecd.org/edu/school/TALIS%202013%20Conceptual%20Framework.pdf.

OECD (2009), *Creating Effective Teaching and Learning Environments: First Results from TALIS,* OECD Publishing, Paris, *http://dx.doi.org/10.1787/9789264072992-en.*

Rockoff, J. (2008), "Does mentoring reduce turnover and improve skills of new employees? Evidence from teachers in New York City", *www0.gsb.columbia.edu/faculty/jrockoff/rockoff_mentoring_february_08.pdf.*

Rockoff, J. and **C. Speroni** (2011), "Subjective and objective evaluations of teacher effectiveness: Evidence from New York City", *Labour Economics,* Vol. 18, pp. 687-696.

Schleicher, A. (ed.) (2012), *Preparing Teachers and Developing School Leaders for the 21st Century: Lessons from around the World,* OECD Publishing, *http://dx.doi.org/10.1787/9789264174559-en.*

Strong, M. (2009), *Effective Teacher Induction and Mentoring: Assessing the Evidence,* Teachers College Press, New York, NY.

Yoon, K.S. et al. (2007), "Reviewing the evidence on how teacher professional development affects student achievement", *Issues & Answers,* REL 2007 – No. 033, Institute of Education Sciences, National Center for Education Evaluation and Regional Assistance, Regional Educational Laboratory Southwest, U.S. Department of Education, Washington, D.C., *http://ies.ed.gov/ncee/edlabs/regions/southwest/pdf/REL_2007033.pdf.*

5

Improving Teaching Using Appraisal and Feedback

Teacher appraisal and feedback are important components of teachers' careers and development. The primary purpose is to provide teachers with valuable input to better understand and improve their teaching practice. However, teacher appraisal and feedback can also be used to identify professional development or career opportunities for teachers. This chapter looks at teachers' access to both formal appraisal and formal and informal feedback from sources internal and external to their schools. The chapter explores the focus and content of the appraisal and feedback that teachers receive, as well as any consequences that result. Finally, the chapter discusses whether other factors, such as increased school autonomy, have an influence on the nature and occurrence of teacher appraisal and feedback.

Highlights

- Teachers receive feedback from multiple sources. On average across countries and economies participating in the OECD Teaching and Learning International Survey (TALIS), nearly 80% of teachers report getting feedback following classroom observation, and nearly two-thirds report receiving feedback following analysis of student test scores. These are encouraging reports given that classroom observation and data-based feedback and decision making have been shown to be important levers for improving teaching.

- Teachers report that the feedback they receive in their schools focuses on several aspects of their teaching. Nearly nine in ten teachers on average report that student performance, teachers' pedagogical competency in their subject field and classroom management are strongly emphasised in the feedback they receive. Feedback from students and parents is somewhat less frequently reported to be considered with moderate or high importance.

- Teachers feel that the appraisals they receive lead to positive changes in their work. More than six in ten teachers report that appraisals lead to positive changes in their teaching practices, and more than half report that appraisals lead to positive changes in both their use of student assessments and their classroom-management practices.

- The formal appraisal of teachers has little to do with giving financial recognition to high-performing teachers or advancing the careers of high performers over low performers. Annual increments in teacher pay are awarded regardless of the outcome of the formal teacher appraisal in all but about one-fifth of teachers' schools. Moreover, 44% of teachers work in schools where the school principal reports that formal teacher appraisal never results in a change in a teacher's likelihood of career advancement.

- Formal teacher appraisal does appear to have a developmental focus in most schools where teachers work. More than eight in ten teachers work in schools where formal appraisals at least sometimes lead to teacher development or training plans.

- While most teachers receive various forms of feedback (many of which are connected to classroom teaching), comprehensive systems of teacher appraisal and feedback that are effectively connected to improving teaching practices and student learning in schools are much less common. Indeed, on average across TALIS countries, nearly half of teachers report that teacher appraisal and feedback systems in their school are largely undertaken simply to fulfil administrative requirements.

INTRODUCTION

Research suggests that high-performing school systems make it a priority to develop effective teachers and put systems in place to ensure that all children are able to benefit from good teaching practices (Barber and Mourshed, 2007). Teacher appraisal and feedback are important components of teachers' careers and development. They can significantly improve teachers' understanding of their teaching methods, teaching practices and student learning (Santiago and Benavides, 2009). In addition to being used to enhance professional development opportunities for teachers, appraisal and feedback systems can also be used to recognise performance.

Statistically, it can be difficult to prove a direct correlation between teacher appraisal and student achievement (Isore, 2009; Figlio and Kenny, 2006; OECD, 2013a). But when teachers receive continuous feedback on their teaching, it creates opportunities for them to improve teaching practices, which, in turn, can have a powerful impact on student learning and outcomes (Fuchs and Fuchs, 1985, 1986; Hattie, 2009; Gates Foundation, 2010).

Meaningful appraisal and feedback are geared to teacher development and improvements in learning (Jacob and Lefgren, 2008; OECD, 2013a). They help teachers improve their teaching skills by identifying and developing specific aspects of their teaching and can improve the way teachers relate to students (Gates Foundation, 2010). Much of this improvement depends on the extent to which appraisal and feedback are formative and can therefore play an important role in teacher development (OECD, 2005, 2013a; Isore, 2009). Yet for such feedback to affect teaching practices, links between performance assessments and professional learning should be actively developed and cultivated. Information gleaned from appraisal and feedback also provides an opportunity to spread effective practices across schools. The OECD Review *Synergies for Better Learning: An International Perspective on Evaluation and Assessment* examined various components of evaluation and assessment frameworks used to bring about better outcomes across school systems (OECD, 2013a).

One of the key components examined was teacher evaluation. Box 5.1 presents the main challenges and policy directions regarding teacher appraisal identified by the OECD review. A number of the challenges identified by the review are also identified by teachers and principals in TALIS and discussed in this chapter.

Box 5.1. **The OECD Review on Evaluation and Assessment Framework for Improving School Outcomes**

The OECD Review *Synergies for Better Learning: An International Perspective on Evaluation and Assessment* examined policies across 25 school systems in 24 countries. In all countries, there is widespread recognition that evaluation and assessment frameworks are key to building stronger and fairer school systems. Countries also emphasise the importance of seeing evaluation and assessment not as ends in themselves, but instead as important tools for achieving improved student outcomes. However, there are a range of challenges in ensuring that evaluation and assessment reach this ultimate objective. Although each country context is unique, some common policy challenges emerge for this work. The following challenges relating specifically to teacher appraisal were identified:

- Developing a shared understanding of high-quality teaching
- Balancing the developmental and accountability functions of teacher appraisal
- Accounting for student results in the appraisal of teachers
- Developing adequate skills for teacher appraisal
- Using teacher appraisal results to shape incentives for teachers

To meet these challenges, a number of policy options regarding teacher appraisal and enhancing teacher professionalism are suggested:

- Resolve tensions between the developmental and accountability functions of teacher appraisal
- Consolidate regular developmental appraisal at the school level
- Establish periodic career-progression appraisal involving external evaluators
- Establish teaching standards to guide teacher appraisal and professional development
- Prepare teachers for appraisal processes and strengthen the capacity of school leaders for teacher appraisal
- Ensure that teacher appraisal feeds into professional development and school development
- Establish links between teacher appraisal and career-advancement decisions

Source: OECD, 2013a.

Recognising teachers' performance is also an important consequence of effective appraisal and feedback (Jensen and Reichl, 2011). Teacher appraisal and feedback can recognise (in various ways) and celebrate great teaching while simultaneously challenging teachers to address weaknesses in their pedagogical practices (Santiago and Benavides, 2009).

Teacher appraisal and feedback have been shown to have a positive effect on teachers' level of job satisfaction, making it a vital element of effective educational environments (Michaelowa, 2002). TALIS data reinforce this, indicating that teacher appraisal and feedback are related not only to job satisfaction but also to teachers' feelings of self-efficacy (see Chapter 7). Teachers, particularly those new to the profession, can be reassured by the feedback they receive (Kyriacou, 1995). They are able to test innovations, address problems and develop their teaching with greater certainty. Such appraisal and feedback can increase collaboration in schools, particularly through mechanisms such as observation, which can encourage sharing of teaching and learning experiences across the school. Collaboration is important not only for teachers' job satisfaction (see Chapter 7) but for improving teaching and learning in schools (Bolam et al., 2005).

Increased collaboration among teachers is important. Teachers who exchange ideas and coordinate practices report higher levels of job satisfaction and self-efficacy (see Chapter 7 and Vieluf et al., 2012) and better teacher-student relationships, all of which are significant predictors of student achievement (Caprara et al., 2006; Clement and Vandenberghe, 2000).

People are more likely to make fundamental shifts in teaching when they are exposed to new ideas, practice new behaviours and observe others practising those behaviours, and when they are being observed and want to be seen as successful (Elmore, 2004; Berry, Johnson and Montgomery, 2005; Andrews and Lewis, 2002 cited in Sargent and Hannum, 2009). Collaboration can also enhance professionalism and prevent stress and burnout (Rosenholtz, 1989; Clement and Vandenberghe, 2000).

Since the objective of teaching is to promote student learning, the manner in which students learn and the interactions between teaching and learning should be a key component of appraisal and feedback (Jensen et al., 2012). Such appraisal and feedback can take many forms and be provided by different people within schools. It can encompass various forms of classroom observation, feedback from students and assessments of teachers' performance and student learning (Gates Foundation, 2013).

Figure 5.1 is adapted from the conceptual framework used in the OECD Review *Synergies for Better Learning: An International Perspective on Evaluation and Assessment* (OECD, 2013a) and illustrates the elements of teacher appraisal and feedback examined by TALIS in this chapter.

■ Figure 5.1 ■
Elements of teacher appraisal examined in TALIS

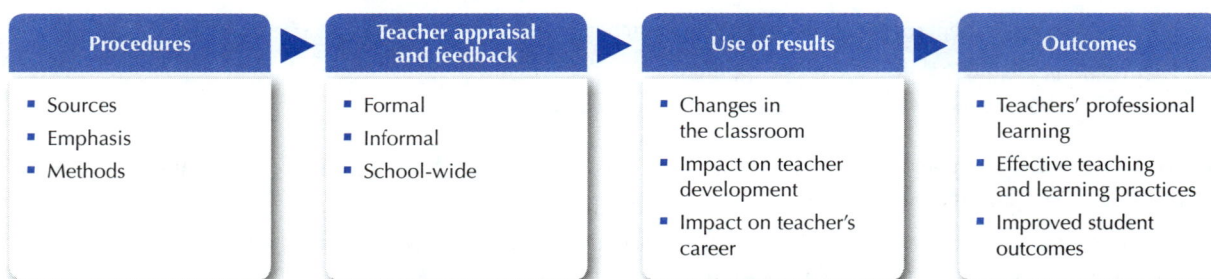

Procedures	Teacher appraisal and feedback	Use of results	Outcomes
▪ Sources ▪ Emphasis ▪ Methods	▪ Formal ▪ Informal ▪ School-wide	▪ Changes in the classroom ▪ Impact on teacher development ▪ Impact on teacher's career	▪ Teachers' professional learning ▪ Effective teaching and learning practices ▪ Improved student outcomes

DEFINING TEACHER APPRAISAL AND FEEDBACK

Teacher appraisal and feedback can encompass a number of activities. TALIS distinguishes between formal teacher appraisal, feedback to individual teachers and teacher appraisal and feedback systems in the school overall. They are defined here as:

▪ **Formal teacher appraisal:** This occurs when a teacher's work is reviewed by the principal, an external inspector or by the teacher's colleagues. Formal teacher appraisal is part of a formalised performance-management system, often involving set procedures and criteria, rather than a more informal approach (e.g. through informal discussions). In TALIS, information about formal teacher appraisal was provided by principals.

▪ **Teacher feedback:** This is broadly defined and includes any communication teachers receive about their teaching, based on some form of interaction with their work (e.g. observing classrooms and the teaching of students, discussing teachers' curriculum or the results of their students). This feedback can be provided through informal discussions or as part of a more formal and structured arrangement. In TALIS, teachers were asked specifically about the teacher feedback they personally receive in their school.

▪ **Teacher appraisal and feedback provided in the school more generally:** This is defined as reviews of teachers' work, which can be conducted in a range of ways, from a more formal approach (e.g. as part of a formal performance-management system, involving set procedures and criteria) to a more informal approach (e.g. through informal discussions). In TALIS, teachers were asked about this type of teacher appraisal and feedback provided in the school as a whole, rather than to themselves specifically.

Organisation of the chapter

This chapter begins by examining the formal appraisal of teachers. The discussion then moves to feedback provided to individual teachers, beginning with a look at who provides feedback to teachers and the number of people (e.g. school principals, mentors, other teachers) who provide this feedback. The methods used to develop feedback to teachers

(e.g. classroom observation, student surveys, self-assessment) are then examined. The next section describes the outcomes of teacher appraisal (formal and informal) and feedback. This includes the effects of outcomes on teachers and their careers and the impact on classroom teaching (as reported by teachers).

Teachers' perceptions of appraisal and feedback systems in their schools are then considered in order to paint a picture of how these systems operate in schools. Finally, some exploratory analyses examine how teacher appraisal and feedback differ between schools with different levels of autonomy. In analysing this issue, it is important to note that the structure of teachers' employment can impact appraisal and feedback alongside governance issues such as the level of school autonomy. For example, in some systems teachers are employed as civil servants. Specific regulatory and procedural requirements for civil servants can affect teacher appraisal and feedback in these systems. This analysis is preliminary in the sense that it looks at a single aspect of school autonomy but highlights the potential for further analysis.

Formal teacher appraisal

From a policy perspective, formal teacher appraisal may encompass greater involvement and regulation from government or a central administrative body. If so, formal teacher appraisal can offer a policy lever to policy makers to influence teaching and learning in schools. But not all systems have regulated frameworks for teacher appraisal and feedback systems. Box 5.2 provides examples from Finland and Sweden, where there are no nationally regulated frameworks for teacher evaluation, but where teachers receive feedback through more informal pathways.

Box 5.2. **Finland and Sweden:**
Working without a nationally regulated framework for teacher evaluation

Finland's Ministry of Education and Culture has no role in teacher appraisal. Guidelines are set in the contract between the local government employer and the teachers' trade union. School principals are seen as the pedagogical leaders of the school, responsible for the teachers in their school and for the implementation of measures needed to enhance teaching quality. Teachers are appraised against the goals and contents of the national core curriculum and, to some extent, against their school's development plan for the year. As a result of a fairly low organisational structure, school leaders can have a significant number of teachers directly under them with whom they conduct face-to-face dialogue.

Teacher appraisal in Sweden is similarly not regulated by law and there are no formal procedures for evaluating the performance of fully qualified teachers. While teachers may be evaluated collectively as part of school self-evaluation and school inspection, there is no official method to appraise individual teachers.

As with Finland, the main form of feedback for permanent teachers is through dialogue with the school leader. School leaders and teachers may hold "individual development dialogues" that focus on teachers' work, working conditions and training. There is little guidance provided by central authorities on how to appraise teacher performance. Each municipality, in collaboration with local stakeholders, defines its own appraisal criteria linked to local objectives. Most municipalities have established some teacher-appraisal procedures with the expectation that schools further refine and develop the procedures to suit their needs.

Sources: Finnish government response to OECD survey; Nusche et al., 2011a.

TALIS 2013 asked school principals about formal teacher appraisal in their school, obtaining information on its frequency, methods and outcomes.

As shown in Table 5.1, 93% of teachers on average across TALIS countries and economies work in schools where principals report some form of formal appraisal. In Italy, the situation is somewhat different, where 70% of teachers work in schools where the principal reports that there is generally no formal teacher appraisal. The same is true for approximately one-third of teachers in Spain and one-quarter of teachers in Finland.

Most teachers are likely to have their work formally appraised by their school leaders: On average across TALIS countries, only 14% of teachers work in schools where the school principal reports that he or she never formally appraises teachers (Figure 5.2). Just under one-third of teachers work in schools where the school principal reports that teachers are never

formally appraised by other members of the school management team. In contrast, just less than half of teachers, on average across TALIS countries, work in schools in which teachers are formally appraised by other teachers. (See also Table 5.1.Web.)

■ Figure 5.2 ■

Teachers who never received formal appraisal

Percentage of lower secondary education teachers whose school principal reports that their teachers were never appraised by the following bodies

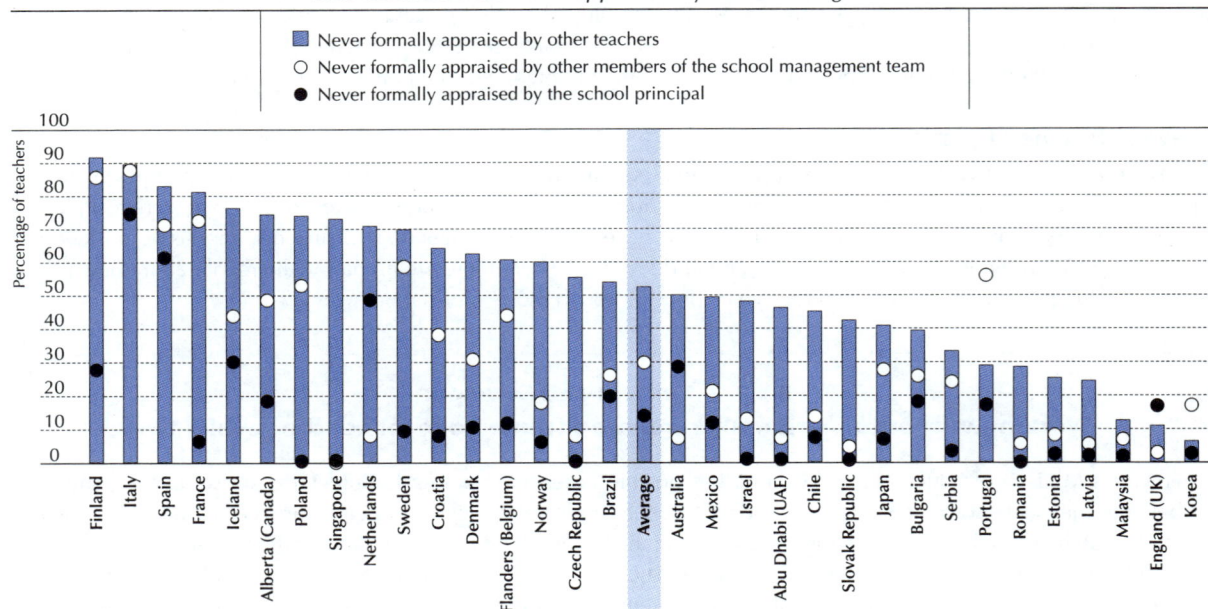

Countries are ranked in descending order, based on the percentage of lower secondary education teachers whose school principal reports that their teachers were never formally appraised by other teachers.
Source: OECD, TALIS 2013 Database, Table 5.1.
StatLink ᐧ᠊ᔒᐧ http://dx.doi.org/10.1787/888933041706

The most commonly reported methods of formally appraising teachers' work are based on collecting evidence of good practice, and thus they focus on classroom observation and analysis of student results (Figure 5.3). On average across TALIS countries, of those teachers who work in schools with formal teacher appraisal systems, 95% work in schools where formal teacher appraisal includes direct observations of their classroom teaching and 95% work in schools where formal teacher appraisal includes an analysis of student test scores (Table 5.2).

One of the findings from TALIS 2008 that is confirmed with TALIS 2013 data (Figure 5.4) is that formal appraisal often does not result in financial recognition for high-performing teachers or in differentiating them from underperforming teachers (OECD, 2009). This may be because school principals are reticent to take such actions or they may be constrained by legal or regulatory requirements. As shown in Table 5.3, on average across TALIS countries, 34% of teachers work in schools where the school principal reports that formal teacher appraisal leads to a change in teachers' salary or payment of a financial bonus. This means that, as illustrated in Figure 5.4, two-thirds of teachers work in schools where formal teacher appraisal never leads to a change in teachers' salary or payment of a financial bonus. In addition, 78% of teachers work in schools where the school principal reports that material sanctions such as reduced annual increases in pay are never imposed on poor-performing teachers following formal teacher appraisal.

Moreover, 44% of teachers work in schools where the school principal reports that formal teacher appraisal never leads to a change in the likelihood of a teacher's career advancement. In a number of countries the figure is much higher. In Italy, Japan, Norway and Spain, 70% or more of teachers work in schools where the school principal reports that teacher appraisal never leads to a change in the likelihood of a teacher's career advancement. This contrasts with Singapore, where only 3% of teachers work in schools where the school principal reports that formal teacher appraisal never results in a change in the likelihood of career advancement, and where 28% work in schools where the school principal reports this connection happens most of the time or always (Table 5.3.Web).

■ Figure 5.3 ■

Methods of formally appraising teachers

Percentage of lower secondary education teachers whose school principal reports that teachers are formally appraised with the following methods[1,2]

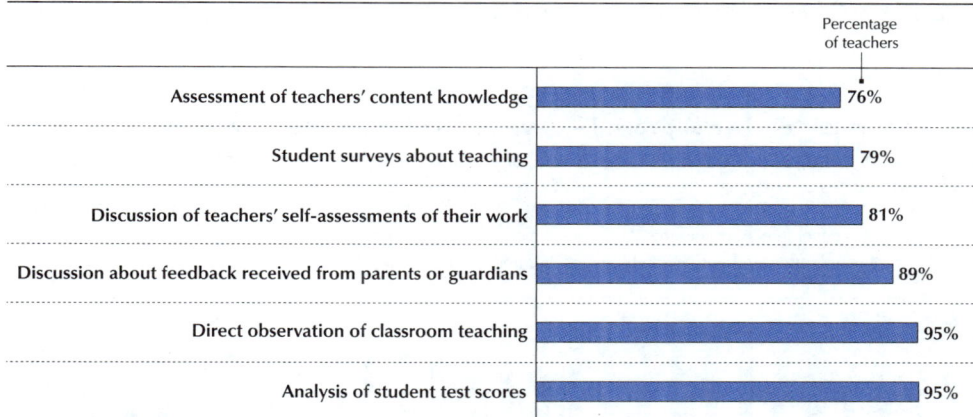

Percentage
of teachers

Method	Percentage
Assessment of teachers' content knowledge	76%
Student surveys about teaching	79%
Discussion of teachers' self-assessments of their work	81%
Discussion about feedback received from parents or guardians	89%
Direct observation of classroom teaching	95%
Analysis of student test scores	95%

1. Percentage of teachers working in schools where the principal reports that teachers are appraised with the following methods by at least one body, including: external individuals or bodies, principal, member(s) of school management team, assigned mentors or other teachers.
2. Data derived from the principal questionnaire (question 28). Please note that schools that are not using formal teacher appraisal were filtered in question 27, meaning that these schools are not covered in question 28.
Items are ranked in ascending order, based on the percentage of lower secondary education teachers whose principal reports that teachers are formally appraised with this specific method.
Source: OECD, TALIS 2013 Database, Table 5.2.
StatLink ⬛🇸🇵 http://dx.doi.org/10.1787/888933041725

■ Figure 5.4 ■

Outcomes of formal teacher appraisal

Percentage of lower secondary education teachers whose school principal reports that the following outcomes occured "sometimes", "most of the time" or "always" after formal teacher appraisal[1]

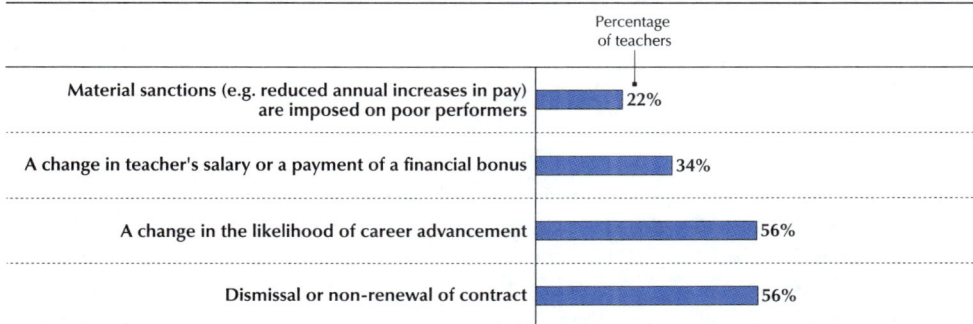

Percentage
of teachers

Outcome	Percentage
Material sanctions (e.g. reduced annual increases in pay) are imposed on poor performers	22%
A change in teacher's salary or a payment of a financial bonus	34%
A change in the likelihood of career advancement	56%
Dismissal or non-renewal of contract	56%

1. Data derived from the principal questionnaire (question 29). Please note that schools that are not using formal teacher appraisal were filtered in question 27, meaning that these schools are not covered in question 29.
Items are ranked in ascending order, based on the percentage of teachers who work in schools whose school principal reports that the outcome occured "sometimes", "most of the time" or "always" after formal teacher appraisal.
Source: OECD, TALIS 2013 Database, Table 5.3.
StatLink ⬛🇸🇵 http://dx.doi.org/10.1787/888933041744

However, formal teacher appraisal is sometimes used as an intervention of last resort. On average across TALIS countries, 56% of teachers work in schools where teacher appraisal at least sometimes helps school principals make the decision whether to dismiss teachers or not renew their contract.

But, as shown in Figure 5.5, it appears that overall, formal teacher appraisal has more of a developmental focus. Most teachers work in schools where formal teacher appraisal is used to create teacher development or training plans and assign mentors to help teachers improve their teaching. On average across TALIS countries, 84% of teachers work in schools where the school principal uses formal teacher appraisal to aid in the creation of teacher development plans.

In addition, on average across TALIS countries, 73% of teachers work in schools where the school principal uses formal teacher appraisal to assign mentors to teachers in need of development. However, these outcomes appear to be much less common in Spain, where fewer than half of the teachers work in schools where the principal reports that a development plan is created for teachers and approximately one in four teachers work in a school where the principal reports that a mentor is appointed to help the teacher improve their teaching (Figure 5.5).

■ Figure 5.5 ■

Outcomes of formal teacher appraisal – development plan and mentoring

Percentage of lower secondary education teachers whose school principal reports that the following outcomes occured "sometimes", "most of the time" or "always" after formal teacher appraisal[1]

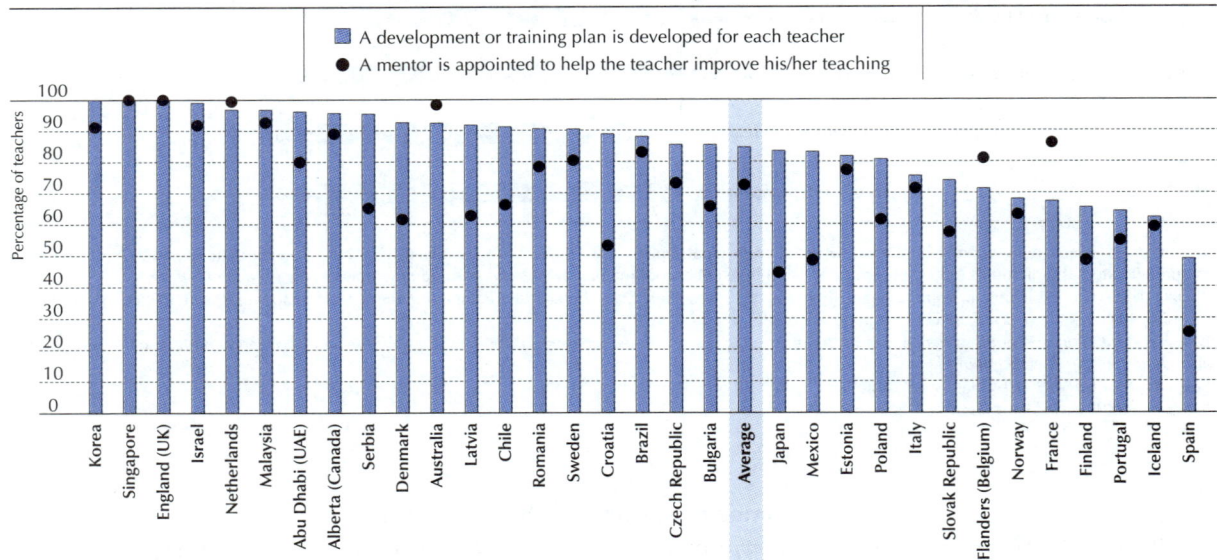

1. Data derived from the principal questionnaire (question 29). Please note that schools that are not using formal teacher appraisal were filtered in question 27, meaning that these schools are not covered in question 29.
Countries are ranked in descending order, based on the percentage of teachers who work in schools whose principal reports that a development or training plan is developed for each teacher "sometimes", "most of the time" or "always" after formal teacher appraisal.
Source: OECD, TALIS 2013 Database, Table 5.3.
StatLink ⌐⌐⌐ http://dx.doi.org/10.1787/888933041763

It should be noted that the authority of school principals differs across (and sometimes within) countries. For example, some school principals have the power to influence the career progression of teachers while others do not. This may influence the extent to which appraisal is likely to affect teachers' career advancement. Further, any discussion of changing the intended outcomes of teacher appraisal and feedback should take into consideration the influence of different government arrangements on schools and school systems. The findings presented here should not be interpreted as indicative of whether school leaders act on – or prefer to ignore – the results of teacher appraisal. A more nuanced understanding is required that reflects differences in governance, context and institutional settings.

Who provides feedback to teachers

Teacher appraisal should have a greater impact if it is accompanied by feedback that improves teaching and learning. It is therefore important to analyse how teacher feedback operates within schools and different school systems. TALIS 2013 asked teachers directly about the feedback they receive regarding their work in their school. This differs from the discussion above, which distinguishes formal appraisal from teacher feedback. This section reports on the multiple possible sources of feedback and distinguishes between feedback from peers, teacher mentors, principals and, in some cases, external evaluators or agencies (Figure 5.6 and Table 5.4).

In all TALIS countries, the majority of teachers report receiving feedback on their teaching. On average, 88% of teachers say that they receive feedback in their school. However, in some countries, a significant percentage of teachers report not receiving feedback on their teaching in their school. For example, in Denmark, Finland, Iceland, Italy, Spain and Sweden, between 22% and 45% of teachers say that they have never received feedback in their current school (Table 5.4).

■ Figure 5.6 ■
Teachers' feedback by source of feedback
Percentage of lower secondary education teachers who report receiving feedback from various sources[1]

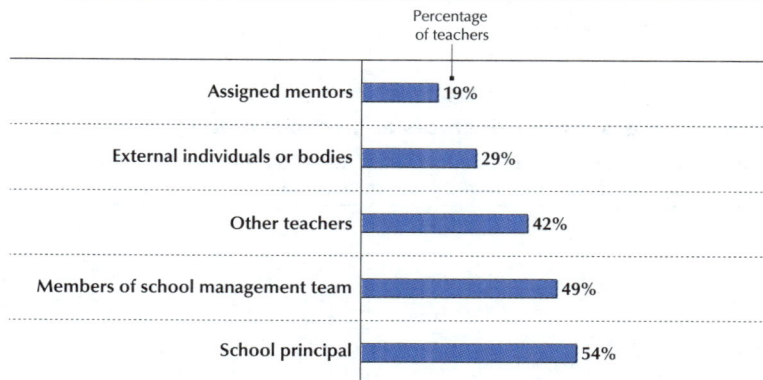

Percentage
of teachers

Source	Percentage
Assigned mentors	19%
External individuals or bodies	29%
Other teachers	42%
Members of school management team	49%
School principal	54%

1. Feedback is defined broadly as any communication of the results of a review of an individual's work, often with the purpose of noting good performance or identifying areas for development. The feedback may be provided formally or informally.
Items are ranked in ascending order, based on the source teachers report receiving feedback from.
Source: OECD, TALIS 2013 Database, Table 5.4.
StatLink http://dx.doi.org/10.1787/888933041782

Peer feedback from other teachers can improve learning and teaching in classrooms and promote collaboration among staff (Kumrow and Dahlen, 2002; MacBeath and McGlynn, 2002). Some studies show that feedback from mentors has a positive impact (Smith and Ingersoll, 2004; Rockoff, 2008).

School leaders have been found to have a good understanding of teachers' effectiveness and are often in a good position to provide effective feedback to improve learning and teaching (Jacob and Lefgren, 2008). More than half of teachers report receiving feedback from their school principal (54% of teachers on average across TALIS countries) or members of the school management team (49% of teachers).

Peer feedback is somewhat less common. On average across TALIS countries, 42% of teachers report that they received feedback on their teaching from other teachers. Feedback from individuals or bodies external to teachers' schools is even less frequently reported by teachers (29% on average).

Feedback from mentors is also not common: On average across TALIS countries, 19% of teachers report that they receive feedback from assigned mentors in their school. However, there is wide variation among the countries. Less than 5% of teachers in Finland, Iceland, Italy, Norway and Sweden report receiving feedback from an assigned mentor compared with more than 40% of teachers in Portugal, Romania and Abu Dhabi (United Arab Emirates). Of course, the percentage of teachers who receive feedback from their mentor is a product of both the nature of the mentor relationship and whether teachers have mentors in the first place (see Chapter 4).

Differences in who provides feedback to teachers within schools may provide an indication of the distribution of responsibilities in schools or, at least, of how the responsibility of providing feedback to teachers is delegated within schools. Some countries have introduced programmes aimed at easing the leadership burden of principals (by disseminating responsibility for appraisal to teachers) and to take advantage of better informed peer appraisals. Programmes of this nature in the United States have also been successful in assessing teacher effectiveness (Goldstein 2004, 2007).

Figure 5.7 (top-left quadrant) shows a group of seven countries (Australia, Chile, Estonia, Malaysia, the Netherlands, Singapore and England [United Kingdom]) where teachers are more likely than average to report receiving feedback from members of the school management team, but less likely than average to report receiving feedback specifically from their school principals (see also Table 5.4). Conversely, in five school systems – Bulgaria, Poland, Serbia, Alberta (Canada) and Flanders (Belgium) – more teachers than average report that they receive feedback from their school principal, but fewer than average report receiving feedback from members of the school management team (see bottom-right quadrant of Figure 5.7). For example, in Bulgaria, 94% of teachers report they received feedback from their school principal,

but only 31% report that they received it from members of the school management team. Differences between these groups may reflect differences in distributed leadership within schools and how the responsibility for providing feedback for teachers is delegated across staff. It may also reflect differences in collaboration between different groups of educators and staff within schools. Further analysis may shed light on these issues and also on how the above differences may be the result of legal or regulatory requirements in countries.

■ Figure 5.7 ■

Teachers' feedback from principals and school management team

*Percentage of lower secondary education teachers who report receiving feedback
from members of the school management team and the school principal*

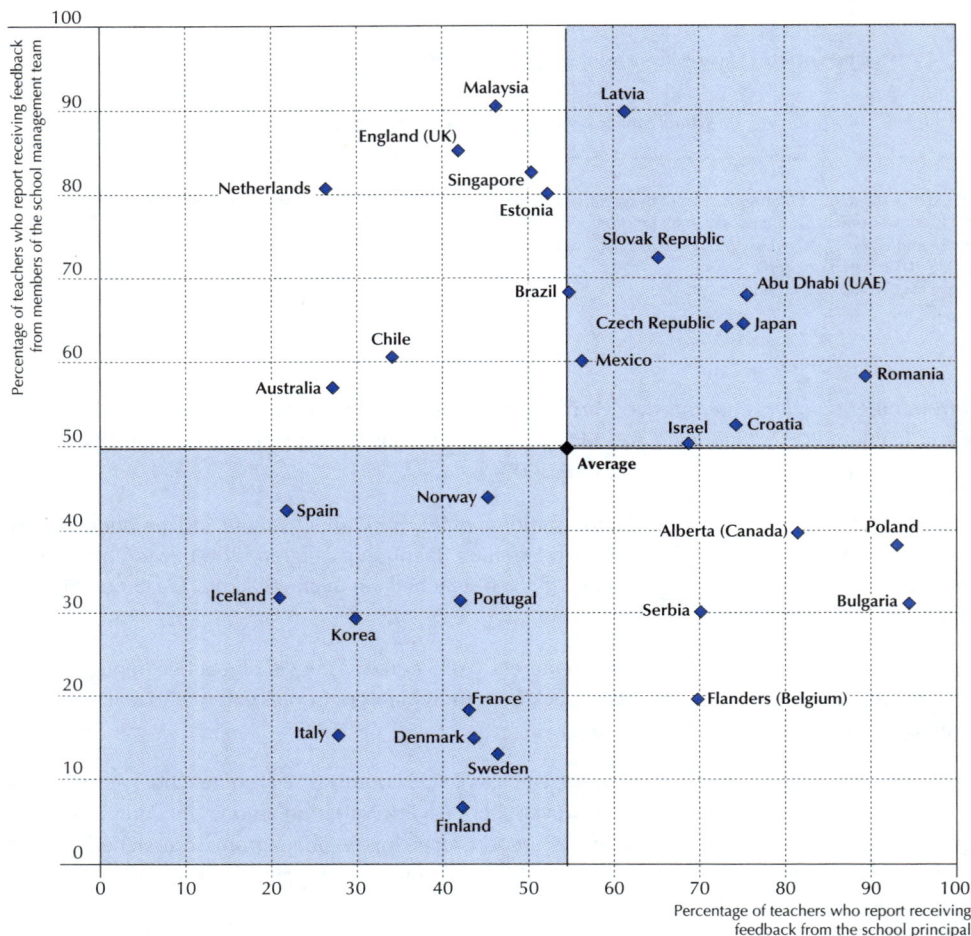

Source: OECD, TALIS 2013 Database, Table 5.4.
StatLink ⟨⟩ http://dx.doi.org/10.1787/888933041801

Multiple sources of teacher feedback

Clearly, teachers receive feedback from different people, but most receive feedback from more than one person. Figure 5.8 shows the number of sources of teacher feedback. The TALIS survey asked teachers whether they received feedback on their teaching from external individuals and bodies, their school principal, other members of the school management team, assigned mentors, or other teachers. Teachers who reported receiving feedback from all of these sources are represented in Figure 5.8 as having received feedback from five different sources.

On average across TALIS countries, more than half of teachers (56%) report that they receive feedback from one or two sources. Twenty percent report receiving feedback from three sources, 9% report receiving feedback from four sources and only 2% report receiving feedback from all five sources.

■ Figure 5.8 ■
Sources for teachers' feedback

*Percentage of lower secondary education teachers who report receiving feedback
from zero, one, two, three, four or all of the five bodies that could provide feedback to teachers[1,2]*

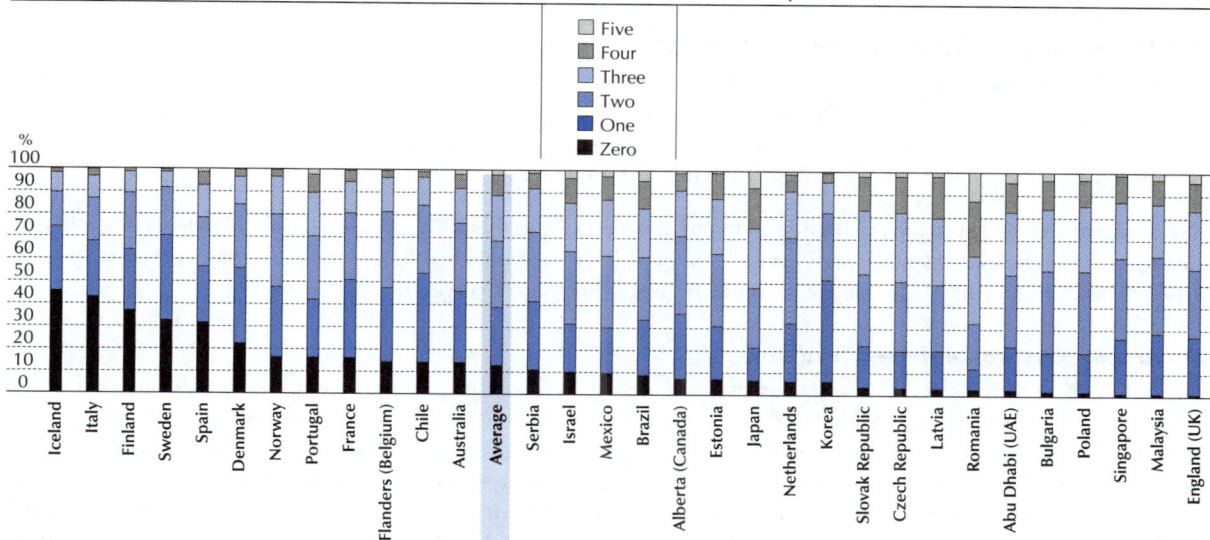

1. Croatia is not presented in this graph because the question on "feedback following assessment of teachers' content knowledge" was excluded as not applicable for this country.
2. The five bodies included in the survey are: external individuals or bodies, school principal, member(s) of the school management team, assigned mentors and other teachers (not a part of the management team).
Countries are ranked in descending order, based on the percentage of teachers who report not having received any feedback.
Source: OECD, TALIS 2013 Database, Table 5.10.Web.
StatLink http://dx.doi.org/10.1787/888933041820

In Finland, Iceland, Italy, Sweden and Spain, more than 30% of teachers report that they did not receive feedback on their teaching in their school from any of the five sources identified in the TALIS survey. In contrast, at least 20% of teachers in Japan, Latvia and Romania report receiving feedback from at least four sources.

Box 5.3 presents the reported sources of feedback by teachers in primary and upper secondary schools for those countries that implemented TALIS at these levels.

Box 5.3. **Sources of feedback for primary and upper secondary teachers**

Tables 5.4.a and 5.4.b present teachers' reports of the sources of the feedback they receive in their school in primary (ISCED 1) and upper secondary (ISCED 3) education, respectively. There are some interesting differences in the feedback that teachers at different levels of school education report receiving.

On average across the six countries with available data, primary school teachers are more likely to report receiving feedback from their principal than their colleagues in lower secondary schools (67% compared with 58% for these six countries). The difference between lower secondary teachers and upper secondary teachers is much smaller: On average across the 10 countries with available data, 44% of upper secondary school teachers report the same, compared with 48% on average for these countries in lower secondary schools.

Although there is not much difference in terms of the percentages of teachers in primary schools compared with lower secondary schools who report having received feedback from members of the school management team (29% and 31%, respectively), teachers in upper secondary schools are more likely than teachers in lower secondary schools to report the same in the ten countries with available data (49% compared with 42%). This may reflect the larger size of upper secondary schools (see Chapter 2), which may have a larger school management team. This may have consequences for the workloads of school principals at different levels of education and also for the structure of teacher feedback.

More sources of feedback does not automatically equate to better feedback. More information about the precise feedback received by teachers would be needed to make such an assertion. However, multiple sources of feedback could be an indicator of some types of teacher collaboration or distributed leadership within schools (Boston Consulting Group, 2003).

Methods for providing teacher feedback

Feedback to teachers has the greatest impact on classroom learning and teaching when it is based on a comprehensive appraisal of teachers' work (Jacob and Lefgren, 2008). A survey such as TALIS cannot provide complete data on the extent to which a comprehensive appraisal of teachers' work in school is undertaken before providing feedback. However, various inferences can be drawn by analysing the methods of providing feedback to teachers.

TALIS asked teachers about the methods used to provide feedback to them. These methods included feedback following classroom observation, student surveys, assessments of teachers' content knowledge, analysis of student test scores, self-assessments of their work and feedback from parents (including parent surveys).

Classroom observation-based feedback

Classroom observation can act as a quality-assurance mechanism, as people monitor teaching practices and ensure consistency in the quality of teaching across a school (Goldstein, 2004, 2007). Classroom observations that provide constructive and immediate feedback for teachers to improve their teaching can have a significant impact on student learning (Zwart et al., 2007). While observation is possibly perceived as threatening or confrontational for some, teachers say that this method improves teaching and learning and collegiality in schools (Kumrow and Dahlen, 2002). In time, it can help create a culture of sharing and for exchanging ideas across and between schools (Blackwell and McLean, 1996; Munson, 1998).

Table 5.5 shows that on average across TALIS countries, nearly 80% of teachers report that they receive feedback following some sort of classroom observation. In 12 countries (Bulgaria, the Czech Republic, Korea, Latvia, Malaysia, Poland, Romania, Singapore, the Slovak Republic, Abu Dhabi [United Arab Emirates] and England [United Kingdom]), at least 90% of teachers receive feedback following a classroom observation. Given the evidence showing positive links between observation and feedback and improvements in teaching and learning, this should be a positive indicator of teacher development and school improvement. In contrast, less than half of teachers in Finland, Iceland, Italy and Spain report receiving feedback following a classroom observation. As mentioned, these countries have comparatively low percentages of teachers who report receiving feedback in their school.

Student test scores as feedback

TALIS data show that the analysis of student test scores is the next most common practice on which feedback to teachers is based. On average across TALIS countries, 64% of teachers report that they receive feedback on their teaching following analysis of their students' test scores. Again, this is a positive finding given the evidence showing the positive impact of data-based feedback on school improvement and system performance (Barber and Mourshed, 2007). But there is substantial variation across countries. In Brazil, Bulgaria, Korea, Latvia, Malaysia, Mexico, Poland, Romania, Singapore and Abu Dhabi (United Arab Emirates), at least eight in ten teachers report that they received feedback on their teaching following analysis of their students' test scores. In contrast, in Finland, Iceland, and Sweden, less than a third of teachers report receiving feedback in this way.

Content knowledge assessments

Just over half of teachers, on average across TALIS countries, report that the feedback they received was based on an assessment of their content knowledge (55% of teachers on average across TALIS countries). This is particularly common in Latvia, Malaysia, Romania and Abu Dhabi (United Arab Emirates), where more than 80% of teachers report that assessments of their content knowledge are used as a basis for feedback on how to improve their teaching. In some countries, this is uncommon. Less than one-quarter of teachers in Iceland, Spain and Sweden report receiving feedback based on an assessment of their content knowledge. This should not be interpreted as conclusive evidence that these countries do not recognise the importance of content knowledge in effective instruction. There are many reasons why content knowledge may not be emphasised in teacher feedback. For example, teachers' content knowledge may be emphasised in other aspects of teacher training and development. Further analysis of countries' policies and field work in schools would reveal the nuances of how content knowledge is developed and assessed in countries and the interplay of various aspects of education systems.

Using student surveys to provide feedback

Students can be a vital source of feedback for teachers about their individual needs, ways of responding to distinct aspects of teaching, their progress, attitudes and learning habits. Student surveys have been important in the development of teaching in some Australian schools and in programmes in the United States and Canada (Peterson et al., 2003; Wilkerson et al., 2000; Bouchamma, 2005; Jensen and Reichl, 2011).

On average across TALIS countries, 53% of teachers report that the feedback they received is based on student surveys. But this varies widely across countries. Less than one-third of teachers in Finland, Iceland and Sweden report that student surveys are used as a basis for feedback on their teaching. On the other hand, more than three-quarters of teachers in Korea, Latvia, Malaysia and Romania report that student surveys are used in the feedback they receive at their school. Further field work could provide interesting information about the content of student surveys and how they are used to improve school culture and instruction in classrooms.

Feedback from parents

A similar percentage of teachers (53% on average across TALIS countries) report surveys or discussions with parents as a source of feedback in their school. Again, there is wide variation among countries that largely reflects patterns of the use of student surveys for teacher feedback.

One-third or fewer teachers in Iceland, Israel and Sweden report that parent surveys or discussions with parents are used as a basis for the feedback they receive in their school. Again, some other countries are much more likely to use feedback from parents in assessing teachers. For example, more than three-quarters of teachers in Latvia, Malaysia, Romania and Abu Dhabi (United Arab Emirates) report that surveys of and discussions with parents are used as a basis for the feedback they receive on their teaching in their school. Similar patterns are evident with feedback following teachers' self-assessment. On average across TALIS countries, 53% of teachers report receiving feedback following a self-assessment.

Box 5.4 presents the main findings regarding the reported methods of providing feedback to primary and upper secondary teachers for those countries with available data.

Box 5.4. **Methods for providing feedback to primary and upper secondary teachers**

Tables 5.5.a and 5.5.b present data about the methods for providing feedback to primary school (ISCED 1) teachers and upper secondary school (ISCED 3) teachers, respectively. Overall, the methods of providing feedback to teachers are similar across different levels of school education, although some differences are apparent.

On average, primary school teachers are more likely than teachers at other levels to receive feedback based on surveys of or discussions with parents. Across the six countries with available data, 58% of primary school teachers report receiving feedback based on parent interactions, compared with 50% on average for these same countries in lower secondary schools. On average, 41% of upper secondary school teachers across the ten countries with available data report the same (compared with 51% on average for these same countries in lower secondary schools).

Conversely, feedback based on student surveys was more common in upper secondary schools. On average across the ten countries with available data, 59% of upper secondary school teachers report the use of feedback from student surveys. This compares with 48% for these same countries in lower secondary education. On average across the six countries with available data in primary schools, 46% of teachers report receiving feedback based on student surveys. Presumably, this reflects the challenges associated with surveying students in the earlier years of school education. But in upper secondary schools, student surveys may be preferred to parent feedback because the connection between schools and parents can lessen as students get older.

To provide an overall picture of the nature of teacher feedback in schools, Figure 5.9 presents the percentage of teachers, on average across TALIS countries, who receive feedback from different people based on various mechanisms for providing feedback. For example, the top-left corner of the figure shows that 16% of teachers on average receive feedback from an individual or body external to the school following an observation of the teacher's classroom. The figure highlights that the majority of feedback comes from teachers' school principals and other members of the school management team. Teachers report that these school leaders most frequently use classroom observation as the basis for the feedback they provide to them. On average across TALIS countries, 39% of teachers report receiving feedback at their school in this manner.

In addition, on average across TALIS countries, 32% of teachers report receiving feedback, again based on classroom observations, from other members of the school management team.

■ Figure 5.9 ■

Teachers' feedback by source and type

Percentage of lower secondary education teachers who report having received the following feedback from different bodies and the percentage of teachers who report not having received the following feedback[1]

	Feedback following classroom observation	Feedback from student surveys	Feedback following assessment of teachers' content knowledge	Feedback following analysis of student test scores	Feedback following self-assessment of teachers' work	Feedback from surveys or discussion with parents
	%	%	%	%	%	%
External individuals or bodies	16	8	11	9	6	8
School principal	39	19	20	24	24	23
Member(s) of school management team	32	22	20	27	22	22
Assigned mentors	12	6	9	7	7	5
Other teachers (not a part of the management team)	24	15	15	18	12	14
I have never received this type of feedback in this school	21	45	44	35	46	45

1. Teachers can receive feedback from more than one body at the same time, meaning that percentages will not add up to 100%.
Source: OECD, TALIS 2013 Database, Tables 5.5.Web.1, 5.5.Web.2, 5.5.Web.3, 5.5.Web.4, 5.5.Web.5 and 5.5.Web.6.
StatLink ⌐□□ http://dx.doi.org/10.1787/888933041839

Peer feedback

Peer feedback can increase collaboration, which, in turn, helps improve student learning as teachers jointly reflect on diagnosing student learning, lesson design and teaching approaches (Richards and Lockhart, 1992). Teachers discuss alternative teaching approaches, observe each other's classes, re-examine content and identify and solve problems in teaching the content (Kennedy, 2005).

Across countries, peer feedback is less commonly reported by teachers than feedback from school leaders, but it is still an important avenue of feedback for a number of teachers (Table 5.4). On average, nearly one-quarter of teachers (24%) report receiving feedback from peers following an observation of their classroom teaching. In the Netherlands and Norway, however, this number is 40%, and in Korea 73% of teachers report receiving feedback from their colleagues after an observation. Between 12-18% of teachers, on average across TALIS countries, report receiving feedback from peers based on other sources of information, such as an analysis of student test scores, an assessment of teachers' content knowledge or discussions with parents.

Multiple sources of feedback

Given the complexity of teachers' roles and responsibilities, it may be most accurate and instructive to gather multiple sources of evidence about teacher practices (Danielson, 2007; Peterson, Wahlquist and Bone, 2000; Marshall, 2005). However, this doesn't necessarily mean that more methods of providing feedback result in higher-quality feedback. For example, multiple sources of feedback may increase the likelihood of conflicting messages. The quality of the feedback provided is paramount, but TALIS does not collect the information required to make detailed assessments of the quality of feedback.

However, TALIS does ask teachers about the number of methods used to provide feedback on their teaching (Figure 5.10). Specifically, teachers are asked whether they receive any of six specific methods of feedback: feedback following classroom observation, student surveys, assessment of teachers' content knowledge, analysis of student test scores, self-assessment of teachers' work and surveys of or discussion with parents. Teachers receiving feedback based on all six methods, as indicated in Figure 5.10, may be receiving more comprehensive feedback on their teaching than teachers receiving it from a single source.

There is a relatively even distribution across the number of sources of feedback for teachers. On average across TALIS countries, 13% of teachers report receiving no feedback on their teaching, and between 10%-13% of teachers report receiving feedback from either one (10% of teachers), two (12% of teachers), three (13% of teachers), four (12% of teachers) or five (11% of teachers) different sources. However, 30% of teachers report receiving feedback from all six sources identified in the TALIS survey. In addition, at least half of teachers in Korea, Latvia, Malaysia, Romania and Abu Dhabi (United Arab Emirates) report receiving feedback on their teaching from all six sources.

■ Figure 5.10 ■
Methods for teachers' feedback

*Percentage of lower secondary education teachers who report receiving feedback
for zero, one, two, three, four, five or all of the six methods surveyed for teacher feedback[1,2]*

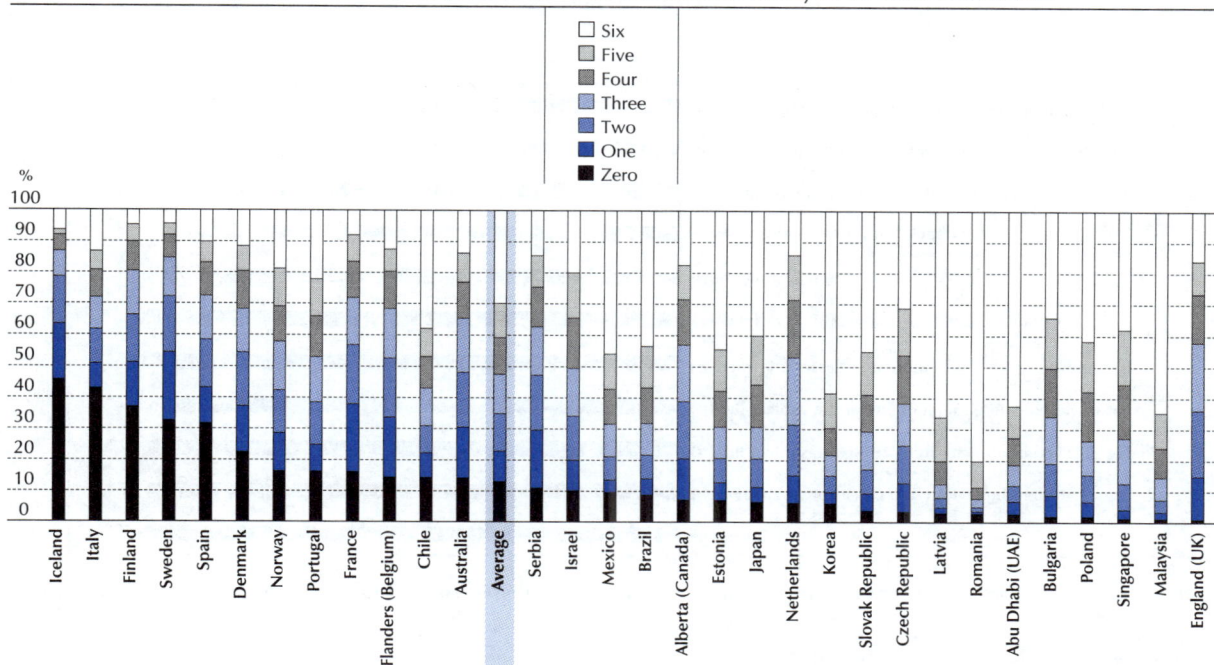

1. Croatia is not presented in this graph because the question on "feedback following assessment of teachers' content knowledge" was excluded as not applicable for this country.
2. Surveyed items are: "feedback following direct observation of your classroom teaching", "feedback from student surveys about your teaching", "feedback following an assessment of your content knowledge", "feedback following an analysis of your students' test scores", "feedback following your self-assessment of your work (e.g. presentation of a portfolio assessment)" and "feedback following surveys or discussions with parents or guardians".
Countries are ranked in descending order, based on the percentage of teachers who report not receiving any feedback.
Source: OECD, TALIS 2013 Database, Table 5.11.Web.
StatLink ⟨⟩ http://dx.doi.org/10.1787/888933041858

Teachers receiving feedback from all six sources may be working in schools with well-functioning systems of teacher feedback. Yet caution should be applied in interpreting the data in this way. TALIS does not have data on the frequency of teacher feedback. Hence, even though 30% of teachers report that they receive feedback in their school from all six sources identified in the TALIS survey, there may be substantial variation in the frequency of feedback received by this percentage of teachers. And, as mentioned previously, TALIS does not measure the quality of such feedback.

Focus of teacher feedback

What the data cited in the previous section do show is that on average across TALIS countries, a sizable proportion of teachers is getting feedback from multiple sources based on a number of different methods for appraising teaching (e.g. classroom observation). But what is the focus of such feedback? Table 5.6 and Figure 5.11 present teachers' reports of the different areas that have been emphasised in the feedback they receive at their school. It distinguishes between eleven aspects of school education and teaching and learning in classrooms: student performance, knowledge and understanding of subject fields, pedagogy, student assessment, student behaviour and classroom management, teaching students with special learning needs, teaching in a multicultural or multilingual setting, feedback that is developmental, feedback from parents, feedback from students and professional collaboration. (For the exact wording of the questions posed to teachers in these areas, see the questionnaires in the *TALIS Technical Report* [OECD, 2014]).

On average across TALIS countries, most teachers report that virtually all of the 11 aspects of teachers' work are emphasised (with moderate or high importance) in the feedback they receive in their school. Nearly nine in ten teachers, on average across TALIS countries, report that student performance, teachers' pedagogical competency in their subject field, and student behaviour and classroom management are strongly emphasised in the feedback they receive in their school.

■ Figure 5.11 ■

Emphasis of teacher feedback

Percentage of lower secondary education teachers who report that the feedback they received emphasised the following issues with a "moderate" or "high" importance

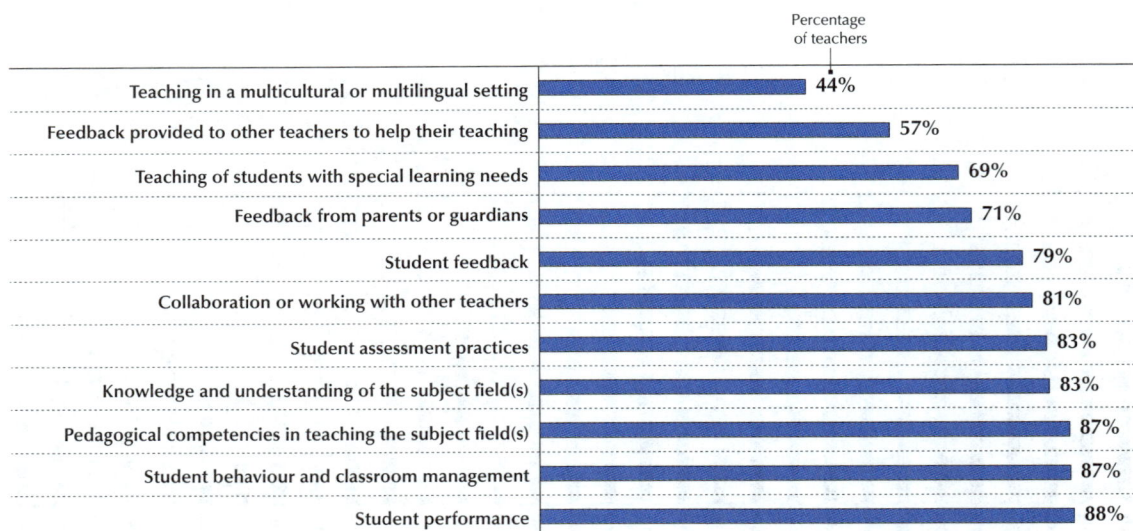

Percentage
of teachers

Teaching in a multicultural or multilingual setting	44%
Feedback provided to other teachers to help their teaching	57%
Teaching of students with special learning needs	69%
Feedback from parents or guardians	71%
Student feedback	79%
Collaboration or working with other teachers	81%
Student assessment practices	83%
Knowledge and understanding of the subject field(s)	83%
Pedagogical competencies in teaching the subject field(s)	87%
Student behaviour and classroom management	87%
Student performance	88%

Items are ranked in ascending order, based on the percentage of teachers who report that the feedback they received emphasised the issue with a "moderate" or "high" importance.
Source: OECD, TALIS 2013 Database, Table 5.6.
StatLink ⟨⟩ http://dx.doi.org/10.1787/888933041877

Feedback from students is reported as having a moderate or high emphasis in the feedback teachers receive for 79% of teachers, on average across TALIS countries. Fewer teachers (71%) report that parent surveys are emphasised with moderate or high importance in the feedback teachers receive about their work. Box 5.5 provides concrete examples from Norway and Sweden of how student feedback has been used to help teachers improve their teaching.

Box 5.5. **Using student feedback to help teachers improve their teaching in Norway and Sweden**

In Norway, principles and guidelines have been developed for teacher appraisal by students. Student surveys are provided for teachers who want to use them and focus on teaching practices that are relevant for student learning, such as adapted education and feedback to students, as well as questions on the general context of teaching, such as materials and physical conditions. Students' self-assessment and assessment of peers also permits analysis of how student effort and motivation influences the learning environment.

The teacher and a group of students prepare a report on their analysis of results and changes they have agreed to make. This report, together with relevant data, is submitted to the teachers' closest supervisor. While not all stakeholders agree with the recommendations that have emerged from this project, most have accepted the general idea that student views are an important source of feedback that teachers can use to improve their practice.

Reflecting the student-centred approach to education in Sweden, teachers often conduct surveys among their students with the aim of obtaining feedback on their teaching practices. These surveys are organised at the teachers' own initiative and results are used exclusively by the teacher concerned, often in interaction with the students.

Sources: Nusche et al., 2011a; Nusche et al., 2011b.

Box 5.6 presents comparisons of the emphasis of teacher feedback between TALIS 2008 and TALIS 2013 data for those countries that participated in both cycles.

Box 5.6. **Comparing the emphasis of teacher feedback, TALIS 2008 and TALIS 2013**

Table 5.6.c provides a comparison between the percentage of teachers in 2008 and 2013 who report receiving feedback that focuses, with moderate or high importance, on student performance, knowledge and understanding of their subject field(s), teaching students with special learning needs, teaching in a multicultural or multilingual setting, and student feedback. On average for countries that participated in both cycles, a larger number of teachers in 2013 than in 2008 report an emphasis placed on student performance in the feedback. However, on average for countries that participated in both cycles, there is very little difference in the percentage of teachers reporting a strong focus on most of the other areas in the feedback they receive, although more data are needed to identify long-term trends.

The only clear exception is the emphasis on student performance in the feedback teachers report receiving. On average across TALIS countries that participated in both TALIS cycles, 67% of teachers reported a strong emphasis on student performance in TALIS 2008. This percentage reaches 87% in TALIS 2013. This difference is particularly evident in the following countries:

- **Australia:** 51% of teachers reported a moderate or high importance placed on student performance in the feedback they received in TALIS 2008 compared with 88% of teachers in TALIS 2013

- **Denmark:** 29% of teachers in TALIS 2008 compared with 72% of teachers in TALIS 2013

- **Iceland:** 45% of teachers in TALIS 2008 compared with 78% of teachers in TALIS 2013

- **Italy:** 62% of teachers in TALIS 2008 compared with 95% of teachers in TALIS 2013

- **Norway:** 47% of teachers in TALIS 2008 compared with 73% of teachers in TALIS 2013

- **Portugal:** 64% of teachers in TALIS 2008 compared with 95% of teachers in TALIS 2013

This may reflect the greater emphasis placed on student performance by governments and administrators in many countries over this period. For example, in Australia, national student assessments were introduced in 2008 and have played a significant role in education reform and school improvement debates across the country (Zanderigo, Dowd and Turner, 2012). A natural consequence is for this to have an impact on the feedback teachers receive. If the feedback is constructive and implemented as part of an effective programme, it might be possible to trace the links between reforms to introduce student assessments, a greater emphasis in teacher feedback and an improvement in teaching that lifts student performance. TALIS does not collect data on teaching effectiveness but does highlight potential links between policy reforms and teacher feedback and development.

In most countries, there is also a higher reported emphasis placed on teaching students with special learning needs in teachers' feedback. On average across TALIS countries, 68% of teachers reported that teaching students with special learning needs is given a strong emphasis in the feedback they receive in their school. This compares with 58% in TALIS 2008. This finding is also interesting given the needs that teachers expressed for professional development in this area in both cycles of TALIS. (See Chapter 4.)

Box 5.7 examines the focus of teacher feedback as reported by teachers in primary and upper secondary schools for those countries that implemented TALIS at these levels of education and highlights the main differences found between levels of education.

Box 5.7. **Focus of feedback for primary and upper secondary teachers**

Tables 5.6.a and 5.6.b present data on the focus of feedback for teachers in primary (ISCED 1) and upper secondary (ISCED 3) education, respectively. Again, the data reinforce that the structure of teacher feedback is similar across different levels of education. However, there are some noteworthy differences.

On average, upper secondary school teachers report that the feedback they receive has considerably less emphasis on teaching students with special learning needs compared with primary school teachers and lower-secondary school teachers. On average across the six countries with available data, 74% of primary school teachers report

. . .

Box 5.7. **Focus of feedback for primary and upper secondary teachers** (cont.)

receiving feedback on their teaching with a moderate or high importance placed on teaching students with special learning needs. This compares with 61% on average for these same countries for lower secondary teachers. In the ten countries with available data in upper secondary schools, only 49% of teachers on average report the same (compared with 62% for these same countries in lower secondary schools).

Again, the emphasis on parents' feedback is lower for upper seconadary school teachers. On average across the ten countries with available data, 54% of upper secondary school teachers report receiving feedback at their school based on feedback from parents or guardians. This compares with an average of 70% for their colleagues in lower secondary schools in these same countries. Across the six countries with available data in primary schools, 74% of primary school teachers on average report the same (compared with 65% for the same countries in lower secondary schools).

OUTCOMES OF TEACHER APPRAISAL AND FEEDBACK

It is interesting to learn that teachers across countries are receiving appraisal and feedback, in many instances from a variety of sources and using several methods. But an equally important discussion concerns the outcomes of teacher appraisal and feedback. In other words, where does all of this lead? Research shows that feedback to teachers can have a number of positive impacts, ranging from a personal impact on teachers to an impact on their career, their development and their teaching. Each of these areas highlights the benefits of feedback in school education (Hattie, 2009).

First, feedback to teachers plays a positive role in recognising the work of teachers and in improving the enjoyment of their jobs. As shown in Table 5.7, on average across TALIS countries, 61% of teachers report moderate or large change in public recognition after the feedback they receive in their schools. Between countries, this ranges from at least three-quarters of teachers in Bulgaria, Japan, Malaysia and Romania, to less than half of teachers in Australia, Iceland, Portugal, Singapore, Alberta (Canada) and England (United Kingdom).

Slightly more teachers (63% on average across TALIS countries) report an increase in job satisfaction and job motivation (65% on average across TALIS countries). This is particularly pronounced in Bulgaria, Chile, Italy, Japan, Malaysia, Mexico and Romania, where more than three-quarters of teachers report an increase in job satisfaction and motivation. In addition, on average across TALIS countries, 71% of teachers report that the confidence they have in their teaching abilities increases after receiving feedback on their work in their school.

Nearly three-quarters of teachers, on average across TALIS countries, report a moderate or large increase in their confidence as a teacher after receiving feedback on their work. This outcome was common across all TALIS countries, with only Australia, Iceland, the Netherlands, Portugal, Spain and England (United Kingdom) having less than 60% of teachers report such an increase in confidence following feedback on their work.

Box 5.8. **Using appraisal results for professional development in Korea**

In Korea's Teacher Appraisal for Professional Development programme, a report collates teacher evaluation sheets. This includes the results of peer reviews conducted within each school. Using the evaluation sheets, each teacher writes a "plan for professional development (including training attendance plans)" and submits it to the appraisal management committee, which then compiles a report for the principal and vice-principal.

Based on appraisal results, local education authorities grant those teachers considered to be excellent a "study and research year" (similar to the sabbatical year given to university faculty) as an opportunity to participate in professional development activities. Underperforming teachers are obliged to participate in short- to long-term training programmes according to their appraisal results. Regardless of appraisal outcomes, local education offices support teachers with customised self-training programmes, fostering an atmosphere of self-study and self-improvement among teachers.

Source: Kim et al., 2010.

Some of the main policy recommendations regarding teacher appraisal stemming from the OECD Review *Synergies for Better Learning: An International Perspective on Evaluation and Assessment* include ensuring that teacher appraisal feeds into professional development and school development and establishing links between teacher appraisal and career-advancement decisions (OECD, 2013a). TALIS data show that these policy directions are not in place in all participating countries. Just under half of teachers on average report that their feedback has directly led to a positive change in the amount of professional development they undertake. This positive outcome is less common in Australia, the Czech Republic, Finland, France, Iceland, Norway, Sweden and England (United Kingdom), where less than one-third of teachers report this as a positive outcome of their feedback. Box 5.8 presents an example of how appraisal results are used for teachers' professional development in Korea.

Teacher feedback is also linked to teachers' careers and their jobs. On average across TALIS countries, just over one-third of teachers report that the feedback they receive is linked to the likelihood of their career advancement.

More than half of teachers (55% on average across TALIS countries) report that the feedback they receive in their school has an impact on their job responsibilities. This is especially encouraging for school improvement if feedback is based on a comprehensive appraisal of teachers' work, and then, after feedback is provided, teachers' job responsibilities are altered to better match their skills to specific jobs in schools. This would, in theory, increase school effectiveness.

While teacher feedback is related to changes in job responsibilities for most teachers, and career advancement for just over one-third of teachers on average, fewer teachers report that it is linked to their salary. On average across TALIS countries, 25% of teachers report that the feedback they receive has had a moderate or large positive impact on their salary (or they have received a financial bonus).

Box 5.9 provides an example of how teacher appraisal can be directly linked not only to financial bonuses but to specific career pathways that reflect teachers' strengths and interests.

Box 5.9. **Singapore: Linking teacher appraisal to career pathways**

Singapore's Enhanced Performance Management System (EPMS) is a developmental tool to help teachers achieve their aspirations in the Education Service. It was established after an extensive and comprehensive process of consultation with teachers from all levels. It is a structured process for setting work targets, appraising performance based on expected competencies and helping teachers identify areas for growth and plan for development accordingly. Regular discussions between teachers and their supervisors using the EPMS ensure that teachers who have done well are recognised and rewarded, while those who need to improve their performance are coached. This process thus helps teachers progress along their career track.

The Ministry of Education provides teachers with three career tracks to meet different professional aspirations and interests:

- The Teaching Track provides advancement opportunities for teachers who are keen to pursue a career in classroom teaching through progression to senior teacher, lead teacher, master teacher or principal master teacher. These senior teachers will take on mentoring roles as they impart their expertise and experience to their colleagues and develop new pedagogies to meet learning needs.

- The Leadership Track presents teachers with opportunities to take on management and leadership positions in schools or at the Ministry of Education.

- The Senior Specialist Track is for teachers who are more inclined towards more specialised areas where deep knowledge and skills are essential for breaking new ground in educational developments.

Source: Ministry of Education, Singapore.

The impact of teacher feedback on classroom teaching is the most important part of this analysis given the influence of effective teaching on student learning. It is encouraging that most teachers report that the feedback they receive results in changes in classroom teaching (Figure 5.12). On average across TALIS countries, 62% of teachers report that the feedback they receive in their school led to a moderate or large positive change in their teaching practices (Table 5.7).

■ Figure 5.12 ■

Outcomes of teacher feedback

Percentage of lower secondary education teachers who report a "moderate" or "large" positive change in the following practices after they received feedback on their work at their school

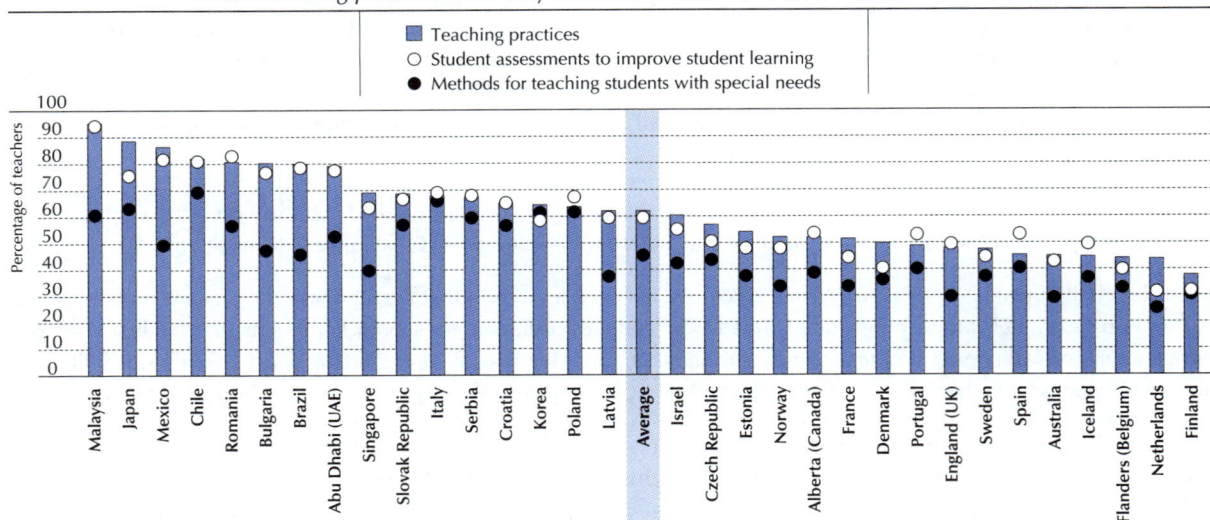

Countries are ranked in descending order, based on the percentage of teachers who report a "moderate" or "large" positive change in their teaching practices after they received feedback on their work at their school.
Source: OECD, TALIS 2013 Database, Table 5.7.
StatLink ⬛ http://dx.doi.org/10.1787/888933041896

Looking at the details of specific teaching practices, more than half of teachers report that the feedback they received in their school led to moderate or large positive changes in their use of student assessments to improve student learning (59% of teachers) and classroom-management practices (56% of teachers). Moreover, 45% of teachers on average report that the feedback they receive leads to moderate or large positive changes in their methods for teaching students with special needs.

These findings emphasise the developmental nature of feedback and how it can have a direct impact on classroom teaching. This doesn't mean that all feedback has a direct impact on teaching. Some feedback will be particularly beneficial to teachers and some may have little impact. For example, on average across TALIS countries, 69% of teachers report receiving feedback that emphasised teaching students with special learning needs. However, only 45% report that the feedback they receive resulted in a moderate or large change in their teaching of students with special learning needs.

Box 5.10 presents the positive outcomes of the feedback reported by teachers in primary and upper secondary schools for those countries with available data.

Box 5.10. **Outcomes of feedback for primary and upper secondary education teachers**

Tables 5.7.a and 5.7.b present teachers' reports of the outcomes of the feedback they receive in their school in primary (ISCED 1) and upper secondary (ISCED 2) education, respectively. Both largely reflect the findings of lower seccondary teachers, with one clear exception.

On average across the six countries with available data, a larger proportion of primary school teachers report that the feedback they receive leads to a moderate or large change in the methods they use to teach students with special learning needs (52%), compared with the average in those same countries for lower secondary schools (41%). In the ten countries with available data in upper secondary schools, even fewer teachers report this outome following the feedback they receive (35% compared with 43% for these same countries in lower secondary schools). This aligns with the data presented in Tables 5.6.a and 5.6.b, which show, on average, that the feedback that upper secondary school teachers receive has less of an emphasis on teaching students with special learning needs.

Box 5.11 presents comparisons of teachers' reports of the outcomes of the feedback they received in 2008 during the first cycle of TALIS and the responses obtained from teachers in 2013 for those countries that participated in both surveys.

> ### Box 5.11. **Comparing the outcomes of teacher feedback, TALIS 2008 and TALIS 2013**
>
> Table 5.7.c compares teachers' reports in TALIS 2008 and TALIS 2013 on the likelihood that the appraisal and feedback they receive in their school leads to a moderate or large change in the likelihood of their career advancement. Comparing countries that participated in both TALIS cycles, in 2008, just 17% of teachers reported that appraisal and feedback was linked to their career advancement, compared with 35% of teachers in TALIS 2013. While two data points are too few to identify a trend, it can be seen as encouraging that in a relatively short time, the percentage of teachers who receive feedback linked to their career advancement has more than doubled.

Similar findings are evident in the outcomes of formal teacher appraisal as reported by school leaders and presented earlier in this chapter (Table 5.3). For example, on average across TALIS countries, one-third of teachers work in schools where their school principal reports that formal teacher appraisal at least sometimes results in a change in teachers' salary or pay. In addition, 70% of teachers work in schools where their school principal reports that formal teacher appraisal is linked to changes in teachers' job responsibilities. At least when it comes to outcomes, there are strong similarities in teachers' reports of the feedback they receive in their school and what school principals report about formal appraisal in their school.

PERCEPTIONS OF TEACHER APPRAISAL AND FEEDBACK SYSTEMS IN SCHOOLS

A number of teachers perceive that systems of teacher appraisal and feedback in their school are more generally often disconnected from both the development of teaching and learning in classrooms and systems of teacher recognition. As shown in Table 5.8 and Figure 5.13, on average across TALIS countries, 43% of teachers report that the teacher appraisal and feedback system in their school has little impact on classroom teaching.

■ Figure 5.13 ■
Impact of teacher appraisal and feedback systems in schools
Percentage of lower secondary education teachers who "agree" or "strongly agree" with the following statements about teacher appraisal and feedback systems in their school

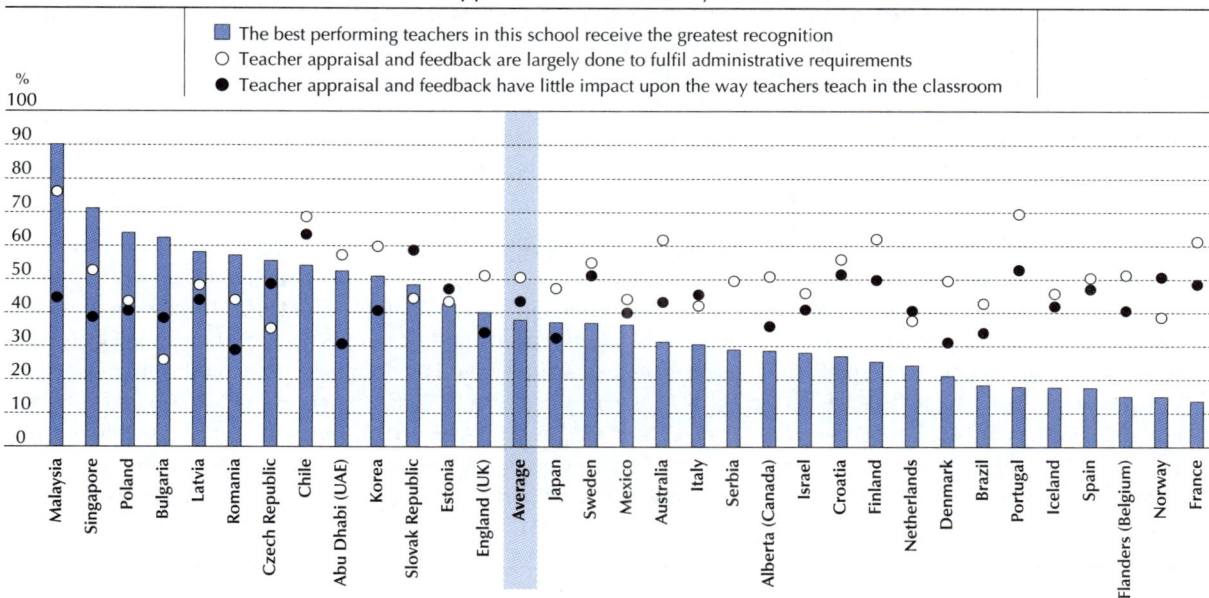

Countries are ranked in descending order, based on the percentage of teachers who "agree" or "strongly agree" that the best performing teachers in their school receive the greatest recognition.
Source: OECD, TALIS 2013 Database, Table 5.8.
StatLink http://dx.doi.org/10.1787/888933041915

On average across TALIS countries, just more than half of teachers report that teacher appraisal and feedback in the school is largely undertaken to fulfil administrative requirements (Table 5.8 and Figure 5.13). Only in Bulgaria do less than 30% of teachers report that appraisal and feedback are largely done to fulfil administrative requirements, whereas in Malaysia more than three-quarters of teachers report the same.

This is highly informative for policy makers. For many teachers, appraisal and feedback systems are in place in the school but only provide an administrative exercise that is not having the desired impact on classroom teaching (and therefore on student learning). This may indicate that policies that require teacher appraisal and feedback are not having their desired impact. Reform-minded policy makers may need to recognise that implementing new systems of teacher appraisal and feedback – or any form of performance management – is a difficult process in any setting, let alone in schools that do not have a history of effective teacher appraisal and feedback. These cases may necessitate a focus on the behavioural and often cultural change that is required in schools for these reforms (Fullan, 2010).

Teachers report that teacher appraisal and feedback in their school does not lead to any positive or negative consequences for the majority of teachers. On average across TALIS countries, less than 40% of teachers report that the best-performing teachers in their schools receive the greatest recognition (e.g. rewards, additional training or responsibilities) or that a teacher would be dismissed for consistently underperforming (31%).[1]

It may not be surprising, given the evidence showing that relatively few teachers are dismissed due to poor performance (Boston Consulting Group, 2003), that most teachers report that sustained underperformance does not lead to dismissal of teachers in their school. But the lack of connection between teacher appraisal and feedback and recognising good performance may be disappointing to many policy makers and those interested in teacher development and professional recognition.

Recognition can take numerous forms, such as additional development opportunities and changes in job responsibilities. The perceived separation between teacher appraisal and feedback and teacher recognition reinforces the finding that the former is not being sufficiently linked to the improvement and development of teaching practices in schools. But comprehensive appraisal and feedback systems not only direct improvements in classroom teaching, they also inform how human resources are employed within schools. It appears this is not occurring in most schools, which could lead to an inefficient use of teachers' talents and skills, particularly if such skills are not being developed effectively.

Box 5.12. **Comparing outcomes of teacher appraisal and feedback, TALIS 2008 and TALIS 2013**

While two data points are not enough to identify a trend, it seems that across the countries that participated in both cycles of TALIS, more teachers in TALIS 2013 than in TALIS 2008 report that the best-performing teachers are being recognised in their school. Table 5.8.c shows that in TALIS 2008, only 26% of teachers reported that the best teachers in their school receive the greatest recognition. In 2013, 36% of teachers report that the best teachers in their school received the greatest recognition. This difference was most pronounced in Australia (9% of teachers in TALIS 2008 reported that the best-performing teachers in their school received the greatest recognition, compared with 31% of teachers in 2013), Korea (10% of teachers in TALIS 2008 compared with 51% in TALIS 2013) and Malaysia (53% of teachers in TALIS 2008 compared with 90% in TALIS 2013).

Also, in a number of countries, fewer teachers report that in their school, underperforming (on a sustained basis) teachers will be dismissed. While there is little difference on average across TALIS countries between 2008 and 2013, there are substantial differences in teacher reports in some countries in TALIS 2013 compared with TALIS 2008. For example, there were differences in teachers' reports in Bulgaria (65% of teachers in TALIS 2008 reported that consistently underperforming teachers in their school would be dismissed, compared with only 48% in TALIS 2013), Iceland (36% of teachers in TALIS 2008 compared with 24% of teachers in TALIS 2013) and Poland (34% of teachers in TALIS 2008 compared with 17% of teachers in TALIS 2013). This does not necessarily mean that schools in these countries are comprehensively addressing underperformance. That would require a mix of appraisal, feedback and development opportunities, and TALIS did not collect comprehensive data on complete systems of addressing underperformance.

This situation builds on issues identified in TALIS 2008. TALIS 2008 found that teacher appraisal and feedback have a strong positive influence on teachers and their work. Teachers reported that appraisal and feedback increased their job satisfaction and, to some degree, their job security, and that these assessments significantly increased their

development as effective teachers. However, teachers' reports from TALIS 2008 also showed that teacher appraisal and feedback are underdeveloped in many countries (OECD, 2009). Box 5.12 provides some comparisons between teachers' perceptions of the outcomes of appraisal and feedback systems in their school between TALIS 2008 and TALIS 2013.

DOES SCHOOL AUTONOMY MAKE A DIFFERENCE TO TEACHER APPRAISAL AND FEEDBACK?

Considerable analyses have been made of the impact of school autonomy on student performance (e.g. OECD 2010, 2011, 2013b). Some schools excel when given increased autonomy (Caldwell and Spinks, 2013). They innovate and reform schooling in numerous ways (Hargreaves, 2010, 2012). Much of this research does not claim that a causal link exists between school autonomy and student performance. Instead, it emphasises the advantages of school autonomy as part of a comprehensive strategy for school and system improvement (Caldwell and Spinks, 2008).

The reports from the OECD Programme for International Student Assessment (PISA) have estimated the impact of school autonomy on student performance and found a positive relationship (OECD 2010, 2013). But little is understood of how autonomy changes the way schools operate. TALIS provides some opportunities to analyse this issue with the present data and in the future.

A complete analysis of all aspects of school autonomy and its impact on how schools operate is not possible with the current TALIS data. But it is possible to explore how this issue could be analysed by examining the relationship between one aspect of school autonomy and how it relates to differences in teacher appraisal and feedback.

In theory, schools with greater decision-making responsibilities for teacher performance management should be able to develop their own effective systems of teacher appraisal and feedback. This reflects a number of arguments have been made in favour of autonomy:

- **Schools have local knowledge:** School leaders know more about their school than a centralised authority does. They can therefore make more informed decisions (Woessmann et al., 2009; Hoxby, 1999). For example, a school principal may know better which teachers should receive the greatest increases in salary.

- **Each school must respond to its specific circumstances:** Central policies designed for all schools may not be the best fit for individual schools (Chubb and Moe, 1990, p. 14; Angus and Olney, 2011, pp. 11-12). In addition, school autonomy can help empower school leaders to develop the policies that best improve learning and teaching in their specific school (Caldwell and Spinks, 2008).

- **Autonomy allows schools to experiment and find what works:** Innovation can increase as school leaders use their greater freedom to come up with new solutions and programmes (Greene et al., 2010, p. 6; Witte, 1990, p. 39).

- **Using local information can lead to more efficient outcomes:** Budgets determined at the local level can lead to more specific expenditures that better suit each school, with fewer resources spent on non-essential items (Odden and Busch, 1998; Clark, 2009).

- **Schools will become more accountable for outcomes:** Autonomous leaders often feel more responsibility for school performance. For example, a school autonomy pilot programme in the Australian state of New South Wales found that many principals understood the accountability that came with greater autonomy (Department of Education and Communities [NSW], 2011, p. 26).

- **Autonomy should foster a sense of ownership in school management:** Greater school autonomy and accountability can engender a strong sense of ownership among staff. Ownership can increase innovation and effective reforms in schools (Triant, 2001, p. 4; Hargreaves and Hopkins, 1991, p. 7).

Given the perceived benefits of school autonomy, it is pertinent to analyse how schools with different levels of autonomy appraise and provide feedback to their teachers.

School autonomy is more complex than is often portrayed. It is not the case that a school simply has autonomy or does not. Schools have different levels of autonomy over different aspects of decision making (see Chapters 2 and 3 for the TALIS 2013 data in this area). A more nuanced understanding can be gained from examining how schools operate and respond to various aspects of autonomy. In this case, a specific aspect of autonomy was selected for further analysis.

Table 5.9 presents differences in levels of school autonomy over the responsibility for determining teachers' salary increases and teachers' reports of teacher appraisal and feedback in schools with different levels of school autonomy.

On average across TALIS countries, 29% of teachers work in schools where their school principal reports that significant responsibility for determining teachers' salary increases resides at the school level. Only 8% of school principals report that this responsibility was shared between the school and higher levels, while 62% of school principals report that the responsibility for determining teachers' salary increases lies at a higher administrative level. There is therefore a clear contrast between the 29% of schools that have responsibility for determining teachers' salary increases (and therefore have a high level of autonomy in this areas) and the 62% that do not (which have a low level of autonomy in this area).

But there is variation among countries. More than 80% of school principals reported that significant responsibility for determining teachers' salary increases resides at the school level in the Czech Republic, the Netherlands, the Slovak Republic, Sweden and England (United Kingdom). And in Bulgaria, Estonia and Latvia, at least one-quarter of school principals reported that significant responsibilities for determining teachers' salary increases is shared between the school and higher administrative levels (Table 5.9).

Such differences can arise for a number of reasons, including administrative, institutional, historical and regulatory differences, and can affect the level of autonomy in schools. The question then becomes how and whether this level of autonomy impacts the way in which schools operate. To start to analyse this issue, comparisons can be made between teacher appraisal and feedback in schools with low and high levels of autonomy.

The second portion of Table 5.9 compares teachers' reports of teacher appraisal and feedback in these two categories of schools. There is little overall difference in teachers' reports of appraisal and feedback in schools with different levels of this aspect of autonomy. For example, on average across TALIS countries, 38% of teachers in schools with autonomy over teachers' salary decisions report that the best-performing teachers in their school receive the greatest recognition, compared with 37% of teachers in schools with no autonomy over teachers' salary increases. Similar findings are evident in regard to the association between teacher appraisal and feedback on teachers' classroom teaching practices, the extent that teacher feedback is based on a thorough assessment of teachers' teaching, whether a development or training plan is established for teachers and whether teacher appraisal and feedback is largely done to fulfil administrative requirements. In other words, a school's autonomy over teacher's salary decision has little to no impact over these aspects of a teacher's appraisal and feedback.

The greatest difference overall is evident in the dismissal of teachers who are consistently underperforming. On average across TALIS countries, 40% of teachers in schools with high autonomy over teacher salaries report that in their school, consistently underperforming teachers would be dismissed. In schools with low autonomy over teachers' salary increases, only 30% of teachers report that consistently underperforming teachers would be dismissed in their school. This difference is greatest in Brazil (79% of teachers in high-autonomy schools compared with 27% of teachers in low-autonomy schools); Japan (35% of teachers in high-autonomy schools compared with 11% of teachers in low-autonomy schools); Mexico (69% of teachers in high-autonomy schools compared with 16% of teachers in low-autonomy schools); and Abu Dhabi (United Arab Emirates) (59% of teachers in high-autonomy schools compared with 29% of teachers in low-autonomy schools).

The finding that school autonomy over determining teachers' salary increases does not, on average, relate to differences in most aspects of teacher appraisal and feedback may provide some context for mixed findings in previous research on the relationship between autonomy and performance (Clark, 2009). But, of course, caution should be taken in drawing too much from this analysis of one aspect of autonomy.

Policy makers have often struggled with ineffective staffing practices, which are often concentrated on the hiring and firing decisions of a central body. Increasing school autonomy has often been a response to this (OECD, 2011). However, Table 5.9 shows that autonomous schools (with respect to determining teachers' salaries) generally have the same practices in important areas of teacher appraisal and feedback as those with low autonomy over determining teachers' salary increases. Regardless of the level of autonomy, there are still rights and obligations that a school principal must follow, and these may impact teacher appraisal and feedback more than different levels of school autonomy would. Therefore, an effective school improvement strategy needs to recognise that empowering school leaders is about much more than simple autonomy (Caldwell and Spinks, 2008).

SUMMARY AND MAIN POLICY IMPLICATIONS

Effective appraisal and feedback is an essential element in improving the performance of individual teachers in the classroom – and therefore in improving student learning. Appraisal and feedback systems can achieve this by increasing teacher motivation and through direct links to teachers' professional learning (Lustick and Sykes, 2006). Effective appraisal and feedback can also support teachers in the advancement of their careers and lead teachers to take on new roles and responsibilities within their school. This chapter provides an in-depth analysis of teachers' and principals' accounts of the process by which teachers receive appraisal and feedback in their school and of the perceived impacts and outcomes of this feedback.

TALIS provides valuable information on the appraisal and feedback systems that are at work in schools, and the findings presented in this chapter have important implications for possible policy avenues that may further support the continuous improvement of schools and teachers and lead to better student outcomes.

Ensure that multiple avenues are in place for teachers to receive feedback on their work

Teacher feedback systems are operating across most schools and have features associated with effective school improvement. Teachers report that the feedback they receive comes from multiple sources. More than half of the teachers on average report receiving feedback from at least two different types of people, and one in ten teachers reports receiving feedback from at least four different people. Approximately half of the teachers on average say that this feedback comes from their principal or other members of their school management team. Fewer, however, say that this feedback comes from colleagues or other teachers in the school. Research has shown that such collaborative exchanges between teachers offer good opportunities to provide teachers with evidence about their practice and also for providing support for professional growth (Goldstein, 2007; Milanowski, 2005). Clearly, it is important that school leaders, in addition to providing direct feedback to individual teachers, should encourage a climate in which peer appraisal can take place.

Promote the use of comprehensive sources of data for teacher appraisals

Teachers report that the appraisal they receive is based on important aspects of their work. For example, nearly 80% of teachers, on average across TALIS countries, report getting feedback following classroom observation, and nearly two-thirds report receiving feedback following analysis of student test scores. As reported in the OECD Review *Synergies for Better Learning: An International Perspective on Evaluation and Assessment* (OECD, 2013a), comprehensive appraisal models that take into account multiple sources of evidence provide the most solid basis for teacher appraisals. Furthermore, one of the main conclusions of the Measures of Effective Teaching (MET) study is the importance of using multiple measures and sources of evidence, such as classroom observations and student surveys, to ensure a valid assessment of teachers' performance (Gates Foundation, 2013).

School leaders can ensure that regular classroom observations take place in a trusting environment where teachers can receive constructive feedback on their teaching. Effective classroom observations may require some capacity building within the school, as well as active engagement on the part of teachers to ensure that the responsibility does not fall solely on the school leader. With the addition of multiple measures for teacher appraisal naturally come additional tasks for teachers and school leaders. School leaders may want to consider distributing some of these tasks to other members of staff in leadership positions in order to manage their own time (see Chapter 3). For this additional work to be seen by teachers as beneficial and not just as a time burden, the different methods of appraisal and feedback need to be made an integral part of the teachers' practice, and the link to improving the core work of teachers needs to be made clear.

As mentioned earlier, the ultimate goal of effective teacher appraisal is improving student learning. Therefore, student learning outcomes should be an essential component of teacher appraisal. However, using student test results simplistically for high-stakes decisions can be counterproductive and lead to cases where teachers are "teaching to test". Rather, teacher appraisals should consider the use of a variety of types of evidence of student progress (OECD, 2013a).

Ensure that formal teacher appraisal feeds into professional development

It is difficult to imagine an effective teacher appraisal system that is not adequately linked to teachers' further development. One of the key policy recommendations offered in the OECD Review *Synergies for Better Learning: An International Perspective on Evaluation and Assessment* (OECD, 2013a) is to ensure that teacher appraisal, and the accompanying feedback on teacher work, play a central developmental role in teachers' careers. TALIS shows that just under half of teachers on average report that the feedback they receive leads to a positive change in the amount of professional development they undertake. Moreover, just more than four teachers in ten work in schools where their principal reports

that a development plan is created most of the time or always for teachers following formal appraisal. There is clearly some room to improve the link between teachers' feedback and their further development plans. A key to ensuring this success is the adequate preparation of the school leader to help teachers identify their individual needs and incorporate these needs into the school's priorities in order to provide relevant professional development opportunities for their teaching staff (see also Chapter 4).

Establish a comprehensive and coherent framework for teacher appraisal

Teachers perceive that overall systems of appraisal and feedback in their schools are not operating well. On average across TALIS countries, 43% of teachers report that the teacher appraisal and feedback systems in their schools are not strongly related to classroom teaching, and more than half of teachers report that they are largely undertaken simply to fulfil administrative requirements (Table 5.8).

There may be impediments that preclude appraisal and feedback from being constructive. These may be structural or regulatory (e.g. regulations that prevent feedback from being linked to teacher appraisal) or cultural (e.g. a lack of active professional collaboration in schools) or reflect a strategic failure to connect positive school practices such as teacher feedback to desired improvements in teaching and learning.

Numerous analyses have emphasised the importance of effective implementation of policy reform to have the desired result of improving student learning (Barber, 2008). Effective implementation is often the result of a carefully constructed strategy that aligns different policies and programmes around clear objectives to improve learning and teaching. In so doing, comprehensive implementation programmes can connect policies to the classroom, improving teaching and learning across schools (Fullan, 2009; OECD, 2013a). Furthermore, research suggests that it is important that appraisal and feedback systems are viewed as an integrated element of the school culture rather than as an "add-on" to existing systems (Santiago and Benavides, 2009; Marshall, 2005). This could partly explain why, on average across TALIS countries, only just more than one-third of teachers report that the best-performing teachers in their schools receive the greatest recognition. Further analysis is required to ascertain whether this is occurring and how policy makers, school leaders and school management can have a stronger impact on improving teaching through various teacher appraisal and feedback mechanisms.

New analyses in TALIS 2013 show that schools with very different levels of autonomy over changes in teachers' salary do not differ in the effects that feedback has on a variety of aspects related to teaching. For example, on average across TALIS countries, 38% of teachers in schools with autonomy over teachers' salary decisions report that the best-performing teachers in their school receive the greatest recognition, compared with 37% of teachers in schools with no autonomy over teachers' salary increases. Thus, a simple change in school autonomy with regard to teachers' salaries does not appear to be the answer.

View teacher appraisal as a tool to improve student learning

Teacher feedback is reportedly producing some positive changes in teaching. On average across TALIS countries, 62% of teachers report that the feedback they received in their school led to a moderate or large positive change in teaching practices. Feedback is also positively associated with teachers' jobs. On average across TALIS countries, 63% of teachers report an increase in job satisfaction, and 65% report an increase in job motivation from the feedback they receive about their teaching. Such job-related outcomes can lead to improvements in teaching – and in student learning. On average across TALIS countries, 71% of teachers also report that the confidence they have as a teacher increases after receiving feedback on their work in their school.

These positive findings suggest great opportunities for school leaders to improve both teaching and teachers' confidence and job satisfaction. Efforts to increase collaboration and programmes to increase feedback are having a large positive impact, according to teachers. Cultural change can be a large stumbling block in schools that are not used to collaboration or programmes such as classroom observation and feedback. But the programmes themselves don't have to be complicated; it is more about providing teachers the time, resources and space for collaboration and emphasising feedback on how to improve learning in schools.

Note

1. It is important to note that this is based on teachers' personal judgments of the "best performing teachers". The TALIS study did not seek to define teacher performance but asked teachers their impression of how performance (as they define it) is recognised in their school.

A note regarding Israel

The statistical data for Israel are supplied by and under the responsibility of the relevant Israeli authorities. The use of such data by the OECD is without prejudice to the status of the Golan Heights, East Jerusalem and Israeli settlements in the West Bank under the terms of international law.

References

Angus, M. and **H. Olney** (2011), "Targeting support for high-need students in primary schools: Report of the TRIPS Study", Australian Primary Principals Association, *www.appa.asn.au/reports/TRIPS-study.pdf* (accessed 23 April 2013).

Barber, M. (2008), *Instruction to Deliver: Fighting to Transform Britain's Public Services*, Methuen Publishers Ltd, York.

Barber, M. and **M. Mourshed** (2007), *How the World's Best-Performing Schools Come Out on Top*, McKinsey and Company.

Berry, B., D. Johnson and **D. Montgomery** (2005), "The power of teacher leadership", *Educational Leadership*, Vol. 62/3, p. 56.

Blackwell, R. and **M. McLean** (1996), "Peer observation of teaching and staff development", *Higher Education Quarterly,* Vol. 50/2, p. 156.

Bolam, R. et al. (2005), "Creating and sustaining effective professional learning communities", University of Bristol, *www.educationscotland. gov.uk/Images/Creating%20and%20Sustaining%20PLCs_tcm4-631034.pdf.*

Boston Consulting Group (2003). *Schools Strategy Workforce Development*, Melbourne.

Bouchamma, Y. (2005), "Evaluating teaching personnel. Which model of supervision do Canadian teachers prefer?", *Journal of Personnel Evaluation and Education*, Vol. 18, pp. 289-308.

Caldwell, B.J. and **J.M. Spinks** (2008), *Raising the Stakes: From Improvement to Transformation in the Reform of Schools*, Routledge, Abingdon.

Caldwell, B.J. and **J.M. Spinks** (2013), *The Self-Transforming School*, Routledge, Abingdon.

Caprara, G.V. et al. (2006), "Teachers' self-efficacy beliefs as determinants of job satisfaction and students' academic achievement: A study at the school level", *Journal of School Psychology,* Vol. 44/6, pp. 473-490.

Chubb, J.E. and **T.M. Moe** (1990), *Politics, Markets and America's Schools*, The Brookings Institution, Washington, DC.

Clark, D. (2009), "The performance and competitive effects of school autonomy", *Journal of Political Economy*, Vol. 117/4, pp. 745-783.

Clement, M. and **R. Vandenberghe** (2000), "Teachers' professional development: A solitary or collegial (ad)venture", *Teaching and Teacher Education,* Vol. 16, pp. 81–101.

Danielson, C. (2007), *Enhancing Professional Practice: A Framework for Teaching, 1st and 2nd Editions*, Association for Supervision and Curriculum Development (ASCD), Alexandria, VA.

Department of Education and Communities (NSW) (2011), "Independent review of the school based management pilot", *www.det.nsw. edu.au/media/downloads/about-us/statistics-and-research/key-statistics-and-reports/irsb-management-pilot.pdf* (accessed 20 February 2013).

Elmore, R.F. (2004), *School Reform from the Inside Out: Policy, Practice and Performance,* Harvard University Press, Cambridge, MA.

Figlio, D. and **L. Kenny** (2006), "Individual teacher incentives and student performance", NBER Working Paper, No. 12627.

Fuchs, L.S. and **D. Fuchs** (1985), "A quantitative synthesis of effects of formative evaluation on achievement", 69th Annual Meeting of the American Educational Research Association, Chicago, IL.

Fuchs, L.S. and **D. Fuchs** (1986), "Effects of systematic formative evaluation: A meta-analysis", *Exceptional Children,* Vol. 53/3, pp. 199-208.

Fullan, M. (2009), "Large-scale reform comes of age", *Journal of Educational Change*, Vol. 10/2-3, pp. 101-113, *http://michaelfullan. ca/Articles_09/LargeScaleReform.pdf.*

Fullan, M. (2010), "The big ideas behind whole system reform", *Education Canada*, Vol. 50/3, pp. 24-30.

Gates Foundation (2010). *Learning about Teaching: Initial Findings from the Measures of Effective Teaching Project,* Bill and Melinda Gates Foundation, Seattle, WA.

Gates Foundation (2013), *Ensuring Fair and Reliable Measures of Effective Teaching: Culminating Findings for the MET Project's Three-Year Study*, Bill and Melinda Gates Foundation, Seattle, WA.

Goldstein, J. (2007), "Easy to dance to: Solving the problems of teacher evaluation with peer assistance and review", *American Journal of Education*, Vol. 113/3: pp. 479-508.

Goldstein, J. (2004), "Making sense of distributed leadership: The case of peer assistance and review", *Educational Evaluation and Policy Analysis*, Vol. 26/2, pp.173-197.

Greene, J. et al. (2010), "Expanding choice in elementary and secondary education: A report on rethinking the federal role in education", The Brookings Institution, *www.brookings.edu/~/media/research/files/reports/2010/2/02%20school%20choice/0202_school_choice. pdf* (accessed 7 May 2014).

Hargreaves, D.H. (2012), "A self-improving school system: towards maturity", *http://dera.ioe.ac.uk/15804/1/a-self-improving-school-system-towards-maturity.pdf* (accessed 7 May 2014).

Hargreaves, D.H. (2010), "Creating a self-improving school system", *http://dera.ioe.ac.uk/2093/1/download%3Fid%3D133672%26 filename%3Dcreating-a-self-improving-school-system.pdf* (accessed 7 May 2014).

Hargreaves, D.H. and D. Hopkins (1991), *The Empowered School: The Management and Practice of Development Planning*, Cromwell Press, Trowbridge.

Hattie, J. (2009), *Visible Learning. A Synthesis of Over 800 Meta-Analyses Relating to Achievement*, Routledge, Milton Park.

Hoxby, C.M. (1999), "The effects of school choice on curriculum and atmosphere", in *Earning and Learning: How Schools Matter*, S.E. Mayer and P.E. Peterson (eds.), Brookings Institution Press, Washington, DC., pp. 281-316.

Isoré, M. (2009), "Teacher evaluation: Current practices in OECD countries and a literature review", *OECD Education Working Papers*, No. 23, OECD Publishing, Paris, *http://dx.doi.org/10.1787/223283631428*.

Jacob, B. and L. Lefgren (2008), "Can principals identify effective teachers? Evidence on subjective performance evaluation in education", *Journal of Labor Economics*, Vol. 26/1, pp. 101-136.

Jensen, B. and J. Reichl (2011), *Better Teacher Appraisal and Feedback: Improving Performance*, Grattan Institute, Melbourne.

Jensen, B. et al. (2012), *Catching Up: Learning from the Best School Systems in East Asia,* Grattan Institute, Melbourne.

Kennedy, M.M. (2005), *Inside Teaching: How Classroom Life Undermines Reform*, Harvard University Press, Cambridge, MA.

Kim, K. et al. (2010), *OECD Review on Evaluation and Assessment Frameworks for Improving School Outcomes: Country Background Report for Korea*, Korean Educational Development Institute (KEDI), Seoul.

Kumrow, D. and B. Dahlen (2002), "Is peer review an effective approach for evaluating teachers?", *The Clearing House*, Vol. 75/5, p. 238.

Kyriacou, C. (1995), "An evaluation of teacher appraisal in schools within one local education authority", *School Leadership and Management*, Vol.15, pp. 109-116.

Lustick, D. and G. Sykes (2006), "National Board Certification as professional development: What are teachers learning?", *Education Policy Analysis Archives,* Vol. 14/5.

MacBeath, J. and A. McGlynn (2002), *Self-Evaluation–What's In It for Schools?,* Routledge Falmer, London.

Marshall, K. (2005), "It's time to rethink teacher supervision and evaluation", *Phi Delta Kappan,* Vol. 86/10, pp. 727-735.

Michaelowa, K. (2002), *Teacher Job Satisfaction, Student Achievement, and the Cost of Primary Education in Francophone Sub-Saharan Africa*, Hamburg Institute of International Economics.

Milanowski, A. (2005), "Split roles in performance evaluation: A field study involving new teachers", *Journal of Personnel Evaluation in Education,* Vol. 18/3, pp. 153-159.

Munson, B.R. (1998), "Peers observing peers: The better way to observe teachers", *Contemporary Education*, Vol. 69/2: pp. 108-110.

Nusche, D.L. et al. (2011a), *OECD Reviews of Evaluation and Assessment in Education: Norway*, OECD Publishing, Paris, *http://dx.doi. org/10.1787/9789264117006-en*.

Nusche, D. et al. (2011b), *OECD Reviews of Evaluation and Assessment in Education: Sweden,* OECD Publishing, Paris, *http://dx.doi.org/10.1787/9789264116610-en.*

Odden, A. and **C. Busch** (1998), *Financing Schools for High Performance: Strategies for Improving the Use of Educational Resources,* Jossey-Bass, San Francisco, CA.

OECD (2014), *TALIS 2013 Technical Report, www.oecd.org/edu/school/TALIS-technical-report-2013.pdf.*

OECD (2013a), *Synergies for Better Learning: An International Perspective on Evaluation and Assessment,* OECD Reviews of Evaluation and Assessment in Education, OECD Publishing, Paris, *http://dx.doi.org/10.1787/9789264190658-en.*

OECD (2013b), *PISA 2012 Results: What Makes Schools Successful? Resources, Policies and Practices (Volume IV)*, PISA, OECD Publishing, Paris, *http://dx.doi.org/10.1787/9789264201156-en.*

OECD (2011), *Lessons from PISA for the United States,* Strong Performers and Successful Reformers in Education, OECD Publishing, Paris, *http://dx.doi.org/10.1787/9789264096660-en.*

OECD (2010), *PISA Results 2009: What Makes a School Successful (Volume IV)*, OECD Publishing, Paris, *http://dx.doi.org/10.1787/9789264091559-en.*

OECD (2009), *Creating Effective Teaching and Learning Environments: First Results from TALIS*, OECD Publishing, Paris, *http://dx.doi.org/10.1787/9789264072992-en.*

OECD (2005), *Teachers Matter: Attracting, Developing and Retaining Effective Teachers,* Education and Training Policy, OECD Publishing, Paris, *http://dx.doi.org/10.1787/9789264018044-en.*

Peterson, K., C. Wahlquist and **K. Bone** (2000), "Student surveys for school teacher evaluation", *Journal of Personnel Evaluation in Education* 14/2, pp.135-153.

Peterson, K. et al. (2003), "Parent surveys for teacher evaluation", *Journal of Personnel Evaluation in Education*, Vol. 17, pp. 317-330.

Richards, J.C. and **C. Lockhart** (1992), "Teacher development through peer observation", *TESOL Journal*, Vol. 1/2, pp. 7-10.

Rockoff, J.E. (2008), "Does mentoring reduce turnover and improve skills of new employees: Evidence from teachers in New York City", NBER Working Paper, No. 13868.

Rosenholtz, S. (1989), *Teachers' Workplace: The Social Organization of Schools,* Longman, New York, NY.

Santiago, P. and **F. Benavides** (2009), *Teacher Evaluation: A Conceptual Framework and Examples of Country Practices*, OECD Publishing, Paris, *http://www.oecd.org/education/school/44568106.pdf.*

Sargent, T.C. and **E. Hannum** (2009), "Doing more with less: Teacher professional learning communities in resource-constrained primary schools in rural China", *Journal of Teacher Education*, Vol. 60/3, pp. 258-276, *http://dx.doi.org.ezp.lib.unimelb.edu.au/10.1177/0022487109337279.*

Smith, T. and **R. Ingersoll** (2004), "What are the effects of induction and mentoring on beginning teacher turnover?", *American Educational Research Journal*, Vol. 41, pp. 681-714.

Triant, B. (2001), "Autonomy and innovation: How do Massachusetts charter school principals use their freedom?", Thomas B. Fordham Foundation, *www.edexcellence.net/publications/autonomy.html* (accessed 20 Feb 2013).

Vieluf, S., et al. (2012), *Teaching Practices and Pedagogical Innovation: Evidence from TALIS,* OECD Publishing, Paris, *http://dx.doi.org/10.1787/9789264123540-en.*

Wilkerson, D. et al. (2000), "Validation of student, principal, and self-ratings in 360 feedback for teacher evaluation", *Journal of Personnel Evaluation in Education*, Vol. 14/2, pp.179-192.

Witte, J.F. (1990), "Choice and control: An analytical overview", in *Choice and Control in American Education Volume 1: The Theory of Choice and Control in Education,* W.H. Clune and J.F. Witte (eds.), Falmer Press, London, pp. 11-46.

Woessmann, L. et al. (2009), *School Accountability, Autonomy and Choice Around the World,* Edward Elgar Publishing, Cheltenham.

Zanderigo, T., E. Dowd and **S. Turner** (2012), *Delivering School Transparency in Australia: National Reporting through My School,* Strong Performers and Successful Reformers in Education, OECD Publishing, Paris, *http://dx.doi.org/10.1787/9789264175884-en.*

Zwart, R.C. et al. (2007), "Experienced teacher learning within the context of reciprocal peer coaching", *Teachers and Teaching: Theory and Practice*, Vol. 13/2, pp. 165-187, *http://expertisecentrumlerenvandocenten.nl/files/TTTP_collegiale_coaching_0.pdf.*

6

Examining Teacher Practices and Classroom Environment

This chapter examines different types of teaching practices, teachers' beliefs and classroom environments. Specifically, the chapter examines the teaching and professional practices that teachers report using in their work and their beliefs about the nature of teaching and learning. The chapter provides analyses of teaching environments and explores the relationship between teaching practices, teachers' beliefs, classroom environments and school leadership. Implications for policy and practice are discussed based on the results presented.

Highlights

- Teachers who report participation in professional development activities involving individual and collaborative research, observation visits to other schools or a network of teachers are more likely to report using teaching practices that involve small groups, projects requiring more than a week for students to complete and information and computer technology (ICT).

- Roughly two-thirds of teachers report a positive classroom climate, which corresponds to a greater likelihood of using teaching practices involving small groups, projects requiring more than a week and ICT. Thus, the majority of teachers perceive that they experience a good learning environment in which to engage students in learning.

- Regarding student assessment practices, teachers generally report frequent observation of student work accompanied by immediate feedback and development and administration of their own assessments. However, wide variations across countries were reported on these and other assessment practices.

- Teachers' beliefs about teaching and learning are mostly a function of differences in the teachers themselves. School environment variables are not a major factor in explaining teachers' beliefs about teaching and learning.

- Overall, teachers spend about 80% of their time on actual teaching and learning. However, approximately one in four teachers in more than half of the participating countries report losing at least 30% of their time to classroom disruptions and administrative tasks. These findings indicate that teachers in several countries could benefit from help with respect to managing classroom disruptions.

INTRODUCTION

Quality instruction encompasses the use of different teaching practices, and the teaching practices deployed by teachers can play a role in student learning and motivation to learn (Seidel and Shavelson, 2007). Furthermore, teachers' decisions on what to do in the classroom are dependent on many factors. For example, teachers often make decisions about pedagogical practices to use in the classroom based on their beliefs about the nature of teaching and learning (Beyer and Davis, 2008; Pajares, 1992; Speer, 2008). Moreover, many teaching practices may be affected by other factors, including teacher characteristics (such as, gender, subjects taught, level of formal education and training and professional development training), school climate and classroom climate (OECD, 2009; Richardson, 1996; Richardson et al., 1991; Shapiro and Kilbey, 1990). A positive classroom climate is cultivated when teachers work with their students to develop a safe, respectful and supportive environment that facilitates student motivation and learning, while a positive school climate reflects a good atmosphere and social networks in a school (Brophy and Good, 1986; Loukas and Murphy, 2007; Woolfolk, 2010). Positive school and classroom climates will result in less disruptive behaviours and result in more time for teaching and learning (Guardino and Fullerton, 2010; Martella, Nelson and Marchand-Martella, 2003).

Another related aspect of teachers' professional practice is the degree to which teachers work together to improve student learning. Co-operation among teachers can facilitate resource sharing, including the exchange of ideas (Clement and Vandenberghe, 2000; Murawski and Swanson, 2001). Teachers' professional practices are also related to some of the factors previously identified. For example, teachers who receive more professional development are more likely to co-operate with other teachers for teaching support and on ideas to improve teaching (OECD, 2009).

Figure 6.1 provides a framework for the relationship between teaching practices, teacher beliefs, school- and classroom-level environments and impacts on student learning and teachers' job-related attitudes. The non-directionality of the relationships shown in the figure is indicative of the bidirectional nature of the relationships between the variables.[1]

Theoretical background, review of literature and analytical framework

One of the key goals of the OECD Teaching and Learning International Survey (TALIS) is to examine teaching practices that teachers report using in the classroom and how these practices relate to the beliefs that teachers hold and the environments in which teachers work. Hence, this section of the chapter presents a framework for the relationship between teaching practices, teachers' beliefs, classroom environment, school climate and job-related attitudes. Although TALIS is not designed to explore student achievement and motivation to learn, as shown in the previous TALIS report (OECD, 2009), the framework provides a holistic picture of how teacher-related factors can enhance student learning and motivation.

■ Figure 6.1 ■
Framework for the analysis of teaching pratices and beliefs[1]

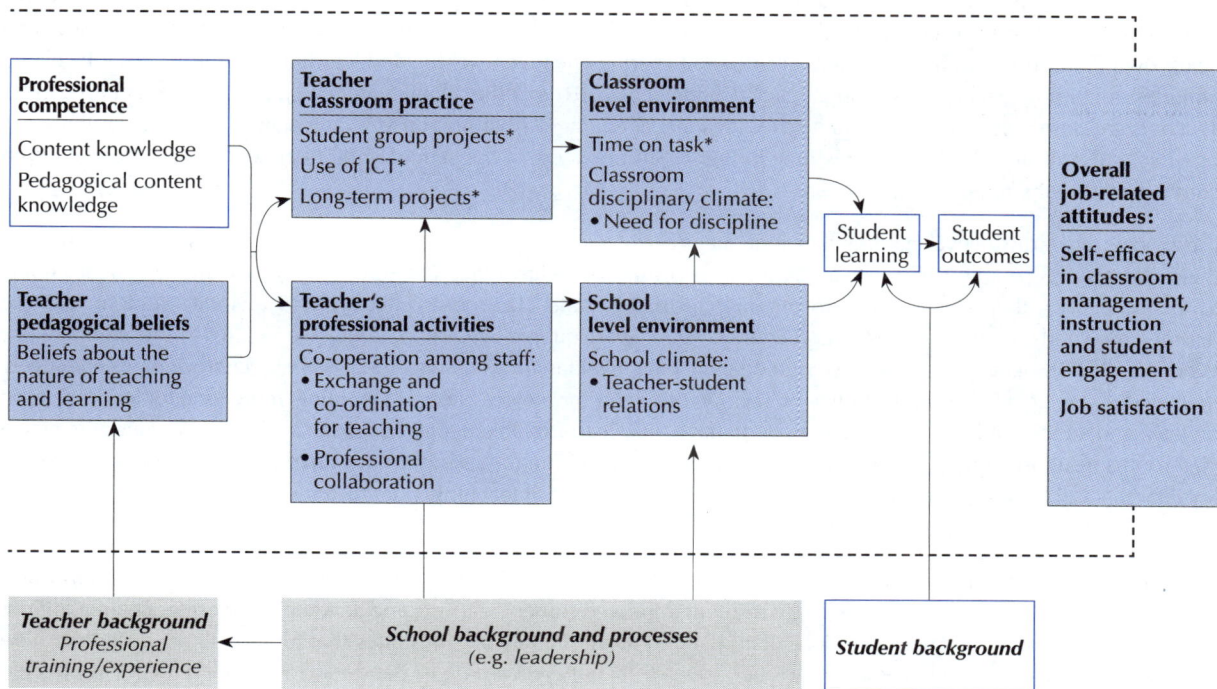

1. Constructs that are covered by the survey are highlighted in blue; single-item measures are indicated with an asterisk (*).

Because teaching shapes the future of the young, educators and policy makers in many countries seek to understand and support effective teaching practices that can facilitate student learning and achievement. Certain teaching practices (or strategies) engender effective classroom learning (Hattie, 2003; Hattie and Timperley, 2007; Marzano, 1998; Marzano, Pickering, and Pollock, 2001). For example, in a report on research-based strategies, Marzano, Pickering and Pollock (2001) reported on effective teaching practices for increasing student achievement. These include co-operative learning activities, summarising and note taking, the use of questioning and so forth. One important distinction is between active and passive teaching strategies, which differ in the degree to which students are engaged in the process of learning. When teaching is characterised mainly by strategies involving lecturing, with very little student involvement, such strategies are said to be passive. Conversely, when teachers design instructions such that students play a central role in the learning process, such strategies are known as active teaching practices (or strategies). In active teaching, a teacher may ask students to discuss a concept in groups or engage in concept mapping or some reflective activities that require deep thinking (Adesope and Nesbit, 2013; Orlich et al., 2013). A number of studies point to the positive effect of using active teaching strategies in the classroom. Indeed, there is widespread use of active, co-operative and project-based learning strategies that have been found to improve student learning (Dunlosky et al., 2013; Johnson and Johnson, 2009).

Although there is no doubt that effective teaching practices engender student learning and motivation, the teaching practices that teachers actually use in the classroom hinge on several important factors, including teachers' beliefs about teaching and learning. Teachers tend to structure their classrooms according to their beliefs about effective teaching and learning, including how they should carry out their work, how their students learn and how to structure lessons and classrooms to enhance learning. Teachers who believe, for example, that students learn better through group work on projects might engage students more in small group projects or project-based activities. Beliefs that do not align with evidence-based, effective theories of teaching and learning may lead to teaching practices that are inappropriate and ineffective (Lefrançois, 2000). Hence, a related goal of this chapter is to uncover how teaching practices are related to teachers' beliefs.

Teaching practices and teachers' beliefs are sometimes rooted in personal experiences that are shaped by cultural norms and also can be formed through information acquired via educational training as well as socialisation in the school in which a teacher works. Hence, this chapter explores teaching practices and how they are influenced by teacher characteristics and backgrounds as well as where variances in responses lie (teacher, school or country level). The framework also explores the relationship between teacher co-operation and school leadership factors. Research has shown that school climate plays a major role in fostering effective teaching and learning and influences job-related attitudes, including teacher stress and efficacy (Chong et al., 2010; Collie, Shapka and Perry, 2012; Cohen et al., 2009). Teachers are positively influenced when school leaders encourage collaboration among teachers, students, families and other school staff. Such collaborations may influence all members of the school and enhance not only the classroom climate but also the entire school climate.

Classrooms have distinctive features that influence learning. Teachers are often concerned with how best to manage their classrooms, promote learning and minimise disruptive behaviours. The term "classroom management" refers to all the actions that teachers take to organise instruction and classrooms effectively to facilitate student learning (Emmer and Evertson, 2009; Evertson and Emmer, 2009; Evertson and Weinstein, 2006; Moore, 2014; Woolfolk, 2010). Woolfolk (2010) suggests three positive outcomes of effective classroom management. When classrooms are effectively managed and relatively free of disruptive behaviours, students have more access to learning, more time for learning (time on task) and a better ability to self-regulate or manage their learning. Taken together, these positive outcomes of effective classrooms result in higher academic achievement for students. The framework in this chapter also explores classroom-level factors, such as how teachers spend their class time in terms of teaching, administrative tasks and keeping order in the classroom, as well as the classroom disciplinary climate.

Student academic performance and learning is beyond the scope of TALIS. Nevertheless, the framework demonstrates how the previously mentioned factors might result in improved student learning and academic performance. In addition, although this chapter does not cover job-related attitudes, the framework illustrates that all the factors described here can result in improved teacher self-efficacy and job satisfaction. According to Bandura (1990), self-efficacy is affected through reciprocal interaction between cognition, behaviour and the environment. Thus, social cognitive theory predicts that a teacher's behaviour will be shaped through the interactions between their beliefs, behaviour (practices) and environment (classrooms) (Bandura, 1989). Indeed, Klassen and Chiu (2010) found that teachers experience an ongoing commitment towards the profession when they have high self-efficacy, believing in their capabilities to apply appropriate learning strategies. (See Chapter 7 for a discussion of such job-related attitudes.)

The relationships between teaching practices and associated factors are not linear. For example, successful teaching practices may lead to changes in beliefs, and the beliefs that teachers hold can in turn drive teaching practices (Pajares, 1992; Sheen and O'Neill, 2005; Smagorinsky et al., 2004). The chapter uses representative data from TALIS countries to explore the relationships between teaching practices and the previously mentioned factors. Specifically, this chapter seeks to understand the profiles of teaching practices and how those profiles relate to teaching beliefs and teacher characteristics (including initial training and professional development). In addition, the chapter presents profiles of teachers' professional practices (including teacher collaboration) and how these relate to teacher characteristics and school climate.

Organisation of the chapter

This chapter begins by looking at the profiles of teachers' teaching and professional practices (which include teacher collaboration) and then explores how teaching practices relate to teaching beliefs, teacher characteristics (including initial training and professional development) and classroom context. The chapter continues with a discussion of how teachers' professional practices relate to teacher characteristics, school leadership and school climate. The next section looks at how teachers spend their time and then discusses the relationship between teachers' working time and the school climate. The analyses in this chapter also try to take into account the degree to which teacher, school or country factors contribute to the variances in teachers' beliefs, teacher co-operation and classroom environment.

Classroom teaching practices

Teaching practices are linked to a host of factors such as teaching beliefs, professional development training and teacher characteristics (OECD, 2009; Vieluf et al., 2012). Teaching practices deployed by teachers can play a significant role in the degree to which students learn. This section provides a description of teaching practices reported by teachers participating in TALIS.

The TALIS survey asked teachers to identify a particular class from their teaching schedule and then respond to a series of questions about the frequency with which they used a number of practices in this target class (Table 6.1). As shown in Figure 6.2, of the eight practices examined, the two types of practices that teachers report using most frequently on average across countries are presenting a summary of recently learned content and checking students' exercise books or homework. On average, more than 70% of teachers across TALIS countries report engaging in any of these types of practices frequently or in all or nearly all lessons. Teachers in Iceland, however, report presenting a summary of recently learned content in their classes much less frequently than average (only 38% report doing this frequently or in all their lessons). Similarly, compared with the average, many fewer teachers in Iceland (47%), but also in Korea (53%), Sweden (51%) and Flanders (Belgium) (53%), report checking students' exercise books or homework frequently or in all lessons.

On average, more than two-thirds of teachers (68%) across countries report that they frequently refer to a problem from everyday life to demonstrate why new knowledge is useful. Using this practice can provide students with an idea of why the topic they are learning about is relevant and how it might be useful in their own lives. However, less than half of the teachers in Iceland (40%), Korea (50%) and Sweden (49%) report doing this.

More than two-thirds of teachers (67%) on average report that they frequently let students practice similar tasks until every student has understood the subject matter, though less than half of the teachers in Iceland (48%), Japan (32%) and Korea (48%) report this.

Less than half of teachers (44%) on average report regularly giving different work to those students having difficulties learning and/or those who can advance faster. The use of this practice especially seems to vary among countries, with only 20% of teachers in Korea and the Netherlands using it frequently or in every lesson, while 67% of teachers in Norway and Abu Dhabi (United Arab Emirates) report doing so. This can be a challenging – yet increasingly necessary – task for teachers. It also requires additional planning and preparation for each lesson to provide multiple tasks for students that progress at different rates.

The three remaining practices presented in Table 6.1 and Figure 6.2 are discussed in more detail below.

■ Figure 6.2 ■

Teaching practices

Percentage of lower secondary education teachers who report using the following teaching practices[1]

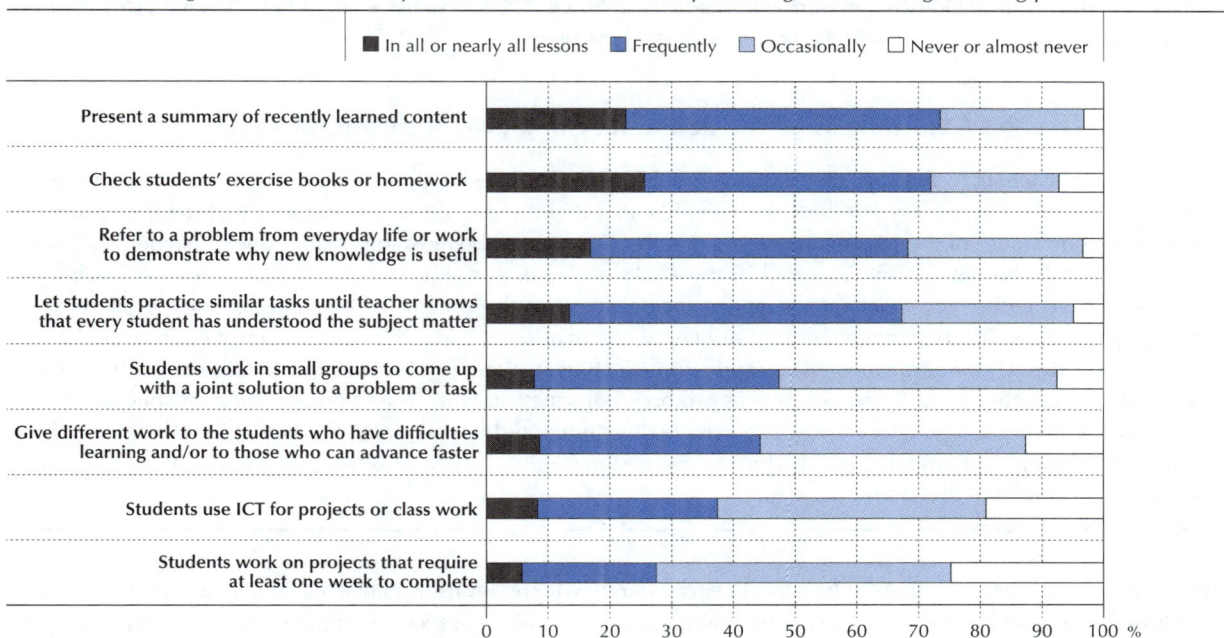

1. These data are reported by teachers and refer to a randomly chosen class they currently teach from their weekly timetable.
Items are ranked in descending order, based on the percentage of lower secondary education teachers who use the following teaching practices "frequently" or "in all or nearly all lessons".
Source: OECD, TALIS 2013 Database, Tables 6.1 and 6.1.Web.
StatLink ⟨⟩ http://dx.doi.org/10.1787/888933041934

Box 6.1 discusses the teaching practices reported by primary and upper secondary school teachers for those countries with available data.

Box 6.1. **Teaching practices used in primary and upper secondary schools**

Tables 6.1.a and 6.1.b report the percentages of teachers who use certain teaching practices frequently or in all or nearly all of their lessons in primary and upper secondary education.

On average across the countries that participated in both the primary and lower secondary surveys, a higher percentage of primary school teachers (84%) than lower secondary school teachers (72%) report checking students' exercise books or homework. More teachers at a primary level also report giving different work to students who can advance faster or have learning difficulties (66%) than their peers in lower secondary schools (44%). This difference is especially apparent in Flanders (Belgium), where 74% of primary teachers report using this practice frequently or in every lesson, whereas only 28% of lower secondary teachers do. As with lower secondary school teachers, the practices reported by the fewest primary teachers as being used frequently include giving students projects that take a week to complete and using ICT. The notable exception is found with primary teachers in Mexico, 84% of whom report assigning projects that require more than a week to their pupils (as opposed to 31% of primary teachers across the six countries surveyed).

Less variation is seen between teachers of upper and lower secondary schools. Across countries where data are available for both levels, fewer upper secondary school teachers report frequently giving different work to struggling or advanced students (35% vs. 44%) and more upper secondary school teachers than lower secondary school teachers report that students frequently use ICT (57% vs. 37%).

The three practices remaining – involving students working in small groups, projects that take more than a week to complete and projects requiring students to work with ICT) – are those on which this chapter focuses. As discussed earlier in this chapter, the literature suggests that these practices can be conceptualised as active practices. The choice of these teaching practices does not suggest that they are always effective for learning. As with other teaching strategies, their effectiveness largely depends on how they are implemented in the classroom (Chang and Lee, 2010; Johnson and Johnson, 2009; Parsons, Dodman and Burrowbridge, 2013; Prince, 2004; Schmidt et al., 2009). Box 6.2 provides more details regarding the rationale behind the choice of these three practices.

Box 6.2. **Analysis of the active teaching practice items in TALIS**

TALIS asked teachers to indicate the frequency with which they used eight teaching practices throughout the year in a specific target class. An item analysis indicated that three of the eight practices had the largest item discrimination values of the set. This suggested that these items may be most informative about teachers' beliefs compared with the other items included in the TALIS questionnaire. Additionally, the literature on teaching practices cited earlier in this chapter supports the selection of these items as being representative of active teaching practices. The three items were *(a)* students work on projects that require at least one week to complete, *(b)* students use ICT for projects or class work, and *(c)* students work in small groups to come up with a joint solution to a problem or task. These practices promote skills that students should possess for academic success and may be highly sought after in post-secondary education and the workplace. See Box 2.5 in Chapter 2 for more information regarding interpreting logistic regression results and Annex B for more information about the analyses performed in this chapter.

Figure 6.3 displays the proportions of teachers in each country who report using active teaching practices frequently or in all lessons (see also Table 6.1). As the figure shows, teachers in most countries report more use of practices involving small-group work compared with ICT or projects lasting longer than one week. Nearly half (47%) of the teachers on average report frequently using practices involving students working in small groups. In contrast, just over a third of teachers on average (37%) report using practices involving ICT frequently, and just over one-quarter (27%) report using practices involving projects that required at least one week to complete. In Australia, Chile, Denmark, Mexico, Norway

and Abu Dhabi (United Arab Emirates), at least two of the active teaching practices were reported to be used frequently by more than half of the teachers. Box 6.3 provides an example of government support for programmes dedicated to improving classroom practice using ICT.

■ Figure 6.3 ■
Teaching practices by country

Percentage of lower secondary education teachers who report using the following teaching practices "frequently" or "in all or nearly all lessons"[1]

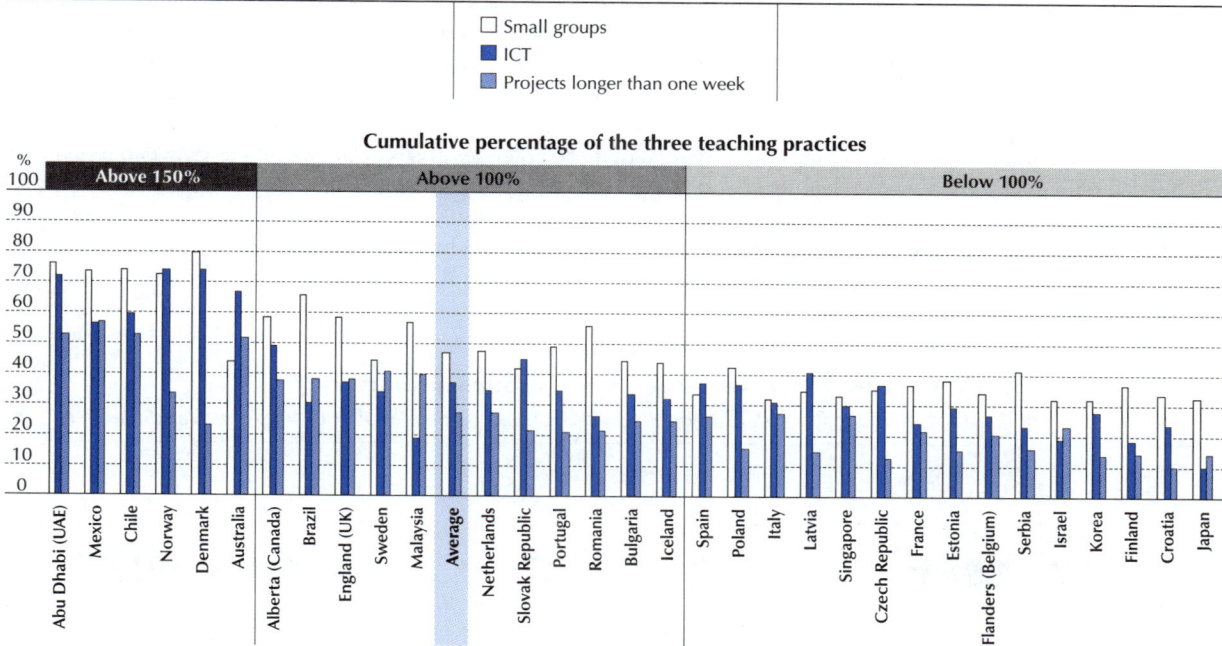

☐ Small groups
■ ICT
☐ Projects longer than one week

Cumulative percentage of the three teaching practices

1. These data are reported by teachers and refer to a randomly chosen class they currently teach from their weekly timetable.
Countries are ranked in descending order, based on the overall percentage of teachers who are using the three teaching practices "frequently" or "in all or nearly all lessons".
Source: OECD, TALIS 2013 Database, Table 6.1.
StatLink http://dx.doi.org/10.1787/888933041953

Box 6.3. Government support for system-wide use of ICT in the classroom: Portugal

From 2007 to 2011, Portugal made significant investments in technology for education, equipping schools with lab computers, interactive whiteboards, wireless networks and fiber broadband connections. This investment was a top priority for the government under its "Technological Plan", which also provided laptops for more than 1.5 million primary and secondary school students and teachers through the well-publicised Magellan and e-escola programmes. This unprecedented access to technology sparked a wave of innovative teaching practices in many classrooms across the country, creating new opportunities for use of and access to technology, particularly for students coming from lower income backgrounds. Post implementation, it was noted that further adoption of these innovative practices could have been facilitated by increased teacher professional development and exchange of good practices.

Although the government is no longer funding these initiatives, the classroom innovations remain, and the country has seen a difference in their students' results on the 2009 Programme for International Student Assessment (PISA), in particular. Students in Portugal ranked first in terms of their reported level of confidence in completing high-level ICT tasks, as well as in other ICT-related skills, such as the ability to create multimedia presentations (OECD, 2010).

Source: Portuguese Government, 2014.

What accounts for the variance in teaching practices?

The analyses in this section examine the extent to which the variance observed in teaching practices is accounted for by factors at the country, school or teacher level. In other words, is the variation in use of these practices accounted for more by factors related to the country, the school where a teacher works (e.g. the culture or composition of teachers in the school) or by characteristics of each individual teacher? Knowing the source of variation contributes to the understanding of which variables (e.g. school climate or individual teacher behaviour) may explain practices and where efforts should be directed to change practices.[2]

Figure 6.4 displays variance at the country, school and teacher level for teaching practices involving the use of small groups of students, projects requiring more than a week to complete and the integration of technology into the classroom. This figure displays how much of the variation in responses to these teaching practice items is accounted for at each level of the sample. Such figures point to whether the differences in responses are mostly due to factors at the teacher level, the school level or the country level. Across all three teaching practices, the conclusion is the same: Most of the total variance seen in teachers' reports of these practices arises from differences between individual teachers. Variance attributable to school-level and country-level differences is minimal. Therefore, efforts to change teaching practices are more likely to have an impact if directed towards individual teachers. The variance components for the remaining five teaching practices examined in TALIS are similar in breakdown to the three practices on which this chapter focuses.

■ Figure 6.4 ■

Distribution of variance – small groups, projects, ICT

Distribution of variance in lower secondary education across the three levels of country, school and teacher

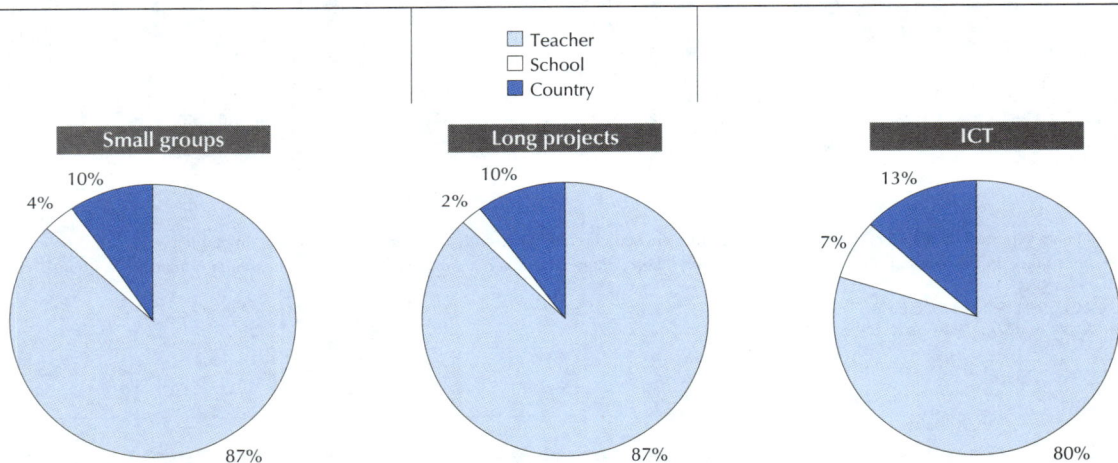

It is noteworthy that the use of practices involving ICT seems to be more dependent on school factors than the other two types of practices examined, ostensibly because ICT requires a lot of financial commitment by the school. Variability in the reported use of practices involving small groups and projects requiring more than one week appears to be explained almost exclusively at the teacher level. In contrast, up to one-fifth of the variability in the use of technology is accounted for by school-level factors (7%) and by country-level factors (13%). So, although in general the use of specific practices tends to be mostly a function of the individual teacher, when it comes to practices that require more resources, such as the use of ICT, school- and country-level factors tend to play slightly more of a role.

These findings are consistent with the TALIS 2008 report, which concluded that most of the variability in teachers' reported use of teaching practices originated at the individual teacher level. Future work examining which school-level factors account for the differences between schools is forthcoming in subsequent TALIS publications, which will use school-level data available from PISA 2012.

Given the importance of teacher characteristics in shaping teachers' use of teaching practices, the following section examines the relationships between these active practices and teacher characteristics, teachers' professional development and classroom context. Box 6.2 provides details on the specific teaching practices items retained for these analyses and on the analyses conducted.

Teacher characteristics

This section examines the possible relationships between each of the three types of practices and teacher characteristics, such as gender, subjects taught, years of experience, level of education and feelings of preparedness for the content, pedagogy and practice in the subject taught.

In some countries, gender appears to be related to the likelihood of teachers reporting using these practices frequently, all other factors being equal (Tables 6.2 to 6.4). In 14 countries, female teachers are more likely than their male counterparts to report frequently using practices that involve having students work in small groups (Table 6.2). Similarly, female teachers in nine countries are more likely to report frequently using practices that involved projects that require at least one week to complete, although the opposite was the case in Flanders (Belgium) (Table 6.3). Finally, male teachers in four countries (Finland, France, Japan and Korea) are more likely to report frequently using ICT, while female teachers are more likely to use this practice in three countries (Brazil, Bulgaria and Mexico) (Table 6.4).

TALIS data suggest that a teacher's subject field appears to be related to the teacher's choice of teaching practices. With some exceptions, humanities, mathematics and science teachers are less likely than teachers in other subject fields to report using practices involving small group work. Although in seven countries, humanities teachers are more likely to report the frequent use of practices involving small groups, in ten other countries they are less likely to report this. In only two countries (Iceland and Abu Dhabi [United Arab Emirates]) are mathematics and science teachers more likely to report frequently using small group work, while in 15 other countries these teachers are actually less likely to do so (Table 6.2).[3]

As mentioned earlier, fewer teachers on average report that they frequently use projects requiring more than a week than report using other types of practices (Table 6.1). In all countries, mathematics and science teachers, compared with teachers in other subjects, are less likely to report using projects that require at least one week to complete (Table 6.3). Similarly, humanities teachers in most countries are also less likely to report using these types of projects than are teachers in other subject areas. Given the low likelihood of teachers reporting the use of these practices in mathematics, science and humanities, compared with other content areas, a finer-grained analysis could be useful to examine the malleable factors within each content area that are related to the use of these practices. For instance, there may be factors related to teaching mathematics that are not present in other domains, such as the humanities, that create barriers to using such techniques. Future studies examining these three teaching practices and related classroom- and teacher-level variables within individual mathematics, science and humanities content areas would provide a clearer picture of their use.

Moreover, the frequent use of ICT in the classroom also does not appear to be taking place in mathematics and science. Only in Denmark and Norway are mathematics or science teachers more likely than their colleagues in other subject areas to report using practices with ICT. In 19 other countries, mathematics and science teachers are significantly less likely to report frequent use of ICT in their practices. In a few countries, teachers of humanities are more likely than other teachers to report frequent use of ICT by students (Australia, Denmark, Iceland, Norway, Sweden and Alberta [Canada]), but in 14 other countries, the opposite is the case (Table 6.4).

Teachers' years of experience does not appear to be related to the likelihood that they will report using any of these types of practices. Significant (though small and inconsistent) results were found in only a small number of countries.

Only a handful of countries exhibit a relationship between teachers' highest level of education and their likelihood to report frequently using these three types of practices, but this relationship is inconsistent across these countries. For example, in the Czech Republic, teachers with higher levels of education (i.e. the equivalent of ISCED level 5A – a Bachelor's degree – or above) are about 40% less likely to report the frequent use of practices involving small groups and about 28% less likely to use ICT than are teachers with lower levels of education, while in Chile, teachers with higher levels of education are 53% more likely to report frequently using ICT, and in Mexico they are 65% more likely to report frequently using practices involving small group work. The inconsistency of the relationships precludes drawing any major inferences across the countries. Future research specifically with TALIS may further examine the relationship between teachers' level of education and the use of certain teaching practices.

Finally, the analyses examined the associations between teachers' reported use of classroom practices and how well prepared teachers feel they are in the areas of content, pedagogy and classroom practices. Of these three relationships, teachers' feelings of preparedness for pedagogy appear to be the most related to the reported frequent use of practices involving small group work (Tables 6.2 and 6.4). In contrast, teachers' feelings of preparedness for content are not highly related to teachers' reports of frequent use of the selected practices in their classroom. Finally, positive associations between feelings of preparedness for classroom practice and reported frequent use of these three selected practices can be observed in a small number of countries. In Japan, Korea and Singapore, teachers who feel more prepared for classroom practice are more likely (in these cases between 46% and 64% more likely) to report frequently using small group work in their classroom (Table 6.2). Moreover, in Singapore, Spain and England (United Kingdom), teachers who feel more prepared for classroom practice are more likely to report frequently using projects that require more than one week to complete (Table 6.3). Finally, in Croatia, the Czech Republic, Korea, Spain and England (United Kingdom), positive associations were observed for the reported frequent use of ICT (Table 6.4). In these countries, enhancing teachers' feelings of preparedness for classroom practice may help promote the frequent use of multiple forms of classroom practice. Observing colleagues' teaching, team teaching and being observed by and reflecting on teaching practices with a mentor might be ways that schools and countries could offer more support in the area of developing a teacher's confidence around his or her teaching practice.

The most consistent factor associated with the use of active learning is the subject matter taught. The consistent connection across all countries is related to the use of projects requiring a longer time to complete and teaching mathematics or humanities. In addition, gender may play a role in this relationship but only for a minority of countries. What is clear is that the use of active learning is largely related to the nature of the subject matter taught and whether it lends itself easily to the use of active learning. Teachers' reported confidence in preparedness in pedagogy of the subject matter they teach is more likely to be of relevance than is preparedness for the content or classroom practices. Future work may examine these examples to understand what unique training teachers receive and to encourage such feelings and use of teaching practices.

Professional development

Professional development examined in TALIS includes participation in workshops, conferences, classroom observations, qualification programmes, networking, collaboration and mentoring (see Chapter 4). TALIS data show that in many countries, teachers who participated in professional development activities are more likely to report the frequent use of the three types of teaching practices – involving small groups, projects taking longer than one week and the use of ICT (see Tables 6.5, 6.6 and 6.7).

As shown in Figure 6.5, the most consistent relationships across countries can be seen between participation in individual or collaborative research on a topic of interest and the reported use of practices involving projects that require at least one week to complete and practices involving the use of ICT. Participation in a network of teachers appears to be mostly relevant for the frequent use of practices involving small group work and projects involving the use of ICT (significant relationships found in 12 and 11 countries, respectively). Fewer, but still between five and seven countries, showed significant relationships between participation in mentoring or peer observation and coaching and the reported frequent use of all three types of active practices.

In countries where significant relationships were found, teachers who participated in these development activities were as much as twice as likely to report using the three teaching practices as were those teachers who did not engage in such development activities. Individual or collaborative research on a topic of interest showed positive associations across most countries, but especially in Norway, where teachers who took part in this activity were more likely to report frequently using all three practices compared with teachers not using such research: These teachers were 77% more likely to report frequently making use of practices involving small groups and projects requiring more than a week and almost twice as likely to report frequently using ICT practices. In Finland, teachers who took part in individual or collaborative research on a topic of interest were approximately twice as likely to report using practices involving small group work and ICT.

Across a number of countries, participation in a network of teachers is also related to an increased likelihood of reporting the frequent use of these three teaching practices. Similarly, in some countries, participation in observation visits to other schools is also positively related to the reported frequent use of the three practices (Tables 6.5 to 6.7). It is perhaps not surprising that teachers who participated in development activities were more likely to report frequently using the three teaching practices (practices involving small groups, projects requiring more than a week and the use of ICT).

■ Figure 6.5 ■

Relationships between teaching practices and professional development activities

Number of countries where a significant positive relationship is found between the reported use of the following teaching pratices and the reported participation in the following professional development activities in lower secondary education

	Small group practice	Projects that require at least one week to complete	Use of ICT
Participation in a network of teachers formed specifically for the professional development of teachers	12	6	11
Individual or collaborative research on a topic of interest	10	16	17
Mentoring and/or peer observation and coaching	7	7	5

Cells are shaded based on the number of countries where a significant positive relationship is found between the use of the teaching pratice and the professional development activity. Darker tones indicate a higher number of countries where a significant positive relationship is found.
Source: OECD, TALIS 2013 Database, Tables 6.5, 6.6 and 6.7.
StatLink http://dx.doi.org/10.1787/888933041991

It is likely that when teachers participate in observation visits to others schools, they may be exposed to other ways of using these teaching strategies and return to their classroom with more ideas on how to use them. Indeed, many countries are advancing professional development on effective use of these teaching practices. For example, there is a growing interest in making competency in the use of ICT a requirement for many teachers (Dexter and Riedel, 2003; Phelps and Graham, 2004).

Classroom context

The classroom context is an important factor to consider in examining the use of specific teaching practices, as it may well influence a teacher's choice of practices. Several contextual factors were examined in relation to the three selected teaching practices. Factors such as class size, the proportion of students in the class whose first language is different from the language of instruction, the proportion of low academic achievers or gifted students, the proportion of students with special needs and the classroom disciplinary climate (e.g. waiting for students to quiet down) were included in the analysis to examine their relationship to teachers' reported use of specific practices (Box 6.4). Note that these classroom-level data, including the reported teaching practices used, were all collected regarding a specific target class (results from these analyses are presented in Tables 6.8 to 6.10).

Box 6.4. **How classroom context is described in TALIS**

The TALIS questionnaire asks teachers about specific characteristics regarding a random class they teach. Details are gathered about class size, student composition (proportions of students whose first language is different from the language of instruction; low academic achievers or gifted students; and students with special needs or behavioural problems or who come from a disadvantaged socio-economic status (SES) and classroom disciplinary climate.

To assess the classroom disciplinary climate, TALIS asked teachers to indicate how strongly they agreed – on a four-point scale ranging from strongly disagree to strongly agree – with the following statements about the target class:

▪ When the lesson begins, I have to wait quite a long time for students to quiet down

▪ Students in this class take care to create a pleasant learning atmosphere

▪ I lose quite a lot of time because of students interrupting the lesson

▪ There is much disruptive noise in this classroom

See Annex B for more information about the construction of this complex index.

Of the factors examined across countries, classroom disciplinary climate was most consistently associated with the likelihood of reporting the frequent use of the three teaching practices across countries (Tables 6.8, 6.9 and 6.10). In almost all countries, teachers who reported a more positive classroom disciplinary climate were also more likely to report a frequent use of practices involving small group work and ICT. A relationship with the reported use of projects

requiring more than one week was found in fewer countries. One possible explanation of this less-prevalent link is that longer projects require work outside the classroom, and thus the likelihood of teachers using this tool may be less affected by classroom context. Not surprisingly, maintaining a well-behaved student body and classroom environment is related to being able to use practices involving small groups and ICT. When students are actively engaged, there are fewer classroom distractions and disciplinary issues. Teaching practices involving small groups, project-based learning or hands-on or experiential learning keep students engaged and may thus promote a positive classroom climate. Technology, when used effectively, can also promote experiential learning and keep students engaged.

When examining the relationships between the characteristics of students in a class (e.g. proportions of high or low achievers or of students with special needs)[4] and the use of the three teaching practices, analyses displayed interesting relationships. Teachers in a number of countries who reported a higher proportion of gifted students in their classrooms were more likely to report the frequent use of these teaching practices (ranging from 9 to 11 countries, depending on the practice). In contrast, classrooms with higher proportions of low academic achievers are associated with a lower likelihood that teachers in a number of countries reported the frequent use of these practices (between 6 and 10 countries, depending on the practice). This may be linked with the general climate of the classroom and the amount of time teachers have to spend on management rather than on teaching. Alternatively, teachers in these classrooms may believe that such active practices are not best suited for these students. Teachers with students of different ability distributions in their classroom may need different teaching practices to facilitate effective learning. In addition, while many countries are providing teachers with additional support to meet the needs of special-needs students, such support may not be provided for teachers who work with low-achieving students. Finally, in six countries (Finland, France, Israel, Japan, Norway and Flanders [Belgium]), teachers who report larger proportions of students with special needs in their target class are also more likely to report the frequent use of practices involving ICT in the classroom. A number of special-needs students depend on assistive technology devices to learn, so it is not uncommon for schools to invest in such technologies to support those students and for their teachers to develop teaching practices that involve the use of technology.

Class size seems to have a different relationship depending on the type of practice in question. For example, in five countries (the Czech Republic, France, Israel, Korea and Poland), teachers working in classes with more students tend to be slightly less likely to report the frequent use of practices involving small group work, while in five countries (Denmark, Estonia, Israel, Latvia and Sweden), teachers working with larger classes are slightly more likely to report the frequent use of ICT in their classroom (Tables 6.8 and 6.10). These results are not surprising considering the challenges of promoting small group discussions and student engagement when class size is large. In addition, teachers may use technologies such as clickers (or personal response systems) in large classes (Mayer et al., 2009).

TEACHERS' USE OF STUDENT ASSESSMENT

An important function of student assessment is to allow all students to show what they know and can do in an equitable way (Binkley et al., 2010; Gipps and Stobart, 2004). One way to ensure this is to use multiple assessment approaches and opportunities, including engaging students in their own assessment (OECD, 2013a). Also important is to ensure that teachers are well prepared to effectively ensure formative and summative assessment of students (OECD, 2013a). As seen in Chapter 4, a number of teachers report an unmet need for professional development in student evaluation and assessment practices (see Table 4.13). In particular, more than one in four teachers in Japan, Korea, Malaysia and Sweden identified this as an issue.

Although a full investigation of student assessment practices and their outcomes is beyond the scope of this cycle of TALIS, teachers were asked about the frequency with which they use different types of student assessment practices in a specific target class. This section reports on teachers' use of student assessment practices.

Figure 6.6 shows the average proportions of teachers who report using different student assessment practices in their classroom (see also Table 6.11). Teachers report making frequent use of a variety of assessment practices. On average, teachers in participating countries were most likely to report frequent observation of students accompanied by immediate feedback (80%) and the development and administration of their own assessments (68%). Roughly half of teachers report frequently providing written feedback in addition to summative marks on their students' assignments (55%), and roughly half of teachers also report calling on individual students to answer questions in front of the class (49%). Assessment practices that are used less frequently, including allowing students to evaluate their own progress (38%) and the administration of standardised tests (38%), are still reported by more than a third of teachers. The overall pattern of reported assessment practices suggests larger proportions of teachers are employing forms of assessment that would likely be formative in nature (e.g. observing students and providing immediate feedback) than primarily summative

(e.g. administering a standardised test), but that both forms of assessment are used widely. It appears that many teachers in the participating countries are using multiple assessment approaches and opportunities, which is more likely to gather a complete picture of student learning (OECD, 2013a).

■ Figure 6.6 ■
Teachers' use of student assessment practices

Percentage of lower secondary education teachers who report using the following methods of assessing student learning[1]

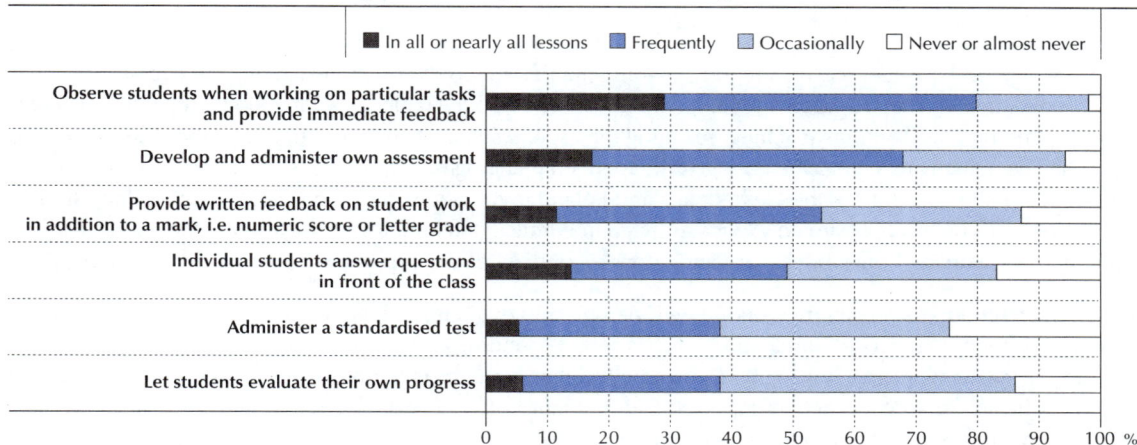

1. These data are reported by teachers and refer to a randomly chosen class they currently teach from their weekly timetable.
Items are ranked in descending order, based on the percentage of teachers who use the following methods of assessing student learning "frequently" or "in all or nearly all lessons".
Source: OECD, TALIS 2013 Database, Tables 6.11 and 6.11.Web.
StatLink ⬛⬛⬛ http://dx.doi.org/10.1787/888933042010

The reported use of assessment practices varies widely among countries. The proportions of teachers reporting frequent development and administration of their own assessments ranges from 29% in Japan to 93% in Brazil. Frequent standardised test administration is reported by 8% of teachers in France, compared with 71% in Latvia and Singapore. Only 5% of teachers in Iceland report calling on individual students to answer questions in front of the class, while 80% of the teachers in Italy do. The use of frequent written feedback on student work ranges from 22% in Latvia to 82% in Abu Dhabi (United Arab Emirates) and England (United Kingdom). In France and Iceland, 17% of teachers report frequently allowing students to evaluate their own progress. In England (United Kingdom), 69% of teachers report the frequent use of this practice. Finally, frequent student observation with immediate feedback is reported by 43% of the teachers in Japan, a higher proportion at the low end relative to the reports of other assessment practices, and 94% of those in Malaysia. Considering the power of feedback on student learning (Hattie and Timperley, 2007; Butler and Winne, 1995), teachers may be given additional support on how and when to give feedback to maximise learning.

Box 6.5 provides examples of systems where innovative forms of student assessment are promoted.

Box 6.5. Promoting the use of innovative assessments by teachers in Flanders (Belgium) and Mexico

In the Flemish Community of Belgium, the central education authorities are promoting a shift towards a "broad assessment culture", which includes a focus on formative assessment and new assessment approaches. It implies the use of "alternative" assessment approaches (compared with tests), including observation, portfolios, reflection sheets and self- and peer-assessment activities (Flemish Ministry of Education and Training, 2010).

In Mexico, the national curriculum (study plan) states that rubrics, checklists, registries of observations, written pieces of work, team projects, conceptual maps, portfolios and written and oral tests should be used. It also requires that students should be frequently involved in self-assessment and peer-assessment activities (Santiago et al., 2012).

Source: OECD 2013a.

TIME SPENT ON VARIOUS TASKS

Teachers' work is composed of a multitude of often competing responsibilities. This section examines teachers' reported working hours overall as well as the time they report spending on various work-related tasks during a typical week. It is important to note that these findings are meant to paint a picture of the typical work week across the entire teacher population in each country and therefore include responses from teachers working full time and part time. Of course, how teachers' working hours are regulated varies among countries and will also have an impact on their actual working hours (see OECD, 2013b). Table 6.12 presents teachers' reports on the number of hours they spend on various tasks throughout the work week.[5] Across countries, teachers report spending an average of 38 total hours working, ranging from 29 hours in Chile and Italy to 54 hours in Japan.[6]

Figure 6.7 shows that, as expected, teachers report spending the majority of their time teaching. The overall average is 19 hours per week, ranging from 15 hours in Norway to 27 hours in Chile (Table 6.12). It is noteworthy that teachers in Japan report spending only 18 hours teaching, meaning they spend substantially more time on other tasks related to their job than they do actually teaching. The average time spent on planning or preparing lessons is seven hours, ranging from five hours in Finland, Israel, Italy, the Netherlands and Poland to ten hours in Croatia. Time spent marking student work averages five hours but is approximately twice as much in Portugal (ten hours) and Singapore (nine hours). Box 6.6 discusses the reported working hours for primary and upper secondary teachers for those countries with available data.

Other tasks, such as school management, working with parents and extracurricular activities, take only an average of two hours per week each. Teachers in Korea and Malaysia report spending twice as much time than the TALIS average on general administrative work (six hours). It is also notable that extracurricular activities are an important aspect of teachers' work in Japan, where teachers report spending eight hours on extracurricular activities, far above the TALIS average of two hours. Box 6.7 provides an example of a Polish study of teachers' working time.

■ Figure 6.7 ■

Teachers' working hours

Average number of 60-minute hours lower secondary education teachers report having spent on the following activities during the most recent complete calendar week[1]

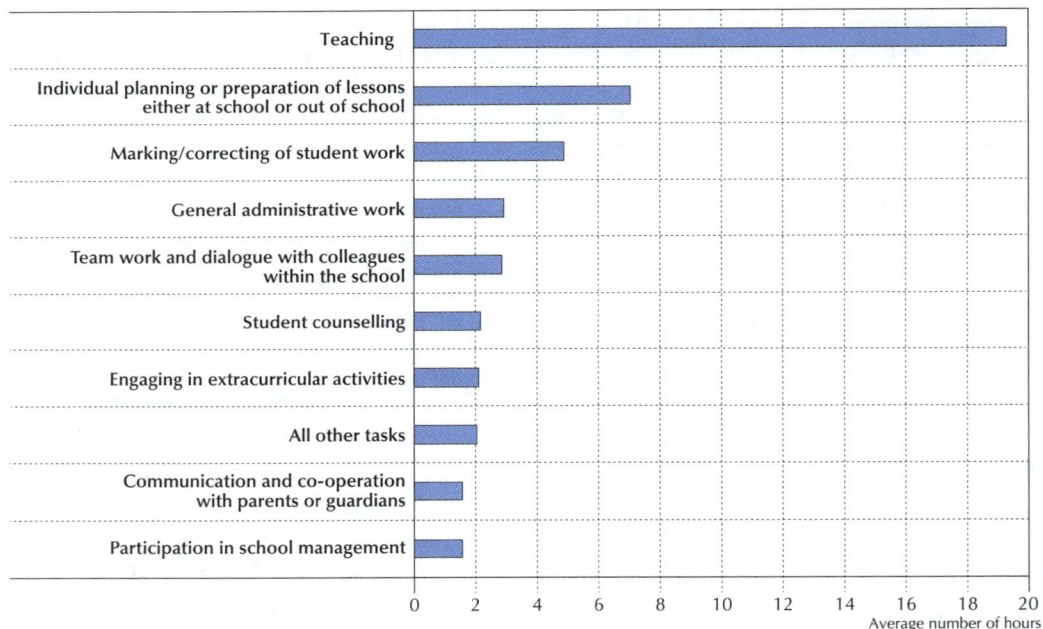

1. A "complete" calendar week is one that was not shortened by breaks, public holidays, sick leave, etc. Also includes tasks that took place during weekends, evenings or other off-classroom hours.
Items are ranked in descending order, based on the average number of 60-minute hours spent on the following activities during the most recent complete calendar week.
Source: OECD, TALIS 2013 Database, Table 6.12.
StatLink ⎘ http://dx.doi.org/10.1787/888933042029

Box 6.6. **Working hours in primary and upper secondary education**

Tables 6.12.a and 6.12.b show the working hours for teachers at the primary (ISCED 1) and upper secondary (ISCED 3) levels.

Across the countries with data for both levels, primary school teachers report having very similar working hours to their lower secondary school colleagues. The only difference of note is that, on average, primary school teachers report spending 2 hours more teaching per week (21 hours) than their peers in lower secondary schools (19 hours).

The division of teachers' time is also similar for upper secondary teachers, with the exception of time spent on teaching, where upper secondary teachers teach on average 1 hour less per week (18 hours) than their colleagues in lower secondary education (19 hours). In Denmark, Finland, Iceland and Mexico, upper secondary teachers report spending two to three hours less than their peers in lower secondary schools on teaching.

Box 6.7. **Teacher working time study in Poland**

A large survey on teachers' working time was conducted in Poland between November 2011 and December 2012. It covered teachers of general curriculum subjects from primary, lower secondary and upper secondary schools. Teachers took part in one of two components of the study: 2 617 teachers from 477 schools responded to a questionnaire administered by professional pollsters about their work activities during their previous day, and 4 762 teachers from 921 schools filled in an online self-report questionnaire. The analysis focused on five main tasks: Preparing and conducting classes, preparing and conducting extracurricular activities and marking students' assignments.

An important finding of this study was the non-linear relationship between time spent on teaching and total time spent on other major activities. For teachers who teach less than 18 hours a week, this relationship was proportional. In other words, the more time they teach, the more time they spend on other tasks, such as class preparation. But for teachers who teach 18 hours or more, the time spent on the four other key activities remained constant. In other words, for this group of teachers, teaching more hours per week did not lead to them reporting more hours on tasks such as class preparation or marking students assignments.

Source: Federowicz et al. (2013).

BELIEFS ABOUT THE NATURE OF TEACHING AND LEARNING

Teachers come into the classroom with pre-existing beliefs about how teaching and learning should be carried out. Such beliefs may be rooted in the teachers' prior experiences, including their pre-service training and in-service professional development (Kennedy, 1997; Richardson, 1996) and may affect practices teachers enact and how classroom environments are structured to promote student learning (Ertmer, 2005; Hofer and Pintrich, 1997). Some researchers have claimed that the teaching practices that teachers employ are shaped both by their teaching experiences in the classrooms and their pre-service training (Zeichner and Tabachnick, 1981). Although the literature on teacher education is replete with debates on the effectiveness of teacher education programmes, there is consensus that research efforts should be devoted to understanding the different components that make up high-quality programmes (Brouwer and Korthagen, 2005; Zeichner and Schulte, 2001). One such component is the need for teacher education programmes to attend to the beliefs of pre-service teachers about the nature of teaching and learning. For example, teacher preparation programmes may prepare teachers for learner-centred classrooms where learners are exposed to inquiry forms of learning. Pre-service teachers trained under such a model might likely adopt (or believe in) more constructivist, student-centred forms of learning. Indeed, there is evidence that teachers' beliefs as well as content and pedagogical knowledge can influence student learning (Darling-Hammond, 1998; Staub and Stern, 2002; Tatto and Coupland, 2003). In this section, the relationship between teachers' beliefs and school-level factors is examined along with the general profile of beliefs about learning.

Table 6.13 reports the percentages of teachers who agree with certain statements about how students learn and the role of the teacher in that process. As shown in Figure 6.8, overall there is strong agreement among teachers that it is their role to facilitate inquiry in the student (94% on average). Also, a majority of teachers believe that students should be allowed to think of solutions themselves before teachers show them (93%). The rate of agreement was mixed across the other variables, but it was generally above 80% across countries for beliefs related to students being able to find their own solutions and that thinking and reasoning skills are more important than content. Notable differences were in Italy, Norway and Sweden, where only between 45% and 59% of teachers agree that students learn best by trying to solve problems on their own. Along the same lines, the Netherlands shows the lowest average percentage of teachers who agree that reasoning skills are more important than content. Box 6.8 describes the data on teaching beliefs reported by primary and upper secondary teachers from those countries with available data.

■ Figure 6.8 ■
Teachers' beliefs about teaching and learning

Percentage of lower secondary education teachers who "agree" or "strongly agree" with the following statements

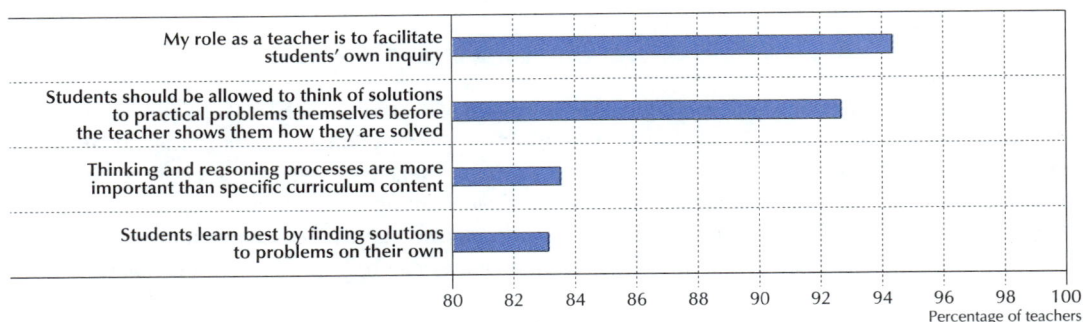

Items are ranked in descending order, based on the percentage of teachers who "agree" or "strongly agree" with the statement.
Source: OECD, TALIS 2013 Database, Table 6.13.
StatLink ᴹˢᴾ http://dx.doi.org/10.1787/888933042048

Box 6.8. **Beliefs about teaching in primary and upper secondary education**

Tables 6.13.a and 6.13.b present the percentages of primary (ISCED 1) and upper secondary (ISCED 3) teachers who agree with various statements regarding their beliefs about teaching.

Across levels of schooling, there is very little difference in teachers' beliefs about how students learn and how teachers contribute to that learning. This is true both across countries participating at each ISCED level and at the individual country level. The differences are at most three to four percentage points and are seen at the upper secondary level. For example, 53% of lower secondary school teachers in Norway believe that students learn best by finding solutions to problems on their own, while 57% of upper secondary school teachers in Norway have this belief. In Iceland, 91% of lower secondary school teachers believe that students should be allowed to think of solutions to problems before they are shown by the teacher, while only 87% of upper secondary school teachers feel this way. This similarity in response across level indicates that teachers' beliefs are more likely shaped by national culture than by the level of students they teach.

What accounts for the variance in teachers' beliefs?

As was done for the teaching practices earlier in this chapter, the variance was partitioned at the country, school and teacher level for the index of constructivist beliefs (Box 6.9). This enabled the determination of the extent to which these beliefs are related to the country in which a teacher resides, a school where the teacher works or the individual teacher. Understanding where the source of variance in teaching beliefs resides can assist in understanding what level of information is needed to better explain or understand these beliefs. For example, if the variance is associated mainly with the school in which a teacher is employed, to change beliefs it may be best to focus on interventions that change the school climate.

Box 6.9. **Description of the index of constructivist beliefs**

To assess the kinds of beliefs teachers hold about how students learn, TALIS 2013 employed an index of constructivist beliefs that asked teachers both about the ways they believe students learn best and how they as teachers might facilitate this learning. Teachers were asked on a four-point scale (ranging from strongly disagree to strongly agree) to indicate how strongly they agreed with the following items:

- My role as a teacher is to facilitate students' own inquiry
- Students learn best by finding solutions to problems on their own
- Students should be allowed to think of solutions to practical problems themselves before the teacher shows them how they are solved
- Thinking and reasoning processes are more important than specific curriculum content

See Annex B for more information about the construction and validation of this index

---

Figure 6.9 shows the separation of variance into three components for constructivist beliefs. As mentioned previously regarding Figure 6.4, the variance component figures display how much of the variation (in responses to the items that make up the index) is accounted for at each level of the sample. The majority (87%) of the total variance in constructivist beliefs lies in individual differences among teachers. Little variation can be attributed to school or country effects. Variance at the country level is approximately 12% and at the school level only 2%. These results imply that the socialisation that occurs within a school is minimally related to teachers' beliefs. Perhaps these beliefs are formed early in training and are stable. If changes in teachers' beliefs are needed, pre-service training or in-service interventions targeting the individual teacher may be most effective.

■ Figure 6.9 ■
Distribution of variance – constructivist beliefs
Distribution of variance in lower secondary education across the three levels of country, school and teacher.

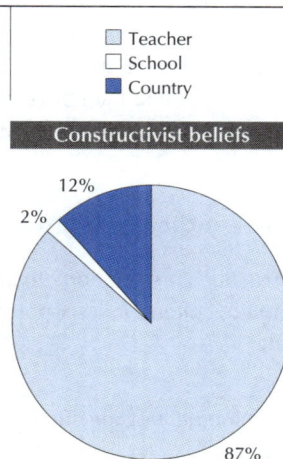

Source: OECD, TALIS 2013 Database.
StatLink http://dx.doi.org/10.1787/888933042067

BRINGING BELIEFS AND PRACTICES TOGETHER

The relationships between constructivist beliefs and the use of active teaching practices were explored in multiple regression models (see Box 3.5 for a general description of multiple regressions).[7] Table 6.14 presents the results of the analyses. In the examination of the regression models, a few findings emerged from the three predictors after background variables were controlled for. Across all countries, the practice of students working in small groups was significantly and positively related to constructivist teaching beliefs. In other words, teachers who report using practices that involved students working in small groups frequently or in all their lessons have stronger constructivist beliefs when compared with teachers who report using these types of practices never or occasionally.

Across countries, the reported frequency of having students persist in a project for more than one week is less strongly related to constructivist beliefs than is the practice of students working in small groups. Positive relationships were found in 15 countries, and a negative relationship was found in Korea. Teachers' reported frequency of using practices that require students to use ICT is positively related to their constructivist beliefs in 16 countries. In terms of magnitude of effect across variables, the reported use of practices involving small group work shows the strongest relationship, being moderately linked to constructivist beliefs, on average.

TEACHER PROFESSIONAL PRACTICES: CO-OPERATION AMONG STAFF

Many studies have examined the effect of productive co-operation among teachers as well as among students (DuFour, 2004; DuFour and Burnette, 2002; Murawski and Swanson, 2001; Slavin, 1995, 2009, 2013). DuFour (2004) used the term "professional learning communities" to depict a group of educators working "together to analyse and improve their classroom practice…engaging in an ongoing cycle of questions that promote deep team learning" (p. 9). However, some researchers have claimed that the effectiveness of co-operative practices depends on the structure of the collaboration (Clement and Vandenberghe, 2000). This section looks at the profiles of teachers' professional practices (including teacher collaboration) and how they might relate to teacher characteristics, school leadership and school climate.

Professional collaboration behaviours can be said to be more aligned with progressive forms of professionalism that emphasise an exchange of ideas at a deeper level (OECD, 2009). TALIS data show that these behaviours occur at lower rates when compared with simple exchange and co-ordination between teachers (this includes surface-level behaviours such as exchanging teaching materials with colleagues, having discussions about students or attending conferences together). Thus, it may be useful to consider how these behaviours can be improved within and across countries so that they occur at least as much as the other behaviours.

Table 6.15 and Figure 6.10 present percentages of responses from teachers who report never engaging in the activities captured in the eight items across the two co-operation indices (see Box 6.10 for a description of these indices). As shown in Figure 6.10, teachers are much more likely to report never engaging in activities associated with more complex forms of collaboration (on the right side of the figure) than in activities representing simpler forms of exchange and co-ordination (on the left side of the figure). This is consistent with the findings from TALIS 2008 (Vieluf et al., 2012).

It is striking that on average more than four teachers in ten report never teaching jointly (42%) or never observing other teachers' classes to provide feedback (45%). In particular, more than two-thirds of teachers in Bulgaria, the Netherlands and Spain report never engaging in joint teaching, while more than three-quarters of teachers in Brazil, France, Iceland, Spain and Flanders (Belgium) report never observing other teachers' classes.

Box 6.10. **Description of the indices used to measure co-operation**

TALIS 2013 used two indices to measure teacher co-operation. To measure exchange and co-ordination for teaching, teachers were asked to respond as to how often (on a six-point scale ranging from never to once a week or more) they do the following in their school:

- Exchange teaching materials with colleagues
- Engage in discussions about the learning development of specific students
- Work with other teachers in my school to ensure common standards in evaluations for assessing student progress
- Attend team conferences

To measure professional collaboration, teachers were asked to respond as to how often (on a six-point scale ranging from never to once a week or more) they do the following in their school:

- Teach jointly as a team in the same class
- Observe other teachers' classes and provide feedback
- Engage in joint activities across different classes and age groups (e.g. projects)
- Take part in collaborative professional learning

Further details on the indices can be found in Annex B.

■ Figure 6.10 ■
Teacher co-operation

Percentage of lower secondary education teachers who report never doing the following activities

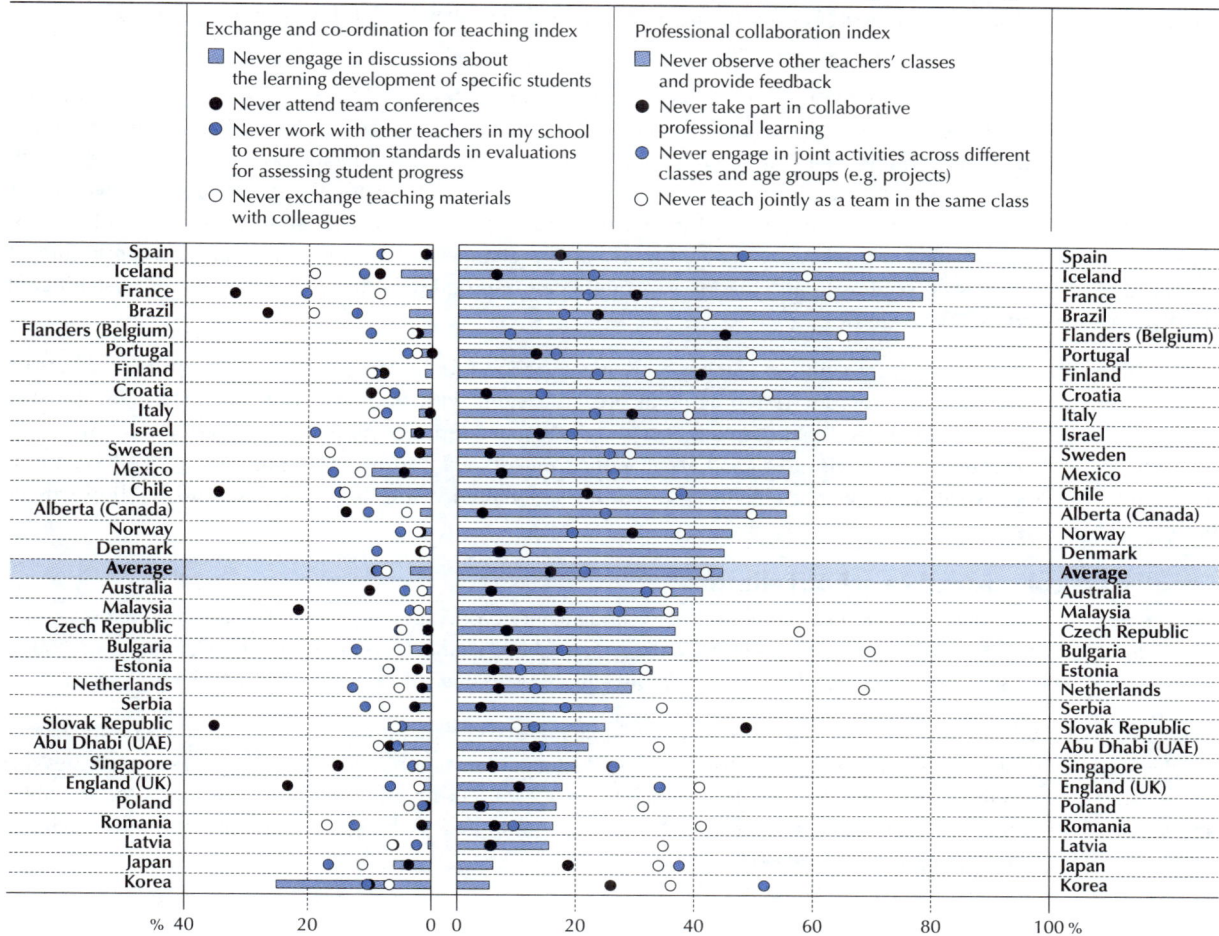

Countries are ranked in descending order, based on the percentage of teachers who report never observing other teachers' classes and providing feedback.
Source: OECD, TALIS 2013 Database, Table 6.15.
StatLink ⟨⟨⟩⟩ http://dx.doi.org/10.1787/888933042086

Box 6.11 examines primary school and upper secondary school teachers' participation in co-operative and collaborative activities.

Box 6.11. **Primary and upper secondary teachers' engagement in co-operation activities**

Tables 6.15.a and 6.15.b show the percentages of teachers in primary (ISCED 1) and upper secondary (ISCED 3) education who report never participating in the activities in the two co-operation indices.

The largest between-country differences in participation in co-operation activities between the levels and countries surveyed appear with primary teachers. A larger proportion of primary school teachers (80%) report teaching jointly with other teachers in the same class, as compared with 68% of lower secondary school teachers. This difference is especially apparent in Flanders (Belgium), where only 35% of lower secondary school teachers report engaging in joint teaching, whereas 69% of primary school teachers do.

The most obvious differences in co-operation activities for the upper secondary level occur with engaging in joint activities across different classes and age groups. It appears that this activity is slightly less common at the upper secondary level, where 30% of teachers report never participating, than it is at the lower secondary level, where only 20% of teachers report that they never participate.

Tables 6.16 and 6.17 report on the results from two multiple regressions to examine the relationships between teacher co-operation (as defined in Box 6.10) and teachers' professional development activities.[8] Results from these analyses show that in most countries all variables have a positive relationship to both outcomes (although some more than others), indicating that these forms of professional development activities may lead to better professional collaboration of teachers.

Instead of focusing on the magnitude of effects of these variables, the analyses focus on the general trends of findings across countries. In doing so, for both professional collaboration and exchange and co-ordination for teaching, the three professional development activities with the highest number of significant positive relationships with the dependent variables are participation in a network of teachers for professional development, individual or collaborative research on a topic of interest and mentoring and/or peer observation and coaching. Mentoring or coaching is positively related to professional collaboration and exchange and co-ordination for teaching in almost all of the TALIS countries. In contrast, participation in a qualification programme has the least number of significant positive relationships across countries.

Mentoring or coaching and participation in teacher networks are found to be consistently positive predictors across countries for co-operation behaviours, outcomes that are consistent with findings from the first cycle of TALIS (OECD, 2009). These findings suggest that participation in collaborative forms of professional development may help promote further collaborative behaviour in teachers. If policy makers want to promote professional collaboration, these types of professional development activities, which are associated with this outcome, could be the focus of future policy efforts.

Creating a collaborative school climate

As noted previously in this chapter, the relationship between teacher co-operation and school leadership factors can be critical to the school environment and affect teaching and learning (Chong et al., 2010). As reported in Caprara et al. (2003), quality school leadership can lead to teachers exerting more effort toward their school's success (see also Chapter 3).

One important aspect of school leadership that may be an indicator of a collaborative climate in the school is the extent to which principals give other stakeholders opportunities to participate in school decisions. This section examines the relationship between this aspect of school leadership (see Box 6.12 for a description of how this is measured in TALIS) and teacher co-operation within the school (professional collaboration and exchange and co-ordination for teaching; see Box 6.10 for a description of these indices).

Box 6.12. Description of the index of participation among stakeholders

To measure participation among stakeholders, teachers were asked the extent to which they agreed or disagreed with the following statements about their school:

- This school provides staff with opportunities to actively participate in school decisions
- This school provides parents or guardians with opportunities to actively participate in school decisions
- This school provides students with opportunities to actively participate in school decisions
- This school has a culture of shared responsibility for school issues
- There is a collaborative school culture that is characterised by mutual support

Further details on the construction of this index can be found in Annex B.

As shown in Tables 6.18 and 6.19, across all participating countries, the relationship between participation among stakeholders in the school and teacher co-operation is positive. The average correlation across all countries between participation among stakeholders and both of the teacher co-operation index measures is about 0.25. However, teachers in three countries (Chile, Mexico and Abu Dhabi [United Arab Emirates]) report a higher positive relationship (at least 0.35) between at least one form of teacher co-operation and participation among stakeholders in the school. These findings suggest that a school leadership structure that promotes involvement among a wide range of stakeholders in the school may also promote teacher co-operation within the school. In turn, such co-operative activities among teachers may help foster a positive school climate and develop robust classroom environments that could facilitate student learning.

What accounts for the variance in teacher co-operation?

The analyses in this section were performed in the same manner as those looking at teacher practices and teachers' beliefs earlier in the chapter. Namely, the variance was partitioned by country, school and teacher levels for professional collaboration and exchange and co-ordination for teaching.[9] These analyses can have clear implications for targeting interventions or professional development opportunities at the appropriate level of implementation. If, for example, co-operation is explained best at the school level, professional development may be most effective for school administrators or the teaching faculty as a whole. In contrast, directing such efforts at school administrators or the teaching faculty as a whole may not be as effective if the variability in responses lies within individual teachers, regardless of school in which they work.

Figure 6.11 provides the separation of variance into three components for professional collaboration and exchange and co-ordination for teaching. The variance at the school level is approximately 8% across both variables. The consistent finding is that the majority of the variance for both constructs remains at the individual level (i.e. with the teacher). Teachers differ from each other in their co-operation responses even within the same school. Therefore, if there is a need to increase co-operative behaviours, the focus of change and training should be on the teacher, as an individual, and not on the school in which the teacher works. However, teacher co-operation appears to have a higher portion of variance explained at the country level compared with other variables examined in this chapter. Country-level variance for professional collaboration and exchange and co-ordination for teaching is 26% and 19%, respectively. This finding suggests that the propensity for teachers to exhibit these co-operation behaviours may be at least partly cultural.

■ Figure 6.11 ■
Distribution of variance – teacher co-operation indices:
Professional collaboration and exchange and co-ordination
Distribution of variance in lower secondary education across the three levels of country, school and teacher

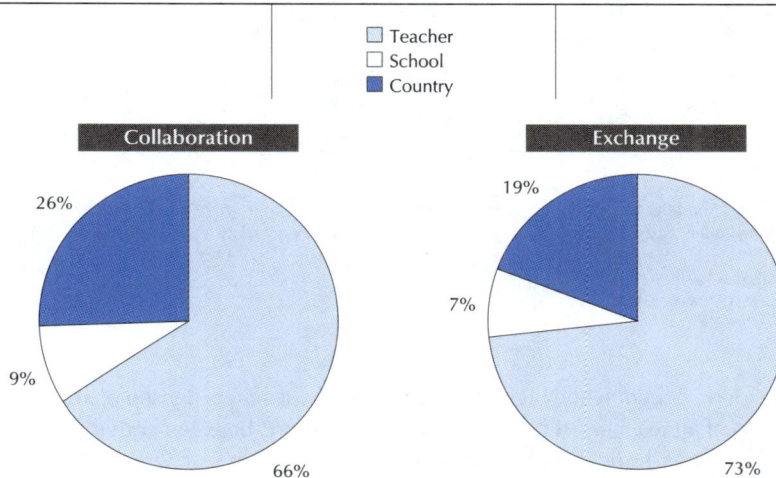

Source: OECD, TALIS 2013 Database.
StatLink http://dx.doi.org/10.1787/888933042105

CLASSROOM ENVIRONMENT

There is evidence that classroom climate can influence student learning and socio-emotional behaviours (Brophy and Good, 1986; Brown et al., 2010). For example, researchers have found that a positive classroom climate is associated with both cognitive and motivational outcomes, including improved academic performance, motivation, engagement, school satisfaction, self-esteem and fewer disruptive behaviours (Baker, 1999; Patrick, Kaplan and Ryan, 2011; Reyes et al., 2012). Indeed, disruptive behaviours result in less time for teaching and ultimately interfere with student learning (Guardino and Fullerton, 2010; Martella, Nelson and Marchand-Martella, 2003). This chapter uses classroom disciplinary climate measures as indicators of classroom climate (see Box 6.4 for a description of the classroom climate index).

Country differences in classroom environment

This section describes how teachers typically spend their class time. Figure 6.12 displays the distribution of class time teachers report spending on three types of activities: Teaching and learning activities, administrative tasks and keeping order (or behaviour management of individual students or the entire class). Across countries, teachers report spending the majority of their time (79%) on teaching and learning activities (Table 6.20). However, proportions vary, from 87% in Bulgaria to 67% in Brazil.

■ Figure 6.12 ■

Distribution of class time during an average lesson

Average proportion of time lower secondary education teachers report spending on each of these activities in an average lesson[1]

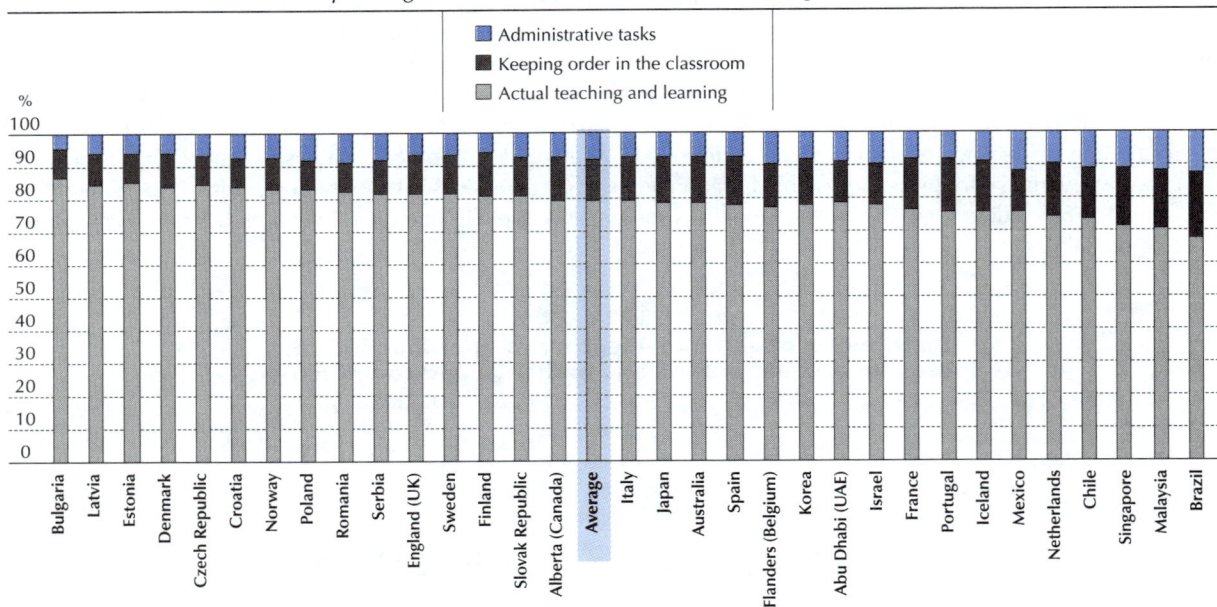

1. These data are reported by teachers and refer to a randomly chosen class they currently teach from their weekly timetable.
Countries are ranked in descending order, based on the average proportion of time teachers in lower secondary education report spending on actual teaching and learning.
Source: OECD, TALIS 2013 Database, Table 6.20.
StatLink http://dx.doi.org/10.1787/888933042124

Keeping order in the classroom, generally the biggest concern for new teachers (Jensen et al., 2012; Woolfolk, 2010), occupies an average of 13% of all teachers' time across countries. Reports between countries vary from 8% in Poland to 20% in Brazil. Administrative tasks require the least amount of time from teachers (8%) compared with the other two broad categories. Teachers in Bulgaria and Estonia report spending 5% of their class time on administrative tasks, while teachers in Brazil, Malaysia and Mexico report that 12% of their class time was devoted to such tasks. There is no doubt that teaching and learning should make up the major component of teachers' class time each day. TALIS results corroborate this, as teachers report spending an average of 79% of their class time on actual teaching and learning. However, teachers and students could further benefit from developing ways that reduce the amount of class time spent on administrative tasks and on keeping order so that they devote more time to teaching and learning. Box 6.13 presents the distribution of class time reported by primary and upper secondary teacher in those countries with available data.

Looking at the TALIS 2013 data further, variations can be seen within countries as to how teachers are reporting spending their class time. Figure 6.13 displays the distributions of responses for the 25th to the 75th percentiles of teachers within each country regarding the proportion of class time they report spending on teaching and learning. Short bars in the figure, such as those for Croatia, Norway, Poland, Romania and Serbia, suggest relative uniformity in how teachers report spending their class time on teaching and learning. Longer bars, such as those for Brazil, Chile, Japan and Singapore, suggest more variation in the proportion of class time teachers report spending on teaching and learning.

Box 6.13. **Distribution of class time for primary and upper secondary teachers**

Tables 6.20.a and 6.20.b look at the distribution of class time activities reported by primary (ISCED 1) and upper secondary (ISCED 3) teachers.

Across participating countries, primary school teachers report spending approximately the same proportions of time for each activity. However, primary school teachers in Denmark and Norway report spending more class time keeping order in the classroom than do their lower secondary school colleagues (14% vs. 10% in Denmark and 12% vs. 9% in Norway).

In contrast, across the countries surveyed, teachers in upper secondary schools seem to spend less class time keeping order (9%) than do their lower secondary school colleagues (13%). These findings are not surprising considering the age of students and their experience in school at each level.

■ Figure 6.13 ■

Percentiles of time spent on teaching and learning

Distribution within each country of the percentage of class time teachers report spending on teaching and learning in lower secondary education[1]

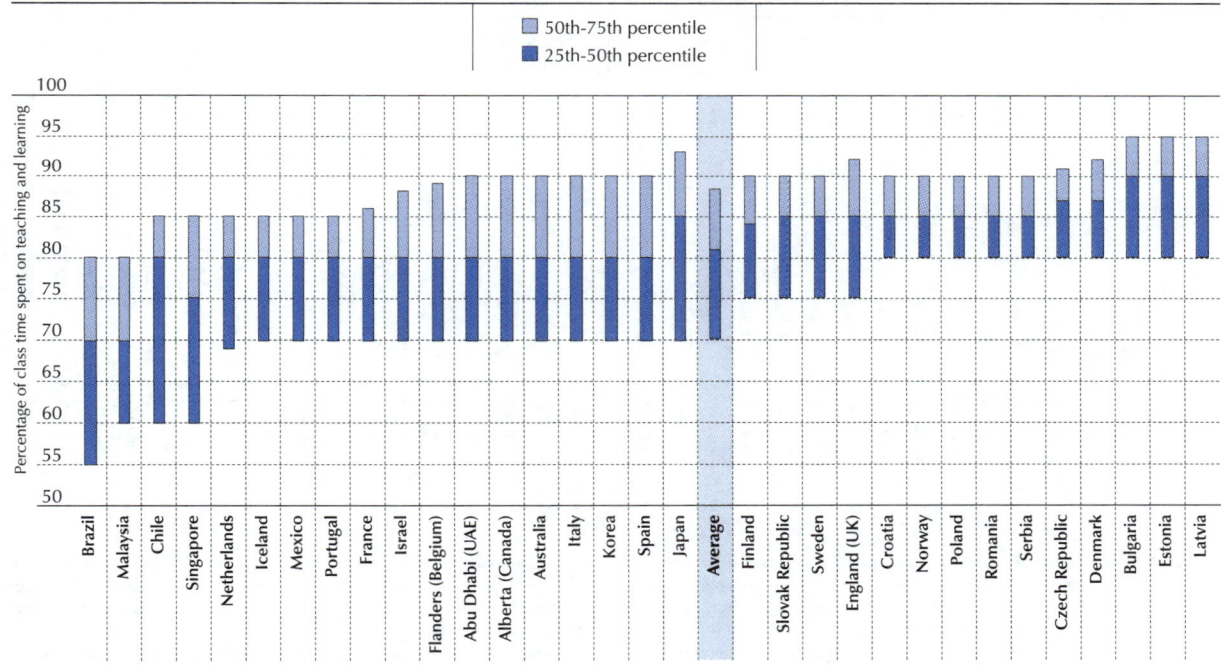

1. The chart shows the percentage of time spent on actual teaching and learning for the second and the third quartile (middle) of the distribution within each country. For example, in Brazil, 25% of teachers report spending between 55% and 70% of the class time on teaching and learning, and another quarter of the Brazilian teachers report spending between 70% to 80% of the class time on teaching and learning.
Countries are ranked in ascending order, based on the 25th percentile of the time teachers report spending on actual teaching and learning in lower secondary education.
Source: OECD, TALIS 2013 Database.
StatLink ⟲ http://dx.doi.org/10.1787/888933042143

Looking across the countries listed in Figure 6.13, one can see that in a majority of participating countries, half of the teachers report spending 80% or more of their class time on teaching and learning (this is the case for countries where the bar representing the 50th-75th percentile of teachers is entirely contained at 80% or above). These teachers could be considered to be making effective use of lesson time, given that some class time can be expected to be spent on administrative tasks and keeping order in the classroom. As also shown in Figure 6.13, in about half of the participating countries, 25% of teachers report spending at least 30% of their time on classroom disruptions and administrative tasks (this is the case for countries where the lower part of the bar representing the 25th-50th percentile of teachers reaches 70% or less). Most notably, in Brazil, Chile, Malaysia and Singapore, one in four teachers reports spending at least 40% of their class time on classroom disruptions and administrative tasks. This indicates that teachers in several countries could benefit from interventions that facilitate more effective use of class time. Aims of such interventions would be to maximise the class-time learning opportunities for all students.

Important variations can also be seen within countries regarding the proportion of time teachers report spending on keeping order in the classroom (Figure 6.14). Similar to Figure 6.13, Figure 6.14 displays the distributions of responses for the 25th to the 75th percentiles of teachers within each country regarding the proportion of class time they report spending on keeping order in the classroom. As shown in the figure, there is more variation in teachers' responses in a country such as Brazil than in countries such as Croatia, Norway, Romania or Serbia.

Moreover, Figure 6.14 shows that half of the teachers in Brazil, Malaysia and Singapore report spending 15% or more of their class time on keeping order in the classroom. In contrast, half of the teachers in Bulgaria, Croatia, the Czech Republic, Estonia, Latvia, Poland and Romania report spending 5% or less of their class time on keeping order in the classroom.

■ Figure 6.14 ■

Percentiles of time spent on keeping order in the classroom

Distribution within each country of the percentage of class time teachers report spending on keeping order in the classroom in lower secondary education[1]

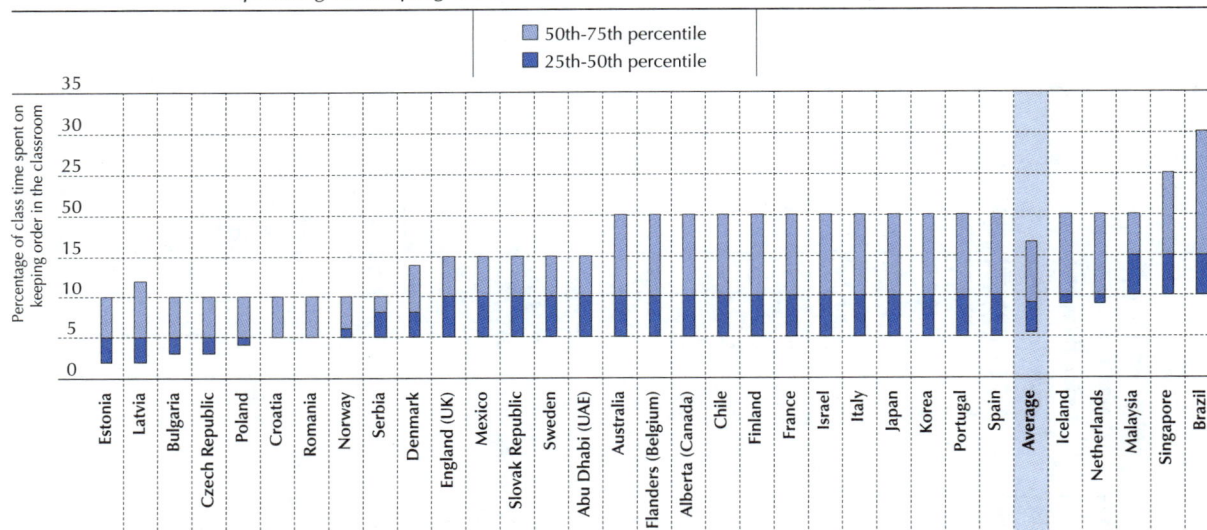

1. The chart shows the percentage of time spent on keeping order in the classroom for the second and the third quartile (middle) of the distribution within each country. For example, in Estonia, 25% of teachers report spending between 2% to 5% of the class time on keeping order in the classroom and another quarter of teachers report spending between 5% to 10% of the class time on the same task. In Croatia and Romania, 25th-50th percentile is not showing because there is no variation between them, both are at 5% of the class time spent on keeping order in the classroom.
Countries are ranked in ascending order, based on the 25th percentile of the time teachers report spending on keeping order in the classroom in lower secondary education.
Source: OECD, TALIS 2013 Database.
StatLink ▉[S] http://dx.doi.org/10.1787/888933042162

Table 6.21 displays descriptive information for each country for classroom disciplinary climate. As the table shows, a majority of teachers in all countries report that students do contribute to a positive environment (average agreement of 71%). Nearly a third of teachers on average report losing quite a lot of time to behavioural problems or waiting for students to settle down. Just more than one in four teachers (26%) reports that there is a lot of disruptive noise in their classrooms. These issues seem particularly problematic for teachers in Brazil, where more than half of the teachers agree that these are issues they deal with in their classroom.

Table 6.22 shows the correlations between the proportion of time reported to be spent on teaching and learning and classroom disciplinary climate (see Box 6.4). Findings suggest a moderate relationship between these variables (the average correlation across countries is high at 0.48). In countries such as Australia, Finland, France, Iceland, Spain and

Sweden, there is a stronger link between time on teaching and learning and the classroom environment. However, this relationship is weaker in countries such as Chile, Japan, Korea and Mexico. In such countries, future work could explore what might explain the time teachers spend on teaching and learning as opposed to managing students.

On average, the correlation between classroom disciplinary climate and time spent on teaching and learning was nearly 0.5. This positive relationship supports the idea that a better classroom climate is associated with more time on teaching and learning for the teacher. It also indicates that there is much left to explain regarding the influences of time spent on teaching and learning after considering classroom climate.

Time spent on learning and teaching tasks is a fundamental and essential component of effective educational environments and should also lead to better classroom environments. Targeted efforts to assist teachers with increasing their skills to effectively manage the classroom to lower irrelevant distractions and noise should promote more time for learning tasks. Ultimately, this should lead to increased learning opportunities for students, regardless of the country in which they reside. This aligns with results in Chapter 4 showing that one of the most frequently reported needs for professional development by teachers on average was for professional development around managing student behaviour (see Table 4.12).

What accounts for the variance in classroom climate?

To gain more information about the constructs of classroom disciplinary climate within schools, the variance was again portioned by three levels for the index of classroom disciplinary climate, as explained earlier in the chapter. The interest was specifically focused on understanding the extent to which this variable was a school- or country-level factor rather than a teacher-level factor to gain insight regarding teachers' responses to the classroom climate indices. That is, are the responses explained by factors related to school or country or by the uniqueness of the individual teacher? Knowing this allows for future interventions to target the level where change needs to occur to influence climate.

Figure 6.15 shows the separation of the variance into three components for classroom disciplinary climate. As mentioned earlier, the variance component figures display how much of the variation in responses to these items is accounted for at each level of the sample.[10] The variance accounted for at the school level (7%) and at the country level (8%) is minimal. These proportions indicate that the majority of variance (84%) in classroom disciplinary climate responses lies with the individual teacher. That is, there is little difference in teachers' responses between schools or countries, yet there is much variability within schools and countries that can be explored. A classroom that is well controlled and orderly is basic to instruction. Indeed, it is the teacher who is in control of this environment, and making sure that teachers have the tools to manage the environment depends on the teacher. The disciplinary climate depends less on the socialisation of the school or the country within which a teacher resides than on the practices put in place in the classroom itself.

■ Figure 6.15 ■
Distribution of variance – classroom discipline
Distribution of variance in lower secondary education across the three levels of country, school and teacher

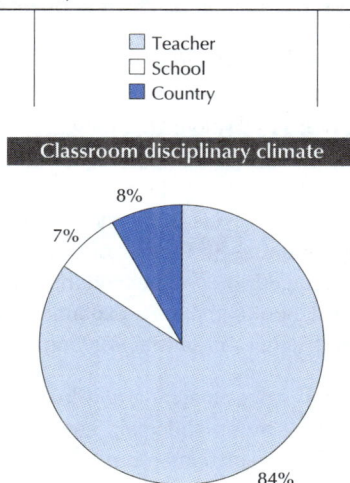

Legend:
- Teacher
- School
- Country

Classroom disciplinary climate

- 8%
- 7%
- 84%

Source: OECD, TALIS 2013 Database.
StatLink ⟨⟩ http://dx.doi.org/10.1787/888933042181

SUMMARY AND IMPLICATIONS FOR POLICY AND PRACTICE

This chapter presented information and analysis on teachers' reported teaching and professional practices, beliefs about the nature of teaching and learning, professional development, professional collaborative practices, working time, school leadership factors and the classroom environment in which teachers work. With accountability increasing in many countries, one can argue that teachers are in the spotlight more than ever. However, increasing accountability provides a unique opportunity for teachers, as many policy makers and educators are eager to understand the conditions under which their teachers work and the barriers to teachers' quest to educate the next generation of active citizens. Future research work should focus on individual factors, while policy work should include individual factors and, equally importantly, factors at the school and country level.

Provide further support (either through professional development or initial teacher education) to encourage teachers' use of active teaching practices

Educational research literature is replete with evidence showing the effectiveness of such teaching practices as well as the need to effectively enact these practices to engender learning (Johnson and Johnson, 2009; Mayer, 2014; Woolfolk, 2010). For example, nearly three decades of research in media and technology has shown that technology, in and of itself, will not facilitate learning. However, the affordances of technologies and multimedia can enhance learning when enacted with theoretically and empirically sound pedagogical strategies (Clark, 1983, 1994; Mayer, 2003, 2014). Indeed, Kozma (1994, p. 1) proclaimed a need to better understand "media and the methods that employ them as they interact with the cognitive and social processes by which knowledge is constructed". Research since then has focused more on pedagogical strategies for setting up a computer-based learning environment. It is not surprising that teachers with pedagogical knowledge of their topics are well positioned to inculcate these three teaching practices, especially the use of information technologies or computing in their classrooms. It is perhaps more surprising that in most countries, TALIS data indicate that class size does not seem to have a strong relationship with teachers' reported use of practices involving small group activities, project-based tasks or ICT. Rather, the composition of students in a class seems to be a more important factor in teachers' choices of teaching practices.

Although many factors may determine teachers' use of active teaching practices, teachers are encouraged to develop pedagogical knowledge in the subjects they teach, as possessing such pedagogical knowledge may free them to explore the use of active teaching practices. Teachers who are struggling with pedagogical knowledge may find it challenging to incorporate teaching strategies that require additional time and resources to implement.

Professional development is one way to deepen teachers' knowledge and interest in using these three contemporary teaching practices. Professional development includes participation in workshops, conferences, observation, qualification programmes, networking, individual and collaborative research and mentoring. Indeed, TALIS results show that across many countries, teachers who engage in some of these types of professional development activities are more likely to report using at least one of these three teaching practices. Policy makers and educators are encouraged to provide teachers with professional development opportunities and encourage their teachers to develop pedagogical knowledge on the subject as well as to effectively deploy these teaching practices in their classrooms. In addition, teachers are encouraged to develop professional practices that will deepen their knowledge in the use of active teaching practices.

Promote teacher co-operation and a positive school climate

Ample research evidence shows that a powerful movement of change takes place when teachers co-operate and work together, resulting in effective schools, classrooms and student learning (DuFour, 2004). Results from TALIS align with the general finding in the literature. Specifically, TALIS data indicate that teachers collaborated more with their colleagues especially when professional development activities afforded them the opportunity to network with other teachers and provide mentoring and coaching. Hence, policy makers and school leaders can support professional development activities where teachers are given more opportunities to mentor one another and develop a strong network with one another. In addition, teachers are also encouraged to seek networking and mentoring opportunities to enhance co-operation, build trust and promote a positive school climate. As explained in Chapter 7, it is possible for such strategic mentoring programmes to result in improved teacher job satisfaction and self-efficacy.

School climate is another major factor that influences teaching and learning (Chong et al., 2010; Collie, Shapka and Perry, 2012). Research has shown that effective school leadership engenders both self-efficacy and collective teacher efficacy geared toward creating effective schools and classrooms (Barouch-Gilbert, Adesope and Schroeder, 2013; Caprara et al., 2003). Results from TALIS align with findings in extant literature. Indeed, TALIS results show a positive moderate relationship between school leadership that promotes participation among a wide variety of stakeholders in

the school and teacher co-operation. This indicates that when the school climate is good, teachers are more willing to co-operate with one another. Also, teacher co-operation can promote a positive school climate. When the school climate is good and teachers work together productively, these may translate into robust classroom environments that facilitate student learning.

Provide development opportunities or feedback to improve teachers' classroom-management skills

A positive classroom disciplinary climate results in a higher proportions of class time spent on actual teaching rather than on attending to undesirable behaviours (Brown et al., 2010; Reyes et al., 2012). Results from TALIS analyses are consistent with general findings in classroom climate research. Significant practical and policy implications are associated with these findings. Educators, school leaders and policy makers can improve classroom climate by providing teachers with interventions or professional development opportunities that focus on more effective use of lesson time. In addition, teachers should seek opportunities to promote healthy positive classroom climate. For example, teachers may build a strong relationship and trust with parents and children, as such an approach has been found to be effective for promoting positive classroom climate and minimising undesirable behaviours in the classroom (El Nokali, Bachman and Votruba-Drzal, 2010). The overarching goal would be to maximise lesson-time learning opportunities for all students.

Notes

1. The figure was adapted from OECD, 2009, Chapter 4.

2. For distribution of variance in each country, see Table 6.23.Web.

3. Note that references to teachers as humanities or mathematics and science teachers throughout this chapter are based on the target class that teachers were asked to respond about in the TALIS questionnaire. See Annex B for the definition of humanities teachers used in TALIS.

4. For the purpose of the analyses, the items from the teacher questionnaire pertaining to the student composition of the target class were collapsed from five to two categories. The collapsing of the categories was determined by reviewing the distribution of responses and selecting a point where both representation of the responses and sufficient variability to be meaningful were maintained. This strategy was the same as followed in Chapter 2. Responses were divided into two categories, one for up to 10% of students and one for greater than 10% of students in the target class. See Annex B for more information.

5. This includes hours reported by teachers working full time and part time.

6. Teachers were asked to report the number of 60-minute hours they spent during their most recent complete calendar week on teaching, planning lessons, marking, collaborating with other teachers, participating in staff meetings and other tasks related to their work at this particular school. In this total, they were requested to include any tasks that took place during weekends, evenings or other off-classroom hours.

7. Multiple regression analysis was performed using the constructivist beliefs index scale as the dependent variable and the following three teaching practices as predictors: use of practices involving small groups, projects that take more than a week to complete and use of ICT. The background variables controlled for included gender, total years working as a teacher, level of education and type of target class taught. See Annex B for more information about these analyses.

8. The variables included *(a)* participation in courses and workshops, *(b)* participation in education conferences, *(c)* observation visits to other schools, *(d)* participation in qualification programmes, *(e)* participation in a network of teachers for professional development, *(f)* individual or collaborative research on a topic of interest, and *(g)* mentoring and/or peer observation and coaching. The analyses controlled for teacher gender, years of experience, highest level of education and subject taught in the target class. See Annex B for more details about the analyses performed.

9. For distribution of variance in each country, see Table 6.23.Web.

10. For the distribution of variance in each country, see Table 6.23.Web.

A note regarding Israel

The statistical data for Israel are supplied by and under the responsibility of the relevant Israeli authorities. The use of such data by the OECD is without prejudice to the status of the Golan Heights, East Jerusalem and Israeli settlements in the West Bank under the terms of international law.

References

Adesope, O.O. and **J.C. Nesbit** (2013), "Learning with animated and static concept maps", *Learning and Instruction,* Vol. 27, pp. 1-10.

Baker, J.A. (1999), "Teacher–student interaction in urban at-risk classrooms: Differential behaviour, relationship quality, and student satisfaction with school", *Elementary School Journal,* Vol. 100/1, pp. 57-70.

Bandura, A. (1990), "Perceived self-efficacy in the exercise of personal agency", *Journal of Applied Sport Psychology,* Vol. 2, pp. 128-163.

Bandura, A. (1989), "Human agency in social cognitive theory", *American Psychologist*, Vol. 44, pp. 1175-1184.

Barouch-Gilbert, R., **O.O. Adesope** and **N.L. Schroeder** (2013), "Efficacy beliefs, job satisfaction, stress and their influences on retention of English-medium content teachers in the Dominican Republic", *Educational Psychology: An International Journal of Experimental Educational Psychology*, *http://dx.doi.org/10.1080/01443410.2013.814193.*

Beyer, C.J. and **E.A. Davis** (2008), "Fostering second graders' scientific explanations: A beginning elementary teacher's knowledge, beliefs, and practice", *The Journal of the Learning Sciences,* Vol. 17/3, pp. 381-414.

Binkley, M. et al. (2010), "Defining 21st Century Skills", draft white paper, *http://atc21s.org/wp-content/uploads/2011/11/1-Defining-21st-Century-Skills.pdf.*

Brophy, J. and **T. Good** (1986), "Teacher behaviour and student achievement", in *Handbook of Research on Teaching*, 3rd edition, M. Wittrock (ed.), Macmillan, New York, NY, pp. 328-375.

Brouwer, N. and **F. Korthagen** (2005), "Can teacher education make a difference?", *American Educational Research Journal*, Vol. 42, pp. 153-224.

Brown, J.L. et al. (2010), "Improving classroom quality: Teacher influences and experimental impacts of the 4Rs program", *Journal of Educational Psychology,* Vol. 102/1, pp. 153-167.

Butler, D.L. and **P.H. Winne** (1995), "Feedback and self-regulated learning: A theoretical synthesis", *Review of Educational Research*, Vol. 65/3, 245 -281.

Caprara, G.V. et al. (2003), "Efficacy beliefs as determinants of teachers' job satisfaction", *Journal of Educational Psychology,* Vol. 95, pp. 821-832.

Chang, L.C. and **G.C. Lee** (2010), "A team-teaching model for practicing project-based learning in high school: Collaboration between computer and subject teachers", *Computers & Education,* Vol. 55, pp. 961-969.

Chong, W.H. et al. (2010), "The relationships among school types, teacher efficacy beliefs, and academic climate: Perspective from Asian middle schools", *The Journal of Educational Research,* Vol. 103, pp. 183-190.

Clark, R.E. (1994), "Media will never influence learning", *Educational Technology Research and Development,* Vol. 42, pp. 21-29.

Clark, R.E. (1983), "Reconsidering research on learning from media", *Review of Educational Research,* Vol. 53, pp. 445-59.

Clement, M. and **Vandenberghe** (2000), "Teachers' professional development: A solitary or collegial (ad)venture?", *Teaching and Teacher Education*, Vol. 16, pp. 81-101.

Cohen, J. et al. (2009), "School climate: Research, policy, practice, and teacher education", *Teachers College Record,* Vol. 111, pp. 180-213.

Collie, R.J., **J.D. Shapka** and **N.E. Perry** (2012), "School climate and socio-emotional learning: Predicting teacher stress, job satisfaction, and teaching efficacy", *Journal of Educational Psychology,* Vol. 104/4, pp. 1189-1204.

Darling-Hammond, L. (1998), "Teachers and teaching: Testing policy hypotheses from a national commission report", *Educational Researcher,* Vol. 27/1, pp. 5-15.

Dexter, S. and **E. Riedel** (2003), "Why improving preservice teacher educational technology preparation must go beyond the College's walls", *Journal of Teacher Education,* Vol. 54/4, pp. 334-346.

DuFour, R. (2004), "What is a 'professional learning community'?", *Educational Leadership,* Vol. 61, 6-11.

DuFour, R. and **B. Burnette** (2002), "Pull out negativity by its roots", *Journal of Staff Development,* Vol. 23/3, pp. 27-30.

Dunlosky et al. (2013), "Improving students' learning with effective learning techniques: Promising directions from cognitive and educational psychology", *Psychological Science in the Public Interest,* Vol. 14, pp. 4-58.

El Nokali, N.E., H.J. Bachman and E. Votruba-Drzal (2010), "Parent involvement and children's academic and social development in elementary school", *Child Development*, Vol. 81/3, pp. 988-1005.

Ertmer, P.A. (2005). "Teacher pedagogical beliefs: The final frontier in our quest for technology integration?", *Educational Technology Research and Development*, Vol. 53, pp. 25-39.

Emmer, E.T. and C.S. Evertson (2009), *Classroom Management for Middle and High School Teachers*, 8th edition, Merrill, Upper Saddle River, NJ.

Evertson, C. and E.T. Emmer (2009), *Classroom Management for Elementary Teachers*, 8th edition, Pearson Merrill, Upper Saddle River, NJ.

Evertson, C.M. and C.S. Weinstein (2006), *A Handbook of Classroom Management: Research, Practice, and Contemporary Issues*, Lawrence Erlbaum Associates, Mahwah, NJ.

Federowicz, M. et al. (2013), *Czas pracy i warunki pracy w relacjach nauczycieli*, Instytut Badań Edukacyjnych, Warsaw.

Flemish Ministry of Education and Training and the University of Antwerp Edubron Research Group (2010), *OECD Review on Evaluation and Assessment Frameworks for Improving School Outcomes: Country Background Report for the Flemish Community of Belgium*, www.oecd.org/edu/evaluationpolicy.

Gipps, C. and G. Stobart (2004), "Fairness in assessment", in *Perspectives on Pupil Assessment*, General Teaching Council for England (GTC), London.

Guardino, C.A. and E. Fullerton (2010), "Changing behaviours by changing the classroom environment", *Teaching Exceptional Children*, Vol. 42/6, pp. 8-13.

Hattie, J. (2003), "Teachers make a difference: Building teacher quality", ACER Annual Conference, Auckland.

Hattie, J. and H. Timperley (2007), "The power of feedback", *Review of Educational Research*, Vol. 77/1, pp. 81-112.

Hofer, B.K. and P.R. Pintrich (1997). "The development of epistemological theories: Beliefs about knowledge and knowing and their relation to learning", *Review of Educational Research*, Vol. 67/1, pp. 88-140.

Jensen, B. et al. (2012), *The Experience of New Teachers: Results from TALIS 2008*, OECD Publishing, Paris, http://dx.doi.org/10.1787/9789264120952-en.

Johnson, D.W. and R.T. Johnson (2009), "An educational psychology success story: Social interdependence theory and cooperative learning", *Educational Researcher*, Vol. 38/5, pp. 365-379.

Kennedy, M.M. (1997), *Defining an Ideal Teacher Education Program*, National Council for the Accreditation of Teacher Education, Washington, D.C.

Klassen, R.M. and M.M. Chiu (2010), "Effects on teachers' self-efficacy and job satisfaction: Teacher gender, years of experience, and job stress", *Journal of Educational Psychology* Vol. 102/3, pp. 741-756.

Kozma, R. (1994), "Will media influence learning? Reframing the debate", *Educational Technology Research and Development*, Vol. 42, pp. 1-19.

Lefrançois, G.R. (2000), *Psychology for Teaching*, 8th edition, Wadsworth/Thomson Learning, University of Alberta, Canada.

Loukas, A. and J.L. Murphy (2007), "Middle school student perceptions of school climate: Examining protective functions on subsequent adjustment problems", *Journal of School Psychology*, Vol. 45, pp. 293-309.

Martella, R.C., J.R. Nelson and N.E. Marchand-Martella (2003), *Managing Disruptive Behaviour in the Schools: A Schoolwide, Classroom, and Individualized Social Learning Approach*, Allyn and Bacon, Boston, MA.

Marzano, R.J. (1998), *A Theory-Based Meta-Analysis of Research on Instruction*, Mid-Continent Regional Educational Laboratory, Aurora, CO.

Marzano, R.J., D.J. Pickering and J.E. Pollock (2001), *Classroom Instruction That Works*, ASCD, Alexandria, VA.

Mayer, R.E. (ed.) (2014), *The Cambridge Handbook of Multimedia Learning*, 2nd edition, Cambridge University Press, New York, NY.

Mayer, R.E. et al. (2009), "Clickers in college classrooms: Fostering learning with questioning methods in large lecture classes", *Contemporary Educational Psychology*, Vol. 34, pp. 51-57.

Mayer, R.E. (2003), "The promise of multimedia learning: Using the same instructional design methods across different media", *Learning and Instruction*, Vol. 13(2), pp. 125-139.

Moore, K.D. (2014), *Effective Instructional Strategies: From Theory to Practice*, Sage Publications, Thousand Oaks, CA.

Murawski, W.W. and H.L. Swanson (2001), "A meta-analysis of co-teaching research", *Remedial and Special Education*, Vol. 22, pp. 258-267.

OECD (2013a), *OECD Reviews of Evaluation and Assessment in Education: Synergies for Better Learning, An International Perspective on Evaluation and Assessment*, OECD Publishing, Paris, http://dx.doi.org/10.1787/9789264190658-en.

OECD (2013b), *Education at a Glance 2013: OECD Indicators*, OECD Publishing, Paris, http://dx.doi.org/10.1787/eag-2013-en.

OECD (2010), *PISA 2009 Results: Learning Trends: Changes in Student Performance Since 2000, (Volume V)*, PISA, OECD Publishing, Paris, http://dx.doi.org/10.1787/9789264091580-en.

OECD (2009), *Creating Effective Teaching and Learning Environments: First Results from TALIS*, OECD Publishing, Paris, http://dx.doi.org/10.1787/9789264068780-en.

Orlich, D.C. et al. (2013), *Teaching Strategies: A Guide to Effective Instruction*, 10th edition, Wadsworth, Cengage Learning, Boston, Massachusetts.

Pajares, M.F. (1992), "Teachers' beliefs and educational research: Cleaning up a messy construct", *Review of Educational Research*, Vol. 62/3, pp. 307-333.

Parsons, S.A., S.L. Dodman and S.C. Burrowbridge (2013), "Broadening the view of differentiated instruction", *Phi Delta Kappan*, Vol. 95, pp. 38-42.

Patrick, H., A. Kaplan and A.M. Ryan (2011), "Positive classroom motivational environments: Convergence between mastery goal structure and classroom social climate", *Journal of Educational Psychology*, Vol. 103/2, pp. 367-382.

Phelps, R. and A. Graham (2004), "Teachers and ICT: Exploring a metacognitive approach to professional development", *Australasian Journal of Educational Technology*, Vol. 20/1, pp. 49-68.

Prince, M. (2004), "Does active learning work? A review of the research", *Journal of Engineering Education*, Vol. 93/3, pp. 223-231.

Reyes, M.R. et al. (2012), "Classroom emotional climate, student engagement, and academic achievement", *Journal of Educational Psychology*, Vol. 104/3, pp. 700-712.

Richardson, V. (1996), "The role of attitudes and beliefs in learning to teach", in *Handbook of Research on Teacher Education*, J. Sikula, T.J. Buttery and E. Guyton (eds.), 2nd edition, Macmillan, New York, NY, pp. 102-119.

Richardson, V. et al. (1991), "The relationship between teachers' beliefs and practices in reading comprehension instruction", *American Educational Research Journal*, Vol. 28/3, pp. 559-586.

Santiago, P. et al. (2012), *OECD Reviews of Evaluation and Assessment in Education: Mexico 2012*, OECD Reviews of Evaluation and Assessment in Education, OECD Publishing, Paris, http://dx.doi.org/10.1787/9789264172647-en.

Schmidt, H.G. et al. (2009), "Constructivist, problem-based learning does work: A meta-analysis of curricular comparisons involving a single medical school", *Educational Psychologist*, Vol. 44, pp. 227-249.

Seidel, T. and R.J. Shavelson (2007), "Teaching effectiveness research in the past decade: The role of theory and research design in disentangling meta-analysis research", *Review of Educational Research*, Vol. 77, pp. 454-499.

Shapiro, J. and D. Kilbey (1990), "Closing the gap between theory and practice: Teacher beliefs, instructional decisions and critical thinking", *Reading Horizons*, Vol. 31, pp. 59-73.

Sheen, R. and R. O'Neill (2005), "Tangled up in form: Critical comments on 'Teachers' stated beliefs about incidental focus on form and their classroom practices' by Basturkmen, Loewen, and Ellis", *Applied Linguistics*, Vol. 26/2, pp. 268-274.

Slavin, R.E. (2013), "Classroom applications of cooperative learning", in *APA Handbook of Educational Psychology*, S. Graham (ed.), American Psychological Association, Washington, D.C.

Slavin, R.E. (2009), "Cooperative learning", in *International Encyclopedia of Education*, G. McCulloch and D. Crook (eds.), Routledge, Abington.

Slavin, R.E. (1995), *Cooperative Learning: Theory, Research, and Practice*, 2nd edition, Allyn and Bacon, Boston, MA.

Smagorinsky, P. et al. (2004), "Tensions in learning to teach: Accommodation and development of a teaching identity", *Journal of Teacher Education*, Vol. 55/1, pp. 8-24.

Speer, N.M. (2008), "Connecting beliefs and practices: A fine-grained analysis of a college mathematics teacher's collections of beliefs and their relationship to his instructional practices", *Cognition and Instruction*, Vol. 26/2, pp. 218-267.

Staub, F.C. and **E. Stern** (2002), "The nature of teachers' pedagogical content beliefs matters for students' achievement gains: Quasi-experimental evidence from elementary mathematics", *Journal of Educational Psychology,* Vol. 94/2, pp. 344-355.

Tatto, M.T. and **D.B. Coupland** (2003), "Teacher education and teachers' beliefs: Theoretical and measurement concerns", in *Teacher Beliefs and Classroom Performance: The Impact of Teacher Education*, J. Raths (ed.), Information Age Publishing, Greenwich, CT, pp. 123-184.

Vieluf, S. et al. (2012), *Teaching Practices and Pedagogical Innovation: Evidence from TALIS*, OECD Publishing, Paris, *http://dx.doi.org/10.1787/9789264123540-en.*

Woolfolk, A. (2010), *Educational Psychology*, 11th edition, Pearson/Allyn and Bacon, Columbus, OH.

Zeichner, K. and **A. Schulte** (2001), "What we know and don't know from peer-reviewed research about alternative teacher certification programs", *Journal of Teacher Education*, Vol. 52/4, pp. 266-282.

Zeichner, K.M. and **B.R. Tabachnick** (1981), "Are the effects of university teacher education 'washed out' by school experience?", *Journal of Teacher Education,* Vol. 32/3, pp. 7-11.

7

Teacher Self-Efficacy and Job Satisfaction: Why They Matter

This chapter focuses on teachers' feelings of self-efficacy and job satisfaction. Self-efficacy refers to the level of confidence teachers have in their abilities, while job satisfaction is the sense of fulfilment and gratification that teachers get from working. The chapter looks at some of the themes previously examined in this report (professional development, appraisal and feedback, school leadership, teacher characteristics) and investigates whether they influence teachers' feelings of self-efficacy and job satisfaction. The discussion then considers teacher and school characteristics that might serve to lessen the effects of potentially challenging classroom circumstances for teachers. It concludes with recommendations for policy makers, school leaders and teachers.

Highlights

- Less than a third of all teachers across TALIS countries believe that teaching is a valued profession in society. In all but one TALIS country, the extent to which teachers can participate in decision making has a strong positive association with the likelihood of reporting teaching is valued profession in society.

- Furthermore, teachers who report that they are provided with opportunities to participate in decision making at a school level have higher reported levels of job satisfaction in all TALIS countries and higher feelings of self-efficacy in most countries. The relationship between job satisfaction and teacher participation in school decision making is particularly strong for all countries.

- With more teaching experience comes higher levels of self-efficacy, but in some cases lower levels of job satisfaction. Teachers with more than five years of work experience report higher levels of self-efficacy than their less-experienced colleagues in 26 countries but lower levels of job satisfaction in 12 TALIS countries.

- Challenging classroom circumstances can affect teachers' self-efficacy and job satisfaction. In particular, an increase in the percentage of students with behavioural problems is associated with a strong decrease in teachers' reported levels of job satisfaction in almost all countries.

- Teachers' perception that appraisal and feedback lead to changes in their teaching practice is related to higher job satisfaction in nearly all countries, whereas the perception that appraisal and feedback is performed merely for administrative purposes relates to lower levels of job satisfaction in all TALIS countries.

- The relationships that teachers develop with their school leader, other teachers or with students in their schools are valuable. Positive interpersonal relationships can negate the otherwise detrimental effects that challenging classrooms of students might have on a teacher's job satisfaction or feelings of self-efficacy. Relationships between teachers and students have an exceptionally powerful relation with teachers' job satisfaction.

- Collaboration among teachers, whether through professional learning or collaborative practices, is also influential. Collaborative practices are related to both higher levels of self-efficacy and job satisfaction. In particular, teachers who report participating in collaborative professional learning five times a year or more also report significantly enhanced levels of self-efficacy in almost all countries and higher job satisfaction in two-thirds of the countries.

INTRODUCTION

According to Bandura's (1986) social cognitive theory, self-efficacy refers to individuals' beliefs about their capabilities to successfully accomplish a particular course of action. In education, research has shown that students' self-efficacy has an important influence on their academic achievement and behaviour. Yet there is increasing evidence that teachers' sense of self-efficacy, consisting of efficacy in instruction, student engagement and classroom management, also is an important factor in influencing academic outcomes of students, and simultaneously enhances teachers' job satisfaction (Caprara et al., 2006; Klassen and Chiu, 2010). Job satisfaction, in turn, refers to a sense of fulfilment and gratification from working in an occupation (Locke, 1969), and teacher job satisfaction consists of satisfaction with the profession and satisfaction with the current work environment. Research shows that while teachers are generally satisfied with the aspects of their jobs that relate to their teaching work, such as work tasks and professional growth, they tend to be dissatisfied with other aspects surrounding the performance of their job – for example, working conditions, interpersonal relations and salary (Butt et al., 2005; Crossman and Harris, 2006; Dinham and Scott, 1998).

A number of studies have demonstrated positive associations between teachers' self-efficacy and higher levels of student achievement and motivation and teachers' instructional practices, enthusiasm, commitment, job satisfaction and teaching behaviour (Skaalvik and Skaalvik, 2007; Tschannen-Moran and Woolfolk Hoy, 2001; Tschannen-Moran and Barr, 2004; Caprara et al., 2006). Lower levels of teachers' self-efficacy, on the other hand, have been linked to teachers experiencing more difficulties with student misbehaviour, being more pessimistic about student learning and experiencing higher levels of job-related stress and lower levels of job satisfaction (Caprara et al., 2003; Caprara et al., 2006; Klassen and Chiu, 2010; Collie, Shapka and Perry, 2012). Furthermore, teachers' self-efficacy appears to be a valid construct across countries differing in language and culture, and there is evidence that teachers' self-efficacy shows a similar positive relationship with teachers' job satisfaction across cultural settings (Klassen et al., 2009; OECD, 2009).

This positive relationship between teachers' self-efficacy and job satisfaction is particularly important because there is empirical evidence supporting the positive association between job satisfaction and job performance across a wide range of work settings (Judge et al., 2001). Job commitment has been found to have an important role in this relationship, as job satisfaction leads to enhanced commitment, which in turns leads to better job performance (Lee, Carswell and Allen, 2000; Kardos and Johnson, 2007). Moreover, job satisfaction plays a key role in teachers' attitudes and efforts in their daily work with children (Caprara et al., 2003). Exploring the relationship between teachers' self-efficacy and job satisfaction may therefore have implications for teachers' retention and commitment to the school, job performance and, by extension, the academic achievement of students (Klassen et al., 2009; Price and Collett, 2012; Somech and Bogler, 2002; Brief and Weiss, 2002).

Although the described studies show associations between teacher self-efficacy and student achievement, most of these studies did not research the direction or causality of these associations. Caprara et al. (2006) investigated the direction of causality and found that teachers' personal efficacy beliefs affected their job satisfaction and students' academic achievement when controlling for previous levels of student achievement. Yet Holzberger, Philipp and Kunter (2013) only partially confirmed a causal effect of teachers' self-efficacy on later instructional quality. (Their analyses revealed that instructional quality also effects teacher self-efficacy.) This means that it remains a possibility that "good teaching" causes higher teacher self-efficacy and that further research is needed to better understand these relationships.

Analytical model

This chapter examines relationships between teachers' self-efficacy, job satisfaction and other themes discussed in the previous chapters of this report, such as school leadership, teacher professional development and teacher appraisal and feedback (see Box 7.1 for information about how self-efficacy and job satisfaction are measured in TALIS). Figure 7.1 illustrates the hypothesised relationships between the variables of interest in this final chapter. Though "teacher stress", "teacher retention", and "student outcomes" are not directly measured by TALIS, they are included in the figure to show how the TALIS data fit into the bigger story for teachers, their attitudes and student outcomes. Figure 7.1 also illustrates the research questions this chapter considers.

■ Figure 7.1 ■

Framework for the analyses of teachers' self-efficacy and job satisfaction

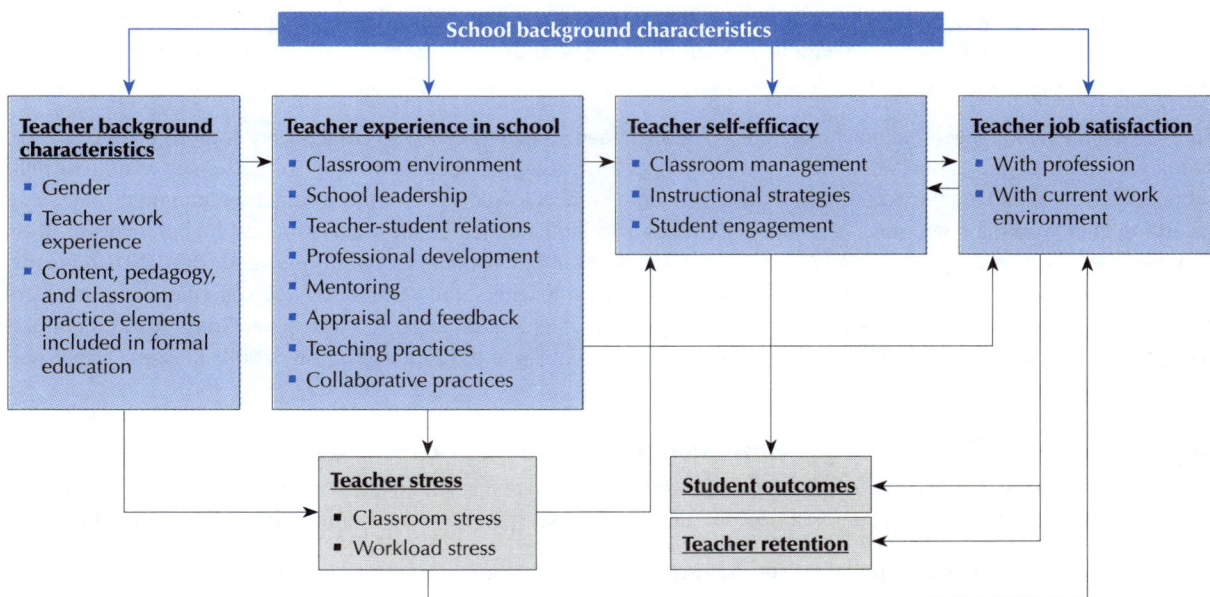

Note: Constructs that are covered by the survey are in blue; others are in grey.
Source: Adapted from Klassen, R.M. & Chiu (2010).

Organisation of this chapter

This chapter uses the literature, as well as the themes discussed in previous chapters of this report, to examine different aspects of teacher self-efficacy and job satisfaction. First, this chapter examines how teachers' self-efficacy and job satisfaction are related to school and teacher background characteristics. For example, does teacher self-efficacy vary according to teacher gender, work experience and training in different elements of subjects taught (i.e. Wolters and Daugherty, 2007; Kooij et al., 2008)? Following the few studies available in the literature, the chapter also looks at how and whether teachers' job satisfaction is influenced by teachers' self-efficacy and vice versa (i.e. Caprara et al., 2003; Liu and Ramsey, 2008). Furthermore, what are the effects of relationships teachers form in the school, school leadership styles, teachers' perceptions of classroom and school environment and teachers' beliefs and practices on teachers' job satisfaction and self-efficacy (i.e. Collie, Shapka and Perry, 2012; Calik et al., 2012; Wahlstrom and Louis, 2008)? Finally, this chapter considers the extent to which professional development, mentoring and collaborative practices have a positive impact on teachers' self-efficacy and job satisfaction (i.e. Lumpe et al., 2012; LoCasale-Crouch et al., 2012; Devos et al., 2012). At the end of this chapter, key policy implications derived from TALIS findings are highlighted.

A PROFILE OF TEACHERS' SELF-EFFICACY AND JOB SATISFACTION

Despite the emerging evidence of the relationship between teachers' self-efficacy and student learning (Caprara et al., 2003; Caprara et al., 2006; Klassen and Chiu, 2010; Collie, Shapka and Perry, 2012), still relatively little is known about how teachers' job satisfaction and self-efficacy are related to each other and to important demographic characteristics such as years of experience, gender, educational attainment and teaching level. This is important information because self-efficacy beliefs and job satisfaction in the workplace are not static and reflect a lifelong process of development that fluctuates in line with personal characteristics and changing circumstances (Klassen and Chiu, 2010).

Research seems to suggest that teachers' self-efficacy is most malleable in the early stage of a teacher's career, after which it increases and becomes more stable and established as teachers gain experience (Tschannen-Moran and Woolfolk Hoy, 2007; Wolters and Daugherty, 2007). However, Klassen and Chiu (2010) reported a non-linear relationship between teachers' self-efficacy and years of experience, with teacher's self-efficacy increasing with experience for teachers in the early and middle stages of their careers but declining for teachers in late career stages. It seems that the middle and late career stages bring their own challenges that can affect self-efficacy and job satisfaction. For teachers, the combination of successful past experience; verbal support from principals, students, peers, and parents; and opportunities for observation of successful peers builds self-efficacy for teaching (Tschannen-Moran, Woolfolk Hoy and Hoy, 1998). The influence of the sources of self-efficacy are likely to change over the course of a teacher's career though, with verbal persuasion and contextual factors playing a more important role for novice teachers than for veteran teachers (Tschannen-Moran and Woolfolk Hoy, 2007). In one of the few studies researching the relationship between teacher training and self-efficacy, Woolfolk Hoy and Burke Spero (2005) reported a significant increase in teachers' self-efficacy during teacher training, followed by a decline at the end of the first teaching year.

Furthermore, teaching level and teacher gender have also been shown to be related to teachers' attitudes. For example, primary school teachers report higher levels of self-efficacy for student engagement than do teachers in middle or high school (Wolters and Daugherty, 2007). Additionally, women report lower levels of job satisfaction than men, especially regarding their working conditions. A number of studies also indicate that female teachers report higher levels of stress than male teachers (e.g. Antoniou, Polychroni and Vlachakis, 2006; Chaplain, 2008; Klassen and Chiu, 2010). Finally, while Klassen et al. (2009) found similar relationships between teachers' job satisfaction and self-efficacy for teachers from five North American and Asian countries, findings from other studies suggest that teachers' national and cultural background can influence the relationship between these variables (e.g. Liu and Ramsey, 2008; Klassen, Usher and Bong, 2010).[1]

Individual self-efficacy and job satisfaction items across countries

Before addressing teacher and school characteristics in relation to teacher self-efficacy and job satisfaction, this section first provides an overview of teachers' responses to questions about specific aspects of their self-efficacy (see Box 7.1).

The individual items that make up the indices discussed in Box 7.1 are interesting in and of themselves. Table 7.1 shows that in the majority of TALIS countries, most teachers report holding beliefs that suggest high levels of self-efficacy. On average across countries, between 80% and 92% of teachers report that they can often get students to believe they can do well in school work, help students value learning, craft good questions for students, control disruptive behaviour in the classroom, make expectations about student behaviour clear, help students think critically, get students

to follow classroom rules, calm a student who is disruptive, use a variety of assessment strategies and provide alternative explanations when students are confused.[2] In comparison, motivating students who show low interest in school work (70%) and implementing alternative instructional strategies (77%) both seem relatively more difficult on average for teachers across the TALIS countries.

Box 7.1. **Teacher self-efficacy and job satisfaction indices**

TALIS measures three aspects of teacher self-efficacy: classroom management, instruction and student engagement. Similarly, TALIS measures two aspects of teacher job satisfaction: satisfaction with profession and satisfaction with current work environment. See Annex B for more details on the construction of these indices.

Efficacy in classroom management

- Control disruptive behaviour in the classroom
- Make my expectations about student behaviour clear
- Get students to follow classroom rules
- Calm a student who is disruptive or noisy

Efficacy in instruction

- Craft good questions for my students
- Use a variety of assessment strategies
- Provide an alternative explanation, for example, when students are confused
- Implement alternative instructional strategies in my classroom

Efficacy in student engagement

- Get students to believe they can do well in school work
- Help my students value learning
- Motivate students who show low interest in school work
- Help students think critically

Satisfaction with current work environment

- I would like to change to another school if that were possible
- I enjoy working at this school
- I would recommend my school as a good place to work
- All in all, I am satisfied with my job

Satisfaction with profession

- The advantages of being a teacher clearly outweigh the disadvantages
- If I could decide again, I would still choose to work as a teacher
- I regret that I decided to become a teacher
- I wonder whether it would have been better to choose another profession

---

Yet in some countries, compared with the overall average, teachers seem to believe significantly and consistently less in their ability to have a positive influence in these domains. Notably, teachers in Japan show lower levels of confidence in their ability across domains as compared with the TALIS average. The averages range from a low of only 16% of teachers in Japan believing they can often help students think critically, to a high of 54% thinking they can provide alternative explanations when students are confused. Teachers in the Czech Republic also report lower levels of confidence in their abilities in some areas: For example, only 30% of teachers in the Czech Republic believe they can motivate students who show low interest in school work, while 39% think they can help students value learning. The patterns are less consistent for teachers in Croatia, Norway and Spain, but percentages in each country are 53% or less for one or more of the elements used to measure self-efficacy.

The extent to which teachers across countries hold beliefs that relate to job satisfaction is displayed in Table 7.2 and Figure 7.2. On average, 91% of teachers across countries report overall satisfaction with their job, 93% of all teachers report being satisfied with their performance in their current school, 84% would recommend their school as a good place to work and 90% say they enjoy working at their current school. However, consistent with the findings for elements measuring self-efficacy in Table 7.1, only 50% of teachers in Japan report being satisfied with their performance in their current school, and 62% would recommend their school as a good place to work. Nevertheless, more than three-quarters (78%) of teachers in Japan say they enjoy working in their current school. While results in most countries centre around 77% of teachers reporting that the advantages of being a teacher clearly outweigh the disadvantages, in Brazil, the Czech Republic, France and the Slovak Republic, only 60% or less of teachers believe this.

■ Figure 7.2 ■

Teachers' job satisfaction

Percentage of lower secondary education teachers who "strongly disagree", "disagree", "agree" or "strongly agree" with the following statements

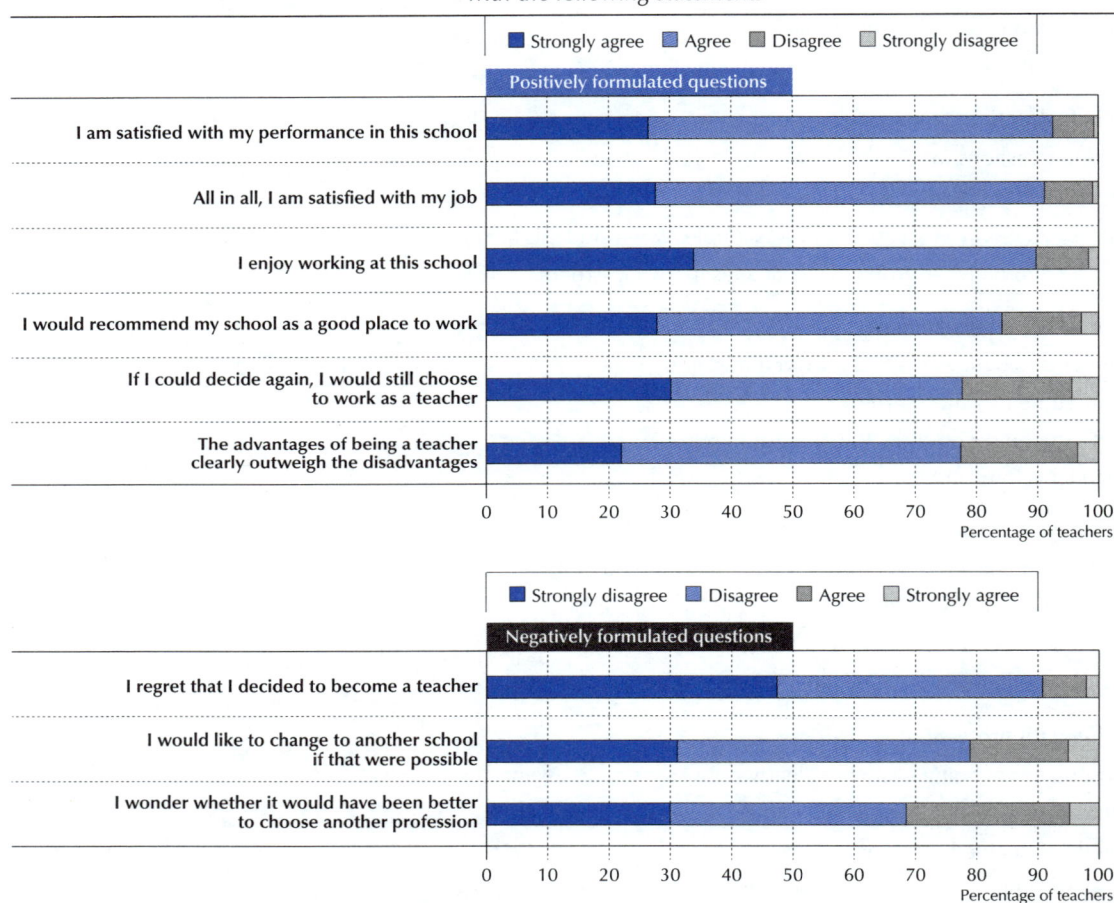

Items are ranked in descending order, based on the percentage of teachers who "strongly agree" or "agree" with the statement for positively formulated questions. For negatively formulated questions the order is reversed, meaning it is in descending order based on the percentage of teachers who "strongly disagree" or "disagree" with the statement.
Source: OECD, TALIS 2013 Database, Tables 7.2 and 7.2.Web.
StatLink ⟐⟐⟐ http://dx.doi.org/10.1787/888933042200

Yet these results do not dissuade teachers in these four countries from reporting that they would choose to become a teacher if they could decide again: Approximately 70% or more of the teachers in these countries say that if they could decide again, they would still choose to work as a teacher (the TALIS average is 78%). More than 9 in 10 teachers in Malaysia and Mexico would choose to be teachers again, but in Japan (58%), Korea (63%) and Sweden (53%), fewer teachers agree. Noticeably more teachers in Korea (20%) and Sweden (18%) also report that they regret becoming a

teacher compared with the international average (9%). Again, significantly more teachers in Korea and Sweden, along with five other countries (Bulgaria, Iceland, Portugal, Singapore and the Slovak Republic), also report that they wonder if it would have been better to choose a different profession (40% or more versus the international average of 32%).

Finally, on average, less than a third of all teachers across countries believe that teaching is a valued profession in society (Figure 7.3). This is a significant finding on its own, as even the perception of whether a profession is valued can affect recruitment or retention of candidates in the profession. Large variations among the TALIS countries are observed, however. This issue is particularly problematic in Croatia, France, the Slovak Republic, Spain and Sweden, where less than 10% of teachers believe that teaching is valued. In Korea, Malaysia, Singapore and Abu Dhabi (United Arab Emirates), however, the majority of teachers feel differently, with two-thirds or more of teachers reporting that their society values teaching as a profession.

■ Figure 7.3 ■
Teachers' view of the way society values the teaching profession

Percentage of lower secondary education teachers who "strongly disagree", "disagree", "agree" or "strongly agree" with the following statement: I think that the teaching profession is valued in society

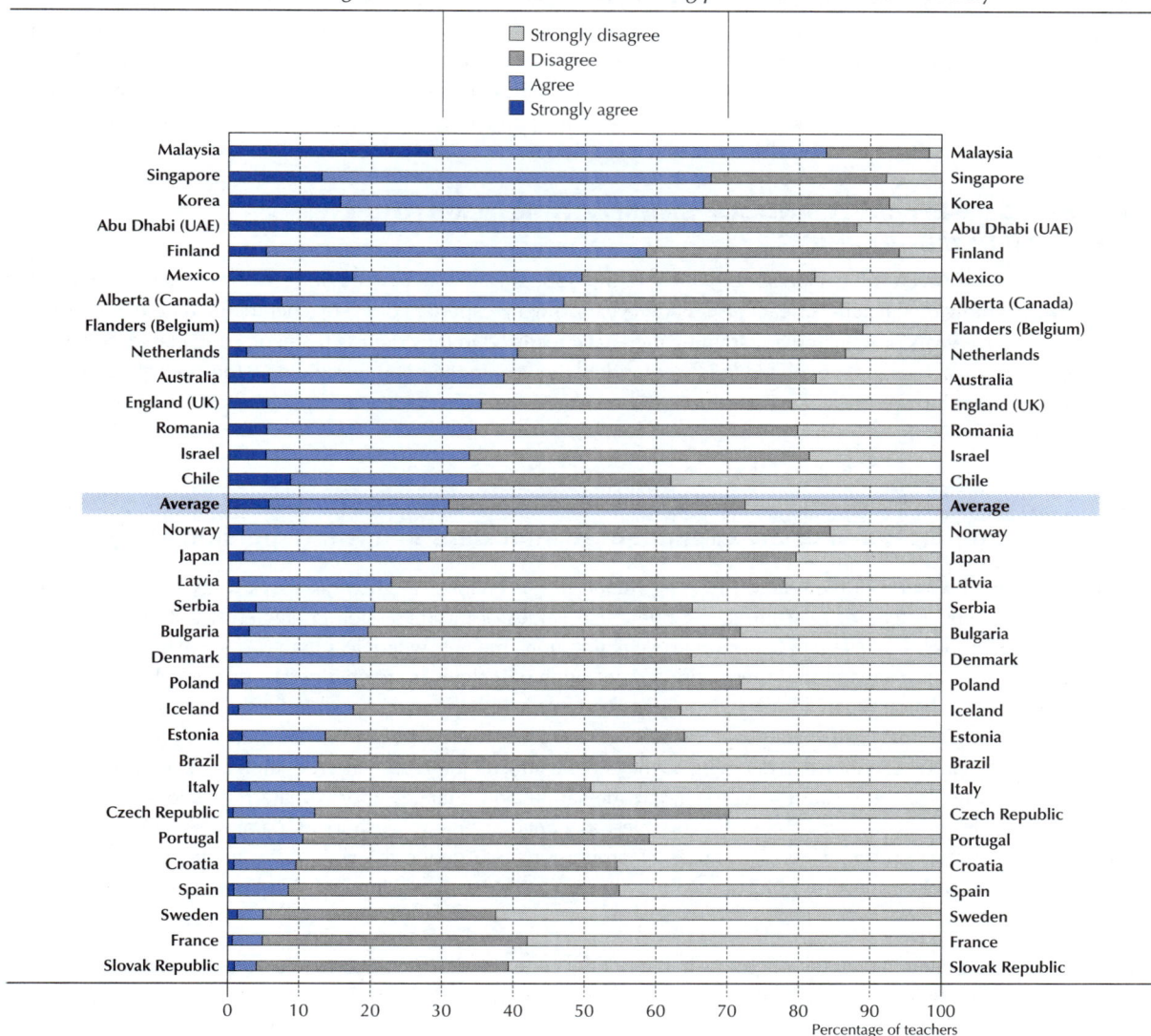

Countries are ranked in descending order, based on the percentage of teachers who "strongly agree" or "agree" that they think that the teaching profession is valued in society.

Source: OECD, TALIS 2013 Database, Tables 7.2 and 7.2.Web.

StatLink ⌷⌷⌷ http://dx.doi.org/10.1787/888933042219

Additional analyses shed more light on what factors might influence teachers' perceptions in this area.[3] A weak relation to gender appears, as male teachers are more likely than female teachers to perceive teaching as valued in nine countries. In addition, experience may play a role in shaping this belief: In 13 countries, teachers with more than five years of teaching experience perceive their profession to be less valued than do their less-experienced colleagues (Table 7.3). In Bulgaria, Croatia, Serbia and Spain, teachers with more than five years of teaching experience are at least half as likely to report teaching is a valued profession in society compared with their less-experienced peers. In Chile, Singapore and Flanders (Belgium), however, teachers with more than five years of teaching report better societal perceptions of teaching than do their less-experienced colleagues.

Interestingly, in 28 of the TALIS countries, the extent to which teachers can participate in decision making has a strong positive association with the likelihood of reporting teaching as a valued profession in society. In Bulgaria, Croatia and Latvia, when teachers are part of decision-making processes in their school, they are three times as likely to report that teaching is a valued profession in society, while teachers in Chile are more than five times as likely to do so.

Thus, while TALIS data show that the vast majority of teachers across countries are satisfied with their jobs, less than a third believe that teaching is a valued profession in their societies. This perception is striking and can negatively impact the teaching profession in those countries. A negative view of the teaching profession, either by society as a whole or when perceived by teachers themselves, can impact the recruitment of high-quality professionals into the teaching profession. It can also affect whether teachers stay in the profession. Many countries have enacted policies aimed to increase the prestige of the teaching profession in order to avoid these issues (Schleicher, 2011). Countries may want to conduct further analyses to look at the origins of these negative perceptions and to specify what it is specifically about the teaching profession that engenders these negative perceptions.

TEACHERS' SELF-EFFICACY AND JOB SATISFACTION IN RELATION TO TEACHER DEMOGRAPHICS

To a certain extent, levels of teachers' self-efficacy and job satisfaction can be influenced by the demographic characteristics of individual teachers. Teachers' gender, years of work experience as a teacher (defined here as more than five years versus five years or less) and any training they have received in the content, pedagogy and classroom practice of the subjects they teach can all be related to how confident they are in their abilities and how they feel about their job. The possible relationships of these demographic factors with teacher self-efficacy and job satisfaction are investigated in this section (Box 7.2).

Box 7.2. **Interpretation of the strength of relationships in linear regression analyses**

To facilitate interpretation of the relationships examined in this chapter, the text discusses weak, moderate, and strong relationships instead of referring to the numerical values of the regression coefficients. Cut-off points for these three categories were 0.2 and 0.3 standard deviation unit changes, where less than 0.2 is weak, 0.2-0.299 is moderate and 0.3 or higher is strong. These standard deviation unit changes are obtained by dividing the regression coefficient of the relation between the independent variable and dependent variable by the standard deviation of the dependent variable. This means that for every country, the distribution of self-efficacy and job satisfaction scores were taken into account when deciding on the classification of their regression coefficients. For dichotomous independent variables, these 0.2 and 0.3 standard deviation unit changes approximate regression coefficients of 0.3 and 0.5, respectively. For continuous variables, a change in one unit is not comparable to a dichotomous change. For variables such as class size, hours or proportions, we define the size of the relationship as weak, moderate, and strong at the threshold of 10 times the unit ($\beta1*10$ more students, 10 more hours, 10% more time spent).

For index scores, we define the cut-off points in relation to a one standard deviation increase on that measure. This means that the coefficient on the non-dichotomous independent variables is first translated into standard deviation units by ($\beta1*\sigma x1$). We then discuss a weak, moderate and strong relationship from this threshold.

The calculation and categorisation of all weak, moderate and strong classifications are displayed in the web tables following each regression table.

Table 7.4 shows the associations between these demographic characteristics and teacher self-efficacy, and Table 7.5 shows the same connections with job satisfaction. In 18 countries, male teachers reported lower levels of self-efficacy. Male teachers displayed lower self-efficacy (moderate relationship[4]) in particular in Australia, Denmark, Estonia and the Slovak Republic. These results are interesting to note given the finding in Chapter 2 that overall, the minority of lower secondary school teachers are male. In Japan, which is one of the few countries in which the majority (61%) of lower secondary teachers are male, the opposite is found: Male teachers report higher levels of self-efficacy (the strength of this relationship is moderate; in other countries where male teachers show higher self-efficacy it is weak). A similar pattern was observed for job satisfaction (Table 7.5). Again, in 13 countries male teachers report lower job satisfaction levels. This finding is especially noticeable among male teachers in Croatia and Iceland.

Tables 7.4 and 7.5 also show that teaching experience relates differently to self-efficacy versus job satisfaction. More-experienced teachers tend to have higher self-efficacy in most countries but lower levels of job satisfaction in 12 TALIS countries. Particularly notable relationships were found in Denmark, France, Italy, Japan, Latvia, Singapore, Sweden, Abu Dhabi (United Arab Emirates), Alberta (Canada) and Flanders (Belgium), where teachers' self-efficacy was much higher for those teachers with more than five years of experience as a teacher than it was for their colleagues with less experience. In contrast, in Finland, Korea, the Netherlands, Poland, Serbia and Flanders (Belgium), job satisfaction is moderately lower for more-experienced teachers as compared with their less-experienced counterparts.

Figures 7.4 and 7.5 illustrate the relationship of work experience as a teacher with self-efficacy and job satisfaction, respectively. In five-year intervals, these figures compare the attitude of teachers with different levels of experience. Though it is important to keep in mind that these figures illustrate only a small variation on the indices, the different linear trends do provide interesting information. For teacher self-efficacy (Figure 7.4), there is a general upward trend by experience intervals, though there appears to be a slight stagnation for teachers with 11-20 years of experience, followed by a spike at 21-25 years. This is in line with the literature that reports that the middle and late career stages bring their own challenges that can affect self-efficacy and job satisfaction (Klassen and Chiu, 2010; Tschannen-Moran et al., 1998). Interestingly though, the relation between teaching experience and job satisfaction seems to tell a different story. Figure 7.5 shows a U-shaped relationship. This means that teachers' job satisfaction, on average across countries, slightly decreases through the first 15 years of teaching. Thereafter, however, a positive association emerges. This means that for the highly experienced teachers across TALIS countries, more years of work experience as a teacher is linked to slightly higher job satisfaction.

■ Figure 7.4 ■

Teachers' self-efficacy and experience

Teachers' self-efficacy level in lower secondary education according to the years of experience as a teacher in total

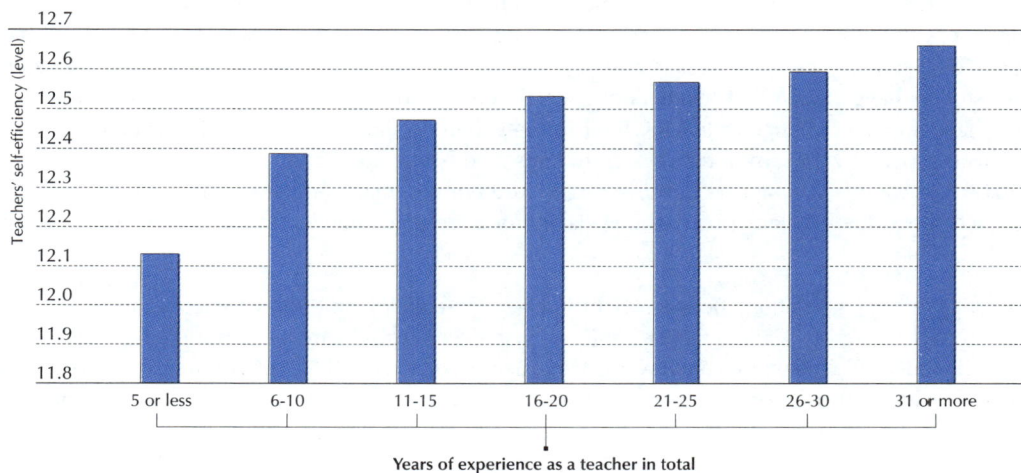

Source: OECD, TALIS 2013 Database.
StatLink ᴍꜱᴾ http://dx.doi.org/10.1787/888933042238

■ Figure 7.5 ■
Teachers' job satisfaction and experience

Teachers' job satisfaction level in lower secondary education according to the years of experience as a teacher in total

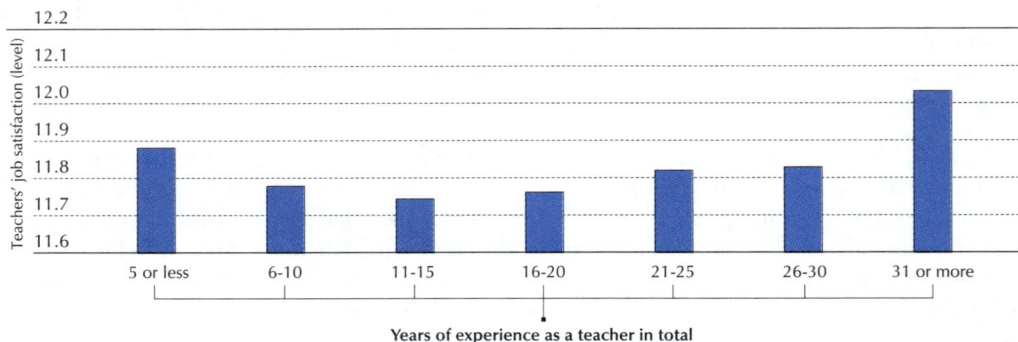

Source: OECD, TALIS 2013 Database.
StatLink ⌨ http://dx.doi.org/10.1787/888933042257

The extent to which content, pedagogy and classroom practice elements are included in a teacher's formal training has a smaller but significant effect on teacher self-efficacy and job satisfaction (Tables 7.4 and 7.5). For almost all countries the same pattern is observed: The less teachers report the inclusion of these three elements in formal training, the lower their levels of self-efficacy and job satisfaction. These findings emphasise the importance of tailoring the content, pedagogy and classroom practice elements of a teachers' formal education to the specific subjects they will teach.

Finally, Tables 7.4 and 7.5 show the mutual effects that job satisfaction and self-efficacy have on each other, when controlling for the other variables included in the model. As expected, for all countries, an increase in a teacher's job satisfaction is associated with higher reported self-efficacy and vice versa. While the associations in the two different directions are very similar, a teacher's reported confidence levels seem to carry slightly more weight, as in most countries the effect of self-efficacy on job satisfaction is slightly higher than the other way around.[5]

TEACHERS' SELF-EFFICACY AND JOB SATISFACTION IN RELATION TO CLASSROOM ENVIRONMENT

Certain classroom characteristics can make a teacher's work more challenging. Teaching classes in which a high proportion of students have different achievement levels, special needs or behavioural problems can affect a teacher's self-efficacy and job satisfaction, especially if the teacher is not properly prepared or supported (Major, 2012). Most of the empirical evidence in this area comes from studies focused on teachers of children with special needs. Chapter 4 identified that teaching special-needs students is one of the areas in which teachers need professional development the most. Other studies have shown that teachers of special-needs students are prone to low job satisfaction and self-efficacy and have a greater chance of leaving their schools than do their colleagues who teach classes without such students. This is especially the case if they teach students with behavioural and emotional problems (Emery and Vandenberg, 2010; Katsiyannis, Zhang and Conroy, 2003). Furthermore, many educators of emotionally challenged children experience stress due to a lack of specific skills and/or experience needed to teach these kinds of children (Henderson et al., 2005).

This section investigates the associations between both teacher self-efficacy and job satisfaction and class size and challenging classroom characteristics. Similar to the analyses in Chapter 6, classrooms are considered to be challenging if more than 10% of students in the classroom are low academic achievers or more than 10% of students have behavioural problems.[6] Classrooms in which 10% or more of the students are academically gifted are also included in this category, as teaching to a wide range of student abilities in one classs can also be a challenge (Major, 2012).

The strength and significance of the associations of these variables with teacher self-efficacy and job satisfaction can be seen in Tables 7.6 and 7.7, respectively. A finding of special interest, given the discussion of optimal class size that occurs in many countries, is that class size seems to have only a minimal effect on either teaching efficacy or

job satisfaction in just a few countries. Further TALIS data indicate that it is not the number of students but the type of students that are in a teacher's class that has the largest association with teachers' self-efficacy and job satisfaction. An example of this is provided in Figure 7.6, where the minimal effect of class size on teachers' job satisfaction is contrasted with the stronger influence of teaching students with behavioural problems. Analyses in this section will elaborate on this finding.

■ Figure 7.6 ■
Teachers' job satisfaction and class composition

Teachers' job satisfaction level in lower secondary education according to the number of students in the classroom and according to the percentage of students with behavioural problems[1]

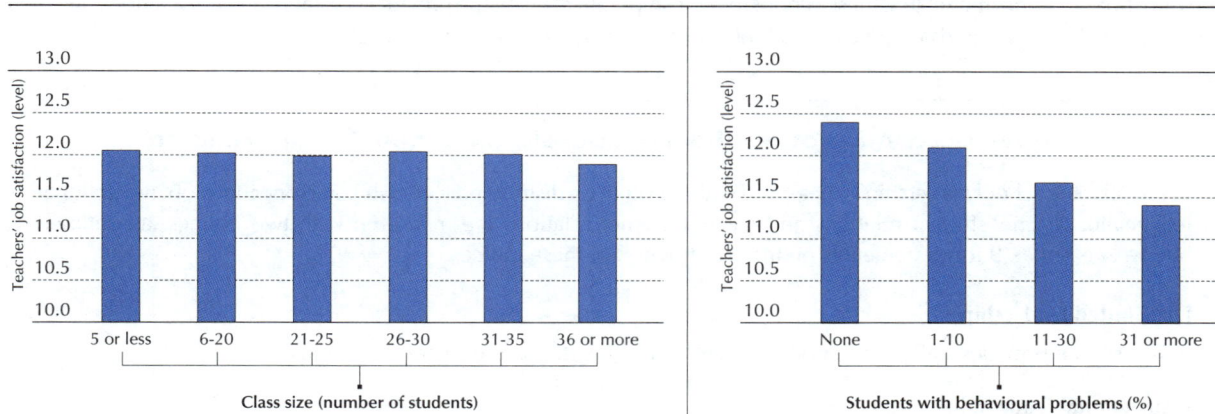

1. Data on class size and students with behavioural problems are reported by teachers and refer to a randomly chosen class they currently teach from their weekly timetable.
Source: OECD, TALIS 2013 Database.
StatLink ⬛🇮🇸📈 http://dx.doi.org/10.1787/888933042276

The associations between challenging classroom characteristics and teacher self-efficacy and job satisfaction tell an interesting story across TALIS countries. Teachers teaching classes where more than a tenth of the students are low academic achievers or have behavioural problems show significantly lower self-efficacy and job satisfaction levels in many of the TALIS countries (Tables 7.6 and 7.7). For self-efficacy, the negative relation with teaching more low academic achievers is present only in 9 countries, but for job satisfaction in 24 countries. Furthermore, teaching in classes composed of more students with behavioural problems is associated with lower self-efficacy in 16 countries and lower job satisfaction in 29 countries. These associations are of at least moderate strength in 7 countries for self-efficacy and moderate or strong in 24 countries for job satisfaction (Tables 7.6.Web and 7.7.Web). An illustration of the relationship between teaching students with behavioural problems and job satisfaction can be seen in Figure 7.6. In contrast, teaching in classrooms where more than a tenth of students are academically gifted relates to higher levels of teachers' self-efficacy in 17 countries and higher levels of job satisfaction in 23 countries. For teachers in the Czech Republic and Japan, this aspect has a particularly strong relationship with self-efficacy, and the same association is observed in Bulgaria with job satisfaction.

TEACHERS' SELF-EFFICACY AND JOB SATISFACTION IN RELATION TO SCHOOL LEADERSHIP AND IN-SCHOOL RELATIONS

Teachers' perceptions of school climate, collaborative culture and school leadership greatly impact their levels of stress, teaching efficacy and job satisfaction (Collie et al., 2012; Demir, 2008). For example, perceived stress due to students' behaviour has been found to relate negatively to teaching efficacy, and perceived stress related to workload and teacher self-efficacy appears to be directly related to teachers' job satisfaction (Collie, Shapka and Perry, 2012; Klassen and Chiu, 2010; Taylor and Tashakkori, 1994). These relationships are further reinforced by instructional leadership, defined as providing an effective teaching and learning environment and thereby increasing school quality and student achievement (see Chapter 3). Distributed leadership also has a reinforcing impact, in addition to reducing teacher isolation and increasing commitment to the common good (see Chapter 3; Wahlstrom and Louis, 2008; Pounder, 1999).

Yet, what is even more important than principal leadership styles is the relationships teachers have with other teachers (in the TALIS questionnaire, this is defined by different ways of co-operating), their school leaders and their students as a foundation to improve their instruction (Louis, 2006). Next to teachers' specific classroom management self-efficacy (Box 7.1), teachers' satisfaction with these relationships seems to be the most crucial indicator of teachers' overall job satisfaction and self-efficacy (Holzberger, Philipp and Kunter, 2013; Caprara et al., 2006; Klassen and Chiu, 2010).

In this section, the association between these in-school relationships and teacher self-efficacy and job satisfaction is explored. Teacher-leader relations are examined separately from teacher-teacher and teacher-student relations. Two aspects of the teacher-leader relationship are important and examined in this chapter: The level of opportunities that teachers have to share in the decision making in their schools and the instructional leadership that school principals provide (Box 7.3). The impact that these school relationships can have on the previously established associations between challenging classrooms and self-efficacy and job satisfaction (Tables 7.6 and 7.7) is also discussed.

Box 7.3. **Description of in-school relationships examined in this chapter**

In this chapter, school leadership is measured with one item on distributed leadership and one index on instructional leadership. Teacher-student relations and teacher-teacher relations are measured with two indices, as outlined below. See Annex B for more details on the construction of these indices.[7]

Distributed leadership
- This school provides staff with opportunities to actively participate in school decisions

Instructional leadership
- I took actions to support co-operation among teachers to develop new teaching practices
- I took actions to ensure that teachers take responsibility for improving their teaching skills
- I took actions to ensure that teachers feel responsible for their students' learning outcomes

Teacher-student relationships
- In this school, teachers and students usually get on well with each other
- Most teachers in this school believe that the students' well-being is important
- Most teachers in this school are interested in what students have to say
- If a student from this school needs extra assistance, the school provides it

Teacher-teacher relationships
- Teach jointly as a team in the same class
- Observe other teachers' classes and provide feedback
- Engage in joint activities across different classes and age groups (e.g. projects)
- Exchange teaching materials with colleagues
- Engage in discussions about the learning development of specific students
- Work with other teachers in my school to ensure common standards in evaluations for assessing student progress
- Attend team conferences
- Take part in collaborative professional learning

In all countries, when teachers report more positive relationships with students and collaborative relationships with other teachers, they report significantly higher levels of self-efficacy (Table 7.8). The association appears to be stronger for teacher-teacher relations than for teacher-student relations in many countries.

Teacher-teacher collaborative relationships are also weakly to moderately associated with higher levels of teacher job satisfaction (Table 7.9). In terms of increasing job satisfaction, the teacher-student relations are exceptionally powerful (in many cases, the teacher-student association is two to three times greater than the teacher-teacher relationship).

In general, then, teachers' reports of the quality of their relationships with other teachers in the school seems to be particularly important for teachers' feelings of self-efficacy, while for teachers' job satisfaction, their perception of the quality of the student-teacher relationships in the school appears to matter most.

In 20 countries, teachers who agree that the staff at their school are provided with opportunities to participate in decision making report higher self-efficacy scores (Table 7.8). These relationships are especially strong in Israel and Romania. An even more uniform and strong relationship is observed with job satisfaction. The ability to participate in decision making at school is significantly related to a strong improvement in teachers' job satisfaction across all countries (Table 7.9). Surprisingly, in contrast to the literature reviewed in this section, instructional leadership as measured in TALIS appears to have a minimal association with teachers' self-efficacy and job satisfaction.

The take-away points from these analyses are four-fold. First, in-school relations are important for teachers' self-efficacy and job satisfaction. Second, school leaders should try to focus on encouraging collaborative relationships among teachers and positive relationships between teachers and students in their schools. Next, school leaders who work to provide school staff with opportunities to share in decision making may gain returns in the realm of higher job satisfaction. And finally, there is little evidence that instructional leadership is associated with higher self-efficacy or job satisfaction among teachers.

The role of in-school relationships in accounting for the impact of classroom composition

This section examines the role that teachers' in-school relationships can play in impeding or alleviating the influences that the composition of students in the classroom might have on teachers' self-efficacy and job satisfaction. Figure 7.7 provides an illustration of the relationships that are covered in this section.

■ Figure 7.7 ■
The influence of class composition on teachers' attitudes and relationships

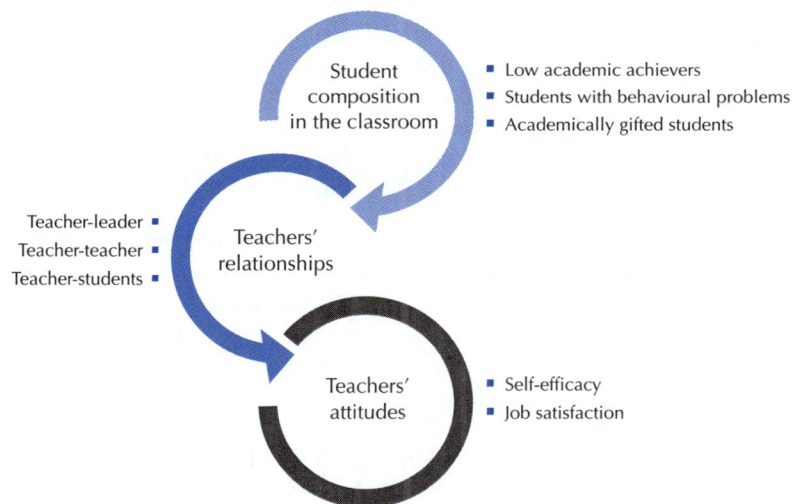

At least in some countries, the relationships teachers have in their school do appear to alter the associations between many classroom composition characteristics and self-efficacy and job satisfaction reported earlier in this chapter (Tables 7.6 and 7.7). The previously reported finding that teachers working in classrooms containing more than 10% low-achieving students tend to show lower levels of teachers' self-efficacy and job satisfaction still holds after accounting for teachers' in-school relationships, but the strength of this relationship is reduced in many countries (see Tables 7.8.Web.1 and 7.9.Web.1 for teacher-student and teacher-teacher relationships and Tables 7.8.Web.2 and 7.9.Web.2 for teacher-leader relationships, columns highlighted in light blue).[8] Specifically, for teachers' self-efficacy, in Brazil, France, Italy, Mexico, Portugal, Romania, Serbia, Spain and Abu Dhabi (United Arab Emirates), the strength of the association between self-efficacy and teaching more low academic achievers is weaker or no longer significant. In relation to job satisfaction, the strength of the association is reduced in nearly all countries. In these cases, the relationships teachers have with their principal, their colleagues and their students can help alleviate the lower levels of self-efficacy and job satisfaction experienced by teachers working in classrooms with higher proportions of low-achieving students.

Overall, teachers' in-school relationships do not seem to override the associations reported earlier in the chapter between behaviour problems in classrooms and teachers' self-efficacy. Nonetheless, taking into account teachers' in-school relationships, the strength of the associations decreases in Australia, Croatia, the Czech Republic, Denmark, Israel, Poland, Portugal, Romania, Spain, Abu Dhabi (United Arab Emirates) and England (United Kingdom). In nearly all countries where teaching in classrooms with more behavioural problem students was significantly associated with lower levels of job satisfaction, positive in-school relationships help decrease the magnitude of this association (Tables 7.8.Web.1, 7.8.Web.2, 7.9.Web.1 and 7.9.Web.2).

These data show that the relationships that teachers develop with others in their schools are incredibly valuable, for many reasons. These interpersonal relationships can be so powerful that they can negate the normally detrimental relationships between challenging classrooms of students and a teacher's job satisfaction or feelings of self-efficacy. The kinds of changes that are needed to foster more productive interpersonal relationships in a school are not ones that can be dictated by policy makers. They need to occur within schools, supported by school leaders and initiated by teachers themselves. Policies can offer principals organisational leeway to shape their teacher team in such a way that these interpersonal relationships can grow and be nurtured.

TEACHERS' SELF-EFFICACY AND JOB SATISFACTION IN RELATION TO PROFESSIONAL DEVELOPMENT OF TEACHERS

In summarising research on effective teacher professional development, Darling-Hammond and Richardson (2009) contend that successful programmes are sustained over time, are collaborative and focused on the content to be taught and provide multiple opportunities for classroom application. Since teaching beliefs such as self-efficacy constitute an important factor in the goal of facilitating student learning, they recently became the target of professional development programming. Studies have shown that professional development activities that are focused on the three components of teachers' self-efficacy – classroom management, instruction and student engagement – increase such beliefs as well as teachers' beliefs about student learning (Rosenfeld and Rosenfeld, 2008; Ross and Bruce, 2007a; Powell-Moman and Brown-Schild, 2011; Karimi, 2011). Studies remain equivocal as to whether the duration of the professional development programme or the teacher's years of work experience affect any impact that a professional development programme might have on teachers' self-efficacy beliefs and students' achievement (Lumpe et al., 2012; Wayne et al., 2008; Powell-Moman and Brown-Schild, 2011; Rosenfeld and Rosenfeld, 2008). When mentoring is considered, however, it seems that for new teachers specifically, time spent with a mentor, participation in mentor-facilitated professional development activities and the quality of mentors' interactions are significantly related to the teachers' self-efficacy and their development of effective collaborative relationships (LoCasale-Crouch et al., 2012).

As discussed in Chapter 4, there are several facets to professional development. There can be formally organised professional development, which could include induction programmes, mentoring programmes, classroom observation visits, workshops and conferences. There can also be more informally organised professional development, which could also include a mentoring relationship in which a teacher can be the recipient or the mentor in the relationship. This section examines the relationship between teachers' participation in different types and aspects of professional development with their self-efficacy and job satisfaction.

In 14 of the participating countries, teachers who report having participated in a formal induction programme have higher levels of self-efficacy, though the opposite is the case in France (Table 7.10). In Chile, the Czech Republic, Latvia and Norway, the strength of the relationship is moderate, while the relationship is especially strong in Poland. In eight countries, teachers who report having participated in a formal induction programme also tend to report higher levels of job satisfaction, though the opposite again occurs in France and also in Japan (Table 7.11). The strength of the relationship between participation in formal induction and increased job satisfaction is moderate for teachers in Bulgaria, Norway and Poland. Interestingly, participation in informal induction activities is more consistently associated with higher job satisfaction across countries than it is self-efficacy.

The relationship between mentorship[9] and self-efficacy varies widely across TALIS countries (Table 7.10). Across countries, acting as a mentor is more consistently related to higher levels of self-efficacy than is being mentored, and this relationship is especially strong in France, Japan and Korea. In these countries, teachers who report that they are providing mentorship to other colleagues tend to have much higher levels of self-efficacy.

Teachers' reports of participation in mentorship activities are related to higher job satisfaction in about a quarter of the countries. Reports of receiving mentorship are connected to higher job satisfaction in seven countries, whereas being

a mentor relates to higher job satisfaction in eight countries (Table 7.11). For the latter, the strength of the association is moderate in six of these countries, while in Sweden it is strong.

Teachers' reports of participation in mentorship, observation or coaching programmes as part of a formal school arrangement are never significantly related to lower self-efficacy or job satisfaction in any of the countries. There is a positive association with self-efficacy in 14 countries; for France, Israel, Spain, Sweden and Abu Dhabi (United Arab Emirates), these associations are moderate in strength. There is only a weak positive relationship between this form of professional development and job satisfaction in 7 countries.

Teachers who report having participated in courses, workshops and/or conferences show higher levels of self-efficacy and job satisfaction in only very few countries. Yet, the associations for self-efficacy are of moderate strength in Abu Dhabi (United Arab Emirates). Similarly, in Australia and England (United Kingdom), teachers participating in such activities report moderately higher levels of job satisfaction.

These findings suggest that for most countries informal induction matters more for teachers' job satisfaction, while formal induction matters more for teachers' feelings of self-efficacy. Providing or receiving mentorship can relate to an increase in teachers' job satisfaction, while associations with teacher self-efficacy do not show as consistent a pattern across countries. Professional development activities that are part of a formal school arrangement have a positive relationship with job satisfaction only for a few countries, although they relate positively to self-efficacy in twice as many countries.[10]

TEACHERS' SELF-EFFICACY AND JOB SATISFACTION IN RELATION TO TEACHER APPRAISAL AND FEEDBACK

As mentioned in Chapter 5, teacher appraisal and feedback can be used to recognise and celebrate teachers' strengths while simultaneously challenging teachers to address weaknesses in their pedagogical practices. Appraisal and feedback can have a significant impact on classroom instruction, teacher motivation and attitudes, as well as on student outcomes. Specifically, appraisal and feedback can play an important role in teachers' job satisfaction and self-efficacy. Although no research has directly investigated this yet, the impact of different sources of feedback and appraisal are expected to vary greatly. Whereas teachers say they derive little value from student ratings, teacher-solicited feedback is generally regarded as the most useful source of feedback for improving teaching (Wininger and Birkholz, 2013; Ross and Bruce, 2007b; Michaelowa, 2002).

There are many methods and approaches that can be used to appraise and provide feedback to teachers. Given the findings in Chapter 5, it is important to look at whether teachers receive feedback from more than one appraiser as well as the type of feedback they receive (such as results of student surveys or students' test scores or feedback on classroom management). In addition, teachers' perceptions of the impact of the appraisal are relevant (for example, are appraisals perceived as impacting classroom teaching or simply as an activity for administrative purposes). Box 7.4 explains how the TALIS questionnaire items on appraisal and feedback were compressed into six measures highlighted in this section.

In 13 of the participating countries, teachers who report having at least two evaluators also report higher levels of self-efficacy (Table 7.12). These associations are moderate or strong in Finland, Iceland, Malaysia, Norway and Spain. For job satisfaction, there is a positive relationship between teachers with at least two evaluators in 23 countries (Table 7.13). The association is weak to moderate in most cases, but it is again strong in Finland and Iceland. Receiving feedback from student surveys is associated with higher levels of teacher self-efficacy in almost all TALIS countries and with job satisfaction in 20 countries. It is interesting to note the possible relationships here, which could be interpreted in two ways. Teachers might learn from these student surveys in ways that help them feel more confident in their abilities and more satisfied with their jobs. Alternatively, it might be that the teachers who are more confident and content with their roles are those who administer student surveys in the first place.

Teachers who receive feedback about student test scores report higher levels of self-efficacy in 24 countries (Table 7.12). The association is particularly strong in Brazil, Norway, Romania, the Slovak Republic and Abu Dhabi (United Arab Emirates). This type of feedback is also related to higher job satisfaction in 17 participating countries (Table 7.13). In Brazil and Korea this relationship is especially strong, while it is negative, albeit weak, for teachers in Spain. Further, receiving feedback on classroom management is positively related to self-efficacy in 17 participating countries. This association is again strong in Brazil, Bulgaria, Italy, Korea, Serbia and the Slovak Republic. Teachers who receive feedback on classroom management also report higher levels of job satisfaction for 23 countries, and for half of these it is a strong association: Brazil, Bulgaria, Chile, Croatia, the Czech Republic, Estonia, Norway, Portugal, Serbia, the Slovak Republic and Abu Dhabi (United Arab Emirates).

Box 7.4. **Appraisal and feedback measures used in this chapter**

Six measures of appraisal and feedback are used in this chapter. The selection of these measures is based on the findings presented in Chapter 5.

Number of evaluators

The first measure identifies whether teachers were appraised by more than one evaluator.

Types of feedback

The next three measures identify the types, or sources, of feedback teachers received. Teacher responses were categorised according to whether they considered that the feedback they received considered the following three elements with moderate or high importance:

- Student surveys
- Students' test scores
- Feedback on their classroom management of student behaviour

Teachers' perceptions of appraisal and feedback

The last two measures concern teachers' perceptions related to their appraisal and feedback. The first measure relates to teachers' responses about the extent to which they agreed that their appraisal impacted their teaching. The second measure concerns the extent to which teachers agreed that their appraisal was performed primarily for administrative purposes.

The way teachers perceive the appraisal and feedback they receive in relation to their attitudes is also highly informative. In ten countries, teachers who perceive feedback as impacting their classroom teaching also report higher levels of self-efficacy (Table 7.12). This association is moderate or strong in Finland, Romania and Abu Dhabi (United Arab Emirates). The perception that appraisal and feedback influences teaching practices also positively relates to job satisfaction in nearly all TALIS countries (Table 7.13). For 11 countries this constitutes a strong relationship: Bulgaria, the Czech Republic, Italy, Malaysia, Mexico, Norway, Poland, Romania, Singapore, Abu Dhabi (United Arab Emirates) and England (United Kingdom). In contrast, when teachers perceive their appraisal and feedback to be only an administrative exercise, there is an associated decrease in teachers' self-efficacy in 14 countries. In Israel, Portugal, the Slovak Republic and England (United Kingdom), this reduction is particularly pronounced. Moreover, such a perception of appraisal and feedback is linked to a decrease in job satisfaction in all TALIS countries. This negative association with job satisfaction is strong in most countries and weak only in Brazil.

Taken together, the analyses found that the six appraisal and feedback measures contribute to meaningful differences in self-efficacy and job satisfaction in most countries.[11] It is particularly noteworthy for policy makers and school leaders that when teachers perceive that appraisal and feedback are being provided only for administrative reasons, there is a marked drop in their levels of self-efficacy and job satisfaction. Thus it would seem that in addition to the aforementioned benefits of meaningful appraisal and feedback for improving teaching practice (see Chapter 5), countries and schools may also want to consider the relationship that appraisal and feedback have with teachers' self-efficacy and job satisfaction.

TEACHERS' SELF-EFFICACY AND JOB SATISFACTION IN RELATION TO TEACHERS' BELIEFS AND PRACTICES

To equip students with the skills and competencies needed in the 21st century, the use of a variety of teaching practices has been encouraged world wide, ranging from more traditional practices (such as direct transmission), to more recently conceived, constructivist practices. The latter form of teaching and learning develops students' skills to manage complex situations and learn both independently and continuously, and it has been argued to enhance motivation and achievement of students (Nie and Lau, 2010; Guthrie, Wigfield and VonSecker, 2000; Hacker and Tenent, 2002; Nie et al., 2013). Research advocating constructivist approaches also suggests that teacher self-efficacy is higher for teachers who use constructivist instruction techniques than for those teachers who use reception or direct transmission instruction techniques (Luke et al., 2005; Nie et al., 2013). Using TALIS 2008 data, Vieluf et al. (2012) reported that the impact of direct transmission versus constructivist approaches depends on different factors, such as subjects taught and classroom variables. In fact, it was not the use of one kind of practice over another per se, but the variety of practices employed that was found to be related to higher teacher self-efficacy, among other things.

Given the findings in Chapter 6 and the reviewed research, this section focusses on the level of constructivist pedagogical beliefs teachers report integrating into their teaching. It then looks at the practices, as measured by the reported total working hours in a week and the proportion of time devoted to teaching, keeping order in the classroom and performing administrative tasks. This section first examines the relationship between these reported beliefs and practices and teachers' self-efficacy and job satisfaction and then examines whether these beliefs and practices can alleviate some of the negative relationships found between challenging classrooms and self-efficacy and job satisfaction.

TALIS data indicate that in most countries, constructivist beliefs have a positive association with teachers' self-efficacy and job satisfaction (Tables 7.14 and 7.15). Teachers who report more highly constructivist beliefs have higher levels of self-efficacy (and only slightly higher levels of job satisfaction).

The number of hours spent teaching in a typical work week has more significant associations with self-efficacy than with job satisfaction, although all of these associations are weak (Tables 7.14.Web.2 and 7.15.Web.2). Interestingly, the associations with self-efficacy and job satisfaction tend to be opposite. In 23 countries, teachers who report teaching more hours are slightly more likely to have higher levels of self-efficacy. In contrast, in five countries (Bulgaria, Estonia, Portugal, Singapore and Flanders [Belgium]), teachers who report teaching more hours tend to report slightly lower levels of job satisfaction. The proportion of time teachers report spending on keeping order in the classroom is related to lower levels of self-efficacy and job satisfaction in almost all countries. Although this relationship tends to be weak in most countries (Table 7.14.Web.3), teachers in Norway who report spending more time keeping order in the classroom report much lower levels of self-efficacy, and in six other countries this relationship is moderate (Bulgaria, Croatia, the Czech Republic, Denmark, Israel and Serbia). Finally, the proportion of time spent on administrative tasks in the classroom seems to have a weak negative association with job satisfaction for about half of the countries, while it relates negatively to self-efficacy in 12 countries. Of these countries, Australia and Bulgaria show the most pronounced effects (Tables 7.14.Web.4 and 7.15.Web.4).

The main message from these findings is that when teachers' report more constructivist beliefs, they universally report higher levels of self-efficacy and job satisfaction. This relationship between teachers' beliefs about how their students learn and how they feel about their own abilities and work might be interesting to explore further. Contrary to what might be expected, the number of hours that teachers report teaching is somewhat less significant in explaining these outcomes, although time spent keeping order in the classroom does tend to be associated with lower levels of self-efficacy and job satisfaction. Finally, the time spent on administrative tasks has similar negative relations with teacher attitudes, although the associations are less widespread and weaker across countries.

The role of beliefs and practices in accounting for the impact of classroom composition

This section examines the role that can be played by teachers' constructivist beliefs, teaching practices and the time they report spending on tasks such as teaching, keeping order or performing administrative tasks (Figure 7.8) in terms of impeding or alleviating the associations reported earlier in this chapter between the student composition in the classroom and teachers' self-efficacy and job satisfaction (Tables 7.6 and 7.7).

The proportion of time spent keeping order in the classroom plays the most crucial role in these relationships (Table 7.14.Web.3). For teachers in classrooms with higher proportions of low academic achievers who exhibited lower self-efficacy, looking at the proportion of time these teachers report spending on keeping order accounts fully for the negative association in four countries (Italy, Serbia, Spain and Sweden) and reduces the magnitude of the relationship in Brazil, France, Mexico, Portugal and Romania. In other words, it is not so much that these teachers teach in classrooms with more low academic achievers that relates to their lower levels of self-efficacy, but rather the higher proportion of time they report spending on keeping order in the classroom.

A similar finding emerges for teachers who work in classrooms with higher proportions of students with behaviour problems and who show lower levels of self-efficacy. The proportion of time these teachers spend keeping order accounts fully for this negative association in ten countries and reduces the magnitude of the association in Poland, Romania and Abu Dhabi (United Arab Emirates). What this means is that in many countries, the relationship between teaching in challenging classrooms (i.e. classrooms containing more low achievers or students with behavioural problems) and lower self-efficacy can be explained by the amount of time that teacher spends keeping order in the class.

The proportion of time keeping order in the classroom also accounts for some of the associations between teaching in challenging classrooms and lower teacher job satisfaction. Whether challenging classrooms are defined as ones

with higher proportions of low academic achievers or by higher proportions of students with behavioural problems, including the proportion of time keeping order fully or partially accounts for the negative association in almost countries (Table 7.15.Web.3). In other words, it is not the percentage of students with behavioural problems or low achievement levels in a classroom that is the most important influence on a teacher's self-efficacy or job satisfaction. Rather, it is the time the teacher spends dealing with the classroom-management issues that these students – or other students in these classes – may cause.

■ Figure 7.8 ■
The influence of class composition on teachers' attitudes, beliefs and practices

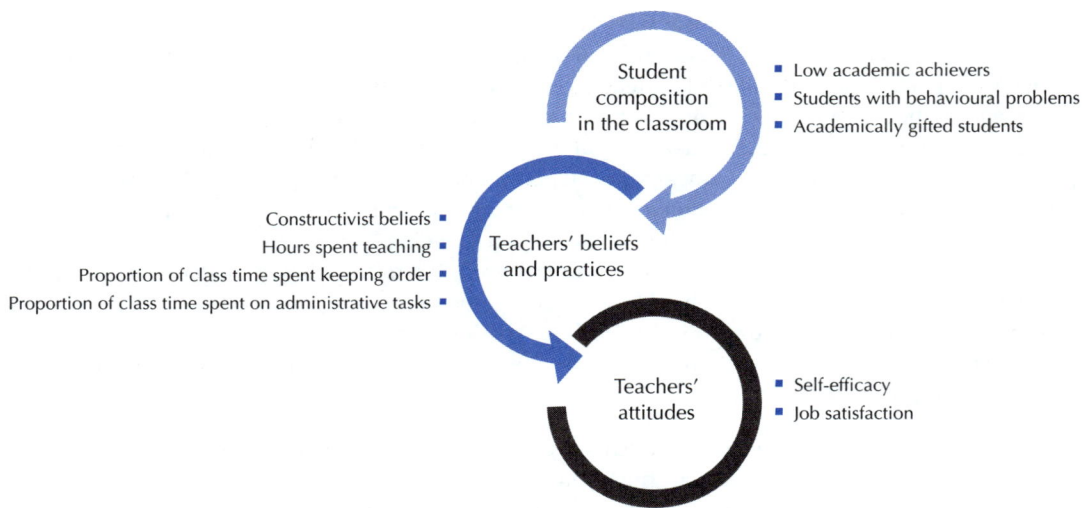

TEACHERS' SELF-EFFICACY AND JOB SATISFACTION IN RELATION TO TEACHERS' PROFESSIONAL COLLABORATIVE PRACTICES

Formal collaborative learning generally entails teachers meeting on a regular basis to develop shared responsibility for their students' school success (Chong and Kong, 2012). Although an increasing number of teacher professional development experiences are structured around collaboration, evidence on conditions for successful collaboration and positive outcomes related to collaborative practices remains relatively little and inconclusive (Nelson et al., 2008). Yet a myriad of different structures and processes to create a collaborative culture among teachers in schools have been described (Erickson et al., 2005; Nelson et al., 2008). Empirical evidence shows that teacher collaboration may enhance teacher efficacy, which in turn may improve student achievement and sustain positive teacher behaviours (Liaw, 2009; Puchner and Taylor, 2006). In a meta-review of empirical studies, Cordingley et al. (2003) reported that collaborative professional development is related to a positive impact upon teachers' range of teaching practices and instructional strategies, to their ability to match these to their students' needs and to their self-esteem and self-efficacy. There is also evidence that such collaborative professional development is linked to a positive influence upon student learning processes, motivation and outcomes.

This section analyses the associations between several collaborative practices and teacher self-efficacy and job satisfaction. Specifically, the following indicators for collaborative practices were used: teaching jointly in the same class, observing and providing feedback on other teachers' classes, engaging in joint activities across different classes and age groups and taking part in collaborative professional learning. Teachers who report engaging in these activities five times a year or more are compared with those who report engaging in them less frequently..

Table 7.16 shows the associations between the aforementioned collaborative practices and teacher self-efficacy. With the exception of only a few countries, it seems that teachers who report using collaborative practices five times a year or more also report higher levels of self-efficacy. For many countries this association is weak, but for a few countries a more pronounced realtionship emerges. For example, in Chile, Croatia and the Slovak Republic, teaching as a team in the same class five times a year or more has a pronounced positive association with self-efficacy. Observing other teachers' classes and providing feedback is at least moderately related to an increase in teachers' self-efficacy in the Netherlands, Serbia

and Sweden (Table 7.16.Web). Similarly, engaging in joint activities across different classes and age groups relates to moderately higher self-efficacy in 11 countries and to a strong rise in self-efficacy scores in Croatia, the Czech Republic, Finland and Iceland. Yet the strongest relationship with teachers' self-efficacy is taking part in collaborative professional learning. For almost all countries, teachers who engage in this activity five times a year or more also show higher levels of self-efficacy, and for half of the countries this relationship is of moderate strength. Particularly strong associations emerged for Bulgaria, Chile, Estonia, Finland, Israel and Korea.

Table 7.17 shows the relationships between these collaborative practices and teacher job satisfaction. Similar to the results for teacher self-efficacy, almost all countries showed a positive relationship between teacher collaboration and job satisfaction. Some relationships are particularly prominent. For example, for teachers in Chile and Estonia, the association of jointly teaching the same class with teachers' job satisfaction stands out (Table 7.17.Web). Similar moderate relationships emerge for eight countries with respect to observing other teachers' classes. Furthermore, in Abu Dhabi (United Arab Emirates), teacher job satisfaction is moderately higher when teachers engage in joint activities across different classes and age groups. Comparable to teacher self-efficacy, the strongest association with job satisfaction appears for teachers taking part in collaborative professional learning five times a year or more. For two-thirds of the countries this is related to enhanced job satisfaction significantly. Of these, 12 countries show moderately strong associations, and Brazil and Chile show exceptionally strong associations. This means that teachers who take part in collaborative learning more frequently also show much higher levels of job satisfaction than those who do not.

The relationships between collaborative practices and teacher self-efficacy and job satisfaction, on average across countries, are illustrated in Figures 7.9 and 7.10, respectively. When looking at all TALIS countries, an upward trend can be seen for the frequency of collaborative practices and the positive link to teacher self-efficacy.

For job satisfaction, the positive association appears to stagnate slightly for higher frequencies. Overall however, more engagement in collaborative practices seems to be, on average, associated with higher self-efficacy and job satisfaction for teachers across the TALIS countries.

These findings, along with those in the previous section on interpersonal relationships in schools, underscore the need for a new model of teaching. The traditional picture of a single classroom with one teacher in isolation is not good enough for a variety of reasons. Relationship building and fostering collaborative practices in schools, whether these be through collaborative professional development activities, systems of peer feedback or collaborative teaching activities, are highly beneficial to teacher self-efficacy and job satisfaction.

■ Figure 7.9 ■

Teachers' self-efficacy and professional collaboration

Teachers' self-efficacy level according to the frequency of teacher professional collaboration for the following items for lower secondary education teachers

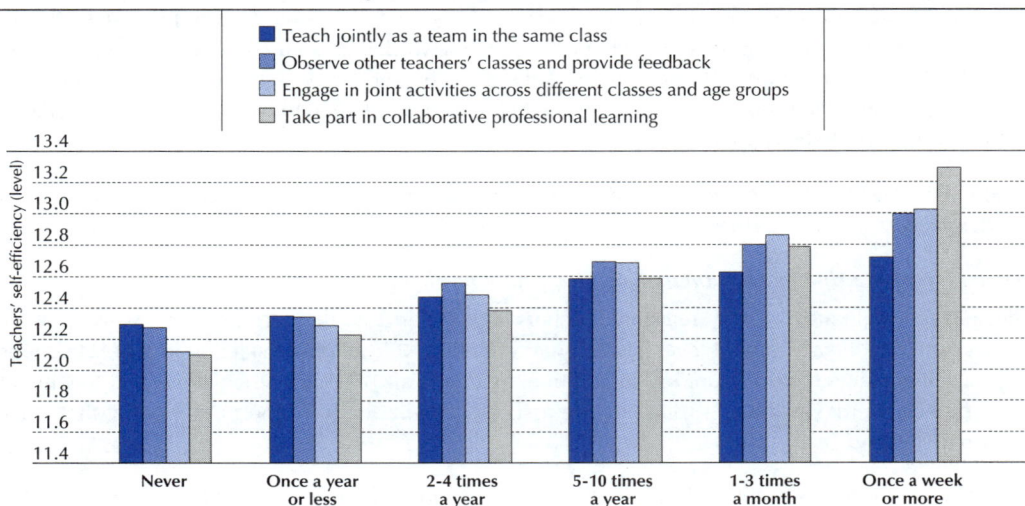

Legend:
- Teach jointly as a team in the same class
- Observe other teachers' classes and provide feedback
- Engage in joint activities across different classes and age groups
- Take part in collaborative professional learning

Source: OECD, TALIS 2013 Database.
StatLink ⬛⬛⬛ http://dx.doi.org/10.1787/888933042295

■ Figure 7.10 ■

Teachers' job satisfaction and professional collaboration

*Teachers' job satisfaction level according to the frequency of teacher professional collaboration
for the following items for lower secondary education teachers*

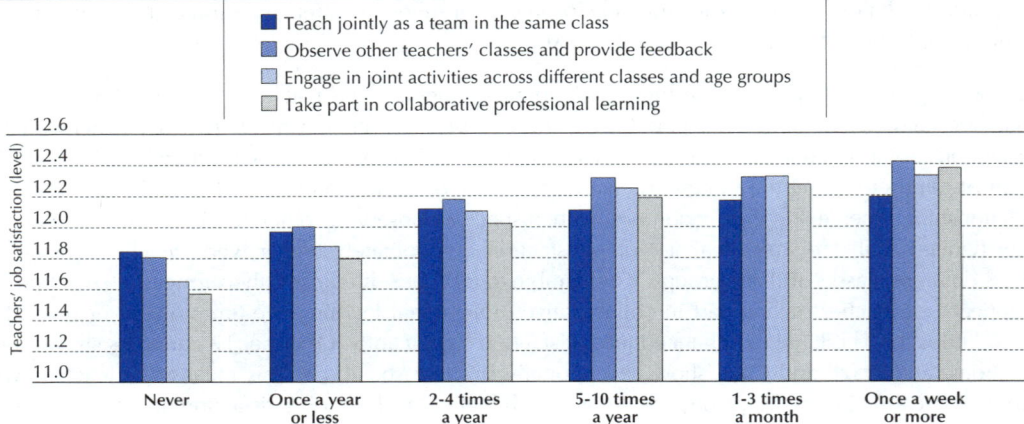

Source: OECD, TALIS 2013 Database.
StatLink ᵃᵉᶠᶫ http://dx.doi.org/10.1787/888933042314

SUMMARY AND MAIN POLICY IMPLICATIONS

The concepts of teacher self-efficacy and job satisfaction are more important to schools and education systems than a surface-level reading might indicate. In other words, it is not just about making sure teachers are happy and feel good about themselves and their teaching, although, of course, that is important as well. Research cited in this chapter indicates the positive associations between both self-efficacy and job satisfaction and student achievement. High levels of teacher self-efficacy are also associated with student motivation and other positive teacher behaviours. Although perhaps more importantly, low levels of self-efficacy can be linked with high levels of stress for teachers and problems dealing with students who misbehave. The TALIS data also demonstrate that in most countries, increasing teacher self-efficacy is slightly more likely to result in an increase in teachers' job satisfaction than the other way around. Job satisfaction is important in itself as it relates to teacher retention and teachers' level of commitment.

The data presented in this chapter indicate that on average, nine of ten teachers are satisfied with their jobs and 70-92% of teachers are confident in their abilities in the areas measured. The biggest differences come at the country level. The differences in reported levels of efficacy and job satisfaction come from a variety of sources, depending on the country, but across countries challenging classroom circumstances play a large role. This is hardly a surprise given the amount of time a teacher spends in his/her classroom and the importance of the work that occurs – or should be occurring – there. If a teacher spends an inordinate amount of time keeping order or if a higher percentage of his or her students experience behavioural issues, it is natural to think that this teacher might be less confident in his or her abilities or feel less positive about his or her job. The TALIS data support this.

Fortunately, the TALIS data also illuminate positive influences on teacher self-efficacy and job satisfaction that can aid in policy or programme development in these areas.

Empower teachers to play a role in decision making at a school level

Teacher leadership is important for many reasons. Teachers who report that they are provided with opportunities to participate in decision making at a school level have higher reported levels of job satisfaction in all TALIS countries and higher feelings of self-efficacy in most countries. In addition, in almost all TALIS countries, the extent to which teachers can participate in decision making has a strong positive association with the likelihood of reporting that teaching is a valued profession in society.

As discussed in Chapter 3, the concept of distributed leadership is not only important for helping to alleviate some of the burden school leaders face, but it can be beneficial to teachers as well. Furthermore, teachers are uniquely placed to aid in school-level decision making because they might be closer to students and parents, more familiar with how

curriculum is implemented and more able to discuss student assessments and results than their school principals might be. Thus, it is not only worth school principals devolving some of the responsibility for school-level decisions to teachers, but policy makers should consider providing guidance on distributed leadership and distributed decision making at a system level.

Build teacher capacity to more successfully and efficiently handle behaviour problems

TALIS data indicate that as the percentage of students with behavioural problems increases, there is a strong decrease in teachers' reported levels of job satisfaction. In addition, teachers who spend more time keeping order in the classroom report lower levels of self-efficacy and job satisfaction in most countries. When these relationships were examined further, the analyses found that these negative relationships between both self-efficacy and job satisfaction and specific classroom climate issues can also be elucidated by a teacher's reports of keeping order in class. In other words, it is not the percentage of students with behavioural problems or low achievement levels in a classroom that is the most important influence on a teacher's self-efficacy or job satisfaction. Rather, it is the time the teacher spends dealing with the classroom-management issues that these students – or other students in these classes – may cause.

Though causal inferences cannot be made, analyses reported in this chapter provide preliminary support for building teacher capacity so that the impact of behavioural problems on teaching and learning can be reduced. This could benefit not only the teacher but also the student learning that occurs. Professional development detailing classroom management or a variety of instructional strategies might be one answer, especially for newer teachers. Addressing teacher resource issues by providing additional classroom or pedagogical support for particularly challenging classes might be another. It is equally important to be sure that during initial teacher education, teachers have several, sufficiently long periods of teaching practice in a variety of schools to ensure that beginning teachers do not enter the profession until they have developed adequate classroom competencies. More flexible classroom situations, such as team teaching, which can provide other benefits discussed later, might also enable teachers to share the tasks of teaching and attending to potential discipline issues.

Support the development of interpersonal relationships within the school environment

The findings in this chapter show that the interpersonal relationships in a school have powerful mediating effects on some of the challenging classroom circumstances that teachers might face. In addition, relationships that teachers have with their students have a strong association with teachers' level of job satisfaction.

School leaders need to provide opportunities and support for relationship building at a school level. This support could be in the form of resources such as physical space in which teachers can meet with each other or time away from class or other administrative work to allow teachers to meet and develop relationships with students or colleagues. The leadership team needs to make itself available to its teaching staff as well. Government policies can also offer school leaders the organisational freedom to develop strategies in these areas and to make changes in the school day or school building to help. Perhaps most important, however, are teachers themselves, who need to be open and willing to engage with their colleagues, their administration and with the learners.

Institute meaningful systems of appraisal and feedback that have connections with teachers' practice

In previous chapters this report has discussed the importance of appraisal and feedback on many aspects of a teacher's work. This chapter further shows that teachers' perceptions of these systems in their school can make a difference. In all TALIS countries, teachers' perception that appraisal and feedback leads to changes in their teaching practice is related to higher job satisfaction, whereas the perception that appraisal and feedback is performed merely for administrative purposes leads to lower levels of job satisfaction.

This is yet another reason that policy makers and schools should support the development of teacher appraisal and feedback systems that are actually linked to improving teaching. (See the policy recommendations in Chapters 5 and 6 for more specific details in this area.)

Encourage collaboration among teachers, either through professional development or classroom practices

Collaboration among teachers is important not just for building the interpersonal relationships among staff that are valuable but also in and of itself. It is clear from the TALIS data that teachers benefit from even minimal amounts of collaboration with colleagues. The data show that participating in collaborative professional development or engaging in collaborative practices five times a year or more has a positive relationship with both teacher self-efficacy and job satisfaction. Many of the collaborative practices mentioned in TALIS could – and should – be done at a school level,

such as observing other teacher' classes and providing feedback or teaching as a team in the same class. But these activities in particular serve a variety of purposes, such as providing professional development for teachers in the context within which they work or offering teachers another source of feedback on their work. Some work needs to be done by school leaders to make more flexible time tabling to allow for team teaching, for example, but the benefits are likely to outweigh any burden.

Notes

1. Most of the studies cited in this chapter are based on research conducted in the United States. Examining the proposed relationships with the large international TALIS database therefore sheds a new, more cross-culturally nuanced light on teacher attitudes.

2. Teachers responded that they could perform these actions quite a bit or a lot, which has here been summarised by "often".

3. These analyses were made up of binary logistic regressions conducted for each country separately. The combined Strongly Disagree-Disagree group was chosen as a reference category for the analysis examining the extent to which teachers feel that teaching is a valued profession in society. Please see Annex B for further technical details about the analyses performed and the interpretation of the associated results tables.

4. To facilitate interpretation, the text discusses weak, moderate and strong relationships instead of the numerical values of the regression coefficients. Cut-off points for these three categories were standard deviation unit changes of 0.2 and 0.3. Please see Box 7.2 for more information.

5. This conclusion holds when looking at the different associations in terms of standard deviation unit changes (see Annex B).

6. Similarly, the cut-off points were determined by reviewing the distribution of responses and selecting a point where both representation of the responses and sufficient variability to be meaningful were maintained.

7. As discussed in Box 7.2, for non-dichotomous variables we use a threshold marker of one standard deviation higher than the mean to discuss substantive differences in coefficient sizes, since a "one-unit" change on these indices holds little meaning. A teacher with a score that is one standard deviation higher than average will be referenced in the text as a teacher with a high score on that measure. For example, a teacher with a "high teacher-student relationship score" references a teacher with a teacher-student relationship score at least one standard deviation higher than the average mean score.

8. Note that the baseline classroom composition coefficients used in Tables 7.8 to 7.15 are slightly different from those presented in Tables 7.6 and 7.7. This is due to differences in the analyses performed. See Annex B for more information.

9. Note that there are many countries with low participation in mentorship (see Chapter 4). For robustness of analyses, only countries with more than minimal mentorship participation (a threshold minimum of 5% was used) are discussed.

10. In supplementary analyses (not shown here), there does not appear to be consistent or significant changes in classroom composition correlations with self-efficacy or job satisfaction when professional development is accounted for.

11. In supplementary analyses (not shown here), there does not appear to be consistent or significant changes in classroom composition correlations with self-efficacy or job satisfaction when these appraisal or feedback measures are accounted for.

A note regarding Israel

The statistical data for Israel are supplied by and under the responsibility of the relevant Israeli authorities. The use of such data by the OECD is without prejudice to the status of the Golan Heights, East Jerusalem and Israeli settlements in the West Bank under the terms of international law.

References

Antoniou, A.S., F. Polychroni and **A.N. Vlachakis** (2006), "Gender and age differences in occupational stress and professional burnout between primary and high-school teachers in Greece", *Journal of Managerial Psychology,* Vol. 21, pp. 682-690.

Bandura, A. (1986), *Social Foundations of Thought and Action: A Social Cognitive Theory,* Prentice Hall, Englewood Cliffs, NJ.

Brief, A.P. and **H.M. Weiss** (2002), "Organizational behavior: Affect in the workplace", *Annual Review of Psychology,* Vol. 53, pp. 279-307.

Butt, G. et al. (2005), "Teacher job satisfaction: Lessons from the TSW pathfinder project", *School Leadership and Management,* Vol. 25, pp. 455-471.

Calik, T. et al. (2012), "Examination of relationships between instructional leadership of school principals and self-efficacy of teachers and collective teacher efficacy", *Educational Sciences: Theory and Practice,* Vol. 12/4, pp. 2498-2504.

Caprara, G.V. et al. (2003), "Efficacy beliefs as determinants of teachers' job satisfaction", *Journal of Educational Psychology,* Vol. 95/4, pp. 821-832.

Caprara, G.V. et al. (2006), "Teachers' self-efficacy beliefs as determinants of job satisfaction and students' academic achievement: A study at the school level", *Journal of School Psychology,* Vol. 44/6, pp. 473-490.

Chaplain, R.P. (2008), "Stress and psychological distress among trainee and secondary teachers in England", *Educational Psychology,* Vol. 28, pp. 195-209.

Chong, W.H. and **C.A. Kong** (2012), "Teacher collaborative learning and teacher self-efficacy: The case of lesson study", *Journal of Experimental Education,* Vol. 80/3, pp. 263-283.

Collie, R.J., J.D. Shapka and **N.E. Perry** (2012), "School climate and socio-emotional learning: Predicting teacher stress, job satisfaction, and teaching efficacy", *Journal of Educational Psychology,* Vol. 104/4, pp. 1189-1204.

Cordingley P. et al. (2003), "The impact of collaborative CPD on classroom teaching and learning", in *Research Evidence in Education Library,* EPPI-Centre, Social Science Research Unit, Institute of Education, University of London, London.

Crossman, A. and **P. Harris** (2006), "Job satisfaction of secondary school teachers", *Educational Management Administration and Leadership,* Vol. 34, pp. 29-46.

Darling-Hammond, L. and **N. Richardson** (2009), "Teacher learning: What matters?", *Educational Leadership,* Vol. 66/5, pp. 46-53.

Demir, K. (2008), "Transformational leadership and collective efficacy: The moderating roles of collaborative culture and teachers' self-efficacy", *Egitim, Arastirmalari – Eurasian Journal of Educational Research,* Vol. 33, pp. 93-112.

Devos, C., V. Dupriez and **L. Paguay** (2012), "Does the social working environment predict beginning teachers' self-efficacy and feelings of depression?", *Teaching and Teacher Education: An International Journal of Research and Studies,* 28(2), pp. 206-217.

Dinham, S. and **C. Scott** (1998), "A three-domain model of teacher and school executive career satisfaction", *Journal of Educational Administration,* Vol. 36, pp. 362-378.

Emery, D.W. and **B. Vandenberg** (2010), "Special education teacher burnout and ACT", *International Journal of Special Education,* Vol. 25/3, pp. 119-131.

Erickson, G. et al. (2005), "Collaborative teacher learning: Findings from two professional development projects", *Teacher and Teacher Education,* Vol. 21, pp. 787-798.

Guthrie, J.T., A. Wigfield and **C. VonSecker** (2000), "Effects of integrated instruction on motivation and strategy use in reading", *Journal of Educational Psychology,* Vol. 92, pp. 331-341.

Hacker, D.J. and **A. Tenent** (2002), "Implementing reciprocal teaching in the classroom: Overcoming obstacles and making modifications", *Journal of Educational Psychology,* Vol. 94, pp. 699-718.

Henderson, K. et al. (2005), "Teachers of children with emotional disturbance: A national look at preparation, teaching conditions, and practices", *Behavioral Disorders,* Vol. 31/1, pp. 6-17.

Holzberger, D., A. Philipp and **M. Kunter** (2013), "How teachers' self-efficacy is related to instructional quality: A longitudinal analysis", *Journal of Educational Psychology,* online first publication, April 29, *http://dx.doi.org/10.1037/a0032198.*

Judge, T.A. et al. (2001), "The job satisfaction-job performance relationship: A qualitative and quantitative review", *Psychological Bulletin,* Vol. 127/3, pp. 376-407.

Kardos, S.M. and **S.M. Johnson** (2007), "On their own and presumed expert: New teachers' experiences with their colleagues", *Teachers College Record,* Vol. 109, pp. 2083-2106.

Karimi, M.N. (2011), "The effects of professional development initiatives on EFL teachers' degree of self-efficacy", *Australian Journal of Teacher Education,* Vol. 36/6, pp. 50-62.

Katsiyannis, A., D. Zhang and **M.A. Conroy** (2003), "Availability of special education teachers", *Remedial and Special Education,* Vol. 24/4, pp. 246-253.

Klassen, R.M. et al. (2009), "Exploring the validity of a teachers' self-efficacy scale in five countries", *Contemporary Educational Psychology,* Vol. 34/1, pp. 67-76.

Klassen, R.M. and **M.M. Chiu** (2010), "Effect on teachers' self-efficacy and job satisfaction: Teacher gender, years of experience, and job stress", *Journal of Educational Psychology,* Vol. 102/3, pp. 741-756.

Klassen, R.M., E.L. Usher and **M. Bong** (2010), "Teachers' collective efficacy, job satisfaction, and job stress in cross-cultural context", *Journal of Experimental Education,* Vol. 78, pp. 464-486.

Kooij, D. et al. (2008), "Older workers' motivation to continue to work: Five meanings of age", *Journal of Managerial Psychology,* Vol. 23, pp. 364-394.

Lee, K., J.J. Carswell and **N.J. Allen** (2000), "A meta-analytic review of occupational commitment: Relations with person- and work-related variables", *Journal of Applied Psychology,* Vol. 85, pp. 799-811.

Liaw, E.C. (2009), "Teacher efficacy of pre-service teachers in Taiwan: The influence of classroom teaching and group discussions", *Teaching and Teacher Education,* Vol. 25, pp. 176-180.

Liu, X.S. and **J. Ramsey** (2008), "Teachers' job satisfaction: Analyses of the Teacher Follow-up Survey in the United States for 2000-2001", *Teaching and Teacher Education,* Vol. 24, pp. 1173-1184.

LoCasale-Crouch, J. et al. (2012), "The role of the mentor in supporting new teachers: Associations with self-efficacy, reflection, and quality", *Mentoring and Tutoring: Partnership in Learning,* Vol. 20/3, pp. 303-323.

Locke, E. (1969), "What is job satisfaction?" *Organizational Behavior and Human Performance,* Vol. 4, pp. 309-336.

Louis, K.S. (2006), "Changing the culture of schools: Professional community, organizational learning, and trust", *Journal of School Leadership,* Vol. 16, pp. 477-487.

Luke, A. et al. (2005), *Innovation and Enterprise in Classroom Practice: A Discussion of Enabling and Disenabling Pedagogical Factors in P5 and S3 Classrooms,* Centre for Research in Instruction and Practice, Singapore.

Lumpe, A. et al. (2012), "Beliefs about teaching science: The relationship between elementary teachers' participation in professional development and student achievement", *International Journal of Science Education,* Vol. 34/2, pp. 153-166.

Major, A.E. (2012), "Job design for special education teachers", *Current Issues in Education,* Vol. 15/2, *http://cie.asu.edu/ojs/index.php/cieatasu/article/view/900/333.*

Michaelowa, K. (2002), *Teacher Job Satisfaction, Student Achievement, and the Cost of Primary Education in Francophone Sub-Saharan Africa,* Hamburg Institute of International Economics.

Nelson, T.H. et al. (2008), "A culture of collaborative inquiry: Learning to develop and support professional learning communities", *Teachers College Record,* Vol. 110, pp. 1269-1303.

Nie, Y. and **S. Lau** (2010), "Differential relations of traditional and constructivist instruction to students' cognition, motivation, and achievement", *Learning and Instruction,* Vol. 20, pp. 411-423.

Nie, Y. et al. (2013), "The roles of teacher efficacy in instructional innovation: Its predictive relations to constructivist and didactic instruction", *Educational Research for Policy and Practice,* Vol. 12/1, pp. 67-77.

OECD (2009), *Creating Effective Teaching and Learning Environments: First Results from TALIS,* OECD Publishing, Paris, *http://dx.doi.org/10.1787/9789264068780-en.*

Pounder, D.G. (1999), "Teacher teams: Exploring job characteristics and work-related outcomes of work group enhancement", *Educational Administration Quarterly,* Vol. 35/3, pp. 317-348.

Powell-Moman, A.D. and **V.B. Brown-Schild** (2011), "The influence of a two-year professional development institute on teacher self-efficacy and use of inquiry-based instruction", *Science Educator,* Vol. 20/2, pp. 47-53.

Price, H. and **J. Collett** (2012), "The role of exchange and emotion on commitment: A study using teachers", *Social Science Research,* Vol. 41, pp. 1469-1479.

Puchner, L.D. and **A.R. Taylor** (2006), "Lesson study, collaboration and teacher efficacy: Stories from two-school based math lesson study groups", *Teaching and Teacher Education,* Vol. 22, pp. 922-934.

Rosenfeld, M. and **Rosenfeld** (2008), "Developing effective teacher beliefs about learners: The role of sensitizing teachers to individual learning differences", *Educational Psychology,* Vol. 28/3, pp. 245-272.

Ross, J. and **C. Bruce** (2007a), "Professional development effects on teacher efficacy: Results of a randomized field trial", *Journal of Educational Research,* Vol. 101/1, pp. 50-60.

Ross, J. and **C. Bruce** (2007b), "Teacher self-assessment: A mechanism for facilitating professional growth", *Teaching and Teacher Education,* Vol. 23, pp. 146-159.

Schleicher, A. (2011), *Building a High-Quality Teaching Profession: Lessons from around the World,* OECD Publishing, Paris, *http://dx.doi.org/10.1787/9789264113046-en.*

Skaalvik, E.M. and **S. Skaalvik** (2007), "Dimensions of teacher self-efficacy and relations with strain factors, perceived collective teacher efficacy, and teacher burnout", *Journal of Educational Psychology,* Vol. 99/3, pp. 611-625.

Somech, A. and **R. Bogler** (2002), "Antecedents and consequences of teacher organizational and professional commitment", *Educational Administration Quarterly,* Vol. 38, pp. 555-577.

Taylor, D.L. and **A. Tashakkori** (1994), "Predicting teachers' sense of efficacy and job satisfaction using school climate and participatory decision making", presented at the Annual Meeting of the Southwest Educational Research Association, January 1994, San Antonio, TX.

Tschannen-Moran, M. and **M. Barr** (2004), "Fostering student achievement: The relationship between collective teacher efficacy and student achievement", *Leadership and Policy in Schools,* Vol. 3/3, pp. 187-207.

Tschannen-Moran, M. and **A. Woolfolk Hoy** (2001), "Teacher efficacy: Capturing an elusive construct", *Teaching and Teacher Education,* Vol. 17/7, pp. 783-805.

Tschannen-Moran, M. and **A. Woolfolk Hoy** (2007), "The differential antecedents of self-efficacy beliefs of novice and experienced teachers", *Teaching and Teacher Education,* Vol. 23/6, pp. 944-956.

Tschannen-Moran, M., A. Woolfolk Hoy and **W.K. Hoy** (1998), "Teacher efficacy: Its meaning and measure", *Review of Educational Research,* Vol. 68, pp. 202-248.

Wolters, C.A. and **S.G. Daugherty** (2007), "Goal structures and teachers' sense of efficacy: Their relation and association to teaching experience and academic level", *Journal of Educational Psychology,* Vol. 99, pp. 181-193.

Vieluf, S. et al. (2012), *Teaching Practices and Pedagogical Innovation: Evidence from TALIS,* OECD Publishing, *http://dx.doi.org/10.1787/9789264123540-en.*

Wahlstrom, K.L. and **K.S. Louis** (2008), "How teachers experience principal leadership: The roles of professional community, trust, efficacy, and shared responsibility", *Educational Administration Quarterly,* Vol. 44, pp. 458-495.

Wayne, A.J. et al. (2008), "Experimenting with teacher professional development: Motives and methods", *Educational Researcher,* Vol. 37/8, pp. 469-479.

Wininger, S.R. and **P.M. Birkholz** (2013), "Sources of instructional feedback, job satisfaction, and basic psychological needs", *Innovative Higher Education,* Vol. 38, pp. 159-170.

Woolfolk Hoy, A. and **R. Burke Spero** (2005), "Changes in teacher efficacy during the early years of teaching: A comparison of four measures", *Teaching and Teacher Education,* Vol. 21, pp. 343-356.

Annex A

TECHNICAL NOTES ON SAMPLING PROCEDURES AND RESPONSE RATES FOR TALIS 2013

ANNEX A

TECHNICAL NOTES ON SAMPLING PROCEDURES AND RESPONSE RATES FOR TALIS 2013

Sampling procedures and response rates

The objective of the Teaching and Learning International Survey (TALIS) in 2013 was to obtain, in each participating country, a representative sample of teachers for each ISCED level in which the country participated. Moreover, a representative sample of teachers teaching students of the appropriate age in schools selected for Programme for International Student Assessment (PISA) in 2012 was required for each country that opted to participate in the TALIS-PISA link. TALIS 2013 identified policy issues that encompass the classroom, teachers, schools and school management, so the coverage of TALIS 2013 extends to all teachers of each concerned ISCED level and to the principals of the schools where they teach. The international sampling plan prepared for TALIS 2013 used a stratified two-stage probability sampling design. This means that teachers (second stage units, or secondary sampling units) were to be randomly selected from the list of in-scope teachers in each of the randomly selected schools (first stage units, or primary sampling units). A more detailed description of the survey design and its implementation can be found in the TALIS Technical Report (2014).

A teacher of ISCED level 1, 2 or 3 is one who, as part of his or her regular duties in their school, provides instruction in programmes at that ISCED level. Teachers who teach a mixture of programmes at different ISCED levels in the target school are included in the TALIS universe. There is no minimum cut-off for how much teaching these teachers need to be engaged in at any of the three ISCED levels.

The international target population of TALIS 2013 restricts the survey to those teachers who teach regular classes in ordinary schools and to the principals of those schools. Teachers teaching to adults and teachers working in schools exclusively devoted to children with special needs are not part of the international target population and are deemed out of scope. Unlike in TALIS 2008, however, teachers working with special-needs students in a regular school setting were considered in-scope in TALIS 2013. When a school is made up exclusively of these teachers, the school itself is said to be out of scope. Teacher aides, pedagogical support staff (e.g. guidance counsellors and librarians) and health and social support staff (e.g. doctors, nurses, psychiatrists, psychologists, occupational therapists and social workers) were not considered to be teachers and thus not part of the TALIS international target population.

For national reasons, participating countries could choose to restrict the coverage of their national implementation of TALIS 2013 to parts of the country. For example, a province or state experiencing civil unrest or an area struck by a natural disaster could be removed from the international target population to create a national target population. Participating countries were invited to keep these exclusions to a minimum.

TALIS 2013 recognised that attempting to survey teachers in very small schools can be inefficient and difficult. For each ISCED level, surveying teachers in schools with no more than three teachers at a specific ISCED level and those teaching in schools located in geographically remote areas could be a costly, time-consuming and statistically inefficient exercise. Therefore, participating countries were allowed to exclude those teachers for TALIS 2013 data collection, thus creating a national survey population different from the national target population. The National Project Manager (NPM) for each country was required to document the reasons for exclusion, the size, the location, the clientele and so on, of each excluded school. This documentation was required for each ISCED level in which a country participated. The school exclusions for the TALIS-PISA link were the same as those used in PISA 2012.

Within a selected in-scope school, the following categories of teachers were excluded from the sample:

- Teachers teaching in schools exclusively serving special-needs students. Teachers who also act as school principals: no teacher data collected, but school principal data collected.

- Substitute, emergency or occasional teachers.

- Teachers on long-term leave.

- Teachers teaching exclusively to adults.

- Teachers who had taken part in the TALIS 2013 field trial.

Sample size requirements

For each ISCED level, the same requirements for sample size and precision of estimates were established. To allow for reliable estimation and modelling, while allowing for some amount of non-response, the minimum sample size was set at 20 teachers within each participating school. A minimum sample of 200 schools was to be drawn from the population of in-scope schools. Thus, the nominal international sample size was a minimum of 4 000 teachers for each ISCED level in which a country participated. Participating countries could choose to augment their national sample by selecting more schools, by selecting more teachers within each selected school or by increasing both. Some countries were asked to increase the within-school sample to counterbalance the effect of selecting too many schools with fewer than 20 teachers. The sample size requirement was reduced for some participating countries because of the smaller number of schools available for sampling. In a few cases, because the average number of teachers in the schools was less than expected in the international plan, the number of schools sampled was increased to maintain a minimum total number of participating teachers.

In many countries, the separation of grades in ISCED levels does not correspond to a physical separation of school buildings or administrations: Schools that offer grades 8 to 12 could straddle ISCED levels 2 and 3, but all of ISCED level 2 would not be covered by those schools. In countries that participated in more than one ISCED level, arrangements were made with the NPM and their team to optimise the selection of the school sample by either minimising the overlap of the respective samples (one school is selected for participation in only one ISCED level) or maximising the sample overlap (a selected school contributes to all concerned ISCED levels). However, in the case of maximised overlap, teachers who taught at more than one level would be asked to participate in only one. In all countries that participated in the TALIS-PISA link, the strategy was to minimise the overlap of the TALIS sample and the PISA 2012 sample.

Participation rates

The quality requirements for TALIS 2013 translate into participation rates (response rates) for schools and for teachers. Reaching these levels of participation does not preclude that some amount of bias may be present in the results, but it should minimise the negative effect of non-response biases. As TALIS 2013 built on the knowledge gained during TALIS 2008, some assumptions of "reasonable" response rates for the populations of teachers can be formulated. Thus, for the sake of continuity, the participation requirements for TALIS 2013 were kept at the 2008 level even though most participating countries far exceed those requirements.

For each ISCED level, the minimum school participation rate was set at 75% after replacement. Though replacement schools could be called upon as substitutes for non-responding schools, NPMs were encouraged to do all they could to obtain the participation of the schools in the original sample. Responding schools that yielded at least 50% of responding teachers were considered to be participating schools; schools that failed to meet that threshold were considered to be non-participating, even though the number of responding teachers may have been enough to contribute to some of the analyses.

The minimum teacher participation rate was 75% of the selected teachers in participating schools (original sample or replacement schools). Teacher participation was calculated over all participating schools, whether the schools were in the original sample or used as a replacement, and thus the participation rate for teachers is a requirement at the national level but not at the school level. The overall unweighted and weighted participation rates are the product of the respective school and teacher participation rates. Tables A.1 to A.4 present the unweighted school participation rates before and after replacement of non-participating schools, the unweighted teacher participation rate, the unweighted overall participation rates by country, and a weighted estimated size of the teacher population for ISCED level 1, ISCED level 2, ISCED level 3 and the TALIS-PISA link, respectively. Nearly 108 000 ISCED level 2 teachers participated from 34 countries, which corresponds to 82% of all teachers sampled.

Definition of teachers

TALIS 2013 followed the INES (International Indicator of Educational System) data collection definition of a teacher for sampling and analysis:

> The formal definition of a classroom teacher is a person whose professional activity involves the planning, organising and conducting of group activities whereby students' knowledge, skills and attitudes develop as stipulated by educational programmes. In short, it is one whose main activity is teaching (OECD, 2004).

Notes regarding the interpretation of the data

This section lists issues to be noted regarding the sampling or field operations that should be considered when interpreting the data reported for these countries.

- Flanders (Belgium): The ISCED level 2 sampling was done based on "administrative units" rather than on schools; users should therefore be careful when comparing "school-level" estimates.

- Israel: The sampling excluded Ultra-Orthodox schools.

- Japan: In a number of schools, some teachers who should have been included were mistakenly excluded (e.g. part time, special needs).

- Korea: The data collection occurred in the early part of the year following the TALIS reference year.

- Mexico: In the ISCED 3 sample, six schools were rejected because of unapproved teacher sampling procedures.

- Malaysia: Many issues were discovered with coverage (established at about 90%), reconciliation of the sampled schools with the sampling frame, teacher sampling, data inconsistencies and deviations from the prescribed protocols of the survey. Schools where information could not be corrected or confirmed were rejected.

- Portugal: Azores and Madeira were excluded from data collection.

- Singapore: The ISCED 2 and ISCED 3 coverage falls below 95% after the exclusion of 27 private schools.

- Serbia: Users should use caution because not all school listings could be confirmed and differences between school listings and sampling frame information could not be explained.

- United States: Data from the United States are located below the line in selected tables in this report and not included in the calculations for the international average. This is because the United States did not meet the international standards for participation rates, as shown in Table A.2. As mentioned previously, to maintain a minimum level of reliability, the TALIS Technical Standards require that at least 75% of schools (after replacement) and at least 75% of teachers within the selected schools participate in the survey.

[Part 1/1]

Table A.1 **Participation and estimated size of teacher population – ISCED 1**

	Number of participating schools	Responding teachers in participating schools	School participation before replacement %	School participation after replacement %	Teacher participation in participating schools %	Overall participation %	Weighted estimated size of teacher population
Denmark	161	2 088	52	82	79	65	35 946
Finland	193	2 922	89	100	93	92	25 425
Mexico	183	1 291	95	96	96	92	458 616
Norway	144	2 450	52	75	85	64	42 459
Poland	169	3 151	78	87	98	85	211 617
Sub-national entities							
Flanders (Belgium)	198	2 681	52	83	91	75	29 149

Source: OECD, TALIS 2013 Database.

StatLink ᐸᐸᐸ http://dx.doi.org/10.1787/888933048280

[Part 1/1]

Table A.2 **Participation and estimated size of teacher population – ISCED 2**

	Number of participating schools	Responding teachers in participating schools	School participation before replacement %	School participation after replacement %	Teacher participation in participating schools %	Overall participation %	Weighted estimated size of teacher population
Australia	123	2 059	58	81	87	70	106 225
Brazil	1 070	14 291	97	97	94	91	594 874
Bulgaria	197	2 975	95	99	97	96	26 501
Chile	178	1 676	88	91	93	85	51 632
Croatia	199	3 675	99	99	96	95	16 714
Cyprus*	98	1 867	99	99	95	95	3 754
Czech Republic	220	3 219	99	100	98	98	37 419
Denmark	148	1 649	53	81	77	62	25 125
Estonia	197	3 129	93	100	99	99	7 728
Finland	146	2 739	91	99	91	90	18 386
France	204	3 002	79	82	75	61	198 232
Iceland	129	1 430	95	95	80	76	1 901
Israel	195	3 403	98	98	86	85	33 065
Italy	194	3 337	76	98	90	88	178 382
Japan	192	3 484	88	96	99	95	222 809
Korea	177	2 933	68	89	88	78	85 184
Latvia	116	2 126	77	80	96	77	12 894
Malaysia	150	2 984	75	75	97	73	92 735
Mexico	187	3 138	95	96	91	87	250 831
Netherlands	127	1 912	54	81	75	61	58 190
Norway	145	2 981	56	73	80	58	22 631
Poland	195	3 858	83	100	97	97	132 502
Portugal	185	3 628	91	93	92	86	44 496
Romania	197	3 286	100	100	98	98	68 810
Serbia	191	3 857	80	96	97	92	23 179
Singapore	159	3 109	100	100	99	99	9 583
Slovak Republic	193	3 493	87	99	96	95	27 163
Spain	192	3 339	97	97	91	88	204 508
Sweden	186	3 319	93	96	87	84	30 043
Sub-national entities							
Abu Dhabi (United Arab Emirates)	166	2 433	89	89	83	74	7 919
Alberta (Canada)	182	1 773	76	94	93	87	10 208
England (United Kingdom)	154	2 496	56	75	83	63	216 131
Flanders (Belgium)	168	3 129	68	84	89	75	19 184
United States	122	1 926	39	62	83	51	1 052 144

* See notes at the beginning of this Annex.

Source: OECD, TALIS 2013 Database.

StatLink ᐸᐸᐸ http://dx.doi.org/10.1787/888933048299

[Part 1/1]

Table A.3   **Participation and estimated size of teacher population – ISCED 3**

	Number of participating schools	Responding teachers in participating schools	School participation before replacement %	School participation after replacement %	Teacher participation in participating schools %	Overall participation %	Weighted estimated size of teacher population
Australia	124	1 982	60	81	84	68	76 666
Denmark	113	1 514	64	77	75	58	19 914
Finland	146	2 412	92	96	90	87	22 527
Iceland	29	1 104	94	94	78	73	1 504
Italy	210	3 659	75	97	89	86	273 498
Mexico	190	2 940	93	96	91	88	232 835
Norway	106	2 658	55	73	73	53	22 727
Poland	162	3 289	75	84	96	81	174 108
Singapore	159	3 131	100	100	99	99	12 047
Sub-national entities							
Abu Dhabi (United Arab Emirates)	165	2 472	88	88	80	71	6 414

Source: OECD, TALIS 2013 Database.

StatLink http://dx.doi.org/10.1787/888933048318

[Part 1/1]

Table A.4   **Participation and estimated size of teacher population – TALIS-PISA link**

	Number of participating schools	Responding teachers in participating schools	School participation before replacement %	School participation after replacement %	Teacher participation in participating schools %	Overall participation %	Weighted estimated size of teacher population
Australia	122	2 719	58	82	84	69	85 750
Finland	147	3 326	97	98	94	92	18 254
Latvia	118	2 123	82	85	97	82	10 228
Mexico	152	2 167	97	99	90	90	378 222
Portugal	141	3 152	93	93	93	87	52 101
Romania	147	3 275	98	98	98	96	86 051
Singapore	166	4 130	100	100	99	99	12 052
Spain	310	6 130	99	99	93	92	173 216

Source: OECD, TALIS 2013 Database.

StatLink http://dx.doi.org/10.1787/888933048337

Annex B

TECHNICAL NOTES ON INDICES AND ANALYSIS USED IN TALIS 2013

ANNEX B

TECHNICAL NOTES ON INDICES AND ANALYSIS USED IN TALIS 2013

This annex provides information on how the indices (or scales) and other measures derived from the TALIS 2013 teacher and principal questionnaires were constructed. It also provides technical details of some of the more advanced statistical analyses presented throughout the report. Additional technical details on these matters can be found in the *TALIS 2013 Technical Report*.

Construction of indices and other derived measures

This section examines in some detail the composition of indices and other measures used in this report that were derived from the TALIS 2013 teacher and principal and PISA mathematics teacher questionnaires. The section begins with important considerations regarding the reliability and validity of the indices across participating countries and economies.

Reliability and validity of the indices across countries and economies

TALIS measures the self-reported beliefs, attitudes and practices of teachers and school principals in participating countries across a range of topics. The development of these beliefs, attitudes and practices is influenced by individual characteristics but also by the cultural background and the school system. Furthermore, individual and cultural factors affect the interpretation of questions and the ways in which responses are given (Van de Vijver and Leung, 1997). These influences may produce differences in levels of endorsement or frequency in survey responses, but they may also affect the index structure used to compile responses and thus limit the comparability of the resulting scores. As a consequence, social surveys and cross-cultural studies in particular entail special methodological challenges.

Commonly observed inconsistencies and uncertainties in social and cross-cultural research include acquiescence (the tendency for a respondent to agree with a survey statement independent of item content), extremity responding (the tendency to choose extreme response options independent of item content) and social desirability (the tendency to favour response options that are perceived to be socially most adequate). When developing the TALIS 2013 questionnaires, care was taken to ensure that items were compatible with the culture and school system of each TALIS country and economy and that the items had high-quality translation and verification. Moreover, as in the previous cycle of TALIS, the extent to which acquiescence and extremity responding were present in survey responses was examined. The degree of internal consistency and validity of the operationalised teacher and principal indices or derived scales are quantified from the evaluation of the item statistics, the relationship between the scale items and the factor structure of the indices. These psychometric properties of the scale are tested for each participating country. Social desirability response bias was examined in the field-trial phase and findings and implications from these analyses are reported in the *TALIS 2013 Technical Report* (OECD, 2014). Finally, the cross-cultural comparability – or "invariance" – of the indices measuring beliefs, attitudes and practices throughout the report was evaluated simultaneously across countries by means of multi-group confirmatory factor analysis (MGCFA).

Cross-cultural survey methods often differentiate three hierarchical levels of invariance: configural, metric and scalar.

- **Configural invariance** is established when the same items are associated with the same underlying factors in all participating countries. This implies an acceptable fit of confirmatory factor analysis models using the same factor structure for all countries.
- **Metric invariance** is achieved when the strength of the associations between each of the items and the underlying factors is also equivalent across countries.
- **Scalar invariance** is the most rigorous form of invariance. It implies that cross-country differences in the means of the observed items are a result of differences in the means of their corresponding factors. At least partial scalar invariance is needed to make meaningful comparisons of mean scores across countries (e.g. Baumgartner and Steenkamp, 2001).

In invariance tests, metric invariance requires configural invariance, and scalar invariance requires both configural and metric invariance. The ISCED 2 samples were used as reference populations for evaluating configural, metric and scalar invariance. Results for these invariances tests are presented in the *TALIS 2013 Technical Report*. All of the scales achieved metric or loose metric invariance, but none of them reached the scalar level of invariance. The *TALIS 2013 Technical Report* discusses the construction of the indices reported and the results from the invariance analysis in greater detail (OECD, 2014).

Because the level of invariance (namely scalar) required to perform cross-country comparison of indices scores was not reached, a pooled sample with data from all ISCED 2 countries was created and a confirmatory factor analysis (CFA) was conducted using this pooled sample. Weights were rescaled so that each country would contribute equally to the analysis.

The estimated intercepts and loadings from the CFA using the pooled sample (presented in the technical documentation for each scale in the *TALIS 2013 Technical Report*) were used as fixed parameters to calculate factor scores for each country separately per population (ISCED levels 1, 2 and 3, as well as the TALIS-PISA link populations) by using the weighted robust likelihood estimation method. After factor scores with determinacies greater than .80 were computed, they were rescaled to have a standard deviation of 2 on the pooled sample used for estimating the loadings and intercepts (ISCED 2 countries), and the value 10 on the scale was made to coincide with the midpoint of the scale in the response options for the questions that make up the scale. In the cases of scales made up of items with response options ranging from 1-strongly disagree to 4-strongly agree, a score higher than 10, even if below the empirical scale average, indicates agreement with the items in the scale. A score below 10 indicates disagreement with the items in the scale.

This way, although a scalar level of invariance was not achieved using MGCFA, this scaling approach allowed factor scores to be obtained from the same loadings and intercepts across all countries and populations (ISCED levels 1, 2 and 3 and the TALIS-PISA link populations).

However, not all scales the study planned to produce yielded suitable data for MGCFA. The data from school questionnaire items related to the lack of resources and autonomy indices did not fit the CFA models and had to be produced using a simpler technique. For the autonomy scales, if the principal selected principal, school management team or teacher as those having significant responsibility for the specified task, we considered the task a school responsibility (autonomous). If the principal selected school governing board or external authority, we considered the task an external responsibility (not autonomous). If the school principal selected from both lists, we considered it a shared responsibility (mixed). For each scale, if more than half the tasks were classified as autonomous, the school was classified as autonomous for that scale. If more than half the tasks were classified as not autonomous, the school was classified as not autonomous. If neither criterion was met, the school was classified as mixed. The categories for this index are 1 for "no autonomy", 2 for "mixed autonomy", 3 for "autonomy".

Scores for the lack of resources indices were computed in a different way. If all responses to the component variables for the particular index were "not at all" or "very little", the index was set to 1. If all responses to the component variables for the particular index were "to some extent" or "a lot", the index was set to 3. All other combinations were coded as 2. The categories for this index are 1 for "not a problem", 2 for "a bit of a problem", and 3 for "a problem".

The list and description of the indices constructed from the teacher, school principals and PISA mathematics teacher questionnaires' data follow here. A summary table is presented below. Moreover, tables containing the fit indices for each index for each population are available in the *TALIS 2013 Technical Report*. See the *Technical Report* for the TALIS questionnaires (OECD, 2014).

Summary of the indices constructed from teacher, school principal and PISA mathematics teacher questionnaires

Construct	Scale Description	Scale Name	Items
Teacher Questionnaire			
Teacher self-efficacy	Self- efficacy in classroom management	TSELEFFS, SECLSS	TT2G34D; TT2G34F; TT2G34H; TT2G34I
Teacher self-efficacy	Self-efficacy in instruction	TSELEFFS, SEINSS	TT2G34C; TT2G34J; TT2G34K; TT2G34L
Teacher self-efficacy	Self-efficacy in student engagement	TSELEFFS, SEENGS	TT2G34A; TT2G34B; TT2G34E; TT2G34G
Teacher job satisfaction	Satisfaction with current work environment	TJOBSATS, TJSENVS	TT2G46C; TT2G46E; TT2G46G; TT2G46J
Teacher job satisfaction	Satisfaction with profession	TJOBSATS, TJSPROS	TT2G46A; TT2G46B; TT2G46D; TT2G46F
School climate	Participation among stakeholders	TSCSTAKES	TT2G44A; TT2G44B; TT2G44C; TT2G44D; TT2G44E
School climate	Teacher-student relations	TSCTSTUDS	TT2G45A; TT2G45B; TT2G45C; TT2G45D
Classroom disciplinary climate	Classroom disciplinary climate—need for discipline	TCDISCS	TT2G41A; TT2G41B; TT2G41C; TT2G41D
Teacher pedagogical beliefs	Constructivist beliefs	TCONSBS	TT2G32A; TT2G32B; TT2G32C; TT2G32D
Teacher co-operation	Exchange and coordination for teaching	TCOOPS, TCEXCHS	TT2G33D; TT2G33E; TT2G33F; TT2G33G
Teacher co-operation	Professional collaboration	TCOOPS, TCCOLLS	TT2G33A; TT2G33B; TT2G33C; TT2G33H
Effective professional development (PD)	Effective professional development	TEFFPROS	TT2G25A; TT2G25B; TT2G25C; TT2G25D
Needs for professional development	Need for PD in subject matter and pedagogy	TPDPEDS	TT2G26A; TT2G26B; TT2G26C; TT2G26D; TT2G26F
Needs for professional development	Need for PD for teaching for diversity	TPDDIVS	TT2G26H; TT2G26I; TT2G26J; TT2G26K; TT2G26L; TT2G26N
Principal/School Questionnaire			
School climate	School climate—delinquency and violence	PSCDELIQS	TC2G32D; TC2G32E; TC2G32F; TC2G32G
School climate	School climate—mutual respect	PSCMUTRS	TC2G30C; TC2G30D; TC2G30E; TC2G30F
Distributed leadership	Degree of distributed leadership in the school	PDISLEADS	TC2G22A; TC2G22B; TC2G22C
Job satisfaction	Satisfaction with current work environment	PJOBSATS, PJSENVS	TC2G39E; TC2G39F; TC2G39H; TC2G39I
Job satisfaction	Satisfaction with profession	PJOBSATS, PJSPROS	TC2G39A; TC2G39B; TC2G39D
School leadership	Instructional leadership	PINSLEADS	TC2G21C; TC2G21D; TC2G21E
School resources	Lack of pedagogical personnel	PLACKPER	TC2G31A; TC2G31B; TC2G31C
School resources	Lack of material resources	PLACKMAT	TC2G31D; TC2G31E; TC2G31F; TC2G31G; TC2G31H
School autonomy	School autonomy for staffing	PSASTAFF	TC2G18A; TC2G18B
School autonomy	School autonomy for budgeting	PSBUDGET	TC2G18C; TC2G18D; TC2G18E
School autonomy	School autonomy for instructional policies	PSINSPOL	TC2G18F; TC2G18G; TC2G18J; TC2G18K

Source: OECD, TALIS 2013 Database.

Teacher indices

Teacher self-efficacy

To assess teachers' self-efficacy, TALIS asked teachers to indicate to what extent they can do certain activities (on a four-point scale ranging from "not at all" to "a lot") by responding to a number of statements about their work in the school in terms of classroom management, instruction and student engagement.

A test of reliability in each country revealed that these groups of items consistently measure the same constructs. The CFA fit indices in each country have shown that the internal structure of the indices is supported (OECD, 2014).

The questionnaire items forming these indices are as follows:

Efficacy in classroom management

- Control disruptive behaviour in the classroom
- Make my expectations about student behaviour clear
- Get students to follow classroom rules
- Calm a student who is disruptive or noisy

Efficacy in instruction

- Craft good questions for my students
- Use a variety of assessment strategies
- Provide an alternative explanation for an example when students are confused
- Implement alternative instructional strategies in my classroom

Efficacy in student engagement

- Get students to believe they can do well in school work
- Help my students value learning
- Motivate students who show low interest in school work
- Help students think critically

Each index was calculated to have a standard deviation of 2, and the mid-point of 10 on the index coincides with the average response scale of 2.5. The index of teacher self-efficacy is summarised across the three indices.

Teacher job satisfaction

To assess teachers' job satisfaction, TALIS asked teachers to indicate how satisfied they feel about their job (on a four-point scale ranging from "strongly disagree" to "strongly agree") by responding to a number of statements about their work environment and the teaching profession.

A test of reliability in each country revealed that these groups of items consistently measure the same constructs. The CFA fit indices in each country have shown that the internal structure of the indices is supported (OECD, 2014).

The questionnaire items forming these indices are as follows:

Satisfaction with current work environment

- I would like to change to another school if that were possible
- I enjoy working at this school
- I would recommend my school as a good place to work
- All in all, I am satisfied with my job

Satisfaction with profession

- The advantages of being a teacher clearly outweigh the disadvantages
- If I could decide again, I would still choose to work as a teacher
- I regret that I decided to become a teacher
- I wonder whether it would have been better to choose another profession

Each index was calculated to have a standard deviation of 2, and the mid-point of 10 on the index coincides with the average response scale of 2.5. The index of teacher job satisfaction is summarised across the two indices.

School climate

To assess teachers' opinions on school climate, TALIS asked teachers to indicate how they felt (on a four-point scale ranging from "strongly disagree" to "strongly agree") regarding different aspects about the participation of different stakeholders in their school's life and the relations between teachers and students.

A test of reliability in each country revealed that these groups of items consistently measure the same constructs. The CFA fit indices in each country have shown that the internal structure of the indices is supported (OECD, 2014).

The questionnaire items forming these indices are as follows:

Participation among stakeholders

- This school provides staff with opportunities to actively participate in school decisions
- This school provides parents or guardians with opportunities to actively participate in school decisions
- This school provides students with opportunities to actively participate in school decisions
- This school has a culture of shared responsibility for school issues
- There is a collaborative school culture that is characterised by mutual support

Teacher-student relations

- In this school, teachers and students usually get on well with each other
- Most teachers in this school believe that the students' well-being is important
- Most teachers in this school are interested in what students have to say
- If a student from this school needs extra assistance, the school provides it

Each index was calculated to have a standard deviation of 2, and the mid-point of 10 on the index coincides with the average response scale of 2.5.

Classroom disciplinary climate

To assess the classroom disciplinary climate, TALIS asked teachers to indicate how strongly they agreed (on a four-point scale ranging from "strongly disagree" to "strongly agree") with a number of statements about a target class that they taught. This target class was defined as the first ISCED level 2 class that the teacher (typically) taught in the school where she or he works after 11 a.m. the previous Tuesday.

A test of reliability in each country revealed that these items consistently measure the same construct. The CFA fit indices in each country have shown that the internal structure of the index is supported (OECD, 2014).

The questionnaire items forming this index are as follows:

- When the lesson begins, I have to wait quite a long time for students to quiet down
- Students in this class take care to create a pleasant learning atmosphere
- I lose quite a lot of time because of students interrupting the lesson
- There is much disruptive noise in this classroom

The index was calculated to have a standard deviation of 2, and the mid-point of 10 on the index coincides with the average response scale of 2.5.

Teacher constructivist beliefs

To assess teachers' constructivist beliefs about teaching and learning, TALIS asked teachers to indicate how strongly they agreed (on a four-point scale ranging from "strongly disagree" to "strongly agree") with a number of statements.

In short, constructivist beliefs are characterised by a view of the teacher as the facilitator of learning with more autonomy given to students, whereas a direct transmission view sees the teacher as the instructor, providing information and demonstrating solutions.

A test of reliability in each country revealed that these items consistently measure the same construct. The CFA fit indices in each country have shown that the internal structure of the index is supported (OECD, 2014).

The questionnaire items forming this index are as follows:

- My role as a teacher is to facilitate students' own inquiry
- Students learn best by finding solutions to problems on their own
- Students should be allowed to think of solutions to practical problems themselves before the teacher shows them how they are solved
- Thinking and reasoning processes are more important than specific curriculum content

The index was calculated to have a standard deviation of 2, and the mid-point of 10 on the index coincides with the average response scale of 2.5.

Teacher co-operation

To assess co-operation among teaching staff, TALIS asked teachers to indicate the frequency with which they undertook specified activities (using a six-point scale ranging from "never" to "weekly"). Teacher co-operation was measured by two indices: exchange and coordination for teaching and professional collaboration.

A test of reliability in each country revealed that these groups of items consistently measure the same constructs. The CFA fit indices in each country have shown that the internal structure of the indices is supported (OECD, 2014).

The questionnaire items forming these two indices are as follows:

Exchange and coordination for teaching

- Exchange teaching materials with colleagues
- Engage in discussions about the learning development of specific students
- Work with other teachers in my school to ensure common standards in evaluations for assessing student progress
- Attend team conferences

Professional collaboration

- Teach jointly as a team in the same class
- Observe other teachers' classes and provide feedback
- Engage in joint activities across different classes and age groups (e.g. projects)
- Take part in collaborative professional learning

Each index was calculated to have a standard deviation of 2, and the mid-point of 10 on the index coincides with the average response scale of 3.5. The index of teacher co-operation is summarised across the two indices.

Effective professional development

To assess teachers' effective professional development, TALIS asked teachers to indicate the extent of their professional development activities (on a four-point scale ranging from "not in any" to "yes, in all") by responding to a number of statements regarding certain components.

A test of reliability in each country revealed that these groups of items consistently measure the same construct. The CFA fit indices in each country have shown that the internal structure of the index is supported (OECD, 2014).

The questionnaire items forming this index are as follows:

- A group of colleagues from my school or subject group
- Opportunities for active learning methods (not only listening to a lecturer)
- Collaborative learning activities or research with other teachers
- An extended time period (several occasions spread over several weeks or months)

The index was calculated to have a standard deviation of 2, and the mid-point of 10 on the index coincides with the average response scale of 2.5.

Needs for professional development

To assess teachers' need for professional development, TALIS asked teachers to indicate the degree to which they need such (on a four-point scale ranging from "no need at present" to "high level of need") by responding to a number of statements about professional development in subject matter and pedagogy and about professional development for teaching for diversity.

A test of reliability in each country revealed that these groups of items consistently measure the same constructs. The CFA fit indices in each country have shown that the internal structure of the indices is supported (OECD 2014).

The questionnaire items forming these indices are as follows:

Need for professional development in subject matter and pedagogy

- Knowledge and understanding of my subject field(s)
- Pedagogical competencies in teaching my subject field(s)
- Knowledge of the curriculum
- Student evaluation and assessment practice
- Student behaviour and classroom management

Need for professional development for teaching for diversity
- Approaches to individualised learning
- Teaching students with special needs (see Question 9 for the definition)
- Teaching in a multicultural or multilingual setting
- Teaching cross-curricular skills (e.g. problem solving, learning-to-learn)
- Approaches to developing cross-occupational competencies for future work or future studies
- Student career guidance and counselling

Each index was calculated to have a standard deviation of 2, and the mid-point of 10 on the index coincides with the average response scale of 2.5.

School indices

School climate

To assess principals' opinions on school climate, TALIS asked school principals to provide information regarding a number of statements about different aspects of the climate in their school in terms of delinquency and mutual respect. For the index of delinquency and violence, TALIS asked the principals to indicate the frequency (on a five-point scale ranging from "never" to "daily") with which certain acts occurred in their school. For the index of mutual respect, TALIS asked school principals to indicate how strongly they agreed (on a four-point scale ranging from "strongly disagree" to "strongly agree") with a number of statements about the mutual respect of teachers and students in their school.

A test of reliability in each country revealed that these groups of items consistently measure the same constructs. The CFA fit indices in each country have shown that the internal structure of the indices is supported (OECD, 2014).

The questionnaire items forming these indices are as follows:
Delinquency and violence
- Vandalism and theft
- Intimidation or verbal abuse among students (or other forms of non-physical bullying)
- Physical injury caused by violence among students
- Intimidation or verbal abuse of teachers or staff

Mutual respect
- School staff have an open discussion about difficulties
- There is mutual respect for colleagues' ideas
- There is a culture of sharing success
- The relationships between teachers and students are good

The index of delinquency and violence was calculated to have a standard deviation of 2, and the mid-point of 10 on the index coincides with the average response scale of 3.0. The index of mutual respect was calculated to have a standard deviation of 2, and the mid-point of 10 on the index coincides with the average response scale of 2.5.

Distributed leadership

To assess the distributed leadership in schools, TALIS asked school principals to indicate the distribution of the opportunities for it (on a four-point scale ranging from "strongly disagree" to "strongly agree") by responding to a number of statements.

A test of reliability in each country revealed that these groups of items consistently measure the same construct. The CFA fit indices in each country have shown that the internal structure of the index is supported (OECD, 2014).

The questionnaire items forming this index are as follows:
- This school provides staff with opportunities to actively participate in school decisions
- This school provides parents or guardians with opportunities to actively participate in school decisions
- This school provides students with opportunities to actively participate in school decisions

Each index was calculated to have a standard deviation of 2, and the mid-point of 10 on the index coincides with the average response scale of 2.5.

Job satisfaction

To assess principals' job satisfaction, TALIS asked school principals to indicate how satisfied they feel with their job (on a four-point scale ranging from "strongly disagree" to "strongly agree") by responding to a number of statements about their work environment and their profession.

A test of reliability in each country revealed that these groups of items consistently measure the same constructs. The CFA fit indices in each country have shown that the internal structure of the indices is supported (OECD, 2014).

The questionnaire items forming these indices are as follows:

Satisfaction with current work environment

- I enjoy working at this school
- I would recommend my school as a good place to work
- I am satisfied with my performance in this school
- All in all, I am satisfied with my job

Satisfaction with profession

- The advantages of this profession clearly outweigh the disadvantages
- If I could decide again, I would still choose this job/position
- I regret that I decided to become a principal

Each index was calculated to have a standard deviation of 2, and the mid-point of 10 on the index coincides with the average response scale of 2.5. The index of principal job satisfaction is summarised across the two indices.

Instructional leadership

To assess principals' role in school leadership, TALIS asked school principals to indicate the frequency with which they took on certain activities (on a four-point scale ranging from "never or rarely" to "very often") by responding to a number of statements.

A test of reliability in each country revealed that these groups of items consistently measure the same construct. The CFA fit indices in each country have shown that the internal structure of the index is supported (OECD, 2014).

The questionnaire items forming this index are as follows:

- I took actions to support co-operation among teachers to develop new teaching practices
- I took actions to ensure that teachers take responsibility for improving their teaching skills
- I took actions to ensure that teachers feel responsible for their students' learning outcomes

The index was calculated to have a standard deviation of 2, and the mid-point of 10 on the index coincides with the average response scale of 2.5.

School resources

To assess principals' opinion on the lack of resources in their schools, TALIS asked school principals to indicate to what extent the quality of instruction is hindered in their schools (on a four-point scale ranging from "not at all" to "a lot") by responding to a number of statements regarding pedagogical personnel and material resources.

Simple categorisation technique is used for the index because of many items with low item-total correlations and mixed factor structures from the factor analysis models (see OECD, 2014). If all responses to the component variables for the particular index were "not at all" or "very little", the index was set to 1. If all responses to the component variables for the particular index were "to some extent" or "a lot", the index was set to 3. All other combinations were coded as 2. The categories for this index are 1 for "not a problem", 2 for "a bit of a problem", and 3 for "a problem".

The questionnaire items forming these indices are as follows:

Lack of pedagogical personnel

- Shortage of qualified and/or well-performing teachers
- Shortage of teachers with competence in teaching students with special needs
- Shortage of vocational teachers

Lack of material

- Shortage or inadequacy of instructional materials (e.g. textbooks)
- Shortage or inadequacy of computers for instruction
- Insufficient Internet access
- Shortage or inadequacy of computer software for instruction
- Shortage or inadequacy of library materials

School autonomy

To assess principals' autonomy in governing their schools, TALIS asked school principals to indicate who has significant responsibility on making decisions at the school level by responding to a number of statements. The school principals answered the statements with "yes" or "no" depending on who has the significant responsibility for making the decisions: the principal, other members of the school management team, teachers, school governing boards or local authorities.

Simple categorisation technique is used for the index. If the principal selected principal, school management team or teacher as those having significant responsibility for the specified task, the task was considered a school responsibility (autonomous). If the principal selected school governing board or external authority, the task was considered an external responsibility (not autonomous). If the school principal selected from both lists, it was considered a shared responsibility (mixed). For each scale, if more than half the tasks were classified as autonomous, the school was classified as autonomous for that scale. If more than half the tasks were classified as not autonomous, the school was classified as not autonomous. If neither criterion was met, the school was classified as mixed.

The questionnaire items forming these indices are as follows:

School autonomy for staffing

- Appointing or hiring teachers
- Dismissing or suspending teachers from employment

School autonomy for budgeting

- Establishing teachers' starting salaries, including setting pay scales
- Determining teachers' salary increases
- Deciding on budget allocations within the school

School autonomy for instructional policies

- Establishing student disciplinary policies and procedures
- Establishing student assessment policies, including national/regional assessments
- Determining course content, including national/regional curricula
- Deciding which courses are offered

The categories for each index are 1 for "no autonomy", 2 for "mixed autonomy", and 3 for "autonomy".

Ratios derived from TALIS data

Student-teacher ratio

The student-teacher ratio was derived from school principals' responses to a question about the number of staff (head counts) currently working in the school and the total number of students (head counts) of all grades in the school. The measure is not therefore restricted to those teaching or supporting ISCED level 2 education in the school but covers education at all levels provided in the school. The ratio is derived by dividing the number of students by the number of teachers (those whose main activity is the provision of instruction to students). The analyses reporting this ratio in Chapter 2 were done at the school level and therefore used the final school estimation weight (SCHWGT).

Ratio of teachers to number of personnel for pedagogical support

This ratio was derived from school principals' responses to a question about the number of staff (head counts) currently working in the whole school and is therefore not restricted only to those teaching or supporting ISCED level 2 education in the school. The ratio is derived by dividing the number of teachers (those whose main activity is the provision of instruction to students) by the sum of school administrative personnel and management personnel. School administrative personnel include receptionists, secretaries and administration assistants, and management personnel include principals, assistant principals and other staff whose main activity is management. The analyses reporting this ratio in Chapter 2 were done at the school level and therefore used the final school estimation weight (SCHWGT).

Ratio of teachers to number of school administrative or management personne

This ratio was derived from school principals' responses to a question about the number of staff (headcounts) currently working in the school. The measure is not therefore restricted to those teaching or supporting ISCED level 2 education in the school but covers education at all levels provided in the school. The ratio is derived by dividing the number of teachers (those whose main activity is the provision of instruction to students) by the sum of school administrative personnel and management personnel. School administrative personnel include receptionists, secretaries and administration assistants while management personnel include principals, assistant principals, and other management staff whose main activity is management. The analyses reporting this ratio in Chapter 2 were done at the school level and therefore used the final school estimation weight (SCHWGT).

Average class size

In the section of the teacher questionnaire that asked teachers about their classroom teaching practices, teachers were asked to report on a target class that they taught. This target class was defined as the first ISCED level 2 class that the teacher taught in the school after 11 a.m. on the previous Tuesday. To characterise the target class, teachers were asked to report the number of students currently enrolled in this class. The average class size is obtained by making the average of the class sizes reported by the individual teachers. The analyses reporting this ratio in Chapter 2 were done at the teacher level and therefore used the final teacher estimation weight (TCHWGT).

Technical notes on analyses
Technical note on the logistic regression analyses presented in Chapter 2

Logistic regression analysis enables the estimation of the relationship between one or more independent variables (or predictors) on categorical dependent (or predicted) variables with two categories (binary logistic regression) or more categories (multinomial logistic regression). Regression analysis was carried out for each country separately, as prior analysis showed noticeable differences in regression coefficients between countries.

Multinomial logistic regression compares multiple groups through a combination of binary logistic regressions. To calculate logistic regressions, three transformations of data take place: from probability to odds, from odds to log odds and from log odds to odds ratios. The transformation from probability to odds is a monotonic transformation, meaning that the odds increase as the probability increases or vice versa. Probabilities range from 0 to 1. Odds range from 0 to positive infinity. The transformation from odds to log of odds is the log transformation; this is also a monotonic transformation. Log odds range from negative infinity to positive infinity. One of the main reasons that probabilities need to be transformed to log odds is that among all of the infinitely many choices of transformation, the log of odds is one of the easiest to understand and interpret (UCLA: Institute for Digital Research and Education).

Namely, log odds model the logit-transformed probability as a linear relationship with the predictor variables. More formally, let y be the binary outcome variable indicating failure/success with 0/1, and p be the probability of y to be 1, so that $p = prob(y=1)$. Let x_1, .., x_k be a set of predictor variables. Then, the logistic regression of y on x1, ..., xk estimates parameter values for $ß_0$, $ß_1$, . . . , $ß_k$ via the maximum likelihood method of the following equation:

$$logit(p) = log(p/(1-p)) = ß_0 + ß_1{}^*x_1 + ... + ß_k{}^*x_k$$

Hence, when a categorical outcome variable is modelled using logistic regression, it is assumed that the logit transformation of the outcome variable has a linear relationship with the predictor variables. To make data even more interpretable in terms of probability, the final transformation takes place: from log odds to odds ratios. Odds ratios are the exponentiated coefficients of the predictor variables, where categories of these variables are compared with a predetermined reference category.

Then, in terms of probabilities, the equation above is translated into the following:

$$p = exp(ß_0 + ß_1{}^*x_1 + ... + ß_k{}^*x_k)/(1+exp(ß_0 + ß_1{}^*x_1 + ... + ß_k{}^*x_k))$$

The teacher and school variables included in the regression analysis in Chapter 2 are presented in Table B.1, and the percentages of missing cases for each variable are included in Table B.2. It was necessary to have different reference categories for the binary logistic regressions and the multinomial logistic regressions because of statistical power. This means that for the binary logistic regressions, the first, or zero-coded, category of every binary variable was the baseline category, whereas for multinomial regressions, the last category of every categorical variable was selected as the reference category. Concretely, this means that whereas for Table 2.12 the less-educated and less-experienced teachers were chosen as the reference category, for Table 2.14 it was the opposite: The more highly educated and experienced teachers were the basis for comparison. For the latter table, for example, this means that odds ratios can be interpreted in such a way that for a unit change in the predictor variable (e.g. having attained an educational degree of ISCED level 5B and lower versus 5A and higher), the odds ratio of the outcome variable (e.g. teaching in a small city or large city) relative to the reference category (e.g. teaching in a town) is expected to change by a factor of the respective parameter estimate, given that the variables in the model are held constant.

For all the teacher-level regressions in Chapter 2, of which the results are presented in Tables 2.5, 2.12, and 2.14, gender and subjects taught were included as control variables. For Table 2.5, a teacher's level of education and years of work experience also functioned as control variables, whereas these were the main predictor variables for Tables 2.12 and 2.14. For Table 2.5, TT2G12A, TT2G12B, and TT2G12C were the main predictor variables in each of the models, respectively.

When a logistic regression is calculated, SPSS output generates first the regression coefficient (ß – the estimated increase in the log odds of the outcome per unit increase in the value of the predictor variable. Additionally, the exponential function of the regression coefficient (exp(ß)) is obtained, which is the odds ratio associated with a one-unit increase in the predictor variable. Three outcomes are possible for the odds ratios:

- OR=1 Predictor variable does not affect odds of outcome
- OR>1 Predictor variable associated with higher odds of outcome
- OR<1 Predictor variable associated with lower odds of outcome

In the text, the language of odds ratios was made more accessible by reformulating and rounding up in terms of likelihood and probabilities.

Technical notes on the analyses performed in Chapter 3

Principals in participating countries were asked to provide input into educational policy development by answering a questionnaire developed for this purpose.

Multiple linear regression analyses were computed using the International Database (IDB) Analyzer version 3.1.8. The IDB Analyzer uses SPSS as an engine to compute population estimates and design-based standard errors (IDB Analyzer User Guide, p. 10). Regression analyses were carried out for each country separately. The teacher and school variables included in the regression analyses in Chapter 3 are presented in Table B.3, and the percentages of missing cases for each variable are included in Table B.4.

Multiple linear regression analyses were employed using data from the principal questionnaire to explore the extent to which various factors (independent variables) associate with instructional leadership, distributed leadership or principal job satisfaction (dependent variables). Regression analysis allows for exploring how the value of the dependent variable changes when any one of the independent variables varies while all other independent variables are held constant. A relationship is considered significant if the T-value is equal to or greater than 1.96. The following equation depicts the relationship between dependent variable and independent variables in a multiple regression model (an example is provided for a regression model with instructional leadership as the dependent variable and principal background as independent variables).

$$Y = \beta_0 + \beta_1 X_1 + \beta_2 X_2 + \beta_3 X_3 + \beta_4 X_4 + \beta_5 X_5 + \varepsilon$$

For example, for the results presented in Table 3.5, Y is the use of distributed leadership and the independent variables are X_1 for gender, X_2 for years of experience as a principal and X_3 for years of experience as a teacher. Principal age and educational attainment were included as control variables. For the regression results presented in Tables 3.6 and 3.7 and Tables 3.16 through 3.23, principal gender, age and educational attainment were controlled for. Since there are other factors that could not be controlled, these factors are part of the error term.

In general, when everything else held constant, a one-unit increase in X_j on average Y increases by β_j units.

A regression coefficient represents the change in the dependent variable that is associated with a change in the predictor variable when all other variables are held constant. When interpreting multiple regression coefficients, it is important to keep in mind that each coefficient is influenced by the other independent variables in a regression model. The influence depends on the extent to which predictor variables are correlated, which is often the case. Therefore, each regression coefficient does not explain the total effect of independent variables on dependent variables. Rather, each coefficient represents the additional effect of adding that variable to the model, if the effects of all other variables in the model are already accounted for. It should be noted that no adjustments were made to correct for the multiple analyses, increasing the likelihood that a relationship will be considered significant simply by chance. It is also important to note that because cross-sectional survey data were used for the analyses, no causal conclusions could be drawn.

Technical notes on the analyses performed in Chapter 4

Please refer to the technical notes for Chapter 2 earlier in this annex for a general description of the use of logistic regressions. This portion of the annex provides further details about the use of logistic regressions in Chapter 4.

In this chapter on professional development, regression analyses were carried out both at an aggregate level and for each country separately. After analysing this background model on professional development participation (see Table 4.21.Web), the predictor variables considered to be relevant based on theoretical considerations were added.

The teacher and school variables included in the regression analysis in Chapter 4 are presented in Table B.5, and the percentages of missing cases for each variable are included in Table B.6. For the results presented in Table 4.13, the following variables were controlled for: teacher gender, age, years of experience, part-time/full-time employment status, permanent/fixed term and percentage of students from disadvantaged homes. For the regression results presented in Table 4.29.Web, the following control variables were included: teacher gender, age, years of experience, part-time/full-time employment status, permanent/fixed term contract status, whether a teacher completed a teacher education or training programme, hours worked in a week, principal working on a school development plan for the school, public/private school, size of the school location and percentage of students from disadvantaged homes. In Table 4.30.Web, the control variables used were teacher gender, age, years of experience, part-time/full-time employment status, permanent/fixed term contract status, whether a teacher completed a teacher education or training programme, hours worked in a week, serving as a mentor, principal working on a school development plan for the school, public/private school, size of the school location and percentage of students from disadvantaged homes.

Regression analyses for Chapter 4 were computed with the programme STATA using population weights and BRR methodology with Fay's adjustment for variance estimation, given the complex sample design of TALIS.

Technical notes on the analyses performed in Chapter 6

Logistic regression and odds ratios

Please refer to the technical notes for Chapter 2 earlier for a general description of the use of logistic regressions. This portion of the annex provides further details about the use of logistic regressions in Chapter 6. The teacher and school variables included in the regression analyses in Chapter 6 are presented in Table B.7, and the percentages of missing cases for each variable are included in Table B.8.

All logistic regressions on the data presented in Chapter 6 were performed using SAS PROC SURVEYLOGISTIC and were all performed for each country separately. The SURVEYLOGIST procedure permitted the use of the BRR replicate weights in the data set (accounting for the complex sample design), as well as the final teacher weight TCHWGT. More information about the use of sampling and replicate weights in TALIS analyses can be found in the *TALIS 2013 Technical Report* (OECD, 2014). Effect coding was employed with CLASS variables, and point estimates from the SAS output were reported as the odds ratios instead of the exp(ß) values. Effect coding is used on CLASS variables to make comparisons easier between reference categories. Detailed information on effect coding, point estimates and their interpretation can be found in the SAS documentation at the following link:

http://support.sas.com/documentation/cdl/en/statug/63033/HTML/default/viewer.htm#statug_logistic_sect053.htm

The exp(ß) value provides an odds ratio that is interpretable as the change in odds for each level change in the independent variable. However, when using effect coding for CLASS variables, a variable such as gender is coded internally to SAS as 1= female and –1= male. In this instance, a one-unit change makes no logical sense because there is no category for 0. Therefore, the exp(ß) is not a meaningful odds ratio to make use of. The point estimates derived from SAS are odds ratios where a reference category is employed for all comparisons and effect coding is accounted for. For continuous variables, the "point estimate odds ratio" will be equivalent to the exp(ß).

For the logistic regression involving the three active teaching practices (namely, students work on projects that require at least one week to complete, students use ICT for projects or class work and students work in small groups to come up with a joint solution to a problem or task), the distribution of responses on these items justified dichotomising them (splitting the responses into two categories) for use as dependent variables. The three teaching items were therefore dichotomised by combining the categories for "Never" and "Occasionally" into one category named "Occasionally" and by combining the categories for "Frequently" and "In all lessons" into one category named "Frequently". None of these newly created response categories held less than 27% of the responses, therefore avoiding the problem of low cell counts in the analyses.

To perform the logistic regressions, a separate model was constructed for each of the three dichotomised teaching practice dependent variables. The background variables were entered into the model in their own block and tested before entering the predictor variables of theoretical interest. Only background variables significant at the α = .05 level were retained in the model when the predictor variables were entered. Thus, all results reflect net effects of the relevant predictor variables. Teacher characteristics included gender, type of target class taught (mathematics or science or humanities), years of experience, highest level of education and how well prepared teachers felt for the content, pedagogy and classroom practice in the target subject taught. Humanities teachers were defined as in TALIS 2008 as teachers who taught reading, writing and literature, social studies, modern foreign languages, Ancient Greek and/or Latin and religion and/or ethics. These dichotomised control variables are standardised around the mean of 0, where the absence of a characteristic is recoded to –1 and the presence of a characteristic is recoded to 1.

For Tables 6.2 to 6.4, the predictor variables for teaching practices were modified slightly to substitute TT2G13A, B and C in place of TT1G12A, B and C. The TT2G13 set of questions asked teachers how well prepared they felt for the teaching elements of content, pedagogy and classroom practice. This set of variables provided more interesting content and variability across responses than the TT2G12 series of questions, which asked whether the three elements were included in a teacher's formal education and training. Logistic regressions that were run using the TT2G13 series of questions explained roughly 20% more variance in the predicted variable than those using the TT2G12 series.

Control variables were employed in most of the logistic regressions. For the analyses outlined in Tables 6.5 to 6.10 and Tables 6.14, 6.16 and 6.17, controls included teacher gender, years of experience, highest level of education and subject taught in the target class. For Tables 6.2 to 6.4, these same control variables were the predictor variables of interest, and no other control variables were employed for those analyses. Control variables were tested in their own analysis block and non-significant terms were removed before entering the block of predictor variables of interest for the analysis. Please see Table B.7 for specific control variable names.

Multiple linear regression analysis

All multiple linear regressions were performed using the SPSS macros derived from the IEA IDB Analyzer programme or using SAS PROC SURVEYREG. Both of these programmes made use of the BRR replicate weights to account for the complex sample design as well as the final teacher weight TCHWGT. All multiple regressions were performed for each country separately. When these three teaching practices are used as independent variables in the models, the original four answer categories are preserved and not dichotomised as previously when they were used as dependent variables.

Control variables were employed in the linear regressions. Specifically, teacher gender, years of experience working as a teacher, highest level of education and subject taught in the target class were controlled for. These variables are standardised with 0 as the mean. Control variables were tested in their own analysis block and non-significant terms were removed before entering the block of predictor variables of interest for the analysis. All reported effects are net effects instead of gross effects. Please see Table B.7 for specific control variable names.

Multilevel analysis for distribution of variance

The analyses that report the distribution of variance by three levels (country, school and teacher) utilised baseline models in a multilevel modeling framework. This allowed the portioning of the variance into the three different levels. To take a simple example of a two-level model (teachers nested in schools), such a baseline model contains no predictor variables and simply separates the variance into the within-group variance (σ^2_w) and the between-group variance (σ^2_b), such as is completed in a random effects one-way ANOVA model. These components can be used to form the intraclass correlation coefficient (ICC, ρ) that represents the portion of variance that lies between the cluster variable: in this two-level case, that would be schools. This is formed as $\rho = \sigma^2_b / (\sigma^2_b + \sigma^2_w)$. When the ICC is small (e.g. < 0.05 or 5%), groups such as schools are only slightly different from one another. When that value increases (e.g. 0.25), the difference between groups increases, be it at the second level (school) or third level (country). In a baseline model for three levels, the within-variance component remains, and instead of a single estimate for between-group variance, this becomes two variance components, representing level 2 and level 3, respectively. The ICC is calculated in the same fashion as before, with all three variance components as the denominator, and the numerator being the variance component of interest.

Technical notes on the analyses performed in Chapter 7

To investigate what factors influence teachers' perception of society's view of the teaching profession, binary logistic regression analyses were carried out for each country separately (see Table 7.3). Please refer to the technical notes on Chapter 2 earlier for more information on logistic regression analyses. Regression analyses for this chapter were computed using population weights and BRR methodology with Fay's adjustment for variance estimation, given the complex sample design of TALIS.

The combined "Strongly Disagree-Disagree" group was chosen as a reference category for the analysis examining the extent to which teachers feel that teaching is a valued profession in society. The variables included as control variables were teacher gender, years of experience, level of education and the extent to which content, pedagogy and classroom practice elements of subjects currently taught by the teacher were included in his or her formal education.

The rest of the chapter used multiple linear regressions. First, multicollinearity was tested for by correlating all dependent and independent variables with each other. Country-specific multiple linear regressions were then run to test the effects of various independent variables on teacher self-efficacy and job satisfaction levels. Multiple linear regression attempts were made to model the relationship between two or more independent variables and a dependent variable (self-efficacy and job satisfaction) by fitting a linear equation to the TALIS data. Every value of the independent variable x is associated with a value of the dependent variable y in the TALIS data that is intended to mirror values in the wider population that the country samples represent.

For each country, the population regression line for k explanatory variables $x_1, x_2, \ldots, x_k$ is defined to be $y = \beta_0 + \beta_1 * x_1 + \ldots + \beta_k * x_k$, where β_0 is the intercept and β_1 the slope of the line. Statistical software such as SPSS provides fitted values $b_0, b_1, \ldots, b_k$ that estimate the parameters $\beta_0, \beta_1, \ldots, \beta_k$ of the population regression line for the TALIS data. This line describes how the mean response of the chosen dependent variable changes with the explanatory variables in the TALIS database. For example, the slope for the relationship between being female and job satisfaction could be 0.30 in country A, meaning that female teachers in country A on average have job satisfaction levels that are higher by 0.30 points than for male teachers. For continuous variables, the slope reflects the effect on the dependent variable of a one-unit increase in the independent variable.

To facilitate interpretation, the text in the chapter discusses weak, moderate, and strong relationships instead of the numerical values of the regression coefficients. Cut-off points for these three categories were regression coefficients that translated into 0.2 and 0.3 standard deviation unit changes, where less than 0.2 is weak, 0.2-0.299 is moderate and 0.3 or higher is strong. These standard deviation unit changes for dichotomous independent variables are obtained by dividing the regression coefficient of the relation (b_k) between the independent variable (x_k) and dependent variable (y) by the standard deviation of the dependent variable for country A (σ_{yA}). This allows for the magnitude of the relation between x_k and y as weak, moderate, or strong to be discussed in comparable standard deviation units, accounting for every country's distribution of self-efficacy and job satisfaction scores. For many countries, these 0.2 and 0.3 standard deviation unit changes on dichotomous independent variables approximate regression coefficients of 0.3 and 0.5, respectively.

For continuous variables such as hours or proportions, the size of the relationship was defined as weak, moderate, or strong at the threshold of ten times the unit ($\beta_1 * 10$ more students, 10 more hours, 10% more time spent). For index scores, we define the cut-off points in relation to a one standard deviation increase on that measure. This means that the coefficient on these continuous-scale indexed independent variables is first translated into standard deviation units by ($\beta_1 * \sigma_{x1}$) and then divided by the standard deviation of the country's dependent variable (σ_{yA}). We discuss a weak, moderate, or strong relationship from this threshold based on one standard deviation change in the indexed independent variable.

Besides key predictor variables, several control variables were included in the regression analyses in this chapter. The teacher and school variables included in the analyses in Chapter 7 are presented in Table B.9, and the percentages of missing cases for each variable are included in Table B.10. For Tables 7.4 and 7.5, educational level of the teacher was controlled. For Tables 7.8 to 7.15, teacher characteristics of gender, educational level, work experience as a teacher and the inclusion of content, pedagogy and classroom practice elements in the formal education of the teacher were controlled. Moreover, the classroom characteristics identifying the target classroom size as well as the composition consisting of more than 10% low-achieving students, more than 10% behaviour problem students and more than 10% gifted students were included as control variables. For Tables 7.16 and 7.17, gender, educational level, work experience as a teacher, the inclusion of content/pedagogy/classroom practice elements in the formal education of the teacher, class size and the classroom composition variables of low academic achievers, behavioural problem students and academically gifted students were controlled for. For Tables 7.8 to 7.15, nested regression modelling techniques are used to demonstrate the relationship of teachers' leadership and school relations (Tables 7.8 and 7.9), professional development (Tables 7.10 and 7.11), appraisal and feedback (Tables 7.12 and 7.13) and beliefs and practices (Tables 7.14 and 7.15) to self-efficacy and job satisfaction. These techniques were also used to test whether these independent variables change any of the classroom composition associations (shown in Tables 7.6 and 7.7) with self-efficacy and job satisfaction. Nesting these key independent variables within the classroom composition models reveals whether the association of classroom composition to the dependent variable is affected by the association of these key independent variables. If there is a substantial reduction in the previously established significant classroom composition coefficient (where the coefficient value is reduced or is no longer significantly related to the dependent variable), then there is reason to conclude that the classroom composition association is partially related to the key independent variable modelled.

To specify this relationship, the sample is restricted by listwise-deleting any missing cases. Due to this, the baseline classroom composition coefficients used in Tables 7.8 to 7.11 and Tables 7.14 and 7.15 are slightly different from those presented in Tables 7.6 and 7.7 (see Tables B2.11.Web to B2.18.Web for each baseline model). Namely, "nesting models", where one model builds off another, requires the n-count (or sample size) to be identical in all the models per country. To do this, all the cases that were in the final model were tagged, that is, the full model which has all the controls + classroom composition variables + focal independent variables (in-school relationships, professional development, or beliefs and practices). The syntax then keeps only these cases and listwise-deletes the other cases that may have missing data on any of those variables. The "baseline" models (controls + classroom composition variables) are consequently rerun on the dependent variable. This is the same model as Tables 7.6 and 7.7 but with a different n-count per model per country. The final models are then run (controls + classroom composition variables + focal independent variables). Because these models compare with the same cases, it can be stated that the changes are due to the inclusion of the focal independent variables. However, this poses the problem that the "baseline" values of the nesting models do not directly align with the ones in Tables 7.6 and 7.7.

Note that with cross-sectional data such as the TALIS data, no direction of impact can be established. Hence, it is not possible to distinguish empirically between, for example, a model that describes teachers' self-efficacy as dependent on teachers' work experience and a model that describes teachers' work experience as dependent on their self-efficacy. The perspective taken, i.e. the choice of independent and dependent variables, is entirely based on theoretical considerations.

References

Baumgartner, H. and J.B. E.M. Steenkamp (2001), "Response styles in marketing research: A cross-national investigation", *Journal of Marketing Research*, No. 18, pp. 143-156.

OECD (2014), *TALIS 2013 Technical Report*, OECD Publishing, Paris.

Van de Vijver, F.J.R. and K. Leung (1997), "Methods and data-analysis for cross-cultural research", in *Cross-Cultural Psychology Series*, W.J. Lonner and J.W. Berry (eds.), Sage Publication, Thousand Oaks, CA.

UCLA: Institute for Digital Research and Education, "Interpreting odds ratios in logistic regression", *http://www.ats.ucla.edu/stat/mult_pkg/faq/general/odds_ratio.htm* (accessed 6 November, 2013).

[Part 1/1]

Table B.1   List of variables in the Chapter 2 regression analyses

Variable	Level	Type of variable	Based on variable(s) in the data set
Teacher background			
Feeling prepared for content elements of subjects I teach (0 = not at all/somewhat; 1 = well/very well)	Teacher	Dependent	TT2G13A
Feeling prepared for pedagogy elements of subjects I teach (0 = not at all/somewhat; 1 = well/very well)	Teacher	Dependent	TT2G13B
Feeling prepared for classroom practice elements of subjects I teach (0 = not at all/somewhat; 1 = well/very well)	Teacher	Dependent	TT2G13C
Teacher's gender (1 = female; 2 = male)	Teacher	Independent	TT2G01
Number of years of teaching (0 = 5 years or less; 1 = more than 5 years)	Teacher	Independent	TT2G05B
Teacher's education (0 = ISCED 5B or below; 1 = ISCED 5A or higher)	Teacher	Independent	TT2G10
Inclusion of content elements in formal training (1 = yes for all of the subjects I teach; 2 = yes for some of the subjects I teach; 3 = no)	Teacher	Independent	TT2G12A
Inclusion of pedagogy elements in formal training (1 = yes for all of the subjects I teach; 2 = yes for some of the subjects I teach; 3 = no)	Teacher	Independent	TT2G12B
Inclusion of classroom practice elements in formal training (1 = yes for all of the subjects I teach; 2 = yes for some of the subjects I teach; 3 = no)	Teacher	Independent	TT2G12C
Subjects taught (those with 0% cell count were excluded, original coding)	Teacher	Independent	TT2G15A, 15B, 15C, 15D, 15E, 15F, 15G, 15H, 15I, 15J, 15K, 15L
School background			
Size of school location (1 = 15 000 people or less; 2 = between 15 001 and 100 000 people; 3 = more than 100 000 people)	Teacher	Dependent	TC2G09
Percentage of students whose first language is different from the language of instruction (0 = 10% or below; 1 = above 10%)	Teacher	Dependent	TC2G15A
Percentage of students with special needs (0 = 10% or below; 1 = above 10%)	Teacher	Dependent	TC2G15B
Percentage of students from socio-economically disadvantaged homes (0 = 30% or below; 1 = above 30%)	Teacher	Dependent	TC2G15C

Source: OECD, TALIS 2013 Database.

StatLink http://dx.doi.org/10.1787/888933048356

[Part 1/3]

The percentage of missing cases for each country for each variable included in the Chapter 2 regression analyses

Table B.2

	Number of responding teachers (unweighted)	Teacher background							
		Feeling prepared for the content of the subject(s) taught	Feeling prepared for the pedagogy of the subject(s) taught	Feeling prepared for classroom practice in the subject(s) taught	Gender	Year(s) working as a teacher in total	Highest level of education of teacher	Content of the subject(s) taught was included in formal education or training	Pedagogy of the subject(s) taught was included in formal education or training
		Teacher %							
		TT2G13A	TT2G13B	TT2G13C	TT2G01	TT2G05B	TT2G10	TT2G12A	TT2G12B
Australia	2 059	1.4	1.7	1.6	0.0	2.6	0.8	1.0	1.0
Brazil	14 291	9.5	13.2	9.9	0.0	17.5	7.8	8.1	8.3
Bulgaria	2 975	1.7	3.0	3.8	0.0	14.4	0.5	0.5	0.5
Chile	1 676	2.4	3.8	4.2	0.0	10.8	1.5	3.3	3.3
Croatia	3 675	0.8	2.3	2.6	0.0	20.2	0.5	1.4	1.5
Czech Republic	3 219	0.1	0.4	0.4	0.0	1.7	0.1	0.1	0.1
Denmark	1 649	0.7	0.9	0.8	0.0	2.4	0.6	1.9	1.9
Estonia	3 129	1.3	1.9	2.1	0.0	3.7	0.5	0.8	0.8
Finland	2 739	0.7	0.8	0.9	0.0	2.2	0.3	0.3	0.3
France	3 002	1.2	1.7	1.5	0.0	1.7	0.6	1.0	1.0
Iceland	1 430	2.2	2.3	2.7	0.0	5.0	1.8	1.5	1.6
Israel	3 403	2.0	2.4	2.2	0.0	3.0	1.1	1.2	1.4
Italy	3 337	0.8	1.0	1.3	0.0	1.2	0.4	0.9	0.9
Japan	3 484	0.4	0.4	0.4	0.0	2.6	0.4	1.8	1.8
Korea	2 933	0.8	1.9	1.9	0.0	3.4	0.1	0.2	0.2
Latvia	2 126	1.0	1.1	1.4	0.0	5.3	0.6	0.7	0.7
Malaysia	2 984	0.5	0.5	0.6	0.0	1.0	0.5	0.4	0.4
Mexico	3 138	2.0	3.2	3.2	0.1	21.4	0.7	1.5	1.7
Netherlands	1 912	0.9	0.9	1.0	0.0	1.1	0.5	0.9	0.9
Norway	2 981	1.3	1.3	1.5	0.0	2.7	0.7	1.4	1.4
Poland	3 858	0.6	0.5	0.7	0.0	5.7	0.2	0.3	0.3
Portugal	3 628	0.2	0.4	0.4	0.0	3.2	0.3	0.2	0.3
Romania	3 286	0.6	1.1	0.9	0.0	1.9	0.5	0.6	0.7
Serbia	3 857	3.3	4.1	2.9	0.0	12.4	0.5	3.9	3.9
Singapore	3 109	0.2	0.3	0.2	0.0	1.0	0.0	0.1	0.1
Slovak Republic	3 493	0.4	0.7	1.0	0.0	1.5	0.1	0.5	0.6
Spain	3 339	0.4	0.5	0.7	0.0	1.1	0.3	0.5	0.5
Sweden	3 319	0.7	1.1	1.1	0.0	1.7	0.6	0.6	0.7
Sub-national entities									
Abu Dhabi (United Arab Emirates)	2 433	2.8	4.6	3.9	0.0	5.1	1.3	2.2	2.2
Alberta (Canada)	1 773	0.2	0.3	0.3	0.0	1.9	0.2	0.2	0.2
England (United Kingdom)	2 496	0.8	1.0	1.0	0.0	3.6	0.8	0.9	0.9
Flanders (Belgium)	3 129	0.6	0.8	0.7	0.0	2.9	0.3	0.4	0.4

Note: Percentages in this table represent the weighted proportion of missing cases.
Source: OECD, TALIS 2013 Database.
StatLink ⟐ http://dx.doi.org/10.1787/888933048375

[Part 2/3]

The percentage of missing cases for each country for each variable included in the Chapter 2 regression analyses

Table B.2

	Teacher background								
	Classroom practice in the subject(s) taught was included in formal education or training	Teaching reading, writing and literature	Teaching mathematics	Teaching science	Teaching social studies	Teaching modern foreign languages	Teaching ancient Greek and/or Latin	Teaching technology	Teaching arts
	Teacher %								
	TT2G12C	TT2G15A	TT2G15B	TT2G15C	TT2G15D	TT2G15E	TT2G15F	TT2G15G	TT2G15H
Australia	1.0	2.5	2.6	2.6	2.6	2.6	2.7	2.5	2.6
Brazil	8.3	6.6	6.7	6.6	6.7	6.7	6.6	6.6	6.6
Bulgaria	0.5	1.9	2.0	2.0	1.9	2.0	2.1	2.1	2.1
Chile	3.3	7.4	7.4	7.3	7.5	7.4	7.4	7.3	7.4
Croatia	1.4	1.3	1.3	1.4	1.3	1.4	1.3	1.3	1.3
Czech Republic	0.1	0.3	0.3	0.3	0.3	0.3	0.3	0.3	0.3
Denmark	1.9	1.1	1.1	1.0	1.1	1.1	1.1	1.1	1.1
Estonia	0.8	1.1	1.1	1.1	1.1	1.1	1.1	1.1	1.1
Finland	0.3	0.6	0.6	0.7	0.6	0.6	0.7	0.7	0.6
France	1.0	1.7	1.8	1.9	1.8	1.8	1.8	1.8	1.8
Iceland	1.6	4.5	4.5	4.5	4.5	4.4	4.5	4.6	4.4
Israel	1.4	2.8	2.8	2.8	2.9	2.8	0.0	2.8	2.8
Italy	0.9	0.8	0.8	0.8	0.8	0.8	0.8	0.8	0.8
Japan	1.8	0.4	0.4	0.4	0.3	0.4	100.0	0.4	0.4
Korea	0.2	1.2	1.2	1.2	1.2	1.2	1.3	1.2	1.1
Latvia	0.8	1.7	1.8	1.6	1.6	1.6	1.8	1.6	1.8
Malaysia	0.4	0.7	0.7	0.7	0.7	0.7	0.7	0.6	0.7
Mexico	1.6	1.3	1.3	1.4	1.4	1.4	1.3	1.4	1.4
Netherlands	0.9	2.6	2.5	2.5	2.5	2.5	2.5	2.5	2.4
Norway	1.4	1.1	1.2	1.2	1.3	1.1	1.3	1.3	1.2
Poland	0.3	0.7	0.7	0.7	0.7	0.7	0.8	0.8	0.7
Portugal	0.2	0.9	0.9	1.0	0.9	0.9	0.9	0.9	0.9
Romania	0.7	0.9	1.0	1.0	1.0	1.0	1.0	1.0	1.0
Serbia	3.9	1.6	1.6	1.7	1.6	1.7	1.7	1.7	1.7
Singapore	0.1	0.4	0.6	0.6	0.6	0.7	0.7	0.6	0.7
Slovak Republic	0.6	0.6	0.6	0.5	0.5	0.6	0.6	0.6	0.5
Spain	0.5	1.1	1.1	1.1	1.1	1.1	1.1	1.1	1.1
Sweden	0.7	1.3	1.3	1.3	1.3	1.3	0.0	1.3	1.3
Sub-national entities									
Abu Dhabi (United Arab Emirates)	2.2	7.1	7.3	7.3	7.4	7.4	7.6	7.4	7.5
Alberta (Canada)	0.2	1.2	1.2	1.2	1.1	1.2	1.2	1.2	1.3
England (United Kingdom)	0.9	1.7	1.7	1.7	1.7	1.7	1.7	1.6	1.6
Flanders (Belgium)	0.4	0.9	0.9	0.9	0.9	0.9	0.9	0.9	0.9

Note: Percentages in this table represent the weighted proportion of missing cases.
Source: OECD, TALIS 2013 Database.
StatLink ⟰ http://dx.doi.org/10.1787/888933048375

[Part 3/3]

The percentage of missing cases for each country for each variable included in the Chapter 2

Table B.2   **regression analyses**

	Teacher background				School background			
	Teaching physical education	Teaching religion and/or ethics	Teaching practical and vocational skills	Teaching other subject	School location size	Students whose first language is different from the language of instruction	Students with special needs	Students from socio-economically disadvantaged homes
	Teacher %							
	TT2G15I	TT2G15J	TT2G15K	TT2G15L	TC2G09	TC2G15A	TC2G15B	TC2G15C
Australia	2.5	2.6	2.6	2.7	7.5	8.7	8.7	8.7
Brazil	6.6	6.6	6.6	6.7	1.6	4.6	2.3	3.3
Bulgaria	2.1	2.2	2.2	2.1	0.0	4.5	3.3	3.3
Chile	7.4	7.4	7.3	7.5	16.9	17.6	16.9	16.3
Croatia	1.3	1.2	1.3	1.3	2.4	4.5	2.6	3.2
Czech Republic	0.3	0.3	0.3	0.3	0.0	0.0	0.0	0.1
Denmark	1.0	1.1	1.1	1.0	16.7	16.5	16.5	17.0
Estonia	1.1	1.1	1.1	1.1	1.0	1.5	1.5	1.5
Finland	0.7	0.7	0.7	0.7	0.0	0.0	0.0	0.0
France	1.8	1.8	1.8	1.9	13.1	14.0	14.7	14.3
Iceland	4.5	4.5	4.4	4.5	19.2	20.5	20.8	21.6
Israel	2.9	2.9	2.8	3.0	6.7	8.0	8.5	8.4
Italy	0.8	0.8	0.8	0.8	0.5	1.1	0.7	0.7
Japan	0.4	0.3	0.4	0.3	0.0	0.6	0.6	0.6
Korea	1.3	1.2	1.2	1.2	7.6	7.7	7.7	7.7
Latvia	1.8	1.7	1.7	2.1	6.5	6.5	6.7	6.5
Malaysia	0.6	0.7	0.6	0.6	2.2	2.9	2.9	2.9
Mexico	1.5	1.4	1.4	1.4	0.4	1.5	0.4	0.4
Netherlands	2.5	2.5	2.5	2.0	6.5	8.8	8.8	8.8
Norway	1.3	1.3	1.3	1.2	23.1	26.8	26.8	26.8
Poland	0.7	0.8	0.8	0.8	3.6	5.0	4.9	4.9
Portugal	1.0	0.9	0.9	1.0	3.7	4.5	5.3	5.6
Romania	0.9	1.0	1.0	1.0	0.0	0.3	0.7	0.3
Serbia	1.7	1.7	1.7	1.7	2.9	7.2	7.0	6.6
Singapore	0.6	0.6	0.6	0.7	9.0	10.2	10.2	9.6
Slovak Republic	0.6	0.5	0.6	0.5	3.3	5.0	4.4	4.4
Spain	1.1	1.1	1.1	1.0	0.5	1.1	1.1	1.1
Sweden	1.3	1.3	1.3	1.3	8.4	8.3	7.9	8.3
Sub-national entities								
Abu Dhabi (United Arab Emirates)	7.4	7.3	7.5	7.5	23.6	26.6	26.6	26.6
Alberta (Canada)	1.1	1.2	1.2	1.4	1.8	1.8	1.8	2.4
England (United Kingdom)	1.7	1.7	1.7	1.8	1.7	4.3	4.3	4.3
Flanders (Belgium)	0.9	0.9	0.9	0.9	8.3	11.2	11.6	11.2

Note: Percentages in this table represent the weighted proportion of missing cases.

Source: OECD, TALIS 2013 Database.

StatLink http://dx.doi.org/10.1787/888933048375

[Part 1/1]

Table B.3   List of variables in the Chapter 3 regression analyses

Variable	Level	Type of variable	Based on variable(s) in the data set
Principals' background			
Principal's gender (0 = female; 1 = male)	Principal	Independent	TC2G01
Principal's age (continuous)	Principal	Independent	TC2G02
Principal's educational attainment (1 = below ISCED level 5; 2 = ISCED level 5B; 3 = ISCED level 5A; 4 = ISCED level 6)	Principal	Independent	TC2G03
Principal's years of experience as a principal in total (continuous)	Principal	Independent	TC2G04B
Principal's years of experience as a teacher in total (continuous)	Principal	Independent	TC2G04D
School background			
Ratio of teacher to administrative or management personnel (continuous)	Principal	Independent	TARATIO
School locality (0 = school in a location of 15 000 people or less; 1 = school in location of 15 001 people or more)	Principal	Independent	TC2G09
Publicly managed school (0 = privately managed; 1 = publicly managed)	Principal	Independent	TC2G10
50% or more of the school's funding comes from the government (0 = public funding not 50% or more; 1 = public funding is 50% or more)	Principal	Independent	TC2G11A
Number of teachers (continuous)	Principal	Independent	TC2G12A
Number of students (continuous)	Principal	Independent	TC2G14
More than 10% of students have a different first language than the language(s) of instruction (0 = 10% or below; 1 = above 10%)	Principal	Independent	TC2G15A
More than 10% of students have special needs (0 = 10% or below; 1 = above 10%)	Principal	Independent	TC2G15B
More than 30% of students are from disadvantaged homes (0 = 30% or below; 1 = above 30%)	Principal	Independent	TC2G15C
Ratio of teacher to pedagogical support personnel (continuous)	Principal	Independent	TPRATIO
School leadership			
Distributed leadership (continuous)	Principal	Dependent	PDISLEADS
Percentage of time the principal spends on curriculum and teaching-related tasks and meetings (continuous)	Principal	Dependent	TC2G19B
Principal used student performance and student evaluation results to develop the school's educational goals and programmes (0 = no; 1 = yes)	Principal	Dependent	TC2G20A
Principal worked on a professional development plan for this school (0 = no; 1 = yes)	Principal	Dependent	TC2G20B
Principal observing instruction in the classroom (0 = sometimes or never or rarely; 1 = often or very often)	Principal	Dependent	TC2G21B
Instructional leadership (continuous)	Principal	Dependent, independent	PINSLEADS
Inadequate school budget and resources (0 = not at all or very little; 1 = to some extent or a lot)	Principal	Independent	TC2G26A
Government regulation and policy (0 = not at all or very little; 1 = to some extent or a lot)	Principal	Independent	TC2G26B
Teachers' absence (0 = not at all or very little; 1 = to some extent or a lot)	Principal	Independent	TC2G26C
Lack of parent/guardian involvement (0 = not at all or very little; 1 = to some extent or a lot)	Principal	Independent	TC2G26D
Teachers' career-based wage system (0 = not at all or very little; 1 = to some extent or a lot)	Principal	Independent	TC2G26E
Lack of support for own professional development (0 = not at all or very little; 1 = to some extent or a lot)	Principal	Independent	TC2G26F
Lack of support for teachers' professional development (0 = not at all or very little; 1 = to some extent or a lot)	Principal	Independent	TC2G26G
High workload and level of responsibility (0 = not at all or very little; 1 = to some extent or a lot)	Principal	Independent	TC2G26H
Lack of shared leadership with other school staff members (0 = not at all or very little; 1 = to some extent or a lot)	Principal	Independent	TC2G26I
Teacher formal appraisal			
After teacher appraisal, measures to remedy any weaknesses in teaching are discussed with the teacher (0 = never; 1 = sometimes, most of the time or always)	Principal	Dependent	TC2G29A
After teacher appraisal, a development or training plan is developed for each teacher (0 = never; 1 = sometimes, most of the time or always)	Principal	Dependent	TC2G29B
If a teacher is found to be a poor performer, material sanctions such as reduced annual increases in pay are imposed on the teacher (0 = never; 1 = sometimes, most of the time or always)	Principal	Dependent	TC2G29C
After teacher appraisal, a mentor is appointed to help the teacher improve his/her teaching (0 = never; 1 = sometimes, most of the time or always)	Principal	Dependent	TC2G29D
After teacher appraisal, there is a change in a teacher's work responsibilities (0 = never; 1 = sometimes, most of the time or always)	Principal	Dependent	TC2G29E
After teacher appraisal, there is a change in a teacher's salary or a payment of a financial bonus (0 = never; 1 = sometimes, most of the time or always)	Principal	Dependent	TC2G29F
After teacher appraisal, there is a change in the likelihood of a teacher's career advancement (0 = never; 1 = sometimes, most of the time or always)	Principal	Dependent	TC2G29G
After teacher appraisal, dismissal or non-renewal of contract occurs (0 = never; 1 = sometimes, most of the time or always)	Principal	Dependent	TC2G29H
School climate			
School climate - mutual respect (continuous)	Principal	Dependent, independent	PSCMUTRS
Lack of material resources, a bit of a problem (0 = not a problem or a problem; 1 = a bit of a problem)	Principal	Independent	PLACKMAT
Lack of material resources, a problem (0 = Not a problem or a bit of a problem; 1 = a problem)	Principal	Independent	PLACKMAT
Lack of pedagogical personnel, a bit of a problem (0 = not a problem or a problem; 1 = a bit of a problem)	Principal	Independent	PLACKPER
Lack of pedagogical personnel, a problem (0 = not a problem or a bit of a problem; 1 = a problem)	Principal	Independent	PLACKPER
School delinquency and violence (continuous)	Principal	Independent	PSCDELIQS
Job satisfaction			
Principal job satisfaction (continuous)	Principal	Dependent, independent	PJOBSATS

Source: OECD, TALIS 2013 Database.

StatLink ⟢ http://dx.doi.org/10.1787/888933048394

[Part 1/6]

The percentage of missing cases for each country for each variable included in the Chapter 3 regression analyses

Table B.4

	Number of responding principals (unweighted)	Principals' background				
		Gender	Age	Highest level of education of principal	Number of year(s) of experience working as a principal in total	Number of year(s) of experience working as a teacher in total
		Principal %				
		TC2G01	TC2G02	TC2G03	TC2G04B	TC2G04D
Australia	123	6.3	7.4	6.3	10.9	10.5
Brazil	1 070	1.1	2.4	3.8	24.1	13.7
Bulgaria	197	0.0	0.0	0.0	7.8	4.1
Chile	178	17.5	18.0	15.7	28.2	27.0
Croatia	199	1.9	2.7	1.9	9.0	7.7
Czech Republic	220	0.0	0.0	0.0	0.7	0.7
Denmark	148	16.9	16.9	16.9	18.9	18.2
Estonia	197	0.5	0.0	0.0	0.0	0.5
Finland	146	0.0	0.0	0.0	1.3	2.1
France	204	11.6	10.9	11.4	12.2	14.1
Iceland	129	16.3	16.3	16.3	19.4	18.6
Israel	195	7.7	4.5	4.5	4.9	4.4
Italy	194	0.7	0.7	0.7	1.4	0.7
Japan	192	0.0	0.0	0.0	0.8	2.4
Korea	177	6.7	6.7	6.7	7.0	8.7
Latvia	116	7.5	7.4	6.9	7.3	8.3
Malaysia	150	3.2	2.5	2.5	1.8	1.8
Mexico	187	1.6	2.6	1.8	8.5	7.2
Netherlands	127	5.4	5.4	5.4	5.4	5.4
Norway	145	21.5	21.9	21.5	23.6	23.6
Poland	195	2.1	2.1	2.1	7.6	2.4
Portugal	185	3.6	3.6	5.3	12.9	5.4
Romania	197	0.0	0.0	0.0	0.2	0.6
Serbia	191	3.3	2.9	3.4	12.6	5.3
Singapore	159	10.2	9.6	9.6	10.8	10.8
Slovak Republic	193	3.1	2.3	2.3	2.6	2.5
Spain	192	0.8	2.9	0.6	2.4	2.1
Sweden	186	10.5	10.5	10.5	12.6	13.2
Sub-national entities						
Abu Dhabi (United Arab Emirates)	166	19.7	22.1	20.8	22.0	21.9
Alberta (Canada)	182	3.8	3.8	3.8	5.3	4.7
England (United Kingdom)	154	2.0	2.3	2.0	5.4	1.4
Flanders (Belgium)	168	5.8	7.2	6.8	7.2	7.6

Note: Percentages in this table represent the weighted proportion of missing cases.
Source: OECD, TALIS 2013 Database.
StatLink ᔕ http://dx.doi.org/10.1787/888933048413

[Part 2/6]

Table B.4 The percentage of missing cases for each country for each variable included in the Chapter 3 regression analyses

	School background									
	Ratio of teacher to administrative or management personnel	School location size	Public/private schools	Public funding above 50%	Number of teachers	Number of students	Students whose first language is different from the language of instruction	Students with special needs	Students from socio-economically disadvantaged homes	Ratio of teacher to pedagogical support personnel
	Principal %									
	TARATIO	TC2G09	TC2G10	TC2G11A	TC2G12A	TC2G14	TC2G15A	TC2G15B	TC2G15C	TPRATIO
Australia	9.9	8.4	8.4	9.4	9.9	8.8	9.9	9.9	9.9	10.0
Brazil	7.9	2.0	1.4	3.6	5.7	4.0	5.1	2.4	4.0	7.3
Bulgaria	7.9	0.0	0.0	0.0	6.4	1.9	3.7	2.9	2.9	6.4
Chile	24.4	16.0	13.6	16.4	23.2	22.0	16.0	15.3	14.7	26.3
Croatia	6.6	2.4	1.9	1.9	6.6	3.5	5.5	2.8	3.3	9.8
Czech Republic	0.2	0.0	0.0	0.3	0.2	0.0	0.0	0.0	0.0	0.7
Denmark	18.9	17.5	17.6	16.9	18.2	16.9	16.9	16.9	17.5	18.9
Estonia	1.5	0.5	0.5	0.5	1.5	1.0	1.0	1.0	1.0	2.5
Finland	0.0	0.0	0.0	0.0	0.0	0.0	0.0	0.0	0.0	2.1
France	15.2	12.4	11.9	12.4	14.1	12.4	13.0	13.6	13.4	15.4
Iceland	17.8	17.1	17.1	18.6	17.8	17.8	17.8	18.6	18.6	20.9
Israel	8.8	5.5	4.1	4.7	8.6	9.2	5.8	6.4	6.1	9.5
Italy	2.1	0.7	0.0	0.0	0.3	0.0	0.8	0.4	0.4	0.3
Japan	2.7	0.0	0.0	0.0	2.3	0.0	0.4	0.4	0.4	3.5
Korea	7.4	7.5	7.0	7.0	7.4	7.4	7.4	7.4	7.4	9.6
Latvia	6.9	6.9	6.9	6.9	6.9	6.9	6.9	7.3	6.9	7.3
Malaysia	2.6	2.6	2.6	3.2	2.6	2.6	3.1	3.1	3.1	2.6
Mexico	5.2	0.8	0.8	1.6	2.6	2.0	1.5	0.8	0.8	4.2
Netherlands	6.4	5.4	5.4	5.4	6.4	5.4	7.3	7.3	7.3	6.9
Norway	22.9	21.5	21.5	21.5	22.9	21.9	24.7	24.7	24.7	22.9
Poland	4.2	2.5	2.1	2.4	2.7	3.8	4.3	3.3	3.3	7.4
Portugal	9.3	4.0	4.0	4.8	8.3	7.5	4.8	5.6	6.1	8.9
Romania	0.0	0.0	0.0	0.0	0.0	0.0	0.1	0.9	0.1	1.8
Serbia	6.6	3.2	2.9	3.1	5.6	4.8	6.8	6.5	6.4	7.2
Singapore	11.4	9.6	10.2	10.2	10.2	10.8	10.8	10.8	10.2	10.2
Slovak Republic	4.1	2.5	3.1	2.5	2.5	2.5	4.3	3.6	3.6	2.5
Spain	0.8	0.6	0.9	0.6	0.8	0.6	0.9	0.9	0.9	1.2
Sweden	11.8	11.2	10.5	10.5	11.5	12.0	10.9	10.5	10.9	12.6
Sub-national entities										
Abu Dhabi (United Arab Emirates)	23.9	21.2	20.8	21.5	23.5	22.2	22.2	22.2	22.2	26.7
Alberta (Canada)	3.8	3.8	4.3	3.8	3.8	3.8	3.8	3.8	4.2	8.5
England (United Kingdom)	6.9	1.4	1.4	1.4	3.3	3.1	3.4	3.4	3.4	4.0
Flanders (Belgium)	9.3	7.4	7.4	5.8	8.6	7.4	10.0	10.6	10.0	19.5

Note: Percentages in this table represent the weighted proportion of missing cases.
Source: OECD, TALIS 2013 Database.
StatLink ⟲ http://dx.doi.org/10.1787/888933048413

[Part 3/6]

Table B.4

The percentage of missing cases for each country for each variable included in the Chapter 3 regression analyses

	School leadership						
	Distributed leadership	Percentage of time the principal spends on curriculum and teaching-related tasks and meetings	Principal used student performance and student evaluation results to develop the school's educational goals and programmes	Principal worked on a professional development plan for this school	Principal observing instruction in the classroom	Instructional leadership	Inadequate school budget and resources
				Principal %			
	PDISLEADS	TC2G19B	TC2G20A	TC2G20B	TC2G21B	PINSLEADS	TC2G26A
Australia	9.9	9.9	9.9	9.9	9.9	9.9	10.9
Brazil	1.3	9.4	4.5	4.6	3.0	1.4	6.9
Bulgaria	0.0	0.6	1.8	1.8	0.0	0.0	0.8
Chile	17.0	23.0	20.1	20.1	16.5	16.5	17.8
Croatia	1.9	5.7	5.9	5.9	1.9	1.9	3.4
Czech Republic	0.0	0.6	0.6	0.6	0.0	0.0	0.0
Denmark	16.9	16.9	18.2	18.2	16.9	16.9	16.9
Estonia	0.5	1.0	1.0	1.0	1.0	0.5	1.0
Finland	0.6	0.0	0.0	0.0	0.0	0.0	0.0
France	13.3	13.9	15.9	15.9	14.8	13.7	13.8
Iceland	17.8	19.4	17.8	17.8	17.8	17.8	17.8
Israel	4.7	9.8	8.6	8.6	8.2	8.2	9.7
Italy	0.3	1.2	1.7	1.7	1.1	0.3	0.0
Japan	0.0	0.0	0.6	0.6	0.0	0.0	0.0
Korea	8.3	10.4	9.3	9.3	8.3	8.3	8.3
Latvia	6.9	6.9	10.6	10.6	6.9	6.9	6.9
Malaysia	3.0	4.6	2.6	2.6	2.6	2.6	2.6
Mexico	0.8	5.2	1.2	1.2	1.3	1.0	1.6
Netherlands	17.3	11.9	11.5	11.5	17.3	17.3	17.3
Norway	21.9	22.6	21.9	21.9	21.9	21.9	21.9
Poland	2.5	3.1	2.7	2.7	3.7	3.3	2.5
Portugal	4.8	6.5	6.0	6.0	4.8	4.8	7.5
Romania	0.2	2.4	0.6	0.6	0.2	0.2	0.2
Serbia	4.0	9.8	5.3	5.3	4.6	3.8	4.7
Singapore	10.8	10.8	11.4	11.4	11.4	11.4	10.8
Slovak Republic	2.5	2.8	2.5	2.5	2.5	2.5	2.5
Spain	0.6	0.9	1.2	1.2	0.6	0.6	0.6
Sweden	10.7	11.6	11.1	11.1	12.0	12.0	10.7
Sub-national entities							
Abu Dhabi (United Arab Emirates)	21.5	29.8	22.9	22.9	22.2	22.2	23.6
Alberta (Canada)	3.8	7.4	4.9	4.9	4.3	4.3	4.9
England (United Kingdom)	3.8	4.4	2.8	2.8	4.1	2.7	2.7
Flanders (Belgium)	7.4	9.0	7.9	7.9	7.4	7.4	7.9

Note: Percentages in this table represent the weighted proportion of missing cases.
Source: OECD, TALIS 2013 Database.
StatLink ⟨⟩ http://dx.doi.org/10.1787/888933048413

[Part 4/6]
Table B.4 The percentage of missing cases for each country for each variable included in the Chapter 3 regression analyses

	School leadership							
	Government regulation and policy	Teachers' absences	Lack of parent or guardian involvement and support	Teachers' career-based wage system	Lack of opportunities for my own professional development	Lack of opportunities for teachers' professional development	High workload and level of responsibilities in teachers' job	Lack of shared leadership with other school staff members
	Principal %							
	TC2G26B	TC2G26C	TC2G26D	TC2G26E	TC2G26F	TC2G26G	TC2G26H	TC2G26I
Australia	10.9	10.9	10.9	10.9	10.9	10.9	10.9	10.9
Brazil	7.9	9.0	5.8	6.7	6.2	6.7	5.6	6.6
Bulgaria	2.3	0.8	0.6	0.0	1.6	1.3	1.3	1.3
Chile	18.5	18.4	17.8	19.0	17.8	17.8	17.8	17.8
Croatia	1.9	3.3	2.2	2.7	1.9	1.9	1.9	1.9
Czech Republic	0.0	0.7	0.0	0.1	0.1	0.0	0.0	0.1
Denmark	16.9	16.9	16.9	16.9	16.9	16.9	16.9	16.9
Estonia	1.0	0.5	1.0	1.0	1.0	1.0	1.0	1.5
Finland	0.0	0.8	0.0	0.0	0.0	0.6	0.0	0.6
France	14.1	13.5	13.5	14.5	14.1	13.5	13.5	13.5
Iceland	17.8	17.8	18.6	19.4	19.4	19.4	18.6	18.6
Israel	13.2	9.3	9.3	9.9	9.9	10.5	10.1	9.9
Italy	0.0	0.8	0.0	0.0	0.2	0.0	0.0	0.0
Japan	0.0	0.0	0.3	0.0	0.0	0.0	0.0	0.0
Korea	8.3	8.3	8.3	8.3	8.8	8.3	8.3	8.3
Latvia	6.9	6.9	6.9	6.9	6.9	6.9	6.9	6.9
Malaysia	2.6	2.6	2.6	3.1	2.6	2.6	2.6	2.6
Mexico	2.8	3.8	2.3	1.6	3.3	2.3	2.9	2.3
Netherlands	17.3	17.7	17.3	17.3	17.3	17.3	17.3	17.7
Norway	23.3	21.9	21.9	22.2	21.9	21.9	21.9	21.9
Poland	2.5	2.8	4.0	2.5	2.8	2.5	2.5	2.5
Portugal	5.9	7.2	5.9	7.2	5.9	6.3	5.9	6.3
Romania	0.2	0.2	0.2	0.2	0.2	0.2	0.2	0.2
Serbia	5.5	4.4	5.7	6.0	4.8	5.0	3.9	4.5
Singapore	10.8	10.8	10.8	10.8	10.8	10.8	10.8	10.8
Slovak Republic	2.9	2.5	2.5	2.5	2.5	2.5	2.5	2.5
Spain	0.6	0.6	0.6	0.6	0.6	0.7	0.6	0.6
Sweden	10.7	10.7	10.7	100.0	11.7	10.7	10.7	10.7
Sub-national entities								
Abu Dhabi (United Arab Emirates)	24.7	23.6	23.6	23.6	24.2	23.6	23.6	24.0
Alberta (Canada)	4.9	4.3	4.3	4.9	4.3	4.3	4.3	4.3
England (United Kingdom)	3.1	3.3	2.7	3.3	2.7	2.7	2.7	3.5
Flanders (Belgium)	7.9	7.9	7.9	7.9	7.9	7.9	8.2	7.9

Note: Percentages in this table represent the weighted proportion of missing cases.
Source: OECD, TALIS 2013 Database.
StatLink http://dx.doi.org/10.1787/888933048413

[Part 5/6]
The percentage of missing cases for each country for each variable included in the Chapter 3 regression analyses

Table B.4

	Teacher formal appraisal							
	After teacher appraisal, measures to remedy any weaknesses in teaching are discussed with the teacher	After teacher appraisal, a development or training plan is developed for each teacher	If a teacher is found to be a poor performer, material sanctions such as reduced annual increases in pay are imposed on the teacher	After teacher appraisal, a mentor is appointed to help the teacher improve his/her teaching	After teacher appraisal, there is a change in a teacher's work responsibilities	After teacher appraisal, there is a change in a teacher's salary or a payment of a financial bonus	After teacher appraisal, there is a change in the likelihood of a teacher's career advancement	After teacher appraisal, dismissal or non-renewal of contract occurs
	Principal %							
	TC2G29A	TC2G29B	TC2G29C	TC2G29D	TC2G29E	TC2G29F	TC2G29G	TC2G29H
Australia	14.0	14.0	14.0	14.0	14.0	14.0	14.0	14.5
Brazil	17.8	18.1	17.9	18.1	18.5	18.2	19.0	18.0
Bulgaria	13.1	13.1	13.7	14.2	13.1	13.1	13.9	13.1
Chile	31.7	31.7	31.7	31.7	31.7	32.3	32.3	31.7
Croatia	4.2	4.2	100.0	4.2	5.0	100.0	5.7	4.6
Czech Republic	0.6	0.6	0.6	0.6	0.6	0.6	0.6	0.6
Denmark	23.5	23.5	23.5	23.5	23.5	24.3	23.5	23.5
Estonia	3.0	3.0	3.0	3.0	3.5	3.0	3.0	3.0
Finland	27.4	27.4	27.4	27.4	27.4	27.4	27.4	27.4
France	15.0	15.5	15.0	15.0	15.7	15.0	15.4	15.4
Iceland	34.9	34.9	34.9	34.9	34.9	35.7	34.9	34.9
Israel	8.4	10.3	8.9	8.4	8.9	8.9	9.5	9.3
Italy	69.1	69.1	69.1	69.3	69.7	69.1	69.1	69.1
Japan	4.2	4.6	4.2	4.2	4.2	4.2	4.2	4.2
Korea	8.9	8.9	9.8	8.9	9.4	9.4	9.4	9.2
Latvia	9.1	9.1	9.1	9.1	9.1	9.1	9.1	9.1
Malaysia	4.0	4.0	4.0	4.0	4.0	4.0	4.0	4.0
Mexico	4.0	4.5	4.0	4.0	4.0	4.4	4.0	4.8
Netherlands	18.9	18.9	18.9	18.9	18.9	20.2	18.9	18.9
Norway	28.0	28.0	28.0	28.0	28.0	28.0	28.0	28.0
Poland	4.0	4.8	4.0	4.0	4.5	4.0	4.5	4.0
Portugal	9.5	10.0	9.5	9.5	9.5	9.5	9.5	9.5
Romania	2.8	2.2	2.1	2.1	2.1	2.1	2.1	2.1
Serbia	7.1	7.9	7.8	7.8	7.3	7.7	7.1	7.1
Singapore	12.0	11.4	11.4	11.4	11.4	11.4	11.4	11.4
Slovak Republic	2.8	2.8	3.4	3.4	4.1	3.4	3.4	3.4
Spain	37.6	37.6	37.6	37.6	37.6	37.6	37.6	37.6
Sweden	14.8	14.8	14.8	14.8	14.8	15.4	15.8	15.1
Sub-national entities								
Abu Dhabi (United Arab Emirates)	24.2	24.2	24.2	24.2	25.1	24.2	24.7	24.2
Alberta (Canada)	15.9	15.9	15.9	15.9	15.9	16.5	16.9	16.5
England (United Kingdom)	4.6	4.6	4.6	4.6	4.6	5.0	4.6	4.6
Flanders (Belgium)	9.7	9.7	10.2	9.7	10.3	10.2	10.2	10.2

Note: Percentages in this table represent the weighted proportion of missing cases.
Source: OECD, TALIS 2013 Database.
StatLink 🔗 http://dx.doi.org/10.1787/888933048413

[Part 6/6]

The percentage of missing cases for each country for each variable included in the Chapter 3
Table B.4 **regression analyses**

	School climate				Job satisfaction
	School climate - mutual respect	Lack of pedagogical personnel index	Lack of material resources index	School delinquency and violence	Principal job satisfaction
	Principal %				
	PSCMUTRS	PLACKMAT	PLACKPER	PSCDELIQS	PJOBSATS
Australia	12.2	10.9	10.9	13.3	10.9
Brazil	1.3	2.5	1.8	2.5	1.6
Bulgaria	0.0	2.1	0.0	0.6	1.6
Chile	17.0	18.2	18.2	18.2	17.0
Croatia	1.9	1.9	1.9	1.9	1.9
Czech Republic	0.1	0.1	0.1	0.0	0.6
Denmark	16.9	16.9	16.9	16.9	17.6
Estonia	1.0	1.0	1.0	1.0	1.0
Finland	0.6	0.0	0.0	0.0	0.6
France	14.3	14.0	13.7	14.1	13.7
Iceland	17.8	18.6	18.6	18.6	19.4
Israel	7.4	7.6	7.1	10.8	4.7
Italy	0.0	0.0	0.0	0.7	0.6
Japan	0.0	0.0	0.0	0.0	0.0
Korea	8.8	8.8	8.8	8.3	7.8
Latvia	6.9	7.3	6.9	6.9	6.9
Malaysia	4.4	3.2	3.2	3.7	3.2
Mexico	0.8	0.8	0.8	0.8	0.8
Netherlands	17.3	17.3	17.3	17.3	17.3
Norway	21.9	21.9	21.9	24.3	21.9
Poland	2.5	2.5	2.5	2.5	2.5
Portugal	4.8	4.8	4.8	4.8	4.8
Romania	1.4	1.7	1.7	1.7	2.2
Serbia	3.6	3.6	3.6	3.6	3.6
Singapore	11.4	10.8	10.8	10.8	10.8
Slovak Republic	2.5	2.5	2.5	2.5	2.5
Spain	1.1	0.0	0.0	0.4	0.3
Sweden	10.7	10.7	10.7	10.7	10.7
Sub-national entities					
Abu Dhabi (United Arab Emirates)	22.6	21.9	21.9	23.3	21.9
Alberta (Canada)	4.9	6.0	6.0	4.9	4.9
England (United Kingdom)	2.3	2.3	2.3	2.3	2.7
Flanders (Belgium)	8.9	8.9	8.9	8.9	8.9

Note: Percentages in this table represent the weighted proportion of missing cases.
Source: OECD, TALIS 2013 Database.
StatLink http://dx.doi.org/10.1787/888933048413

[Part 1/1]
Table B.5   **List of variables in the Chapter 4 regression analyses**

Variable	Level	Type of variable	Based on variable(s) in the data set
Teacher background			
Teacher's participation in different professional development programmes (0 = no; 1 = yes)	Teacher	Dependent, independent	TT2G21A1, TT2G21B1, TT2G21C1, TT2G21D1, TT2G21E1, TT2G21F, TT2G21G, TT2G21H, TT2G21I
Teacher's gender (0 = male; 1 = female)	Teacher	Independent	TT2G01
Teacher's age (discretised in three dichotomous variables: age 16-29, age 30-39, age 40 or more)	Teacher	Independent	TT2G02
Teacher's employment status (0 = full time; 1 = part time)	Teacher	Independent	TT2G03
Number of years of teaching at this school (discretised in three dichotomous variables: 0-2 years, 3-5 years, 6 or more years)	Teacher	Independent	TT2G05A
Teacher's employment status at the school (0 = permanent; 1 = fixed-term)	Teacher	Independent	TT2G06
Teacher's education (dichotomised: 0 = ISCED 5B or below; 1 = ISCED 5A or higher)	Teacher	Independent	TT2G10
Teacher's background includes a training programme (0 = no; 1 = yes)	Teacher	Independent	TT2G11
Subjects taught (discretised in four dichotomous variables: Reading & writing, mathematics, science, no specialisation)	Teacher	Independent	TT2G15A; 15B; 15C
Number of hours worked in the most recent complete calendar week (discretised in three dichotomous variables: 0-30 hours, 31-50 hours, 51 or more hours)	Teacher	Independent	TT2G16
Professional development			
Index of needs for teaching for diversity (continuous)	Teacher	Independent	TPDDIV
Index of pedagogical needs (continuous)	Teacher	Independent	TPDPED
Teacher's participation in formal professional development programmes (0 = no; 1 = yes)	Teacher	Independent	TT2G19A
Teacher serving as a mentor (0 = no; 1 = yes)	Teacher	Independent	TT2G20B
School background			
Management of the school (0 = public; 1 = private)	Teacher	Independent	TC2G10
School's enrollment (discretised in three dichotomous variables: 1-365 students; 366-1065 students; 1066 or more students)	Teacher	Independent	TC2G14
Percentage of students from socio-economically disadvantaged homes (0 = above 30%; 1 = 30% or below)	Teacher	Independent	TC2G15C
School leadership			
Principal working on a professional development plan for their school (0 = no; 1 = yes)	Teacher	Independent	TC2G20B
Teacher induction and mentoring			
Access to mentoring system for teachers in the school (0 = no; 1 = yes)	Teacher	Independent	TC2G36

Source: OECD, TALIS 2013 Database.
StatLink ⬛⬛ http://dx.doi.org/10.1787/888933048432

[Part 1/4]

Table B.6 The percentage of missing cases for each country for each variable included in the Chapter 4 regression analyses

	Number of responding teachers (unweighted)	Teacher background					
		Participation in courses/ workshops	Participation in education conferences or seminars	Participation in observation visits to other schools	Participation in observation visits to business premises, public organisations, non-governmental organisations	Participation in in-service training courses in business premises, public organisations, non-governmental organisations	Participation in a qualification programme
		Teacher %					
		TT2G21A1	TT2G21B1	TT2G21C1	TT2G21D1	TT2G21E1	TT2G21F
Australia	2 059	4.5	4.5	4.5	4.5	4.5	4.5
Brazil	14 291	6.7	6.8	6.7	6.7	6.8	6.5
Bulgaria	2 975	2.0	2.2	2.0	1.9	2.0	1.9
Chile	1 676	7.6	7.5	7.6	7.7	7.8	7.5
Croatia	3 675	1.4	1.5	1.5	1.5	1.5	1.3
Czech Republic	3 219	0.3	0.3	0.3	0.3	0.3	0.3
Denmark	1 649	2.7	2.7	2.7	2.7	2.7	2.6
Estonia	3 129	1.9	2.1	2.0	2.0	2.1	1.8
Finland	2 739	1.2	1.2	1.3	1.2	1.4	1.2
France	3 002	4.1	4.2	4.1	4.3	4.2	4.0
Iceland	1 430	11.2	11.3	11.4	11.2	11.2	11.3
Israel	3 403	4.0	4.1	4.1	4.1	4.1	4.2
Italy	3 337	1.8	1.8	1.7	1.9	1.9	1.7
Japan	3 484	1.0	1.1	1.1	1.1	1.0	0.8
Korea	2 933	2.3	2.3	2.3	2.4	2.4	2.2
Latvia	2 126	1.3	1.3	1.3	1.3	1.4	1.2
Malaysia	2 984	0.6	0.6	0.6	0.6	0.6	0.6
Mexico	3 138	0.5	0.5	0.5	0.5	0.5	0.4
Netherlands	1 912	2.6	2.7	2.7	2.7	2.6	2.6
Norway	2 981	3.5	3.5	3.5	3.5	3.5	3.5
Poland	3 858	0.8	0.8	0.8	0.8	0.8	1.0
Portugal	3 628	0.9	0.9	0.9	0.9	0.9	0.9
Romania	3 286	1.6	1.7	1.7	1.8	1.8	1.6
Serbia	3 857	1.6	1.7	1.5	1.4	1.4	1.4
Singapore	3 109	0.3	0.3	0.3	0.3	0.4	0.3
Slovak Republic	3 493	0.7	0.7	0.7	0.8	0.8	0.7
Spain	3 339	1.3	1.4	1.4	1.4	1.4	1.3
Sweden	3 319	3.0	3.0	3.0	3.0	3.0	2.9
Sub-national entities							
Abu Dhabi (United Arab Emirates)	2 433	5.9	6.0	6.2	6.0	6.2	6.2
Alberta (Canada)	1 773	1.9	2.0	2.0	1.9	1.9	1.9
England (United Kingdom)	2 496	2.9	2.9	2.9	2.9	3.0	2.9
Flanders (Belgium)	3 129	1.3	1.4	1.3	1.4	1.4	1.4

Note: Percentages in this table represent the weighted proportion of missing cases.
Source: OECD, TALIS 2013 Database.
StatLink ⌨ http://dx.doi.org/10.1787/888933048451

[Part 2/4]

The percentage of missing cases for each country for each variable included in the Chapter 4 regression analyses

Table B.6

	Teacher background						
	Participation in a network of teachers formed specifically for the professional development of teachers	Participation in individual or collaborative research on a topic of interest to you professionally	Participation in mentoring and/or peer observation and coaching, as part of a formal school arrangement	Gender	Age	Employement status (full-time or part-time)	Number of years teaching at this school
	Teacher %						
	TT2G21G	TT2G21H	TT2G21I	TT2G01	TT2G02	TT2G03	TT2G05A
Australia	4.5	4.5	4.5	0.0	0.4	0.6	1.4
Brazil	6.6	6.7	6.7	0.0	0.1	11.2	23.8
Bulgaria	2.0	2.0	2.2	0.0	0.1	1.8	6.7
Chile	7.6	7.6	7.6	0.0	0.8	1.7	8.5
Croatia	1.4	1.4	1.4	0.0	0.1	0.9	14.1
Czech Republic	0.4	0.4	0.4	0.0	0.6	0.1	0.1
Denmark	2.8	2.8	2.7	0.0	0.0	0.4	0.8
Estonia	2.0	2.0	2.0	0.0	1.6	0.6	1.1
Finland	1.2	1.3	1.2	0.0	0.0	0.2	0.8
France	4.2	4.2	4.3	0.0	0.0	0.2	0.6
Iceland	11.5	11.3	11.4	0.0	0.3	0.4	1.5
Israel	4.2	4.2	4.2	0.0	0.2	0.8	1.8
Italy	1.8	1.7	1.8	0.0	0.0	0.4	1.4
Japan	0.9	0.9	0.9	0.0	0.1	0.6	1.0
Korea	2.3	2.2	2.3	0.0	0.0	0.8	1.2
Latvia	1.2	1.2	1.2	0.0	1.1	0.8	2.0
Malaysia	0.6	0.6	0.6	0.0	0.0	0.8	0.7
Mexico	0.5	0.5	0.5	0.1	0.2	2.3	12.7
Netherlands	2.6	2.6	2.6	0.0	0.1	0.1	0.7
Norway	3.5	3.5	3.5	0.0	0.1	0.4	0.7
Poland	1.0	1.0	1.0	0.0	0.0	0.3	3.5
Portugal	0.9	0.9	0.9	0.0	0.0	0.6	7.5
Romania	1.7	1.7	1.6	0.0	0.0	0.8	1.3
Serbia	1.6	1.6	1.6	0.0	0.1	1.8	8.2
Singapore	0.3	0.3	0.3	0.0	0.2	0.1	0.3
Slovak Republic	0.7	0.8	0.8	0.0	0.3	0.1	0.6
Spain	1.5	1.3	1.4	0.0	0.0	0.5	0.5
Sweden	2.9	3.1	3.0	0.0	0.1	0.1	0.7
Sub-national entities							
Abu Dhabi (United Arab Emirates)	6.3	6.2	6.2	0.0	0.3	1.8	2.9
Alberta (Canada)	1.9	1.9	1.9	0.0	0.4	0.2	1.0
England (United Kingdom)	2.9	2.9	3.0	0.0	0.3	0.1	1.4
Flanders (Belgium)	1.5	1.4	1.4	0.0	0.0	0.1	0.8

Note: Percentages in this table represent the weighted proportion of missing cases.
Source: OECD, TALIS 2013 Database.
StatLink http://dx.doi.org/10.1787/888933048451

[Part 3/4]

Table B.6   **The percentage of missing cases for each country for each variable included in the Chapter 4 regression analyses**

	Teacher background						
	Employement status (permanent or fixed-term)	Highest level of education of teacher	Completion of teacher education or training programme	Teaching reading, writing and literature	Teaching mathematics	Teaching science	Number of hours worked in the most recent complete calendar week
	Teacher %						
	TT2G06	TT2G10	TT2G11	TT2G15A	TT2G15B	TT2G15C	TT2G16
Australia	0.8	0.8	0.9	2.5	2.6	2.6	2.9
Brazil	10.1	7.8	7.4	6.6	6.7	6.6	8.8
Bulgaria	0.5	0.5	0.6	1.9	2.0	2.0	2.5
Chile	1.7	1.5	2.5	7.4	7.4	7.3	7.9
Croatia	0.6	0.5	1.5	1.3	1.3	1.4	3.6
Czech Republic	0.1	0.1	0.5	0.3	0.3	0.3	0.3
Denmark	0.3	0.6	0.5	1.1	1.1	1.0	1.9
Estonia	0.5	0.5	0.6	1.1	1.1	1.1	1.5
Finland	0.2	0.3	0.3	0.6	0.6	0.7	1.2
France	0.4	0.6	1.0	1.7	1.8	1.9	2.6
Iceland	0.7	1.8	0.9	4.5	4.5	4.5	6.4
Israel	1.2	1.1	1.0	2.8	2.8	2.8	3.8
Italy	0.4	0.4	0.4	0.8	0.8	0.8	1.0
Japan	1.2	0.4	1.0	0.4	0.4	0.4	2.0
Korea	0.3	0.1	0.2	1.2	1.2	1.2	1.1
Latvia	0.6	0.6	0.5	1.7	1.8	1.6	1.3
Malaysia	0.5	0.5	0.6	0.7	0.7	0.7	1.0
Mexico	1.4	0.7	1.1	1.3	1.3	1.4	1.7
Netherlands	0.1	0.5	0.7	2.6	2.5	2.5	1.8
Norway	0.5	0.7	0.8	1.1	1.2	1.2	2.1
Poland	0.1	0.2	0.2	0.7	0.7	0.7	0.6
Portugal	0.4	0.3	2.2	0.9	0.9	1.0	1.2
Romania	0.7	0.5	0.5	0.9	1.0	1.0	0.8
Serbia	0.4	0.5	5.2	1.6	1.6	1.7	3.8
Singapore	0.1	0.0	0.1	0.4	0.6	0.6	0.4
Slovak Republic	0.3	0.1	0.2	0.6	0.6	0.5	0.7
Spain	0.5	0.3	0.3	1.1	1.1	1.1	0.8
Sweden	0.3	0.6	0.5	1.3	1.3	1.3	2.1
Sub-national entities							
Abu Dhabi (United Arab Emirates)	1.7	1.3	1.7	7.1	7.3	7.3	5.0
Alberta (Canada)	0.5	0.2	0.3	1.2	1.2	1.2	1.3
England (United Kingdom)	0.7	0.8	1.0	1.7	1.7	1.7	2.2
Flanders (Belgium)	0.2	0.3	0.3	0.9	0.9	0.9	0.9

Note: Percentages in this table represent the weighted proportion of missing cases.
Source: OECD, TALIS 2013 Database.
StatLink ⟨⟩ http://dx.doi.org/10.1787/888933048451

[Part 4/4]

The percentage of missing cases for each country for each variable included in the Chapter 4 regression analyses

Table B.6

	Professional development				School background			School leadership	Teacher induction and mentoring
	Index of needs for teaching for diversity	Index of pedagogical needs	Participation in formal induction programme	Serving as a mentor	Public/ private schools	Number of students	Students from socio-economically disadvantaged homes	Principal working on a professional development plan for their school	Teachers' access to mentoring system
	Teacher %								
	TPDDIV	**TPDPED**	**TT2G19A**	**TT2G20B**	**TC2G10**	**TC2G14**	**TC2G15C**	**TC2G20B**	**TC2G36**
Australia	6.1	5.8	3.4	4.2	7.5	8.1	8.7	8.9	9.5
Brazil	7.5	7.5	7.4	9.7	0.9	4.8	3.3	3.5	5.1
Bulgaria	3.0	2.9	0.8	5.0	0.0	1.3	3.3	2.3	1.5
Chile	8.5	7.9	4.1	6.6	14.5	22.7	16.3	21.5	22.7
Croatia	2.4	2.1	1.7	9.7	1.9	3.2	3.2	7.5	5.4
Czech Republic	0.6	0.5	0.4	1.0	0.0	0.0	0.1	0.5	1.0
Denmark	3.7	3.7	2.2	2.7	17.2	16.5	17.0	17.6	16.5
Estonia	2.3	2.1	1.6	2.4	1.0	1.5	1.5	1.6	1.6
Finland	1.6	1.5	1.2	1.5	0.0	0.0	0.0	0.0	0.0
France	5.7	5.8	2.9	3.7	12.7	13.1	14.3	17.4	16.2
Iceland	15.8	15.5	7.8	8.7	19.2	20.5	21.6	20.5	20.5
Israel	5.9	5.7	4.2	4.9	5.9	10.6	8.4	8.8	7.4
Italy	2.1	1.9	1.5	3.4	0.0	0.0	0.7	1.4	0.0
Japan	0.7	0.7	0.3	0.6	0.0	0.0	0.6	1.8	4.3
Korea	2.9	2.7	1.9	2.9	7.2	7.7	7.7	9.5	8.8
Latvia	2.1	1.8	1.3	2.7	6.5	6.5	6.5	11.4	6.5
Malaysia	0.8	0.8	0.6	0.7	2.2	2.2	2.9	2.2	3.7
Mexico	1.0	0.8	0.8	3.2	0.4	2.0	0.4	1.5	6.1
Netherlands	4.9	4.8	2.0	2.5	6.5	6.5	8.8	12.0	13.3
Norway	5.1	4.9	2.8	3.5	23.1	23.6	26.8	23.6	23.6
Poland	1.8	2.0	0.8	2.6	3.3	4.7	4.9	4.2	5.0
Portugal	1.6	1.3	1.1	2.3	3.7	7.1	5.6	5.9	6.9
Romania	1.7	1.7	1.3	2.8	0.0	0.0	0.3	1.4	1.3
Serbia	1.7	1.5	1.7	8.3	2.4	4.4	6.6	5.0	8.3
Singapore	0.5	0.4	0.2	0.6	9.6	10.1	9.6	10.9	9.6
Slovak Republic	1.4	1.2	0.9	1.2	4.1	3.3	4.4	3.3	3.9
Spain	2.0	1.7	1.1	1.8	1.1	0.5	1.1	1.1	0.6
Sweden	4.5	4.2	3.0	3.2	7.9	8.9	8.3	8.9	9.0
Sub-national entities									
Abu Dhabi (United Arab Emirates)	7.9	8.0	5.4	6.6	23.5	26.3	26.6	26.6	26.2
Alberta (Canada)	3.2	3.3	1.7	2.0	2.2	1.8	2.4	3.9	2.1
England (United Kingdom)	4.9	5.1	2.5	3.5	1.7	3.6	4.3	3.9	5.5
Flanders (Belgium)	2.4	2.3	1.4	1.5	8.3	8.3	11.2	8.7	10.0

Note: Percentages in this table represent the weighted proportion of missing cases.
Source: OECD, TALIS 2013 Database.
StatLink ⟨⟩ http://dx.doi.org/10.1787/888933048451

[Part 1/1]

Table B.7   List of variables in the Chapter 6 regression analyses

Variable	Level	Type of variable	Based on variable(s) in the data set
Teachers' background			
Teacher gender (-1=male; 1 = female)	Teacher	Independent	TT2G01
Years of experience (continuous)	Teacher	Independent	TT2G05B
Education (-1 = below ISCED 5A; 1 = ISCED 5A or above)	Teacher	Independent	TT2G10
Feel prepared for the content of the subject(s) taught (-1 = not at all/somewhat; 1 = well/very well)	Teacher	Independent	TT2G13A
Feel prepared for the pedagogy of the subject(s) taught (-1 = not at all/somewhat; 1 = well/very well)	Teacher	Independent	TT2G13B
Feel prepared for classroom practice in the subject(s) taught (-1 = not at all/somewhat; 1 = well/very well)	Teacher	Independent	TT2G13C
Professional development[1]			
Courses/workshops (-1 = no; 1 = yes)	Teacher	Independent	TT2G21A1
Education conferences or seminars (-1 = no; 1 = yes)	Teacher	Independent	TT2G21B1
Observation visits to other schools (-1 = no; 1 = yes)	Teacher	Independent	TT2G21C1
Qualification programme (-1 = no; 1 = yes)	Teacher	Independent	TT2G21F
Participation in a network of teachers formed specifically for the professional development of teachers (-1 = no; 1 = yes)	Teacher	Independent	TT2G21G
Individual or collaborative research on a topic of interest (-1 = no; 1 = yes)	Teacher	Independent	TT2G21H
Mentoring and/or peer observation and coaching (-1 = no; 1 = yes)	Teacher	Independent	TT2G21I
Classroom context			
Classroom climate (continuous)	Teacher	Independent	TCDISCS
Students whose first language is different from the language(s) of instruction (-1 = 10% or below; 1 = More than 10%)	Teacher	Independent	TT2G35A
Low academic achievers (-1 = 10% or below; 1 = more than 10%)	Teacher	Independent	TT2G35B
Students with special needs (-1 = 10% or below; 1 = more than 10%)	Teacher	Independent	TT2G35C
Students with behavioural problems (-1 = 10% or below; 1 = more than 10%)	Teacher	Independent	TT2G35D
Students from socio-economically disadvantaged homes (-1 = 10% or below; 1 = more than 10%)	Teacher	Independent	TT2G35E
Academically gifted students (-1 = 10% or below; 1 = more than 10%)	Teacher	Independent	TT2G35F
Target class subject: Math or Science (-1 = other; 1 = math/science)	Teacher	Independent	TT2G37
Target class subject: Humanities (-1 = other; 1 = humanities[2])	Teacher	Independent	TT2G37
Target class size (continuous)	Teacher	Independent	TT2G38
Teaching practices			
Professional collaboration (continuous)	Teacher	Dependent	TCCOLLS
Exchange and coordination for teaching (continuous)	Teacher	Dependent	TCEXCHS
Constructivist beliefs (continuous)	Teacher	Dependent	TCONSBS
Students work in small groups to come up with a joint solution to a problem (1 = frequently/In all or nearly all lessons; 2 = never or almost never/occasionally)	Teacher	Dependent	TT2G42B
Students work on projects that require at least one week to complete (1 = frequently/In all or nearly all lessons; 2 = never or almost never/occasionally)	Teacher	Dependent	TT2G42G
Students use ICT for projects or class work (1 = frequently/In all or nearly all lessons; 2 = never or almost never/occasionally)	Teacher	Dependent	TT2G42H
Students work in small groups to come up with a joint solution to a problem (original coding for TT2G42B)	Teacher	Independent	TT2G42B
Students work on projects that require at least one week to complete (original coding for TT2G42G)	Teacher	Independent	TT2G42G
Students use ICT for projects or class work (original coding for TT2G42H)	Teacher	Independent	TT2G42H

1. For the linear regression tables, the professional development variables are recoded "0 = no, 1 = yes" instead of "-1 = no, 1 = yes".

2. Humanities combines the following subject categories: reading, writing and literature, social studies, modern foreign languages, ancient Greek and/or Latin and religion and/or ethics.

Source: OECD, TALIS 2013 Database.

StatLink ⧉ http://dx.doi.org/10.1787/888933048470

[Part 1/4]

The percentage of missing cases for each country for each variable included in the Chapter 6 regression analyses

Table B.8

	Number of responding teachers (unweighted)	Teacher background					
		Gender	Year(s) working as a teacher in total	Highest level of education of teacher	Feeling prepared for the content of the subject(s) taught	Feeling prepared for the pedagogy of the subject(s) taught	Feeling prepared for classroom practice in the subject(s) taught
		Teacher %					
		TT2G01	TT2G05B	TT2G10	TT2G13A	TT2G13B	TT2G13C
Australia	2 059	0.0	2.6	0.8	1.4	1.7	1.6
Brazil	14 291	0.0	17.5	7.8	9.5	13.2	9.9
Bulgaria	2 975	0.0	14.4	0.5	1.7	3.0	3.8
Chile	1 676	0.0	10.8	1.5	2.4	3.8	4.2
Croatia	3 675	0.0	20.2	0.5	0.8	2.3	2.6
Czech Republic	3 219	0.0	1.7	0.1	0.1	0.4	0.4
Denmark	1 649	0.0	2.4	0.6	0.7	0.9	0.8
Estonia	3 129	0.0	3.7	0.5	1.3	1.9	2.1
Finland	2 739	0.0	2.2	0.3	0.7	0.8	0.9
France	3 002	0.0	1.7	0.6	1.2	1.7	1.5
Iceland	1 430	0.0	5.0	1.8	2.2	2.3	2.7
Israel	3 403	0.0	3.0	1.1	2.0	2.4	2.2
Italy	3 337	0.0	1.2	0.4	0.8	1.0	1.3
Japan	3 484	0.0	2.6	0.4	0.4	0.4	0.4
Korea	2 933	0.0	3.4	0.1	0.8	1.9	1.9
Latvia	2 126	0.0	5.3	0.6	1.0	1.1	1.4
Malaysia	2 984	0.0	1.0	0.5	0.5	0.5	0.6
Mexico	3 138	0.1	21.4	0.7	2.0	3.2	3.2
Netherlands	1 912	0.0	1.1	0.5	0.9	0.9	1.0
Norway	2 981	0.0	2.7	0.7	1.3	1.3	1.5
Poland	3 858	0.0	5.7	0.2	0.6	0.5	0.7
Portugal	3 628	0.0	3.2	0.3	0.2	0.4	0.4
Romania	3 286	0.0	1.9	0.5	0.6	1.1	0.9
Serbia	3 857	0.0	12.4	0.5	3.3	4.1	2.9
Singapore	3 109	0.0	1.0	0.0	0.2	0.3	0.2
Slovak Republic	3 493	0.0	1.5	0.1	0.4	0.7	1.0
Spain	3 339	0.0	1.1	0.3	0.4	0.5	0.7
Sweden	3 319	0.0	1.7	0.6	0.7	1.1	1.1
Sub-national entities							
Abu Dhabi (United Arab Emirates)	2 433	0.0	5.1	1.3	2.8	4.6	3.9
Alberta (Canada)	1 773	0.0	1.9	0.2	0.2	0.3	0.3
England (United Kingdom)	2 496	0.0	3.6	0.8	0.8	1.0	1.0
Flanders (Belgium)	3 129	0.0	2.9	0.3	0.6	0.8	0.7

Note: Percentages in this table represent the weighted proportion of missing cases.
Source: OECD, TALIS 2013 Database.
StatLink ᵐˢᵖ http://dx.doi.org/10.1787/888933048489

TALIS 2013 RESULTS: AN INTERNATIONAL PERSPECTIVE ON TEACHING AND LEARNING

[Part 2/4]

The percentage of missing cases for each country for each variable included in the Chapter 6 regression analyses

Table B.8

	Professional development						
	Participation in courses/ workshops	Participation in education conferences or seminars	Participation in observation visits to other schools	Participation in a qualification programme	Participation in a network of teachers formed specifically for the professional development of teachers	Participation in individual or collaborative research on a topic of interest to you professionally	Participation in mentoring and/or peer observation and coaching, as part of a formal school arrangement
				Teacher %			
	TT2G21A1	TT2G21B1	TT2G21C1	TT2G21F	TT2G21G	TT2G21H	TT2G21I
Australia	4.5	4.5	4.5	4.5	4.5	4.5	4.5
Brazil	6.7	6.8	6.7	6.5	6.6	6.7	6.7
Bulgaria	2.0	2.2	2.0	1.9	2.0	2.0	2.2
Chile	7.6	7.5	7.6	7.5	7.6	7.6	7.6
Croatia	1.4	1.5	1.5	1.3	1.4	1.4	1.4
Czech Republic	0.3	0.3	0.3	0.3	0.4	0.4	0.4
Denmark	2.7	2.7	2.7	2.6	2.8	2.8	2.7
Estonia	1.9	2.1	2.0	1.8	2.0	2.0	2.0
Finland	1.2	1.2	1.3	1.2	1.2	1.3	1.2
France	4.1	4.2	4.1	4.0	4.2	4.2	4.3
Iceland	11.2	11.3	11.4	11.3	11.5	11.3	11.4
Israel	4.0	4.1	4.1	4.2	4.2	4.2	4.2
Italy	1.8	1.8	1.7	1.7	1.8	1.7	1.8
Japan	1.0	1.1	1.1	0.8	0.9	0.9	0.9
Korea	2.3	2.3	2.3	2.2	2.3	2.2	2.3
Latvia	1.3	1.3	1.3	1.2	1.2	1.2	1.2
Malaysia	0.6	0.6	0.6	0.6	0.6	0.6	0.6
Mexico	0.5	0.5	0.5	0.4	0.5	0.5	0.5
Netherlands	2.6	2.7	2.7	2.6	2.6	2.6	2.6
Norway	3.5	3.5	3.5	3.5	3.5	3.5	3.5
Poland	0.8	0.8	0.8	1.0	1.0	1.0	1.0
Portugal	0.9	0.9	0.9	0.9	0.9	0.9	0.9
Romania	1.6	1.7	1.7	1.6	1.7	1.7	1.6
Serbia	1.6	1.7	1.5	1.4	1.6	1.6	1.6
Singapore	0.3	0.3	0.3	0.3	0.3	0.3	0.3
Slovak Republic	0.7	0.7	0.7	0.7	0.7	0.8	0.8
Spain	1.3	1.4	1.4	1.3	1.5	1.3	1.4
Sweden	3.0	3.0	3.0	2.9	2.9	3.1	3.0
Sub-national entities							
Abu Dhabi (United Arab Emirates)	5.9	6.0	6.2	6.2	6.3	6.2	6.2
Alberta (Canada)	1.9	2.0	2.0	1.9	1.9	1.9	1.9
England (United Kingdom)	2.9	2.9	2.9	2.9	2.9	2.9	3.0
Flanders (Belgium)	1.3	1.4	1.3	1.4	1.5	1.4	1.4

Note: Percentages in this table represent the weighted proportion of missing cases.
Source: OECD, TALIS 2013 Database.
StatLink ᴍᴨᴘ http://dx.doi.org/10.1787/888933048489

Table B.8

[Part 3/4]
The percentage of missing cases for each country for each variable included in the Chapter 6 regression analyses

	Classroom context								
	Classroom disciplinary climate	Students whose first language is different from language of instruction (target class)	Low academic achievers (target class)	Students with special needs (target class)	Students with behavioural problems (target class)	Students from socio-economically disadvantaged homes (target class)	Academically gifted students (target class)	Subject category of the target class	Class size (target class)
	Teacher %								
	TCDISCS	TT2G35A	TT2G35B	TT2G35C	TT2G35D	TT2G35E	TT2G35F	TT2G37	TT2G38
Australia	17.6	9.1	9.1	9.2	9.1	9.5	9.2	17.6	17.7
Brazil	20.8	10.2	9.9	10.5	9.4	9.2	9.4	27.6	22.4
Bulgaria	1.4	3.5	3.3	4.3	3.2	4.0	3.3	10.9	4.5
Chile	30.9	11.1	10.0	10.9	9.9	10.4	10.2	38.8	35.2
Croatia	14.5	3.2	3.7	3.1	3.5	3.6	3.3	18.3	16.6
Czech Republic	5.7	0.8	0.7	0.8	0.7	0.8	0.8	5.9	6.2
Denmark	16.5	4.9	5.1	5.2	5.2	5.5	4.9	16.2	16.3
Estonia	16.2	2.9	3.1	3.2	2.9	3.7	3.1	17.4	16.6
Finland	16.3	2.1	2.4	2.6	2.4	3.1	2.4	16.5	16.8
France	14.0	7.4	7.7	7.7	7.4	8.0	7.5	13.7	13.9
Iceland	31.5	18.0	17.8	18.0	18.2	19.8	18.3	31.9	33.1
Israel	23.8	7.3	7.7	7.7	7.4	8.0	7.5	24.0	24.0
Italy	20.8	2.8	2.9	2.8	2.9	3.0	2.8	20.9	21.2
Japan	11.9	0.7	0.8	0.7	0.7	0.9	1.0	21.5	12.7
Korea	20.3	4.6	4.8	4.7	4.9	4.8	4.9	20.0	20.5
Latvia	9.5	3.2	3.3	4.1	3.2	3.5	3.7	9.2	9.7
Malaysia	38.6	1.2	1.1	1.3	1.1	1.2	1.3	38.6	38.8
Mexico	12.1	1.6	1.5	2.0	1.5	1.5	1.5	24.9	13.8
Netherlands	24.1	8.5	8.3	8.3	8.5	8.6	8.4	24.1	24.3
Norway	23.8	8.7	9.2	8.5	8.5	10.1	8.8	27.3	26.9
Poland	12.7	2.4	2.3	2.1	2.2	2.6	2.3	13.3	13.1
Portugal	5.6	2.0	2.0	2.2	1.9	2.0	1.9	8.6	5.8
Romania	18.7	1.7	1.5	1.7	1.8	1.5	1.7	18.8	19.4
Serbia	7.6	2.8	5.0	3.1	2.8	3.1	3.1	9.6	10.3
Singapore	7.3	0.7	1.0	1.0	0.8	0.8	0.8	7.7	8.8
Slovak Republic	14.4	1.2	1.4	1.4	1.5	1.4	1.4	14.5	15.3
Spain	12.8	3.8	3.7	3.9	3.7	4.6	4.0	12.9	13.2
Sweden	29.7	6.0	6.1	6.1	6.3	7.1	6.2	29.1	30.4
Sub-national entities									
Abu Dhabi (United Arab Emirates)	29.7	12.4	12.5	13.2	12.6	14.0	12.3	29.7	31.1
Alberta (Canada)	17.1	4.1	4.4	4.2	4.1	4.4	4.2	17.1	17.2
England (United Kingdom)	21.6	6.9	7.2	7.1	7.3	7.2	7.2	21.4	22.0
Flanders (Belgium)	15.4	3.1	3.2	3.5	3.2	3.5	3.6	15.4	16.1

Note: Percentages in this table represent the weighted proportion of missing cases.
Source: OECD, TALIS 2013 Database.
StatLink ⟨⟩ http://dx.doi.org/10.1787/888933048489

[Part 4/4]

Table B.8 The percentage of missing cases for each country for each variable included in the Chapter 6 regression analyses

	Teaching practices					
	Professional collaboration	Teacher co-operation sub-scale/exchange and coordination for teaching	Constructivist beliefs	Students work in small groups to come up with a joint solution to a problem (target class)	Students work on projects that require at least one week to complete (target class)	Students use ICT for projects or class work (target class)
	Teacher %					
	TCCOLLS	TCEXCHS	TCONSBS	TT2G42B	TT2G42G	TT2G42H
Australia	8.1	8.1	7.7	17.8	17.7	17.7
Brazil	6.9	6.9	6.7	21.3	21.9	22.1
Bulgaria	0.7	0.7	0.6	2.3	4.9	4.8
Chile	9.4	9.4	8.4	31.7	32.4	32.1
Croatia	1.5	1.5	1.4	14.4	15.1	15.1
Czech Republic	0.4	0.4	0.5	6.0	6.0	6.1
Denmark	3.9	3.9	3.9	16.7	16.9	16.8
Estonia	2.2	2.2	2.0	16.9	17.1	17.1
Finland	1.7	1.7	1.9	16.7	17.0	17.0
France	6.3	6.3	6.3	14.6	15.9	15.3
Iceland	15.3	15.3	14.2	33.6	34.8	34.4
Israel	5.9	5.9	6.3	25.2	26.0	25.6
Italy	2.0	2.0	2.2	21.2	21.5	21.4
Japan	0.4	0.4	0.4	12.0	12.1	12.2
Korea	4.3	4.3	4.0	21.2	20.9	20.9
Latvia	2.3	2.3	1.9	10.1	10.7	10.4
Malaysia	1.0	1.0	1.0	38.7	38.8	38.7
Mexico	0.9	0.9	0.7	12.4	12.5	12.4
Netherlands	6.8	6.8	6.3	24.5	24.6	24.7
Norway	7.1	7.1	6.2	24.4	24.3	24.3
Poland	1.3	1.3	1.2	13.1	13.8	13.7
Portugal	1.1	1.1	1.1	5.9	6.6	6.4
Romania	1.3	1.3	1.3	19.1	19.2	19.2
Serbia	0.8	0.8	0.9	8.1	9.5	9.5
Singapore	0.3	0.3	0.3	7.6	7.7	7.6
Slovak Republic	0.8	0.8	0.7	14.9	14.8	14.8
Spain	2.4	2.4	2.2	13.3	13.5	13.3
Sweden	5.1	5.1	5.0	30.2	30.4	30.2
Sub-national entities						
Abu Dhabi (United Arab Emirates)	8.3	8.3	7.7	30.4	30.5	30.6
Alberta (Canada)	3.1	3.1	3.3	17.5	18.0	17.7
England (United Kingdom)	6.3	6.3	5.9	22.0	22.1	22.0
Flanders (Belgium)	2.2	2.2	2.2	15.9	16.4	16.3

Note: Percentages in this table represent the weighted proportion of missing cases.

Source: OECD, TALIS 2013 Database.

StatLink ⬛⬛ http://dx.doi.org/10.1787/888933048489

[Part 1/1]

Table B.9   List of independent variables in the Chapter 7 regression analyses

Variable	Level	Type of variable	Based on variable(s) in the data set
Teacher background			
Teacher's gender (1 = female; 2 = male)	Teacher	Independent	TT2G01
Number of years of teaching (0 = 5 years or less; 1 = more than 5 years)	Teacher	Independent	TT2G05B
Teacher's education (0 = ISCED 5B or below; 1 = ISCED 5A or higher)	Teacher	Independent	TT2G10
Inclusion of content/pedagogy/classroom practice elements in formal training (continuous variable where the scores on the three variables were combined following the questionnaire coding: 1 = yes for all of the subjects I teach; 2 = yes for some of the subjects I teach; 3 = no)	Teacher	Independent	TT2G12A, TT2G12B, TT2G12C
Subjects taught (0 = yes; 1 = no)	Teacher	Independent	TT2G15A, TT2G15B, TT2G15C, TT2G15E, TT2G15G, TT2G15H
Number of hours worked in the most recent complete calendar week (more than 90 hours were excluded) (continuous)	Teacher	Independent	TT2G16
Professional development			
Teacher's participation in formal professional development programmes (0 = no; 1 = yes)	Teacher	Independent	TT2G19A
Teacher's participation in informal professional development programmes (0 = no; 1 = yes)	Teacher	Independent	TT2G19B
Teacher assigned a mentor (0 = no; 1 = yes)	Teacher	Independent	TT2G20A
Teacher serving as a mentor (0 = no; 1 = yes)	Teacher	Independent	TT2G20B
Formal participation in mentoring and coaching (0 = no; 1 = yes)	Teacher	Independent	TT2G21I
Professional development participation in conferences, courses and workshops (summation: 0 = no; 1 or higher = yes)	Teacher	Independent	TT2G21A1, TT2G21B1
Teacher feedback			
Feedback from at least two evaluators on classroom observation (0 = recorded receiving feedback from 1 or 0 evaluators; 1 = received feedback from 2 or more evaluators)	Teacher	Independent	TT2G28B1, TT2G28B2, TT2G28B3, TT2G28B4, TT2G28B5
Feedback from student surveys (0 = did not record receiving any student survey feedback; 1 = received 1 or more types of student survey feedback)	Teacher	Independent	TT2G28A1, TT2G28A2, TT2G28A3, TT2G28A4, TT2G28A5
Feedback from test scores (0 = did not record receiving any test score feedback; 1 = received 1 or more types of test score feedback)	Teacher	Independent	TT2G28D1, TT2G28D2, TT2G28D3, TT2G28D4, TT2G28D5
Feedback on student behavior in the classroom (0 = low to no importance; 1 = moderate to high importance)	Teacher	Independent	TT2G29E
Appraisal is only for administrative purposes (0 = disagree/strongly disagree; 1 = agree/strongly agree)	Teacher	Independent	TT2G31C
Appraisal impacts teaching (0 = disagree/strongly disagree; 1 = agree/strongly agree)	Teacher	Independent	TT2G31B
Teaching practices			
Teacher self-efficacy (continuous)	Teacher	Dependent	TSELEFFS
Teacher co-operation (continuous)	Teacher	Independent	TCOOPS
Constructivist beliefs (continuous)	Teacher	Independent	TCONSB
Teach jointly as a team in the same class (0 = less than five times a year; 1 = five times a year or more)	Teacher	Independent	TT2G33A
Observe other teachers' classes and provide feedback (0 = less than five times a year; 1 = five times a year or more)	Teacher	Independent	TT2G33B
Engage in joint activities across different classes and age groups (e.g. projects) (0 = less than five times a year; 1 = five times a year or more)	Teacher	Independent	TT2G33C
Take part in collaborative professional learning (0 = less than five times a year; 1 = five times a year or more)	Teacher	Independent	TT2G33H
Classroom context			
Low academic achievers (0 = 10% or below; 1= above 10%)	Teacher	Independent	TT2G35B
Students with behavioural problems (0 = 10% or below; 1 = above 10%)	Teacher	Independent	TT2G35D
Academically gifted students (0 = 10% or below; 1 = above 10%)	Teacher	Independent	TT2G35F
Target class size (continuous: number of students)	Teacher	Independent	TT2G38
Proportion of time doing adminstrative tasks (continuous)	Teacher	Independent	TT2G39A
Proportion of time keeping order (continuous)	Teacher	Independent	TT2G39B
School climate and job satisfaction			
Teacher job satisfaction (continuous)	Teacher	Dependent	TJOBSATS
I think that teaching is a valued profession in society (0 = strongly disagree or disagree; 1 = strongly agree or agree)	Teacher	Dependent	TT2G46H
Teacher-student relations (continuous)	Teacher	Independent	TSCTSTU
This school provides staff with opportunities to actively participate in school decisions (0 = strongly disagree or disagree; 1 = strongly agree or agree)	Teacher	Independent	TT2G44A
School background			
Instructional leadership (continuous)	Principal	Independent	PINSLEAD

Source: OECD, TALIS 2013 Database.

StatLink http://dx.doi.org/10.1787/888933048508

TALIS 2013 RESULTS: AN INTERNATIONAL PERSPECTIVE ON TEACHING AND LEARNING

[Part 1/7]

The percentage of missing cases for each country for each variable included in the Chapter 7 regression analyses

Table B.10

	Number of responding teachers (unweighted)	Teacher background					
		Gender	Year(s) working as a teacher in total	Highest level of education of teacher	Content of the subject(s) taught was included in formal education or training	Pedagogy of the subject(s) taught was included in formal education or training	Classroom practice in the subject(s) taught was included in formal education or training
					Teacher %		
		TT2G01	TT2G05B	TT2G10	TT2G12A	TT2G12B	TT2G12C
Australia	2 059	0.0	2.6	0.8	1.0	1.0	1.0
Brazil	14 291	0.0	17.5	7.8	8.1	8.3	8.3
Bulgaria	2 975	0.0	14.4	0.5	0.5	0.5	0.5
Chile	1 676	0.0	10.8	1.5	3.3	3.3	3.3
Croatia	3 675	0.0	20.2	0.5	1.4	1.5	1.4
Czech Republic	3 219	0.0	1.7	0.1	0.1	0.1	0.1
Denmark	1 649	0.0	2.4	0.6	1.9	1.9	1.9
Estonia	3 129	0.0	3.7	0.5	0.8	0.8	0.8
Finland	2 739	0.0	2.2	0.3	0.3	0.3	0.3
France	3 002	0.0	1.7	0.6	1.0	1.0	1.0
Iceland	1 430	0.0	5.0	1.8	1.5	1.6	1.6
Israel	3 403	0.0	3.0	1.1	1.2	1.4	1.4
Italy	3 337	0.0	1.2	0.4	0.9	0.9	0.9
Japan	3 484	0.0	2.6	0.4	1.8	1.8	1.8
Korea	2 933	0.0	3.4	0.1	0.2	0.2	0.2
Latvia	2 126	0.0	5.3	0.6	0.7	0.7	0.8
Malaysia	2 984	0.0	1.0	0.5	0.4	0.4	0.4
Mexico	3 138	0.1	21.4	0.7	1.5	1.7	1.6
Netherlands	1 912	0.0	1.1	0.5	0.9	0.9	0.9
Norway	2 981	0.0	2.7	0.7	1.4	1.4	1.4
Poland	3 858	0.0	5.7	0.2	0.3	0.3	0.3
Portugal	3 628	0.0	3.2	0.3	0.2	0.3	0.2
Romania	3 286	0.0	1.9	0.5	0.6	0.7	0.7
Serbia	3 857	0.0	12.4	0.5	3.9	3.9	3.9
Singapore	3 109	0.0	1.0	0.0	0.1	0.1	0.1
Slovak Republic	3 493	0.0	1.5	0.1	0.5	0.6	0.6
Spain	3 339	0.0	1.1	0.3	0.5	0.5	0.5
Sweden	3 319	0.0	1.7	0.6	0.6	0.7	0.7
Sub-national entities							
Abu Dhabi (United Arab Emirates)	2 433	0.0	5.1	1.3	2.2	2.2	2.2
Alberta (Canada)	1 773	0.0	1.9	0.2	0.2	0.2	0.2
England (United Kingdom)	2 496	0.0	3.6	0.8	0.9	0.9	0.9
Flanders (Belgium)	3 129	0.0	2.9	0.3	0.4	0.4	0.4

Note: Percentages in this table represent the weighted proportion of missing cases.
Source: OECD, TALIS 2013 Database.
StatLink http://dx.doi.org/10.1787/888933048527

[Part 2/7]

Table B.10 **The percentage of missing cases for each country for each variable included in the Chapter 7 regression analyses**

	Teacher background						
	Teaching reading, writing and literature	Teaching mathematics	Teaching science	Teaching modern foreign languages	Teaching technology	Teaching arts	Number of hours worked in the most recent complete calendar week
	Teacher %						
	TT2G15A	TT2G15B	TT2G15C	TT2G15E	TT2G15G	TT2G15H	TT2G16
Australia	2.5	2.6	2.6	2.6	2.5	2.6	3.0
Brazil	6.6	6.7	6.6	6.7	6.6	6.6	9.1
Bulgaria	1.9	2.0	2.0	2.0	2.1	2.1	2.6
Chile	7.4	7.4	7.3	7.4	7.3	7.4	8.2
Croatia	1.3	1.3	1.4	1.4	1.3	1.3	3.6
Czech Republic	0.3	0.3	0.3	0.3	0.3	0.3	0.4
Denmark	1.1	1.1	1.0	1.1	1.1	1.1	1.9
Estonia	1.1	1.1	1.1	1.1	1.1	1.1	1.6
Finland	0.6	0.6	0.7	0.6	0.7	0.6	1.2
France	1.7	1.8	1.9	1.8	1.8	1.8	2.6
Iceland	4.5	4.5	4.5	4.4	4.6	4.4	6.4
Israel	2.8	2.8	2.8	2.8	2.8	2.8	3.9
Italy	0.8	0.8	0.8	0.8	0.8	0.8	1.1
Japan	0.4	0.4	0.4	0.4	0.4	0.4	2.6
Korea	1.2	1.2	1.2	1.2	1.2	1.1	1.2
Latvia	1.7	1.8	1.6	1.6	1.6	1.8	1.3
Malaysia	0.7	0.7	0.7	0.7	0.6	0.7	1.7
Mexico	1.3	1.3	1.4	1.4	1.4	1.4	1.9
Netherlands	2.6	2.5	2.5	2.5	2.5	2.4	1.8
Norway	1.1	1.2	1.2	1.1	1.3	1.2	2.1
Poland	0.7	0.7	0.7	0.7	0.8	0.7	0.6
Portugal	0.9	0.9	1.0	0.9	0.9	0.9	1.6
Romania	0.9	1.0	1.0	1.0	1.0	1.0	0.8
Serbia	1.6	1.6	1.7	1.7	1.7	1.7	3.8
Singapore	0.4	0.6	0.6	0.7	0.6	0.7	1.3
Slovak Republic	0.6	0.6	0.5	0.6	0.6	0.5	0.8
Spain	1.1	1.1	1.1	1.1	1.1	1.1	0.8
Sweden	1.3	1.3	1.3	1.3	1.3	1.3	2.1
Sub-national entities							
Abu Dhabi (United Arab Emirates)	7.1	7.3	7.3	7.4	7.4	7.5	5.1
Alberta (Canada)	1.2	1.2	1.2	1.2	1.2	1.3	1.6
England (United Kingdom)	1.7	1.7	1.7	1.7	1.6	1.6	2.4
Flanders (Belgium)	0.9	0.9	0.9	0.9	0.9	0.9	0.9

Note: Percentages in this table represent the weighted proportion of missing cases.
Source: OECD, TALIS 2013 Database.
StatLink ⟨≣≣⟩ http://dx.doi.org/10.1787/888933048527

[Part 3/7]

Table B.10 The percentage of missing cases for each country for each variable included in the Chapter 7 regression analyses

	Professional development					
	Participation in formal induction programme	Teacher's participation in informal professional development programmes	Teacher assigned a mentor	Serving as a mentor	Participation in mentoring and/or peer observation and coaching, as part of a formal school arrangement	Professional development participation in conferences, courses and workshops (combined TT2G21A1, TT2G21B1)
			Teacher %			
	TT2G19A	TT2G19B	TT2G20A	TT2G20B	TT2G21I	TT2G21A1, TT2G21B1
Australia	3.4	3.6	3.6	4.2	4.5	4.4
Brazil	7.4	8.7	8.7	9.7	6.7	6.6
Bulgaria	0.8	1.0	1.0	5.0	2.2	1.8
Chile	4.1	5.0	5.0	6.6	7.6	7.5
Croatia	1.7	2.2	2.2	9.7	1.4	1.4
Czech Republic	0.4	0.6	0.6	1.1	0.4	0.3
Denmark	2.2	3.1	3.1	2.7	2.7	2.6
Estonia	1.6	2.6	2.6	2.4	2.0	1.9
Finland	1.2	1.4	1.4	1.5	1.2	1.2
France	2.9	3.4	3.4	3.7	4.3	4.1
Iceland	7.8	8.9	8.9	8.7	11.4	11.1
Israel	4.2	4.8	4.8	4.9	4.2	4.0
Italy	1.5	1.8	1.8	3.4	1.8	1.7
Japan	0.3	0.4	0.4	0.6	0.9	1.0
Korea	1.9	2.0	2.0	2.9	2.3	2.3
Latvia	1.3	2.0	2.0	2.7	1.2	1.2
Malaysia	0.6	0.8	0.8	0.7	0.6	0.6
Mexico	0.9	1.4	1.4	3.2	0.5	0.4
Netherlands	2.1	2.6	2.6	2.5	2.6	2.6
Norway	2.8	4.0	4.0	3.5	3.5	3.5
Poland	0.8	2.0	2.0	2.6	1.0	0.8
Portugal	1.1	1.9	1.9	2.3	0.9	0.9
Romania	1.3	1.4	1.4	2.8	1.7	1.7
Serbia	1.7	2.9	2.9	8.3	1.6	1.4
Singapore	0.2	0.3	0.3	0.6	0.3	0.3
Slovak Republic	0.9	1.1	1.1	1.2	0.8	0.7
Spain	1.1	1.8	1.8	1.8	1.4	1.3
Sweden	3.0	3.7	3.7	3.2	3.0	3.0
Sub-national entities						
Abu Dhabi (United Arab Emirates)	5.4	5.5	5.5	6.6	6.2	5.8
Alberta (Canada)	1.7	1.8	1.8	2.0	1.9	1.9
England (United Kingdom)	2.5	2.7	2.7	3.5	3.0	2.9
Flanders (Belgium)	1.4	1.7	1.7	1.5	1.4	1.3

Note: Percentages in this table represent the weighted proportion of missing cases.
Source: OECD, TALIS 2013 Database.
StatLink ⟪⟫ http://dx.doi.org/10.1787/888933048527

[Part 4/7]

Table B.10

The percentage of missing cases for each country for each variable included in the Chapter 7 regression analyses

	Professional development					
	Feedback from at least two evaluators on classroom observation (combined TT2G28B1 to TT2G28B5)	Feedback from student surveys (combined TT2G28A1 to TT2G28A5)	Feedback from test scores (combined TT2G28D1 to TT2G28D5)	Feedback on student behavior in the classroom	Appraisal is only for administrative purposes	Appraisal impacts teaching
	Teacher %					
	TT2G28B1 to TT2G28B5	TT2G28A1 to TT2G28A5	TT2G28D1 to TT2G28D5	TT2G29E	TT2G31C	TT2G31B
Australia	7.1	9.4	8.3	22.0	9.5	9.3
Brazil	9.0	11.6	10.4	20.0	17.7	14.0
Bulgaria	1.6	1.6	1.6	8.6	6.7	5.9
Chile	10.9	12.3	12.3	26.9	10.9	10.6
Croatia	0.1	0.1	0.1	12.3	6.9	7.2
Czech Republic	0.8	3.6	3.7	4.8	2.4	2.2
Denmark	4.2	6.6	5.3	26.6	10.5	7.6
Estonia	3.2	5.6	6.6	11.1	4.7	4.6
Finland	2.4	3.4	2.9	39.7	6.5	4.8
France	7.9	16.5	15.4	22.7	12.1	11.1
Iceland	18.7	20.5	20.1	56.1	26.5	22.5
Israel	6.9	11.0	9.8	19.8	9.6	9.3
Italy	4.0	5.6	5.7	45.3	8.8	8.1
Japan	0.6	0.6	0.6	8.3	7.0	6.3
Korea	3.5	5.5	5.5	10.0	6.0	5.5
Latvia	2.9	6.1	5.0	7.5	3.9	3.3
Malaysia	1.2	1.8	1.8	2.9	1.2	1.1
Mexico	1.5	3.2	2.3	13.8	4.5	4.9
Netherlands	6.2	7.6	7.5	12.9	8.3	8.4
Norway	6.3	11.8	10.3	25.4	14.4	13.3
Poland	1.6	6.5	4.5	6.3	4.9	4.0
Portugal	2.6	7.1	5.2	20.4	3.9	3.7
Romania	1.7	4.2	3.8	5.0	3.0	2.7
Serbia	4.6	4.8	4.8	9.1	5.1	5.8
Singapore	0.9	3.1	2.4	3.0	1.4	1.3
Slovak Republic	1.2	4.1	4.1	6.2	2.7	2.4
Spain	2.9	4.0	3.4	35.7	6.4	6.1
Sweden	5.4	6.6	6.5	38.8	10.2	10.0
Sub-national entities						
Abu Dhabi (United Arab Emirates)	8.1	10.7	9.9	13.3	11.4	10.4
Alberta (Canada)	3.8	6.0	5.7	12.3	5.2	5.2
England (United Kingdom)	4.9	8.1	6.8	7.4	6.7	6.8
Flanders (Belgium)	3.1	6.2	6.0	20.0	4.8	4.7

Note: Percentages in this table represent the weighted proportion of missing cases.
Source: OECD, TALIS 2013 Database.
StatLink ⟋⟍ http://dx.doi.org/10.1787/888933048527

[Part 5/7]

Table B.10 The percentage of missing cases for each country for each variable included in the Chapter 7 regression analyses

	Teaching practices						
	Teacher self-efficacy	Teacher co-operation index	Constructivist beliefs	Teach jointly as a team in the same class	Observe other teachers' classes and provide feedback	Engage in joint activities across different classes and age groups	Take part in collaborative professional learning
	Teacher %						
	TSELEFFS	TCOOPS	TCONSBS	TT2G33A	TT2G33B	TT2G33C	TT2G33H
Australia	8.2	8.1	7.7	8.2	8.3	8.2	8.4
Brazil	6.8	7.0	6.7	9.4	9.0	8.5	8.8
Bulgaria	0.7	0.7	0.6	2.6	2.4	4.6	3.1
Chile	8.7	9.4	8.4	13.0	10.9	12.1	12.8
Croatia	1.4	1.5	1.4	4.3	2.9	3.2	2.2
Czech Republic	0.3	0.4	0.5	0.7	0.7	0.6	1.1
Denmark	4.2	3.9	3.9	4.0	4.2	4.1	4.3
Estonia	2.2	2.2	2.0	6.0	3.2	3.4	3.9
Finland	1.9	1.7	1.9	1.9	2.1	1.9	2.5
France	7.0	6.3	6.3	7.1	7.2	7.1	7.8
Iceland	15.1	15.3	14.2	16.8	16.0	16.7	16.8
Israel	6.6	5.9	6.3	6.6	6.7	7.4	8.2
Italy	2.3	2.0	2.2	2.5	3.2	2.7	3.5
Japan	0.6	0.4	0.4	1.6	0.4	1.0	0.7
Korea	4.2	4.3	4.0	4.6	5.4	4.9	5.2
Latvia	2.3	2.3	1.9	4.9	3.0	3.2	3.7
Malaysia	1.1	1.0	1.0	1.1	1.2	1.1	1.1
Mexico	0.8	0.9	0.7	4.8	2.1	1.7	1.6
Netherlands	7.3	6.8	6.3	7.6	7.0	7.0	7.3
Norway	7.3	7.1	6.2	10.1	8.5	8.5	9.0
Poland	1.2	1.3	1.2	5.2	2.1	2.0	2.8
Portugal	1.5	1.1	1.1	1.6	1.6	1.7	2.0
Romania	1.6	1.3	1.3	1.8	1.8	1.8	1.7
Serbia	0.8	0.8	0.9	3.7	2.0	2.4	1.9
Singapore	0.4	0.4	0.3	0.8	0.7	0.6	0.7
Slovak Republic	1.0	0.8	0.7	1.4	1.6	1.0	2.3
Spain	2.4	2.4	2.2	2.8	2.9	3.0	3.6
Sweden	5.5	5.1	5.0	5.3	5.4	5.5	5.6
Sub-national entities							
Abu Dhabi (United Arab Emirates)	8.5	8.3	7.7	10.5	10.5	9.9	10.5
Alberta (Canada)	3.7	3.1	3.3	3.2	3.1	3.1	3.3
England (United Kingdom)	6.5	6.4	5.9	6.4	6.7	6.5	7.0
Flanders (Belgium)	2.5	2.2	2.2	2.9	2.6	2.8	5.5

Note: Percentages in this table represent the weighted proportion of missing cases.
Source: OECD, TALIS 2013 Database.
StatLink ᕦ http://dx.doi.org/10.1787/888933048527

[Part 6/7]

The percentage of missing cases for each country for each variable included in the Chapter 7 regression analyses

Table B.10

	Classroom context					
	Low academic achievers (target class)	Students with behavioural problems (target class)	Academically gifted students (target class)	Class size (target class)	Proportion of time doing adminstrative tasks	Proportion of time keeping order
	Teacher %					
	TT2G35B	TT2G35D	TT2G35F	TT2G38	TT2G39A	TT2G39B
Australia	9.1	9.1	9.2	17.7	18.1	18.1
Brazil	9.9	9.4	9.4	22.4	26.3	26.3
Bulgaria	3.3	3.2	3.3	4.5	2.9	2.9
Chile	10.0	9.9	10.2	35.2	36.4	36.4
Croatia	3.7	3.5	3.3	16.6	15.3	15.3
Czech Republic	0.7	0.7	0.8	6.2	6.2	6.2
Denmark	5.1	5.2	4.9	16.3	16.7	16.7
Estonia	3.1	2.9	3.1	16.6	17.0	17.0
Finland	2.4	2.4	2.4	16.8	16.8	16.8
France	7.7	7.4	7.5	13.9	14.6	14.6
Iceland	17.8	18.2	18.3	33.1	34.6	34.6
Israel	7.7	7.4	7.5	24.0	25.9	25.9
Italy	2.9	2.9	2.8	21.2	23.4	23.4
Japan	0.8	0.7	1.0	12.7	13.1	13.1
Korea	4.8	4.9	4.9	20.5	21.9	21.9
Latvia	3.3	3.2	3.7	9.7	11.8	11.8
Malaysia	1.1	1.1	1.3	38.8	41.0	41.0
Mexico	1.5	1.5	1.5	13.8	14.6	14.6
Netherlands	8.3	8.5	8.4	24.3	24.5	24.5
Norway	9.2	8.5	8.8	26.9	25.7	25.7
Poland	2.3	2.2	2.3	13.1	13.2	13.2
Portugal	2.0	1.9	1.9	5.8	6.2	6.2
Romania	1.5	1.8	1.7	19.4	20.4	20.4
Serbia	5.0	2.8	3.1	10.3	10.3	10.3
Singapore	1.0	0.8	0.8	8.8	9.8	9.8
Slovak Republic	1.4	1.5	1.4	15.3	15.6	15.6
Spain	3.7	3.7	4.0	13.2	14.0	14.0
Sweden	6.1	6.3	6.2	30.4	31.2	31.2
Sub-national entities						
Abu Dhabi (United Arab Emirates)	12.5	12.6	12.3	31.1	37.5	37.5
Alberta (Canada)	4.4	4.1	4.2	17.2	18.3	18.3
England (United Kingdom)	7.2	7.3	7.2	22.0	21.9	21.9
Flanders (Belgium)	3.2	3.2	3.6	16.1	17.1	17.1

Note: Percentages in this table represent the weighted proportion of missing cases.

Source: OECD, TALIS 2013 Database.

StatLink http://dx.doi.org/10.1787/888933048527

[Part 7/7]

Table B.10 The percentage of missing cases for each country for each variable included in the Chapter 7 regression analyses

	School climate and job satisfaction				School background
	Teacher job satisfaction	I think that teaching is a valued profession in society	Teacher-student relations index	This school provides staff with opportunities to actively participate in school decisions	Instructional leadership
	Teacher %				
	TJOBSATS	TT2G46H	TSCTSTU	TT2G44A	PINSLEAD
Australia	9.0	9.2	8.6	8.7	8.9
Brazil	7.2	8.1	7.3	8.0	1.1
Bulgaria	0.7	1.4	0.8	1.1	0.0
Chile	8.7	10.1	8.6	9.4	17.2
Croatia	1.3	1.7	1.5	2.1	1.9
Czech Republic	0.5	0.7	0.4	0.7	0.0
Denmark	4.2	4.4	4.2	4.6	16.5
Estonia	2.2	2.5	2.1	2.8	1.0
Finland	2.1	2.5	2.2	2.4	0.0
France	6.7	7.1	6.9	8.8	14.6
Iceland	15.5	15.9	15.4	16.9	20.5
Israel	6.3	6.8	6.1	7.2	8.4
Italy	2.2	2.5	2.3	3.1	0.5
Japan	0.4	0.7	0.5	0.7	0.0
Korea	4.6	5.1	4.6	4.8	8.8
Latvia	2.0	2.4	2.2	2.6	6.5
Malaysia	1.0	1.0	1.0	1.1	2.3
Mexico	1.3	1.5	1.1	1.3	0.9
Netherlands	7.6	7.7	7.4	7.9	13.3
Norway	7.7	8.4	7.6	8.8	23.6
Poland	1.1	1.5	1.1	1.6	4.6
Portugal	1.4	1.5	1.4	2.0	4.5
Romania	1.4	1.6	1.3	1.6	0.3
Serbia	0.9	1.5	0.8	1.5	3.5
Singapore	0.5	0.8	0.5	0.9	10.9
Slovak Republic	0.9	1.4	0.9	1.4	3.3
Spain	2.6	3.0	2.6	3.3	0.5
Sweden	5.8	5.8	5.8	6.3	9.4
Sub-national entities					
Abu Dhabi (United Arab Emirates)	8.9	9.8	8.7	9.9	26.6
Alberta (Canada)	3.7	3.8	3.8	4.0	3.1
England (United Kingdom)	6.8	6.8	6.9	7.1	3.5
Flanders (Belgium)	2.7	3.3	2.7	3.3	8.3

Note: Percentages in this table represent the weighted proportion of missing cases.
Source: OECD, TALIS 2013 Database.
StatLink ⬛⬛⬛ http://dx.doi.org/10.1787/888933048527

Annex C

TALIS 2013 DATA

All tables in Annex C are available on line

Notes regarding Cyprus

Note by Turkey: The information in this document with reference to "Cyprus" relates to the southern part of the Island. There is no single authority representing both Turkish and Greek Cypriot people on the Island. Turkey recognises the Turkish Republic of Northern Cyprus (TRNC). Until a lasting and equitable solution is found within the context of the United Nations, Turkey shall preserve its position concerning the "Cyprus issue".

Note by all the European Union Member States of the OECD and the European Union: The Republic of Cyprus is recognised by all members of the United Nations with the exception of Turkey. The information in this document relates to the area under the effective control of the Government of the Republic of Cyprus.

A note regarding Israel

The statistical data for Israel are supplied by and under the responsibility of the relevant Israeli authorities. The use of such data by the OECD is without prejudice to the status of the Golan Heights, East Jerusalem and Israeli settlements in the West Bank under the terms of international law.

[Part 1/1]
Gender and age distribution of teachers
Percentage of lower secondary education teachers with the following characteristics and average age of teachers

Table 2.1

| | Female | | \multicolumn{12}{c}{Percentage of teachers in each age group} | | | | | | | | | | Average age | |
| | | | Under 25 years | | 25-29 years | | 30-39 years | | 40-49 years | | 50-59 years | | 60 years or more | | | |
	%	S.E.	%	S.E.	%	S.E.	%	S.E.	%	S.E.	%	S.E.	%	S.E.	Average	S.E.
Australia	59.2	(1.4)	4.2	(0.5)	11.5	(0.9)	22.9	(1.1)	24.3	(1.3)	30.2	(1.5)	6.9	(0.6)	43.4	(0.3)
Brazil	71.1	(0.7)	4.6	(0.4)	13.0	(0.6)	36.2	(0.7)	30.2	(0.7)	13.7	(0.5)	2.3	(0.2)	39.2	(0.2)
Bulgaria	81.2	(0.8)	0.6	(0.2)	2.8	(0.4)	18.3	(0.9)	31.5	(1.1)	40.9	(1.2)	5.8	(0.5)	47.4	(0.2)
Chile	62.8	(1.3)	2.9	(0.5)	18.2	(1.1)	28.5	(1.3)	20.2	(1.1)	23.3	(1.3)	7.1	(0.9)	41.3	(0.5)
Croatia	74.3	(0.8)	0.4	(0.2)	13.3	(0.6)	34.4	(0.8)	21.5	(0.8)	17.8	(0.8)	12.6	(0.6)	42.6	(0.2)
Cyprus*	70.1	(1.1)	0.6	(0.2)	6.0	(0.5)	37.0	(1.3)	26.2	(1.1)	28.2	(1.1)	2.0	(0.3)	42.7	(0.2)
Czech Republic	76.5	(0.7)	0.8	(0.1)	10.0	(0.6)	26.5	(0.9)	27.4	(0.9)	27.4	(0.9)	7.8	(0.5)	44.2	(0.2)
Denmark	59.6	(1.2)	0.4	(0.1)	5.6	(0.8)	29.7	(1.4)	28.5	(1.5)	24.7	(1.3)	11.1	(0.9)	45.0	(0.3)
Estonia	84.5	(0.6)	1.3	(0.2)	6.1	(0.5)	17.2	(0.8)	27.2	(0.9)	31.9	(1.0)	16.3	(1.0)	47.9	(0.3)
Finland	72.4	(0.7)	0.3	(0.1)	7.4	(0.5)	28.4	(0.9)	31.0	(0.9)	27.4	(1.0)	5.4	(0.5)	44.1	(0.2)
France	66.0	(0.7)	0.7	(0.2)	7.8	(0.7)	32.6	(1.0)	32.7	(0.9)	21.5	(0.8)	4.7	(0.4)	42.6	(0.3)
Iceland	71.9	(1.2)	0.6	(0.2)	5.7	(0.6)	28.2	(1.3)	33.8	(1.3)	22.1	(1.2)	9.6	(0.8)	44.6	(0.3)
Israel	76.3	(1.4)	1.6	(0.3)	12.1	(1.2)	29.6	(1.0)	29.4	(1.0)	21.3	(0.9)	6.0	(0.6)	42.1	(0.4)
Italy	78.5	(0.7)	0.0	(0.0)	1.0	(0.2)	15.7	(0.7)	32.9	(0.9)	39.2	(1.0)	11.1	(0.5)	48.9	(0.2)
Japan	39.0	(0.8)	5.3	(0.4)	13.3	(0.6)	23.4	(0.8)	27.1	(1.0)	28.1	(1.1)	2.8	(0.4)	41.9	(0.2)
Korea	68.2	(1.1)	1.2	(0.3)	9.7	(0.6)	28.4	(1.2)	33.5	(1.1)	26.4	(1.3)	0.9	(0.2)	42.4	(0.3)
Latvia	88.7	(0.6)	1.6	(0.4)	3.3	(0.5)	17.9	(1.2)	33.6	(1.6)	33.1	(1.1)	10.5	(0.8)	47.1	(0.3)
Malaysia	70.5	(1.0)	0.6	(0.2)	17.7	(0.8)	34.2	(0.9)	34.9	(1.0)	12.6	(0.6)	0.0	(0.0)	38.9	(0.2)
Mexico	53.8	(1.1)	2.6	(0.4)	10.0	(0.2)	29.2	(1.1)	32.3	(1.0)	21.9	(1.0)	4.0	(0.5)	43.2	(0.4)
Netherlands	54.6	(1.3)	4.4	(0.9)	12.7	(0.9)	23.4	(1.2)	22.6	(1.1)	29.4	(1.4)	7.5	(0.6)	43.2	(0.4)
Norway	61.0	(1.0)	1.5	(0.4)	9.7	(0.8)	28.5	(1.0)	26.4	(1.1)	18.8	(0.8)	15.2	(1.3)	44.2	(0.4)
Poland	74.9	(1.0)	0.8	(0.2)	7.8	(0.6)	35.0	(0.9)	33.0	(1.2)	21.6	(0.9)	1.8	(0.3)	41.9	(0.2)
Portugal	73.2	(0.8)	0.0	(0.0)	1.2	(0.2)	24.2	(0.9)	46.6	(0.9)	25.5	(0.9)	2.4	(0.3)	44.7	(0.2)
Romania	69.2	(1.0)	3.6	(0.6)	9.9	(0.7)	38.6	(1.1)	21.0	(0.9)	17.9	(0.8)	9.0	(0.7)	41.6	(0.3)
Serbia	65.6	(0.7)	1.2	(0.2)	9.1	(0.6)	34.4	(1.0)	25.1	(0.8)	20.4	(0.7)	9.9	(0.6)	43.1	(0.2)
Singapore	65.0	(0.9)	5.0	(0.4)	26.8	(0.8)	37.9	(0.9)	18.6	(0.7)	8.6	(0.5)	3.0	(0.3)	36.0	(0.2)
Slovak Republic	81.9	(0.8)	0.5	(0.1)	10.8	(0.7)	30.9	(0.9)	25.3	(0.9)	25.4	(1.0)	7.1	(0.6)	43.4	(0.3)
Spain	58.8	(1.0)	0.2	(0.1)	2.6	(0.4)	23.2	(1.0)	38.8	(0.8)	31.8	(1.0)	3.5	(0.3)	45.6	(0.2)
Sweden	66.5	(0.8)	0.6	(0.2)	4.4	(0.5)	25.7	(1.0)	31.4	(1.0)	24.5	(0.8)	13.3	(0.7)	46.0	(0.3)
Sub-national entities																
Abu Dhabi (United Arab Emirates)	58.9	(1.9)	1.4	(0.3)	10.6	(0.9)	45.3	(1.5)	31.0	(1.1)	10.1	(0.8)	1.6	(0.3)	38.7	(0.3)
Alberta (Canada)	60.3	(1.3)	2.3	(0.5)	16.1	(1.0)	33.3	(1.4)	26.9	(1.3)	18.6	(1.2)	2.8	(0.4)	40.1	(0.3)
England (United Kingdom)	63.2	(1.1)	3.8	(0.4)	17.1	(0.8)	34.4	(1.2)	24.6	(0.8)	17.9	(0.7)	2.2	(0.4)	39.2	(0.3)
Flanders (Belgium)	68.1	(1.4)	5.8	(0.5)	17.8	(0.7)	30.5	(1.1)	22.0	(1.0)	23.2	(0.9)	0.7	(0.2)	39.3	(0.2)
Average	68.1	(0.2)	1.9	(0.1)	10.0	(0.1)	29.2	(0.2)	28.8	(0.2)	23.8	(0.2)	6.3	(0.1)	42.9	(0.0)
United States	64.4	(1.1)	3.1	(0.5)	12.6	(1.3)	28.6	(1.1)	25.4	(1.1)	22.7	(1.1)	7.7	(0.7)	42.2	(0.4)

* See notes at the beginning of this Annex.
Source: OECD, TALIS 2013 Database.
StatLink http://dx.doi.org/10.1787/888933042333

[Part 1/1]

Gender and age distribution of primary teachers

Table 2.1.a *Percentage of primary education teachers with the following characteristics and average age of teachers*

	Female		Under 25 years		25-29 years		30-39 years		40-49 years		50-59 years		60 years or more		Average age	
	%	S.E.	%	S.E.	%	S.E.	%	S.E.	%	S.E.	%	S.E.	%	S.E.	Average	S.E.
Denmark	75.8	(0.8)	0.2	(0.1)	5.5	(0.6)	29.1	(1.1)	28.5	(0.9)	25.8	(1.0)	11.0	(0.7)	45.4	(0.2)
Finland	81.5	(0.7)	0.4	(0.1)	8.2	(0.7)	26.1	(0.9)	35.2	(1.1)	25.5	(1.1)	4.5	(0.5)	43.9	(0.3)
Mexico	66.8	(1.5)	5.5	(0.9)	14.2	(1.4)	33.5	(1.5)	25.8	(1.6)	19.1	(1.4)	2.0	(0.6)	39.6	(0.5)
Norway	80.2	(1.4)	0.7	(0.2)	6.5	(0.6)	24.8	(1.2)	31.4	(1.1)	23.1	(0.9)	13.5	(1.4)	45.3	(0.4)
Poland	85.5	(0.8)	0.4	(0.2)	7.2	(0.7)	26.5	(1.1)	40.2	(1.1)	24.5	(1.2)	1.1	(0.2)	42.9	(0.3)
Sub-national entities																
Flanders (Belgium)	82.6	(0.9)	6.3	(0.6)	16.0	(0.9)	31.8	(1.1)	24.9	(1.0)	20.7	(1.0)	0.4	(0.1)	39.0	(0.3)
Average	78.7	(0.4)	2.2	(0.2)	9.6	(0.3)	28.6	(0.5)	31.0	(0.5)	23.1	(0.5)	5.4	(0.3)	42.7	(0.1)

Source: OECD, TALIS 2013 Database.
StatLink ⟶ http://dx.doi.org/10.1787/888933042352

[Part 1/1]

Gender and age distribution of upper secondary teachers

Table 2.1.b *Percentage of upper secondary education teachers with the following characteristics and average age of teachers*

	Female		Under 25 years		25-29 years		30-39 years		40-49 years		50-59 years		60 years or more		Average age	
	%	S.E.	%	S.E.	%	S.E.	%	S.E.	%	S.E.	%	S.E.	%	S.E.	Average	S.E.
Australia	57.4	(1.2)	2.9	(0.4)	10.2	(0.8)	24.3	(1.2)	26.3	(1.0)	27.5	(1.1)	8.8	(0.9)	44.0	(0.3)
Denmark	48.5	(1.5)	0.2	(0.1)	5.7	(0.5)	25.6	(1.2)	26.1	(1.2)	25.1	(0.8)	17.3	(1.1)	46.9	(0.3)
Finland	61.9	(2.6)	0.5	(0.3)	3.5	(0.4)	20.6	(1.3)	31.8	(0.9)	32.3	(1.4)	11.3	(1.4)	47.1	(0.4)
Iceland	56.0	(1.4)	0.0	(0.0)	2.3	(0.4)	18.8	(1.1)	26.6	(1.3)	32.0	(1.4)	20.3	(1.2)	49.4	(0.3)
Italy	65.0	(1.0)	0.1	(0.1)	1.3	(0.2)	15.5	(0.7)	29.1	(0.7)	44.0	(0.8)	9.9	(0.6)	49.1	(0.2)
Mexico	48.2	(1.2)	2.9	(0.5)	11.4	(0.9)	31.4	(1.4)	27.5	(1.0)	21.1	(1.0)	5.6	(0.6)	41.7	(0.4)
Norway	52.0	(1.2)	0.3	(0.1)	5.5	(0.7)	20.0	(1.1)	30.2	(1.1)	26.7	(1.2)	17.3	(1.0)	47.4	(0.4)
Poland	67.9	(1.2)	0.4	(0.1)	7.0	(0.5)	33.9	(1.2)	32.0	(1.2)	22.3	(0.9)	4.4	(0.5)	42.8	(0.3)
Singapore	64.5	(0.9)	4.1	(0.4)	22.3	(0.8)	40.8	(0.9)	21.0	(0.8)	10.0	(0.5)	1.9	(0.3)	36.6	(0.2)
Sub-national entities																
Abu Dhabi (United Arab Emirates)	52.5	(1.4)	0.9	(0.2)	8.1	(0.8)	40.1	(1.1)	32.9	(0.9)	15.6	(0.8)	2.4	(0.4)	40.7	(0.3)
Average	57.4	(0.5)	1.2	(0.1)	7.7	(0.2)	27.1	(0.4)	28.4	(0.3)	25.7	(0.3)	9.9	(0.3)	44.6	(0.1)

Source: OECD, TALIS 2013 Database.
StatLink ⟶ http://dx.doi.org/10.1787/888933042371

[Part 1/1]
Gender and age distribution of teachers, 2008 and 2013
Table 2.1.c *Percentage of lower secondary education teachers with the following characteristics[1, 2]*

	Female		Percentage of teachers in each age group											
			Under 25 years		25-29 years		30-39 years		40-49 years		50-59 years		60 years or more	
	2008	2013	2008	2013	2008	2013	2008	2013	2008	2013	2008	2013	2008	2013
	% S.E.	% S.E.	% S.E.	% S.E.	% S.E.	% S.E.	% S.E.	% S.E.	% S.E.	% S.E.	% S.E.	% S.E.	% S.E.	% S.E.
Australia	59.2 (1.1)	59.2 (1.4)	4.5 (0.5)	4.2 (0.5)	13.7 (0.7)	11.5 (0.9)	22.6 (1.1)	23.0 (1.1)	26.5 (1.0)	24.3 (1.4)	28.9 (1.2)	30.0 (1.5)	3.8 (0.4)	6.9 (0.6)
Brazil	73.6 (1.0)	71.2 (0.7)	6.1 (0.8)	4.7 (0.4)	15.9 (0.9)	13.0 (0.6)	34.1 (1.1)	36.1 (0.7)	31.5 (1.0)	30.1 (0.7)	11.2 (0.6)	13.9 (0.5)	1.2 (0.2)	2.3 (0.2)
Bulgaria	82.7 (1.0)	81.2 (0.8)	1.7 (0.6)	0.6 (0.2)	5.2 (0.9)	2.8 (0.4)	23.9 (1.2)	18.3 (0.9)	32.9 (2.0)	31.5 (1.1)	33.2 (1.4)	40.9 (1.2)	3.1 (0.4)	5.8 (0.5)
Denmark	58.1 (1.2)	59.9 (1.4)	0.9 (0.2)	0.4 (0.1)	7.3 (0.6)	5.6 (0.7)	30.0 (1.3)	30.4 (1.4)	23.3 (1.5)	28.6 (1.4)	30.8 (1.3)	24.4 (1.4)	7.8 (0.8)	10.6 (0.8)
Estonia	83.7 (0.6)	84.6 (0.6)	2.5 (0.3)	1.4 (0.2)	8.4 (0.5)	6.1 (0.6)	18.2 (0.8)	17.2 (0.9)	32.0 (0.9)	27.2 (0.9)	27.1 (1.0)	31.8 (1.0)	11.7 (0.6)	16.2 (1.0)
Iceland	69.1 (1.5)	72.2 (1.2)	2.6 (0.4)	0.6 (0.2)	10.9 (0.9)	5.4 (0.6)	26.0 (1.2)	28.3 (1.3)	31.0 (1.2)	34.0 (1.4)	23.0 (1.1)	21.9 (1.2)	6.6 (0.7)	9.7 (0.8)
Italy	77.7 (0.7)	78.6 (0.7)	0.1 (0.1)	0.0 (0.0)	2.4 (0.3)	1.0 (0.2)	17.2 (0.8)	15.8 (0.7)	28.7 (0.8)	32.9 (0.9)	44.8 (1.1)	39.1 (1.0)	6.7 (0.4)	11.1 (0.5)
Korea	64.4 (1.3)	68.3 (1.1)	0.6 (0.1)	1.2 (0.3)	11.9 (0.9)	9.6 (0.5)	25.4 (1.0)	28.5 (1.2)	45.4 (1.2)	33.6 (1.1)	15.7 (0.5)	26.3 (1.3)	1.1 (0.2)	0.9 (0.2)
Malaysia	66.0 (1.0)	70.6 (1.0)	1.6 (0.3)	0.6 (0.2)	16.9 (0.7)	17.7 (0.8)	42.2 (0.9)	34.4 (0.9)	31.5 (0.8)	34.9 (1.0)	7.6 (0.5)	12.4 (0.6)	0.1 (0.1)	0.0 (0.0)
Mexico	53.2 (1.3)	54.0 (1.1)	3.0 (0.5)	2.5 (0.4)	11.7 (1.0)	10.0 (0.7)	25.8 (1.0)	29.4 (1.1)	37.3 (1.1)	32.3 (1.0)	18.7 (0.9)	21.9 (1.0)	3.5 (0.5)	3.9 (0.5)
Norway	60.4 (1.1)	60.9 (1.0)	0.8 (0.2)	1.5 (0.4)	8.4 (0.7)	9.8 (0.8)	31.1 (1.1)	28.6 (1.1)	19.8 (0.9)	26.3 (1.1)	27.9 (1.1)	18.7 (0.8)	12.0 (0.7)	15.1 (1.3)
Poland	76.3 (0.7)	74.9 (1.0)	1.7 (0.3)	0.8 (0.2)	13.5 (0.7)	7.8 (0.6)	36.0 (0.9)	35.1 (0.9)	34.5 (1.1)	33.0 (1.2)	13.4 (0.7)	21.5 (0.9)	0.9 (0.2)	1.8 (0.3)
Portugal	70.7 (0.9)	73.4 (0.8)	0.5 (0.1)	0.0 (0.0)	7.4 (0.5)	1.2 (0.2)	40.0 (1.2)	24.2 (0.9)	36.3 (1.1)	46.8 (0.9)	14.2 (1.0)	25.4 (1.0)	1.7 (0.3)	2.3 (0.3)
Slovak Republic	81.7 (0.8)	82.0 (0.8)	3.4 (0.5)	0.5 (0.1)	12.7 (0.8)	10.9 (0.7)	25.6 (1.2)	30.8 (0.9)	22.8 (0.9)	25.4 (0.9)	30.1 (1.1)	25.3 (1.0)	5.3 (0.7)	7.2 (0.6)
Spain	56.9 (1.0)	58.5 (1.0)	0.4 (0.2)	0.2 (0.1)	6.2 (0.5)	2.6 (0.4)	29.7 (1.1)	23.2 (1.0)	33.8 (0.9)	39.0 (0.8)	25.8 (1.1)	31.7 (1.0)	4.1 (0.4)	3.4 (0.4)
Sub-national entities														
Flanders (Belgium)	68.9 (1.4)	68.0 (1.4)	8.3 (0.7)	5.9 (0.5)	18.4 (0.8)	17.7 (0.8)	26.3 (0.8)	30.6 (1.1)	23.6 (1.2)	22.0 (1.0)	22.9 (0.9)	23.1 (0.9)	0.5 (0.2)	0.7 (0.2)
Average	68.9 (0.3)	69.8 (0.3)	2.4 (0.1)	1.6 (0.1)	10.7 (0.2)	8.3 (0.2)	28.4 (0.3)	27.1 (0.3)	30.7 (0.3)	31.4 (0.3)	23.5 (0.3)	25.5 (0.3)	4.4 (0.1)	6.1 (0.2)

1. The teacher population coverage was slightly different between 2008 and 2013. In order to have comparable populations for the tables comparing results from TALIS 2008 and TALIS 2013, teachers who teach exclusively to students with special needs were excluded from the 2013 data in these tables.
2. The wording and order of questions may have changed slightly between the 2008 and 2013 surveys.
Source: OECD, TALIS 2008 and TALIS 2013 Databases.
StatLink ⬛📈 http://dx.doi.org/10.1787/888933042390

[Part 1/1]
Teachers' educational attainment
Table 2.2   *Percentage of lower secondary education teachers by highest level of formal education completed[1]*

	Highest level of formal education completed							
	Below ISCED level 5		ISCED level 5B[2]		ISCED level 5A		ISCED level 6	
	%	S.E.	%	S.E.	%	S.E.	%	S.E.
Australia	0.1	(0.1)	0.0	(0.0)	98.9	(0.2)	0.9	(0.2)
Brazil	4.5	(0.5)	1.8	(0.2)	93.5	(0.6)	0.3	(0.1)
Bulgaria	1.0	(0.2)	7.8	(0.8)	90.8	(0.8)	0.4	(0.2)
Chile	0.5	(0.2)	17.9	(1.3)	81.1	(1.3)	0.5	(0.2)
Croatia	a	a	17.7	(0.8)	81.9	(0.8)	0.4	(0.1)
Cyprus*	a	a	0.7	(0.2)	96.2	(0.5)	3.1	(0.5)
Czech Republic	4.4	(0.4)	1.9	(0.3)	89.2	(0.6)	4.5	(0.4)
Denmark	2.1	(0.5)	0.6	(0.2)	97.1	(0.5)	0.2	(0.1)
Estonia	5.2	(0.5)	5.9	(0.5)	88.5	(0.7)	0.4	(0.1)
Finland	1.1	(0.2)	2.9	(0.4)	94.5	(0.5)	1.4	(0.3)
France	0.9	(0.2)	3.6	(0.5)	93.4	(0.5)	2.2	(0.3)
Iceland	10.0	(0.9)	4.7	(0.5)	85.3	(1.0)	0.0	(0.0)
Israel	0.8	(0.2)	1.5	(0.3)	96.4	(0.4)	1.3	(0.2)
Italy	3.6	(0.4)	15.8	(0.6)	78.1	(0.7)	2.5	(0.4)
Japan	0.1	(0.0)	3.5	(0.4)	95.8	(0.4)	0.6	(0.2)
Korea	0.1	(0.1)	0.1	(0.1)	98.0	(0.3)	1.8	(0.3)
Latvia	1.4	(0.3)	1.5	(0.3)	97.0	(0.4)	0.1	(0.1)
Malaysia	1.7	(0.4)	6.8	(0.7)	91.4	(0.7)	0.1	(0.1)
Mexico	8.7	(0.6)	1.5	(0.2)	89.1	(0.7)	0.7	(0.2)
Netherlands	4.1	(0.8)	0.7	(0.2)	94.6	(0.8)	0.7	(0.2)
Norway	2.0	(0.4)	a	a	97.9	(0.4)	0.1	(0.1)
Poland	0.1	(0.0)	0.0	(0.0)	98.8	(0.2)	1.1	(0.2)
Portugal[3]	0.3	(0.1)	2.4	(0.2)	84.8	(0.6)	12.4	(0.6)
Romania	1.2	(0.3)	5.4	(0.5)	92.3	(0.6)	1.1	(0.2)
Serbia	1.6	(0.3)	15.5	(0.8)	82.7	(0.8)	0.1	(0.0)
Singapore	1.8	(0.2)	5.5	(0.4)	92.4	(0.5)	0.3	(0.1)
Slovak Republic	1.6	(0.3)	0.2	(0.1)	97.5	(0.4)	0.7	(0.1)
Spain	3.4	(0.3)	1.0	(0.2)	91.4	(0.5)	4.2	(0.4)
Sweden	3.8	(0.4)	7.7	(0.5)	87.9	(0.7)	0.6	(0.1)
Sub-national entities								
Abu Dhabi (United Arab Emirates)	1.8	(0.7)	4.7	(0.6)	92.6	(0.9)	0.9	(0.3)
Alberta (Canada)	0.1	(0.1)	1.0	(0.3)	97.5	(0.4)	1.4	(0.3)
England (United Kingdom)	1.4	(0.3)	1.7	(0.3)	95.2	(0.5)	1.6	(0.3)
Flanders (Belgium)	2.6	(0.3)	85.4	(0.8)	11.8	(0.8)	0.2	(0.1)
Average[4]	2.3	(0.1)	7.1	(0.1)	89.5	(0.1)	1.4	(0.0)
United States	0.1	(0.1)	0.4	(0.2)	98.0	(0.5)	1.4	(0.4)

1. Education categories are based on the International Standard Classification of Education (ISCED 1997). ISCED level 5A programmes are generally longer and more theory-based, while 5B programmes are typically shorter and more practical and skills oriented. No distinction was made between ISCED level 5A (Bachelor) and ISCED level 5A (Master).

2. Includes Bachelor's degrees in some countries.

3. In Portugal, the teachers with a "Pre-Bologna Master's degree" are counted as ISCED level 6. The way the question is presented prevents the disaggregation between "Pre-Bologna Master's degree" and "Doctorate degree".

4. The averages do not add up to 100 across categories because of the presence of cells that are not applicable "a" in some countries.

* See notes at the beginning of this Annex.

Source: OECD, TALIS 2013 Database.

StatLink ⌨ http://dx.doi.org/10.1787/888933042409

[Part 1/1]
Primary teachers' educational attainment

Table 2.2.a   *Percentage of primary education teachers by highest level of formal education completed[1]*

	Highest level of formal education completed							
	Below ISCED level 5		ISCED level 5B[2]		ISCED level 5A		ISCED level 6	
	%	S.E.	%	S.E.	%	S.E.	%	S.E.
Denmark	1.5	(0.3)	0.3	(0.1)	98.1	(0.4)	0.1	(0.0)
Finland	1.0	(0.4)	3.0	(0.5)	95.4	(0.8)	0.5	(0.2)
Mexico	19.0	(1.5)	1.0	(0.3)	79.5	(1.6)	0.5	(0.2)
Norway	1.6	(0.3)	a	a	98.3	(0.3)	0.1	(0.1)
Poland	0.2	(0.1)	0.6	(0.2)	99.1	(0.2)	0.2	(0.1)
Sub-national entities								
Flanders (Belgium)	0.3	(0.1)	93.7	(0.6)	6.0	(0.6)	0.0	(0.0)
Average[3]	3.9	(0.3)	19.7	(0.2)	79.4	(0.3)	0.2	(0.1)

1. Education categories are based on the International Standard Classification of Education (ISCED 1997). ISCED level 5A programmes are generally longer and more theory-based, while 5B programmes are typically shorter and more practical and skills oriented. No distinction was made between ISCED level 5A (Bachelor) and ISCED level 5A (Master).
2. Includes Bachelor's degrees in some countries.
3. The averages do not add up to 100 across categories because of the presence of cells that are not applicable "a" in some countries.
Source: OECD, TALIS 2013 Database.
StatLink ᴍ🖰🖷 http://dx.doi.org/10.1787/888933042428

[Part 1/1]
Upper secondary teachers' educational attainment

Table 2.2.b   *Percentage of upper secondary education teachers by highest level of formal education completed[1]*

	Highest level of formal education completed							
	Below ISCED level 5		ISCED level 5B[2]		ISCED level 5A		ISCED level 6	
	%	S.E.	%	S.E.	%	S.E.	%	S.E.
Australia	0.1	(0.1)	0.2	(0.1)	98.6	(0.3)	1.1	(0.2)
Denmark	6.8	(1.3)	3.8	(0.6)	87.4	(1.2)	2.0	(0.4)
Finland	1.4	(0.4)	11.9	(2.2)	84.5	(2.0)	2.2	(0.4)
Iceland	4.7	(0.6)	11.7	(0.8)	81.1	(1.1)	2.5	(0.4)
Italy	6.1	(0.4)	4.6	(0.3)	85.6	(0.7)	3.7	(0.5)
Mexico	4.9	(0.6)	2.4	(0.4)	91.4	(0.8)	1.4	(0.2)
Norway	4.8	(0.6)	a	a	94.5	(0.6)	0.7	(0.2)
Poland	0.5	(0.2)	0.8	(0.2)	97.3	(0.4)	1.4	(0.3)
Singapore	0.7	(0.2)	3.5	(0.4)	95.5	(0.4)	0.3	(0.1)
Sub-national entities								
Abu Dhabi (United Arab Emirates)	0.6	(0.2)	3.1	(0.4)	94.5	(0.4)	1.8	(0.2)
Average[3]	3.1	(0.2)	4.7	(0.3)	91.0	(0.3)	1.7	(0.1)

1. Education categories are based on the International Standard Classification of Education (ISCED 1997). ISCED level 5A programmes are generally longer and more theory-based, while 5B programmes are typically shorter and more practical and skills oriented. No distinction was made between ISCED level 5A (Bachelor) and ISCED level 5A (Master).
2. Includes Bachelor's degrees in some countries.
3. The averages do not add up to 100 across categories because of the presence of cells that are not applicable "a" in some countries.
Source: OECD, TALIS 2013 Database.
StatLink ᴍ🖰🖷 http://dx.doi.org/10.1787/888933042447

[Part 1/1]
Teachers' educational attainment, 2008 and 2013
Table 2.2.c   *Percentage of lower secondary education teachers by highest level of formal education completed[1, 2, 3]*

	Highest level of formal education completed															
	Below ISCED level 5				ISCED level 5B[4]				ISCED level 5A				ISCED level 6			
	2008		2013		2008		2013		2008		2013		2008		2013	
	%	S.E.	%	S.E.	%	S.E.	%	S.E.	%	S.E.	%	S.E.	%	S.E.	%	S.E.
Australia	0.3	(0.1)	0.1	(0.1)	1.0	(0.3)	0.0	(0.0)	96.5	(0.5)	99.0	(0.2)	2.2	(0.3)	0.9	(0.2)
Brazil	8.6	(1.0)	4.4	(0.5)	0.2	(0.1)	1.8	(0.2)	91.1	(1.0)	93.5	(0.6)	0.1	(0.0)	0.2	(0.1)
Bulgaria	3.7	(1.1)	1.0	(0.2)	15.7	(1.7)	7.8	(0.8)	80.4	(1.9)	90.8	(0.8)	0.2	(0.1)	0.4	(0.2)
Denmark	1.9	(0.4)	2.0	(0.5)	0.2	(0.1)	0.6	(0.2)	97.8	(0.4)	97.1	(0.5)	0.0	(0.0)	0.3	(0.1)
Estonia	7.0	(0.5)	5.2	(0.5)	6.5	(0.5)	5.9	(0.5)	86.2	(0.7)	88.5	(0.7)	0.3	(0.1)	0.4	(0.1)
Iceland	12.1	(0.8)	10.3	(0.9)	20.8	(1.1)	4.6	(0.5)	66.9	(1.2)	85.1	(1.0)	0.2	(0.1)	0.0	(0.0)
Korea	0.3	(0.1)	0.1	(0.1)	0.3	(0.1)	0.1	(0.1)	98.7	(0.2)	98.0	(0.3)	0.7	(0.2)	1.8	(0.3)
Malaysia	1.0	(0.1)	1.7	(0.4)	12.1	(0.6)	6.8	(0.7)	86.9	(0.6)	91.5	(0.7)	0.0	(0.0)	0.1	(0.1)
Mexico	10.4	(0.9)	8.7	(0.6)	3.0	(0.4)	1.5	(0.2)	86.3	(1.1)	89.1	(0.7)	0.3	(0.1)	0.7	(0.2)
Norway	0.9	(0.2)	2.0	(0.4)	0.0	(0.0)	a	a	99.0	(0.2)	97.8	(0.4)	0.0	(0.0)	0.1	(0.1)
Poland	0.3	(0.1)	0.1	(0.0)	1.2	(0.3)	0.0	(0.0)	98.0	(0.3)	98.9	(0.2)	0.5	(0.2)	1.1	(0.2)
Portugal[5]	0.4	(0.1)	0.3	(0.1)	4.3	(0.4)	2.4	(0.2)	95.1	(0.5)	85.0	(0.6)	0.2	(0.1)	12.3	(0.6)
Slovak Republic	2.5	(0.4)	1.6	(0.3)	0.0	(0.0)	0.2	(0.1)	96.6	(0.4)	97.6	(0.4)	0.8	(0.2)	0.7	(0.1)
Spain	3.5	(0.3)	3.3	(0.3)	1.6	(0.2)	1.0	(0.2)	90.2	(0.5)	91.5	(0.5)	4.7	(0.4)	4.3	(0.4)
Sub-national entities																
Flanders (Belgium)	3.4	(0.4)	2.6	(0.3)	84.2	(1.0)	85.5	(0.8)	12.3	(0.9)	11.7	(0.8)	0.1	(0.1)	0.2	(0.1)
Average[6]	3.8	(0.1)	2.9	(0.1)	10.1	(0.2)	8.4	(0.1)	85.5	(0.2)	87.7	(0.2)	0.7	(0.0)	1.6	(0.1)

1. The teacher population coverage was slightly different between TALIS 2008 and TALIS 2013. In order to have comparable populations for the tables comparing results from 2008 and 2013, teachers who teach exclusively to students with special needs were excluded from the 2013 data in these tables.

2. The wording and order of questions may have changed slightly between the 2008 and 2013 surveys.

3. Education categories are based on the International Standard Classification of Education (ISCED 1997). ISCED level 5A programmes are generally longer and more theory-based, while 5B programmes are typically shorter and more practical and skills oriented. No distinction was made between ISCED level 5A (Bachelor) and ISCED level 5A (Master).

4. Includes Bachelor's degrees in some countries.

5. In Portugal, the teachers with a "Pre-Bologna Master's degree" are counted as ISCED level 5A in TALIS 2008, and as ISCED level 6 in TALIS 2013. The way the question is presented in TALIS 2013 prevents the disaggregation between "Pre-Bologna Master's degree" and "Doctorate degree".

6. The averages do not add up to 100 across categories because of the presence of cells that are not applicable "a" in some countries.

Source: OECD, TALIS 2008 and TALIS 2013 Databases.

StatLink ᴬᴵˢᵖ http://dx.doi.org/10.1787/888933042466

[Part 1/1]
Completion and content of teacher education or training programme
Percentage of lower secondary education teachers who completed a teacher education or training
Table 2.3 *programme and for whom the following elements were included in their formal education and training*

	Completion of teacher education or training programme		Elements included in formal education and training									
			Content of the subject(s) being taught				Pedagogy of the subject(s) being taught				Practice in the subject(s) being taught			
			For all subjects		For some subjects		For all subjects		For some subjects		For all subjects		For some subjects	
	%	S.E.	%	S.E.	%	S.E.	%	S.E.	%	S.E.	%	S.E.	%	S.E.
Australia	97.6	(0.3)	62.2	(1.1)	31.1	(1.2)	64.0	(1.2)	31.1	(1.0)	70.1	(1.2)	26.8	(1.3)
Brazil	75.8	(0.8)	62.3	(0.9)	27.4	(0.8)	50.9	(0.8)	27.7	(0.8)	61.3	(0.8)	26.8	(0.7)
Bulgaria	97.7	(0.3)	87.3	(0.9)	9.7	(0.8)	86.8	(1.0)	8.7	(0.7)	84.4	(1.1)	10.0	(0.8)
Chile	85.7	(1.1)	61.0	(1.6)	31.0	(1.6)	60.0	(1.7)	29.4	(1.6)	56.8	(1.6)	27.2	(1.4)
Croatia	94.9	(0.5)	93.5	(0.4)	5.0	(0.4)	88.4	(0.6)	5.5	(0.4)	85.9	(0.7)	6.1	(0.4)
Cyprus*	89.7	(0.6)	69.8	(1.2)	27.1	(1.2)	61.7	(1.3)	29.5	(1.2)	56.1	(1.3)	30.7	(1.2)
Czech Republic	76.7	(0.8)	57.2	(1.4)	37.8	(1.3)	55.4	(1.4)	36.0	(1.2)	51.8	(1.4)	34.3	(1.1)
Denmark	93.5	(0.9)	60.2	(1.1)	36.3	(1.0)	60.3	(1.1)	35.3	(1.0)	52.3	(1.4)	40.7	(1.3)
Estonia	94.4	(0.4)	78.2	(1.0)	17.4	(0.9)	78.2	(0.9)	16.2	(0.8)	69.0	(1.0)	19.8	(0.8)
Finland	92.5	(0.7)	77.1	(0.9)	19.0	(0.7)	75.1	(0.9)	21.3	(0.8)	69.2	(1.0)	25.2	(0.8)
France	90.1	(0.5)	85.0	(0.7)	10.6	(0.6)	66.0	(1.0)	10.6	(0.6)	72.5	(0.9)	8.6	(0.6)
Iceland	92.4	(0.7)	41.7	(1.2)	45.1	(1.2)	43.1	(1.3)	45.2	(1.4)	42.2	(1.2)	44.6	(1.3)
Israel	93.6	(0.5)	77.1	(1.1)	19.2	(1.1)	74.8	(1.1)	20.8	(1.1)	75.7	(1.0)	19.7	(1.0)
Italy	79.1	(0.8)	69.4	(1.0)	22.1	(0.9)	62.6	(1.0)	21.9	(0.8)	35.5	(0.9)	12.4	(0.6)
Japan	87.8	(0.7)	71.2	(0.9)	27.3	(0.9)	67.6	(0.9)	29.7	(0.9)	69.5	(0.8)	28.2	(0.8)
Korea	96.1	(0.3)	90.4	(0.6)	8.9	(0.5)	83.6	(0.7)	12.5	(0.7)	79.0	(0.8)	13.0	(0.7)
Latvia	90.8	(0.8)	86.4	(0.9)	10.4	(0.7)	85.1	(0.7)	11.3	(0.7)	80.4	(0.9)	11.9	(0.7)
Malaysia	92.1	(1.1)	77.0	(1.3)	21.2	(1.2)	75.8	(1.1)	22.9	(1.1)	75.0	(1.1)	23.3	(1.2)
Mexico	61.5	(1.2)	67.4	(1.0)	23.2	(0.8)	64.3	(1.1)	24.9	(1.1)	57.7	(1.2)	23.9	(1.0)
Netherlands	91.5	(1.1)	84.5	(1.4)	12.3	(1.2)	86.5	(1.1)	10.8	(1.0)	82.4	(1.2)	10.6	(1.1)
Norway	92.5	(0.9)	51.4	(1.3)	45.1	(1.3)	50.6	(1.3)	45.2	(1.2)	50.7	(1.5)	42.5	(1.5)
Poland	99.4	(0.1)	95.0	(0.4)	3.5	(0.4)	94.7	(0.4)	3.9	(0.4)	88.1	(0.6)	7.7	(0.5)
Portugal	82.1	(0.8)	76.4	(0.7)	21.5	(0.7)	74.2	(0.8)	21.5	(0.7)	71.0	(0.8)	21.0	(0.7)
Romania	97.1	(0.4)	84.2	(1.0)	12.1	(0.9)	82.4	(1.1)	13.2	(0.9)	81.6	(1.1)	11.8	(0.8)
Serbia	71.4	(1.0)	80.4	(0.9)	12.5	(0.7)	75.0	(0.9)	13.7	(0.6)	65.0	(1.0)	13.1	(0.7)
Singapore	99.1	(0.2)	77.8	(0.7)	19.4	(0.7)	82.0	(0.7)	16.2	(0.7)	82.6	(0.7)	15.8	(0.7)
Slovak Republic	89.4	(0.7)	65.4	(1.0)	27.7	(0.9)	63.2	(0.9)	25.2	(0.9)	54.2	(1.1)	25.3	(0.8)
Spain	97.5	(0.3)	64.5	(0.9)	29.7	(0.8)	44.3	(1.0)	30.8	(0.8)	44.0	(0.9)	31.2	(0.9)
Sweden	89.9	(0.7)	72.2	(1.0)	24.2	(0.9)	67.8	(1.0)	24.9	(1.0)	68.6	(1.0)	22.2	(1.0)
Sub-national entities														
Abu Dhabi (United Arab Emirates)	83.3	(1.1)	72.2	(1.5)	20.2	(1.3)	67.1	(1.5)	20.9	(1.1)	70.9	(1.6)	17.9	(1.2)
Alberta (Canada)	98.3	(0.4)	44.2	(1.6)	48.8	(1.5)	49.1	(1.5)	45.9	(1.5)	51.5	(1.4)	41.6	(1.4)
England (United Kingdom)	91.9	(0.6)	71.9	(1.1)	22.4	(1.3)	75.6	(1.0)	19.6	(1.0)	80.6	(0.9)	16.2	(0.9)
Flanders (Belgium)	98.3	(0.3)	76.5	(1.1)	17.0	(0.8)	80.5	(1.0)	15.5	(0.8)	77.6	(1.0)	16.4	(0.8)
Average	89.8	(0.1)	72.5	(0.2)	22.6	(0.2)	69.6	(0.2)	22.7	(0.2)	67.1	(0.2)	22.0	(0.2)
United States	94.9	(0.7)	77.6	(1.2)	16.5	(0.9)	74.1	(1.2)	17.7	(1.0)	74.8	(1.3)	15.0	(0.8)

* See notes at the beginning of this Annex.
Source: OECD, TALIS 2013 Database.
StatLink ⌨ http://dx.doi.org/10.1787/888933042485

[Part 1/1]
Teachers' feelings of preparedness for teaching
Percentage of lower secondary education teachers who feel prepared or not
for the following elements of their teaching

Table 2.4

	Extent to which teachers feel prepared for the following elements in their teaching					
	Content of the subject(s) being taught		Pedagogy of the subject(s) being taught		Practice in the subject(s) being taught	
	Not at all or somewhat prepared	Well or very well prepared	Not at all or somewhat prepared	Well or very well prepared	Not at all or somewhat prepared	Well or very well prepared
	%	S.E.	%	S.E.	%	S.E.	%	S.E.	%	S.E.	%	S.E.
Australia	7.4	(0.8)	92.6	(0.8)	9.4	(0.8)	90.6	(0.8)	8.7	(0.9)	91.3	(0.9)
Brazil	1.6	(0.2)	98.4	(0.2)	7.2	(0.4)	92.8	(0.4)	3.5	(0.3)	96.5	(0.3)
Bulgaria	7.9	(0.6)	92.1	(0.6)	11.1	(0.7)	88.9	(0.7)	12.7	(0.8)	87.3	(0.8)
Chile	3.4	(0.6)	96.6	(0.6)	3.2	(0.6)	96.8	(0.6)	3.0	(0.5)	97.0	(0.5)
Croatia	1.7	(0.3)	98.3	(0.3)	7.6	(0.5)	92.4	(0.5)	10.8	(0.5)	89.2	(0.5)
Cyprus*	1.1	(0.3)	98.9	(0.3)	3.3	(0.5)	96.7	(0.5)	3.3	(0.4)	96.7	(0.4)
Czech Republic	1.4	(0.3)	98.6	(0.3)	8.5	(0.6)	91.5	(0.6)	10.7	(0.6)	89.3	(0.6)
Denmark	7.3	(0.8)	92.7	(0.8)	15.5	(0.9)	84.5	(0.9)	12.0	(0.8)	88.0	(0.8)
Estonia	2.1	(0.3)	97.9	(0.3)	3.1	(0.3)	96.9	(0.3)	6.2	(0.5)	93.8	(0.5)
Finland	27.8	(1.1)	72.2	(1.1)	36.0	(0.9)	64.0	(0.9)	34.0	(0.9)	66.0	(0.9)
France	9.6	(0.6)	90.4	(0.6)	39.7	(1.0)	60.3	(1.0)	42.1	(0.9)	57.9	(0.9)
Iceland	16.9	(1.0)	83.1	(1.0)	21.5	(1.1)	78.5	(1.1)	21.7	(1.1)	78.3	(1.1)
Israel	0.9	(0.2)	99.1	(0.2)	1.1	(0.2)	98.9	(0.2)	1.9	(0.3)	98.1	(0.3)
Italy	4.3	(0.4)	95.7	(0.4)	9.7	(0.5)	90.3	(0.5)	8.8	(0.5)	91.2	(0.5)
Japan	24.0	(0.9)	76.0	(0.9)	30.1	(1.0)	69.9	(1.0)	32.0	(0.9)	68.0	(0.9)
Korea	16.8	(0.7)	83.2	(0.7)	19.3	(0.7)	80.7	(0.7)	21.9	(0.8)	78.1	(0.8)
Latvia	1.4	(0.3)	98.6	(0.3)	3.1	(0.4)	96.9	(0.4)	4.8	(0.6)	95.2	(0.6)
Malaysia	0.3	(0.1)	99.7	(0.1)	0.9	(0.2)	99.1	(0.2)	0.5	(0.1)	99.5	(0.1)
Mexico	23.7	(0.9)	76.3	(0.9)	24.0	(0.8)	76.0	(0.8)	24.7	(0.9)	75.3	(0.9)
Netherlands	7.0	(0.7)	93.0	(0.7)	14.7	(1.0)	85.3	(1.0)	18.5	(1.2)	81.5	(1.2)
Norway	7.0	(0.9)	93.0	(0.9)	11.4	(1.1)	88.6	(1.1)	8.9	(1.1)	91.1	(1.1)
Poland	1.6	(0.6)	98.4	(0.6)	2.6	(0.6)	97.4	(0.6)	4.3	(0.7)	95.7	(0.7)
Portugal	1.8	(0.2)	98.2	(0.2)	5.0	(0.4)	95.0	(0.4)	4.8	(0.4)	95.2	(0.4)
Romania	0.2	(0.1)	99.8	(0.1)	1.5	(0.3)	98.5	(0.3)	1.9	(0.4)	98.1	(0.4)
Serbia	1.1	(0.2)	98.9	(0.2)	3.0	(0.4)	97.0	(0.4)	2.3	(0.3)	97.7	(0.3)
Singapore	14.2	(0.7)	85.8	(0.7)	19.8	(0.8)	80.2	(0.8)	21.2	(0.7)	78.8	(0.7)
Slovak Republic	1.0	(0.2)	99.0	(0.2)	2.8	(0.3)	97.2	(0.3)	4.7	(0.5)	95.3	(0.5)
Spain	1.1	(0.2)	98.9	(0.2)	8.8	(0.6)	91.2	(0.6)	7.4	(0.6)	92.6	(0.6)
Sweden	3.1	(0.4)	96.9	(0.4)	10.1	(0.6)	89.9	(0.6)	9.9	(0.6)	90.1	(0.6)
Sub-national entities												
Abu Dhabi (United Arab Emirates)	3.0	(0.4)	97.0	(0.4)	3.9	(0.5)	96.1	(0.5)	2.6	(0.4)	97.4	(0.4)
Alberta (Canada)	11.5	(0.7)	88.5	(0.7)	11.1	(0.7)	88.9	(0.7)	9.7	(0.6)	90.3	(0.6)
England (United Kingdom)	6.9	(0.6)	93.1	(0.6)	9.5	(0.8)	90.5	(0.8)	7.2	(0.6)	92.8	(0.6)
Flanders (Belgium)	4.5	(0.4)	95.5	(0.4)	7.4	(0.6)	92.6	(0.6)	9.9	(0.6)	90.1	(0.6)
Average	**6.8**	**(0.1)**	**93.2**	**(0.1)**	**11.1**	**(0.1)**	**88.9**	**(0.1)**	**11.4**	**(0.1)**	**88.6**	**(0.1)**
United States	5.0	(0.7)	95.0	(0.7)	8.4	(0.9)	91.6	(0.9)	8.6	(0.9)	91.4	(0.9)

*See notes at the beginning of this Annex.
Source: OECD, TALIS 2013 Database.
StatLink ⬛ http://dx.doi.org/10.1787/888933042504

[Part 1/1]

Analysis of teachers' feelings of preparedness for teaching

Multinomial logistic regression analysis for feeling prepared for the following elements of teaching in lower secondary education[1,2]

Table 2.5

	Feeling prepared for the content of the subject(s) taught[3]				Feeling prepared for the pedagogy of the subject(s) taught[3]				Feeling prepared for classroom practice in the subject(s) taught[3]			
	Dependent on:											
	Content of the subject(s) taught was included in formal education or training for all subject(s) taught		Content of the subject(s) taught was included in formal education or training for some subject(s) taught		Pedagogy of the subject(s) taught was included in formal education or training for all subject(s) taught		Pedagogy of the subject(s) taught was included in formal education or training for some subject(s) taught		Classroom practice in the subject(s) taught was included in formal education or training for all subject(s) taught		Classroom practice in the subject(s) taught was included in formal education or training for some subject(s) taught	
	ß	Odds ratios[4]	ß	Odds ratios[4]	ß	Odds ratios[4]	ß	Odds ratios[4]	ß	Odds ratios[4]	ß	Odds ratios[4]
Australia	1.5	4.6	0.6	1.8	1.9	6.7	1.2	3.4	1.2	3.5	1.0	2.7
Brazil	1.8	5.9	0.5	1.6	2.0	7.2	0.8	2.3	0.7	2.0	0.4	1.6
Bulgaria	3.1	22.6	1.5	4.6	2.9	18.7	1.6	4.9	2.7	14.9	1.6	5.2
Chile	0.9	2.4	-0.9	0.4	2.2	8.7	0.9	2.4	1.0	2.8	-0.2	0.8
Croatia	2.0	7.2			1.0	2.7	0.5	1.6	1.2	3.5	0.3	1.4
Czech Republic	2.1	7.8	1.3	3.7	0.7	2.1	0.5	1.7	0.3	1.3		
Denmark	1.0	2.7	0.4	1.4	0.9	2.5			0.7	2.0	0.2	1.3
Estonia	1.7	5.6	0.6	1.8	1.7	5.5	1.2	3.4	2.2	9.4	1.4	4.0
Finland	1.9	6.5	1.1	3.0	1.7	5.5	0.9	2.4	2.0	7.1	1.6	4.8
France	2.6	13.0	1.3	3.5	1.6	4.8	0.7	1.9	1.1	2.9	0.3	1.3
Iceland	1.4	3.9	0.5	1.7	2.2	8.6	1.1	2.9	1.1	3.1	0.5	1.6
Israel	2.0	7.2	0.9	2.3	2.9	17.6	1.6	4.7	2.3	9.9	1.1	3.0
Italy	0.4	1.5	-0.8	0.4	1.3	3.9	0.7	2.0	0.5	1.7	-0.1	0.9
Japan	0.6	1.9	0.1	1.1	0.3	1.4	-0.2	0.8	0.7	2.0	0.2	1.3
Korea	1.2	3.3			1.6	5.0	0.6	1.7	1.4	4.0	0.3	1.4
Latvia	2.5	11.7	0.7	2.0	2.2	9.0			1.7	5.5	1.2	3.5
Malaysia												
Mexico	-0.4	0.7	0.2	1.2	-0.2	0.8	0.2	1.2	-0.3	0.8	0.1	1.1
Netherlands	1.3	3.8	0.5	1.6	0.4	1.5			1.0	2.7	0.8	2.3
Norway	0.7	2.0			2.3	9.5	1.1	2.9	1.9	6.9	0.9	2.6
Poland	2.2	8.6	1.0	2.7	1.7	5.6	1.5	4.4	1.7	5.6	1.2	3.2
Portugal	1.4	4.1			2.3	9.9	1.0	2.8	1.7	5.4	0.4	1.5
Romania	1.4	4.1	1.7	5.6	3.3	26.4	2.4	11.4	2.4	10.6	1.7	5.4
Serbia												
Singapore	1.0	2.9			1.0	2.7			0.9	2.5		
Slovak Republic	1.5	4.6	0.6	1.8	1.5	4.5	1.2	3.4	1.6	4.8	1.5	4.4
Spain	2.1	8.0	1.3	3.6	1.8	5.9	0.8	2.2	1.2	3.3	0.4	1.5
Sweden	2.2	8.6	1.6	4.8	2.1	8.2	1.2	3.2	0.8	2.3	0.2	1.1
Sub-national entities												
Abu Dhabi (United Arab Emirates)	1.2	3.2	0.8	2.3	1.9	6.9	1.1	3.1	1.2	3.2		
Alberta (Canada)	1.7	5.2	0.5	1.7	2.1	8.5	0.9	2.3	1.1	3.1		
England (United Kingdom)	1.8	5.8	0.8	2.2	1.9	6.7	1.0	2.6	1.4	4.1	0.7	2.0
Flanders (Belgium)	2.3	9.5	1.4	3.9	1.5	4.4	1.2	3.2	1.4	4.2	1.1	3.1

1. Cells are blank where no significant relationship was found. Significance was tested at the 5% level. Controlling for teacher gender, years of experience, level of education and subjects taught. Where there was 0% of the teachers in a particular country teaching a particular subject (e.g. Ancient Greek/Latin), this subject was left out of the regression for this country.

2. Cells with data representing less than 5% of the cases are shaded in grey and should be interpreted with caution. These results are not highlighted in the text of the report.

3. The reference category is the combination of teachers who answered "not at all prepared" or "somewhat prepared".

4. This is the exponentiated beta. See Box 2.5 for interpretation of odds ratios.

Source: OECD, TALIS 2013 Database.

StatLink http://dx.doi.org/10.1787/888933042542

[Part 1/1]
Work experience of teachers
Table 2.6   *Average years of working experience among lower secondary education teachers in various roles*

	Average years of working experience as a teacher at this school		Average years of working experience as a teacher in total		Average years of working experience in other education roles		Average years of working experience in other jobs	
	Average	S.E.	Average	S.E.	Average	S.E.	Average	S.E.
Australia	8.7	(0.2)	16.7	(0.3)	1.8	(0.1)	5.6	(0.2)
Brazil	7.0	(0.2)	13.6	(0.2)	3.7	(0.1)	6.6	(0.1)
Bulgaria	14.5	(0.3)	21.5	(0.2)	3.3	(0.3)	5.7	(0.2)
Chile	9.8	(0.4)	15.1	(0.5)	6.3	(0.3)	4.2	(0.2)
Croatia	12.8	(0.2)	15.7	(0.3)	1.5	(0.2)	3.8	(0.2)
Cyprus*	4.8	(0.1)	13.4	(0.2)	4.0	(0.2)	5.9	(0.2)
Czech Republic	12.7	(0.2)	17.7	(0.3)	1.2	(0.1)	1.8	(0.1)
Denmark	12.0	(0.4)	16.1	(0.3)	1.9	(0.1)	4.4	(0.2)
Estonia	14.4	(0.3)	21.6	(0.3)	3.4	(0.2)	4.2	(0.2)
Finland	10.5	(0.2)	15.5	(0.2)	1.2	(0.1)	3.2	(0.1)
France	9.4	(0.2)	17.1	(0.3)	2.0	(0.1)	1.6	(0.1)
Iceland	10.0	(0.2)	14.3	(0.3)	4.0	(0.2)	9.6	(0.3)
Israel	10.7	(0.3)	16.1	(0.4)	3.0	(0.1)	3.6	(0.1)
Italy	8.1	(0.2)	19.8	(0.3)	1.2	(0.1)	2.9	(0.1)
Japan	4.5	(0.1)	17.4	(0.2)	0.6	(0.0)	0.8	(0.1)
Korea	3.9	(0.2)	16.4	(0.3)	0.9	(0.1)	0.7	(0.0)
Latvia	15.6	(0.4)	22.0	(0.4)	3.4	(0.2)	3.6	(0.2)
Malaysia	7.2	(0.2)	13.6	(0.3)	1.2	(0.1)	0.7	(0.0)
Mexico	11.3	(0.3)	15.8	(0.3)	4.5	(0.3)	7.4	(0.4)
Netherlands	10.7	(0.3)	15.7	(0.3)	3.3	(0.2)	5.0	(0.3)
Norway	10.8	(0.4)	15.5	(0.4)	1.9	(0.1)	4.2	(0.2)
Poland	11.2	(0.2)	17.1	(0.2)	2.1	(0.1)	1.8	(0.1)
Portugal	10.4	(0.2)	19.4	(0.2)	3.4	(0.2)	1.8	(0.1)
Romania	10.4	(0.2)	16.5	(0.3)	4.5	(0.3)	2.5	(0.1)
Serbia	11.1	(0.2)	14.9	(0.2)	9.6	(0.4)	4.7	(0.2)
Singapore	5.6	(0.1)	9.7	(0.2)	1.2	(0.1)	1.9	(0.1)
Slovak Republic	12.2	(0.3)	17.7	(0.3)	1.4	(0.1)	2.0	(0.1)
Spain	9.2	(0.2)	18.3	(0.3)	2.8	(0.1)	3.2	(0.1)
Sweden	9.8	(0.2)	16.4	(0.3)	2.6	(0.1)	5.7	(0.1)
Sub-national entities								
Abu Dhabi (United Arab Emirates)	5.5	(0.2)	12.8	(0.2)	1.4	(0.1)	1.4	(0.1)
Alberta (Canada)	7.1	(0.3)	12.9	(0.3)	2.4	(0.1)	7.0	(0.2)
England (United Kingdom)	7.9	(0.3)	12.4	(0.2)	1.6	(0.1)	5.3	(0.2)
Flanders (Belgium)	12.7	(0.2)	15.2	(0.2)	0.8	(0.1)	2.1	(0.1)
Average	9.8	(0.0)	16.2	(0.0)	2.7	(0.0)	3.8	(0.0)
United States	8.7	(0.3)	13.8	(0.4)	3.0	(0.2)	8.1	(0.3)

*See notes at the beginning of this Annex.
Source: OECD, TALIS 2013 Database.
StatLink ⌨ http://dx.doi.org/10.1787/888933042580

[Part 1/1]
Work experience of primary teachers
Table 2.6.a   *Average years of working experience among primary education teachers in various roles*

	Average years of working experience as a teacher at this school		Average years of working experience as a teacher in total		Average years of working experience in other education roles		Average years of working experience in other jobs	
	Average	S.E.	Average	S.E.	Average	S.E.	Average	S.E.
Denmark	11.1	(0.3)	15.8	(0.2)	1.9	(0.1)	5.0	(0.2)
Finland	8.9	(0.2)	15.4	(0.3)	1.9	(0.1)	3.0	(0.1)
Mexico	7.9	(0.4)	15.9	(0.5)	3.0	(0.4)	4.6	(0.5)
Norway	11.1	(0.9)	15.9	(0.7)	3.0	(0.2)	4.2	(0.2)
Poland	14.3	(0.2)	18.8	(0.3)	2.1	(0.2)	2.3	(0.2)
Sub-national entities								
Flanders (Belgium)	13.5	(0.3)	16.3	(0.3)	0.6	(0.1)	1.0	(0.1)
Average	11.2	(0.2)	16.3	(0.2)	2.1	(0.1)	3.3	(0.1)

Source: OECD, TALIS 2013 Database.
StatLink ⌨ http://dx.doi.org/10.1787/888933042599

[Part 1/1]
Work experience of upper secondary teachers
Table 2.6.b   *Average years of working experience among upper secondary education teachers in various roles*

	Average years of working experience as a teacher at this school		Average years of working experience as a teacher in total		Average years of working experience in other education roles		Average years of working experience in other jobs	
	Average	S.E.	Average	S.E.	Average	S.E.	Average	S.E.
Australia	8.9	(0.2)	17.4	(0.3)	1.7	(0.1)	5.2	(0.2)
Denmark	11.7	(0.4)	14.8	(0.4)	2.4	(0.2)	6.1	(0.4)
Finland	12.5	(0.6)	16.2	(0.3)	2.0	(0.2)	6.7	(0.3)
Iceland	12.1	(0.3)	16.4	(0.4)	3.3	(0.2)	10.6	(0.3)
Italy	9.7	(0.2)	20.1	(0.2)	1.1	(0.1)	3.4	(0.1)
Mexico	11.1	(0.3)	14.2	(0.4)	4.3	(0.3)	10.5	(0.3)
Norway	11.1	(0.3)	15.6	(0.4)	3.0	(0.2)	7.0	(0.3)
Poland	12.6	(0.2)	16.9	(0.2)	3.1	(0.3)	4.3	(0.3)
Singapore	6.4	(0.1)	10.5	(0.2)	1.3	(0.1)	1.6	(0.1)
Sub-national entities								
Abu Dhabi (United Arab Emirates)	5.7	(0.2)	14.8	(0.2)	1.6	(0.1)	1.8	(0.1)
Average	9.4	(0.1)	15.4	(0.1)	2.4	(0.1)	4.8	(0.1)

Source: OECD, TALIS 2013 Database.
StatLink http://dx.doi.org/10.1787/888933042618

[Part 1/1]
Employment status of teachers, full time or part time
Percentage of lower secondary education teachers who are employed full time and part time
Table 2.7   *(taking into account all their current teaching jobs) and the reasons for part-time employment[1]*

	Full time (more than 90% of full-time hours)		Part time (71% to 90% of full-time hours)		Part time (50% to 70% of full-time hours)		Part time (less than 50% of full-time hours)		Reason stated for working part time			
									Teacher chose to work part time		There was no possibility to work full time	
	%	S.E.	%	S.E.	%	S.E.	%	S.E.	%	S.E.	%	S.E.
Australia	84.3	(1.2)	7.9	(0.5)	5.3	(0.6)	2.5	(0.5)	89.9	(1.5)	10.1	(1.5)
Brazil	40.3	(1.2)	15.9	(0.6)	30.5	(0.9)	13.3	(0.6)	50.9	(1.4)	49.1	(1.4)
Bulgaria	92.8	(0.7)	3.3	(0.5)	3.0	(0.4)	0.9	(0.3)	24.8	(4.1)	75.2	(4.1)
Chile	68.5	(1.6)	18.2	(1.3)	9.2	(0.8)	4.1	(0.6)	35.8	(2.5)	64.2	(2.5)
Croatia	87.3	(0.7)	4.4	(0.4)	4.6	(0.4)	3.7	(0.4)	11.2	(1.5)	88.8	(1.5)
Cyprus*	95.0	(0.6)	2.5	(0.4)	1.1	(0.3)	1.4	(0.3)	12.2	(3.2)	87.8	(3.2)
Czech Republic	81.1	(0.9)	6.8	(0.6)	6.3	(0.5)	5.9	(0.5)	60.6	(2.4)	39.4	(2.4)
Denmark	89.6	(1.0)	7.6	(0.8)	1.6	(0.3)	1.2	(0.3)	86.3	(2.5)	13.7	(2.5)
Estonia	65.4	(1.5)	12.5	(0.8)	11.8	(0.7)	10.4	(0.7)	35.0	(1.8)	65.0	(1.8)
Finland	94.2	(0.6)	2.7	(0.3)	1.9	(0.3)	1.2	(0.3)	55.2	(4.1)	44.8	(4.1)
France	84.8	(0.9)	10.3	(0.7)	4.5	(0.5)	0.4	(0.1)	85.7	(2.2)	14.3	(2.2)
Iceland	83.6	(0.8)	7.8	(0.6)	5.5	(0.6)	3.1	(0.4)	74.7	(3.0)	25.3	(3.0)
Israel	73.3	(1.5)	11.5	(1.3)	9.0	(0.5)	6.2	(0.7)	53.4	(2.5)	46.6	(2.5)
Italy	89.1	(0.7)	3.3	(0.4)	5.2	(0.5)	2.5	(0.3)	49.0	(3.2)	51.0	(3.2)
Japan	96.2	(0.6)	1.3	(0.3)	1.2	(0.2)	1.3	(0.3)	67.2	(5.3)	32.8	(5.3)
Korea	99.3	(0.2)	0.2	(0.1)	0.4	(0.1)	0.1	(0.1)	63.7	(13.4)	36.3	(13.4)
Latvia	82.4	(0.9)	6.5	(0.4)	6.1	(0.6)	5.1	(0.6)	27.8	(2.9)	72.2	(2.9)
Malaysia	97.3	(0.4)	1.9	(0.4)	0.7	(0.2)	0.1	(0.0)	52.2	(6.3)	47.8	(6.3)
Mexico	40.4	(1.6)	14.5	(0.7)	21.1	(1.0)	24.0	(1.1)	19.4	(1.6)	80.6	(1.6)
Netherlands	43.4	(1.8)	28.6	(1.5)	18.5	(1.2)	9.5	(1.4)	87.0	(1.7)	13.0	(1.7)
Norway	79.9	(1.4)	11.2	(1.0)	7.0	(0.4)	1.9	(0.3)	84.8	(2.3)	15.2	(2.3)
Poland	81.0	(1.3)	4.5	(0.4)	8.7	(0.7)	5.7	(0.9)	23.4	(2.8)	76.6	(2.8)
Portugal	94.5	(0.5)	2.4	(0.3)	1.3	(0.2)	1.8	(0.3)	7.4	(1.7)	92.6	(1.7)
Romania	91.6	(0.8)	2.0	(0.4)	3.3	(0.4)	3.1	(0.6)	23.8	(3.8)	76.2	(3.8)
Serbia	81.3	(1.0)	8.7	(0.6)	5.1	(0.5)	4.9	(0.4)	3.8	(0.8)	96.2	(0.8)
Singapore	96.5	(0.3)	1.9	(0.2)	1.6	(0.2)	0.1	(0.1)	93.7	(2.1)	6.3	(2.1)
Slovak Republic	88.3	(0.7)	3.1	(0.4)	2.9	(0.3)	5.7	(0.5)	45.0	(2.8)	55.0	(2.8)
Spain	89.2	(0.9)	3.3	(0.4)	4.5	(0.5)	3.0	(0.4)	28.3	(2.9)	71.7	(2.9)
Sweden	78.3	(1.0)	14.4	(0.8)	5.7	(0.4)	1.6	(0.3)	78.9	(2.0)	21.1	(2.0)
Sub-national entities												
Abu Dhabi (United Arab Emirates)	98.7	(0.3)	0.9	(0.2)	0.3	(0.2)	0.1	(0.0)	60.5	(9.8)	39.5	(9.8)
Alberta (Canada)	91.1	(1.1)	3.4	(0.6)	4.2	(0.5)	1.3	(0.3)	66.2	(4.3)	33.8	(4.3)
England (United Kingdom)	86.4	(0.9)	5.2	(0.5)	6.7	(0.6)	1.7	(0.3)	89.7	(2.8)	10.3	(2.8)
Flanders (Belgium)	74.7	(1.1)	12.1	(0.7)	11.0	(0.8)	2.3	(0.4)	75.4	(1.7)	24.6	(1.7)
Average	82.4	(0.2)	7.3	(0.1)	6.4	(0.1)	3.9	(0.1)	52.2	(0.7)	47.8	(0.7)
United States	96.3	(0.9)	1.1	(0.2)	1.9	(0.6)	0.6	(0.3)	64.9	(10.0)	35.1	(10.0)

1. Cells with data representing less than 5% of the cases are shaded in grey and should be interpreted with caution. These results are not highlighted in the text of the report.
* See notes at the beginning of this Annex.
Source: OECD, TALIS 2013 Database.
StatLink http://dx.doi.org/10.1787/888933042656

[Part 1/1]

Employment status of teachers, full time or part time, 2008 and 2013

Percentage of lower secondary education teachers who are employed full time and part time

Table 2.7.c *(taking into account all their current teaching jobs)[1, 2]*

	Full time[3]				Part time (50% to 90% of full-time hours)				Part time (less than 50% of full-time hours)			
	2008		2013		2008		2013		2008		2013	
	%	S.E.	%	S.E.	%	S.E.	%	S.E.	%	S.E.	%	S.E.
Australia	86.9	(1.0)	84.3	(1.2)	11.0	(0.9)	13.2	(1.0)	2.1	(0.4)	2.5	(0.5)
Brazil	51.6	(1.5)	40.2	(1.2)	37.5	(1.5)	46.5	(1.1)	10.9	(0.7)	13.3	(0.6)
Bulgaria	95.0	(0.8)	92.8	(0.7)	4.2	(0.8)	6.3	(0.7)	0.8	(0.2)	0.9	(0.3)
Denmark	91.2	(0.9)	89.7	(0.9)	7.5	(0.9)	9.3	(0.8)	1.3	(0.3)	1.0	(0.3)
Estonia	71.8	(1.2)	65.4	(1.5)	20.7	(1.1)	24.4	(1.2)	7.5	(0.5)	10.2	(0.7)
Iceland	81.1	(1.0)	83.7	(0.8)	14.8	(0.9)	13.2	(0.8)	4.1	(0.5)	3.1	(0.4)
Italy	89.3	(0.8)	89.1	(0.7)	10.7	(0.8)	8.4	(0.7)	0.0	(0.0)	2.5	(0.3)
Korea	98.8	(0.2)	99.3	(0.2)	1.2	(0.2)	0.6	(0.2)	0.0	(0.0)	0.1	(0.1)
Malaysia	98.7	(0.2)	97.3	(0.4)	1.0	(0.2)	2.6	(0.4)	0.3	(0.1)	0.1	(0.0)
Mexico	35.0	(1.6)	40.4	(1.6)	37.6	(1.2)	35.5	(1.1)	27.4	(1.4)	24.1	(1.1)
Norway	81.7	(0.9)	79.9	(1.4)	17.0	(0.9)	18.1	(1.2)	1.3	(0.3)	1.9	(0.3)
Poland	80.4	(1.6)	81.0	(1.3)	14.2	(1.0)	13.3	(0.8)	5.4	(0.7)	5.7	(0.9)
Portugal	91.2	(0.7)	94.5	(0.5)	5.9	(0.5)	3.7	(0.4)	2.9	(0.4)	1.8	(0.3)
Slovak Republic	90.4	(0.7)	88.4	(0.7)	6.0	(0.6)	6.0	(0.5)	3.6	(0.4)	5.7	(0.5)
Spain	89.0	(0.9)	89.1	(0.9)	9.0	(0.8)	7.8	(0.6)	2.0	(0.3)	3.0	(0.4)
Sub-national entities												
Flanders (Belgium)	77.6	(1.2)	74.8	(1.1)	20.8	(1.1)	23.1	(0.9)	1.6	(0.3)	2.2	(0.4)
Average	81.9	(0.3)	80.6	(0.3)	13.7	(0.2)	14.5	(0.2)	4.5	(0.1)	4.9	(0.1)

1. The teacher population coverage was slightly different between 2008 and 2013. In order to have comparable populations for the tables comparing results from TALIS 2008 and TALIS 2013, teachers who teach exclusively to students with special needs were excluded from the 2013 data in these tables.

2. The wording and order of questions may have changed slightly between the 2008 and 2013 surveys.

3. Full-time employment is defined here as more than 90% of full-time hours.

Source: OECD, TALIS 2008 and TALIS 2013 Databases.

StatLink ⏩ http://dx.doi.org/10.1787/888933042675

[Part 1/1]
Employment contract status of teacher
Table 2.8 *Percentage of lower secondary education teachers with the following employment characteristics*

	Permanently employed		Fixed-term contract: More than 1 school year		Fixed-term contract: 1 school year or less	
	%	S.E.	%	S.E.	%	S.E.
Australia	87.4	(1.1)	3.8	(0.5)	8.9	(0.9)
Brazil	76.5	(0.9)	7.8	(0.5)	15.7	(0.8)
Bulgaria	87.1	(1.1)	4.5	(0.5)	8.4	(0.8)
Chile	62.9	(1.7)	18.6	(1.4)	18.5	(1.4)
Croatia	92.5	(0.6)	3.5	(0.4)	4.0	(0.4)
Cyprus*	73.1	(1.0)	6.8	(0.5)	20.1	(1.0)
Czech Republic	82.3	(0.9)	5.2	(0.5)	12.5	(0.8)
Denmark	95.7	(0.6)	1.0	(0.3)	3.3	(0.6)
Estonia	84.5	(0.8)	6.0	(0.6)	9.5	(0.6)
Finland	76.9	(1.1)	3.9	(0.4)	19.2	(0.9)
France	95.8	(0.5)	0.4	(0.1)	3.8	(0.4)
Iceland	85.1	(0.9)	5.1	(0.6)	9.8	(0.7)
Israel	78.6	(1.4)	4.7	(0.5)	16.7	(1.3)
Italy	81.5	(0.9)	a	a	18.5	(0.9)
Japan	80.1	(0.9)	6.3	(0.5)	13.6	(0.7)
Korea	82.6	(0.9)	12.0	(0.8)	5.4	(0.5)
Latvia	93.1	(0.6)	4.1	(0.4)	2.8	(0.5)
Malaysia	99.8	(0.1)	0.1	(0.1)	0.0	(0.0)
Mexico	76.2	(1.1)	12.5	(0.7)	11.2	(1.0)
Netherlands	84.0	(1.0)	2.5	(0.5)	13.5	(1.0)
Norway	87.1	(1.0)	3.3	(0.5)	9.6	(0.8)
Poland	84.5	(1.6)	2.3	(0.4)	13.2	(1.6)
Portugal	75.7	(1.0)	9.1	(0.5)	15.2	(0.9)
Romania	69.5	(1.3)	5.6	(0.5)	25.0	(1.3)
Serbia	82.1	(1.0)	4.4	(0.4)	13.5	(0.9)
Singapore	90.1	(0.5)	7.1	(0.5)	2.8	(0.3)
Slovak Republic	80.9	(1.1)	4.6	(0.5)	14.5	(0.9)
Spain	81.5	(1.0)	2.7	(0.3)	15.8	(1.0)
Sweden	89.1	(0.7)	1.8	(0.3)	9.1	(0.6)
Sub-national entities						
Abu Dhabi (United Arab Emirates)	50.0	(2.7)	26.0	(1.9)	23.9	(2.2)
Alberta (Canada)	80.2	(1.3)	3.1	(0.4)	16.7	(1.2)
England (United Kingdom)	93.6	(0.5)	1.7	(0.3)	4.6	(0.5)
Flanders (Belgium)	83.2	(1.0)	4.2	(0.5)	12.6	(0.7)
Average[1]	82.5	(0.2)	5.8	(0.1)	11.9	(0.2)
United States	67.1	(2.6)	8.2	(1.5)	24.7	(2.3)

1. The averages do not add up to 100 across categories because of the presence of cells that are not applicable "a" in some countries.
*See notes at the beginning of this Annex.
Source: OECD, TALIS 2013 Database.
StatLink ᴍᴤ http://dx.doi.org/10.1787/888933042694

[Part 1/1]
Employment contract status of teachers, 2008 and 2013
Table 2.8.c *Percentage of lower secondary education teachers with the following employment characteristics[1, 2]*

	Permanently employed				Fixed-term contract: More than 1 school year				Fixed-term contract: 1 school year or less			
	2008		2013		2008		2013		2008		2013	
	%	S.E.	%	S.E.	%	S.E.	%	S.E.	%	S.E.	%	S.E.
Australia	86.8	(1.0)	87.3	(1.1)	4.3	(0.7)	3.8	(0.5)	8.9	(0.7)	8.9	(0.9)
Brazil	74.2	(1.5)	76.4	(0.9)	7.1	(0.8)	7.8	(0.5)	18.7	(1.4)	15.7	(0.8)
Bulgaria	84.6	(1.2)	87.1	(1.1)	4.4	(0.7)	4.5	(0.5)	11.0	(1.1)	8.4	(0.8)
Denmark	96.6	(0.6)	96.0	(0.5)	0.3	(0.1)	1.0	(0.3)	3.1	(0.6)	3.0	(0.5)
Estonia	84.2	(1.1)	84.8	(0.8)	5.0	(0.5)	5.9	(0.5)	10.8	(0.9)	9.3	(0.6)
Iceland	74.6	(1.1)	85.2	(1.0)	6.2	(0.7)	5.1	(0.6)	19.2	(1.0)	9.6	(0.8)
Italy	80.6	(0.8)	81.5	(0.9)	a	a	a	a	19.4	(0.8)	18.5	(0.9)
Korea	95.6	(0.4)	82.6	(0.9)	4.2	(0.4)	12.0	(0.8)	0.2	(0.1)	5.4	(0.5)
Malaysia	97.8	(0.3)	99.8	(0.1)	1.9	(0.3)	0.1	(0.1)	0.4	(0.2)	0.0	(0.0)
Mexico	86.8	(1.9)	76.3	(1.1)	5.0	(0.6)	12.5	(0.7)	8.2	(1.7)	11.2	(1.0)
Norway	89.9	(0.9)	87.0	(1.0)	1.8	(0.3)	3.3	(0.5)	8.3	(0.8)	9.7	(0.8)
Poland	77.1	(1.1)	84.5	(1.6)	5.1	(0.7)	2.3	(0.4)	17.8	(0.9)	13.2	(1.6)
Portugal	67.6	(1.4)	75.8	(1.0)	15.0	(0.9)	9.1	(0.5)	17.4	(1.0)	15.1	(0.9)
Slovak Republic	82.1	(1.1)	80.9	(1.1)	3.8	(0.5)	4.6	(0.5)	14.1	(1.0)	14.5	(0.9)
Spain	75.6	(1.1)	81.7	(1.0)	6.5	(0.4)	2.5	(0.3)	17.9	(1.0)	15.8	(1.0)
Sub-national entities												
Flanders (Belgium)	80.7	(0.9)	83.2	(1.0)	4.8	(0.4)	4.1	(0.5)	14.6	(0.8)	12.6	(0.7)
Average[3]	83.4	(0.3)	84.4	(0.2)	5.0	(0.1)	5.3	(0.1)	11.9	(0.2)	10.7	(0.2)

1. The teacher population coverage was slightly different between 2008 and 2013. In order to have comparable populations for the tables comparing results from TALIS 2008 and TALIS 2013, teachers who teach exclusively to students with special needs were excluded from the 2013 data in these tables.
2. The wording and order of questions may have changed slightly between the 2008 and 2013 surveys.
3. The averages do not add up to 100 across categories because of the presence of cells that are not applicable "a" in some countries.
Source: OECD, TALIS 2008 and TALIS 2013 Databases.
StatLink http://dx.doi.org/10.1787/888933042713

[Part 1/1]

Teachers working in schools with high or low percentage of students with different first language

Percentage of lower secondary education teachers with the following characteristics whose principals report that more than 10% or 10% or less of the students have a first language that is different from the language of instruction[1,2]

Table 2.9

| | Teachers working in schools with more than 10% of students whose first language is different from the language of instruction[3] | | Teachers with 5 years teaching experience or less | | | | Teachers with more than 5 years teaching experience | | | | Teachers with a highest level of education of ISCED 5B or below[4,5] | | | | Teachers with a highest level of education of ISCED 5A or above[4] | | | |
| | | | Working in schools with more than 10% of students whose first language is different from the language of instruction | | Working in schools with 10% or less of students whose first language is different from the language of instruction | | Working in schools with more than 10% of students whose first language is different from the language of instruction | | Working in schools with 10% or less of students whose first language is different from the language of instruction | | Working in schools with more than 10% of students whose first language is different from the language of instruction | | Working in schools with 10% or less of students whose first language is different from the language of instruction | | Working in schools with more than 10% of students whose first language is different from the language of instruction | | Working in schools with 10% or less of students whose first language is different from the language of instruction | |
	%	S.E.	%	S.E.	%	S.E.	%	S.E.	%	S.E.	%	S.E.	%	S.E.	%	S.E.	%	S.E.
Australia	32.8	(5.0)	19.8	(2.0)	18.9	(1.5)	80.2	(2.0)	81.1	(1.5)	0.3	(0.2)	0.1	(0.1)	99.7	(0.2)	99.9	(0.1)
Brazil	2.1	(1.0)	17.4	(4.9)	20.9	(1.0)	82.6	(4.9)	79.1	(1.0)	8.2	(5.3)	6.0	(0.6)	91.8	(5.3)	94.0	(0.6)
Bulgaria	32.6	(2.8)	7.1	(1.3)	8.1	(1.0)	92.9	(1.3)	91.9	(1.0)	14.9	(1.9)	6.4	(0.9)	85.1	(1.9)	93.6	(0.9)
Chile	3.9	(1.7)	31.4	(7.9)	30.9	(1.9)	68.6	(7.9)	69.1	(1.9)	29.4	(3.4)	17.2	(1.5)	70.6	(3.4)	82.8	(1.5)
Croatia	5.6	(1.8)	29.3	(6.3)	23.1	(0.9)	70.7	(6.3)	76.9	(0.9)	12.6	(3.2)	17.8	(0.7)	87.4	(3.2)	82.2	(0.7)
Cyprus*	33.2	(0.2)	17.5	(1.7)	13.3	(1.1)	82.5	(1.7)	86.7	(1.1)	1.3	(0.4)	0.4	(0.2)	98.7	(0.4)	99.6	(0.2)
Czech Republic	3.6	(1.4)	17.8	(4.5)	15.5	(0.8)	82.2	(4.5)	84.5	(0.8)	8.9	(3.8)	6.2	(0.5)	91.1	(3.8)	93.8	(0.5)
Denmark	26.2	(5.1)	12.8	(2.5)	19.3	(1.6)	87.2	(2.5)	80.7	(1.6)	0.6	(0.4)	3.4	(0.8)	99.4	(0.4)	96.6	(0.8)
Estonia	9.7	(2.0)	10.8	(2.2)	10.6	(0.7)	89.2	(2.2)	89.4	(0.7)	14.0	(2.7)	10.8	(0.7)	86.0	(2.7)	89.2	(0.7)
Finland	9.2	(2.4)	21.7	(2.8)	18.6	(0.9)	78.3	(2.8)	81.4	(0.9)	3.6	(0.9)	4.1	(0.5)	96.4	(0.9)	95.9	(0.5)
France	17.8	(2.7)	13.7	(2.3)	11.0	(0.9)	86.3	(2.3)	89.0	(0.9)	3.9	(1.1)	4.6	(0.5)	96.1	(1.1)	95.4	(0.5)
Iceland	20.9	(0.1)	23.6	(3.4)	18.6	(1.5)	76.4	(3.4)	81.4	(1.5)	18.5	(2.8)	14.0	(1.1)	81.5	(2.8)	86.0	(1.1)
Israel	24.9	(4.1)	21.4	(2.8)	21.6	(1.5)	78.6	(2.8)	78.4	(1.5)	2.8	(0.7)	2.1	(0.4)	97.2	(0.7)	97.9	(0.4)
Italy	31.7	(3.1)	9.5	(1.1)	8.2	(0.7)	90.5	(1.1)	91.8	(0.7)	16.2	(0.9)	20.8	(0.8)	83.8	(0.9)	79.2	(0.8)
Japan	2.1	(1.0)	30.4	(3.2)	20.0	(0.8)	69.6	(3.2)	80.0	(0.8)	2.7	(1.5)	3.6	(0.4)	97.3	(1.5)	96.4	(0.4)
Korea	0.0	(0.0)	0.0	(0.0)	20.8	(1.1)	0.0	(0.0)	79.2	(1.1)	0.0	(0.0)	0.2	(0.1)	0.0	(0.0)	99.8	(0.1)
Latvia	20.9	(3.9)	7.6	(1.8)	6.8	(0.8)	92.4	(1.8)	93.2	(0.8)	1.2	(0.5)	3.3	(0.5)	98.8	(0.5)	96.7	(0.5)
Malaysia	55.5	(3.7)	26.2	(1.4)	18.2	(1.8)	73.8	(1.4)	81.8	(1.8)	10.2	(1.1)	6.3	(0.9)	89.8	(1.1)	93.7	(0.9)
Mexico	2.5	(1.3)	15.5	(3.1)	18.9	(0.9)	84.5	(3.1)	81.1	(0.9)	4.1	(1.9)	10.3	(0.7)	95.9	(1.9)	89.7	(0.7)
Netherlands	14.3	(4.5)	23.7	(2.6)	21.1	(1.9)	76.3	(2.6)	78.9	(1.9)	4.9	(1.1)	4.8	(1.0)	95.1	(1.1)	95.2	(1.0)
Norway	21.8	(4.4)	29.2	(3.8)	23.9	(2.1)	70.8	(3.8)	76.1	(2.1)	1.2	(0.5)	2.3	(0.7)	98.8	(0.5)	97.7	(0.7)
Poland	0.3	(0.3)	0.0	(0.0)	10.4	(0.9)	100.0	(0.0)	89.6	(0.9)	0.0	(0.0)	0.1	(0.0)	100.0	(0.0)	99.9	(0.0)
Portugal	2.7	(1.1)	2.0	(1.4)	2.9	(0.3)	98.0	(1.4)	97.1	(0.3)	4.8	(1.2)	2.7	(0.3)	95.2	(1.2)	97.3	(0.3)
Romania	9.8	(2.2)	23.6	(2.0)	16.8	(1.1)	76.4	(2.0)	83.2	(1.1)	9.1	(3.3)	6.3	(0.6)	90.9	(3.3)	93.7	(0.6)
Serbia	9.3	(2.0)	24.2	(2.4)	18.6	(1.0)	75.8	(2.4)	81.4	(1.0)	16.7	(3.1)	17.2	(0.9)	83.3	(3.1)	82.8	(0.9)
Singapore	89.2	(0.1)	43.7	(1.0)	37.5	(2.6)	56.3	(1.0)	62.5	(2.6)	6.7	(0.5)	9.7	(1.6)	93.3	(0.5)	90.3	(1.6)
Slovak Republic	10.5	(2.3)	17.1	(2.4)	17.4	(0.8)	82.9	(2.4)	82.6	(0.8)	4.1	(1.4)	1.5	(0.4)	95.9	(1.4)	98.5	(0.4)
Spain	30.0	(3.1)	8.2	(1.3)	8.6	(0.9)	91.8	(1.3)	91.4	(0.9)	4.9	(0.7)	4.2	(0.4)	95.1	(0.7)	95.8	(0.4)
Sweden	41.9	(4.1)	14.2	(1.6)	10.7	(0.9)	85.8	(1.6)	89.3	(0.9)	12.5	(1.2)	11.0	(0.9)	87.5	(1.2)	89.0	(0.9)
Sub-national entities																		
Abu Dhabi (United Arab Emirates)	43.6	(4.3)	25.5	(2.3)	12.7	(1.3)	74.5	(2.3)	87.3	(1.3)	8.2	(2.1)	5.1	(0.8)	91.8	(2.1)	94.9	(0.8)
Alberta (Canada)	41.1	(5.0)	24.3	(1.7)	26.0	(1.8)	75.7	(1.7)	74.0	(1.8)	0.5	(0.2)	1.4	(0.5)	99.5	(0.2)	98.6	(0.5)
England (United Kingdom)	27.6	(4.3)	33.1	(1.9)	24.0	(0.9)	66.9	(1.9)	76.0	(0.9)	2.8	(0.7)	3.3	(0.5)	97.2	(0.7)	96.7	(0.5)
Flanders (Belgium)	26.9	(3.6)	26.6	(1.7)	18.3	(1.0)	73.4	(1.7)	81.7	(1.0)	82.9	(1.9)	90.1	(0.7)	17.1	(1.9)	9.9	(0.7)
Average	21.3	(0.5)	19.1	(0.5)	17.3	(0.2)	77.9	(0.5)	82.7	(0.2)	9.5	(0.3)	9.0	(0.1)	87.5	(0.3)	91.0	(0.1)
United States	21.7	(4.0)	24.7	(3.2)	21.3	(1.9)	75.3	(3.2)	78.7	(1.9)	0.0	(0.0)	0.6	(0.3)	100.0	(0.0)	99.4	(0.3)

1. The first column presents the global proportion of teachers working in schools with more than 10% of students whose first language is different from the language of instruction. For example, in Australia, 32.8% of teachers work in schools with more than 10% of students whose first language is different from the language of instruction. The other columns look at the distribution of teachers across schools with more than 10% or 10% or less of students whose first language is different from the language of instruction (more or less challenging schools). Of particular interest is the comparison in the proportions of highly experienced (or educated) teachers in more or less challenging schools. The table is formatted in such a way as to facilitate making this comparison. In Australia, for example, among teachers working in more challenging schools, 80.2% have more than five years teaching experience. In comparison, among teachers working in less challenging schools, 81.1% have more than five years of teaching experience. There is, therefore, not a large difference in the proportion of highly experienced teachers between more and less challenging schools in Australia. Columns with similar shading within the teacher experience and teacher education variables add up to 100%.

2. Cells with data representing less than 5% of the cases are shaded in grey and should be interpreted with caution. These results are not highlighted in the text of the report.

3. These data are broad estimates reported by principals.

4. Education categories are based on the International Standard Classification of Education (ISCED 1997). ISCED level 5A programmes are generally longer and more theory-based, while 5B programmes are typically shorter and more practical and skills oriented. No distinction was made between ISCED level 5A (Bachelor) and ISCED level 5A (Master).

5. Includes Bachelor's degrees in some countries.

*See notes at the beginning of this Annex.

Source: OECD, TALIS 2013 Database.

StatLink ⟐ http://dx.doi.org/10.1787/888933042732

[Part 1/1]

Teachers working in schools with high or low percentage of students with special needs

Percentage of lower secondary education teachers with the following characteristics whose principals report that more than 10% or 10% or less of the students have special needs[1,2]

Table 2.10

| | Teachers working in schools with more than 10% of students with special needs[3,4] | | Teachers with 5 years teaching experience or less | | | | Teachers with more than 5 years teaching experience | | | | Teachers with a highest level of education of ISCED 5B or below[5,6] | | | | Teachers with a highest level of education of ISCED 5A or above[5] | | | |
| | | | Working in schools with more than 10% of students with special needs[4] | | Working in schools with 10% or less of students with special needs[4] | | Working in schools with more than 10% of students with special needs[4] | | Working in schools with 10% or less of students with special needs[4] | | Working in schools with more than 10% of students with special needs[4] | | Working in schools with 10% or less of students with special needs[4] | | Working in schools with more than 10% of students with special needs[4] | | Working in schools with 10% or less of students with special needs[4] | |
	%	S.E.	%	S.E.	%	S.E.	%	S.E.	%	S.E.	%	S.E.	%	S.E.	%	S.E.	%	S.E.
Australia	23.6	(4.5)	20.2	(2.2)	18.9	(1.5)	79.8	(2.2)	81.1	(1.5)	0.2	(0.2)	0.1	(0.1)	99.8	(0.2)	99.9	(0.1)
Brazil	4.9	(1.1)	14.0	(2.0)	21.3	(1.0)	86.0	(2.0)	78.7	(1.0)	2.7	(0.9)	6.2	(0.6)	97.3	(0.9)	93.8	(0.6)
Bulgaria	1.5	(0.8)	14.6	(3.1)	7.7	(1.0)	85.4	(3.1)	92.3	(0.8)	27.0	(9.8)	8.8	(0.8)	73.0	(9.8)	91.2	(0.8)
Chile	27.5	(3.6)	27.7	(3.3)	31.7	(2.3)	72.3	(3.3)	68.3	(2.3)	22.6	(2.5)	16.1	(1.7)	77.4	(2.5)	83.9	(1.7)
Croatia	9.4	(2.0)	20.7	(2.5)	23.6	(1.0)	79.3	(2.5)	76.4	(1.0)	20.0	(2.3)	17.3	(0.8)	80.0	(2.3)	82.7	(0.8)
Cyprus*	12.1	(0.2)	15.0	(2.7)	15.0	(1.0)	85.0	(2.7)	85.0	(1.0)	1.4	(0.5)	0.6	(0.2)	98.6	(0.5)	99.4	(0.2)
Czech Republic	21.4	(2.4)	19.5	(1.8)	14.6	(0.9)	80.5	(1.8)	85.4	(0.9)	9.7	(1.5)	5.4	(0.6)	90.3	(1.5)	94.6	(0.6)
Denmark	32.4	(5.7)	13.3	(2.2)	19.6	(1.7)	86.7	(2.2)	80.4	(1.7)	3.0	(1.5)	2.5	(0.5)	97.0	(1.5)	97.5	(0.5)
Estonia	28.8	(3.9)	12.7	(1.6)	9.7	(0.7)	87.3	(1.6)	90.3	(0.7)	12.9	(1.5)	10.4	(0.9)	87.1	(1.5)	89.6	(0.9)
Finland	26.8	(3.6)	20.9	(1.5)	18.1	(1.0)	79.1	(1.5)	81.9	(1.0)	4.7	(0.8)	3.8	(0.5)	95.3	(0.8)	96.2	(0.5)
France	38.5	(3.8)	12.6	(1.3)	10.8	(1.0)	87.4	(1.3)	89.2	(1.0)	4.7	(0.7)	4.3	(0.6)	95.3	(0.7)	95.7	(0.6)
Iceland	59.5	(0.2)	21.8	(1.7)	16.6	(1.8)	78.2	(1.7)	83.4	(1.8)	16.4	(1.4)	13.0	(1.5)	83.6	(1.4)	87.0	(1.5)
Israel	41.0	(4.3)	19.4	(2.1)	23.2	(1.8)	80.6	(2.1)	76.8	(1.8)	2.1	(0.6)	2.4	(0.4)	97.9	(0.6)	97.6	(0.4)
Italy	28.5	(3.5)	7.9	(1.0)	8.8	(0.7)	92.1	(1.0)	91.2	(0.7)	19.7	(1.1)	19.3	(0.8)	80.3	(1.1)	80.7	(0.8)
Japan	9.2	(2.0)	25.8	(2.8)	19.7	(0.8)	74.2	(2.8)	80.3	(0.8)	1.8	(0.7)	3.8	(0.4)	98.2	(0.7)	96.2	(0.4)
Korea	8.1	(2.3)	22.1	(3.3)	20.7	(1.2)	77.9	(3.3)	79.3	(1.2)	0.7	(0.6)	0.2	(0.1)	99.3	(0.6)	99.8	(0.1)
Latvia	8.4	(2.6)	10.0	(3.7)	6.7	(0.8)	90.0	(3.7)	93.3	(0.8)	4.0	(1.7)	2.7	(0.4)	96.0	(1.7)	97.3	(0.4)
Malaysia	4.1	(1.5)	12.3	(3.8)	23.1	(1.2)	87.7	(3.8)	76.9	(1.2)	8.9	(3.2)	8.4	(0.8)	91.1	(3.2)	91.6	(0.8)
Mexico	7.3	(2.0)	23.2	(5.1)	18.5	(0.9)	76.8	(5.1)	81.5	(0.9)	11.9	(2.7)	10.0	(0.7)	88.1	(2.7)	90.0	(0.7)
Netherlands	45.6	(4.6)	22.7	(2.6)	20.4	(2.1)	77.3	(2.6)	79.6	(2.1)	6.7	(1.6)	3.2	(0.6)	93.3	(1.6)	96.8	(0.6)
Norway	50.0	(5.3)	27.2	(2.8)	23.0	(2.2)	72.8	(2.8)	77.0	(2.2)	1.9	(0.9)	2.2	(0.5)	98.1	(0.9)	97.8	(0.5)
Poland	57.9	(4.5)	13.6	(1.3)	6.1	(0.8)	86.4	(1.3)	93.9	(0.8)	0.1	(0.1)	0.0	(0.0)	99.9	(0.1)	100.0	(0.0)
Portugal	14.2	(2.7)	2.1	(0.7)	3.0	(0.3)	97.9	(0.7)	97.0	(0.3)	3.1	(0.8)	2.6	(0.3)	96.9	(0.8)	97.4	(0.3)
Romania	3.5	(1.6)	26.4	(5.6)	17.0	(1.0)	73.6	(5.6)	83.0	(1.0)	6.4	(2.7)	6.6	(0.7)	93.6	(2.7)	93.4	(0.7)
Serbia	5.5	(1.5)	18.4	(3.1)	18.7	(1.0)	81.6	(3.1)	81.3	(1.0)	22.5	(3.9)	16.8	(0.9)	77.5	(3.9)	83.2	(0.9)
Singapore	1.3	(0.0)	42.9	(9.0)	43.0	(0.9)	57.1	(9.0)	57.0	(0.9)	7.9	(4.5)	7.0	(0.5)	92.1	(4.5)	93.0	(0.5)
Slovak Republic	15.9	(3.0)	20.4	(2.8)	16.7	(0.9)	79.6	(2.8)	83.3	(0.9)	3.7	(1.4)	1.4	(0.3)	96.3	(1.4)	98.6	(0.3)
Spain	16.4	(3.1)	9.4	(3.1)	8.3	(0.7)	90.6	(3.1)	91.7	(0.7)	3.9	(0.8)	4.5	(0.4)	96.1	(0.8)	95.5	(0.4)
Sweden	63.0	(3.8)	11.7	(1.0)	13.5	(1.6)	88.3	(1.0)	86.5	(1.6)	12.3	(0.9)	10.4	(0.9)	87.7	(0.9)	89.6	(0.9)
Sub-national entities																		
Abu Dhabi (United Arab Emirates)	4.7	(2.0)	24.8	(6.9)	17.9	(1.4)	75.2	(6.9)	82.1	(1.4)	14.7	(2.3)	6.0	(1.1)	85.3	(2.3)	94.0	(1.1)
Alberta (Canada)	51.0	(4.6)	24.7	(1.6)	25.9	(2.1)	75.3	(1.6)	74.1	(2.1)	1.2	(0.6)	0.9	(0.3)	98.8	(0.6)	99.1	(0.3)
England (United Kingdom)	66.5	(4.0)	27.4	(1.4)	24.6	(2.3)	72.6	(1.4)	75.4	(2.3)	3.0	(0.5)	3.5	(1.0)	97.0	(0.5)	96.5	(1.0)
Flanders (Belgium)	54.0	(4.6)	22.9	(1.3)	17.8	(1.4)	77.1	(1.3)	82.2	(1.4)	89.0	(1.2)	87.5	(1.0)	11.0	(1.2)	12.5	(1.0)
Average	25.5	(0.6)	19.0	(0.6)	17.7	(0.2)	81.0	(0.6)	82.3	(0.2)	10.6	(0.4)	8.7	(0.1)	89.4	(0.4)	91.3	(0.1)
United States	63.1	(5.8)	21.4	(2.0)	23.1	(2.4)	78.6	(2.0)	76.9	(2.4)	0.4	(0.2)	0.7	(0.6)	99.6	(0.2)	99.3	(0.6)

1. The first column presents the global proportion of teachers working in school with more than 10% of students with special needs. For example, in Australia, 23.6% of teachers work in schools with more than 10% of students with special needs. The other columns look at the distribution of teachers across schools with more than 10% or with 10% or less of students with special needs (more or less challenging schools). Of particular interest is the comparison in the proportions of highly experienced (or educated) teachers in more or less challenging schools. The table is formatted in such a way as to facilitate making this comparison. In Australia, for example, among teachers working in schools with more than 10% of students with special needs, 79.8% have more than five years teaching experience. In comparison, among teachers working in schools with 10% or less of students with special needs, 81.1% have more than five years of teaching experience. There is, therefore, not a large difference in the proportion of highly experienced teachers between more and less challenging schools in Australia. Columns with similar shading within the teacher experience and teacher education variables add up to 100%.

2. Cells with data representing less than 5% of the cases are shaded in grey and should be interpreted with caution. These results are not highlighted in the text of the report.

3. These data are broad estimates reported by principals.

4. Special-needs students are not well defined internationally but usually cover those for whom a special learning need has been formally identified because they are mentally, physically or emotionally disadvantaged. Often, special-needs students will be those for whom additional public or private resources (personnel, material or financial) have been provided to support their education. "Gifted students" are not considered to have special needs under the definition used here and in other OECD work. Some teachers perceive all students as unique learners and thus having some special learning needs. For the purpose of this survey, it is important to assure a more objective judgment of who is a special-needs student and who is not. That is why a formal identification is stressed above.

5. Education categories are based on the International Standard Classification of Education (ISCED 1997). ISCED level 5A programmes are generally longer and more theory-based, while 5B programmes are typically shorter and more practical and skills oriented. No distinction was made between ISCED level 5A (Bachelor) and ISCED level 5A (Master).

6. Includes Bachelor's degrees in some countries.

* See notes at the beginning of this Annex.

Source: OECD, TALIS 2013 Database.

StatLink ⬛⬛⬛ http://dx.doi.org/10.1787/888933042751

[Part 1/1]

Teachers working in schools with high or low percentage of students from disadvantaged homes

Percentage of lower secondary education teachers with the following characteristics whose principals report that more than 30% or 30% or less of the students are from socioeconomically disadvantaged homes[1, 2]

Table 2.11

	Teachers working in schools with more than 30% of students from socio-economically disadvantaged homes[3, 4]		Teachers with 5 years teaching experience or less				Teachers with more than 5 years teaching experience				Teachers with a highest level of education of ISCED 5B or below[5, 6]				Teachers with a highest level of education of ISCED 5A or above[5]			
			Working in schools with more than 30% of students from socio-economically disadvantaged homes[4]		Working in schools with 30% or less of students from socio-economically disadvantaged homes[4]		Working in schools with more than 30% of students from socio-economically disadvantaged homes[4]		Working in schools with 30% or less of students from socio-economically disadvantaged homes[4]		Working in schools with more than 30% of students from socio-economically disadvantaged homes[4]		Working in schools with 30% or less of students from socio-economically disadvantaged homes[4]		Working in schools with more than 30% of students from socio-economically disadvantaged homes[4]		Working in schools with 30% or less of students from socio-economically disadvantaged homes[4]	
	%	S.E.	%	S.E.	%	S.E.	%	S.E.	%	S.E.	%	S.E.	%	S.E.	%	S.E.	%	S.E.
Australia	26.0	(3.8)	21.3	(2.2)	18.5	(1.6)	78.7	(2.2)	81.5	(1.6)	0.4	(0.2)	0.1	(0.1)	99.6	(0.2)	99.9	(0.1)
Brazil	40.4	(2.1)	17.4	(1.2)	23.3	(1.3)	82.6	(1.2)	76.7	(1.3)	6.1	(0.8)	6.1	(0.9)	93.9	(0.8)	93.9	(0.9)
Bulgaria	23.9	(3.1)	8.6	(1.8)	7.6	(0.9)	91.4	(1.8)	92.4	(0.9)	14.2	(2.5)	7.5	(0.8)	85.8	(2.5)	92.5	(0.8)
Chile	54.6	(4.1)	30.1	(2.5)	32.0	(2.8)	69.9	(2.5)	68.0	(2.8)	22.8	(2.0)	11.8	(1.7)	77.2	(2.0)	88.2	(1.7)
Croatia	7.3	(1.9)	20.4	(2.6)	23.6	(1.0)	79.6	(2.6)	76.4	(1.0)	18.5	(2.2)	17.5	(0.8)	81.5	(2.2)	82.5	(0.8)
Cyprus*	7.8	(0.1)	14.6	(3.4)	14.6	(1.0)	85.4	(3.4)	85.4	(1.0)	1.6	(0.5)	0.6	(0.2)	98.4	(0.5)	99.4	(0.2)
Czech Republic	3.9	(1.4)	13.8	(4.8)	15.7	(0.8)	86.2	(4.8)	84.3	(0.8)	13.6	(3.1)	6.0	(0.5)	86.4	(3.1)	94.0	(0.5)
Denmark	2.5	(1.3)	37.6	(8.4)	17.1	(1.4)	62.4	(8.4)	82.9	(1.4)	24.3	(13.0)	2.1	(0.4)	75.7	(13.0)	97.9	(0.4)
Estonia	10.9	(2.2)	14.4	(2.1)	10.1	(0.7)	85.6	(2.1)	89.9	(0.7)	14.2	(2.1)	10.7	(0.8)	85.8	(2.1)	89.3	(0.8)
Finland	3.1	(1.8)	18.3	(3.0)	18.9	(0.9)	81.7	(3.0)	81.1	(0.9)	2.6	(2.0)	4.1	(0.4)	97.4	(2.0)	95.9	(0.4)
France	44.6	(3.7)	11.9	(1.1)	11.1	(1.2)	88.1	(1.1)	88.9	(1.2)	3.8	(0.6)	4.9	(0.6)	96.2	(0.6)	95.1	(0.6)
Iceland	2.4	(0.1)	27.9	(10.0)	19.3	(1.3)	72.1	(10.0)	80.7	(1.3)	12.7	(5.1)	15.2	(1.0)	87.3	(5.1)	84.8	(1.0)
Israel	46.2	(3.7)	24.4	(2.6)	19.4	(1.2)	75.6	(2.6)	80.6	(1.2)	1.9	(0.5)	2.6	(0.5)	98.1	(0.5)	97.4	(0.5)
Italy	9.5	(2.0)	8.8	(2.7)	8.5	(0.6)	91.2	(2.7)	91.5	(0.6)	20.7	(1.6)	19.2	(0.7)	79.3	(1.6)	80.8	(0.7)
Japan	5.8	(1.8)	24.7	(3.1)	20.0	(0.8)	75.3	(3.1)	80.0	(0.8)	1.4	(1.0)	3.7	(0.4)	98.6	(1.0)	96.3	(0.4)
Korea	8.5	(2.3)	17.0	(3.0)	21.1	(1.2)	83.0	(3.0)	78.9	(1.2)	0.0	(0.0)	0.2	(0.1)	100.0	(0.0)	99.8	(0.1)
Latvia	18.3	(4.2)	6.2	(1.5)	7.1	(0.9)	93.8	(1.5)	92.9	(0.9)	3.9	(1.1)	2.6	(0.6)	96.1	(1.1)	97.4	(0.6)
Malaysia	57.9	(4.1)	23.4	(1.7)	21.6	(1.9)	76.6	(1.7)	78.4	(1.9)	9.7	(1.1)	6.7	(1.1)	90.3	(1.1)	93.3	(1.1)
Mexico	44.2	(3.5)	18.4	(1.3)	19.1	(1.4)	81.6	(1.3)	80.9	(1.4)	9.8	(1.0)	10.4	(1.0)	90.2	(1.0)	89.6	(1.0)
Netherlands	11.6	(4.0)	19.1	(2.6)	21.8	(1.7)	80.9	(2.6)	78.2	(1.7)	4.3	(1.4)	4.9	(0.9)	95.7	(1.4)	95.1	(0.9)
Norway	3.9	(1.7)	29.0	(8.3)	24.9	(1.9)	71.0	(8.3)	75.1	(1.9)	0.6	(0.5)	2.1	(0.5)	99.4	(0.5)	97.9	(0.5)
Poland	18.1	(3.4)	11.8	(2.1)	10.1	(1.0)	88.2	(2.1)	89.9	(1.0)	0.0	(0.0)	0.1	(0.1)	100.0	(0.0)	99.9	(0.1)
Portugal	48.5	(4.1)	2.7	(0.8)	3.1	(0.8)	97.3	(0.8)	96.9	(0.8)	3.0	(0.4)	2.7	(0.4)	97.0	(0.4)	97.3	(0.4)
Romania	27.7	(3.7)	21.7	(1.9)	15.8	(1.2)	78.3	(1.9)	84.2	(1.2)	7.0	(1.1)	6.5	(0.8)	93.0	(1.1)	93.5	(0.8)
Serbia	6.8	(2.0)	19.2	(3.8)	18.8	(1.0)	80.8	(3.8)	81.2	(1.0)	17.0	(3.2)	17.0	(0.9)	83.0	(3.2)	83.0	(0.9)
Singapore	6.4	(0.1)	45.6	(4.1)	42.8	(1.0)	54.4	(4.1)	57.2	(1.0)	8.9	(2.1)	7.0	(0.5)	91.1	(2.1)	93.0	(0.5)
Slovak Republic	10.4	(2.2)	18.4	(3.6)	17.2	(0.8)	81.6	(3.6)	82.8	(0.8)	4.9	(2.3)	1.4	(0.3)	95.1	(2.3)	98.6	(0.3)
Spain	13.9	(2.6)	10.4	(3.6)	8.2	(0.7)	89.6	(3.6)	91.8	(0.7)	4.7	(1.1)	4.4	(0.4)	95.3	(1.1)	95.6	(0.4)
Sweden	10.4	(2.4)	19.7	(4.2)	11.5	(0.8)	80.3	(4.2)	88.5	(0.8)	13.9	(2.0)	11.3	(0.7)	86.1	(2.0)	88.7	(0.7)
Sub-national entities																		
Abu Dhabi (United Arab Emirates)	10.8	(2.8)	19.3	(4.5)	18.1	(1.4)	80.7	(4.5)	81.9	(1.4)	6.9	(1.8)	6.4	(1.1)	93.1	(1.8)	93.6	(1.1)
Alberta (Canada)	20.3	(3.9)	30.8	(2.5)	24.2	(1.5)	69.2	(2.5)	75.8	(1.5)	1.0	(0.6)	1.0	(0.4)	99.0	(0.6)	99.0	(0.4)
England (United Kingdom)	24.4	(2.9)	30.1	(2.2)	25.3	(1.1)	69.9	(2.2)	74.7	(1.1)	3.6	(0.9)	3.0	(0.4)	96.4	(0.9)	97.0	(0.4)
Flanders (Belgium)	16.0	(2.9)	28.6	(2.2)	19.0	(0.9)	71.4	(2.2)	81.0	(0.9)	84.8	(3.0)	88.8	(0.7)	15.2	(3.0)	11.2	(0.7)
Average	19.6	(0.5)	20.2	(0.7)	17.9	(0.2)	79.8	(0.7)	82.1	(0.2)	10.4	(0.5)	8.8	(0.1)	89.6	(0.5)	91.2	(0.1)
United States	64.5	(6.2)	21.2	(1.9)	23.6	(3.1)	78.8	(1.9)	76.4	(3.1)	0.2	(0.2)	1.0	(0.6)	99.8	(0.2)	99.0	(0.6)

1. The first column presents the global proportion of teachers working in school with more than 30% of students from socioeconomically disadvantaged homes. For example, in Australia, 26.0% of teachers work in schools with more than 30% of students from socioeconomically disadvantaged homes. The other columns look at the distribution of teachers across schools with more than 30% or with 30% or less of students from socioeconomically disadvantaged homes (more or less challenging schools). Of particular interest is the comparison in the proportions of highly experienced (or educated) teachers in more or less challenging schools. The table is formatted in such a way as to facilitate making this comparison. In Australia, for example, among teachers working in schools with more than 30% of students from socioeconomically disadvantaged homes, 78.7% have more than five years teaching experience. In comparison, among teachers working in schools with 30% or less of students from socioeconomically disadvantaged homes, 81.5% have more than five years of teaching experience. There is, therefore, not a large difference in the proportion of highly experienced teachers between more and less challenging schools in Australia. Columns with similar shading within the teacher experience and teacher education variables add up to 100%.

2. Cells with data representing less than 5% of the cases are shaded in grey and should be interpreted with caution. These results are not highlighted in the text of the report.

3. These data are broad estimates reported by principals.

4. "Socioeconomically disadvantaged homes" refers to homes lacking the basic necessities or advantages of life, such as adequate housing, nutrition or medical care. They are those that receive or are eligible to receive subsidies or other welfare benefits. The type of benefits accorded to disadvantaged homes may vary among the countries. The disadvantaged homes may in some countries correspond to those that are eligible for free school meals, in others to those that get housing allowance, or other social assistance.

5. Education categories are based on the International Standard Classification of Education (ISCED 1997). ISCED level 5A programmes are generally longer and more theory-based, while 5B programmes are typically shorter and more practical and skills oriented. No distinction was made between ISCED level 5A (Bachelor) and ISCED level 5A (Master).

6. Includes Bachelor's degrees in some countries.

* See notes at the beginning of this Annex.

Source: OECD, TALIS 2013 Database.

StatLink http://dx.doi.org/10.1787/888933042770

[Part 1/1]
Analysis of the distribution of teachers in more challenging schools

Binary logistic regression analysis for the distribution of teachers in more challenging schools based on years of experience as a teacher and on highest level of education completed[1,2]

Table 2.12

	Teachers working in schools with more than 10% of students whose first language is different from the language of instruction[3]				Teachers working in schools with more than 10% of students with special needs[4]				Teachers working in schools with more than 30% of students from socioeconomically disadvantaged homes[5]			
	Dependent on:											
	Teachers with a highest level of education of ISCED 5A or above[6]		Teachers with more than 5 years teaching experience[7]		Teachers with a highest level of education of ISCED 5A or above[6]		Teachers with more than 5 years teaching experience[7]		Teachers with a highest level of education of ISCED 5A or above[6]		Teachers with more than 5 years teaching experience[7]	
	ß	Odds ratios[8]	ß	Odds ratios[8]	ß	Odds ratios[8]	ß	Odds ratios[8]	ß	Odds ratios[8]	ß	Odds ratios[8]
Australia	-1.1	0.3	0.0	1.0					-1.8	0.2	-0.1	0.9
Brazil	-0.3	0.7	0.2	1.3	1.2	3.2	0.4	1.5	-0.1	0.9	0.4	1.5
Bulgaria	-0.6	0.5			-0.8	0.4	-1.0	0.4	-0.5	0.6	-0.1	0.9
Chile	-0.6	0.5	-0.2	0.8	-0.4	0.7	0.1	1.1	-0.8	0.5		
Croatia	0.4	1.5	-0.3	0.8	-0.2	0.8						
Czech Republic	-0.3	0.8	-0.2	0.9	-0.6	0.6	-0.3	0.7	-1.0	0.4	0.2	1.2
Denmark	1.6	5.0	0.5	1.7			0.6	1.8	-1.4	0.2	-0.9	0.4
Estonia	-0.4	0.7			-0.2	0.8	-0.3	0.7			-0.4	0.7
Finland			-0.2	0.8			-0.2	0.8				
France	0.1	1.1	-0.3	0.8	-0.3	0.8	-0.2	0.8	0.3	1.4	-0.1	0.9
Iceland			-0.4	0.7			-0.3	0.7				
Israel	-0.5	0.6					0.2	1.3	0.3	1.4	-0.3	0.7
Italy	0.4	1.5	-0.1	0.9	0.0	1.0	0.1	1.1	0.2	1.2		
Japan	0.3	1.3	-0.6	0.6	0.7	1.9	-0.3	0.7	1.4	3.9	-0.3	0.8
Korea					-1.4	0.2						
Latvia	0.9	2.5	-0.2	0.8			-0.4	0.7	-0.4	0.7	0.2	1.2
Malaysia	-0.7	0.5	-0.6	0.6			0.8	2.2	-0.4	0.7	-0.2	0.8
Mexico	3.0	20.2	0.5	1.7	-0.2	0.8	-0.3	0.7	0.1	1.1	0.1	1.1
Netherlands	0.5	1.6	-0.2	0.8	-0.6	0.5	-0.1	1.0			0.1	1.1
Norway	0.8	2.3	-0.3	0.7			-0.2	0.8	1.4	4.0	-0.2	0.8
Poland												
Portugal	-0.5	0.6	0.5	1.6	-0.3	0.8	0.3	1.4				
Romania	-0.3	0.7	-0.4	0.7	0.2	1.2	-0.5	0.6	-0.1	0.9	-0.4	0.7
Serbia			-0.3	0.7	-0.5	0.6						
Singapore	0.5	1.6	-0.3	0.8					-0.3	0.7		
Slovak Republic	-0.9	0.4			-1.0	0.4	-0.3	0.8	-1.5	0.2		
Spain	-0.2	0.8	0.1	1.1	0.3	1.3	-0.1	0.9	-0.2	0.8	-0.2	0.8
Sweden	-0.1	0.9	-0.3	0.7	-0.2	0.8	0.2	1.2	-0.2	0.8	-0.6	0.5
Sub-national entities												
Abu Dhabi (United Arab Emirates)	-0.5	0.6	-0.8	0.4	-1.1	0.3	-0.4	0.6				
Alberta (Canada)	1.0	2.8									-0.4	0.7
England (United Kingdom)			-0.4	0.6			-0.2	0.8	-0.3	0.7	-0.3	0.8
Flanders (Belgium)	0.8	2.3	-0.4	0.7	0.2	1.3	-0.3	0.8	0.7	1.9	-0.4	0.6

1. Cells are blank where no significant relationship was found. Significance was tested at the 5% level. Controlling for teacher gender and subjects taught. Where there was 0% of the teachers in a particular country teaching a particular subject (e.g. Ancient Greek/Latin), this subject was left out of the regression for this country.

2. Cells with data representing less than 5% of the cases are shaded in grey and should be interpreted with caution. These results are not highlighted in the text of the report.

3. The reference category is 10% or less of students whose first language is different from the language of instruction.

4. The reference category is 10% or less of students with special needs.

5. The reference category is 30% or less of students from socioeconomically disadvantaged homes.

6. For the educational attainment dummy variable, ISCED level 5B or below was the reference category. Coefficients and odds ratios therefore represent the association of having a degree of ISCED 5A or higher, in comparison to ISCED level 5B or below, with the school in which the teacher works being more challenging.

7. For the work experience dummy variable, less than five years was the reference category. Coefficients and odds ratios therefore represent the association of having worked as a teacher in total for five years or more in comparison to less than five years, with the school in which the teacher works being more challenging.

8. This is the exponentiated beta. See Box 2.5 for interpretation of odds ratios.

Source: OECD, TALIS 2013 Database.

StatLink ⟶ http://dx.doi.org/10.1787/888933042789

[Part 1/3]

Distribution of teachers in urban and rural schools based on teachers' experience and education

Percentage of lower secondary education teachers with the following characteristics working in schools located in areas with 15 000 people or less[1]

Table 2.13

	Teachers working in schools located in areas with 15 000 people or fewer		Within schools located in areas with 15 000 people or fewer							
			Teachers with 5 years teaching experience or less		Teachers with more than 5 years teaching experience		Teachers with a highest level of education of ISCED 5B or below[2,3]		Teachers with a highest level of education of ISCED 5A or above[2]	
	%	S.E.	%	S.E.	%	S.E.	%	S.E.	%	S.E.
Australia	10.5	(1.9)	26.3	(3.4)	73.7	(3.4)	0.0	(0.0)	100.0	(0.0)
Brazil	35.8	(2.2)	21.1	(1.6)	78.9	(1.6)	9.7	(1.4)	90.3	(1.4)
Bulgaria	46.3	(2.6)	8.7	(1.4)	91.3	(1.4)	13.2	(1.5)	86.8	(1.5)
Chile	31.6	(4.1)	31.1	(3.5)	68.9	(3.5)	20.6	(2.5)	79.4	(2.5)
Croatia	62.9	(2.1)	25.9	(1.2)	74.1	(1.2)	18.5	(1.0)	81.5	(1.0)
Cyprus*	42.6	(0.2)	15.2	(1.5)	84.8	(1.5)	0.9	(0.3)	99.1	(0.3)
Czech Republic	54.5	(3.6)	15.3	(1.1)	84.7	(1.1)	6.4	(0.8)	93.6	(0.8)
Denmark	52.3	(4.4)	20.2	(2.0)	79.8	(2.0)	4.1	(1.0)	95.9	(1.0)
Estonia	58.9	(2.6)	10.9	(1.0)	89.1	(1.0)	13.7	(1.0)	86.3	(1.0)
Finland	41.7	(3.7)	17.5	(1.2)	82.5	(1.2)	4.4	(0.7)	95.6	(0.7)
France	55.7	(2.8)	10.1	(0.9)	89.9	(0.9)	5.0	(0.7)	95.0	(0.7)
Iceland	69.6	(0.1)	20.8	(1.5)	79.2	(1.5)	14.7	(1.2)	85.3	(1.2)
Israel	29.9	(3.1)	20.4	(2.6)	79.6	(2.6)	3.0	(0.6)	97.0	(0.6)
Italy	44.6	(3.0)	8.9	(1.0)	91.1	(1.0)	19.5	(1.0)	80.5	(1.0)
Japan	7.4	(1.4)	20.7	(3.8)	79.3	(3.8)	6.8	(1.8)	93.2	(1.8)
Korea	17.9	(2.4)	21.1	(3.4)	78.9	(3.4)	0.3	(0.3)	99.7	(0.3)
Latvia	59.7	(1.7)	5.7	(0.9)	94.3	(0.9)	3.5	(0.6)	96.5	(0.6)
Malaysia	47.8	(4.2)	21.1	(1.7)	78.9	(1.7)	9.5	(1.1)	90.5	(1.1)
Mexico	29.3	(3.3)	20.0	(1.4)	80.0	(1.4)	9.8	(1.3)	90.2	(1.3)
Netherlands	8.5	(3.1)	19.3	(3.8)	80.7	(3.8)	5.9	(1.9)	94.1	(1.9)
Norway	58.2	(4.3)	25.0	(2.8)	75.0	(2.8)	2.9	(0.9)	97.1	(0.9)
Poland	54.4	(2.4)	8.6	(0.8)	91.4	(0.8)	0.1	(0.1)	99.9	(0.1)
Portugal	55.9	(3.6)	2.0	(0.4)	98.0	(0.4)	3.2	(0.4)	96.8	(0.4)
Romania	62.0	(2.2)	21.8	(1.3)	78.2	(1.3)	7.5	(0.9)	92.5	(0.9)
Serbia	48.1	(3.1)	23.3	(1.7)	76.7	(1.7)	19.4	(1.5)	80.6	(1.5)
Singapore	a	a	a	a	a	a	a	a	a	a
Slovak Republic	57.7	(2.9)	18.1	(1.2)	81.9	(1.2)	2.3	(0.5)	97.7	(0.5)
Spain	33.2	(2.8)	11.5	(1.5)	88.5	(1.5)	4.4	(0.6)	95.6	(0.6)
Sweden	34.0	(3.8)	10.5	(1.0)	89.5	(1.0)	12.4	(1.5)	87.6	(1.5)
Sub-national entities										
Abu Dhabi (United Arab Emirates)	25.5	(4.0)	12.6	(2.0)	87.4	(2.0)	6.1	(1.4)	93.9	(1.4)
Alberta (Canada)	40.3	(2.7)	27.7	(2.5)	72.3	(2.5)	1.3	(0.7)	98.7	(0.7)
England (United Kingdom)	24.4	(3.8)	24.5	(2.9)	75.5	(2.9)	4.3	(0.9)	95.7	(0.9)
Flanders (Belgium)	41.4	(4.5)	18.6	(1.4)	81.4	(1.4)	90.1	(0.9)	9.9	(0.9)
Average	**42.0**	**(0.5)**	**17.6**	**(0.4)**	**82.4**	**(0.4)**	**10.1**	**(0.2)**	**89.9**	**(0.2)**
United States	43.7	(6.0)	20.7	(2.5)	79.3	(2.5)	0.5	(0.5)	99.5	(0.5)

1. Cells with data representing less than 5% of the cases are shaded in grey and should be interpreted with caution. These results are not highlighted in the text of the report.

2. Education categories are based on the International Standard Classification of Education (ISCED 1997). ISCED level 5A programmes are generally longer and more theory-based, while 5B programmes are typically shorter and more practical and skills oriented. No distinction was made between ISCED level 5A (Bachelor) and ISCED level 5A (Master).

3. Includes Bachelor's degrees in some countries.

* See notes at the beginning of this Annex.

Source: OECD, TALIS 2013 Database.

StatLink http://dx.doi.org/10.1787/888933042846

[Part 2/3]
Distribution of teachers in urban and rural schools based on teachers' experience and education
Percentage of lower secondary education teachers with the following characteristics working in schools located in areas with 15 000 people or less[1]

Table 2.13

| | Teachers working in schools located in areas with 15 001 to 100 000 people | | Within schools located in areas with 15 001 to 100 000 people | | | | | | | |
| | | | Teachers with 5 years teaching experience or less | | Teachers with more than 5 years teaching experience | | Teachers with a highest level of education of ISCED 5B or below[2,3] | | Teachers with a highest level of education of ISCED 5A or above[2] | |
	%	S.E.	%	S.E.	%	S.E.	%	S.E.	%	S.E.
Australia	18.0	(4.8)	16.1	(2.9)	83.9	(2.9)	0.0	(0.0)	100.0	(0.0)
Brazil	26.4	(2.3)	20.3	(1.7)	79.7	(1.7)	5.8	(1.0)	94.2	(1.0)
Bulgaria	26.6	(2.9)	6.5	(1.1)	93.5	(1.1)	6.7	(1.2)	93.3	(1.2)
Chile	21.6	(2.8)	30.0	(2.6)	70.0	(2.6)	16.1	(2.5)	83.9	(2.5)
Croatia	17.6	(1.7)	22.3	(2.8)	77.7	(2.8)	18.5	(1.6)	81.5	(1.6)
Cyprus*	32.5	(0.2)	14.6	(1.7)	85.4	(1.7)	0.4	(0.2)	99.6	(0.2)
Czech Republic	27.3	(3.1)	15.9	(1.6)	84.1	(1.6)	6.3	(1.1)	93.7	(1.1)
Denmark	37.6	(5.5)	12.5	(2.0)	87.5	(2.0)	0.7	(0.5)	99.3	(0.5)
Estonia	14.2	(2.3)	10.0	(1.6)	90.0	(1.6)	8.2	(1.6)	91.8	(1.6)
Finland	25.7	(3.9)	20.5	(2.0)	79.5	(2.0)	3.8	(0.9)	96.2	(0.9)
France	31.8	(3.2)	14.4	(1.7)	85.6	(1.7)	3.6	(0.6)	96.4	(0.6)
Iceland	19.0	(0.1)	13.0	(2.3)	87.0	(2.3)	17.8	(2.5)	82.2	(2.5)
Israel	45.4	(4.0)	22.7	(2.0)	77.3	(2.0)	1.9	(0.5)	98.1	(0.5)
Italy	36.5	(3.0)	8.7	(0.8)	91.3	(0.8)	20.0	(1.0)	80.0	(1.0)
Japan	28.1	(2.9)	19.0	(1.4)	81.0	(1.4)	3.7	(0.7)	96.3	(0.7)
Korea	4.2	(1.6)	18.0	(8.3)	82.0	(8.3)	0.7	(0.7)	99.3	(0.7)
Latvia	13.9	(2.0)	5.3	(1.8)	94.7	(1.8)	1.6	(0.9)	98.4	(0.9)
Malaysia	36.0	(3.9)	22.8	(2.0)	77.2	(2.0)	7.4	(1.3)	92.6	(1.3)
Mexico	14.4	(2.5)	17.7	(3.2)	82.3	(3.2)	11.2	(1.7)	88.8	(1.7)
Netherlands	61.4	(4.9)	22.5	(2.4)	77.5	(2.4)	5.1	(1.2)	94.9	(1.2)
Norway	27.9	(3.9)	20.5	(2.2)	79.5	(2.2)	1.4	(0.6)	98.6	(0.6)
Poland	18.2	(3.2)	12.5	(2.4)	87.5	(2.4)	0.2	(0.2)	99.8	(0.2)
Portugal	30.8	(3.7)	3.2	(1.2)	96.8	(1.2)	2.1	(0.4)	97.9	(0.4)
Romania	15.6	(2.5)	11.5	(2.4)	88.5	(2.4)	5.5	(1.1)	94.5	(1.1)
Serbia	24.1	(3.0)	16.7	(1.7)	83.3	(1.7)	19.6	(1.5)	80.4	(1.5)
Singapore	a	a	a	a	a	a	a	a	a	a
Slovak Republic	33.5	(2.8)	16.1	(1.3)	83.9	(1.3)	0.6	(0.3)	99.4	(0.3)
Spain	31.1	(3.2)	6.2	(1.7)	93.8	(1.7)	4.7	(0.7)	95.3	(0.7)
Sweden	39.7	(3.7)	12.9	(1.4)	87.1	(1.4)	11.4	(1.1)	88.6	(1.1)
Sub-national entities										
Abu Dhabi (United Arab Emirates)	19.1	(4.0)	14.7	(3.0)	85.3	(3.0)	4.5	(1.5)	95.5	(1.5)
Alberta (Canada)	20.6	(4.5)	24.7	(2.8)	75.3	(2.8)	1.0	(0.5)	99.0	(0.5)
England (United Kingdom)	38.3	(4.4)	25.4	(1.9)	74.6	(1.9)	3.5	(0.9)	96.5	(0.9)
Flanders (Belgium)	43.3	(4.5)	19.1	(1.2)	80.9	(1.2)	89.0	(1.2)	11.0	(1.2)
Average	27.5	(0.6)	16.1	(0.4)	83.9	(0.4)	8.8	(0.2)	91.2	(0.2)
United States	24.2	(5.1)	16.3	(3.0)	83.7	(3.0)	0.5	(1.1)	98.9	(0.6)

1. Cells with data representing less than 5% of the cases are shaded in grey and should be interpreted with caution. These results are not highlighted in the text of the report.
2. Education categories are based on the International Standard Classification of Education (ISCED 1997). ISCED level 5A programmes are generally longer and more theory-based, while 5B programmes are typically shorter and more practical and skills oriented. No distinction was made between ISCED level 5A (Bachelor) and ISCED level 5A (Master).
3. Includes Bachelor's degrees in some countries.
*See notes at the beginning of this Annex.
Source: OECD, TALIS 2013 Database.
StatLink http://dx.doi.org/10.1787/888933042846

[Part 3/3]
Distribution of teachers in urban and rural schools based on teachers' experience and education
Percentage of lower secondary education teachers with the following characteristics working in schools located in areas with 15 000 people or less[1]

Table 2.13

| | Teachers working in schools located in areas with more than 100 000 people | | Within schools located in areas with more than 100 000 people | | | | | | | |
| | | | Teachers with 5 years teaching experience or less | | Teachers with more than 5 years teaching experience | | Teachers with a highest level of education of ISCED 5B or below[2,3] | | Teachers with a highest level of education of ISCED 5A or above[2] | |
	%	S.E.	%	S.E.	%	S.E.	%	S.E.	%	S.E.
Australia	71.5	(4.7)	18.8	(1.3)	81.2	(1.3)	0.2	(0.1)	99.8	(0.1)
Brazil	37.8	(2.4)	20.7	(1.7)	79.3	(1.7)	3.1	(0.7)	96.9	(0.7)
Bulgaria	27.0	(2.5)	7.0	(1.3)	93.0	(1.3)	3.3	(0.9)	96.7	(0.9)
Chile	46.8	(4.2)	29.3	(3.0)	70.7	(3.0)	17.3	(2.3)	82.7	(2.3)
Croatia	19.6	(1.3)	16.6	(1.5)	83.4	(1.5)	13.8	(1.4)	86.2	(1.4)
Cyprus*	24.9	(0.2)	14.5	(1.7)	85.5	(1.7)	0.7	(0.3)	99.3	(0.3)
Czech Republic	18.2	(2.6)	16.2	(1.8)	83.8	(1.8)	6.0	(1.5)	94.0	(1.5)
Denmark	10.1	(3.4)	22.4	(4.3)	77.6	(4.3)	2.7	(1.4)	97.3	(1.4)
Estonia	26.9	(2.1)	10.2	(1.2)	89.8	(1.2)	6.9	(1.0)	93.1	(1.0)
Finland	32.6	(4.1)	19.4	(1.6)	80.6	(1.6)	3.8	(0.8)	96.2	(0.8)
France	12.5	(2.5)	9.8	(1.7)	90.2	(1.7)	4.9	(1.3)	95.1	(1.3)
Iceland	11.4	(0.1)	21.8	(4.0)	78.2	(4.0)	11.2	(2.8)	88.8	(2.8)
Israel	24.8	(3.5)	21.0	(2.6)	79.0	(2.6)	2.6	(0.8)	97.4	(0.8)
Italy	18.9	(2.9)	7.8	(1.3)	92.2	(1.3)	18.8	(1.2)	81.2	(1.2)
Japan	64.5	(2.7)	20.8	(1.0)	79.2	(1.0)	3.2	(0.4)	96.8	(0.4)
Korea	77.9	(2.8)	20.9	(1.2)	79.1	(1.2)	0.2	(0.1)	99.8	(0.1)
Latvia	26.4	(2.4)	10.8	(1.8)	89.2	(1.8)	2.1	(0.8)	97.9	(0.8)
Malaysia	16.2	(3.2)	28.5	(3.5)	71.5	(3.5)	7.4	(2.0)	92.6	(2.0)
Mexico	56.3	(3.7)	18.5	(1.4)	81.5	(1.4)	10.1	(0.9)	89.9	(0.9)
Netherlands	30.1	(4.6)	19.3	(1.5)	80.7	(1.5)	3.5	(0.7)	96.5	(0.7)
Norway	13.8	(2.7)	30.7	(4.7)	69.3	(4.7)	1.0	(0.5)	99.0	(0.5)
Poland	27.4	(3.7)	12.6	(2.0)	87.4	(2.0)	0.0	(0.0)	100.0	(0.0)
Portugal	13.2	(2.8)	5.6	(2.5)	94.4	(2.5)	2.5	(0.6)	97.5	(0.6)
Romania	22.5	(2.1)	9.4	(1.0)	90.6	(1.0)	4.9	(0.8)	95.1	(0.8)
Serbia	27.8	(2.5)	14.6	(1.1)	85.4	(1.1)	11.1	(1.0)	88.9	(1.0)
Singapore	100.0	(0.0)	43.0	(0.9)	57.0	(0.9)	7.1	(0.5)	92.9	(0.5)
Slovak Republic	8.8	(2.0)	18.9	(2.3)	81.1	(2.3)	3.2	(1.3)	96.8	(1.3)
Spain	35.7	(3.2)	7.6	(0.6)	92.4	(0.6)	4.2	(0.6)	95.8	(0.6)
Sweden	26.4	(2.6)	14.2	(1.8)	85.8	(1.8)	10.7	(1.1)	89.3	(1.1)
Sub-national entities										
Abu Dhabi (United Arab Emirates)	55.4	(5.1)	21.6	(2.2)	78.4	(2.2)	7.6	(1.9)	92.4	(1.9)
Alberta (Canada)	39.2	(4.2)	23.2	(1.7)	76.8	(1.7)	0.8	(0.3)	99.2	(0.3)
England (United Kingdom)	37.2	(3.5)	29.7	(1.9)	70.3	(1.9)	2.2	(0.5)	97.8	(0.5)
Flanders (Belgium)	15.3	(3.6)	27.8	(3.3)	72.2	(3.3)	79.3	(2.4)	20.7	(2.4)
Average	32.6	(0.5)	18.6	(0.4)	81.4	(0.4)	7.8	(0.2)	92.2	(0.2)
United States	32.1	(4.3)	27.8	(2.6)	72.2	(2.6)	0.1	(0.1)	99.9	(0.1)

1. Cells with data representing less than 5% of the cases are shaded in grey and should be interpreted with caution. These results are not highlighted in the text of the report.
2. Education categories are based on the International Standard Classification of Education (ISCED 1997). ISCED level 5A programmes are generally longer and more theory-based, while 5B programmes are typically shorter and more practical and skills oriented. No distinction was made between ISCED level 5A (Bachelor) and ISCED level 5A (Master).
3. Includes Bachelor's degrees in some countries.
* See notes at the beginning of this Annex.
Source: OECD, TALIS 2013 Database.
StatLink http://dx.doi.org/10.1787/888933042846

[Part 1/1]
Analysis of the distribution of teachers in urban and rural schools

Multinomial logistic regression analysis for the distribution of lower secondary education teachers in urban and rural schools based on years of experience as a teacher and on highest level of education completed[1,2]

Table 2.14

	Schools located in small cities with between 15 001 and 100 000 people[3]				Schools located in large cities with more than 100 000 people[3]			
	Dependent on:							
	Teachers with a highest level of education of ISCED 5B or below[4]		Teachers with 5 years teaching experience or less[5]		Teachers with a highest level of education of ISCED 5B or below[4]		Teachers with 5 years teaching experience or less[5]	
	ß	Odds ratios[6]	ß	Odds ratios[6]	ß	Odds ratios[6]	ß	Odds ratios[6]
Australia			-0.5	0.6			-0.3	0.8
Brazil	-0.4	0.7			-0.9	0.4	0.0	1.0
Bulgaria	-0.4	0.7	-0.4	0.7	-1.0	0.4	-0.3	0.7
Chile	-0.3	0.8	-0.1	0.9	-0.2	0.9	-0.1	0.9
Croatia			-0.2	0.8	-0.4	0.6	-0.6	0.5
Czech Republic	-0.1	0.9			-0.2	0.9	0.1	1.1
Denmark	-1.5	0.2	-0.5	0.6	-0.3	0.7	0.2	1.2
Estonia	-0.5	0.6			-0.8	0.5		
Finland			0.2	1.2			0.1	1.1
France	-0.3	0.7	0.4	1.5				
Iceland			-0.7	0.5				
Israel	-0.5	0.6	0.1	1.1				
Italy							-0.1	1.0
Japan	-0.4	0.7	-0.2	0.8	-0.6	0.5	-0.1	0.9
Korea	0.9	2.3	-0.2	0.8	-0.6	0.6	0.0	1.0
Latvia	-0.6	0.5			-0.5	0.6	0.9	2.5
Malaysia	-0.2	0.8	0.0	1.0	-0.1	0.9	0.3	1.4
Mexico	0.1	1.1	-0.2	0.8			-0.1	0.9
Netherlands	-0.3	0.7	0.2	1.2	-0.6	0.6		
Norway	-0.8	0.5	-0.3	0.8	-1.4	0.2	0.3	1.4
Poland	1.1	3.0	0.4	1.6			0.4	1.5
Portugal	-0.5	0.6	0.4	1.5	-0.4	0.7	1.1	2.9
Romania	-0.3	0.7	-0.8	0.5	-0.4	0.7	-1.1	0.3
Serbia			-0.4	0.7	-0.6	0.5	-0.6	0.5
Singapore								
Slovak Republic	-1.4	0.2	-0.1	0.9	0.4	1.5		
Spain			-0.7	0.5			-0.5	0.6
Sweden			0.2	1.3	-0.2	0.8	0.3	1.4
Sub-national entities								
Abu Dhabi (United Arab Emirates)	-0.4	0.6					0.6	1.9
Alberta (Canada)			-0.1	0.9			-0.2	0.8
England (United Kingdom)	-0.1	0.9			-0.7	0.5	0.2	1.3
Flanders (Belgium)	-0.1	0.9			-0.7	0.5	0.5	1.6

1. Cells are blank where no significant relationship was found. Significance was tested at the 5% level. Controlling for teacher gender and subjects taught. Where there was 0% of the teachers in a particular country teaching a particular subject (e.g. Ancient Greek/Latin), this subject was left out of the regression for this country.

2. Cells with data representing less than 5% of the cases are shaded in grey and should be interpreted with extreme caution. These results are not highlighted in the text of the report.

3. The reference category for school location is 15 000 or fewer inhabitants.

4. For the educational attainment dummy variable, ISCED 5A or higher was the reference category. Coefficients and odds ratios therefore represent the association of having a degree of ISCED 5B and below, in comparison to ISCED level 5A or higher, with the school location in which the teacher works.

5. For the work experience dummy variable, five years or more was the reference category. Coefficients and odds ratios therefore represent the association of having worked as a teacher in total for less than five years or less in comparison to more than five years or more, with the school location in which the teacher works.

6. This is the exponentiated beta. Please refer to Box 2.5 for interpretation of odds ratios.

Source: OECD, TALIS 2013 Database.

StatLink ᵐˢᵖ http://dx.doi.org/10.1787/888933042865

[Part 1/2]

Education and training completed in selected subjects taught

Percentage of lower secondary education teachers who received the following types of formal education or training in the subject fields they currently teach[1]

Table 2.15

| | Currently teaching reading, writing and literature[2] | | Of whom received the following types of formal education or training in this subject category | | | | | | Currently teaching mathematics[5] | | Of whom received the following types of formal education or training in this subject category | | | | | |
| | | | ISCED level 4 or above or a subject specialisation as part of the teacher training[3] | | In-service or professional development stage | | No formal education or training at ISCED level 4 or higher or at the professional development stage for this subject category[4] | | | | ISCED level 4 or above or a subject specialisation as part of the teacher training[3] | | In-service or professional development stage | | No formal education or training at ISCED level 4 or higher or at the professional development stage for this subject category[4] | |
	%	S.E.	%	S.E.	%	S.E.	%	S.E.	%	S.E.	%	S.E.	%	S.E.	%	S.E.
Australia	37.6	(1.0)	90.2	(1.3)	40.0	(2.0)	7.2	(1.2)	25.5	(1.1)	92.7	(1.3)	34.0	(3.1)	5.3	(1.1)
Brazil	35.7	(0.7)	88.1	(1.0)	41.1	(1.4)	4.4	(0.5)	23.3	(0.5)	88.8	(0.7)	37.8	(1.5)	5.3	(0.6)
Bulgaria	17.5	(0.4)	99.0	(0.5)	35.1	(2.9)	0.9	(0.4)	15.7	(0.4)	97.7	(0.8)	34.4	(2.8)	1.0	(0.5)
Chile	24.3	(1.1)	95.9	(1.2)	12.1	(1.8)	2.0	(0.8)	20.7	(0.7)	97.3	(0.9)	11.5	(2.1)	2.1	(0.8)
Croatia	20.2	(0.6)	96.3	(0.8)	24.1	(1.5)	3.3	(0.8)	13.9	(0.4)	95.7	(1.2)	20.5	(2.0)	4.0	(1.2)
Cyprus*	32.8	(1.3)	94.7	(1.1)	33.0	(2.3)	2.9	(0.8)	12.9	(0.8)	97.0	(1.1)	29.0	(3.2)	1.6	(0.8)
Czech Republic	21.9	(0.6)	92.3	(1.2)	26.9	(2.1)	2.7	(0.7)	21.5	(0.5)	89.8	(1.3)	23.2	(1.9)	6.1	(1.1)
Denmark	43.2	(1.3)	92.9	(1.0)	5.2	(0.9)	5.2	(0.8)	33.2	(0.9)	87.2	(1.5)	4.4	(0.9)	10.7	(1.4)
Estonia	21.7	(0.7)	91.3	(1.1)	27.7	(2.1)	5.3	(1.0)	14.3	(0.5)	94.5	(1.2)	22.4	(2.1)	3.2	(0.9)
Finland	23.2	(0.7)	85.3	(1.6)	13.7	(1.4)	10.8	(1.4)	28.8	(0.7)	84.0	(1.3)	10.8	(1.0)	11.5	(1.2)
France	21.9	(0.7)	92.8	(1.0)	16.4	(1.5)	5.8	(0.8)	17.1	(0.6)	96.1	(0.9)	13.6	(1.6)	3.8	(0.9)
Iceland	34.3	(1.3)	82.6	(1.8)	39.0	(2.3)	7.0	(1.2)	29.7	(1.2)	76.5	(2.1)	36.5	(2.7)	10.6	(1.4)
Israel	23.9	(0.9)	89.2	(2.2)	32.6	(2.1)	3.9	(0.9)	19.1	(0.5)	89.9	(2.1)	37.1	(2.2)	3.5	(0.9)
Italy	35.6	(0.6)	90.6	(0.9)	26.1	(1.5)	6.6	(0.8)	23.0	(0.6)	72.4	(1.9)	26.4	(2.0)	19.9	(1.6)
Japan	17.3	(0.5)	87.5	(1.5)	43.5	(1.9)	9.5	(1.2)	22.1	(0.6)	80.8	(1.4)	36.7	(1.9)	16.4	(1.3)
Korea	38.2	(0.8)	88.4	(1.1)	24.5	(1.3)	5.1	(0.7)	25.3	(0.7)	87.3	(1.3)	22.2	(1.5)	7.8	(1.0)
Latvia	26.8	(0.9)	91.9	(1.6)	34.5	(2.6)	3.3	(0.9)	15.8	(0.6)	91.3	(2.2)	40.3	(4.3)	3.8	(1.0)
Malaysia	56.1	(1.0)	86.1	(1.0)	37.8	(1.8)	9.6	(0.8)	27.3	(0.8)	87.4	(1.3)	34.4	(2.0)	7.3	(1.0)
Mexico	30.2	(0.9)	89.4	(1.2)	27.0	(1.5)	3.6	(0.7)	19.7	(0.7)	91.6	(1.4)	30.5	(2.1)	3.2	(0.9)
Netherlands[8]	13.7	(0.9)	81.3	(3.3)	a	a	18.7	(3.3)	12.8	(0.9)	78.3	(4.2)	a	a	21.7	(4.2)
Norway	42.4	(1.3)	82.9	(1.1)	13.7	(1.3)	11.4	(1.1)	36.3	(0.8)	87.3	(1.2)	11.2	(1.3)	7.5	(1.1)
Poland	21.3	(0.7)	90.4	(1.4)	46.0	(2.6)	5.3	(1.0)	14.0	(0.5)	95.9	(0.8)	47.4	(2.5)	1.8	(0.6)
Portugal	21.2	(0.5)	95.6	(0.8)	41.0	(1.7)	3.3	(0.7)	13.8	(0.4)	97.7	(0.7)	35.9	(2.4)	1.9	(0.7)
Romania	20.5	(0.6)	95.8	(0.9)	43.7	(2.9)	2.9	(0.8)	15.2	(0.5)	96.3	(1.3)	38.8	(2.6)	2.5	(0.8)
Serbia	19.0	(0.5)	96.3	(0.7)	16.7	(1.5)	0.7	(0.2)	13.1	(0.3)	96.7	(0.9)	13.5	(1.9)	1.3	(0.5)
Singapore	42.9	(0.8)	97.3	(0.5)	50.2	(1.5)	1.3	(0.3)	19.6	(0.8)	96.0	(0.9)	45.9	(2.2)	2.4	(0.6)
Slovak Republic	25.7	(0.7)	83.3	(1.6)	16.4	(1.3)	13.5	(1.6)	24.9	(0.6)	85.0	(1.5)	19.5	(1.6)	12.9	(1.3)
Spain	23.8	(0.6)	92.4	(0.9)	30.2	(1.7)	4.1	(0.7)	21.4	(0.7)	93.3	(1.0)	24.8	(1.9)	5.1	(1.0)
Sweden	30.2	(0.7)	82.1	(1.3)	13.4	(1.1)	11.2	(1.1)	28.4	(0.8)	84.6	(1.3)	11.9	(1.1)	10.1	(1.0)
Sub-national entities																
Abu Dhabi (United Arab Emirates)	36.0	(1.2)	90.3	(1.3)	36.3	(2.6)	3.3	(0.6)	15.9	(0.9)	92.0	(1.9)	35.9	(3.9)	3.2	(1.1)
Alberta (Canada)	41.4	(1.6)	91.3	(1.0)	38.9	(1.7)	3.8	(0.7)	30.4	(1.2)	78.0	(1.9)	38.1	(2.5)	9.2	(1.2)
England (United Kingdom)	27.9	(1.0)	89.2	(1.1)	39.2	(1.8)	5.8	(0.8)	19.4	(0.7)	90.5	(1.3)	33.2	(2.1)	5.9	(1.1)
Flanders (Belgium)	25.1	(0.7)	95.7	(1.0)	22.7	(1.9)	3.7	(1.0)	16.8	(0.6)	93.3	(1.3)	15.9	(2.2)	4.6	(1.0)
Average	28.9	(0.2)	90.6	(0.2)	29.6	(0.3)	5.7	(0.2)	20.9	(0.1)	89.8	(0.3)	27.4	(0.4)	6.6	(0.2)
United States	35.7	(1.7)	97.1	(0.7)	61.4	(2.8)	1.4	(0.5)	27.6	(1.5)	96.0	(0.9)	42.6	(2.3)	2.3	(0.7)

1. Cells with data representing less than 5% of the cases are shaded in grey and should be interpreted with caution. These results are not highlighted in the text of the report.

2. Subjects include reading and writing (and literature) in the mother tongue, in the language of instruction or in the tongue of the country (region) as a second language (for non-natives); language studies, public speaking, literature.

3. This category includes "in ISCED level 4 or 5B", "in ISCED level 5A or above" and "in subject specialisation as part of the teacher training". Education categories are based on the International Standard Classification of Education (ISCED 1997). ISCED level 5A programmes are generally longer and more theory-based, while 5B programmes are typically shorter and more practical and skills oriented. No distinction was made between ISCED level 5A (Bachelor) and ISCED level 5A (Master).

4. This category includes those respondents who responded to this question but who did not select a response option for that particular subject.

5. Subjects include mathematics, mathematics with statistics, geometry, algebra, etc.

6. Subjects include science, physics, physical science, chemistry, biology, human biology, environmental science, agriculture/forestry.

7. Subjects include languages different from the language of instruction.

8. For the Netherlands, the category "at the in-service or professional development stage" was excluded.

* See notes at the beginning of this Annex.

Source: OECD, TALIS 2013 Database.

StatLink ⌦ http://dx.doi.org/10.1787/888933042922

[Part 2/2]

Education and training completed in selected subjects taught

Table 2.15

Percentage of lower secondary education teachers who received the following types of formal education or training in the subject fields they currently teach[1]

| | Currently teaching science[6] | | Of whom received the following types of formal education or training in this subject category | | | | | | Currently teaching modern foreign languages[7] | | Of whom received the following types of formal education or training in this subject category | | | | | |
| | | | ISCED level 4 or above or a subject specialisation as part of the teacher training[3] | | In-service or professional development stage | | No formal education or training at ISCED level 4 or higher or at the professional development stage for this subject category[4] | | | | ISCED level 4 or above or a subject specialisation as part of the teacher training[3] | | In-service or professional development stage | | No formal education or training at ISCED level 4 or higher or at the professional development stage for this subject category[4] | |
	%	S.E.	%	S.E.	%	S.E.	%	S.E.	%	S.E.	%	S.E.	%	S.E.	%	S.E.
Australia	20.0	(0.9)	93.4	(1.4)	31.4	(3.3)	5.6	(1.1)	6.4	(0.6)	89.6	(2.7)	30.1	(5.4)	8.7	(2.5)
Brazil	22.8	(0.5)	79.8	(1.2)	30.9	(1.4)	12.3	(1.0)	13.8	(0.4)	82.9	(1.5)	35.4	(1.9)	9.6	(1.1)
Bulgaria	18.5	(0.6)	93.7	(1.7)	31.2	(2.4)	4.4	(1.4)	18.5	(0.6)	92.6	(1.5)	30.5	(2.3)	4.1	(1.2)
Chile	18.3	(0.9)	94.7	(1.5)	14.1	(2.2)	4.1	(1.3)	11.8	(0.8)	89.7	(2.4)	15.0	(2.9)	6.2	(1.8)
Croatia	18.5	(0.5)	92.0	(1.1)	17.1	(1.6)	6.6	(1.0)	18.5	(0.4)	91.3	(1.3)	19.0	(1.5)	8.1	(1.3)
Cyprus*	13.9	(0.9)	94.6	(1.7)	27.6	(2.8)	3.0	(1.4)	12.1	(0.8)	81.3	(2.7)	22.1	(3.3)	14.4	(2.4)
Czech Republic	34.3	(0.7)	83.7	(1.2)	24.0	(1.4)	10.0	(1.0)	31.9	(0.6)	76.9	(1.6)	36.4	(1.5)	7.9	(0.8)
Denmark	33.4	(1.0)	84.7	(1.9)	3.7	(0.9)	14.9	(1.9)	38.0	(1.0)	77.4	(1.9)	3.8	(0.8)	20.8	(1.9)
Estonia	18.5	(0.6)	91.8	(1.3)	20.4	(1.7)	4.2	(1.0)	20.4	(0.6)	89.4	(1.3)	24.0	(1.7)	5.5	(0.9)
Finland	28.7	(0.7)	87.4	(1.2)	8.0	(1.0)	10.5	(1.1)	28.4	(0.7)	81.7	(1.5)	10.8	(1.2)	15.2	(1.4)
France	13.7	(0.5)	95.7	(1.2)	15.0	(1.9)	3.7	(1.1)	19.7	(0.6)	93.4	(1.1)	11.0	(1.6)	5.7	(1.0)
Iceland	18.4	(1.2)	70.6	(2.7)	26.0	(2.7)	20.8	(2.3)	31.2	(1.3)	66.0	(2.6)	29.1	(2.2)	21.7	(2.2)
Israel	16.1	(0.7)	89.5	(2.7)	35.9	(2.5)	4.5	(1.2)	17.1	(0.6)	89.1	(1.6)	27.8	(2.1)	8.8	(1.4)
Italy	22.7	(0.6)	79.7	(1.5)	25.8	(2.1)	14.7	(1.4)	18.9	(0.6)	82.5	(1.4)	24.2	(1.8)	14.1	(1.2)
Japan	15.6	(0.4)	88.5	(1.5)	38.6	(2.1)	6.9	(1.1)	18.6	(0.4)	89.1	(1.3)	43.1	(2.1)	8.0	(1.1)
Korea	24.5	(0.7)	87.1	(1.2)	22.6	(1.7)	8.3	(1.1)	17.6	(0.6)	81.7	(1.7)	15.8	(1.8)	12.3	(1.5)
Latvia	17.7	(0.8)	86.5	(2.0)	37.9	(2.3)	5.1	(1.0)	15.3	(0.6)	87.4	(2.2)	31.9	(3.2)	10.3	(2.0)
Malaysia	24.9	(0.8)	86.4	(1.3)	33.7	(2.1)	9.5	(1.3)	13.3	(0.8)	75.6	(2.1)	28.1	(2.6)	20.3	(2.1)
Mexico	23.7	(0.6)	90.6	(1.2)	25.4	(2.0)	3.6	(0.8)	10.8	(0.6)	90.2	(2.0)	24.3	(2.8)	4.7	(1.2)
Netherlands[8]	14.1	(0.7)	90.1	(2.2)	a	a	9.9	(2.2)	20.2	(1.4)	94.6	(1.3)	a	a	5.4	(1.3)
Norway	26.1	(0.7)	84.0	(1.8)	8.4	(0.9)	11.9	(1.4)	33.2	(0.8)	75.2	(2.2)	16.4	(2.4)	14.9	(1.2)
Poland	19.3	(0.5)	91.6	(1.2)	35.5	(2.3)	5.1	(1.1)	18.9	(0.6)	90.9	(1.2)	25.4	(2.2)	6.7	(1.1)
Portugal	20.6	(0.5)	96.4	(0.8)	33.9	(2.1)	3.0	(0.7)	16.4	(0.4)	96.8	(0.7)	36.1	(2.3)	3.1	(0.8)
Romania	17.3	(0.6)	90.9	(1.7)	38.6	(2.9)	7.4	(1.6)	19.9	(0.6)	92.3	(1.4)	38.6	(2.1)	6.4	(1.3)
Serbia	18.8	(0.5)	94.0	(0.9)	12.4	(1.2)	3.2	(0.8)	17.0	(0.5)	94.0	(0.9)	16.0	(1.6)	3.2	(0.7)
Singapore	18.4	(0.7)	96.9	(0.8)	45.5	(2.0)	2.2	(0.6)	0.6	(0.1)	66.7	(10.3)	5.3	(5.3)	33.3	(10.3)
Slovak Republic	34.0	(0.8)	82.2	(1.3)	17.2	(1.2)	15.1	(1.4)	30.5	(0.7)	77.0	(1.4)	26.4	(1.7)	11.3	(1.0)
Spain	18.1	(0.5)	93.4	(1.1)	25.0	(1.8)	4.8	(1.1)	18.9	(0.5)	92.4	(1.1)	32.2	(2.5)	4.2	(0.8)
Sweden	21.2	(0.6)	89.3	(1.5)	7.4	(1.2)	8.1	(1.3)	31.9	(0.7)	84.2	(1.3)	6.5	(1.0)	13.3	(1.3)
Sub-national entities																
Abu Dhabi (United Arab Emirates)	18.5	(0.7)	92.7	(1.8)	39.6	(3.5)	3.3	(1.0)	11.4	(0.9)	82.4	(2.8)	28.4	(3.3)	13.6	(2.4)
Alberta (Canada)	29.4	(1.2)	81.4	(1.8)	32.0	(2.7)	10.1	(1.2)	10.5	(0.6)	75.6	(3.0)	28.1	(3.5)	17.0	(3.1)
England (United Kingdom)	16.1	(0.6)	94.1	(1.1)	36.6	(2.6)	5.6	(1.0)	9.0	(0.5)	98.1	(0.8)	37.8	(4.5)	1.9	(0.8)
Flanders (Belgium)	15.9	(0.6)	90.0	(1.5)	16.3	(2.0)	7.4	(1.4)	17.7	(0.5)	92.5	(1.0)	24.3	(2.4)	6.3	(1.1)
Average	21.0	(0.1)	89.0	(0.3)	25.6	(0.4)	7.6	(0.2)	18.7	(0.1)	85.5	(0.4)	24.5	(0.5)	10.5	(0.4)
United States	19.8	(1.0)	95.5	(1.2)	36.0	(3.3)	3.3	(1.0)	5.6	(0.6)	91.7	(4.2)	30.2	(7.3)	7.4	(4.2)

1. Cells with data representing less than 5% of the cases are shaded in grey and should be interpreted with caution. These results are not highlighted in the text of the report.

2. Subjects include reading and writing (and literature) in the mother tongue, in the language of instruction or in the tongue of the country (region) as a second language (for non-natives); language studies, public speaking, literature.

3. This category includes "in ISCED level 4 or 5B", "in ISCED level 5A or above" and "in subject specialisation as part of the teacher training". Education categories are based on the International Standard Classification of Education (ISCED 1997). ISCED level 5A programmes are generally longer and more theory-based, while 5B programmes are typically shorter and more practical and skills oriented. No distinction was made between ISCED level 5A (Bachelor) and ISCED level 5A (Master).

4. This category includes those respondents who responded to this question but who did not select a response option for that particular subject.

5. Subjects include mathematics, mathematics with statistics, geometry, algebra, etc.

6. Subjects include science, physics, physical science, chemistry, biology, human biology, environmental science, agriculture/forestry.

7. Subjects include languages different from the language of instruction.

8. For the Netherlands, the category "at the in-service or professional development stage" was excluded.

* See notes at the beginning of this Annex.

Source: OECD, TALIS 2013 Database.

StatLink ᴍ⬛ http://dx.doi.org/10.1787/888933042922

[Part 1/1]

Education and training completed in selected subjects not currently taught

Percentage of lower secondary education teachers who received some formal education or training in the following subjects but who are not currently teaching these subject fields[1]

Table 2.16

	Received formal education or training at ISCED level 4 or above or a subject specialisation as part of the teacher training in reading, writing and literature[2,6]		Of whom not currently teaching reading, writing and literature		Received formal education or training at ISCED level 4 or above or a subject specialisation as part of the teacher training in mathematics[3,6]		Of whom not currently teaching mathematics		Received formal education or training at ISCED level 4 or above or a subject specialisation as part of the teacher training in science[4,6]		Of whom not currently teaching science		Received formal education or training at ISCED level 4 or above or a subject specialisation as part of the teacher training in modern foreign languages[5,6]		Of whom not currently teaching modern foreign languages	
	%	S.E.	%	S.E.	%	S.E.	%	S.E.	%	S.E.	%	S.E.	%	S.E.	%	S.E.
Australia	79.4	(1.0)	57.1	(1.3)	69.6	(1.3)	66.1	(1.5)	68.0	(1.4)	72.4	(1.3)	40.7	(1.4)	86.1	(1.4)
Brazil	66.0	(0.8)	52.0	(0.9)	42.9	(0.6)	51.6	(1.1)	37.8	(0.7)	51.8	(1.1)	35.6	(0.7)	67.6	(1.0)
Bulgaria	34.5	(0.9)	49.7	(1.4)	30.6	(0.8)	49.9	(1.6)	32.1	(0.9)	46.5	(1.5)	42.1	(1.1)	59.6	(1.4)
Chile	65.6	(2.1)	64.3	(1.7)	58.6	(1.9)	65.4	(1.3)	50.7	(1.8)	66.0	(1.6)	39.2	(1.7)	72.8	(2.0)
Croatia	42.3	(0.7)	54.3	(1.2)	29.7	(0.7)	55.7	(1.3)	32.5	(0.8)	48.0	(1.3)	35.4	(0.8)	52.5	(1.1)
Cyprus*	52.8	(1.4)	41.7	(1.8)	37.6	(1.2)	66.5	(2.1)	34.3	(1.2)	60.7	(2.4)	38.5	(1.2)	75.1	(1.7)
Czech Republic	43.1	(1.0)	52.8	(1.3)	38.7	(1.0)	50.2	(1.5)	45.5	(0.9)	37.1	(1.3)	47.5	(0.9)	48.5	(1.1)
Denmark	71.0	(1.1)	43.2	(1.6)	57.7	(1.2)	49.7	(1.2)	46.6	(1.2)	38.4	(1.5)	36.7	(1.2)	19.8	(2.0)
Estonia	59.8	(1.1)	66.6	(1.2)	52.7	(1.1)	74.1	(0.9)	53.8	(1.1)	68.1	(1.1)	56.7	(1.0)	67.9	(0.9)
Finland	44.6	(0.9)	55.8	(1.3)	37.8	(0.9)	36.7	(1.4)	38.0	(0.8)	34.0	(1.3)	42.5	(1.0)	45.7	(1.4)
France	45.0	(0.9)	54.8	(1.3)	33.5	(0.8)	50.7	(1.3)	33.9	(0.7)	61.0	(1.5)	49.4	(0.9)	63.4	(1.2)
Iceland	65.9	(1.3)	56.8	(1.7)	56.1	(1.2)	59.5	(1.9)	42.7	(1.4)	69.6	(2.1)	41.8	(1.4)	50.9	(2.4)
Israel	49.2	(1.2)	56.6	(1.4)	39.5	(1.2)	56.0	(1.5)	32.8	(0.9)	55.7	(1.7)	42.9	(1.0)	64.4	(1.1)
Italy	53.2	(0.9)	39.4	(1.1)	26.3	(0.7)	36.5	(1.6)	28.3	(0.8)	35.8	(1.4)	35.0	(0.9)	55.3	(1.4)
Japan	44.4	(1.0)	66.0	(0.9)	42.7	(1.0)	58.4	(1.2)	39.6	(0.9)	65.2	(1.1)	51.5	(0.9)	67.9	(0.9)
Korea	70.9	(0.9)	52.3	(1.0)	66.6	(1.1)	66.9	(1.0)	66.0	(1.0)	67.8	(1.1)	59.2	(1.1)	75.8	(0.9)
Latvia	55.8	(0.9)	55.9	(1.7)	44.8	(1.0)	67.4	(1.1)	44.3	(1.1)	65.1	(1.6)	42.6	(1.4)	68.9	(1.3)
Malaysia	69.0	(1.2)	29.8	(1.1)	57.5	(1.2)	58.5	(1.4)	47.9	(1.0)	55.2	(1.5)	41.8	(1.4)	76.0	(1.5)
Mexico	77.5	(1.0)	65.1	(1.1)	66.9	(1.2)	73.0	(1.0)	59.2	(1.0)	63.9	(1.0)	57.0	(1.3)	83.1	(0.9)
Netherlands	26.8	(1.5)	58.8	(2.7)	19.6	(1.5)	48.9	(3.9)	21.0	(1.2)	39.0	(3.8)	26.3	(1.5)	28.1	(3.4)
Norway	63.4	(1.3)	44.6	(1.8)	59.7	(1.9)	46.7	(1.4)	49.4	(1.8)	55.5	(1.4)	32.0	(1.0)	22.1	(1.5)
Poland	41.8	(0.8)	53.7	(1.3)	33.3	(0.8)	59.8	(1.6)	35.2	(0.9)	49.8	(1.3)	52.0	(1.4)	67.0	(1.1)
Portugal	40.9	(0.9)	50.0	(1.4)	39.5	(0.8)	66.0	(1.0)	34.6	(0.7)	42.8	(1.4)	32.4	(0.9)	50.7	(1.5)
Romania	41.3	(1.0)	52.4	(1.2)	29.6	(1.0)	50.3	(1.7)	30.0	(1.0)	47.8	(1.9)	46.3	(1.3)	60.3	(1.3)
Serbia	40.4	(0.7)	54.5	(1.3)	30.7	(0.7)	58.7	(1.2)	34.5	(0.8)	48.9	(1.3)	48.3	(1.1)	66.9	(0.9)
Singapore	84.1	(0.7)	50.3	(1.0)	70.0	(0.9)	73.1	(1.0)	60.7	(0.9)	70.6	(1.0)	20.2	(0.7)	98.1	(0.4)
Slovak Republic	53.8	(1.0)	60.3	(1.3)	52.8	(1.0)	60.1	(1.0)	55.2	(1.0)	49.4	(1.1)	49.0	(1.1)	52.2	(1.4)
Spain	54.8	(0.9)	59.6	(1.2)	49.8	(0.7)	60.1	(1.3)	42.9	(0.7)	60.5	(1.1)	54.3	(1.0)	67.6	(0.8)
Sweden	38.7	(0.9)	35.3	(1.5)	35.8	(0.8)	32.3	(1.8)	33.5	(0.9)	43.1	(1.5)	36.1	(0.9)	25.5	(1.6)
Sub-national entities																
Abu Dhabi (United Arab Emirates)	62.1	(1.4)	47.8	(1.7)	44.1	(1.2)	67.4	(1.7)	43.2	(1.0)	60.8	(1.5)	37.4	(1.5)	75.4	(1.8)
Alberta (Canada)	82.1	(1.0)	53.8	(1.8)	58.6	(1.3)	59.6	(1.6)	59.8	(1.1)	60.1	(1.5)	26.4	(1.1)	70.0	(1.9)
England (United Kingdom)	69.9	(0.8)	64.3	(1.2)	54.1	(1.0)	67.6	(1.3)	46.2	(1.0)	67.0	(1.3)	25.3	(0.7)	64.9	(1.7)
Flanders (Belgium)	74.1	(1.0)	67.4	(0.9)	36.5	(0.8)	56.9	(1.5)	45.2	(0.8)	68.2	(1.2)	38.8	(0.9)	57.6	(1.4)
Average	56.5	(0.2)	53.5	(0.2)	45.6	(0.2)	57.6	(0.3)	43.2	(0.2)	55.3	(0.3)	41.2	(0.2)	60.8	(0.3)
United States	93.5	(0.7)	63.0	(1.6)	90.0	(0.9)	70.5	(1.6)	88.2	(1.0)	78.5	(1.2)	70.2	(1.2)	92.7	(0.9)

1. In-service or professional development stage is not included in this table.

2. Subjects include reading and writing (and literature) in the mother tongue, in the language of instruction or in the tongue of the country (region) as a second language (for non-natives); language studies, public speaking, literature.

3. Subjects include mathematics, mathematics with statistics, geometry, algebra, etc.

4. Subjects include science, physics, physical science, chemistry, biology, human biology, environmental science, agriculture/forestry.

5. Subjects include languages different from the language of instruction.

6. Education categories are based on the International Standard Classification of Education (ISCED 1997). ISCED level 5A programmes are generally longer and more theory-based, while 5B programmes are typically shorter and more practical and skills oriented. No distinction was made between ISCED level 5A (Bachelor) and ISCED level 5A (Master).

* See notes at the beginning of this Annex.

Source: OECD, TALIS 2013 Database.

StatLink ⟋⟍⟍ http://dx.doi.org/10.1787/888933042960

[Part 1/1]
School type and school competition

Table 2.17 *Percentage of lower secondary education teachers who work in schools where principals report the following school characteristics*

	Public schools[1]		Private schools[2]		Schools that compete with two or more other schools for at least some of their students		Schools that compete with one other school for at least some of their students		Schools that do not compete with other schools for their students	
	%	S.E.	%	S.E.	%	S.E.	%	S.E.	%	S.E.
Australia	51.9	(3.6)	48.1	(3.6)	91.3	(1.9)	4.4	(1.5)	4.3	(1.2)
Brazil	81.6	(0.8)	18.4	(0.8)	62.0	(2.4)	19.7	(2.4)	18.3	(2.0)
Bulgaria	99.2	(0.6)	0.8	(0.6)	66.4	(3.2)	12.9	(2.6)	20.7	(2.8)
Chile	39.7	(2.9)	60.3	(2.9)	84.0	(3.4)	9.4	(3.2)	6.6	(1.8)
Croatia	98.4	(1.1)	1.6	(1.1)	39.1	(3.7)	20.2	(3.4)	40.7	(3.8)
Cyprus*	80.3	(0.1)	19.7	(0.1)	42.1	(0.2)	17.2	(0.2)	40.7	(0.2)
Czech Republic	95.7	(0.3)	4.3	(0.3)	66.3	(3.2)	15.5	(2.4)	18.2	(2.8)
Denmark	75.6	(2.8)	24.4	(2.8)	75.8	(4.4)	9.4	(2.6)	14.8	(3.8)
Estonia	95.2	(1.6)	4.8	(1.6)	62.1	(3.6)	21.9	(3.4)	16.0	(2.5)
Finland	95.3	(1.6)	4.7	(1.6)	50.1	(4.3)	18.4	(3.5)	31.5	(3.5)
France	81.5	(1.2)	18.5	(1.2)	48.4	(3.9)	27.2	(3.7)	24.3	(3.4)
Iceland	98.4	(0.0)	1.6	(0.0)	33.4	(0.1)	8.2	(0.0)	58.3	(0.1)
Israel	89.7	(2.8)	10.3	(2.8)	64.7	(3.6)	20.5	(2.8)	14.8	(2.9)
Italy	95.5	(0.2)	4.5	(0.2)	53.3	(4.1)	14.5	(2.8)	32.1	(3.7)
Japan	89.9	(0.9)	10.1	(0.9)	28.2	(2.6)	5.7	(1.8)	66.1	(3.0)
Korea	81.5	(0.8)	18.5	(0.8)	46.8	(4.2)	9.6	(2.6)	43.7	(4.2)
Latvia	98.6	(1.5)	1.4	(1.5)	78.6	(3.9)	11.2	(2.9)	10.2	(2.9)
Malaysia	100.0	(0.0)	0.0	(0.0)	77.0	(4.1)	11.2	(3.0)	11.8	(3.0)
Mexico	82.1	(1.0)	17.9	(1.0)	76.4	(3.5)	16.4	(2.9)	7.2	(2.1)
Netherlands	22.1	(5.2)	77.9	(5.2)	69.7	(5.7)	19.8	(4.9)	10.5	(3.3)
Norway	94.6	(3.1)	5.4	(3.1)	37.1	(5.6)	19.5	(5.0)	43.3	(6.4)
Poland	94.7	(1.4)	5.3	(1.4)	66.3	(3.1)	18.3	(2.4)	15.3	(2.5)
Portugal	88.5	(0.9)	11.5	(0.9)	57.2	(3.9)	20.7	(3.5)	22.1	(3.3)
Romania	100.0	(0.0)	a	a	59.4	(4.0)	13.1	(2.7)	27.5	(3.7)
Serbia	100.0	(0.0)	a	a	45.7	(3.5)	15.4	(3.5)	39.0	(3.4)
Singapore	100.0	(0.0)	0.0	(0.0)	98.4	(0.1)	0.0	(0.0)	1.6	(0.1)
Slovak Republic	91.2	(1.6)	8.8	(1.6)	63.7	(3.4)	14.1	(2.7)	22.2	(3.0)
Spain	73.7	(1.9)	26.3	(1.9)	68.2	(3.0)	15.8	(2.9)	16.0	(2.6)
Sweden	86.6	(1.3)	13.4	(1.3)	69.0	(3.6)	9.0	(2.5)	22.1	(3.4)
Sub-national entities										
Abu Dhabi (United Arab Emirates)	44.8	(2.8)	55.2	(2.8)	54.1	(4.2)	18.8	(4.2)	27.1	(4.2)
Alberta (Canada)	95.1	(1.3)	4.9	(1.3)	64.2	(4.1)	20.9	(3.3)	14.9	(3.0)
England (United Kingdom)	51.4	(3.9)	48.6	(3.9)	92.4	(2.4)	4.9	(1.8)	2.7	(1.2)
Flanders (Belgium)	26.5	(1.3)	73.5	(1.3)	89.6	(2.9)	7.4	(2.4)	3.0	(1.5)
Average[3]	81.8	(0.3)	19.4	(0.4)	63.1	(0.6)	14.3	(0.5)	22.7	(0.5)
United States	87.3	(3.2)	12.7	(3.2)	62.0	(5.4)	8.8	(3.7)	29.2	(5.6)

1. Refers to the percentage of teachers in lower secondary education who work in schools where principals reported that their school was publicly managed. This is a school managed by a public education authority, government agency, municipality or governing board appointed by government or elected by public franchise.
2. Refers to the percentage of teachers in lower secondary education who work in schools where principals reported that their school was privately managed. This is a school managed by a non-government organisation; e.g. a church, trade union, business or other private institution. In some countries, the privately-managed-schools category includes schools that receive significant funding from the governments (government-dependent private schools).
3. The averages do not add up to 100 across categories because of the presence of cells that are not applicable "a" in some countries.
* See notes at the beginning of this Annex.
Source: OECD, TALIS 2013 Database.
StatLink ⟶ http://dx.doi.org/10.1787/888933042998

[Part 1/1]
Primary school type and school competition
Percentage of primary education teachers who work in schools where principals report
the following school characteristics

Table 2.17.a

	Public schools[1]		Private schools[2]		Schools that compete with two or more other schools for at least some of their students		Schools that compete with one other school for at least some of their students		Schools that do not compete with other schools for their students	
	%	S.E.	%	S.E.	%	S.E.	%	S.E.	%	S.E.
Denmark	82.5	(1.8)	17.5	(1.8)	73.1	(4.4)	11.4	(3.2)	15.5	(3.7)
Finland	98.4	(1.2)	1.6	(1.2)	80.0	(3.0)	3.0	(1.2)	17.0	(2.8)
Mexico	84.6	(1.7)	15.4	(1.7)	59.8	(4.9)	18.4	(4.1)	21.8	(3.5)
Norway	98.1	(1.4)	1.9	(1.4)	51.5	(4.4)	18.6	(9.0)	29.9	(8.1)
Poland	95.8	(1.0)	4.2	(1.0)	58.8	(4.4)	26.1	(4.3)	15.1	(3.3)
Sub-national entities										
Flanders (Belgium)	38.5	(2.2)	61.5	(2.2)	77.7	(3.7)	16.3	(3.3)	6.0	(2.2)
Average	83.0	(0.7)	17.0	(0.7)	66.8	(1.7)	15.6	(2.0)	17.5	(1.8)

1. Refers to the percentage of teachers in primary education who work in schools where principals reported that their school was publicly managed. This is a school managed by a public education authority, government agency, municipality or governing board appointed by government or elected by public franchise.

2. Refers to the percentage of teachers in primary education who work in schools where principals reported that their school was privately managed. This is a school managed by a non-government organisation; e.g. a church, trade union, business or other private institution. In some countries, the privately-managed-schools category includes schools that receive significant funding from the governments (government-dependent private schools).

Source: OECD, TALIS 2013 Database.

StatLink http://dx.doi.org/10.1787/888933043017

[Part 1/1]
Upper secondary school type and school competition
Percentage of upper secondary education teachers who work in schools where principals report
the following school characteristics

Table 2.17.b

	Public schools[1]		Private schools[2]		Schools that compete with two or more other schools for at least some of their students[3]		Schools that compete with one other school for at least some of their students[3]		Schools that do not compete with other schools for their students[3]	
	%	S.E.	%	S.E.	%	S.E.	%	S.E.	%	S.E.
Australia	55.8	(4.0)	44.2	(4.0)	92.3	(2.7)	4.3	(2.1)	3.5	(1.8)
Denmark	97.1	(1.6)	2.9	(1.6)	88.8	(4.0)	9.3	(3.5)	1.9	(1.9)
Finland	85.3	(3.9)	14.7	(3.9)	53.2	(6.3)	17.0	(3.9)	29.8	(5.1)
Iceland	85.8	(0.1)	14.2	(0.1)	75.2	(0.1)	13.4	(0.1)	11.4	(0.1)
Italy	90.4	(1.4)	9.6	(1.4)	56.5	(4.9)	22.9	(4.9)	20.5	(3.4)
Mexico	70.4	(1.7)	29.6	(1.7)	79.2	(4.0)	14.5	(3.5)	6.3	(1.9)
Norway	92.7	(2.1)	7.3	(2.1)	56.6	(7.5)	18.2	(6.1)	25.3	(6.1)
Poland	97.2	(1.4)	2.8	(1.4)	84.0	(3.7)	11.6	(3.0)	4.5	(2.1)
Singapore	100.0	(0.0)	0.0	(0.0)	98.3	(0.0)	0.0	(0.0)	1.7	(0.0)
Sub-national entities										
Abu Dhabi (United Arab Emirates)	43.0	(3.3)	57.0	(3.3)	60.3	(4.3)	17.9	(4.0)	21.8	(4.0)
Average	81.8	(0.7)	18.2	(0.7)	74.4	(1.4)	12.9	(1.1)	12.7	(1.0)

1. Refers to the percentage of teachers in upper secondary education who work in schools where principals reported that their school was publicly managed. This is a school managed by a public education authority, government agency, municipality or governing board appointed by government or elected by public franchise.

2. Refers to the percentage of teachers in upper secondary education who work in schools where principals reported that their school was privately managed. This is a school managed by a non-government organisation; e.g. a church, trade union, business or other private institution. In some countries, the privately-managed-schools category includes schools that receive significant funding from the governments (government-dependent private schools).

3. For general education programmes.

Source: OECD, TALIS 2013 Database.

StatLink http://dx.doi.org/10.1787/888933043036

[Part 1/1]
School and class size

Table 2.18 *Average number of students and staff and average staff ratios in schools where lower secondary education teachers work (includes both public and private schools), and average class size in lower secondary education*

	Number of students in schools[1]		Number of teachers in schools[1]		Ratio of students to number of teachers[2]		Ratio of teachers to number of personnel for pedagogical support		Ratio of teachers to number of school administrative or management personnel		Average class size[3]	
	Average	S.E.	Average	S.E.	Average	S.E.	Average	S.E.	Average	S.E.	Average	S.E.
Australia	814.2	(51.5)	66.6	(4.2)	12.3	(0.2)	8.1	(1.0)	4.4	(0.3)	24.7	(0.7)
Brazil	586.0	(12.8)	33.8	(1.3)	19.1	(0.6)	13.8	(0.7)	4.5	(0.2)	30.8	(0.3)
Bulgaria	345.0	(9.7)	25.9	(0.6)	12.5	(0.3)	9.4	(0.7)	2.3	(0.1)	21.7	(0.2)
Chile	483.7	(20.2)	25.7	(1.2)	20.4	(1.8)	5.4	(0.4)	3.7	(0.2)	31.8	(0.6)
Croatia	433.0	(20.6)	39.4	(1.8)	10.8	(0.6)	14.8	(0.5)	11.1	(0.4)	20.0	(0.2)
Cyprus*	364.1	(20.0)	49.5	(1.8)	7.1	(0.2)	22.5	(2.1)	4.9	(0.2)	20.7	(0.1)
Czech Republic	341.7	(7.7)	26.0	(0.6)	13.0	(0.2)	16.6	(0.9)	5.3	(0.1)	21.1	(0.2)
Denmark	401.4	(13.2)	32.8	(1.3)	12.1	(0.2)	10.3	(0.9)	6.5	(0.2)	21.2	(0.2)
Estonia	297.3	(17.3)	32.2	(1.2)	7.7	(0.2)	9.5	(0.4)	6.7	(0.2)	17.3	(0.3)
Finland	348.0	(12.3)	33.1	(0.9)	10.0	(0.2)	8.2	(0.5)	12.4	(0.4)	17.8	(0.2)
France	542.9	(16.3)	39.9	(1.1)	13.6	(0.3)	5.6	(0.5)	6.8	(0.2)	25.5	(0.1)
Iceland	247.8	(13.2)	27.0	(1.2)	8.4	(0.2)	4.3	(0.3)	6.9	(0.2)	19.6	(0.3)
Israel	494.2	(35.4)	47.7	(3.4)	10.8	(0.5)	6.8	(0.8)	3.9	(0.3)	27.6	(0.4)
Italy	794.6	(29.3)	85.8	(2.5)	9.8	(0.3)	60.1	(3.6)	11.4	(0.3)	21.8	(0.2)
Japan	357.3	(9.7)	24.2	(0.6)	20.3	(3.6)	11.5	(0.6)	6.0	(0.1)	31.2	(0.3)
Korea	567.2	(14.0)	31.7	(0.7)	15.5	(0.3)	8.6	(0.5)	3.8	(0.1)	32.4	(0.3)
Latvia	295.1	(10.3)	32.8	(1.1)	9.1	(0.8)	8.1	(0.4)	5.2	(0.3)	17.7	(0.4)
Malaysia	1 151.1	(20.6)	82.7	(1.1)	13.6	(0.2)	53.1	(2.8)	5.9	(0.2)	32.1	(0.3)
Mexico	416.8	(23.2)	25.4	(0.9)	15.1	(0.7)	12.1	(0.8)	4.4	(0.3)	33.0	(0.6)
Netherlands	869.9	(71.4)	74.4	(6.1)	11.4	(0.7)	9.8	(1.2)	7.5	(0.5)	25.4	(0.3)
Norway	257.0	(13.6)	29.1	(1.5)	8.5	(0.2)	5.4	(0.3)	5.4	(0.3)	22.5	(0.5)
Poland	220.6	(9.4)	27.2	(0.9)	7.9	(0.3)	11.6	(0.7)	6.2	(0.3)	21.4	(0.2)
Portugal	1 152.5	(51.9)	109.5	(4.7)	10.5	(0.2)	7.5	(1.2)	8.5	(0.3)	22.6	(0.2)
Romania	474.0	(21.6)	31.6	(1.4)	15.1	(0.5)	22.0	(1.7)	7.9	(0.3)	21.7	(0.4)
Serbia	554.6	(21.4)	45.1	(1.7)	11.8	(0.4)	24.1	(1.3)	9.9	(0.4)	21.9	(0.3)
Singapore	1 251.4	(34.9)	91.1	(3.2)	14.0	(0.2)	11.9	(1.0)	2.7	(0.1)	35.5	(0.2)
Slovak Republic	314.3	(9.0)	25.0	(0.6)	12.1	(0.2)	16.9	(0.7)	4.0	(0.2)	19.1	(0.2)
Spain	545.4	(26.3)	44.5	(1.8)	11.8	(0.3)	19.2	(1.1)	5.6	(0.2)	23.6	(0.2)
Sweden	373.5	(17.5)	35.1	(1.4)	10.8	(0.4)	7.1	(0.4)	10.5	(0.4)	21.4	(0.3)
Sub-national entities												
Abu Dhabi (United Arab Emirates)	887.6	(44.3)	61.6	(2.8)	14.0	(0.7)	12.7	(1.6)	5.9	(0.3)	25.1	(0.6)
Alberta (Canada)	334.9	(11.5)	18.4	(0.7)	18.0	(0.6)	3.8	(0.2)	4.2	(0.1)	25.8	(0.4)
England (United Kingdom)	890.2	(27.4)	67.5	(2.8)	13.6	(0.2)	4.1	(0.2)	3.3	(0.2)	23.9	(0.3)
Flanders (Belgium)	623.7	(49.8)	78.6	(4.9)	7.9	(0.5)	31.3	(3.5)	10.0	(0.6)	17.3	(0.3)
Average	546.4	(4.8)	45.5	(0.4)	12.4	(0.1)	14.4	(0.2)	6.3	(0.0)	24.1	(0.1)
United States	566.5	(43.6)	38.2	(2.3)	14.9	(1.0)	8.0	(1.4)	6.4	(0.3)	27.0	(0.6)

1. These data are reported by principals and represent the average of school-level data in each country. For example, in Australia, 814.2 represents the average number of students per school where lower secondary teachers work and 66.6 represents the average number of teachers in schools where lower secondary teachers work. The education provision in these schools may extend across ISCED levels (e.g. in schools that offer both lower and upper secondary education) and therefore may not apply only to teachers or students in lower secondary education.

2. The average ratio of students to number of teachers is derived from the principal questionnaire. It is calculated by making the average of the school ratios in each country and can therefore be different from the ratio of the averages you could calculate from this table.

3. These data are reported by lower secondary teachers and refer to a randomly chosen class they currently teach from their weekly timetable.

* See notes at the beginning of this Annex.

Source: OECD, TALIS 2013 Database.

StatLink ⬛☷⬛ http://dx.doi.org/10.1787/888933043055

[Part 1/1]
Primary school and class size

Average number of students and staff and average staff ratios in schools where primary education teachers work (includes both public and private schools), and average class size in primary education

Table 2.18.a

	Number of students in schools[1]		Number of teachers in schools[1]		Ratio of students to number of teachers[2]		Ratio of teachers to number of personnel for pedagogical support		Ratio of teachers to number of school administrative or management personnel		Average class size[3]	
	Average	S.E.	Average	S.E.	Average	S.E.	Average	S.E.	Average	S.E.	Average	S.E.
Denmark	387.4	(12.2)	31.8	(1.1)	12.6	(0.2)	9.8	(0.9)	6.6	(0.2)	21.4	(0.2)
Finland	180.2	(6.1)	14.1	(0.6)	12.6	(0.3)	3.0	(0.2)	7.4	(0.4)	17.8	(0.3)
Mexico	195.4	(9.8)	8.4	(0.4)	24.1	(1.1)	6.0	(0.3)	5.6	(0.3)	26.3	(0.6)
Norway	220.1	(17.4)	22.6	(1.8)	9.6	(0.3)	3.4	(0.2)	5.2	(0.3)	19.3	(0.4)
Poland	201.6	(5.7)	21.0	(0.7)	8.6	(0.2)	9.7	(0.5)	6.0	(0.4)	18.8	(0.2)
Sub-national entities												
Flanders (Belgium)	301.8	(7.6)	22.8	(0.6)	13.4	(0.2)	15.2	(0.7)	8.5	(0.3)	18.0	(0.2)
Average	247.8	(4.3)	20.1	(0.4)	13.5	(0.2)	7.9	(0.2)	6.5	(0.1)	20.3	(0.1)

1. These data are reported by principals and represent the average of school-level data in each country. For example, in Denmark, 387.4 represents the average number of students per school where primary teachers work and 31.8 represents the average number of teachers in schools where primary teachers work. The education provision in these schools may extend across ISCED levels (e.g. in schools that offer both primary and lower secondary education) and therefore may not apply only to teachers or students in primary education.

2. The average ratio of students to number of teachers is derived from the principal questionnaire. It is calculated by making the average of the school ratios in each country and can therefore be different from the ratio of the averages you could calculate from this table.

3. These data are reported by primary education teachers and refer to a randomly chosen class they currently teach from their weekly timetable.

Source: OECD, TALIS 2013 Database.

StatLink ⟨⟩ http://dx.doi.org/10.1787/888933043074

[Part 1/1]
Upper secondary school and class size

Average number of students and staff and average staff ratios in schools where upper secondary education teachers work (includes both public and private schools), and average class size in upper secondary education

Table 2.18.b

	Number of students in schools[1]		Number of teachers in schools[1]		Ratio of students to number of teachers[2]		Ratio of teachers to number of personnel for pedagogical support		Ratio of teachers to number of school administrative or management personnel		Average class size[3]	
	Average	S.E.	Average	S.E.	Average	S.E.	Average	S.E.	Average	S.E.	Average	S.E.
Australia	817.2	(48.1)	65.5	(4.2)	12.7	(0.2)	8.4	(0.6)	4.4	(0.2)	18.5	(0.4)
Denmark	960.5	(106.7)	96.7	(9.1)	10.0	(0.2)	38.9	(3.3)	6.2	(0.3)	23.5	(0.3)
Finland	1 091.9	(229.2)	87.1	(14.8)	12.5	(0.7)	12.6	(0.9)	8.1	(0.3)	20.0	(0.4)
Iceland	724.6	(63.7)	56.1	(3.6)	12.2	(0.7)	20.0	(3.4)	8.3	(0.5)	22.6	(0.4)
Italy	717.2	(26.2)	80.4	(3.1)	9.2	(0.3)	18.1	(1.0)	8.4	(0.3)	21.9	(0.2)
Mexico	380.6	(25.3)	23.9	(1.2)	16.4	(0.9)	12.7	(0.9)	2.8	(0.1)	33.9	(0.6)
Norway	507.7	(29.5)	69.6	(4.0)	7.4	(0.2)	13.2	(2.0)	5.5	(0.2)	19.4	(0.4)
Poland	387.4	(26.8)	43.2	(2.1)	8.6	(0.5)	17.9	(1.2)	4.4	(0.2)	23.1	(0.3)
Singapore	1 257.4	(30.8)	92.4	(2.8)	13.9	(0.2)	12.0	(1.0)	2.8	(0.1)	33.4	(0.2)
Sub-national entities												
Abu Dhabi (United Arab Emirates)	1 039.6	(61.0)	73.1	(3.2)	13.1	(0.3)	13.8	(1.6)	6.4	(0.4)	24.0	(0.4)
Average	788.4	(27.9)	68.8	(2.0)	11.6	(0.2)	16.8	(0.6)	5.7	(0.1)	24.0	(0.1)

1. These data are reported by principals and represent the average of school-level data in each country. For example, in Australia, 817.2 represents the average number of students per school where upper secondary teachers work and 65.5 represents the average number of teachers in schools where upper secondary teachers work. The education provision in these schools may extend across ISCED levels (e.g. in schools that offer both lower and upper secondary education) and therefore may not apply only to teachers or students in upper secondary education.

2. The average ratio of students to number of teachers is derived from the principal questionnaire. It is calculated by making the average of the school ratios in each country and can therefore be different from the ratio of the averages you could calculate from this table.

3. These data are reported by upper secondary teachers and refer to a randomly chosen class they currently teach from their weekly timetable.

Source: OECD, TALIS 2013 Database.

StatLink ⟨⟩ http://dx.doi.org/10.1787/888933043093

TALIS 2013 RESULTS: AN INTERNATIONAL PERSPECTIVE ON TEACHING AND LEARNING

[Part 1/1]
School resources
Percentage of lower secondary education teachers whose school principal reports that the following resources issues hinder the school's capacity to provide quality instruction[1]

Table 2.19

	Shortage of qualified and/or well-performing teachers		Shortage of teachers with competences in teaching students with special needs		Shortage of vocational teachers		Shortage or inadequacy of instructional materials		Shortage or inadequacy of computers for instruction		Insufficient internet access		Shortage or inadequacy of computer software for instruction		Shortage or inadequacy of library materials		Shortage of support personnel	
	%	S.E.	%	S.E.	%	S.E.	%	S.E.	%	S.E.	%	S.E.	%	S.E.	%	S.E.	%	S.E.
Australia	47.8	(6.3)	37.4	(6.1)	27.6	(5.8)	13.9	(3.9)	8.0	(2.3)	14.6	(3.2)	12.0	(3.5)	6.5	(1.9)	28.2	(4.6)
Brazil	49.2	(2.6)	55.3	(2.5)	33.2	(2.6)	27.2	(2.2)	44.9	(2.6)	48.8	(2.5)	55.9	(2.3)	43.8	(2.5)	57.1	(2.3)
Bulgaria	27.3	(3.0)	28.6	(2.9)	11.2	(2.3)	34.5	(3.5)	41.0	(3.4)	12.6	(2.5)	30.6	(3.3)	35.9	(3.4)	13.4	(2.4)
Chile	56.7	(4.6)	51.5	(4.9)	46.4	(4.6)	23.2	(3.7)	29.1	(4.1)	37.6	(4.8)	36.1	(4.9)	34.6	(4.4)	42.6	(4.3)
Croatia	24.7	(2.8)	63.1	(3.6)	4.9	(1.7)	27.4	(3.4)	52.0	(3.9)	32.8	(3.4)	53.0	(3.9)	44.6	(4.0)	38.2	(3.4)
Cyprus*	38.3	(0.2)	40.9	(0.3)	31.5	(0.2)	30.9	(0.2)	39.9	(0.2)	32.7	(0.2)	43.5	(0.2)	35.6	(0.2)	44.2	(0.2)
Czech Republic	27.3	(3.4)	24.8	(3.4)	8.1	(1.9)	28.3	(3.5)	33.2	(3.3)	11.0	(2.4)	27.6	(3.4)	33.0	(3.6)	47.5	(3.7)
Denmark	14.8	(3.5)	40.5	(5.1)	11.3	(3.1)	19.8	(3.7)	40.6	(4.9)	37.5	(4.9)	29.6	(4.2)	18.4	(4.0)	48.3	(5.3)
Estonia	50.4	(4.4)	61.3	(4.0)	12.9	(2.9)	51.1	(4.2)	34.8	(3.9)	12.7	(2.3)	33.2	(3.9)	29.4	(3.4)	49.0	(4.1)
Finland	17.1	(3.3)	56.0	(4.8)	4.9	(1.8)	22.3	(4.2)	46.4	(4.4)	32.8	(4.2)	45.8	(4.1)	25.6	(4.1)	51.5	(4.2)
France	31.7	(3.8)	76.4	(2.8)	9.1	(2.3)	23.6	(3.5)	24.3	(3.3)	23.9	(3.4)	30.5	(3.7)	19.3	(3.4)	58.9	(4.0)
Iceland	13.9	(0.1)	28.4	(0.1)	29.1	(0.1)	13.8	(0.1)	49.4	(0.1)	29.6	(0.1)	54.1	(0.1)	17.1	(0.1)	23.3	(0.1)
Israel	53.5	(4.4)	52.1	(4.2)	45.8	(4.3)	29.3	(4.0)	59.1	(4.3)	50.1	(4.3)	54.1	(4.5)	43.6	(4.6)	58.4	(4.2)
Italy	38.3	(3.5)	58.0	(3.7)	12.1	(2.3)	56.4	(3.9)	56.0	(3.9)	47.4	(3.9)	53.8	(3.9)	43.6	(3.7)	77.5	(2.9)
Japan	79.7	(2.7)	76.0	(3.2)	37.3	(3.3)	17.2	(2.8)	28.3	(3.4)	29.8	(3.7)	40.1	(3.6)	40.2	(3.6)	72.4	(3.0)
Korea	36.7	(4.2)	50.4	(3.9)	35.7	(3.9)	15.0	(2.6)	12.5	(2.8)	7.7	(2.0)	9.9	(2.4)	18.4	(3.4)	54.7	(4.1)
Latvia	24.6	(4.6)	26.2	(4.1)	4.1	(1.9)	29.1	(4.3)	36.7	(4.8)	15.6	(3.8)	30.4	(4.3)	29.8	(4.2)	36.1	(4.4)
Malaysia	31.1	(4.0)	21.3	(3.5)	15.6	(3.2)	15.7	(3.3)	52.6	(4.3)	56.9	(4.0)	41.3	(4.4)	35.2	(4.3)	37.1	(4.5)
Mexico	56.0	(3.8)	58.1	(3.9)	29.1	(3.2)	38.9	(3.4)	66.7	(3.2)	64.9	(3.6)	65.5	(3.3)	51.0	(3.5)	59.6	(3.5)
Netherlands	71.1	(4.6)	71.4	(5.0)	9.6	(3.7)	16.6	(3.9)	47.4	(5.7)	30.8	(5.4)	53.7	(5.1)	16.8	(4.2)	45.7	(5.6)
Norway	43.1	(7.3)	64.8	(6.6)	2.1	(1.2)	15.1	(4.3)	48.4	(6.9)	37.8	(5.6)	35.3	(5.5)	29.7	(5.8)	46.4	(5.6)
Poland	12.7	(2.7)	19.8	(3.1)	2.2	(1.0)	11.7	(2.7)	29.0	(4.0)	21.2	(3.7)	40.1	(4.0)	21.7	(3.6)	32.3	(4.2)
Portugal	27.2	(3.9)	43.4	(4.1)	24.0	(3.3)	12.2	(2.4)	17.4	(3.0)	12.9	(3.0)	27.3	(3.6)	16.9	(3.3)	66.8	(3.8)
Romania	58.1	(3.7)	56.1	(3.8)	42.6	(3.9)	77.1	(3.1)	75.8	(3.7)	64.1	(3.9)	74.7	(3.4)	66.6	(3.7)	65.4	(3.8)
Serbia	19.8	(3.3)	65.1	(4.0)	6.0	(2.5)	20.1	(3.2)	36.5	(3.9)	32.8	(4.1)	44.7	(4.1)	33.1	(4.0)	22.1	(3.7)
Singapore	50.5	(0.3)	48.4	(0.3)	9.6	(0.1)	1.3	(0.0)	4.3	(0.0)	6.5	(0.1)	7.1	(0.2)	4.6	(0.1)	29.3	(0.2)
Slovak Republic	29.9	(3.4)	32.6	(3.5)	10.5	(2.4)	82.1	(2.9)	37.2	(3.5)	14.1	(2.3)	31.8	(3.5)	45.7	(3.6)	44.4	(3.5)
Spain	34.1	(3.6)	61.6	(3.6)	12.3	(2.2)	23.5	(2.9)	35.3	(3.6)	36.0	(4.0)	41.9	(3.7)	26.6	(3.3)	72.1	(3.5)
Sweden	32.4	(3.4)	49.9	(4.1)	8.7	(2.2)	23.4	(3.3)	52.7	(3.7)	32.9	(3.7)	36.2	(3.8)	13.1	(2.7)	61.0	(4.2)
Sub-national entities																		
Abu Dhabi (United Arab Emirates)	59.8	(5.0)	51.3	(4.6)	35.8	(4.9)	28.5	(3.8)	35.0	(4.1)	33.8	(4.1)	39.4	(4.1)	39.3	(4.5)	52.7	(4.7)
Alberta (Canada)	30.3	(4.4)	45.5	(5.1)	30.7	(4.2)	15.0	(3.8)	33.4	(4.1)	24.9	(3.5)	25.0	(3.7)	17.3	(3.3)	46.4	(4.8)
England (United Kingdom)	46.1	(4.4)	26.5	(3.7)	12.5	(3.0)	13.4	(2.8)	21.6	(3.1)	15.4	(3.0)	14.4	(3.2)	18.4	(3.6)	18.8	(3.7)
Flanders (Belgium)	33.4	(4.8)	42.7	(4.7)	22.2	(3.8)	10.1	(2.5)	29.5	(4.4)	25.8	(4.4)	19.0	(3.8)	12.3	(2.7)	45.3	(4.4)
Average	38.4	(0.7)	48.0	(0.7)	19.3	(0.5)	26.3	(0.6)	38.1	(0.7)	29.9	(0.6)	37.5	(0.6)	29.3	(0.6)	46.9	(0.7)
United States	34.3	(5.4)	32.6	(5.0)	19.0	(4.9)	24.8	(4.2)	34.7	(5.1)	24.7	(5.2)	26.9	(5.6)	14.9	(3.3)	47.1	(5.1)

1. Includes principals reporting that the resources issue hindered quality instruction "a lot" or "to some extent".

*See notes at the beginning of this Annex.

Source: OECD, TALIS 2013 Database.

StatLink ᴍᴪᴸ http://dx.doi.org/10.1787/888933043112

[Part 1/1]
School climate – Student-related factors
Percentage of lower secondary education teachers whose school principal considers the following student behaviours to occur at least weekly in their school

Table 2.20

	Arriving late at school		Absenteeism		Cheating		Vandalism and theft		Intimidation or verbal abuse among students		Physical injury caused by violence among students		Intimidation or verbal abuse of teachers or staff		Use/possession of drugs and/or alcohol	
	%	S.E.	%	S.E.	%	S.E.	%	S.E.	%	S.E.	%	S.E.	%	S.E.	%	S.E.
Australia	66.1	(4.9)	58.9	(5.2)	2.5	(1.8)	3.1	(1.6)	25.2	(4.4)	3.5	(1.6)	9.7	(2.8)	0.0	(0.0)
Brazil	51.4	(2.5)	38.4	(2.2)	17.4	(1.7)	11.8	(1.6)	34.4	(2.1)	6.7	(1.0)	12.5	(1.5)	6.9	(1.4)
Bulgaria	40.7	(3.5)	25.2	(3.0)	12.4	(2.9)	6.3	(1.4)	20.9	(3.3)	5.3	(2.1)	2.1	(1.1)	0.8	(0.5)
Chile	72.6	(4.1)	52.6	(4.2)	16.5	(3.3)	3.1	(1.6)	17.6	(3.6)	4.4	(1.9)	6.3	(2.4)	1.1	(1.1)
Croatia	19.9	(3.0)	10.7	(2.2)	30.6	(3.6)	1.3	(0.7)	16.1	(2.5)	1.5	(0.9)	1.8	(0.9)	0.0	(0.0)
Cyprus*	59.0	(0.2)	51.3	(0.2)	8.7	(0.2)	8.2	(0.1)	23.2	(0.2)	7.3	(0.2)	5.4	(0.1)	0.0	(0.0)
Czech Republic	39.4	(3.8)	5.7	(1.5)	12.9	(2.4)	3.9	(1.5)	4.9	(1.6)	0.0	(0.0)	0.5	(0.4)	0.9	(0.6)
Denmark	37.7	(5.3)	30.5	(4.7)	4.4	(2.5)	0.0	(0.0)	9.4	(3.4)	2.4	(1.4)	2.1	(1.3)	0.0	(0.0)
Estonia	53.4	(4.3)	48.6	(4.2)	34.3	(4.3)	1.5	(0.8)	23.5	(3.7)	1.7	(1.1)	11.0	(2.7)	1.4	(0.8)
Finland	86.5	(3.0)	64.0	(4.0)	2.0	(1.5)	2.4	(1.5)	27.8	(3.8)	0.0	(0.0)	3.6	(1.6)	1.0	(0.7)
France	61.6	(3.6)	50.9	(3.5)	16.5	(2.8)	6.8	(2.0)	23.7	(3.0)	7.0	(1.9)	3.0	(1.3)	0.9	(0.6)
Iceland	34.6	(0.1)	26.9	(0.1)	0.0	(0.0)	0.0	(0.0)	6.0	(0.1)	0.0	(0.0)	2.2	(0.0)	0.8	(0.0)
Israel	57.7	(4.0)	49.3	(4.1)	9.9	(2.2)	7.9	(2.2)	12.8	(2.7)	5.9	(1.5)	0.3	(0.3)	0.6	(0.6)
Italy	32.2	(3.5)	10.0	(2.5)	20.9	(2.9)	3.5	(1.8)	10.1	(2.6)	1.5	(1.4)	2.1	(1.6)	0.0	(0.0)
Japan	50.6	(3.8)	40.4	(3.5)	0.0	(0.0)	3.1	(1.3)	3.6	(1.5)	1.6	(0.9)	2.2	(1.1)	0.0	(0.0)
Korea	26.1	(3.7)	19.9	(3.2)	0.8	(0.8)	3.3	(1.5)	8.2	(2.4)	2.0	(1.1)	0.0	(0.0)	0.0	(0.0)
Latvia	47.3	(4.6)	39.4	(4.4)	34.0	(5.2)	0.8	(0.8)	18.2	(4.2)	0.0	(0.0)	5.0	(2.4)	0.0	(0.0)
Malaysia	56.9	(3.9)	57.6	(3.9)	9.0	(2.7)	10.8	(2.9)	0.0	(0.0)	0.0	(0.0)	0.0	(0.0)	0.0	(0.0)
Mexico	46.4	(4.0)	45.5	(3.3)	18.2	(3.0)	13.2	(2.8)	29.5	(3.7)	10.8	(2.3)	3.0	(1.0)	3.6	(1.4)
Netherlands	75.7	(4.6)	52.9	(5.4)	58.5	(5.4)	8.4	(3.1)	21.9	(4.5)	1.3	(1.3)	2.8	(2.0)	3.0	(1.8)
Norway	60.8	(7.4)	45.7	(5.4)	2.9	(1.8)	1.8	(1.0)	15.3	(5.7)	0.0	(0.0)	3.9	(2.4)	0.8	(0.8)
Poland	51.5	(4.4)	38.0	(4.0)	40.0	(3.9)	4.0	(1.5)	8.0	(2.2)	0.0	(0.0)	0.3	(0.3)	0.3	(0.3)
Portugal	58.1	(3.3)	33.3	(3.4)	13.0	(2.8)	7.4	(2.2)	14.6	(2.8)	5.0	(1.7)	5.5	(1.7)	3.6	(1.5)
Romania	28.7	(3.5)	29.6	(3.7)	5.4	(1.7)	1.9	(0.9)	9.0	(2.0)	0.9	(0.8)	0.0	(0.0)	0.0	(0.0)
Serbia	43.7	(4.2)	36.0	(3.9)	9.0	(2.0)	2.2	(1.1)	12.6	(2.5)	0.5	(0.5)	1.6	(0.5)	0.0	(0.0)
Singapore	51.8	(0.3)	35.0	(0.3)	0.0	(0.0)	0.0	(0.0)	1.8	(0.0)	0.0	(0.0)	0.6	(0.0)	0.0	(0.0)
Slovak Republic	40.0	(3.5)	14.1	(2.2)	15.3	(2.7)	4.5	(1.6)	2.2	(1.1)	0.0	(0.0)	0.6	(0.6)	0.0	(0.0)
Spain	37.6	(3.8)	24.8	(3.1)	11.1	(2.3)	4.9	(1.5)	13.9	(2.7)	0.1	(0.1)	1.9	(1.0)	3.6	(1.4)
Sweden	78.4	(3.2)	67.2	(3.7)	7.2	(2.0)	3.6	(1.4)	31.1	(3.7)	0.8	(0.8)	4.9	(1.8)	0.5	(0.5)
Sub-national entities																
Abu Dhabi (United Arab Emirates)	52.1	(4.6)	38.7	(4.9)	4.1	(2.0)	4.3	(1.8)	6.5	(2.2)	0.6	(0.5)	0.0	(0.0)	0.0	(0.0)
Alberta (Canada)	70.1	(4.4)	61.8	(4.6)	5.2	(1.9)	1.6	(1.2)	28.7	(4.7)	2.0	(1.2)	2.6	(1.3)	6.0	(2.2)
England (United Kingdom)	55.6	(4.8)	42.5	(4.3)	0.0	(0.0)	2.4	(1.1)	15.7	(2.6)	1.3	(0.8)	6.5	(1.8)	0.0	(0.0)
Flanders (Belgium)	65.1	(3.8)	30.1	(4.3)	12.3	(3.2)	7.4	(2.6)	30.7	(4.2)	1.3	(1.0)	9.1	(2.0)	3.9	(1.7)
Average	51.8	(0.7)	38.7	(0.6)	13.2	(0.5)	4.4	(0.3)	16.0	(0.5)	2.3	(0.2)	3.4	(0.3)	1.2	(0.1)
United States	73.3	(5.0)	60.7	(5.5)	17.4	(4.7)	5.5	(2.6)	20.9	(4.3)	1.7	(1.7)	4.7	(2.1)	3.5	(2.3)

* See notes at the beginning of this Annex.
Source: OECD, TALIS 2013 Database.
StatLink ⟡ http://dx.doi.org/10.1787/888933043150

[Part 1/1]
School climate – Teacher-related factors
Percentage of lower secondary education teachers whose school principal considers the following
Table 2.21 *teacher behaviours to occur at least weekly in their school*

	Arriving late at school		Absenteeism		Discrimination	
	%	S.E.	%	S.E.	%	S.E.
Australia	15.6	(4.7)	15.6	(5.6)	0.0	(0.0)
Brazil	29.5	(2.4)	17.6	(1.8)	0.4	(0.2)
Bulgaria	1.1	(0.8)	0.0	(0.0)	0.0	(0.0)
Chile	34.5	(4.5)	17.9	(3.7)	1.8	(1.1)
Croatia	2.9	(1.2)	0.0	(0.0)	0.0	(0.0)
Cyprus*	17.7	(0.2)	17.3	(0.2)	0.6	(0.0)
Czech Republic	0.5	(0.4)	0.0	(0.0)	0.0	(0.0)
Denmark	1.6	(0.9)	0.7	(0.7)	0.0	(0.0)
Estonia	3.5	(1.8)	0.0	(0.0)	0.0	(0.0)
Finland	11.4	(2.7)	0.7	(0.7)	0.0	(0.0)
France	13.1	(2.5)	7.0	(2.2)	0.6	(0.6)
Iceland	4.1	(0.1)	0.0	(0.0)	0.0	(0.0)
Israel	22.0	(4.2)	13.2	(3.6)	0.0	(0.0)
Italy	5.3	(1.6)	1.7	(1.3)	0.5	(0.5)
Japan	1.9	(1.0)	0.0	(0.0)	0.0	(0.0)
Korea	1.0	(0.7)	0.0	(0.0)	0.0	(0.0)
Latvia	0.9	(0.9)	0.7	(0.7)	0.0	(0.0)
Malaysia	14.4	(2.9)	1.5	(1.2)	0.3	(0.3)
Mexico	27.5	(3.3)	20.6	(3.3)	2.2	(1.1)
Netherlands	12.9	(3.7)	1.7	(1.7)	0.0	(0.0)
Norway	21.4	(4.7)	0.0	(0.0)	0.0	(0.0)
Poland	2.7	(1.1)	1.1	(1.1)	0.0	(0.0)
Portugal	18.2	(3.2)	4.3	(1.7)	0.9	(0.9)
Romania	1.5	(0.9)	0.0	(0.0)	0.0	(0.0)
Serbia	5.6	(1.7)	0.6	(0.6)	0.0	(0.0)
Singapore	9.0	(0.1)	1.4	(0.0)	0.0	(0.0)
Slovak Republic	1.5	(0.8)	0.0	(0.0)	0.0	(0.0)
Spain	8.9	(2.0)	0.9	(0.8)	0.6	(0.6)
Sweden	12.2	(2.4)	0.4	(0.4)	0.4	(0.4)
Sub-national entities						
Abu Dhabi (United Arab Emirates)	20.0	(4.1)	11.3	(3.1)	0.5	(0.5)
Alberta (Canada)	5.4	(1.8)	5.2	(1.6)	0.0	(0.0)
England (United Kingdom)	5.1	(1.9)	10.7	(2.6)	0.0	(0.0)
Flanders (Belgium)	25.2	(3.7)	2.1	(0.9)	0.0	(0.0)
Average	10.9	(0.4)	4.7	(0.3)	0.3	(0.1)
United States	21.8	(5.1)	12.6	(4.2)	0.0	(0.0)

*See notes at the beginning of this Annex.
Source: OECD, TALIS 2013 Database.
StatLink http://dx.doi.org/10.1787/888933043188

[Part 1/1]
Professional climate – Communication, shared beliefs and respect amongst colleagues
Percentage of lower secondary education teachers whose school principal reports that these statements apply to their school[1]

Table 2.22

	The school staff share a common set of beliefs about schooling/learning		There is a high level of co-operation between the school and the local community		School staff have an open discussion about difficulties		There is mutual respect for colleagues' ideas		There is a culture of sharing success	
	%	S.E.	%	S.E.	%	S.E.	%	S.E.	%	S.E.
Australia	89.2	(4.9)	82.1	(5.6)	87.3	(4.9)	95.2	(2.2)	92.1	(4.3)
Brazil	91.1	(1.6)	70.3	(2.0)	96.4	(1.0)	92.7	(1.5)	90.7	(1.5)
Bulgaria	80.9	(3.0)	89.1	(2.5)	96.0	(1.5)	79.6	(2.6)	86.9	(2.8)
Chile	91.2	(2.5)	71.1	(4.1)	96.0	(1.9)	90.3	(2.5)	87.7	(2.5)
Croatia	57.0	(3.8)	88.0	(2.3)	91.0	(2.1)	90.7	(2.3)	93.4	(1.9)
Cyprus2,3	93.5	(0.1)	84.6	(0.2)	96.0	(0.1)	95.3	(0.1)	96.9	(0.1)
Czech Republic	91.6	(1.9)	75.5	(3.2)	92.3	(2.2)	93.9	(1.8)	89.0	(2.3)
Denmark	76.3	(4.2)	45.6	(5.3)	92.5	(2.3)	93.3	(2.3)	89.1	(2.8)
Estonia	95.2	(2.5)	75.4	(3.2)	89.3	(2.9)	92.7	(2.0)	84.4	(3.0)
Finland	89.7	(2.3)	66.1	(4.0)	94.6	(2.2)	92.8	(2.5)	84.6	(3.2)
France	75.4	(3.3)	77.8	(3.1)	81.7	(3.2)	87.1	(2.6)	78.9	(3.2)
Iceland	86.3	(0.1)	81.0	(0.1)	95.1	(0.1)	90.6	(0.2)	93.1	(0.1)
Israel	94.6	(2.3)	84.7	(3.2)	98.2	(1.2)	94.7	(2.1)	96.1	(1.7)
Italy	90.6	(2.3)	74.2	(3.4)	87.7	(2.4)	86.0	(2.4)	81.1	(2.8)
Japan	98.1	(1.0)	75.3	(3.2)	96.1	(1.4)	95.2	(1.6)	96.4	(1.4)
Korea	96.2	(1.6)	91.4	(2.3)	93.5	(2.1)	100.0	(0.0)	96.2	(1.6)
Latvia	96.2	(2.0)	85.1	(3.6)	95.6	(2.1)	96.7	(1.9)	97.4	(1.5)
Malaysia	83.1	(2.6)	86.4	(2.7)	87.5	(2.7)	98.0	(0.8)	100.0	(0.0)
Mexico	66.2	(3.6)	70.1	(3.6)	88.4	(2.6)	91.6	(2.4)	87.2	(2.8)
Netherlands	72.2	(4.9)	21.2	(4.2)	79.0	(4.8)	87.5	(4.5)	75.5	(5.1)
Norway	87.1	(3.6)	40.8	(5.3)	96.7	(1.6)	97.5	(1.3)	86.0	(4.5)
Poland	91.6	(2.0)	85.1	(3.1)	92.2	(2.1)	91.6	(1.9)	88.6	(2.3)
Portugal	89.9	(2.4)	86.7	(2.8)	88.8	(2.6)	92.0	(2.0)	84.2	(2.8)
Romania	93.6	(1.9)	97.7	(1.1)	99.2	(0.5)	99.1	(0.9)	97.6	(1.2)
Serbia	72.4	(3.4)	81.0	(3.1)	92.3	(2.2)	90.6	(2.5)	82.4	(3.6)
Singapore	97.4	(0.0)	85.8	(0.2)	96.1	(0.1)	99.3	(0.0)	97.3	(0.0)
Slovak Republic	78.4	(2.8)	77.5	(3.4)	100.0	(0.0)	97.3	(1.2)	97.8	(1.0)
Spain	87.3	(2.9)	64.9	(3.9)	92.6	(2.5)	91.6	(2.5)	84.7	(2.9)
Sweden	80.5	(3.0)	33.5	(3.6)	94.3	(1.8)	87.1	(2.8)	76.3	(2.9)
Sub-national entities										
Abu Dhabi (United Arab Emirates)	94.2	(2.5)	88.5	(3.5)	95.2	(2.5)	95.7	(2.2)	92.2	(2.7)
Alberta (Canada)	96.3	(1.9)	88.6	(3.2)	95.0	(2.2)	95.5	(1.5)	95.6	(1.8)
England (United Kingdom)	96.0	(1.8)	87.5	(3.6)	90.2	(2.9)	96.7	(1.7)	96.2	(1.7)
Flanders (Belgium)	96.1	(1.6)	61.5	(5.2)	91.7	(2.0)	95.3	(1.6)	93.5	(2.1)
Average	87.1	(0.5)	75.0	(0.6)	92.7	(0.4)	93.1	(0.4)	90.0	(0.4)
United States	97.6	(1.3)	83.2	(3.9)	83.4	(5.0)	92.6	(2.6)	88.7	(3.8)

1. Includes principals who "agree" and "strongly agree" that these statements apply to their school.
* See notes at the beginning of this Annex.
Source: OECD, TALIS 2013 Database.
StatLink ᵐˢᵖ http://dx.doi.org/10.1787/888933043226

[Part 1/1]
School climate – Teacher-student relations
*Percentage of lower secondary education teachers who "agree" or "strongly agree" that
the following statements apply to their school and the percentage of teachers in lower secondary education
working in schools where the principals "agree" or "strongly agree" that the relationships
between teachers and students are good*

Table 2.23

| | Teachers who report that the following statements apply | | | | | | | | Principals who report that the following statement applies | |
| | In this school, teachers and students usually get on well with each other | | Most teachers in this school believe that the students' well-being is important | | Most teachers in this school are interested in what students have to say | | If a student from this school needs extra assistance, the school provides it | | The relationships between teachers and students are good | |
	%	S.E.	%	S.E.	%	S.E.	%	S.E.	%	S.E.
Australia	96.9	(0.6)	98.5	(0.3)	95.4	(0.5)	94.3	(0.8)	100.0	(0.0)
Brazil	91.9	(0.5)	94.5	(0.4)	85.9	(0.6)	76.7	(0.9)	94.1	(1.3)
Bulgaria	95.2	(0.6)	96.3	(0.4)	94.1	(0.6)	98.5	(0.3)	96.6	(1.3)
Chile	94.2	(0.8)	95.8	(0.6)	90.5	(0.9)	89.8	(1.1)	95.0	(2.3)
Croatia	93.8	(0.6)	96.7	(0.4)	87.7	(0.8)	93.6	(0.6)	98.1	(1.1)
Cyprus*	93.0	(0.7)	95.5	(0.5)	87.4	(0.9)	93.9	(0.6)	96.4	(0.1)
Czech Republic	95.6	(0.5)	94.6	(0.5)	89.4	(0.8)	98.0	(0.3)	98.4	(0.9)
Denmark	99.2	(0.2)	99.5	(0.2)	95.5	(0.7)	80.7	(1.5)	100.0	(0.0)
Estonia	96.3	(0.4)	96.9	(0.3)	91.8	(0.6)	97.4	(0.5)	98.0	(0.8)
Finland	96.5	(0.5)	98.1	(0.3)	94.9	(0.5)	97.2	(0.3)	98.0	(1.1)
France	93.7	(0.6)	93.5	(0.5)	89.7	(0.7)	92.8	(0.6)	96.5	(1.4)
Iceland	98.2	(0.4)	98.8	(0.4)	96.4	(0.6)	88.2	(0.9)	99.0	(0.0)
Israel	95.0	(0.6)	91.5	(0.6)	88.9	(0.7)	92.6	(0.9)	99.2	(0.6)
Italy	91.3	(0.7)	95.9	(0.4)	89.5	(0.6)	87.3	(0.7)	97.9	(1.1)
Japan	94.8	(0.6)	93.6	(0.5)	94.2	(0.5)	93.9	(0.5)	97.1	(1.2)
Korea	94.5	(0.6)	90.6	(0.7)	92.2	(0.6)	76.5	(0.9)	99.3	(0.7)
Latvia	95.9	(0.6)	96.5	(0.5)	94.5	(0.6)	98.1	(0.4)	99.1	(0.9)
Malaysia	95.8	(0.5)	98.7	(0.2)	89.5	(0.6)	94.7	(0.6)	100.0	(0.0)
Mexico	88.0	(0.8)	94.0	(0.6)	81.3	(0.9)	71.7	(1.5)	93.7	(2.0)
Netherlands	98.4	(0.6)	98.6	(0.4)	95.2	(1.0)	91.8	(1.3)	96.8	(2.2)
Norway	99.2	(0.3)	99.5	(0.2)	97.9	(0.8)	90.3	(0.9)	100.0	(0.0)
Poland	94.9	(0.5)	91.8	(0.7)	91.9	(0.7)	97.5	(0.4)	99.0	(0.7)
Portugal	97.8	(0.3)	98.3	(0.2)	92.7	(0.5)	96.1	(0.4)	99.4	(0.6)
Romania	95.7	(0.6)	96.4	(0.4)	89.4	(0.8)	91.1	(0.8)	98.9	(0.7)
Serbia	93.1	(0.5)	96.6	(0.3)	88.0	(0.6)	91.8	(0.6)	96.4	(1.4)
Singapore	96.4	(0.3)	97.6	(0.3)	91.8	(0.5)	98.3	(0.2)	100.0	(0.0)
Slovak Republic	92.2	(0.8)	95.5	(0.4)	89.7	(0.7)	97.0	(0.4)	98.0	(1.2)
Spain	96.0	(0.4)	96.2	(0.4)	89.8	(0.5)	88.3	(0.7)	97.0	(1.2)
Sweden	98.2	(0.2)	99.2	(0.2)	94.7	(0.5)	74.2	(1.7)	98.4	(1.2)
Sub-national entities										
Abu Dhabi (United Arab Emirates)	93.5	(0.7)	97.5	(0.4)	91.8	(0.7)	93.3	(0.8)	97.2	(1.8)
Alberta (Canada)	97.0	(0.4)	99.2	(0.2)	98.0	(0.4)	95.9	(0.7)	98.0	(1.3)
England (United Kingdom)	96.8	(0.4)	98.7	(0.3)	96.7	(0.5)	95.7	(0.6)	99.3	(0.7)
Flanders (Belgium)	97.3	(0.4)	98.4	(0.2)	94.9	(0.5)	98.2	(0.3)	99.5	(0.3)
Average	**95.3**	**(0.1)**	**96.5**	**(0.1)**	**91.8**	**(0.1)**	**91.4**	**(0.1)**	**98.0**	**(0.2)**
United States	94.6	(0.8)	98.4	(0.4)	94.4	(0.8)	95.3	(0.6)	96.9	(1.6)

* See notes at the beginning of this Annex.
Source: OECD, TALIS 2013 Database.
StatLink ᴍᴤᴘ http://dx.doi.org/10.1787/888933043264

[Part 1/1]

School climate – Teacher-student relations, 2008 and 2013

Percentage of lower secondary education teachers who report that the following statements apply to their school[1, 2, 3]

Table 2.23.c

	In this school, teachers and students usually get on well with each other				Most teachers in this school believe that the students' well-being is important				Most teachers in this school are interested in what students have to say				If a student from this school needs extra assistance, the school provides it			
	2008		2013		2008		2013		2008		2013		2008		2013	
	%	S.E.	%	S.E.	%	S.E.	%	S.E.	%	S.E.	%	S.E.	%	S.E.	%	S.E.
Australia	94.7	(0.6)	96.9	(0.6)	97.1	(0.5)	98.5	(0.3)	93.0	(0.6)	95.4	(0.5)	91.6	(0.7)	94.3	(0.8)
Brazil	90.1	(0.7)	91.9	(0.5)	94.1	(0.5)	94.4	(0.4)	85.6	(0.8)	85.9	(0.6)	70.8	(1.6)	76.6	(0.9)
Bulgaria	94.5	(0.8)	95.2	(0.6)	96.7	(0.3)	96.3	(0.4)	94.8	(0.4)	94.1	(0.6)	98.3	(0.3)	98.5	(0.3)
Denmark	97.6	(0.6)	99.2	(0.2)	98.1	(0.5)	99.4	(0.2)	93.8	(0.8)	95.4	(0.8)	82.1	(1.3)	81.0	(1.5)
Estonia	92.3	(0.7)	96.4	(0.3)	93.8	(0.5)	96.9	(0.4)	84.3	(0.8)	91.8	(0.6)	95.7	(0.4)	97.4	(0.5)
Iceland	96.8	(0.5)	98.5	(0.4)	98.4	(0.4)	98.8	(0.4)	95.1	(0.6)	96.3	(0.6)	85.2	(1.1)	87.9	(0.9)
Italy	93.6	(0.5)	91.3	(0.7)	94.8	(0.4)	95.9	(0.4)	91.8	(0.5)	89.5	(0.6)	85.8	(0.7)	87.3	(0.7)
Korea	89.9	(0.9)	94.5	(0.6)	86.8	(0.7)	90.6	(0.7)	90.9	(0.7)	92.2	(0.6)	85.6	(0.8)	76.4	(0.9)
Malaysia	82.2	(0.9)	95.8	(0.5)	96.2	(0.4)	98.7	(0.2)	88.4	(0.7)	89.4	(0.6)	94.1	(0.4)	94.6	(0.6)
Mexico	85.0	(0.9)	87.9	(0.8)	90.3	(0.7)	94.0	(0.6)	79.2	(1.0)	81.4	(0.9)	77.1	(1.1)	71.7	(1.5)
Norway	97.5	(0.4)	99.3	(0.3)	98.6	(0.3)	99.5	(0.2)	95.2	(0.5)	97.9	(0.8)	83.1	(1.2)	90.2	(0.9)
Poland	90.6	(0.9)	94.8	(0.5)	90.4	(0.8)	91.8	(0.7)	91.5	(0.8)	91.8	(0.7)	94.7	(0.5)	97.5	(0.4)
Portugal	95.2	(0.6)	97.8	(0.3)	98.2	(0.3)	98.3	(0.2)	92.4	(0.6)	92.6	(0.5)	91.9	(0.7)	96.1	(0.4)
Slovak Republic	87.5	(1.3)	92.3	(0.8)	93.8	(0.6)	95.5	(0.4)	86.5	(1.0)	89.6	(0.7)	95.4	(0.6)	97.0	(0.4)
Spain	91.7	(0.8)	96.0	(0.4)	93.0	(0.5)	96.3	(0.4)	83.7	(0.8)	89.9	(0.5)	86.9	(0.8)	88.3	(0.7)
Sub-national entities																
Flanders (Belgium)	95.0	(0.5)	97.4	(0.4)	97.2	(0.3)	98.4	(0.2)	93.2	(0.5)	94.9	(0.5)	97.4	(0.4)	98.2	(0.3)
Average	92.1	(0.2)	95.3	(0.1)	94.8	(0.1)	96.5	(0.1)	90.0	(0.2)	91.8	(0.2)	88.5	(0.2)	89.6	(0.2)

1. The teacher population coverage was slightly different between 2008 and 2013. In order to have comparable populations for the tables comparing results from TALIS 2008 and TALIS 2013, teachers who teach exclusively to students with special needs were excluded from the 2013 data in these tables.

2. The wording and order of questions may have changed slightly between the 2008 and 2013 surveys.

3. Includes teachers who responded that they "agree" or "strongly agree" that the statements apply to their school.

Source: OECD, TALIS 2008 and TALIS 2013 Databases.

StatLink ⊞⊟ http://dx.doi.org/10.1787/888933043283

[Part 1/1]
School autonomy
Percentage of lower secondary education teachers whose school principal reports
Table 2.24 *that considerable responsibility for the following tasks is held at the school level[1]*

	Appointing or hiring teachers		Dismissing or suspending teachers from employment		Establishing teachers' starting salaries, including setting pay scales		Determining teachers' salary increases		Deciding on budget allocations within the school		Establishing student disciplinary policies and procedures		Establishing student assessment policies, including national/ regional assessments		Approving students for admission to the school		Choosing which learning materials are used		Determining course content, including national/ regional curricula		Deciding which courses are offered	
	%	S.E.	%	S.E.	%	S.E.	%	S.E.	%	S.E.	%	S.E.	%	S.E.	%	S.E.	%	S.E.	%	S.E.	%	S.E.
Australia	90.9	(2.2)	72.9	(4.0)	33.2	(4.5)	29.5	(3.8)	93.9	(3.5)	98.4	(1.1)	90.7	(3.2)	98.7	(0.6)	100.0	(0.0)	86.0	(3.0)	100.0	(0.0)
Brazil	37.6	(1.6)	38.0	(1.8)	18.8	(1.1)	18.3	(1.3)	66.0	(2.3)	94.3	(1.1)	65.3	(2.4)	76.9	(1.6)	95.8	(1.1)	55.1	(2.0)	46.1	(2.2)
Bulgaria	100.0	(0.0)	100.0	(0.0)	81.6	(3.0)	88.9	(2.7)	97.6	(1.4)	98.9	(0.8)	78.1	(3.2)	88.0	(2.3)	97.7	(1.2)	66.0	(3.5)	76.6	(2.7)
Chile	73.6	(3.3)	71.9	(3.4)	61.6	(3.3)	61.4	(3.3)	66.3	(3.2)	97.0	(1.2)	88.2	(2.7)	95.8	(1.5)	96.8	(1.3)	78.2	(3.3)	84.9	(2.6)
Croatia	100.0	(0.0)	96.3	(1.4)	2.9	(1.3)	2.0	(1.1)	82.4	(2.8)	96.1	(1.4)	66.3	(3.2)	59.0	(3.4)	89.8	(2.3)	33.9	(3.5)	18.7	(2.7)
Cyprus*	24.9	(0.2)	23.8	(0.1)	23.1	(0.1)	23.1	(0.1)	50.4	(0.2)	93.9	(0.1)	82.9	(0.2)	32.4	(0.2)	60.1	(0.2)	35.4	(0.2)	29.7	(0.2)
Czech Republic	100.0	(0.0)	100.0	(0.0)	98.2	(1.1)	96.6	(2.0)	100.0	(0.0)	100.0	(0.0)	99.4	(0.5)	100.0	(0.0)	100.0	(0.0)	100.0	(0.0)	100.0	(0.0)
Denmark	100.0	(0.0)	97.7	(2.2)	45.3	(5.2)	48.6	(5.5)	100.0	(0.0)	100.0	(0.0)	93.6	(2.1)	92.2	(3.9)	100.0	(0.0)	94.5	(2.0)	91.1	(3.9)
Estonia	100.0	(0.0)	99.7	(0.3)	95.4	(1.4)	83.8	(2.9)	97.5	(1.1)	100.0	(0.0)	100.0	(0.0)	98.1	(0.9)	100.0	(0.0)	96.3	(1.2)	98.4	(0.7)
Finland	79.5	(3.3)	54.2	(4.2)	24.4	(3.6)	29.0	(4.3)	95.7	(1.7)	97.8	(1.3)	74.6	(4.0)	84.8	(3.4)	99.4	(0.6)	75.9	(3.8)	89.9	(2.9)
France	31.4	(2.7)	16.2	(2.2)	1.2	(0.7)	1.8	(0.8)	97.5	(1.3)	100.0	(0.0)	70.5	(3.5)	61.5	(3.8)	99.6	(0.4)	21.8	(3.4)	47.3	(3.9)
Iceland	100.0	(0.0)	100.0	(0.0)	14.5	(0.1)	28.0	(0.2)	70.2	(0.1)	100.0	(0.0)	93.1	(0.1)	84.1	(0.1)	98.5	(0.0)	70.1	(0.1)	91.1	(0.1)
Israel	85.9	(1.9)	75.9	(2.8)	16.3	(4.0)	23.8	(4.2)	73.8	(3.9)	99.6	(0.4)	89.6	(2.6)	83.2	(2.6)	93.8	(1.6)	79.1	(2.9)	93.0	(1.7)
Italy	76.8	(3.3)	56.0	(4.0)	7.7	(1.6)	8.0	(1.7)	94.4	(1.7)	100.0	(0.0)	89.7	(2.3)	98.3	(1.0)	100.0	(0.0)	94.8	(1.7)	100.0	(0.0)
Japan	18.0	(2.4)	17.4	(2.4)	6.5	(1.2)	16.1	(2.5)	59.5	(3.7)	98.5	(0.9)	89.6	(2.0)	45.9	(3.6)	43.4	(3.2)	53.5	(3.4)	55.8	(3.7)
Korea	42.1	(3.2)	32.8	(3.3)	11.6	(2.6)	8.7	(2.2)	95.4	(1.8)	97.2	(1.5)	51.5	(4.1)	85.5	(3.0)	99.2	(0.8)	66.9	(3.8)	95.1	(1.7)
Latvia	99.5	(0.5)	100.0	(0.0)	75.9	(4.3)	72.3	(4.4)	94.7	(2.5)	97.6	(1.8)	91.9	(3.1)	99.3	(0.7)	98.8	(0.9)	76.2	(4.4)	96.2	(2.2)
Malaysia	7.1	(2.4)	6.5	(2.1)	0.0	(0.0)	11.3	(2.7)	40.1	(4.3)	64.7	(4.0)	20.7	(3.5)	27.8	(3.8)	88.4	(2.9)	10.5	(2.7)	84.3	(3.2)
Mexico	30.7	(3.1)	29.2	(2.8)	18.1	(1.1)	18.5	(1.0)	52.2	(3.2)	87.3	(2.8)	45.9	(4.1)	72.2	(3.5)	93.4	(1.8)	22.8	(2.3)	36.5	(3.4)
Netherlands	100.0	(0.0)	100.0	(0.0)	95.4	(2.3)	91.6	(2.8)	100.0	(0.0)	100.0	(0.0)	98.4	(1.6)	100.0	(0.0)	100.0	(0.0)	100.0	(0.0)	100.0	(0.0)
Norway	96.2	(3.3)	77.8	(6.4)	17.4	(4.5)	19.4	(5.4)	95.8	(2.0)	92.9	(2.2)	83.2	(4.3)	56.7	(7.3)	99.0	(0.7)	83.9	(4.4)	78.9	(4.8)
Poland	99.4	(0.6)	99.0	(0.7)	49.3	(4.3)	32.8	(4.2)	90.6	(1.9)	100.0	(0.0)	98.5	(0.9)	98.3	(1.2)	100.0	(0.0)	79.0	(2.9)	68.7	(3.6)
Portugal	90.6	(2.0)	57.0	(3.5)	11.4	(1.8)	8.8	(1.6)	86.4	(2.7)	98.9	(0.8)	71.7	(3.6)	99.5	(0.5)	99.5	(0.5)	43.7	(3.5)	94.8	(1.5)
Romania	67.4	(3.9)	71.7	(3.7)	10.0	(2.3)	11.6	(2.5)	44.3	(3.9)	100.0	(0.0)	56.8	(3.8)	77.2	(3.5)	94.3	(1.7)	48.2	(4.0)	83.5	(3.1)
Serbia	97.7	(1.2)	96.6	(1.3)	19.8	(3.3)	17.9	(2.7)	87.3	(2.5)	94.4	(1.8)	69.2	(3.6)	87.3	(2.5)	97.4	(1.2)	51.3	(3.8)	88.1	(2.4)
Singapore	39.9	(0.3)	37.1	(0.2)	9.7	(0.1)	17.8	(0.1)	97.4	(0.0)	100.0	(0.0)	97.3	(0.0)	91.4	(0.1)	99.1	(0.0)	86.0	(0.2)	92.8	(0.1)
Slovak Republic	100.0	(0.0)	99.4	(0.6)	92.8	(1.9)	92.9	(1.9)	98.9	(0.8)	100.0	(0.0)	100.0	(0.0)	99.6	(0.4)	100.0	(0.0)	99.5	(0.5)	99.5	(0.5)
Spain	26.8	(2.0)	25.8	(2.0)	5.0	(1.4)	5.5	(1.3)	54.7	(4.1)	93.4	(1.6)	37.1	(3.4)	53.3	(4.0)	98.2	(0.5)	32.5	(3.5)	39.0	(3.2)
Sweden	98.6	(1.3)	87.3	(2.3)	79.8	(2.7)	96.1	(1.5)	97.0	(1.3)	97.8	(1.1)	80.9	(2.9)	97.0	(1.4)	99.2	(0.6)	68.2	(3.7)	67.9	(3.9)
Sub-national entities																						
Abu Dhabi (United Arab Emirates)	55.4	(3.0)	54.9	(3.0)	53.4	(3.0)	54.1	(2.8)	56.8	(2.9)	67.6	(3.7)	61.4	(3.6)	70.6	(3.7)	61.6	(4.0)	49.9	(3.6)	51.6	(4.2)
Alberta (Canada)	96.4	(1.4)	62.2	(4.8)	3.9	(1.5)	5.0	(1.7)	89.8	(2.5)	97.1	(1.4)	77.6	(4.1)	92.2	(2.6)	98.2	(0.7)	41.0	(4.4)	95.6	(1.5)
England (United Kingdom)	100.0	(0.0)	100.0	(0.0)	94.4	(2.0)	97.4	(1.3)	100.0	(0.0)	100.0	(0.0)	99.4	(0.6)	84.6	(2.8)	100.0	(0.0)	96.7	(1.6)	100.0	(0.0)
Flanders (Belgium)	100.0	(0.0)	100.0	(0.0)	6.0	(2.2)	4.1	(1.9)	95.1	(2.2)	96.6	(1.7)	96.2	(1.8)	88.9	(3.3)	100.0	(0.0)	34.1	(4.7)	79.0	(3.6)
Average	74.7	(0.3)	68.4	(0.5)	35.9	(0.5)	37.1	(0.5)	82.5	(0.4)	95.8	(0.3)	79.1	(0.5)	81.2	(0.5)	94.0	(0.2)	64.6	(0.5)	78.0	(0.5)
United States	96.2	(2.1)	88.1	(3.4)	53.5	(5.4)	58.8	(5.7)	88.1	(3.6)	87.4	(3.5)	64.0	(5.6)	79.9	(4.5)	84.7	(3.5)	60.3	(5.3)	87.3	(3.4)

1. School level includes either the school principal, other members of the school management team, teachers or the school governing board.
* See notes at the beginning of this Annex.
Source: OECD, TALIS 2013 Database.
StatLink http://dx.doi.org/10.1787/888933043321

[Part 1/1]
Principals' working time

Table 3.1   *Average proportion of time lower secondary education principals report spending on the following activities*

	Administrative and leadership tasks and meetings[1]		Curriculum and teaching-related tasks and meetings[2]		Student interactions[3]		Parents or guardian interactions[4]		Interactions with local and regional community, business and industry		Other	
	Average	S.E.	Average	S.E.	Average	S.E.	Average	S.E.	Average	S.E.	Average	S.E.
Australia	46.9	(2.3)	17.0	(1.5)	14.3	(0.8)	12.1	(0.8)	6.9	(0.4)	2.8	(0.5)
Brazil	33.9	(0.8)	21.3	(0.5)	18.8	(0.5)	14.2	(0.3)	8.0	(0.2)	4.2	(0.3)
Bulgaria	44.0	(1.1)	23.1	(0.8)	12.5	(0.5)	9.9	(0.3)	7.1	(0.3)	3.3	(0.3)
Chile	30.3	(1.2)	26.5	(1.0)	17.9	(0.8)	13.7	(0.6)	7.5	(0.5)	4.2	(0.9)
Croatia	37.4	(1.2)	22.3	(0.6)	13.1	(0.6)	10.9	(0.4)	9.7	(0.4)	6.5	(0.6)
Cyprus*	42.6	(1.5)	16.3	(0.7)	18.5	(0.8)	13.6	(0.6)	6.5	(0.4)	2.5	(0.3)
Czech Republic	50.2	(1.1)	21.5	(0.7)	10.3	(0.4)	8.4	(0.3)	4.9	(0.2)	4.7	(0.4)
Denmark	50.5	(1.2)	17.6	(0.8)	11.7	(0.6)	10.4	(0.4)	5.9	(0.4)	3.8	(0.5)
Estonia	47.3	(1.1)	16.9	(0.6)	14.4	(0.6)	9.2	(0.4)	7.7	(0.4)	4.5	(0.3)
Finland	47.9	(1.3)	18.4	(0.8)	13.9	(0.6)	10.2	(0.5)	5.5	(0.3)	4.1	(0.5)
France	41.2	(1.2)	21.1	(0.6)	17.1	(0.9)	10.9	(0.3)	6.8	(0.3)	3.0	(0.3)
Iceland	40.5	(1.4)	17.8	(1.0)	17.6	(0.8)	11.3	(0.5)	7.0	(0.5)	6.0	(0.9)
Israel	34.6	(2.4)	24.1	(1.0)	18.8	(1.0)	12.2	(0.8)	7.1	(0.6)	3.2	(0.6)
Italy	36.1	(1.1)	24.6	(0.7)	12.6	(0.6)	14.4	(0.5)	9.6	(0.3)	2.6	(0.4)
Japan	35.6	(1.0)	25.2	(0.7)	14.6	(0.5)	11.2	(0.4)	8.3	(0.4)	5.0	(0.6)
Korea	35.0	(1.3)	26.9	(1.0)	14.1	(0.6)	11.0	(0.4)	8.2	(0.5)	4.7	(0.7)
Latvia	39.7	(1.2)	17.1	(0.7)	17.4	(0.7)	13.0	(0.8)	8.1	(0.5)	4.6	(0.6)
Malaysia	40.6	(1.2)	29.7	(1.0)	13.9	(0.5)	7.6	(0.4)	5.0	(0.2)	3.3	(0.3)
Mexico	37.9	(1.2)	22.1	(0.8)	18.2	(0.6)	13.3	(0.5)	6.6	(0.4)	2.2	(0.2)
Netherlands	53.6	(2.3)	18.3	(2.1)	6.9	(0.7)	8.7	(0.6)	7.2	(0.5)	5.2	(0.8)
Norway	39.9	(1.7)	17.7	(1.0)	12.7	(0.7)	9.9	(0.7)	11.6	(0.7)	8.2	(1.2)
Poland	42.0	(1.2)	22.9	(0.8)	15.0	(0.7)	10.5	(0.4)	6.7	(0.3)	2.9	(0.3)
Portugal	44.8	(1.7)	18.5	(0.8)	14.4	(0.8)	10.8	(0.5)	6.7	(0.4)	4.9	(0.6)
Romania	37.0	(1.0)	24.1	(0.7)	13.8	(0.5)	11.3	(0.4)	8.6	(0.4)	5.2	(0.5)
Serbia	38.2	(1.2)	22.4	(0.7)	12.6	(0.4)	10.9	(0.4)	10.4	(0.4)	5.6	(0.4)
Singapore	43.9	(1.4)	21.8	(0.7)	15.8	(0.6)	9.7	(0.4)	6.1	(0.3)	2.7	(0.4)
Slovak Republic	44.7	(1.1)	21.2	(0.7)	13.3	(0.6)	10.4	(0.5)	6.6	(0.3)	3.8	(0.4)
Spain	36.1	(1.2)	24.6	(1.1)	15.6	(0.9)	13.7	(0.6)	6.0	(0.4)	4.0	(0.7)
Sweden	50.9	(1.3)	18.5	(1.0)	13.6	(0.6)	10.3	(0.4)	2.8	(0.2)	3.8	(0.5)
Sub-national entities												
Abu Dhabi (United Arab Emirates)	34.0	(1.3)	23.4	(0.9)	17.6	(0.8)	13.5	(0.7)	7.7	(0.5)	3.9	(0.6)
Alberta (Canada)	38.7	(1.2)	23.1	(1.0)	21.1	(0.9)	11.7	(0.5)	4.2	(0.3)	1.3	(0.3)
England (United Kingdom)	42.8	(1.2)	21.2	(0.7)	15.8	(0.7)	9.7	(0.5)	6.3	(0.5)	4.4	(0.8)
Flanders (Belgium)	45.5	(1.4)	18.1	(0.9)	14.7	(0.8)	10.7	(0.7)	5.5	(0.3)	5.6	(1.0)
Average	41.3	(0.2)	21.4	(0.2)	14.9	(0.1)	11.2	(0.1)	7.1	(0.1)	4.1	(0.1)
United States	30.0	(1.6)	24.8	(1.3)	20.5	(1.4)	11.4	(0.8)	4.2	(0.4)	9.2	(0.9)

1. Including human resource/personnel issues, regulations, reports, school budget, preparing timetables and class composition, strategic planning, leadership and management activities, responding to requests from district, regional, state, or national education officials.

2. Including developing curriculum, teaching, classroom observations, student evaluation, mentoring teachers, teacher professional development.

3. Including counseling and conversations outside structured learning activities.

4. Including formal and informal interactions.

* See notes at the beginning of this Annex.

Source: OECD, TALIS 2013 Database.

StatLink ᴬᴿᴵᴹ http://dx.doi.org/10.1787/888933043359

[Part 1/1]
Principals' working time in primary education

Table 3.1.a *Average proportion of time primary education principals report spending on the following activities*

	Administrative and leadership tasks and meetings[1]		Curriculum and teaching-related tasks and meetings[2]		Student interactions[3]		Parents or guardian interactions[4]		Interactions with local and regional community, business and industry		Other	
	Average	S.E.	Average	S.E.	Average	S.E.	Average	S.E.	Average	S.E.	Average	S.E.
Denmark	51.1	(1.4)	18.7	(0.8)	10.0	(0.5)	10.0	(0.4)	6.2	(0.3)	4.1	(0.5)
Finland	40.4	(1.8)	28.8	(2.5)	12.5	(1.1)	10.6	(0.8)	4.3	(0.3)	3.4	(0.5)
Mexico	31.6	(1.1)	25.8	(1.0)	18.0	(0.7)	14.8	(0.5)	7.1	(0.4)	2.8	(0.7)
Norway	42.4	(1.4)	18.6	(1.8)	10.9	(0.6)	8.6	(0.4)	13.6	(0.8)	6.0	(0.7)
Poland	41.6	(1.3)	24.3	(1.1)	13.4	(0.8)	10.1	(0.6)	7.0	(0.4)	3.6	(0.4)
Sub-national entities												
Flanders (Belgium)	45.9	(1.3)	19.6	(0.7)	12.3	(0.5)	11.9	(0.6)	5.2	(0.3)	5.0	(0.7)
Average	42.2	(0.6)	22.6	(0.6)	12.9	(0.3)	11.0	(0.2)	7.2	(0.2)	4.2	(0.2)

1. Including human resource/personnel issues, regulations, reports, school budget, preparing timetables and class composition, strategic planning, leadership and management activities, responding to requests from district, regional, state, or national education officials.
2. Including developing curriculum, teaching, classroom observations, student evaluation, mentoring teachers, teacher professional development.
3. Including counseling and conversations outside structured learning activities.
4. Including formal and informal interactions.
Source: OECD, TALIS 2013 Database.
StatLink 🔗 http://dx.doi.org/10.1787/888933043378

[Part 1/1]
Principals' working time in upper secondary education

Table 3.1.b *Average proportion of time upper secondary education principals report spending on the following activities*

	Administrative and leadership tasks and meetings[1]		Curriculum and teaching-related tasks and meetings[2]		Student interactions[3]		Parents or guardian interactions[4]		Interactions with local and regional community, business and industry		Other	
	Average	S.E.	Average	S.E.	Average	S.E.	Average	S.E.	Average	S.E.	Average	S.E.
Australia	49.0	(2.0)	16.7	(1.0)	15.0	(1.3)	11.7	(0.7)	5.8	(0.3)	1.9	(0.4)
Denmark	50.7	(1.9)	19.4	(1.2)	11.0	(0.7)	3.7	(0.4)	10.5	(0.9)	4.7	(0.6)
Finland	54.9	(1.4)	16.6	(0.9)	10.0	(0.7)	4.6	(0.3)	10.2	(1.4)	3.9	(0.5)
Iceland	50.0	(4.0)	15.5	(1.5)	14.2	(1.7)	5.3	(0.5)	7.5	(1.1)	7.5	(2.0)
Italy	37.2	(1.4)	23.3	(0.7)	16.3	(0.7)	12.3	(0.6)	8.7	(0.4)	2.2	(0.5)
Mexico	35.2	(1.5)	21.6	(1.0)	20.1	(1.0)	12.4	(0.5)	7.8	(0.5)	3.1	(0.4)
Norway	44.4	(1.7)	12.8	(1.0)	10.3	(0.6)	5.7	(0.4)	17.9	(1.2)	8.7	(1.2)
Poland	42.6	(1.4)	20.9	(0.8)	14.1	(1.0)	9.6	(0.5)	8.4	(0.4)	4.5	(0.5)
Singapore	44.5	(1.3)	21.9	(0.7)	15.5	(0.6)	9.4	(0.4)	6.0	(0.3)	2.8	(0.4)
Sub-national entities												
Abu Dhabi (United Arab Emirates)	34.0	(1.4)	22.8	(0.8)	19.2	(0.7)	13.4	(0.6)	7.6	(0.4)	3.0	(0.4)
Average	44.2	(0.6)	19.1	(0.3)	14.6	(0.3)	8.8	(0.2)	9.0	(0.3)	4.2	(0.3)

1. Including human resource/personnel issues, regulations, reports, school budget, preparing timetables and class composition, strategic planning, leadership and management activities, responding to requests from district, regional, state, or national education officials.
2. Including developing curriculum, teaching, classroom observations, student evaluation, mentoring teachers, teacher professional development.
3. Including counseling and conversations outside structured learning activities.
4. Including formal and informal interactions.
Source: OECD, TALIS 2013 Database.
StatLink 🔗 http://dx.doi.org/10.1787/888933043397

[Part 1/1]
Principals' leadership
*Percentage of lower secondary education principals who report having engaged "often" or "very often"
in the following leadership activities during the 12 months prior to the survey*

Table 3.2

	Collaborate with teachers to solve classroom discipline problems		Observe instruction in the classroom		Take action to support co-operation among teachers to develop new teaching practices		Take action to ensure that teachers take responsibility for improving their teaching skills		Take action to ensure that teachers feel responsible for their students' learning outcomes		Provide parents or guardians with information on the school and student performance		Check for mistakes and errors in school administrative procedures and reports		Resolve problems with the lesson timetable in the school		Collaborate with principals from other schools	
	%	S.E.	%	S.E.	%	S.E.	%	S.E.	%	S.E.	%	S.E.	%	S.E.	%	S.E.	%	S.E.
Australia	35.3	(6.4)	33.1	(6.6)	64.0	(5.6)	76.1	(5.1)	82.5	(5.2)	78.1	(5.5)	62.5	(6.8)	25.9	(6.0)	59.3	(6.0)
Brazil	82.6	(1.8)	60.0	(2.6)	75.3	(2.1)	75.3	(2.0)	83.7	(1.9)	89.0	(1.4)	80.4	(2.0)	63.6	(2.6)	38.4	(2.5)
Bulgaria	78.6	(3.6)	89.1	(2.5)	69.4	(3.8)	88.3	(2.7)	96.9	(1.3)	78.5	(3.2)	82.6	(3.0)	56.0	(4.4)	56.9	(4.2)
Chile	80.0	(3.4)	71.8	(3.7)	84.5	(2.8)	87.9	(2.6)	92.9	(2.1)	89.5	(2.7)	92.1	(2.2)	74.0	(3.5)	42.2	(3.8)
Croatia	73.7	(3.1)	51.2	(3.9)	61.7	(3.6)	64.8	(3.7)	72.1	(3.4)	38.5	(3.7)	64.0	(3.8)	45.4	(3.8)	77.6	(2.9)
Cyprus*	85.7	(3.2)	63.3	(5.0)	50.0	(5.3)	76.3	(3.7)	82.5	(4.0)	88.8	(3.4)	73.5	(4.1)	52.0	(4.7)	62.2	(4.0)
Czech Republic	69.9	(3.1)	51.7	(3.7)	69.0	(3.5)	70.1	(3.4)	72.6	(3.4)	54.7	(3.4)	94.1	(1.7)	20.3	(2.7)	37.2	(3.5)
Denmark	56.0	(4.9)	17.1	(3.3)	43.9	(4.4)	53.6	(4.3)	45.5	(4.5)	28.0	(4.0)	24.4	(3.8)	39.9	(4.7)	58.3	(4.3)
Estonia	41.3	(3.4)	6.7	(1.5)	41.3	(3.7)	52.0	(3.3)	53.0	(3.5)	42.6	(3.7)	35.8	(3.4)	19.3	(2.8)	62.3	(3.3)
Finland	70.2	(3.7)	10.7	(2.8)	56.6	(3.8)	40.0	(3.6)	44.0	(4.4)	24.6	(3.2)	45.5	(4.2)	75.5	(3.4)	82.4	(3.3)
France	67.5	(4.1)	7.7	(2.5)	59.9	(4.1)	51.6	(4.8)	64.2	(4.0)	41.9	(4.1)	86.5	(2.5)	64.7	(3.9)	72.3	(3.6)
Iceland	41.5	(4.7)	15.1	(3.7)	56.7	(4.3)	57.5	(5.2)	76.4	(4.4)	49.1	(4.8)	18.3	(3.8)	48.1	(5.1)	67.0	(4.9)
Israel	81.1	(3.4)	47.6	(6.2)	67.6	(6.2)	76.0	(4.4)	81.8	(3.5)	66.5	(5.7)	54.3	(6.2)	57.4	(5.6)	37.5	(5.6)
Italy	83.6	(3.7)	33.7	(4.2)	64.9	(4.8)	59.8	(5.1)	71.0	(4.4)	72.3	(4.6)	71.9	(4.8)	49.7	(5.1)	51.4	(4.9)
Japan	33.2	(4.3)	66.8	(3.4)	33.9	(4.3)	38.9	(4.0)	32.6	(3.5)	51.2	(3.5)	36.6	(3.4)	8.8	(2.6)	54.8	(4.2)
Korea	78.3	(4.7)	69.4	(3.8)	73.6	(4.6)	77.8	(3.8)	80.5	(3.9)	76.6	(4.3)	73.7	(4.5)	47.7	(3.9)	74.1	(4.9)
Latvia	68.5	(5.6)	45.0	(4.9)	63.4	(5.6)	74.8	(4.6)	83.6	(4.1)	54.3	(6.9)	74.9	(5.2)	19.2	(5.1)	76.4	(4.8)
Malaysia	90.6	(2.6)	88.2	(3.3)	97.9	(1.1)	95.5	(1.6)	99.6	(0.4)	86.3	(2.9)	91.4	(2.4)	75.4	(3.5)	88.8	(2.7)
Mexico	75.0	(3.7)	64.3	(4.2)	72.2	(4.1)	75.1	(3.6)	86.1	(2.6)	93.3	(2.1)	89.5	(2.5)	68.7	(3.6)	56.9	(4.0)
Netherlands	27.8	(6.0)	43.1	(6.0)	42.8	(7.1)	69.1	(6.6)	86.9	(3.3)	71.0	(4.8)	38.1	(6.2)	22.0	(6.1)	86.2	(4.0)
Norway	78.2	(3.7)	21.2	(6.5)	55.6	(8.0)	47.5	(7.4)	41.1	(6.8)	36.6	(6.1)	31.0	(5.9)	43.0	(8.5)	71.3	(6.7)
Poland	70.7	(3.7)	61.9	(4.9)	62.8	(4.3)	72.0	(4.4)	91.6	(3.0)	80.7	(3.3)	60.9	(4.8)	41.5	(4.4)	61.1	(4.5)
Portugal	70.0	(4.2)	5.2	(1.8)	61.0	(4.2)	63.3	(4.4)	74.5	(4.1)	84.0	(3.2)	36.8	(4.2)	66.8	(3.5)	57.0	(4.2)
Romania	93.1	(2.6)	82.2	(3.2)	79.8	(3.5)	85.4	(2.5)	90.2	(2.3)	91.1	(2.7)	93.7	(2.3)	83.7	(3.2)	87.4	(2.9)
Serbia	80.4	(3.4)	70.4	(3.3)	85.7	(3.0)	81.5	(3.2)	82.1	(2.9)	77.8	(3.2)	81.4	(3.5)	69.5	(3.8)	95.8	(1.5)
Singapore	63.8	(4.0)	58.5	(4.3)	65.4	(4.4)	84.4	(3.0)	91.1	(2.5)	68.1	(4.0)	68.7	(4.2)	32.6	(4.4)	36.1	(3.7)
Slovak Republic	78.8	(3.3)	61.8	(4.2)	81.5	(3.3)	79.3	(3.3)	82.7	(3.2)	66.9	(4.0)	48.4	(4.0)	24.5	(3.4)	58.6	(4.3)
Spain	82.9	(3.1)	29.5	(4.0)	59.4	(5.1)	55.8	(4.8)	69.3	(4.3)	83.1	(2.6)	65.3	(4.7)	52.5	(4.7)	45.0	(5.0)
Sweden	50.3	(4.2)	27.8	(5.0)	53.9	(4.9)	44.1	(4.9)	63.9	(4.5)	29.8	(4.0)	26.4	(4.5)	30.7	(4.3)	50.2	(4.5)
Sub-national entities																		
Abu Dhabi (United Arab Emirates)	86.0	(3.3)	88.0	(3.1)	91.3	(2.9)	93.4	(2.4)	93.2	(2.6)	89.2	(3.3)	84.8	(3.4)	74.1	(4.4)	57.8	(4.8)
Alberta (Canada)	81.1	(3.3)	76.0	(3.1)	71.1	(3.0)	79.1	(3.5)	84.8	(3.1)	75.2	(3.1)	46.7	(3.6)	42.5	(4.0)	63.5	(3.6)
England (United Kingdom)	39.7	(5.9)	78.4	(4.9)	61.4	(3.9)	75.3	(4.3)	82.9	(4.9)	70.9	(5.1)	40.8	(4.5)	18.4	(2.6)	58.2	(4.6)
Flanders (Belgium)	53.5	(5.4)	21.4	(4.2)	36.5	(4.8)	41.5	(4.8)	57.0	(3.7)	42.8	(3.8)	34.5	(4.0)	33.5	(4.7)	64.3	(4.4)
Average	68.2	(0.7)	49.0	(0.7)	64.1	(0.8)	68.6	(0.7)	75.5	(0.6)	65.8	(0.7)	60.9	(0.7)	46.9	(0.8)	62.1	(0.7)
United States	79.3	(5.4)	78.5	(5.7)	75.0	(4.9)	78.2	(5.5)	87.0	(4.9)	72.6	(6.4)	40.6	(5.7)	31.5	(5.6)	52.6	(6.9)

*See notes at the beginning of this Annex.
Source: OECD, TALIS 2013 Database.
StatLink ⌸ http://dx.doi.org/10.1787/888933043416

[Part 1/1]
Principals' leadership in primary education
Percentage of primary education principals who report having engaged "often" or "very often"
in the following leadership activities during the 12 months prior to the survey

Table 3.2.a

	Collaborate with teachers to solve classroom discipline problems		Observe instruction in the classroom		Take action to support co-operation among teachers to develop new teaching practices		Take action to ensure that teachers take responsibility for improving their teaching skills		Take action to ensure that teachers feel responsible for their students' learning outcomes		Provide parents or guardians with information on the school and student performance		Check for mistakes and errors in school administrative procedures and reports		Resolve problems with the lesson timetable in the school		Collaborate with principals from other schools	
	%	S.E.	%	S.E.	%	S.E.	%	S.E.	%	S.E.	%	S.E.	%	S.E.	%	S.E.	%	S.E.
Denmark	58.5	(3.8)	17.6	(3.2)	36.6	(3.8)	43.1	(4.3)	40.1	(4.2)	22.0	(3.7)	18.3	(3.3)	35.4	(4.1)	63.6	(3.9)
Finland	64.8	(4.8)	7.3	(2.2)	42.8	(4.6)	27.3	(3.9)	36.4	(5.2)	36.2	(5.9)	41.3	(4.4)	50.5	(4.9)	79.1	(3.3)
Mexico	73.4	(3.6)	54.1	(3.8)	65.0	(3.7)	66.8	(3.4)	75.3	(2.9)	84.3	(2.6)	68.7	(3.5)	38.6	(4.0)	45.8	(3.9)
Norway	48.0	(8.2)	18.1	(3.3)	51.4	(4.7)	41.3	(3.8)	36.6	(4.9)	34.6	(6.5)	27.4	(7.2)	50.4	(8.8)	70.4	(7.9)
Poland	65.9	(4.7)	72.2	(5.1)	71.4	(4.4)	79.6	(4.1)	87.2	(3.7)	81.8	(4.0)	64.4	(4.8)	46.8	(5.2)	79.4	(4.3)
Sub-national entities																		
Flanders (Belgium)	43.8	(4.1)	29.1	(3.8)	46.3	(4.6)	50.4	(4.4)	60.7	(4.4)	45.3	(4.3)	33.0	(3.8)	38.8	(4.3)	72.0	(3.9)
Average	59.1	(2.1)	33.1	(1.5)	52.3	(1.8)	51.4	(1.6)	56.0	(1.7)	50.7	(1.9)	42.2	(1.9)	43.4	(2.2)	68.4	(1.9)

Source: OECD, TALIS 2013 Database.
StatLink http://dx.doi.org/10.1787/888933043454

[Part 1/1]
Principals' leadership in upper secondary education
Percentage of upper secondary education principals who report having engaged "often" or "very often"
in the following leadership activities during the 12 months prior to the survey

Table 3.2.b

	Collaborate with teachers to solve classroom discipline problems		Observe instruction in the classroom		Take action to support co-operation among teachers to develop new teaching practices		Take action to ensure that teachers take responsibility for improving their teaching skills		Take action to ensure that teachers feel responsible for their students' learning outcomes		Provide parents or guardians with information on the school and student performance		Check for mistakes and errors in school administrative procedures and reports		Resolve problems with the lesson timetable in the school		Collaborate with principals from other schools	
	%	S.E.	%	S.E.	%	S.E.	%	S.E.	%	S.E.	%	S.E.	%	S.E.	%	S.E.	%	S.E.
Australia	35.0	(6.1)	27.2	(5.5)	58.8	(5.6)	79.4	(5.1)	75.9	(3.9)	74.4	(4.7)	54.0	(6.1)	9.9	(3.0)	61.4	(5.9)
Denmark	26.4	(5.4)	17.3	(4.2)	50.6	(5.1)	53.4	(5.6)	51.3	(5.1)	11.8	(3.5)	23.8	(4.6)	42.1	(5.8)	64.6	(6.3)
Finland	14.4	(2.7)	3.6	(1.5)	55.4	(6.0)	58.4	(5.0)	60.1	(5.0)	12.9	(2.9)	51.5	(4.8)	48.3	(4.4)	85.1	(3.6)
Iceland	21.1	(7.4)	12.7	(7.0)	57.8	(10.9)	49.3	(7.4)	70.4	(9.3)	33.8	(9.6)	22.0	(8.7)	21.1	(9.2)	78.9	(6.4)
Italy	76.0	(3.9)	43.9	(4.1)	62.9	(4.3)	63.7	(4.1)	65.1	(4.1)	82.0	(3.3)	73.9	(3.4)	41.1	(4.3)	45.4	(4.6)
Mexico	63.5	(5.3)	47.5	(4.1)	67.1	(4.2)	76.8	(3.9)	82.5	(3.4)	83.7	(3.0)	80.1	(4.1)	59.2	(4.5)	44.1	(4.1)
Norway	27.6	(5.9)	6.5	(2.9)	51.1	(7.0)	54.1	(5.2)	55.2	(6.3)	15.8	(3.4)	33.6	(5.7)	23.4	(4.8)	56.5	(6.4)
Poland	46.9	(5.0)	65.7	(3.0)	59.6	(4.9)	76.1	(5.5)	85.1	(3.5)	77.0	(4.3)	54.9	(7.4)	27.7	(6.1)	68.8	(6.9)
Singapore	61.5	(4.3)	58.2	(4.1)	66.9	(3.9)	84.5	(3.3)	91.3	(2.4)	67.4	(4.3)	66.1	(4.2)	31.8	(3.9)	35.8	(4.0)
Sub-national entities																		
Abu Dhabi (United Arab Emirates)	84.3	(3.6)	85.9	(2.9)	93.0	(2.5)	93.8	(2.0)	93.0	(2.5)	89.5	(2.7)	82.5	(3.9)	76.2	(3.7)	57.5	(4.9)
Average	45.7	(1.6)	36.8	(1.3)	62.3	(1.9)	68.9	(1.6)	73.0	(1.6)	54.8	(1.5)	54.2	(1.7)	38.1	(1.7)	59.8	(1.7)

Source: OECD, TALIS 2013 Database.
StatLink http://dx.doi.org/10.1787/888933043492

[Part 1/1]

Principals' participation in a school development plan

Percentage of lower secondary education principals who report having engaged in the following activities related to a school development plan in the 12 months prior to the survey

Table 3.3

	Used student performance and student evaluation results (including national/international assessments) to develop the school's educational goals and programmes		Worked on a professional development plan for the school	
	%	S.E.	%	S.E.
Australia	94.7	(2.5)	89.2	(4.6)
Brazil	87.3	(1.8)	71.0	(2.2)
Bulgaria	95.0	(1.6)	62.5	(3.7)
Chile	86.1	(3.0)	78.3	(3.5)
Croatia	75.4	(3.5)	89.2	(2.7)
Cyprus*	66.3	(4.8)	71.6	(4.5)
Czech Republic	88.7	(2.4)	88.1	(2.5)
Denmark	84.0	(3.4)	72.6	(4.1)
Estonia	81.5	(2.7)	58.0	(3.6)
Finland	73.7	(3.6)	39.7	(4.6)
France	87.2	(2.8)	46.0	(4.1)
Iceland	82.1	(3.8)	81.1	(4.1)
Israel	94.3	(2.7)	86.5	(4.9)
Italy	90.8	(2.3)	77.2	(3.6)
Japan	93.0	(2.1)	95.1	(2.5)
Korea	95.3	(2.3)	91.4	(3.1)
Latvia	94.4	(2.0)	92.9	(2.9)
Malaysia	99.5	(0.5)	97.4	(1.2)
Mexico	96.3	(1.5)	86.1	(3.1)
Netherlands	84.1	(3.7)	57.8	(7.8)
Norway	97.7	(1.5)	81.8	(4.8)
Poland	94.8	(2.1)	94.7	(2.2)
Portugal	92.1	(2.1)	61.0	(4.6)
Romania	88.7	(3.0)	83.8	(3.5)
Serbia	89.7	(2.6)	94.9	(1.8)
Singapore	99.3	(0.7)	98.6	(1.0)
Slovak Republic	88.4	(2.5)	95.6	(1.7)
Spain	90.3	(2.5)	39.8	(4.7)
Sweden	89.6	(3.3)	61.4	(4.9)
Sub-national entities				
Abu Dhabi (United Arab Emirates)	93.8	(2.1)	97.0	(1.4)
Alberta (Canada)	96.8	(1.3)	97.5	(1.5)
England (United Kingdom)	99.5	(0.5)	94.8	(2.8)
Flanders (Belgium)	58.5	(4.6)	78.1	(4.0)
Average	88.8	(0.5)	79.1	(0.6)
United States	95.0	(2.8)	93.5	(3.7)

*See notes at the beginning of this Annex.

Source: OECD, TALIS 2013 Database.

StatLink ⬛🔗 http://dx.doi.org/10.1787/888933043530

[Part 1/1]

Primary principals' participation in a school development plan

Percentage of primary education principals who report having engaged in the following activities
Table 3.3.a *related to a school development plan in the 12 months prior to the survey*

	Used student performance and student evaluation results (including national/international assessments) to develop the school's educational goals and programmes		Worked on a professional development plan for the school	
	%	S.E.	%	S.E.
Denmark	75.4	(3.9)	77.0	(2.6)
Finland	56.3	(6.3)	32.2	(3.5)
Mexico	95.8	(1.8)	76.0	(3.5)
Norway	97.1	(1.5)	74.2	(5.6)
Poland	93.9	(2.5)	97.2	(1.2)
Sub-national entities				
Flanders (Belgium)	74.0	(4.1)	89.0	(2.7)
Average	82.1	(1.5)	74.3	(1.4)

Source: OECD, TALIS 2013 Database.
StatLink ⟶ http://dx.doi.org/10.1787/888933043549

[Part 1/1]

Upper secondary principals' participation in a school development plan

Percentage of upper secondary education principals who report having engaged in the following activities
Table 3.3.b *related to a school development plan in the 12 months prior to the survey*

	Used student performance and student evaluation results (including national/international assessments) to develop the school's educational goals and programmes		Worked on a professional development plan for the school	
	%	S.E.	%	S.E.
Australia	94.4	(3.5)	93.4	(3.6)
Denmark	78.0	(5.0)	79.6	(4.2)
Finland	75.9	(5.4)	53.5	(4.7)
Iceland	78.9	(8.2)	78.9	(9.2)
Italy	90.5	(2.5)	72.6	(3.3)
Mexico	92.7	(2.6)	84.6	(3.5)
Norway	100.0	(0.0)	80.8	(4.4)
Poland	84.1	(4.1)	95.2	(2.1)
Singapore	99.3	(0.7)	98.7	(1.0)
Sub-national entities				
Abu Dhabi (United Arab Emirates)	95.5	(2.0)	99.1	(0.9)
Average	88.9	(1.3)	83.6	(1.4)

Source: OECD, TALIS 2013 Database.
StatLink ⟶ http://dx.doi.org/10.1787/888933043568

[Part 1/2]
Responsibility for leadership activities
Percentage of lower secondary education principals who report a shared responsibility
for the following tasks[1]

Table 3.4

	Appointing or hiring teachers		Dismissing or suspending teachers from employment		Establishing teachers' starting salaries, including setting payscales		Determining teachers' salary increases		Deciding on budget allocations within the school		Establishing student disciplinary policies and procedures	
	%	S.E.	%	S.E.	%	S.E.	%	S.E.	%	S.E.	%	S.E.
Australia	50.9	(5.7)	26.2	(5.2)	15.3	(4.2)	18.5	(4.8)	55.4	(6.2)	62.5	(6.5)
Brazil	24.1	(2.1)	22.4	(2.4)	4.8	(1.4)	4.8	(1.4)	32.5	(2.6)	53.1	(2.7)
Bulgaria	19.5	(3.5)	13.6	(3.0)	38.8	(3.8)	37.0	(3.6)	50.2	(3.8)	50.6	(4.0)
Chile	31.3	(3.6)	24.9	(3.2)	10.8	(2.4)	13.5	(2.4)	20.2	(3.1)	48.1	(4.1)
Croatia	80.4	(3.4)	70.3	(3.7)	1.9	(1.2)	1.2	(0.9)	58.5	(4.1)	67.3	(3.6)
Cyprus*	19.8	(3.1)	16.7	(2.9)	10.4	(2.6)	7.4	(2.4)	34.4	(5.0)	66.7	(4.7)
Czech Republic	27.4	(2.8)	19.1	(2.4)	21.9	(2.7)	29.1	(3.2)	63.3	(3.5)	78.4	(2.9)
Denmark	83.7	(3.2)	58.3	(4.1)	22.4	(4.0)	26.7	(3.9)	84.4	(3.6)	88.6	(2.8)
Estonia	63.8	(3.5)	35.9	(3.5)	33.3	(3.3)	55.6	(3.4)	67.7	(3.2)	75.3	(3.2)
Finland	39.5	(4.1)	23.3	(3.6)	6.4	(2.2)	14.3	(3.2)	36.9	(4.0)	58.3	(4.3)
France	15.1	(3.0)	11.0	(2.1)	0.9	(0.6)	1.6	(0.8)	52.1	(4.3)	59.0	(3.8)
Iceland	38.7	(4.8)	26.0	(4.4)	6.8	(2.6)	11.8	(3.0)	31.7	(4.3)	75.5	(4.6)
Israel	51.4	(6.6)	36.9	(6.1)	10.1	(5.6)	14.3	(6.0)	43.7	(6.7)	75.3	(4.0)
Italy	35.1	(4.2)	25.2	(3.8)	3.7	(1.4)	2.9	(1.2)	62.9	(4.8)	73.1	(4.0)
Japan	7.0	(2.4)	9.1	(2.8)	1.5	(1.0)	9.2	(2.3)	26.2	(3.7)	43.6	(4.5)
Korea	12.0	(3.0)	7.9	(2.7)	1.3	(0.8)	0.0	(0.0)	20.1	(4.0)	20.8	(4.1)
Latvia	53.1	(5.5)	45.5	(6.3)	52.5	(5.9)	50.4	(5.4)	75.2	(4.5)	73.6	(4.8)
Malaysia	2.7	(1.2)	4.4	(1.8)	0.0	(0.0)	9.2	(2.6)	25.0	(3.7)	42.1	(4.3)
Mexico	16.4	(2.5)	14.2	(2.3)	6.0	(2.2)	8.3	(2.3)	18.0	(3.4)	40.7	(4.3)
Netherlands	77.9	(4.6)	63.0	(7.7)	34.2	(6.8)	46.1	(7.5)	69.3	(5.1)	67.9	(7.9)
Norway	56.3	(7.0)	41.9	(6.3)	15.2	(4.7)	16.1	(5.2)	52.1	(6.5)	75.5	(5.4)
Poland	23.5	(3.7)	11.7	(3.3)	20.5	(4.4)	23.7	(4.4)	50.6	(5.3)	65.4	(4.5)
Portugal	53.2	(4.3)	24.3	(4.3)	4.1	(2.1)	1.8	(0.9)	33.1	(4.2)	49.7	(4.6)
Romania	36.0	(4.1)	24.1	(4.0)	4.0	(1.8)	4.9	(1.7)	23.0	(3.9)	49.6	(4.5)
Serbia	66.4	(4.0)	53.5	(3.6)	10.6	(2.7)	7.3	(2.1)	65.4	(4.0)	59.9	(3.7)
Singapore	36.8	(4.0)	31.5	(4.0)	6.0	(1.9)	14.7	(3.0)	69.7	(4.1)	83.9	(3.4)
Slovak Republic	42.6	(3.7)	38.1	(3.4)	24.5	(4.0)	33.9	(4.0)	62.9	(3.7)	72.0	(3.4)
Spain	21.9	(4.2)	19.9	(3.4)	2.8	(1.2)	3.2	(1.2)	28.4	(4.6)	62.1	(4.8)
Sweden	23.9	(4.1)	16.5	(2.9)	26.8	(4.3)	29.9	(3.9)	25.7	(4.0)	34.7	(4.1)
Sub-national entities												
Abu Dhabi (United Arab Emirates)	33.3	(4.0)	32.6	(4.2)	18.4	(3.7)	20.1	(3.5)	22.6	(3.4)	41.6	(4.4)
Alberta (Canada)	45.6	(3.7)	29.7	(3.6)	0.4	(0.4)	0.4	(0.4)	47.4	(3.3)	61.6	(3.0)
England (United Kingdom)	66.0	(4.3)	54.6	(5.0)	51.4	(5.8)	60.6	(5.4)	73.6	(4.2)	72.6	(5.0)
Flanders (Belgium)	33.1	(5.4)	39.6	(5.3)	0.0	(0.0)	0.0	(0.0)	60.5	(4.9)	64.7	(4.3)
Average	39.0	(0.7)	29.5	(0.7)	14.2	(0.6)	17.5	(0.6)	46.7	(0.8)	61.0	(0.8)
United States	43.0	(5.8)	41.2	(6.0)	0.0	(0.0)	0.6	(0.6)	33.8	(6.3)	51.9	(5.5)

1. A shared responsibility occurs when an active role is played in decision making by the principal and one of the following entities: "other members of the school management team", "teachers (not as part of the school management team)", "school governing board", "local, municipality/regional, state, or national/federal authority".
* See notes at the beginning of this Annex.
Source: OECD, TALIS 2013 Database.
StatLink http://dx.doi.org/10.1787/888933043587

© OECD 2014   TALIS 2013 RESULTS: AN INTERNATIONAL PERSPECTIVE ON TEACHING AND LEARNING

[Part 2/2]
Responsibility for leadership activities
Percentage of lower secondary education principals who report a shared responsibility
for the following tasks[1]

Table 3.4

	Establishing student assessment policies, including national/regional assessments		Approving students for admission to the school		Choosing which learning materials are used		Determining course content, including national/regional curricula		Deciding which courses are offered	
	%	S.E.	%	S.E.	%	S.E.	%	S.E.	%	S.E.
Australia	55.4	(5.5)	39.9	(6.2)	34.5	(5.9)	42.7	(5.7)	75.8	(4.9)
Brazil	41.9	(2.6)	39.6	(2.8)	52.1	(2.8)	30.0	(2.5)	27.4	(2.7)
Bulgaria	42.1	(4.2)	34.5	(3.3)	27.0	(3.6)	32.0	(3.7)	25.3	(3.2)
Chile	43.4	(3.9)	40.5	(4.0)	45.3	(4.2)	35.9	(3.9)	47.1	(3.9)
Croatia	35.0	(3.8)	33.8	(3.7)	25.5	(3.4)	16.3	(2.9)	11.2	(2.4)
Cyprus*	50.5	(5.4)	28.4	(4.1)	37.2	(4.6)	22.9	(3.3)	22.9	(2.6)
Czech Republic	78.2	(2.8)	25.1	(2.8)	72.8	(3.1)	78.1	(3.0)	77.9	(3.0)
Denmark	81.9	(3.4)	59.2	(4.6)	53.2	(4.5)	57.4	(4.6)	80.4	(3.6)
Estonia	69.2	(3.5)	50.8	(3.6)	53.6	(3.5)	36.1	(3.4)	74.8	(2.9)
Finland	43.0	(4.1)	26.0	(3.7)	47.6	(4.0)	34.5	(3.8)	59.9	(4.0)
France	51.0	(3.8)	29.3	(3.9)	62.5	(4.0)	8.9	(2.4)	35.6	(4.2)
Iceland	73.3	(4.5)	47.2	(5.4)	51.9	(4.9)	56.2	(4.7)	76.7	(4.3)
Israel	61.6	(5.3)	59.2	(6.3)	64.2	(5.2)	51.6	(5.9)	76.8	(3.4)
Italy	65.2	(3.8)	32.1	(4.1)	57.0	(4.9)	59.1	(4.1)	76.1	(3.6)
Japan	39.9	(4.3)	17.5	(3.4)	23.0	(3.4)	25.6	(3.5)	23.6	(3.6)
Korea	18.6	(3.8)	11.6	(3.0)	18.5	(3.8)	19.1	(3.8)	13.8	(3.7)
Latvia	56.9	(6.0)	28.0	(3.9)	58.9	(6.1)	40.0	(6.0)	64.1	(5.9)
Malaysia	17.0	(3.6)	18.7	(3.7)	43.0	(4.8)	6.6	(2.2)	46.8	(4.5)
Mexico	31.2	(3.6)	33.2	(4.0)	38.5	(3.9)	18.5	(2.8)	26.2	(3.7)
Netherlands	71.3	(5.8)	82.2	(4.5)	34.4	(7.2)	56.1	(5.8)	92.3	(2.6)
Norway	74.0	(4.8)	32.8	(7.5)	73.9	(6.1)	60.3	(5.2)	65.4	(6.7)
Poland	67.6	(4.2)	19.1	(2.5)	59.4	(4.9)	40.0	(4.9)	49.0	(4.3)
Portugal	36.3	(4.2)	42.5	(4.7)	36.6	(4.2)	21.2	(4.2)	49.9	(4.4)
Romania	32.2	(4.0)	31.3	(3.9)	34.1	(3.9)	17.7	(3.3)	27.6	(3.3)
Serbia	34.4	(3.9)	31.9	(3.1)	32.7	(4.1)	15.9	(3.6)	44.4	(4.6)
Singapore	81.1	(3.4)	66.3	(4.0)	40.2	(3.9)	40.9	(4.1)	75.8	(4.0)
Slovak Republic	67.5	(4.0)	27.5	(3.3)	69.2	(4.0)	71.0	(3.6)	77.3	(3.1)
Spain	27.6	(4.1)	21.2	(3.7)	39.5	(4.4)	15.0	(3.8)	28.5	(3.7)
Sweden	41.8	(4.6)	19.5	(3.8)	17.2	(3.6)	26.4	(4.1)	28.3	(4.1)
Sub-national entities										
Abu Dhabi (United Arab Emirates)	38.2	(3.9)	43.3	(4.3)	37.6	(4.2)	28.1	(3.6)	30.0	(4.1)
Alberta (Canada)	59.2	(3.3)	44.5	(3.8)	62.0	(3.5)	30.7	(3.7)	66.8	(3.3)
England (United Kingdom)	68.1	(5.3)	49.4	(4.7)	34.1	(6.2)	40.5	(6.1)	66.0	(5.5)
Flanders (Belgium)	69.2	(4.5)	50.1	(5.0)	37.0	(4.0)	7.8	(2.6)	66.1	(4.7)
Average	52.2	(0.7)	36.9	(0.7)	44.7	(0.8)	34.6	(0.7)	51.8	(0.7)
United States	41.8	(6.0)	35.4	(6.3)	51.2	(6.2)	42.0	(6.8)	67.2	(6.0)

1. A shared responsibility occurs when an active role is played in decision making by the principal and one of the following entities: "other members of the school management team", "teachers (not as part of the school management team)", "school governing board", "local, municipality/regional, state, or national/federal authority".
* See notes at the beginning of this Annex.
Source: OECD, TALIS 2013 Database.
StatLink http://dx.doi.org/10.1787/888933043587

[Part 1/1]

Relationship between distributed leadership and principals' characteristics

Significant results of the multiple linear regressions of principals' characteristics and distributed leadership in lower secondary education[1]

Table 3.5

	Use of distributed leadership[2]					
	Dependent on:					
	Male[3]		Years of experience as a principal (in total)[4]		Years of experience as a teacher[5]	
	ß	S.E.	ß	S.E.	ß	S.E.
Australia						
Brazil						
Bulgaria						
Chile			0.07	(0.03)		
Croatia						
Czech Republic						
Denmark						
Estonia					-0.02	(0.01)
Finland						
France			-0.07	(0.03)		
Iceland						
Israel						
Italy						
Japan					0.04	(0.02)
Korea						
Latvia						
Malaysia	0.53	(0.23)				
Mexico						
Netherlands					0.07	(0.03)
Norway					-0.03	(0.01)
Poland						
Portugal						
Romania						
Serbia						
Singapore						
Slovak Republic			0.04	(0.02)		
Spain						
Sweden						
Sub-national entities						
Abu Dhabi (United Arab Emirates)	-1.43	(0.43)				
Alberta (Canada)	-0.65	(0.33)				
England (United Kingdom)	-1.12	(0.48)			-0.08	(0.03)
Flanders (Belgium)					0.07	(0.02)

1. Cells are blank where no significant relationship was found. Significance was tested at the 5% level, controlling for principal age and educational attainment.
2. Continuous variable. See the textbox describing this index and Annex B for more details.
3. Male is a dichotomous variable where the reference category is female.
4. Years of experience as a principal (in total) is a continuous variable.
5. Years of experience as a teacher is a continuous variable.

Source: OECD, TALIS 2013 Database.

StatLink http://dx.doi.org/10.1787/888933043625

[Part 1/1]
Relationship between principals' distributed leadership and school characteristics
Significant results of the multiple linear regressions of principals' distributed leadership

Table 3.6 *and school characteristics in lower secondary education[1]*

	Use of distributed leadership[2]															
	Dependent on:															
	School locality (15 001 people or more)[3]		Publicly managed school[4]		50% or more of the school's funding comes from the government[5]		Number of teachers[6]		Number of students[7]		More than 10% of students have a different first language than the language(s) of instruction[8]		More than 10% of students have special needs[9]		More than 30% of students are from disadvantaged homes[10]	
	ß	S.E.	ß	S.E.	ß	S.E.	ß	S.E.	ß	S.E.	ß	S.E.	ß	S.E.	ß	S.E.
Australia			0.53	(0.17)												
Brazil			2.10	(0.59)												
Bulgaria	-1.06	(0.37)			-1.46	(0.52)	-0.04	(0.02)	0.00	(0.00)			-2.27	(0.95)		
Chile															1.12	(0.49)
Croatia																
Czech Republic																
Denmark																
Estonia															1.14	(0.30)
Finland																
France			1.36	(0.60)												
Iceland					2.55	(1.22)	-0.08	(0.03)	0.01	(0.00)					3.02	(1.25)
Israel																
Italy																
Japan	-0.82	(0.33)			1.12	(0.55)	0.03	(0.01)	0.00	(0.00)						
Korea			1.04	(0.48)	1.97	(0.34)										
Latvia																
Malaysia																
Mexico			2.23	(0.81)									1.30	(0.64)		
Netherlands																
Norway	0.36	(0.17)	-0.45	(0.22)					0.00	(0.00)						
Poland											4.38	(0.41)				
Portugal																
Romania																
Serbia					1.07	(0.32)	-0.02	(0.01)					-1.14	(0.46)		
Singapore					-1.12	(0.52)							0.76	(0.26)		
Slovak Republic																
Spain					1.65	(0.67)										
Sweden			-1.07	(0.51)					0.00	(0.00)	-0.55	(0.27)			1.07	(0.49)
Sub-national entities																
Abu Dhabi (United Arab Emirates)			1.72	(0.63)	-1.78	(0.69)										
Alberta (Canada)					1.95	(0.81)										
England (United Kingdom)	-1.47	(0.53)	0.86	(0.36)												
Flanders (Belgium)																

1. Cells are blank where no significant relationship was found. Significance was tested at the 5% level, controlling for principal gender, age and educational attainment. Cells with data representing less than 10% of the cases are shaded in grey and should be interpreted with caution. These results are not highlighted in the text of the report. Please note that 10% is the threshold used when reporting directly on principals' results. It is higher than what is used for teachers because the sample size of principals is smaller than that of teachers.

2. Continuous variable. See the textbox describing this index and Annex B for more details.

3. School locality is a dichotomous variable where the reference category is less than 15 000 people.

4. Publicly managed school is a dichotomous variable where the reference category is privately managed school.

5. School's funding is a dichotomous variable where the reference category is 50% or more of the school's funding does not come from the government.

6. Number of teachers is a continuous variable.

7. Number of students is a continuous variable.

8. Students who have a different first language than the language(s) of instruction is a dichotomous variable where the reference category is 10% or less of students have a different first language than the language(s) of instruction.

9. Students with special needs is a dichotomous variable where the reference category is 10% or less of students have special needs.

10. Students from disadvantaged homes is a dichotomous variable where the reference category is 30% or less of students are from disadvantaged homes.

Source: OECD, TALIS 2013 Database.

StatLink ᴥᴥᴥ http://dx.doi.org/10.1787/888933043663

[Part 1/1]

Relationship between principals' distributed leadership and school climate

Significant results of the multiple linear regressions of distributed leadership and school climate in lower secondary education[1]

Table 3.7

	Use of distributed leadership[2]															
	Dependent on:															
	Lack of material resources (a bit of a problem)[3]		Lack of material resources (a problem)[4]		Lack of pedagogical personnel (a bit of a problem)[5]		Lack of pedagogical personnel (a problem)[6]		School delinquency and violence[7]		School climate – mutual respect[8]		Ratio of teacher to administrative or management personnel[9]		Ratio of teacher to pedagogical support personnel[10]	
	ß	S.E.	ß	S.E.	ß	S.E.	ß	S.E.	ß	S.E.	ß	S.E.	ß	S.E.	ß	S.E.
Australia											0.10	(0.05)				
Brazil									0.13	(0.03)	0.34	(0.06)			0.02	(0.01)
Bulgaria	-0.93	(0.36)														
Chile			1.87	(0.79)	-1.30	(0.62)									-0.10	(0.05)
Croatia											0.24	(0.06)				
Czech Republic			-1.20	(0.51)			1.61	(0.72)								
Denmark	-0.63	(0.27)														
Estonia			-1.00	(0.42)							0.28	(0.07)				
Finland											0.22	(0.07)				
France			1.76	(0.81)							0.26	(0.10)				
Iceland			-3.57	(0.59)					-0.28	(0.12)			-0.11	(0.05)		
Israel							0.89	(0.35)					0.14	(0.07)		
Italy					-0.43	(0.15)					0.09	(0.04)				
Japan											0.49	(0.11)				
Korea	0.79	(0.37)									0.44	(0.09)				
Latvia											0.24	(0.08)				
Malaysia											0.18	(0.05)			0.01	(0.00)
Mexico																
Netherlands											0.21	(0.10)				
Norway							-0.74	(0.25)			0.23	(0.06)				
Poland											0.35	(0.11)				
Portugal			3.48	(1.10)					-0.19	(0.08)						
Romania											0.19	(0.10)				
Serbia											0.34	(0.10)	-0.06	(0.03)		
Singapore			1.15	(0.41)					-0.38	(0.13)	0.23	(0.07)				
Slovak Republic											0.36	(0.07)				
Spain							2.21	(1.00)	0.23	(0.11)	0.31	(0.10)				
Sweden			-1.81	(0.46)	-0.65	(0.29)					0.14	(0.06)				
Sub-national entities																
Abu Dhabi (United Arab Emirates)	-0.92	(0.45)							-0.52	(0.15)	0.22	(0.06)				
Alberta (Canada)											0.15	(0.07)				
England (United Kingdom)					-0.78	(0.36)					0.30	(0.11)				
Flanders (Belgium)											0.40	(0.12)				

1. Cells are blank where no significant relationship was found. Significance was tested at the 5% level, controlling for principal gender, age and educational attainment. Cells with data representing less than 10% of the cases are shaded in grey and should be interpreted with caution. These results are not highlighted in the text of the report. Please note that 10% is the threshold used when reporting directly on principals' results. It is higher than what is used for teachers because the sample size of principals is smaller than that of teachers.

2. Continuous variable. See the textbox describing this index and Annex B for more details.

3. Lack of material resources index is a dichotomous variable where the reference category is "not a problem" or "a problem". The index is combining the answers of the following questions: i) shortage or inadequacy of instructional materials (e.g. textbooks), ii) shortage or inadequacy of computers for instruction, iii) insufficient Internet access, iv) shortage or inadequacy of computer software for instruction, and v) shortage or inadequacy of library materials.

4. Lack of material resources index is a dichotomous variable where the reference category is "not a problem" or "a bit of a problem". The index is combining the answers of the following questions: i) shortage or inadequacy of instructional materials (e.g. textbooks), ii) shortage or inadequacy of computers for instruction, iii) insufficient Internet access, iv) shortage or inadequacy of computer software for instruction, and v) shortage or inadequacy of library materials.

5. Lack of pedagogical personnel index is a dichotomous variable where the reference category is "not a problem" or "a problem". The index is combining the answers of the following questions: i) shortage of qualified and/or well performing teachers, ii) shortage of teachers with competence in teaching students with special needs, and iii) shortage of vocational teachers.

6. Lack of pedagogical personnel index is a dichotomous variable where the reference category is "not a problem" or "a bit of a problem". The index is combining the answers of the following questions: i) shortage of qualified and/or well performing teachers, ii) shortage of teachers with competence in teaching students with special needs, and iii) shortage of vocational teachers.

7. School delinquency and violence index is a continuous variable combining answers of the following questions: i) frequency of vandalism and theft, ii) frequency of intimidation or verbal abuse among students (or other forms of non-physical bullying), iii) frequency of physical injury caused by violence among students, and iv) frequency of intimidation or verbal abuse of teachers or staff.

8. School climate - mutual respect index is a continuous variable combining answers of the following questions: i) school staff have an open discussion about difficulties, ii) there is mutual respect for colleagues' ideas, iii) there is a culture of sharing success, and iv) the relationships between teachers and students are good.

9. Ratio of teacher to administrative or management personnel is a continous variable.

10. Ratio of teacher to pedagogical support personnel is a continuous variable.

Source: OECD, TALIS 2013 Database.

StatLink http://dx.doi.org/10.1787/888933043701

[Part 1/1]
Gender and age of principals
Percentage of lower secondary education principals with the following characteristics and mean age
Table 3.8   *of principals*

| | Female | | Mean age | | Percentage of principals in each age group | | | | | | | | | |
| | | | | | Under 30 years | | 30-39 years | | 40-49 years | | 50-59 years | | 60 years or more | |
	%	S.E.	Average	S.E.	%	S.E.	%	S.E.	%	S.E.	%	S.E.	%	S.E.
Australia	38.6	(5.5)	53.2	(1.0)	0.0	(0.0)	4.7	(4.5)	21.8	(5.2)	55.2	(6.3)	18.3	(4.5)
Brazil	74.5	(2.1)	45.0	(0.4)	2.0	(0.7)	27.8	(1.9)	39.7	(2.3)	24.3	(1.8)	6.2	(1.4)
Bulgaria	71.5	(3.5)	51.1	(0.5)	0.0	(0.0)	4.6	(1.6)	35.2	(3.0)	47.2	(3.9)	13.0	(2.6)
Chile	53.4	(3.9)	53.7	(0.7)	0.0	(0.0)	6.4	(2.1)	24.2	(3.3)	39.3	(3.9)	30.2	(4.0)
Croatia	59.9	(3.7)	52.0	(0.7)	0.0	(0.0)	8.7	(2.1)	25.5	(3.7)	43.7	(4.0)	22.2	(3.5)
Cyprus*	53.1	(4.3)	55.2	(0.5)	0.0	(0.0)	3.2	(1.8)	8.5	(2.6)	73.4	(4.3)	14.9	(3.4)
Czech Republic	48.4	(3.6)	50.3	(0.5)	0.0	(0.0)	6.3	(1.8)	38.8	(3.1)	44.6	(3.4)	10.3	(2.2)
Denmark	32.4	(4.4)	52.9	(0.6)	0.0	(0.0)	4.1	(1.8)	24.3	(3.7)	52.1	(4.9)	19.5	(3.9)
Estonia	60.2	(3.4)	52.2	(0.6)	0.0	(0.0)	5.1	(1.6)	29.4	(3.3)	43.2	(3.5)	22.3	(2.9)
Finland	40.6	(4.0)	51.2	(0.6)	0.6	(0.6)	8.0	(2.3)	33.0	(3.8)	45.6	(4.1)	12.8	(3.0)
France	41.7	(3.7)	52.0	(0.5)	0.0	(0.0)	1.7	(1.0)	32.0	(4.1)	56.0	(4.6)	10.3	(2.3)
Iceland	54.6	(4.7)	50.9	(0.8)	0.0	(0.0)	7.4	(2.6)	36.1	(4.5)	40.7	(4.5)	15.7	(3.8)
Israel	52.6	(6.0)	48.9	(0.9)	0.2	(0.2)	11.8	(3.5)	45.5	(6.7)	32.8	(5.8)	9.7	(2.7)
Italy	55.2	(4.2)	57.0	(0.5)	0.0	(0.0)	1.0	(0.6)	13.2	(2.4)	39.4	(4.8)	46.5	(4.9)
Japan	6.0	(1.9)	57.0	(0.3)	0.0	(0.0)	0.0	(0.0)	1.6	(1.0)	80.4	(3.0)	18.0	(3.1)
Korea	13.3	(2.2)	58.8	(0.2)	0.0	(0.0)	0.0	(0.0)	0.0	(0.0)	54.4	(4.2)	45.6	(4.2)
Latvia	77.0	(4.2)	52.9	(0.8)	0.0	(0.0)	4.1	(1.7)	26.9	(5.1)	51.9	(4.5)	17.1	(3.4)
Malaysia	49.1	(4.6)	53.5	(0.3)	0.0	(0.0)	0.0	(0.0)	13.1	(3.2)	86.9	(3.2)	0.0	(0.0)
Mexico	40.8	(3.7)	51.9	(0.6)	0.0	(0.0)	8.7	(2.5)	28.2	(3.6)	46.7	(4.3)	16.3	(2.8)
Netherlands	30.8	(7.7)	52.2	(1.1)	0.0	(0.0)	6.4	(4.2)	26.4	(8.0)	49.2	(7.0)	18.0	(5.1)
Norway	58.2	(8.0)	52.1	(1.0)	0.0	(0.0)	3.7	(1.6)	39.8	(8.1)	35.9	(8.0)	20.6	(5.4)
Poland	66.6	(4.3)	49.9	(0.6)	0.8	(0.6)	5.6	(2.6)	38.5	(4.5)	48.4	(4.8)	6.8	(2.4)
Portugal	39.4	(4.3)	52.1	(0.5)	0.0	(0.0)	4.9	(1.6)	24.9	(3.9)	57.4	(3.9)	12.8	(3.1)
Romania	63.9	(4.3)	46.7	(0.9)	0.7	(0.7)	30.6	(4.0)	26.9	(3.7)	36.9	(4.6)	5.0	(1.7)
Serbia	55.3	(3.4)	49.0	(0.6)	0.0	(0.0)	13.8	(2.7)	39.2	(4.3)	35.1	(4.1)	11.9	(2.2)
Singapore	52.5	(4.8)	48.3	(0.5)	0.0	(0.0)	10.7	(2.7)	39.4	(4.5)	47.9	(4.3)	2.0	(1.2)
Slovak Republic	60.0	(4.2)	52.5	(0.6)	0.0	(0.0)	9.7	(2.5)	23.3	(3.5)	49.6	(3.7)	17.4	(3.0)
Spain	44.7	(5.0)	49.4	(0.8)	0.0	(0.0)	13.8	(3.7)	33.7	(4.9)	44.7	(5.1)	7.8	(1.9)
Sweden	54.9	(4.9)	50.7	(0.7)	0.0	(0.0)	4.2	(1.8)	45.0	(5.0)	38.0	(4.6)	12.9	(3.0)
Sub-national entities														
Abu Dhabi (United Arab Emirates)	60.9	(3.6)	49.0	(0.8)	0.0	(0.0)	9.2	(2.7)	49.1	(4.3)	27.4	(4.0)	14.3	(3.8)
Alberta (Canada)	43.1	(3.8)	49.3	(0.7)	0.0	(0.0)	10.9	(2.4)	41.4	(3.6)	39.3	(4.0)	8.4	(2.6)
England (United Kingdom)	38.1	(4.1)	49.4	(0.5)	0.0	(0.0)	7.8	(2.4)	43.7	(3.9)	45.7	(3.5)	2.8	(1.2)
Flanders (Belgium)	38.8	(5.1)	49.5	(0.6)	1.0	(1.0)	9.8	(2.4)	30.8	(5.0)	53.6	(4.7)	4.8	(2.2)
Average	49.4	(0.8)	51.5	(0.1)	0.2	(0.0)	7.7	(0.4)	29.7	(0.7)	47.5	(0.8)	15.0	(0.6)
United States	48.6	(5.7)	48.3	(1.1)	1.1	(1.1)	19.2	(5.0)	32.9	(4.0)	36.1	(5.7)	10.7	(4.1)

* See notes at the beginning of this Annex.
Source: OECD, TALIS 2013 Database.
StatLink ⬛⬛⬛ http://dx.doi.org/10.1787/888933043739

[Part 1/1]
Gender and age of primary principals

Table 3.8.a *Percentage of primary education principals with the following characteristics and mean age of principals*

| | Female | | Mean age | | Percentage of principals in each age group | | | | | | | | | |
| | | | | | Under 30 years | | 30-39 years | | 40-49 years | | 50-59 years | | 60 years or more | |
	%	S.E.	Average	S.E.	%	S.E.	%	S.E.	%	S.E.	%	S.E.	%	S.E.
Denmark	37.4	(4.4)	53.0	(0.7)	0.0	(0.0)	8.0	(2.4)	20.2	(3.3)	51.5	(4.3)	20.2	(3.2)
Finland	47.2	(4.1)	49.1	(1.1)	0.0	(0.0)	14.2	(4.5)	31.2	(4.4)	49.4	(5.7)	5.1	(1.8)
Mexico	42.8	(3.9)	45.3	(0.8)	13.8	(2.6)	14.6	(2.9)	30.4	(3.6)	34.5	(3.4)	6.8	(2.0)
Norway	60.2	(7.9)	53.6	(0.9)	0.0	(0.0)	5.9	(3.1)	20.9	(3.2)	50.0	(5.3)	23.2	(4.7)
Poland	72.5	(4.0)	50.2	(0.7)	0.0	(0.0)	3.6	(1.3)	34.7	(5.2)	57.6	(4.7)	4.1	(2.1)
Sub-national entities														
Flanders (Belgium)	59.1	(3.9)	47.6	(0.6)	0.0	(0.0)	16.8	(3.4)	34.6	(4.0)	48.6	(4.5)	0.0	(0.0)
Average	53.2	(2.0)	49.8	(0.3)	2.3	(0.4)	10.5	(1.3)	28.7	(1.6)	48.6	(1.9)	9.9	(1.1)

Source: OECD, TALIS 2013 Database.
StatLink ⟨⟩ http://dx.doi.org/10.1787/888933043758

[Part 1/1]
Gender and age of upper secondary principals

Table 3.8.b *Percentage of upper secondary education principals with the following characteristics and mean age of principals*

| | Female | | Mean age | | Percentage of principals in each age group | | | | | | | | | |
| | | | | | Under 30 years | | 30-39 years | | 40-49 years | | 50-59 years | | 60 years or more | |
	%	S.E.	Average	S.E.	%	S.E.	%	S.E.	%	S.E.	%	S.E.	%	S.E.
Australia	39.5	(5.8)	54.4	(0.8)	0.0	(0.0)	5.0	(2.3)	16.3	(4.7)	58.8	(5.8)	19.8	(5.1)
Denmark	46.0	(5.6)	52.1	(0.8)	0.0	(0.0)	4.6	(2.3)	31.1	(4.9)	51.9	(5.4)	12.3	(3.3)
Finland	44.9	(4.5)	53.1	(0.7)	0.0	(0.0)	6.6	(1.7)	24.0	(4.6)	43.4	(4.2)	26.1	(4.0)
Iceland	42.2	(11.2)	55.6	(1.1)	0.0	(0.0)	0.0	(0.0)	16.9	(7.6)	59.1	(9.7)	24.0	(8.7)
Italy	48.1	(4.0)	58.5	(0.8)	0.0	(0.0)	0.3	(0.3)	10.9	(3.3)	38.7	(3.5)	50.1	(4.5)
Mexico	40.9	(4.6)	45.8	(0.9)	7.0	(2.1)	24.6	(4.2)	31.5	(4.6)	23.1	(3.8)	13.8	(2.9)
Norway	49.2	(5.0)	53.7	(0.8)	0.0	(0.0)	4.1	(2.3)	24.4	(5.2)	46.5	(5.3)	24.9	(5.3)
Poland	52.6	(5.0)	50.0	(1.1)	0.0	(0.0)	8.4	(4.6)	36.5	(3.8)	47.7	(6.2)	7.3	(1.9)
Singapore	54.0	(4.3)	48.3	(0.5)	0.0	(0.0)	10.5	(2.7)	40.5	(4.4)	45.6	(4.1)	3.4	(1.8)
Sub-national entities														
Abu Dhabi (United Arab Emirates)	46.6	(4.0)	49.5	(0.7)	0.0	(0.0)	7.4	(2.4)	46.5	(3.7)	32.0	(4.1)	14.1	(3.1)
Average	46.4	(1.8)	52.1	(0.3)	0.7	(0.2)	7.1	(0.8)	27.9	(1.5)	44.7	(1.7)	19.6	(1.4)

Source: OECD, TALIS 2013 Database.
StatLink ⟨⟩ http://dx.doi.org/10.1787/888933043777

[Part 1/1]
Gender and age of principals, 2008 and 2013

Table 3.8.c *Percentage of lower secondary education principals with the following characteristics[1]*

	Female				Percentage of principals in each age group											
					Under 40 years				40-49 years				50-59 years				60 years or more			
	2008		2013		2008		2013		2008		2013		2008		2013		2008		2013	
	%	S.E.	%	S.E.	%	S.E.	%	S.E.	%	S.E.	%	S.E.	%	S.E.	%	S.E.	%	S.E.	%	S.E.
Australia	38.2	(4.8)	38.6	(5.5)	8.6	(5.2)	4.7	(4.5)	25.4	(4.3)	21.8	(5.2)	57.5	(6.1)	55.2	(6.3)	8.4	(2.4)	18.3	(4.5)
Brazil	76.0	(2.8)	74.5	(2.1)	36.3	(2.6)	29.9	(1.8)	41.0	(3.3)	39.7	(2.3)	18.4	(2.3)	24.3	(1.8)	4.3	(1.4)	6.2	(1.4)
Bulgaria	69.0	(6.0)	71.5	(3.5)	12.0	(5.7)	4.6	(1.6)	45.6	(7.7)	35.2	(3.0)	38.0	(7.6)	47.2	(3.9)	4.5	(3.3)	13.0	(2.6)
Denmark	37.8	(5.3)	32.4	(4.4)	2.6	(1.3)	4.1	(1.8)	19.1	(4.2)	24.3	(3.7)	64.6	(5.4)	52.1	(4.9)	13.8	(4.5)	19.5	(3.9)
Estonia	56.4	(3.2)	60.2	(3.4)	11.3	(2.6)	5.1	(1.6)	42.0	(4.1)	29.4	(3.5)	37.3	(4.0)	43.2	(3.5)	9.4	(2.2)	22.3	(2.9)
Iceland	49.1	(5.2)	54.6	(4.7)	9.9	(3.1)	7.4	(2.6)	35.7	(4.9)	36.1	(4.5)	44.4	(4.5)	40.7	(4.5)	9.9	(2.8)	15.7	(3.8)
Italy	45.8	(4.9)	55.2	(4.2)	3.1	(1.4)	1.0	(0.6)	11.9	(2.1)	13.2	(2.4)	51.0	(3.6)	39.4	(4.8)	34.1	(4.1)	46.5	(4.9)
Korea	15.0	(4.2)	13.3	(2.2)	0.5	(0.5)	0.0	(0.0)	0.0	(0.0)	0.0	(0.0)	63.9	(4.3)	54.4	(4.2)	35.7	(4.3)	45.6	(4.2)
Malaysia	42.3	(3.7)	49.1	(4.6)	2.6	(1.1)	0.0	(0.0)	27.2	(3.4)	13.1	(3.2)	69.5	(3.4)	86.9	(3.2)	0.8	(0.5)	0.0	(0.0)
Mexico	34.7	(5.1)	40.8	(3.7)	8.9	(1.7)	8.7	(2.5)	33.9	(3.0)	28.2	(3.6)	45.3	(3.9)	46.7	(4.3)	11.9	(2.1)	16.3	(2.8)
Norway	41.4	(4.1)	58.2	(8.0)	8.2	(2.5)	3.7	(1.6)	19.2	(3.2)	39.8	(8.1)	55.3	(4.5)	35.9	(8.0)	17.4	(3.2)	20.6	(5.4)
Poland	68.7	(3.7)	66.6	(4.3)	14.7	(3.3)	6.3	(2.7)	52.5	(4.6)	38.5	(4.5)	28.9	(4.7)	48.4	(4.8)	3.9	(1.3)	6.8	(2.4)
Portugal	40.0	(4.1)	39.4	(4.3)	10.1	(2.8)	4.9	(1.6)	42.1	(4.1)	24.9	(3.9)	45.1	(4.0)	57.4	(3.9)	2.6	(0.9)	12.8	(3.1)
Slovak Republic	60.3	(4.9)	60.0	(4.2)	4.6	(2.0)	9.7	(2.5)	33.0	(4.8)	23.3	(3.5)	50.6	(4.8)	49.6	(3.7)	11.7	(3.4)	17.4	(3.0)
Spain	39.6	(5.3)	44.7	(5.0)	10.6	(2.9)	13.8	(3.7)	34.4	(4.0)	33.7	(4.9)	43.4	(3.7)	44.7	(5.1)	11.5	(2.8)	7.8	(1.9)
Sub-national entities																				
Flanders (Belgium)	38.2	(4.3)	38.8	(5.1)	8.7	(2.3)	10.8	(2.2)	30.5	(4.6)	30.8	(5.0)	56.2	(4.8)	53.6	(4.7)	4.7	(1.6)	4.8	(2.2)
Average	47.0	(1.1)	49.9	(1.1)	9.5	(0.7)	7.2	(0.6)	30.8	(1.0)	27.0	(1.0)	48.1	(1.2)	48.7	(1.2)	11.5	(0.7)	17.1	(0.8)

1. The wording and order of questions may have changed slightly between the 2008 and 2013 surveys.
Source: OECD, TALIS 2008 and TALIS 2013 Databases.
StatLink ⟨⟩ http://dx.doi.org/10.1787/888933043796

[Part 1/1]
Principals' educational attainment

Table 3.9 *Percentage of lower secondary education principals by highest level of formal education completed[1]*

	Highest level of formal education completed							
	Below ISCED level 5		ISCED level 5B[2]		ISCED level 5A		ISCED level 6	
	%	S.E.	%	S.E.	%	S.E.	%	S.E.
Australia	0.0	(0.0)	0.0	(0.0)	97.0	(1.6)	3.0	(1.6)
Brazil	2.1	(0.8)	1.8	(0.6)	96.1	(1.0)	0.0	(0.0)
Bulgaria	0.0	(0.0)	0.0	(0.0)	99.2	(0.6)	0.8	(0.6)
Chile	0.0	(0.0)	24.5	(3.6)	73.4	(3.6)	2.0	(1.2)
Croatia	a	a	18.0	(3.1)	81.1	(3.2)	0.8	(0.8)
Cyprus*	0.0	(0.0)	0.0	(0.0)	87.8	(3.5)	12.2	(3.5)
Czech Republic	0.0	(0.0)	0.0	(0.0)	91.8	(1.8)	8.2	(1.8)
Denmark	0.8	(0.8)	0.0	(0.0)	99.2	(0.8)	0.0	(0.0)
Estonia	0.0	(0.0)	2.5	(1.1)	95.9	(1.4)	1.5	(0.9)
Finland	0.0	(0.0)	0.0	(0.0)	95.5	(1.7)	4.5	(1.7)
France	1.4	(0.7)	12.9	(2.7)	84.8	(2.8)	0.9	(0.6)
Iceland	8.3	(2.7)	1.9	(1.3)	89.8	(3.0)	0.0	(0.0)
Israel	0.0	(0.0)	0.5	(0.5)	94.8	(1.9)	4.7	(1.9)
Italy	0.0	(0.0)	1.2	(0.9)	95.2	(1.5)	3.6	(1.3)
Japan	0.5	(0.5)	0.4	(0.4)	98.4	(0.6)	0.7	(0.0)
Korea	0.0	(0.0)	0.0	(0.0)	96.5	(1.0)	3.5	(1.0)
Latvia	0.0	(0.0)	0.0	(0.0)	100.0	(0.0)	0.0	(0.0)
Malaysia	0.0	(0.0)	0.0	(0.0)	100.0	(0.0)	0.0	(0.0)
Mexico	0.8	(0.8)	0.0	(0.0)	93.5	(1.7)	5.7	(1.5)
Netherlands	0.0	(0.0)	0.0	(0.0)	98.5	(0.6)	1.5	(0.6)
Norway	0.0	(0.0)	a	a	100.0	(0.0)	0.0	(0.0)
Poland	0.0	(0.0)	0.0	(0.0)	99.2	(0.6)	0.8	(0.6)
Portugal[3]	0.0	(0.0)	2.8	(1.5)	70.4	(4.3)	26.8	(4.3)
Romania	0.0	(0.0)	4.6	(1.9)	94.1	(2.0)	1.3	(0.6)
Serbia	0.0	(0.0)	2.3	(1.7)	97.1	(1.8)	0.6	(0.4)
Singapore	0.0	(0.0)	0.0	(0.0)	97.3	(1.3)	2.7	(1.3)
Slovak Republic	0.0	(0.0)	0.0	(0.0)	98.1	(0.9)	1.9	(0.9)
Spain	a	a	1.6	(2.0)	94.2	(2.2)	4.3	(1.4)
Sweden	2.9	(2.5)	7.9	(2.0)	89.0	(3.1)	0.2	(0.2)
Sub-national entities								
Abu Dhabi (United Arab Emirates)	0.0	(0.0)	0.9	(0.9)	92.2	(2.9)	7.0	(2.8)
Alberta (Canada)	0.0	(0.0)	0.0	(0.0)	95.8	(1.8)	4.2	(1.8)
England (United Kingdom)	0.7	(0.7)	0.0	(0.0)	97.1	(1.4)	2.2	(1.2)
Flanders (Belgium)	1.0	(1.0)	39.7	(4.6)	58.6	(4.7)	0.7	(0.5)
Average	0.6	(0.1)	3.9	(0.3)	92.5	(0.4)	3.2	(0.3)
United States	0.0	(0.0)	0.0	(0.0)	84.3	(4.6)	15.7	(4.6)

1. Education categories are based on the International Standard Classification of Education (ISCED 1997). ISCED level 5A programmes are generally longer and more theory-based, while 5B programmes are typically shorter and more practical and skills oriented. No distinction was made between ISCED level 5A (Bachelor) and ISCED level 5A (Master).

2. Includes Bachelor's degrees in some countries.

3. In Portugal, the principals with a "pre-Bologna Master's degree" are counted as ISCED level 6. The way the question is presented prevents the disaggregation between "pre-Bologna Master's degree" and "Doctorate degree".

* See notes at the beginning of this Annex.

Source: OECD, TALIS 2013 Database.

StatLink 📊 http://dx.doi.org/10.1787/888933043815

[Part 1/1]
Primary education principals' educational attainment

Table 3.9.a *Percentage of primary education principals by level of education and training completed[1]*

	Highest level of formal education completed							
	Below ISCED level 5		ISCED level 5B[2]		ISCED level 5A		ISCED level 6	
	%	S.E.	%	S.E.	%	S.E.	%	S.E.
Denmark	0.7	(0.7)	0.0	(0.0)	99.3	(0.7)	0.0	(0.0)
Finland	0.0	(0.0)	0.3	(0.3)	98.9	(0.6)	0.9	(0.5)
Mexico	14.0	(2.4)	0.0	(0.0)	83.8	(2.7)	2.3	(1.1)
Norway	0.0	(0.0)	a	a	100.0	(0.0)	0.0	(0.0)
Poland	0.0	(0.0)	2.0	(2.8)	96.4	(3.0)	1.6	(1.2)
Sub-national entities								
Flanders (Belgium)	0.7	(0.7)	89.8	(2.9)	9.5	(2.8)	0.0	(0.0)
Average[3]	2.6	(0.4)	18.4	(0.8)	81.3	(0.8)	0.8	(0.3)

1. Education categories are based on the International Standard Classification of Education (ISCED 1997). ISCED level 5A programmes are generally longer and more theory-based, while 5B programmes are typically shorter and more practical and skills oriented. No distinction was made between ISCED level 5A (Bachelor) and ISCED level 5A (Master).
2. Includes Bachelor's degrees in some countries.
3. The averages do not add up to 100 across categories because of the presence of cells that are not applicable "a" in some countries.
Source: OECD, TALIS 2013 Database.
StatLink ⌨ http://dx.doi.org/10.1787/888933043834

[Part 1/1]
Upper secondary education principals' educational attainment

Table 3.9.b *Percentage of upper secondary education principals by level of education and training completed[1]*

	Highest level of formal education completed							
	Below ISCED level 5		ISCED level 5B[2]		ISCED level 5A		ISCED level 6	
	%	S.E.	%	S.E.	%	S.E.	%	S.E.
Australia	0.0	(0.0)	0.0	(0.0)	96.1	(1.6)	3.9	(1.6)
Denmark	1.8	(1.3)	2.5	(1.2)	91.1	(2.9)	4.6	(2.3)
Finland	0.0	(0.0)	2.1	(1.6)	86.8	(2.6)	11.1	(3.3)
Iceland	0.0	(0.0)	0.0	(0.0)	95.8	(4.3)	4.2	(4.3)
Italy	0.3	(0.3)	0.4	(0.5)	97.0	(1.4)	2.4	(1.2)
Mexico	2.9	(2.1)	0.0	(0.0)	93.1	(2.8)	3.9	(1.9)
Norway	0.0	(0.0)	a	a	100.0	(0.0)	0.0	(0.0)
Poland	0.2	(0.2)	0.0	(0.0)	99.2	(0.5)	0.7	(0.5)
Singapore	0.0	(0.0)	0.0	(0.0)	97.4	(1.3)	2.6	(1.3)
Sub-national entities								
Abu Dhabi (United Arab Emirates)	0.0	(0.0)	3.3	(1.6)	88.5	(2.6)	8.2	(2.3)
Average	0.5	(0.2)	0.9	(0.3)	94.5	(0.7)	4.2	(0.7)

1. Education categories are based on the International Standard Classification of Education (ISCED 1997). ISCED level 5A programmes are generally longer and more theory-based, while 5B programmes are typically shorter and more practical and skills oriented. No distinction was made between ISCED level 5A (Bachelor) and ISCED level 5A (Master).
2. Includes Bachelor's degrees in some countries.
Source: OECD, TALIS 2013 Database.
StatLink ⌨ http://dx.doi.org/10.1787/888933043853

[Part 1/1]
Principals' educational attainment, 2008 and 2013

Table 3.9.c *Percentage of lower secondary education principals by level of education and training completed[1, 2]*

	Highest level of formal education completed															
	Below ISCED level 5				ISCED level 5B[3]				ISCED level 5A				ISCED level 6			
	2008		2013		2008		2013		2008		2013		2008		2013	
	%	S.E.	%	S.E.	%	S.E.	%	S.E.	%	S.E.	%	S.E.	%	S.E.	%	S.E.
Australia	5.6	(5.1)	0.0	(0.0)	0.0	(0.0)	0.0	(0.0)	90.1	(5.1)	97.0	(1.6)	4.4	(1.4)	3.0	(1.6)
Brazil	5.0	(1.7)	2.1	(0.8)	0.5	(0.4)	1.8	(0.6)	94.4	(1.7)	96.1	(1.0)	0.2	(0.1)	0.0	(0.0)
Bulgaria	0.0	(0.0)	0.0	(0.0)	0.0	(0.0)	0.0	(0.0)	99.0	(1.0)	99.2	(0.6)	1.0	(1.0)	0.8	(0.6)
Denmark	1.4	(1.4)	0.8	(0.8)	0.0	(0.0)	0.0	(0.0)	97.3	(1.7)	99.2	(0.8)	1.3	(1.0)	0.0	(0.0)
Estonia	0.0	(0.0)	0.0	(0.0)	1.2	(0.8)	2.5	(1.1)	97.6	(1.1)	95.9	(1.4)	1.2	(0.8)	1.5	(0.9)
Iceland	0.0	(0.0)	8.3	(2.7)	15.0	(3.6)	1.9	(1.3)	85.0	(3.6)	89.8	(3.0)	0.0	(0.0)	0.0	(0.0)
Italy	0.0	(0.0)	0.0	(0.0)	0.0	(0.0)	1.2	(0.9)	99.7	(0.2)	95.2	(1.5)	0.3	(0.2)	3.6	(1.3)
Korea	3.1	(1.9)	0.0	(0.0)	0.3	(0.3)	0.0	(0.0)	94.9	(2.1)	96.5	(1.0)	1.7	(0.9)	3.5	(1.0)
Malaysia	0.4	(0.4)	0.0	(0.0)	0.9	(0.9)	0.0	(0.0)	98.7	(0.9)	100.0	(0.0)	0.0	(0.0)	0.0	(0.0)
Mexico	0.3	(0.3)	0.8	(0.8)	1.1	(1.1)	0.0	(0.0)	96.9	(1.4)	93.5	(1.7)	1.8	(0.8)	5.7	(1.5)
Norway	0.0	(0.0)	0.0	(0.0)	a	a	a	a	98.8	(1.2)	100.0	(0.0)	1.2	(1.2)	0.0	(0.0)
Poland	0.0	(0.0)	0.0	(0.0)	0.4	(0.4)	0.0	(0.0)	98.0	(0.9)	99.2	(0.6)	1.6	(1.1)	0.8	(0.6)
Portugal[4]	0.0	(0.0)	0.0	(0.0)	7.3	(2.7)	2.8	(1.5)	92.3	(2.7)	70.4	(4.3)	0.3	(0.3)	26.8	(4.3)
Slovak Republic	0.0	(0.0)	0.0	(0.0)	0.0	(0.0)	0.0	(0.0)	99.4	(0.3)	98.1	(0.9)	0.6	(0.3)	1.9	(0.9)
Spain	12.8	(4.8)	a	a	1.1	(0.6)	1.6	(2.0)	83.2	(5.0)	94.2	(2.2)	2.9	(1.3)	4.3	(1.4)
Sub-national entities																
Flanders (Belgium)	0.0	(0.0)	1.0	(1.0)	37.4	(3.9)	39.7	(4.6)	59.5	(4.0)	58.6	(4.7)	3.1	(2.4)	0.7	(0.5)
Average	1.8	(0.5)	0.9	(0.2)	4.3	(0.4)	3.4	(0.4)	92.8	(0.6)	92.7	(0.5)	1.3	(0.3)	3.3	(0.3)

1. The wording and order of questions may have changed slightly between the 2008 and 2013 surveys.

2. Education categories are based on the International Standard Classification of Education (ISCED 1997). ISCED level 5A programmes are generally longer and more theory-based, while 5B programmes are typically shorter and more practical and skills oriented. No distinction was made between ISCED level 5A (Bachelor) and ISCED level 5A (Master).

3. Includes Bachelor's degrees in some countries.

4. In Portugal, the principals with a "pre-Bologna Master's degree" are counted as ISCED level 5A in TALIS 2008, and as ISCED level 6 in TALIS 2013. The way the question is presented in TALIS 2013 prevents the disaggregation between "pre-Bologna Master's degree" and "Doctorate degree".

Source: OECD, TALIS 2008 and TALIS 2013 Databases.

StatLink ⟨⟩ http://dx.doi.org/10.1787/888933043872

[Part 1/1]

Principals' formal education

Percentage of lower secondary education principals who report that the following elements were included in their formal education

Table 3.10

	School administration or principal training programme or course				Teacher training/education programme or course				Instructional leadership training or course			
	Before taking up position as principal	After taking up position as principal	Before and after taking up position as principal	Never	Before taking up position as principal	After taking up position as principal	Before and after taking up position as principal	Never	Before taking up position as principal	After taking up position as principal	Before and after taking up position as principal	Never
	% (S.E.)	% (S.E.)	% (S.E.)	% (S.E.)	% (S.E.)	% (S.E.)	% (S.E.)	% (S.E.)	% (S.E.)	% (S.E.)	% (S.E.)	% (S.E.)
Australia	22.7 (5.0)	24.0 (4.7)	17.4 (4.7)	35.9 (5.5)	84.7 (3.3)	1.9 (1.1)	9.2 (2.2)	4.2 (2.1)	20.2 (3.8)	27.0 (4.8)	21.7 (5.1)	31.1 (6.2)
Brazil	24.2 (2.4)	38.8 (2.4)	25.2 (2.2)	11.9 (1.5)	43.8 (2.5)	16.5 (2.3)	35.8 (2.6)	3.8 (0.8)	24.0 (2.4)	33.0 (2.8)	27.7 (2.6)	15.4 (1.7)
Bulgaria	11.2 (2.7)	66.2 (3.9)	11.3 (2.4)	11.3 (2.7)	55.8 (4.6)	16.2 (3.4)	18.2 (3.1)	9.8 (2.2)	7.2 (2.2)	61.3 (4.1)	10.7 (2.6)	20.8 (3.5)
Chile	44.8 (4.1)	18.4 (3.1)	25.6 (3.4)	11.1 (2.3)	49.2 (4.5)	13.1 (2.9)	32.5 (4.4)	5.2 (1.9)	30.0 (3.8)	28.1 (3.9)	33.0 (3.7)	8.9 (2.4)
Croatia	0.0 (0.0)	36.8 (3.8)	5.1 (1.4)	58.1 (3.8)	58.1 (3.9)	3.3 (1.4)	18.8 (3.2)	19.8 (3.0)	5.5 (2.0)	43.1 (4.0)	10.7 (2.5)	40.8 (4.0)
Cyprus*	13.8 (3.2)	40.4 (5.2)	28.7 (4.5)	17.0 (3.4)	48.3 (5.1)	16.9 (4.3)	20.2 (4.1)	14.6 (4.0)	27.8 (4.6)	34.4 (5.4)	20.0 (4.0)	17.8 (4.1)
Czech Republic	18.6 (3.1)	52.7 (3.5)	18.9 (2.7)	9.7 (2.2)	48.2 (3.7)	5.0 (1.5)	15.1 (2.7)	31.7 (3.5)	22.0 (3.2)	33.9 (3.4)	13.2 (2.3)	30.9 (3.5)
Denmark	3.3 (1.6)	41.4 (4.3)	10.7 (2.2)	44.6 (4.3)	82.6 (3.6)	4.3 (1.9)	0.8 (0.8)	12.2 (2.9)	16.9 (3.5)	40.1 (5.0)	30.2 (4.0)	12.8 (3.2)
Estonia	28.4 (3.2)	46.2 (3.4)	23.4 (3.0)	2.0 (1.1)	61.1 (3.6)	6.7 (1.5)	27.2 (3.4)	5.1 (1.4)	26.2 (3.2)	26.1 (3.1)	36.4 (3.5)	11.3 (2.2)
Finland	70.1 (3.9)	8.1 (2.3)	18.3 (2.9)	3.5 (1.6)	95.2 (1.8)	0.0 (0.0)	3.3 (1.5)	1.5 (1.1)	13.8 (3.3)	30.2 (3.8)	27.7 (4.1)	28.3 (3.6)
France	42.0 (4.4)	23.8 (3.8)	31.9 (3.9)	2.4 (1.4)	56.3 (4.0)	11.2 (2.2)	17.0 (3.0)	15.6 (2.9)	28.2 (3.5)	19.0 (3.2)	22.8 (3.4)	29.9 (3.4)
Iceland	21.9 (4.2)	40.0 (4.8)	21.0 (4.2)	17.1 (3.8)	87.0 (3.3)	1.9 (1.3)	7.4 (2.8)	3.7 (1.9)	31.1 (4.5)	30.2 (4.6)	30.2 (4.5)	8.5 (2.8)
Israel	46.3 (5.5)	32.7 (7.4)	10.4 (2.9)	10.6 (2.9)	80.9 (4.8)	0.8 (0.5)	10.6 (4.5)	7.7 (2.2)	30.1 (5.3)	27.2 (5.7)	9.4 (2.9)	33.3 (5.7)
Italy	21.3 (4.4)	41.3 (5.3)	33.6 (4.2)	3.8 (1.4)	54.7 (4.4)	17.8 (3.7)	17.9 (3.3)	9.6 (3.3)	17.3 (2.8)	31.2 (4.5)	25.1 (4.3)	26.5 (4.0)
Japan	13.9 (2.3)	45.4 (4.4)	37.1 (3.8)	3.5 (1.3)	48.4 (4.3)	25.0 (4.2)	21.2 (3.3)	5.4 (1.7)	51.1 (4.1)	23.1 (4.0)	19.7 (3.1)	6.2 (1.9)
Korea	37.3 (5.3)	15.8 (3.4)	43.4 (5.5)	3.5 (2.1)	55.5 (5.9)	6.1 (2.7)	34.0 (5.3)	4.4 (2.7)	50.3 (5.8)	4.9 (1.7)	37.7 (4.9)	7.1 (2.8)
Latvia	13.9 (3.5)	47.0 (6.7)	12.4 (3.0)	26.7 (5.6)	63.5 (6.5)	4.6 (2.5)	24.8 (5.5)	7.1 (4.4)	18.6 (4.3)	46.1 (5.0)	18.5 (3.6)	16.8 (4.5)
Malaysia	4.9 (2.0)	58.2 (5.1)	21.8 (4.2)	15.0 (3.4)	57.4 (4.1)	12.2 (2.5)	22.1 (3.9)	8.3 (2.1)	13.5 (3.2)	51.3 (4.6)	29.8 (4.3)	5.4 (1.5)
Mexico	16.5 (3.2)	46.8 (3.9)	27.0 (3.2)	9.8 (2.4)	68.3 (3.5)	3.3 (1.4)	13.4 (2.4)	15.1 (2.8)	18.8 (3.5)	43.4 (4.0)	27.0 (4.0)	10.8 (2.6)
Netherlands	30.1 (6.0)	37.4 (7.1)	28.8 (4.9)	3.6 (1.4)	87.7 (3.9)	0.8 (0.8)	0.9 (0.6)	10.6 (3.8)	23.0 (4.9)	36.3 (7.4)	31.3 (5.3)	9.3 (2.8)
Norway	17.5 (6.1)	37.8 (7.2)	28.7 (3.7)	15.9 (4.4)	98.6 (0.8)	0.0 (0.0)	0.9 (0.7)	0.5 (0.5)	35.3 (7.9)	13.7 (4.3)	23.3 (3.3)	27.6 (6.9)
Poland	60.3 (4.2)	26.1 (4.6)	13.7 (2.9)	0.0 (0.0)	37.1 (4.3)	7.4 (3.0)	39.1 (4.4)	16.5 (3.7)	14.1 (4.1)	18.2 (2.9)	10.3 (3.2)	57.4 (4.7)
Portugal	28.6 (4.1)	32.2 (4.0)	14.0 (2.6)	25.2 (4.0)	23.5 (4.3)	13.8 (3.5)	17.7 (3.4)	45.0 (5.2)	12.6 (3.1)	38.3 (4.2)	13.7 (3.2)	35.5 (4.8)
Romania	14.3 (3.1)	48.9 (4.4)	26.9 (3.9)	9.9 (3.2)	50.2 (4.7)	6.2 (2.7)	43.2 (4.4)	0.4 (0.4)	31.7 (4.5)	24.5 (4.0)	27.7 (3.7)	16.1 (3.1)
Serbia	6.1 (2.2)	34.8 (4.1)	8.4 (2.4)	50.7 (4.4)	45.6 (4.2)	5.2 (1.9)	35.3 (4.4)	14.0 (2.8)	2.5 (1.4)	35.9 (4.1)	8.1 (2.3)	53.4 (4.6)
Singapore	65.2 (3.9)	6.0 (2.2)	22.1 (3.7)	6.8 (2.2)	85.9 (2.8)	0.7 (0.7)	10.0 (2.7)	3.4 (1.5)	48.4 (4.5)	6.0 (2.2)	36.8 (4.3)	8.8 (2.5)
Slovak Republic	17.9 (2.9)	57.8 (4.0)	20.1 (3.2)	4.2 (1.7)	47.2 (4.0)	19.4 (3.3)	25.8 (3.7)	7.6 (2.1)	20.2 (3.2)	30.6 (3.9)	13.8 (2.9)	35.4 (4.1)
Spain	20.6 (3.3)	40.8 (4.8)	21.2 (3.5)	17.3 (3.2)	44.6 (4.1)	12.5 (2.9)	34.5 (4.5)	8.5 (2.3)	11.8 (2.9)	37.3 (4.0)	10.3 (2.6)	40.7 (4.7)
Sweden	8.2 (2.1)	61.5 (4.6)	21.4 (3.5)	8.9 (2.7)	90.6 (3.2)	0.7 (0.7)	1.4 (1.2)	7.2 (2.9)	48.1 (4.9)	14.4 (3.2)	27.8 (4.3)	9.7 (3.4)
Sub-national entities												
Abu Dhabi (United Arab Emirates)	21.0 (3.8)	34.8 (4.7)	33.1 (3.9)	11.2 (2.6)	44.3 (4.4)	16.5 (3.4)	29.6 (4.0)	9.6 (2.9)	21.4 (3.6)	36.6 (4.8)	34.6 (4.5)	7.4 (2.6)
Alberta (Canada)	38.7 (3.8)	21.0 (3.5)	23.4 (3.3)	17.0 (2.4)	86.7 (2.6)	0.0 (0.0)	11.4 (2.2)	1.9 (1.4)	34.1 (3.4)	24.2 (4.1)	33.4 (3.9)	8.2 (2.1)
England (United Kingdom)	39.2 (3.6)	11.0 (4.4)	25.7 (4.4)	24.1 (5.7)	87.1 (4.7)	4.3 (3.3)	5.0 (2.4)	3.6 (2.3)	39.2 (5.9)	9.0 (3.4)	18.1 (4.7)	33.7 (4.9)
Flanders (Belgium)	16.3 (2.5)	62.7 (4.0)	13.1 (3.3)	7.9 (3.0)	96.2 (2.0)	0.7 (0.5)	1.3 (0.7)	1.8 (1.8)	10.7 (2.5)	49.6 (4.3)	12.2 (2.8)	27.6 (4.6)
Average	25.4 (0.6)	37.5 (0.8)	21.9 (0.6)	15.2 (0.5)	64.4 (0.7)	7.7 (0.4)	18.3 (0.6)	9.6 (0.5)	24.4 (0.7)	30.6 (0.7)	22.8 (0.7)	22.2 (0.7)
United States	68.5 (6.5)	9.1 (4.1)	22.4 (5.9)	0.0 (0.0)	84.2 (4.5)	2.5 (2.0)	13.3 (4.1)	0.0 (0.0)	56.7 (6.4)	10.8 (4.1)	32.2 (5.9)	0.3 (0.3)

*See notes at the beginning of this Annex.

Source: OECD, TALIS 2013 Database.

StatLink http://dx.doi.org/10.1787/888933043891

[Part 1/1]
Primary education principals' formal education
Percentage of primary education principals who report that the following elements were included in their formal education

Table 3.10.a

	School administration or principal training programme or course				Teacher training/education programme or course				Instructional leadership training or course			
	Before taking up position as principal	After taking up position as principal	Before and after taking up position as principal	Never	Before taking up position as principal	After taking up position as principal	Before and after taking up position as principal	Never	Before taking up position as principal	After taking up position as principal	Before and after taking up position as principal	Never
	% S.E.	% S.E.	% S.E.	% S.E.	% S.E.	% S.E.	% S.E.	% S.E.	% S.E.	% S.E.	% S.E.	% S.E.
Denmark	7.0 (2.2)	49.5 (4.4)	7.7 (2.1)	35.9 (3.9)	86.3 (3.3)	0.7 (0.7)	0.0 (0.0)	13.0 (3.2)	7.6 (2.2)	51.1 (4.3)	22.4 (3.4)	18.9 (3.8)
Finland	57.8 (5.3)	14.4 (3.2)	17.8 (3.1)	10.1 (4.5)	97.1 (2.4)	0.0 (0.0)	0.6 (0.6)	2.4 (2.4)	9.6 (2.0)	37.7 (5.8)	18.6 (2.8)	34.0 (5.6)
Mexico	18.5 (3.5)	39.0 (3.8)	14.6 (2.7)	27.9 (3.5)	78.4 (3.2)	2.2 (1.3)	12.9 (2.5)	6.4 (1.7)	17.4 (3.3)	39.3 (4.0)	19.3 (3.0)	23.9 (3.5)
Norway	12.2 (2.7)	45.6 (3.2)	19.4 (3.2)	22.8 (3.2)	95.5 (1.3)	0.6 (0.6)	0.9 (0.9)	3.0 (0.8)	21.1 (3.3)	23.6 (5.4)	16.1 (7.2)	39.1 (8.9)
Poland	57.2 (4.5)	27.0 (3.8)	15.1 (3.7)	0.7 (0.5)	36.9 (6.2)	5.9 (2.8)	34.1 (5.7)	23.1 (5.6)	5.3 (1.5)	17.8 (3.0)	10.8 (3.3)	66.2 (4.3)
Sub-national entities												
Flanders (Belgium)	21.7 (3.2)	46.4 (4.4)	22.5 (3.5)	9.4 (2.6)	97.1 (1.5)	0.4 (0.4)	1.6 (1.1)	0.9 (0.9)	18.2 (3.2)	44.5 (4.0)	15.3 (3.3)	22.0 (3.5)
Average	29.1 (1.5)	37.0 (1.6)	16.2 (1.3)	17.8 (1.3)	81.9 (1.4)	1.6 (0.5)	8.3 (1.1)	8.1 (1.2)	13.2 (1.1)	35.7 (1.9)	17.1 (1.7)	34.0 (2.2)

Source: OECD, TALIS 2013 Database.
StatLink http://dx.doi.org/10.1787/888933043910

[Part 1/1]
Upper secondary education principals' formal education
Percentage of upper secondary education principals who report that the following elements were included in their formal education

Table 3.10.b

	School administration or principal training programme or course				Teacher training/education programme or course				Instructional leadership training or course			
	Before taking up position as principal	After taking up position as principal	Before and after taking up position as principal	Never	Before taking up position as principal	After taking up position as principal	Before and after taking up position as principal	Never	Before taking up position as principal	After taking up position as principal	Before and after taking up position as principal	Never
	% S.E.	% S.E.	% S.E.	% S.E.	% S.E.	% S.E.	% S.E.	% S.E.	% S.E.	% S.E.	% S.E.	% S.E.
Australia	21.4 (3.9)	23.6 (5.6)	27.7 (6.5)	27.3 (4.5)	87.1 (4.3)	1.6 (1.1)	9.0 (3.7)	2.3 (1.9)	23.4 (4.8)	26.7 (4.8)	23.3 (5.0)	26.6 (5.5)
Denmark	13.2 (4.0)	21.3 (5.3)	4.1 (2.0)	61.4 (6.6)	73.6 (4.5)	0.7 (0.7)	4.2 (2.2)	21.6 (4.2)	7.9 (3.0)	50.5 (6.0)	18.6 (4.2)	23.0 (4.3)
Finland	57.7 (6.1)	11.6 (2.6)	16.6 (5.3)	14.1 (4.5)	95.3 (1.9)	2.0 (1.6)	1.6 (1.0)	1.1 (0.8)	14.2 (3.6)	29.1 (5.1)	26.5 (5.9)	30.1 (5.3)
Iceland	28.2 (9.6)	25.3 (9.9)	12.7 (4.4)	33.8 (9.6)	76.0 (9.7)	4.2 (4.3)	15.5 (7.7)	4.2 (4.3)	38.0 (11.5)	21.1 (9.5)	28.2 (9.0)	12.7 (7.6)
Italy	26.4 (3.2)	27.7 (4.0)	37.8 (4.2)	8.1 (2.1)	49.7 (4.1)	18.3 (2.9)	24.1 (3.5)	7.9 (2.2)	20.8 (3.3)	24.5 (3.9)	26.3 (4.1)	28.4 (3.6)
Mexico	17.2 (3.1)	32.8 (4.8)	27.4 (4.0)	22.5 (4.2)	38.6 (4.9)	9.7 (3.3)	5.8 (2.5)	46.0 (5.0)	23.1 (4.2)	36.3 (4.9)	22.5 (3.6)	18.0 (4.4)
Norway	21.2 (5.2)	33.5 (6.5)	23.5 (5.1)	21.8 (5.2)	82.4 (5.6)	1.8 (1.8)	4.1 (2.5)	11.7 (4.6)	40.0 (6.2)	15.5 (4.9)	21.4 (5.5)	23.2 (5.2)
Poland	68.0 (6.9)	18.0 (6.2)	13.2 (4.2)	0.9 (0.9)	42.5 (4.2)	5.0 (2.3)	47.4 (5.1)	5.1 (1.7)	13.2 (5.1)	17.5 (5.8)	16.3 (4.8)	53.0 (7.6)
Singapore	63.8 (4.4)	5.4 (2.1)	23.5 (3.7)	7.3 (2.2)	86.0 (2.6)	0.7 (0.7)	10.0 (2.6)	3.3 (1.5)	47.9 (4.5)	4.6 (1.8)	38.2 (4.0)	9.3 (2.5)
Sub-national entities												
Abu Dhabi (United Arab Emirates)	29.1 (4.2)	23.5 (3.9)	38.2 (3.9)	9.2 (2.1)	42.8 (4.2)	16.4 (3.1)	34.1 (4.2)	6.7 (2.4)	26.3 (4.0)	29.6 (4.0)	37.5 (4.1)	6.7 (2.3)
Average	34.6 (1.7)	22.3 (1.7)	22.5 (1.4)	20.6 (1.5)	67.4 (1.6)	6.0 (0.8)	15.6 (1.2)	11.0 (1.0)	25.5 (1.7)	25.5 (1.7)	25.9 (1.7)	23.1 (1.6)

Source: OECD, TALIS 2013 Database.
StatLink http://dx.doi.org/10.1787/888933043929

[Part 1/1]
Principals' formal education including leadership training
Percentage of lower secondary education principals who report having received leadership training in their formal education[1]

Table 3.11

	No leadership training in formal education (0)		Weak leadership training in formal education (1)		Average leadership training in formal education (2)		Strong leadership training in formal education (3)	
	%	S.E.	%	S.E.	%	S.E.	%	S.E.
Australia	0.3	(0.3)	26.5	(6.0)	17.5	(3.7)	55.6	(5.8)
Brazil	2.4	(0.8)	5.3	(1.0)	14.6	(1.9)	77.7	(2.1)
Bulgaria	4.9	(1.8)	8.8	(2.4)	13.6	(2.8)	72.8	(3.7)
Chile	2.8	(1.4)	4.3	(1.7)	9.0	(2.4)	84.0	(2.9)
Croatia	14.0	(2.6)	29.1	(4.3)	25.4	(3.4)	31.6	(3.7)
Czech Republic	2.7	(1.2)	19.7	(3.0)	25.2	(3.3)	52.4	(3.9)
Denmark	1.8	(1.3)	12.2	(2.9)	42.7	(5.0)	43.3	(4.5)
Estonia	1.5	(0.9)	1.5	(1.0)	10.8	(2.3)	86.2	(2.3)
Finland	0.0	(0.0)	3.1	(1.6)	27.1	(3.7)	69.8	(3.8)
France	0.1	(0.1)	10.7	(2.8)	25.9	(3.3)	63.2	(3.4)
Iceland	0.0	(0.0)	6.7	(2.5)	16.2	(3.5)	77.1	(4.3)
Israel	0.2	(0.2)	10.6	(2.3)	29.8	(6.1)	59.5	(6.3)
Italy	0.3	(0.3)	2.9	(1.1)	33.2	(4.1)	63.6	(4.2)
Japan	2.1	(1.1)	3.1	(1.3)	2.9	(1.2)	91.9	(2.1)
Korea	1.9	(1.9)	2.1	(1.9)	5.2	(1.4)	90.9	(3.0)
Latvia	4.4	(3.8)	13.2	(4.5)	11.0	(4.2)	71.3	(5.7)
Malaysia	2.5	(1.1)	1.6	(0.8)	18.2	(3.8)	77.8	(3.8)
Mexico	0.5	(0.5)	8.5	(2.6)	18.0	(3.3)	73.1	(3.4)
Netherlands	1.4	(0.9)	0.9	(0.8)	17.6	(4.1)	80.1	(4.1)
Norway	0.0	(0.0)	9.5	(3.6)	25.0	(6.1)	65.5	(7.1)
Poland	0.0	(0.0)	15.6	(3.8)	43.4	(4.3)	41.0	(4.6)
Portugal	22.5	(4.4)	12.7	(3.2)	25.2	(4.5)	39.6	(5.6)
Romania	0.0	(0.0)	4.7	(2.1)	16.9	(3.7)	78.4	(3.9)
Serbia	12.5	(2.9)	32.6	(4.9)	19.1	(3.5)	35.8	(4.0)
Singapore	3.4	(1.5)	1.4	(1.0)	6.1	(2.1)	89.2	(2.7)
Slovak Republic	0.4	(0.4)	8.5	(2.4)	29.1	(3.6)	62.0	(4.1)
Spain	3.7	(1.8)	11.7	(2.8)	31.9	(4.4)	52.7	(4.1)
Sweden	0.0	(0.0)	4.9	(2.8)	16.6	(3.7)	78.5	(3.8)
Sub-national entities								
Abu Dhabi (United Arab Emirates)	1.9	(1.2)	4.5	(2.2)	13.6	(3.5)	79.9	(3.8)
Alberta (Canada)	0.0	(0.0)	6.8	(2.2)	13.6	(2.4)	79.7	(2.6)
England (United Kingdom)	1.1	(0.6)	14.8	(3.9)	29.1	(6.1)	54.9	(6.1)
Flanders (Belgium)	1.8	(1.8)	3.9	(2.1)	24.5	(4.0)	69.8	(4.8)
Average	2.8	(0.3)	9.4	(0.5)	20.6	(0.7)	67.1	(0.8)

1. Leadership training index was constructed from the following variables: *i)* school administration or principal training programme or course, *ii)* teacher training/education programme or course, *iii)* instructional leadership training or course. Responses indicating "never" were coded as zero (0) and responses indicating that the training had occurred "before," "after," or "before and after" were coded as one (1). Each respondent's codes were summed to produce the following categories: 0 (no training), 1 (weak leadership training), 2 (average leadership training) and 3 (strong leadership training). See the textbox describing this index and Annex B for more details.
Source: OECD, TALIS 2013 Database.

StatLink ⟨⟩ http://dx.doi.org/10.1787/888933043948

[Part 1/2]
Work experience of principals
Percentage of lower secondary education principals with the following work experience and average years
Table 3.12 *of experience in each role*

	Years working as a principal					Years working in other school management roles				
	Average years of experience	Less than 3 years experience	3-10 years experience	11-20 years experience	More than 20 years experience	Average years of experience	Less than 3 years experience	3-10 years experience	11-20 years experience	More than 20 years experience
	Average S.E.	% S.E.	% S.E.	% S.E.	% S.E.	Average S.E.	% S.E.	% S.E.	% S.E.	% S.E.
Australia	8.0 (0.6)	14.9 (3.0)	57.3 (5.7)	23.7 (5.1)	4.2 (1.7)	10.5 (0.6)	7.2 (3.6)	48.2 (6.0)	36.8 (5.4)	7.8 (2.3)
Brazil	7.3 (0.4)	24.9 (2.4)	51.5 (2.9)	17.1 (2.3)	6.4 (1.6)	6.0 (0.5)	41.8 (3.0)	39.2 (2.6)	14.1 (1.9)	4.9 (1.3)
Bulgaria	12.5 (0.7)	16.0 (3.1)	27.3 (3.3)	37.6 (4.4)	19.1 (3.5)	2.0 (0.3)	79.3 (3.6)	13.7 (3.2)	6.1 (2.1)	0.9 (0.5)
Chile	11.3 (0.9)	17.3 (3.2)	44.4 (5.0)	19.1 (3.1)	19.2 (3.8)	5.7 (0.7)	55.9 (4.1)	26.0 (3.9)	9.3 (2.7)	8.7 (2.6)
Croatia	10.4 (0.6)	13.9 (2.9)	46.5 (3.8)	26.3 (3.6)	13.3 (2.8)	3.9 (0.7)	75.0 (3.8)	11.5 (2.8)	5.1 (2.0)	8.3 (2.4)
Cyprus*	4.7 (0.5)	43.3 (4.9)	45.4 (5.3)	8.2 (2.9)	3.1 (1.8)	9.4 (0.7)	7.4 (2.4)	71.3 (4.3)	9.6 (2.8)	11.7 (3.2)
Czech Republic	9.7 (0.5)	18.4 (2.6)	42.1 (3.7)	27.5 (3.4)	12.0 (2.3)	3.6 (0.3)	57.5 (3.5)	32.2 (3.4)	10.2 (2.0)	0.1 (0.1)
Denmark	12.6 (0.5)	2.5 (1.5)	36.7 (4.6)	48.3 (4.6)	12.4 (2.7)	3.3 (0.5)	62.0 (4.2)	28.8 (3.8)	7.6 (2.1)	1.7 (1.2)
Estonia	12.1 (0.7)	19.3 (2.9)	34.0 (3.3)	23.3 (2.8)	23.3 (2.9)	4.1 (0.5)	59.9 (3.6)	24.4 (2.9)	11.2 (2.4)	4.6 (1.5)
Finland	11.3 (0.6)	13.7 (2.6)	37.1 (4.4)	36.4 (4.1)	12.8 (2.9)	2.9 (0.5)	68.8 (4.1)	22.8 (3.7)	6.1 (2.1)	2.3 (1.3)
France	7.5 (0.4)	19.3 (3.2)	56.3 (4.0)	20.4 (3.5)	4.0 (1.0)	6.0 (0.4)	27.2 (2.9)	57.7 (3.8)	12.7 (2.7)	2.4 (1.3)
Iceland	10.6 (0.9)	21.2 (4.3)	38.5 (5.2)	26.9 (4.5)	13.5 (3.7)	4.7 (0.6)	45.3 (5.2)	43.4 (5.1)	10.4 (2.8)	0.9 (0.9)
Israel	9.8 (0.9)	17.9 (3.8)	42.3 (5.8)	30.5 (7.1)	9.4 (2.4)	7.1 (0.7)	27.9 (4.6)	49.4 (6.5)	17.4 (4.5)	5.3 (2.4)
Italy	10.8 (0.8)	14.6 (3.2)	53.4 (4.6)	11.8 (2.5)	20.2 (3.8)	8.7 (0.6)	21.1 (4.2)	47.4 (4.6)	25.9 (4.1)	5.5 (2.0)
Japan	4.5 (0.2)	29.7 (3.2)	67.5 (3.3)	2.8 (1.1)	0.0 (0.0)	4.9 (0.2)	19.6 (3.2)	77.0 (3.4)	3.5 (1.5)	0.0 (0.0)
Korea	3.1 (0.2)	46.5 (5.1)	53.5 (5.1)	0.0 (0.0)	0.0 (0.0)	4.6 (0.7)	39.2 (4.7)	56.8 (5.3)	0.4 (0.4)	3.5 (2.1)
Latvia	13.0 (0.8)	9.2 (2.8)	31.7 (6.0)	43.2 (6.5)	15.9 (3.6)	6.5 (1.0)	48.0 (4.9)	28.3 (5.8)	14.2 (4.3)	9.5 (3.7)
Malaysia	6.5 (0.4)	28.1 (4.3)	52.3 (4.8)	17.3 (3.1)	2.3 (1.5)	9.4 (0.5)	17.0 (3.0)	42.7 (4.1)	36.5 (3.9)	3.7 (1.1)
Mexico	10.8 (0.8)	14.8 (3.0)	46.2 (4.2)	24.5 (3.5)	14.5 (3.4)	6.6 (0.8)	46.2 (4.2)	31.8 (3.8)	13.4 (3.3)	8.6 (2.7)
Netherlands	10.0 (1.3)	16.6 (5.8)	42.9 (7.9)	31.5 (5.3)	8.9 (3.8)	7.6 (0.7)	14.2 (2.6)	59.9 (6.5)	24.2 (5.9)	1.8 (1.4)
Norway	8.7 (1.2)	17.7 (4.7)	48.9 (7.6)	20.0 (5.7)	13.3 (6.2)	3.8 (0.4)	49.4 (6.7)	42.0 (6.7)	8.6 (2.6)	0.0 (0.0)
Poland	11.2 (0.9)	14.9 (3.7)	34.1 (4.5)	38.0 (4.4)	12.9 (3.8)	2.3 (0.4)	73.0 (4.0)	19.2 (3.3)	7.4 (2.1)	0.4 (0.4)
Portugal	6.6 (0.7)	39.0 (4.8)	36.0 (4.0)	18.5 (3.6)	6.5 (1.9)	6.8 (0.5)	24.8 (4.1)	50.4 (4.9)	23.4 (4.0)	1.4 (0.8)
Romania	7.0 (0.6)	33.5 (4.0)	38.8 (3.9)	24.2 (4.1)	3.5 (1.4)	6.2 (0.6)	40.0 (4.2)	41.1 (4.5)	13.4 (2.8)	5.4 (2.1)
Serbia	7.4 (0.4)	15.9 (2.9)	56.1 (4.3)	26.2 (3.8)	1.8 (0.9)	2.7 (0.5)	69.1 (5.1)	21.7 (4.4)	7.4 (2.7)	1.8 (1.1)
Singapore	7.7 (0.4)	17.0 (3.3)	54.1 (4.4)	27.6 (3.7)	1.4 (1.0)	7.7 (0.5)	8.8 (2.5)	70.9 (4.0)	18.3 (3.4)	2.0 (1.2)
Slovak Republic	11.0 (0.6)	8.6 (1.9)	47.9 (3.8)	26.7 (3.6)	16.9 (3.0)	3.6 (0.4)	61.2 (4.1)	27.0 (3.7)	11.1 (2.6)	0.7 (0.7)
Spain	7.9 (0.8)	21.0 (3.7)	50.7 (4.5)	24.4 (4.1)	3.9 (2.3)	4.5 (0.6)	45.4 (4.5)	43.9 (4.4)	7.3 (2.4)	3.4 (1.7)
Sweden	7.0 (0.5)	18.3 (3.6)	57.7 (5.0)	23.6 (4.6)	0.4 (0.4)	3.5 (0.4)	54.1 (4.5)	38.0 (4.5)	7.2 (1.9)	0.7 (0.7)
Sub-national entities										
Abu Dhabi (United Arab Emirates)	10.9 (0.8)	12.5 (3.1)	44.5 (4.8)	30.0 (4.4)	13.0 (3.7)	7.0 (0.7)	23.5 (4.2)	54.9 (4.8)	14.5 (3.8)	7.1 (2.7)
Alberta (Canada)	8.0 (0.5)	16.6 (2.9)	57.0 (3.6)	21.0 (3.3)	5.4 (2.2)	5.6 (0.4)	33.0 (3.5)	52.9 (3.8)	12.5 (2.3)	1.6 (0.9)
England (United Kingdom)	7.5 (0.5)	20.3 (2.9)	54.5 (4.7)	23.7 (4.3)	1.4 (0.8)	11.8 (0.6)	4.2 (2.8)	45.4 (4.9)	39.1 (5.6)	11.3 (2.5)
Flanders (Belgium)	7.3 (0.4)	22.2 (4.1)	48.8 (5.2)	28.5 (3.9)	0.5 (0.5)	4.2 (0.5)	46.1 (5.0)	44.9 (4.9)	8.2 (3.0)	0.8 (0.6)
Average	8.9 (0.1)	20.0 (0.6)	46.5 (0.8)	24.5 (0.7)	9.0 (0.5)	5.7 (0.1)	41.0 (0.7)	41.4 (0.8)	13.7 (0.6)	3.9 (0.3)
United States	7.2 (0.6)	19.8 (5.3)	57.5 (5.7)	22.7 (5.9)	0.0 (0.0)	4.4 (0.6)	44.6 (6.8)	45.8 (7.0)	5.2 (2.8)	4.4 (2.7)

*See notes at the beginning of this Annex.
Source: OECD, TALIS 2013 Database.
StatLink ⟦⟧ http://dx.doi.org/10.1787/888933043967

[Part 2/2]

Table 3.12 Work experience of principals

Percentage of lower secondary education principals with the following work experience and average years of experience in each role

	Years working as a teacher										Years working in other jobs									
	Average years of experience		Less than 3 years experience		3-10 years experience		11-20 years experience		More than 20 years experience		Average years of experience		Less than 3 years experience		3-10 years experience		11-20 years experience		More than 20 years experience	
	Average	S.E.	%	S.E.	%	S.E.	%	S.E.	%	S.E.	Average	S.E.	%	S.E.	%	S.E.	%	S.E.	%	S.E.
Australia	26.7	(1.0)	1.2	(1.0)	6.9	(1.9)	15.5	(5.3)	76.4	(5.3)	2.7	(0.5)	69.7	(6.0)	24.4	(5.7)	4.8	(2.3)	1.0	(1.0)
Brazil	14.2	(0.5)	7.2	(1.7)	31.2	(2.5)	37.6	(2.3)	23.9	(2.3)	4.7	(0.4)	55.0	(3.3)	29.2	(3.0)	11.8	(1.7)	4.0	(1.0)
Bulgaria	20.2	(0.9)	1.4	(0.9)	20.5	(3.4)	28.5	(3.5)	49.5	(4.2)	3.4	(0.5)	61.2	(3.5)	33.4	(4.0)	3.1	(1.5)	2.3	(1.4)
Chile	25.2	(1.0)	3.2	(1.6)	8.3	(2.2)	22.4	(3.6)	66.1	(4.2)	3.1	(0.6)	74.9	(3.9)	11.4	(2.8)	9.7	(2.6)	4.0	(1.8)
Croatia	15.9	(0.7)	7.6	(2.2)	24.2	(3.4)	37.0	(3.7)	31.2	(3.6)	4.1	(0.7)	72.0	(3.8)	12.3	(2.9)	7.5	(2.4)	8.3	(2.3)
Cyprus*	27.8	(0.6)	1.0	(1.0)	3.1	(1.8)	15.5	(3.0)	80.4	(3.0)	2.6	(0.6)	82.4	(3.5)	10.6	(3.1)	3.5	(2.0)	3.5	(2.0)
Czech Republic	17.7	(0.7)	2.0	(1.0)	26.4	(3.3)	35.5	(3.6)	36.1	(3.6)	1.3	(0.2)	83.1	(2.8)	14.3	(2.6)	2.1	(0.6)	0.6	(0.6)
Denmark	18.1	(0.9)	1.7	(1.2)	27.2	(4.0)	31.4	(4.5)	39.8	(4.8)	3.6	(0.5)	65.6	(4.3)	24.0	(4.3)	6.9	(2.4)	3.5	(1.2)
Estonia	22.4	(0.8)	5.1	(1.7)	12.7	(2.2)	24.5	(3.1)	57.7	(3.3)	5.5	(0.6)	57.9	(3.9)	21.3	(3.1)	13.2	(2.3)	7.6	(1.9)
Finland	17.2	(0.9)	3.1	(1.4)	25.9	(4.0)	36.3	(4.0)	34.7	(4.0)	2.2	(0.2)	70.4	(4.0)	26.6	(3.7)	3.0	(1.5)	0.0	(0.0)
France	14.8	(0.8)	19.7	(3.1)	18.5	(2.7)	33.4	(4.0)	28.4	(3.9)	5.6	(0.7)	57.3	(4.5)	22.0	(4.0)	13.4	(2.8)	7.3	(2.0)
Iceland	14.5	(0.9)	3.8	(1.9)	39.0	(5.1)	35.2	(4.9)	21.9	(4.3)	4.8	(0.6)	53.5	(4.9)	33.7	(4.7)	9.9	(2.8)	3.0	(1.7)
Israel	23.4	(0.8)	0.0	(0.0)	8.8	(3.0)	25.4	(4.8)	65.8	(5.6)	3.6	(0.6)	63.4	(5.5)	27.9	(5.3)	3.0	(1.3)	5.7	(2.4)
Italy	22.2	(0.7)	0.0	(0.0)	9.7	(2.7)	31.9	(4.4)	58.4	(4.6)	2.0	(0.4)	80.7	(3.3)	14.0	(2.7)	3.1	(1.2)	2.2	(1.2)
Japan	29.6	(0.6)	1.0	(0.7)	0.3	(0.3)	6.3	(2.1)	92.3	(2.1)	1.7	(0.6)	86.0	(3.2)	10.1	(2.6)	1.0	(0.6)	2.8	(1.9)
Korea	29.2	(0.6)	0.6	(0.6)	1.0	(1.0)	8.8	(3.1)	89.6	(3.3)	1.4	(0.4)	86.1	(3.6)	11.8	(3.3)	0.5	(0.5)	1.6	(1.2)
Latvia	25.0	(1.2)	3.6	(2.5)	8.6	(3.6)	21.4	(4.4)	66.4	(5.2)	4.6	(0.7)	61.2	(4.0)	22.3	(5.1)	10.1	(3.7)	6.4	(2.8)
Malaysia	26.4	(0.6)	0.0	(0.0)	5.2	(1.9)	11.2	(2.6)	83.5	(3.2)	1.0	(0.4)	93.6	(1.8)	2.6	(1.5)	2.0	(1.3)	1.9	(1.1)
Mexico	23.8	(0.8)	2.2	(1.4)	12.4	(2.6)	23.6	(3.3)	61.8	(3.9)	6.4	(0.9)	58.9	(4.6)	18.0	(3.9)	12.6	(2.9)	10.4	(3.2)
Netherlands	19.9	(1.5)	4.5	(3.2)	14.7	(2.2)	35.7	(5.5)	45.1	(7.7)	1.5	(0.4)	83.9	(2.5)	12.9	(1.9)	3.2	(1.7)	0.0	(0.0)
Norway	15.4	(0.7)	1.0	(0.6)	30.5	(4.2)	46.1	(4.4)	22.4	(3.2)	5.8	(1.5)	47.3	(7.0)	31.8	(5.7)	16.0	(5.5)	4.9	(4.9)
Poland	25.5	(0.7)	0.7	(0.7)	2.9	(1.8)	17.4	(3.9)	79.0	(4.1)	1.8	(0.4)	80.3	(3.9)	13.8	(3.4)	4.5	(1.8)	1.4	(0.9)
Portugal	21.5	(0.7)	1.2	(0.7)	12.5	(2.9)	30.0	(3.6)	56.3	(3.8)	1.9	(0.4)	80.3	(3.9)	14.7	(3.6)	2.7	(1.5)	2.3	(1.2)
Romania	23.3	(1.0)	1.8	(1.8)	2.1	(1.0)	37.0	(4.4)	59.1	(4.6)	2.8	(0.6)	78.2	(3.3)	11.9	(2.8)	5.8	(2.4)	4.0	(1.7)
Serbia	14.7	(0.6)	1.8	(0.9)	31.0	(4.0)	44.7	(3.8)	22.5	(3.1)	2.8	(0.5)	71.3	(4.3)	20.2	(3.9)	7.7	(2.6)	0.7	(0.5)
Singapore	14.5	(0.8)	1.4	(1.0)	38.6	(4.2)	35.8	(3.8)	24.2	(3.6)	1.0	(0.2)	87.0	(2.8)	11.6	(2.6)	1.4	(1.0)	0.0	(0.0)
Slovak Republic	21.2	(0.8)	0.5	(0.4)	18.8	(2.7)	30.8	(3.5)	49.9	(3.8)	2.0	(0.5)	84.3	(2.8)	9.6	(2.1)	2.9	(1.5)	3.2	(1.5)
Spain	23.2	(1.0)	0.5	(0.5)	8.7	(2.9)	29.0	(4.5)	61.8	(4.9)	3.9	(0.5)	65.0	(4.0)	23.7	(3.8)	5.3	(1.6)	6.0	(2.0)
Sweden	13.9	(0.7)	7.0	(2.9)	31.9	(4.3)	40.5	(5.1)	20.6	(3.1)	6.7	(0.7)	44.7	(4.3)	28.8	(3.8)	19.6	(4.7)	6.9	(3.0)
Sub-national entities																				
Abu Dhabi (United Arab Emirates)	11.5	(0.9)	11.3	(3.2)	51.5	(4.5)	19.3	(3.4)	17.9	(3.7)	1.5	(0.5)	85.7	(3.8)	10.6	(3.2)	1.9	(1.4)	1.8	(1.8)
Alberta (Canada)	20.8	(0.8)	0.0	(0.0)	18.2	(3.3)	29.1	(3.5)	52.7	(3.8)	5.3	(0.7)	52.2	(3.9)	33.9	(3.7)	7.2	(2.3)	6.7	(2.1)
England (United Kingdom)	24.5	(0.7)	2.2	(1.3)	5.6	(2.6)	23.1	(3.6)	69.2	(4.0)	2.4	(0.5)	77.0	(3.8)	17.6	(3.4)	2.1	(1.1)	3.3	(1.4)
Flanders (Belgium)	17.9	(0.7)	0.5	(0.5)	17.6	(3.7)	51.3	(6.2)	30.6	(5.2)	1.9	(0.4)	78.8	(4.1)	14.4	(3.3)	6.4	(2.5)	0.5	(0.5)
Average	20.7	(0.1)	3.0	(0.3)	17.4	(0.5)	28.8	(0.7)	50.8	(0.7)	3.2	(0.1)	71.2	(0.7)	19.0	(0.6)	6.3	(0.4)	3.6	(0.3)
United States	13.3	(0.9)	1.1	(1.1)	51.8	(6.6)	30.6	(7.5)	16.5	(4.9)	3.7	(0.7)	60.3	(5.1)	31.4	(4.1)	5.4	(3.0)	2.9	(2.0)

* See notes at the beginning of this Annex.
Source: OECD, TALIS 2013 Database.
StatLink http://dx.doi.org/10.1787/888933043967

[Part 1/1]
Work experience of primary education principals
Percentage of primary education principals with the following work experience and average years of experience in each role

Table 3.12.a

	Years working as a principal					Years working in other school management roles				
	Average years of experience	Less than 3 years experience	3-10 years experience	11-20 years experience	More than 20 years experience	Average years of experience	Less than 3 years experience	3-10 years experience	11-20 years experience	More than 20 years experience
	Average / S.E.	% / S.E.	% / S.E.	% / S.E.	% / S.E.	Average / S.E.	% / S.E.	% / S.E.	% / S.E.	% / S.E.
Denmark	12.3 (0.6)	4.2 (1.7)	42.8 (3.8)	37.7 (4.3)	15.3 (3.1)	2.8 (0.4)	62.2 (4.0)	32.7 (3.6)	4.4 (2.0)	0.7 (0.7)
Finland	11.7 (1.2)	18.7 (4.4)	31.0 (5.1)	32.3 (5.2)	18.0 (4.4)	2.1 (0.3)	70.0 (4.4)	27.5 (4.3)	2.3 (0.9)	0.2 (0.2)
Mexico	10.4 (0.8)	16.9 (2.7)	45.8 (3.9)	20.7 (3.3)	16.6 (3.1)	3.4 (0.7)	72.1 (4.4)	18.4 (3.8)	2.9 (1.6)	6.7 (2.4)
Norway	8.7 (0.7)	12.8 (2.7)	58.7 (4.0)	20.9 (3.3)	7.6 (2.3)	4.0 (0.5)	43.5 (8.7)	51.9 (8.7)	4.6 (1.2)	0.0 (0.0)
Poland	12.2 (0.8)	4.1 (1.2)	34.4 (5.9)	48.2 (5.8)	13.2 (3.8)	1.9 (0.3)	80.6 (3.1)	11.3 (2.3)	7.4 (2.0)	0.7 (0.7)
Sub-national entities										
Flanders (Belgium)	7.8 (0.5)	16.4 (3.2)	53.5 (4.3)	27.1 (3.9)	3.0 (1.4)	3.2 (0.6)	73.1 (4.3)	17.3 (3.6)	4.6 (1.9)	5.0 (1.9)
Average	10.5 (0.3)	12.2 (1.2)	44.4 (1.9)	31.2 (1.8)	12.3 (1.3)	2.9 (0.2)	66.9 (2.1)	26.5 (2.0)	4.3 (0.7)	2.2 (0.5)

	Years working as a teacher					Years working in other jobs				
	Average years of experience	Less than 3 years experience	3-10 years experience	11-20 years experience	More than 20 years experience	Average years of experience	Less than 3 years experience	3-10 years experience	11-20 years experience	More than 20 years experience
	Average / S.E.	% / S.E.	% / S.E.	% / S.E.	% / S.E.	Average / S.E.	% / S.E.	% / S.E.	% / S.E.	% / S.E.
Denmark	19.7 (0.8)	0.7 (0.7)	23.9 (3.7)	33.8 (3.7)	41.6 (4.2)	4.3 (0.7)	65.0 (4.2)	22.8 (3.6)	4.7 (1.9)	7.5 (2.0)
Finland	20.0 (1.2)	1.5 (1.0)	22.6 (4.9)	30.4 (4.9)	45.4 (6.0)	2.1 (0.4)	74.2 (5.1)	24.7 (5.1)	0.8 (0.5)	0.3 (0.3)
Mexico	20.9 (0.8)	3.5 (1.3)	21.2 (2.8)	22.2 (3.6)	53.1 (4.0)	2.6 (0.5)	69.5 (5.2)	23.3 (4.6)	7.2 (2.8)	0.0 (0.0)
Norway	17.6 (1.2)	0.9 (0.9)	25.5 (4.9)	32.3 (5.3)	41.4 (6.3)	2.3 (0.5)	73.5 (7.9)	21.4 (7.7)	3.9 (1.6)	1.2 (0.8)
Poland	27.2 (0.6)	0.0 (0.0)	1.2 (0.7)	10.0 (3.1)	88.9 (3.2)	2.0 (0.5)	79.7 (4.0)	16.8 (3.7)	0.0 (0.0)	3.5 (1.6)
Sub-national entities										
Flanders (Belgium)	18.0 (0.7)	3.1 (1.0)	16.3 (3.2)	43.3 (4.3)	37.3 (4.3)	1.4 (0.4)	88.1 (2.8)	6.9 (2.1)	2.6 (1.3)	2.3 (1.6)
Average	20.6 (0.4)	1.6 (0.4)	18.4 (1.5)	28.7 (1.7)	51.3 (2.0)	2.4 (0.2)	75.0 (2.1)	19.3 (2.0)	3.2 (0.7)	2.5 (0.5)

Source: OECD, TALIS 2013 Database.
StatLink http://dx.doi.org/10.1787/888933043986

[Part 1/1]

Work experience of upper secondary education principals

Percentage of upper secondary education principals with the following work experience and average years of experience in each role

Table 3.12.b

	Years working as a principal					Years working in other school management roles				
	Average years of experience	Less than 3 years experience	3-10 years experience	11-20 years experience	More than 20 years experience	Average years of experience	Less than 3 years experience	3-10 years experience	11-20 years experience	More than 20 years experience
	Average S.E.	% S.E.	% S.E.	% S.E.	% S.E.	Average S.E.	% S.E.	% S.E.	% S.E.	% S.E.
Australia	7.6 (0.5)	19.0 (5.0)	56.2 (6.2)	23.1 (4.4)	1.7 (1.0)	11.9 (0.9)	11.1 (4.0)	38.7 (5.5)	37.6 (5.8)	12.5 (4.9)
Denmark	11.2 (0.8)	12.0 (3.6)	40.7 (5.9)	35.4 (5.9)	11.9 (3.4)	5.0 (0.7)	49.2 (5.3)	34.7 (5.4)	15.5 (5.2)	0.6 (0.6)
Finland	11.1 (0.9)	17.7 (4.5)	32.9 (3.9)	36.4 (4.4)	13.0 (3.0)	3.6 (0.5)	65.3 (4.5)	22.8 (3.6)	9.4 (3.0)	2.5 (1.3)
Iceland	9.0 (1.6)	26.5 (9.6)	35.3 (9.6)	33.9 (10.7)	4.4 (4.5)	4.6 (0.9)	42.2 (8.4)	45.1 (10.6)	12.7 (7.4)	0.0 (0.0)
Italy	12.2 (0.8)	3.7 (1.6)	55.5 (4.5)	19.2 (3.7)	21.6 (3.4)	7.9 (0.7)	25.1 (3.6)	44.8 (5.0)	23.6 (3.6)	6.5 (2.5)
Mexico	9.3 (0.8)	21.8 (3.6)	48.0 (4.1)	17.2 (3.2)	13.0 (3.0)	5.3 (0.6)	50.2 (4.3)	31.2 (3.9)	12.9 (2.7)	5.7 (2.0)
Norway	7.8 (0.7)	21.2 (5.7)	54.1 (6.3)	20.0 (4.2)	4.7 (2.4)	7.7 (0.8)	22.4 (5.0)	49.9 (5.9)	23.0 (5.4)	4.7 (2.4)
Poland	9.3 (0.8)	20.6 (6.3)	42.4 (6.4)	25.4 (5.2)	11.7 (2.9)	5.7 (1.0)	53.9 (6.8)	19.0 (3.5)	21.4 (6.6)	5.6 (1.3)
Singapore	7.5 (0.4)	19.6 (3.3)	53.0 (4.5)	26.1 (3.7)	1.3 (0.9)	7.6 (0.5)	10.1 (2.4)	69.8 (4.0)	18.1 (3.5)	2.0 (1.2)
Sub-national entities										
Abu Dhabi (United Arab Emirates)	9.3 (0.7)	18.2 (3.4)	45.4 (4.4)	27.3 (4.0)	9.1 (2.8)	7.1 (0.6)	16.7 (3.2)	65.0 (4.3)	10.7 (2.7)	7.6 (2.2)
Average	9.4 (0.3)	18.0 (1.6)	46.3 (1.8)	26.4 (1.7)	9.3 (0.9)	6.6 (0.2)	34.6 (1.6)	42.1 (1.8)	18.5 (1.5)	4.8 (0.7)

	Years working as a teacher					Years working in other jobs				
	Average years of experience	Less than 3 years experience	3-10 years experience	11-20 years experience	More than 20 years experience	Average years of experience	Less than 3 years experience	3-10 years experience	11-20 years experience	More than 20 years experience
	Average S.E.	% S.E.	% S.E.	% S.E.	% S.E.	Average S.E.	% S.E.	% S.E.	% S.E.	% S.E.
Australia	24.8 (1.2)	1.6 (1.6)	10.2 (3.2)	20.5 (4.1)	67.7 (4.9)	2.7 (0.8)	69.7 (6.0)	23.5 (5.0)	4.1 (2.5)	2.7 (2.7)
Denmark	16.5 (1.0)	9.8 (4.5)	18.8 (3.5)	39.9 (5.2)	31.4 (4.3)	4.6 (0.8)	51.7 (5.1)	36.9 (5.6)	7.8 (4.0)	3.6 (2.5)
Finland	13.6 (0.8)	7.1 (2.4)	41.4 (4.5)	29.2 (4.2)	22.3 (3.6)	4.4 (0.5)	47.0 (4.7)	42.7 (6.0)	8.0 (3.4)	2.3 (1.2)
Iceland	18.7 (2.4)	0.0 (0.0)	21.1 (8.2)	40.9 (11.2)	38.0 (11.0)	7.5 (1.6)	39.7 (10.9)	35.3 (10.7)	16.2 (5.2)	8.8 (5.2)
Italy	22.0 (0.7)	0.0 (0.0)	9.1 (2.5)	33.9 (4.3)	57.0 (4.3)	1.9 (0.4)	79.2 (3.6)	16.4 (3.2)	2.8 (1.5)	1.6 (1.3)
Mexico	17.1 (0.9)	7.2 (2.3)	27.9 (5.0)	32.1 (4.7)	32.8 (4.0)	10.0 (1.2)	38.6 (4.9)	25.8 (4.1)	17.0 (3.8)	18.6 (3.6)
Norway	17.0 (1.0)	4.1 (2.4)	25.4 (4.6)	40.4 (4.7)	30.0 (5.5)	4.9 (0.7)	51.1 (6.1)	35.3 (5.7)	10.0 (2.9)	3.5 (2.0)
Poland	23.7 (1.0)	0.8 (0.8)	4.5 (3.1)	29.6 (6.2)	65.1 (5.5)	2.4 (0.6)	76.1 (7.1)	19.6 (6.9)	2.4 (1.2)	1.9 (1.1)
Singapore	14.9 (0.8)	1.3 (0.9)	38.1 (4.2)	35.6 (3.9)	25.0 (4.0)	1.3 (0.4)	86.7 (2.8)	11.3 (2.6)	1.3 (0.9)	0.7 (0.7)
Sub-national entities										
Abu Dhabi (United Arab Emirates)	13.4 (0.8)	5.0 (2.0)	49.7 (3.8)	24.3 (4.0)	21.1 (3.8)	2.1 (0.5)	79.5 (3.7)	14.4 (3.1)	4.4 (1.9)	1.8 (1.2)
Average	18.2 (0.4)	3.7 (0.7)	24.6 (1.4)	32.6 (1.8)	39.0 (1.7)	4.2 (0.3)	61.9 (1.9)	26.1 (1.8)	7.4 (1.0)	4.6 (0.8)

Source: OECD, TALIS 2013 Database.

StatLink ⟶ http://dx.doi.org/10.1787/888933044005

[Part 1/1]
Employment status of principals

Table 3.13 *Percentage of lower secondary education principals with the following characteristics*

	Full time without teaching obligations[1]		Full time with teaching obligations[1]		Part time without teaching obligations[2]		Part time with teaching obligations[2]	
	%	S.E.	%	S.E.	%	S.E.	%	S.E.
Australia	78.9	(5.1)	20.6	(5.1)	0.5	(0.5)	0.0	(0.0)
Brazil	52.5	(2.8)	36.3	(2.7)	7.3	(1.5)	3.8	(0.9)
Bulgaria	8.4	(2.4)	91.6	(2.4)	0.0	(0.0)	0.0	(0.0)
Chile	75.1	(3.5)	20.8	(3.2)	1.3	(0.9)	2.8	(1.4)
Croatia	99.2	(0.8)	0.8	(0.8)	a	a	a	a
Cyprus*	88.8	(2.7)	11.2	(2.7)	a	a	a	a
Czech Republic	a	a	97.6	(1.0)	a	a	2.4	(1.0)
Denmark	67.2	(3.5)	32.8	(3.5)	0.0	(0.0)	0.0	(0.0)
Estonia	69.5	(3.1)	25.4	(2.8)	2.0	(1.0)	3.0	(1.3)
Finland	25.2	(3.3)	71.1	(3.5)	1.6	(1.2)	2.1	(1.2)
France	84.6	(2.0)	15.4	(2.0)	0.0	(0.0)	0.0	(0.0)
Iceland	58.3	(3.9)	36.1	(4.1)	0.9	(0.9)	4.6	(2.1)
Israel	24.6	(4.7)	74.6	(4.8)	0.8	(0.8)	0.0	(0.0)
Italy	95.8	(1.1)	4.2	(1.1)	a	a	a	a
Japan	97.8	(1.0)	2.2	(1.0)	0.0	(0.0)	0.0	(0.0)
Korea	98.4	(0.8)	1.6	(0.8)	0.0	(0.0)	0.0	(0.0)
Latvia	28.7	(5.3)	67.0	(6.5)	0.0	(0.0)	4.3	(3.8)
Malaysia	5.0	(1.9)	95.0	(1.9)	0.0	(0.0)	0.0	(0.0)
Mexico	71.8	(3.8)	20.7	(3.4)	5.5	(2.1)	2.0	(0.1)
Netherlands	85.5	(6.5)	12.6	(6.5)	1.5	(1.4)	0.4	(0.4)
Norway	76.3	(7.4)	17.1	(5.7)	0.0	(0.0)	6.6	(5.0)
Poland	20.3	(3.6)	71.4	(4.9)	1.5	(1.5)	6.8	(3.0)
Portugal[3]	87.0	(3.5)	10.4	(3.3)	0.8	(0.6)	1.8	(1.1)
Romania	2.2	(0.9)	68.6	(4.2)	0.2	(0.2)	29.0	(4.3)
Serbia	99.2	(0.8)	0.8	(0.8)	0.0	(0.0)	0.0	(0.0)
Singapore	99.3	(0.7)	0.7	(0.7)	0.0	(0.0)	0.0	(0.0)
Slovak Republic	5.0	(1.9)	91.3	(2.4)	0.0	(0.0)	3.7	(1.5)
Spain	8.0	(2.2)	71.1	(3.6)	1.6	(1.1)	19.3	(3.7)
Sweden	92.4	(3.8)	7.2	(3.8)	0.0	(0.0)	0.5	(0.5)
Sub-national entities								
Abu Dhabi (United Arab Emirates)	92.5	(2.9)	5.9	(2.4)	1.7	(1.7)	0.0	(0.0)
Alberta (Canada)	38.5	(3.3)	50.4	(4.1)	3.8	(2.0)	7.4	(2.7)
England (United Kingdom)	63.2	(4.9)	34.9	(4.8)	1.6	(0.9)	0.3	(0.3)
Flanders (Belgium)	98.0	(1.1)	1.2	(0.9)	0.8	(0.6)	0.0	(0.0)
Average[3]	62.4	(0.6)	35.4	(0.6)	1.2	(0.2)	3.4	(0.3)
United States	93.4	(3.6)	3.5	(3.0)	3.1	(2.2)	0.0	(0.0)

1. Full-time employment is defined as 90% or more of full-time hours.
2. Part-time employment is defined as less than 90% of full-time hours.
3. The averages do not add up to 100 across categories because of the presence of cells that are not applicable "a" in some countries.
*See notes at the beginning of this Annex.
Source: OECD, TALIS 2013 Database.
StatLink http://dx.doi.org/10.1787/888933044024

[Part 1/1]
Principals' recent professional development
Participation rates, types and average number of days of professional development reported
to be undertaken by lower secondary education principals in the 12 months prior to the survey[1, 2]

Table 3.14

	Percentage of principals who did not participate in any professional development[3]		Percentage of principals who participated in a professional network, mentoring or research activity		Average number of days among those who participated		Percentage of principals who participated in courses, conferences or observation visits		Average number of days among those who participated		Percentage of principals who participated in other types of professional development activities		Average number of days among those who participated	
	%	S.E.	%	S.E.	Average	S.E.	%	S.E.	Average	S.E.	%	S.E.	Average	S.E.
Australia	3.1	(3.0)	84.2	(3.7)	7.6	(0.6)	93.4	(3.5)	8.1	(0.6)	36.4	(5.1)	4.5	(0.7)
Brazil	14.5	(1.8)	39.1	(2.6)	50.5	(6.5)	71.0	(2.2)	37.4	(4.0)	36.8	(2.6)	29.2	(5.6)
Bulgaria	6.0	(2.1)	37.1	(3.6)	13.1	(2.5)	93.5	(2.1)	9.8	(1.5)	15.3	(2.9)	7.8	(1.2)
Chile	23.5	(3.1)	35.0	(3.6)	51.2	(13.7)	64.9	(3.7)	24.8	(5.3)	24.0	(3.5)	31.2	(10.3)
Croatia	0.8	(0.6)	68.8	(3.5)	4.9	(0.4)	81.0	(3.1)	7.3	(0.6)	39.0	(3.5)	4.2	(0.8)
Cyprus*	32.6	(4.8)	21.1	(3.7)	22.9	(15.0)	51.6	(5.2)	21.9	(9.1)	16.3	(3.6)	14.0	(7.0)
Czech Republic	13.4	(2.4)	28.1	(3.3)	11.8	(2.5)	82.2	(2.7)	9.0	(1.2)	33.7	(3.6)	7.1	(1.8)
Denmark	10.7	(2.9)	54.4	(4.3)	6.5	(0.8)	82.0	(2.9)	6.4	(0.5)	26.1	(4.0)	8.1	(1.9)
Estonia	5.1	(1.7)	54.1	(3.7)	7.7	(0.8)	93.9	(1.8)	10.2	(0.7)	48.0	(3.7)	6.9	(1.0)
Finland	8.3	(2.4)	48.1	(4.1)	4.4	(0.3)	87.7	(2.9)	5.8	(0.4)	36.2	(3.8)	3.7	(0.4)
France	24.1	(3.6)	46.2	(4.4)	7.2	(1.6)	54.5	(4.3)	3.8	(0.4)	21.8	(3.6)	8.5	(3.3)
Iceland	3.7	(1.8)	37.0	(4.3)	17.4	(9.2)	94.4	(1.7)	7.1	(0.7)	42.6	(4.6)	9.6	(3.9)
Israel	6.2	(1.9)	59.1	(6.6)	13.4	(2.4)	86.2	(2.9)	13.1	(2.1)	26.6	(4.5)	10.6	(2.4)
Italy	5.4	(1.6)	40.2	(4.1)	28.2	(10.7)	93.5	(1.7)	9.0	(0.9)	19.1	(3.4)	8.0	(1.2)
Japan	14.6	(3.3)	56.9	(4.2)	6.1	(0.7)	83.1	(3.4)	9.5	(0.7)	17.7	(2.8)	3.8	(0.7)
Korea	5.6	(2.3)	65.6	(5.2)	11.9	(1.7)	86.6	(3.6)	14.1	(2.3)	48.8	(5.0)	7.6	(1.1)
Latvia	0.7	(0.7)	53.6	(5.3)	12.0	(2.2)	98.0	(1.2)	15.2	(3.1)	52.2	(6.0)	8.6	(1.9)
Malaysia	1.5	(0.9)	78.0	(3.3)	12.1	(1.6)	98.1	(1.0)	14.8	(1.8)	58.4	(4.1)	9.8	(1.5)
Mexico	5.3	(1.8)	33.6	(3.7)	56.3	(10.6)	87.2	(2.7)	24.3	(3.0)	27.4	(3.7)	37.3	(11.0)
Netherlands	0.4	(0.4)	87.5	(6.6)	10.8	(2.5)	97.4	(0.9)	7.3	(1.0)	22.9	(6.0)	5.1	(0.9)
Norway	9.5	(3.8)	54.1	(5.6)	9.2	(0.8)	83.3	(5.1)	8.6	(0.8)	33.0	(4.9)	8.3	(1.1)
Poland	0.7	(0.5)	31.2	(5.1)	14.5	(6.2)	95.6	(2.4)	9.1	(1.4)	51.2	(5.1)	8.0	(1.5)
Portugal	23.5	(4.0)	10.8	(2.7)	128.0	(74.2)	67.1	(4.3)	23.9	(5.9)	24.3	(3.6)	17.6	(6.5)
Romania	12.5	(2.9)	29.4	(3.7)	24.6	(4.0)	75.0	(4.2)	21.9	(2.9)	41.8	(3.7)	14.8	(2.5)
Serbia	24.2	(3.9)	20.6	(3.4)	26.3	(12.6)	57.5	(4.6)	11.2	(2.8)	38.4	(4.3)	8.6	(1.8)
Singapore	0.0	(0.0)	92.5	(2.1)	15.5	(2.6)	99.3	(0.7)	13.4	(1.3)	44.0	(4.2)	14.1	(5.8)
Slovak Republic	16.4	(3.0)	63.6	(3.5)	10.1	(1.0)	62.2	(4.0)	7.8	(0.9)	28.4	(3.7)	6.2	(1.1)
Spain	22.9	(3.7)	27.8	(3.2)	25.7	(9.6)	67.6	(4.0)	11.8	(2.3)	39.5	(4.4)	10.4	(2.8)
Sweden	3.6	(1.9)	41.6	(4.6)	6.6	(1.2)	93.5	(2.3)	7.7	(0.6)	30.3	(4.0)	7.2	(1.6)
Sub-national entities														
Abu Dhabi (United Arab Emirates)	4.7	(1.9)	64.2	(5.1)	26.5	(11.1)	91.0	(2.4)	17.6	(7.1)	45.1	(5.2)	8.0	(1.2)
Alberta (Canada)	4.3	(1.5)	76.5	(3.4)	10.0	(1.8)	88.4	(2.8)	9.3	(1.2)	30.1	(3.6)	6.5	(1.0)
England (United Kingdom)	3.2	(1.4)	78.7	(3.5)	6.4	(0.6)	94.4	(1.9)	5.3	(0.3)	26.1	(4.0)	4.1	(0.8)
Flanders (Belgium)	0.9	(0.9)	67.3	(4.5)	6.2	(0.6)	97.4	(1.3)	8.3	(0.5)	24.3	(4.0)	4.9	(0.7)
Average	9.5	(0.4)	51.1	(0.7)	20.2	(2.5)	83.4	(0.5)	12.6	(0.5)	33.5	(0.7)	10.4	(0.7)
United States	6.0	(4.5)	68.2	(5.4)	23.6	(9.7)	91.0	(4.8)	18.4	(6.8)	42.3	(6.3)	21.8	(14.6)

1. Professional development aimed at principals.

2. Cells with data representing less than 10% of the cases are shaded in grey and should be interpreted with caution. These results are not highlighted in the text of the report. Please note that 10% is the threshold used when reporting directly on principals' results. It is higher than what is used for teachers because the sample size of principals is smaller than that of teachers.

3. This represents the percentage of principals who answered that they did not participate in any of the elements surveyed in questions 7a, 7b and 7c of the principal questionnaire.

* See notes at the beginning of this Annex.

Source: OECD, TALIS 2013 Database.

StatLink http://dx.doi.org/10.1787/888933044043

[Part 1/1]
Barriers to principals' participation in professional development
Percentage of lower secondary education principals who "agree" or "strongly agree" that the following presented barriers to their participation in professional development

Table 3.15

	Missing prerequisites		Too expensive		Lack of employer support		Conflicts with work schedule		Conflicts with family responsibilities		No relevant opportunities available		No incentives	
	%	S.E.	%	S.E.	%	S.E.	%	S.E.	%	S.E.	%	S.E.	%	S.E.
Australia	0.6	(0.6)	31.6	(6.1)	9.2	(2.9)	60.9	(5.9)	28.2	(6.1)	10.5	(4.7)	34.2	(5.5)
Brazil	7.5	(1.4)	24.1	(2.1)	33.4	(2.1)	38.6	(2.6)	13.1	(1.9)	20.7	(1.9)	31.5	(2.5)
Bulgaria	7.0	(1.9)	38.0	(3.7)	3.6	(1.4)	59.0	(4.3)	8.1	(2.3)	19.3	(2.9)	54.1	(3.3)
Chile	13.0	(2.8)	53.7	(4.3)	35.1	(3.9)	50.7	(3.9)	20.6	(3.3)	44.0	(4.2)	58.9	(4.0)
Croatia	4.7	(1.7)	49.4	(4.2)	13.6	(2.6)	6.3	(1.9)	2.4	(1.1)	23.5	(3.3)	29.2	(3.0)
Cyprus*	13.7	(3.2)	34.7	(4.9)	38.3	(4.7)	48.4	(4.7)	22.6	(4.1)	47.4	(4.9)	53.6	(4.6)
Czech Republic	2.6	(1.1)	20.5	(2.8)	8.7	(2.1)	34.3	(3.6)	6.8	(1.7)	9.1	(2.0)	20.0	(3.1)
Denmark	5.0	(2.0)	25.4	(4.1)	10.8	(2.7)	29.5	(4.6)	15.6	(3.4)	18.3	(3.1)	18.9	(3.5)
Estonia	7.1	(1.9)	22.5	(3.1)	9.2	(2.0)	14.8	(2.6)	5.6	(1.6)	16.3	(2.4)	9.7	(2.2)
Finland	2.3	(1.2)	9.8	(2.7)	8.8	(2.3)	42.2	(4.0)	17.8	(2.7)	16.1	(3.0)	30.1	(3.6)
France	6.9	(2.0)	18.8	(3.4)	13.8	(2.3)	59.9	(4.6)	9.9	(2.8)	19.8	(3.1)	37.5	(3.6)
Iceland	6.5	(2.5)	27.1	(4.5)	14.0	(3.5)	56.1	(4.9)	22.4	(4.2)	16.8	(3.5)	29.0	(4.4)
Israel	1.4	(0.7)	5.1	(1.9)	12.0	(2.7)	56.8	(6.8)	21.9	(4.6)	20.9	(4.6)	42.0	(5.7)
Italy	3.9	(1.5)	32.8	(4.7)	57.7	(4.2)	56.6	(4.4)	5.2	(1.6)	51.7	(4.7)	73.3	(4.3)
Japan	11.4	(2.3)	43.1	(4.8)	35.0	(4.3)	78.2	(3.5)	15.3	(3.1)	29.8	(4.0)	26.3	(3.9)
Korea	31.2	(4.7)	17.5	(4.1)	36.3	(4.4)	67.3	(4.7)	3.6	(2.0)	18.0	(4.3)	40.9	(4.1)
Latvia	2.0	(1.2)	20.6	(6.0)	9.6	(3.6)	26.2	(5.6)	10.9	(3.2)	8.6	(2.1)	13.9	(3.2)
Malaysia	9.6	(2.6)	8.9	(2.3)	6.9	(2.2)	42.4	(4.3)	1.5	(1.1)	15.4	(2.7)	18.7	(3.1)
Mexico	22.5	(3.5)	36.9	(3.9)	46.6	(4.0)	41.3	(4.1)	13.0	(2.8)	37.2	(3.8)	47.5	(3.9)
Netherlands	5.1	(2.8)	19.4	(8.0)	12.1	(6.8)	20.8	(6.6)	4.7	(2.6)	13.6	(3.7)	17.5	(6.8)
Norway	0.5	(0.5)	24.0	(3.4)	20.1	(7.3)	44.9	(4.8)	15.1	(4.3)	5.5	(2.1)	18.7	(5.5)
Poland	6.6	(3.0)	42.7	(4.5)	19.8	(2.9)	29.6	(4.7)	15.0	(3.1)	36.8	(5.1)	36.9	(4.7)
Portugal	23.1	(3.1)	64.2	(3.9)	81.8	(3.6)	41.1	(4.3)	12.3	(2.8)	54.1	(4.3)	71.4	(4.3)
Romania	7.6	(2.3)	40.4	(4.3)	7.5	(2.3)	28.6	(4.1)	14.9	(3.4)	3.9	(1.2)	43.5	(4.6)
Serbia	4.2	(2.1)	70.1	(3.7)	39.6	(4.1)	8.4	(2.2)	6.4	(2.0)	41.4	(3.3)	55.3	(3.9)
Singapore	2.7	(1.4)	3.4	(1.5)	2.0	(1.2)	42.9	(3.9)	8.2	(2.4)	8.7	(2.4)	7.5	(2.3)
Slovak Republic	4.0	(1.7)	18.6	(3.2)	2.8	(1.3)	22.4	(3.4)	5.1	(1.8)	25.8	(3.7)	40.2	(3.2)
Spain	3.6	(1.8)	33.2	(4.1)	27.4	(3.2)	56.2	(4.3)	29.0	(4.2)	53.3	(4.7)	79.1	(4.2)
Sweden	1.7	(0.8)	27.5	(4.7)	14.8	(3.1)	61.3	(5.0)	12.1	(2.7)	6.8	(2.0)	10.5	(2.7)
Sub-national entities														
Abu Dhabi (United Arab Emirates)	6.6	(2.7)	41.1	(5.1)	25.4	(4.1)	33.7	(4.3)	9.1	(2.8)	24.4	(3.8)	50.9	(4.6)
Alberta (Canada)	4.2	(2.0)	32.2	(3.8)	15.2	(3.1)	63.0	(3.5)	35.8	(3.8)	11.6	(2.8)	39.9	(3.8)
England (United Kingdom)	3.2	(2.5)	29.7	(4.0)	3.7	(1.9)	56.8	(5.9)	17.0	(2.8)	7.7	(2.1)	18.1	(2.9)
Flanders (Belgium)	4.9	(1.6)	21.1	(3.9)	8.1	(2.7)	43.4	(4.5)	9.2	(2.9)	0.9	(0.6)	10.8	(2.5)
Average	7.2	(0.4)	29.9	(0.7)	20.7	(0.6)	43.1	(0.8)	13.3	(0.5)	22.4	(0.6)	35.4	(0.7)
United States	4.2	(2.4)	39.1	(7.7)	11.0	(3.4)	66.9	(5.4)	24.3	(5.3)	10.1	(5.3)	25.8	(4.6)

* See notes at the beginning of this Annex.
Source: OECD, TALIS 2013 Database.
StatLink ⟐ http://dx.doi.org/10.1787/888933044062

[Part 1/2]
Impact of instructional leadership on teacher appraisal and school planning
Significant results of logistic regressions of instructional leadership and development of a school plan and educational goals and programmes, observing instruction in the classroom and teacher appraisal outcomes in lower secondary education[1]

Table 3.16

	Principal used student performance and student evaluation results to develop the school's educational goals and programmes[2]	Principal worked on a professional development plan for this school[3]	Principal observing instruction in the classroom[4]	After teacher appraisal measures to remedy any weaknesses in teaching are discussed with the teacher[5]	After teacher appraisal a development or training plan is developed for each teacher[5]	If a teacher is found to be a poor performer, material sanctions such as reduced annual increases in pay are imposed on the teacher[5]
	Model 1	Model 2	Model 3	Model 4	Model 5	Model 6
			Dependent on:			
	Use of instructional leadership[6]	Use of instructional leadership[6]	Use of instructional leadership[6]	Use of instructional leadership[6]	Use of instructional leadership[6]	Use of instructional leadership[6]
Australia		+	+			
Brazil	+	+	+			
Bulgaria	+	+		+	+	
Chile			+			
Croatia	+	+	+			
Czech Republic			+		+	
Denmark						
Estonia	+	+		−	+	+
Finland	+	+				
France		+			+	
Iceland						
Israel	+		+	+	+	
Italy	+	+	+			
Japan			+			
Korea		+				
Latvia					+	
Malaysia	+		+	+		
Mexico		+	+		+	
Netherlands		+	+			
Norway			+		+	+
Poland						
Portugal	+	+	+	+	+	
Romania			+	−	+	
Serbia	+					
Singapore			+			
Slovak Republic			+			
Spain		+	+	+	+	
Sweden			+			
Sub-national entities						
Abu Dhabi (United Arab Emirates)					+	
Alberta (Canada)	+	+	+		+	
England (United Kingdom)			+			
Flanders (Belgium)	+	+	+			+

1. Cells are blank where no significant relationship was found. Variables where a significant positive relationship was found are indicated by a "+", while those where a significant negative relationship was found are shown with a "–". Significance was tested at the 5% level, controlling for principal gender, age and educational attainment. Cells with data representing less than 10% of the cases are shaded in grey and should be interpreted with caution. These results are not highlighted in the text of the report. Please note that 10% is the threshold used when reporting directly on principals' results. It is higher than what is used for teachers because the sample size of principals is smaller than that of teachers.
2. Dichotomous variable where the reference category is principal who did not use student performance and student evaluation results to develop the school's educational goals and programmes.
3. Dichotomous variable where the reference category is principal who did not work on a professional development plan for their school.
4. Dichotomous variable where the reference category is principal observing instruction in the classroom "sometimes", "never" or "rarely".
5. Dichotomous variable where the reference category is "never occurs".
6. Continuous variable. See the textbox describing this index and Annex B for more details.
Source: OECD, TALIS 2013 Database.
StatLink http://dx.doi.org/10.1787/888933044100

[Part 2/2]
Impact of instructional leadership on teacher appraisal and school planning
Significant results of logistic regressions of instructional leadership and development of a school plan and educational goals and programmes, observing instruction in the classroom and teacher appraisal outcomes in lower secondary education[1]

Table 3.16

	After teacher appraisal a mentor is appointed to help the teacher improve his/her teaching[5]	After teacher appraisal there is a change in a teacher's work responsibilities[5]	After teacher appraisal there is a change in a teacher's salary or a payment of a financial bonus[5]	After teacher appraisal there is a change in the likelihood of a teacher's career advancement[5]	After teacher appraisal dismissal or non-renewal of contract occurs[5]
	Model 7	Model 8	Model 9	Model 10	Model 11
	Dependent on:				
	Use of instructional leadership[6]	Use of instructional leadership[6]	Use of instructional leadership[6]	Use of instructional leadership[6]	Use of instructional leadership[6]
Australia					
Brazil					
Bulgaria	+				+
Chile					−
Croatia					
Czech Republic				+	
Denmark	+				
Estonia	+				
Finland	+		+		
France					
Iceland					
Israel				+	
Italy					
Japan	+	+		+	
Korea					
Latvia					
Malaysia					+
Mexico		+			
Netherlands	+	−		+	+
Norway	+			+	
Poland		+			
Portugal					
Romania	+				
Serbia					
Singapore			+		
Slovak Republic				+	
Spain		+			+
Sweden	+				
Sub-national entities					
Abu Dhabi (United Arab Emirates)					
Alberta (Canada)	+				
England (United Kingdom)					
Flanders (Belgium)			−		

1. Cells are blank where no significant relationship was found. Variables where a significant positive relationship was found are indicated by a "+", while those where a significant negative relationship was found are shown with a "−". Significance was tested at the 5% level, controlling for principal gender, age and educational attainment. Cells with data representing less than 10% of the cases are shaded in grey and should be interpreted with caution. These results are not highlighted in the text of the report. Please note that 10% is the threshold used when reporting directly on principals' results. It is higher than what is used for teachers because the sample size of principals is smaller than that of teachers.
2. Dichotomous variable where the reference category is principal who did not use student performance and student evaluation results to develop the school's educational goals and programmes.
3. Dichotomous variable where the reference category is principal who did not work on a professional development plan for their school.
4. Dichotomous variable where the reference category is principal observing instruction in the classroom "sometimes", "never" or "rarely".
5. Dichotomous variable where the reference category is "never occurs".
6. Continuous variable. See the textbox describing this index and Annex B for more details.
Source: OECD, TALIS 2013 Database.
StatLink http://dx.doi.org/10.1787/888933044100

[Part 1/1]

Impact of instructional leadership on school climate, job satisfaction and principals' use of time

*Significant results of the multiple linear regressions of instructional leadership with school climate,
job satisfaction and percentage of time the principal reports spending on curriculum and teaching-related tasks
and meetings in lower secondary education[1]*

Table 3.17

	Percentage of time the principal spends on curriculum and teaching-related tasks and meetings[2]		Principal job satisfaction[3]		School climate – mutual respect[3]	
	Model 1		Model 2		Model 3	
	Dependent on:					
	Use of instructional leadership[3]		Use of instructional leadership[3]		Use of instructional leadership[3]	
	ß	S.E.	ß	S.E.	ß	S.E.
Australia	1.55	(0.37)			0.34	(0.11)
Brazil			0.21	(0.04)	0.31	(0.04)
Bulgaria			0.64	(0.15)	0.48	(0.13)
Chile						
Croatia					0.19	(0.08)
Czech Republic			0.19	(0.06)	0.14	(0.06)
Denmark	1.14	(0.42)				
Estonia			0.21	(0.06)		
Finland						
France						
Iceland						
Israel	1.23	(0.44)	0.18	(0.07)	0.14	(0.06)
Italy			0.26	(0.08)	0.32	(0.10)
Japan			0.39	(0.11)	0.31	(0.10)
Korea			0.26	(0.10)	0.34	(0.11)
Latvia						
Malaysia			0.33	(0.08)	0.40	(0.11)
Mexico			0.14	(0.05)	0.21	(0.10)
Netherlands	1.45	(0.58)	0.24	(0.10)		
Norway			0.17	(0.08)		
Poland			0.29	(0.10)		
Portugal	0.95	(0.37)	0.28	(0.06)	0.22	(0.07)
Romania			0.31	(0.10)	0.25	(0.11)
Serbia			0.48	(0.10)	0.26	(0.13)
Singapore					0.21	(0.07)
Slovak Republic					0.16	(0.08)
Spain	0.86	(0.37)			0.22	(0.08)
Sweden	2.08	(0.47)	0.23	(0.07)		
Sub-national entities						
Abu Dhabi (United Arab Emirates)			0.22	(0.09)	0.25	(0.12)
Alberta (Canada)			0.15	(0.07)	0.24	(0.08)
England (United Kingdom)						
Flanders (Belgium)	1.54	(0.64)				

1. Cells are blank where no significant relationship was found. Significance was tested at the 5% level, controlling for principal gender, age and educational attainment.

2. Continuous variable representing the proportion of time principals spend on this activity. Including developing curriculum, teaching, classroom observations, student evaluation, mentoring teachers, and teacher professional development.

3. Continuous variable. See the textbox describing this index and Annex B for more details.

Source: OECD, TALIS 2013 Database.

StatLink http://dx.doi.org/10.1787/888933044138

[Part 1/1]
Relationship between principals' instructional leadership and school climate
Significant results of the multiple linear regressions of principals' instructional leadership and school climate in lower secondary education[1]

Table 3.18

	Use of distributed leadership[2]							
	Dependent on:							
	Lack of material resources (a bit of a problem)[3]	Lack of material resources (a problem)[4]	Lack of pedagogical personnel (a bit of a problem)[5]	Lack of pedagogical personnel (a problem)[6]	School delinquency and violence[7]	School climate – mutual respect[8]	Ratio of teacher to administrative or management personnel[9]	Ratio of teacher to pedagogical support personnel[10]
	ß S.E.	ß S.E.	ß S.E.	ß S.E.	ß S.E.	ß S.E.	ß S.E.	ß S.E.
Australia					0.30 (0.08)	0.34 (0.11)		
Brazil						0.32 (0.05)		
Bulgaria						0.19 (0.06)		
Chile		1.58 (0.46)						
Croatia					0.13 (0.06)	0.14 (0.06)		
Czech Republic					-0.25 (0.08)			
Denmark								-0.03 (0.01)
Estonia		1.24 (0.53)						
Finland								
France						0.12 (0.06)		
Iceland		-1.41 (0.57)						-0.09 (0.04)
Israel						0.34 (0.13)		
Italy						0.18 (0.07)		
Japan			0.90 (0.45)	0.99 (0.47)		0.28 (0.07)		
Korea						0.22 (0.08)		0.04 (0.02)
Latvia								
Malaysia						0.23 (0.07)		
Mexico								
Netherlands								
Norway	-0.90 (0.44)					0.31 (0.13)		0.09 (0.04)
Poland								
Portugal						0.22 (0.09)		
Romania	-1.65 (0.35)	-1.47 (0.37)				0.17 (0.08)		
Serbia					-0.21 (0.07)			
Singapore						0.22 (0.09)		0.02 (0.01)
Slovak Republic						0.20 (0.08)		
Spain						0.22 (0.11)		
Sweden								
Sub-national entities								
Abu Dhabi (United Arab Emirates)								
Alberta (Canada)						0.21 (0.07)		
England (United Kingdom)								
Flanders (Belgium)								

1. Cells are blank where no significant relationship was found. Significance was tested at the 5% level, controlling for principal gender, age and educational attainment. Cells with data representing less than 10% of the cases are shaded in grey and should be interpreted with caution. These results are not highlighted in the text of the report. Please note that 10% is the threshold used when reporting directly on principals' results. It is higher than what is used for teachers because the sample size of principals is smaller than that of teachers.

2. Continuous variable. See the textbox describing this index and Annex B for more details.

3. Lack of material resources index is a dichotomous variable where the reference category is "not a problem" or "a problem". The index is combining the answers of the following questions: *i)* shortage or inadequacy of instructional materials (e.g. textbooks), *ii)* shortage or inadequacy of computers for instruction, *iii)* insufficient Internet access, *iv)* shortage or inadequacy of computer software for instruction, and *v)* shortage or inadequacy of library materials.

4. Lack of material resources index is a dichotomous variable where the reference category is "not a problem" or "a bit of a problem". The index is combining the answers of the following questions: *i)* shortage or inadequacy of instructional materials (e.g. textbooks), *ii)* shortage or inadequacy of computers for instruction, *iii)* insufficient Internet access, *iv)* shortage or inadequacy of computer software for instruction, and *v)* shortage or inadequacy of library materials.

5. Lack of pedagogical personnel index is a dichotomous variable where the reference category is "not a problem" or "a problem". The index is combining the answers of the following questions: *i)* shortage of qualified and/or well performing teachers, *ii)* shortage of teachers with competence in teaching students with special needs, and *iii)* shortage of vocational teachers.

6. Lack of pedagogical personnel index is a dichotomous variable where the reference category is "not a problem" or "a bit of a problem". The index is combining the answers of the following questions: *i)* shortage of qualified and/or well performing teachers, *ii)* shortage of teachers with competence in teaching students with special needs, and *iii)* shortage of vocational teachers.

7. School delinquency and violence index is a continuous variable combining answers of the following questions: *i)* frequency of vandalism and theft, *ii)* frequency of intimidation or verbal abuse among students (or other forms of non-physical bullying), *iii)* frequency of physical injury caused by violence among students, and *iv)* frequency of intimidation or verbal abuse of teachers or staff.

8. School climate - mutual respect index is a continuous variable combining answers of the following questions: *i)* school staff have an open discussion about difficulties, *ii)* there is mutual respect for colleagues' ideas, *iii)* there is a culture of sharing success, and *iv)* the relationships between teachers and students are good.

9. Ratio of teacher to administrative or management personnel is a continous variable.

10. Ratio of teacher to pedagogical support personnel is a continuous variable.

Source: OECD, TALIS 2013 Database.

StatLink ⬛🖘 http://dx.doi.org/10.1787/888933044176

[Part 1/1]

Relationship between principals' leadership style and job satisfaction

Significant results of the multiple linear regressions of instructional or distributed leadership and principals' job satisfaction in lower secondary education[1]

Table 3.19

	Instructional leadership[2]		Distributed leadership[2]	
	Model 1		Model 2	
	Dependent on:			
	Principal job satisfaction[2]		Principal job satisfaction[2]	
	ß	S.E.	ß	S.E.
Australia				
Brazil	0.25	(0.04)	0.21	(0.07)
Bulgaria	0.20	(0.04)	0.33	(0.08)
Chile				
Croatia			0.17	(0.08)
Czech Republic	0.28	(0.09)	0.18	(0.09)
Denmark				
Estonia	0.21	(0.07)	0.21	(0.05)
Finland			0.14	(0.05)
France				
Iceland				
Israel	0.38	(0.15)		
Italy	0.23	(0.09)	0.10	(0.04)
Japan	0.18	(0.05)	0.35	(0.08)
Korea	0.17	(0.08)	0.25	(0.10)
Latvia				
Malaysia	0.34	(0.15)		
Mexico	0.37	(0.14)	0.66	(0.13)
Netherlands	0.21	(0.10)		
Norway	0.24	(0.12)	0.13	(0.05)
Poland	0.16	(0.07)	0.45	(0.10)
Portugal	0.46	(0.10)	0.30	(0.10)
Romania	0.36	(0.09)		
Serbia	0.27	(0.06)	0.29	(0.09)
Singapore				
Slovak Republic	0.17	(0.08)		
Spain				
Sweden	0.26	(0.10)	0.26	(0.11)
Sub-national entities				
Abu Dhabi (United Arab Emirates)	0.20	(0.09)	0.25	(0.11)
Alberta (Canada)	0.22	(0.10)		
England (United Kingdom)				
Flanders (Belgium)			0.37	(0.10)

1. Cells are blank where no significant relationship was found. Significance was tested at the 5% level, controlling for principal gender, age and educational attainment.

2. Continuous variable. See the textbox describing this index and Annex B for more details.

Source: OECD, TALIS 2013 Database.

StatLink ⟜ http://dx.doi.org/10.1787/888933044214

[Part 1/1]
Relationship between principals' job satisfaction and principals' characteristics
Significant results of the multiple linear regressions of principals' job satisfaction and principals' characteristics in lower secondary education[1]

Table 3.20

	Principal job satisfaction[2]					
	Dependent on:					
	Male[3]		Years of experience as a principal[4]		Years of experience as a teacher[5]	
	ß	S.E.	ß	S.E.	ß	S.E.
Australia						
Brazil						
Bulgaria						
Chile						
Croatia			0.04	(0.02)		
Czech Republic						
Denmark						
Estonia						
Finland						
France	0.96	(0.33)				
Iceland						
Israel						
Italy	-0.69	(0.33)	0.04	(0.02)		
Japan					-0.04	(0.02)
Korea						
Latvia						
Malaysia	0.65	(0.30)				
Mexico						
Netherlands					0.04	(0.02)
Norway						
Poland	-0.93	(0.35)				
Portugal						
Romania					0.05	(0.02)
Serbia						
Singapore						
Slovak Republic	-0.80	(0.25)	0.09	(0.02)		
Spain			0.06	(0.03)		
Sweden						
Sub-national entities						
Abu Dhabi (United Arab Emirates)	-1.65	(0.42)			0.05	(0.02)
Alberta (Canada)	-0.68	(0.28)				
England (United Kingdom)						
Flanders (Belgium)						

1. Cells are blank where no significant relationship was found. Significance was tested at the 5% level, controlling for principal gender, age and educational attainment.
2. Continuous variable. See the textbox describing this index and Annex B for more details.
3. Male is a dichotomous variable where the reference category is female.
4. Years of experience as a principal (in total) is a continuous variable.
5. Years of experience as a teacher is a continuous variable.
Source: OECD, TALIS 2013 Database.
StatLink http://dx.doi.org/10.1787/888933044252

[Part 1/1]
Relationship between principals' job satisfaction and school characteristics
Significant results of the multiple linear regressions of principals' job satisfaction and school characteristics
Table 3.21 *in lower secondary education[1]*

	School locality (15 001 people or more)[3]		Publicly managed school[4]		50% or more of the school's funding comes from the government[5]		Number of teachers[6]		Number of students[7]		More than 10% of students have a different first language than the language(s) of instruction[8]		More than 10% of students have special needs[9]		More than 30% of students are from disadvantaged homes[10]	
	ß	S.E.	ß	S.E.	ß	S.E.	ß	S.E.	ß	S.E.	ß	S.E.	ß	S.E.	ß	S.E.
Australia													0.69	(0.26)	-0.74	(0.34)
Brazil																
Bulgaria					-4.37	(0.64)			0.00	(0.00)			-1.80	(0.59)		
Chile																
Croatia																
Czech Republic			-0.93	(0.46)							1.35	(0.61)	0.75	(0.25)		
Denmark																
Estonia							0.04	(0.01)					-0.63	(0.27)		
Finland																
France					-1.39	(0.50)										
Iceland															1.96	(0.88)
Israel																
Italy																
Japan									0.00	(0.00)						
Korea																
Latvia																
Malaysia					-1.06	(0.24)			0.00	(0.00)						
Mexico													0.66	(0.20)		
Netherlands																
Norway															-2.44	(1.11)
Poland	0.73	(0.30)									2.75	(0.40)				
Portugal	0.80	(0.25)					-0.01	(0.00)	0.00	(0.00)						
Romania													-0.93	(0.29)		
Serbia																
Singapore					1.91	(0.55)			0.00	(0.00)			1.56	(0.38)		
Slovak Republic																
Spain							-0.03	(0.01)	0.00	(0.00)	-0.93	(0.38)				
Sweden																
Sub-national entities																
Abu Dhabi (United Arab Emirates)			1.13	(0.57)							1.01	(0.50)				
Alberta (Canada)			1.35	(0.50)												
England (United Kingdom)													-0.68	(0.30)		
Flanders (Belgium)													-1.24	(0.54)		

1. Cells are blank where no significant relationship was found. Significance was tested at the 5% level, controlling for principal gender, age and educational attainment. Cells with data representing less than 10% of the cases are shaded in grey and should be interpreted with caution. These results are not highlighted in the text of the report. Please note that 10% is the threshold used when reporting directly on principals' results. It is higher than what is used for teachers because the sample size of principals is smaller than that of teachers.

2. Continuous variable. See the textbox describing this index and Annex B for more details.

3. School locality is a dichotomous variable where the reference category is less than 15 000 people.

4. Publicly managed school is a dichotomous variable where the reference category is privately managed school.

5. School's funding is a dichotomous variable where the reference category is 50% or more of the school's funding does not come from the government.

6. Number of teachers is a continuous variable.

7. Number of students is a continuous variable.

8. Students who have a different first language than the language(s) of instruction is a dichotomous variable where the reference category is 10% or less of students have a different first language than the language(s) of instruction.

9. Students with special needs is a dichotomous variable where the reference category is 10% or less of students have special needs.

10. Students from disadvantaged homes is a dichotomous variable where the reference category is 30% or less of students are from disadvantaged homes.

Source: OECD, TALIS 2013 Database.

StatLink http://dx.doi.org/10.1787/888933044290

[Part 1/1]
Relationship between principals' job satisfaction and school climate
Significant results of the multiple linear regressions of principals' job satisfaction and school climate in lower secondary education[1]

Table 3.22

| | Principal job satisfaction[2] | | | | | | | |
| | Dependent on: | | | | | | | |
	Lack of material resources (a bit of a problem)[3]		Lack of material resources (a problem)[4]		Lack of pedagogical personnel (a bit of a problem)[5]		Lack of pedagogical personnel (a problem)[6]		School delinquency and violence[7]		School climate – mutual respect[8]		Ratio of teacher to administrative or management personnel[9]		Ratio of teacher to pedagogical support personnel[10]	
	ß	S.E.	ß	S.E.	ß	S.E.	ß	S.E.	ß	S.E.	ß	S.E.	ß	S.E.	ß	S.E.
Australia											0.19	(0.08)				
Brazil									-0.06	(0.03)	0.37	(0.05)				
Bulgaria	-0.76	(0.30)	-1.97	(0.62)							0.32	(0.10)				
Chile											0.19	(0.05)				
Croatia											0.45	(0.07)				
Czech Republic											0.24	(0.08)				
Denmark									-0.20	(0.10)	0.27	(0.08)				
Estonia											0.39	(0.11)			0.05	(0.02)
Finland							-1.33	(0.39)	-0.22	(0.10)	0.21	(0.08)			0.08	(0.02)
France									-0.23	(0.10)	0.22	(0.10)				
Iceland							-1.89	(0.70)								
Israel											0.47	(0.09)				
Italy											0.18	(0.07)				
Japan									-0.28	(0.07)	0.38	(0.11)				
Korea			-1.44	(0.45)							0.35	(0.09)				
Latvia	-0.52	(0.23)														
Malaysia					0.68	(0.23)	1.17	(0.36)			0.37	(0.06)				
Mexico					0.80	(0.25)	0.69	(0.34)			0.19	(0.05)				
Netherlands											0.47	(0.12)				
Norway			-3.63	(0.68)					0.38	(0.17)	0.54	(0.12)				
Poland			-1.13	(0.28)							0.35	(0.07)				
Portugal			-1.56	(0.66)							0.20	(0.06)	-0.09	(0.04)		
Romania							0.99	(0.30)			0.36	(0.07)				
Serbia	-1.03	(0.32)									0.18	(0.09)				
Singapore			-2.12	(0.57)							0.22	(0.07)				
Slovak Republic											0.27	(0.10)				
Spain											0.31	(0.07)				
Sweden																
Sub-national entities																
Abu Dhabi (United Arab Emirates)	-0.91	(0.40)	-1.57	(0.48)					-0.35	(0.12)	0.25	(0.10)				
Alberta (Canada)							-1.05	(0.38)			0.20	(0.06)				
England (United Kingdom)											0.24	(0.10)				
Flanders (Belgium)			1.58	(0.54)							0.29	(0.08)				

1. Cells are blank where no significant relationship was found. Significance was tested at the 5% level, controlling for principal gender, age and educational attainment. Cells with data representing less than 10% of the cases are shaded in grey and should be interpreted with caution. These results are not highlighted in the text of the report. Please note that 10% is the threshold used when reporting directly on principals' results. It is higher than what is used for teachers because the sample size of principals is smaller than that of teachers.

2. Continuous variable. See the textbox describing this index and Annex B for more details.

3. Lack of material resources index is a dichotomous variable where the reference category is "not a problem" or "a problem". The index is combining the answers of the following questions: i) shortage or inadequacy of instructional materials (e.g. textbooks), ii) shortage or inadequacy of computers for instruction, iii) insufficient Internet access, iv) shortage or inadequacy of computer software for instruction, and v) shortage or inadequacy of library materials.

4. Lack of material resources index is a dichotomous variable where the reference category is "not a problem" or "a bit of a problem". The index is combining the answers of the following questions: i) shortage or inadequacy of instructional materials (e.g. textbooks), ii) shortage or inadequacy of computers for instruction, iii) insufficient Internet access, iv) shortage or inadequacy of computer software for instruction, and v) shortage or inadequacy of library materials.

5. Lack of pedagogical personnel index is a dichotomous variable where the reference category is "not a problem" or "a problem". The index is combining the answers of the following questions: i) shortage of qualified and/or well performing teachers, ii) shortage of teachers with competence in teaching students with special needs, and iii) shortage of vocational teachers.

6. Lack of pedagogical personnel index is a dichotomous variable where the reference category is "not a problem" or "a bit of a problem". The index is combining the answers of the following questions: i) shortage of qualified and/or well performing teachers, ii) shortage of teachers with competence in teaching students with special needs, and iii) shortage of vocational teachers.

7. School delinquency and violence index is a continuous variable combining answers of the following questions: i) frequency of vandalism and theft, ii) frequency of intimidation or verbal abuse among students (or other forms of non-physical bullying), iii) frequency of physical injury caused by violence among students, and iv) frequency of intimidation or verbal abuse of teachers or staff.

8. School climate - mutual respect index is a continuous variable combining answers of the following questions: i) school staff have an open discussion about difficulties, ii) there is mutual respect for colleagues' ideas, iii) there is a culture of sharing success, and iv) the relationships between teachers and students are good..

9. Ratio of teacher to administrative or management personnel is a continous variable.

10. Ratio of teacher to pedagogical support personnel is a continuous variable.

Source: OECD, TALIS 2013 Database.

StatLink ⟐⟐ http://dx.doi.org/10.1787/888933044328

[Part 1/1]

Relationship between principals' job satisfaction and barriers for principals' effectiveness

Significant results of the multiple linear regressions of principals' job satisfaction and barriers for principals'

Table 3.23 *effectiveness in lower secondary education[1]*

	Principal job satisfaction[2]																	
	Dependent on:																	
	Inadequate school budget and resources[3]		Government regulation and policy[3]		Teachers' absence[3]		Lack of parent/ guardian involvement[3]		Teachers' career-based wage system[3]		Lack of support for own professional development[3]		Lack of support for teachers' professional development[3]		High workload and level of responsibility[3]		Lack of shared leadership with other school staff members[3]	
	ß	S.E.	ß	S.E.	ß	S.E.	ß	S.E.	ß	S.E.	ß	S.E.	ß	S.E.	ß	S.E.	ß	S.E.
Australia																	-1.04	(0.48)
Brazil											-0.48	(0.22)					-0.51	(0.21)
Bulgaria									-1.23	(0.44)					-0.99	(0.35)	-0.70	(0.33)
Chile																		
Croatia	1.14	(0.54)	-0.99	(0.37)													-1.15	(0.27)
Czech Republic																		
Denmark	-0.61	(0.29)			-1.21	(0.35)												
Estonia			-0.83	(0.30)	0.42	(0.21)									-0.78	(0.25)		
Finland			-0.56	(0.26)			-1.25	(0.29)									-0.65	(0.32)
France					-0.96	(0.36)					-1.09	(0.53)						
Iceland			1.07	(0.54)											-1.09	(0.43)		
Israel															-0.65	(0.31)		
Italy															-0.99	(0.30)		
Japan															-0.60	(0.29)		
Korea																		
Latvia	-1.26	(0.51)																
Malaysia			0.58	(0.28)											-0.74	(0.29)		
Mexico																		
Netherlands									0.85	(0.36)					-1.65	(0.36)		
Norway															-0.99	(0.50)		
Poland											-0.86	(0.42)						
Portugal													0.66	(0.30)				
Romania			-0.75	(0.34)														
Serbia																		
Singapore																		
Slovak Republic	-1.16	(0.33)									0.85	(0.31)	-0.79	(0.26)	-0.93	(0.33)	-0.84	(0.25)
Spain									0.81	(0.29)							-1.16	(0.44)
Sweden	-0.75	(0.27)											-0.75	(0.29)	-0.95	(0.30)	-0.70	(0.35)
Sub-national entities																		
Abu Dhabi (United Arab Emirates)											1.27	(0.58)	-1.03	(0.50)	-1.10	(0.48)		
Alberta (Canada)	-0.85	(0.34)											0.78	(0.35)				
England (United Kingdom)							-1.70	(0.82)							-1.40	(0.34)		
Flanders (Belgium)															-1.15	(0.44)	-0.93	(0.32)

1. Cells are blank where no significant relationship was found. Significance was tested at the 5% level, controlling for principal gender, age and educational attainment. Cells with data representing less than 10% of the cases are shaded in grey and should be interpreted with caution. These results are not highlighted in the text of the report. Please note that 10% is the threshold used when reporting directly on principals' results. It is higher than what is used for teachers because the sample size of principals is smaller than that of teachers.

2. Continuous variable. See the textbox describing this index and Annex B for more details.

3. The answers from principals are combined into two categories for the regressions where the reference category is principals who answered that the barrier was "not at all" limiting their effectiveness or "very little".

Source: OECD, TALIS 2013 Database.

StatLink http://dx.doi.org/10.1787/888933044366

[Part 1/1]

Access to and participation in induction programmes

Percentage of lower secondary education teachers whose school principal reports the existence of induction processes for new teachers in the school and the percentage who report having taken part in an induction programme during their first regular employment as a teacher

Table 4.1

	Access to induction programmes or activities (reported by principals)										Participation in induction programmes or activities (reported by teachers)					
	Formal induction						Informal induction activities (not part of an induction programme) for new teachers		General and/or administrative introduction to the school for new teachers		Took part in a formal induction programme		Took part in informal induction activities not part of an induction programme		Took part in a general and/or administrative introduction to the school	
	For all new teachers to the school[1]		Only for teachers new to teaching[1]		No induction programme for new teachers[1]											
	%	S.E.	%	S.E.	%	S.E.	%	S.E.	%	S.E.	%	S.E.	%	S.E.	%	S.E.
Australia	91.5	(2.6)	3.7	(1.9)	4.9	(1.6)	90.3	(3.1)	97.2	(1.3)	52.6	(1.6)	51.4	(1.2)	61.1	(1.1)
Brazil	22.8	(2.2)	4.5	(0.9)	72.7	(2.1)	48.3	(2.8)	65.6	(2.3)	32.4	(0.8)	33.0	(0.9)	32.8	(1.0)
Bulgaria	62.5	(3.8)	22.7	(3.0)	14.8	(3.0)	87.9	(1.9)	96.4	(1.1)	68.9	(1.5)	62.0	(1.3)	81.3	(1.1)
Chile	37.1	(4.6)	3.0	(1.6)	59.9	(4.6)	64.0	(4.1)	79.6	(3.4)	36.6	(2.0)	39.6	(1.7)	36.4	(1.4)
Croatia	30.5	(3.4)	60.3	(3.6)	9.2	(2.2)	73.7	(3.3)	94.6	(1.8)	68.0	(0.8)	54.0	(0.9)	59.7	(0.9)
Cyprus*	22.8	(0.2)	38.1	(0.2)	39.1	(0.2)	77.8	(0.2)	74.0	(0.2)	51.1	(1.2)	35.4	(1.2)	30.9	(1.0)
Czech Republic	30.9	(3.7)	7.4	(1.9)	61.7	(3.8)	81.2	(2.8)	97.1	(1.2)	45.2	(1.1)	55.6	(1.1)	45.0	(1.0)
Denmark	55.7	(5.7)	6.4	(2.4)	37.9	(5.7)	78.3	(4.3)	85.1	(3.5)	26.6	(1.6)	39.5	(1.6)	27.8	(1.3)
Estonia	31.9	(4.5)	9.5	(2.4)	58.6	(4.3)	88.4	(2.3)	84.2	(2.8)	19.4	(1.1)	34.8	(1.1)	37.3	(1.2)
Finland	52.6	(4.6)	1.0	(1.0)	46.5	(4.4)	92.7	(2.5)	89.7	(2.2)	16.3	(1.1)	51.5	(1.0)	42.5	(1.2)
France	20.0	(3.1)	57.8	(3.9)	22.3	(3.3)	49.9	(3.6)	95.0	(1.6)	55.1	(1.2)	41.9	(0.9)	49.0	(1.1)
Iceland	26.9	(0.2)	26.8	(0.1)	46.2	(0.1)	95.1	(0.1)	97.1	(0.1)	29.5	(1.2)	34.6	(1.3)	36.4	(1.4)
Israel	63.4	(4.3)	18.9	(3.0)	17.7	(3.8)	76.2	(3.6)	94.9	(2.2)	51.5	(1.2)	29.5	(1.1)	30.1	(0.9)
Italy	11.4	(2.5)	74.7	(3.1)	14.0	(2.2)	68.5	(3.3)	63.0	(3.6)	49.4	(1.1)	32.7	(1.0)	49.7	(1.0)
Japan	17.2	(2.6)	70.6	(2.8)	12.2	(2.2)	37.0	(3.4)	81.5	(2.8)	83.3	(0.8)	18.4	(0.8)	69.3	(1.0)
Korea	58.0	(3.8)	22.0	(3.2)	20.0	(3.3)	69.9	(3.7)	92.5	(2.2)	72.3	(0.8)	60.1	(0.9)	71.1	(1.0)
Latvia	22.9	(4.3)	12.7	(3.2)	64.4	(5.2)	84.1	(3.9)	98.0	(1.7)	35.9	(1.2)	46.3	(1.2)	40.8	(1.3)
Malaysia	50.7	(4.5)	45.3	(4.5)	4.0	(1.7)	91.8	(2.4)	99.0	(0.3)	87.4	(0.8)	60.6	(1.3)	80.8	(0.9)
Mexico	24.2	(3.1)	3.8	(1.6)	72.0	(3.1)	38.8	(3.3)	49.1	(3.7)	57.2	(1.2)	52.4	(1.1)	44.9	(1.1)
Netherlands	93.3	(3.2)	1.1	(1.1)	5.6	(3.0)	88.8	(2.7)	100.0	(0.0)	45.6	(1.5)	46.5	(1.3)	60.0	(1.7)
Norway	28.9	(7.1)	26.5	(5.0)	44.6	(7.8)	83.5	(4.1)	55.0	(6.5)	10.3	(1.5)	35.5	(1.4)	20.0	(1.4)
Poland	16.2	(3.0)	7.3	(2.9)	76.5	(3.9)	88.9	(2.2)	79.3	(3.3)	37.8	(1.4)	59.7	(1.2)	50.3	(1.1)
Portugal	17.5	(2.8)	2.7	(1.5)	79.7	(3.0)	84.4	(2.9)	87.2	(2.9)	35.5	(1.0)	39.6	(1.0)	21.0	(0.8)
Romania	19.0	(3.0)	26.6	(3.2)	54.3	(3.8)	65.5	(3.8)	59.6	(4.0)	51.2	(1.2)	58.7	(1.4)	59.4	(1.2)
Serbia	30.4	(3.9)	53.3	(4.3)	16.2	(3.2)	74.8	(3.3)	83.4	(2.6)	59.1	(1.1)	35.7	(0.9)	44.0	(1.1)
Singapore	99.3	(0.0)	0.7	(0.0)	0.0	(0.0)	98.6	(0.0)	100.0	(0.0)	80.0	(0.8)	60.3	(1.0)	82.6	(0.8)
Slovak Republic	35.9	(3.9)	46.9	(3.8)	17.2	(3.0)	81.8	(3.0)	87.1	(2.8)	60.5	(1.2)	46.0	(1.1)	31.2	(1.1)
Spain	21.9	(3.1)	2.7	(1.2)	75.4	(3.3)	54.3	(3.6)	79.1	(3.0)	35.3	(1.2)	35.0	(1.0)	21.8	(1.0)
Sweden	29.8	(3.6)	33.5	(3.7)	36.7	(3.6)	63.5	(3.7)	80.2	(3.5)	10.7	(0.7)	19.1	(0.8)	22.8	(0.9)
Sub-national entities																
Abu Dhabi (United Arab Emirates)	73.6	(4.4)	4.5	(1.8)	21.9	(4.0)	85.1	(3.0)	96.4	(1.0)	70.9	(2.0)	53.7	(1.4)	58.7	(1.3)
Alberta (Canada)	51.5	(4.7)	33.5	(4.0)	15.0	(3.1)	80.9	(3.6)	93.8	(2.0)	51.0	(1.7)	42.7	(1.4)	55.4	(1.3)
England (United Kingdom)	94.3	(2.0)	5.2	(1.9)	0.6	(0.6)	88.4	(2.9)	94.6	(2.1)	75.8	(0.9)	46.5	(1.3)	57.5	(1.2)
Flanders (Belgium)	93.3	(2.0)	1.5	(1.1)	5.2	(1.7)	90.7	(2.6)	99.2	(0.6)	42.5	(1.0)	40.4	(0.9)	54.4	(1.1)
Average	43.6	(0.6)	22.3	(0.5)	34.2	(0.6)	76.5	(0.5)	85.7	(0.5)	48.6	(0.2)	44.0	(0.2)	47.5	(0.2)
United States	68.7	(4.8)	19.0	(3.6)	12.3	(4.3)	82.0	(3.8)	94.6	(2.0)	59.3	(2.0)	44.1	(2.1)	57.6	(1.2)

1. The data presented in the column entitled "For all new teachers to the school" are derived from questions 33A and 34 of the principal questionnaire (PQ). It present the percentage of teachers working in schools where the principal report that there is an induction programme for new teachers (PQ33A) and who report that all teachers who are new to the school are offered an induction programme (PQ34). The data presented in the column entitled "Only for teachers new to teaching" are also derived from questions PQ33A and PQ34. They present the percentage of teachers working in schools where the principal report that there is an induction programme for new teachers (PQ33A) and who report that only teachers who are new to teaching are offered an induction programme (PQ34). The data presented in the column entitled "No induction programme for new teachers" are derived from question PQ33A and represent the percentage of teachers working in schools where the principal report that there is no induction programme for new teachers. The percentages presented in these three columns add up to 100%.

* See notes at the beginning of this Annex.

Source: OECD, TALIS 2013 Database.

StatLink 🔗 http://dx.doi.org/10.1787/888933044727

[Part 1/1]

Access to and participation in induction programmes in primary education

Percentage of primary education teachers whose school principal reports the existence of induction processes for new teachers in the school and the percentage of teachers who report having taken part in an induction programme during their first regular employment as a teacher

Table 4.1.a

	Access to induction programmes or activities (reported by principals)					Participation in induction programmes or activities (reported by teachers)		
	Formal induction			Informal induction activities (not part of an induction programme) for new teachers	General and/or administrative introduction to the school for new teachers	Took part in a formal induction programme	Took part in informal induction activities not part of an induction programme	Took part in a general and/or administrative introduction to the school
	For all new teachers to the school[1]	Only for teachers new to teaching[1]	No induction programme for new teachers[1]					
	%	S.E.	%	S.E.	%	S.E.	%	S.E.	%	S.E.	%	S.E.	%	S.E.	%	S.E.
Denmark	53.5	(4.9)	9.2	(2.7)	37.3	(4.7)	80.0	(3.6)	82.0	(4.0)	28.4	(1.4)	37.6	(1.0)	25.3	(0.9)
Finland	43.4	(3.5)	2.3	(1.2)	54.3	(3.6)	91.8	(1.7)	93.4	(1.9)	15.9	(0.9)	51.1	(1.4)	45.1	(1.2)
Mexico	12.5	(2.6)	1.3	(1.1)	86.2	(2.8)	28.7	(4.2)	33.4	(4.4)	59.6	(1.8)	47.5	(2.0)	46.6	(2.0)
Norway	19.1	(3.8)	39.9	(5.0)	41.0	(5.0)	86.7	(3.1)	44.3	(4.5)	10.1	(0.7)	31.3	(1.3)	16.5	(0.9)
Poland	18.7	(3.4)	7.0	(2.0)	74.3	(3.6)	84.3	(3.1)	75.9	(4.1)	45.1	(1.0)	59.0	(1.2)	50.9	(1.2)
Sub-national entities																
Flanders (Belgium)	74.1	(3.6)	7.4	(2.3)	18.5	(3.2)	78.3	(3.6)	83.3	(3.1)	18.8	(1.1)	22.6	(0.9)	26.9	(1.0)
Average	36.9	(1.5)	11.2	(1.1)	52.0	(1.6)	75.0	(1.3)	68.7	(1.5)	29.6	(0.5)	41.5	(0.5)	35.2	(0.5)

1. The data presented in the column entitled "For all new teachers to the school" are derived from questions 33A and 34 of the principal questionnaire (PQ). The data present the percentage of teachers working in schools where the principal reports that there is an induction programme for new teachers (PQ33A) and who reports that all teachers who are new to the school are offered an induction programme (PQ34). The data presented in the column entitled "Only for teachers new to teaching" are also derived from questions PQ33A and PQ34. They present the percentage of teachers working in schools where the principal reports that there is an induction programme for new teachers (PQ33A) and who reports that only teachers who are new to teaching are offered an induction programme (PQ34). The data presented in the column entitled "No induction programme for new teachers" are derived from question PQ33A and represent the percentage of teachers working in schools where the principal reports that there is no induction programme for new teachers. The percentages presented in these three columns add up to 100%.

Source: OECD, TALIS 2013 Database.

StatLink http://dx.doi.org/10.1787/888933044746

[Part 1/1]

Access to and participation in induction programmes in upper secondary education

Percentage of upper secondary education teachers whose school principal reports the existence of induction processes for new teachers in the school and the percentage of teachers who report having taken part in an induction programme during their first regular employment as a teacher

Table 4.1.b

	Access to induction programmes or activities (reported by principals)					Participation in induction programmes or activities (reported by teachers)		
	Formal induction			Informal induction activities (not part of an induction programme) for new teachers	General and/or administrative introduction to the school for new teachers	Took part in a formal induction programme	Took part in informal induction activities not part of an induction programme	Took part in a general and/or administrative introduction to the school
	For all new teachers to the school[1]	Only for teachers new to teaching[1]	No induction programme for new teachers[1]					
	%	S.E.	%	S.E.	%	S.E.	%	S.E.	%	S.E.	%	S.E.	%	S.E.	%	S.E.
Australia	92.9	(3.1)	6.1	(2.9)	1.0	(1.0)	89.4	(3.2)	97.7	(1.3)	53.2	(1.4)	52.8	(1.6)	61.9	(1.3)
Denmark	90.8	(3.6)	4.8	(3.3)	4.4	(1.8)	78.8	(4.9)	99.6	(0.4)	45.0	(1.6)	55.7	(1.6)	44.3	(1.8)
Finland	71.4	(4.4)	0.2	(0.2)	28.4	(4.4)	87.9	(4.8)	94.4	(3.3)	24.7	(1.3)	55.5	(2.9)	46.8	(2.0)
Iceland	50.2	(0.2)	6.6	(0.1)	43.2	(0.2)	93.4	(0.1)	83.3	(0.1)	17.9	(1.3)	42.4	(1.6)	36.3	(1.7)
Italy	21.5	(2.9)	55.8	(3.6)	22.7	(2.6)	73.7	(2.9)	71.6	(3.3)	46.5	(1.0)	31.1	(0.8)	48.7	(1.0)
Mexico	46.1	(4.0)	3.4	(1.6)	50.5	(3.9)	60.0	(4.4)	75.3	(3.3)	64.2	(1.3)	57.1	(1.2)	52.4	(1.3)
Norway	69.5	(6.2)	11.4	(4.6)	19.2	(4.9)	75.4	(6.6)	74.1	(5.9)	12.0	(1.0)	44.2	(1.3)	25.0	(1.1)
Poland	20.4	(5.2)	5.2	(2.2)	74.5	(5.6)	90.1	(3.4)	82.5	(4.4)	35.9	(1.6)	57.9	(1.3)	50.2	(1.4)
Singapore	99.3	(0.0)	0.7	(0.0)	0.0	(0.0)	98.6	(0.0)	100.0	(0.0)	76.2	(0.8)	60.3	(0.9)	80.0	(0.8)
Sub-national entities																
Abu Dhabi (United Arab Emirates)	77.2	(4.2)	1.6	(1.2)	21.3	(4.1)	89.5	(2.8)	97.8	(1.1)	71.5	(1.4)	52.1	(1.5)	56.9	(1.2)
Average	63.9	(1.2)	9.6	(0.8)	26.5	(1.1)	83.7	(1.2)	87.6	(1.0)	44.7	(0.4)	50.9	(0.5)	50.3	(0.4)

1. The data presented in the column entitled "For all new teachers to the school" are derived from questions 33A and 34 of the principal questionnaire (PQ). The data present the percentage of teachers working in schools where the principal reports that there is an induction programme for new teachers (PQ33A) and who reports that all teachers who are new to the school are offered an induction programme (PQ34). The data presented in the column entitled "Only for teachers new to teaching" are also derived from questions PQ33A and PQ34. They present the percentage of teachers working in schools where the principal reports that there is an induction programme for new teachers (PQ33A) and who reports that only teachers who are new to teaching are offered an induction programme (PQ34). The data presented in the column entitled "No induction programme for new teachers" are derived from question PQ33A and represent the percentage of teachers working in schools where the principal reports that there is no induction programme for new teachers. The percentages presented in these three columns add up to 100%.

Source: OECD, TALIS 2013 Database.

StatLink http://dx.doi.org/10.1787/888933044765

[Part 1/1]

Teachers' participation in formal induction programmes, by work status and gender

Percentage of lower secondary education teachers with the following characteristics who report having participated in a formal induction programme in their first regular employment as a teacher[1, 2]

Table 4.2

	Gender				Experience				Work status				Hours of work per week[4]			
	Male teachers		Female teachers		Teachers with 5 years teaching experience or less		Teachers with more than 5 years teaching experience		Permanent teachers		Fixed-term teachers[3]		Teachers working less than 30 hours per week		Teachers working 30 hours per week or more	
	%	S.E.	%	S.E.	%	S.E.	%	S.E.	%	S.E.	%	S.E.	%	S.E.	%	S.E.
Australia	54.7	(2.2)	51.1	(2.3)	71.5	(3.0)	48.0	(1.7)	52.7	(1.8)	51.9	(2.2)	58.1	(3.5)	51.2	(1.7)
Brazil	30.3	(1.3)	33.2	(0.9)	27.3	(1.8)	33.1	(1.0)	32.5	(1.0)	32.1	(1.4)	31.1	(1.2)	32.8	(1.0)
Bulgaria	72.9	(2.2)	68.0	(1.7)	81.1	(3.4)	67.3	(1.6)	68.0	(1.7)	74.5	(3.0)	72.0	(2.3)	68.2	(1.7)
Chile	38.2	(3.1)	35.6	(2.1)	30.2	(3.2)	38.2	(2.2)	35.3	(2.1)	37.7	(3.3)	34.3	(2.4)	36.5	(2.6)
Croatia	67.9	(1.8)	68.1	(0.9)	68.0	(1.9)	67.9	(1.0)	68.8	(0.8)	59.5	(3.3)	61.2	(2.2)	69.6	(0.9)
Cyprus*	51.3	(2.3)	51.1	(1.5)	47.7	(3.6)	51.6	(1.4)	51.6	(1.5)	49.9	(2.3)	45.3	(2.4)	54.0	(1.5)
Czech Republic	42.1	(2.1)	46.1	(1.3)	37.2	(2.7)	46.6	(1.2)	45.9	(1.3)	41.7	(2.2)	45.4	(2.9)	46.2	(1.2)
Denmark	27.2	(2.3)	26.2	(1.9)	39.9	(3.0)	23.8	(1.8)	26.6	(1.6)	25.3	(5.9)	22.8	(3.9)	26.9	(1.6)
Estonia	18.7	(2.3)	19.6	(1.2)	28.1	(3.0)	18.0	(1.3)	18.4	(1.2)	24.9	(2.7)	21.7	(1.7)	18.4	(1.2)
Finland	20.6	(1.9)	14.7	(1.2)	22.2	(2.5)	15.2	(1.1)	15.4	(1.1)	19.3	(2.3)	15.2	(1.5)	16.9	(1.4)
France	56.3	(1.9)	54.4	(1.4)	67.5	(2.6)	53.7	(1.3)	56.6	(1.3)	20.4	(3.9)	46.3	(2.5)	57.3	(1.3)
Iceland	24.2	(2.4)	31.6	(1.4)	23.2	(2.8)	30.9	(1.4)	31.0	(1.4)	21.3	(2.8)	24.8	(2.4)	30.9	(1.4)
Israel	55.5	(2.7)	50.3	(1.4)	72.0	(2.3)	45.9	(1.3)	48.0	(1.2)	65.1	(2.5)	49.9	(1.8)	53.4	(1.4)
Italy	43.6	(1.9)	51.0	(1.2)	18.6	(2.3)	52.4	(1.1)	58.6	(1.1)	9.0	(1.2)	42.9	(1.6)	54.4	(1.5)
Japan	84.7	(1.0)	81.0	(1.1)	66.4	(2.1)	87.7	(0.8)	91.8	(0.6)	48.2	(2.1)	77.3	(2.6)	83.9	(0.8)
Korea	72.5	(1.6)	72.2	(1.0)	69.2	(2.3)	73.4	(1.0)	75.6	(0.9)	56.1	(2.3)	71.9	(1.9)	72.3	(1.0)
Latvia	28.7	(3.1)	36.8	(1.3)	26.2	(4.5)	36.4	(1.3)	35.8	(1.2)	37.1	(5.2)	32.5	(2.2)	37.5	(1.6)
Malaysia	86.0	(1.4)	88.0	(0.9)	95.6	(1.1)	85.0	(0.9)	87.5	(0.8)	80.9	(20.9)	83.3	(1.9)	88.5	(0.8)
Mexico	59.5	(1.5)	55.1	(1.6)	57.0	(2.6)	57.4	(1.4)	55.5	(1.2)	62.8	(2.5)	55.5	(1.5)	58.0	(1.7)
Netherlands	42.4	(2.2)	48.3	(1.7)	64.5	(3.8)	40.6	(1.3)	42.1	(1.5)	64.4	(4.9)	50.4	(3.3)	44.0	(1.7)
Norway	10.6	(1.8)	10.2	(1.5)	27.5	(4.1)	5.0	(0.7)	9.1	(1.2)	18.6	(5.0)	8.9	(1.5)	10.7	(1.8)
Poland	43.0	(2.9)	36.1	(1.4)	32.7	(2.9)	37.5	(1.5)	38.7	(1.6)	33.0	(2.0)	35.8	(2.3)	38.6	(1.6)
Portugal	37.6	(1.7)	34.7	(1.1)	31.6	(4.9)	35.6	(1.0)	37.4	(1.1)	29.6	(1.9)	30.1	(2.4)	36.2	(1.0)
Romania	53.1	(2.3)	50.4	(1.4)	48.0	(2.9)	51.5	(1.5)	50.9	(1.7)	51.6	(1.9)	48.2	(2.2)	52.3	(1.6)
Serbia	59.2	(1.5)	59.0	(1.2)	55.6	(2.3)	60.6	(1.2)	64.8	(1.2)	33.5	(2.1)	53.8	(1.7)	62.3	(1.3)
Singapore	81.9	(1.3)	79.0	(1.0)	94.6	(0.7)	69.2	(1.3)	80.8	(0.8)	73.0	(2.9)	80.5	(1.9)	79.9	(0.8)
Slovak Republic	56.7	(2.7)	61.3	(1.2)	58.7	(2.3)	60.8	(1.4)	62.0	(1.4)	53.8	(2.3)	51.6	(2.0)	63.3	(1.4)
Spain	36.2	(1.9)	34.6	(1.4)	35.5	(5.1)	35.1	(1.1)	36.1	(1.3)	31.5	(2.2)	35.3	(3.7)	35.3	(1.1)
Sweden	12.5	(1.1)	9.9	(0.8)	21.9	(2.3)	9.1	(0.6)	9.7	(0.7)	19.2	(2.4)	14.3	(2.2)	10.4	(0.7)
Sub-national entities																
Abu Dhabi (United Arab Emirates)	76.8	(1.9)	66.9	(2.7)	65.3	(2.9)	72.1	(2.1)	66.9	(3.1)	75.1	(1.7)	69.0	(2.1)	71.6	(2.5)
Alberta (Canada)	51.7	(2.3)	50.6	(2.0)	66.3	(3.2)	45.6	(1.7)	48.6	(1.7)	61.2	(3.8)	54.5	(4.2)	50.4	(1.8)
England (United Kingdom)	74.6	(1.5)	76.5	(1.2)	92.9	(1.1)	69.4	(1.2)	75.8	(0.9)	76.8	(3.7)	67.0	(4.9)	77.1	(0.8)
Flanders (Belgium)	43.1	(1.7)	42.2	(1.2)	67.8	(1.9)	36.3	(1.2)	37.4	(1.2)	68.2	(2.0)	34.4	(2.2)	44.6	(1.2)
Average	48.9	(0.4)	48.3	(0.3)	51.9	(0.5)	47.3	(0.2)	49.0	(0.2)	45.7	(0.8)	46.1	(0.4)	49.5	(0.3)
United States	63.7	(2.6)	57.0	(2.2)	67.7	(4.1)	57.1	(2.2)	59.8	(2.5)	58.3	(2.9)	55.7	(3.5)	60.1	(2.2)

1. Cells with data representing less than 5% of the cases are shaded in grey and should be interpreted with caution. These results are not highlighted in the text of the report.

2. The percentages presented in this table reflect the level of participation in induction programmes based on different characteristics of the teachers. It is important to note that participation in informal induction activities not part of an induction programme and participation in a general and/or administrative introduction to the school are not taken into account in the percentages presented in this table.

3. Including teachers with fixed-term contract for a period of more than one school year and teachers with fixed-term contract for a period of one school year or less.

4. Refers to question 16 of the teacher questionnaire where teachers were asked about the approximate number of hours they spent in total on teaching, planning lessons, marking, collaborating with other teachers, participating in staff meetings and on other tasks related to their job at their school during their most recent calendar week.

* See notes at the beginning of this Annex.

Source: OECD, TALIS 2013 Database.

StatLink http://dx.doi.org/10.1787/888933044784

[Part 1/1]
Mentoring programmes in lower secondary education
Percentage of lower secondary education teachers whose school principal reports the existence of a mentoring system in the school, the characteristics of the mentors and the percentage of teachers in lower secondary education who are involved in mentoring activities[1]

Table 4.3

	Access to mentoring programmes (reported by principals)														Participation in mentoring programmes (reported by teachers)			
	Target group of mentoring system								The subject field(s) of the mentor is the same as that of the teacher being mentored								Teachers who presently have an assigned mentor to support them		Teachers who serve as an assigned mentor for one or more teachers
	Only for teachers who are new to teaching		For all teachers who are new to the school		For all teachers in the school		There is no access to a mentoring system for teachers in the school		Most of the time		Sometimes		Rarely or never				
	%	S.E.	%	S.E.	%	S.E.	%	S.E.	%	S.E.	%	S.E.	%	S.E.	%	S.E.	%	S.E.
Australia	18.6	(4.5)	39.3	(5.6)	39.5	(6.0)	2.6	(1.4)	55.3	(6.5)	42.8	(6.6)	1.9	(1.2)	16.7	(1.4)	28.0	(1.1)
Brazil	3.6	(1.0)	10.3	(1.8)	59.7	(2.3)	26.4	(2.3)	40.2	(2.9)	42.7	(3.2)	17.2	(2.6)	33.7	(1.0)	6.4	(0.4)
Bulgaria	16.5	(2.8)	27.3	(3.1)	43.3	(3.6)	12.9	(2.4)	73.0	(3.7)	23.5	(3.8)	3.6	(1.2)	6.1	(0.7)	10.2	(0.7)
Chile	1.6	(1.2)	13.9	(3.5)	10.2	(2.6)	74.3	(4.0)	49.7	(8.5)	46.8	(9.0)	3.5	(3.6)	4.5	(0.9)	6.6	(0.7)
Croatia	68.7	(3.3)	14.0	(2.6)	16.2	(2.7)	1.1	(0.4)	98.4	(0.8)	1.6	(0.8)	0.0	(0.0)	5.6	(0.4)	13.8	(0.7)
Cyprus*	40.3	(0.2)	12.7	(0.1)	13.2	(0.1)	33.8	(0.2)	96.6	(0.1)	1.2	(0.0)	2.2	(0.1)	6.4	(0.5)	5.2	(0.5)
Czech Republic	16.5	(2.7)	21.8	(2.9)	29.3	(3.3)	32.3	(3.9)	87.8	(2.4)	10.4	(2.2)	1.8	(1.0)	3.8	(0.4)	7.7	(0.7)
Denmark	23.4	(4.1)	45.0	(5.5)	5.7	(2.0)	25.8	(4.9)	45.2	(5.8)	53.3	(5.9)	1.6	(1.2)	4.2	(0.7)	12.7	(0.9)
Estonia	31.3	(4.0)	28.0	(4.0)	15.1	(3.1)	25.6	(3.4)	68.7	(4.8)	21.8	(4.0)	9.5	(2.7)	3.3	(0.5)	9.1	(0.8)
Finland	5.4	(1.9)	23.2	(3.8)	6.0	(2.1)	65.4	(3.7)	76.6	(6.5)	19.0	(5.9)	4.4	(2.8)	2.8	(0.5)	3.8	(0.5)
France	68.5	(3.4)	5.4	(1.7)	2.5	(1.3)	23.6	(3.3)	95.2	(1.8)	4.8	(1.8)	0.0	(0.0)	3.5	(0.4)	5.5	(0.4)
Iceland	36.6	(0.1)	19.2	(0.1)	36.5	(0.1)	7.7	(0.0)	52.0	(0.2)	45.2	(0.2)	2.8	(0.0)	5.8	(0.7)	12.3	(0.8)
Israel	26.2	(3.8)	49.7	(4.4)	10.9	(2.3)	13.2	(3.0)	85.3	(3.4)	12.9	(3.3)	1.8	(1.0)	20.2	(0.8)	23.3	(1.0)
Italy	60.5	(3.6)	6.7	(1.9)	1.6	(0.9)	31.2	(3.6)	88.8	(2.8)	9.2	(2.7)	2.0	(0.9)	4.5	(0.4)	5.1	(0.4)
Japan	50.3	(3.3)	10.1	(2.3)	19.4	(2.7)	20.2	(2.7)	57.9	(3.9)	33.2	(3.9)	8.8	(2.2)	33.2	(1.1)	16.5	(0.8)
Korea	34.0	(3.5)	20.8	(2.9)	31.1	(3.8)	14.1	(2.8)	75.9	(3.8)	13.5	(3.2)	10.7	(2.5)	18.5	(0.7)	34.3	(0.9)
Latvia	16.4	(3.9)	18.6	(4.0)	23.6	(4.6)	41.4	(5.6)	57.5	(7.1)	39.8	(7.0)	2.7	(1.7)	4.1	(0.6)	7.0	(0.7)
Malaysia	48.6	(4.4)	25.0	(4.0)	18.4	(3.4)	8.0	(2.1)	71.0	(4.2)	29.0	(4.2)	0.0	(0.0)	26.5	(1.4)	26.5	(1.2)
Mexico	8.1	(2.6)	7.2	(1.9)	24.4	(3.4)	60.3	(4.3)	55.2	(6.5)	39.5	(6.3)	5.3	(2.7)	17.0	(1.0)	10.9	(0.8)
Netherlands	0.6	(0.6)	25.4	(4.6)	70.6	(5.0)	3.5	(2.7)	19.2	(4.4)	47.9	(6.2)	32.9	(5.8)	16.6	(1.2)	19.4	(1.4)
Norway	29.4	(4.3)	20.1	(5.2)	10.5	(6.1)	40.0	(7.6)	45.1	(8.5)	45.9	(8.2)	9.0	(4.5)	6.9	(2.8)	7.7	(0.7)
Poland	20.4	(3.9)	24.2	(3.2)	21.4	(3.4)	34.0	(4.3)	81.1	(4.2)	17.2	(4.1)	1.6	(1.2)	11.6	(0.6)	14.9	(0.7)
Portugal	4.0	(1.5)	11.4	(2.7)	18.8	(3.2)	65.7	(3.8)	82.5	(5.9)	17.5	(5.9)	0.0	(0.0)	4.3	(0.4)	7.6	(0.5)
Romania	10.7	(2.2)	15.0	(2.8)	53.2	(3.9)	21.0	(3.3)	77.1	(3.9)	15.3	(3.2)	7.6	(2.6)	8.0	(0.7)	8.2	(0.8)
Serbia	86.4	(2.8)	9.8	(2.5)	0.0	(0.0)	3.8	(1.6)	98.1	(1.1)	1.9	(1.1)	0.0	(0.0)	8.2	(0.5)	13.5	(0.6)
Singapore	20.5	(0.1)	47.1	(0.3)	31.6	(0.2)	0.8	(0.0)	85.5	(0.1)	13.2	(0.1)	1.3	(0.0)	39.6	(0.9)	39.4	(0.9)
Slovak Republic	16.8	(2.5)	18.5	(3.2)	47.1	(3.7)	17.6	(2.9)	94.9	(2.1)	3.9	(1.7)	1.2	(1.2)	4.2	(0.4)	8.9	(0.5)
Spain	15.1	(2.4)	10.7	(2.2)	15.5	(2.6)	58.7	(3.4)	68.0	(5.3)	24.7	(4.7)	7.3	(3.3)	3.8	(0.4)	6.8	(0.5)
Sweden	46.8	(3.8)	12.4	(2.4)	0.0	(0.0)	40.8	(3.7)	60.3	(4.7)	32.1	(4.8)	7.5	(2.7)	3.7	(0.4)	5.5	(0.4)
Sub-national entities																		
Abu Dhabi (United Arab Emirates)	7.6	(2.8)	17.8	(4.2)	63.2	(4.8)	11.4	(3.2)	74.3	(5.0)	24.6	(5.0)	1.1	(0.8)	51.9	(1.8)	29.2	(1.1)
Alberta (Canada)	27.0	(4.1)	26.7	(3.7)	33.4	(4.4)	12.9	(3.7)	67.6	(4.6)	30.0	(4.6)	2.5	(1.1)	13.0	(1.3)	20.7	(1.3)
England (United Kingdom)	26.1	(4.3)	30.6	(3.6)	42.7	(4.8)	0.6	(0.6)	39.7	(4.3)	53.7	(4.1)	6.6	(2.3)	19.1	(1.2)	31.4	(1.0)
Flanders (Belgium)	6.1	(1.8)	65.0	(4.0)	7.4	(2.2)	21.4	(3.0)	25.0	(4.6)	41.3	(4.9)	33.7	(4.5)	10.2	(0.8)	10.2	(1.0)
Average	**27.0**	**(0.5)**	**22.2**	**(0.6)**	**24.9**	**(0.6)**	**25.8**	**(0.6)**	**68.1**	**(0.8)**	**26.0**	**(0.8)**	**5.8**	**(0.4)**	**12.8**	**(0.2)**	**14.2**	**(0.1)**
United States	29.8	(5.2)	45.3	(5.3)	18.1	(3.8)	6.8	(2.7)	71.4	(5.9)	26.0	(5.8)	2.6	(1.6)	12.2	(1.1)	16.8	(1.3)

1. Refers to mentoring by or for teachers at the school. Does not refer to students within teacher education programmes who are practising as teachers at the school.
* See notes at the beginning of this Annex.
Source: OECD, TALIS 2013 Database.
StatLink ⟐ http://dx.doi.org/10.1787/888933044803

[Part 1/1]

Mentoring programmes in primary education

Percentage of primary education teachers whose school principal reports the existence of a mentoring system in the school, the characteristics of the mentors and the percentage of primary education teachers who report being involved in mentoring activities[1]

Table 4.3.a

	Access to mentoring programmes (reported by principals)													Participation in mentoring programmes (reported by teachers)			
	Target group of mentoring system								The subject field(s) of the mentor is the same as that of the teacher being mentored								
	Only for teachers who are new to teaching		For all teachers who are new to the school		For all teachers in the school		There is no access to a mentoring system for teachers in the school		Most of the time		Sometimes		Rarely or never		Teachers who presently have an assigned mentor to support them		Teachers who serve as an assigned mentor for one or more teachers	
	%	S.E.	%	S.E.	%	S.E.	%	S.E.	%	S.E.	%	S.E.	%	S.E.	%	S.E.	%	S.E.
Denmark	26.5	(3.9)	36.5	(3.8)	2.4	(1.3)	34.6	(4.4)	28.3	(5.6)	62.0	(5.6)	9.7	(3.1)	3.4	(0.5)	9.1	(0.7)
Finland	2.9	(1.1)	21.1	(2.8)	11.9	(2.4)	64.1	(3.3)	88.2	(4.0)	7.1	(3.1)	4.7	(2.8)	3.6	(0.5)	3.3	(0.4)
Mexico	2.4	(1.9)	3.1	(1.7)	20.4	(3.9)	74.1	(4.2)	60.0	(9.0)	35.0	(7.8)	5.0	(6.1)	21.7	(2.1)	7.8	(1.2)
Norway	47.5	(4.8)	20.6	(3.8)	2.2	(1.5)	29.6	(4.3)	70.4	(6.8)	29.6	(6.8)	0.0	(0.0)	3.6	(0.5)	7.6	(0.6)
Poland	16.9	(3.0)	30.1	(4.3)	28.4	(3.9)	24.6	(3.8)	76.5	(3.8)	20.8	(3.9)	2.7	(1.7)	10.8	(0.8)	16.2	(1.0)
Sub-national entities																	
Flanders (Belgium)	9.3	(2.4)	25.9	(4.0)	10.8	(2.5)	54.0	(4.5)	75.7	(5.6)	21.6	(5.3)	2.7	(1.9)	6.3	(0.6)	9.5	(0.6)
Average	17.6	(1.3)	22.9	(1.4)	12.7	(1.1)	46.9	(1.7)	66.5	(2.5)	29.4	(2.3)	4.1	(1.3)	8.2	(0.4)	8.9	(0.3)

1. Refers to mentoring by or for teachers at the school. Does not refer to students within teacher education programmes who are practising as teachers at the school.
Source: OECD, TALIS 2013 Database.
StatLink http://dx.doi.org/10.1787/888933044822

[Part 1/1]

Mentoring programmes in upper secondary education

Percentage of upper secondary education teachers whose school principal reports the existence of a mentoring system in the school, the characteristics of the mentors and the percentage of upper secondary education teachers who report being involved in mentoring activities[1]

Table 4.3.b

	Access to mentoring programmes (reported by principals)													Participation in mentoring programmes (reported by teachers)			
	Target group of mentoring system								The subject field(s) of the mentor is the same as that of the teacher being mentored								
	Only for teachers who are new to teaching		For all teachers who are new to the school		For all teachers in the school		There is no access to a mentoring system for teachers in the school		Most of the time		Sometimes		Rarely or never		Teachers who presently have an assigned mentor to support them		Teachers who serve as an assigned mentor for one or more teachers	
	%	S.E.	%	S.E.	%	S.E.	%	S.E.	%	S.E.	%	S.E.	%	S.E.	%	S.E.	%	S.E.
Australia	27.3	(4.8)	32.7	(4.7)	29.0	(5.2)	11.0	(4.1)	59.6	(5.6)	32.9	(5.7)	7.5	(3.0)	14.2	(1.1)	30.4	(1.2)
Denmark	11.7	(3.3)	59.4	(6.1)	15.9	(4.2)	13.1	(3.6)	82.6	(5.2)	17.4	(5.2)	0.0	(0.0)	10.6	(1.1)	25.2	(1.5)
Finland	5.4	(3.0)	21.0	(3.2)	17.5	(4.2)	56.2	(6.0)	65.8	(5.7)	31.4	(5.4)	2.8	(1.5)	3.9	(1.3)	4.7	(0.7)
Iceland	2.1	(0.1)	42.8	(0.2)	33.2	(0.1)	21.9	(0.1)	78.8	(0.1)	17.3	(0.1)	3.9	(0.0)	7.0	(0.8)	12.9	(1.1)
Italy	49.4	(3.7)	14.5	(2.5)	1.8	(0.9)	34.3	(3.3)	92.0	(2.3)	5.0	(1.8)	3.0	(1.5)	2.6	(0.4)	4.0	(0.4)
Mexico	5.6	(1.9)	12.3	(2.6)	18.3	(3.2)	63.8	(3.9)	63.0	(6.9)	25.1	(5.8)	11.9	(4.3)	13.1	(1.1)	11.7	(1.0)
Norway	37.5	(6.7)	27.9	(6.2)	7.2	(3.4)	27.4	(6.5)	70.7	(7.5)	29.3	(7.5)	0.0	(0.0)	6.8	(0.6)	12.3	(0.9)
Poland	10.6	(2.7)	38.9	(4.4)	21.6	(3.1)	28.9	(4.6)	83.9	(6.6)	16.1	(6.6)	0.0	(0.0)	11.6	(0.8)	16.2	(1.0)
Singapore	22.1	(0.1)	47.9	(0.1)	29.2	(0.1)	0.7	(0.0)	85.5	(0.1)	13.1	(0.1)	1.4	(0.0)	34.5	(1.0)	44.1	(0.8)
Sub-national entities																	
Abu Dhabi (United Arab Emirates)	3.1	(2.0)	16.6	(3.9)	70.0	(4.6)	10.3	(3.3)	68.6	(5.4)	28.4	(5.2)	3.0	(1.7)	48.9	(1.9)	30.1	(1.0)
Average	17.5	(1.1)	31.4	(1.3)	24.4	(1.1)	26.8	(1.3)	75.1	(1.6)	21.6	(1.6)	3.3	(0.6)	15.3	(0.3)	19.2	(0.3)

1. Refers to mentoring by or for teachers at the school. Does not refer to students within teacher education programmes who are practising as teachers at the school.
Source: OECD, TALIS 2013 Database.
StatLink http://dx.doi.org/10.1787/888933044841

[Part 1/1]

Teachers having a mentor, by work status, experience and gender

Percentage of lower secondary education teachers with the following characteristics

Table 4.4 *who report having an assigned mentor[1, 2]*

	Gender				Experience				Work status				Hours of work per week[4]			
	Male teachers		Female teachers		Teachers with 5 years teaching experience or less		Teachers with more than 5 years teaching experience		Permanent teachers		Fixed-term teachers[3]		Teachers working less than 30 hours per week		Teachers working 30 hours per week or more	
	%	S.E.	%	S.E.	%	S.E.	%	S.E.	%	S.E.	%	S.E.	%	S.E.	%	S.E.
Australia	16.4	(2.0)	16.9	(1.6)	31.9	(3.0)	13.2	(1.5)	15.2	(1.4)	27.7	(3.4)	12.7	(2.1)	17.8	(1.7)
Brazil	29.5	(1.5)	35.4	(1.1)	31.9	(1.7)	33.3	(1.1)	32.9	(1.2)	37.2	(1.6)	33.3	(1.5)	33.7	(1.1)
Bulgaria	5.9	(1.1)	6.1	(0.8)	14.5	(3.3)	4.9	(0.6)	4.9	(0.7)	13.7	(2.1)	6.5	(1.5)	6.1	(0.7)
Chile	5.2	(1.7)	4.1	(0.7)	5.9	(2.2)	4.3	(0.8)	4.9	(1.1)	3.8	(0.9)	5.8	(1.6)	3.6	(0.8)
Croatia	6.8	(0.9)	5.1	(0.5)	20.7	(1.9)	0.6	(0.2)	3.7	(0.4)	27.6	(2.9)	10.5	(1.4)	4.7	(0.5)
Cyprus*	6.2	(1.0)	6.4	(0.6)	17.8	(2.5)	3.5	(0.5)	2.3	(0.4)	17.0	(1.6)	3.9	(0.8)	7.4	(0.7)
Czech Republic	4.5	(0.8)	3.6	(0.5)	16.5	(2.3)	1.5	(0.2)	2.0	(0.3)	12.4	(1.9)	3.7	(0.9)	3.9	(0.5)
Denmark	3.5	(0.8)	4.6	(0.8)	9.6	(2.2)	2.9	(0.7)	3.5	(0.6)	19.2	(5.9)	6.1	(2.2)	3.9	(0.7)
Estonia	4.2	(1.1)	3.2	(0.5)	15.9	(2.6)	1.8	(0.3)	2.4	(0.4)	8.5	(1.8)	3.3	(0.7)	3.4	(0.6)
Finland	3.1	(0.7)	2.7	(0.6)	8.3	(1.7)	1.6	(0.4)	1.4	(0.3)	7.6	(1.5)	2.5	(0.7)	2.9	(0.6)
France	4.6	(0.7)	3.0	(0.5)	19.4	(2.5)	1.4	(0.3)	3.5	(0.4)	3.8	(1.9)	3.5	(0.9)	3.5	(0.5)
Iceland	4.2	(1.2)	6.4	(0.7)	18.4	(2.7)	3.0	(0.5)	4.1	(0.6)	14.7	(2.5)	7.6	(1.5)	5.0	(0.7)
Israel	22.8	(2.1)	19.4	(0.9)	44.4	(2.3)	13.6	(0.8)	14.0	(0.7)	43.5	(2.3)	20.0	(1.4)	20.6	(1.1)
Italy	5.6	(0.9)	4.1	(0.5)	9.1	(1.8)	4.0	(0.4)	4.8	(0.5)	3.0	(0.6)	4.6	(0.7)	4.3	(0.5)
Japan	34.6	(1.4)	31.0	(1.3)	42.9	(2.3)	31.0	(1.2)	33.4	(1.1)	32.1	(1.9)	27.7	(2.4)	34.0	(1.2)
Korea	19.5	(1.3)	18.0	(0.9)	28.7	(2.6)	15.8	(0.7)	16.1	(0.7)	29.9	(2.5)	20.3	(1.5)	17.8	(0.8)
Latvia	7.5	(1.8)	3.6	(0.6)	16.9	(3.7)	2.9	(0.4)	3.6	(0.5)	10.0	(4.2)	5.1	(0.9)	3.6	(0.6)
Malaysia	25.5	(2.1)	26.9	(1.5)	43.4	(2.3)	21.5	(1.5)	26.4	(1.4)	82.3	(17.8)	23.0	(2.1)	27.3	(1.5)
Mexico	18.3	(1.3)	15.9	(1.4)	17.5	(2.1)	16.7	(1.2)	16.0	(1.1)	20.5	(1.9)	15.4	(1.2)	18.2	(1.5)
Netherlands	15.6	(1.9)	17.5	(1.8)	34.9	(3.7)	11.9	(1.0)	10.5	(1.0)	49.7	(4.1)	20.0	(2.8)	15.2	(1.3)
Norway	8.1	(3.7)	6.2	(2.3)	17.4	(5.7)	3.6	(1.9)	5.1	(2.3)	19.3	(6.5)	3.2	(0.8)	7.7	(3.5)
Poland	11.4	(1.1)	11.6	(0.6)	37.6	(2.7)	8.3	(0.6)	10.3	(0.5)	18.4	(2.6)	12.8	(1.4)	11.2	(0.7)
Portugal	5.2	(0.8)	3.9	(0.5)	8.8	(2.9)	4.1	(0.4)	4.1	(0.5)	4.8	(0.7)	4.2	(1.1)	4.2	(0.4)
Romania	7.7	(1.1)	8.1	(0.9)	16.1	(2.3)	5.9	(0.8)	6.2	(0.9)	12.2	(1.3)	8.8	(1.2)	7.6	(0.8)
Serbia	7.6	(0.9)	8.6	(0.7)	26.0	(2.5)	3.5	(0.5)	7.2	(0.6)	12.8	(1.9)	9.0	(0.9)	7.9	(0.6)
Singapore	40.8	(1.5)	39.0	(1.0)	64.7	(1.3)	20.8	(1.0)	39.2	(0.9)	43.8	(3.3)	39.0	(2.5)	39.9	(1.0)
Slovak Republic	5.1	(0.9)	4.0	(0.4)	14.7	(1.7)	1.7	(0.3)	1.9	(0.3)	13.7	(1.4)	6.3	(1.0)	3.5	(0.4)
Spain	3.3	(0.5)	4.2	(0.6)	10.0	(1.9)	3.3	(0.4)	3.4	(0.4)	5.5	(1.1)	4.8	(0.9)	3.6	(0.5)
Sweden	5.1	(0.8)	3.0	(0.4)	16.9	(1.9)	1.7	(0.3)	2.5	(0.3)	13.0	(1.8)	1.9	(0.8)	3.9	(0.4)
Sub-national entities																
Abu Dhabi (United Arab Emirates)	58.6	(2.4)	47.2	(2.2)	51.8	(3.1)	52.0	(1.9)	49.4	(2.2)	54.5	(2.3)	48.8	(2.2)	53.1	(2.3)
Alberta (Canada)	11.4	(1.6)	14.0	(1.5)	29.2	(3.2)	7.5	(1.1)	7.1	(1.0)	36.6	(3.7)	14.7	(2.7)	12.6	(1.4)
England (United Kingdom)	20.7	(2.2)	18.2	(1.2)	39.0	(2.0)	12.2	(1.1)	16.6	(1.3)	55.4	(6.6)	16.9	(2.4)	19.5	(1.3)
Flanders (Belgium)	9.6	(1.1)	10.4	(1.0)	37.7	(2.6)	3.0	(0.5)	3.1	(0.4)	45.4	(2.8)	8.7	(1.3)	10.6	(0.9)
Average	13.3	(0.3)	12.5	(0.2)	24.8	(0.5)	9.6	(0.2)	11.0	(0.2)	24.2	(0.7)	12.6	(0.3)	12.8	(0.2)
United States	14.8	(1.8)	10.8	(1.5)	37.0	(2.9)	5.4	(0.9)	7.3	(0.8)	21.9	(2.7)	11.0	(2.1)	12.5	(1.1)

1. Cells with data representing less than 5% of the cases are shaded in grey and should be interpreted with caution. These results are not highlighted in the text of the report.

2. Percentages presented in this table reflect the proportion of teachers who report having an assigned mentor based on different characteristics of the teachers. For example, 16.4% of male teachers in Australia report having an assigned mentor.

3. Including teachers with fixed-term contract for a period of more than one school year and teachers with fixed-term contract for a period of one school year or less.

4. Refers to question 16 of the teacher questionnaire where teachers were asked about the approximate number of hours they spent in total on teaching, planning lessons, marking, collaborating with other teachers, participating in staff meetings and on other tasks related to their job at their school during their most recent calendar week.

* See notes at the beginning of this Annex.

Source: OECD, TALIS 2013 Database.

StatLink 🔗 http://dx.doi.org/10.1787/888933044860

[Part 1/1]
Teachers serving as mentor, by work status, experience and gender
Percentage of lower secondary education teachers with the following characteristics
Table 4.5 *who report serving as a mentor for one or more teachers[1, 2]*

	Gender				Experience				Work status				Hours of work per week[4]			
	Male teachers		Female teachers		Teachers with 5 years teaching experience or less		Teachers with more than 5 years teaching experience		Permanent teachers		Fixed-term teachers[3]		Teachers working less than 30 hours per week		Teachers working 30 hours per week or more	
	%	S.E.	%	S.E.	%	S.E.	%	S.E.	%	S.E.	%	S.E.	%	S.E.	%	S.E.
Australia	27.6	(1.9)	28.2	(1.8)	9.8	(1.7)	32.3	(1.3)	30.4	(1.5)	10.9	(2.3)	25.9	(2.7)	28.6	(1.2)
Brazil	6.5	(0.7)	6.3	(0.6)	4.6	(0.7)	6.9	(0.5)	6.5	(0.5)	5.5	(0.7)	5.8	(0.5)	6.5	(0.6)
Bulgaria	7.0	(1.3)	11.0	(0.8)	4.8	(2.0)	10.8	(0.9)	11.4	(0.8)	2.0	(0.9)	10.9	(2.3)	10.1	(0.8)
Chile	7.1	(1.3)	6.3	(0.9)	6.2	(1.3)	7.3	(0.9)	8.3	(1.1)	3.6	(1.0)	7.7	(1.1)	6.2	(1.1)
Croatia	14.7	(1.3)	13.5	(0.8)	4.0	(0.8)	16.8	(1.0)	14.9	(0.8)	1.4	(0.6)	10.8	(1.2)	14.6	(0.8)
Cyprus*	4.5	(0.9)	5.6	(0.7)	3.1	(1.2)	5.1	(0.6)	4.6	(0.6)	7.1	(1.0)	4.5	(0.9)	5.5	(0.7)
Czech Republic	5.3	(1.0)	8.5	(0.8)	3.7	(0.9)	8.6	(0.8)	8.8	(0.8)	3.0	(0.8)	4.8	(1.1)	8.4	(0.7)
Denmark	13.9	(1.5)	11.9	(1.4)	7.4	(2.2)	13.8	(1.1)	13.1	(1.0)	5.3	(2.5)	13.3	(2.9)	12.8	(1.0)
Estonia	5.6	(1.4)	9.7	(0.9)	3.1	(1.4)	9.7	(0.9)	9.7	(0.9)	5.7	(1.2)	8.5	(0.9)	9.3	(1.0)
Finland	4.4	(1.1)	3.6	(0.5)	2.0	(0.7)	4.3	(0.6)	4.5	(0.7)	1.7	(0.5)	2.8	(0.9)	4.2	(0.6)
France	6.3	(0.9)	5.2	(0.5)	0.7	(0.5)	6.2	(0.5)	5.7	(0.5)	1.0	(0.8)	4.5	(0.9)	5.9	(0.5)
Iceland	12.4	(1.8)	12.3	(1.0)	4.1	(1.2)	14.5	(1.0)	13.6	(1.0)	5.5	(1.7)	13.8	(1.9)	12.0	(1.0)
Israel	22.2	(1.9)	23.7	(1.1)	9.1	(1.4)	27.4	(1.2)	26.4	(1.1)	12.6	(1.5)	21.3	(1.6)	25.0	(1.3)
Italy	3.5	(0.7)	5.5	(0.5)	0.8	(0.6)	5.5	(0.5)	6.1	(0.5)	1.0	(0.5)	4.5	(0.7)	5.6	(0.6)
Japan	19.3	(1.0)	12.1	(0.9)	3.8	(0.8)	19.9	(1.0)	19.0	(0.9)	6.8	(1.0)	11.3	(2.1)	17.2	(0.8)
Korea	40.8	(1.6)	31.2	(1.1)	13.3	(1.5)	39.4	(1.1)	36.4	(1.0)	23.3	(2.3)	37.8	(1.8)	33.0	(1.1)
Latvia	4.3	(1.4)	7.4	(0.7)	1.6	(1.1)	7.1	(0.7)	7.2	(0.7)	5.0	(2.2)	4.1	(1.0)	8.4	(0.9)
Malaysia	24.9	(1.7)	27.1	(1.4)	14.7	(1.8)	30.2	(1.3)	26.5	(1.2)	a	a	26.1	(2.2)	26.5	(1.3)
Mexico	12.1	(1.1)	9.8	(1.0)	5.7	(1.1)	12.9	(1.0)	10.8	(0.9)	11.8	(1.4)	9.0	(1.0)	12.1	(1.1)
Netherlands	19.6	(1.5)	19.2	(2.1)	7.5	(2.1)	22.5	(1.4)	21.3	(1.4)	9.4	(3.1)	12.6	(1.6)	21.6	(1.5)
Norway	7.8	(0.8)	7.6	(0.9)	3.2	(0.8)	9.2	(0.8)	8.6	(0.8)	1.7	(0.6)	8.5	(1.6)	7.5	(0.7)
Poland	10.1	(1.5)	16.5	(1.0)	0.4	(0.2)	16.6	(0.9)	16.6	(0.8)	5.1	(1.3)	8.2	(1.1)	17.2	(0.8)
Portugal	10.0	(1.0)	6.7	(0.5)	4.0	(2.2)	7.4	(0.5)	9.3	(0.6)	2.3	(0.6)	6.3	(1.3)	7.6	(0.5)
Romania	7.2	(1.0)	8.7	(1.0)	1.0	(0.6)	9.8	(0.9)	10.7	(1.0)	2.6	(0.7)	6.2	(1.2)	8.9	(0.9)
Serbia	15.9	(1.1)	12.2	(0.7)	1.5	(0.5)	15.6	(0.8)	16.2	(0.7)	1.3	(0.6)	12.0	(1.1)	14.2	(0.8)
Singapore	39.2	(1.4)	39.5	(1.3)	20.3	(1.3)	53.8	(1.2)	41.5	(1.0)	20.1	(2.3)	34.8	(1.9)	40.4	(1.0)
Slovak Republic	5.5	(0.9)	9.6	(0.6)	2.7	(0.9)	10.2	(0.6)	10.2	(0.6)	3.4	(1.1)	7.9	(0.9)	9.3	(0.6)
Spain	6.7	(0.7)	6.8	(0.7)	5.3	(1.6)	6.9	(0.5)	7.2	(0.6)	4.9	(1.0)	6.2	(1.1)	6.9	(0.6)
Sweden	4.6	(0.6)	6.0	(0.6)	2.8	(1.1)	6.0	(0.5)	5.9	(0.5)	1.8	(0.7)	4.1	(1.1)	5.7	(0.5)
Sub-national entities																
Abu Dhabi (United Arab Emirates)	30.8	(1.6)	28.1	(1.7)	18.0	(2.5)	31.1	(1.3)	34.3	(2.0)	24.3	(1.4)	28.2	(1.8)	29.3	(1.3)
Alberta (Canada)	19.9	(1.6)	21.2	(1.6)	8.6	(1.4)	25.2	(1.5)	24.6	(1.5)	4.8	(1.6)	21.7	(2.9)	20.5	(1.3)
England (United Kingdom)	33.2	(1.6)	30.3	(1.1)	16.9	(1.7)	36.6	(1.1)	33.0	(1.0)	7.7	(2.6)	26.5	(2.5)	32.3	(1.1)
Flanders (Belgium)	10.9	(1.5)	9.9	(1.0)	2.8	(0.9)	12.2	(1.2)	11.9	(1.2)	1.8	(0.6)	7.7	(1.3)	10.8	(1.1)
Average	14.0	(0.2)	14.0	(0.2)	6.0	(0.2)	16.4	(0.2)	15.6	(0.2)	6.4	(0.3)	12.7	(0.3)	14.7	(0.2)
United States	14.2	(1.8)	18.2	(1.5)	8.3	(1.5)	19.3	(1.6)	18.0	(1.5)	14.4	(2.1)	13.4	(2.3)	17.5	(1.4)

1. Cells with data representing less than 5% of the cases are shaded in grey and should be interpreted with caution. These results are not highlighted in the text of the report.

2. Percentages presented in this table reflect the proportion of teachers who report serving as a mentor based on different characteristics of the teachers. For example, 27.6% of male teachers in Australia report serving as a mentor for one or more teachers.

3. Including teachers with fixed-term contract for a period of more than one school year and teachers with fixed-term contract for a period of one school year or less.

4. Refers to question 16 of the teacher questionnaire where teachers were asked about the approximate number of hours they spent in total on teaching, planning lessons, marking, collaborating with other teachers, participating in staff meetings and on other tasks related to their job at their school during their most recent calendar week.

*See notes at the beginning of this Annex.

Source: OECD, TALIS 2013 Database.

StatLink ᴍᴤᴾ http://dx.doi.org/10.1787/888933044879

[Part 1/1]

Teachers' recent professional development and personal cost involved

Participation rates and reported personal financial cost of professional development activities undertaken by lower secondary education teachers in the 12 months prior to the survey

Table 4.6

	Percentage of teachers who undertook some professional development activities in the previous 12 months[1]		Percentage of teachers who undertook some professional development activities in the previous 12 months without any type of support[2]		Percentage of teachers who had to pay for none, some or all of the professional development activities undertaken					
					None		Some		All	
	%	S.E.	%	S.E.	%	S.E.	%	S.E.	%	S.E.
Australia	96.6	(0.5)	1.2	(0.4)	75.0	(1.5)	23.5	(1.3)	1.5	(0.4)
Brazil	91.5	(0.5)	14.7	(0.9)	58.4	(1.1)	21.8	(0.7)	19.8	(1.0)
Bulgaria	85.2	(1.1)	1.4	(0.3)	84.9	(1.2)	12.1	(1.0)	3.0	(0.5)
Chile	71.7	(1.8)	11.2	(1.1)	58.9	(1.8)	23.9	(1.6)	17.2	(1.5)
Croatia	96.8	(0.3)	1.3	(0.2)	73.3	(0.9)	22.9	(0.8)	3.8	(0.4)
Cyprus*	89.1	(0.7)	4.7	(0.7)	81.8	(1.2)	9.7	(0.9)	8.5	(0.9)
Czech Republic	82.5	(1.0)	2.3	(0.4)	77.2	(1.1)	17.5	(0.9)	5.4	(0.6)
Denmark	86.4	(1.1)	1.5	(0.3)	84.9	(1.2)	13.3	(1.1)	1.8	(0.5)
Estonia	93.0	(0.5)	0.4	(0.1)	69.1	(1.1)	29.0	(1.0)	1.9	(0.3)
Finland	79.3	(1.0)	4.1	(0.5)	72.6	(1.1)	21.6	(1.0)	5.8	(0.6)
France	76.4	(0.9)	2.7	(0.4)	75.8	(1.1)	18.8	(1.0)	5.4	(0.6)
Iceland	91.1	(0.8)	2.6	(0.6)	60.8	(1.4)	32.9	(1.4)	6.3	(0.8)
Israel	91.1	(0.6)	10.0	(0.7)	45.0	(1.3)	40.0	(1.2)	15.0	(0.7)
Italy	75.4	(0.9)	9.5	(0.8)	69.2	(1.2)	16.6	(0.9)	14.2	(0.9)
Japan	83.2	(0.8)	6.7	(0.6)	56.4	(1.4)	32.9	(1.2)	10.7	(0.8)
Korea	91.4	(0.6)	7.5	(0.6)	25.2	(1.1)	64.1	(1.3)	10.8	(0.8)
Latvia	96.1	(0.6)	2.1	(0.5)	71.1	(1.7)	24.7	(1.6)	4.3	(0.6)
Malaysia	96.6	(0.4)	0.3	(0.1)	46.8	(1.4)	49.7	(1.4)	3.5	(0.3)
Mexico	95.6	(0.4)	10.0	(0.8)	59.5	(1.2)	26.3	(1.1)	14.3	(0.9)
Netherlands	93.2	(0.6)	2.5	(0.6)	77.5	(1.1)	18.0	(0.9)	4.5	(0.6)
Norway	87.0	(0.9)	2.5	(0.4)	81.0	(1.2)	15.3	(1.0)	3.7	(0.4)
Poland	93.7	(0.7)	7.8	(0.6)	60.9	(1.2)	26.9	(1.1)	12.2	(0.8)
Portugal	88.5	(0.7)	28.6	(1.1)	42.8	(1.3)	24.4	(0.8)	32.8	(1.1)
Romania	83.3	(1.2)	20.9	(1.1)	30.7	(1.2)	41.0	(1.3)	28.3	(1.4)
Serbia	92.9	(0.5)	5.5	(0.6)	52.7	(1.4)	36.7	(1.1)	10.6	(1.0)
Singapore	98.0	(0.3)	0.2	(0.1)	89.7	(0.5)	9.5	(0.5)	0.8	(0.1)
Slovak Republic	73.3	(1.0)	6.8	(0.9)	54.3	(1.8)	31.6	(1.4)	14.0	(1.3)
Spain	84.3	(1.0)	10.5	(0.7)	57.0	(1.2)	30.9	(1.0)	12.1	(0.8)
Sweden	83.4	(1.0)	1.6	(0.3)	86.3	(0.7)	10.7	(0.6)	3.0	(0.4)
Sub-national entities										
Abu Dhabi (United Arab Emirates)	92.0	(1.3)	1.7	(0.3)	62.5	(1.8)	33.9	(1.8)	3.6	(0.5)
Alberta (Canada)	97.7	(0.4)	1.1	(0.2)	61.9	(1.5)	36.3	(1.5)	1.8	(0.4)
England (United Kingdom)	91.7	(0.7)	0.8	(0.3)	92.7	(0.7)	6.4	(0.6)	0.9	(0.3)
Flanders (Belgium)	88.2	(0.9)	2.4	(0.3)	86.8	(0.7)	9.7	(0.7)	3.5	(0.4)
Average	88.4	(0.1)	5.7	(0.1)	66.1	(0.2)	25.2	(0.2)	8.6	(0.1)
United States	95.2	(0.8)	1.7	(0.5)	74.1	(1.5)	22.8	(1.2)	3.2	(0.6)

1. Percentage of teachers who report having participated in at least one of the following professional development activities in the 12 months prior to the survey: "courses/workshops", "education conferences or seminars", "observation visits to other schools", "observation visits to business premises, public organisations or non-governmental organisations", "in-service training courses in business premises, public organisations or non-governmental organisations", "qualification programme (e.g. a degree programme)", "participation in a network of teachers formed specifically for the professional development of teachers", "individual or collaborative research", or "mentoring and/or peer observation and coaching".

2. Percentage of teachers participating in professional development activities without receiving financial support, time for activities that took place during the regular working hours at their school or non-monetary support for activites outside working hours.

* See notes at the beginning of this Annex.

Source: OECD, TALIS 2013 Database.

StatLink http://dx.doi.org/10.1787/888933044898

[Part 1/1]
Primary teachers' recent professional development and personal cost involved
Participation rates and reported personal financial cost of professional development activities undertaken
by primary education teachers in the 12 months prior to the survey

Table 4.6.a

| | Percentage of teachers who undertook some professional development activities in the previous 12 months[1] | | Percentage of teachers who had to pay for none, some or all of the professional development activities undertaken | | | | | |
| | | | None | | Some | | All | |
	%	S.E.	%	S.E.	%	S.E.	%	S.E.
Denmark	87.6	(1.0)	84.8	(1.0)	14.0	(0.9)	1.2	(0.3)
Finland	80.6	(1.0)	78.7	(1.3)	17.7	(1.3)	3.6	(0.6)
Mexico	96.9	(0.6)	66.9	(2.6)	23.6	(1.8)	9.5	(1.5)
Norway	89.1	(0.9)	85.7	(0.8)	11.0	(0.7)	3.3	(0.4)
Poland	95.0	(0.5)	59.7	(1.6)	29.2	(1.4)	11.1	(0.9)
Sub-national entities								
Flanders (Belgium)	88.9	(0.8)	88.8	(0.8)	8.3	(0.7)	2.9	(0.4)
Average	89.7	(0.3)	77.4	(0.6)	17.3	(0.5)	5.3	(0.3)

1. Percentage of teachers who report having participated in at least one of the following professional development activities in the 12 months prior to the survey: "courses/workshops", "education conferences or seminars", "observation visits to other schools", "observation visits to business premises, public organisations or non-governmental organisations", "in-service training courses in business premises, public organisations or non-governmental organisations", "qualification programme (e.g. a degree programme)", "participation in a network of teachers formed specifically for the professional development of teachers", "individual or collaborative research", or "mentoring and/or peer observation and coaching".
Source: OECD, TALIS 2013 Database.
StatLink http://dx.doi.org/10.1787/888933044917

[Part 1/1]
Upper secondary teachers' recent professional development and personal cost involved
Participation rates and reported personal financial cost of professional development activities undertaken
by upper secondary education teachers in the 12 months prior to the survey

Table 4.6.b

| | Percentage of teachers who undertook some professional development activities in the previous 12 months[1] | | Percentage of teachers who had to pay for none, some or all of the professional development activities undertaken | | | | | |
| | | | None | | Some | | All | |
	%	S.E.	%	S.E.	%	S.E.	%	S.E.
Australia	97.0	(0.5)	73.2	(1.3)	25.7	(1.2)	1.1	(0.3)
Denmark	94.1	(0.8)	85.7	(1.0)	12.6	(1.1)	1.7	(0.5)
Finland	84.1	(1.9)	67.5	(1.8)	28.7	(1.8)	3.8	(0.8)
Iceland	85.5	(1.1)	59.7	(1.7)	31.3	(1.6)	9.1	(1.1)
Italy	76.0	(1.1)	59.5	(1.2)	21.9	(1.0)	18.6	(0.9)
Mexico	94.0	(0.7)	58.9	(1.6)	27.4	(1.3)	13.7	(1.0)
Norway	91.4	(0.8)	76.1	(1.1)	20.2	(0.9)	3.7	(0.4)
Poland	93.3	(0.5)	59.6	(1.6)	29.1	(1.4)	11.3	(0.8)
Singapore	97.9	(0.3)	90.5	(0.5)	9.0	(0.5)	0.5	(0.1)
Sub-national entities								
Abu Dhabi (United Arab Emirates)	94.0	(0.8)	61.2	(1.7)	35.3	(1.7)	3.5	(0.5)
Average	90.7	(0.3)	69.2	(0.4)	24.1	(0.4)	6.7	(0.2)

1. Percentage of teachers who report having participated in at least one of the following professional development activities in the 12 months prior to the survey: "courses/workshops", "education conferences or seminars", "observation visits to other schools", "observation visits to business premises, public organisations or non-governmental organisations", "in-service training courses in business premises, public organisations or non-governmental organisations", "qualification programme (e.g. a degree programme)", "participation in a network of teachers formed specifically for the professional development of teachers", "individual or collaborative research", or "mentoring and/or peer observation and coaching".
Source: OECD, TALIS 2013 Database.
StatLink http://dx.doi.org/10.1787/888933044936

[Part 1/1]

Teachers' recent professional development and personal cost involved, 2008 and 2013

Participation rates and reported personal financial cost of professional development activities undertaken by lower secondary education teachers in the 12 months prior to the survey[1,2]

Table 4.6.c

	Percentage of teachers who undertook some professional development activities in the previous 12 months (or 18 months)[3]				Percentage of teachers who had to pay for none, some or all of the professional development activities undertaken												
					None				Some				All			
	2008		2013[4]		2008		2013		2008		2013		2008		2013	
	%	S.E.	%	S.E.	%	S.E.	%	S.E.	%	S.E.	%	S.E.	%	S.E.	%	S.E.
Australia	96.7	(0.2)	95.8	(0.5)	74.5	(1.2)	75.0	(1.5)	24.3	(1.2)	23.5	(1.3)	1.2	(0.3)	1.5	(0.4)
Brazil	83.0	(0.8)	89.5	(0.6)	54.8	(1.6)	58.3	(1.1)	26.9	(1.4)	22.0	(0.7)	18.3	(1.2)	19.7	(1.0)
Bulgaria	88.3	(2.0)	83.1	(1.2)	73.4	(2.1)	84.9	(1.2)	20.5	(2.2)	12.1	(1.0)	6.1	(0.7)	3.0	(0.5)
Denmark	75.6	(0.4)	86.1	(1.2)	77.3	(1.5)	85.1	(1.2)	16.3	(1.1)	13.2	(1.1)	6.4	(0.9)	1.8	(0.5)
Estonia	92.7	(0.3)	92.0	(0.5)	72.5	(1.0)	69.2	(1.1)	25.6	(0.9)	28.9	(1.0)	2.0	(0.3)	1.9	(0.3)
Iceland	77.1	(0.6)	90.7	(0.8)	67.8	(1.3)	61.3	(1.4)	27.8	(1.4)	32.7	(1.4)	4.5	(0.6)	6.0	(0.8)
Italy	84.6	(1.2)	74.9	(0.9)	68.7	(1.0)	69.2	(1.2)	13.7	(0.6)	16.6	(0.9)	17.6	(0.8)	14.2	(0.9)
Korea	91.9	(0.6)	91.2	(0.6)	27.1	(1.1)	25.2	(1.1)	58.5	(1.1)	64.1	(1.3)	14.4	(0.8)	10.7	(0.8)
Malaysia	91.7	(0.3)	96.0	(0.5)	43.5	(1.5)	46.9	(1.4)	52.7	(1.5)	49.6	(1.4)	3.9	(0.4)	3.5	(0.3)
Mexico	91.5	(1.8)	95.2	(0.5)	43.2	(1.3)	59.3	(1.2)	38.0	(1.1)	26.4	(1.1)	18.8	(1.1)	14.3	(0.9)
Norway	86.7	(0.3)	86.5	(0.9)	79.8	(1.1)	80.8	(1.3)	17.0	(1.0)	15.5	(1.1)	3.3	(0.4)	3.7	(0.4)
Poland	90.4	(1.2)	93.5	(0.7)	44.2	(1.3)	61.0	(1.2)	45.1	(1.1)	26.8	(1.1)	10.7	(0.9)	12.2	(0.8)
Portugal	85.8	(1.0)	84.8	(0.7)	50.3	(1.4)	42.9	(1.3)	25.2	(1.1)	24.4	(0.8)	24.5	(1.2)	32.7	(1.1)
Slovak Republic	75.0	(0.4)	72.9	(1.0)	70.4	(1.4)	54.4	(1.8)	24.1	(1.2)	31.6	(1.4)	5.5	(0.6)	14.0	(1.4)
Spain	100.0	(0.5)	83.7	(1.1)	54.8	(1.3)	57.0	(1.2)	29.6	(1.0)	31.0	(1.0)	15.6	(0.9)	12.1	(0.8)
Sub-national entities																
Flanders (Belgium)	90.3	(0.4)	87.2	(0.9)	81.4	(1.3)	87.0	(0.7)	15.3	(1.1)	9.6	(0.6)	3.2	(0.5)	3.5	(0.4)
Average	87.6	(0.2)	87.7	(0.2)	61.5	(0.3)	63.6	(0.3)	28.8	(0.3)	26.7	(0.3)	9.7	(0.2)	9.7	(0.2)

1. The teacher population coverage was slightly different between 2008 and 2013. In order to have comparable populations for the tables comparing results from 2008 and 2013, teachers who teach exclusively to students with special needs were excluded from the 2013 data in these tables.

2. The wording and order of questions may have changed slightly between the 2008 and 2013 surveys. In 2008, teachers were asked about their participation in professional development activities in the previous 18 months.

3. In 2008, teachers were asked about their participation in professional development activities in the 18 months prior to the survey. In 2013, teachers were asked the same question but for the 12 months prior to the survey.

4. To have comparable data between 2008 and 2013, questions 21d and 21e were excluded from the derived variable looking at the percentage of teachers who participated in at least one professional development activity in the 12 months prior to the 2013 survey. The professional development activities included in the derived variable for this table are: "courses/workshops", "education conferences or seminars", "observation visits to other schools", "qualification programme (e.g. a degree programme)", "participation in a network of teachers formed specifically for the professional development of teachers", "individual or collaborative research" and "mentoring and/or peer observation and coaching".

Source: OECD, TALIS 2008 and 2013 Databases.

StatLink ⟨⟩ http://dx.doi.org/10.1787/888933044955

[Part 1/1]

Teachers' recent professional development, by work status, experience and gender
Percentage of lower secondary education teachers with the following characteristics who participated
Table 4.7 *in professional development activities in the 12 months prior to the survey[1, 2]*

	Gender				Experience				Work status				Hours of work per week[4]			
	Male teachers		Female teachers		Teachers with 5 years teaching experience or less		Teachers with more than 5 years teaching experience		Permanent teachers		Fixed-term teachers[3]		Teachers working less than 30 hours per week		Teachers working 30 hours per week or more	
	%	S.E.	%	S.E.	%	S.E.	%	S.E.	%	S.E.	%	S.E.	%	S.E.	%	S.E.
Australia	96.0	(0.7)	97.1	(0.5)	97.0	(1.0)	96.5	(0.6)	96.9	(0.5)	95.3	(1.6)	94.6	(1.2)	97.1	(0.4)
Brazil	90.6	(0.9)	91.9	(0.6)	90.8	(1.1)	91.7	(0.6)	91.4	(0.6)	92.1	(0.9)	90.9	(0.8)	91.9	(0.5)
Bulgaria	82.0	(1.8)	85.9	(1.1)	77.7	(4.6)	86.1	(1.1)	86.4	(1.0)	77.7	(3.1)	81.6	(2.0)	86.0	(1.2)
Chile	69.1	(2.5)	73.2	(2.0)	73.3	(2.8)	71.6	(2.1)	70.5	(1.9)	73.9	(2.5)	70.9	(2.5)	74.5	(2.1)
Croatia	95.7	(0.8)	97.1	(0.3)	97.4	(0.6)	96.6	(0.5)	97.1	(0.3)	93.0	(1.8)	94.6	(1.1)	97.3	(0.3)
Cyprus*	87.5	(1.7)	89.9	(0.9)	88.3	(2.0)	89.4	(0.9)	90.1	(0.9)	87.0	(1.4)	87.3	(1.4)	90.3	(0.8)
Czech Republic	80.2	(1.6)	83.2	(1.1)	83.3	(1.8)	82.3	(1.1)	84.1	(1.1)	74.6	(2.1)	71.9	(2.4)	84.8	(1.1)
Denmark	85.7	(1.6)	86.9	(1.2)	81.7	(2.5)	87.3	(1.2)	87.5	(1.2)	63.2	(5.4)	76.4	(3.7)	87.4	(1.2)
Estonia	87.7	(1.7)	94.0	(0.5)	92.2	(1.6)	93.2	(0.5)	93.6	(0.5)	90.0	(1.5)	88.8	(1.1)	94.8	(0.5)
Finland	74.7	(2.1)	81.0	(1.1)	75.0	(2.1)	80.3	(1.1)	80.7	(1.1)	74.5	(1.9)	75.1	(2.1)	80.9	(1.1)
France	77.4	(1.5)	75.8	(1.0)	78.0	(2.2)	76.2	(1.0)	76.5	(0.9)	74.2	(3.4)	72.1	(2.3)	77.5	(1.0)
Iceland	89.8	(1.7)	91.6	(0.9)	80.0	(2.7)	93.4	(0.8)	93.3	(0.8)	78.5	(2.8)	88.1	(1.8)	92.1	(0.9)
Israel	88.5	(1.2)	91.9	(0.8)	91.0	(1.2)	91.2	(0.7)	91.4	(0.7)	90.4	(1.3)	90.3	(0.9)	91.8	(0.7)
Italy	68.7	(1.9)	77.2	(1.0)	72.1	(3.0)	75.7	(1.0)	76.9	(1.0)	69.0	(2.5)	71.0	(1.4)	78.8	(1.1)
Japan	82.0	(0.9)	85.0	(1.2)	80.1	(1.7)	84.2	(0.7)	85.0	(0.8)	75.4	(2.3)	69.2	(2.6)	84.8	(0.7)
Korea	91.6	(1.1)	91.3	(0.7)	84.1	(1.7)	93.3	(0.5)	93.0	(0.6)	83.7	(2.0)	88.1	(1.4)	92.6	(0.6)
Latvia	94.5	(1.2)	96.3	(0.6)	89.1	(3.2)	96.6	(0.6)	95.9	(0.6)	98.1	(1.0)	93.3	(1.1)	97.4	(0.6)
Malaysia	95.0	(0.9)	97.2	(0.5)	96.7	(0.8)	96.5	(0.5)	96.6	(0.5)	100.0	(0.0)	94.6	(1.0)	97.0	(0.5)
Mexico	95.2	(0.6)	96.0	(0.5)	94.8	(1.3)	96.2	(0.5)	95.5	(0.5)	95.9	(0.9)	94.7	(0.8)	96.3	(0.5)
Netherlands	93.7	(1.0)	92.8	(0.7)	92.7	(1.7)	93.2	(0.8)	93.9	(0.7)	89.4	(2.2)	87.5	(1.2)	95.2	(0.7)
Norway	87.1	(1.7)	87.0	(0.9)	90.2	(1.5)	86.3	(1.2)	87.5	(1.0)	83.6	(2.5)	79.2	(2.4)	88.9	(0.9)
Poland	91.8	(1.3)	94.3	(0.7)	93.7	(1.3)	93.6	(0.7)	93.8	(0.7)	92.9	(1.5)	91.5	(1.9)	94.4	(0.6)
Portugal	86.8	(1.3)	89.2	(0.7)	89.0	(3.6)	88.5	(0.6)	88.9	(0.8)	87.4	(1.2)	87.5	(2.2)	88.6	(0.7)
Romania	79.6	(2.0)	84.9	(1.3)	77.7	(2.4)	84.5	(1.2)	87.4	(1.2)	73.7	(2.0)	74.8	(2.6)	86.5	(1.2)
Serbia	91.3	(1.0)	93.7	(0.6)	90.6	(1.4)	93.4	(0.6)	94.2	(0.5)	86.6	(1.5)	89.0	(1.1)	94.6	(0.5)
Singapore	97.9	(0.5)	98.1	(0.3)	98.4	(0.4)	97.8	(0.4)	98.6	(0.2)	92.4	(1.5)	95.0	(0.9)	98.6	(0.2)
Slovak Republic	66.4	(2.3)	74.8	(1.0)	70.8	(2.2)	73.8	(1.1)	75.9	(1.1)	62.6	(2.3)	66.7	(2.0)	75.5	(1.2)
Spain	82.2	(1.9)	85.7	(1.0)	88.8	(5.8)	83.9	(0.9)	83.9	(1.2)	85.5	(1.8)	80.5	(3.8)	85.0	(0.9)
Sweden	82.2	(1.5)	84.1	(1.2)	82.3	(2.5)	83.7	(1.1)	84.0	(1.1)	78.9	(2.8)	74.3	(2.8)	84.5	(1.0)
Sub-national entities																
Abu Dhabi (United Arab Emirates)	95.0	(0.9)	89.9	(2.0)	80.9	(2.9)	94.3	(1.2)	91.6	(1.8)	92.3	(1.5)	91.4	(1.7)	92.0	(1.6)
Alberta (Canada)	97.8	(0.6)	97.7	(0.6)	96.6	(1.1)	98.1	(0.4)	98.1	(0.4)	96.1	(1.5)	95.8	(1.7)	98.0	(0.4)
England (United Kingdom)	91.7	(1.3)	91.8	(0.7)	91.9	(1.6)	91.7	(0.7)	91.7	(0.8)	92.4	(2.1)	88.6	(1.7)	92.2	(0.8)
Flanders (Belgium)	88.1	(1.2)	88.2	(1.0)	88.4	(1.8)	88.4	(0.8)	87.9	(0.9)	89.8	(1.7)	83.6	(2.0)	89.4	(0.9)
Average	86.8	(0.3)	88.9	(0.2)	86.5	(0.4)	88.8	(0.2)	89.1	(0.2)	84.6	(0.4)	84.2	(0.3)	89.6	(0.2)
United States	96.0	(1.4)	94.8	(0.9)	97.8	(0.6)	94.5	(1.0)	94.0	(1.0)	97.8	(0.8)	95.7	(1.3)	95.1	(0.8)

1. Cells with data representing less than 5% of the cases are shaded in grey and should be interpreted with caution. These results are not highlighted in the text of the report.

2. Percentages presented in this table reflect the proportion of teachers who reported having participated in professional development activities in the 12 months prior to the survey based on different characteristics of the teachers. For example, 96% of male teachers in Australia reported participating in professional development activities in the 12 months prior to the survey. Professional development activities could be one of the following: "courses/workshops", "education conferences or seminars", "observation visits to other schools", "observation visits to business premises, public organisations or non-governmental organisations", "in-service training courses in business premises, public organisations or non-governmental organisations", "qualification programme (e.g. a degree programme)", "participation in a network of teachers formed specifically for the professional development of teachers", "individual or collaborative research", or "mentoring and/or peer observation and coaching".

3. Including teachers with fixed-term contract for a period of more than one school year and teachers with fixed-term contract for a period of one school year or less.

4. Refers to question 16 of the teacher questionnaire where teachers were asked about the approximate number of hours they spent in total on teaching, planning lessons, marking, collaborating with other teachers, participating in staff meetings and other tasks related to their job at their school during their most recent calendar week.

* See notes at the beginning of this Annex.

Source: OECD, TALIS 2013 Database.

StatLink ᵃˢᵖ http://dx.doi.org/10.1787/888933044974

[Part 1/1]
Teachers' recent professional development by school type and location

Table 4.8

Percentage of lower secondary education teachers who work in schools with the following characteristics and who participated in professional development in the 12 months prior to the survey[1, 2]

	School type				School location					
	Teachers working in public schools[3]		Teachers working in private schools[4]		Teachers working in schools located in areas with 15 000 people or less		Teachers working in schools located in areas with 15 001 to 100 000 people		Teachers working in schools located in areas with more than 100 000 people	
	%	S.E.	%	S.E.	%	S.E.	%	S.E.	%	S.E.
Australia	96.7	(0.8)	96.5	(0.7)	97.0	(1.2)	97.9	(1.0)	96.2	(0.7)
Brazil	91.0	(0.5)	94.3	(1.2)	93.4	(0.8)	92.5	(0.8)	89.1	(0.8)
Bulgaria	85.3	(1.1)	66.4	(18.4)	83.0	(1.9)	87.8	(1.6)	86.3	(1.8)
Chile	72.0	(3.1)	71.7	(2.3)	63.3	(4.4)	75.4	(3.8)	75.4	(2.5)
Croatia	96.9	(0.3)	90.7	(2.7)	96.7	(0.4)	96.1	(0.8)	97.8	(0.7)
Cyprus*	89.7	(0.9)	86.8	(1.3)	88.5	(1.2)	92.0	(1.3)	88.6	(1.4)
Czech Republic	82.3	(1.1)	85.6	(2.0)	83.9	(1.3)	79.4	(2.1)	82.8	(2.8)
Denmark	87.5	(1.2)	82.7	(3.0)	85.1	(1.8)	87.5	(2.4)	88.2	(3.1)
Estonia	92.8	(0.5)	98.5	(0.9)	91.8	(0.7)	93.0	(1.7)	95.8	(0.6)
Finland	79.4	(1.0)	77.6	(6.8)	79.8	(1.5)	74.9	(2.1)	82.0	(2.1)
France	78.6	(1.1)	69.2	(2.4)	77.1	(1.3)	76.8	(1.9)	75.3	(3.2)
Iceland	90.9	(0.8)	93.5	(6.5)	90.3	(1.0)	90.1	(1.8)	96.0	(1.4)
Israel	91.6	(0.7)	87.0	(2.7)	90.4	(1.0)	90.7	(0.9)	92.8	(1.5)
Italy	75.1	(0.9)	81.0	(4.1)	77.4	(1.4)	74.0	(1.6)	73.3	(2.3)
Japan	84.9	(0.8)	67.6	(2.6)	88.2	(2.5)	83.8	(1.5)	82.3	(1.0)
Korea	91.8	(0.7)	90.3	(1.6)	93.1	(2.0)	91.1	(4.5)	91.2	(0.6)
Latvia	96.3	(0.6)	95.3	(2.8)	96.5	(0.8)	96.2	(1.2)	95.7	(1.1)
Malaysia	96.5	(0.5)	a	a	96.3	(0.7)	96.4	(0.8)	97.3	(0.7)
Mexico	95.5	(0.5)	96.1	(1.2)	96.9	(0.6)	96.1	(1.0)	94.8	(0.6)
Netherlands	92.6	(1.1)	93.0	(0.7)	92.9	(1.7)	92.9	(0.8)	93.0	(1.3)
Norway	88.0	(1.0)	86.3	(6.9)	87.9	(1.3)	86.2	(1.9)	91.2	(1.9)
Poland	93.6	(0.7)	94.5	(1.7)	92.5	(1.2)	94.7	(1.2)	95.1	(0.8)
Portugal	88.0	(0.7)	92.2	(1.8)	87.3	(0.9)	88.7	(1.1)	92.7	(1.1)
Romania	83.3	(1.2)	a	a	80.1	(1.8)	86.8	(1.7)	89.6	(1.4)
Serbia	92.9	(0.5)	a	a	92.4	(0.8)	92.7	(1.2)	94.0	(0.8)
Singapore	98.2	(0.3)	a	a	a	a	a	a	98.2	(0.3)
Slovak Republic	72.6	(1.2)	78.4	(2.4)	71.7	(1.6)	74.4	(1.7)	76.4	(1.7)
Spain	82.9	(1.1)	87.8	(3.0)	85.0	(1.4)	82.7	(2.6)	84.9	(1.5)
Sweden	84.7	(1.2)	76.6	(2.9)	82.7	(2.2)	85.4	(1.5)	81.8	(2.1)
Sub-national entities										
Abu Dhabi (United Arab Emirates)	97.3	(0.9)	90.6	(1.9)	94.4	(2.3)	94.7	(1.5)	93.0	(1.7)
Alberta (Canada)	97.9	(0.4)	92.7	(3.8)	98.3	(0.6)	97.7	(0.9)	97.1	(0.7)
England (United Kingdom)	92.6	(0.9)	90.9	(1.2)	91.5	(1.9)	91.2	(1.0)	92.6	(1.2)
Flanders (Belgium)	88.9	(1.1)	88.4	(1.0)	88.5	(1.2)	88.9	(1.0)	87.2	(2.0)
Average	88.7	(0.2)	86.3	(0.8)	87.9	(0.3)	88.4	(0.3)	89.3	(0.3)
United States	95.4	(0.7)	91.9	(4.0)	93.8	(1.4)	96.4	(0.9)	95.5	(1.3)

1. Cells with data representing less than 5% of the cases are shaded in grey and should be interpreted with caution. These results are not highlighted in the text of the report.

2. Percentages presented in this table reflect the proportion of teachers who reported participating in professional development activities in the 12 months prior to the survey based school characteristics where teachers work. For example, 96.7% of teachers working in public schools in Australia reported having participated in professional development activities in the 12 months prior to the survey. Professional development activities could be one of the following: "courses/workshops", "education conferences or seminars", "observation visits to other schools", "observation visits to business premises, public organisations or non-governmental organisations", "in-service training courses in business premises, public organisations or non-governmental organisations", "qualification programme (e.g. a degree programme)", "participation in a network of teachers formed specifically for the professional development of teachers", "individual or collaborative research", or "mentoring and/or peer observation and coaching".

3. Public schools refer to the percentage of teachers in lower secondary education who work in schools where principal reports that their school is publically managed. This is a school managed by a public education authority, government agency, municipality, or governing board appointed by government or elected by public franchise.

4. Private schools refer to the percentage of teachers in lower secondary education who work in schools where principal reports that their school is privately managed. This is a school managed by a non-government organisation; e.g. a church, trade union, business or other private institution.

* See notes at the beginning of this Annex.

Source: OECD, TALIS 2013 Database.

StatLink http://dx.doi.org/10.1787/888933044993

[Part 1/1]

Type of professional development recently undertaken by teachers

Participation rates for each type of professional development reported to be undertaken by lower secondary education teachers in the 12 months prior to the survey

Table 4.9

	Courses/ workshops		Education conferences or seminars where teachers and/or researchers present their research results and discuss educational issues		Observation visits to other schools		Observation visits to business premises, public organisations, non-governmental organisations		In-service training courses in business premises, public organisations, non-governmental organisations		Qualification programme (e.g. a degree programme)		Participation in a network of teachers formed specifically for the professional development of teachers		Individual or collaborative research on a topic of interest to the teacher		Mentoring and/or peer observation and coaching, as part of a formal school arrangement	
	%	S.E.	%	S.E.	%	S.E.	%	S.E.	%	S.E.	%	S.E.	%	S.E.	%	S.E.	%	S.E.
Australia	85.7	(0.9)	56.3	(1.6)	14.7	(1.0)	13.6	(0.9)	24.4	(1.8)	10.0	(0.7)	51.5	(1.6)	37.4	(1.4)	44.4	(1.8)
Brazil	65.8	(0.9)	38.9	(0.9)	12.2	(0.7)	16.5	(0.7)	37.7	(1.0)	36.5	(0.9)	25.6	(0.8)	46.5	(0.8)	34.9	(1.0)
Bulgaria	60.3	(1.6)	39.8	(1.2)	15.2	(1.2)	7.3	(0.7)	23.8	(0.9)	49.0	(1.7)	21.6	(1.1)	22.6	(1.2)	30.9	(1.4)
Chile	55.3	(1.9)	29.8	(1.5)	9.0	(1.0)	9.4	(0.9)	8.1	(0.8)	16.7	(1.1)	21.7	(1.4)	32.8	(1.3)	14.1	(1.1)
Croatia	79.1	(0.9)	79.4	(0.8)	6.7	(0.5)	6.1	(0.5)	6.6	(0.4)	6.5	(0.4)	62.6	(0.9)	35.0	(0.8)	19.7	(0.8)
Cyprus*	60.6	(1.2)	63.0	(1.3)	18.3	(0.9)	11.4	(0.8)	13.2	(0.9)	8.7	(0.7)	24.7	(1.1)	24.5	(1.0)	18.7	(0.9)
Czech Republic	69.7	(1.5)	22.4	(1.0)	13.9	(0.9)	18.3	(0.8)	14.4	(0.7)	17.6	(0.8)	17.4	(0.9)	15.8	(0.7)	34.3	(1.5)
Denmark	72.9	(1.7)	36.4	(1.3)	5.7	(0.8)	12.4	(1.1)	5.3	(0.6)	10.2	(0.9)	40.8	(1.9)	19.0	(1.2)	18.3	(1.5)
Estonia	82.0	(1.0)	51.3	(1.2)	31.5	(1.3)	15.8	(0.8)	22.8	(1.0)	19.1	(0.8)	51.3	(0.9)	34.0	(1.1)	21.8	(1.4)
Finland	60.1	(1.3)	35.5	(1.2)	20.0	(1.1)	15.9	(1.1)	8.8	(0.7)	11.3	(0.7)	20.5	(1.0)	7.6	(0.6)	5.1	(0.7)
France	53.7	(1.2)	19.8	(0.9)	9.2	(0.7)	5.3	(0.5)	2.7	(0.3)	5.5	(0.5)	18.3	(0.8)	41.2	(1.0)	13.4	(0.6)
Iceland	70.0	(1.3)	58.2	(1.4)	52.1	(1.3)	15.1	(1.2)	9.3	(0.9)	10.6	(0.9)	56.6	(1.3)	20.7	(1.2)	15.2	(1.0)
Israel	76.3	(1.0)	45.0	(1.1)	14.3	(1.1)	7.2	(0.5)	5.4	(0.6)	26.4	(1.2)	40.3	(1.1)	26.0	(1.0)	32.4	(1.1)
Italy	50.9	(1.4)	31.3	(1.0)	12.5	(0.7)	5.2	(0.5)	3.4	(0.3)	9.8	(0.6)	21.8	(0.9)	45.6	(1.2)	12.3	(0.7)
Japan	59.8	(1.0)	56.5	(1.1)	51.4	(1.3)	6.5	(0.5)	4.6	(0.4)	6.2	(0.5)	23.1	(1.0)	22.6	(1.0)	29.8	(1.1)
Korea	78.1	(0.9)	45.3	(1.2)	31.9	(1.3)	10.2	(0.6)	13.9	(0.7)	18.9	(0.8)	54.6	(1.1)	43.2	(1.2)	52.8	(1.2)
Latvia	88.8	(1.1)	60.1	(1.5)	52.4	(1.6)	20.6	(1.1)	9.3	(0.9)	12.7	(1.3)	36.6	(1.5)	28.6	(1.1)	17.4	(1.3)
Malaysia	91.3	(0.7)	32.9	(1.3)	19.9	(1.4)	19.2	(1.1)	23.7	(0.9)	10.1	(0.7)	55.6	(1.2)	24.9	(1.1)	34.9	(1.2)
Mexico	90.3	(0.7)	38.6	(1.2)	10.7	(0.7)	11.7	(0.7)	19.1	(0.9)	42.7	(1.2)	41.1	(1.2)	48.9	(1.1)	21.4	(1.0)
Netherlands	78.4	(1.2)	45.7	(1.7)	15.8	(1.2)	20.1	(1.3)	23.4	(1.2)	20.0	(1.1)	30.3	(1.3)	38.3	(1.5)	33.6	(2.0)
Norway	64.2	(1.4)	40.0	(2.5)	7.5	(1.0)	8.2	(1.3)	3.9	(0.4)	17.9	(1.2)	37.8	(1.7)	15.1	(1.0)	32.4	(1.9)
Poland	81.0	(1.0)	52.4	(1.2)	11.7	(0.9)	9.0	(0.7)	16.3	(0.8)	30.6	(1.0)	40.6	(1.3)	37.8	(1.3)	44.7	(1.2)
Portugal	66.5	(1.1)	40.4	(1.2)	16.7	(0.8)	39.1	(1.1)	12.8	(0.6)	28.6	(1.0)	19.1	(0.8)	36.6	(0.9)	12.9	(0.7)
Romania	51.9	(1.4)	28.6	(1.3)	33.3	(1.2)	12.4	(0.8)	16.3	(1.0)	37.5	(1.1)	50.4	(1.3)	39.2	(1.2)	39.3	(1.5)
Serbia	69.9	(1.1)	60.4	(1.2)	14.6	(0.8)	12.4	(0.7)	11.1	(0.6)	7.6	(0.6)	33.1	(0.9)	31.9	(0.9)	28.2	(1.0)
Singapore	92.9	(0.5)	61.4	(1.0)	24.1	(0.8)	20.8	(0.8)	16.5	(0.7)	10.1	(0.5)	52.7	(1.0)	45.4	(0.9)	65.2	(1.0)
Slovak Republic	38.5	(1.2)	25.0	(0.9)	4.1	(0.4)	2.1	(0.3)	4.0	(0.4)	23.2	(0.9)	34.3	(1.4)	11.2	(0.6)	40.4	(1.3)
Spain	66.6	(1.4)	24.4	(0.9)	9.1	(0.5)	8.4	(0.5)	7.6	(0.5)	21.2	(0.8)	28.3	(1.0)	41.5	(1.1)	21.3	(0.9)
Sweden	58.1	(1.3)	45.1	(1.3)	13.5	(0.9)	9.5	(0.9)	7.4	(0.7)	10.4	(0.8)	41.5	(1.7)	9.6	(0.6)	17.5	(1.3)
Sub-national entities																		
Abu Dhabi (United Arab Emirates)	81.6	(2.2)	49.8	(1.4)	28.1	(1.7)	28.8	(1.5)	31.7	(1.4)	16.8	(1.2)	44.6	(1.7)	48.9	(1.9)	60.5	(2.2)
Alberta (Canada)	84.9	(1.0)	73.6	(1.3)	19.8	(1.5)	8.1	(0.7)	21.4	(1.0)	10.8	(0.9)	62.9	(1.5)	48.9	(1.6)	35.0	(1.5)
England (United Kingdom)	75.0	(1.3)	29.4	(1.2)	19.5	(1.1)	5.6	(0.6)	22.4	(1.1)	10.0	(0.9)	33.3	(1.2)	26.6	(1.1)	57.0	(1.2)
Flanders (Belgium)	78.8	(1.2)	23.0	(1.0)	8.2	(0.9)	9.2	(0.7)	11.3	(0.6)	16.5	(0.8)	23.4	(1.0)	18.8	(0.8)	12.7	(0.8)
Average	70.9	(0.2)	43.6	(0.2)	19.0	(0.2)	12.8	(0.1)	14.0	(0.1)	17.9	(0.2)	36.9	(0.2)	31.1	(0.2)	29.5	(0.2)
United States	84.2	(1.4)	48.8	(2.2)	13.3	(1.2)	7.0	(0.7)	15.4	(1.1)	16.4	(1.2)	47.4	(1.8)	41.1	(1.6)	32.5	(1.8)

* See notes at the beginning of this Annex.

Source: OECD, TALIS 2013 Database.

StatLink ᴍᴘᴧ http://dx.doi.org/10.1787/888933045012

[Part 1/3]
Content and positive impact of professional development activities
*Percentage of lower secondary education teachers who report having participated
in professional development with the following content in the 12 months prior to the survey
and who report a "moderate" or "large" positive impact of this professional development on their teaching[1]*

Table 4.10

	Knowledge and understanding of subject field(s)				Pedagogical competencies in teaching subject field(s)				Knowledge of the curriculum				Student evaluation and assessment practices				ICT skills for teaching			
	Percentage of teachers		Moderate or large positive impact		Percentage of teachers		Moderate or large positive impact		Percentage of teachers		Moderate or large positive impact		Percentage of teachers		Moderate or large positive impact		Percentage of teachers		Moderate or large positive impact	
	%	S.E.	%	S.E.	%	S.E.	%	S.E.	%	S.E.	%	S.E.	%	S.E.	%	S.E.	%	S.E.	%	S.E.
Australia	77.9	(1.3)	84.2	(1.0)	65.5	(1.2)	75.0	(1.6)	71.7	(1.7)	77.6	(1.1)	58.6	(1.3)	71.9	(2.0)	71.7	(1.7)	70.5	(1.8)
Brazil	86.3	(0.8)	92.0	(0.6)	81.1	(0.8)	89.2	(0.6)	68.4	(0.9)	86.6	(0.8)	73.1	(0.9)	86.4	(0.6)	45.7	(1.0)	78.8	(1.0)
Bulgaria	60.1	(1.5)	92.4	(1.1)	62.7	(1.5)	89.2	(1.2)	46.4	(1.8)	92.7	(1.0)	47.4	(1.6)	87.8	(1.4)	55.6	(1.8)	84.6	(1.5)
Chile	67.9	(1.6)	94.5	(1.0)	65.5	(1.4)	91.6	(1.2)	54.8	(1.8)	86.4	(1.6)	52.5	(2.3)	86.8	(1.5)	51.4	(2.2)	86.9	(1.7)
Croatia	86.6	(0.6)	85.3	(0.8)	82.1	(0.7)	81.8	(0.9)	68.4	(1.0)	81.1	(1.1)	81.6	(0.8)	85.0	(0.8)	58.2	(1.5)	73.3	(1.1)
Cyprus*	78.3	(1.2)	89.7	(1.2)	73.4	(1.3)	87.2	(1.4)	76.6	(1.3)	92.0	(1.1)	60.8	(1.6)	84.6	(1.5)	53.8	(1.6)	81.1	(1.9)
Czech Republic	65.1	(1.3)	88.5	(0.8)	50.7	(1.2)	85.4	(1.1)	20.3	(1.0)	77.7	(2.3)	29.3	(1.1)	79.2	(1.9)	53.4	(1.6)	82.8	(1.3)
Denmark	62.0	(1.9)	89.7	(1.0)	60.8	(1.7)	86.5	(1.4)	24.8	(1.4)	80.0	(2.1)	31.8	(1.5)	78.8	(2.3)	48.7	(1.9)	81.0	(1.6)
Estonia	79.8	(0.9)	93.4	(0.6)	69.4	(1.0)	87.9	(1.0)	79.6	(1.0)	85.3	(0.8)	71.1	(1.1)	83.4	(1.2)	63.3	(1.3)	83.7	(1.1)
Finland	78.1	(0.9)	81.9	(1.2)	56.5	(1.3)	74.4	(1.2)	31.3	(1.4)	58.9	(2.5)	28.8	(1.2)	62.4	(2.5)	47.6	(1.9)	67.7	(1.9)
France	51.3	(1.4)	86.6	(1.0)	62.7	(1.3)	83.2	(1.0)	45.7	(1.3)	81.7	(1.4)	50.7	(1.5)	77.7	(1.4)	39.8	(1.4)	77.0	(1.7)
Iceland	58.5	(1.6)	94.6	(0.9)	52.4	(1.4)	93.0	(1.4)	73.8	(1.4)	77.1	(1.6)	61.7	(1.6)	79.9	(1.6)	43.9	(1.4)	78.4	(1.9)
Israel	80.2	(1.1)	90.9	(0.7)	74.0	(0.9)	86.1	(0.9)	66.8	(1.2)	86.8	(0.9)	55.8	(1.1)	83.4	(1.3)	60.2	(1.6)	78.8	(1.5)
Italy	62.6	(1.2)	90.2	(0.8)	60.3	(1.2)	88.9	(0.8)	37.2	(1.3)	84.1	(1.5)	42.0	(1.2)	84.9	(1.4)	53.2	(1.3)	82.2	(1.4)
Japan	88.3	(0.7)	90.0	(0.7)	86.4	(0.8)	89.3	(0.8)	47.4	(1.4)	73.0	(1.6)	59.0	(1.3)	76.8	(1.2)	36.0	(1.4)	69.1	(1.9)
Korea	80.8	(0.7)	95.6	(0.5)	81.0	(0.9)	95.4	(0.5)	73.3	(1.0)	93.6	(0.6)	48.9	(1.0)	93.4	(0.8)	54.1	(1.3)	90.3	(0.8)
Latvia	86.4	(1.1)	94.8	(0.7)	83.8	(0.8)	91.5	(0.9)	61.4	(1.4)	86.1	(1.1)	68.5	(1.3)	87.3	(1.3)	72.1	(1.5)	86.9	(1.2)
Malaysia	93.8	(0.6)	97.3	(0.4)	83.5	(0.9)	94.5	(0.5)	90.3	(0.6)	95.2	(0.4)	91.2	(0.6)	93.8	(0.5)	70.8	(1.3)	87.7	(0.8)
Mexico	88.3	(0.7)	95.0	(0.5)	88.8	(0.8)	93.1	(0.7)	89.7	(0.7)	91.0	(0.7)	80.6	(1.0)	88.1	(0.8)	72.6	(1.0)	83.7	(1.0)
Netherlands	69.0	(2.0)	89.5	(1.2)	62.2	(1.6)	82.6	(1.3)	42.5	(1.6)	81.1	(1.9)	37.5	(1.4)	76.1	(1.8)	48.1	(1.9)	72.8	(1.9)
Norway	66.2	(1.9)	92.6	(0.8)	57.6	(2.1)	90.4	(1.1)	37.3	(2.5)	80.4	(2.4)	65.0	(2.5)	86.2	(1.7)	32.8	(2.1)	78.3	(2.3)
Poland	66.0	(1.3)	90.8	(0.7)	61.5	(1.1)	88.5	(0.9)	56.6	(1.4)	87.2	(1.1)	57.6	(1.2)	85.3	(0.9)	51.5	(1.5)	84.9	(1.1)
Portugal	68.6	(0.8)	95.0	(0.5)	64.4	(1.0)	92.5	(0.7)	42.6	(0.9)	91.4	(0.9)	33.2	(1.2)	88.1	(1.1)	49.1	(1.6)	91.8	(0.9)
Romania	75.0	(1.1)	95.9	(0.4)	77.7	(0.9)	94.3	(0.7)	67.1	(1.2)	92.6	(0.9)	66.0	(1.2)	93.2	(0.9)	60.5	(1.4)	91.1	(1.0)
Serbia	71.2	(1.1)	91.1	(0.7)	66.3	(1.1)	88.5	(0.8)	33.1	(1.0)	80.9	(1.5)	72.0	(1.1)	85.9	(0.9)	46.2	(1.2)	84.4	(1.2)
Singapore	88.4	(0.7)	89.0	(0.6)	85.8	(0.6)	86.8	(0.7)	79.8	(0.8)	86.8	(0.7)	69.6	(0.8)	84.5	(0.8)	67.9	(0.8)	72.6	(1.0)
Slovak Republic	59.9	(1.3)	95.7	(0.6)	58.2	(1.3)	93.7	(0.7)	36.3	(1.4)	88.3	(1.0)	38.1	(1.2)	88.5	(1.2)	60.4	(1.3)	91.6	(0.8)
Spain	52.6	(1.1)	91.8	(0.8)	58.1	(1.1)	87.2	(0.8)	33.3	(1.3)	84.8	(1.3)	30.8	(1.5)	82.8	(1.7)	68.2	(1.6)	86.5	(0.9)
Sweden	58.6	(1.4)	84.4	(1.2)	45.4	(1.1)	77.8	(1.3)	70.5	(1.2)	80.3	(1.1)	64.0	(1.5)	75.0	(1.2)	46.8	(1.6)	66.4	(1.9)
Sub-national entities																				
Abu Dhabi (United Arab Emirates)	77.3	(1.2)	94.3	(0.9)	78.1	(1.3)	92.0	(1.0)	70.4	(1.6)	93.3	(0.8)	83.2	(1.5)	92.3	(0.8)	76.5	(1.4)	89.5	(1.0)
Alberta (Canada)	83.2	(1.1)	82.3	(1.2)	67.3	(1.3)	73.9	(1.6)	55.3	(1.7)	75.7	(1.5)	72.9	(1.6)	71.2	(1.4)	52.9	(1.9)	69.3	(1.7)
England (United Kingdom)	57.0	(1.1)	87.4	(1.1)	54.7	(1.3)	82.1	(1.5)	49.8	(1.2)	84.0	(1.2)	64.4	(1.3)	77.1	(1.1)	38.9	(1.7)	64.2	(1.5)
Flanders (Belgium)	74.8	(0.9)	89.7	(0.8)	61.9	(1.2)	84.3	(0.8)	54.3	(1.1)	89.5	(1.1)	40.4	(1.3)	79.2	(1.4)	37.2	(1.8)	80.1	(1.5)
Average	**72.7**	**(0.2)**	**90.8**	**(0.1)**	**67.9**	**(0.2)**	**87.2**	**(0.2)**	**56.3**	**(0.2)**	**84.3**	**(0.2)**	**57.2**	**(0.2)**	**82.9**	**(0.2)**	**54.2**	**(0.3)**	**80.3**	**(0.3)**
United States	70.3	(1.3)	82.9	(1.4)	60.7	(2.0)	77.3	(1.5)	65.7	(1.8)	78.4	(1.7)	72.2	(1.7)	71.7	(1.6)	49.5	(2.0)	72.8	(1.8)

1. Cells with data representing less than 5% of the cases are shaded in grey and should be interpreted with caution. These results are not highlighted in the text of the report.

2. Special needs students are not well defined internationally but usually cover those for whom a special learning need has been formally identified because they are mentally, physically or emotionally disadvantaged. Often, special needs students will be those for whom additional public or private resources (personnel, material or financial) have been provided to support their education. "Gifted students" are not considered to have special needs under the definition used here and in other OECD work. Some teachers perceive all students as unique learners and thus having some special learning needs. For the purpose of this survey, it is important to ensure a more objective judgment of who is a special needs student and who is not. That is why a formal identification is stressed above.

* See notes at the beginning of this Annex.

Source: OECD, TALIS 2013 Database.

StatLink ▦▨ http://dx.doi.org/10.1787/888933045050

[Part 2/3]
Content and positive impact of professional development activities
Percentage of lower secondary education teachers who report having participated in professional development with the following content in the 12 months prior to the survey and who report a "moderate" or "large" positive impact of this professional development on their teaching[1]

Table 4.10

	Student behaviour and classroom management				School management and administration				Approaches to individual learning				Teaching students with special needs[2]				Teaching in a multicultural or multilingual setting			
	Percentage of teachers		Moderate or large positive impact		Percentage of teachers		Moderate or large positive impact		Percentage of teachers		Moderate or large positive impact		Percentage of teachers		Moderate or large positive impact		Percentage of teachers		Moderate or large positive impact	
	%	S.E.	%	S.E.	%	S.E.	%	S.E.	%	S.E.	%	S.E.	%	S.E.	%	S.E.	%	S.E.	%	S.E.
Australia	35.0	(1.9)	65.2	(2.3)	25.8	(1.2)	63.9	(2.8)	52.4	(1.5)	63.5	(2.3)	32.3	(1.6)	60.0	(2.4)	13.3	(1.5)	64.5	(3.5)
Brazil	53.9	(1.1)	80.2	(1.0)	23.6	(0.8)	77.0	(1.8)	56.4	(1.1)	84.8	(0.8)	30.8	(1.0)	69.5	(1.5)	19.1	(0.9)	71.8	(1.5)
Bulgaria	44.6	(1.8)	83.5	(1.8)	11.8	(1.0)	76.9	(3.8)	26.8	(1.5)	86.1	(1.7)	25.7	(1.8)	75.5	(2.3)	20.5	(1.4)	81.7	(2.4)
Chile	41.1	(1.9)	91.0	(1.6)	25.5	(1.7)	85.3	(2.5)	33.0	(1.7)	89.4	(1.9)	32.8	(1.8)	87.0	(1.9)	17.8	(1.5)	84.5	(2.9)
Croatia	47.4	(1.2)	77.7	(1.2)	11.3	(0.7)	65.9	(3.3)	46.7	(1.2)	77.1	(1.3)	46.1	(1.4)	77.0	(1.3)	9.1	(0.7)	73.7	(2.2)
Cyprus*	53.9	(1.8)	81.6	(1.6)	20.2	(1.4)	80.4	(3.0)	33.9	(1.5)	80.3	(2.2)	24.1	(1.4)	73.2	(2.8)	25.9	(1.4)	76.5	(3.1)
Czech Republic	29.9	(1.5)	80.8	(1.5)	10.5	(0.6)	83.9	(2.3)	23.2	(0.9)	81.2	(1.6)	23.8	(1.1)	80.8	(1.9)	11.4	(0.8)	80.5	(2.4)
Denmark	37.3	(2.1)	78.5	(2.8)	5.3	(0.5)	71.3	(6.0)	19.5	(1.4)	74.4	(3.0)	25.3	(1.4)	75.0	(2.5)	11.4	(2.3)	69.8	(3.5)
Estonia	49.8	(1.7)	78.4	(1.4)	9.9	(0.7)	73.1	(2.5)	36.6	(1.4)	85.0	(1.6)	36.9	(1.7)	76.8	(1.8)	21.9	(1.6)	78.3	(2.0)
Finland	33.3	(1.4)	63.2	(2.0)	9.4	(0.8)	62.0	(4.6)	40.5	(1.3)	66.6	(1.7)	34.7	(1.3)	66.1	(1.6)	14.4	(1.1)	63.7	(2.9)
France	23.3	(1.2)	70.2	(2.5)	4.5	(0.5)	61.7	(5.1)	29.1	(1.3)	72.7	(2.0)	23.2	(1.3)	72.5	(2.4)	3.6	(0.4)	80.5	(4.7)
Iceland	31.2	(1.5)	81.8	(2.1)	5.3	(0.7)	77.9	(5.7)	36.6	(1.7)	77.4	(2.3)	25.5	(1.5)	82.1	(2.2)	13.1	(1.1)	66.7	(4.0)
Israel	45.0	(1.5)	83.6	(1.7)	27.8	(1.1)	81.7	(1.8)	38.1	(1.4)	79.9	(1.4)	32.0	(1.3)	79.1	(2.0)	17.6	(1.1)	79.7	(2.6)
Italy	34.7	(1.2)	85.5	(1.3)	10.0	(0.7)	74.0	(3.2)	36.6	(1.4)	87.9	(1.4)	44.3	(1.4)	87.1	(1.1)	14.9	(0.9)	86.2	(1.9)
Japan	44.5	(1.3)	81.4	(1.3)	22.7	(1.1)	72.8	(2.1)	51.5	(1.3)	76.9	(1.3)	44.5	(1.5)	82.2	(1.2)	10.2	(0.7)	71.6	(3.3)
Korea	63.8	(1.0)	94.2	(0.8)	34.5	(1.0)	88.6	(1.1)	50.1	(1.3)	92.6	(0.9)	56.8	(1.2)	93.2	(0.8)	25.9	(1.1)	87.8	(1.7)
Latvia	45.6	(1.8)	79.4	(1.6)	13.1	(0.8)	81.2	(2.8)	60.0	(1.7)	84.8	(1.2)	31.1	(2.7)	82.5	(1.8)	21.4	(1.6)	82.1	(1.9)
Malaysia	74.9	(0.9)	94.0	(0.6)	65.5	(1.1)	88.4	(0.8)	69.0	(1.1)	91.2	(0.6)	17.9	(0.9)	71.2	(2.2)	24.7	(1.2)	78.0	(1.7)
Mexico	67.0	(1.2)	88.3	(1.0)	35.7	(1.5)	75.3	(2.0)	54.4	(1.1)	82.2	(1.2)	28.8	(1.4)	67.0	(2.2)	26.9	(1.1)	76.9	(1.9)
Netherlands	51.6	(1.6)	80.3	(1.6)	13.1	(1.2)	64.3	(4.3)	41.0	(1.9)	70.2	(2.1)	35.8	(1.7)	73.1	(2.6)	13.0	(1.4)	68.7	(5.3)
Norway	41.3	(3.0)	82.7	(1.6)	9.4	(1.0)	80.0	(3.1)	17.9	(0.8)	86.7	(2.5)	24.3	(1.4)	85.2	(2.5)	7.9	(0.8)	77.8	(3.8)
Poland	43.0	(1.4)	81.4	(1.4)	9.7	(0.6)	76.9	(2.8)	52.8	(1.4)	83.1	(1.2)	57.6	(1.7)	84.4	(1.1)	4.9	(0.5)	85.3	(2.9)
Portugal	30.2	(1.2)	88.3	(1.2)	6.9	(0.6)	86.4	(3.1)	19.5	(0.9)	88.6	(1.6)	16.5	(1.3)	85.8	(1.8)	9.6	(0.6)	87.4	(2.1)
Romania	62.2	(1.2)	92.6	(0.7)	19.6	(1.1)	86.3	(2.0)	55.7	(1.2)	91.9	(0.8)	23.6	(1.3)	87.6	(1.9)	18.2	(1.1)	85.3	(1.7)
Serbia	50.0	(1.3)	86.2	(1.1)	13.8	(0.8)	78.2	(2.5)	43.8	(1.3)	81.1	(1.4)	38.9	(1.5)	77.9	(1.6)	11.3	(0.8)	78.5	(2.4)
Singapore	45.4	(0.9)	79.0	(1.2)	33.1	(0.8)	72.2	(1.4)	39.1	(1.0)	75.3	(1.4)	23.0	(0.7)	69.9	(1.8)	19.3	(0.8)	75.2	(2.0)
Slovak Republic	25.5	(1.5)	88.4	(1.5)	14.3	(0.9)	85.7	(1.9)	28.1	(1.2)	88.7	(1.4)	22.3	(1.1)	84.6	(1.9)	13.2	(1.1)	89.4	(1.9)
Spain	30.5	(1.2)	84.2	(1.4)	11.1	(0.7)	81.9	(2.5)	23.6	(0.9)	83.2	(2.0)	19.6	(1.1)	83.0	(1.9)	25.1	(1.0)	79.1	(2.0)
Sweden	27.8	(1.5)	69.4	(1.8)	7.1	(0.8)	69.3	(4.5)	24.9	(1.1)	65.1	(2.2)	24.1	(1.4)	64.6	(2.4)	12.7	(1.3)	61.9	(2.9)
Sub-national entities																				
Abu Dhabi (United Arab Emirates)	78.7	(2.6)	90.0	(0.9)	40.2	(1.9)	85.8	(1.3)	65.1	(1.7)	88.4	(1.1)	41.6	(2.1)	79.7	(2.0)	43.1	(1.7)	84.9	(1.4)
Alberta (Canada)	32.9	(1.6)	64.1	(2.4)	16.9	(0.9)	70.8	(3.0)	64.3	(1.4)	64.7	(1.6)	40.2	(2.1)	63.6	(2.0)	19.1	(1.2)	60.2	(3.0)
England (United Kingdom)	37.3	(1.9)	63.5	(1.9)	28.8	(1.4)	68.0	(2.4)	51.3	(1.6)	72.0	(1.4)	38.3	(1.9)	67.9	(2.2)	12.9	(1.1)	63.7	(4.1)
Flanders (Belgium)	29.5	(1.3)	80.9	(1.5)	9.8	(0.6)	75.3	(2.8)	20.9	(0.8)	80.8	(1.8)	23.1	(1.3)	87.1	(1.7)	8.3	(0.8)	78.9	(3.0)
Average	43.7	(0.3)	80.9	(0.3)	18.4	(0.2)	76.4	(0.5)	40.7	(0.2)	80.4	(0.3)	31.7	(0.3)	77.3	(0.3)	16.4	(0.2)	76.7	(0.5)
United States	38.1	(2.1)	66.6	(2.3)	16.4	(1.1)	64.2	(3.8)	57.8	(1.8)	69.4	(1.6)	38.6	(1.6)	67.2	(1.9)	23.7	(2.3)	61.4	(2.6)

1. Cells with data representing less than 5% of the cases are shaded in grey and should be interpreted with caution. These results are not highlighted in the text of the report.

2. Special needs students are not well defined internationally but usually cover those for whom a special learning need has been formally identified because they are mentally, physically or emotionally disadvantaged. Often, special needs students will be those for whom additional public or private resources (personnel, material or financial) have been provided to support their education. "Gifted students" are not considered to have special needs under the definition used here and in other OECD work. Some teachers perceive all students as unique learners and thus having some special learning needs. For the purpose of this survey, it is important to ensure a more objective judgment of who is a special needs student and who is not. That is why a formal identification is stressed above.

*See notes at the beginning of this Annex.

Source: OECD, TALIS 2013 Database.

StatLink http://dx.doi.org/10.1787/888933045050

[Part 3/3]

Content and positive impact of professional development activities

Percentage of lower secondary education teachers who report having participated in professional development with the following content in the 12 months prior to the survey and who report a "moderate" or "large" positive impact of this professional development on their teaching[1]

Table 4.10

	Teaching cross-curricular skills (e.g. problem solving, learning-to-learn)				Approaches to developing cross-occupational competencies for future work or future studies				New technologies in the workplace				Student career guidance and counselling			
	Percentage of teachers		Moderate or large positive impact		Percentage of teachers		Moderate or large positive impact		Percentage of teachers		Moderate or large positive impact		Percentage of teachers		Moderate or large positive impact	
	%	S.E.	%	S.E.	%	S.E.	%	S.E.	%	S.E.	%	S.E.	%	S.E.	%	S.E.
Australia	37.1	(1.3)	61.8	(2.5)	11.2	(1.1)	58.4	(4.4)	56.8	(1.8)	67.5	(2.0)	13.4	(0.8)	73.1	(3.8)
Brazil	50.9	(1.1)	80.6	(1.0)	47.3	(1.1)	78.7	(1.1)	52.8	(1.2)	79.3	(1.0)	18.9	(1.0)	73.4	(2.0)
Bulgaria	37.0	(1.6)	84.1	(1.7)	27.7	(1.4)	79.1	(2.2)	52.6	(1.7)	82.0	(1.5)	31.8	(1.6)	84.7	(2.2)
Chile	45.6	(2.0)	91.5	(1.5)	28.9	(1.9)	90.6	(1.8)	38.0	(1.8)	86.1	(2.3)	29.5	(1.8)	88.4	(2.1)
Croatia	37.1	(1.1)	77.8	(1.4)	23.7	(0.9)	78.0	(1.6)	41.1	(1.3)	74.2	(1.3)	17.5	(0.9)	79.4	(2.0)
Cyprus*	37.3	(1.6)	79.3	(2.4)	11.6	(1.1)	76.5	(4.1)	47.6	(1.4)	78.2	(2.1)	16.8	(1.2)	77.4	(3.4)
Czech Republic	28.3	(1.3)	80.6	(1.9)	17.0	(1.0)	78.8	(2.1)	42.2	(1.4)	81.6	(1.5)	10.0	(0.6)	86.3	(2.5)
Denmark	16.6	(0.9)	77.8	(2.7)	10.9	(0.9)	72.5	(4.2)	28.8	(2.0)	78.3	(2.3)	6.6	(0.8)	70.2	(6.2)
Estonia	46.6	(1.3)	84.1	(1.2)	24.4	(1.1)	84.2	(1.9)	47.1	(1.7)	83.9	(1.3)	20.0	(1.0)	78.5	(1.9)
Finland	25.4	(1.0)	61.9	(2.6)	10.9	(0.8)	61.1	(4.0)	42.2	(1.7)	63.1	(2.3)	6.9	(0.6)	64.0	(4.4)
France	22.8	(1.2)	68.6	(2.3)	8.9	(0.8)	69.7	(3.6)	10.5	(0.8)	74.4	(3.1)	14.4	(1.1)	72.7	(2.9)
Iceland	16.6	(1.2)	74.6	(3.5)	12.2	(1.1)	80.1	(4.1)	34.1	(1.5)	80.5	(2.4)	7.0	(0.9)	71.9	(5.8)
Israel	44.6	(1.2)	84.2	(1.3)	33.8	(1.1)	83.1	(1.7)	47.7	(1.4)	78.4	(1.4)	31.1	(1.1)	81.9	(1.9)
Italy	34.0	(1.2)	85.9	(1.4)	11.8	(0.8)	84.4	(2.6)	44.7	(1.4)	80.0	(1.6)	30.7	(1.1)	86.6	(1.4)
Japan	54.6	(1.3)	81.1	(1.2)	15.9	(1.0)	77.1	(2.3)	14.8	(0.9)	68.6	(2.5)	40.8	(1.2)	79.7	(1.3)
Korea	47.5	(1.1)	91.7	(1.0)	39.2	(1.0)	89.6	(1.0)	37.4	(1.0)	91.3	(0.8)	74.0	(0.9)	93.4	(0.6)
Latvia	51.9	(1.4)	82.5	(1.7)	20.9	(1.3)	78.6	(2.3)	58.7	(1.6)	86.3	(1.3)	30.7	(1.5)	86.2	(1.9)
Malaysia	70.6	(1.1)	89.0	(0.7)	44.2	(1.2)	84.2	(1.1)	55.5	(1.3)	83.1	(1.1)	44.0	(1.1)	83.4	(1.2)
Mexico	67.5	(1.0)	85.4	(0.9)	39.1	(1.0)	82.8	(1.4)	55.0	(1.4)	80.9	(1.1)	42.5	(1.1)	82.4	(1.2)
Netherlands	33.2	(1.4)	77.6	(2.1)	17.2	(1.0)	76.9	(4.7)	29.8	(2.1)	71.2	(2.6)	30.3	(1.5)	82.5	(2.3)
Norway	28.2	(1.4)	86.4	(2.6)	17.8	(1.4)	85.6	(3.1)	6.8	(1.0)	77.0	(4.8)	11.9	(1.2)	85.0	(3.8)
Poland	31.6	(1.0)	83.4	(1.3)	7.6	(0.7)	82.5	(2.8)	41.5	(1.5)	83.7	(1.4)	13.6	(0.8)	80.8	(2.2)
Portugal	31.5	(1.0)	90.8	(1.3)	12.3	(0.7)	86.0	(1.9)	35.6	(1.4)	92.0	(1.1)	19.5	(1.2)	91.0	(1.4)
Romania	50.4	(1.2)	92.5	(0.9)	28.5	(1.2)	91.1	(1.3)	30.4	(1.2)	87.6	(1.4)	50.1	(1.2)	93.0	(1.0)
Serbia	32.3	(1.1)	84.3	(1.5)	11.9	(0.7)	79.8	(2.5)	33.1	(1.3)	82.9	(1.3)	29.1	(0.9)	87.0	(1.4)
Singapore	36.1	(0.9)	74.7	(1.4)	16.7	(0.7)	74.1	(2.2)	39.8	(0.9)	69.0	(1.5)	28.5	(0.9)	69.3	(1.6)
Slovak Republic	31.7	(1.4)	89.6	(1.3)	13.6	(0.8)	88.5	(2.0)	33.2	(1.4)	89.6	(1.2)	8.0	(0.6)	90.1	(2.5)
Spain	36.3	(1.3)	84.0	(1.5)	15.1	(0.9)	82.5	(1.9)	55.7	(1.5)	85.7	(1.1)	15.9	(0.8)	82.1	(1.9)
Sweden	16.2	(0.9)	65.2	(2.4)	9.0	(0.7)	71.4	(3.0)	37.1	(1.7)	65.4	(2.2)	4.0	(0.4)	56.7	(5.1)
Sub-national entities																
Abu Dhabi (United Arab Emirates)	67.4	(1.6)	87.7	(1.1)	60.2	(2.0)	89.8	(0.9)	69.0	(1.7)	88.3	(1.0)	51.7	(1.8)	89.0	(1.2)
Alberta (Canada)	41.1	(1.6)	61.7	(2.3)	15.4	(1.1)	65.6	(3.1)	53.7	(2.1)	64.9	(2.0)	11.7	(0.9)	72.3	(3.7)
England (United Kingdom)	37.4	(1.8)	69.8	(1.6)	10.7	(0.8)	65.9	(3.7)	31.6	(1.7)	64.1	(2.1)	9.8	(0.6)	63.1	(3.9)
Flanders (Belgium)	24.5	(1.0)	85.8	(1.7)	6.1	(0.5)	86.0	(3.1)	13.3	(0.8)	81.8	(2.4)	7.6	(0.7)	81.9	(3.1)
Average	**38.5**	**(0.2)**	**80.5**	**(0.3)**	**20.7**	**(0.2)**	**79.2**	**(0.5)**	**40.0**	**(0.3)**	**78.8**	**(0.3)**	**23.6**	**(0.2)**	**79.9**	**(0.5)**
United States	49.5	(2.0)	64.5	(1.4)	17.4	(1.1)	69.1	(3.1)	57.4	(2.2)	73.5	(1.6)	11.2	(0.8)	65.1	(5.2)

1. Cells with data representing less than 5% of the cases are shaded in grey and should be interpreted with caution. These results are not highlighted in the text of the report.

2. Special needs students are not well defined internationally but usually cover those for whom a special learning need has been formally identified because they are mentally, physically or emotionally disadvantaged. Often, special needs students will be those for whom additional public or private resources (personnel, material or financial) have been provided to support their education. "Gifted students" are not considered to have special needs under the definition used here and in other OECD work. Some teachers perceive all students as unique learners and thus having some special learning needs. For the purpose of this survey, it is important to ensure a more objective judgment of who is a special needs student and who is not. That is why a formal identification is stressed above.

* See notes at the beginning of this Annex.

Source: OECD, TALIS 2013 Database.

StatLink ⬛📈 http://dx.doi.org/10.1787/888933045050

[Part 1/1]
Support received by teachers for professional development
Percentage of lower secondary education teachers who report having received the following types of support for the professional development undertaken in the 12 months prior to the survey

Table 4.11

	Scheduled time for activities that took place during regular working hours at this school		Salary supplement for activities outside working hours		Non-monetary support for activities outside working hours (reduced teaching, days off, study leave, etc.)	
	%	S.E.	%	S.E.	%	S.E.
Australia	79.5	(1.2)	3.9	(0.4)	17.4	(1.2)
Brazil	43.9	(1.1)	11.0	(0.9)	14.3	(0.7)
Bulgaria	51.4	(1.7)	26.2	(1.3)	16.4	(1.1)
Chile	44.4	(1.8)	11.9	(1.3)	17.8	(1.4)
Croatia	73.5	(1.1)	10.6	(0.7)	11.1	(0.6)
Cyprus*	58.5	(1.5)	2.4	(0.5)	13.6	(1.0)
Czech Republic	60.5	(1.3)	14.3	(0.9)	15.0	(0.9)
Denmark	61.9	(1.5)	11.6	(1.3)	10.1	(0.8)
Estonia	81.8	(1.1)	14.5	(1.1)	27.3	(1.2)
Finland	51.3	(1.6)	5.3	(0.7)	12.9	(0.8)
France	46.1	(1.2)	4.8	(0.5)	16.8	(0.8)
Iceland	74.5	(1.2)	6.5	(0.8)	15.3	(1.2)
Israel	32.9	(1.2)	13.0	(0.7)	12.3	(0.9)
Italy	26.9	(1.2)	5.7	(0.6)	11.3	(0.7)
Japan	58.4	(1.3)	6.5	(0.7)	11.2	(0.9)
Korea	28.3	(0.9)	23.1	(0.9)	10.7	(0.7)
Latvia	63.7	(1.5)	5.6	(0.7)	13.8	(1.1)
Malaysia	88.0	(0.7)	14.0	(1.0)	19.1	(1.1)
Mexico	48.2	(1.3)	3.6	(0.5)	11.8	(0.8)
Netherlands	70.0	(1.9)	3.3	(0.6)	13.5	(1.0)
Norway	60.1	(1.9)	7.5	(0.9)	23.0	(1.4)
Poland	39.1	(1.3)	5.2	(0.7)	11.1	(0.7)
Portugal	15.1	(0.9)	0.7	(0.1)	3.9	(0.4)
Romania	18.4	(1.2)	1.4	(0.3)	7.5	(0.6)
Serbia	46.8	(1.2)	1.8	(0.3)	13.8	(0.7)
Singapore	70.3	(0.8)	7.3	(0.5)	16.6	(0.7)
Slovak Republic	54.0	(1.5)	14.4	(0.8)	16.0	(1.0)
Spain	22.6	(1.3)	2.4	(0.4)	6.4	(0.5)
Sweden	64.3	(1.4)	4.3	(0.6)	31.1	(1.1)
Sub-national entities						
Abu Dhabi (United Arab Emirates)	61.3	(1.5)	5.5	(0.9)	14.9	(1.3)
Alberta (Canada)	73.9	(1.2)	8.2	(0.8)	16.9	(1.2)
England (United Kingdom)	66.1	(1.5)	4.1	(0.5)	9.1	(0.6)
Flanders (Belgium)	61.5	(1.7)	0.7	(0.2)	3.0	(0.4)
Average	54.5	(0.2)	7.9	(0.1)	14.1	(0.2)
United States	65.6	(2.0)	21.9	(1.8)	14.9	(1.4)

*See notes at the beginning of this Annex.
Source: OECD, TALIS 2013 Database.
StatLink http://dx.doi.org/10.1787/888933045088

[Part 1/2]
Teachers' needs for professional development
Percentage of lower secondary education teachers indicating they have a high level of need
Table 4.12   *for professional development in the following areas*

	Knowledge and understanding of the subject field(s)		Pedagogical competencies in teaching subject field(s)		Knowledge of the curriculum		Student evaluation and assessment practice		ICT skills for teaching		Student behaviour and classroom management		School management and administration	
	%	S.E.	%	S.E.	%	S.E.	%	S.E.	%	S.E.	%	S.E.	%	S.E.
Australia	2.4	(0.5)	2.8	(0.5)	3.7	(0.5)	3.3	(0.4)	13.6	(0.9)	3.8	(0.6)	4.9	(0.7)
Brazil	6.7	(0.4)	6.9	(0.4)	7.0	(0.5)	10.2	(0.4)	27.5	(0.7)	19.6	(0.8)	25.5	(0.7)
Bulgaria	12.4	(0.8)	11.8	(0.8)	14.5	(1.0)	13.4	(0.8)	20.3	(0.9)	15.8	(0.8)	9.1	(0.7)
Chile	5.7	(0.7)	6.1	(0.6)	7.0	(0.7)	9.7	(0.7)	12.8	(0.9)	12.1	(0.9)	16.5	(1.1)
Croatia	5.7	(0.4)	8.6	(0.5)	3.6	(0.3)	13.5	(0.7)	19.7	(0.9)	19.9	(0.8)	5.8	(0.5)
Cyprus*	2.4	(0.4)	4.3	(0.6)	8.3	(0.8)	4.8	(0.6)	12.5	(0.7)	7.5	(0.8)	11.7	(0.9)
Czech Republic	8.5	(0.5)	6.1	(0.4)	3.0	(0.3)	5.3	(0.5)	14.8	(0.7)	13.6	(0.7)	4.0	(0.4)
Denmark	6.4	(0.8)	6.0	(0.7)	3.2	(0.4)	7.5	(0.8)	18.7	(1.2)	6.9	(0.7)	3.1	(0.6)
Estonia	11.5	(0.7)	11.9	(0.7)	12.7	(0.7)	13.8	(0.8)	24.1	(0.9)	16.7	(1.0)	3.5	(0.3)
Finland	3.8	(0.4)	3.4	(0.4)	3.4	(0.3)	3.9	(0.4)	17.5	(1.0)	7.8	(0.6)	1.9	(0.3)
France	5.4	(0.4)	9.2	(0.6)	2.9	(0.3)	13.6	(0.7)	25.1	(0.9)	9.3	(0.7)	4.2	(0.4)
Iceland	9.0	(0.8)	8.5	(0.8)	22.7	(1.2)	18.2	(1.1)	28.6	(1.5)	14.2	(1.0)	4.9	(0.8)
Israel	9.3	(0.6)	10.5	(0.7)	7.9	(0.6)	10.2	(0.6)	24.5	(1.2)	12.3	(0.6)	10.0	(0.6)
Italy	16.6	(0.7)	23.5	(1.0)	11.3	(0.6)	22.9	(1.0)	35.9	(0.8)	28.6	(1.0)	9.9	(0.7)
Japan	51.0	(0.9)	56.9	(0.9)	20.6	(0.9)	39.6	(0.9)	25.9	(0.9)	43.0	(0.9)	14.6	(0.7)
Korea	25.2	(0.9)	31.3	(1.0)	23.5	(0.9)	25.3	(1.1)	24.9	(1.1)	30.4	(1.1)	17.5	(0.8)
Latvia	3.7	(0.5)	4.3	(0.5)	3.2	(0.5)	6.3	(0.6)	19.4	(1.1)	15.0	(1.0)	4.3	(0.5)
Malaysia	28.8	(1.0)	25.2	(1.0)	23.4	(0.9)	39.7	(1.3)	37.6	(1.2)	21.3	(1.1)	17.8	(0.9)
Mexico	4.4	(0.6)	8.0	(0.8)	5.0	(0.5)	8.0	(0.6)	21.0	(1.0)	8.6	(0.6)	15.4	(0.8)
Netherlands	6.9	(0.7)	5.6	(0.5)	4.3	(0.5)	6.6	(0.8)	14.9	(1.1)	9.0	(1.0)	4.2	(0.5)
Norway	7.1	(0.7)	7.9	(0.7)	4.5	(0.4)	12.4	(1.2)	18.3	(1.4)	4.3	(0.5)	2.5	(0.3)
Poland	1.8	(0.3)	1.8	(0.3)	2.1	(0.3)	3.3	(0.4)	10.6	(0.8)	13.1	(0.7)	6.0	(0.4)
Portugal	4.7	(0.4)	4.2	(0.4)	2.9	(0.3)	4.8	(0.4)	9.2	(0.5)	10.4	(0.6)	14.1	(0.6)
Romania	5.4	(0.5)	7.2	(0.5)	6.7	(0.6)	7.5	(0.5)	18.6	(0.9)	13.6	(0.7)	18.2	(0.9)
Serbia	5.4	(0.4)	6.6	(0.5)	7.1	(0.5)	9.1	(0.6)	19.5	(0.8)	14.5	(0.8)	6.9	(0.5)
Singapore	6.2	(0.4)	9.9	(0.6)	7.1	(0.4)	11.9	(0.6)	11.8	(0.6)	9.3	(0.5)	7.4	(0.4)
Slovak Republic	9.1	(0.6)	8.0	(0.6)	11.9	(0.8)	9.3	(0.6)	18.6	(0.9)	14.5	(0.7)	7.9	(0.5)
Spain	1.8	(0.2)	5.0	(0.5)	1.3	(0.2)	4.3	(0.6)	14.1	(0.7)	8.4	(0.6)	10.2	(0.5)
Sweden	9.6	(0.6)	9.1	(0.6)	16.5	(0.8)	26.4	(0.9)	25.5	(0.8)	9.1	(0.6)	3.1	(0.3)
Sub-national entities														
Abu Dhabi (United Arab Emirates)	2.3	(0.4)	4.0	(0.6)	3.3	(0.4)	4.7	(0.5)	9.5	(0.8)	6.1	(0.6)	12.2	(0.8)
Alberta (Canada)	2.6	(0.5)	2.4	(0.5)	2.3	(0.4)	4.5	(0.6)	9.3	(0.8)	3.8	(0.5)	4.1	(0.5)
England (United Kingdom)	1.8	(0.3)	1.6	(0.3)	1.9	(0.5)	2.4	(0.3)	7.7	(0.7)	2.9	(0.3)	3.5	(0.4)
Flanders (Belgium)	3.0	(0.3)	2.9	(0.4)	2.7	(0.3)	6.9	(0.6)	10.5	(0.7)	4.9	(0.4)	1.8	(0.3)
Average	8.7	(0.1)	9.7	(0.1)	7.9	(0.1)	11.6	(0.1)	18.9	(0.2)	13.1	(0.1)	8.7	(0.1)
United States	1.6	(0.3)	2.2	(0.4)	3.3	(0.5)	4.2	(0.7)	8.1	(0.8)	5.1	(0.6)	4.1	(0.5)

1. Special needs students are not well defined internationally but usually cover those for whom a special learning need has been formally identified because they are mentally, physically or emotionally disadvantaged. Often, special needs students will be those for whom additional public or private resources (personnel, material or financial) have been provided to support their education. "Gifted students" are not considered to have special needs under the definition used here and in other OECD work. Some teachers perceive all students as unique learners and thus having some special learning needs. For the purpose of this survey, it is important to ensure a more objective judgment of who is a special needs student and who is not. That is why a formal identification is stressed above.

*See notes at the beginning of this Annex.

Source: OECD, TALIS 2013 Database.

StatLink ᴹˢᴾ http://dx.doi.org/10.1787/888933045107

[Part 2/2]
Teachers' needs for professional development
Percentage of lower secondary education teachers indicating they have a high level of need
Table 4.12 *for professional development in the following areas*

	Approaches to individualised learning		Teaching students with special needs[1]		Teaching in a multicultural or multilingual setting		Teaching cross-curricular skills (e.g. problem solving, learning-to-learn)		Approaches to developing cross-occupational competencies for future work or future studies		New technologies in the workplace		Student career guidance and counselling	
	%	S.E.	%	S.E.	%	S.E.	%	S.E.	%	S.E.	%	S.E.	%	S.E.
Australia	6.2	(0.8)	8.2	(0.8)	4.4	(0.7)	3.1	(0.4)	4.2	(0.5)	12.5	(0.8)	5.9	(1.0)
Brazil	12.0	(0.4)	60.1	(0.9)	46.4	(0.9)	19.0	(0.6)	21.7	(0.7)	36.9	(0.9)	36.0	(0.8)
Bulgaria	10.1	(0.9)	22.8	(1.0)	16.6	(1.0)	9.1	(0.7)	13.2	(0.9)	22.7	(1.3)	9.5	(0.6)
Chile	12.6	(0.8)	25.8	(1.5)	24.4	(1.3)	11.6	(1.0)	11.9	(1.0)	16.7	(1.1)	17.4	(1.2)
Croatia	19.0	(0.7)	32.7	(0.9)	11.3	(0.7)	13.1	(0.7)	13.0	(0.7)	23.8	(0.9)	10.6	(0.6)
Cyprus*	9.2	(0.8)	27.0	(1.0)	17.5	(0.9)	9.0	(0.7)	15.2	(0.9)	20.0	(1.0)	17.1	(0.8)
Czech Republic	5.6	(0.4)	8.0	(0.5)	5.1	(0.4)	5.6	(0.5)	4.5	(0.4)	10.2	(0.7)	3.7	(0.4)
Denmark	4.3	(0.6)	27.7	(1.3)	6.8	(0.7)	5.1	(0.6)	5.6	(0.7)	14.0	(1.1)	3.6	(0.5)
Estonia	9.9	(0.6)	19.7	(0.9)	9.2	(0.7)	14.7	(0.8)	8.0	(0.6)	20.9	(1.0)	7.9	(0.7)
Finland	8.3	(0.6)	12.6	(0.8)	5.4	(0.6)	4.3	(0.5)	1.3	(0.2)	13.9	(0.8)	1.5	(0.3)
France	19.1	(0.9)	27.4	(0.9)	11.4	(0.7)	11.2	(0.7)	11.6	(0.6)	17.0	(0.7)	20.5	(0.9)
Iceland	11.8	(1.0)	16.1	(1.1)	8.9	(0.8)	6.6	(0.7)	7.8	(0.8)	19.1	(1.2)	6.4	(0.7)
Israel	12.7	(0.6)	22.8	(1.0)	13.0	(0.8)	14.4	(0.8)	13.2	(0.8)	22.9	(0.9)	13.9	(0.7)
Italy	22.1	(0.8)	32.3	(1.0)	27.4	(0.9)	22.3	(0.7)	16.4	(0.8)	32.2	(0.9)	18.7	(0.8)
Japan	40.2	(0.9)	40.6	(1.1)	10.7	(0.6)	34.5	(1.0)	22.0	(0.8)	16.0	(0.7)	42.9	(0.9)
Korea	25.1	(0.9)	36.0	(1.0)	18.9	(0.9)	27.5	(1.0)	25.0	(0.9)	18.9	(1.0)	42.6	(1.1)
Latvia	13.6	(1.0)	12.1	(1.3)	4.8	(0.7)	11.3	(0.9)	5.0	(0.6)	24.3	(1.0)	9.7	(0.7)
Malaysia	22.4	(1.0)	10.0	(0.7)	10.4	(0.8)	23.7	(1.1)	21.1	(1.0)	30.8	(1.0)	17.3	(1.0)
Mexico	13.6	(0.8)	47.4	(1.2)	33.2	(1.0)	11.2	(0.7)	17.8	(0.8)	28.1	(1.1)	21.2	(1.0)
Netherlands	14.0	(1.0)	10.7	(1.0)	3.1	(0.5)	6.8	(0.9)	4.3	(0.5)	11.5	(1.2)	6.4	(0.7)
Norway	5.2	(0.5)	12.4	(0.9)	7.4	(1.0)	8.0	(0.9)	6.7	(0.5)	8.7	(0.5)	5.0	(0.6)
Poland	9.2	(0.5)	14.4	(0.8)	5.5	(0.5)	7.2	(0.6)	3.9	(0.3)	13.2	(0.8)	7.2	(0.6)
Portugal	8.4	(0.5)	26.5	(1.0)	16.8	(0.7)	6.8	(0.5)	10.5	(0.5)	9.2	(0.6)	6.9	(0.4)
Romania	15.1	(0.8)	27.0	(1.0)	19.7	(0.9)	13.7	(0.8)	17.4	(0.8)	22.0	(0.9)	15.2	(0.8)
Serbia	15.1	(0.7)	35.4	(1.1)	10.2	(0.6)	10.0	(0.5)	7.4	(0.5)	21.4	(0.8)	12.2	(0.7)
Singapore	10.1	(0.6)	15.0	(0.5)	4.9	(0.4)	8.3	(0.5)	9.2	(0.6)	9.8	(0.6)	7.8	(0.5)
Slovak Republic	10.6	(0.6)	18.8	(0.9)	7.8	(0.6)	9.0	(0.5)	6.6	(0.5)	14.5	(0.7)	6.6	(0.5)
Spain	8.5	(0.5)	21.8	(1.0)	19.0	(1.0)	7.9	(0.5)	9.4	(0.7)	14.0	(0.7)	8.1	(0.5)
Sweden	15.3	(0.9)	19.8	(1.0)	11.3	(0.9)	12.0	(0.6)	7.7	(0.5)	18.1	(0.8)	2.8	(0.4)
Sub-national entities														
Abu Dhabi (United Arab Emirates)	8.2	(0.6)	22.6	(1.1)	12.9	(0.9)	7.1	(0.6)	11.1	(0.8)	17.7	(1.3)	11.8	(0.9)
Alberta (Canada)	5.3	(0.6)	8.7	(0.7)	3.8	(0.6)	3.3	(0.5)	3.6	(0.5)	11.8	(0.9)	3.9	(0.5)
England (United Kingdom)	3.4	(0.4)	6.4	(0.6)	6.9	(0.6)	3.6	(0.5)	4.1	(0.5)	8.4	(0.6)	5.7	(0.4)
Flanders (Belgium)	6.6	(0.6)	5.3	(0.5)	3.1	(0.5)	3.2	(0.3)	2.1	(0.3)	4.8	(0.5)	2.1	(0.3)
Average	12.5	(0.1)	22.3	(0.2)	12.7	(0.1)	11.0	(0.1)	10.4	(0.1)	17.8	(0.2)	12.4	(0.1)
United States	5.1	(0.7)	8.2	(1.0)	5.0	(0.7)	4.7	(0.8)	7.0	(0.9)	14.6	(1.0)	4.3	(0.7)

1. Special needs students are not well defined internationally but usually cover those for whom a special learning need has been formally identified because they are mentally, physically or emotionally disadvantaged. Often, special needs students will be those for whom additional public or private resources (personnel, material or financial) have been provided to support their education. "Gifted students" are not considered to have special needs under the definition used here and in other OECD work. Some teachers perceive all students as unique learners and thus having some special learning needs. For the purpose of this survey, it is important to ensure a more objective judgment of who is a special needs student and who is not. That is why a formal identification is stressed above.
* See notes at the beginning of this Annex.
Source: OECD, TALIS 2013 Database.
StatLink http://dx.doi.org/10.1787/888933045107

[Part 1/1]

Teachers' needs for professional development in primary education

Percentage of primary education teachers indicating they have a high level of need

Table 4.12.a   *for professional development in the following areas*

	Knowledge and understanding of the subject field(s)		Pedagogical competencies in teaching subject field(s)		Knowledge of the curriculum		Student evaluation and assessment practice		ICT skills for teaching		Student behaviour and classroom management		School management and administration	
	%	S.E.	%	S.E.	%	S.E.	%	S.E.	%	S.E.	%	S.E.	%	S.E.
Denmark	7.1	(0.8)	7.0	(0.7)	2.6	(0.4)	7.7	(0.6)	23.4	(1.2)	12.8	(1.0)	2.1	(0.4)
Finland	2.0	(0.3)	3.0	(0.5)	2.6	(0.4)	5.2	(0.4)	19.1	(1.3)	9.0	(0.7)	2.6	(0.4)
Mexico	4.7	(0.8)	7.3	(1.1)	7.4	(0.9)	9.7	(1.3)	24.3	(1.5)	9.2	(1.0)	14.8	(1.2)
Norway	7.0	(0.6)	6.6	(0.6)	4.7	(0.4)	17.3	(1.2)	24.9	(1.1)	5.6	(0.7)	2.9	(0.6)
Poland	1.2	(0.3)	1.8	(0.3)	2.4	(0.3)	4.2	(0.5)	11.6	(0.8)	10.9	(0.8)	6.3	(0.7)
Sub-national entities														
Flanders (Belgium)	1.2	(0.2)	1.6	(0.3)	1.2	(0.2)	6.1	(0.7)	17.2	(0.9)	6.3	(0.6)	2.3	(0.4)
Average	3.9	(0.2)	4.5	(0.3)	3.5	(0.2)	8.4	(0.3)	20.1	(0.5)	9.0	(0.3)	5.2	(0.3)

	Approaches to individualised learning		Teaching students with special needs[1]		Teaching in a multicultural or multilingual setting		Teaching cross-curricular skills (e.g. problem solving, learning-to-learn)		Approaches to developing cross-occupational competencies for future work or future studies		New technologies in the workplace		Student career guidance and counselling	
	%	S.E.	%	S.E.	%	S.E.	%	S.E.	%	S.E.	%	S.E.	%	S.E.
Denmark	5.8	(0.5)	34.1	(1.3)	8.7	(0.8)	5.7	(0.5)	4.0	(0.5)	13.4	(0.9)	1.8	(0.3)
Finland	7.5	(0.7)	16.7	(1.1)	4.9	(0.6)	4.0	(0.4)	1.0	(0.2)	13.1	(1.1)	0.8	(0.2)
Mexico	13.8	(1.2)	41.6	(2.1)	39.3	(1.9)	13.2	(1.2)	21.1	(1.6)	34.9	(1.9)	21.8	(1.6)
Norway	6.4	(0.6)	13.6	(0.8)	11.8	(1.0)	9.7	(0.9)	4.8	(0.5)	6.5	(0.5)	3.5	(0.4)
Poland	10.1	(0.7)	18.2	(1.3)	5.2	(0.5)	6.1	(0.5)	3.1	(0.3)	11.2	(0.9)	4.0	(0.6)
Sub-national entities														
Flanders (Belgium)	7.8	(0.6)	8.8	(0.7)	4.2	(0.5)	4.1	(0.5)	a	a	a	a	1.8	(0.3)
Average	8.6	(0.3)	22.2	(0.5)	12.4	(0.4)	7.1	(0.3)	6.8	(0.4)	15.8	(0.5)	5.6	(0.3)

1. Special needs students are not well defined internationally but usually cover those for whom a special learning need has been formally identified because they are mentally, physically or emotionally disadvantaged. Often, special needs students will be those for whom additional public or private resources (personnel, material or financial) have been provided to support their education. "Gifted students" are not considered to have special needs under the definition used here and in other OECD work. Some teachers perceive all students as unique learners and thus having some special learning needs. For the purpose of this survey, it is important to ensure a more objective judgment of who is a special needs student and who is not. That is why a formal identification is stressed above.

Source: OECD, TALIS 2013 Database.

StatLink ⌐ http://dx.doi.org/10.1787/888933045126

[Part 1/1]
Teachers' needs for professional development in upper secondary education
*Percentage of upper secondary education teachers indicating they have a high level of need
for professional development in the following areas*

Table 4.12.b

	Knowledge and understanding of the subject field(s)		Pedagogical competencies in teaching subject field(s)		Knowledge of the curriculum		Student evaluation and assessment practice		ICT skills for teaching		Student behaviour and classroom management		School management and administration	
	%	S.E.	%	S.E.	%	S.E.	%	S.E.	%	S.E.	%	S.E.	%	S.E.
Australia	1.6	(0.3)	1.7	(0.3)	2.0	(0.4)	2.7	(0.4)	13.5	(0.9)	2.6	(0.4)	3.6	(0.5)
Denmark	4.4	(0.5)	8.1	(0.9)	3.5	(0.6)	5.1	(0.6)	11.0	(1.1)	7.8	(0.8)	2.9	(0.6)
Finland	4.7	(0.8)	4.0	(0.7)	4.0	(0.8)	3.2	(0.5)	16.0	(0.9)	8.4	(0.9)	3.6	(0.7)
Iceland	9.1	(0.9)	8.5	(0.9)	14.8	(1.2)	13.4	(1.0)	20.4	(1.3)	12.7	(1.1)	4.3	(0.7)
Italy	19.0	(0.7)	22.6	(0.8)	8.5	(0.6)	22.4	(0.9)	36.1	(1.2)	22.6	(0.8)	10.4	(0.6)
Mexico	4.4	(0.5)	11.0	(1.0)	5.5	(0.6)	8.4	(0.7)	14.9	(0.9)	8.8	(0.7)	12.8	(0.7)
Norway	7.7	(0.5)	7.0	(0.6)	5.1	(0.6)	10.8	(0.7)	11.5	(0.7)	5.4	(0.4)	2.7	(0.4)
Poland	2.5	(0.4)	2.4	(0.3)	3.6	(0.5)	3.5	(0.7)	10.3	(0.7)	11.1	(0.7)	6.7	(0.5)
Singapore	4.7	(0.4)	7.7	(0.5)	6.0	(0.5)	10.6	(0.6)	12.1	(0.6)	7.1	(0.4)	6.9	(0.5)
Sub-national entities														
Abu Dhabi (United Arab Emirates)	3.1	(0.5)	4.3	(0.5)	4.0	(0.5)	5.9	(0.6)	11.5	(0.9)	6.0	(0.6)	11.1	(0.8)
Average	6.1	(0.2)	7.7	(0.2)	5.7	(0.2)	8.6	(0.2)	15.7	(0.3)	9.3	(0.2)	6.5	(0.2)

	Approaches to individualised learning		Teaching students with special needs[1]		Teaching in a multicultural or multilingual setting		Teaching cross-curricular skills (e.g. problem solving, learning-to-learn)		Approaches to developing cross-occupational competencies for future work or future studies		New technologies in the workplace		Student career guidance and counselling	
	%	S.E.	%	S.E.	%	S.E.	%	S.E.	%	S.E.	%	S.E.	%	S.E.
Australia	5.4	(0.7)	7.1	(0.6)	3.9	(0.5)	4.2	(0.4)	4.9	(0.7)	13.0	(1.0)	4.3	(0.6)
Denmark	5.1	(0.6)	10.4	(1.2)	4.3	(0.7)	4.8	(0.6)	3.8	(0.6)	8.9	(0.7)	3.2	(0.7)
Finland	7.8	(0.7)	9.8	(0.6)	6.1	(0.7)	4.3	(0.7)	3.1	(0.6)	14.2	(1.2)	2.2	(0.6)
Iceland	8.9	(0.9)	11.1	(1.0)	9.1	(1.0)	6.9	(0.8)	8.7	(0.9)	15.4	(1.1)	5.5	(0.7)
Italy	17.6	(0.8)	25.3	(1.0)	25.6	(0.8)	21.6	(0.8)	20.2	(0.7)	35.7	(0.9)	19.2	(0.8)
Mexico	12.1	(0.8)	36.3	(1.3)	28.9	(1.4)	11.4	(0.8)	16.1	(1.0)	22.0	(1.1)	16.4	(0.9)
Norway	4.5	(0.4)	10.1	(0.9)	7.6	(0.8)	7.6	(0.6)	8.1	(0.6)	11.0	(0.9)	5.0	(0.5)
Poland	6.4	(0.6)	12.9	(0.9)	7.0	(0.5)	6.2	(0.5)	5.2	(0.6)	12.2	(0.7)	7.0	(0.8)
Singapore	8.8	(0.5)	12.2	(0.6)	4.6	(0.4)	7.9	(0.5)	8.7	(0.5)	9.6	(0.6)	6.9	(0.5)
Sub-national entities														
Abu Dhabi (United Arab Emirates)	6.9	(0.7)	20.7	(1.0)	11.3	(0.8)	7.1	(0.7)	12.5	(0.9)	19.2	(1.0)	12.7	(0.8)
Average	8.4	(0.2)	15.6	(0.3)	10.8	(0.3)	8.2	(0.2)	9.1	(0.2)	16.1	(0.3)	8.2	(0.2)

1. Special needs students are not well defined internationally but usually cover those for whom a special learning need has been formally identified because they are mentally, physically or emotionally disadvantaged. Often, special needs students will be those for whom additional public or private resources (personnel, material or financial) have been provided to support their education. "Gifted students" are not considered to have special needs under the definition used here and in other OECD work. Some teachers perceive all students as unique learners and thus having some special learning needs. For the purpose of this survey, it is important to ensure a more objective judgment of who is a special needs student and who is not. That is why a formal identification is stressed above.

Source: OECD, TALIS 2013 Database.

StatLink 🔗 http://dx.doi.org/10.1787/888933045145

[Part 1/1]

Teachers' needs for professional development, 2008 and 2013

Percentage of lower secondary education teachers indicating they have a high level of need

Table 4.12.c *for professional development in the following areas[1, 2]*

	Knowledge and understanding of the subject field(s)				ICT skills for teaching				School management and administration				Teaching students with special needs[3]				Teaching in a multicultural or multilingual setting			
	2008		2013		2008		2013		2008		2013		2008		2013		2008		2013	
	%	S.E.	%	S.E.	%	S.E.	%	S.E.	%	S.E.	%	S.E.	%	S.E.	%	S.E.	%	S.E.	%	S.E.
Australia	5.0	(0.5)	2.3	(0.5)	17.8	(0.9)	13.6	(0.9)	5.9	(0.5)	4.8	(0.7)	15.1	(1.0)	8.2	(0.8)	4.0	(0.4)	4.5	(0.7)
Brazil	14.9	(1.1)	6.7	(0.4)	35.6	(1.3)	27.5	(0.7)	20.0	(0.8)	25.5	(0.7)	63.2	(1.2)	60.0	(0.9)	33.2	(1.2)	46.3	(0.9)
Bulgaria	21.2	(1.5)	12.4	(0.8)	26.9	(1.6)	20.3	(0.9)	8.5	(0.9)	9.1	(0.7)	24.4	(1.5)	22.8	(1.0)	15.5	(2.3)	16.6	(1.0)
Denmark	4.6	(0.5)	6.3	(0.8)	20.1	(1.7)	18.7	(1.1)	3.9	(0.5)	3.2	(0.6)	24.6	(1.4)	28.0	(1.3)	7.1	(1.0)	7.0	(0.7)
Estonia	22.6	(1.0)	11.6	(0.7)	27.9	(0.9)	24.2	(0.9)	4.6	(0.4)	3.5	(0.3)	28.1	(0.9)	19.6	(0.9)	9.7	(0.8)	9.3	(0.7)
Iceland	10.3	(0.9)	9.0	(0.9)	17.3	(1.1)	28.3	(1.4)	7.9	(0.8)	4.5	(0.8)	23.2	(1.2)	15.5	(1.1)	14.0	(0.9)	8.9	(0.8)
Italy	34.0	(0.7)	16.5	(0.7)	25.8	(0.8)	35.9	(0.8)	8.6	(0.5)	9.9	(0.7)	35.3	(1.0)	32.3	(1.0)	25.3	(0.9)	27.4	(0.9)
Korea	38.3	(1.0)	25.1	(0.9)	17.7	(0.7)	24.9	(1.1)	10.8	(0.6)	17.4	(0.8)	25.6	(0.9)	36.0	(1.0)	10.4	(0.6)	18.9	(0.9)
Malaysia	56.8	(1.5)	28.7	(1.0)	43.8	(1.2)	37.5	(1.2)	29.9	(1.1)	17.8	(0.9)	25.9	(1.1)	9.9	(0.7)	30.3	(1.3)	10.4	(0.8)
Mexico	11.0	(0.9)	4.3	(0.5)	24.9	(1.1)	20.9	(1.0)	11.9	(0.7)	15.3	(0.8)	38.8	(1.3)	47.4	(1.2)	18.2	(0.9)	33.2	(1.0)
Norway	8.6	(0.7)	7.0	(0.7)	28.1	(1.2)	18.2	(1.4)	5.8	(0.6)	2.5	(0.3)	29.2	(1.0)	12.3	(0.9)	8.3	(0.8)	7.4	(1.1)
Poland	17.0	(0.9)	1.8	(0.3)	22.2	(0.9)	10.6	(0.8)	7.8	(0.6)	5.9	(0.4)	29.4	(1.3)	14.5	(0.8)	6.6	(0.6)	5.6	(0.5)
Portugal	4.8	(0.4)	4.7	(0.4)	24.2	(0.9)	9.3	(0.5)	18.2	(0.9)	13.9	(0.6)	50.0	(1.1)	26.3	(1.0)	17.0	(0.7)	16.8	(0.7)
Slovak Republic	17.2	(1.0)	9.1	(0.6)	14.8	(1.0)	18.7	(0.9)	4.8	(0.5)	7.9	(0.5)	20.1	(1.0)	18.9	(0.9)	4.6	(0.5)	7.8	(0.6)
Spain	5.0	(0.5)	1.8	(0.2)	26.2	(1.1)	14.0	(0.7)	14.2	(0.6)	10.0	(0.5)	35.8	(1.0)	21.9	(1.0)	17.5	(0.7)	19.0	(1.0)
Sub-national entities																				
Flanders (Belgium)	17.5	(0.7)	3.0	(0.3)	14.8	(0.7)	10.6	(0.7)	2.4	(0.3)	1.8	(0.3)	12.8	(0.8)	5.3	(0.5)	3.7	(0.5)	3.1	(0.5)
Average	18.0	(0.2)	9.4	(0.2)	24.2	(0.3)	20.8	(0.2)	10.3	(0.2)	9.6	(0.2)	30.1	(0.3)	23.7	(0.2)	14.1	(0.2)	15.1	(0.2)

1. The teacher population coverage was slightly different between 2008 and 2013. In order to have comparable populations for the tables comparing results from 2008 and 2013, teachers who teach exclusively to students with special needs were excluded from the 2013 data in these tables.

2. The wording and order of questions may have changed slightly between the 2008 and 2013 surveys.

3. Special needs students are not well defined internationally but usually cover those for whom a special learning need has been formally identified because they are mentally, physically or emotionally disadvantaged. Often, special needs students will be those for whom additional public or private resources (personnel, material or financial) have been provided to support their education. "Gifted students" are not considered to have special needs under the definition used here and in other OECD work. Some teachers perceive all students as unique learners and thus having some special learning needs. For the purpose of this survey, it is important to ensure a more objective judgment of who is a special needs student and who is not. That is why a formal identification is stressed above.

Source: OECD, TALIS 2008 and 2013 Databases.

StatLink http://dx.doi.org/10.1787/888933045164

[Part 1/2]

Professional development participation resulting from needs for pedagogy and teaching diversity

Significant results of the logistic regression of participation in the following professional development activities during the 12 months prior to the survey and the index of pedagogical needs or the index of needs for teaching diversity[1,2]

Table 4.13

	Participation in courses/workshops, education conferences or seminars[3]		Participation in observation visits to other schools, business premises, public organisations or non-governmental organisations[4]		Participation in in-service training courses in business premises, public organisations, non-governmental organisations		Participation in qualification programme	
	Model 1[5]	Model 2[5]	Model 3[5]	Model 4[5]	Model 5[5]	Model 6[5]	Model 7[5]	Model 8[5]
	Dependent on:							
	Index of pedagogical needs[6]	Index of needs for teaching for diversity[7]	Index of pedagogical needs[6]	Index of needs for teaching for diversity[7]	Index of pedagogical needs[6]	Index of needs for teaching for diversity[7]	Index of pedagogical needs[6]	Index of needs for teaching for diversity[7]
Australia						+		
Brazil					+		+	
Bulgaria	+	+	+	+	+	+	+	+
Chile				-				
Croatia	+	+	+	+	+	+		
Czech Republic	+	+	+	+	+	+	+	+
Denmark								
Estonia	+	+	+	+		+	+	+
Finland	+	+	+	+			+	+
France	+			+				
Iceland	+							
Israel	+	+					+	
Italy	+						+	+
Japan	+	+	+	+	+	+		
Korea	+	+	+	+	+	+	+	+
Latvia	+	+		+				
Malaysia	+	+		+	+	+		+
Mexico								-
Netherlands				+	+	+		+
Norway	+							
Poland	+	+	+	+	+		+	+
Portugal	+							
Romania	+	+				+	+	+
Serbia	+	+		+		+		+
Singapore				+				+
Slovak Republic	+	+		+	+	+	+	+
Spain	+	+	+		+	+	+	
Sweden	+							
Sub-national entities								
Abu Dhabi (United Arab Emirates)								
Alberta (Canada)	+	+		+		+		
England (United Kingdom)					+	+		
Flanders (Belgium)	+	+		+		+	+	+

1. Cells are blank where no significant relationship was found (significance was tested at the 5% level). Variables where a significant positive relationship was found are indicated by a "+" while those where a significant negative relationship was found are shown with a "–". Participation in professional development activities tends to be positively predicted by the index of pedagogical needs and the index of needs for teaching for diversity. For example, in Bulgaria an increase in the index of pedagogical needs is positively associated with the likelihood of teachers reporting participating in professional development activities.

2. Cells with data representing less than 5% of the cases are shaded in grey and should be interpreted with caution. These results are not highlighted in the text of the report.

3. This is the combination of two different questions: *(i)* courses/workshops (e.g. on subject matter or methods and/or other education-related topics) and *(ii)* education conferences or seminars (where teachers and/or researchers present their research results and discuss educational issues).

4. This is the combination of two different questions: *(i)* observation visits to other schools and *(ii)* observation visits to business premises, public organisations or non-governmental organisations.

5. Controlling for teacher gender, age, years of experience, part-time/full-time, permanent/fixed term and the percentage of students from disadvantaged homes in each model. Each model was run independently.

6. The index for pedagogical needs considers professional development needs for: *(i)* knowledge and understanding of my subject field(s); *(ii)* pedagogical competencies in the specific teacher field(s); *(iii)* knowledge of the curriculum; *(iv)* student evaluation and assessment practice; and *(v)* student behaviour and classroom management.

7. The index of needs for teaching for diversity considers professional development needs for: *(i)* approaches to individualised learning; *(ii)* teaching students with special needs; *(iii)* teaching in a multicultural or multilingual setting; *(iv)* teaching cross-curricular skills; *(v)* approaches to developing cross-occupational competencies for future work or future studies; and *(vi)* student career guidance and counselling.

Source: OECD, TALIS 2013 Database.

StatLink ⎘ http://dx.doi.org/10.1787/888933045202

[Part 2/2]

Professional development participation resulting from needs for pedagogy and teaching diversity

Significant results of the logistic regression of participation in the following professional development activities during the 12 months prior to the survey and the index of pedagogical needs or the index of needs for teaching diversity[1,2]

Table 4.13

	Participation in a network of teachers formed specifically for the professional development of teachers		Participation in individual or collaborative research on a topic of interest to you professionally		Participation in mentoring and/or peer observation and coaching, as part of a formal school arrangement	
	Model 9[5]	Model 10[5]	Model 11[5]	Model 12[5]	Model 13[5]	Model 14[5]
	Dependent on:					
	Index of pedagogical needs[6]	Index of needs for teaching for diversity[7]	Index of pedagogical needs[6]	Index of needs for teaching for diversity[7]	Index of pedagogical needs[6]	Index of needs for teaching for diversity[7]
Australia	+	+				+
Brazil		-		-		-
Bulgaria	+	+	+	+	+	+
Chile						
Croatia	+	+	+	+		
Czech Republic		+	+	+	+	+
Denmark						
Estonia	+	+	+	+		+
Finland	+	+	+	+		+
France	+		+	+		+
Iceland						
Israel	+	+				
Italy	+	+	+	+		
Japan	+	+	+	+	+	+
Korea	+	+	+	+	+	+
Latvia		+		+		+
Malaysia	+	+	+	+		+
Mexico	-		-	-		-
Netherlands	+	+		+		
Norway						
Poland		+		+	+	+
Portugal						
Romania	+	+				
Serbia	+	+		+	+	+
Singapore			+		+	
Slovak Republic	+	+			+	+
Spain	+	+			+	
Sweden					-	
Sub-national entities						
Abu Dhabi (United Arab Emirates)						
Alberta (Canada)		+		+		+
England (United Kingdom)				+		
Flanders (Belgium)	+	+		+		

1. Cells are blank where no significant relationship was found (significance was tested at the 5% level). Variables where a significant positive relationship was found are indicated by a "+" while those where a significant negative relationship was found are shown with a "–". Participation in professional development activities tends to be positively predicted by the index of pedagogical needs and the index of needs for teaching for diversity. For example, in Bulgaria an increase in the index of pedagogical needs is positively associated with the likelihood of teachers reporting participating in professional development activities.

2. Cells with data representing less than 5% of the cases are shaded in grey and should be interpreted with caution. These results are not highlighted in the text of the report.

3. This is the combination of two different questions: *(i)* courses/workshops (e.g. on subject matter or methods and/or other education-related topics) and *(ii)* education conferences or seminars (where teachers and/or researchers present their research results and discuss educational issues).

4. This is the combination of two different questions: *(i)* observation visits to other schools and *(ii)* observation visits to business premises, public organisations or non-governmental organisations.

5. Controlling for teacher gender, age, years of experience, part-time/full-time, permanent/fixed term and the percentage of students from disadvantaged homes in each model. Each model was run independently.

6. The index for pedagogical needs considers professional development needs for: *(i)* knowledge and understanding of my subject field(s); *(ii)* pedagogical competencies in the specific teacher field(s); *(iii)* knowledge of the curriculum; *(iv)* student evaluation and assessment practice; and *(v)* student behaviour and classroom management.

7. The index of needs for teaching for diversity considers professional development needs for: *(i)* approaches to individualised learning; *(ii)* teaching students with special needs; *(iii)* teaching in a multicultural or multilingual setting; *(iv)* teaching cross-curricular skills; *(v)* approaches to developing cross-occupational competencies for future work or future studies; and *(vi)* student career guidance and counselling.

Source: OECD, TALIS 2013 Database.

StatLink ᴬᴸᴾ http://dx.doi.org/10.1787/888933045202

[Part 1/1]
Barriers to teachers' participation in professional development
Percentage of lower secondary education teachers indicating that they "agree" or "strongly agree"
Table 4.14 *that the following reasons represent barriers to their participation in professional development*

	Do not have the pre-requisites (e.g. qualifications, experience, seniority)		Professional development is too expensive/ unaffordable		There is a lack of employer support		Professional development conflicts with my work schedule		Lack of time due to family responsibilities		There is no relevant professional development offered		There are no incentives for participating in such activities	
	%	S.E.	%	S.E.	%	S.E.	%	S.E.	%	S.E.	%	S.E.	%	S.E.
Australia	6.5	(0.5)	38.8	(1.6)	23.9	(1.4)	58.0	(1.4)	32.7	(1.8)	24.6	(1.1)	39.6	(1.5)
Brazil	8.1	(0.4)	44.0	(0.8)	61.2	(1.0)	54.8	(0.9)	25.8	(0.8)	39.8	(0.9)	52.8	(1.1)
Bulgaria	10.4	(1.0)	58.1	(1.3)	12.7	(0.9)	51.3	(1.5)	28.8	(1.1)	45.4	(1.4)	65.7	(1.5)
Chile	24.8	(1.6)	72.8	(1.4)	52.8	(2.0)	62.3	(1.6)	45.8	(1.6)	63.6	(1.4)	73.1	(1.5)
Croatia	3.8	(0.4)	47.9	(1.1)	19.5	(0.9)	22.3	(0.9)	21.8	(0.9)	34.9	(0.9)	39.8	(0.9)
Cyprus*	12.2	(0.8)	44.1	(1.3)	41.3	(1.2)	45.1	(1.3)	52.3	(1.3)	43.0	(1.2)	61.3	(1.2)
Czech Republic	7.2	(0.5)	36.1	(1.3)	21.1	(1.4)	45.0	(1.2)	31.8	(0.9)	25.9	(0.8)	37.8	(1.2)
Denmark	11.0	(0.8)	55.6	(1.3)	26.0	(1.3)	40.2	(1.5)	20.3	(1.2)	38.3	(1.3)	39.2	(1.5)
Estonia	12.0	(0.8)	37.3	(1.1)	16.4	(0.9)	35.4	(1.3)	24.0	(1.1)	29.4	(1.0)	19.3	(0.9)
Finland	7.1	(0.6)	23.1	(1.3)	23.2	(1.6)	51.9	(1.2)	37.0	(1.2)	39.8	(1.2)	42.9	(1.4)
France	9.8	(0.7)	24.4	(0.9)	14.3	(0.7)	42.6	(1.0)	43.9	(1.1)	42.5	(1.3)	49.8	(1.1)
Iceland	5.5	(0.7)	43.1	(1.4)	14.5	(1.2)	57.9	(1.3)	40.7	(1.4)	40.7	(1.4)	40.7	(1.7)
Israel	8.3	(0.6)	28.8	(1.1)	25.9	(1.3)	50.4	(1.2)	49.5	(1.0)	27.3	(0.9)	57.2	(1.1)
Italy	14.0	(0.6)	53.0	(1.1)	39.8	(1.1)	59.6	(1.1)	39.2	(1.1)	66.6	(1.0)	83.4	(0.8)
Japan	26.7	(0.8)	62.1	(1.1)	59.5	(1.0)	86.4	(0.6)	52.4	(0.9)	37.3	(0.9)	38.0	(0.9)
Korea	29.6	(1.0)	47.9	(0.9)	70.2	(1.0)	83.1	(0.8)	47.4	(1.0)	43.4	(1.1)	57.0	(1.1)
Latvia	4.7	(0.5)	30.0	(1.5)	11.2	(0.9)	28.8	(1.2)	21.6	(1.1)	23.2	(1.1)	22.0	(1.1)
Malaysia	9.3	(0.6)	21.8	(1.0)	17.7	(1.0)	55.5	(1.1)	26.6	(0.9)	23.4	(0.8)	36.8	(1.2)
Mexico	26.5	(1.0)	53.7	(1.3)	63.6	(1.2)	53.6	(1.2)	27.6	(1.0)	56.2	(1.4)	63.7	(1.3)
Netherlands	8.2	(0.8)	26.3	(1.5)	26.9	(1.4)	38.3	(1.3)	26.9	(1.5)	39.3	(1.5)	30.9	(1.8)
Norway	8.7	(0.7)	37.1	(1.7)	28.5	(2.1)	48.6	(2.1)	38.2	(1.6)	19.3	(1.0)	31.8	(1.4)
Poland	4.0	(0.4)	53.1	(1.1)	19.9	(1.0)	33.0	(1.2)	43.9	(1.0)	46.6	(1.6)	39.0	(1.2)
Portugal	13.2	(0.6)	80.7	(0.9)	92.1	(0.5)	74.8	(0.9)	48.2	(1.0)	67.5	(1.1)	85.2	(0.7)
Romania	13.1	(1.0)	55.5	(1.3)	18.8	(1.0)	41.8	(1.3)	35.0	(1.4)	21.5	(1.0)	59.9	(1.3)
Serbia	8.7	(0.6)	58.1	(1.2)	34.5	(1.2)	27.4	(1.0)	22.3	(1.0)	47.7	(0.9)	51.9	(1.3)
Singapore	15.6	(0.8)	19.8	(0.7)	21.0	(0.8)	62.2	(0.8)	45.2	(0.9)	22.4	(0.8)	37.3	(0.9)
Slovak Republic	11.0	(0.6)	49.7	(1.5)	17.5	(1.1)	34.2	(1.1)	36.3	(1.1)	43.0	(1.3)	41.6	(1.3)
Spain	7.8	(0.5)	38.1	(1.0)	30.6	(1.0)	59.7	(1.1)	57.5	(1.0)	61.5	(1.1)	80.3	(1.2)
Sweden	7.7	(0.5)	60.6	(1.2)	35.4	(1.3)	58.1	(1.1)	22.6	(0.8)	46.1	(1.2)	38.2	(1.3)
Sub-national entities														
Abu Dhabi (United Arab Emirates)	4.5	(0.5)	41.2	(1.5)	39.6	(1.8)	45.2	(1.5)	27.1	(1.2)	40.9	(1.9)	57.9	(1.7)
Alberta (Canada)	5.8	(0.7)	42.4	(1.6)	21.6	(1.3)	61.2	(1.5)	44.1	(1.3)	32.0	(1.4)	47.6	(1.4)
England (United Kingdom)	10.1	(0.8)	43.4	(1.7)	27.4	(1.4)	60.4	(1.4)	27.0	(1.1)	24.8	(1.1)	38.1	(1.2)
Flanders (Belgium)	9.1	(0.5)	16.8	(0.9)	15.3	(0.9)	42.0	(1.2)	34.3	(1.1)	28.6	(1.0)	25.0	(0.9)
Average	**11.1**	**(0.1)**	**43.8**	**(0.2)**	**31.6**	**(0.2)**	**50.6**	**(0.2)**	**35.7**	**(0.2)**	**39.0**	**(0.2)**	**48.0**	**(0.2)**
United States	5.3	(0.8)	30.7	(2.2)	20.7	(1.4)	45.6	(1.4)	38.7	(1.2)	27.6	(1.6)	44.0	(1.6)

*See notes at the beginning of this Annex.
Source: OECD, TALIS 2013 Database.
StatLink ⟐ http://dx.doi.org/10.1787/888933045240

[Part 1/1]
Teachers who never received formal appraisal
*Percentage of lower secondary education teachers whose school principal reports that their teachers
were never appraised by the following bodies or never appraised at all*

Table 5.1

	Never formally appraised by the school principal		Never formally appraised by other members of the school management team		Never formally appraised by the teacher's mentor		Never formally appraised by other teachers		Never formally appraised by external individuals or bodies		Generally never formally appraised	
	%	S.E.	%	S.E.	%	S.E.	%	S.E.	%	S.E.	%	S.E.
Australia	28.5	(5.8)	7.1	(2.3)	25.9	(4.4)	50.1	(6.4)	77.9	(4.4)	2.8	(1.4)
Brazil	19.6	(1.6)	25.9	(2.0)	41.0	(2.5)	53.9	(2.6)	58.0	(2.7)	13.4	(1.4)
Bulgaria	18.0	(3.2)	25.7	(3.2)	50.6	(3.6)	39.3	(3.6)	14.7	(2.8)	10.2	(2.4)
Chile	7.3	(2.3)	13.6	(3.0)	60.3	(4.1)	45.1	(5.0)	52.9	(4.0)	4.1	(1.7)
Croatia	7.8	(1.9)	38.1	(3.3)	21.2	(2.9)	64.3	(4.0)	13.9	(2.6)	2.6	(1.0)
Cyprus*	3.7	(0.1)	43.3	(0.2)	46.3	(0.2)	59.5	(0.2)	19.7	(0.1)	0.0	(0.0)
Czech Republic	0.2	(0.2)	7.7	(1.6)	67.2	(4.1)	55.4	(4.0)	6.9	(1.7)	0.2	(0.2)
Denmark	10.3	(3.2)	30.7	(4.4)	82.0	(4.1)	62.6	(4.9)	76.1	(4.3)	9.0	(3.0)
Estonia	2.4	(1.1)	8.1	(1.7)	30.8	(3.4)	25.1	(3.2)	8.4	(2.4)	1.7	(1.0)
Finland	27.6	(3.9)	85.8	(3.2)	92.4	(2.5)	91.9	(2.5)	77.7	(4.0)	25.9	(4.2)
France	6.2	(2.0)	72.7	(3.3)	62.2	(4.1)	81.4	(3.1)	7.2	(2.0)	0.7	(0.7)
Iceland	30.0	(0.1)	43.8	(0.1)	84.4	(0.1)	76.5	(0.1)	52.3	(0.1)	20.7	(0.1)
Israel	0.9	(0.7)	12.8	(2.6)	24.4	(3.9)	48.2	(4.1)	28.5	(3.9)	0.9	(0.7)
Italy	74.7	(3.1)	88.0	(2.2)	89.9	(2.2)	89.7	(2.0)	88.8	(2.2)	70.1	(3.2)
Japan	6.8	(1.7)	27.6	(3.3)	44.4	(4.1)	40.8	(3.7)	32.4	(3.2)	3.8	(1.1)
Korea	2.5	(1.3)	16.9	(3.0)	35.8	(4.0)	6.2	(2.0)	42.7	(4.2)	0.0	(0.0)
Latvia	2.0	(1.5)	5.3	(2.4)	53.5	(5.2)	24.3	(3.9)	10.9	(3.6)	2.0	(1.5)
Malaysia	1.7	(1.2)	6.8	(2.1)	15.7	(3.2)	12.5	(2.4)	0.9	(0.9)	0.9	(0.9)
Mexico	11.7	(2.9)	21.2	(3.2)	53.3	(4.0)	49.4	(3.9)	19.4	(3.0)	4.6	(1.9)
Netherlands	48.6	(5.7)	7.9	(2.7)	84.3	(3.8)	71.0	(5.1)	46.8	(5.4)	2.4	(1.2)
Norway	5.9	(2.0)	17.7	(4.4)	52.6	(5.4)	60.1	(7.5)	56.3	(7.9)	5.9	(2.0)
Poland	0.4	(0.4)	53.0	(4.3)	75.5	(3.2)	74.1	(3.4)	16.0	(3.3)	0.0	(0.0)
Portugal	17.1	(2.8)	56.0	(4.1)	26.1	(3.8)	28.9	(3.6)	62.2	(4.2)	2.4	(1.1)
Romania	0.0	(0.0)	5.5	(1.7)	42.9	(4.1)	28.5	(3.3)	5.3	(1.7)	0.0	(0.0)
Serbia	3.3	(1.3)	23.9	(3.2)	9.9	(2.3)	33.2	(4.2)	8.7	(2.3)	2.2	(1.0)
Singapore	0.6	(0.0)	0.0	(0.0)	46.3	(0.3)	73.1	(0.2)	53.4	(0.2)	0.0	(0.0)
Slovak Republic	0.6	(0.5)	4.5	(1.8)	61.5	(3.3)	42.4	(3.8)	17.8	(2.5)	0.0	(0.0)
Spain	61.5	(3.4)	71.3	(3.3)	80.7	(2.8)	83.1	(2.7)	52.8	(3.5)	36.3	(3.5)
Sweden	9.2	(2.4)	58.7	(3.1)	75.4	(3.1)	69.9	(3.4)	29.3	(3.2)	3.6	(1.5)
Sub-national entities												
Abu Dhabi (United Arab Emirates)	0.8	(0.8)	7.2	(2.4)	25.5	(4.4)	46.2	(4.6)	36.6	(4.2)	0.0	(0.0)
Alberta (Canada)	18.3	(3.9)	48.6	(4.8)	77.3	(3.6)	74.5	(3.7)	81.4	(3.2)	16.1	(3.7)
England (United Kingdom)	16.7	(4.0)	2.8	(1.4)	22.0	(4.2)	10.9	(2.4)	41.8	(5.1)	0.0	(0.0)
Flanders (Belgium)	11.6	(3.1)	43.9	(4.5)	40.7	(3.7)	60.8	(4.2)	38.7	(4.0)	2.1	(1.3)
Average	13.8	(0.4)	29.8	(0.5)	51.6	(0.6)	52.5	(0.7)	37.5	(0.6)	7.4	(0.3)
United States	1.3	(1.3)	31.9	(6.6)	48.6	(6.0)	63.7	(5.2)	72.5	(4.6)	0.0	(0.0)

*See notes at the beginning of this Annex.
Source: OECD, TALIS 2013 Database.
StatLink ⬛⬛ http://dx.doi.org/10.1787/888933045582

[Part 1/1]
Methods of formally appraising teachers

Percentage of lower secondary education teachers whose school principal reports that appraisal is used

Table 5.2 *in their school and report that teachers are formally appraised with the following methods[1, 2]*

	Appraisal used in the school where the teacher works		Direct observation of classroom teaching		Student surveys about teaching		Assessment of teachers' content knowledge		Analysis of student test scores		Discussion of teachers' self-assessments of their work		Discussion about feedback received from parents or guardians	
	%	S.E.	%	S.E.	%	S.E.	%	S.E.	%	S.E.	%	S.E.	%	S.E.
Australia	97.2	(1.4)	94.6	(2.3)	75.9	(4.2)	76.6	(5.5)	94.2	(2.3)	87.9	(2.7)	86.9	(3.4)
Brazil	86.6	(1.4)	92.9	(1.3)	88.4	(1.8)	78.9	(2.2)	98.1	(0.6)	79.6	(1.9)	91.6	(1.1)
Bulgaria	89.8	(2.4)	100.0	(0.0)	82.6	(3.1)	85.0	(3.0)	97.1	(1.8)	68.5	(4.0)	85.1	(2.4)
Chile	95.9	(1.7)	100.0	(0.0)	58.2	(4.8)	80.1	(4.0)	97.4	(1.3)	83.6	(3.6)	90.8	(2.7)
Croatia	97.4	(1.0)	99.6	(0.4)	95.0	(1.6)	a	a	93.7	(1.7)	80.0	(2.7)	92.9	(1.8)
Cyprus*	100.0	(0.0)	97.6	(0.1)	50.5	(0.2)	83.5	(0.2)	84.0	(0.2)	61.3	(0.2)	62.7	(0.2)
Czech Republic	99.8	(0.2)	100.0	(0.0)	96.8	(1.3)	74.7	(3.3)	99.6	(0.4)	93.5	(2.0)	97.8	(1.1)
Denmark	91.0	(3.0)	90.7	(3.1)	78.8	(5.6)	66.5	(5.4)	95.7	(1.3)	79.1	(4.2)	95.3	(1.9)
Estonia	98.3	(1.0)	98.6	(1.0)	96.6	(1.1)	88.9	(2.7)	98.0	(2.1)	96.0	(1.5)	98.8	(0.8)
Finland	74.1	(4.2)	78.3	(4.0)	85.3	(4.0)	37.8	(4.9)	73.8	(5.0)	60.1	(4.5)	97.9	(1.6)
France	99.3	(0.7)	95.5	(1.5)	29.9	(3.8)	74.0	(3.6)	93.5	(2.0)	43.7	(4.2)	85.2	(3.1)
Iceland	79.3	(0.1)	72.0	(0.1)	71.8	(0.1)	41.3	(0.2)	92.1	(0.1)	61.3	(0.2)	77.4	(0.1)
Israel	99.1	(0.7)	97.9	(1.4)	84.1	(3.3)	83.4	(3.7)	97.9	(1.6)	91.5	(2.2)	80.3	(4.0)
Italy	29.9	(3.2)	73.7	(5.9)	52.3	(7.5)	45.2	(7.0)	88.4	(4.3)	62.2	(7.2)	82.8	(5.3)
Japan	96.2	(1.1)	98.4	(1.2)	86.5	(2.7)	63.6	(3.7)	97.6	(1.1)	92.1	(2.2)	86.8	(2.4)
Korea	100.0	(0.0)	100.0	(0.0)	93.8	(2.0)	82.2	(3.3)	98.7	(0.9)	79.9	(3.3)	81.4	(3.2)
Latvia	98.0	(1.5)	100.0	(0.0)	100.0	(0.0)	76.5	(4.8)	100.0	(0.0)	99.1	(0.9)	100.0	(0.0)
Malaysia	99.1	(0.9)	100.0	(0.0)	78.9	(3.5)	92.6	(2.3)	100.0	(0.0)	93.4	(2.0)	98.1	(1.2)
Mexico	95.4	(1.9)	99.5	(0.5)	88.2	(2.4)	89.5	(2.6)	99.1	(0.7)	89.4	(2.3)	90.9	(1.8)
Netherlands	97.6	(1.2)	98.8	(1.2)	94.4	(2.6)	88.6	(3.5)	94.3	(2.1)	88.0	(3.9)	74.7	(5.0)
Norway	94.1	(2.0)	96.0	(1.5)	76.7	(5.3)	69.3	(6.2)	99.8	(0.2)	84.0	(3.6)	90.3	(4.3)
Poland	100.0	(0.0)	100.0	(0.0)	99.1	(0.6)	88.1	(2.4)	100.0	(0.0)	89.9	(1.8)	98.0	(0.9)
Portugal	97.6	(1.1)	96.2	(1.8)	48.2	(3.6)	56.8	(4.0)	90.3	(2.1)	85.3	(3.1)	72.5	(3.4)
Romania	100.0	(0.0)	100.0	(0.0)	94.3	(1.8)	98.6	(0.7)	100.0	(0.0)	97.6	(1.1)	100.0	(0.0)
Serbia	97.8	(1.0)	97.6	(1.2)	57.0	(4.1)	80.2	(2.9)	86.8	(2.6)	70.6	(4.2)	86.3	(3.0)
Singapore	100.0	(0.0)	100.0	(0.0)	74.5	(0.2)	96.8	(0.1)	98.5	(0.0)	97.1	(0.0)	92.6	(0.1)
Slovak Republic	100.0	(0.0)	100.0	(0.0)	92.5	(2.3)	78.9	(3.1)	100.0	(0.0)	85.1	(2.8)	95.3	(1.6)
Spain	63.7	(3.5)	59.3	(4.7)	72.4	(4.4)	34.3	(4.1)	97.1	(1.5)	78.9	(3.4)	90.1	(2.5)
Sweden	96.4	(1.5)	96.3	(1.6)	91.5	(2.2)	63.4	(3.8)	99.4	(0.6)	69.3	(3.9)	87.4	(2.7)
Sub-national entities														
Abu Dhabi (United Arab Emirates)	100.0	(0.0)	100.0	(0.0)	92.6	(2.8)	97.7	(1.6)	99.1	(0.9)	92.3	(3.1)	99.8	(0.2)
Alberta (Canada)	83.9	(3.7)	99.8	(0.2)	69.7	(4.6)	80.9	(3.8)	92.4	(2.3)	85.7	(3.3)	92.8	(3.0)
England (United Kingdom)	100.0	(0.0)	100.0	(0.0)	81.7	(3.4)	84.2	(3.3)	99.4	(0.6)	88.6	(2.3)	79.1	(4.1)
Flanders (Belgium)	97.9	(1.3)	99.2	(0.8)	61.2	(4.8)	81.5	(3.7)	87.3	(3.4)	60.6	(4.1)	87.0	(3.0)
Average	92.6	(0.3)	94.9	(0.3)	78.8	(0.6)	75.6	(0.6)	95.3	(0.3)	81.1	(0.5)	88.7	(0.5)
United States	100.0	(0.0)	100.0	(0.0)	60.1	(5.7)	72.1	(5.2)	93.3	(3.8)	73.7	(5.5)	90.5	(3.2)

1. Percentage of teachers working in schools where the principal is reporting that teachers are appraised with the following methods by at least one body, including: external individuals or bodies, principal, member(s) of school management team, assigned mentors or other teachers.

2. Data derived from the principal questionnaire (question 28). Please note that schools that are not using formal teacher appraisal were filtered in question 27, meaning that these schools are not covered in question 28.

*See notes at the beginning of this Annex.

Source: OECD, TALIS 2013 Database.

StatLink ⟡ http://dx.doi.org/10.1787/888933045620

[Part 1/1]
Outcomes of formal teacher appraisal
Percentage of lower secondary education teachers whose school principal reports that the following outcomes occured "sometimes", "most of the time" or "always" after formal teacher appraisal[1]

Table 5.3

	Measures to remedy any weaknesses in teaching are discussed with the teacher		A development or training plan is developed for each teacher		Material sanctions (e.g. reduced annual increases in pay) are imposed on poor performers		A mentor is appointed to help the teacher improve his/her teaching		A change in teachers' work responsibilities		A change in teachers' salary or a payment of a financial bonus		A change in the likelihood of career advancement		Dismissal or non-renewal of contract	
	%	S.E.	%	S.E.	%	S.E.	%	S.E.	%	S.E.	%	S.E.	%	S.E.	%	S.E.
Australia	100.0	(0.0)	92.4	(3.2)	5.4	(2.3)	98.3	(1.2)	79.8	(4.7)	14.2	(5.2)	80.4	(3.8)	68.3	(5.4)
Brazil	100.0	(0.0)	87.9	(1.8)	11.5	(1.7)	82.9	(2.2)	50.4	(2.4)	25.4	(2.3)	46.7	(3.1)	59.4	(2.4)
Bulgaria	96.2	(1.9)	85.3	(3.1)	22.6	(3.4)	65.6	(4.0)	71.4	(3.6)	83.5	(2.9)	63.9	(3.9)	76.8	(3.5)
Chile	98.0	(1.6)	91.1	(2.7)	20.4	(4.1)	66.2	(5.2)	61.5	(4.8)	22.8	(4.5)	47.1	(5.4)	68.6	(4.8)
Croatia	100.0	(0.0)	88.7	(2.4)	a	a	53.0	(3.7)	56.1	(3.6)	a	a	62.7	(3.8)	13.9	(2.8)
Cyprus*	100.0	(0.0)	88.0	(0.1)	8.2	(0.1)	85.1	(0.2)	50.0	(0.3)	6.6	(0.1)	69.9	(0.2)	40.4	(0.2)
Czech Republic	100.0	(0.0)	85.3	(3.0)	60.6	(3.7)	73.1	(3.2)	59.8	(4.2)	93.6	(1.8)	55.1	(3.7)	78.6	(3.4)
Denmark	99.7	(0.3)	92.6	(2.0)	a	a	61.5	(5.7)	86.7	(3.2)	7.3	(2.2)	54.4	(5.7)	68.8	(4.2)
Estonia	99.7	(0.3)	81.7	(2.8)	15.6	(3.0)	77.2	(3.5)	90.2	(2.4)	73.9	(3.3)	63.7	(4.0)	69.9	(3.7)
Finland	100.0	(0.0)	65.3	(5.2)	6.4	(2.8)	48.3	(5.0)	73.4	(4.5)	49.1	(5.5)	39.2	(5.2)	70.3	(5.0)
France	97.3	(1.2)	67.2	(3.7)	11.2	(2.6)	85.9	(2.8)	48.9	(4.0)	26.5	(3.2)	65.8	(3.7)	27.1	(3.4)
Iceland	98.2	(0.1)	62.1	(0.2)	6.1	(0.1)	59.1	(0.2)	62.3	(0.2)	16.6	(0.1)	55.2	(0.2)	76.6	(0.2)
Israel	99.5	(0.5)	99.0	(0.7)	5.1	(1.7)	91.7	(1.9)	90.3	(2.5)	14.1	(3.2)	72.3	(4.2)	72.7	(4.0)
Italy	94.2	(2.9)	75.4	(5.6)	6.5	(3.0)	71.4	(6.4)	50.0	(7.3)	22.9	(5.4)	6.0	(2.2)	29.4	(5.6)
Japan	98.3	(1.0)	83.4	(2.8)	8.7	(1.8)	44.5	(3.5)	52.7	(3.6)	11.4	(2.1)	14.5	(2.4)	9.0	(2.1)
Korea	99.4	(0.6)	100.0	(0.0)	5.1	(1.7)	91.1	(2.4)	96.7	(1.4)	49.3	(4.4)	68.2	(3.9)	23.2	(3.7)
Latvia	100.0	(0.0)	91.7	(2.9)	34.4	(4.6)	62.7	(4.7)	93.9	(2.0)	68.0	(4.1)	57.0	(5.7)	58.4	(4.6)
Malaysia	99.7	(0.3)	96.7	(1.7)	10.5	(2.4)	92.6	(2.2)	97.9	(1.1)	19.9	(3.7)	54.2	(4.5)	2.6	(1.5)
Mexico	97.0	(1.4)	83.1	(3.0)	8.5	(2.0)	48.4	(3.9)	37.0	(3.5)	15.5	(2.5)	39.9	(3.8)	23.5	(2.8)
Netherlands	100.0	(0.0)	96.8	(2.0)	18.5	(4.4)	99.4	(0.6)	82.8	(4.2)	39.2	(5.4)	71.9	(5.6)	96.2	(2.7)
Norway	100.0	(0.0)	68.0	(7.1)	5.4	(3.3)	63.0	(7.2)	87.9	(2.9)	2.6	(1.6)	29.7	(7.2)	59.4	(8.0)
Poland	98.3	(1.0)	80.7	(3.6)	12.3	(2.7)	61.4	(3.8)	66.3	(4.2)	62.7	(4.3)	37.7	(3.6)	79.8	(2.9)
Portugal	90.7	(2.6)	64.1	(3.8)	0.0	(0.0)	54.7	(4.3)	48.9	(3.8)	3.6	(1.9)	35.6	(3.9)	24.2	(3.5)
Romania	98.9	(0.8)	90.4	(2.1)	47.7	(3.7)	78.3	(3.1)	55.7	(3.6)	38.2	(3.2)	87.9	(2.3)	49.3	(3.9)
Serbia	100.0	(0.0)	95.4	(1.3)	26.3	(3.4)	65.1	(3.2)	64.0	(4.3)	11.5	(2.5)	38.0	(4.1)	22.2	(3.4)
Singapore	100.0	(0.0)	100.0	(0.0)	78.6	(0.2)	100.0	(0.0)	100.0	(0.0)	87.6	(0.2)	96.7	(0.1)	86.7	(0.2)
Slovak Republic	100.0	(0.0)	73.9	(3.5)	56.3	(4.0)	57.3	(3.7)	65.3	(3.8)	75.7	(3.5)	57.1	(4.0)	83.2	(2.6)
Spain	85.9	(3.4)	48.8	(4.7)	0.9	(0.7)	25.4	(3.7)	42.3	(4.5)	2.9	(1.5)	26.9	(3.9)	28.3	(3.6)
Sweden	100.0	(0.0)	90.3	(2.2)	78.8	(2.8)	80.3	(3.4)	86.8	(3.0)	45.4	(3.8)	63.0	(4.2)	73.5	(4.0)
Sub-national entities																
Abu Dhabi (United Arab Emirates)	98.5	(1.1)	96.2	(2.2)	21.7	(4.3)	79.9	(4.1)	76.4	(3.7)	38.1	(4.1)	60.7	(4.0)	55.1	(4.6)
Alberta (Canada)	99.9	(0.1)	95.6	(1.7)	4.5	(1.6)	88.9	(3.0)	71.3	(4.2)	3.0	(1.6)	69.3	(4.6)	80.3	(3.4)
England (United Kingdom)	100.0	(0.0)	100.0	(0.0)	78.2	(3.2)	100.0	(0.0)	91.1	(2.2)	66.1	(5.0)	96.6	(1.7)	81.4	(4.0)
Flanders (Belgium)	100.0	(0.0)	71.3	(3.7)	2.3	(1.4)	81.0	(3.4)	65.3	(3.9)	0.9	(0.9)	50.1	(4.7)	89.3	(3.1)
Average	98.5	(0.2)	84.5	(0.5)	21.9	(0.5)	72.5	(0.6)	70.1	(0.6)	34.3	(0.6)	55.7	(0.7)	56.0	(0.7)
United States	100.0	(0.0)	96.6	(2.5)	23.2	(5.9)	86.5	(4.0)	66.4	(5.4)	14.0	(4.4)	68.1	(6.0)	94.6	(2.1)

1. Data derived from the principal questionnaire (question 29). Please note that schools that are not using formal teacher appraisal were filtered in question 27, meaning that these schools are not covered in question 29.

* See notes at the beginning of this Annex.

Source: OECD, TALIS 2013 Database.

StatLink http://dx.doi.org/10.1787/888933045753

[Part 1/1]
Teachers' feedback by source of feedback
Percentage of lower secondary education teachers who report receiving feedback from various sources
Table 5.4 *and teachers who report never having received feedback in their school[1]*

| | Have received feedback from[2] | | | | | | | | | | Have never received feedback in their current school[3] | |
| | External individuals or bodies | | School principal | | Members of school management team | | Assigned mentors | | Other teachers | | | |
	%	S.E.	%	S.E.	%	S.E.	%	S.E.	%	S.E.	%	S.E.
Australia	14.8	(1.0)	27.2	(1.6)	57.0	(2.0)	24.1	(1.5)	50.6	(2.0)	14.1	(1.5)
Brazil	27.6	(0.9)	54.8	(1.0)	68.3	(1.1)	37.8	(1.2)	29.0	(0.8)	8.7	(0.5)
Bulgaria	56.6	(1.6)	94.5	(0.7)	31.1	(1.3)	16.0	(0.9)	43.5	(1.7)	1.8	(0.4)
Chile	20.1	(1.3)	34.1	(1.8)	60.6	(1.9)	13.6	(1.1)	23.4	(1.5)	14.0	(1.4)
Croatia[4]	36.4	(0.9)	74.3	(1.3)	52.5	(1.4)	14.4	(0.7)	31.7	(1.0)	5.6	(0.5)
Cyprus*	46.5	(1.1)	47.0	(1.3)	35.1	(1.2)	15.6	(1.0)	38.1	(1.5)	17.5	(1.0)
Czech Republic	48.1	(1.2)	73.2	(1.4)	64.2	(1.6)	7.9	(0.6)	52.5	(1.4)	3.3	(0.5)
Denmark	19.2	(1.3)	43.7	(2.5)	14.9	(1.1)	5.6	(0.9)	58.2	(1.6)	22.3	(1.3)
Estonia	28.2	(1.1)	52.3	(2.0)	80.1	(1.3)	5.8	(0.8)	45.8	(1.4)	7.0	(0.7)
Finland	18.5	(0.9)	42.4	(1.4)	6.6	(0.7)	0.7	(0.2)	43.0	(1.1)	36.9	(1.2)
France	70.3	(1.1)	43.1	(1.3)	18.2	(0.9)	6.1	(0.6)	20.7	(1.0)	16.1	(0.8)
Iceland	11.8	(1.0)	21.0	(1.3)	31.8	(1.3)	4.6	(0.6)	23.8	(1.2)	45.4	(1.6)
Israel	34.2	(1.1)	68.7	(1.3)	50.3	(1.5)	29.5	(1.2)	29.7	(1.2)	10.0	(0.7)
Italy	21.9	(0.8)	27.8	(1.0)	15.2	(0.8)	2.4	(0.3)	39.2	(1.0)	42.8	(0.9)
Japan	30.9	(1.2)	75.2	(1.2)	64.5	(1.1)	39.1	(1.1)	47.2	(1.0)	6.3	(0.5)
Korea	13.0	(0.7)	29.8	(1.3)	29.3	(1.1)	9.4	(0.6)	84.4	(0.7)	6.0	(0.6)
Latvia	34.2	(1.3)	61.3	(2.0)	89.8	(1.4)	6.5	(0.6)	57.5	(1.6)	2.9	(0.4)
Malaysia	25.6	(1.1)	46.3	(1.5)	90.5	(0.7)	28.8	(1.4)	33.3	(0.9)	1.1	(0.2)
Mexico	38.9	(1.1)	56.3	(1.8)	60.1	(1.4)	24.0	(1.2)	34.7	(1.0)	9.5	(0.8)
Netherlands	18.1	(1.7)	26.4	(1.7)	80.7	(1.7)	19.1	(1.6)	57.0	(1.5)	6.1	(0.8)
Norway	9.8	(1.2)	45.3	(1.7)	43.9	(2.8)	3.2	(0.8)	57.4	(2.1)	16.2	(1.2)
Poland	32.3	(1.2)	93.0	(0.8)	38.2	(1.8)	26.2	(1.1)	50.7	(1.2)	1.7	(0.3)
Portugal	9.9	(0.6)	42.1	(1.1)	31.4	(1.0)	45.4	(1.2)	55.4	(0.9)	16.2	(0.8)
Romania	64.5	(1.3)	89.4	(0.9)	58.2	(1.5)	43.0	(1.4)	47.3	(1.2)	2.7	(0.4)
Serbia	34.5	(0.9)	70.2	(1.2)	30.1	(1.0)	12.0	(0.7)	37.5	(1.3)	4.4	(0.4)
Singapore	10.8	(0.6)	50.4	(0.9)	82.6	(0.8)	38.3	(0.9)	42.6	(1.0)	1.2	(0.2)
Slovak Republic	32.3	(1.4)	65.2	(1.5)	72.4	(1.1)	14.1	(0.7)	54.6	(1.3)	3.6	(0.4)
Spain	17.3	(0.9)	21.8	(1.3)	42.4	(1.3)	25.9	(1.1)	34.7	(0.9)	31.5	(1.1)
Sweden	10.4	(0.7)	46.4	(1.5)	13.0	(1.2)	3.3	(0.5)	33.7	(1.2)	32.5	(1.2)
Sub-national entities												
Abu Dhabi (United Arab Emirates)	25.0	(1.6)	75.6	(2.9)	67.9	(1.5)	54.4	(1.9)	19.9	(1.3)	2.6	(0.6)
Alberta (Canada)	28.9	(1.4)	81.4	(1.3)	39.7	(1.7)	9.4	(1.1)	35.8	(1.3)	7.1	(0.5)
England (United Kingdom)	28.9	(1.6)	41.9	(1.6)	85.2	(0.9)	28.9	(1.0)	51.1	(1.4)	0.9	(0.3)
Flanders (Belgium)	33.8	(2.0)	69.8	(1.7)	19.6	(1.3)	18.2	(1.3)	19.7	(1.0)	14.3	(1.1)
Average	**28.9**	**(0.2)**	**54.3**	**(0.3)**	**49.3**	**(0.2)**	**19.2**	**(0.2)**	**41.9**	**(0.2)**	**12.5**	**(0.1)**
United States	23.6	(1.3)	84.6	(2.5)	48.2	(2.4)	10.5	(1.0)	27.4	(2.0)	1.9	(0.7)

1. Feedback is defined broadly as any communication of the results of a review of an individual's work, often with the purpose of noting good performance or identifying areas for development. The feedback may be provided formally or informally.

2. Referring to the percentage of teachers receiving feedback from respective bodies for at least one item from question 28 of the teacher questionnaire. The same teacher can receive feedback from different bodies via different methods.

3. Referring to the percentage of teachers reporting never having received feedback in their school for any of the items surveyed in question 28 from the teacher questionnaire.

4. The question on "feedback following assessment of teachers' content knowledge" was excluded as not applicable for Croatia.

* See notes at the beginning of this Annex.

Source: OECD, TALIS 2013 Database.

StatLink ▦ http://dx.doi.org/10.1787/888933045791

[Part 1/1]
Teachers' feedback by source of feedback in primary education
Percentage of primary education teachers who report receiving feedback from various sources and teachers who report never having received feedback in their school[1]

Table 5.4.a

| | Have received feedback from[2] | | | | | | | | | | Have never received feedback in their current school[3] | |
| | External individuals or bodies | | School principal | | Members of school management team | | Assigned mentors | | Other teachers | | | |
	%	S.E.	%	S.E.	%	S.E.	%	S.E.	%	S.E.	%	S.E.
Denmark	20.2	(1.1)	47.2	(1.9)	15.5	(1.4)	5.5	(0.6)	64.8	(1.5)	17.1	(1.0)
Finland	24.8	(1.1)	55.1	(1.4)	7.5	(0.8)	1.3	(0.2)	57.1	(1.4)	24.1	(1.4)
Mexico	41.9	(2.1)	72.1	(2.2)	43.3	(2.0)	20.6	(1.6)	31.6	(1.7)	11.3	(1.4)
Norway	13.8	(1.0)	52.4	(3.9)	40.2	(3.1)	2.4	(0.4)	62.7	(2.0)	10.7	(1.4)
Poland	35.5	(1.5)	95.4	(0.5)	30.5	(1.5)	24.1	(1.2)	45.2	(1.5)	1.2	(0.3)
Sub-national entities												
Flanders (Belgium)	31.8	(1.2)	81.0	(1.4)	36.9	(1.1)	6.7	(0.7)	19.2	(1.1)	9.6	(0.9)
Average	28.0	(0.6)	67.2	(0.9)	29.0	(0.7)	10.1	(0.4)	46.7	(0.6)	12.3	(0.5)

1. Feedback is defined broadly as any communication of the results of a review of an individual's work, often with the purpose of noting good performance or identifying areas for development. The feedback may be provided formally or informally.
2. Referring to the percentage of teachers receiving feedback from respective bodies for at least one item from question 28 of the teacher questionnaire. The same teacher can receive feedback from different bodies via different methods.
3. Referring to the percentage of teachers reporting never having received feedback in their school for any of the items surveyed in question 28 from the teacher questionnaire.
Source: OECD, TALIS 2013 Database.
StatLink http://dx.doi.org/10.1787/888933045810

[Part 1/1]
Teachers' feedback by source of feedback in upper secondary education
Percentage of upper secondary education teachers who report receiving feedback from various sources and teachers who report never having received feedback in their school[1]

Table 5.4.b

| | Have received feedback from[2] | | | | | | | | | | Have never received feedback in their current school[3] | |
| | External individuals or bodies | | School principal | | Members of school management team | | Assigned mentors | | Other teachers | | | |
	%	S.E.	%	S.E.	%	S.E.	%	S.E.	%	S.E.	%	S.E.
Australia	19,0	(1,0)	26,7	(1,9)	58,5	(1,6)	19,8	(1,3)	53,8	(1,9)	12,8	(1,0)
Denmark	14,8	(1,3)	40,4	(2,3)	19,3	(1,7)	13,0	(1,4)	44,7	(1,9)	25,6	(1,9)
Finland	15,7	(1,5)	31,2	(2,2)	18,4	(2,1)	3,5	(0,8)	48,2	(2,0)	28,2	(1,4)
Iceland	4,7	(0,8)	41,7	(1,5)	44,6	(1,7)	5,4	(0,8)	19,4	(1,3)	21,2	(1,2)
Italy	14,4	(0,7)	25,3	(1,3)	17,6	(0,9)	2,1	(0,3)	35,9	(1,2)	45,0	(1,3)
Mexico	26,7	(1,2)	40,8	(2,1)	64,0	(1,6)	20,8	(1,0)	32,9	(1,3)	10,8	(0,9)
Norway	9,8	(0,8)	15,9	(1,0)	71,4	(2,1)	4,5	(0,7)	46,9	(1,5)	10,7	(1,3)
Poland	25,9	(1,2)	87,0	(1,2)	52,4	(2,4)	23,1	(1,3)	44,2	(1,3)	3,2	(0,6)
Singapore	11,6	(0,6)	53,9	(0,9)	81,6	(0,8)	36,2	(0,9)	43,7	(1,0)	1,0	(0,2)
Sub-national entities												
Abu Dhabi (United Arab Emirates)	25,1	(1,4)	77,3	(1,9)	66,7	(1,5)	51,5	(1,8)	19,8	(1,0)	3,4	(0,6)
Average	16,8	(0,4)	44,0	(0,5)	49,5	(0,5)	18,0	(0,4)	39,0	(0,5)	16,2	(0,4)

1. Feedback is defined broadly as any communication of the results of a review of an individual's work, often with the purpose of noting good performance or identifying areas for development. The feedback may be provided formally or informally.
2. Referring to the percentage of teachers receiving feedback from respective bodies for at least one item from question 28 of the teacher questionnaire. The same teacher can receive feedback from different bodies via different methods.
3. Referring to the percentage of teachers reporting never having received feedback in their school for any of the items surveyed in question 28 from the teacher questionnaire.
Source: OECD, TALIS 2013 Database.
StatLink http://dx.doi.org/10.1787/888933045829

[Part 1/1]
Methods for providing feedback to teachers

Table 5.5   *Percentage of lower secondary education teachers who report receiving feedback via the following methods[1, 2]*

	Feedback following classroom observation		Feedback from student surveys		Feedback following assessment of teachers' content knowledge		Feedback following analysis of student test scores		Feedback following self-assessment of teachers' work		Feedback from surveys or discussion with parents	
	%	S.E.	%	S.E.	%	S.E.	%	S.E.	%	S.E.	%	S.E.
Australia	69.6	(2.0)	39.8	(2.3)	33.0	(1.6)	56.0	(1.9)	44.6	(2.2)	39.8	(1.3)
Brazil	80.7	(0.8)	67.2	(0.9)	68.4	(0.9)	83.2	(0.7)	59.0	(1.1)	70.1	(0.8)
Bulgaria	96.2	(0.5)	60.0	(1.7)	73.4	(1.5)	84.3	(1.0)	51.3	(1.7)	55.5	(1.6)
Chile	78.5	(1.7)	53.2	(2.1)	59.8	(1.7)	69.7	(1.6)	60.2	(1.7)	56.4	(1.8)
Croatia	89.7	(0.7)	56.5	(1.2)	a	a	52.2	(1.1)	40.8	(1.2)	55.9	(1.0)
Cyprus*	74.5	(1.0)	33.2	(1.3)	49.7	(1.4)	48.7	(1.4)	41.9	(1.3)	46.3	(1.4)
Czech Republic	94.5	(0.7)	65.4	(1.2)	57.4	(1.1)	73.6	(1.2)	49.5	(1.3)	62.0	(1.2)
Denmark	57.7	(1.9)	41.3	(1.3)	33.5	(1.3)	49.2	(1.6)	37.2	(1.4)	37.4	(1.4)
Estonia	88.5	(0.8)	69.8	(1.3)	73.0	(1.1)	71.6	(1.3)	70.9	(1.3)	61.9	(1.4)
Finland	46.2	(1.4)	26.2	(1.1)	25.9	(1.3)	27.6	(1.1)	20.8	(1.1)	37.4	(1.1)
France	79.2	(0.9)	37.7	(1.0)	48.4	(1.0)	43.0	(1.1)	15.7	(0.9)	34.3	(1.0)
Iceland	35.9	(1.6)	17.3	(1.1)	18.1	(1.2)	26.6	(1.3)	15.3	(1.0)	31.3	(1.4)
Israel	79.6	(1.0)	49.2	(1.4)	61.4	(1.4)	67.3	(1.3)	56.4	(1.2)	32.7	(1.3)
Italy	40.5	(1.0)	35.2	(0.9)	26.0	(0.9)	44.2	(1.0)	25.2	(1.0)	41.3	(1.0)
Japan	86.9	(0.9)	66.4	(1.4)	67.4	(1.1)	63.3	(1.0)	77.6	(1.1)	65.3	(1.1)
Korea	91.2	(0.7)	77.3	(0.9)	78.1	(1.1)	84.0	(0.9)	75.3	(1.0)	70.5	(1.0)
Latvia	94.9	(0.6)	81.2	(1.3)	83.5	(1.1)	91.0	(0.7)	89.0	(0.9)	80.7	(1.2)
Malaysia	97.5	(0.3)	77.3	(0.9)	89.3	(0.8)	93.2	(0.6)	78.7	(1.1)	78.4	(1.1)
Mexico	82.1	(1.1)	63.2	(1.1)	68.5	(1.1)	80.6	(1.0)	69.8	(1.2)	67.7	(1.3)
Netherlands	86.5	(1.3)	67.6	(2.7)	51.3	(2.1)	52.9	(2.2)	46.6	(1.8)	34.6	(1.8)
Norway	73.2	(1.6)	53.7	(1.8)	40.8	(1.6)	52.9	(1.4)	47.5	(1.8)	48.4	(2.0)
Poland	97.3	(0.3)	64.9	(1.1)	72.1	(1.1)	83.7	(0.8)	62.3	(1.3)	73.1	(1.0)
Portugal	65.8	(1.2)	43.1	(1.2)	48.1	(1.1)	64.4	(1.1)	63.7	(1.1)	46.4	(1.1)
Romania	95.8	(0.5)	92.3	(0.6)	91.0	(0.8)	90.0	(0.6)	93.4	(0.6)	87.7	(0.8)
Serbia	75.1	(1.2)	34.9	(1.1)	52.8	(1.2)	47.8	(1.2)	38.0	(1.1)	40.4	(1.0)
Singapore	96.8	(0.4)	61.8	(0.8)	70.5	(0.9)	81.3	(0.7)	87.2	(0.6)	51.7	(0.9)
Slovak Republic	93.4	(0.6)	71.5	(1.1)	71.1	(1.0)	77.2	(1.1)	65.9	(1.1)	68.7	(1.1)
Spain	42.6	(1.3)	35.8	(1.4)	20.9	(1.0)	53.6	(1.2)	27.3	(1.3)	45.6	(1.1)
Sweden	51.1	(1.7)	26.6	(1.4)	16.7	(0.9)	28.3	(1.0)	20.2	(0.9)	29.3	(0.9)
Sub-national entities												
Abu Dhabi (United Arab Emirates)	95.0	(0.7)	72.8	(1.9)	81.9	(1.3)	85.5	(1.1)	83.0	(1.5)	78.5	(1.3)
Alberta (Canada)	84.2	(1.0)	40.6	(1.6)	39.2	(1.3)	61.2	(1.4)	44.3	(1.3)	57.1	(1.3)
England (United Kingdom)	98.9	(0.3)	42.3	(1.7)	38.5	(1.6)	69.8	(1.5)	45.9	(1.6)	40.9	(1.2)
Flanders (Belgium)	81.4	(1.4)	34.9	(1.6)	42.6	(1.4)	41.9	(1.3)	35.4	(1.5)	34.1	(1.2)
Average	78.8	(0.2)	53.3	(0.2)	54.8	(0.2)	63.6	(0.2)	52.7	(0.2)	53.4	(0.2)
United States	97.7	(0.7)	26.3	(1.5)	46.3	(2.1)	63.8	(2.4)	48.6	(2.5)	41.0	(2.2)

1. Feedback is defined broadly as any communication of the results of a review of an individual's work, often with the purpose of noting good performance or identifying areas for development. The feedback may be provided formally or informally.
2. Percentage of teachers reporting receiving feedback via the following methods by at least one body, including: external individuals or bodies, principal, member(s) of school management team, assigned mentors or other teachers.
* See notes at the beginning of this Annex.
Source: OECD, TALIS 2013 Database.
StatLink http://dx.doi.org/10.1787/888933045848

[Part 1/1]
Methods for providing feedback to teachers in primary education

Table 5.5.a *Percentage of primary education teachers who report receiving feedback via the following methods[1, 2]*

	Feedback following classroom observation		Feedback from student surveys		Feedback following assessment of teachers' content knowledge		Feedback following analysis of student test scores		Feedback following self-assessment of teachers' work		Feedback from surveys or discussion with parents	
	%	S.E.	%	S.E.	%	S.E.	%	S.E.	%	S.E.	%	S.E.
Denmark	63.8	(1.7)	42.6	(1.4)	33.5	(1.2)	56.2	(1.3)	42.6	(1.2)	39.3	(1.2)
Finland	59.6	(1.5)	31.4	(1.1)	35.0	(1.4)	38.2	(1.5)	28.9	(1.3)	52.4	(1.6)
Mexico	81.7	(1.9)	65.9	(2.2)	76.9	(2.0)	80.0	(1.7)	75.8	(1.9)	73.8	(2.1)
Norway	79.3	(1.5)	47.1	(1.2)	45.2	(1.8)	67.3	(2.2)	55.8	(1.7)	56.5	(1.2)
Poland	97.8	(0.4)	62.2	(1.5)	75.9	(1.2)	83.6	(0.9)	66.2	(1.4)	76.3	(1.2)
Sub-national entities												
Flanders (Belgium)	83.5	(1.2)	28.9	(1.3)	36.8	(1.2)	63.7	(1.1)	43.4	(1.5)	50.2	(1.5)
Average	77.6	(0.6)	46.4	(0.6)	50.5	(0.6)	64.8	(0.6)	52.1	(0.6)	58.1	(0.6)

1. Feedback is defined broadly as any communication of the results of a review of an individual's work, often with the purpose of noting good performance or identifying areas for development. The feedback may be provided formally or informally.
2. Percentage of teachers reporting receiving feedback via the following methods by at least one body, including: external individuals or bodies, principal, member(s) of school management team, assigned mentors or other teachers.
Source: OECD, TALIS 2013 Database.
StatLink http://dx.doi.org/10.1787/888933045867

[Part 1/1]
Methods for providing feedback to teachers in upper secondary education

Table 5.5.b *Percentage of upper secondary education teachers who report receiving feedback via the following methods[1, 2]*

	Feedback following classroom observation		Feedback from student surveys		Feedback following assessment of teachers' content knowledge		Feedback following analysis of student test scores		Feedback following self-assessment of teachers' work		Feedback from surveys or discussion with parents	
	%	S.E.	%	S.E.	%	S.E.	%	S.E.	%	S.E.	%	S.E.
Australia	68.3	(1.8)	37.2	(2.0)	34.1	(1.3)	63.0	(1.3)	48.1	(1.7)	40.1	(1.3)
Denmark	57.9	(2.2)	47.7	(2.2)	28.5	(1.7)	24.6	(1.9)	32.9	(2.1)	7.7	(1.0)
Finland	52.0	(2.3)	49.3	(2.4)	39.3	(1.6)	27.9	(1.1)	23.6	(2.1)	23.6	(1.5)
Iceland	34.2	(1.7)	74.3	(1.4)	20.1	(1.4)	28.4	(1.6)	16.2	(1.3)	18.0	(1.3)
Italy	36.9	(1.1)	34.6	(1.1)	25.2	(1.1)	40.6	(1.3)	21.1	(1.0)	37.5	(1.3)
Mexico	75.1	(1.4)	76.6	(1.7)	66.0	(1.4)	74.8	(1.3)	68.2	(1.4)	59.5	(1.6)
Norway	69.7	(2.2)	77.9	(1.5)	44.0	(1.7)	57.4	(1.8)	50.3	(1.6)	34.1	(1.6)
Poland	95.8	(0.6)	61.9	(1.6)	69.8	(1.5)	75.4	(1.1)	57.2	(1.8)	65.8	(1.1)
Singapore	96.4	(0.4)	63.8	(0.9)	68.3	(0.8)	82.7	(0.7)	87.2	(0.7)	52.1	(1.0)
Sub-national entities												
Abu Dhabi (United Arab Emirates)	94.6	(0.8)	69.5	(1.9)	79.1	(1.3)	83.5	(1.5)	82.0	(1.6)	74.1	(1.6)
Average	68.1	(0.5)	59.3	(0.5)	47.4	(0.4)	55.8	(0.4)	48.7	(0.5)	41.2	(0.4)

1. Feedback is defined broadly as any communication of the results of a review of an individual's work, often with the purpose of noting good performance or identifying areas for development. The feedback may be provided formally or informally.
2. Percentage of teachers reporting receiving feedback via the following methods by at least one body, including: external individuals or bodies, principal, member(s) of school management team, assigned mentors or other teachers.
Source: OECD, TALIS 2013 Database.
StatLink http://dx.doi.org/10.1787/888933045886

[Part 1/2]

Emphasis of teacher feedback

Percentage of lower secondary education teachers who report the feedback they received emphasised the following issues with a "moderate" or "high" importance[1]

Table 5.6

	Student performance		Knowledge and understanding of the subject field(s)		Pedagogical competencies in teaching the subject field(s)		Student assessment practices		Student behaviour and classroom management		Teaching of students with special learning needs	
	%	S.E.	%	S.E.	%	S.E.	%	S.E.	%	S.E.	%	S.E.
Australia	87.5	(1.4)	69.1	(1.5)	74.9	(1.2)	76.5	(1.5)	70.0	(1.6)	50.8	(1.8)
Brazil	95.8	(0.3)	92.6	(0.4)	92.7	(0.4)	93.6	(0.4)	91.2	(0.5)	76.6	(0.9)
Bulgaria	91.9	(0.7)	89.1	(0.8)	90.2	(0.7)	83.3	(0.9)	80.2	(1.2)	56.2	(2.0)
Chile	90.1	(0.9)	91.8	(0.9)	92.3	(0.9)	90.1	(1.0)	91.2	(1.0)	79.7	(1.5)
Croatia	92.1	(0.5)	83.7	(0.8)	89.1	(0.7)	91.2	(0.6)	89.6	(0.6)	82.3	(0.9)
Cyprus*	91.2	(0.9)	91.7	(0.8)	93.8	(0.6)	87.2	(0.8)	92.0	(0.8)	68.3	(1.3)
Czech Republic	94.4	(0.6)	88.7	(0.7)	91.4	(0.6)	90.7	(0.7)	93.5	(0.5)	81.6	(1.2)
Denmark	71.6	(1.9)	80.9	(1.2)	83.5	(1.2)	60.9	(1.5)	84.8	(1.2)	60.6	(1.6)
Estonia	87.4	(0.8)	83.2	(0.9)	87.3	(0.8)	81.2	(0.9)	87.3	(0.9)	64.8	(1.4)
Finland	75.0	(1.2)	77.4	(1.1)	79.0	(1.0)	63.5	(1.6)	82.0	(1.1)	58.6	(1.3)
France	69.7	(0.9)	86.1	(0.9)	93.5	(0.5)	83.4	(0.7)	94.2	(0.5)	65.6	(1.0)
Iceland	77.5	(1.8)	67.7	(1.9)	71.8	(1.8)	68.0	(1.9)	75.6	(1.7)	62.8	(1.9)
Israel	88.7	(0.8)	87.4	(0.8)	88.8	(0.8)	76.8	(1.1)	86.7	(0.8)	60.2	(1.2)
Italy	95.1	(0.7)	89.9	(0.8)	89.8	(0.9)	87.3	(0.8)	92.7	(0.8)	87.5	(0.8)
Japan	77.6	(0.9)	85.6	(0.7)	92.7	(0.5)	82.5	(0.8)	86.4	(0.7)	71.4	(1.1)
Korea	82.2	(0.9)	85.4	(0.7)	88.5	(0.7)	84.3	(0.9)	85.5	(0.7)	83.5	(0.7)
Latvia	96.4	(0.4)	92.4	(0.8)	95.5	(0.6)	94.5	(0.5)	91.4	(0.8)	65.7	(2.0)
Malaysia	99.7	(0.1)	99.6	(0.1)	98.9	(0.2)	98.8	(0.2)	97.9	(0.3)	69.7	(1.3)
Mexico	90.8	(0.8)	86.3	(0.8)	85.6	(0.9)	85.0	(0.9)	82.9	(0.9)	51.1	(1.5)
Netherlands	81.6	(1.1)	75.6	(1.4)	94.6	(0.8)	73.8	(1.5)	92.6	(0.7)	60.9	(2.3)
Norway	73.0	(1.2)	71.8	(1.5)	73.4	(1.5)	68.0	(1.4)	87.3	(1.0)	60.2	(2.6)
Poland	90.8	(0.8)	85.9	(0.8)	85.6	(0.7)	88.5	(0.8)	87.4	(0.7)	79.5	(1.1)
Portugal	94.8	(0.5)	89.4	(0.6)	93.1	(0.5)	92.6	(0.5)	93.7	(0.5)	84.2	(0.8)
Romania	97.6	(0.3)	96.3	(0.4)	95.5	(0.5)	95.5	(0.5)	95.8	(0.5)	73.4	(1.5)
Serbia	95.2	(0.4)	92.0	(0.5)	91.8	(0.5)	91.6	(0.5)	91.9	(0.5)	90.4	(0.6)
Singapore	94.7	(0.4)	87.6	(0.6)	91.0	(0.6)	88.2	(0.6)	86.3	(0.7)	47.2	(1.0)
Slovak Republic	94.9	(0.4)	92.7	(0.7)	93.7	(0.5)	92.4	(0.5)	93.7	(0.5)	85.0	(0.8)
Spain	87.9	(0.8)	63.8	(1.4)	63.6	(1.4)	66.8	(1.4)	79.8	(0.9)	66.9	(1.4)
Sweden	74.7	(1.3)	59.0	(1.3)	72.3	(1.2)	68.7	(1.3)	77.7	(1.2)	60.0	(1.5)
Sub-national entities												
Abu Dhabi (United Arab Emirates)	88.9	(0.7)	84.2	(0.8)	84.3	(1.0)	86.0	(0.8)	84.9	(0.7)	65.1	(1.5)
Alberta (Canada)	87.6	(0.8)	75.1	(1.1)	78.6	(1.1)	86.1	(0.9)	75.7	(1.2)	65.2	(1.9)
England (United Kingdom)	96.9	(0.4)	75.8	(1.3)	80.4	(0.9)	90.4	(0.8)	85.3	(1.1)	73.7	(1.1)
Flanders (Belgium)	74.6	(1.2)	76.5	(1.1)	85.8	(0.7)	72.9	(1.2)	81.2	(0.9)	57.3	(1.3)
Average	87.5	(0.2)	83.5	(0.2)	86.8	(0.2)	83.0	(0.2)	86.9	(0.2)	68.7	(0.2)
United States	91.6	(0.7)	78.1	(1.4)	80.4	(1.4)	81.2	(1.5)	81.8	(1.2)	63.4	(1.6)

1. Feedback is defined broadly as any communication of the results of a review of an individual's work, often with the purpose of noting good performance or identifying areas for development. The feedback may be provided formally or informally.

* See notes at the beginning of this Annex.

Source: OECD, TALIS 2013 Database.

StatLink ᵍᵉᵖ http://dx.doi.org/10.1787/888933046019

[Part 2/2]

Emphasis of teacher feedback

Percentage of lower secondary education teachers who report the feedback they received emphasised the following issues with a "moderate" or "high" importance[1]

Table 5.6

	Teaching in a multicultural or multilingual setting		Feedback provided to other teachers to help their teaching		Feedback from parents or guardians		Student feedback		Collaboration or working with other teachers	
	%	S.E.	%	S.E.	%	S.E.	%	S.E.	%	S.E.
Australia	30.1	(1.9)	46.6	(1.4)	55.1	(2.0)	62.9	(2.2)	71.3	(1.4)
Brazil	64.7	(0.9)	79.3	(0.7)	85.2	(0.7)	87.6	(0.6)	90.3	(0.5)
Bulgaria	52.8	(1.8)	62.6	(1.6)	64.3	(1.5)	76.6	(1.2)	82.7	(1.1)
Chile	58.6	(2.1)	69.6	(1.6)	68.3	(1.6)	82.4	(1.5)	78.5	(1.7)
Croatia	32.1	(1.2)	64.9	(1.1)	81.3	(0.8)	87.0	(0.7)	82.1	(0.6)
Cyprus*	67.4	(1.3)	59.4	(1.6)	66.5	(1.4)	77.1	(1.4)	81.8	(1.1)
Czech Republic	47.8	(1.3)	65.1	(1.2)	83.1	(0.9)	88.3	(0.8)	87.5	(0.8)
Denmark	34.8	(2.2)	58.8	(1.7)	72.3	(1.5)	83.5	(1.3)	88.3	(1.1)
Estonia	35.1	(1.9)	50.4	(1.4)	71.9	(1.2)	82.0	(1.1)	80.4	(1.0)
Finland	25.6	(2.0)	34.4	(1.4)	76.2	(1.2)	78.2	(1.0)	80.2	(1.0)
France	22.7	(1.0)	26.5	(0.9)	49.7	(1.2)	55.9	(1.3)	77.2	(1.0)
Iceland	33.9	(2.0)	36.3	(1.9)	58.8	(2.0)	61.2	(2.1)	73.1	(1.6)
Israel	39.1	(1.5)	48.5	(1.4)	55.6	(1.3)	76.0	(1.1)	79.7	(1.0)
Italy	68.4	(1.4)	69.8	(1.3)	89.9	(0.9)	91.2	(0.8)	90.5	(0.8)
Japan	28.4	(1.0)	56.6	(1.1)	70.9	(0.9)	80.9	(0.8)	79.9	(0.9)
Korea	60.0	(1.0)	74.4	(1.0)	69.1	(1.1)	82.2	(0.9)	80.5	(0.9)
Latvia	44.6	(2.5)	71.2	(1.4)	85.3	(1.1)	90.6	(0.7)	88.4	(1.0)
Malaysia	70.2	(1.1)	93.2	(0.4)	95.6	(0.4)	98.0	(0.2)	98.8	(0.2)
Mexico	38.9	(1.2)	53.5	(1.2)	62.8	(1.2)	79.4	(1.0)	70.9	(1.2)
Netherlands	23.7	(1.9)	40.2	(1.2)	57.8	(1.5)	83.5	(1.6)	82.7	(1.1)
Norway	24.3	(1.4)	43.8	(1.9)	63.9	(2.1)	75.2	(1.3)	77.8	(1.2)
Poland	18.1	(0.8)	53.0	(1.2)	70.1	(1.1)	74.6	(1.1)	75.4	(1.1)
Portugal	61.5	(1.1)	76.7	(0.8)	84.3	(0.7)	91.2	(0.6)	94.1	(0.5)
Romania	59.2	(1.3)	77.0	(0.9)	91.7	(0.6)	96.9	(0.5)	94.4	(0.5)
Serbia	66.0	(1.1)	73.8	(1.0)	87.8	(0.7)	92.6	(0.5)	89.8	(0.6)
Singapore	39.6	(1.0)	58.2	(1.0)	64.6	(0.8)	74.2	(0.8)	75.2	(0.9)
Slovak Republic	57.0	(1.3)	72.3	(0.9)	87.2	(0.7)	93.1	(0.5)	91.2	(0.5)
Spain	49.5	(1.7)	55.1	(1.2)	72.3	(1.1)	72.3	(1.1)	71.7	(1.3)
Sweden	27.5	(1.8)	36.3	(1.4)	61.4	(1.4)	75.3	(1.1)	71.4	(1.3)
Sub-national entities										
Abu Dhabi (United Arab Emirates)	62.5	(1.6)	74.6	(1.4)	82.9	(1.4)	81.8	(1.3)	85.3	(1.2)
Alberta (Canada)	36.2	(1.8)	37.8	(1.7)	62.5	(1.5)	67.6	(1.5)	68.1	(1.5)
England (United Kingdom)	33.2	(1.7)	44.2	(1.3)	43.2	(1.2)	55.4	(1.6)	48.8	(1.5)
Flanders (Belgium)	29.1	(1.8)	29.7	(1.0)	44.7	(1.1)	55.9	(1.4)	74.5	(1.1)
Average	**43.7**	**(0.3)**	**57.4**	**(0.2)**	**70.8**	**(0.2)**	**79.1**	**(0.2)**	**80.7**	**(0.2)**
United States	38.2	(2.3)	31.9	(1.5)	47.7	(1.3)	47.7	(1.6)	60.7	(1.8)

1. Feedback is defined broadly as any communication of the results of a review of an individual's work, often with the purpose of noting good performance or identifying areas for development. The feedback may be provided formally or informally.

* See notes at the beginning of this Annex.

Source: OECD, TALIS 2013 Database.

StatLink ⬛⬛ http://dx.doi.org/10.1787/888933046019

[Part 1/1]
Emphasis of teacher feedback in primary education
Percentage of primary education teachers who report the feedback they received emphasised the following issues with a "moderate" or "high" importance[1]

Table 5.6.a

	Student performance		Knowledge and understanding of the subject field(s)		Pedagogical competencies in teaching the subject field(s)		Student assessment practices		Student behaviour and classroom management		Teaching of students with special learning needs	
	%	S.E.	%	S.E.	%	S.E.	%	S.E.	%	S.E.	%	S.E.
Denmark	70.7	(1.3)	80.7	(1.0)	86.7	(0.9)	64.9	(1.3)	87.0	(0.9)	73.6	(1.5)
Finland	75.8	(1.4)	79.3	(1.2)	82.6	(1.1)	61.6	(1.7)	86.6	(1.1)	72.8	(1.4)
Mexico	95.2	(0.7)	93.9	(0.8)	92.1	(1.1)	91.3	(1.0)	86.7	(1.5)	67.5	(2.0)
Norway	83.9	(1.2)	75.4	(0.9)	74.4	(1.2)	69.0	(1.8)	88.9	(1.0)	71.2	(1.5)
Poland	93.5	(0.7)	88.8	(0.7)	89.2	(0.9)	91.0	(0.8)	90.7	(1.0)	84.1	(1.2)
Sub-national entities												
Flanders (Belgium)	79.3	(1.0)	71.0	(1.2)	82.7	(1.0)	72.8	(1.2)	81.7	(1.0)	73.6	(1.1)
Average	83.1	(0.4)	81.5	(0.4)	84.6	(0.4)	75.1	(0.5)	86.9	(0.5)	73.8	(0.6)

	Teaching in a multicultural or multilingual setting		Feedback provided to other teachers to help their teaching		Feedback from parents or guardians		Student feedback		Collaboration or working with other teachers	
	%	S.E.	%	S.E.	%	S.E.	%	S.E.	%	S.E.
Denmark	39.7	(2.1)	63.2	(1.4)	78.1	(1.0)	81.8	(0.9)	90.2	(0.9)
Finland	27.3	(1.7)	45.0	(1.7)	83.8	(1.2)	73.5	(1.2)	85.8	(1.2)
Mexico	45.4	(2.3)	67.6	(2.0)	78.8	(1.6)	88.5	(1.1)	81.9	(1.4)
Norway	32.6	(2.0)	50.6	(1.1)	73.1	(2.1)	72.4	(2.0)	81.7	(1.5)
Poland	18.2	(1.3)	59.2	(1.5)	77.5	(1.0)	78.0	(1.1)	79.6	(1.0)
Sub-national entities										
Flanders (Belgium)	34.0	(1.9)	31.5	(1.2)	55.3	(1.4)	55.9	(1.3)	77.8	(1.1)
Average	32.9	(0.8)	52.9	(0.6)	74.4	(0.6)	75.0	(0.5)	82.8	(0.5)

1. Feedback is defined broadly as any communication of the results of a review of an individual's work, often with the purpose of noting good performance or identifying areas for development. The feedback may be provided formally or informally.
Source: OECD, TALIS 2013 Database.
StatLink http://dx.doi.org/10.1787/888933046038

[Part 1/1]
Emphasis of teacher feedback in upper secondary education
Percentage of upper secondary education teachers who report the feedback they received emphasised the following issues with a "moderate" or "high" importance[1]

Table 5.6.b

	Student performance		Knowledge and understanding of the subject field(s)		Pedagogical competencies in teaching the subject field(s)		Student assessment practices		Student behaviour and classroom management		Teaching of students with special learning needs	
	%	S.E.	%	S.E.	%	S.E.	%	S.E.	%	S.E.	%	S.E.
Australia	88.4	(1.1)	71.1	(1.2)	73.6	(1.2)	77.2	(1.4)	67.4	(1.4)	46.7	(1.8)
Denmark	53.6	(2.0)	73.3	(1.8)	86.8	(1.1)	58.1	(2.2)	83.8	(1.5)	35.0	(2.0)
Finland	81.5	(1.6)	80.3	(1.2)	78.6	(1.6)	66.9	(1.9)	64.3	(1.4)	50.2	(3.7)
Iceland	59.8	(1.7)	51.0	(2.2)	60.1	(2.0)	48.9	(2.1)	45.0	(2.2)	26.3	(1.5)
Italy	94.9	(0.5)	88.6	(0.9)	86.1	(1.0)	87.2	(0.9)	91.0	(0.8)	78.2	(1.4)
Mexico	87.4	(0.8)	83.7	(0.9)	81.0	(0.9)	80.5	(0.9)	81.1	(1.1)	38.6	(1.4)
Norway	69.8	(1.6)	67.3	(1.5)	67.1	(1.9)	74.8	(1.6)	82.4	(1.4)	44.8	(1.8)
Poland	89.3	(0.8)	85.6	(0.9)	85.4	(1.0)	89.7	(0.8)	86.1	(1.0)	70.8	(1.2)
Singapore	94.4	(0.5)	86.8	(0.6)	89.4	(0.5)	86.0	(0.5)	85.1	(0.7)	42.6	(1.0)
Sub-national entities												
Abu Dhabi (United Arab Emirates)	89.3	(0.8)	81.9	(1.1)	83.9	(0.9)	85.2	(1.1)	83.6	(1.0)	55.5	(1.6)
Average	80.9	(0.4)	77.0	(0.4)	79.2	(0.4)	75.4	(0.5)	77.0	(0.4)	48.9	(0.6)

	Teaching in a multicultural or multilingual setting		Feedback provided to other teachers to help their teaching		Feedback from parents or guardians		Student feedback		Collaboration or working with other teachers	
	%	S.E.	%	S.E.	%	S.E.	%	S.E.	%	S.E.
Australia	26.5	(1.7)	49.0	(1.9)	57.2	(1.4)	65.2	(1.6)	71.0	(1.9)
Denmark	27.6	(2.0)	48.8	(2.2)	19.1	(1.6)	83.2	(1.6)	79.8	(1.4)
Finland	31.1	(2.9)	34.3	(2.5)	54.6	(2.9)	88.3	(1.5)	78.6	(1.4)
Iceland	17.7	(1.6)	20.9	(1.7)	19.0	(1.4)	78.0	(1.6)	44.0	(1.9)
Italy	54.6	(1.6)	66.3	(1.3)	86.8	(0.7)	91.7	(0.6)	87.9	(0.9)
Mexico	34.6	(1.3)	52.3	(1.3)	53.2	(1.6)	81.0	(1.0)	68.1	(1.5)
Norway	22.6	(1.4)	34.5	(1.6)	41.9	(1.5)	82.4	(1.4)	71.1	(1.2)
Poland	17.1	(0.8)	54.8	(1.5)	67.2	(1.1)	74.0	(0.9)	73.5	(1.3)
Singapore	36.6	(1.0)	60.4	(1.0)	61.3	(0.9)	75.3	(0.9)	74.5	(0.7)
Sub-national entities										
Abu Dhabi (United Arab Emirates)	59.0	(1.2)	69.2	(1.2)	79.4	(1.2)	80.6	(1.2)	81.0	(1.1)
Average	32.7	(0.5)	49.0	(0.5)	54.0	(0.5)	79.9	(0.4)	73.0	(0.4)

1. Feedback is defined broadly as any communication of the results of a review of an individual's work, often with the purpose of noting good performance or identifying areas for development. The feedback may be provided formally or informally.
Source: OECD, TALIS 2013 Database.
StatLink ⟐ http://dx.doi.org/10.1787/888933046057

[Part 1/1]
Emphasis of teacher feedback, 2008 and 2013
*Percentage of lower secondary education teachers who report the feedback they received emphasised
the following issues with a "moderate" or "high" importance*[1, 2, 3]

Table 5.6.c

	Student performance				Knowledge and understanding of the subject field(s)				Teaching of students with special learning needs				Teaching in a multicultural or multilingual setting				Student feedback			
	2008		2013		2008		2013		2008		2013		2008		2013		2008		2013	
	%	S.E.	%	S.E.	%	S.E.	%	S.E.	%	S.E.	%	S.E.	%	S.E.	%	S.E.	%	S.E.	%	S.E.
Australia	51.4	(1.6)	87.7	(1.4)	72.4	(1.2)	69.1	(1.4)	41.2	(1.9)	50.7	(1.8)	29.1	(1.6)	30.0	(1.9)	58.4	(1.9)	62.9	(2.3)
Brazil	78.0	(1.2)	95.8	(0.3)	92.5	(0.5)	92.5	(0.4)	68.0	(1.4)	76.6	(0.9)	76.5	(1.3)	64.7	(0.9)	88.4	(0.9)	87.7	(0.6)
Bulgaria	88.4	(2.3)	91.9	(0.7)	91.4	(1.1)	89.1	(0.8)	61.7	(1.9)	56.2	(2.0)	68.9	(2.3)	52.8	(1.8)	81.0	(2.2)	76.6	(1.2)
Denmark	28.6	(1.7)	72.0	(1.9)	47.1	(1.9)	80.8	(1.2)	39.5	(1.8)	59.4	(1.6)	22.9	(1.7)	34.2	(2.1)	60.7	(1.5)	83.2	(1.3)
Estonia	72.1	(1.4)	87.5	(0.8)	86.0	(0.9)	83.3	(0.9)	60.2	(1.4)	64.5	(1.4)	33.9	(1.9)	35.0	(1.9)	79.2	(1.2)	82.1	(1.1)
Iceland	44.9	(2.0)	77.6	(1.8)	66.4	(1.8)	68.5	(2.0)	48.8	(1.9)	62.2	(1.9)	22.9	(1.9)	34.1	(2.1)	78.6	(1.5)	61.4	(2.2)
Italy	62.5	(1.8)	95.0	(0.7)	92.2	(0.7)	89.9	(0.8)	81.5	(1.2)	87.5	(0.8)	70.6	(1.6)	68.4	(1.4)	85.9	(1.2)	91.1	(0.8)
Korea	66.3	(1.2)	82.2	(0.9)	64.8	(1.0)	85.5	(0.8)	45.8	(1.2)	83.5	(0.7)	31.8	(1.1)	59.9	(1.0)	62.2	(1.2)	82.2	(0.9)
Malaysia	95.7	(0.4)	99.7	(0.1)	97.8	(0.3)	99.6	(0.1)	49.2	(2.3)	69.6	(1.3)	81.9	(1.5)	70.2	(1.1)	94.1	(0.4)	98.0	(0.2)
Mexico	84.5	(0.9)	90.7	(0.8)	88.1	(0.8)	86.3	(0.8)	64.2	(1.6)	50.9	(1.5)	67.8	(1.4)	38.9	(1.2)	82.9	(1.1)	79.3	(1.0)
Norway	47.3	(1.6)	73.0	(1.2)	72.1	(1.1)	71.6	(1.5)	55.2	(1.2)	59.6	(2.6)	21.0	(1.5)	24.2	(1.4)	59.9	(1.6)	75.3	(1.3)
Poland	87.2	(1.0)	90.8	(0.8)	94.6	(0.7)	85.9	(0.8)	71.5	(1.8)	79.4	(1.1)	40.0	(1.7)	18.1	(0.8)	82.8	(1.2)	74.5	(1.1)
Portugal	64.4	(1.5)	94.8	(0.5)	78.6	(1.1)	89.4	(0.6)	58.2	(1.6)	84.3	(0.8)	47.9	(1.5)	61.5	(1.1)	82.7	(1.0)	91.2	(0.6)
Slovak Republic	76.0	(1.2)	94.8	(0.4)	82.7	(1.0)	92.7	(0.7)	62.2	(1.6)	85.0	(0.8)	44.0	(1.7)	56.8	(1.3)	81.7	(1.0)	93.1	(0.5)
Spain	69.5	(1.4)	87.8	(0.8)	65.6	(1.7)	63.9	(1.4)	66.2	(1.7)	66.7	(1.4)	56.0	(1.8)	49.3	(1.7)	54.9	(1.7)	72.3	(1.1)
Sub-national entities																				
Flanders (Belgium)	53.2	(1.8)	74.7	(1.1)	73.3	(1.4)	76.4	(1.1)	54.3	(1.6)	57.3	(1.3)	31.6	(1.9)	29.0	(1.8)	59.1	(1.4)	56.0	(1.4)
Average	66.9	(0.4)	87.2	(0.3)	79.1	(0.3)	82.8	(0.3)	58.0	(0.4)	68.3	(0.4)	46.7	(0.4)	45.4	(0.4)	74.5	(0.3)	79.2	(0.3)

1. Feedback is defined broadly as any communication of the results of a review of an individual's work, often with the purpose of noting good performance or identifying areas for development. The feedback may be provided formally or informally.

2. The teacher population coverage was slightly different between 2008 and 2013. In order to have comparable populations for the tables comparing results from 2008 and 2013, teachers who teach exclusively to students with special needs were excluded from the 2013 data in these tables.

3. The wording and order of questions may have changed slightly between the 2008 and 2013 surveys. Moreover, in the 2013 survey, the proposed answer "I do not know if it was considered" was removed from the questionnaire. For needs of comparison between 2008 and 2013, all teachers who chose this answer in 2008 were excluded and are therefore not considered in the percentage presented for 2008.

Source: OECD, TALIS 2008 and 2013 Databases.

StatLink ⊞≋ http://dx.doi.org/10.1787/888933046076

[Part 1/2]
Outcomes of teacher feedback
Percentage of lower secondary education teachers who report a "moderate" or "large" positive change
Table 5.7 *in the following issues after they received feedback on their work at their school[1]*

	Public recognition		Role in school development initiatives		Likelihood of career advancement		Amount of professional development		Job responsibilities		Confidence as a teacher		Salary and/or financial bonus	
	%	S.E.	%	S.E.	%	S.E.	%	S.E.	%	S.E.	%	S.E.	%	S.E.
Australia	39.9	(1.3)	38.6	(1.5)	30.8	(1.3)	31.2	(1.2)	39.5	(1.3)	56.5	(1.7)	11.9	(1.0)
Brazil	71.3	(0.9)	66.9	(0.9)	50.0	(1.0)	70.1	(0.8)	80.3	(0.7)	85.8	(0.6)	27.0	(0.8)
Bulgaria	79.6	(1.2)	60.1	(1.5)	32.0	(1.4)	54.1	(1.6)	82.1	(1.1)	87.0	(0.9)	47.0	(1.6)
Chile	70.3	(1.9)	64.3	(1.9)	64.1	(1.8)	68.3	(1.7)	74.9	(1.7)	86.1	(1.3)	47.0	(2.4)
Croatia	55.7	(1.1)	45.0	(1.1)	33.0	(0.9)	47.4	(1.0)	52.3	(1.0)	73.3	(0.9)	15.4	(0.7)
Cyprus*	61.2	(1.5)	55.6	(1.4)	39.3	(1.5)	52.7	(1.7)	59.3	(1.5)	78.5	(1.1)	10.7	(0.9)
Czech Republic	57.3	(1.3)	38.6	(1.1)	21.6	(1.0)	30.3	(1.1)	43.6	(1.1)	62.4	(1.2)	27.3	(1.1)
Denmark	56.2	(1.7)	44.4	(1.7)	22.7	(1.5)	47.9	(1.8)	47.7	(1.8)	64.7	(1.5)	11.2	(0.9)
Estonia	56.4	(1.4)	43.4	(1.4)	27.8	(1.6)	46.4	(1.5)	47.3	(1.4)	64.3	(1.3)	27.2	(1.2)
Finland	55.9	(1.5)	33.0	(1.4)	14.5	(1.3)	26.9	(1.1)	34.4	(1.4)	63.5	(1.4)	13.1	(1.1)
France	54.2	(1.2)	43.6	(1.1)	36.5	(1.1)	22.0	(1.0)	39.4	(1.1)	64.7	(1.1)	22.5	(1.2)
Iceland	42.9	(2.3)	40.9	(2.3)	13.0	(1.4)	31.8	(1.9)	34.4	(2.1)	58.9	(2.0)	16.5	(1.7)
Israel	70.4	(1.2)	55.5	(1.2)	54.0	(1.5)	50.5	(1.3)	58.4	(1.2)	73.1	(1.1)	24.0	(1.1)
Italy	54.3	(1.3)	45.3	(1.2)	a	a	46.2	(1.2)	a	a	71.9	(1.1)	a	a
Japan	83.0	(0.9)	63.4	(1.1)	33.6	(1.1)	41.9	(1.1)	71.1	(1.0)	85.1	(0.7)	27.9	(1.0)
Korea	59.9	(1.1)	52.9	(1.2)	37.4	(1.2)	55.0	(1.2)	65.1	(1.2)	65.8	(1.0)	38.4	(1.0)
Latvia	58.2	(1.4)	46.3	(1.6)	37.0	(1.6)	45.0	(1.5)	48.6	(1.2)	63.7	(1.6)	21.5	(1.2)
Malaysia	89.8	(0.8)	87.2	(0.8)	81.8	(0.8)	85.5	(0.7)	93.0	(0.6)	96.0	(0.4)	78.0	(1.0)
Mexico	62.0	(1.4)	62.6	(1.3)	51.3	(1.2)	67.8	(1.2)	82.0	(1.0)	89.0	(0.8)	30.9	(1.3)
Netherlands	52.2	(1.7)	45.3	(1.4)	31.1	(1.9)	36.6	(1.6)	44.1	(1.8)	58.7	(2.0)	19.9	(1.6)
Norway	58.9	(1.8)	34.9	(2.1)	15.2	(1.3)	25.4	(1.4)	32.0	(1.8)	68.0	(1.3)	19.9	(1.5)
Poland	72.1	(1.0)	64.4	(1.0)	51.0	(1.1)	53.1	(1.1)	53.3	(1.1)	69.2	(0.8)	32.6	(1.0)
Portugal	47.9	(1.2)	46.2	(1.1)	23.7	(1.0)	38.5	(1.0)	44.9	(1.1)	58.8	(1.0)	6.5	(0.6)
Romania	80.8	(1.0)	68.7	(1.2)	60.0	(1.5)	58.8	(1.3)	76.1	(1.0)	88.1	(0.6)	27.8	(1.3)
Serbia	68.1	(0.9)	51.1	(1.0)	36.2	(1.0)	55.8	(1.0)	66.2	(1.0)	75.7	(0.9)	20.5	(0.9)
Singapore	49.1	(0.9)	49.1	(0.9)	44.3	(0.9)	47.0	(0.9)	57.9	(1.0)	69.2	(0.9)	38.0	(1.0)
Slovak Republic	68.5	(1.0)	62.6	(1.0)	39.6	(1.1)	47.4	(1.2)	60.1	(1.1)	71.9	(0.9)	37.0	(1.4)
Spain	50.8	(1.2)	45.8	(1.2)	28.9	(1.0)	38.2	(1.0)	42.2	(1.2)	59.0	(1.1)	10.5	(0.9)
Sweden	60.0	(1.1)	37.6	(1.2)	20.4	(1.2)	23.6	(1.1)	38.3	(1.5)	61.4	(1.2)	33.2	(1.2)
Sub-national entities														
Abu Dhabi (United Arab Emirates)	74.8	(1.8)	72.7	(1.6)	49.8	(1.8)	67.7	(1.8)	73.2	(1.6)	81.3	(1.4)	31.3	(1.4)
Alberta (Canada)	44.3	(1.6)	43.7	(1.5)	33.7	(1.5)	36.6	(1.6)	44.1	(1.5)	60.5	(1.5)	10.7	(0.9)
England (United Kingdom)	40.6	(1.3)	36.1	(1.4)	33.0	(1.4)	28.0	(1.5)	35.0	(1.3)	53.0	(1.3)	18.4	(1.1)
Flanders (Belgium)	52.4	(1.4)	34.5	(1.2)	17.5	(0.8)	34.0	(1.0)	43.1	(1.0)	63.0	(1.1)	7.0	(0.6)
Average	60.6	(0.2)	50.9	(0.2)	36.4	(0.2)	45.8	(0.2)	55.1	(0.2)	70.6	(0.2)	25.3	(0.2)
United States	42.3	(1.3)	40.2	(1.5)	26.4	(1.0)	31.4	(1.3)	39.4	(1.5)	60.8	(1.6)	12.9	(1.2)

1. Feedback is defined broadly as any communication of the results of a review of an individual's work, often with the purpose of noting good performance or identifying areas for development. The feedback may be provided formally or informally.
* See notes at the beginning of this Annex.
Source: OECD, TALIS 2013 Database.
StatLink http://dx.doi.org/10.1787/888933046095

[Part 2/2]
Outcomes of teacher feedback
Percentage of lower secondary education teachers who report a "moderate" or "large" positive change
Table 5.7 *in the following issues after they received feedback on their work at their school[1]*

	Classroom-management practices		Knowledge and understanding of main subject field(s)		Teaching practices		Methods for teaching students with special needs		Student assessments to improve student learning		Job satisfaction		Motivation	
	%	S.E.	%	S.E.	%	S.E.	%	S.E.	%	S.E.	%	S.E.	%	S.E.
Australia	39.5	(1.7)	33.5	(1.5)	45.0	(1.7)	29.0	(1.4)	42.9	(1.2)	46.9	(1.5)	50.0	(1.5)
Brazil	75.3	(0.7)	77.2	(0.8)	79.9	(0.7)	45.9	(0.9)	78.5	(0.7)	72.4	(0.9)	72.5	(0.9)
Bulgaria	80.4	(1.2)	77.0	(1.1)	80.3	(1.2)	47.4	(1.9)	76.6	(1.2)	78.4	(1.1)	78.9	(1.0)
Chile	84.1	(1.3)	78.7	(1.5)	82.0	(1.3)	69.3	(1.8)	80.9	(1.4)	82.8	(1.7)	83.4	(1.7)
Croatia	56.3	(1.0)	52.6	(1.0)	65.1	(1.0)	56.6	(1.0)	65.1	(1.0)	63.5	(1.1)	66.8	(1.1)
Cyprus*	62.0	(1.5)	52.4	(1.6)	65.0	(1.6)	44.7	(1.5)	60.4	(1.5)	69.6	(1.4)	61.1	(1.6)
Czech Republic	52.7	(1.4)	45.5	(1.1)	56.9	(1.0)	43.5	(1.3)	50.5	(1.2)	55.7	(1.0)	55.2	(1.0)
Denmark	41.5	(1.4)	43.4	(1.5)	49.9	(1.7)	36.0	(1.7)	40.4	(1.5)	58.6	(1.9)	61.7	(1.7)
Estonia	44.2	(1.3)	50.4	(1.2)	54.1	(1.4)	37.4	(1.5)	47.9	(1.5)	54.7	(1.2)	55.7	(1.2)
Finland	32.8	(1.2)	32.8	(1.1)	37.7	(1.2)	30.3	(1.2)	31.8	(1.2)	59.6	(1.3)	61.0	(1.7)
France	42.1	(1.2)	34.9	(1.2)	51.5	(1.2)	33.5	(1.2)	44.5	(1.2)	59.3	(1.1)	62.0	(1.1)
Iceland	39.7	(1.9)	37.4	(2.2)	44.7	(2.1)	36.7	(2.1)	49.5	(2.1)	58.3	(2.2)	57.2	(2.1)
Israel	56.1	(1.2)	54.6	(1.4)	60.3	(1.2)	42.2	(1.3)	55.1	(1.3)	72.4	(1.1)	73.8	(1.0)
Italy	67.4	(1.2)	61.8	(1.2)	67.9	(1.1)	65.9	(1.2)	69.0	(1.1)	75.3	(1.1)	75.0	(1.1)
Japan	71.2	(0.9)	86.2	(0.7)	88.6	(0.6)	63.2	(1.2)	75.5	(0.9)	77.4	(1.0)	81.5	(0.9)
Korea	57.8	(1.1)	62.8	(1.1)	64.4	(1.1)	61.4	(1.1)	58.4	(1.1)	53.0	(1.1)	57.4	(1.1)
Latvia	44.3	(1.6)	55.1	(1.4)	62.1	(1.3)	37.3	(1.8)	59.4	(1.5)	53.6	(1.4)	56.2	(1.4)
Malaysia	92.4	(0.6)	95.5	(0.5)	95.2	(0.5)	60.7	(1.3)	94.2	(0.5)	94.1	(0.5)	94.7	(0.5)
Mexico	82.9	(0.9)	83.4	(0.9)	86.3	(0.9)	49.3	(1.1)	81.6	(0.9)	89.3	(0.7)	86.6	(0.8)
Netherlands	38.9	(1.6)	30.2	(1.4)	43.8	(1.8)	25.1	(1.7)	31.4	(1.3)	45.2	(1.6)	51.6	(1.8)
Norway	47.1	(2.0)	39.7	(1.4)	52.2	(1.5)	33.5	(2.4)	47.9	(2.3)	54.6	(1.4)	52.9	(1.5)
Poland	58.6	(1.0)	52.4	(1.0)	63.5	(1.0)	61.6	(0.9)	67.3	(1.0)	67.8	(0.9)	69.1	(0.8)
Portugal	50.0	(1.1)	37.7	(1.0)	48.9	(1.1)	40.1	(1.2)	53.1	(1.1)	54.7	(1.1)	54.1	(1.0)
Romania	78.6	(1.0)	72.0	(1.0)	80.7	(0.9)	56.7	(1.5)	82.9	(0.8)	84.6	(0.8)	83.6	(0.9)
Serbia	60.9	(1.1)	57.8	(1.1)	67.4	(1.0)	59.5	(1.2)	67.9	(0.9)	67.5	(1.0)	68.4	(1.0)
Singapore	61.6	(0.9)	61.5	(1.0)	69.1	(0.8)	39.7	(0.9)	63.4	(0.9)	61.2	(0.9)	63.2	(1.0)
Slovak Republic	52.5	(1.1)	61.5	(1.1)	68.7	(1.0)	56.9	(1.3)	66.6	(1.1)	68.4	(1.1)	68.9	(1.1)
Spain	44.8	(1.2)	33.4	(1.3)	45.4	(1.3)	40.5	(1.3)	53.2	(1.2)	53.5	(1.2)	55.3	(1.3)
Sweden	45.0	(1.2)	36.7	(1.1)	47.5	(1.2)	37.2	(1.2)	44.7	(1.1)	50.6	(1.4)	53.7	(1.3)
Sub-national entities														
Abu Dhabi (United Arab Emirates)	76.2	(1.6)	70.7	(1.8)	79.1	(1.6)	52.6	(1.7)	77.4	(1.5)	68.0	(1.5)	74.6	(1.5)
Alberta (Canada)	39.0	(1.7)	37.2	(1.7)	52.0	(1.8)	38.6	(1.8)	53.6	(1.7)	51.4	(1.4)	53.2	(1.4)
England (United Kingdom)	41.7	(1.5)	26.7	(1.1)	48.1	(1.7)	29.6	(1.6)	49.5	(1.5)	38.9	(1.5)	41.3	(1.5)
Flanders (Belgium)	37.7	(1.2)	32.6	(0.9)	44.1	(1.1)	32.8	(1.3)	39.9	(1.2)	52.3	(1.2)	55.6	(1.2)
Average	56.2	(0.2)	53.5	(0.2)	62.0	(0.2)	45.3	(0.3)	59.4	(0.2)	63.4	(0.2)	64.7	(0.2)
United States	41.5	(1.4)	35.8	(1.3)	54.5	(1.6)	34.9	(1.4)	49.5	(1.6)	48.9	(1.2)	52.8	(1.5)

1. Feedback is defined broadly as any communication of the results of a review of an individual's work, often with the purpose of noting good performance or identifying areas for development. The feedback may be provided formally or informally.
*See notes at the beginning of this Annex.
Source: OECD, TALIS 2013 Database.
StatLink http://dx.doi.org/10.1787/888933046095

[Part 1/1]
Outcomes of teacher feedback in primary education
Percentage of primary education teachers who report a "moderate" or "large" positive change
Table 5.7.a *in the following issues after they received feedback on their work at their school[1]*

	Public recognition		Role in school development initiatives		Likelihood of career advancement		Amount of professional development		Job responsibilities		Confidence as a teacher		Salary and/or financial bonus	
	%	S.E.	%	S.E.	%	S.E.	%	S.E.	%	S.E.	%	S.E.	%	S.E.
Denmark	60.1	(1.3)	42.0	(1.3)	20.3	(1.1)	47.3	(1.3)	45.0	(1.4)	64.3	(1.3)	8.8	(0.7)
Finland	59.0	(1.8)	36.2	(1.3)	14.6	(1.2)	28.0	(1.4)	40.8	(1.8)	69.0	(1.5)	12.8	(1.0)
Mexico	68.6	(2.1)	72.0	(1.8)	60.9	(2.1)	77.3	(1.7)	89.1	(1.2)	92.7	(1.1)	29.4	(2.2)
Norway	65.3	(1.2)	37.7	(1.7)	16.1	(1.1)	25.2	(1.9)	31.0	(1.6)	71.2	(1.4)	19.2	(1.2)
Poland	72.2	(1.2)	64.7	(1.3)	51.5	(1.5)	56.4	(1.7)	55.9	(1.5)	72.1	(1.2)	32.1	(1.3)
Sub-national entities														
Flanders (Belgium)	54.2	(1.4)	38.2	(1.4)	16.2	(0.9)	39.5	(1.3)	45.7	(1.2)	61.3	(1.3)	4.7	(0.5)
Average	63.2	(0.6)	48.5	(0.6)	29.9	(0.6)	45.6	(0.6)	51.3	(0.6)	71.8	(0.5)	17.8	(0.5)

	Classroom-management practices		Knowledge and understanding of main subject field(s)		Teaching practices		Methods for teaching students with special needs		Student assessments to improve student learning		Job satisfaction		Motivation	
	%	S.E.	%	S.E.	%	S.E.	%	S.E.	%	S.E.	%	S.E.	%	S.E.
Denmark	48.4	(1.3)	44.8	(1.4)	55.5	(1.6)	46.9	(1.3)	43.0	(1.4)	59.4	(1.4)	61.5	(1.2)
Finland	39.0	(1.4)	36.3	(1.5)	42.2	(1.6)	41.1	(1.6)	34.5	(1.2)	65.9	(1.6)	67.7	(1.6)
Mexico	86.1	(1.2)	89.0	(1.3)	91.0	(1.0)	63.5	(2.2)	87.1	(1.4)	92.2	(1.0)	89.0	(1.2)
Norway	54.7	(1.3)	47.6	(1.1)	60.4	(1.3)	47.2	(1.3)	55.7	(1.4)	61.2	(1.1)	60.9	(1.2)
Poland	63.2	(1.3)	55.9	(1.4)	64.2	(1.4)	67.5	(1.1)	70.5	(1.0)	69.8	(1.2)	71.4	(1.1)
Sub-national entities														
Flanders (Belgium)	40.7	(1.2)	33.9	(1.2)	46.3	(1.3)	45.4	(1.2)	44.7	(1.4)	51.4	(1.4)	54.8	(1.3)
Average	55.3	(0.5)	51.3	(0.6)	59.9	(0.6)	52.0	(0.6)	55.9	(0.5)	66.7	(0.5)	67.6	(0.5)

1. Feedback is defined broadly as any communication of the results of a review of an individual's work, often with the purpose of noting good performance or identifying areas for development. The feedback may be provided formally or informally.
Source: OECD, TALIS 2013 Database.
StatLink ⧉ http://dx.doi.org/10.1787/888933046114

[Part 1/1]

Outcomes of teacher feedback in upper secondary education

Percentage of upper secondary education teachers who report a "moderate" or "large" positive change in the following issues after they received feedback on their work at their school[1]

Table 5.7.b

	Public recognition		Role in school development initiatives		Likelihood of career advancement		Amount of professional development		Job responsibilities		Confidence as a teacher		Salary and/or financial bonus	
	%	S.E.	%	S.E.	%	S.E.	%	S.E.	%	S.E.	%	S.E.	%	S.E.
Australia	40.4	(1.7)	40.0	(1.5)	30.6	(1.4)	31.4	(1.4)	39.1	(1.6)	52.6	(1.6)	11.9	(1.0)
Denmark	50.5	(2.4)	34.4	(2.5)	26.7	(2.2)	46.8	(1.6)	39.6	(2.0)	58.0	(2.0)	17.7	(1.7)
Finland	50.7	(1.6)	38.4	(3.7)	19.1	(2.4)	35.1	(2.0)	37.8	(1.5)	60.9	(1.7)	19.2	(1.8)
Iceland	30.4	(2.0)	29.8	(2.0)	11.1	(1.4)	21.4	(1.5)	21.4	(1.8)	51.9	(2.3)	12.1	(1.3)
Italy	51.0	(1.4)	40.9	(1.4)	a	a	43.8	(1.6)	a	a	71.6	(1.2)	a	a
Mexico	60.3	(1.4)	57.6	(1.3)	51.3	(1.6)	64.2	(1.4)	76.4	(1.1)	88.1	(0.9)	32.7	(1.2)
Norway	48.8	(1.1)	30.0	(1.2)	15.8	(1.3)	26.6	(1.5)	24.6	(1.2)	61.7	(1.4)	22.7	(1.1)
Poland	66.3	(1.4)	62.5	(1.2)	49.7	(1.3)	53.4	(1.2)	52.2	(1.5)	66.8	(1.6)	30.0	(1.3)
Singapore	50.8	(0.9)	51.0	(0.9)	46.3	(0.8)	49.8	(0.8)	59.1	(0.9)	69.1	(0.8)	40.2	(0.8)
Sub-national entities														
Abu Dhabi (United Arab Emirates)	71.0	(1.7)	68.4	(1.4)	44.6	(1.6)	63.5	(1.7)	66.9	(1.6)	76.3	(1.4)	29.0	(1.4)
Average	52.0	(0.5)	45.3	(0.6)	32.8	(0.5)	43.6	(0.5)	46.3	(0.5)	65.7	(0.5)	23.9	(0.4)

	Classroom-management practices		Knowledge and understanding of main subject field(s)		Teaching practices		Methods for teaching students with special needs		Student assessments to improve student learning		Job satisfaction		Motivation	
	%	S.E.	%	S.E.	%	S.E.	%	S.E.	%	S.E.	%	S.E.	%	S.E.
Australia	34.8	(1.7)	32.9	(1.4)	42.2	(1.9)	22.4	(1.5)	43.2	(1.7)	43.4	(1.6)	47.1	(1.5)
Denmark	40.3	(2.2)	38.4	(2.3)	52.8	(2.3)	24.7	(1.6)	42.1	(1.8)	51.7	(1.9)	54.8	(1.9)
Finland	28.7	(1.7)	42.3	(2.6)	47.4	(1.7)	27.6	(1.8)	40.7	(2.7)	57.7	(2.1)	58.4	(1.7)
Iceland	32.5	(1.7)	27.2	(1.8)	43.5	(2.1)	19.2	(1.5)	37.9	(1.9)	46.9	(2.1)	46.7	(2.1)
Italy	61.8	(1.4)	55.9	(1.6)	65.2	(1.4)	52.9	(1.5)	64.7	(1.5)	72.4	(1.1)	73.7	(1.1)
Mexico	80.9	(1.1)	80.8	(1.1)	85.9	(1.0)	43.8	(1.3)	81.5	(1.0)	87.8	(0.8)	85.5	(1.0)
Norway	40.1	(1.6)	36.1	(1.7)	45.9	(1.4)	25.4	(1.5)	44.3	(1.4)	49.7	(1.4)	47.9	(1.4)
Poland	56.7	(1.5)	51.4	(1.5)	60.4	(1.4)	52.0	(1.4)	63.2	(1.9)	64.0	(1.3)	65.0	(1.2)
Singapore	59.4	(0.9)	60.3	(0.8)	67.3	(0.8)	36.7	(0.8)	62.2	(0.8)	61.6	(0.9)	63.2	(0.9)
Sub-national entities														
Abu Dhabi (United Arab Emirates)	69.5	(1.6)	60.7	(1.5)	72.4	(1.4)	44.9	(1.6)	73.7	(1.4)	64.1	(1.6)	70.8	(1.6)
Average	50.5	(0.5)	48.6	(0.5)	58.3	(0.5)	35.0	(0.5)	55.4	(0.5)	59.9	(0.5)	61.3	(0.5)

1. Feedback is defined broadly as any communication of the results of a review of an individual's work, often with the purpose of noting good performance or identifying areas for development. The feedback may be provided formally or informally.

Source: OECD, TALIS 2013 Database.

StatLink http://dx.doi.org/10.1787/888933046133

[Part 1/1]
Outcomes of teacher feedback, 2008 and 2013
Percentage of lower secondary education teachers who report a "moderate" or "large" positive change
Table 5.7.c *in the following issues after they received feedback on their work at their school[1, 2, 3]*

| | Likelihood of your career advancement | | | |
| | 2008 | | 2013 | |
	%	S.E.	%	S.E.
Australia	16.9	(0.8)	30.8	(1.3)
Brazil	25.6	(1.2)	49.9	(1.0)
Bulgaria	11.6	(0.9)	32.0	(1.4)
Denmark	4.7	(1.1)	22.9	(1.6)
Estonia	10.5	(0.6)	27.8	(1.6)
Iceland	8.6	(0.9)	12.8	(1.4)
Italy[4]	4.9	(0.5)	a	a
Korea	12.7	(0.8)	37.3	(1.1)
Malaysia	58.2	(1.4)	81.7	(0.8)
Mexico	28.6	(1.3)	51.4	(1.3)
Norway	6.9	(0.6)	15.0	(1.3)
Poland	39.2	(1.2)	51.1	(1.1)
Portugal	6.2	(0.7)	23.7	(1.0)
Slovak Republic	20.8	(1.0)	39.6	(1.1)
Spain	8.6	(0.8)	29.0	(1.0)
Sub-national entities				
Flanders (Belgium)	3.7	(0.4)	17.6	(0.8)
Average	16.7	(0.2)	34.8	(0.3)

1. Feedback is defined broadly as any communication of the results of a review of an individual's work, often with the purpose of noting good performance or identifying areas for development. The feedback may be provided formally or informally.

2. The teacher population coverage was slightly different between 2008 and 2013. In order to have comparable populations for the tables comparing results from 2008 and 2013, teachers who teach exclusively to students with special needs were excluded from the 2013 data in these tables.

3. The wording and order of questions may have changed slightly between the 2008 and 2013 surveys.

4. Question 30c from the teacher questionnaire was not administered in Italy in 2013.

Source: OECD, TALIS 2008 and 2013 Databases.

StatLink http://dx.doi.org/10.1787/888933046152

[Part 1/1]
Impact of teacher appraisal and feedback systems in schools
Percentage of lower secondary education teachers who "agree" or "strongly agree" with the following
Table 5.8 *statements about teacher appraisal and feedback systems in their school*

	The best performing teachers in this school receive the greatest recognition		Teacher appraisal and feedback have little impact upon the way teachers teach in the classroom		Teacher appraisal and feedback are largely done to fulfil administrative requirements		A development or training plan is established to improve their work as a teacher		Feedback is provided to teachers based on a thorough assessment of their teaching		If a teacher is consistently underperforming, he/she would be dismissed		Measures to remedy any weaknesses in teaching are discussed with the teacher		A mentor is appointed to help teachers improve his/her teaching	
	%	S.E.	%	S.E.	%	S.E.	%	S.E.	%	S.E.	%	S.E.	%	S.E.	%	S.E.
Australia	31.3	(2.0)	43.2	(1.2)	61.8	(1.6)	50.5	(1.6)	29.1	(1.7)	24.2	(1.4)	63.2	(1.9)	53.6	(2.1)
Brazil	18.4	(0.7)	33.9	(1.0)	42.8	(0.9)	69.4	(1.1)	45.0	(1.0)	36.8	(0.9)	76.7	(0.8)	63.1	(1.0)
Bulgaria	62.4	(1.7)	38.3	(1.4)	25.8	(1.4)	79.3	(1.3)	64.0	(1.6)	47.7	(1.7)	87.2	(1.0)	65.5	(1.6)
Chile	54.1	(2.3)	63.4	(1.8)	68.7	(1.6)	58.3	(2.1)	60.1	(2.0)	59.6	(2.0)	74.2	(1.6)	48.2	(2.2)
Croatia	27.0	(1.0)	51.5	(1.1)	56.0	(1.2)	59.3	(1.1)	45.2	(1.1)	a	a	65.6	(1.3)	30.7	(1.2)
Cyprus*	27.9	(1.1)	47.3	(1.4)	57.8	(1.3)	64.7	(1.4)	42.8	(1.3)	49.5	(1.5)	78.9	(1.1)	65.2	(1.3)
Czech Republic	55.5	(1.7)	48.6	(1.2)	35.2	(1.4)	59.1	(1.6)	51.8	(1.6)	45.9	(1.3)	83.8	(1.2)	39.4	(1.4)
Denmark	21.1	(1.4)	31.1	(1.6)	49.6	(1.5)	40.5	(1.7)	22.6	(1.3)	35.6	(2.1)	66.8	(1.7)	33.5	(1.6)
Estonia	42.7	(1.5)	47.2	(1.2)	43.3	(1.3)	57.4	(1.3)	50.3	(1.5)	32.8	(1.5)	79.7	(1.0)	40.2	(2.0)
Finland	25.3	(1.3)	49.9	(1.0)	62.0	(1.3)	38.5	(1.5)	16.8	(0.8)	16.4	(1.0)	65.2	(1.2)	16.5	(1.3)
France	13.6	(0.8)	48.6	(1.1)	61.3	(1.2)	42.2	(1.0)	19.4	(0.9)	12.0	(0.7)	57.8	(1.1)	40.8	(1.3)
Iceland	17.8	(1.2)	42.0	(1.6)	45.8	(1.5)	35.5	(1.6)	15.4	(1.1)	24.1	(1.2)	49.1	(1.6)	28.0	(1.5)
Israel	28.0	(1.3)	40.9	(1.0)	45.9	(1.4)	63.4	(1.5)	50.0	(1.5)	40.8	(1.6)	70.6	(1.1)	58.5	(1.1)
Italy	30.5	(1.0)	45.5	(1.0)	42.1	(1.2)	69.8	(1.2)	a	a	a	a	69.2	(1.1)	38.3	(1.0)
Japan	37.1	(1.1)	32.4	(1.0)	47.3	(1.1)	45.6	(1.2)	31.6	(1.1)	13.9	(0.9)	70.6	(0.9)	31.4	(1.2)
Korea	51.0	(1.2)	40.6	(1.0)	59.8	(1.2)	69.4	(1.1)	50.1	(1.2)	18.9	(1.0)	75.4	(1.0)	46.1	(1.3)
Latvia	58.1	(1.5)	43.8	(1.6)	48.3	(1.7)	48.0	(1.8)	73.6	(1.2)	38.7	(2.2)	88.9	(1.0)	36.9	(1.9)
Malaysia	90.1	(0.8)	44.5	(1.1)	76.2	(1.1)	95.9	(0.4)	89.3	(0.8)	17.3	(0.8)	93.4	(0.5)	86.2	(0.7)
Mexico	36.3	(1.2)	40.0	(1.0)	44.1	(1.3)	63.9	(1.3)	42.9	(1.2)	26.0	(1.2)	76.6	(0.9)	50.9	(1.4)
Netherlands	24.2	(1.2)	40.6	(2.0)	37.6	(1.9)	53.6	(2.6)	44.1	(2.5)	34.9	(1.5)	74.3	(1.6)	65.5	(2.4)
Norway	14.9	(0.9)	50.7	(1.8)	38.6	(1.8)	52.4	(2.9)	21.6	(3.2)	11.3	(1.7)	56.0	(2.1)	24.8	(3.5)
Poland	63.9	(1.3)	40.5	(1.1)	43.5	(1.4)	83.1	(1.1)	66.5	(1.4)	17.5	(1.0)	76.6	(1.4)	42.1	(1.7)
Portugal	17.9	(0.9)	52.9	(0.9)	69.5	(0.9)	39.7	(1.1)	53.4	(1.1)	37.3	(1.0)	66.3	(1.1)	49.8	(1.1)
Romania	57.2	(1.3)	28.8	(1.2)	43.8	(1.3)	68.9	(1.3)	72.8	(1.3)	42.9	(1.3)	89.8	(0.8)	66.9	(1.4)
Serbia	28.9	(1.3)	49.6	(1.0)	49.6	(1.2)	72.4	(0.9)	56.5	(1.3)	18.5	(0.7)	80.1	(0.9)	52.5	(1.1)
Singapore	71.2	(0.9)	38.6	(1.0)	52.6	(0.9)	79.6	(0.8)	68.2	(0.9)	45.5	(0.9)	88.0	(0.5)	83.8	(0.7)
Slovak Republic	48.4	(1.3)	58.7	(1.0)	44.3	(0.9)	66.3	(1.3)	65.5	(1.2)	30.8	(1.1)	86.7	(0.8)	35.7	(1.3)
Spain	17.6	(0.9)	47.1	(1.1)	50.5	(1.3)	50.5	(1.3)	17.3	(1.0)	15.2	(1.1)	63.2	(1.0)	14.4	(0.9)
Sweden	36.8	(1.3)	51.1	(1.1)	54.9	(1.2)	49.2	(1.3)	15.4	(1.1)	26.9	(1.2)	61.7	(1.2)	26.8	(1.2)
Sub-national entities																
Abu Dhabi (United Arab Emirates)	52.5	(2.1)	30.6	(1.6)	57.3	(1.9)	77.4	(1.7)	76.2	(1.4)	46.0	(1.5)	82.6	(1.2)	68.2	(1.5)
Alberta (Canada)	28.6	(1.7)	35.9	(1.3)	50.9	(1.8)	51.8	(1.5)	45.6	(1.4)	26.3	(1.3)	69.1	(1.5)	47.3	(1.6)
England (United Kingdom)	40.1	(1.6)	34.0	(1.6)	51.1	(1.7)	65.5	(1.3)	54.8	(1.5)	42.6	(1.5)	83.1	(1.1)	73.0	(1.3)
Flanders (Belgium)	15.0	(0.7)	40.6	(1.1)	51.3	(1.6)	28.9	(1.3)	46.9	(1.4)	33.0	(1.4)	68.0	(1.4)	53.0	(1.5)
Average	37.7	(0.2)	43.4	(0.2)	50.6	(0.2)	59.1	(0.3)	47.0	(0.3)	31.3	(0.2)	73.9	(0.2)	47.8	(0.3)
United States	40.8	(2.1)	39.4	(1.5)	60.1	(1.6)	56.6	(2.0)	53.2	(2.2)	46.9	(2.3)	70.8	(2.0)	53.3	(2.0)

*See notes at the beginning of this Annex.
Source: OECD, TALIS 2013 Database.
StatLink ᵐˢᵖ http://dx.doi.org/10.1787/888933046190

[Part 1/1]

Impact of teacher appraisal and feedback systems in schools, 2008 and 2013

Percentage of lower secondary education teachers who "agree" or "strongly agree" with the following statements about teacher appraisal and feedback in their school[1, 2]

Table 5.8.c

	The best performing teachers in this school receive the greatest recognition				Teacher appraisal and feedback have little impact upon the way teachers teach in the classroom				Teacher appraisal and feedback are largely done to fulfil administrative requirements				A development or training plan is established to improve their work as a teacher				If a teacher is consistently underperforming, he/she would be dismissed			
	2008		2013		2008		2013		2008		2013		2008		2013		2008		2013	
	%	S.E.	%	S.E.	%	S.E.	%	S.E.	%	S.E.	%	S.E.	%	S.E.	%	S.E.	%	S.E.	%	S.E.
Australia	9.2	(0.6)	31.2	(2.0)	61.4	(1.4)	43.2	(1.2)	63.4	(1.5)	61.7	(1.6)	54.5	(1.7)	50.3	(1.7)	29.2	(1.6)	24.1	(1.4)
Brazil	13.2	(0.9)	18.4	(0.7)	35.9	(1.3)	33.9	(1.0)	45.6	(1.2)	42.8	(0.9)	70.9	(1.4)	69.4	(1.1)	30.2	(1.5)	36.8	(0.9)
Bulgaria	50.5	(2.8)	62.4	(1.7)	33.4	(1.3)	38.3	(1.4)	29.4	(1.8)	25.8	(1.4)	77.4	(2.3)	79.3	(1.3)	64.7	(2.4)	47.7	(1.7)
Denmark	15.0	(1.3)	21.2	(1.4)	60.8	(1.7)	31.5	(1.6)	48.1	(1.8)	49.5	(1.5)	54.4	(1.6)	40.7	(1.8)	35.0	(1.8)	35.3	(2.1)
Estonia	37.9	(1.6)	42.7	(1.5)	43.4	(1.1)	47.2	(1.2)	27.8	(1.2)	43.2	(1.3)	64.0	(1.4)	57.1	(1.4)	29.7	(1.2)	32.6	(1.6)
Iceland	18.1	(1.1)	17.4	(1.2)	55.8	(1.4)	42.3	(1.6)	45.8	(1.4)	46.2	(1.6)	45.4	(1.5)	35.7	(1.6)	35.5	(1.3)	23.9	(1.2)
Italy[3]	42.6	(1.3)	30.5	(1.0)	40.9	(1.0)	45.5	(1.0)	32.8	(1.2)	42.2	(1.2)	71.9	(1.1)	69.8	(1.2)	27.3	(1.0)	a	a
Korea	10.0	(0.7)	50.9	(1.2)	51.9	(1.1)	40.6	(1.0)	60.5	(0.9)	59.8	(1.2)	31.3	(1.1)	69.5	(1.1)	10.1	(0.7)	18.8	(1.0)
Malaysia	53.1	(1.3)	90.2	(0.8)	34.7	(1.3)	44.5	(1.1)	50.6	(1.2)	76.2	(1.1)	89.4	(0.7)	95.9	(0.4)	17.7	(0.9)	17.3	(0.8)
Mexico	26.9	(1.2)	36.3	(1.2)	45.3	(1.3)	39.8	(1.0)	50.2	(1.7)	44.0	(1.3)	69.0	(1.4)	63.9	(1.3)	28.9	(1.3)	26.1	(1.2)
Norway	11.5	(0.8)	14.9	(0.9)	64.9	(1.1)	50.7	(1.8)	43.4	(1.2)	38.8	(1.9)	42.4	(1.4)	52.4	(2.9)	10.7	(0.9)	11.3	(1.8)
Poland	59.1	(1.5)	63.9	(1.3)	37.0	(1.4)	40.5	(1.1)	41.8	(1.5)	43.5	(1.4)	78.8	(1.2)	83.1	(1.1)	34.2	(1.2)	17.4	(1.0)
Portugal	11.0	(0.7)	17.9	(0.9)	55.3	(1.2)	52.9	(0.9)	47.9	(1.1)	69.7	(1.0)	49.3	(1.5)	39.6	(1.1)	27.2	(1.1)	37.3	(1.0)
Slovak Republic	48.6	(2.0)	48.4	(1.3)	54.5	(1.5)	58.8	(1.0)	33.8	(1.3)	44.3	(0.9)	73.6	(1.4)	66.3	(1.3)	42.4	(1.7)	30.8	(1.1)
Spain	7.3	(0.6)	17.4	(0.9)	62.2	(1.2)	47.2	(1.1)	48.7	(1.1)	50.4	(1.3)	53.6	(1.7)	50.3	(1.3)	15.1	(0.9)	15.3	(1.1)
Sub-national entities																				
Flanders (Belgium)	5.0	(0.4)	15.0	(0.7)	44.4	(1.4)	40.6	(1.1)	37.9	(1.5)	51.4	(1.6)	45.1	(1.5)	28.9	(1.3)	43.6	(1.6)	33.1	(1.5)
Average	26.2	(0.3)	36.2	(0.3)	48.9	(0.3)	43.6	(0.3)	44.2	(0.3)	49.4	(0.3)	60.7	(0.4)	59.5	(0.4)	30.1	(0.3)	27.2	(0.3)

1. The teacher population coverage was slightly different between 2008 and 2013. In order to have comparable populations for the tables comparing results from 2008 and 2013, teachers who teach exclusively to students with special needs were excluded from the 2013 data in these tables.

2. The wording and order of questions may have changed slightly between the 2008 and 2013 surveys.

3. Question 31f from the teacher questionnaire was not administered in Italy in 2013.

Source: OECD, TALIS 2008 and 2013 Databases.

StatLink ⟨⟩ http://dx.doi.org/10.1787/888933046209

[Part 1/2]
Impact of teacher appraisal and feedback systems in schools
Percentage of lower secondary education teachers who "agree" or "strongly agree" with the following statements about teacher appraisal and feedback systems in their school[1, 2]

Table 5.9

	Significant responsibility for determining teachers' salary increases								The best performing teachers in this school receive the greatest recognition				Teacher appraisal and feedback have little impact upon the way teachers teach in the classroom			
	School level[3]		Shared (school and higher levels)[4]		Higher level(s) (school has no responsibility)[5]		None of the proposed options[6]		School level[3]		Higher level(s) (school has no responsibility)[5]		School level[3]		Higher level(s) (school has no responsibility)[5]	
	%	S.E.	%	S.E.	%	S.E.	%	S.E.	%	S.E.	%	S.E.	%	S.E.	%	S.E.
Australia	26.0	(3.4)	3.5	(1.5)	70.5	(3.8)	0.0	(0.0)	29.6	(2.7)	32.1	(2.8)	46.4	(1.7)	42.9	(1.7)
Brazil	17.2	(1.2)	1.0	(0.5)	81.7	(1.3)	0.0	(0.0)	19.8	(2.1)	18.1	(0.7)	24.1	(2.7)	35.9	(1.1)
Bulgaria	64.4	(3.6)	24.5	(2.7)	9.7	(2.4)	1.4	(1.1)	62.5	(2.0)	64.5	(5.2)	38.4	(1.8)	30.8	(5.4)
Chile	60.7	(3.4)	0.7	(0.7)	36.8	(3.3)	1.9	(0.9)	55.0	(3.8)	54.1	(3.4)	59.9	(3.1)	70.9	(2.5)
Croatia	1.5	(0.9)	0.5	(0.5)	94.1	(1.8)	4.0	(1.4)	15.6	(3.2)	27.0	(1.0)	36.8	(8.6)	51.8	(1.2)
Cyprus*	23.1	(0.1)	0.0	(0.0)	76.9	(0.1)	0.0	(0.0)	31.2	(2.5)	26.8	(1.2)	37.3	(2.6)	50.6	(1.7)
Czech Republic	92.3	(2.8)	4.3	(2.0)	3.4	(2.0)	0.0	(0.0)	56.2	(1.7)	40.0	(11.3)	48.3	(1.2)	58.7	(6.7)
Denmark	35.2	(4.8)	13.4	(3.6)	51.4	(5.5)	0.0	(0.0)	22.2	(2.3)	21.8	(2.3)	32.2	(2.5)	29.7	(2.0)
Estonia	45.3	(4.0)	38.6	(4.1)	16.2	(2.9)	0.0	(0.0)	41.7	(1.9)	41.1	(3.8)	49.6	(1.6)	42.6	(4.1)
Finland	13.6	(3.4)	15.4	(3.6)	71.0	(4.3)	0.0	(0.0)	24.6	(3.2)	25.3	(1.7)	49.6	(3.3)	50.6	(1.4)
France	0.7	(0.5)	1.1	(0.6)	98.2	(0.8)	0.0	(0.0)	42.5	(10.0)	12.9	(2.8)	21.6	(6.9)	48.9	(1.2)
Iceland	15.7	(0.2)	12.3	(0.1)	72.0	(0.2)	0.0	(0.0)	14.6	(3.1)	18.5	(1.7)	40.2	(4.0)	41.1	(2.1)
Israel	14.0	(3.4)	9.9	(2.9)	76.2	(4.2)	0.0	(0.0)	26.8	(3.3)	27.6	(1.5)	41.8	(2.4)	41.0	(1.2)
Italy	6.4	(1.4)	1.6	(1.0)	92.0	(1.7)	0.0	(0.0)	29.0	(2.8)	30.2	(1.1)	36.1	(4.7)	45.8	(1.1)
Japan	9.0	(1.6)	7.8	(2.1)	83.2	(2.5)	0.0	(0.0)	34.6	(4.0)	37.9	(1.2)	31.2	(3.5)	32.4	(1.1)
Korea	8.7	(2.2)	0.0	(0.0)	91.3	(2.2)	0.0	(0.0)	52.5	(4.6)	49.7	(1.4)	39.0	(4.7)	40.5	(1.1)
Latvia	41.8	(4.8)	30.4	(4.5)	27.7	(4.4)	0.0	(0.0)	59.0	(2.8)	57.6	(3.7)	46.3	(2.1)	45.9	(3.0)
Malaysia	2.9	(1.5)	8.4	(2.3)	88.7	(2.7)	0.0	(0.0)	87.9	(2.9)	90.0	(0.9)	42.6	(12.7)	45.0	(1.2)
Mexico	18.5	(1.0)	0.0	(0.0)	81.5	(1.0)	0.0	(0.0)	38.7	(3.2)	35.8	(1.3)	30.9	(2.5)	42.3	(1.2)
Netherlands[7]	83.4	(3.9)	8.2	(2.8)	8.4	(2.8)	0.0	(0.0)	23.5	(1.3)	19.9	(3.0)	41.5	(2.6)	33.8	(6.3)
Norway	3.4	(1.7)	16.0	(5.1)	80.6	(5.4)	0.0	(0.0)	12.6	(4.2)	13.6	(1.1)	52.4	(6.7)	52.2	(2.0)
Poland	16.9	(3.7)	16.0	(3.0)	67.2	(4.2)	0.0	(0.0)	62.2	(3.5)	64.2	(1.6)	40.8	(3.2)	40.1	(1.3)
Portugal	7.3	(1.3)	1.5	(0.9)	91.2	(1.6)	0.0	(0.0)	23.6	(2.9)	17.5	(0.9)	39.3	(4.6)	53.6	(1.0)
Romania	9.0	(2.3)	2.6	(1.1)	88.4	(2.5)	0.0	(0.0)	54.0	(3.9)	57.2	(1.5)	25.2	(2.9)	29.3	(1.4)
Serbia	13.0	(2.2)	4.9	(1.6)	72.2	(3.5)	9.9	(2.9)	30.2	(3.8)	28.6	(1.5)	49.9	(2.8)	48.9	(1.1)
Singapore	7.7	(0.1)	10.1	(0.1)	82.2	(0.1)	0.0	(0.0)	67.1	(3.7)	71.7	(1.1)	36.4	(3.4)	39.5	(1.2)
Slovak Republic	81.2	(3.0)	11.7	(2.5)	7.1	(1.9)	0.0	(0.0)	49.2	(1.5)	39.2	(4.2)	58.3	(1.1)	56.9	(2.6)
Spain	2.1	(1.0)	3.4	(1.0)	94.5	(1.3)	0.0	(0.0)	20.0	(4.1)	17.4	(0.9)	41.5	(3.7)	47.2	(1.2)
Sweden	81.4	(2.9)	14.7	(2.5)	3.9	(1.5)	0.0	(0.0)	38.6	(1.5)	38.0	(9.5)	51.9	(1.1)	46.4	(6.8)
Sub-national entities																
Abu Dhabi (United Arab Emirates)	54.1	(2.8)	0.0	(0.0)	45.9	(2.8)	0.0	(0.0)	52.1	(4.0)	54.1	(2.3)	36.8	(2.8)	24.0	(1.9)
Alberta (Canada)	2.7	(1.3)	2.2	(1.1)	95.0	(1.7)	0.0	(0.0)	12.6	(14.6)	29.4	(1.6)	8.3	(4.7)	36.8	(1.3)
England (United Kingdom)	91.6	(2.3)	5.8	(2.0)	2.6	(1.3)	0.0	(0.0)	40.9	(1.7)	36.3	(5.7)	34.3	(1.8)	33.2	(1.5)
Flanders (Belgium)	4.1	(1.9)	0.0	(0.0)	95.9	(1.9)	0.0	(0.0)	8.4	(1.9)	15.0	(0.8)	51.0	(8.5)	39.8	(1.3)
Average	28.9	(0.5)	8.2	(0.4)	62.4	(0.5)	0.5	(0.1)	37.6	(0.7)	36.8	(0.6)	40.0	(0.8)	43.3	(0.5)
United States	46.9	(6.0)	11.8	(3.6)	41.2	(5.7)	0.0	(0.0)	31.4	(3.6)	46.2	(3.3)	42.0	(2.4)	40.0	(2.6)

1. The first four columns present the proportion of teachers working in school where the principal reports that significant responsibility for determining teachers' salary increases is either "held at the school level", "shared among the school and higher level(s)", "at higher level(s)" or that "none of the proposed options correspond to the level of authority responsible for determining teachers' salary increases". The remaining columns present the percentage of teachers who "agree" or "strongly agree" with different statements about teacher appraisal and feedback systems in their school. These percentages are presented for teachers working in schools where the principal reports that significant responsibility for determining teachers' salary increases is held at the school level and for teachers working in schools where the principal reports that significant responsibility for determining teachers' salary increases is held at higher level(s). For example, in Australia, 26.0% of teachers work in schools where the principal reports that significant responsibility for determining teachers' salary increases is held at the school level and 70.5% of teachers work in schools where the principal reports that significant responsibility for determining teachers' salary increases is held at a higher level(s) (where schools have no responsibility). Among Australian teachers working in schools having responsibility for determining teachers' salary increases, 29.6% "agree" or "strongly agree" that the best performing teachers in their school receive the greatest recognition. In comparison, among Australian teachers working in schools that do not have responsibility for determining teachers' salary increases, 32.1% "agree" or "strongly agree" that the best performing teachers in their school receive the greatest recognition.

2. Cells with data representing less than 5% of the cases are shaded in grey and should be interpreted with caution. These results are not highlighted in the text of the report.

3. School level is defined by cases where the principal reports that significant responsibility for determining teachers' salary increases is held at the school level only, including the principal, other members of the school management team, teachers (not as a part of the school management team) or the school governing board.

4. A shared responsibility is defined by cases where the principal reports that significant responsibility for determining teachers' salary increases is held at the school level (either the principal, other members of the school management team, teachers (not as a part of the school management team) or the school governing board) and at higher level(s) including local, municipality/regional, state, or national/federal authority.

5. Higher level(s) is defined by cases where the principal reports that significant responsibility for determining teachers' salary increases is held at higher level(s) only, including local, municipality/regional, state, or national/federal authority.

6. These are cases where the principal selected some of the proposed options in question 18 but did not select any response option for the specific question on who has significant responsibility for determining teachers' salary increases. The proposed options were: "you, as principal", "other members of the school management team", "teachers (not as a part of the school management team)", "school governing board" or "local, municipality/regional, state, or national/federal authority".

7. The school governing board is commonly seen as part of the school level. In the Netherlands this is a different (higher) level, with often one school board for multiple schools.

* See notes at the beginning of this Annex.

Source: OECD, TALIS 2013 Database.

StatLink ꟿ http://dx.doi.org/10.1787/888933046247

[Part 2/2]
Impact of teacher appraisal and feedback systems in schools
Percentage of lower secondary education teachers who "agree" or "strongly agree" with the following statements about teacher appraisal and feedback systems in their school[1,2]

Table 5.9

	Teacher appraisal and feedback are largely done to fulfil administrative requirements				A development or training plan is established to improve their work as a teacher				Feedback is provided to teachers based on a thorough assessment of their teaching				If a teacher is consistently underperforming, he/she would be dismissed			
	School level[3]		Higher level(s) (school has no responsibility)[5]		School level[3]		Higher level(s) (school has no responsibility)[5]		School level[3]		Higher level(s) (school has no responsibility)[5]		School level[3]		Higher level(s) (school has no responsibility)[5]	
	%	S.E.	%	S.E.	%	S.E.	%	S.E.	%	S.E.	%	S.E.	%	S.E.	%	S.E.
Australia	56.9	(2.3)	63.4	(2.1)	48.3	(2.0)	51.2	(2.5)	30.6	(3.1)	28.6	(2.5)	36.2	(4.4)	19.9	(1.7)
Brazil	38.4	(3.2)	43.5	(0.9)	74.1	(3.5)	68.3	(1.1)	63.8	(3.1)	41.1	(1.1)	79.4	(2.6)	27.2	(0.9)
Bulgaria	25.4	(1.7)	23.3	(3.4)	80.7	(1.6)	77.9	(4.4)	64.3	(2.0)	65.9	(6.0)	47.1	(2.2)	51.9	(5.3)
Chile	66.6	(2.8)	73.4	(2.8)	58.2	(2.9)	56.8	(3.3)	59.7	(3.2)	57.5	(2.9)	62.4	(2.8)	49.2	(3.8)
Croatia	58.4	(12.4)	56.3	(1.3)	54.3	(7.6)	59.5	(1.1)	47.6	(3.0)	45.4	(1.2)	a	a	a	a
Cyprus*	59.2	(2.9)	57.4	(1.5)	66.6	(2.6)	63.9	(1.6)	58.2	(2.5)	38.5	(1.4)	61.3	(2.3)	45.6	(1.8)
Czech Republic	34.3	(1.4)	58.5	(15.7)	60.4	(1.5)	38.6	(17.1)	53.0	(1.5)	29.8	(15.4)	46.4	(1.4)	32.1	(2.2)
Denmark	51.0	(2.5)	51.7	(1.9)	42.2	(2.2)	38.6	(3.0)	24.7	(2.2)	18.5	(1.9)	37.9	(3.9)	34.4	(2.6)
Estonia	46.3	(1.8)	38.8	(3.0)	54.8	(1.8)	56.9	(4.1)	44.8	(2.2)	53.2	(3.7)	30.7	(2.1)	34.1	(3.2)
Finland	59.7	(4.4)	62.8	(1.7)	37.6	(4.3)	38.4	(1.8)	16.5	(1.4)	16.8	(1.1)	17.6	(3.8)	16.0	(1.1)
France	21.6	(6.9)	61.7	(1.3)	25.3	(3.5)	42.2	(1.2)	14.4	(8.7)	19.0	(1.0)	21.8	(1.1)	11.6	(0.8)
Iceland	51.8	(4.2)	41.3	(2.0)	25.9	(4.2)	37.2	(2.0)	14.3	(3.2)	16.3	(1.6)	25.6	(3.8)	24.3	(1.9)
Israel	51.9	(3.1)	46.1	(1.6)	62.4	(4.1)	63.5	(1.7)	43.6	(4.8)	50.7	(1.9)	44.8	(4.3)	39.2	(1.6)
Italy	27.5	(6.1)	43.3	(1.2)	75.7	(2.8)	68.9	(1.3)	a	a	a	a	a	a	a	a
Japan	51.3	(4.7)	46.9	(1.2)	36.2	(3.5)	47.8	(1.4)	24.1	(1.4)	33.6	(1.2)	34.5	(4.9)	11.2	(0.7)
Korea	54.6	(6.8)	60.4	(1.2)	69.4	(3.4)	68.4	(1.3)	52.2	(3.2)	49.8	(1.4)	16.4	(4.3)	18.9	(1.1)
Latvia	52.8	(2.4)	50.4	(3.7)	47.1	(2.4)	47.6	(3.2)	73.4	(1.9)	68.8	(2.3)	36.2	(3.1)	38.9	(4.0)
Malaysia	83.3	(5.3)	76.4	(1.2)	97.3	(2.3)	95.5	(0.5)	81.6	(7.4)	89.5	(0.8)	12.8	(2.3)	17.8	(1.0)
Mexico	32.7	(3.1)	46.6	(1.5)	72.9	(3.8)	62.2	(1.4)	55.1	(2.9)	40.1	(1.3)	69.3	(3.5)	16.0	(1.0)
Netherlands[7]	38.4	(2.4)	34.9	(5.9)	52.0	(2.5)	54.3	(4.9)	42.8	(2.7)	50.8	(6.4)	34.6	(1.9)	39.0	(7.5)
Norway	26.5	(5.8)	37.8	(2.4)	54.9	(8.1)	50.5	(4.0)	24.2	(10.2)	21.6	(5.1)	12.6	(6.2)	9.4	(2.0)
Poland	42.7	(3.9)	41.8	(1.5)	83.8	(2.1)	83.4	(1.3)	67.7	(2.9)	67.3	(1.7)	28.3	(4.5)	16.0	(1.0)
Portugal	45.8	(3.9)	71.6	(1.0)	60.1	(6.0)	38.2	(1.2)	66.4	(3.3)	51.8	(1.2)	50.2	(7.5)	35.9	(1.0)
Romania	43.8	(3.4)	43.7	(1.5)	61.0	(4.3)	70.1	(1.4)	73.3	(4.7)	72.6	(1.4)	45.9	(3.8)	42.8	(1.5)
Serbia	57.0	(2.6)	49.3	(1.4)	71.2	(2.9)	72.5	(1.1)	54.7	(3.8)	56.9	(1.6)	18.0	(2.0)	18.6	(1.0)
Singapore	46.4	(3.8)	53.4	(1.1)	77.6	(3.3)	80.2	(0.9)	64.7	(4.2)	68.1	(1.1)	58.2	(3.8)	45.4	(1.0)
Slovak Republic	43.8	(1.2)	50.3	(5.0)	67.3	(1.4)	60.8	(4.2)	66.3	(1.4)	58.8	(3.8)	31.1	(1.2)	33.1	(4.0)
Spain	42.3	(3.4)	51.3	(1.3)	71.1	(7.8)	49.3	(1.3)	27.2	(3.2)	16.5	(1.1)	31.0	(8.4)	13.7	(1.2)
Sweden	54.7	(1.3)	53.0	(6.7)	48.4	(1.5)	60.0	(4.8)	15.2	(1.1)	18.3	(6.5)	24.9	(1.4)	39.3	(6.3)
Sub-national entities																
Abu Dhabi (United Arab Emirates)	56.2	(3.0)	57.7	(1.9)	75.7	(2.8)	83.3	(1.9)	75.7	(2.1)	79.2	(1.8)	58.8	(2.8)	29.1	(2.1)
Alberta (Canada)	20.2	(15.2)	52.1	(1.7)	54.8	(5.7)	51.8	(1.6)	40.6	(9.7)	45.4	(1.5)	75.0	(14.2)	24.6	(1.3)
England (United Kingdom)	51.1	(1.9)	48.8	(4.3)	65.3	(1.4)	63.5	(8.8)	54.9	(1.7)	46.1	(3.3)	42.9	(1.6)	48.1	(14.4)
Flanders (Belgium)	58.7	(3.1)	51.2	(1.8)	32.0	(12.3)	28.7	(1.5)	53.5	(3.5)	47.7	(1.6)	36.8	(6.5)	32.6	(1.6)
Average	47.0	(0.9)	51.5	(0.7)	59.5	(0.8)	58.5	(0.7)	48.4	(0.7)	45.8	(0.7)	39.6	(0.8)	29.5	(0.7)
United States	64.7	(2.7)	59.0	(3.3)	49.0	(2.8)	57.7	(2.5)	50.1	(3.8)	54.4	(3.0)	40.7	(4.2)	50.2	(3.1)

1. The first four columns present the proportion of teachers working in school where the principal reports that significant responsibility for determining teachers' salary increases is either "held at the school level", "shared among the school and higher level(s)", "at higher level(s)" or that "none of the proposed options correspond to the level of authority responsible for determining teachers' salary increases". The remaining columns present the percentage of teachers who "agree" or "strongly agree" with different statements about teacher appraisal and feedback systems in their school. These percentages are presented for teachers working in schools where the principal reports that significant responsibility for determining teachers' salary increases is held at the school level and for teachers working in schools where the principal reports that significant responsibility for determining teachers' salary increases is held at higher level(s). For example, in Australia, 26.0% of teachers work in schools where the principal reports that significant responsibility for determining teachers' salary increases is held at the school level and 70.5% of teachers work in schools where the principal reports that significant responsibility for determining teachers' salary increases is held at a higher level(s) (where schools have no responsibility). Among Australian teachers working in schools having responsibility for determining teachers' salary increases, 29.6% "agree" or "strongly agree" that the best performing teachers in their school receive the greatest recognition. In comparison, among Australian teachers working in schools that do not have responsibility for determining teachers' salary increases, 32.1% "agree" or "strongly agree" that the best performing teachers in their school receive the greatest recognition.

2. Cells with data representing less than 5% of the cases are shaded in grey and should be interpreted with caution. These results are not highlighted in the text of the report.

3. School level is defined by cases where the principal reports that significant responsibility for determining teachers' salary increases is held at the school level only, including the principal, other members of the school management team, teachers (not as a part of the school management team) or the school governing board.

4. A shared responsibility is defined by cases where the principal reports that significant responsibility for determining teachers' salary increases is held at the school level (either the principal, other members of the school management team, teachers (not as a part of the school management team) or the school governing board) and at higher level(s) including local, municipality/regional, state, or national/federal authority.

5. Higher level(s) is defined by cases where the principal reports that significant responsibility for determining teachers' salary increases is held at higher level(s) only, including local, municipality/regional, state, or national/federal authority.

6. These are cases where the principal selected some of the proposed options in question 18 but did not select any response option for the specific question on who has significant responsibility for determining teachers' salary increases. The proposed options were: "you, as principal", "other members of the school management team", "teachers (not as a part of the school management team)", "school governing board" or "local, municipality/regional, state, or national/federal authority".

7. The school governing board is commonly seen as part of the school level. In the Netherlands this is a different (higher) level, with often one school board for multiple schools.

* See notes at the beginning of this Annex.

Source: OECD, TALIS 2013 Database.

StatLink http://dx.doi.org/10.1787/888933046247

TALIS 2013 RESULTS: AN INTERNATIONAL PERSPECTIVE ON TEACHING AND LEARNING

[Part 1/1]
Teaching practices
Percentage of lower secondary education teachers who report using the following teaching practices
Table 6.1 *"frequently" or "in all or nearly all lessons"[1]*

	Present a summary of recently learned content		Students work in small groups to come up with a joint solution to a problem or task		Give different work to the students who have difficulties learning and/or to those who can advance faster		Refer to a problem from everyday life or work to demonstrate why new knowledge is useful		Let students practice similar tasks until teacher knows that every student has understood the subject matter		Check students' exercise books or homework		Students work on projects that require at least one week to complete		Students use ICT for projects or class work	
	%	S.E.	%	S.E.	%	S.E.	%	S.E.	%	S.E.	%	S.E.	%	S.E.	%	S.E.
Australia	72.3	(1.8)	43.7	(2.1)	45.5	(1.8)	68.6	(1.9)	62.9	(1.7)	65.2	(1.5)	51.8	(1.5)	66.8	(1.9)
Brazil	79.2	(0.7)	65.6	(0.9)	48.6	(0.9)	89.4	(0.6)	74.2	(0.8)	89.7	(0.5)	38.4	(1.0)	30.3	(1.1)
Bulgaria	79.8	(1.1)	44.4	(1.3)	61.5	(1.3)	77.6	(1.1)	78.6	(0.9)	79.2	(0.9)	24.5	(0.9)	33.7	(1.3)
Chile	81.9	(1.4)	73.9	(1.4)	57.2	(2.2)	84.9	(1.2)	86.5	(1.3)	86.2	(1.2)	52.8	(2.1)	59.6	(2.3)
Croatia	59.5	(1.1)	33.3	(1.0)	51.2	(1.1)	78.6	(0.8)	64.4	(1.0)	69.9	(1.0)	9.9	(0.6)	23.5	(0.9)
Cyprus*	83.8	(1.0)	51.3	(1.4)	35.5	(1.5)	82.8	(1.0)	81.2	(1.0)	84.6	(0.9)	26.8	(1.2)	46.4	(1.4)
Czech Republic	87.9	(0.6)	35.2	(1.0)	32.2	(1.0)	69.9	(1.0)	69.7	(1.0)	64.6	(1.1)	12.9	(0.7)	36.5	(1.1)
Denmark	79.5	(1.3)	79.7	(1.2)	44.2	(1.6)	68.7	(1.3)	57.3	(1.4)	60.4	(1.4)	23.1	(1.2)	73.9	(1.9)
Estonia	80.2	(1.0)	37.9	(0.9)	47.0	(1.3)	60.0	(1.1)	67.6	(1.2)	71.2	(0.9)	15.4	(0.8)	29.2	(1.3)
Finland	62.0	(1.1)	36.7	(1.2)	36.6	(1.2)	63.7	(1.1)	50.7	(1.0)	62.4	(0.8)	14.1	(0.8)	18.2	(0.9)
France	74.3	(0.9)	36.8	(1.1)	22.0	(0.8)	56.9	(0.9)	55.5	(1.0)	65.7	(1.0)	21.8	(0.9)	24.2	(1.0)
Iceland	38.0	(1.6)	43.9	(1.4)	49.0	(1.6)	39.6	(1.7)	47.8	(1.7)	47.3	(1.7)	24.7	(1.5)	31.8	(1.4)
Israel	69.4	(0.9)	32.0	(1.5)	33.4	(1.2)	50.2	(1.1)	71.1	(1.3)	65.6	(1.4)	23.2	(1.2)	18.7	(1.3)
Italy	63.8	(1.0)	31.9	(1.2)	58.2	(1.2)	81.0	(0.9)	78.4	(1.0)	84.6	(0.8)	27.5	(1.1)	30.9	(1.4)
Japan	59.8	(1.0)	32.5	(1.2)	21.9	(0.8)	50.9	(1.0)	31.9	(0.9)	61.3	(1.1)	14.1	(0.6)	9.9	(0.6)
Korea	70.8	(0.9)	31.8	(1.2)	20.4	(1.1)	49.5	(1.1)	48.0	(1.1)	53.4	(1.3)	14.0	(0.8)	27.6	(1.2)
Latvia	79.7	(1.3)	34.6	(1.6)	52.8	(1.6)	87.3	(0.8)	83.7	(1.0)	78.7	(1.0)	15.0	(1.0)	40.5	(1.5)
Malaysia	78.2	(1.2)	56.9	(1.7)	39.6	(1.4)	75.7	(1.1)	77.8	(1.2)	93.7	(0.6)	39.7	(1.3)	19.2	(1.3)
Mexico	62.8	(1.1)	73.4	(1.2)	31.9	(1.2)	84.8	(0.8)	79.8	(1.0)	93.7	(0.5)	57.1	(1.0)	56.2	(1.2)
Netherlands	71.5	(1.6)	47.6	(2.0)	20.2	(1.3)	63.4	(1.7)	56.3	(1.8)	65.8	(1.3)	27.1	(1.7)	34.7	(2.1)
Norway	89.2	(0.9)	72.7	(1.7)	67.4	(1.9)	53.6	(1.4)	66.4	(1.2)	71.9	(1.4)	33.7	(1.4)	73.8	(1.7)
Poland	78.1	(1.0)	42.4	(1.3)	55.5	(1.5)	75.5	(1.2)	78.7	(0.9)	63.5	(1.1)	15.8	(0.7)	36.4	(1.5)
Portugal	84.8	(0.7)	49.0	(0.9)	52.7	(0.9)	65.6	(1.0)	60.9	(1.0)	71.0	(0.8)	21.1	(0.8)	34.4	(0.9)
Romania	76.7	(1.1)	55.7	(1.3)	58.0	(1.3)	54.4	(1.1)	80.3	(1.0)	84.0	(0.8)	21.6	(1.0)	26.0	(1.2)
Serbia	62.0	(1.1)	41.5	(1.0)	59.5	(1.1)	83.4	(0.7)	74.7	(0.8)	66.1	(0.9)	15.7	(0.7)	23.1	(0.9)
Singapore	67.2	(1.0)	33.0	(0.9)	21.0	(0.8)	60.6	(0.9)	67.5	(0.9)	83.6	(0.7)	26.6	(0.8)	30.0	(0.8)
Slovak Republic	90.4	(0.6)	41.8	(1.0)	45.2	(1.2)	74.1	(0.9)	74.4	(0.8)	79.0	(0.8)	21.6	(0.9)	44.7	(1.3)
Spain	71.8	(1.1)	33.4	(1.1)	40.3	(1.2)	77.3	(1.2)	70.4	(1.0)	79.7	(1.0)	26.4	(1.0)	37.0	(1.3)
Sweden	72.1	(1.1)	44.4	(1.2)	53.1	(1.2)	48.9	(1.3)	55.2	(1.2)	50.8	(1.2)	40.7	(1.3)	33.8	(1.7)
Sub-national entities																
Abu Dhabi (United Arab Emirates)	83.3	(1.3)	76.1	(2.0)	66.6	(2.3)	71.7	(1.4)	81.6	(1.3)	85.0	(0.9)	53.0	(2.0)	72.1	(1.7)
Alberta (Canada)	79.1	(1.1)	58.4	(1.4)	47.3	(1.8)	73.2	(1.3)	66.1	(1.5)	62.7	(1.5)	37.5	(1.5)	49.3	(1.6)
England (United Kingdom)	75.2	(0.9)	58.4	(1.4)	63.2	(1.4)	62.5	(1.2)	61.8	(1.3)	85.4	(0.9)	38.3	(1.1)	37.1	(1.4)
Flanders (Belgium)	60.4	(1.1)	33.8	(1.0)	27.9	(1.3)	72.0	(1.0)	59.3	(1.2)	52.9	(1.5)	20.6	(1.0)	27.0	(1.1)
Average	73.5	(0.2)	47.4	(0.2)	44.4	(0.2)	68.4	(0.2)	67.3	(0.2)	72.1	(0.2)	27.5	(0.2)	37.5	(0.2)
United States	80.5	(1.2)	54.7	(1.8)	36.2	(1.9)	71.2	(1.1)	70.7	(1.3)	79.1	(1.5)	36.8	(1.7)	45.9	(1.8)

1. These data are reported by teachers and refer to a randomly chosen class they currently teach from their weekly timetable.
* See notes at the beginning of this Annex.
Source: OECD, TALIS 2013 Database.
StatLink ⬛⬛ http://dx.doi.org/10.1787/888933046304

[Part 1/1]
Teaching practices in primary education
Percentage of primary education teachers who report using the following teaching practices "frequently" or "in all or nearly all lessons"[1]

Table 6.1.a

	Present a summary of recently learned content		Students work in small groups to come up with a joint solution to a problem or task		Give different work to the students who have difficulties learning and/or to those who can advance faster		Refer to a problem from everyday life or work to demonstrate why new knowledge is useful		Let students practice similar tasks until teacher knows that every student has understood the subject matter		Check students' exercise books or homework		Students work on projects that require at least one week to complete		Students use ICT for projects or class work	
	%	S.E.	%	S.E.	%	S.E.	%	S.E.	%	S.E.	%	S.E.	%	S.E.	%	S.E.
Denmark	79.0	(0.9)	58.9	(1.3)	62.5	(1.4)	61.1	(1.4)	62.9	(1.3)	70.6	(1.1)	21.9	(1.0)	44.3	(1.7)
Finland	72.7	(1.3)	31.6	(1.5)	59.6	(1.3)	70.0	(1.1)	70.0	(1.5)	80.3	(1.2)	11.9	(0.9)	20.7	(1.3)
Mexico	61.2	(1.9)	84.7	(1.6)	52.1	(2.0)	88.2	(1.2)	89.9	(1.0)	97.7	(0.5)	83.9	(1.3)	39.7	(2.2)
Norway	92.8	(1.4)	64.9	(1.5)	82.5	(1.1)	54.2	(1.6)	83.2	(1.8)	92.8	(0.8)	23.5	(1.3)	57.2	(1.8)
Poland	76.5	(1.0)	46.5	(1.5)	68.0	(1.2)	80.8	(1.0)	85.9	(0.8)	72.5	(1.1)	15.1	(1.0)	29.4	(1.3)
Sub-national entities																
Flanders (Belgium)	67.6	(1.2)	58.7	(1.3)	74.2	(1.2)	77.8	(0.9)	75.8	(1.1)	89.5	(0.7)	32.4	(1.4)	40.4	(1.3)
Average	75.0	(0.5)	57.5	(0.6)	66.5	(0.6)	72.0	(0.5)	78.0	(0.5)	83.9	(0.4)	31.4	(0.5)	38.6	(0.7)

1. These data are reported by teachers and refer to a randomly chosen class they currently teach from their weekly timetable.
Source: OECD, TALIS 2013 Database.
StatLink http://dx.doi.org/10.1787/888933046323

[Part 1/1]
Teaching practices in upper secondary education
Percentage of upper secondary education teachers who report using the following teaching practices "frequently" or "in all or nearly all lessons"[1]

Table 6.1.b

	Present a summary of recently learned content		Students work in small groups to come up with a joint solution to a problem or task		Give different work to the students who have difficulties learning and/or to those who can advance faster		Refer to a problem from everyday life or work to demonstrate why new knowledge is useful		Let students practice similar tasks until teacher knows that every student has understood the subject matter		Check students' exercise books or homework		Students work on projects that require at least one week to complete		Students use ICT for projects or class work	
	%	S.E.	%	S.E.	%	S.E.	%	S.E.	%	S.E.	%	S.E.	%	S.E.	%	S.E.
Australia	76.0	(1.2)	45.9	(1.7)	33.7	(1.3)	72.6	(1.3)	66.8	(1.1)	66.5	(1.5)	50.9	(1.4)	68.8	(1.8)
Denmark	75.5	(1.4)	80.5	(1.2)	22.3	(1.3)	68.3	(1.8)	53.9	(1.7)	45.3	(1.8)	21.9	(1.6)	82.2	(1.4)
Finland	65.7	(1.3)	54.7	(2.2)	28.8	(2.0)	74.4	(2.6)	51.1	(2.1)	36.8	(2.6)	18.0	(1.9)	44.2	(2.5)
Iceland	44.8	(1.8)	47.5	(1.8)	12.2	(1.1)	36.7	(1.8)	53.2	(1.8)	62.9	(1.6)	30.1	(1.4)	52.3	(1.4)
Italy	63.9	(0.9)	34.4	(1.1)	31.8	(1.1)	78.3	(0.9)	65.6	(1.1)	58.2	(0.9)	20.0	(1.0)	28.7	(1.1)
Mexico	70.5	(1.1)	78.1	(1.1)	30.9	(1.3)	88.7	(0.8)	83.4	(0.9)	90.5	(0.9)	48.8	(1.5)	71.0	(1.3)
Norway	86.3	(0.7)	78.1	(1.5)	46.3	(1.7)	59.1	(1.1)	62.9	(1.5)	50.4	(1.3)	34.3	(1.2)	89.8	(0.7)
Poland	75.6	(1.2)	49.0	(1.4)	51.7	(1.4)	75.3	(1.2)	76.4	(1.2)	53.3	(1.5)	15.2	(0.9)	32.6	(1.1)
Singapore	71.2	(0.8)	32.5	(0.9)	25.4	(0.9)	59.0	(1.0)	68.0	(0.9)	82.7	(0.7)	21.1	(0.8)	26.6	(0.9)
Sub-national entities																
Abu Dhabi (United Arab Emirates)	82.4	(1.1)	77.3	(1.4)	64.6	(1.6)	71.2	(1.1)	79.8	(1.2)	84.7	(1.2)	53.9	(1.5)	74.0	(1.1)
Average	71.2	(0.4)	57.8	(0.5)	34.8	(0.4)	68.4	(0.5)	66.1	(0.4)	63.1	(0.5)	31.4	(0.4)	57.0	(0.4)

1. These data are reported by teachers and refer to a randomly chosen class they currently teach from their weekly timetable.
Source: OECD, TALIS 2013 Database.
StatLink http://dx.doi.org/10.1787/888933046342

[Part 1/1]
Relationships between teachers' characteristics and small group practice
Significant results of the logistic regressions of teachers' characteristics with select teaching practices
for teachers in lower secondary education[1]

Table 6.2

	Students work in small groups to come up with a joint solution to a problem or task[2]															
	Dependent on:															
	Female[3]		Teacher of mathematics/ science[4]		Teacher of humanities[5]		Years of experience[6]		Highest level of education (ISCED 5A or above)[7]		Feel prepared for the content of the subject(s) taught[8]		Feel prepared for the pedagogy of the subject(s) taught[9]		Feel prepared for classroom practice in the subject(s) taught[10]	
	ß	Odds ratios[11]	ß	Odds ratios[11]	ß	Odds ratios[11]	ß	Odds ratios[12]	ß	Odds ratios[11]	ß	Odds ratios[11]	ß	Odds ratios[11]	ß	Odds ratios[11]
Australia	0.23	1.57	-0.33	0.51	-0.12	0.78					-0.34	0.51	0.35	2.00		
Brazil	0.24	1.62									-0.31	0.53	0.26	1.67		
Bulgaria			-0.38	0.46												
Chile			-0.24	0.62			0.02	1.02								
Croatia	0.15	1.36	-0.28	0.57	-0.14	0.75							0.20	1.50		
Czech Republic	0.13	1.30	-0.30	0.54					-0.25	0.60	0.42	2.31				
Denmark	0.24	1.61			0.31	1.85										
Estonia					0.20	1.50	0.01	1.01								
Finland	0.15	1.34											0.18	1.43		
France			-0.81	0.20	-0.88	0.17	-0.01	0.99								
Iceland			0.25	1.65	0.31	1.86										
Israel					-0.30	0.55										
Italy	0.17	1.41											0.21	1.51		
Japan							-0.02	0.98							0.25	1.64
Korea			-0.24	0.62	-0.20	0.67							0.24	1.61	0.22	1.54
Latvia					0.27	1.72										
Malaysia							0.01	1.01								
Mexico					-0.26	0.59	0.02	1.02	0.25	1.65						
Netherlands	0.14	1.33	-0.35	0.50	-0.51	0.36							0.22	1.54		
Norway	0.17	1.40			0.27	1.71										
Poland	0.10	1.23	-0.53	0.35	-0.14	0.76										
Portugal			-0.45	0.41	-0.54	0.34									0.23	1.58
Romania													0.66	3.72		
Serbia			-0.25	0.61									0.40	2.23		
Singapore	0.17	1.41	-0.43	0.43									0.31	1.87	0.19	1.46
Slovak Republic			-0.29	0.56			0.01	1.01							0.30	1.81
Spain			-0.36	0.49	-0.39	0.46			0.21	1.51						
Sweden	0.25	1.64			0.21	1.53										
Sub-national entities																
Abu Dhabi (United Arab Emirates)			0.30	1.84												
Alberta (Canada)	0.13	1.30			0.14	1.32										
England (United Kingdom)	0.10	1.23					-0.01	0.99					0.37	2.08		
Flanders (Belgium)			-0.42	0.43			-0.02	0.98								

1. No control variables were used for this regression. Cells are blank when no significant relationship was found. Significance was tested at the 5% level. Cells with data representing less than 5% of the cases are shaded in grey and should be interpreted with caution. These results are not highlighted in the text of the report.

2. The reference category is the combination of teachers who answered that "students work in small groups to come up with a joint solution to a problem or task" happened "frequently" or "in all or nearly all lessons". An odds ratio greater than 1 indicates an increase in the odds of using small groups for the column heading category compared with the reference category, while an odds ratio of less than 1 indicates a decrease in odds of use. For example, in Australia the odds of small group use by female teachers is 57% greater than that of male teachers.

3. Dichotomous variable where the reference category is male.

4. Dichotomous variable where the reference category is non-math/science teachers.

5. Dichotomous variable where the reference category is non-humanities teachers.

6. Continuous variable where the direction of odds ratio is based on increasing years of experience.

7. Dichotomous variable where the reference category is teachers with a highest level of educational attainment below ISCED 5A.

8. Dichotomous variable where the reference category is feeling "not at all" or "somewhat" prepared for content area.

9. Dichotomous variable where the reference category is feeling "not at all" or "somewhat" prepared for pedagogy in subject taught.

10. Dichotomous variable where the reference category is feeling "not at all" or "somewhat" prepared for classroom practice in subject taught.

11. Note that these odds ratios estimates are not corresponding to the exponentiated beta because effect coding was used. Please refer to the technical appendix for a more detailed explanation.

12. This is the exponentiated beta. Please refer to Box 2.5 for interpretation of odds ratios.

Source: OECD, TALIS 2013 Database.

StatLink http://dx.doi.org/10.1787/888933046418

[Part 1/1]

Relationships between teachers' characteristics and use of projects

Significant results of the logistic regressions of teachers' characteristics with select teaching practices for teachers in lower secondary education[1]

Table 6.3

	Students work on projects that require at least one week to complete[2]															
	Dependent on:															
	Female[3]		Teacher of mathematics/ science[4]		Teacher of humanities[5]		Years of experience[6]		Highest level of education (ISCED 5A or above)[7]		Feel prepared for the content of the subject(s) taught[8]		Feel prepared for the pedagogy of the subject(s) taught[9]		Feel prepared for classroom practice in the subject(s) taught[10]	
	ß	Odds ratios[11]	ß	Odds ratios[11]	ß	Odds ratios[11]	ß	Odds ratios[12]	ß	Odds ratios[11]	ß	Odds ratios[11]	ß	Odds ratios[11]	ß	Odds ratios[11]
Australia			-0.97	0.14												
Brazil	0.19	1.45	-0.28	0.57					-0.20	0.68			0.24	1.63		
Bulgaria	0.28	1.75	-0.52	0.35	-0.22	0.65										
Chile			-0.50	0.37	-0.20	0.67										
Croatia			-0.48	0.38	-0.24	0.62										
Czech Republic			-0.76	0.22	-0.35	0.50										
Denmark			-0.45	0.41							-0.29	0.56				
Estonia			-0.70	0.24	-0.50	0.37							-0.48	0.38		
Finland			-1.69	0.03	-0.69	0.25			0.30	1.82						
France			-0.86	0.18	-0.51	0.36					-0.20	0.68				
Iceland			-0.65	0.27	-0.26	0.59	-0.02	0.98								
Israel	0.20	1.51	-0.43	0.42	-0.24	0.61										
Italy			-0.98	0.14	-0.67	0.26										
Japan	0.14	1.33	-0.96	0.15	-0.86	0.18										
Korea			-0.77	0.22	-0.63	0.28										
Latvia			-0.35	0.50												
Malaysia			-0.33	0.52	-0.17	0.71	0.02	1.02			-1.60	0.04				
Mexico	0.14	1.31	-0.26	0.60			0.01	1.01								
Netherlands	0.26	1.70	-1.07	0.12	-0.93	0.16										
Norway			-0.85	0.18			-0.02	0.98					0.37	2.09		
Poland	0.19	1.47	-0.60	0.30	-0.16	0.73									0.51	2.75
Portugal			-0.97	0.14	-0.72	0.24			-0.28	0.57						
Romania	0.18	1.44	-0.23	0.63												
Serbia	0.12	1.28	-0.74	0.23	-0.39	0.46										
Singapore			-0.80	0.20	-0.45	0.41									0.24	1.62
Slovak Republic			-0.37	0.48												
Spain			-0.93	0.16	-0.55	0.34							-0.17	0.71	0.34	1.97
Sweden			-0.97	0.14	-0.19	0.68	-0.01	0.99							-0.20	0.68
Sub-national entities																
Abu Dhabi (United Arab Emirates)			-0.14	0.75												
Alberta (Canada)			-0.77	0.21												
England (United Kingdom)			-1.18	0.10	-0.70	0.24	0.02	1.02							0.34	1.96
Flanders (Belgium)	-0.25	0.60	-1.02	0.13	-1.04	0.13										

1. No control variables were used for this regression. Cells are blank when no significant relationship was found. Significance was tested at the 5% level. Cells with data representing less than 5% of the cases are shaded in grey and should be interpreted with caution. These results are not highlighted in the text of the report.

2. The reference category is the combination of teachers who answered that "students work on projects that require at least one week to complete" happened "frequently" or "in all or nearly all lessons". An odds ratio greater than 1 indicates an increase in the odds of using projects that require at least one week to complete for the column heading category compared with the reference category, while an odds ratio less than 1 indicates a decrease in odds of use. For example, in Brazil the odds of using projects that require at least one week to complete by female teachers is 45% greater than that of male teachers.

3. Dichotomous variable where the reference category is male.

4. Dichotomous variable where the reference category is non-math/science teachers.

5. Dichotomous variable where the reference category is non-humanities teachers.

6. Continuous variable where the direction of odds ratio is based on increasing years of experience.

7. Dichotomous variable where the reference category is teachers with a highest level of educational attainment below ISCED 5A.

8. Dichotomous variable where the reference category is feeling "not at all" or "somewhat" prepared for content area.

9. Dichotomous variable where the reference category is feeling "not at all" or "somewhat" prepared for pedagogy in subject taught.

10. Dichotomous variable where the reference category is feeling "not at all" or "somewhat" prepared for classroom practice in subject taught.

11. Note that these odds ratios estimates are not corresponding to the exponentiated beta because effect coding was used. Please refer to the technical appendix for a more detailed explanation.

12. This is the exponentiated beta. Please refer to Box 2.5 for interpretation of odds ratios.

Source: OECD, TALIS 2013 Database.

StatLink ᵐˢᵖ http://dx.doi.org/10.1787/888933046456

[Part 1/1]

Relationships between teachers' characteristics and use of ICT

Significant results of the logistic regressions of teachers' characteristics with select teaching practices for teachers in lower secondary education[1]

Table 6.4

	Students use ICT (information and communication technology) for projects or class work[2]															
	Dependent on:															
	Female[3]		Teacher of mathematics/ science[4]		Teacher of humanities[5]		Years of experience[6]		Highest level of education (ISCED 5A or above)[7]		Feel prepared for the content of the subject(s) taught[8]		Feel prepared for the pedagogy of the subject(s) taught[9]		Feel prepared for classroom practice in the subject(s) taught[10]	
	ß	Odds ratios[11]	ß	Odds ratios[11]	ß	Odds ratios[11]	ß	Odds ratios[12]	ß	Odds ratios[11]	ß	Odds ratios[11]	ß	Odds ratios[11]	ß	Odds ratios[11]
Australia			-0.24	0.62	0.28	1.76										
Brazil	0.19	1.46	-0.21	0.66											0.36	2.05
Bulgaria	0.24	1.63	-0.42	0.44	-0.24	0.62					-0.43	0.42				
Chile									0.21	1.53						
Croatia			-0.28	0.57	-0.46	0.40									0.26	1.69
Czech Republic			-0.24	0.62					-0.16	0.72			0.17	1.40	0.25	1.64
Denmark			0.32	1.89	0.68	3.93										
Estonia							0.01	1.01								
Finland	-0.19	0.68	-0.45	0.40									0.16	1.37		
France	-0.10	0.82	-0.22	0.65	-0.18	0.69					-0.64	0.28	-0.26	0.59		
Iceland					0.21	1.52							0.28	1.75		
Israel																
Italy							0.01	1.01			0.30	1.84				
Japan	-0.19	0.69	-0.31	0.54	-0.20	0.67	-0.02	0.98								
Korea	-0.16	0.72	-0.35	0.49	-0.21	0.66									0.21	1.53
Latvia																
Malaysia							0.02	1.02								
Mexico	0.11	1.24	-0.44	0.42	-0.29	0.56										
Netherlands			-0.48	0.38							-0.44	0.42	0.29	1.79		
Norway			0.22	1.55	0.76	4.53										
Poland																
Portugal			-0.36	0.49	-0.18	0.69										
Romania			-0.21	0.66	-0.20	0.67									-0.61	0.30
Serbia			-0.54	0.34	-0.46	0.40										
Singapore			-0.32	0.53	-0.13	0.76	0.01	1.01					0.14	1.33		
Slovak Republic			-0.15	0.74	-0.12	0.79							0.32	1.89	0.26	1.70
Spain			-0.48	0.39	-0.22	0.64									0.31	1.85
Sweden					0.38	2.12										
Sub-national entities																
Abu Dhabi (United Arab Emirates)																
Alberta (Canada)					0.60	3.33										
England (United Kingdom)			-0.57	0.32	-0.28	0.58									0.41	2.27
Flanders (Belgium)			-0.55	0.33	-0.36	0.49			-0.24	0.62						

1. No control variables were used for this regression. Cells are blank when no significant relationship was found. Significance was tested at the 5% level. Cells with data representing less than 5% of the cases are shaded in grey and should be interpreted with caution. These results are not highlighted in the text of the report.

2. The reference category is the combination of teachers who answered that "students use ICT (information and communication technology) for projects or class work" happened "frequently" or "in all or nearly all lessons". An odds ratio greater than 1 indicates an increase in the odds of using ICT for the column heading category compared with the reference category, while an odds ratio less than 1 indicates a decrease in odds of use. For example, in Brazil the odds of ICT use by female teachers is 46% greater than that of male teachers.

3. Dichotomous variable where the reference category is male.

4. Dichotomous variable where the reference category is non-math/science teachers.

5. Dichotomous variable where the reference category is non-humanities teachers.

6. Continuous variable where the direction of odds ratio is based on increasing years of experience.

7. Dichotomous variable where the reference category is teachers with a highest level of educational attainment below ISCED 5A.

8. Dichotomous variable where the reference category is feeling "not at all" or "somewhat" prepared for content area.

9. Dichotomous variable where the reference category is feeling "not at all" or "somewhat" prepared for pedagogy in subject taught.

10. Dichotomous variable where the reference category is feeling "not at all" or "somewhat" prepared for classroom practice in subject taught.

11. Note that these odds ratios estimates are not corresponding to the exponentiated beta because effect coding was used. Please refer to the technical appendix for a more detailed explanation.

12. This is the exponentiated beta. Please refer to Box 2.5 for interpretation of odds ratios.

Source: OECD, TALIS 2013 Database.

StatLink http://dx.doi.org/10.1787/888933046494

[Part 1/1]
Relationships between professional development and small group practice
Significant results of the logistic regressions of aspects of teachers' professional development with select teaching practices for teachers in lower secondary education[1]

Table 6.5

	Students work in small groups to come up with a joint solution to a problem or task[2]													
	Dependent on:													
	Courses/ workshops[3]		Education conferences or seminars[4]		Observation visits to other schools[5]		Qualification programme[6]		Participation in a network of teachers formed specifically for the professional development of teachers[7]		Individual or collaborative research on a topic of interest[8]		Mentoring and/or peer observation and coaching[9]	
	ß	Odds ratios[10]	ß	Odds ratios[10]	ß	Odds ratios[10]	ß	Odds ratios[10]	ß	Odds ratios[10]	ß	Odds ratios[10]	ß	Odds ratios[10]
Australia	0.19	1.45			0.21	1.53								
Brazil							0.10	1.23	0.11	1.25			0.14	1.33
Bulgaria									0.15	1.36			0.14	1.33
Chile							0.27	1.72						
Croatia									0.14	1.31	0.15	1.35	0.15	1.35
Czech Republic									0.13	1.29	0.18	1.45	0.09	1.19
Denmark														
Estonia														
Finland					0.11	1.25			0.19	1.46	0.35	2.00		
France									0.21	1.51				
Iceland														
Israel							0.15	1.34						
Italy			0.12	1.28	0.20	1.50							0.17	1.41
Japan	0.10	1.22			0.11	1.24					0.12	1.27	0.12	1.27
Korea					0.13	1.29	0.16	1.38	0.22	1.56	0.12	1.28		
Latvia					0.12	1.27					0.19	1.48		
Malaysia					0.19	1.47								
Mexico									0.14	1.31				
Netherlands									0.18	1.43				
Norway											0.29	1.77		
Poland					0.29	1.79							0.11	1.24
Portugal			0.10	1.22	0.12	1.27	0.16	1.39						
Romania			0.15	1.35										
Serbia	0.10	1.23							0.17	1.40				
Singapore			0.12	1.26							0.10	1.23		
Slovak Republic														
Spain			0.13	1.30	0.18	1.45	0.17	1.42	0.14	1.33				
Sweden							0.21	1.53			0.25	1.66		
Sub-national entities														
Abu Dhabi (United Arab Emirates)	0.28	1.76												
Alberta (Canada)									0.24	1.61	0.13	1.30		
England (United Kingdom)														
Flanders (Belgium)	0.16	1.38												

1. Controlling for teacher gender, years of experience, highest level of education and subject taught in the target class. Cells are blank when no significant relationship was found. Significance was tested at the 5% level.

2. The reference category is the combination of teachers who answered that "students work in small groups to come up with a joint solution to a problem or task" happened "frequently" or "in all or nearly all lessons". An odds ratio greater than 1 indicates an increase in the odds of using small groups for the column heading category compared with the reference category, while an odds ratio less than 1 indicates a decrease in odds of use. For example, in Austrailia the odds of small group use by teachers who attended courses or workshops is 45% greater than that of teachers who did not attend.

3. Dichotomous variable where the reference category is teachers who did not participate in courses/workshops.

4. Dichotomous variable where the reference category is teachers who did not participate in education conferences or seminars.

5. Dichotomous variable where the reference category is teachers who did not participate in observation visits to other schools.

6. Dichotomous variable where the reference category is teachers who did not participate in qualification programmes.

7. Dichotomous variable where the reference category is teachers who did not participate in a network of teachers formed specifically for the professional development of teachers.

8. Dichotomous variable where the reference category is teachers who did not participate in individual or collaborative research.

9. Dichotomous variable where the reference category is teachers who did not participate in mentoring and/or peer observation and coaching.

10. Note that these odds ratios estimates are not corresponding to the exponentiated beta because effect coding was used. Please refer to the technical appendix for a more detailed explanation.

Source: OECD, TALIS 2013 Database.

StatLink http://dx.doi.org/10.1787/888933046532

[Part 1/1]
Relationships between professional development and use of projects
Significant results of the logistic regressions of aspects of teachers' professional development with select teaching practices for teachers in lower secondary education[1]

Table 6.6

	Students work on projects that require at least one week to complete[2]													
	Dependent on:													
	Courses/ workshops[3]		Education conferences or seminars[4]		Observation visits to other schools[5]		Qualification programme[6]		Participation in a network of teachers formed specifically for the professional development of teachers[7]		Individual or collaborative research on a topic of interest[8]		Mentoring and/or peer observation and coaching[9]	
	β	Odds ratios[10]	β	Odds ratios[10]	β	Odds ratios[10]	β	Odds ratios[10]	β	Odds ratios[10]	β	Odds ratios[10]	β	Odds ratios[10]
Australia	0.24	1.60									0.21	1.53		
Brazil					0.12	1.28	0.11	1.24					0.18	1.42
Bulgaria			0.16	1.39							0.26	1.69		
Chile	-0.18	0.69			0.32	1.91	0.21	1.53					0.23	1.58
Croatia											0.25	1.64		
Czech Republic									0.19	1.45	0.22	1.54		
Denmark	-0.17	0.71	0.28	1.76										
Estonia							0.15	1.35						
Finland							0.18	1.42						
France											0.18	1.42		
Iceland														
Israel					0.17	1.40					0.30	1.82	0.17	1.39
Italy									0.13	1.30	0.12	1.27		
Japan														
Korea							0.22	1.55			0.19	1.46		
Latvia											0.28	1.74		
Malaysia									0.12	1.27	0.13	1.30		
Mexico							0.12	1.28						
Netherlands							0.29	1.80						
Norway											0.29	1.77	0.16	1.38
Poland			0.14	1.31			0.14	1.32						
Portugal					0.19	1.46					0.23	1.59	0.14	1.33
Romania			0.24	1.62			0.17	1.41						
Serbia									0.15	1.36	0.31	1.88		
Singapore	-0.24	0.62			0.15	1.34			0.10	1.23				
Slovak Republic			0.22	1.55										
Spain							0.13	1.29	0.14	1.31	0.18	1.42	0.15	1.36
Sweden														
Sub-national entities														
Abu Dhabi (United Arab Emirates)	0.33	1.95									0.16	1.38	0.13	1.30
Alberta (Canada)														
England (United Kingdom)														
Flanders (Belgium)											0.19	1.47		

1. Controlling for teacher gender, years of experience, highest level of education and subject taught in the target class. Cells are blank when no significant relationship was found. Significance was tested at the 5% level.

2. The reference category is the combination of teachers who answered that "students work on projects that require at least one week to complete" happened "frequently" or "in all or nearly all lessons". An odds ratio greater than 1 indicates an increase in the odds of using projects that require at least one week for the column heading category compared with the reference category, while an odds ratio less than 1 indicates a decrease in odds of use. For example, in Austrailia the odds of using projects that require at least one week by teachers who attended courses or workshops is 60% greater than that of teachers who did not attend.

3. Dichotomous variable where the reference category is teachers who did not participate in courses/workshops.

4. Dichotomous variable where the reference category is teachers who did not participate in education conferences or seminars.

5. Dichotomous variable where the reference category is teachers who did not participate in observation visits to other schools.

6. Dichotomous variable where the reference category is teachers who did not participate in qualification programmes.

7. Dichotomous variable where the reference category is teachers who did not participate in a network of teachers formed specifically for the professional development of teachers.

8. Dichotomous variable where the reference category is teachers who did not participate in individual or collaborative research.

9. Dichotomous variable where the reference category is teachers who did not participate in mentoring and/or peer observation and coaching.

10. Note that these odds ratios estimates are not corresponding to the exponentiated beta because effect coding was used. Please refer to the technical appendix for a more detailed explanation.

Source: OECD, TALIS 2013 Database.

StatLink ᴍᴤᴾ http://dx.doi.org/10.1787/888933046570

[Part 1/1]
Relationships between professional development and use of ICT
Significant results of the logistic regressions of aspects of teachers' professional development with select teaching practices for teachers in lower secondary education[1]

Table 6.7

	Students use ICT (information and communication technology) for projects or class work[2]													
	Dependent on:													
	Courses/ workshops[3]		Education conferences or seminars[4]		Observation visits to other schools[5]		Qualification programme[6]		Participation in a network of teachers formed specifically for the professional development of teachers[7]		Individual or collaborative research on a topic of interest[8]		Mentoring and/or peer observation and coaching[9]	
	ß	Odds ratios[10]	ß	Odds ratios[10]	ß	Odds ratios[10]	ß	Odds ratios[10]	ß	Odds ratios[10]	ß	Odds ratios[10]	ß	Odds ratios[10]
Australia														
Brazil			0.11	1.24	0.16	1.37	0.11	1.25	0.11	1.24			0.16	1.39
Bulgaria			0.16	1.37					0.18	1.44	0.16	1.39		
Chile					0.51	2.75	0.33	1.95						
Croatia	0.16	1.39									0.24	1.61		
Czech Republic	0.11	1.25							0.14	1.34	0.14	1.32		
Denmark			0.18	1.44			0.24	1.62					-0.22	0.65
Estonia	-0.20	0.68	0.11	1.24	0.12	1.27					0.16	1.38		
Finland	0.21	1.52							0.18	1.43	0.32	1.90		
France			0.17	1.42	0.30	1.82			0.13	1.29	0.13	1.31		
Iceland									0.21	1.53				
Israel											0.16	1.36		
Italy					0.15	1.35			0.12	1.27				
Japan														
Korea							0.20	1.49			0.13	1.29		
Latvia					0.11	1.26	0.17	1.40						
Malaysia	0.32	1.90	0.19	1.47							0.17	1.40		
Mexico							0.15	1.34					0.17	1.41
Netherlands					0.19	1.46								
Norway											0.34	1.98		
Poland											0.10	1.23	0.08	1.16
Portugal					0.26	1.69			0.10	1.23	0.14	1.32		
Romania			0.18	1.44			0.15	1.36	0.11	1.26				
Serbia									0.13	1.30	0.20	1.48		
Singapore			0.17	1.42										
Slovak Republic	0.14	1.31												
Spain			0.13	1.29					0.14	1.33	0.10	1.23	0.14	1.32
Sweden	0.11	1.25			0.17	1.39					0.20	1.49		
Sub-national entities														
Abu Dhabi (United Arab Emirates)	0.35	2.01									0.16	1.36	0.16	1.39
Alberta (Canada)														
England (United Kingdom)											0.16	1.38		
Flanders (Belgium)							0.12	1.27						

1. Controlling for teacher gender, years of experience, highest level of education and subject taught in the target class. Cells are blank when no significant relationship was found. Significance was tested at the 5% level.

2. The reference category is the combination of teachers who answered that "student use ICT (information and communication technology) for projects or class work" happened "frequently" or "in all or nearly all lessons". An odds ratio greater than 1 indicates an increase in the odds of using ICT for the column heading category compared with the reference category, while an odds ratio less than 1 indicates a decrease in odds of use. For example, in Sweden the odds of ICT use by teachers who attended courses or workshops is 25% greater than that of teachers who did not attend.

3. Dichotomous variable where the reference category is teachers who did not participate in courses/workshops.

4. Dichotomous variable where the reference category is teachers who did not participate in education conferences or seminars.

5. Dichotomous variable where the reference category is teachers who did not participate in observation visits to other schools.

6. Dichotomous variable where the reference category is teachers who did not participate in qualification programmes.

7. Dichotomous variable where the reference category is teachers who did not participate in a network of teachers formed specifically for the professional development of teachers.

8. Dichotomous variable where the reference category is teachers who did not participate in individual or collaborative research.

9. Dichotomous variable where the reference category is teachers who did not participate in mentoring and/or peer observation and coaching.

10. Note that these odds ratios estimates are not corresponding to the exponentiated beta because effect coding was used. Please refer to the technical appendix for a more detailed explanation.

Source: OECD, TALIS 2013 Database.

StatLink ᔑᐂᒣ http://dx.doi.org/10.1787/888933046608

[Part 1/1]
Relationships between classroom context and small groups practice
Significant results of the logistic regressions of aspects of teachers' classroom context with select teaching practices for teachers in lower secondary education[1]

Table 6.8

	Students work in small groups to come up with a joint solution to a problem or task[2]															
	Dependent on:															
	Class size[3]		Students whose first language is different from the language(s) of instruction[4]		Low academic achievers[5]		Students with special needs[6]		Students with behavioural problems[7]		Students from socio-economically disadvantaged homes[8]		Academically gifted students[9]		Classroom climate[10]	
	ß	Odds ratios[11]	ß	Odds ratios[12]	ß	Odds ratios[12]	ß	Odds ratios[12]	ß	Odds ratios[12]	ß	Odds ratios[12]	ß	Odds ratios[12]	ß	Odds ratios[11]
Australia															0.15	1.16
Brazil							0.30	1.83							0.15	1.16
Bulgaria													0.14	1.32		
Chile													0.22	1.56		
Croatia							0.21	1.51					0.14	1.32	0.13	1.14
Czech Republic	-0.02	0.98									0.14	1.32	0.24	1.61	0.17	1.19
Denmark	0.03	1.03											0.31	1.85	0.12	1.13
Estonia															0.13	1.14
Finland			0.22	1.56											0.07	1.08
France	-0.07	0.93													0.08	1.08
Iceland															0.14	1.15
Israel	-0.05	0.96			-0.12	0.78							0.26	1.67		
Italy											0.28	1.77			0.10	1.10
Japan															0.17	1.19
Korea	-0.02	0.98	0.77	4.63	-0.16	0.73			0.21	1.51					0.16	1.17
Latvia															0.12	1.13
Malaysia					-0.21	0.66							0.14	1.31	0.23	1.26
Mexico															0.15	1.17
Netherlands															0.08	1.08
Norway															0.14	1.15
Poland	-0.03	0.97											0.19	1.48	0.17	1.19
Portugal					-0.12	0.79					0.13	1.28			0.06	1.06
Romania					-0.17	0.71									0.23	1.25
Serbia					-0.15	0.75					0.11	1.26			0.13	1.14
Singapore													0.29	1.78	0.19	1.21
Slovak Republic															0.17	1.18
Spain															0.07	1.08
Sweden													0.12	1.26	0.07	1.07
Sub-national entities																
Abu Dhabi (United Arab Emirates)															0.14	1.15
Alberta (Canada)															0.06	1.06
England (United Kingdom)	0.02	1.02													0.14	1.15
Flanders (Belgium)											0.14	1.32	0.45	2.44	0.08	1.08

1. Controlling for teacher gender, years of experience, highest level of education and subject taught in the target class. Cells are blank when no significant relationship was found. Significance was tested at the 5% level. Cells with data representing less than 5% of the cases are shaded in grey and should be interpreted with caution. These results are not highlighted in the text of the report.

2. The reference category is the combination of teachers who answered that "students work in small groups to come up with a joint solution to a problem or task" happened "frequently" or "in all or nearly all lessons". An odds ratio greater than 1 indicates an increase in the odds of small group use for the column heading category compared to the reference category, while an odds ratio less than 1 indicates a decrease in odds of use. For example, in France the odds of small group use decreases by 7% as class size increases.

3. Continuous variable where the direction of odds ratio is based on increasing class size.

4. Dichotomous variable where the reference category is classes with less than 10% of students whose first language is different from the language(s) of instruction.

5. Dichotomous variable where the reference category is classes with less than 10% of low academic achieving students.

6. Dichotomous variable where the reference category is classes with less than 10% of students with special needs.

7. Dichotomous variable where the reference category is classes with less than 10% of students with behavioral problems.

8. Dichotomous variable where the reference category is classes with less than 10% of students from socio-economically disadvantaged homes.

9. Dichotomous variable where the reference category is classes with less than 10% of academically gifted students.

10. Continuous variable where the direction of odds ratio is based on increasing index of classroom disciplinary climate (positive).

11. This is the exponentiated beta. Please refer to text Box 2.5 for interpretation of odds ratios.

12. Note that these odds ratios estimates are not corresponding to the exponentiated beta because effect coding was used. Please refer to the technical appendix for a more detailed explanation.

Source: OECD, TALIS 2013 Database.

StatLink ⟨⟩ http://dx.doi.org/10.1787/888933046646

[Part 1/1]

Relationships between classroom context and use of projects

Significant results of the logistic regressions of aspects of teachers' classroom context with select teaching practices for teachers in lower secondary education[1]

Table 6.9

	Students work on projects that require at least one week to complete[2]														
	Dependent on:														
	Class size[3]		Students whose first language is different from the language(s) of instruction[4]		Low academic achievers[5]		Students with special needs[6]		Students with behavioural problems[7]		Students from socio-economically disadvantaged homes[8]		Academically gifted students[9]		Classroom climate[10]	
	ß	Odds ratios[11]	ß	Odds ratios[12]	ß	Odds ratios[12]	ß	Odds ratios[12]	ß	Odds ratios[12]	ß	Odds ratios[12]	ß	Odds ratios[12]	ß	Odds ratios[11]
Australia															0.08	1.08
Brazil									0.11	1.25					0.05	1.06
Bulgaria			-0.22	0.64	-0.24	0.62			0.19	1.47			0.22	1.56		
Chile																
Croatia					-0.26	0.59					0.25	1.66			0.10	1.11
Czech Republic			0.36	2.07							0.23	1.57				
Denmark															0.09	1.09
Estonia	0.02	1.02														
Finland													0.17	1.42	0.08	1.09
France																
Iceland	-0.03	0.97														
Israel					-0.21	0.66					0.15	1.36	0.27	1.71		
Italy					-0.14	0.76					0.23	1.59	0.10	1.23	0.08	1.08
Japan																
Korea			0.81	5.07	-0.17	0.72										
Latvia																
Malaysia					-0.16	0.73	0.29	1.77					0.15	1.35		
Mexico													0.15	1.35		
Netherlands																
Norway	-0.02	0.98							0.23	1.58						
Poland	0.03	1.03														
Portugal					-0.14	0.76							0.52	2.82		
Romania					-0.24	0.62			0.29	1.77			0.37	2.11	0.15	1.16
Serbia	0.03	1.03	0.27	1.72	-0.18	0.69			0.17	1.42			0.30	1.83		
Singapore	-0.01	0.99	-0.15	0.74									0.29	1.78		
Slovak Republic			-0.24	0.62			0.21	1.52			0.15	1.34				
Spain																
Sweden																
Sub-national entities																
Abu Dhabi (United Arab Emirates)																
Alberta (Canada)					-0.14	0.75										
England (United Kingdom)															0.09	1.10
Flanders (Belgium)																

1. Controlling for teacher gender, years of experience, highest level of education and subject taught in the target class. Cells are blank when no significant relationship was found. Significance was tested at the 5% level. Cells with data representing less than 5% of the cases are shaded in grey and should be interpreted with caution. These results are not highlighted in the text of the report.

2. The reference category is the combination of teachers who answered that "students work on projects that require at least one week to complete" happened "frequently" or "in all or nearly all lessons". For example, in Estonia the odds of using projects that require at least one week increases by 2% as class size increases.

3. Continuous variable where the direction of odds ratio is based on increasing class size.

4. Dichotomous variable where the reference category is classes with less than 10% of students whose first language is different from the language(s) of instruction.

5. Dichotomous variable where the reference category is classes with less than 10% of low academic achieving students.

6. Dichotomous variable where the reference category is classes with less than 10% of students with special needs.

7. Dichotomous variable where the reference category is classes with less than 10% of students with behavioral problems.

8. Dichotomous variable where the reference category is classes with less than 10% of students from socio-economically disadvantaged homes.

9. Dichotomous variable where the reference category is classes with less than 10% of academically gifted students.

10. Continuous variable where the direction of odds ratio is based on increasing index of classroom disciplinary climate (positive).

11. This is the exponentiated beta. Please refer to Box 2.5 for interpretation of odds ratios.

12. Note that these odds ratios estimates are not corresponding to the exponentiated beta because effect coding was used. Please refer to the technical appendix for a more detailed explanation.

Source: OECD, TALIS 2013 Database.

StatLink ⬛⬛ http://dx.doi.org/10.1787/888933046684

[Part 1/1]
Relationships between classroom context and use of ICT
Significant results of the logistic regressions of aspects of teachers' classroom context
with select teaching practices for teachers in lower secondary education[1]

Table 6.10

	Students use ICT (information and communication technology) for projects or class work[2]															
	Dependent on:															
	Class size[3]		Students whose first language is different from the language(s) of instruction[4]		Low academic achievers[5]		Students with special needs[6]		Students with behavioural problems[7]		Students from socio-economically disadvantaged homes[8]		Academically gifted students[9]		Classroom climate[10]	
	ß	Odds ratios[11]	ß	Odds ratios[12]	ß	Odds ratios[12]	ß	Odds ratios[12]	ß	Odds ratios[12]	ß	Odds ratios[12]	ß	Odds ratios[12]	ß	Odds ratios[11]
Australia																
Brazil					-0.21	0.66			0.17	1.40	-0.15	0.75	0.22	1.54	0.12	1.12
Bulgaria			-0.18	0.70					0.20	1.48					0.15	1.17
Chile					-0.21	0.65										
Croatia					-0.11	0.80			0.20	1.48					0.13	1.14
Czech Republic													0.11	1.24	0.09	1.09
Denmark	0.04	1.04	-0.33	0.52												
Estonia	0.02	1.02													0.09	1.09
Finland			0.19	1.46			0.18	1.43					0.19	1.47	0.09	1.09
France							0.15	1.34							0.08	1.08
Iceland																
Israel	0.04	1.04			-0.25	0.60	0.23	1.60					0.23	1.60		
Italy					-0.15	0.74							0.11	1.24	0.07	1.07
Japan							0.26	1.68			0.19	1.45				
Korea			0.60	3.32												
Latvia	0.02	1.02									0.15	1.36			0.16	1.17
Malaysia											-0.17	0.71	0.24	1.61	0.16	1.17
Mexico					-0.14	0.76							0.26	1.68	0.12	1.13
Netherlands													-0.22	0.64		
Norway							0.30	1.82			0.14	1.32				
Poland													0.11	1.24		
Portugal					-0.15	0.74			0.10	1.22	0.10	1.22			0.05	1.05
Romania					-0.16	0.73							0.34	1.97	0.17	1.19
Serbia					-0.14	0.75										
Singapore			-0.13	0.77			0.15	1.35					0.33	1.95	0.09	1.09
Slovak Republic									-0.15	0.75					0.07	1.07
Spain					-0.11	0.80					0.17	1.41				
Sweden	0.01	1.01														
Sub-national entities																
Abu Dhabi (United Arab Emirates)			-0.32	0.53	0.18	1.42									0.09	1.09
Alberta (Canada)																
England (United Kingdom)													0.19	1.47	0.05	1.05
Flanders (Belgium)							0.13	1.29			0.19	1.46				

1. Controlling for teacher gender, years of experience, highest level of education and subject taught in the target class. Cells are blank when no significant relationship was found. Significance was tested at the 5% level. Cells with data representing less than 5% of the cases are shaded in grey and should be interpreted with caution. These results are not highlighted in the text of the report.

2. The reference category is the combination of teachers who answered that "students use ICT for projects or class work" happened "frequently" or "in all or nearly all lessons". For example, in Denmark the odds of using ICT increases by 4% as class size increases.

3. Continuous variable where the direction of odds ratio is based on increasing class size.

4. Dichotomous variable where the reference category is classes with less than 10% of students whose first language is different from the language(s) of instruction.

5. Dichotomous variable where the reference category is classes with less than 10% of low academic achieving students.

6. Dichotomous variable where the reference category is classes with less than 10% of students with special needs.

7. Dichotomous variable where the reference category is classes with less than 10% of students with behavioral problems.

8. Dichotomous variable where the reference category is classes with less than 10% of students from socio-economically disadvantaged homes.

9. Dichotomous variable where the reference category is classes with less than 10% of academically gifted students.

10. Continuous variable where the direction of odds ratio is based on increasing index of classroom disciplinary climate (positive).

11. This is the exponentiated beta. Please refer to Box 2.5 for interpretation of odds ratios.

12. Note that these odds ratios estimates are not corresponding to the exponentiated beta because effect coding was used. Please refer to the technical appendix for a more detailed explanation.

Source: OECD, TALIS 2013 Database.

StatLink ⟰ http://dx.doi.org/10.1787/888933046722

[Part 1/1]
Teachers' use of student assessment practices
Percentage of lower secondary education teachers who report using the following methods of assessing student learning "frequently" or "in all or nearly all lessons"[1]

Table 6.11

	Develop and administer own assessment		Administer a standardised test		Individual students answer questions in front of the class		Provide written feedback on student work in addition to a mark, i.e. numeric score or letter grade		Let students evaluate their own progress		Observe students when working on particular tasks and provide immediate feedback	
	%	S.E.	%	S.E.	%	S.E.	%	S.E.	%	S.E.	%	S.E.
Australia	71.8	(1.7)	31.8	(1.4)	47.6	(2.1)	74.8	(1.7)	31.7	(1.5)	90.0	(0.9)
Brazil	93.4	(0.4)	48.5	(1.0)	36.2	(0.8)	61.7	(0.9)	43.1	(0.8)	80.9	(0.8)
Bulgaria	68.4	(1.2)	55.7	(1.2)	67.3	(1.1)	51.1	(1.2)	24.6	(1.0)	79.6	(0.9)
Chile	92.2	(0.8)	64.3	(2.0)	78.3	(1.3)	66.2	(2.1)	65.8	(1.8)	92.9	(0.8)
Croatia	61.5	(1.1)	23.1	(0.9)	51.7	(1.0)	66.9	(1.2)	42.3	(1.1)	85.3	(0.6)
Cyprus*	80.8	(1.2)	60.8	(1.4)	60.0	(1.5)	60.5	(1.3)	42.1	(1.4)	88.2	(0.9)
Czech Republic	72.2	(0.9)	31.3	(1.1)	45.0	(1.2)	32.3	(0.9)	36.5	(1.3)	82.4	(0.8)
Denmark	56.2	(1.6)	21.5	(1.4)	49.5	(1.6)	60.4	(1.4)	24.3	(1.3)	69.3	(1.3)
Estonia	56.1	(1.3)	32.2	(1.3)	23.2	(1.2)	34.4	(1.1)	29.0	(1.1)	83.5	(1.0)
Finland	66.2	(1.2)	28.0	(1.1)	10.8	(0.7)	25.2	(1.0)	27.2	(1.2)	76.1	(0.8)
France	85.6	(0.7)	8.3	(0.6)	56.9	(1.0)	74.4	(0.9)	16.5	(0.8)	78.2	(0.7)
Iceland	57.0	(1.6)	25.7	(1.5)	5.2	(0.8)	50.2	(1.7)	17.3	(1.3)	63.4	(1.5)
Israel	50.6	(1.4)	63.7	(1.5)	56.0	(1.4)	64.9	(1.3)	23.8	(1.3)	66.4	(1.3)
Italy	69.0	(1.0)	43.1	(1.1)	79.8	(0.8)	52.6	(1.2)	28.6	(1.0)	79.4	(0.9)
Japan	29.1	(0.8)	33.1	(1.0)	53.0	(0.9)	22.9	(1.0)	27.0	(1.1)	43.0	(0.9)
Korea	31.0	(1.0)	51.2	(1.1)	27.4	(1.1)	25.2	(0.9)	21.2	(1.0)	45.8	(1.2)
Latvia	51.0	(1.3)	71.0	(1.5)	23.1	(1.2)	22.1	(1.3)	47.5	(1.6)	84.6	(1.0)
Malaysia	65.5	(1.2)	62.9	(1.3)	66.2	(1.2)	62.7	(1.2)	66.1	(1.4)	93.7	(0.7)
Mexico	78.7	(0.9)	44.0	(1.3)	71.9	(1.0)	73.1	(1.0)	61.5	(1.3)	90.8	(0.6)
Netherlands	66.3	(1.5)	41.0	(1.8)	14.2	(1.2)	39.6	(1.6)	17.6	(1.4)	74.2	(1.3)
Norway	61.4	(1.6)	14.1	(1.0)	53.3	(1.5)	74.7	(1.7)	28.5	(1.5)	67.3	(1.8)
Poland	59.5	(1.0)	51.7	(1.1)	41.1	(1.1)	36.2	(1.1)	38.5	(1.3)	88.9	(0.8)
Portugal	82.5	(0.6)	20.8	(0.8)	65.4	(1.0)	75.5	(0.7)	59.2	(0.9)	89.5	(0.5)
Romania	75.6	(1.1)	19.6	(0.9)	57.7	(1.3)	32.9	(1.3)	40.3	(1.2)	84.2	(0.9)
Serbia	64.6	(1.0)	39.2	(1.0)	47.9	(1.0)	39.6	(1.1)	54.3	(1.0)	84.8	(0.7)
Singapore	64.7	(1.0)	70.5	(0.9)	64.3	(1.0)	72.5	(0.9)	31.9	(0.9)	77.5	(0.8)
Slovak Republic	60.0	(1.0)	39.3	(1.3)	45.3	(1.0)	29.7	(1.2)	61.2	(1.3)	89.2	(0.6)
Spain	76.4	(0.9)	10.1	(0.7)	61.2	(1.0)	69.7	(1.0)	21.6	(0.9)	82.3	(1.2)
Sweden	57.8	(1.2)	13.0	(0.9)	43.6	(1.1)	54.4	(1.4)	32.0	(1.2)	73.6	(1.0)
Sub-national entities												
Abu Dhabi (United Arab Emirates)	87.5	(1.9)	68.1	(1.8)	65.7	(1.7)	82.0	(1.1)	56.2	(2.0)	92.2	(0.9)
Alberta (Canada)	88.1	(1.1)	17.6	(1.3)	36.1	(1.6)	68.0	(1.3)	39.4	(1.7)	88.3	(0.9)
England (United Kingdom)	71.5	(1.2)	39.5	(1.2)	69.1	(1.3)	81.6	(1.1)	69.1	(1.3)	88.8	(0.7)
Flanders (Belgium)	89.1	(0.7)	14.3	(0.9)	40.5	(1.1)	61.3	(1.2)	30.3	(1.2)	77.4	(1.1)
Average	67.9	(0.2)	38.2	(0.2)	48.9	(0.2)	54.5	(0.2)	38.1	(0.2)	79.7	(0.2)
United States	85.0	(1.4)	21.3	(1.2)	47.0	(1.4)	67.3	(1.7)	37.9	(1.9)	88.6	(1.1)

1. These data are reported by teachers and refer to a randomly chosen class they currently teach from their weekly timetable.
* See notes at the beginning of this Annex.
Source: OECD, TALIS 2013 Database.
StatLink ⟶ http://dx.doi.org/10.1787/888933046760

[Part 1/2]
Teachers' working hours

Average number of 60-minute hours lower secondary education teachers report having spent
Table 6.12 *on the following activities during the most recent complete calendar week[1, 2]*

	Total working hours[3]		Hours spent on teaching		Hours spent on individual planning or preparation of lessons either at school or out of school		Hours spent on team work and dialogue with colleagues within the school		Hours spent marking/correcting of student work		Hours spent on student counselling (including student supervision, virtual counselling, career guidance and delinquency guidance)	
	Average	S.E.	Average	S.E.	Average	S.E.	Average	S.E.	Average	S.E.	Average	S.E.
Australia	42.7	(0.5)	18.6	(0.3)	7.1	(0.1)	3.5	(0.1)	5.1	(0.2)	2.3	(0.2)
Brazil	36.7	(0.4)	25.4	(0.2)	7.1	(0.1)	3.3	(0.1)	5.7	(0.1)	2.7	(0.1)
Bulgaria	39.0	(0.4)	18.4	(0.2)	8.1	(0.1)	2.5	(0.1)	4.5	(0.1)	1.7	(0.1)
Chile	29.2	(0.8)	26.7	(0.4)	5.8	(0.2)	2.8	(0.1)	4.1	(0.2)	2.4	(0.1)
Croatia	39.6	(0.2)	19.6	(0.1)	9.7	(0.1)	2.1	(0.1)	3.9	(0.1)	1.8	(0.1)
Cyprus*	33.1	(0.3)	16.2	(0.2)	7.3	(0.1)	2.7	(0.1)	4.9	(0.1)	2.0	(0.1)
Czech Republic	39.4	(0.3)	17.8	(0.1)	8.3	(0.1)	2.2	(0.1)	4.5	(0.1)	2.2	(0.1)
Denmark	40.0	(0.4)	18.9	(0.1)	7.9	(0.1)	3.3	(0.1)	3.5	(0.1)	1.5	(0.1)
Estonia	36.1	(0.5)	20.9	(0.2)	6.9	(0.1)	1.9	(0.0)	4.3	(0.1)	2.1	(0.1)
Finland	31.6	(0.2)	20.6	(0.2)	4.8	(0.1)	1.9	(0.1)	3.1	(0.1)	1.0	(0.1)
France	36.5	(0.3)	18.6	(0.1)	7.5	(0.1)	1.9	(0.0)	5.6	(0.1)	1.2	(0.0)
Iceland	35.0	(0.4)	19.0	(0.2)	7.3	(0.2)	3.3	(0.2)	3.2	(0.1)	1.4	(0.1)
Israel	30.7	(0.5)	18.3	(0.2)	5.2	(0.1)	2.7	(0.1)	4.3	(0.1)	2.1	(0.1)
Italy	29.4	(0.3)	17.3	(0.1)	5.0	(0.1)	3.1	(0.1)	4.2	(0.1)	1.0	(0.0)
Japan	53.9	(0.4)	17.7	(0.1)	8.7	(0.1)	3.9	(0.1)	4.6	(0.1)	2.7	(0.1)
Korea	37.0	(0.4)	18.8	(0.2)	7.7	(0.2)	3.2	(0.1)	3.9	(0.1)	4.1	(0.1)
Latvia	36.1	(0.4)	19.2	(0.3)	6.4	(0.2)	2.3	(0.1)	4.6	(0.1)	3.2	(0.1)
Malaysia	45.1	(0.7)	17.1	(0.3)	6.4	(0.2)	4.1	(0.1)	7.4	(0.2)	2.9	(0.1)
Mexico	33.6	(0.6)	22.7	(0.4)	6.2	(0.1)	2.4	(0.1)	4.3	(0.1)	2.8	(0.1)
Netherlands	35.6	(0.4)	16.9	(0.2)	5.1	(0.1)	3.1	(0.1)	4.2	(0.1)	2.1	(0.1)
Norway	38.3	(0.5)	15.0	(0.2)	6.5	(0.1)	3.1	(0.1)	5.2	(0.2)	2.1	(0.1)
Poland	36.8	(0.5)	18.6	(0.2)	5.5	(0.1)	2.2	(0.1)	4.6	(0.1)	2.1	(0.1)
Portugal	44.7	(0.3)	20.8	(0.1)	8.5	(0.2)	3.7	(0.2)	9.6	(0.2)	2.2	(0.1)
Romania	35.7	(0.5)	16.2	(0.2)	8.0	(0.2)	2.7	(0.1)	4.0	(0.1)	2.6	(0.1)
Serbia	34.2	(0.3)	18.4	(0.2)	7.9	(0.1)	2.3	(0.1)	3.4	(0.1)	2.3	(0.1)
Singapore	47.6	(0.4)	17.1	(0.1)	8.4	(0.1)	3.6	(0.1)	8.7	(0.1)	2.6	(0.0)
Slovak Republic	37.5	(0.4)	19.9	(0.2)	7.5	(0.1)	2.3	(0.1)	3.5	(0.1)	1.9	(0.1)
Spain	37.6	(0.4)	18.6	(0.2)	6.6	(0.1)	2.7	(0.1)	6.1	(0.2)	1.5	(0.0)
Sweden	42.4	(0.2)	17.6	(0.1)	6.7	(0.1)	3.5	(0.1)	4.7	(0.1)	2.7	(0.1)
Sub-national entities												
Abu Dhabi (United Arab Emirates)	36.2	(0.5)	21.2	(0.3)	7.6	(0.3)	3.8	(0.2)	5.4	(0.2)	3.3	(0.1)
Alberta (Canada)	48.2	(0.5)	26.4	(0.3)	7.5	(0.2)	3.0	(0.1)	5.5	(0.2)	2.7	(0.1)
England (United Kingdom)	45.9	(0.4)	19.6	(0.2)	7.8	(0.1)	3.3	(0.1)	6.1	(0.1)	1.7	(0.1)
Flanders (Belgium)	37.0	(0.3)	19.1	(0.2)	6.3	(0.1)	2.1	(0.0)	4.5	(0.1)	1.3	(0.1)
Average	38.3	(0.1)	19.3	(0.0)	7.1	(0.0)	2.9	(0.0)	4.9	(0.0)	2.2	(0.0)
United States	44.8	(0.7)	26.8	(0.5)	7.2	(0.2)	3.0	(0.1)	4.9	(0.1)	2.4	(0.2)

1. A "complete" calendar week is one that was not shortened by breaks, public holidays, sick leave, etc. Also includes tasks that took place during weekends, evenings or other off-classroom hours.

2. The sum of hours spent on different tasks may not be equal to the number of total working hours because teachers were asked about these elements seperately. It is also important to note that data presented in this table represent the averages from all the teachers surveyed, including part-time teachers.

3. Including teaching, planning lessons, marking, collaborating with other teachers, participating in staff meetings and other tasks related to the teacher's job at the school.

* See notes at the beginning of this Annex.

Source: OECD, TALIS 2013 Database.

StatLink ⟐ http://dx.doi.org/10.1787/888933046798

[Part 2/2]
Teachers' working hours
Average number of 60-minute hours lower secondary education teachers report having spent
Table 6.12 *on the following activities during the most recent complete calendar week[1,2]*

	Hours spent in participation in school management		Hours spent on general administrative work (including communication, paperwork, and other clerical duties you undertake in your job as a teacher)		Hours spent on communication and co-operation with parents or guardians		Hours spent engaging in extracurricular activities (e.g. sports and cultural activities after school)		Hours spent on all other tasks	
	Average	S.E.	Average	S.E.	Average	S.E.	Average	S.E.	Average	S.E.
Australia	3.1	(0.2)	4.3	(0.1)	1.3	(0.1)	2.3	(0.2)	2.2	(0.1)
Brazil	1.7	(0.1)	1.8	(0.1)	1.7	(0.1)	2.4	(0.1)	2.2	(0.1)
Bulgaria	1.1	(0.1)	2.7	(0.1)	1.7	(0.0)	2.0	(0.1)	1.7	(0.1)
Chile	2.3	(0.1)	2.9	(0.1)	2.0	(0.1)	2.0	(0.1)	2.2	(0.2)
Croatia	0.5	(0.0)	2.6	(0.1)	1.5	(0.1)	1.9	(0.1)	1.8	(0.1)
Cyprus*	1.3	(0.1)	2.4	(0.1)	1.7	(0.1)	2.5	(0.1)	2.2	(0.2)
Czech Republic	1.1	(0.1)	2.7	(0.1)	0.9	(0.0)	1.3	(0.1)	1.4	(0.1)
Denmark	0.9	(0.1)	2.0	(0.1)	1.8	(0.1)	0.9	(0.1)	2.3	(0.1)
Estonia	0.8	(0.1)	2.3	(0.1)	1.3	(0.1)	1.9	(0.1)	1.5	(0.1)
Finland	0.4	(0.0)	1.3	(0.1)	1.2	(0.0)	0.6	(0.1)	1.0	(0.1)
France	0.7	(0.0)	1.3	(0.0)	1.0	(0.0)	1.0	(0.0)	1.1	(0.0)
Iceland	1.2	(0.1)	2.0	(0.1)	1.4	(0.1)	1.1	(0.1)	2.3	(0.1)
Israel	2.1	(0.1)	1.9	(0.1)	1.8	(0.1)	1.7	(0.1)	3.8	(0.1)
Italy	1.0	(0.0)	1.8	(0.0)	1.4	(0.0)	0.8	(0.1)	0.7	(0.1)
Japan	3.0	(0.1)	5.5	(0.1)	1.3	(0.0)	7.7	(0.2)	2.9	(0.1)
Korea	2.2	(0.1)	6.0	(0.2)	2.1	(0.1)	2.7	(0.1)	2.6	(0.1)
Latvia	1.0	(0.1)	2.4	(0.1)	1.5	(0.1)	2.1	(0.1)	1.4	(0.1)
Malaysia	5.0	(0.2)	5.7	(0.2)	2.4	(0.1)	4.9	(0.2)	4.3	(0.2)
Mexico	1.7	(0.1)	2.3	(0.1)	2.3	(0.1)	2.3	(0.1)	2.0	(0.1)
Netherlands	1.3	(0.1)	2.2	(0.1)	1.3	(0.0)	1.3	(0.1)	2.5	(0.1)
Norway	1.3	(0.1)	2.8	(0.1)	1.4	(0.1)	0.8	(0.1)	1.4	(0.2)
Poland	0.9	(0.1)	2.5	(0.1)	1.3	(0.0)	2.4	(0.1)	1.9	(0.1)
Portugal	1.8	(0.1)	3.8	(0.2)	1.8	(0.1)	2.4	(0.2)	2.6	(0.2)
Romania	0.9	(0.1)	1.5	(0.1)	1.8	(0.1)	2.3	(0.1)	1.8	(0.1)
Serbia	0.8	(0.1)	2.4	(0.1)	1.6	(0.1)	2.2	(0.1)	2.1	(0.1)
Singapore	1.9	(0.1)	5.3	(0.1)	1.6	(0.0)	3.4	(0.1)	2.7	(0.1)
Slovak Republic	1.1	(0.1)	2.7	(0.1)	1.3	(0.1)	2.0	(0.1)	1.6	(0.1)
Spain	1.7	(0.1)	1.8	(0.0)	1.5	(0.0)	0.9	(0.1)	1.5	(0.1)
Sweden	0.8	(0.1)	4.5	(0.1)	1.8	(0.0)	0.4	(0.0)	1.7	(0.1)
Sub-national entities										
Abu Dhabi (United Arab Emirates)	2.7	(0.2)	3.3	(0.2)	2.6	(0.2)	2.5	(0.1)	2.1	(0.1)
Alberta (Canada)	2.2	(0.2)	3.2	(0.1)	1.7	(0.1)	3.6	(0.2)	1.9	(0.1)
England (United Kingdom)	2.2	(0.1)	4.0	(0.1)	1.6	(0.0)	2.2	(0.1)	2.3	(0.1)
Flanders (Belgium)	0.9	(0.0)	2.4	(0.1)	0.7	(0.0)	1.3	(0.1)	1.4	(0.1)
Average	**1.6**	**(0.0)**	**2.9**	**(0.0)**	**1.6**	**(0.0)**	**2.1**	**(0.0)**	**2.0**	**(0.0)**
United States	1.6	(0.1)	3.3	(0.1)	1.6	(0.1)	3.6	(0.3)	7.0	(0.4)

1. A "complete" calendar week is one that was not shortened by breaks, public holidays, sick leave, etc. Also includes tasks that took place during weekends, evenings or other off-classroom hours.

2. The sum of hours spent on different tasks may not be equal to the number of total working hours because teachers were asked about these elements seperately. It is also important to note that data presented in this table represent the averages from all the teachers surveyed, including part-time teachers.

3. Including teaching, planning lessons, marking, collaborating with other teachers, participating in staff meetings and other tasks related to the teacher's job at the school.

* See notes at the beginning of this Annex.

Source: OECD, TALIS 2013 Database.

StatLink ▉▉▉ http://dx.doi.org/10.1787/888933046798

[Part 1/1]

Teachers' working hours in primary education

Average number of 60-minute hours primary education teachers report having spent on the following activities during the most recent complete calendar week[1, 2]

Table 6.12.a

	Total working hours[3]		Hours spent on teaching		Hours spent on individual planning or preparation of lessons either at school or out of school		Hours spent on team work and dialogue with colleagues within the school		Hours spent marking/correcting of student work		Hours spent on student counselling (including student supervision, virtual counselling, career guidance and delinquency guidance)	
	Average	S.E.	Average	S.E.	Average	S.E.	Average	S.E.	Average	S.E.	Average	S.E.
Denmark	39.2	(0.2)	20.3	(0.1)	7.6	(0.1)	3.6	(0.1)	2.5	(0.1)	1.2	(0.0)
Finland	31.2	(0.4)	23.2	(0.2)	4.1	(0.1)	2.1	(0.1)	2.0	(0.1)	0.8	(0.0)
Mexico	34.5	(0.8)	23.7	(0.4)	5.7	(0.2)	2.7	(0.2)	4.0	(0.1)	2.4	(0.2)
Norway	38.0	(0.2)	17.2	(0.2)	7.2	(0.1)	3.8	(0.1)	2.5	(0.1)	1.7	(0.0)
Poland	36.9	(0.3)	18.9	(0.2)	5.6	(0.1)	2.2	(0.1)	4.0	(0.1)	1.9	(0.1)
Sub-national entities												
Flanders (Belgium)	41.0	(0.3)	22.8	(0.1)	6.0	(0.1)	2.1	(0.1)	4.5	(0.1)	1.3	(0.1)
Average	36.8	(0.2)	21.0	(0.1)	6.0	(0.1)	2.8	(0.0)	3.2	(0.0)	1.5	(0.0)

	Hours spent in participation in school management		Hours spent on general administrative work (including communication, paperwork, and other clerical duties you undertake in your job as a teacher)		Hours spent on communication and co-operation with parents or guardians		Hours spent engaging in extracurricular activities (e.g. sports and cultural activities after school)		Hours spent on all other tasks	
	Average	S.E.	Average	S.E.	Average	S.E.	Average	S.E.	Average	S.E.
Denmark	0.7	(0.1)	1.9	(0.1)	1.9	(0.1)	0.7	(0.1)	1.7	(0.1)
Finland	0.4	(0.0)	1.1	(0.0)	1.4	(0.0)	0.4	(0.0)	0.6	(0.0)
Mexico	1.8	(0.1)	2.6	(0.1)	2.4	(0.1)	2.4	(0.1)	2.2	(0.2)
Norway	1.1	(0.1)	2.6	(0.1)	1.6	(0.1)	0.6	(0.0)	1.1	(0.1)
Poland	0.9	(0.1)	2.6	(0.1)	1.6	(0.1)	2.2	(0.1)	1.8	(0.1)
Sub-national entities										
Flanders (Belgium)	1.2	(0.0)	2.6	(0.1)	1.2	(0.1)	1.0	(0.1)	1.4	(0.1)
Average	1.0	(0.0)	2.2	(0.0)	1.7	(0.0)	1.2	(0.0)	1.5	(0.0)

1. A "complete" calendar week is one that was not shortened by breaks, public holidays, sick leave, etc. Also includes tasks that took place during weekends, evenings or other off-classroom hours.

2. The sum of hours spent on different tasks may not be equal to the number of total working hours because teachers were asked about these elements seperately. It is also important to note that data presented in this table represent the averages from all the teachers surveyed, including part-time teachers.

3. Including teaching, planning lessons, marking, collaborating with other teachers, participating in staff meetings and other tasks related to the teacher's job at the school.

Source: OECD, TALIS 2013 Database.

StatLink http://dx.doi.org/10.1787/888933046817

[Part 1/1]

Teachers' working hours in upper secondary education

Average number of 60-minute hours upper secondary education teachers report having spent on the following activities during the most recent complete calendar week[1, 2]

Table 6.12.b

	Total working hours[3]		Hours spent on teaching		Hours spent on individual planning or preparation of lessons either at school or out of school		Hours spent on team work and dialogue with colleagues within the school		Hours spent marking/correcting of student work		Hours spent on student counselling (including student supervision, virtual counselling, career guidance and delinquency guidance)	
	Average	S.E.	Average	S.E.	Average	S.E.	Average	S.E.	Average	S.E.	Average	S.E.
Australia	43.6	(0.4)	18.3	(0.2)	7.5	(0.2)	3.6	(0.1)	5.8	(0.2)	2.3	(0.1)
Denmark	41.9	(0.3)	16.6	(0.3)	11.6	(0.2)	2.9	(0.1)	5.8	(0.2)	2.7	(0.2)
Finland	31.3	(0.5)	17.1	(0.3)	5.4	(0.1)	2.7	(0.1)	3.7	(0.2)	2.3	(0.3)
Iceland	38.3	(0.6)	17.4	(0.3)	8.7	(0.2)	2.6	(0.1)	7.5	(0.2)	1.2	(0.1)
Italy	31.7	(0.3)	17.0	(0.1)	6.3	(0.1)	3.1	(0.1)	5.2	(0.1)	1.1	(0.0)
Mexico	33.6	(0.6)	20.4	(0.5)	7.0	(0.2)	2.4	(0.1)	5.2	(0.2)	3.0	(0.1)
Norway	37.9	(0.2)	14.4	(0.2)	7.9	(0.1)	3.2	(0.1)	5.8	(0.2)	2.3	(0.1)
Poland	37.8	(0.3)	19.3	(0.2)	5.6	(0.1)	2.3	(0.1)	5.1	(0.1)	2.4	(0.1)
Singapore	47.8	(0.3)	17.0	(0.1)	8.2	(0.1)	3.7	(0.1)	9.1	(0.1)	2.6	(0.1)
Sub-national entities												
Abu Dhabi (United Arab Emirates)	37.7	(0.5)	21.0	(0.2)	7.6	(0.2)	4.0	(0.2)	5.3	(0.1)	3.3	(0.1)
Average	38.2	(0.1)	17.9	(0.1)	7.6	(0.1)	3.0	(0.0)	5.8	(0.1)	2.3	(0.0)

	Hours spent in participation in school management		Hours spent on general administrative work (including communication, paperwork, and other clerical duties you undertake in your job as a teacher)		Hours spent on communication and co-operation with parents or guardians		Hours spent engaging in extracurricular activities (e.g. sports and cultural activities after school)		Hours spent on all other tasks	
	Average	S.E.	Average	S.E.	Average	S.E.	Average	S.E.	Average	S.E.
Australia	2.9	(0.2)	4.5	(0.1)	1.3	(0.1)	1.9	(0.1)	2.3	(0.1)
Denmark	0.9	(0.1)	2.6	(0.1)	0.1	(0.0)	0.8	(0.1)	2.2	(0.2)
Finland	0.6	(0.1)	2.6	(0.2)	0.6	(0.1)	0.5	(0.1)	1.9	(0.2)
Iceland	0.7	(0.1)	2.0	(0.1)	0.5	(0.0)	0.6	(0.1)	2.4	(0.2)
Italy	1.1	(0.0)	1.8	(0.1)	1.4	(0.0)	1.0	(0.1)	0.8	(0.1)
Mexico	2.3	(0.1)	3.0	(0.1)	1.5	(0.1)	1.8	(0.1)	2.1	(0.1)
Norway	1.5	(0.1)	3.0	(0.1)	0.6	(0.0)	1.0	(0.1)	1.6	(0.1)
Poland	1.3	(0.1)	2.8	(0.1)	1.4	(0.0)	2.1	(0.1)	1.9	(0.1)
Singapore	2.4	(0.1)	5.4	(0.1)	1.5	(0.0)	3.2	(0.1)	2.5	(0.1)
Sub-national entities										
Abu Dhabi (United Arab Emirates)	2.8	(0.1)	3.5	(0.2)	2.3	(0.1)	2.4	(0.1)	2.3	(0.1)
Average	1.7	(0.0)	3.1	(0.0)	1.1	(0.0)	1.5	(0.0)	2.0	(0.0)

1. A "complete" calendar week is one that was not shortened by breaks, public holidays, sick leave, etc. Also includes tasks that took place during weekends, evenings or other off-classroom hours.

2. The sum of hours spent on different tasks may not be equal to the number of total working hours because teachers were asked about these elements seperately. It is also important to note that data presented in this table represent the averages from all the teachers surveyed, including part-time teachers.

3. Including teaching, planning lessons, marking, collaborating with other teachers, participating in staff meetings and other tasks related to the teacher's job at the school.

Source: OECD, TALIS 2013 Database.

StatLink ᵐˢᵖ http://dx.doi.org/10.1787/888933046836

[Part 1/1]
Teachers' beliefs about teaching and learning
Percentage of lower secondary education teachers who "agree" or "strongly agree" with the following statements

Table 6.13

	My role as a teacher is to facilitate students' own inquiry		Students learn best by finding solutions to problems on their own		Students should be allowed to think of solutions to practical problems themselves before the teacher shows them how they are solved		Thinking and reasoning processes are more important than specific curriculum content	
	%	S.E.	%	S.E.	%	S.E.	%	S.E.
Australia	92.9	(0.5)	71.2	(1.2)	89.3	(1.0)	79.6	(1.2)
Brazil	89.2	(0.6)	85.6	(0.6)	87.9	(0.5)	69.5	(0.8)
Bulgaria	99.0	(0.3)	81.8	(1.1)	93.9	(0.5)	88.5	(0.8)
Chile	94.8	(0.7)	89.6	(1.0)	86.4	(1.1)	88.3	(1.0)
Croatia	94.6	(0.4)	86.1	(0.6)	94.6	(0.4)	90.4	(0.5)
Cyprus*	94.8	(0.5)	89.0	(0.9)	97.0	(0.5)	93.5	(0.6)
Czech Republic	91.2	(0.5)	90.5	(0.7)	96.0	(0.4)	86.7	(0.7)
Denmark	97.7	(0.3)	91.9	(0.7)	96.1	(0.5)	82.9	(1.0)
Estonia	94.2	(0.6)	74.9	(0.9)	95.4	(0.4)	88.9	(0.6)
Finland	97.3	(0.3)	82.2	(0.7)	93.8	(0.4)	91.0	(0.6)
France	92.0	(0.5)	91.3	(0.6)	89.1	(0.7)	71.1	(0.9)
Iceland	98.1	(0.4)	90.9	(0.8)	91.3	(0.7)	90.5	(0.9)
Israel	94.6	(0.4)	88.3	(0.7)	96.5	(0.4)	91.4	(0.6)
Italy	91.5	(0.5)	59.3	(1.0)	69.4	(1.0)	87.4	(0.7)
Japan	93.8	(0.4)	94.0	(0.4)	93.2	(0.5)	70.1	(0.9)
Korea	97.5	(0.3)	95.1	(0.4)	97.2	(0.3)	85.9	(0.6)
Latvia	97.4	(0.4)	88.8	(1.0)	96.9	(0.5)	85.6	(1.0)
Malaysia	89.9	(0.7)	74.3	(0.9)	93.8	(0.6)	85.7	(0.9)
Mexico	93.5	(0.5)	86.0	(0.8)	94.6	(0.5)	72.9	(0.9)
Netherlands	97.9	(0.4)	84.7	(0.8)	96.5	(0.6)	64.0	(1.5)
Norway	94.5	(0.6)	52.6	(1.3)	94.1	(0.6)	78.0	(1.1)
Poland	94.3	(0.4)	86.6	(0.6)	93.2	(0.5)	84.5	(0.7)
Portugal	93.1	(0.5)	89.4	(0.6)	97.0	(0.4)	91.1	(0.6)
Romania	92.0	(0.6)	90.4	(0.5)	93.6	(0.5)	83.0	(0.8)
Serbia	96.9	(0.3)	83.8	(0.7)	94.3	(0.4)	83.3	(0.7)
Singapore	95.0	(0.4)	88.7	(0.7)	97.5	(0.3)	95.0	(0.4)
Slovak Republic	94.0	(0.5)	86.6	(0.7)	95.0	(0.4)	89.5	(0.6)
Spain	90.7	(0.5)	83.5	(0.8)	83.4	(0.9)	85.4	(0.7)
Sweden	83.3	(0.7)	44.9	(1.3)	82.2	(0.7)	82.1	(0.9)
Sub-national entities								
Abu Dhabi (United Arab Emirates)	96.0	(0.5)	89.7	(0.7)	96.1	(0.5)	89.5	(0.9)
Alberta (Canada)	95.8	(0.7)	82.5	(1.2)	94.0	(0.6)	87.3	(1.1)
England (United Kingdom)	96.3	(0.4)	85.7	(0.8)	95.5	(0.6)	73.7	(1.0)
Flanders (Belgium)	98.9	(0.2)	84.5	(0.9)	92.9	(0.5)	70.7	(0.9)
Average	94.3	(0.1)	83.2	(0.1)	92.6	(0.1)	83.5	(0.1)
United States	94.6	(0.6)	81.7	(1.1)	92.6	(0.6)	84.5	(1.0)

*See notes at the beginning of this Annex.
Source: OECD, TALIS 2013 Database.
StatLink ⟐ http://dx.doi.org/10.1787/888933046855

[Part 1/1]

Teachers' beliefs about teaching and learning in primary education

Table 6.13.a *Percentage of primary education teachers who "agree" or "strongly agree" with the following statements*

	My role as a teacher is to facilitate students' own inquiry		Students learn best by finding solutions to problems on their own		Students should be allowed to think of solutions to practical problems themselves before the teacher shows them how they are solved		Thinking and reasoning processes are more important than specific curriculum content	
	%	S.E.	%	S.E.	%	S.E.	%	S.E.
Denmark	98.4	(0.3)	92.1	(0.7)	95.3	(0.5)	82.6	(1.0)
Finland	97.8	(0.3)	85.8	(0.9)	95.4	(0.6)	92.0	(0.7)
Mexico	94.6	(0.7)	86.7	(1.1)	95.9	(0.7)	74.3	(1.6)
Norway	93.5	(1.0)	51.9	(2.1)	95.0	(0.8)	77.3	(0.9)
Poland	93.8	(0.6)	89.5	(0.7)	93.9	(0.5)	87.1	(0.9)
Sub-national entities								
Flanders (Belgium)	99.5	(0.1)	90.9	(0.7)	97.3	(0.4)	78.9	(1.0)
Average	96.3	(0.2)	82.8	(0.5)	95.5	(0.2)	82.0	(0.4)

Source: OECD, TALIS 2013 Database.

StatLink http://dx.doi.org/10.1787/888933046874

[Part 1/1]

Teachers' beliefs about teaching and learning in upper secondary education

Percentage of upper secondary education teachers who "agree" or "strongly agree"

Table 6.13.b *with the following statements*

	My role as a teacher is to facilitate students' own inquiry		Students learn best by finding solutions to problems on their own		Students should be allowed to think of solutions to practical problems themselves before the teacher shows them how they are solved		Thinking and reasoning processes are more important than specific curriculum content	
	%	S.E.	%	S.E.	%	S.E.	%	S.E.
Australia	92.9	(0.7)	73.5	(1.5)	91.3	(0.5)	77.5	(1.4)
Denmark	95.6	(1.0)	90.8	(1.1)	92.6	(0.7)	79.9	(1.1)
Finland	97.6	(0.6)	80.5	(1.4)	91.4	(1.5)	87.2	(0.9)
Iceland	98.6	(0.4)	88.8	(1.0)	87.4	(1.1)	89.7	(1.0)
Italy	91.5	(0.5)	63.0	(0.9)	68.3	(0.9)	86.3	(0.6)
Mexico	92.9	(0.8)	82.6	(1.0)	92.2	(0.7)	75.0	(1.0)
Norway	96.9	(0.3)	56.8	(1.0)	93.6	(0.6)	75.4	(1.1)
Poland	91.9	(0.7)	83.9	(0.9)	91.1	(0.6)	82.6	(0.7)
Singapore	95.7	(0.4)	89.1	(0.6)	97.8	(0.3)	95.1	(0.4)
Sub-national entities								
Abu Dhabi (United Arab Emirates)	96.2	(0.4)	91.1	(0.7)	95.4	(0.4)	89.2	(0.8)
Average	95.0	(0.2)	80.0	(0.3)	90.1	(0.3)	83.8	(0.3)

Source: OECD, TALIS 2013 Database.

StatLink http://dx.doi.org/10.1787/888933046893

[Part 1/1]
Relationship between teaching beliefs and practices
Significant results of the multiple linear regressions of teachers' beliefs with selected teaching practices for lower secondary education teachers[1]

Table 6.14

	Constructivist teaching beliefs[2]					
	Dependent on:					
	Students work in small groups to come up with a joint solution to a problem[3]		Students work on projects that require at least one week to complete[3]		Students use ICT for projects or class work[3]	
	ß	S.E.	ß	S.E.	ß	S.E.
Australia	0.54	(0.09)			0.21	(0.06)
Brazil	0.20	(0.05)	0.16	(0.05)		
Bulgaria	0.22	(0.06)			0.11	(0.05)
Chile	0.30	(0.14)			0.29	(0.10)
Croatia	0.30	(0.07)			0.17	(0.05)
Czech Republic	0.38	(0.06)	0.13	(0.06)	0.12	(0.04)
Denmark	0.30	(0.09)	0.16	(0.07)	0.21	(0.06)
Estonia	0.24	(0.06)	0.10	(0.05)		
Finland	0.20	(0.05)	0.16	(0.05)	0.22	(0.07)
France	0.40	(0.06)	0.13	(0.05)		
Iceland	0.39	(0.10)			0.26	(0.08)
Israel	0.24	(0.08)			0.14	(0.07)
Italy	0.36	(0.07)				
Japan	0.23	(0.04)	0.19	(0.04)		
Korea	0.28	(0.08)	-0.18	(0.08) *		
Latvia	0.23	(0.08)				
Malaysia	0.31	(0.10)	0.15	(0.07)		
Mexico	0.24	(0.07)	0.30	(0.06)		
Netherlands	0.30	(0.08)	0.16	(0.07)	0.21	(0.09)
Norway	0.12	(0.05)				
Poland	0.28	(0.06)			0.18	(0.06)
Portugal	0.22	(0.05)	0.15	(0.05)		
Romania	0.34	(0.09)				
Serbia	0.25	(0.06)			0.17	(0.05)
Singapore	0.23	(0.06)				
Slovak Republic	0.35	(0.07)				
Spain	0.28	(0.07)	0.19	(0.07)		
Sweden	0.13	(0.04)	0.20	(0.04)	0.13	(0.05)
Sub-national entities						
Abu Dhabi (United Arab Emirates)	0.31	(0.11)			0.33	(0.07)
Alberta (Canada)	0.39	(0.08)			0.14	(0.07)
England (United Kingdom)	0.37	(0.06)	0.32	(0.07)		
Flanders (Belgium)	0.36	(0.05)	0.14	(0.05)	0.12	(0.05)

1. Controlling for teacher gender, years of experience, highest level of education and subject taught in the target class. Cells are blank when no significant relationship was found. Significance was tested at the 5% level.

2. Teachers' constructivist beliefs tend to be positively predicted by the use of these three teaching practices. For example, a standard deviation unit increase in the use of small groups in Australia is associated with an increase of 0.54 standard deviation unit in the teacher constructivist beliefs index. See Annex B for more details on this index.

3. Response categories are: "never" or "almost never", "occasionally", "frequently", "in all or nearly all lessons".

Source: OECD, TALIS 2013 Database.

StatLink ⬛⬛ http://dx.doi.org/10.1787/888933046969

[Part 1/1]
Teacher co-operation
Table 6.15 *Percentage of lower secondary education teachers who report never doing the following activities*

	Never teach jointly as a team in the same class		Never observe other teachers' classes and provide feedback		Never engage in joint activities across different classes and age groups (e.g. projects)		Never exchange teaching materials with colleagues		Never engage in discussions about the learning development of specific students		Never work with other teachers in my school to ensure common standards in evaluations for assessing student progress		Never attend team conferences		Never take part in collaborative professional learning	
	%	S.E.	%	S.E.	%	S.E.	%	S.E.	%	S.E.	%	S.E.	%	S.E.	%	S.E.
Australia	35.2	(2.0)	41.3	(2.3)	31.9	(1.3)	1.5	(0.4)	1.4	(0.3)	4.4	(0.9)	10.1	(0.9)	5.7	(0.7)
Brazil	41.9	(1.0)	76.9	(0.7)	17.9	(0.7)	19.2	(0.6)	3.8	(0.4)	12.2	(0.6)	26.7	(0.8)	23.5	(0.6)
Bulgaria	69.7	(1.3)	36.2	(1.6)	17.7	(1.0)	5.2	(0.6)	3.2	(0.5)	12.2	(0.9)	0.7	(0.2)	9.2	(0.7)
Chile	36.4	(1.9)	55.8	(2.0)	37.7	(1.9)	14.1	(1.1)	9.1	(0.8)	14.9	(1.3)	34.5	(1.7)	21.8	(1.2)
Croatia	52.2	(1.4)	69.1	(1.1)	14.0	(1.0)	7.7	(0.6)	2.3	(0.3)	6.2	(0.5)	9.9	(0.7)	4.7	(0.6)
Cyprus*	52.1	(1.5)	41.0	(1.4)	28.5	(1.3)	4.9	(0.5)	2.6	(0.4)	4.4	(0.4)	6.6	(0.6)	21.6	(1.1)
Czech Republic	57.7	(1.1)	36.7	(1.4)	8.2	(0.6)	4.9	(0.5)	1.3	(0.2)	5.3	(0.5)	0.6	(0.1)	8.4	(0.6)
Denmark	11.4	(1.1)	45.0	(1.8)	6.8	(0.9)	1.2	(0.3)	2.0	(0.4)	8.9	(0.8)	1.8	(0.5)	7.1	(0.8)
Estonia	31.7	(1.3)	32.9	(2.1)	10.6	(0.6)	7.0	(0.5)	0.7	(0.2)	6.9	(0.5)	2.3	(0.3)	6.1	(0.6)
Finland	32.3	(1.5)	70.3	(1.6)	23.5	(1.1)	9.8	(0.6)	1.1	(0.3)	9.3	(0.6)	7.9	(0.7)	41.0	(1.1)
France	62.7	(1.2)	78.3	(1.1)	21.9	(0.9)	8.5	(0.6)	0.9	(0.2)	20.4	(0.9)	32.0	(1.1)	30.0	(1.1)
Iceland	58.8	(1.4)	80.9	(1.1)	22.8	(1.2)	19.0	(1.1)	5.1	(0.6)	11.1	(0.9)	8.5	(0.7)	6.4	(0.8)
Israel	61.1	(1.2)	57.4	(1.5)	19.3	(1.0)	5.3	(0.5)	3.5	(0.4)	18.9	(1.2)	2.1	(0.3)	13.7	(1.0)
Italy	38.8	(1.5)	68.9	(0.9)	23.1	(1.0)	9.5	(0.7)	2.1	(0.3)	7.4	(0.6)	0.3	(0.1)	29.4	(1.1)
Japan	34.0	(0.9)	6.1	(0.7)	37.5	(1.1)	11.1	(0.6)	6.0	(0.4)	16.6	(0.8)	3.6	(0.4)	18.8	(0.8)
Korea	36.1	(1.0)	5.5	(0.6)	51.9	(1.1)	6.8	(0.6)	25.0	(1.0)	10.4	(0.7)	9.9	(0.7)	25.9	(0.9)
Latvia	34.8	(1.9)	15.5	(1.5)	5.6	(0.6)	6.3	(0.6)	0.4	(0.1)	2.3	(0.4)	6.1	(0.6)	5.8	(0.6)
Malaysia	35.7	(1.5)	37.2	(1.4)	27.3	(1.0)	2.1	(0.3)	1.0	(0.2)	3.5	(0.4)	21.6	(1.1)	17.3	(0.9)
Mexico	14.9	(0.9)	55.8	(1.4)	26.3	(1.2)	11.6	(0.7)	9.7	(0.8)	16.0	(0.9)	4.5	(0.5)	7.4	(0.6)
Netherlands	68.7	(1.6)	29.4	(1.6)	13.2	(1.2)	5.3	(0.6)	1.8	(0.3)	12.8	(1.0)	1.5	(0.6)	7.0	(0.8)
Norway	37.5	(1.9)	46.3	(2.0)	19.4	(1.3)	2.2	(0.5)	1.6	(0.3)	5.1	(0.7)	1.8	(0.3)	29.5	(1.7)
Poland	31.4	(1.1)	16.8	(1.1)	4.4	(0.5)	3.6	(0.3)	0.5	(0.1)	1.3	(0.2)	0.9	(0.2)	3.8	(0.4)
Portugal	49.5	(1.1)	71.2	(1.1)	16.5	(0.8)	2.5	(0.3)	2.2	(0.3)	4.0	(0.4)	0.0	(0.0)	13.2	(0.7)
Romania	41.2	(1.3)	16.2	(1.0)	9.5	(0.7)	16.8	(1.0)	1.2	(0.2)	12.4	(0.9)	1.5	(0.3)	6.4	(0.6)
Serbia	34.5	(1.2)	26.2	(1.6)	18.3	(0.9)	7.6	(0.6)	2.6	(0.3)	10.7	(0.6)	2.7	(0.3)	4.0	(0.4)
Singapore	26.2	(0.8)	20.0	(0.8)	26.4	(0.8)	1.8	(0.2)	2.8	(0.3)	3.0	(0.3)	15.1	(0.8)	5.9	(0.4)
Slovak Republic	10.0	(0.6)	24.9	(1.2)	12.9	(0.8)	5.9	(0.5)	7.0	(0.5)	4.8	(0.4)	35.2	(1.2)	48.8	(1.3)
Spain	69.3	(1.2)	87.1	(0.8)	48.0	(1.2)	7.5	(0.9)	0.9	(0.2)	8.3	(0.6)	1.0	(0.2)	17.2	(0.9)
Sweden	29.0	(1.0)	56.9	(1.9)	25.6	(1.1)	16.5	(0.8)	1.4	(0.3)	5.3	(0.5)	2.0	(0.3)	5.4	(0.5)
Sub-national entities																
Abu Dhabi (United Arab Emirates)	34.0	(2.2)	22.1	(2.3)	14.0	(1.6)	8.6	(0.9)	4.6	(0.7)	5.5	(0.7)	6.7	(0.8)	13.1	(1.5)
Alberta (Canada)	49.6	(1.8)	55.4	(1.6)	25.0	(1.3)	4.1	(0.5)	1.9	(0.4)	10.3	(0.9)	13.9	(1.0)	4.2	(0.5)
England (United Kingdom)	40.9	(1.3)	17.7	(1.3)	34.2	(1.3)	1.9	(0.4)	1.6	(0.3)	6.6	(0.6)	23.2	(1.1)	10.5	(0.8)
Flanders (Belgium)	64.9	(1.4)	75.2	(1.8)	8.7	(0.7)	3.2	(0.3)	3.1	(0.3)	9.9	(0.8)	2.3	(0.3)	45.1	(1.1)
Average	41.9	(0.2)	44.7	(0.3)	21.5	(0.2)	7.4	(0.1)	3.5	(0.1)	8.8	(0.1)	9.0	(0.1)	15.7	(0.2)
United States	53.7	(1.4)	50.2	(2.4)	42.2	(1.7)	9.2	(0.9)	5.0	(0.7)	13.9	(1.2)	19.5	(1.8)	9.3	(1.3)

*See notes at the beginning of this Annex.
Source: OECD, TALIS 2013 Database.
StatLink http://dx.doi.org/10.1787/888933047007

[Part 1/1]
Teacher co-operation in primary education

Table 6.15.a *Percentage of primary education teachers who report never doing the following activities*

	Never teach jointly as a team in the same class		Never observe other teachers' classes and provide feedback		Never engage in joint activities across different classes and age groups (e.g. projects)		Never exchange teaching materials with colleagues		Never engage in discussions about the learning development of specific students		Never work with other teachers in my school to ensure common standards in evaluations for assessing student progress		Never attend team conferences		Never take part in collaborative professional learning	
	%	S.E.	%	S.E.	%	S.E.	%	S.E.	%	S.E.	%	S.E.	%	S.E.	%	S.E.
Denmark	7.8	(0.9)	41.6	(1.7)	3.5	(0.5)	1.2	(0.3)	0.8	(0.2)	9.4	(0.7)	0.9	(0.3)	5.4	(0.5)
Finland	13.4	(1.3)	64.3	(1.4)	8.5	(0.8)	5.7	(0.8)	0.4	(0.1)	7.7	(0.8)	6.2	(0.8)	31.6	(1.2)
Mexico	9.0	(1.1)	51.3	(2.1)	24.7	(1.6)	7.6	(1.0)	11.6	(1.3)	14.1	(1.6)	3.4	(0.5)	4.7	(0.9)
Norway	32.1	(1.7)	47.6	(2.2)	12.0	(1.6)	1.7	(0.3)	1.7	(0.5)	5.0	(0.5)	4.2	(0.9)	26.6	(1.8)
Poland	27.9	(1.2)	15.9	(1.2)	4.8	(0.5)	3.9	(0.5)	0.5	(0.2)	1.4	(0.3)	1.9	(0.3)	5.1	(0.6)
Sub-national entities																
Flanders (Belgium)	30.6	(1.3)	74.9	(1.5)	3.4	(0.4)	4.3	(0.5)	5.5	(0.4)	15.2	(0.9)	1.4	(0.2)	31.0	(1.1)
Average	20.1	(0.5)	49.3	(0.7)	9.5	(0.4)	4.1	(0.3)	3.4	(0.3)	8.8	(0.4)	3.0	(0.2)	17.4	(0.5)

Source: OECD, TALIS 2013 Database.
StatLink http://dx.doi.org/10.1787/888933047026

[Part 1/1]
Teacher co-operation in upper secondary education

Table 6.15.b *Percentage of upper secondary education teachers who report never doing the following activities*

	Never teach jointly as a team in the same class		Never observe other teachers' classes and provide feedback		Never engage in joint activities across different classes and age groups (e.g. projects)		Never exchange teaching materials with colleagues		Never engage in discussions about the learning development of specific students		Never work with other teachers in my school to ensure common standards in evaluations for assessing student progress		Never attend team conferences		Never take part in collaborative professional learning	
	%	S.E.	%	S.E.	%	S.E.	%	S.E.	%	S.E.	%	S.E.	%	S.E.	%	S.E.
Australia	36.2	(1.9)	37.5	(1.8)	32.1	(1.4)	1.3	(0.3)	1.4	(0.3)	4.5	(0.6)	10.2	(0.8)	4.2	(0.5)
Denmark	23.7	(1.5)	47.3	(1.8)	17.3	(1.0)	1.8	(0.4)	4.3	(0.7)	16.8	(0.9)	3.5	(0.7)	4.1	(0.6)
Finland	35.1	(2.3)	67.1	(2.1)	28.3	(1.7)	11.6	(1.0)	1.2	(0.3)	10.3	(1.5)	4.9	(0.8)	32.3	(1.5)
Iceland	74.4	(1.4)	82.3	(1.2)	74.2	(1.4)	12.6	(1.1)	10.1	(0.9)	18.8	(1.3)	15.5	(1.3)	20.1	(1.3)
Italy	42.2	(1.2)	70.1	(0.9)	29.9	(1.0)	9.4	(0.5)	3.3	(0.3)	10.5	(0.6)	0.2	(0.1)	37.0	(1.2)
Mexico	16.0	(1.0)	55.5	(1.4)	27.8	(1.4)	15.2	(1.0)	15.2	(0.9)	15.5	(1.1)	5.1	(0.7)	10.2	(0.9)
Norway	43.0	(1.5)	48.0	(1.9)	31.5	(1.9)	2.6	(0.4)	2.9	(0.5)	7.5	(0.8)	11.4	(1.1)	32.1	(1.8)
Poland	33.8	(1.3)	15.8	(1.4)	9.8	(0.9)	5.9	(0.7)	1.4	(0.2)	2.2	(0.4)	1.4	(0.4)	6.1	(0.7)
Singapore	25.6	(0.8)	18.1	(0.7)	27.2	(0.8)	1.8	(0.2)	2.4	(0.3)	3.2	(0.3)	15.1	(0.6)	5.6	(0.4)
Sub-national entities																
Abu Dhabi (United Arab Emirates)	34.4	(1.7)	21.1	(1.7)	17.0	(1.2)	7.8	(0.8)	3.2	(0.5)	6.1	(0.7)	6.5	(0.7)	10.2	(1.1)
Average	36.4	(0.5)	46.3	(0.5)	29.5	(0.4)	7.0	(0.2)	4.5	(0.2)	9.5	(0.3)	7.4	(0.3)	16.2	(0.3)

Source: OECD, TALIS 2013 Database.
StatLink http://dx.doi.org/10.1787/888933047045

[Part 1/1]

Relationships between teachers' professional development activities and collaboration

Significant results of the multiple linear regressions of aspects of teachers' professional development with the index for teacher professional collaboration in lower secondary education[1]

Table 6.16

	Professional collaboration[2]													
	Dependent on:													
	Participation in courses/ workshops[3]		Participation in education conferences or seminars[4]		Observation visits to other schools[5]		Qualification programme[6]		Participation in a network of teachers formed specifically for the professional development of teachers[7]		Individual or collaborative research on a topic of interest[8]		Mentoring and/or peer observation and coaching[9]	
	ß	S.E.	ß	S.E.	ß	S.E.	ß	S.E.	ß	S.E.	ß	S.E.	ß	S.E.
Australia					1.18	(0.26)	-0.37	(0.17)			0.39	(0.14)	0.85	(0.13)
Brazil	0.41	(0.08)			0.40	(0.13)	0.26	(0.08)	0.27	(0.09)	0.33	(0.07)	0.76	(0.09)
Bulgaria			0.20	(0.06)	0.22	(0.08)	0.22	(0.09)	0.30	(0.07)	0.36	(0.10)	0.40	(0.07)
Chile			0.66	(0.24)					0.68	(0.26)			1.23	(0.34)
Croatia	0.16	(0.05)	0.19	(0.05)	0.23	(0.09)			0.12	(0.04)	0.29	(0.04)	0.12	(0.05)
Czech Republic	0.23	(0.08)			0.44	(0.10)			0.29	(0.09)	0.34	(0.09)	0.81	(0.07)
Denmark	0.40	(0.12)			0.50	(0.17)			0.29	(0.12)	0.32	(0.13)	0.47	(0.13)
Estonia	0.30	(0.13)	0.33	(0.08)	0.38	(0.09)			0.26	(0.09)	0.40	(0.10)	0.65	(0.10)
Finland	0.41	(0.08)	0.33	(0.08)	0.22	(0.11)			0.43	(0.10)	0.57	(0.21)	0.91	(0.21)
France	0.26	(0.04)	0.21	(0.05)	0.23	(0.09)	0.25	(0.09)	0.26	(0.06)	0.14	(0.05)	0.37	(0.06)
Iceland			0.46	(0.11)					0.42	(0.11)				
Israel	0.33	(0.10)							0.41	(0.07)	0.18	(0.09)	0.97	(0.08)
Italy			0.30	(0.10)	0.79	(0.10)					0.40	(0.09)	0.73	(0.13)
Japan	0.21	(0.06)	0.24	(0.06)	0.24	(0.05)					0.23	(0.06)	0.23	(0.06)
Korea			0.43		0.29	(0.08)	0.35	(0.09)	0.38	(0.08)	0.25	(0.08)	0.48	(0.08)
Latvia			0.21	(0.10)	0.37	(0.08)					0.36	(0.08)	0.39	(0.08)
Malaysia			0.41	(0.12)	0.43	(0.13)			0.48	(0.11)	0.83	(0.11)	0.65	(0.12)
Mexico	0.64	(0.24)	0.39	(0.18)	0.78	(0.22)	0.53	(0.14)	0.47	(0.15)	0.30	(0.11)	0.71	(0.17)
Netherlands									0.36	(0.15)	0.38	(0.09)	0.46	(0.10)
Norway									0.71	(0.11)	0.49	(0.15)	0.74	(0.11)
Poland	0.23	(0.08)	0.16	(0.05)	0.33	(0.09)	0.22	(0.06)	0.37	(0.06)	0.16	(0.07)	0.40	(0.08)
Portugal	0.23	(0.08)	0.23	(0.07)	0.41	(0.09)	0.16	(0.07)	0.28	(0.09)	0.21	(0.07)	0.58	(0.11)
Romania	0.21	(0.09)	0.27	(0.09)	0.34	(0.08)	0.45	(0.10)	0.32	(0.09)	0.19	(0.10)	0.42	(0.09)
Serbia	0.58	(0.09)	0.22	(0.06)	0.53	(0.09)			0.47	(0.08)	0.30	(0.09)	0.45	(0.08)
Singapore			0.27	(0.07)					0.27	(0.07)	0.31	(0.06)	0.77	(0.07)
Slovak Republic			0.27	(0.08)			0.25	(0.06)			0.47	(0.10)	0.44	(0.06)
Spain	0.20	(0.06)	0.25	(0.08)			0.33	(0.10)	0.33	(0.09)	0.21	(0.06)	0.38	(0.08)
Sweden	0.38	(0.06)	0.27	(0.07)	0.36	(0.10)			0.32	(0.08)	0.42	(0.11)	0.61	(0.10)
Sub-national entities														
Abu Dhabi (United Arab Emirates)	0.86	(0.31)	0.47	(0.20)	0.93	(0.16)			0.56	(0.18)	0.51	(0.17)	0.86	(0.20)
Alberta (Canada)			0.52	(0.12)							0.48	(0.10)	0.67	(0.13)
England (United Kingdom)	0.22	(0.10)	0.37	(0.09)	0.41	(0.11)	0.32	(0.16)	0.38	(0.10)	0.33	(0.09)	0.79	(0.10)
Flanders (Belgium)	0.20	(0.06)	0.15	(0.05)	0.33	(0.08)			0.20	(0.04)	0.19	(0.06)	0.53	(0.07)

1. Controlling for teacher gender, years of experience, highest level of education and subject taught in the target class. Cells are blank when no significant relationship was found. Significance was tested at the 5% level.

2. Professional collaboration tends to be positively predicted by the participation in professional development activities. For example, a unit increase in the coefficient of participation in courses/workshops in Brazil is associated with an increase of 0.41 in the professional collaboration index. See Annex B for more details on this index.

3. Dichotomous variable where the reference category is teachers who did not participate in courses/workshops.

4. Dichotomous variable where the reference category is teachers who did not participate in education conferences or seminars.

5. Dichotomous variable where the reference category is teachers who did not participate in observation visits to other schools.

6. Dichotomous variable where the reference category is teachers who did not participate in qualification programmes.

7. Dichotomous variable where the reference category is teachers who did not participate in a network of teachers formed specifically for the professional development of teachers.

8. Dichotomous variable where the reference category is teachers who did not participate in individual or collaborative research.

9. Dichotomous variable where the reference category is teachers who did not participate in mentoring and/or peer observation and coaching.

Source: OECD, TALIS 2013 Database.

StatLink http://dx.doi.org/10.1787/888933047121

[Part 1/1]
Relationships between teachers' professional development activities and co-operation
Significant results of the multiple linear regressions of aspects of teachers' professional development with the index for exchange and co-ordination for lower secondary education teachers[1]

Table 6.17

	Exchange and co-ordination for teaching[2]													
	Dependent on:													
	Participation in courses/ workshops[3]		Participation in education conferences or seminars[4]		Observation visits to other schools[5]		Qualification programme[6]		Participation in a network of teachers formed specifically for the professional development of teachers[7]		Individual or collaborative research on a topic of interest[8]		Mentoring and/or peer observation and coaching[9]	
	ß	S.E.	ß	S.E.	ß	S.E.	ß	S.E.	ß	S.E.	ß	S.E.	ß	S.E.
Australia	0.34	(0.13)			0.55	(0.17)							0.33	(0.10)
Brazil	0.46	(0.09)			0.31	(0.13)	0.24	(0.09)	0.33	(0.09)	0.28	(0.08)	0.73	(0.09)
Bulgaria									0.30	(0.11)	0.45	(0.13)	0.37	(0.09)
Chile			0.52	(0.18)					0.46	(0.22)			0.88	(0.26)
Croatia	0.21	(0.11)	0.35	(0.10)					0.20	(0.08)	0.49	(0.08)		
Czech Republic	0.24	(0.08)			0.26	(0.09)			0.22	(0.09)	0.19	(0.08)	0.71	(0.07)
Denmark	0.37	(0.10)			0.38	(0.16)			0.26	(0.10)	0.23	(0.11)	0.33	(0.12)
Estonia	0.29	(0.12)	0.18	(0.06)	0.19	(0.07)			0.19	(0.07)	0.23	(0.08)	0.36	(0.09)
Finland	0.32	(0.08)	0.26	(0.07)					0.30	(0.08)	0.31	(0.15)	0.50	(0.14)
France	0.22	(0.05)	0.18	(0.06)					0.22	(0.09)	0.16	(0.06)	0.27	(0.08)
Iceland			0.62	(0.15)					0.34	(0.14)				
Israel	0.33	(0.11)							0.41	(0.10)			0.81	(0.10)
Italy			0.21	(0.07)	0.49	(0.07)					0.29	(0.06)	0.44	(0.09)
Japan	0.26	(0.09)	0.32	(0.08)	0.30	(0.07)					0.29	(0.08)	0.31	(0.08)
Korea			0.38	(0.07)	0.22	(0.08)	0.18	(0.09)	0.26	(0.09)	0.21	(0.08)	0.44	(0.09)
Latvia			0.22	(0.11)	0.31	(0.09)					0.29	(0.09)	0.23	(0.09)
Malaysia	0.61	(0.21)	0.31	(0.11)					0.23	(0.11)	0.29	(0.10)	0.43	(0.12)
Mexico	0.59	(0.21)	0.34	(0.17)	0.65	(0.19)	0.46	(0.12)	0.40	(0.13)	0.26	(0.10)	0.62	(0.15)
Netherlands									0.27	(0.13)	0.35	(0.09)	0.28	(0.09)
Norway									0.45	(0.09)	0.35	(0.10)	0.40	(0.09)
Poland	0.21	(0.09)	0.12	(0.06)	0.22	(0.10)	0.15	(0.07)	0.38	(0.07)	0.17	(0.07)	0.37	(0.09)
Portugal	0.23	(0.07)	0.14	(0.07)	0.22	(0.08)			0.18	(0.07)			0.43	(0.09)
Romania			0.16	(0.08)	0.27	(0.08)	0.30	(0.10)	0.30	(0.09)			0.31	(0.09)
Serbia	0.55	(0.09)	0.17	(0.08)	0.36	(0.10)			0.45	(0.09)	0.29	(0.09)	0.40	(0.08)
Singapore			0.28	(0.07)					0.15	(0.07)	0.17	(0.07)	0.67	(0.08)
Slovak Republic			0.30	(0.10)			0.38	(0.09)			0.44	(0.12)	0.50	(0.08)
Spain									0.21	(0.06)	0.18	(0.06)	0.27	(0.06)
Sweden	0.29	(0.06)	0.19	(0.07)	0.30	(0.10)			0.23	(0.07)	0.36	(0.10)	0.45	(0.09)
Sub-national entities														
Abu Dhabi (United Arab Emirates)	0.49	(0.21)	0.30	(0.15)	0.35	(0.14)			0.45	(0.15)			0.53	(0.17)
Alberta (Canada)			0.51	(0.13)							0.45	(0.10)	0.57	(0.13)
England (United Kingdom)	0.25	(0.10)	0.28	(0.10)	0.30	(0.11)			0.25	(0.10)	0.35	(0.09)	0.68	(0.09)
Flanders (Belgium)	0.37	(0.12)	0.20	(0.08)	0.54	(0.11)			0.30	(0.08)	0.28	(0.10)	0.47	(0.11)

1. Controlling for teacher gender, years of experience, highest level of education and subject taught in the target class. Cells are blank when no significant relationship was found. Significance was tested at the 5% level.

2. Exchange and co-ordination for teaching tends to be positively predicted by the participation in professional development activities. For example, a unit increase in the coefficient of participation in courses/workshops in Australia is associated an increase of 0.34 in the exchange and co-ordination for teaching index. See Annex B for more details on this index.

3. Dichotomous variable where the reference category is teachers who did not participate in courses/workshops.

4. Dichotomous variable where the reference category is teachers who did not participate in education conferences or seminars.

5. Dichotomous variable where the reference category is teachers who did not participate in observation visits to other schools.

6. Dichotomous variable where the reference category is teachers who did not participate in qualification programmes.

7. Dichotomous variable where the reference category is teachers who did not participate in a network of teachers formed specifically for the professional development of teachers.

8. Dichotomous variable where the reference category is teachers who did not participate in individual or collaborative research.

9. Dichotomous variable where the reference category is teachers who did not participate in mentoring and/or peer observation and coaching.

Source: OECD, TALIS 2013 Database.

StatLink http://dx.doi.org/10.1787/888933047159

[Part 1/1]

Correlation between participation among stakeholders in the school and teaching co-ordination

Correlation coefficients between participation among stakeholders index and exchange and co-ordination for lower secondary education teachers[1]

Table 6.18

	Participation among stakeholders[2]	
	Correlated with:	
	Exchange and co-ordination for teaching[2]	
	Correlation coefficient (r_{xy})	S.E
Australia	0.18	0.03
Brazil	0.31	0.02
Bulgaria	0.19	0.03
Chile	0.37	0.03
Croatia	0.25	0.02
Czech Republic	0.26	0.02
Denmark	0.22	0.03
Estonia	0.26	0.02
Finland	0.23	0.02
France	0.15	0.02
Iceland	0.16	0.03
Israel	0.28	0.02
Italy	0.21	0.02
Japan	0.20	0.02
Korea	0.25	0.02
Latvia	0.23	0.03
Malaysia	0.23	0.02
Mexico	0.35	0.02
Netherlands	0.24	0.03
Norway	0.20	0.03
Poland	0.18	0.02
Portugal	0.23	0.02
Romania	0.22	0.02
Serbia	0.26	0.02
Singapore	0.22	0.02
Slovak Republic	0.25	0.02
Spain	0.17	0.02
Sweden	0.20	0.02
Sub-national entities		
Abu Dhabi (United Arab Emirates)	0.32	0.04
Alberta (Canada)	0.24	0.03
England (United Kingdom)	0.32	0.02
Flanders (Belgium)	0.13	0.03

1. All correlations are significant at the 5% level. Standardised coefficients are reported in the table.

2. Continuous variable. See Annex B for more details on this index.

Source: OECD, TALIS 2013 Database.

StatLink ⌨ http://dx.doi.org/10.1787/888933047197

[Part 1/1]
Correlation between participation among stakeholders in the school and teacher professional collaboration

Correlation coefficients between participation among stakeholders index and teacher professional collaboration index in lower secondary education[1]

Table 6.19

	Participation among stakeholders[2]	
	Correlated with:	
	Professional collaboration[2]	
	Correlation coefficient (r_{xy})	S.E
Australia	0.20	0.03
Brazil	0.31	0.01
Bulgaria	0.20	0.03
Chile	0.44	0.03
Croatia	0.27	0.02
Czech Republic	0.29	0.02
Denmark	0.25	0.03
Estonia	0.29	0.02
Finland	0.25	0.02
France	0.16	0.02
Iceland	0.22	0.03
Israel	0.30	0.02
Italy	0.21	0.02
Japan	0.21	0.02
Korea	0.28	0.02
Latvia	0.23	0.03
Malaysia	0.26	0.02
Mexico	0.35	0.02
Netherlands	0.26	0.04
Norway	0.23	0.04
Poland	0.18	0.02
Portugal	0.23	0.02
Romania	0.23	0.02
Serbia	0.27	0.02
Singapore	0.25	0.02
Slovak Republic	0.27	0.02
Spain	0.13	0.02
Sweden	0.22	0.02
Sub-national entities		
Abu Dhabi (United Arab Emirates)	0.41	0.03
Alberta (Canada)	0.25	0.03
England (United Kingdom)	0.35	0.02
Flanders (Belgium)	0.15	0.02

1. All correlations are significant at the 5% level. Standardised coefficients are reported in the table.
2. Continuous variable. See Annex B for more details on this index.
Source: OECD, TALIS 2013 Database.
StatLink http://dx.doi.org/10.1787/888933047235

[Part 1/1]
Distribution of class time during an average lesson
Average proportion of time lower secondary education teachers report spending on each of these activities in an average lesson[1, 2]

Table 6.20

	Administrative tasks		Keeping order in the classroom		Actual teaching and learning	
	%	S.E.	%	S.E.	%	S.E.
Australia	7.0	(0.3)	14.5	(0.4)	78.1	(0.6)
Brazil	12.2	(0.1)	19.8	(0.3)	66.7	(0.3)
Bulgaria	4.6	(0.1)	8.8	(0.3)	86.6	(0.3)
Chile	10.8	(0.3)	15.3	(0.6)	73.1	(0.8)
Croatia	7.2	(0.1)	9.1	(0.2)	83.4	(0.3)
Cyprus*	6.8	(0.2)	12.7	(0.3)	80.2	(0.4)
Czech Republic	6.6	(0.1)	8.8	(0.2)	84.0	(0.3)
Denmark	6.0	(0.2)	9.8	(0.3)	84.1	(0.4)
Estonia	5.5	(0.1)	8.8	(0.3)	84.4	(0.4)
Finland	6.0	(0.1)	13.1	(0.3)	80.6	(0.3)
France	7.9	(0.1)	15.7	(0.3)	76.0	(0.4)
Iceland	8.5	(0.3)	15.7	(0.4)	75.5	(0.6)
Israel	9.2	(0.2)	12.8	(0.3)	76.6	(0.5)
Italy	7.5	(0.2)	13.0	(0.3)	78.5	(0.3)
Japan	7.0	(0.2)	14.6	(0.3)	78.3	(0.5)
Korea	8.2	(0.2)	13.6	(0.3)	76.9	(0.4)
Latvia	5.8	(0.2)	9.5	(0.4)	84.5	(0.5)
Malaysia	11.5	(0.3)	17.5	(0.4)	70.8	(0.5)
Mexico	11.6	(0.2)	12.3	(0.3)	75.4	(0.4)
Netherlands	9.5	(0.2)	16.0	(0.4)	73.8	(0.5)
Norway	7.6	(0.2)	8.9	(0.3)	83.0	(0.4)
Poland	8.0	(0.1)	8.5	(0.3)	82.2	(0.4)
Portugal	8.2	(0.1)	15.7	(0.3)	75.8	(0.3)
Romania	8.4	(0.2)	8.7	(0.2)	81.8	(0.4)
Serbia	8.3	(0.1)	9.8	(0.2)	81.7	(0.3)
Singapore	11.1	(0.2)	17.7	(0.2)	70.9	(0.3)
Slovak Republic	7.1	(0.1)	12.1	(0.3)	80.2	(0.4)
Spain	7.4	(0.1)	14.7	(0.3)	77.2	(0.3)
Sweden	6.7	(0.1)	11.5	(0.3)	81.1	(0.4)
Sub-national entities						
Abu Dhabi (United Arab Emirates)	8.3	(0.3)	12.6	(0.6)	76.7	(0.8)
Alberta (Canada)	7.3	(0.2)	13.6	(0.5)	79.0	(0.6)
England (United Kingdom)	6.7	(0.2)	11.4	(0.4)	81.5	(0.5)
Flanders (Belgium)	9.3	(0.2)	13.4	(0.5)	77.0	(0.6)
Average	8.0	(0.0)	12.7	(0.1)	78.7	(0.1)
United States	6.5	(0.2)	13.4	(0.6)	79.7	(0.7)

1. These data are reported by teachers and refer to a randomly chosen class they currently teach from their weekly timetable.
2. The sum of time spent in an average lesson may not add up to 100% because some answers that did not add up to 100% were accepted.
* See notes at the beginning of this Annex.
Source: OECD, TALIS 2013 Database.
StatLink http://dx.doi.org/10.1787/888933047273

TALIS 2013 RESULTS: AN INTERNATIONAL PERSPECTIVE ON TEACHING AND LEARNING

[Part 1/1]
Distribution of class time during an average lesson in primary education
Average proportion of time primary education teachers report spending on each of these activities in an average lesson[1, 2]

Table 6.20.a

	Administrative tasks		Keeping order in the classroom		Actual teaching and learning	
	%	S.E.	%	S.E.	%	S.E.
Denmark	6.1	(0.2)	14.4	(0.3)	79.4	(0.4)
Finland	6.2	(0.1)	14.4	(0.4)	78.9	(0.4)
Mexico	11.6	(0.3)	13.1	(0.3)	75.3	(0.5)
Norway	7.0	(0.2)	11.8	(0.5)	80.8	(0.6)
Poland	7.4	(0.1)	8.7	(0.3)	83.2	(0.3)
Sub-national entities						
Flanders (Belgium)	8.2	(0.2)	12.7	(0.3)	79.0	(0.4)
Average	7.7	(0.1)	12.5	(0.2)	79.4	(0.2)

1. These data are reported by teachers and refer to a randomly chosen class they currently teach from their weekly timetable.
2. The sum of time spent in an average lesson may not add up to 100% because some answers that did not add up to 100% were accepted.
Source: OECD, TALIS 2013 Database.
StatLink ⌦ http://dx.doi.org/10.1787/888933047292

[Part 1/1]
Distribution of class time during an average lesson in upper secondary education
Average proportion of time upper secondary education teachers report spending on each of these activities in an average lesson[1, 2]

Table 6.20.b

	Administrative tasks		Keeping order in the classroom		Actual teaching and learning	
	%	S.E.	%	S.E.	%	S.E.
Australia	6.7	(0.2)	9.2	(0.5)	83.8	(0.6)
Denmark	6.3	(0.2)	6.8	(0.2)	86.7	(0.3)
Finland	7.1	(0.4)	7.1	(0.4)	85.4	(0.7)
Iceland	7.1	(0.2)	8.8	(0.4)	83.8	(0.5)
Italy	7.9	(0.1)	11.7	(0.3)	79.5	(0.4)
Mexico	11.2	(0.2)	10.8	(0.2)	77.5	(0.3)
Norway	7.2	(0.2)	6.8	(0.2)	85.5	(0.4)
Poland	8.3	(0.2)	7.3	(0.3)	83.6	(0.4)
Singapore	10.6	(0.2)	14.2	(0.2)	75.0	(0.3)
Sub-national entities						
Abu Dhabi (United Arab Emirates)	7.8	(0.2)	11.8	(0.5)	78.2	(0.7)
Average	8.0	(0.1)	9.5	(0.1)	81.9	(0.1)

1. These data are reported by teachers and refer to a randomly chosen class they currently teach from their weekly timetable.
2. The sum of time spent in an average lesson may not add up to 100% because some answers that did not add up to 100% were accepted.
Source: OECD, TALIS 2013 Database.
StatLink ⌦ http://dx.doi.org/10.1787/888933047311

[Part 1/1]
Distribution of class time during an average lesson, 2008 and 2013
Average proportion of time lower secondary education teachers report spending on each of these activities in an average lesson[1, 2, 3, 4]

Table 6.20.c

	Administrative tasks				Keeping order in the classroom				Actual teaching and learning			
	2008		2013		2008		2013		2008		2013	
	%	S.E.	%	S.E.	%	S.E.	%	S.E.	%	S.E.	%	S.E.
Australia	8.0	(0.2)	7.0	(0.3)	15.8	(0.5)	14.5	(0.4)	76.2	(0.5)	78.1	(0.6)
Brazil	13.0	(0.3)	12.2	(0.2)	17.8	(0.4)	19.8	(0.3)	69.2	(0.6)	66.8	(0.4)
Bulgaria	5.0	(0.2)	4.6	(0.1)	8.2	(0.3)	8.8	(0.3)	86.9	(0.4)	86.6	(0.3)
Denmark	6.2	(0.2)	6.0	(0.2)	12.3	(0.4)	9.8	(0.3)	81.3	(0.4)	84.2	(0.4)
Estonia	5.5	(0.1)	5.5	(0.1)	9.1	(0.3)	8.8	(0.3)	85.3	(0.3)	84.4	(0.4)
Iceland	8.4	(0.2)	8.5	(0.3)	16.7	(0.4)	15.7	(0.4)	75.0	(0.5)	75.5	(0.6)
Italy	8.8	(0.1)	7.5	(0.2)	14.3	(0.3)	12.9	(0.3)	77.0	(0.3)	78.5	(0.3)
Korea	8.6	(0.2)	8.2	(0.2)	13.7	(0.2)	13.6	(0.3)	77.6	(0.4)	77.0	(0.4)
Malaysia	11.3	(0.2)	11.5	(0.3)	17.1	(0.3)	17.5	(0.4)	71.7	(0.4)	70.8	(0.5)
Mexico	16.5	(0.2)	11.7	(0.2)	13.3	(0.3)	12.3	(0.3)	70.3	(0.4)	75.4	(0.4)
Norway	8.1	(0.2)	7.5	(0.2)	10.9	(0.3)	8.9	(0.3)	81.0	(0.4)	83.1	(0.4)
Poland	8.4	(0.1)	8.0	(0.1)	9.2	(0.2)	8.5	(0.3)	82.3	(0.3)	82.1	(0.4)
Portugal	8.2	(0.2)	8.2	(0.1)	16.1	(0.4)	15.7	(0.3)	75.6	(0.4)	75.8	(0.3)
Slovak Republic	6.7	(0.1)	7.1	(0.1)	10.3	(0.3)	12.1	(0.3)	82.9	(0.4)	80.1	(0.4)
Spain	7.4	(0.1)	7.4	(0.1)	15.7	(0.3)	14.7	(0.3)	76.9	(0.4)	77.3	(0.3)
Sub-national entities												
Flanders (Belgium)	8.7	(0.2)	9.3	(0.2)	13.5	(0.2)	13.4	(0.5)	77.8	(0.3)	77.0	(0.6)
Average	8.7	(0.0)	8.1	(0.0)	13.4	(0.1)	12.9	(0.1)	77.9	(0.1)	78.3	(0.1)

1. The teacher population coverage was slightly different between 2008 and 2013. In order to have comparable populations for the tables comparing results from 2008 and 2013, teachers who teach exclusively to students with special needs were excluded from the 2013 data in these tables.

2. The wording and order of questions may have changed slightly between the 2008 and 2013 surveys.

3. These data are reported by teachers and refer to a randomly chosen class they currently teach from their weekly timetable.

4. The sum of time spent in an average lesson may not add up to 100% because some answers that did not add up to 100% were accepted.

Source: OECD, TALIS 2008 and TALIS 2013 Databases.

StatLink http://dx.doi.org/10.1787/888933047330

[Part 1/1]
Classroom discipline
Percentage of lower secondary education teachers who "agree" or "strongly agree" with the following statements about their target class[1]

Table 6.21

	When the lesson begins, I have to wait quite a long time for students to quiet down		Students in this class take care to create a pleasant atmosphere		I lose quite a lot of time because of students interrupting the lesson		There is much disruptive noise in this classroom	
	%	S.E.	%	S.E.	%	S.E.	%	S.E.
Australia	26.8	(1.6)	66.3	(1.8)	31.5	(1.8)	25.3	(1.5)
Brazil	53.3	(1.0)	52.6	(1.0)	50.0	(1.1)	54.5	(1.0)
Bulgaria	17.3	(1.2)	74.7	(1.3)	26.3	(1.5)	18.4	(1.2)
Chile	49.0	(2.1)	67.8	(1.9)	42.2	(2.1)	43.2	(1.9)
Croatia	14.3	(0.8)	74.9	(1.0)	18.6	(0.9)	18.1	(0.9)
Cyprus*	23.1	(1.2)	68.3	(1.2)	31.8	(1.3)	24.0	(1.3)
Czech Republic	20.2	(1.0)	71.4	(1.2)	21.3	(1.0)	21.9	(1.0)
Denmark	21.3	(1.4)	83.4	(1.1)	23.0	(1.3)	19.3	(1.2)
Estonia	23.9	(1.2)	62.9	(1.3)	21.5	(1.2)	22.4	(1.2)
Finland	30.7	(1.2)	58.5	(1.2)	31.6	(1.2)	32.1	(1.1)
France	37.6	(1.2)	66.8	(1.2)	39.7	(1.3)	29.9	(1.2)
Iceland	46.9	(1.7)	65.5	(1.7)	42.2	(1.7)	27.8	(1.6)
Israel	35.7	(1.2)	75.2	(1.2)	29.7	(1.1)	22.7	(1.2)
Italy	21.8	(1.0)	72.0	(0.9)	24.5	(0.9)	13.2	(0.8)
Japan	14.7	(1.1)	80.6	(1.1)	9.3	(0.8)	13.3	(0.9)
Korea	30.5	(1.3)	76.1	(1.0)	34.9	(1.3)	25.2	(1.1)
Latvia	26.8	(1.4)	65.2	(1.8)	24.9	(1.5)	28.6	(1.5)
Malaysia	25.0	(1.4)	72.4	(1.6)	30.4	(1.4)	22.8	(1.5)
Mexico	19.7	(1.0)	78.1	(1.0)	21.1	(1.1)	20.8	(1.0)
Netherlands	64.2	(1.8)	73.7	(1.4)	34.9	(1.6)	26.3	(1.3)
Norway	37.4	(2.3)	72.8	(1.4)	27.3	(1.8)	22.0	(1.9)
Poland	15.8	(1.2)	74.8	(1.2)	22.7	(1.2)	17.4	(1.2)
Portugal	39.9	(1.0)	66.7	(1.0)	40.4	(0.9)	31.1	(0.9)
Romania	11.6	(1.0)	84.7	(1.0)	15.2	(1.1)	13.6	(1.1)
Serbia	17.1	(0.8)	77.4	(0.9)	20.7	(0.8)	18.2	(0.9)
Singapore	36.3	(0.9)	60.7	(0.8)	37.8	(0.9)	36.2	(0.8)
Slovak Republic	26.9	(1.1)	69.0	(1.2)	35.4	(1.4)	32.5	(1.2)
Spain	43.0	(1.2)	60.6	(1.2)	43.6	(1.3)	39.4	(1.2)
Sweden	28.2	(1.3)	60.4	(1.3)	29.8	(1.3)	34.0	(1.4)
Sub-national entities								
Abu Dhabi (United Arab Emirates)	16.2	(1.0)	80.1	(1.6)	18.5	(1.3)	13.5	(1.0)
Alberta (Canada)	25.1	(1.5)	73.1	(1.6)	29.5	(1.5)	27.7	(1.5)
England (United Kingdom)	21.2	(1.2)	73.9	(1.3)	28.0	(1.3)	21.6	(1.1)
Flanders (Belgium)	30.0	(1.5)	66.9	(1.3)	35.8	(1.7)	27.8	(1.5)
Average	28.8	(0.2)	70.5	(0.2)	29.5	(0.2)	25.6	(0.2)
United States	23.4	(1.3)	69.0	(1.4)	28.4	(1.6)	24.2	(1.4)

1. These data are reported by teachers and refer to a randomly chosen class they currently teach from their weekly timetable.
* See notes at the beginning of this Annex.
Source: OECD, TALIS 2013 Database.
StatLink ⇱ http://dx.doi.org/10.1787/888933047349

[Part 1/1]

Correlation between actual teaching and learning and classroom discipline

Table 6.22 *Correlation coefficient between the percentage of class time dedicated to actual teaching and learning and the classroom disciplinary climate index for lower secondary education teachers[1, 2, 3]*

	Classroom disciplinary climate[4]	
	Correlated with:	
	Percentage of class time dedicated to actual teaching and learning	
	Correlation coefficient (r_{xy})	S.E
Australia	0.65	0.02
Brazil	0.45	0.01
Bulgaria	0.52	0.03
Chile	0.24	0.05
Croatia	0.50	0.02
Czech Republic	0.45	0.02
Denmark	0.57	0.02
Estonia	0.47	0.02
Finland	0.63	0.02
France	0.64	0.01
Iceland	0.61	0.02
Israel	0.52	0.02
Italy	0.49	0.02
Japan	0.21	0.02
Korea	0.29	0.02
Latvia	0.50	0.02
Malaysia	0.40	0.03
Mexico	0.26	0.03
Netherlands	0.54	0.03
Norway	0.49	0.02
Poland	0.44	0.02
Portugal	0.59	0.02
Romania	0.31	0.03
Serbia	0.46	0.02
Singapore	0.52	0.02
Slovak Republic	0.52	0.02
Spain	0.61	0.01
Sweden	0.62	0.01
Sub-national entities		
Abu Dhabi (United Arab Emirates)	0.32	0.04
Alberta (Canada)	0.52	0.03
England (United Kingdom)	0.59	0.02
Flanders (Belgium)	0.58	0.01

1. All correlations are significant at the 5% level. Standardised coefficients are reported in the table.

2. Time on task is defined as the percentage of classroom time spent on teaching and learning.

3. Time spent on actual teaching and learning (as opposed to administrative tasks or keeping order in the classroom) tends to positively correlate with a good classroom disciplinary climate.

4. Continuous variable. See Annex B for more details on this index.

Source: OECD, TALIS 2013 Database.

StatLink http://dx.doi.org/10.1787/888933047387

[Part 1/2]
Teachers' self-efficacy

Table 7.1   *Percentage of lower secondary education teachers who feel they can do the following "quite a bit" or "a lot"*

	Get students to believe they can do well in school work		Help my students value learning		Craft good questions for my students		Control disruptive behaviour in the classroom		Motivate students who show low interest in school work		Make my expectations about student behaviour clear	
	%	S.E.	%	S.E.	%	S.E.	%	S.E.	%	S.E.	%	S.E.
Australia	86.9	(1.1)	81.3	(1.4)	86.0	(0.8)	86.7	(0.7)	65.8	(1.3)	93.4	(0.8)
Brazil	96.5	(0.2)	94.8	(0.3)	97.5	(0.2)	89.7	(0.5)	87.6	(0.6)	96.8	(0.3)
Bulgaria	91.7	(0.7)	94.9	(0.5)	82.3	(0.9)	86.4	(0.8)	67.8	(1.2)	97.1	(0.4)
Chile	90.6	(0.9)	91.0	(1.0)	91.3	(0.9)	90.7	(1.1)	82.9	(1.1)	93.3	(0.8)
Croatia	68.6	(1.0)	52.1	(0.9)	90.3	(0.5)	83.0	(0.7)	50.7	(1.0)	93.6	(0.4)
Cyprus*	95.8	(0.5)	94.2	(0.6)	95.1	(0.5)	93.3	(0.7)	85.3	(0.9)	96.2	(0.5)
Czech Republic	50.5	(0.9)	39.0	(1.0)	70.9	(1.0)	77.1	(0.9)	30.0	(1.0)	71.9	(0.9)
Denmark	99.0	(0.2)	96.6	(0.6)	96.3	(0.5)	96.3	(0.6)	82.5	(0.9)	98.8	(0.3)
Estonia	81.3	(0.8)	86.0	(0.6)	74.4	(0.9)	76.7	(1.0)	75.0	(0.9)	86.9	(0.7)
Finland	83.9	(0.8)	77.3	(0.8)	90.1	(0.5)	86.3	(0.8)	60.4	(1.1)	92.7	(0.5)
France	95.2	(0.5)	87.1	(0.7)	93.8	(0.5)	94.6	(0.5)	76.6	(0.9)	97.7	(0.3)
Iceland	88.6	(1.0)	82.5	(1.1)	96.1	(0.5)	89.9	(0.9)	72.1	(1.3)	91.2	(0.9)
Israel	92.1	(0.5)	85.4	(0.9)	89.8	(0.8)	85.0	(0.9)	74.9	(1.1)	94.1	(0.5)
Italy	98.0	(0.3)	95.6	(0.3)	93.8	(0.5)	93.5	(0.5)	87.3	(0.7)	93.4	(0.5)
Japan	17.6	(0.7)	26.0	(0.9)	42.8	(1.0)	52.7	(1.0)	21.9	(0.8)	53.0	(1.0)
Korea	78.7	(1.0)	78.3	(0.9)	77.4	(0.9)	76.3	(1.1)	59.9	(1.0)	70.5	(1.1)
Latvia	91.0	(0.8)	78.6	(1.2)	93.5	(0.6)	85.2	(1.0)	64.8	(1.5)	94.3	(0.6)
Malaysia	95.9	(0.4)	98.0	(0.3)	95.8	(0.4)	96.3	(0.4)	95.2	(0.4)	92.2	(0.5)
Mexico	87.8	(0.6)	91.0	(0.6)	85.2	(0.8)	86.0	(0.7)	79.1	(0.9)	87.4	(0.8)
Netherlands	90.0	(0.9)	70.2	(1.6)	88.2	(1.1)	89.2	(0.9)	62.5	(1.5)	95.3	(0.6)
Norway	79.9	(1.0)	60.9	(1.9)	79.0	(1.4)	83.8	(0.7)	38.8	(1.0)	89.7	(0.7)
Poland	80.7	(0.8)	67.7	(1.0)	79.4	(0.8)	88.3	(0.9)	59.8	(1.1)	94.6	(0.6)
Portugal	98.9	(0.2)	99.0	(0.2)	98.2	(0.3)	96.1	(0.3)	93.8	(0.5)	96.9	(0.4)
Romania	97.9	(0.4)	95.1	(0.5)	98.9	(0.2)	97.8	(0.3)	88.7	(0.7)	98.5	(0.2)
Serbia	84.9	(0.6)	76.1	(0.7)	90.0	(0.7)	86.1	(0.6)	63.4	(0.9)	91.9	(0.5)
Singapore	83.9	(0.7)	81.5	(0.8)	81.2	(0.7)	79.5	(0.7)	72.1	(0.9)	89.0	(0.6)
Slovak Republic	92.5	(0.5)	88.5	(0.7)	94.5	(0.4)	91.1	(0.7)	84.9	(0.8)	96.9	(0.4)
Spain	71.1	(1.0)	74.1	(0.9)	86.3	(0.7)	81.5	(0.8)	53.4	(1.1)	90.1	(0.7)
Sweden	93.9	(0.5)	76.6	(1.0)	82.0	(0.8)	84.9	(0.8)	64.1	(1.0)	90.6	(0.6)
Sub-national entities												
Abu Dhabi (United Arab Emirates)	96.3	(0.5)	95.4	(0.6)	94.8	(0.5)	94.4	(0.7)	94.9	(0.5)	96.7	(0.4)
Alberta (Canada)	87.0	(0.9)	79.2	(1.1)	84.1	(1.0)	86.9	(0.9)	60.6	(1.3)	95.4	(0.5)
England (United Kingdom)	93.0	(0.6)	87.0	(0.8)	89.8	(0.9)	88.7	(0.8)	75.7	(0.9)	95.6	(0.5)
Flanders (Belgium)	93.1	(0.5)	81.6	(0.8)	95.1	(0.4)	96.4	(0.4)	77.7	(0.9)	97.2	(0.3)
Average	85.8	(0.1)	80.7	(0.2)	87.4	(0.1)	87.0	(0.1)	70.0	(0.2)	91.3	(0.1)
United States	83.7	(1.1)	74.9	(1.3)	88.0	(1.2)	86.2	(1.1)	61.9	(1.4)	94.9	(0.6)

*See notes at the beginning of this Annex.
Source: OECD, TALIS 2013 Database.
StatLink ⇗ http://dx.doi.org/10.1787/888933047463

[Part 2/2]
Teachers' self-efficacy
Table 7.1 *Percentage of lower secondary education teachers who feel they can do the following "quite a bit" or "a lot"*

	Help students think critically		Get students to follow classroom rules		Calm a student who is disruptive or noisy		Use a variety of assessment strategies		Provide an alternative explanation for an example when students are confused		Implement alternative instructional strategies in my classroom	
	%	S.E.	%	S.E.	%	S.E.	%	S.E.	%	S.E.	%	S.E.
Australia	78.4	(1.3)	89.4	(0.9)	83.6	(1.1)	86.3	(1.1)	94.0	(0.7)	82.7	(1.0)
Brazil	95.1	(0.3)	91.7	(0.4)	90.2	(0.5)	91.3	(0.5)	97.7	(0.2)	87.9	(0.6)
Bulgaria	82.5	(0.9)	96.1	(0.4)	87.9	(0.8)	87.8	(0.8)	95.9	(0.4)	69.6	(1.1)
Chile	90.2	(0.9)	92.8	(1.0)	89.2	(1.0)	89.3	(0.9)	95.3	(0.6)	88.9	(1.0)
Croatia	77.9	(0.7)	83.1	(0.6)	81.2	(0.7)	84.6	(0.6)	96.4	(0.4)	92.3	(0.5)
Cyprus*	94.6	(0.6)	96.2	(0.6)	90.2	(0.7)	87.3	(0.9)	97.2	(0.4)	88.1	(0.9)
Czech Republic	51.8	(1.2)	76.4	(1.0)	77.1	(1.0)	72.0	(1.1)	85.2	(0.8)	52.2	(1.1)
Denmark	92.8	(0.7)	94.9	(0.7)	94.3	(0.6)	79.5	(1.1)	98.0	(0.4)	86.6	(1.1)
Estonia	74.8	(0.9)	83.5	(0.8)	73.9	(0.9)	72.3	(0.9)	78.6	(0.9)	59.8	(1.1)
Finland	72.8	(1.0)	86.6	(0.8)	77.1	(0.9)	64.2	(1.1)	76.9	(0.9)	68.2	(1.1)
France	88.7	(0.7)	98.2	(0.3)	94.9	(0.5)	88.3	(0.7)	98.5	(0.2)	82.2	(0.8)
Iceland	74.6	(1.2)	92.1	(0.8)	88.2	(1.0)	85.7	(1.0)	91.8	(0.8)	77.4	(1.2)
Israel	77.6	(1.1)	86.6	(0.8)	81.0	(0.8)	75.0	(1.3)	92.5	(0.5)	77.8	(1.0)
Italy	94.9	(0.4)	96.7	(0.3)	89.7	(0.6)	90.9	(0.6)	98.3	(0.2)	91.3	(0.5)
Japan	15.6	(0.6)	48.8	(1.1)	49.9	(1.1)	26.7	(0.8)	54.2	(0.8)	43.6	(0.9)
Korea	63.6	(1.1)	80.5	(1.0)	73.1	(1.1)	66.6	(1.2)	81.4	(0.9)	62.5	(1.1)
Latvia	83.0	(1.1)	92.0	(0.8)	81.2	(0.9)	90.1	(0.7)	91.4	(0.7)	62.1	(1.4)
Malaysia	91.9	(0.5)	98.0	(0.3)	96.8	(0.3)	88.6	(0.6)	95.8	(0.4)	89.5	(0.5)
Mexico	88.8	(0.7)	85.0	(0.7)	78.0	(1.0)	83.9	(0.8)	93.7	(0.4)	87.5	(0.8)
Netherlands	77.8	(1.2)	90.6	(0.9)	86.7	(0.9)	66.7	(1.6)	93.0	(0.8)	62.2	(1.3)
Norway	66.6	(1.8)	85.6	(0.9)	84.3	(0.8)	73.4	(1.6)	87.8	(1.1)	66.0	(1.5)
Poland	77.5	(0.8)	91.3	(0.7)	87.2	(0.8)	86.7	(0.6)	87.4	(0.6)	66.0	(1.0)
Portugal	97.5	(0.3)	97.5	(0.2)	95.2	(0.4)	98.3	(0.3)	99.2	(0.2)	95.9	(0.3)
Romania	93.4	(0.6)	97.7	(0.4)	97.7	(0.3)	98.0	(0.3)	99.4	(0.2)	93.2	(0.6)
Serbia	84.3	(0.7)	91.1	(0.5)	85.6	(0.6)	86.3	(0.7)	95.3	(0.4)	74.1	(0.8)
Singapore	74.9	(0.7)	83.5	(0.6)	75.3	(0.7)	71.6	(0.9)	88.5	(0.6)	72.8	(0.8)
Slovak Republic	90.2	(0.8)	95.3	(0.4)	92.2	(0.6)	92.0	(0.6)	95.1	(0.4)	80.6	(0.8)
Spain	78.9	(0.9)	83.8	(0.8)	73.7	(0.9)	87.0	(0.6)	96.5	(0.4)	83.2	(0.8)
Sweden	75.1	(0.9)	86.5	(0.7)	82.7	(0.8)	81.4	(0.8)	95.1	(0.5)	71.7	(0.9)
Sub-national entities												
Abu Dhabi (United Arab Emirates)	93.1	(0.7)	96.5	(0.5)	93.4	(0.8)	93.2	(0.6)	96.6	(0.4)	95.1	(0.6)
Alberta (Canada)	82.2	(1.0)	91.1	(0.9)	84.7	(1.0)	86.1	(0.9)	94.3	(0.6)	84.0	(0.8)
England (United Kingdom)	81.4	(1.0)	93.3	(0.6)	86.3	(0.7)	90.2	(0.7)	96.7	(0.4)	84.6	(1.0)
Flanders (Belgium)	87.4	(0.7)	96.6	(0.4)	95.4	(0.5)	80.7	(1.1)	97.7	(0.3)	73.2	(1.1)
Average	80.3	(0.2)	89.4	(0.1)	84.8	(0.1)	81.9	(0.2)	92.0	(0.1)	77.4	(0.2)
United States	83.0	(1.0)	89.3	(1.1)	81.6	(1.4)	82.6	(1.0)	92.9	(0.7)	82.5	(0.9)

*See notes at the beginning of this Annex.
Source: OECD, TALIS 2013 Database.
StatLink http://dx.doi.org/10.1787/888933047463

[Part 1/2]
Teachers' job satisfaction
Percentage of lower secondary education teachers who "agree" or "strongly agree"
with the following statements

Table 7.2

	The advantages of being a teacher clearly outweigh the disadvantages		If I could decide again, I would still choose to work as a teacher		I would like to change to another school if that were possible		I regret that I decided to become a teacher		I enjoy working at this school	
	%	S.E.	%	S.E.	%	S.E.	%	S.E.	%	S.E.
Australia	88.6	(0.8)	81.1	(1.0)	23.0	(1.7)	7.2	(0.6)	91.7	(1.1)
Brazil	60.5	(0.9)	69.7	(0.9)	15.0	(0.7)	13.5	(0.6)	93.7	(0.4)
Bulgaria	62.8	(1.3)	70.2	(1.2)	19.8	(1.2)	14.6	(1.0)	90.6	(0.9)
Chile	78.9	(1.4)	83.8	(1.2)	34.0	(1.9)	13.9	(1.6)	88.2	(1.1)
Croatia	71.9	(0.8)	80.4	(0.7)	16.0	(1.0)	5.7	(0.4)	85.5	(0.8)
Cyprus*	86.9	(0.8)	85.3	(0.8)	23.2	(1.1)	7.1	(0.6)	84.8	(1.0)
Czech Republic	53.0	(1.1)	73.3	(0.8)	10.5	(0.8)	8.2	(0.6)	88.8	(0.8)
Denmark	89.2	(0.9)	78.3	(1.4)	11.2	(1.0)	5.2	(0.7)	94.9	(0.7)
Estonia	69.3	(1.1)	70.3	(0.8)	15.7	(1.1)	10.2	(0.7)	80.7	(1.0)
Finland	95.3	(0.4)	85.3	(0.8)	16.2	(1.0)	5.0	(0.4)	90.8	(0.8)
France	58.5	(1.1)	76.1	(0.8)	26.7	(1.2)	9.4	(0.5)	90.6	(0.7)
Iceland	91.4	(0.9)	70.4	(1.4)	18.3	(1.2)	11.6	(0.9)	94.2	(0.7)
Israel	85.8	(0.7)	82.9	(0.8)	14.3	(0.9)	9.1	(0.6)	91.8	(0.6)
Italy	62.1	(1.0)	86.3	(0.8)	16.4	(1.1)	7.4	(0.5)	90.6	(0.7)
Japan	74.4	(0.9)	58.1	(1.1)	30.3	(1.2)	7.0	(0.5)	78.1	(1.0)
Korea	85.8	(0.8)	63.4	(1.0)	31.2	(1.2)	20.1	(0.8)	74.4	(1.2)
Latvia	60.7	(1.5)	67.6	(1.4)	15.7	(1.1)	12.0	(0.8)	92.4	(0.8)
Malaysia	98.3	(0.2)	92.8	(0.6)	41.3	(1.3)	5.4	(0.4)	94.2	(0.5)
Mexico	80.3	(0.9)	95.5	(0.4)	28.6	(1.3)	3.1	(0.4)	94.4	(0.6)
Netherlands	87.0	(1.0)	81.9	(1.1)	17.2	(1.6)	4.9	(0.8)	93.5	(1.0)
Norway	91.2	(1.1)	76.7	(1.4)	11.6	(1.0)	8.3	(0.6)	96.8	(0.4)
Poland	76.4	(1.0)	79.9	(0.9)	17.1	(1.0)	10.3	(0.6)	90.3	(0.7)
Portugal	70.5	(0.9)	71.6	(0.9)	24.0	(1.1)	16.2	(0.7)	92.8	(0.6)
Romania	64.3	(1.5)	78.5	(1.2)	15.3	(0.9)	10.9	(0.9)	91.3	(0.7)
Serbia	81.4	(0.8)	81.4	(0.7)	21.3	(1.0)	7.0	(0.6)	85.1	(0.8)
Singapore	83.6	(0.6)	82.1	(0.7)	35.1	(0.8)	10.7	(0.5)	85.9	(0.6)
Slovak Republic	58.0	(1.2)	71.5	(0.9)	12.7	(0.9)	13.8	(0.7)	90.5	(0.8)
Spain	79.5	(1.0)	88.2	(0.6)	20.1	(1.2)	6.3	(0.5)	89.4	(0.6)
Sweden	71.2	(1.0)	53.4	(1.1)	21.5	(1.0)	17.8	(0.8)	91.6	(0.6)
Sub-national entities										
Abu Dhabi (United Arab Emirates)	80.1	(1.4)	77.5	(1.4)	30.7	(1.3)	11.7	(0.8)	86.8	(1.0)
Alberta (Canada)	89.7	(0.8)	82.9	(0.9)	23.1	(1.3)	5.6	(0.5)	95.0	(0.8)
England (United Kingdom)	83.6	(0.7)	79.5	(0.9)	31.0	(1.3)	7.9	(0.5)	87.2	(0.8)
Flanders (Belgium)	84.6	(0.9)	85.4	(0.8)	12.8	(0.9)	5.1	(0.6)	94.5	(0.5)
Average	77.4	(0.2)	77.6	(0.2)	21.2	(0.2)	9.5	(0.1)	89.7	(0.1)
United States	87.1	(1.3)	84.0	(1.3)	20.4	(1.5)	6.0	(1.0)	91.2	(1.0)

*See notes at the beginning of this Annex.
Source: OECD, TALIS 2013 Database.
StatLink ᵇᵐᵍᵇ http://dx.doi.org/10.1787/888933047501

[Part 2/2]
Teachers' job satisfaction
*Percentage of lower secondary education teachers who "agree" or "strongly agree"
with the following statements*

Table 7.2

	I wonder whether it would have been better to choose another profession		I would recommend my school as a good place to work		I think that the teaching profession is valued in society		I am satisfied with my performance in this school		All in all, I am satisfied with my job	
	%	S.E.	%	S.E.	%	S.E.	%	S.E.	%	S.E.
Australia	33.7	(1.7)	85.5	(1.5)	38.5	(1.3)	94.2	(0.5)	90.0	(1.0)
Brazil	32.3	(0.9)	88.0	(0.6)	12.6	(0.5)	90.6	(0.5)	87.0	(0.5)
Bulgaria	42.6	(1.4)	89.4	(0.9)	19.6	(1.1)	93.9	(0.6)	94.6	(0.6)
Chile	31.9	(1.6)	85.1	(1.3)	33.6	(2.3)	94.6	(0.6)	94.6	(0.6)
Croatia	31.7	(1.0)	85.4	(1.0)	9.6	(0.5)	93.2	(0.5)	91.4	(0.5)
Cyprus*	25.9	(1.1)	83.4	(0.9)	48.9	(1.2)	96.0	(0.5)	92.9	(0.6)
Czech Republic	29.8	(0.9)	84.5	(1.2)	12.2	(0.6)	95.2	(0.5)	88.6	(0.7)
Denmark	34.1	(1.7)	88.2	(1.4)	18.4	(1.0)	98.3	(0.3)	92.9	(0.9)
Estonia	37.0	(1.0)	79.9	(1.0)	13.7	(1.0)	88.6	(0.7)	90.0	(0.8)
Finland	27.5	(0.9)	87.5	(1.0)	58.6	(1.2)	95.0	(0.4)	91.0	(0.6)
France	26.0	(0.9)	80.1	(1.3)	4.9	(0.4)	87.5	(0.7)	86.4	(0.8)
Iceland	45.4	(1.5)	90.5	(0.9)	17.5	(1.1)	98.1	(0.3)	94.5	(0.8)
Israel	23.8	(0.9)	86.7	(1.0)	33.7	(1.2)	95.2	(0.5)	94.4	(0.6)
Italy	17.6	(0.9)	87.3	(0.9)	12.5	(0.7)	94.7	(0.5)	94.4	(0.5)
Japan	23.3	(0.8)	62.2	(1.7)	28.1	(1.0)	50.5	(1.3)	85.1	(0.7)
Korea	40.2	(1.0)	65.6	(1.6)	66.5	(1.1)	79.4	(1.0)	86.6	(0.8)
Latvia	36.5	(1.1)	86.2	(1.2)	22.8	(1.5)	92.9	(0.6)	91.0	(1.0)
Malaysia	8.8	(0.7)	89.3	(0.8)	83.8	(1.0)	94.7	(0.4)	97.0	(0.3)
Mexico	10.2	(0.7)	89.2	(0.9)	49.5	(1.3)	97.1	(0.3)	97.8	(0.3)
Netherlands	18.5	(1.1)	84.4	(2.3)	40.4	(1.5)	95.3	(0.8)	90.8	(1.1)
Norway	38.2	(1.5)	91.3	(0.9)	30.6	(1.5)	96.0	(0.6)	94.9	(0.7)
Poland	35.3	(1.0)	84.5	(1.1)	17.9	(0.8)	93.5	(0.6)	92.7	(0.6)
Portugal	44.5	(1.0)	88.1	(0.9)	10.5	(0.6)	97.4	(0.3)	94.1	(0.4)
Romania	29.4	(1.3)	87.4	(0.9)	34.7	(1.4)	97.0	(0.4)	91.1	(0.8)
Serbia	27.1	(1.0)	86.1	(0.9)	20.4	(0.9)	93.3	(0.4)	89.5	(0.6)
Singapore	45.9	(0.9)	73.2	(0.8)	67.6	(0.9)	87.1	(0.5)	88.4	(0.6)
Slovak Republic	45.4	(1.2)	81.4	(1.1)	4.0	(0.4)	94.8	(0.5)	89.0	(0.6)
Spain	21.2	(0.9)	86.6	(1.0)	8.5	(0.8)	95.8	(0.4)	95.1	(0.4)
Sweden	50.4	(1.2)	80.1	(1.2)	5.0	(0.5)	95.9	(0.4)	85.4	(0.9)
Sub-national entities										
Abu Dhabi (United Arab Emirates)	35.1	(1.7)	81.9	(1.3)	66.5	(1.7)	96.3	(0.4)	88.9	(0.9)
Alberta (Canada)	34.6	(1.3)	88.8	(1.2)	47.0	(1.4)	97.0	(0.5)	91.9	(0.8)
England (United Kingdom)	34.6	(1.2)	77.7	(1.2)	35.4	(1.5)	92.5	(0.6)	81.8	(0.8)
Flanders (Belgium)	22.7	(0.9)	88.1	(1.2)	45.9	(1.1)	94.8	(0.5)	95.3	(0.5)
Average	31.6	(0.2)	84.0	(0.2)	30.9	(0.2)	92.6	(0.1)	91.2	(0.1)
United States	33.5	(1.5)	85.5	(1.5)	33.7	(1.4)	95.0	(0.9)	89.1	(1.1)

* See notes at the beginning of this Annex.
Source: OECD, TALIS 2013 Database.
StatLink ᴍˢᴾ http://dx.doi.org/10.1787/888933047501

 TALIS 2013 RESULTS: AN INTERNATIONAL PERSPECTIVE ON TEACHING AND LEARNING

[Part 1/1]

Relationship between teacher and school characteristics and societal value of teaching

Significant results in the logistic regressions of teachers' perception of how society views

Table 7.3   *the teaching profession with the following teachers' characteristics in lower secondary education[1]*

	Teachers who think that the teaching profession is valued in society[2]					
	Dependent on:					
	Male[3]		More than 5 years of teaching experience[4]		This school provides staff with opportunities to actively participate in school decisions[5]	
	ß	Odds ratios[6]	ß	Odds ratios[6]	ß	Odds ratios[6]
Australia					1.00	2.71
Brazil	0.59	1.81			0.46	1.59
Bulgaria			-0.71	0.49	1.08	2.96
Chile			0.39	1.48	1.66	5.26
Croatia			-0.67	0.51	1.08	2.96
Czech Republic	0.54	1.72			0.47	1.60
Denmark					0.52	1.68
Estonia			-0.52	0.59	0.96	2.62
Finland			-0.33	0.72	0.46	1.58
France	0.64	1.90	-0.69	0.50	0.61	1.83
Iceland					0.89	2.44
Israel	0.43	1.54	-0.49	0.61	0.68	1.96
Italy	0.37	1.45			0.62	1.86
Japan					0.37	1.44
Korea	0.42	1.53	-0.54	0.58	0.77	2.16
Latvia					1.11	3.03
Malaysia	-0.31	0.73	-0.47	0.63	0.89	2.44
Mexico	0.55	1.73			0.82	2.26
Netherlands					0.56	1.75
Norway			-0.40	0.67	0.67	1.95
Poland	0.37	1.45	-0.41	0.67	0.64	1.89
Portugal	0.62	1.86			0.64	1.90
Romania			-0.36	0.70	0.70	2.01
Serbia			-1.08	0.34	0.97	2.64
Singapore			0.24	1.26	1.03	2.80
Slovak Republic	0.55	1.74	-0.49	0.61		
Spain			-0.75	0.47		
Sweden			-0.60	0.55		
Sub-national entities						
Abu Dhabi (United Arab Emirates)					0.68	1.98
Alberta (Canada)					0.91	2.48
England (United Kingdom)	0.29	1.34	-0.37	0.69	0.78	2.19
Flanders (Belgium)			0.24	1.26	0.50	1.66

1. Cells are blank when no significant relationship was found. Significance was tested at the 5% level, controlling for subject(s) taught and content, pedagogy and classroom practice elements of the subject(s) taught included in formal education or training. Cells with data representing less than 5% of the cases are shaded in grey and should be interpreted with caution. These results are not highlighted in the text of the report.

2. Dichotomous variable where the reference category is the combination of "strongly disagree" and "disagree".

3. Dichotomous variable where the reference category is female.

4. The work experience variable was dichotomised, with five years as a cut-off point. Five years or less was the reference category. Coefficients and odds ratios therefore represent the association of having worked as a teacher in total for more than five years in comparison with five years or less.

5. Dichotomous variable where the reference category is the combination of "strongly disagree" and "disagree".

6. This is the exponentiated beta. Please refer to Box 2.5 for interpretation of odds ratios.

Source: OECD, TALIS 2013 Database.

StatLink ᝏᖰᴸ http://dx.doi.org/10.1787/888933047539

[Part 1/1]
Relationship between teachers' characteristics and their self-efficacy
Significant variables in the multiple linear regressions of teachers' self-efficacy
Table 7.4 *with the following teachers' characteristics in lower secondary education[1]*

	Teachers' self-efficacy[2]							
	Step one[3]						Step two[4]	
	Dependent on:							
	Male[5]		More than 5 years of teaching experience[6]		Content, pedagogy and classroom practice elements of the subject(s) taught included in formal education[7]		Teachers' job satisfaction[2]	
	ß	S.E.	ß	S.E.	ß	S.E.	ß	S.E.
Australia	-0.46	0.09	0.53	0.14	-0.20	0.04	0.21	0.03
Brazil	-0.18	0.06	0.30	0.05	-0.03	0.01	0.23	0.01
Bulgaria			-0.28	0.14	-0.12	0.03	0.22	0.02
Chile					-0.19	0.03	0.23	0.03
Croatia	-0.23	0.06	0.38	0.07			0.26	0.02
Czech Republic			0.35	0.09	-0.10	0.02	0.24	0.02
Denmark	-0.38	0.08	0.47	0.10	-0.11	0.03	0.20	0.02
Estonia	-0.42	0.10			-0.05	0.02	0.19	0.02
Finland			0.30	0.09	-0.13	0.03	0.30	0.02
France	-0.15	0.06	0.54	0.10			0.17	0.01
Iceland			0.36	0.11	-0.13	0.03	0.13	0.03
Israel			0.38	0.11	-0.16	0.03	0.25	0.03
Italy	-0.26	0.06	0.44	0.09	-0.08	0.02	0.20	0.02
Japan	0.48	0.07	0.55	0.07	-0.06	0.02	0.22	0.02
Korea	0.32	0.11	0.50	0.10	-0.19	0.04	0.28	0.02
Latvia			0.48	0.21	-0.11	0.03	0.19	0.03
Malaysia	-0.25	0.08	0.21	0.07	-0.20	0.03	0.38	0.02
Mexico			0.22	0.10	-0.14	0.03	0.32	0.03
Netherlands			0.36	0.10			0.26	0.02
Norway			0.29	0.12	-0.13	0.03	0.23	0.03
Poland	-0.28	0.09					0.26	0.02
Portugal	-0.17	0.05			-0.09	0.02	0.17	0.01
Romania	-0.22	0.07	0.20	0.08	-0.12	0.02	0.20	0.02
Serbia	-0.21	0.05	0.22	0.09	-0.06	0.02	0.29	0.02
Singapore	-0.19	0.08	0.93	0.08	-0.10	0.03	0.23	0.02
Slovak Republic	-0.39	0.09	0.33	0.08	-0.05	0.02	0.25	0.03
Spain	-0.19	0.07			-0.12	0.02	0.32	0.02
Sweden			0.70	0.09	-0.09	0.02	0.19	0.02
Sub-national entities								
Abu Dhabi (United Arab Emirates)			0.50	0.12	-0.09	0.03	0.18	0.02
Alberta (Canada)	-0.30	0.10	0.71	0.11	-0.14	0.03	0.20	0.03
England (United Kingdom)	-0.16	0.08	0.43	0.10	-0.13	0.04	0.21	0.02
Flanders (Belgium)	-0.15	0.06	0.49	0.06			0.16	0.02

1. Cells are blank when no significant relationship was found. Significance was tested at the 5% level. Cells with data representing less than 5% of the cases are shaded in grey and should be interpreted with caution. These results are not highlighted in the text of the report.

2. Continuous variable. See the textbox describing this index and Annex B for more details.

3. The first three variables were entered in the regressions together before adding teachers' job satisfaction; teacher educational attainment was controlled for in this first step.

4. This variable was entered in step 2 of the regressions, meaning teacher gender, educational attainment, work experience, and content, pedagogy and classroom practice elements of the subject(s) taught included in formal education, were controlled for.

5. Dichotomous variable where the reference category is female.

6. The work experience variable was dichotomised, with five years as a cut-off point. Five years or less was the reference category. Coefficients and odds ratios therefore represent the association of having worked as a teacher in total for more than five years in comparison with five years or less.

7. The scores on TT2G12A, 12B and 12C were combined. This variable therefore represents the total extent to which content, pedagogy and classroom practice elements of subject(s) the teacher currently teaches were included in his or her formal education. Because higher scores indicate that these elements were included to a lesser extent or not at all for the subject the teacher currently teaches, negative scores indicate that less preparation is negatively associated with total self-efficacy and job satisfaction scores.

Source: OECD, TALIS 2013 Database.

StatLink http://dx.doi.org/10.1787/888933047577

[Part 1/1]
Relationship between teachers' characteristics and job satisfaction
*Significant variables in the multiple linear regressions of teachers' job satisfaction
with the following teachers' characteristics in lower secondary education[1]*

Table 7.5

	Teachers' job satisfaction[2]							
	Step one[3]						Step two[4]	
	Dependent on:							
	Male[5]		More than 5 years of teaching experience[6]		Content, pedagogy and classroom practice elements of the subject(s) taught included in formal education[7]		Teachers' self-efficacy[2]	
	β	S.E.	β	S.E.	β	S.E.	β	S.E.
Australia					-0.14	0.04	0.26	0.03
Brazil					-0.09	0.02	0.30	0.02
Bulgaria					-0.11	0.03	0.36	0.03
Chile	-0.32	0.09			-0.15	0.03	0.24	0.03
Croatia	-0.49	0.08					0.39	0.02
Czech Republic	-0.24	0.09					0.26	0.02
Denmark					-0.07	0.03	0.38	0.03
Estonia	-0.19	0.08			-0.05	0.02	0.17	0.02
Finland			-0.38	0.09			0.28	0.02
France	-0.18	0.09	-0.33	0.11			0.35	0.03
Iceland	-0.56	0.11	-0.30	0.12			0.13	0.03
Israel							0.28	0.02
Italy					-0.10	0.02	0.26	0.02
Japan	0.24	0.07	-0.20	0.09	-0.07	0.03	0.29	0.02
Korea			-0.51	0.12	-0.12	0.03	0.24	0.02
Latvia	-0.23	0.11					0.22	0.04
Malaysia					-0.16	0.02	0.28	0.02
Mexico					-0.08	0.02	0.24	0.02
Netherlands			-0.41	0.13	-0.16	0.05	0.37	0.04
Norway					-0.11	0.03	0.30	0.03
Poland	-0.27	0.09	-0.49	0.15	-0.14	0.05	0.31	0.02
Portugal			-0.59	0.25	-0.14	0.02	0.35	0.02
Romania	-0.27	0.08					0.39	0.03
Serbia	-0.23	0.08	-0.40	0.08	-0.07	0.02	0.41	0.03
Singapore			0.18	0.06	-0.15	0.03	0.15	0.02
Slovak Republic	-0.21	0.09			-0.03	0.01	0.22	0.02
Spain	-0.28	0.07	-0.33	0.13	-0.06	0.02	0.33	0.02
Sweden	-0.31	0.08	-0.29	0.11			0.29	0.03
Sub-national entities								
Abu Dhabi (United Arab Emirates)	0.32	0.13			-0.15	0.04	0.35	0.04
Alberta (Canada)					-0.14	0.03	0.22	0.03
England (United Kingdom)			-0.29	0.11	-0.14	0.04	0.33	0.03
Flanders (Belgium)			-0.38	0.11	-0.06	0.02	0.25	0.03

1. Cells are blank when no significant relationship was found. Significance was tested at the 5% level. Cells with data representing less than 5% of the cases are shaded in grey and should be interpreted with caution. These results are not highlighted in the text of the report.
2. Continuous variable. See the textbox describing this index and Annex B for more details.
3. The first three variables were entered in the regressions together before adding teachers' job satisfaction; teacher educational attainment was controlled for in this first step.
4. This variable was entered in step 2 of the regressions, meaning teacher gender, educational attainment, work experience, and content, pedagogy and classroom practice elements of the subject(s) taught included in formal education, were controlled for.
5. Dichotomous variable where the reference category is female.
6. The work experience variable was dichotomised, with five years as a cut-off point. Five years or less was the reference category. Coefficients and odds ratios therefore represent the association of having worked as a teacher in total for more than five years in comparison with five years or less.
7. The scores on TT2G12A, 12B and 12C were combined. This variable therefore represents the total extent to which content, pedagogy and classroom practice elements of subject(s) the teacher currently teaches were included in his or her formal education. Because higher scores indicate that these elements were included to a lesser extent or not at all for the subject the teacher currently teaches, negative scores indicate that less preparation is negatively associated with total self-efficacy and job satisfaction scores.
Source: OECD, TALIS 2013 Database.
StatLink http://dx.doi.org/10.1787/888933047615

[Part 1/1]

Relationship between classroom characteristics and teachers' self-efficacy

Significant variables in the multiple linear regressions of teachers' self-efficacy
with the following classroom characteristics in lower secondary education[1]

Table 7.6

	Teachers' self-efficacy[2]							
	Dependent on:							
	Class size[3]		Low academic achievers[4]		Students with behavioural problems[5]		Academically gifted students[6]	
	ß	S.E.	ß	S.E.	ß	S.E.	ß	S.E.
Australia					-0.45	0.18	0.35	0.13
Brazil			-0.29	0.07			0.21	0.10
Bulgaria							0.35	0.08
Chile					-0.33	0.12		
Croatia					-0.39	0.08	0.26	0.06
Czech Republic					-0.22	0.08	0.53	0.10
Denmark					-0.56	0.13	0.37	0.16
Estonia	0.02	0.00						
Finland							0.30	0.08
France			-0.21	0.05	-0.24	0.06		
Iceland	0.01	0.01						
Israel	0.02	0.01			-0.36	0.11	0.42	0.11
Italy			-0.18	0.07				
Japan					-0.21	0.11	0.57	0.10
Korea							0.39	0.11
Latvia							0.25	0.07
Malaysia							0.18	0.08
Mexico			-0.37	0.09				
Netherlands								
Norway	0.01	0.00					0.38	0.08
Poland					-0.46	0.09	0.35	0.07
Portugal			-0.17	0.05	-0.19	0.06		
Romania			-0.28	0.07	-0.57	0.09	0.30	0.10
Serbia			-0.21	0.07			0.16	0.06
Singapore					-0.18	0.09		
Slovak Republic					-0.32	0.09		
Spain			-0.24	0.08	-0.31	0.10		
Sweden			-0.22	0.07				
Sub-national entities								
Abu Dhabi (United Arab Emirates)					-0.33	0.11	0.38	0.08
Alberta (Canada)								
England (United Kingdom)					-0.23	0.10		
Flanders (Belgium)							0.52	0.19

1. Cells are blank when no significant relationship was found. Significance was tested at the 5% level. Cells with data representing less than 5% of the cases are shaded in grey and should be interpreted with caution. These results are not highlighted in the text of the report.

2. Continuous variable. See the textbox describing this index and Annex B for more details.

3. Continuous variable where the data are reported by teachers and refer to a randomly chosen class they currently teach from their weekly timetable.

4. The reference category is 10% or less of students are low academic achievers. Data are reported by teachers and refer to a randomly chosen class they currently teach from their weekly timetable.

5. The reference category is 10% or less of students with behavioural problems. Data are reported by teachers and refer to a randomly chosen class they currently teach from their weekly timetable.

6. The reference category is 10% or less of students are academically gifted. Data are reported by teachers and refer to a randomly chosen class they currently teach from their weekly timetable.

Source: OECD, TALIS 2013 Database.

StatLink ⟐ http://dx.doi.org/10.1787/888933047653

[Part 1/1]
Relationship between classroom characteristics and teachers' job satisfaction
Significant variables in the multiple linear regressions of teachers' job satisfaction
Table 7.7 *with the following classroom characteristics in lower secondary education[1]*

	Teachers' job satisfaction[2]							
	Dependent on:							
	Class size[3]		Low academic achievers[4]		Students with behavioural problems[5]		Academically gifted students[6]	
	ß	S.E.	ß	S.E.	ß	S.E.	ß	S.E.
Australia			-0.32	0.11	-0.55	0.14	0.39	0.13
Brazil			-0.53	0.08	-0.46	0.07	0.26	0.12
Bulgaria			-0.23	0.09	-0.52	0.10	0.59	0.11
Chile					-0.43	0.13	0.31	0.11
Croatia			-0.29	0.08	-0.58	0.11	0.24	0.07
Czech Republic			-0.22	0.08	-0.34	0.10		
Denmark			-0.51	0.09	-0.73	0.17		
Estonia	-0.01	0.00	-0.37	0.09	-0.37	0.08	0.29	0.07
Finland			-0.20	0.08	-0.45	0.09	0.30	0.09
France			-0.33	0.08	-0.71	0.10	0.32	0.08
Iceland			-0.29	0.13			0.26	0.12
Israel					-0.52	0.08	0.23	0.11
Italy			-0.26	0.09	-0.35	0.08	0.27	0.08
Japan			-0.35	0.07	-0.33	0.12	0.49	0.12
Korea			-0.34	0.10	-0.48	0.13	0.43	0.11
Latvia	0.01	0.01			-0.35	0.08	0.36	0.08
Malaysia	-0.01	0.00			-0.32	0.08	0.25	0.07
Mexico			-0.20	0.08	-0.31	0.06	0.18	0.06
Netherlands			-0.37	0.09				
Norway							0.30	0.15
Poland					-0.52	0.09	0.41	0.08
Portugal			-0.40	0.09	-0.41	0.08		
Romania			-0.41	0.09	-0.79	0.13	0.39	0.13
Serbia			-0.32	0.08	-0.54	0.10	0.28	0.07
Singapore			-0.27	0.08	-0.25	0.07		
Slovak Republic			-0.23	0.08	-0.20	0.09	0.16	0.07
Spain			-0.33	0.07	-0.65	0.10		
Sweden			-0.39	0.09	-0.29	0.13		
Sub-national entities								
Abu Dhabi (United Arab Emirates)					-0.99	0.16	0.53	0.16
Alberta (Canada)			-0.29	0.13	-0.35	0.13		
England (United Kingdom)	-0.02	0.01			-0.63	0.14	0.56	0.13
Flanders (Belgium)			-0.30	0.08	-0.50	0.10		

1. Cells are blank when no significant relationship was found. Significance was tested at the 5% level.
2. Continuous variable. See the textbox describing this index and Annex B for more details.
3. Continuous variable where the data are reported by teachers and refer to a randomly chosen class they currently teach from their weekly timetable.
4. The reference category is 10% or less of students are low academic achievers. Data are reported by teachers and refer to a randomly chosen class they currently teach from their weekly timetable.
5. The reference category is 10% or less of students with behavioural problems. Data are reported by teachers and refer to a randomly chosen class they currently teach from their weekly timetable.
6. The reference category is 10% or less of students are academically gifted. Data are reported by teachers and refer to a randomly chosen class they currently teach from their weekly timetable.
Source: OECD, TALIS 2013 Database.
StatLink ⟐ http://dx.doi.org/10.1787/888933047691

[Part 1/2]
Relationship between school environment and teachers' self-efficacy
Significant variables in the multiple linear regressions of teachers' self-efficacy with the following school leadership and school environment variables in lower secondary education[1]

Table 7.8

	Teachers' self-efficacy[2]											
	Model 1[3]											
	Dependent on:											
	Teacher-student relations[5]		Teacher co-operation[6]		Class size[9]		More than 10% of students in the classroom are low academic achievers[10]		More than 10% of the students in the classroom have behavioural problems[11]		More than 10% of the students in the classroom are academically gifted students[12]	
	ß	S.E.	ß	S.E.	ß	S.E.	ß	S.E.	ß	S.E.	ß	S.E.
Australia	0.12	(0.03)	0.19	(0.03)							0.33	(0.12)
Brazil	0.16	(0.01)	0.13	(0.01)			-0.14	(0.07)				
Bulgaria	0.21	(0.03)	0.23	(0.02)							0.21	(0.08)
Chile	0.17	(0.03)	0.11	(0.02)								
Croatia	0.13	(0.02)	0.26	(0.02)					-0.27	(0.09)	0.22	(0.07)
Czech Republic	0.11	(0.02)	0.23	(0.02)					-0.20	(0.08)	0.46	(0.09)
Denmark	0.12	(0.02)	0.11	(0.02)					-0.45	(0.13)		
Estonia	0.14	(0.03)	0.20	(0.02)	0.02	(0.00)						
Finland	0.20	(0.02)	0.24	(0.03)							0.15	(0.08)
France	0.09	(0.02)	0.23	(0.02)			-0.23	(0.06)	-0.21	(0.07)		
Iceland	0.10	(0.03)	0.18	(0.03)								
Israel	0.12	(0.02)	0.25	(0.03)	0.02	(0.01)			-0.29	(0.10)	0.33	(0.10)
Italy	0.11	(0.02)	0.18	(0.02)			-0.14	(0.07)				
Japan	0.08	(0.02)	0.22	(0.02)			-0.14	(0.06)	-0.20	(0.10)	0.45	(0.10)
Korea	0.23	(0.03)	0.21	(0.03)							0.25	(0.11)
Latvia	0.18	(0.04)	0.20	(0.03)							0.24	(0.08)
Malaysia	0.26	(0.02)	0.24	(0.02)								
Mexico	0.11	(0.02)	0.15	(0.02)			-0.26	(0.10)				
Netherlands	0.11	(0.03)	0.19	(0.04)								
Norway	0.10	(0.04)	0.18	(0.04)							0.30	(0.08)
Poland	0.19	(0.03)	0.27	(0.02)					-0.42	(0.08)	0.26	(0.08)
Portugal	0.12	(0.01)	0.17	(0.02)			-0.14	(0.05)	-0.17	(0.06)		
Romania	0.12	(0.02)	0.18	(0.02)			-0.14	(0.06)	-0.42	(0.08)	0.23	(0.09)
Serbia	0.16	(0.02)	0.24	(0.02)								
Singapore	0.21	(0.02)	0.16	(0.03)								
Slovak Republic	0.14	(0.02)	0.27	(0.02)					-0.32	(0.09)		
Spain	0.12	(0.02)	0.26	(0.03)			-0.17	(0.08)	-0.25	(0.10)		
Sweden	0.15	(0.02)	0.19	(0.03)	0.01	(0.00)	-0.15	(0.07)				
Sub-national entities												
Abu Dhabi (United Arab Emirates)	0.12	(0.03)	0.18	(0.02)					-0.27	(0.11)	0.30	(0.12)
Alberta (Canada)	0.17	(0.03)	0.16	(0.04)					0.24	(0.11)		
England (United Kingdom)	0.19	(0.03)	0.20	(0.03)								
Flanders (Belgium)	0.10	(0.02)	0.20	(0.03)							0.51	(0.21)

1. Cells are blank when no significant relationship was found. Significance was tested at the 5% level. The class composition variables (shaded in a different tone) are presented in each model to see how their results vary based on the variables included in each model. Please refer to table B.11.Web in Annex B to see the results of the basic class composition model (not coupled with any other variable). Cells with data representing less than 5% of the cases are shaded in grey and should be interpreted with caution. These results are not highlighted in the text of the report.

2. Continuous variable. See the textbox describing this index and Annex B for more details.

3. First model including teacher-student relations and teacher co-operation. Controlling for teacher gender, experience, educational attainment, formal education or training on content, pedagogy and classroom practice for the subject(s) taught, class size, low academic achievers, students with behavioural problems, and gifted students.

4. Second model including the variables "Staff are provided opportunities to actively participate in school decisions" and "instructional leadership". Controlling for teacher gender, experience, educational attainment, formal education or training on content, pedagogy and classroom practice for the subject(s) taught, class size, low academic achievers, students with behavioural problems, and gifted students.

5. Continuous variable combining answers of question 45 of the teacher questionnaire.

6. Continuous variable combining answers of question 33 of the teacher questionnaire.

7. Dichotomous variable where the reference category is "disagree" or "strongly disagree".

8. Continuous variable. See the textbox describing this index and Annex B for more details.

9. Continuous variable where the data are reported by teachers and refer to a randomly chosen class they currently teach from their weekly timetable.

10. The reference category is 10% or less of students are low academic achievers. Data are reported by teachers and refer to a randomly chosen class they currently teach from their weekly timetable.

11. The reference category is 10% or less of students with behavioural problems. Data are reported by teachers and refer to a randomly chosen class they currently teach from their weekly timetable.

12. The reference category is 10% or less of students are academically gifted. Data are reported by teachers and refer to a randomly chosen class they currently teach from their weekly timetable.

Source: OECD, TALIS 2013 Database.

StatLink http://dx.doi.org/10.1787/888933047729

[Part 2/2]
Relationship between school environment and teachers' self-efficacy
Significant variables in the multiple linear regressions of teachers' self-efficacy with the following school leadership and school environment variables in lower secondary education[1]

Table 7.8

	Teachers' self-efficacy[2]											
	Model 2[4]											
	Dependent on:											
	Staff are provided opportunities to actively participate in school decisions[7]		Instructional leadership[8]		Class size[9]		More than 10% of students in the classroom are low academic achievers[10]		More than 10% of the students in the classroom have behavioural problems[11]		More than 10% of the students in the classroom are academically gifted students[12]	
	β	S.E.	β	S.E.	β	S.E.	β	S.E.	β	S.E.	β	S.E.
Australia			0.06	(0.03)					-0.38	(0.15)	0.40	0.14
Brazil	0.23	(0.06)					-0.23	(0.07)				
Bulgaria			0.14	(0.04)							0.35	0.08
Chile	0.32	(0.13)										
Croatia	0.19	(0.09)							-0.28	(0.09)	0.26	0.07
Czech Republic	0.25	(0.08)							-0.21	(0.08)	0.46	0.10
Denmark	0.21	(0.10)							-0.46	(0.14)		
Estonia					0.02	(0.00)						
Finland	0.25	(0.10)									0.27	0.08
France	0.23	(0.07)					-0.23	(0.06)	-0.23	(0.07)		
Iceland					0.01	(0.01)						
Israel	0.60	(0.09)			0.02	(0.01)			-0.28	(0.11)	0.36	0.11
Italy	0.16	(0.06)					-0.14	(0.07)				
Japan			0.05	(0.03)	0.01	(0.00)					0.48	0.10
Korea	0.22	(0.10)									0.41	0.12
Latvia	0.29	(0.10)									0.30	0.08
Malaysia	0.20	(0.09)										
Mexico							-0.33	(0.10)				
Netherlands												
Norway			0.08	(0.04)							0.38	0.08
Poland	0.34	(0.09)							-0.45	(0.09)	0.35	0.08
Portugal	0.26	(0.05)					-0.18	(0.05)	-0.18	(0.06)		
Romania	0.39	(0.08)					-0.24	(0.06)	-0.49	(0.09)	0.30	0.10
Serbia	0.32	(0.09)					-0.15	(0.07)			0.19	0.07
Singapore	0.38	(0.09)										
Slovak Republic	0.38	(0.08)							-0.31	(0.09)		
Spain							-0.20	(0.08)	-0.30	(0.10)		
Sweden					0.01	(0.00)	-0.19	(0.07)				
Sub-national entities												
Abu Dhabi (United Arab Emirates)	0.43	(0.11)							-0.37	(0.12)	0.36	0.10
Alberta (Canada)									0.24	(0.11)		
England (United Kingdom)	0.29	(0.09)							-0.21	(0.10)		
Flanders (Belgium)											0.57	0.20

1. Cells are blank when no significant relationship was found. Significance was tested at the 5% level. The class composition variables (shaded in a different tone) are presented in each model to see how their results vary based on the variables included in each model. Please refer to table B.11.Web in Annex B to see the results of the basic class composition model (not coupled with any other variable). Cells with data representing less than 5% of the cases are shaded in grey and should be interpreted with caution. These results are not highlighted in the text of the report.

2. Continuous variable. See the textbox describing this index and Annex B for more details.

3. First model including teacher-student relations and teacher co-operation. Controlling for teacher gender, experience, educational attainment, formal education or training on content, pedagogy and classroom practice for the subject(s) taught, class size, low academic achievers, students with behavioural problems, and gifted students.

4. Second model including the variables "Staff are provided opportunities to actively participate in school decisions" and "instructional leadership". Controlling for teacher gender, experience, educational attainment, formal education or training on content, pedagogy and classroom practice for the subject(s) taught, class size, low academic achievers, students with behavioural problems, and gifted students.

5. Continuous variable combining answers of question 45 of the teacher questionnaire.

6. Continuous variable combining answers of question 33 of the teacher questionnaire.

7. Dichotomous variable where the reference category is "disagree" or "strongly disagree".

8. Continuous variable. See the textbox describing this index and Annex B for more details.

9. Continuous variable where the data are reported by teachers and refer to a randomly chosen class they currently teach from their weekly timetable.

10. The reference category is 10% or less of students are low academic achievers. Data are reported by teachers and refer to a randomly chosen class they currently teach from their weekly timetable.

11. The reference category is 10% or less of students with behavioural problems. Data are reported by teachers and refer to a randomly chosen class they currently teach from their weekly timetable.

12. The reference category is 10% or less of students are academically gifted. Data are reported by teachers and refer to a randomly chosen class they currently teach from their weekly timetable.

Source: OECD, TALIS 2013 Database.

StatLink http://dx.doi.org/10.1787/888933047729

[Part 1/2]

Relationship between school environment and teachers' job satisfaction

Significant variables in the multiple linear regressions of teachers' job satisfaction with the following school leadership and school environment variables in lower secondary education[1]

Table 7.9

	Teacher-student relations[5]		Teacher co-operation[6]		Class size[9]		More than 10% of students in the classroom are low academic achievers[10]		More than 10% of the students in the classroom have behavioural problems[11]		More than 10% of the students in the classroom are academically gifted students[12]	
	ß	S.E.	ß	S.E.	ß	S.E.	ß	S.E.	ß	S.E.	ß	S.E.
Australia	0.34	(0.04)	0.14	(0.03)			-0.30	(0.10)				
Brazil	0.26	(0.02)	0.10	(0.02)			-0.32	(0.08)	-0.40	(0.07)		
Bulgaria	0.31	(0.03)	0.10	(0.03)			-0.24	(0.11)	-0.41	(0.10)	0.40	(0.11)
Chile	0.24	(0.03)	0.15	(0.03)					-0.35	(0.14)		
Croatia	0.33	(0.03)	0.16	(0.03)			-0.27	(0.08)	-0.46	(0.12)	0.17	(0.07)
Czech Republic	0.31	(0.02)	0.11	(0.02)			-0.19	(0.07)	-0.27	(0.09)		
Denmark	0.33	(0.03)	0.13	(0.04)			-0.39	(0.09)	-0.58	(0.16)		
Estonia	0.26	(0.02)	0.11	(0.03)	-0.01	(0.00)	-0.30	(0.09)	-0.36	(0.08)	0.26	(0.06)
Finland	0.32	(0.02)	0.11	(0.03)			-0.16	(0.08)	-0.36	(0.08)	0.20	(0.09)
France	0.25	(0.02)	0.22	(0.04)			-0.29	(0.09)	-0.66	(0.10)		
Iceland	0.28	(0.04)	0.13	(0.04)								
Israel	0.34	(0.02)	0.12	(0.02)					-0.38	(0.09)		
Italy	0.28	(0.02)	0.13	(0.02)			-0.22	(0.07)	-0.28	(0.08)	0.17	(0.08)
Japan	0.33	(0.02)	0.15	(0.02)			-0.32	(0.06)	-0.31	(0.10)	0.45	(0.11)
Korea	0.38	(0.02)					-0.23	(0.08)	-0.38	(0.14)	0.26	(0.11)
Latvia	0.28	(0.03)	0.12	(0.03)	0.02	(0.01)			-0.32	(0.08)	0.29	(0.08)
Malaysia	0.33	(0.02)	0.07	(0.02)	-0.01	(0.00)					0.14	(0.07)
Mexico	0.24	(0.02)	0.08	(0.02)	0.01	(0.00)			-0.19	(0.07)		
Netherlands	0.31	(0.04)	0.18	(0.04)			-0.23	(0.10)				
Norway	0.29	(0.03)	0.17	(0.04)			-0.22	(0.10)				
Poland	0.36	(0.02)	0.09	(0.02)					-0.40	(0.08)	0.30	(0.08)
Portugal	0.33	(0.02)	0.12	(0.03)			-0.28	(0.08)	-0.30	(0.08)		
Romania	0.39	(0.02)	0.08	(0.02)			-0.19	(0.07)	-0.49	(0.11)		
Serbia	0.34	(0.02)	0.18	(0.02)			-0.16	(0.08)	-0.46	(0.10)		
Singapore	0.36	(0.02)	0.11	(0.02)	-0.01	(0.00)	-0.17	(0.07)	-0.19	(0.07)		
Slovak Republic	0.25	(0.02)	0.10	(0.02)			-0.18	(0.07)	-0.17	(0.08)		
Spain	0.25	(0.02)	0.17	(0.03)			-0.23	(0.06)	-0.54	(0.09)		
Sweden	0.26	(0.03)	0.27	(0.03)	-0.01	(0.00)	-0.30	(0.09)	-0.27	(0.13)		
Sub-national entities												
Abu Dhabi (United Arab Emirates)	0.42	(0.03)	0.07	(0.03)					-0.80	(0.15)		
Alberta (Canada)	0.31	(0.02)	0.14	(0.03)			-0.25	(0.12)	-0.29	(0.11)		
England (United Kingdom)	0.29	(0.03)	0.21	(0.03)					-0.48	(0.13)	0.47	(0.10)
Flanders (Belgium)	0.26	(0.02)	0.09	(0.04)			-0.28	(0.08)	-0.44	(0.09)		

1. Cells are blank when no significant relationship was found. Significance was tested at the 5% level. The class composition variables (shaded in a different tone) are presented in each model to see how their results vary based on the variables included in each model. Please refer to table B.12.Web in Annex B to see the results of the basic class composition model (not coupled with any other variable).

2. Continuous variable. See the textbox describing this index and Annex B for more details.

3. First model including teacher-student relations and teacher co-operation. Controlling for teacher gender, experience, educational attainment, formal education or training on content, pedagogy and classroom practice for the subject(s) taught, class size, low academic achievers, students with behavioural problems, and gifted students.

4. Second model including the variables "Staff are provided opportunities to actively participate in school decisions" and "instructional leadership". Controlling for teacher gender, experience, educational attainment, formal education or training on content, pedagogy and classroom practice for the subject(s) taught, class size, low academic achievers, students with behavioural problems, and gifted students.

5. Continuous variable combining answers of question 45 of the teacher questionnaire.

6. Continuous variable combining answers of question 33 of the teacher questionnaire.

7. Dichotomous variable where the reference category is "disagree" or "strongly disagree".

8. Continuous variable. See the textbox describing this index and Annex B for more details.

9. Continuous variable where the data are reported by teachers and refer to a randomly chosen class they currently teach from their weekly timetable.

10. The reference category is 10% or less of students are low academic achievers. Data are reported by teachers and refer to a randomly chosen class they currently teach from their weekly timetable.

11. The reference category is 10% or less of students with behavioural problems. Data are reported by teachers and refer to a randomly chosen class they currently teach from their weekly timetable.

12. The reference category is 10% or less of students are academically gifted. Data are reported by teachers and refer to a randomly chosen class they currently teach from their weekly timetable.

Source: OECD, TALIS 2013 Database.

StatLink ᴴᵗᵗᵖ http://dx.doi.org/10.1787/888933047786

[Part 2/2]
Relationship between school environment and teachers' job satisfaction
Significant variables in the multiple linear regressions of teachers' job satisfaction with the following school leadership and school environment variables in lower secondary education[1]

Table 7.9

	Teachers' job satisfaction[2]											
	Model 2[4]											
	Dependent on:											
	Staff are provided opportunities to actively participate in school decisions[7]		Instructional leadership[8]		Class size[9]		More than 10% of students in the classroom are low academic achievers[10]		More than 10% of the students in the classroom have behavioural problems[11]		More than 10% of the students in the classroom are academically gifted students[12]	
	ß	S.E.	ß	S.E.	ß	S.E.	ß	S.E.	ß	S.E.	ß	S.E.
Australia	1.28	(0.13)					-0.39	(0.11)	-0.40	(0.14)	0.34	(0.13)
Brazil	0.93	(0.07)	0.05	(0.02)			-0.41	(0.08)	-0.46	(0.08)	0.25	(0.13)
Bulgaria	1.62	(0.13)					-0.22	(0.10)	-0.47	(0.11)	0.51	(0.11)
Chile	1.04	(0.12)	-0.12	(0.04)					-0.35	(0.14)		
Croatia	1.09	(0.11)					-0.32	(0.08)	-0.44	(0.13)	0.18	(0.08)
Czech Republic	1.32	(0.08)					-0.20	(0.08)	-0.33	(0.09)		
Denmark	1.18	(0.12)					-0.42	(0.09)	-0.60	(0.14)		
Estonia	1.04	(0.09)					-0.32	(0.09)	-0.36	(0.08)	0.28	(0.06)
Finland	0.95	(0.13)					-0.19	(0.08)	-0.40	(0.09)	0.30	(0.09)
France	0.98	(0.09)					-0.28	(0.08)	-0.70	(0.10)	0.20	(0.09)
Iceland	1.07	(0.13)										
Israel	1.26	(0.10)							-0.37	(0.09)		
Italy	1.00	(0.07)					-0.22	(0.08)	-0.32	(0.08)	0.19	(0.08)
Japan	0.80	(0.08)					-0.33	(0.07)	-0.29	(0.12)	0.48	(0.12)
Korea	1.11	(0.08)					-0.27	(0.10)	-0.42	(0.13)	0.36	(0.11)
Latvia	1.10	(0.12)			0.02	(0.01)			-0.29	(0.09)	0.31	(0.08)
Malaysia	0.89	(0.09)	0.06	(0.02)	-0.01	(0.00)			-0.28	(0.08)	0.23	(0.08)
Mexico	0.66	(0.07)							-0.27	(0.07)		
Netherlands	0.96	(0.14)					-0.23	(0.10)				
Norway	0.97	(0.18)										
Poland	1.34	(0.08)							-0.42	(0.09)	0.38	(0.08)
Portugal	1.40	(0.09)					-0.34	(0.09)	-0.32	(0.08)		
Romania	1.36	(0.11)					-0.36	(0.08)	-0.67	(0.12)	0.34	(0.13)
Serbia	1.39	(0.11)					-0.21	(0.08)	-0.47	(0.11)	0.23	(0.09)
Singapore	1.40	(0.06)					-0.28	(0.07)	-0.17	(0.07)		
Slovak Republic	0.96	(0.08)					-0.22	(0.08)	-0.18	(0.09)	0.15	(0.06)
Spain	0.93	(0.08)	0.04	(0.02)			-0.29	(0.07)	-0.61	(0.09)		
Sweden	1.16	(0.11)					-0.30	(0.10)				
Sub-national entities												
Abu Dhabi (United Arab Emirates)	1.32	(0.14)							-0.95	(0.18)		
Alberta (Canada)	1.45	(0.17)					-0.29	(0.13)	-0.33	(0.11)		
England (United Kingdom)	1.34	(0.11)							-0.67	(0.13)	0.45	(0.12)
Flanders (Belgium)	1.19	(0.12)					-0.28	(0.09)	-0.41	(0.11)		

1. Cells are blank when no significant relationship was found. Significance was tested at the 5% level. The class composition variables (shaded in a different tone) are presented in each model to see how their results vary based on the variables included in each model. Please refer to table B.12.Web in Annex B to see the results of the basic class composition model (not coupled with any other variable).
2. Continuous variable. See the textbox describing this index and Annex B for more details.
3. First model including teacher-student relations and teacher co-operation. Controlling for teacher gender, experience, educational attainment, formal education or training on content, pedagogy and classroom practice for the subject(s) taught, class size, low academic achievers, students with behavioural problems, and gifted students.
4. Second model including the variables "Staff are provided opportunities to actively participate in school decisions" and "instructional leadership". Controlling for teacher gender, experience, educational attainment, formal education or training on content, pedagogy and classroom practice for the subject(s) taught, class size, low academic achievers, students with behavioural problems, and gifted students.
5. Continuous variable combining answers of question 45 of the teacher questionnaire.
6. Continuous variable combining answers of question 33 of the teacher questionnaire.
7. Dichotomous variable where the reference category is "disagree" or "strongly disagree".
8. Continuous variable. See the textbox describing this index and Annex B for more details.
9. Continuous variable where the data are reported by teachers and refer to a randomly chosen class they currently teach from their weekly timetable.
10. The reference category is 10% or less of students are low academic achievers. Data are reported by teachers and refer to a randomly chosen class they currently teach from their weekly timetable.
11. The reference category is 10% or less of students with behavioural problems. Data are reported by teachers and refer to a randomly chosen class they currently teach from their weekly timetable.
12. The reference category is 10% or less of students are academically gifted. Data are reported by teachers and refer to a randomly chosen class they currently teach from their weekly timetable.
Source: OECD, TALIS 2013 Database.
StatLink http://dx.doi.org/10.1787/888933047786

[Part 1/1]
Relationship between teacher professional development and teachers' self-efficacy
Significant variables in the multiple linear regressions of teachers' self-efficacy with the following teacher professional development variables in lower secondary education[1]

Table 7.10

	Teachers' self-efficacy[2]											
	Dependent on:											
	Participation in formal induction programme[3]		Participation in informal induction activities[4]		Teachers having a mentor[5]		Teachers serving as mentor[6]		Participation in mentoring and/or peer observation and coaching, as part of a formal school arrangement[7]		Participation in courses/workshops, education conferences or seminars[8]	
	ß	S.E.	ß	S.E.	ß	S.E.	ß	S.E.	ß	S.E.	ß	S.E.
Australia							0.49	0.12				
Brazil	0.21	0.06	0.16	0.06	0.19	0.06						
Bulgaria	0.19	0.09					0.30	0.15				
Chile	0.36	0.14										
Croatia	0.21	0.06							0.22	0.10		
Czech Republic	0.33	0.06			-0.36	0.17			0.24	0.07		
Denmark							0.26	0.11				
Estonia												
Finland							0.48	0.20			0.23	0.09
France	-0.27	0.06					0.44	0.12	0.29	0.09		
Iceland	0.24	0.12										
Israel									0.42	0.09		
Italy	0.19	0.06					0.30	0.14				
Japan			0.28	0.08	-0.18	0.07	0.68	0.08	0.15	0.07		
Korea							0.81	0.10				
Latvia	0.28	0.07							0.26	0.11		
Malaysia					0.27	0.12			0.27	0.08		
Mexico	0.27	0.07					0.37	0.12				
Netherlands												
Norway	0.40	0.20					0.40	0.16				
Poland	0.59	0.07							0.16	0.08		
Portugal			0.19	0.04	0.32	0.13						
Romania	0.19	0.06					0.29	0.11	0.15	0.06		
Serbia	0.17	0.07										
Singapore							0.44	0.08	0.27	0.08		
Slovak Republic							0.35	0.10				
Spain	0.18	0.08							0.34	0.08	0.17	0.09
Sweden									0.38	0.09		
Sub-national entities												
Abu Dhabi (United Arab Emirates)					0.29	0.08	0.18	0.09	0.31	0.08	0.30	0.14
Alberta (Canada)							0.47	0.14				
England (United Kingdom)							0.40	0.08	0.24	0.08		
Flanders (Belgium)					-0.25	0.12	0.20	0.10				

1. Cells are blank when no significant relationship was found. Significance was tested at the 5% level, controlling for teacher gender, experience, educational attainment, formal education or training on content, pedagogy and classroom practice for the subject(s) taught, class size, low academic achievers, students with behavioural problems, and gifted students. Cells with data representing less than 5% of the cases are shaded in grey and should be interpreted with caution. These results are not highlighted in the text of the report.

2. Continuous variable. See the textbox describing this index and Annex B for more details.

3. Dichotomous variable with reference category being teachers who did not participate in a formal induction programme.

4. Dichotomous variable with reference category being teachers who did not participate in informal induction activities.

5. Dichotomous variable with reference category being teachers who do not have a mentor.

6. Dichotomous variable with reference category being teachers who do not serve as a mentor.

7. Dichotomous variable with reference category being teachers who did not participate in mentoring and/or peer observation and coaching, as part of a formal school arrangement.

8. This is the combination of two different questions: "Courses/workshops (e.g. on subject matter or methods and/or other education-related topics)" and "Education conferences or seminars (where teachers and/or researchers present their research results and discuss educational issues)". The reference category is teachers who answered they did not participate in both professional development activities in the 12 months prior to the survey.

Source: OECD, TALIS 2013 Database.

StatLink ⬛⬛⬛ http://dx.doi.org/10.1787/888933047843

[Part 1/1]
Relationship between teacher professional development and teachers' job satisfaction
Significant variables in the multiple linear regressions of teachers' job satisfaction with the following
teacher professional development variables in lower secondary education[1]

Table 7.11

	Teachers' job satisfaction[2] Dependent on:											
	Participation in formal induction programme[3]		Participation in informal induction activities[4]		Teachers having a mentor[5]		Teachers serving as mentor[6]		Participation in mentoring and/or peer observation and coaching, as part of a formal school arrangement[7]		Participation in courses/workshops, education conferences or seminars[8]	
	ß	S.E.	ß	S.E.	ß	S.E.	ß	S.E.	ß	S.E.	ß	S.E.
Australia			0.28	0.14	0.47	0.16			0.28	0.11	0.54	0.20
Brazil	0.20	0.07	0.17	0.07	0.12	0.06					0.22	0.07
Bulgaria	0.45	0.10	0.28	0.09								
Chile												
Croatia	0.21	0.08	0.17	0.08	0.37	0.18						
Czech Republic			0.17	0.07			0.30	0.12				
Denmark	0.30	0.12										
Estonia									0.23	0.08		
Finland			0.24	0.10								
France	-0.24	0.09	0.33	0.08			0.45	0.19				
Iceland												
Israel									0.28	0.10		
Italy							0.41	0.14				
Japan	-0.28	0.10			0.31	0.08						
Korea					0.48	0.11	0.43	0.11				
Latvia							0.41	0.18				
Malaysia			0.15	0.07	0.20	0.08					0.27	0.12
Mexico	0.25	0.07	0.14	0.07								
Netherlands			0.21	0.09								
Norway	0.39	0.15	0.29	0.12			0.37	0.16				
Poland	0.39	0.06					0.39	0.08				
Portugal					0.39	0.17						
Romania												
Serbia												
Singapore			0.19	0.08	0.38	0.08			0.24	0.07		
Slovak Republic												
Spain			0.18	0.07					0.22	0.08		
Sweden			0.30	0.12	0.73	0.28	0.62	0.22	0.39	0.11		
Sub-national entities												
Abu Dhabi (United Arab Emirates)												
Alberta (Canada)									0.31	0.13		
England (United Kingdom)			0.22	0.10							0.50	0.12
Flanders (Belgium)	0.19	0.08										

1. Cells are blank when no significant relationship was found. Significance was tested at the 5% level, controlling for teacher gender, experience, educational attainment, formal education or training on content, pedagogy and classroom practice for the subject(s) taught, class size, low academic achievers, students with behavioural problems, and gifted students. Cells with data representing less than 5% of the cases are shaded in grey and should be interpreted with caution. These results are not highlighted in the text of the report.

2. Continuous variable. See the textbox describing this index and Annex B for more details.

3. Dichotomous variable with reference category being teachers who did not participate in a formal induction programme.

4. Dichotomous variable with reference category being teachers who did not participate in informal induction activities.

5. Dichotomous variable with reference category being teachers who do not have a mentor.

6. Dichotomous variable with reference category being teachers who do not serve as a mentor.

7. Dichotomous variable with reference category being teachers who did not participate in mentoring and/or peer observation and coaching, as part of a formal school arrangement.

8. This is the combination of two different questions: "Courses/workshops (e.g. on subject matter or methods and/or other education-related topics)" and "Education conferences or seminars (where teachers and/or researchers present their research results and discuss educational issues)". The reference category is teachers who answered they did not participate in both professional development activities in the 12 months prior to the survey.

Source: OECD, TALIS 2013 Database.

StatLink http://dx.doi.org/10.1787/888933047881

[Part 1/1]
Relationship between teacher feedback and self-efficacy
Results of the multiple linear regressions of teachers' self-efficacy with the following teacher appraisal and feedback variables in lower secondary education[1]

Table 7.12

	Teachers' self-efficacy[2]											
	Model 1[3]		Model 2[3]		Model 3[3]		Model 4[3]		Model 5[3]		Model 6[3]	
	Dependent on:											
	Teacher receives feedback from direct classroom observation from at least two evaluators[4]		Teacher receives feedback from student surveys[5]		Teacher receives feedback from students' test scores[6]		Teacher feedback emphasised on student behaviour and classroom management[7]		Teacher appraisal and feedback impact classroom teaching[8]		Teacher appraisal and feedback are largely done to fulfil administrative requirements[9]	
	ß	S.E.	ß	S.E.	ß	S.E.	ß	S.E.	ß	S.E.	ß	S.E.
Australia					0.27	(0.11)						
Brazil	0.16	(0.06)	0.48	(0.07)	0.52	(0.11)	0.64	(0.10)	0.18	(0.07)		
Bulgaria	0.24	(0.08)	0.36	(0.08)			0.51	(0.10)	0.19	(0.09)		
Chile			0.28	(0.13)								
Croatia			0.25	(0.07)	0.34	(0.06)					-0.15	(0.06)
Czech Republic	0.20	(0.08)	0.54	(0.06)	0.38	(0.07)	0.29	(0.15)			-0.20	(0.07)
Denmark			0.20	(0.09)	0.26	(0.11)					-0.23	(0.07)
Estonia			0.18	(0.08)	0.18	(0.08)	0.44	(0.12)				
Finland	0.55	(0.13)					0.28	(0.14)	0.47	(0.11)		
France			0.22	(0.06)	0.37	(0.06)					-0.21	(0.07)
Iceland	0.69	(0.24)	0.46	(0.17)			0.44	(0.21)				
Israel			0.52	(0.09)	0.42	(0.10)	0.50	(0.15)			-0.45	(0.10)
Italy			0.48	(0.09)	0.31	(0.11)	0.44	(0.17)	0.17	(0.09)		
Japan	0.14	(0.07)	0.28	(0.07)	0.29	(0.08)						
Korea			0.72	(0.13)	0.54	(0.17)	0.79	(0.15)				
Latvia			0.51	(0.10)	0.34	(0.15)	0.35	(0.13)				
Malaysia	0.37	(0.10)	0.35	(0.09)	0.42	(0.21)	0.94	(0.23)				
Mexico			0.22	(0.10)								
Netherlands												
Norway	0.47	(0.10)	0.40	(0.15)	0.49	(0.12)					-0.16	(0.08)
Poland	0.21	(0.09)	0.35	(0.09)	0.29	(0.13)	0.38	(0.16)	0.24	(0.09)	-0.30	(0.08)
Portugal	0.17	(0.06)	0.34	(0.05)	0.22	(0.06)	0.32	(0.11)	0.18	(0.05)	-0.32	(0.05)
Romania	0.18	(0.07)	0.51	(0.12)	0.47	(0.11)	0.52	(0.14)	0.26	(0.06)	-0.21	(0.06)
Serbia			0.23	(0.08)	0.24	(0.06)	0.51	(0.11)			-0.26	(0.07)
Singapore			0.36	(0.08)	0.48	(0.10)			-0.19	(0.08)		
Slovak Republic			0.39	(0.07)	0.53	(0.08)	0.53	(0.14)			-0.38	(0.06)
Spain	0.43	(0.11)	0.30	(0.09)			0.19	(0.10)	0.31	(0.09)	-0.28	(0.09)
Sweden			0.32	(0.10)	0.44	(0.09)	0.36	(0.13)	0.25	(0.11)	-0.27	(0.09)
Sub-national entities												
Abu Dhabi (United Arab Emirates)	0.24	(0.08)	0.66	(0.09)	0.74	(0.14)	0.38	(0.12)	0.49	(0.11)		
Alberta (Canada)			0.36	(0.11)								
England (United Kingdom)			0.36	(0.09)	0.35	(0.13)					-0.43	(0.10)
Flanders (Belgium)			0.18	(0.07)	0.18	(0.07)						

1. Cells are blank when no significant relationship was found. Significance was tested at the 5% level. Cells with data representing less than 5% of the cases are shaded in grey and should be interpreted with caution. These results are not highlighted in the text of the report.

2. Continuous variable. See the textbox describing this index and Annex B for more details.

3. Controlling for teacher gender, experience, educational attainment, formal education or training on content, pedagogy and classroom practice for the subject(s) taught, class size, low academic achievers, students with behavioural problems, and gifted students in each model. Each model was run independently.

4. Dichotomous variable where the reference category is less than two evaluators. Evaluators can be: *i)* External individuals or bodies, *ii)* School principal, *iii)* Member(s) of the school management team, *iv)* Assigned mentors, or *v)* Other teachers (not part of the school management team). This information is derived from question 28a from the teacher questionnaire.

5. Dichotomous variable where the reference category is "teacher who never received feedback from student surveys about his teaching". The feedback from student surveys can come from: *i)* External individuals or bodies, *ii)* School principal, *iii)* Member(s) of the school management team, *iv)* Assigned mentors, or *v)* Other teachers (not part of the school management team). This information is derived from question 28b of the teacher questionnaire.

6. Dichotomous variable where the reference category is "teacher who never received feedback from his students' test scores". The feedback from students' test scores can come from: *i)* External individuals or bodies, *ii)* School principal, *iii)* Member(s) of the school management team, *iv)* Assigned mentors, or *v)* Other teachers (not part of the school management team). This information is derived from question 28d of the teacher questionnaire.

7. Dichotomous variable where the reference category is the feedback received "did not" consider student behaviour and classroom management or was considered with "low importance". This information is derived from question 29e of the teacher questionnaire.

8. Dichotomous variable where the reference category is teacher "agree" or "strongly agree" that, in his school, teacher appraisal and feedback have little impact upon the way teachers teach in the classroom. This information is derived from question 31b of the teacher questionnaire.

9. Dichotomous variable where the reference category is teacher "disagree" or "strongly disagree" that, in his school, teacher appraisal and feedback are largely done to fulfil administrative requirements. This information is derived from question 31c of the teacher questionnaire.

Source: OECD, TALIS 2013 Database.

StatLink http://dx.doi.org/10.1787/888933047919

[Part 1/1]
Relationship between teacher feedback and job satisfaction
Results of the multiple linear regressions of teachers' job satisfaction with the following teacher appraisal and feedback variables in lower secondary education[1]

Table 7.13

	Teachers' job satisfaction[2]											
	Model 1[3]		Model 2[3]		Model 3[3]		Model 4[3]		Model 5[3]		Model 6[3]	
	Dependent on:											
	Teacher receives feedback from direct classroom observation from at least two evaluators[4]		Teacher receives feedback from student surveys[5]		Teacher receives feedback from students' test scores[6]		Teacher feedback emphasised on student behaviour and classroom management[7]		Teacher appraisal and feedback impact classroom teaching[8]		Teacher appraisal and feedback are largely done to fulfil administrative requirements[9]	
	β	S.E.	β	S.E.	β	S.E.	β	S.E.	β	S.E.	β	S.E.
Australia	0.49	(0.20)					0.46	(0.12)	0.54	(0.12)	-0.83	(0.09)
Brazil	0.44	(0.08)	0.48	(0.08)	0.63	(0.15)	0.81	(0.12)	0.40	(0.08)	-0.19	(0.08)
Bulgaria			0.30	(0.13)	0.42	(0.15)	0.72	(0.13)	0.73	(0.11)	-1.12	(0.13)
Chile	0.35	(0.16)					0.64	(0.27)	0.43	(0.15)	-0.47	(0.15)
Croatia	0.18	(0.09)	0.24	(0.09)	0.32	(0.09)	0.63	(0.13)	0.29	(0.08)	-0.70	(0.08)
Czech Republic	0.28	(0.06)	0.26	(0.08)	0.23	(0.09)	0.58	(0.14)	0.51	(0.07)	-0.79	(0.07)
Denmark					0.23	(0.11)			0.50	(0.12)	-0.64	(0.14)
Estonia	0.16	(0.08)	0.27	(0.09)	0.28	(0.08)	0.50	(0.12)	0.46	(0.06)	-0.65	(0.07)
Finland	0.60	(0.15)					0.37	(0.14)	0.52	(0.13)	-0.65	(0.11)
France					0.21	(0.10)			0.27	(0.09)	-0.52	(0.08)
Iceland	0.76	(0.22)							0.44	(0.17)	-0.79	(0.17)
Israel	0.33	(0.09)	0.20	(0.10)			0.43	(0.13)	0.32	(0.11)	-0.98	(0.11)
Italy			0.26	(0.10)					0.52	(0.11)	-0.80	(0.10)
Japan	0.23	(0.07)			0.26	(0.07)					-0.54	(0.07)
Korea					0.73	(0.18)	0.42	(0.12)	0.20	(0.10)	-0.41	(0.08)
Latvia			0.47	(0.11)					0.28	(0.09)	-0.50	(0.09)
Malaysia	0.32	(0.08)					0.80	(0.29)	0.45	(0.08)	-0.48	(0.09)
Mexico	0.24	(0.08)	0.20	(0.08)			0.31	(0.09)	0.43	(0.06)	-0.46	(0.07)
Netherlands	0.23	(0.10)							0.44	(0.11)	-0.63	(0.12)
Norway	0.40	(0.10)	0.43	(0.16)			0.73	(0.15)	0.58	(0.12)	-0.77	(0.11)
Poland	0.32	(0.10)			0.27	(0.13)	0.41	(0.15)	0.62	(0.08)	-0.72	(0.09)
Portugal	0.51	(0.09)	0.58	(0.08)	0.22	(0.09)	0.61	(0.16)	0.53	(0.08)	-0.79	(0.08)
Romania			0.71	(0.27)	0.49	(0.16)			0.61	(0.10)	-0.41	(0.08)
Serbia			0.20	(0.09)	0.37	(0.10)	0.68	(0.17)	0.42	(0.08)	-0.79	(0.10)
Singapore	0.27	(0.06)	0.24	(0.07)			0.22	(0.09)	0.52	(0.08)	-0.79	(0.07)
Slovak Republic	0.16	(0.06)	0.21	(0.07)	0.28	(0.08)	0.48	(0.16)			-0.54	(0.06)
Spain	0.41	(0.09)	0.27	(0.08)	-0.23	(0.08)	0.23	(0.10)	0.28	(0.09)	-0.79	(0.09)
Sweden			0.42	(0.14)	0.53	(0.11)	0.48	(0.15)	0.28	(0.11)	-1.05	(0.12)
Sub-national entities												
Abu Dhabi (United Arab Emirates)	0.46	(0.10)	0.52	(0.12)	0.49	(0.22)	0.64	(0.17)	0.66	(0.14)	-0.59	(0.13)
Alberta (Canada)	0.43	(0.11)	0.26	(0.12)			0.49	(0.14)	0.48	(0.14)	-0.79	(0.12)
England (United Kingdom)	0.28	(0.12)	0.45	(0.10)	0.35	(0.11)	0.37	(0.12)	0.76	(0.12)	-1.19	(0.10)
Flanders (Belgium)	0.19	(0.09)					0.46	(0.12)	0.31	(0.09)	-0.62	(0.08)

1. Cells are blank when no significant relationship was found. Significance was tested at the 5% level. Cells with data representing less than 5% of the cases are shaded in grey and should be interpreted with caution. These results are not highlighted in the text of the report.

2. Continuous variable. See the textbox describing this index and Annex B for more details.

3. Controlling for teacher gender, experience, educational attainment, formal education or training on content, pedagogy and classroom practice for the subject(s) taught, class size, low academic achievers, students with behavioural problems, and gifted students in each model. Each model was run independently.

4. Dichotomous variable where the reference category is less than two evaluators. Evaluators can be: i) External individuals or bodies, ii) School principal, iii) Member(s) of the school management team, iv) Assigned mentors, or v) Other teachers (not part of the school management team).

5. Dichotomous variable where the reference category is "teacher who never received feedback from student surveys about his teaching". The feedback from student surveys can come from: i) External individuals or bodies, ii) School principal, iii) Member(s) of the school management team, iv) Assigned mentors, or v) Other teachers (not part of the school management team).

6. Dichotomous variable where the reference category is "teacher who never received feedback from his students' test scores". The feedback from students' test scores can come from: i) External individuals or bodies, ii) School principal, iii) Member(s) of the school management team, iv) Assigned mentors, or v) Other teachers (not part of the school management team).

7. Dichotomous variable where the reference category is the feedback received "did not" consider student behaviour and classroom management or was considered with "low importance".

8. Dichotomous variable where the reference category is teacher "agree" or "strongly agree" that, in his school, teacher appraisal and feedback have little impact upon the way teachers teach in the classroom.

9. Dichotomous variable where the reference category is teacher "disagree" or "strongly disagree" that, in his school, teacher appraisal and feedback are largely done to fulfil administrative requirements.

Source: OECD, TALIS 2013 Database.

StatLink ⟲ http://dx.doi.org/10.1787/888933047957

[Part 1/1]

Relationship between teachers' working hours, beliefs and practices and self-efficacy

Significant variables in the multiple linear regressions of teachers' self-efficacy with teachers' working hours, teaching beliefs and practices in lower secondary education[1]

Table 7.14

	Teachers' self-efficacy[2]							
	Model 1[3]		Model 2[3]		Model 3[3]		Model 4[3]	
	Dependent on:							
	Teacher constructivist beliefs[4]		Hours of work per week[5]		Proportion of class time spent on keeping order[6]		Proportion of class time spent on administrative tasks[6]	
	ß	S.E.	ß	S.E.	ß	S.E.	ß	S.E.
Australia	0.16	0.03			-0.03	0.00	-0.04	0.02
Brazil	0.11	0.01	0.00	0.00	-0.02	0.00	-0.01	0.00
Bulgaria	0.24	0.03	0.01	0.00	-0.03	0.01	-0.03	0.01
Chile	0.09	0.03			-0.01	0.01	-0.03	0.01
Croatia	0.14	0.02	0.02	0.00	-0.04	0.01		
Czech Republic	0.15	0.02	0.01	0.00	-0.04	0.00		
Denmark	0.11	0.02			-0.04	0.01		
Estonia	0.29	0.03	0.01	0.00	-0.01	0.00		
Finland	0.23	0.03	0.01	0.00	-0.02	0.00	-0.02	0.01
France	0.07	0.02			-0.02	0.00		
Iceland	0.14	0.03			-0.03	0.01		
Israel	0.22	0.02	0.01	0.00	-0.05	0.01	-0.03	0.01
Italy	0.04	0.02	0.01	0.00	-0.02	0.00		
Japan	0.25	0.02						
Korea	0.17	0.02	0.01	0.00	-0.01	0.01		
Latvia	0.17	0.02	0.01	0.00	-0.02	0.00		
Malaysia	0.19	0.02	0.01	0.00				
Mexico	0.13	0.02	0.01	0.00	-0.03	0.00		
Netherlands	0.12	0.02	0.01	0.01	-0.02	0.00	-0.03	0.01
Norway	0.11	0.04	0.01	0.00	-0.05	0.01	-0.03	0.01
Poland	0.15	0.02	0.01	0.00	-0.03	0.01	-0.02	0.01
Portugal	0.10	0.01	0.00	0.00	-0.02	0.00		
Romania	0.06	0.01			-0.02	0.00		
Serbia	0.20	0.02	0.01	0.00	-0.04	0.00	-0.01	0.01
Singapore	0.17	0.02	0.01	0.00	-0.02	0.00		
Slovak Republic	0.13	0.02	0.00	0.00	-0.03	0.00	-0.02	0.01
Spain	0.07	0.02	0.01	0.00	-0.03	0.00		
Sweden	0.07	0.03			-0.02	0.00		
Sub-national entities								
Abu Dhabi (United Arab Emirates)	0.14	0.02	0.01	0.00	-0.02	0.01		
Alberta (Canada)	0.10	0.03			-0.03	0.00		
England (United Kingdom)	0.11	0.02	0.01	0.00	-0.03	0.00	-0.03	0.01
Flanders (Belgium)	0.14	0.02	0.01	0.00	-0.02	0.00		

1. Cells are blank when no significant relationship was found. Significance was tested at the 5% level.

2. Continuous variable. See the textbox describing this index and Annex B for more details.

3. Controlling for teacher gender, experience, educational attainment, formal education or training on content, pedagogy and classroom practice for the subject(s) taught, class size, low academic achievers, students with behavioural problems, and gifted students in each model. Each model was run independently.

4. Continuous variable combining answers of question 32 of the teacher questionnaire.

5. Continuous variable where 90 hours or more are excluded. This is referring to the most recent complete calendar week the teacher completed prior to the survey. It includes the hours spent on teaching, planning lessons, marking, collaborating with other teachers, participating in staff meetings and other related tasks.

6. Continuous variable from question 39 of the teacher questionnaire.

Source: OECD, TALIS 2013 Database.

StatLink ⟐ http://dx.doi.org/10.1787/888933047995

[Part 1/1]
Relationship between teachers' working hours, beliefs and practices and job satisfaction
Significant variables in the multiple linear regressions of teachers' job satisfaction with teachers' working hours, teaching beliefs and practices in lower secondary education[1]

Table 7.15

	Teachers' job satisfaction[2]							
	Model 1[3]		Model 2[3]		Model 3[3]		Model 4[3]	
	Dependent on:							
	Teacher constructivist beliefs[4]		Hours of work per week[5]		Proportion of class time spent on keeping order[6]		Proportion of class time spent on administrative tasks[6]	
	ß	S.E.	ß	S.E.	ß	S.E.	ß	S.E.
Australia	0.17	0.03			-0.04	0.00		
Brazil	0.07	0.02			-0.02	0.00		
Bulgaria	0.11	0.03	-0.01	0.00	-0.03	0.01		
Chile	0.09	0.03			-0.02	0.01		
Croatia	0.12	0.02			-0.03	0.01	-0.02	0.01
Czech Republic	0.14	0.02			-0.02	0.00	-0.02	0.01
Denmark	0.14	0.04			-0.02	0.01		
Estonia	0.13	0.02	0.00	0.00	-0.02	0.00	-0.02	0.01
Finland					-0.02	0.00	-0.03	0.01
France	0.09	0.02			-0.03	0.00	-0.02	0.01
Iceland	0.06	0.03			-0.01	0.01		
Israel	0.12	0.03			-0.02	0.01		
Italy					-0.01	0.00		
Japan	0.17	0.03			-0.01	0.00		
Korea	0.08	0.02			-0.02	0.01		
Latvia	0.11	0.02			-0.01	0.00		
Malaysia	0.11	0.02			-0.01	0.00	-0.01	0.00
Mexico	0.07	0.02			-0.02	0.00	-0.01	0.00
Netherlands	0.10	0.03	0.01	0.00	-0.02	0.01	-0.02	0.01
Norway	0.19	0.06			-0.03	0.01	-0.03	0.01
Poland	0.11	0.02			-0.03	0.01		
Portugal			-0.01	0.00	-0.03	0.00		
Romania	0.05	0.02			-0.02	0.01		
Serbia	0.12	0.02			-0.03	0.01		
Singapore	0.06	0.02	-0.01	0.00	-0.01	0.00	-0.02	0.00
Slovak Republic	0.04	0.02			-0.02	0.00		
Spain	0.07	0.02			-0.03	0.00	-0.02	0.01
Sweden	0.12	0.04			-0.03	0.00	-0.02	0.01
Sub-national entities								
Abu Dhabi (United Arab Emirates)	0.10	0.04	0.01	0.00	-0.03	0.01	-0.03	0.01
Alberta (Canada)	0.08	0.03			-0.02	0.01	-0.02	0.01
England (United Kingdom)	0.09	0.03			-0.03	0.00	-0.02	0.01
Flanders (Belgium)	0.12	0.03	-0.01	0.00	-0.01	0.00	-0.01	0.01

1. Cells are blank when no significant relationship was found. Significance was tested at the 5% level.

2. Continuous variable. See the textbox describing this index and Annex B for more details.

3. Controlling for teacher gender, experience, educational attainment, formal education or training on content, pedagogy and classroom practice for the subject(s) taught, class size, low academic achievers, students with behavioural problems, and gifted students in each model. Each model was run independently.

4. Continuous variable combining answers of question 32 of the teacher questionnaire.

5. Continuous variable where 90 hours or more are excluded. This is referring to the most recent complete calendar week the teacher completed prior to the survey. It includes the hours spent on teaching, planning lessons, marking, collaborating with other teachers, participating in staff meetings and other related tasks.

6. Continuous variable from question 39 of the teacher questionnaire.

Source: OECD, TALIS 2013 Database.

StatLink http://dx.doi.org/10.1787/888933048090

[Part 1/1]

Relationship between teachers' collaboration and self-efficacy

Significant variables in the multiple linear regressions of teachers' self-efficacy with teachers' professional collaborative practices in lower secondary education[1]

Table 7.16

	Teachers' self-efficacy[2]							
	Dependent on:							
	Teach jointly as a team in the same class 5 times a year or more[3]		Observe other teachers classes and provide feedback 5 times a year or more[3]		Engage in joint activities across different classes and age groups 5 times a year or more[3]		Take part in collaborative professional learning 5 times a year or more[3]	
	ß	S.E.	ß	S.E.	ß	S.E.	ß	S.E.
Australia					0.39	0.15	0.38	0.13
Brazil	0.26	0.07			0.27	0.08	0.37	0.07
Bulgaria					0.33	0.07	0.56	0.08
Chile	0.41	0.13					0.56	0.14
Croatia	0.37	0.16			0.46	0.13	0.33	0.07
Czech Republic			0.21	0.10	0.50	0.07	0.42	0.06
Denmark					0.22	0.09	0.21	0.09
Estonia	0.16	0.08			0.30	0.08	0.50	0.08
Finland	0.29	0.10			0.62	0.12	0.76	0.13
France					0.36	0.07		
Iceland					0.56	0.17	0.31	0.13
Israel					0.30	0.08	0.58	0.08
Italy			0.19	0.10	0.20	0.06	0.37	0.07
Japan	0.17	0.07	0.23	0.07			0.36	0.07
Korea	0.27	0.12					0.75	0.15
Latvia	0.20	0.09	0.18	0.08	0.33	0.11	0.35	0.09
Malaysia	0.23	0.10			0.32	0.11	0.47	0.11
Mexico	0.30	0.09	0.18	0.09			0.40	0.09
Netherlands			0.40	0.13			0.30	0.10
Norway	0.26	0.09					0.35	0.17
Poland	0.17	0.07	0.23	0.09	0.37	0.08	0.34	0.08
Portugal					0.25	0.05	0.29	0.07
Romania	0.20	0.07	0.23	0.06	0.22	0.07	0.21	0.06
Serbia			0.49	0.10	0.40	0.09	0.31	0.08
Singapore	-0.16	0.08	0.32	0.11	0.34	0.12	0.26	0.08
Slovak Republic	0.49	0.07	0.28	0.10	0.35	0.08		
Spain					0.42	0.11	0.47	0.07
Sweden			0.42	0.13	0.41	0.11	0.27	0.07
Sub-national entities								
Abu Dhabi (United Arab Emirates)			0.28	0.09	0.41	0.08	0.33	0.11
Alberta (Canada)					0.28	0.14	0.33	0.09
England (United Kingdom)			0.32	0.09	0.42	0.10	0.34	0.09
Flanders (Belgium)			0.42	0.18	0.16	0.08	0.24	0.12

1. Cells are blank when no significant relationship was found. Significance was tested at the 5% level, controlling for gender, education, work experience as teacher in total, elements included in teacher formal education or training, class size, low academic achievers, students with behavioural problems, and academically gifted students. Cells with data representing less than 5% of the cases are shaded in grey and should be interpreted with caution. These results are not highlighted in the text of the report.

2. Continuous variable. See the textbox describing this index and Annex B for more details.

3. The reference category for this collaborative practice is less than five times a year.

Source: OECD, TALIS 2013 Database.

StatLink ᵐˢᵖ http://dx.doi.org/10.1787/888933048185

[Part 1/1]
Relationship between teachers' collaboration and job satisfaction
Significant variables in the multiple linear regressions of teachers' job satisfaction with teachers' professional
Table 7.17 *collaborative practices in lower secondary education[1]*

	Teach jointly as a team in the same class 5 times a year or more[3]		Observe other teachers classes and provide feedback 5 times a year or more[3]		Engage in joint activities across different classes and age groups 5 times a year or more[3]		Take part in collaborative professional learning 5 times a year or more[3]	
	ß	S.E.	ß	S.E.	ß	S.E.	ß	S.E.
Australia							0.52	0.13
Brazil							0.56	0.08
Bulgaria							0.33	0.13
Chile	0.45	0.13					0.63	0.13
Croatia							0.38	0.09
Czech Republic			0.30	0.09	0.27	0.09	0.35	0.07
Denmark			0.28	0.14			0.29	0.12
Estonia	0.33	0.08					0.35	0.08
Finland			0.39	0.18			0.46	0.13
France	0.24	0.09			0.37	0.09		
Iceland					0.30	0.14	0.49	0.13
Israel			0.30	0.15	0.29	0.12		
Italy					0.33	0.08	0.24	0.09
Japan			0.34	0.09				
Korea			0.54	0.20				
Latvia			0.33	0.13	0.24	0.09		
Malaysia	0.19	0.08						
Mexico							0.37	0.08
Netherlands							0.27	0.11
Norway	0.33	0.12					0.51	0.15
Poland	0.18	0.07	0.38	0.12	0.20	0.08		
Portugal					0.20	0.09	0.40	0.10
Romania			0.30	0.11				
Serbia			0.50	0.12	0.37	0.11	0.32	0.09
Singapore			0.21	0.09	0.23	0.10	0.33	0.07
Slovak Republic			0.36	0.09	0.14	0.07		
Spain					0.29	0.10	0.41	0.06
Sweden			0.49	0.15	0.30	0.14	0.53	0.11
Sub-national entities								
Abu Dhabi (United Arab Emirates)					0.44	0.15		
Alberta (Canada)			0.38	0.15			0.37	0.11
England (United Kingdom)	0.22	0.11	0.39	0.11	0.30	0.14	0.48	0.10
Flanders (Belgium)	-0.28	0.14			0.27	0.12		

1. Cells are blank when no significant relationship was found. Significance was tested at the 5% level, controlling for gender, education, work experience as teacher in total, elements included in teacher formal education or training, class size, low academic achievers, students with behavioural problems, and academically gifted students.
2. Continuous variable. See the textbox describing this index and Annex B for more details.
3. The reference category for this collaborative practice is less than five times a year.
Source: OECD, TALIS 2013 Database.

StatLink http://dx.doi.org/10.1787/888933048223

LIST OF TABLES ONLY AVAILABLE ON LINE

The following tables are available in electronic form only.

Chapter 2 Teachers and their schools

Chapter 3 The importance of school leadership

...

Table 3.18.Web	Relationship between principals' instructional leadership and school climate, detailed results http://dx.doi.org/10.1787/888933044195
Table 3.19.Web	Relationship between principals' leadership style and job satisfaction, detailed results http://dx.doi.org/10.1787/888933044233
Table 3.20.Web	Relationship between principals' job satisfaction and principals' characteristics, detailed results http://dx.doi.org/10.1787/888933044271
Table 3.21.Web	Relationship between principals' job satisfaction and school characteristics, detailed results http://dx.doi.org/10.1787/888933044309
Table 3.22.Web	Relationship between principals' job satisfaction and school climate, detailed results http://dx.doi.org/10.1787/888933044347
Table 3.23.Web	Relationship between principals' job satisfaction and barriers for principals, detailed results http://dx.doi.org/10.1787/888933044385
Table 3.24.Web	Principals' perceived barriers to their effectiveness http://dx.doi.org/10.1787/888933044404
Table 3.24.a.Web	Primary education principals' perceived barriers to their effectiveness http://dx.doi.org/10.1787/888933044423
Table 3.24.b.Web	Upper secondary education principals' perceived barriers to their effectiveness http://dx.doi.org/10.1787/888933044442
Table 3.25.Web	Principals' perceived barriers to their effectiveness, detailed results http://dx.doi.org/10.1787/888933044461
Table 3.26.Web	Principals' job satisfaction, detailed results http://dx.doi.org/10.1787/888933044480
Table 3.27.Web	Principals working in schools with high or low percentage of students with different first language http://dx.doi.org/10.1787/888933044499
Table 3.28.Web	Principals working in schools with high or low percentage of students with special needs http://dx.doi.org/10.1787/888933044518
Table 3.29.Web	Principals working in schools with high or low percentage of students from disadvantaged homes http://dx.doi.org/10.1787/888933044537
Table 3.30.Web	Distribution of principals in urban and rural schools based experience and education http://dx.doi.org/10.1787/888933044556
Table 3.31.Web	School location http://dx.doi.org/10.1787/888933044575
Table 3.32.Web	School governing board http://dx.doi.org/10.1787/888933044594
Table 3.33.Web	Parental involvement opportunities http://dx.doi.org/10.1787/888933044613
Table 3.34.Web	School decisions and collaborative school culture, teacher responses http://dx.doi.org/10.1787/888933044632
Table 3.35.Web	School decisions and collaborative school culture, principal responses http://dx.doi.org/10.1787/888933044651
Table 3.36.Web	Correlation between instructional and distributed leadership of principals http://dx.doi.org/10.1787/888933044670
Table 3.37.Web	Correlation between principals' job satisfaction in profession and work environment http://dx.doi.org/10.1787/888933044689
Table 3.38.Web	Standard deviation for tables related to school leadership http://dx.doi.org/10.1787/888933044708

Chapter 4 Developing and supporting teachers

Table 4.9.Web	Type of professional development recently undertaken by teachers, detailed results http://dx.doi.org/10.1787/888933045031
Table 4.10.Web	Content and positive impact of professional development activities, detailed results http://dx.doi.org/10.1787/888933045069
Table 4.12.Web	Teachers' needs for professional development, detailed results http://dx.doi.org/10.1787/888933045183
Table 4.13.Web	Professional development participation resulting from needs for pedagogy and teaching diversity, detailed results http://dx.doi.org/10.1787/888933045221
Table 4.14.Web	Barriers to teachers' participation in professional development, detailed results http://dx.doi.org/10.1787/888933045259

...

Chapter 5 Improving teaching using appraisal and feedback

...

 TALIS 2013 RESULTS: AN INTERNATIONAL PERSPECTIVE ON TEACHING AND LEARNING

Table 5.5.Web.5	Methods for providing feedback to teachers – Other teachers http://dx.doi.org/10.1787/888933045981
Table 5.5.Web.6	Teachers not receiving feedback – by method http://dx.doi.org/10.1787/888933046000
Table 5.7.Web	Outcomes of teacher feedback, detailed results http://dx.doi.org/10.1787/888933046171
Table 5.8.Web	Impact of teacher appraisal and feedback systems in schools, detailed results http://dx.doi.org/10.1787/888933046228
Table 5.10.Web	Sources for teachers' feedback http://dx.doi.org/10.1787/888933046266
Table 5.11.Web	Methods for teachers' feedback http://dx.doi.org/10.1787/888933046285

Chapter 6 Examining teacher practices and classroom environment

Table 6.1.Web	Teaching practices, detailed results http://dx.doi.org/10.1787/888933046361
Table 6.1.a.Web	Teaching practices in primary education, detailed results http://dx.doi.org/10.1787/888933046380
Table 6.1.b.Web	Teaching practices in upper secondary education, detailed results http://dx.doi.org/10.1787/888933046399
Table 6.2.Web	Relationships between teachers' characteristics and small group practice, detailed results http://dx.doi.org/10.1787/888933046437
Table 6.3.Web	Relationships between teachers' characteristics and use of projects, detailed results http://dx.doi.org/10.1787/888933046475
Table 6.4.Web	Relationships between teachers' characteristics and use of ICT, detailed results http://dx.doi.org/10.1787/888933046513
Table 6.5.Web	Relationships between professional development and small group practice, detailed results http://dx.doi.org/10.1787/888933046551
Table 6.6.Web	Relationships between professional development and use of projects, detailed results http://dx.doi.org/10.1787/888933046589
Table 6.7.Web	Relationships between professional development and use of ICT, detailed results http://dx.doi.org/10.1787/888933046627
Table 6.8.Web	Relationships between classroom context and small groups practice, detailed results http://dx.doi.org/10.1787/888933046665
Table 6.9.Web	Relationships between classroom context and the reported use of projects, detailed results http://dx.doi.org/10.1787/888933046703
Table 6.10.Web	Relationships between classroom context and use of ICT, detailed results http://dx.doi.org/10.1787/888933046741
Table 6.11.Web	Teachers' use of student assessment practices, detailed results http://dx.doi.org/10.1787/888933046779
Table 6.13.Web	Teachers' beliefs about teaching and learning, detailed results http://dx.doi.org/10.1787/888933046912
Table 6.13.a.Web	Teachers' beliefs about teaching and learning in primary education, detailed results http://dx.doi.org/10.1787/888933046931
Table 6.13.b.Web	Teachers' beliefs about teaching and learning in upper secondary education, detailed results http://dx.doi.org/10.1787/888933046950
Table 6.14.Web	Relationship between teaching beliefs and practices, detailed results http://dx.doi.org/10.1787/888933046988
Table 6.15.Web	Teacher co-operation, detailed results http://dx.doi.org/10.1787/888933047064
Table 6.15.a.Web	Teacher co-operation in primary education, detailed results http://dx.doi.org/10.1787/888933047083
Table 6.15.b.Web	Teacher co-operation in upper secondary education, detailed results http://dx.doi.org/10.1787/888933047102
Table 6.16.Web	Relationships between teachers' professional development activities and collaboration, detailed results http://dx.doi.org/10.1787/888933047140
Table 6.17.Web	Relationships between teachers' professional development activities and co-operation, detailed results http://dx.doi.org/10.1787/888933047178

...

Table 6.18.Web	Correlation between participation among stakeholders in the school and teaching co-ordination, detailed results http://dx.doi.org/10.1787/888933047216
Table 6.19.Web	Correlation between participation among stakeholders in the school and teacher professional collaboration, detailed results http://dx.doi.org/10.1787/888933047254
Table 6.21.Web	Classroom discipline, detailed results http://dx.doi.org/10.1787/888933047368
Table 6.22.Web	Correlation between actual teaching and learning and classroom discipline, detailed results http://dx.doi.org/10.1787/888933047406
Table 6.23.Web	Estimates of covariance parameters – intra-class correlation http://dx.doi.org/10.1787/888933047425
Table 6.24.Web	Standard deviation related to teachers' beliefs and practices http://dx.doi.org/10.1787/888933047444

Chapter 7 Teacher self-efficacy and job satisfaction: Why they matter

Table 7.1.Web	Teachers' self-efficacy, detailed results http://dx.doi.org/10.1787/888933047482
Table 7.2.Web	Teachers' job satisfaction, detailed results http://dx.doi.org/10.1787/888933047520
Table 7.3.Web	Relationship between teacher and school characteristics and societal value of teaching, detailed results http://dx.doi.org/10.1787/888933047558
Table 7.4.Web	Relationship between teachers' characteristics and their self-efficacy, detailed results http://dx.doi.org/10.1787/888933047596
Table 7.5.Web	Relationship between teachers' characteristics and job satisfaction, detailed results http://dx.doi.org/10.1787/888933047634
Table 7.6.Web	Relationship between classroom characteristics and teachers' self-efficacy, detailed results http://dx.doi.org/10.1787/888933047672
Table 7.7.Web	Relationship between classroom characteristics and teachers' job satisfaction, detailed results http://dx.doi.org/10.1787/888933047710
Table 7.8.Web.1	Relationship between school environment and teachers' self-efficacy, detailed results http://dx.doi.org/10.1787/888933047748
Table 7.8.Web.2	Relationship between school environment and teachers' self-efficacy, detailed results on school leadership http://dx.doi.org/10.1787/888933047767
Table 7.9.Web.1	Relationship between school environment and teachers' job satisfaction, detailed results http://dx.doi.org/10.1787/888933047805
Table 7.9.Web.2	Relationship between school environment and teachers' job satisfaction, detailed results on school leadership http://dx.doi.org/10.1787/888933047824
Table 7.10.Web	Relationship between teacher professional development and teachers' self-efficacy, detailed results http://dx.doi.org/10.1787/888933047862
Table 7.11.Web	Relationship between teacher professional development and teachers' job satisfaction, detailed results http://dx.doi.org/10.1787/888933047900
Table 7.12.Web	Relationship between teacher feedback and self-efficacy, detailed results http://dx.doi.org/10.1787/888933047938
Table 7.13.Web	Relationship between teacher feedback and job satisfaction, detailed results http://dx.doi.org/10.1787/888933047976
Table 7.14.Web.1	Relationship between teaching beliefs and teachers' self-efficacy, detailed results http://dx.doi.org/10.1787/888933048014
Table 7.14.Web.2	Relationship between teachers' working hours and self-efficacy, detailed results http://dx.doi.org/10.1787/888933048033
Table 7.14.Web.3	Relationship between time spent on keeping order and teachers' self-efficacy, detailed results http://dx.doi.org/10.1787/888933048052
Table 7.14.Web.4	Relationship between time spent on administrative tasks and teachers' self-efficacy, detailed results http://dx.doi.org/10.1787/888933048071
Table 7.15.Web.1	Relationship between teaching beliefs and teachers' job satisfaction, detailed results http://dx.doi.org/10.1787/888933048109
Table 7.15.Web.2	Relationship between teachers' working hours and job satisfaction, detailed results http://dx.doi.org/10.1787/888933048128
Table 7.15.Web.3	Relationship between time spent on keeping order and teachers' job satisfaction, detailed results http://dx.doi.org/10.1787/888933048147

Table 7.15.Web.4	Relationship between time spent on administrative tasks and teachers' job satisfaction, detailed results
	http://dx.doi.org/10.1787/888933048166

Table 7.16.Web	Relationship between teachers' collaboration and self-efficacy, detailed results
	http://dx.doi.org/10.1787/888933048204

Table 7.17.Web	Relationship between teachers' collaboration and job satisfaction, detailed results
	http://dx.doi.org/10.1787/888933048242

Table 7.18.Web	Standard deviation related to teachers' job satisfaction and self-efficacy
	http://dx.doi.org/10.1787/888933048261

Annex B Technical notes on indices and analysis used in TALIS 2013

Table B.11.Web	Baseline model for the relationship between school leadership and school environment and teachers' self-efficacy
	http://dx.doi.org/10.1787/888933048546

Table B.12.Web	Baseline model for the relationship between school leadership and school environment and teachers' job satisfaction
	http://dx.doi.org/10.1787/888933048565

Table B.13.Web	Baseline model for the relationship between teacher professional development and teachers' self-efficacy
	http://dx.doi.org/10.1787/888933048584

Table B.14.Web	Baseline model for the relationship between teacher professional development and teachers' job satisfaction
	http://dx.doi.org/10.1787/888933048603

Table B.15.Web	Baseline model for the relationship between teacher appraisal and feedback and teachers' self-efficacy
	http://dx.doi.org/10.1787/888933048622

Table B.16.Web	Baseline model for the relationship between teacher appraisal and feedback and teachers' job satisfaction
	http://dx.doi.org/10.1787/888933048641

Table B.17.Web	Baseline model for the relationship between teachers' working hours, teaching beliefs and practices and teachers' self-efficacy
	http://dx.doi.org/10.1787/888933048660

Table B.18.Web	Baseline model for the relationship between teachers' working hours, teaching beliefs and practices and teachers' job satisfaction
	http://dx.doi.org/10.1787/888933048679

These tables, as well as additional material, may be found at: *www.oecd.org/edu/school/talis.htm.*

Annex D
LIST OF CONTRIBUTORS

ANNEX D

LIST OF CONTRIBUTORS IN TALIS 2013

TALIS is a collaborative effort, bringing together expertise from participating countries that share an interest in developing a survey programme to inform their policies about teachers, teaching and learning. This report is the product of collaboration and co-operation among the member countries of the OECD and the partner countries participating in the second round of TALIS. Engagement with bodies representing teachers and regular briefings and exchanges with the Trade Union Advisory Council at the OECD have been very important in the development and implementation of TALIS. In particular, the co-operation of the teachers and principals in the participating schools has been crucial in ensuring the success of TALIS.

The TALIS Board of Participating Countries has, in the context of OECD objectives, driven the development of TALIS and has determined its policy objectives. This includes the objectives of the analysis and reports produced, the conceptual framework and the development of the TALIS questionnaires. The Board has also overseen the implementation of the survey.

Participating countries implemented TALIS at the national level at National Project Centres through, among others, National Project Managers (NPMs), National Data Managers (NDMs) and National Sampling Managers (NSMs) who were subject to rigorous technical and operational procedures. The NPMs played a crucial role in helping to secure the co-operation of schools, to validate the questionnaires, to manage the national data collection and processing and to verify the results from TALIS. The NDMs co-ordinated data processing at the national level and liaised in the cleaning of the data. The NSMs were responsible for implementing TALIS, respecting sampling procedures and other rigorous technical and operational procedures.

An Instrument Development Expert Group (IDEG) was established to translate the policy priorities into questionnaires to address the policy and analytical questions that had been agreed by the participating countries. A Technical Advisory Group (TAG) was assembled to advise during the decision-making process for technical or analytical issues. A group of subject-matter experts and analysts were also critical in the analytical phase and drafting of the initial reports.

The co-ordination and management of implementation at the international level was the responsibility of the appointed contractor, the Data Processing and Research Centre of the International Association for the Evaluation of Educational Achievement (IEA DPC). The IEA DPC Secretariat was responsible for overseeing the verification of the translation and for quality control in general. Statistics Canada, as a sub-contractor of the IEA DPC, developed the sampling plan, advised countries on its application, calculated the sampling weights and advised on the calculation of sampling errors.

The OECD Secretariat had overall responsibility for managing the programme, monitoring its implementation on a day-to-day basis and serving as the Secretariat of the Board of Participating Countries.

Members of the TALIS Board of Participating Countries

Chair: Anne-Berit Kavli

Australia: Paul Hunt; Margaret Pearce; Mark Unwin

Abu Dhabi (United Arab Emirates): Masood Badri; Rabih Abouchakra; Tarek El Mourad; Hussein Al-Hindawi

Alberta (Canada): Marie-France Chouinard; Greg Rudolf; Janusz Zieminski

Brazil: Daniel Jaime Capistrano de Olivera; Ana Carolina Silva Cirotto; Juliana Marquez Da Silva

Bulgaria: Neda Oscar Kristanova; Marina Mavrodieva

Chile: Violeta Aranciba Clavel; Carolina Velasco Ortúzar

Croatia: Michelle Bras Roth

Czech Republic: Jana Palečková; Lubomír Martinec

Denmark: Elsebeth Aller

England (United Kingdom): Lorna Bertrand

Estonia: Priit Laanoja

Finland: Kimmo Hämäläinen

Flanders (Belgium): Isabelle Erauw

France: Jean-François Chesné; Catherine Moisan; Florence Lefresne; Caroline Simonis-Sueur

Iceland: Julius Björnsson

Israel: Hany Shilton; Hagit Glickman

Italy: Maria Gemma de Sanctis; Antonella Tozza

Japan: Tsutomu Takaguchi; Akiko Ono; Kenichi Fujioka

Korea: Miran Jang; Doki Kim; Kapsung Kim

Latvia: Ennata Kivrina

Malaysia: Norlida Ab Wahab; Faizulizami Osmin

Mexico: Ana Maria Aceves Estrada; Marina Jazmin Santos Insua

Netherlands: Hans Ruesink

Norway: Anne-Berit Kavli

Poland: Lidia Olak; Magdalena Krawczyk-Radwan; Kamila Hernik

Portugal: Nuno Rodrigues

Romania: Silviu Cristian Mirescu

Serbia: Danijela Petrovic

Singapore: Siew Hoong Wong

Slovak Republic: Romana Kanovska

Spain: Carmen Tovar Sanchez; Javier Munoz Sanchez-Brunete; José Antonio Blanco Fernandez

Sweden: Katalin Bellaagh

United States: Patrick Gonzales

TALIS National Project Managers

Australia: Frances Eveleigh; Christopher Freeman
Abu Dhabi (United Arab Emirates): Tarek El Mourad
Alberta (Canada): Janusz Zieminski
Brazil: Ana Carolina Silva Cirotto; Juliana Marques da Silva (Deputy)
Bulgaria: Marina Mavrodieva
Chile: Carla Guazzini Galdames
Croatia: Michelle Braš Roth
Czech Republic: Vendula Kašparová; Lubomír Martinec
Denmark: Elsebeth Aller
England (United Kingdom): Katharine Brooks; Dawn Pollard
Estonia: Ülle Übius
Finland: Matti Taajamo; Eija Puhakka (Deputy)
Flanders (Belgium): Alexia Deneire; Jan Vanhoof
France: Jean-François Chesné
Iceland: Ragnar Ólafsson
Israel: Lisa Amdur; Hani Shilton
Italy: Maria Gemma De Sanctis
Japan: Akiko Ono; Hiroki Kato; Takashi Fuchigami
Korea: Kapsung Kim
Latvia: Andrejs Geske
Malaysia: Wan Ilias Wan Salleh; Norlida Ab Wahab
Mexico: Ana Maria Aceves Estrada; Marina Jazmin Santos Insua (Deputy)
Netherlands: Mirjam Stuivenberg; Eva van der Boom
Norway: Per Olaf Aamodt
Poland: Kamila Hernik; Rafal Piwowarski
Portugal: Nuno Rodrigues
Romania: Silviu Cristian Mirescu
Serbia: Danijela Petrović; Ivan Anić (Deputy)
Singapore: Siew Yee Lim (2012-2013); Susan Wee; Ivan Lim; Puay Huat Chua (2011-2012)
Slovak Republic: Barbora Mihalikova; Ervin Stava
Spain: Carmen Tovar Sanchez
Sweden: Katalin Bellaagh
United States: Greg Strizek; Erin Roth

TALIS National Data Managers

Australia: Late O'Malley
Abu Dhabi (United Arab Emirates): Tarek El Mourad; Hussein Al-Hindawi (Deputy)
Alberta (Canada): Marilyn Huber
Brazil: Daniel Oliveira; Margarete Souza
Bulgaria: Marina Mavrodieva
Chile: Cristian Pablo Yáñez Navarro; Roberto Schurch Santana
Croatia: Michelle Braš Roth
Czech Republic: Martina Ševců; Jan Hučín
Denmark: Thomas Larsen
England (United Kingdom): Mark Johannesen
Estonia: Lauri Veski
Finland: Eija Puhakka
Flanders (Belgium): Alexia Deneire
France: Sandrine Prost
Iceland: Ragnar Ólafsson

Israel: Lisa Amdur
Italy: Antonio Panaggio
Japan: Kenji Matsubara
Korea: Kapsung Kim
Latvia: Linda Mihno
Malaysia: Norlida Ab Wahab; Faizulizami Osmin
Mexico: Roberto Peña
Netherlands: Mirjam Stuivenberg
Norway: Nils Vibe
Poland: Mikolaj Hnatiuk; Andrzej Wichrowski
Portugal: Joaquim Santos
Romania: Silviu Cristian Mirescu
Serbia: Oliver Toskovic; Smiljana Josic (Deputy)
Singapore: Ching Ling Ang; Sophie Lu; Soon Hock Teo
Slovak Republic: Barbora Mihalikova
Spain: Francisco Javier García Crespo
Sweden: Cecilia Stenman
United States: Greg Strizek

TALIS National Sampling Managers

Australia: Late O'Malley
Abu Dhabi (United Arab Emirates): Tarek El Mourad
Alberta (Canada): Marilyn Huber
Brazil: Daniel Oliveira
Bulgaria: Marina Mavrodieva
Chile: Diego Núñez San Martín
Croatia: Michelle Braš Roth
Czech Republic: Martina Ševců
Denmark: Jesper Lund
England (United Kingdom): David Thomson
Estonia: Lauri Veski
Finland: Eija Puhakka
Flanders (Belgium): Alexia Deneire
France: Pierrette Briant
Iceland: Ragnar Ólafsson
Israel: Lisa Amdur
Italy: Maria Teresa Morana
Japan: Kenji Matsubara
Korea: Kapsung Kim
Latvia: Linda Mihno
Malaysia: Norlida Ab Wahab
Mexico: Moacyr Noe
Netherlands: Mirjam Stuivenberg
Norway: Joakim Caspersen
Poland: Mikolaj Hnatiuk
Portugal: Joaquim Santos
Romania: Silviu Cristian Mirescu
Serbia: Oliver Toskovic
Singapore: Siew Yee Lim
Slovak Republic: Ervin Stava
Spain: Araceli Sánchez
Sweden: Christian Tallberg
United States: Greg Strizek

OECD Secretariat

Core TALIS Team

Julie Bélanger

Michael Davidson

Elizabeth Del Bourgo

Sophie Limoges

Tadakazu Miki

Simon Normandeau

Mathilde Overduin

Delphine Versini

Kristen Weatherby

Other Secretariat Support

Brigitte Beyeler

Louise Binns

Francesca Borgonovi

Célia Braga-Schich

Tracey Burns

Cassandra Davis

Peter Deutscher

Elisa Larrakoetxea

Elizabeth Morgan

Gabriela Moriconi

Isabelle Moulherat

Deborah Nusche

Francesc Pedró

Beatriz Pont

Jaana Puukka

Diana Tramontano

Dirk Van Damme

Pablo Zoido

TALIS Expert Groups

Analysis Expert Group

Chair: Leslie Rutkowski (Indiana University, United States)

Ralph Carstens (IEA DPC)

Eugenio Gonzales (IEA DPC)

Miyako Ikeda (OECD Secretariat)

Heather Price (Basis Policy Research, United States)

Fons van de Vijver (University of Tilburg, the Netherlands)

Instrument Development Expert Group

Chair: Paulina Korsnakova (IEA Secretariat)

Mara Westling Allodie (Stockholm University, Sweden)

Giovanna Barzanò (Ministry of Education, Italy)

Julie Bélanger (OECD Secretariat)

Ralph Carstens (IEA DPC)

Jean Dumais (Statistics Canada)

Ben Jensen (Grattan Institute, Australia)

Eckhard Klieme (German Institute for International Educational Research (DIPF), Germany)

Peter Kloosterman (Indiana University, United States)

Steffen Knoll (IEA DPC)

Sang Wang Park (Pusan National University, Korea)

Susan Seeber (University of Gottingen, Germany)

Svenja Vieluf (German Institute for International Educational Research (DIPF), Germany)

Kristen Weatherby (OECD Secretariat)

Eva Wiren (Swedish National Agency of Education, Stockholm, Sweden)

Technical Advisory Group

Chair: Fons van de Vijver (University of Tilburg, the Netherlands)

Eduardo Backhoff (National Institute for Educational Evaluation (INEE), Mexico)

Jesper Lund (UNI-C, Denmark)

Dennis Mcinerney (Institute of Education, Hong Kong)

Heather Price (Basis Policy Research, United States)

TALIS Consortium

IEA Data Processing Centre (Hamburg, Germany)

Dirk Hastedt (IEA DPC Co-Director)

Steffen Knoll (International Study Director)

Ralph Carstens (International Deputy Study Director)

Friederike Westphal (International Project Manager)

Alena Becker (International Data Manager)

Mark Cockle (International Deputy Project and Data Manager)

IEA Secretariat (Amsterdam, Netherlands)

Paulina Korsnakova (IDEG Chair, Translation Verification and International Quality Control)

Juriaan Hartenberg; Roel Burgers (Manager Financial Control)

Isabelle Braun-Gémin (Assistant Financial Control)

Statistics Canada (Ottawa, Canada)

Jean Dumais (Sampling Referee)

Sylvie LaRoche (Coordinator Sampling and Weighting)

Lori Stratychuk (Sampling and Weighting)

Asma Alavi (Weighting)

Consultants (Indiana University, United States)

Leslie A. Rutkowski (Consultant Scaling, Framework Development)

David J. Rutkowski (Consultant, Framework Development)

Ellen Prusinski (Consultant, Framework Development)

IEA Data Processing and Research Center (Hamburg, Germany)

Andres Sandoval Hernandez (Head of the Research and Analysis Unit)

Deana Desa (Scaling, Data Analysis - Team Leader)

Plamen Mirazchiyski (Scaling, Data Analysis and Quality Control)

Jusuf Karameta (Scaling, Data Analysis)

Agnes Stancel-Piatak (Scaling, Data Analysis)

Christine Busch (Data Processing)

Hannah Köhler (Data Processing)

Sebastian Meyer (Data Processing, National Adaptation Verification)

Pia Möbus (Data Processing)

Dirk Oehler (Data Processing)

Daniel Radtke (Data Processing, National Adaptation Verification)

Bettina Wietzorek (Meeting Organisation)

Anke Sielemann (Meeting Organisation)

Bianca Brandes (Meeting Organisation)

Malte Bahrenfuss (ICT Services)

Matthias Jenßen (ICT Services)

Frank Müller (ICT Services)

Meng Xue (Unithead Software Development)

Harpreet Singh Choudry (Unithead Software Development)

Tim Daniel (Software Development)

Michael Jung (Software Development)

Limiao Duan (Programming)

Christian Harries (Programming)

Vallimeena Chinnamadasamy (Programming)

Maike Junod (Programming)

Deepti Kalamadi (Programming)

Poornima Mamadapur (Programming)

Devi Potham Rajendra Prasath (Programming)

ORGANISATION FOR ECONOMIC CO-OPERATION AND DEVELOPMENT

The OECD is a unique forum where governments work together to address the economic, social and environmental challenges of globalisation. The OECD is also at the forefront of efforts to understand and to help governments respond to new developments and concerns, such as corporate governance, the information economy and the challenges of an ageing population. The Organisation provides a setting where governments can compare policy experiences, seek answers to common problems, identify good practice and work to co-ordinate domestic and international policies.

The OECD member countries are: Australia, Austria, Belgium, Canada, Chile, the Czech Republic, Denmark, Estonia, Finland, France, Germany, Greece, Hungary, Iceland, Ireland, Israel, Italy, Japan, Korea, Luxembourg, Mexico, the Netherlands, New Zealand, Norway, Poland, Portugal, the Slovak Republic, Slovenia, Spain, Sweden, Switzerland, Turkey, the United Kingdom and the United States. The European Union takes part in the work of the OECD.

OECD Publishing disseminates widely the results of the Organisation's statistics gathering and research on economic, social and environmental issues, as well as the conventions, guidelines and standards agreed by its members.

OECD PUBLISHING, 2, rue André-Pascal, 75775 PARIS CEDEX 16
(87 2014 02 1P) ISBN 978-92-64-21133-9 – 2014-02